my first baking book

my first baking book

35 easy and fun recipes for children aged 7 years +

CICO Kidz

Published in 2012 by CICO Kidz
An imprint of Ryland Peters & Small
519 Broadway, 5th Floor, New York NY 10012
20–21 Jockey's Fields, London WC1R 4BW
www.cicobooks.com

10 9 8 7 6 5 4 3 2 1

For recipe credits, see page 128.

A CIP catalog record for this book is available from the Library of Congress and the British Library.

ISBN: 978-1-908170-85-9

Printed in China

Series consultant: Susan Akass
Editors: Susan Akass and Katie Hardwicke
Designer: Elizabeth Healey
Step artworks: Rachel Boulton
Animal artworks: Hannah George
Templates: Simon Roulstone
For photography and styling credits, see page 128.

- All spoon measurements are level unless otherwise specified.

- Both US cup sizes or imperial and metric measurements have been given. Use one set of measurements only and not a mixture of both.

- All eggs are US large (UK medium) unless otherwise stated. This book contains recipes made with raw eggs. It is prudent for more vulnerable people, such as pregnant and nursing mothers, babies and young children, invalids and the elderly, to avoid uncooked dishes made with eggs.

- Some of the recipes contain nuts and should not be consumed by anyone with a nut allergy.

- Ovens should be preheated to the specified temperatures. All ovens work slightly differently. We recommend using an oven thermometer and suggest you consult the maker's handbook for any special instructions, particularly if you are cooking in a fan-assisted oven, as you will need to adjust temperatures according to manufacturer's instructions.

CONTENTS

Introduction

Why learn to bake? There are three great reasons—it's lots of fun; you end up with delicious food to eat; and you create something special to share with your family and friends. What's more, it is a skill that will make you popular all through your life because everyone loves home-baked food.

This book teaches you how to bake by guiding you through each stage of a recipe, showing you how to do everything from greasing a pan to testing if a loaf is baked. It is divided into four chapters: the first, Perfect Pastry, is all about working with pastry to make mouth-watering savory and sweet pastry recipes. In the second chapter, Sweet Treats, you learn how to make cakes, bars, desserts, and cookies all guaranteed to bring your friends running. The third chapter, Delicious Dough, is all about using dough to make buns and bread-based recipes. Finally, Savory Meals and Snacks teaches you how to make some family meal dishes—your parents will be more than happy when you start offering to cook these for supper!

Obviously, you must ask an adult before doing any baking because using knives, stoves, ovens, and electrical equipment can be dangerous. However, the more you learn, the safer it will become. To help you, we have also included a techniques section with more detail about everything you will need to know to cook up the recipes.

We have also graded each recipe with a grading of one, two, or three smiley faces—see below. Level one recipes are the easiest, level two recipes have more stages, and level three recipes are the longest and most difficult—it may be best to leave these for when you have become more of an expert cook.

So, wash your hands, tie on your apron, and start baking!

Project levels

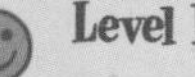

Level 1
These have only a few stages and require just a little adult help.

Level 2
These include more stages, some difficult techniques, and require some adult help.

Level 3
These are longer and require adult help for most of the stages.

Kitchen safety—read this before you start cooking!

- Always wash your hands before you start cooking and after touching raw meat.
- Tie long hair back so that it is out of the way.
- Wear an apron to keep your clothes clean.
- Make sure your ingredients are fresh and within their use-by date.
- When using sharp knives, electrical equipment, or the stovetop (hob), microwave, or oven, always ask an adult to help you.
- Use oven mitts when holding hot pans or dishes.
- Use a chopping board when using a sharp knife or metal cookie cutters—this protects the work surface and will help to stop the knife from slipping.
- Keep your work surface clean and wipe up any spills on the floor so that you don't slip.
- Don't forget to clear up afterward—washing the dishes can be as much fun as baking!

Kitchen equipment

Strainer (sieve)
Colander
Vegetable peeler
Grater
Garlic crusher
Sharp knives
Palette knife

Cutting board
Egg cup
Ovenproof dishes
Plastic wrap (clingfilm)
Baking parchment
Paper towel (kitchen paper)
Mixing bowls in different sizes
Heatproof glass bowls
Microwave-safe bowls
Saucepans
Wooden spoon

Measuring pitcher (jug)
Weighing scales and measuring cups
Measuring spoons
Wire whisk
Spatula
Pastry brush
Rolling pin
6- or 12-hole muffin pans
12-hole mini muffin pan
Paper muffin or cupcake cups
Baking sheets
Cake pans
Wire cooling rack
Cookie cutters
Baking beans

Baking tips and techniques

Using an oven

- The first thing you need to do for most of the baking recipes is turn on the oven. This is because the oven needs to be hot enough to cook the food you put into it and it takes a little while to heat up.
- The recipe instructions always tell you at what temperature to set your oven. Ask an adult to show you how your oven shows you the temperature and how to set the oven to the correct temperature.
- On most ovens there is a light, which goes out when the oven reaches the temperature you have set, and then it is ready to use.
- It is recommended to use the middle shelf of the oven for most baking needs. Make sure that there is space above it for your cakes or bread to rise.
- Always use oven mitts when putting food into the oven or taking it out and put hot dishes onto a heatproof board or trivet so that you don't burn the work surface.

Preparing your pans

After you have switched on the oven, the first thing you need to do in almost every recipe is to prepare your pan. This is an important step to stop the food you are baking from sticking to the pan as it cooks. If it sticks, you won't be able to lift or turn the food out of the pan. To stop it sticking, you can either grease the pan by rubbing all over the inside with a little oil or butter on a paper towel or line the pan with baking parchment or, for some recipes, do both.

Using the stovetop (hob)

Always ask an adult before using the stovetop.

- When using the stovetop, make sure that saucepan handles don't stick out over the front of the stovetop where you could knock them off.
- Don't have the heat too high—it is easy to burn your food.
- Always remember to turn off the heat when you've finished cooking.
- When you take a pan off the stovetop, always put it onto a heatproof board or trivet so that you don't burn the work surface.

Weighing and measuring

Baking is a little like a science experiment and you need to have exact measurements in order for it to work successfully! This means weighing and measuring out the ingredients very carefully. This book uses two different types of measurements. You can follow one method, but don't swap between the two in your recipe. Use either measuring cups or weighing scales for large quantities, and measuring spoons (or normal spoons) for smaller amounts. Check that the ingredients are level with the top of the spoon, unless the instructions tell you otherwise. Use measuring cups or pitchers (jugs) for liquids.

Butter

Many baking recipes use butter and for these, unsalted butter is usually best. For cake recipes that need you to cream the butter with the sugar, it should be nice and soft, so take it out of the fridge in good time. For pastry recipes and other recipes that need you to rub the butter into flour, the butter should be chilled and hard.

Creaming butter and sugar

- Many cake recipes start with creaming butter and sugar, which means beating them together until they are well mixed and become pale and fluffy. This is an important stage because it makes the cakes light in texture.
- Always remember to take the butter out of the fridge at least half an hour before you need it, so it is soft and easy to cream.
- Creaming is much quicker with electric beaters—but always ask an adult to help with using these.

Rubbing in

Many recipes ask you to rub butter into flour. To do this, first cut up the chilled butter into small pieces and add it to the flour. Then, using your fingers, pick up small amounts of butter and flour, and rub them together between your thumb and fingertips. Keep picking up more of the mixture and rubbing it together. In this way, the butter gradually gets mixed into the flour until there are no lumps left and it looks like breadcrumbs.

Tips for rolling out pastry dough

- When you roll out pastry for small tarts, it is easier to roll out 3 or 4 small pieces, one at a time, rather than one big one.
- Use plenty of flour on your work surface to stop the pastry sticking to the surface. Put some on your rolling pin too.
- When you roll pastry, push down and away from you.
- Keep moving the pastry, to make sure it hasn't stuck, and add a little more flour if it does stick.
- Try not to handle the pastry too much—it needs to stay cold and your hands will make it hot!
- Cut circles for tarts as close together as possible, so you fit lots in before you need to gather up the trimmings and roll again.

Making buttermilk substitute

Some recipes ask for buttermilk, but if you don't have this in your fridge you can make your own buttermilk substitute. Put 1 tablespoon of lemon juice in a measuring cup (jug) and add 1 cup (250 ml) of fresh milk. Stir them together and then let the mixture stand for 5 minutes–the milk will curdle, but taste fine.

Folding cake batter

Some recipes ask you to fold in ingredients. Folding is a way of mixing light ingredients into heavier ones without squashing out any air. Use a metal rather than a wooden spoon to cut through the mixture in a gentle figure eight, rather than stirring it round and round as you would with a wooden spoon. Every so often, scrape around the edge of the bowl to make sure all of the ingredients are mixed together.

Proving dough

The yeast in bread dough is alive and needs to grow (prove) in a warm place until the dough has doubled in size. Find the warmest place in your house to put it—in a warm closet, close to a radiator, near a warm oven, on a sunny windowsill, even on a hot water bottle! If the dough is nice and warm, it will take about an hour to prove. It will still prove if it is colder, but will take much longer.

You need to cover your dough with plastic wrap (clingfilm) to stop it drying out as it rises.

Using a microwave

Using a microwave is a quick and easy way to heat and melt ingredients for baking.

Melting chocolate

Put the chopped chocolate in a microwave-safe bowl. Heat on low for 30 seconds, stir, and heat again for another 30 seconds. Keep checking and stirring at regular intervals of 20–30 seconds, and when the chocolate is nearly melted (when there are a few lumps left), remove the bowl from the microwave and stir the melted chocolate until it is smooth. Take care if the bowl is hot and ask an adult to help you take the bowl in and out of the microwave. Take care that the chocolate doesn't overheat.

Microwave safety

- Always use microwave-safe bowls and never put anything metallic in the microwave.
- When heating anything in the microwave, you must take great care to stir the heated ingredient thoroughly before using or eating it—even if it seems lukewarm on the outside, it could be burning hot inside. When you stir melted chocolate or jelly (jam), for example, you will spread the heat evenly and avoid these hot spots. Heat on a medium or low setting for short lengths of time, rather than continuously, and keep checking at regular intervals.
- Timings given in the recipes are general instructions, but as microwave ovens vary, adapt the timings to suit your particular model.

Warming jelly (jam)

Put the jelly in a microwave-safe bowl and heat on medium for 20–30 seconds. Ask an adult to help you take the bowl out of the microwave and stir it gently. You can heat again for a few seconds longer if necessary, but take care that the jelly doesn't overheat—jelly can become burning hot very quickly.

Using knives

Good cooks must learn to use knives properly and you should ask an adult to teach you. If you use it properly, a sharp knife is safer than a blunt one, because it won't slip, but you must hold the food firmly and keep your fingers out if the way. Always use a chopping board and one of the following three techniques:

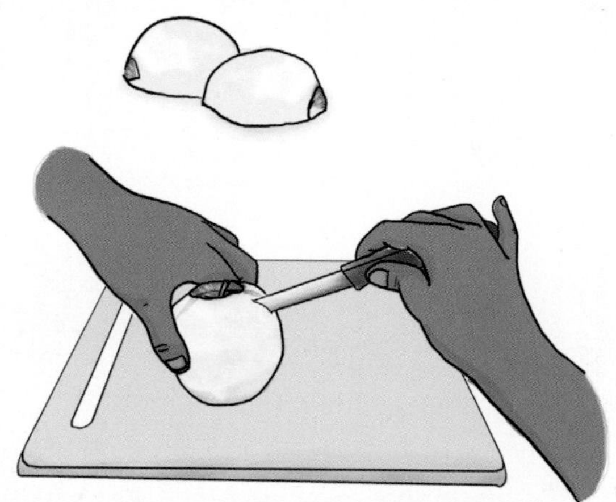

1

"Bridge"

The "Bridge" cutting technique is used for cutting larger things (for example apples, tomatoes, or onions) into smaller pieces:

- Hold the food by forming a bridge with your thumb on one side of the food and your index finger on the other side. Hold the knife in your other hand with the blade facing down, guide the knife under the bridge, and cut through the food.
- For some soft items, such as tomatoes, it might be easier to puncture the tomato skin with the point of the knife before cutting.

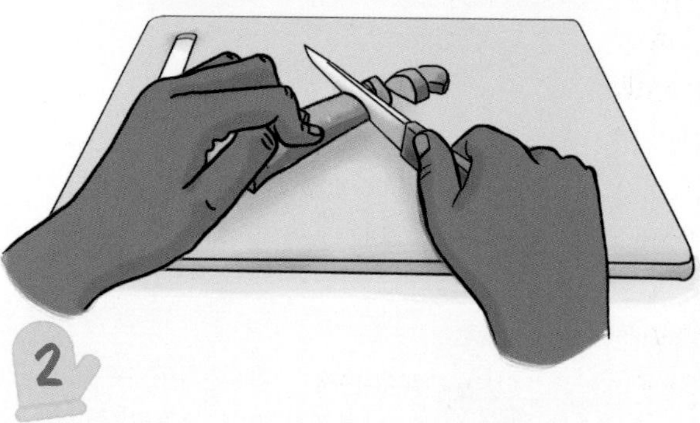

2

"Claw"

The "Claw" cutting technique is used for chopping or slicing foods, such as carrots or onions, into smaller pieces:

- Cut the food in half (using the bridge cutting technique) so that you have a flat side. Place the flat side of the food down on the chopping board so that it is steady.
- Shape the fingers of one hand into a claw shape, tucking the thumb inside the fingers. Rest the claw on the food to be sliced to hold it firm.
- Holding the knife in the other hand, slice the food, making sure to move the "clawed" fingers back as the knife slices closer.

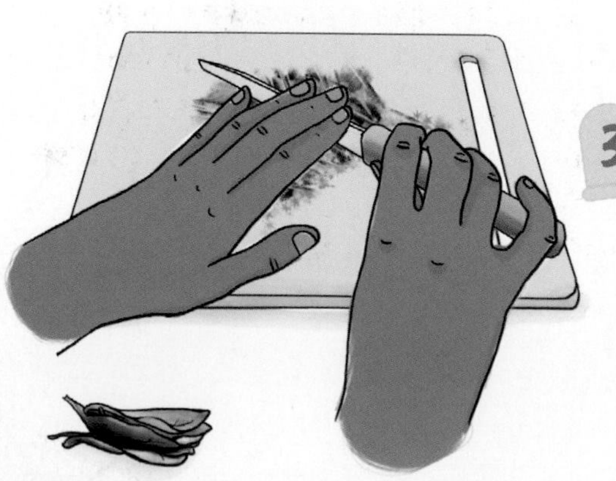

3

Chopping herbs

- Put the pile of herbs on a board. Have the flat of one hand on top of the knife and the other on the handle and rock the knife over the herbs.
- Another way of cutting up herbs is to put them in a small cup and snip them with scissors.

Grating

Cooks grate all sorts of things—cheese, chocolate, carrots, zucchini (courgettes)—to make them small so they will mix into a recipe or be sprinkled on top. Be careful when grating because it is very easy to grate your fingers!

- Stand the grater on a flat chopping board or plate so that it is firm and doesn't wobble. Hold it firmly on the top.
- Hold the food with your fingertips. Grate from top to bottom keeping your fingers well away from the grater.
- Only grate big pieces of food and don't try to grate right to the end—discard the pieces when they get too small to hold safely.

Peeling

To peel carrots (or other vegetables, such as zucchini/courgettes or cucumbers):

- Trim off the ends.
- Hold the carrot at one end and rest the other end on a chopping board.
- Starting halfway along it, run the vegetable peeler down the carrot towards the board and away from your hand.
- Turn the carrot a little and peel the next strip in the same way. Keep turning and peeling until all of one end had been peeled.
- Turn the carrot up the other way, and hold the other end while you peel the second half.

To peel fruit, like apples, or potatoes:

- Rest the apple in the palm of your hand. Starting at the top, run the vegetable peeler around the apple, turning it as you go so that you create a spiral of peel.
- Keep turning the apple as you peel—see how long a strip you can make!

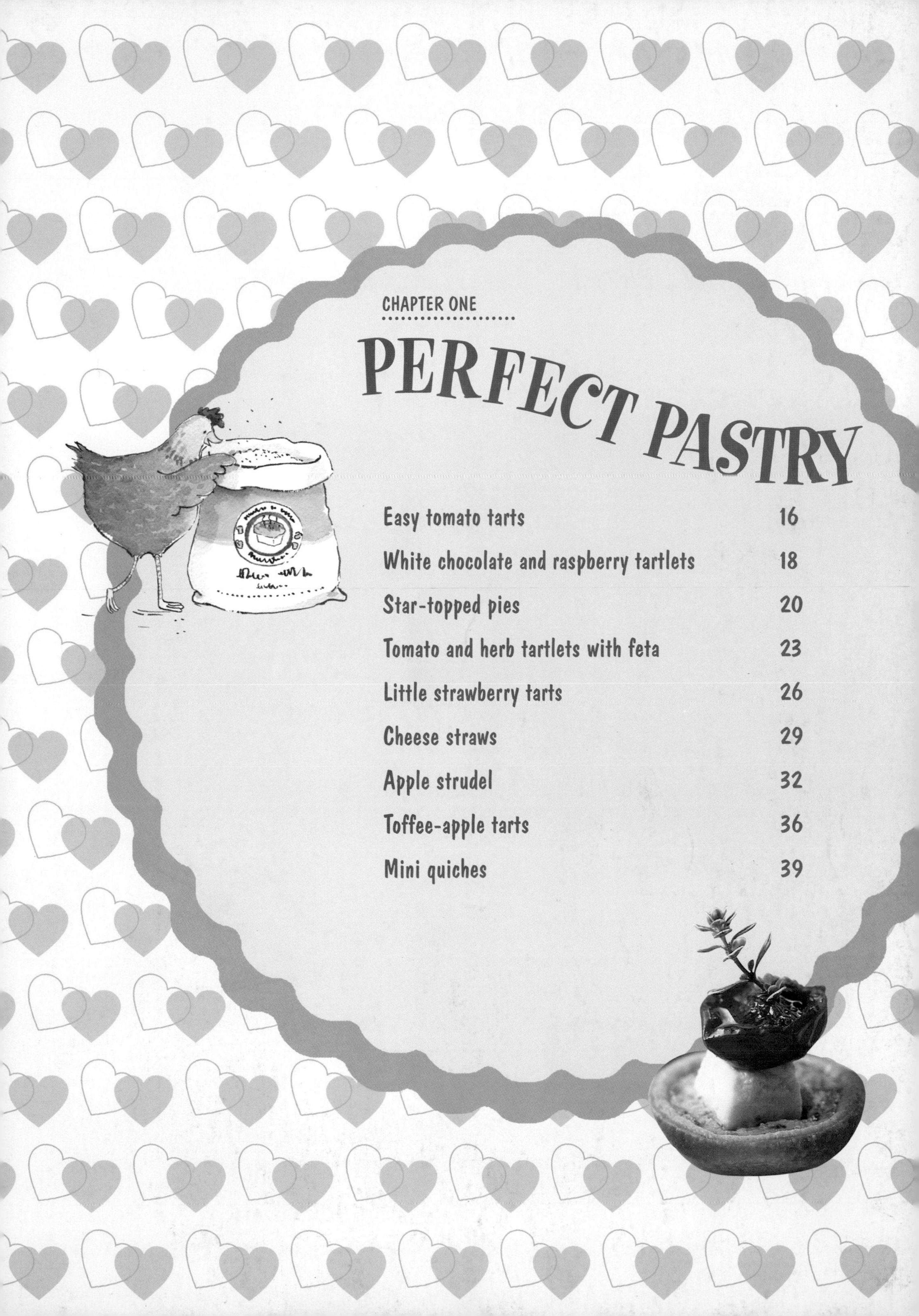

CHAPTER ONE

PERFECT PASTRY

Easy tomato tarts

Puff pastry is such a great ingredient to use. Buy it ready-rolled so that all you have to do is unroll it, cut it into circles, squares, or rectangles, and top with anything you like! This tart is a bit like pizza, but much quicker and easier to make.

You will need

12 oz. (375 g) ready-rolled puff pastry

4 tablespoons sun-dried tomato paste

20 cherry tomatoes

1 ball of mozzarella cheese

a handful of fresh basil leaves

baking sheet

(makes 4 or 6)

Ask an adult to turn the oven on to 400ºF (200ºC) Gas 6. Pour a little olive oil onto a piece of paper towel and rub it over the baking sheets to grease them.

2 Sprinkle a little flour over the work surface. Unroll the puff pastry and using a round-bladed knife, cut it into 4 or 6 (depending on how many people are going to eat them) evenly sized squares or rectangles. Lay them onto the baking sheet.

3 Carefully cut all the tomatoes into three slices. To do this hold a tomato with your hand making a bridge (see page 12). Use a sharp knife to cut down onto a board.

Use a spoon to spread a little sun-dried tomato paste over the pastry but try to leave the very edges bare.

5 Arrange the sliced tomatoes over the tomato paste. Arrange them in one layer rather than piling them up.

6 Tear off little pieces of the mozzarella cheese and put them on top of the tomatoes.

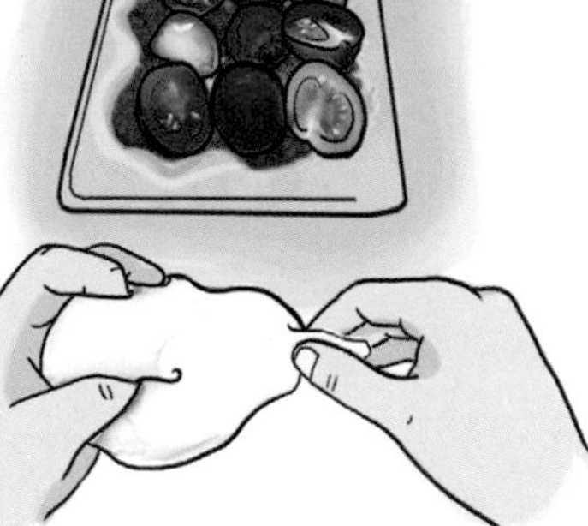

7 Ask an adult to help you put the tarts in the preheated oven and bake for 15 minutes or until the pastry is golden and puffed up and the mozzarella has melted. Ask an adult to help you take the baking sheet out of the oven, and sprinkle fresh basil leaves over the tarts before you serve them.

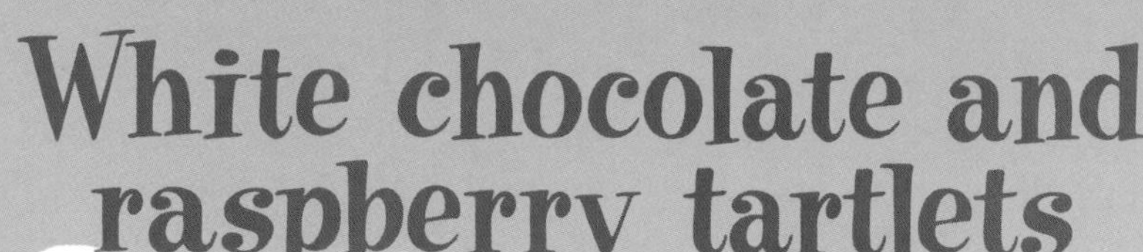

White chocolate and raspberry tartlets

Like the Easy Tomato Tarts on page 16, these summer tartlets are easy to make because they use store-bought, ready-rolled puff pastry. And they're so pretty!

You will need

10 oz. (300 g) ready-rolled puff pastry

3½ oz. (100 g) white chocolate

2 eggs

½ cup (125 ml) heavy (double) cream

¼ cup (50 g) sugar

2 cups (300 g) raspberries

confectioners' (icing) sugar, for dusting

12-hole muffin pan or tartlet pan

cookie cutter, roughly the same size as the muffin pan holes

(makes 12)

1 Ask an adult to turn the oven on to 350°F (180°C) Gas 4. Use a little butter on a piece of paper towel to grease the muffin pan holes to stop the tartlets sticking.

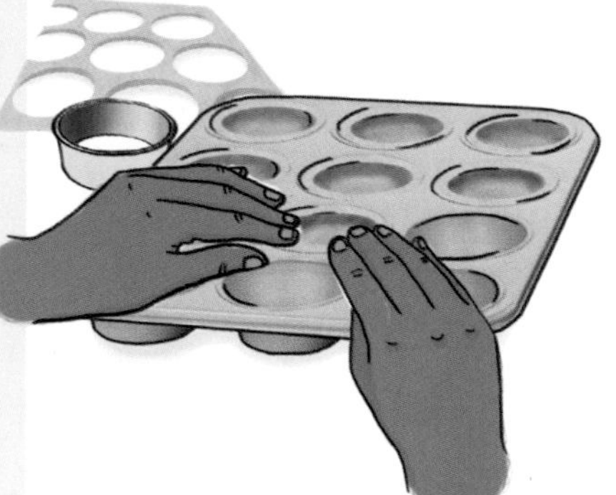

2 Sprinkle a little flour over the work surface. Unroll the puff pastry and cut the dough into 12 circles using the cookie cutter. Gently press each circle into a muffin pan hole.

3 Break the chocolate up into small pieces and put it in a small heatproof bowl. Ask an adult to help you set the bowl over a saucepan of gently simmering water, making sure that the bottom of the bowl does not touch the water. Stir the chocolate with a wooden spoon until it has melted. Take it off the heat and let it cool for a while. (You could melt the chocolate in a microwave instead—see page 11.)

4 Break the eggs into a large bowl, pick out any pieces of shell, then beat them with a fork or whisk until they are well mixed and a little frothy.

5

Pour the cream and sugar into the eggs and whisk them all together. Add the melted chocolate and keep whisking until the mixture is nice and smooth.

6

Carefully spoon the mixture into the tartlets until it is just below the top.

7

Ask an adult to help you put the muffin pan in the preheated oven and bake the tartlets for 15 minutes, or until the pastry is puffy and golden and the filling has risen (don't worry, it will sink as the tarts cool). Ask an adult to help you remove the pan from the oven and let it cool.

8

When cool, take the tartlets out of the muffin pan and put them on a cooling rack. Arrange 3 or 4 raspberries on the top of each tartlet. Put a little confectioners' (icing) sugar into a strainer (sieve) and sift it over the tartlets.

Star-topped pies

Topped with a star, these little pies are prettier than plain apple pies, and with the apple mixture spotted with bright red cranberries, they look even prettier when you take a bite, too.

You will need

2 cooking apples

2 red or sweet eating apples

12 oz. (375 g) store-bought sweet pastry

¼ cup (50 g) superfine (caster) sugar, plus extra for sprinkling

½ teaspoon ground cinnamon, plus extra for sprinkling

juice of ½ lemon

⅓ cup (50 g) dried cranberries

1 tablespoon milk

confectioners' (icing) sugar, for dusting

12-hole tartlet pan

fluted round cookie cutter, just bigger than the tartlet pan holes

star-shaped cookie cutter

(makes 9–12)

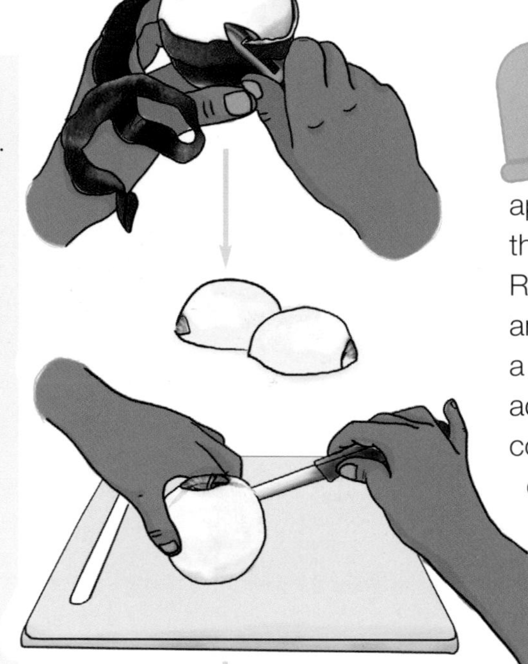

1 First, prepare the apples. Use a potato peeler to peel the skin from both types of apples. Next, use a sharp knife to cut the apples into halves, then quarters. Remember to cut down onto a board and hold the apple with your hand in a bridge shape (see page 12). Ask an adult to help you carefully remove the cores by cutting a V shape into the center of each quarter. Finally, cut the apples into small pieces (see page 12).

How long a piece of APPLE PEEL can you peel?

2 Tip the apples into a medium-sized saucepan and add the sugar, cinnamon, lemon juice, and cranberries. Ask an adult to help you put the pan over a low-medium heat. Stir the mixture from time to time until the apples are soft.

3 Ask an adult to help you remove the pan from the heat. Let it cool a little and then taste the mixture—add a little more sugar if you want it sweeter. Set it aside until it is cold.

4 Ask an adult to turn the oven on to 350°F (180°C) Gas 4.

5 Use a little butter on a piece of paper towel to grease the tartlet holes in the pan. Sprinkle a little flour on a clean work surface. Roll out the pastry until it is about ⅛ in. (3 mm) thick (quite thin). Use the fluted cookie cutter to stamp out 9 circles. Gently press the pastry circles into the pan holes.

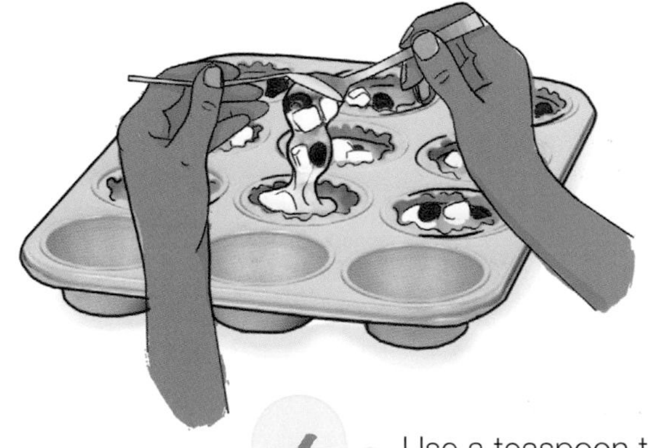

6 Use a teaspoon to put the apple mixture into the pastry cases, filling them almost to the top.

7 Gather up all the scraps of pastry dough, knead them very lightly to bring them together into a ball, and roll the dough out again. Use the star-shaped cutter to stamp out 9 stars for the pie tops.

8 If there is any dough left, gather it together and roll it out again. Make more pairs of circles and stars for more pies.

9 Pour a little milk into a cup. Using a pastry brush, lightly brush the edges of each pie with the milk and top with a pastry star. Press the stars down lightly at the edges to help them stick to the bases. Brush the top of each star with milk.

10 In a small bowl, mix together two tablespoons of sugar with a pinch of ground cinnamon. Sprinkle this over the pies.

11 Ask an adult to help you put the pan on the middle shelf of the preheated oven. Bake for about 25 minutes, or until the pastry is golden brown and the fruit filling is bubbling.

12 Ask an adult to help you remove the pan from the oven. Let the pies cool, then put a little confectioners' (icing) sugar in a strainer (sieve) and sift it over the pies.

Tomato and herb tartlets with feta

Are you or your parents having a party? These sophisticated little tartlets look stunning, taste great, and will impress your friends. Why not have a go?

You will need

12 oz. (375 g) store-bought shortcrust pastry

1 egg, beaten (see page 18)

For the slow-roasted tomatoes:

12 large, ripe cherry tomatoes

4 tablespoons olive oil

1 tablespoon dried oregano

For the herby cheese filling:

1 US extra-large (UK large) egg

⅓ cup (80 g) full-fat cream cheese with garlic and herbs

⅔ cup (150 ml) heavy (double) cream

3 oz. (75 g) feta cheese

salt and freshly ground black pepper

a few fresh herbs such as parsley, basil, or chives (optional)

tiny sprigs of fresh thyme

plain cookie cutter, 2½ in. (6 cm) diameter

2 mini 12-hole muffin pans

foil or baking parchment and baking beans

baking sheet

(makes 24)

1 Put a little butter on a piece of paper towel and grease the holes in the muffin pans. To make the pastry cases, sprinkle some flour onto the work surface and roll out the pastry until it is very thin, about ⅛ in. (3 mm) thick.

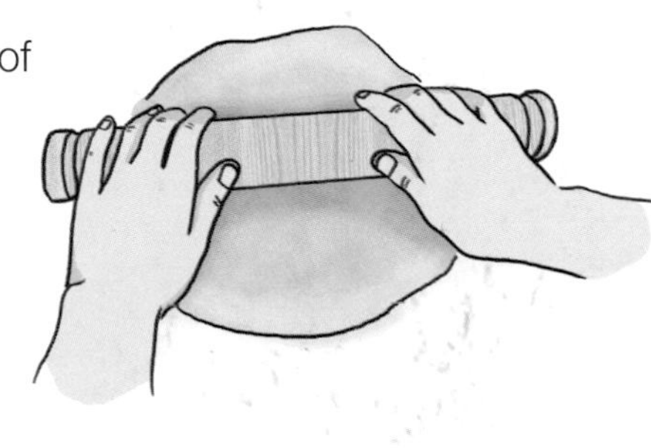

2 Use the cookie cutter to stamp out 24 circles, cutting them close together. You may have to gather the trimmings together and roll them out again.

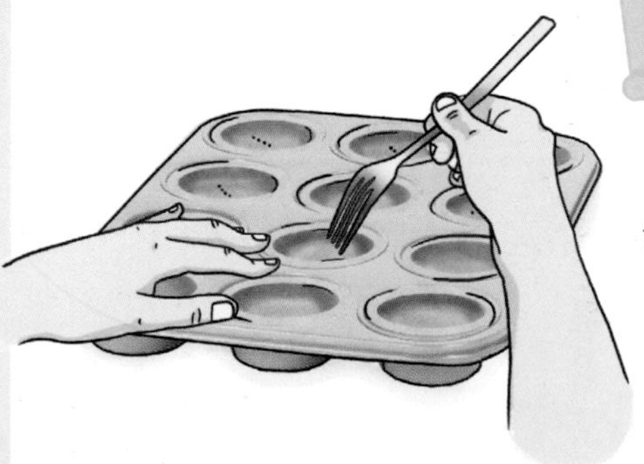

3 Press the circles into the muffin pan holes then prick them all over with a fork, this will stop the pastry from rising. Put them in the fridge for 15 minutes and ask an adult to turn the oven on to 200°C (400°F) Gas 6.

4 To bake blind, put a small cupcake case, or a piece of foil or baking parchment, in each tartlet and fill with baking beans. Ask an adult to help you put the pans in the preheated oven for 8–10 minutes.

5 Ask an adult to remove the muffin pans from the oven and remove the foil or parchment and beans. Return the pans to the oven to bake for 5–7 minutes longer. Now ask an adult to help you brush some beaten egg onto the baked pastry cases and return them to the oven for 5 more minutes until the egg is set and shiny. This will stop the pastry going soggy when you add the filling.

6 Ask an adult to turn the oven down to 325°F (160°C) Gas 3, ready to roast the tomatoes. Put a little olive oil on a paper towel and rub it over the baking sheet to grease it.

7 Carefully cut all the tomatoes in half. To do this, hold a tomato with your hand making a bridge (see page 12). Use a sharp knife and cut down onto a board. Arrange the tomatoes with the cut side up on the baking sheet.

8 Pour the olive oil into a small bowl and add the oregano, a little salt, and lots of ground pepper. Mix it up well and then brush the oil over the cut tomatoes. Ask an adult to put them in the oven and bake them for about 1½–2 hours, checking them every now and then. They should shrivel a bit, but stay bright red—if they get too dark they will be bitter.

CHEESY TARTS with hats on!

9 Now make the cheese filling. First break the egg into a bowl and pick out any bits of shell. Add the cream cheese, the cream, and a little salt and pepper, and beat them together until they are smooth. If you want your tarts to be even herbier, chop the fresh herbs into tiny pieces using a sharp knife and cutting down onto a board (see page 12). Stir them into the cheesy mixture.

10 Cut the feta into 24 small cubes that will fit inside the pastry cases.

11 When it is time for the party, ask an adult to turn the oven on to 350°F (180°C) Gas 4. Arrange the pastry cases on a baking sheet, put a spoonful of herby cheese mixture in each one and top with a cube of feta. Ask an adult to help you put them in the oven and bake for about 15–20 minutes or until the filling is set.

12 Ask an adult to take the tartlets out of the oven and arrange them on a plate. Top each tartlet with a tomato half. Poke a tiny sprig of thyme into the top of each tomato. Pass them around the party while they are still warm.

Little strawberry tarts

What could be nicer on a summer's day than strawberry tarts? These look really professional with their special shiny glaze. They are best eaten on the day you make them—but who could wait anyway?

Put a little butter on a paper towel and rub it all over the baking sheets to grease them.

You will need

1 lb (450 g) store-bought sweet pastry

2 pints (500 g) small fresh strawberries

about ⅔ cup (225 g) raspberry jelly (jam)

2 baking sheets

(makes 4)

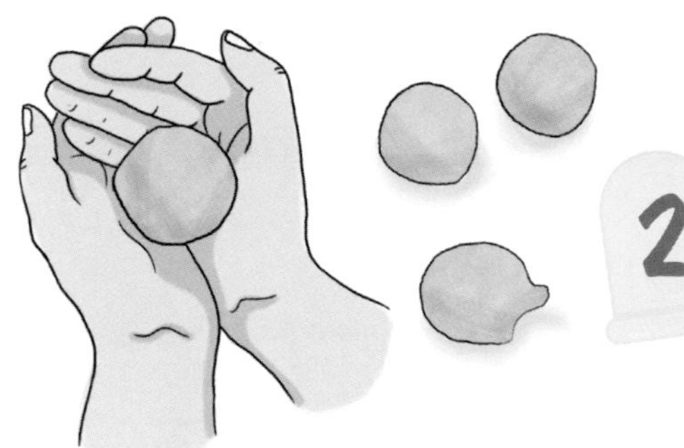

2 Divide the pastry dough into 4 equal pieces and roll each piece of dough into a ball with your hands.

3 Put two pastry balls on each baking sheet, setting them well apart (they will spread in the oven). With your fingers, press and pat out the dough to make circles about ¼ in. (5 mm) thick and about 4 in. (10 cm) across.

4 Pinch the edges of each circle with your fingertips to make a pretty shape, then prick the tart bases all over with a fork (the tiny air holes will stop the base bubbling up in the oven). Chill in the refrigerator for 10 minutes.

5 Ask an adult to turn the oven on to 350°F (180°C) Gas 4. When the dough is chilled, ask an adult to help you put the baking sheets in the preheated oven and bake for 20 minutes until the tart bases are a light golden color. Carefully remove the sheets from the oven and let the bases cool on the sheets.

6 Check over the strawberries and throw out any bad ones. Rinse them in a colander and pat them dry with paper towels. Remove the green stems, leaves, and hulls with your fingers or with a small knife.

7 To make the shiny glaze, spoon the jelly (jam) into a small saucepan. Add 1 tablespoon of water and ask an adult to help you heat it very gently, stirring with a wooden spoon. The solid jelly will melt and become a thick, smooth, hot syrup. Remove from the heat before it starts to boil. (You could also heat the jelly in the microwave, see page 11.)

8 Put each of the baked tart bases on a serving plate. Using a pastry brush, brush a little hot glaze over the middle of each circle leaving the edges bare.

9 Arrange the strawberries on top of the glaze with their pointy ends up. Brush the berries with the rest of the hot glaze so that they are completely covered. If the glaze starts to set before you've finished, gently warm it again.

10 Leave the tartlets until the jelly has set (about 20 minutes) before serving. These are best eaten straight away!

Cheese straws

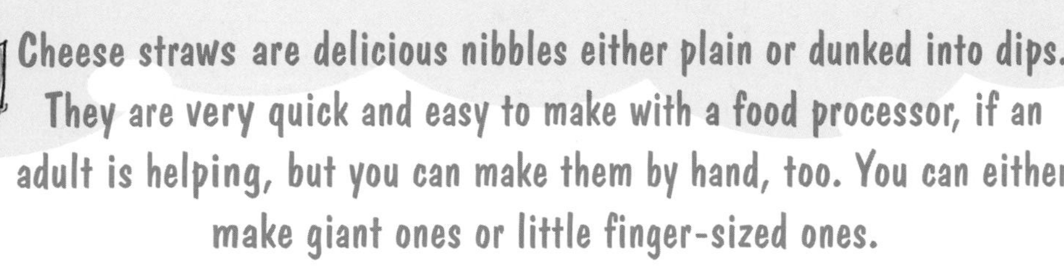

Cheese straws are delicious nibbles either plain or dunked into dips. They are very quick and easy to make with a food processor, if an adult is helping, but you can make them by hand, too. You can either make giant ones or little finger-sized ones.

You will need

1 cup (125 g) whole-wheat (wholemeal) flour

½ stick (65 g) unsalted butter, softened, plus extra for greasing

3 oz. (85 g) Parmesan cheese

1 egg

baking sheet

(makes 20 small straws or 10 giant straws)

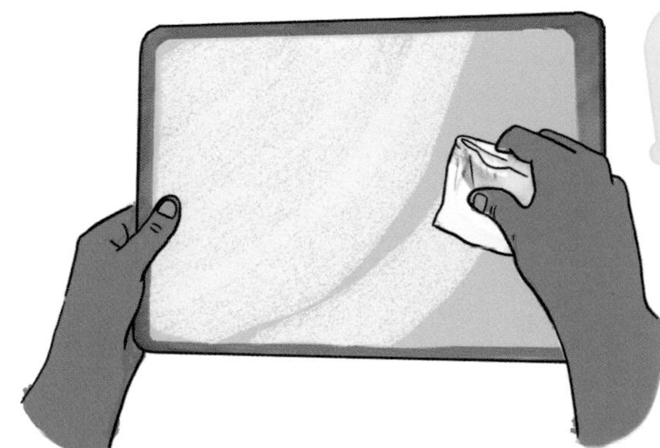

1 Rub the baking sheet with a little soft butter on a paper towel to grease it.

2 Separate the egg yolk from the white. To do this, break the egg onto a small plate, keeping the yolk whole. Now put an egg cup over the yolk and, holding the plate over a bowl, tip the plate so that the egg white slides off. (You don't need the white for this recipe.)

3 If your Parmesan needs grating (you can buy it ready grated), carefully grate it onto a plate using the finest holes on your cheese grater.

GREAT FOR DIPPING!

4 There are two ways to do the next step. If an adult is helping you: blend the flour and butter in a food processor until the mixture looks like fine crumbs. Add two-thirds (2 oz./50 g) of the cheese, the egg yolk, and 2–3 tablespoons water, and process in bursts until the mixture forms a ball.

If you are making the cheese straws by hand: rub the butter into the flour, using your fingers and thumbs (see page 9). Add two-thirds (2 oz./50 g) of the cheese, the egg yolk, and 2–3 tablespoons water. Stir it until the mixture comes together to form a ball. You may find it easier to do this with your hands.

5 Carefully take the dough out of the food processor or bowl, flatten it slightly, wrap it in plastic wrap (clingfilm), and chill in the refrigerator for 30 minutes.

Ask an adult to help you turn the oven on to 400°F (200°C) Gas 6.

7 If you want long straws, lightly sprinkle your work surface with flour and roll the dough out to about ½-in. (1-cm) thickness, making it into a long rectangle the same width as you want your straws to be. Now cut the rectangle into strips about ½ in. (1 cm) wide. Lay the strips on the baking sheet and sprinkle them with the remaining cheese. For short straws, cut the rectangle in half before you cut them.

8 Lay the strips on the baking sheet and sprinkle them with the rest of the grated cheese. Ask an adult to help you put the baking sheet into the preheated oven and bake for 10 minutes or until the straws are golden.

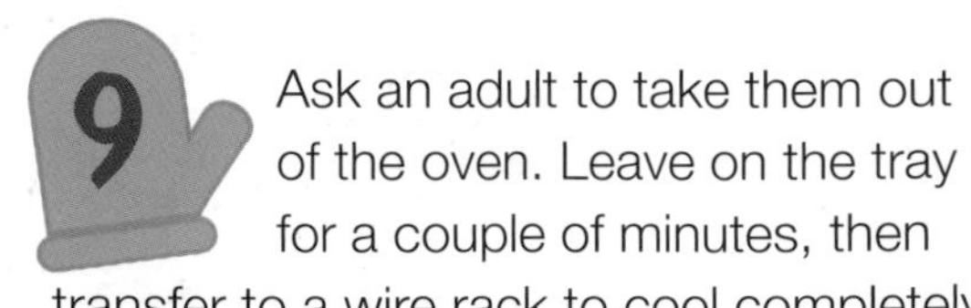

Ask an adult to take them out of the oven. Leave on the tray for a couple of minutes, then transfer to a wire rack to cool completely.

Apple strudel

This recipe uses phyllo (filo) pastry, which is very thin, flaky, and tasty. It comes ready rolled, so it's easy to use, but it looks very impressive. Use sharp apples for this recipe rather than ones that are sweet, but don't have much flavor.

You will need

8 oz. (225 g) ready-rolled phyllo (filo) pastry

9 amaretti cookies

4 medium apples

a generous ⅓ cup (65 g) sugar

1½ teaspoons ground cinnamon

½ stick (60 g) unsalted butter, plus extra for greasing

2 tablespoons slivered (flaked) almonds or raisins, or dried blueberries

confectioners' (icing) sugar, for dusting

cream or yogurt, to serve

large baking sheet

(serves 6)

1. Ask an adult to help you turn the oven on to 400°F (200°C) Gas 6. Rub the baking sheet with a little soft butter on a paper towel. If the phyllo (filo) dough is frozen, let it defrost before you use it. Do not unwrap the dough until you are ready to use it, because it will dry out and become crumbly.

2. Put the amaretti cookies in a plastic bag and tap them with a rolling pin until they have turned to crumbs inside the bag.

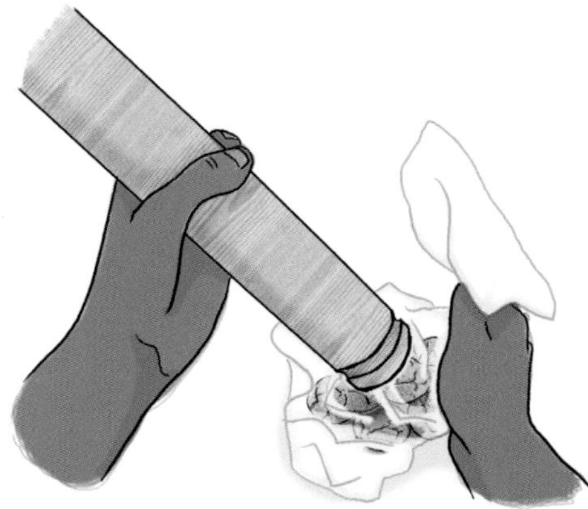

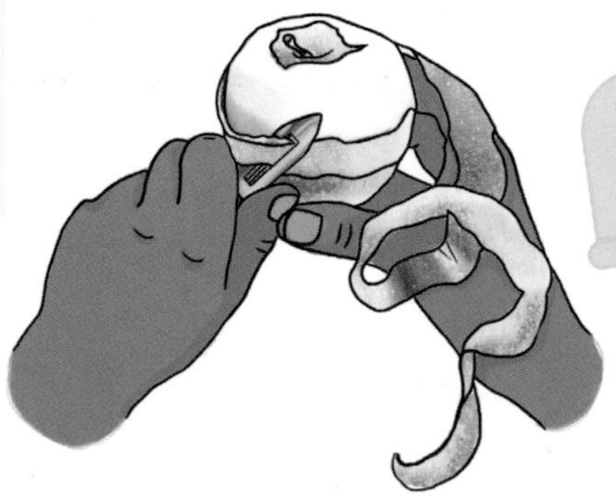

3. Now prepare the apples. First, use a potato peeler to peel them all.

4 Use a sharp knife to cut the apples into halves, then quarters. Remember to cut down onto a board and hold the apple with your hand in a bridge shape (see page 12). Ask an adult to help you carefully remove the cores by cutting a V shape into the center of each quarter. Finally, cut the apples into small pieces (see page 12).

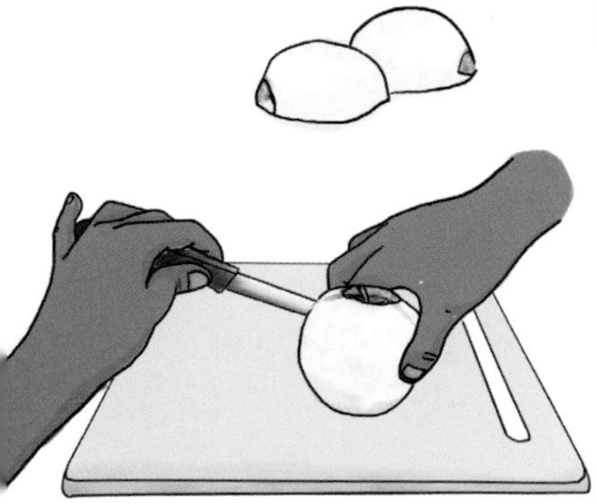

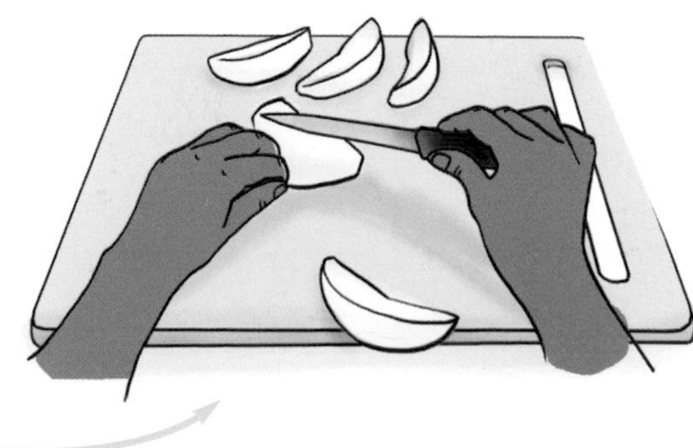

5 Mix the sugar and cinnamon together in a separate small bowl.

6 Ask an adult to help you melt the butter. Either put it in a small saucepan over the lowest possible heat, or put it in a microwave-proof dish and microwave on medium for about 25 seconds.

7 Unwrap the dough and separate the sheets. Put a large piece of baking parchment on the work surface and then lay the pastry sheets on top, overlapping the sheets to make a rectangle about 22 x 28 in. (56 x 71 cm), with a long side toward you. You need about 4–5 sheets.

8 Using a pastry brush, lightly brush about half the melted butter all over the dough.

9 Leaving a clear border of about 2 in. (5 cm) all around the edges, sprinkle the amaretti crumbs onto the pastry, then cover them with the pieces of apple. Sprinkle with the sugar and cinnamon mixture and then add the almonds or dried fruit.

10 Now the really fun part—rolling up the strudel! First, fold over the pastry borders along the two short sides then fold over the pastry border along the long side closest to you. Begin to roll up the strudel from this side, using the baking parchment to help you—but be careful not to roll the paper into the strudel. Don't worry if the pastry splits and the filling falls out, just push it all back together with your hands. Keep rolling until you have a long, thick sausage shape.

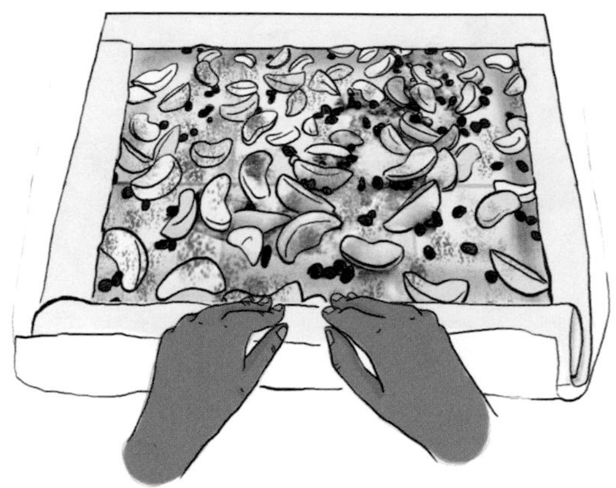

11 It will be difficult to lift the strudel on your own, so ask someone to help you transfer the roll to the buttered baking sheet—use a couple of spatulas to support it. You can lift it in its parchment to help if necessary. If the roll is too big for the size of your tray, you may have to curve the roll into a horseshoe shape. If it splits, press it back together again—it won't show when it's baked! Brush it all over with the rest of the melted butter.

12 Ask an adult to help you put the strudel into the preheated oven. Bake it for 35 minutes, or until golden brown.

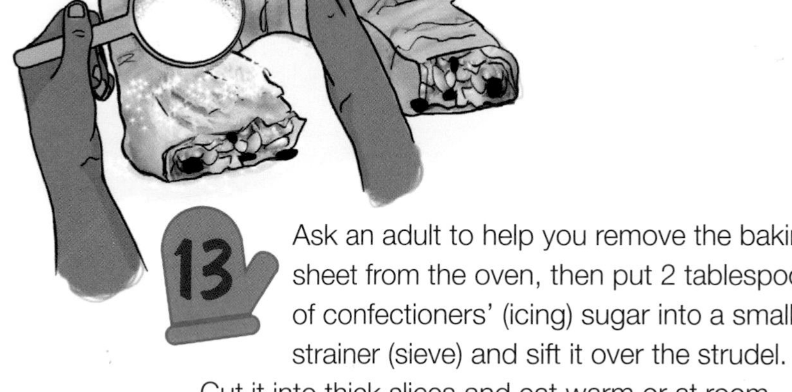

13 Ask an adult to help you remove the baking sheet from the oven, then put 2 tablespoons of confectioners' (icing) sugar into a small strainer (sieve) and sift it over the strudel. Cut it into thick slices and eat warm or at room temperature with cream or yogurt.

CRUNCHY, CRISPY apple strudel!

Toffee-apple tarts

These unusual little tarts are made with real toffees and they are a hit with everyone who makes (and eats) them. It's good to learn how to make pastry and we have given you the recipe here, but you can always cheat and use store-bought sweet pastry instead. And you don't even need to peel the apples!

You will need

For the sweet pastry:

1 stick (125 g) unsalted butter, chilled

1¾ cups (225 g) all-purpose (plain) flour

1 teaspoon sugar

1 egg

1–2 tablespoons cold water

For the filling:

about 6–8 eating apples

12 hard toffee candies

2 x 12-hole muffin pans

3 in. (7.5 cm) round cookie cutter

(makes 24)

1 To make the dough, tip the flour into a mixing bowl. Cut the butter into very small pieces with a round-bladed knife and then rub it into the flour, using your fingers and thumbs, until the mixture looks like fine crumbs (see page 9).

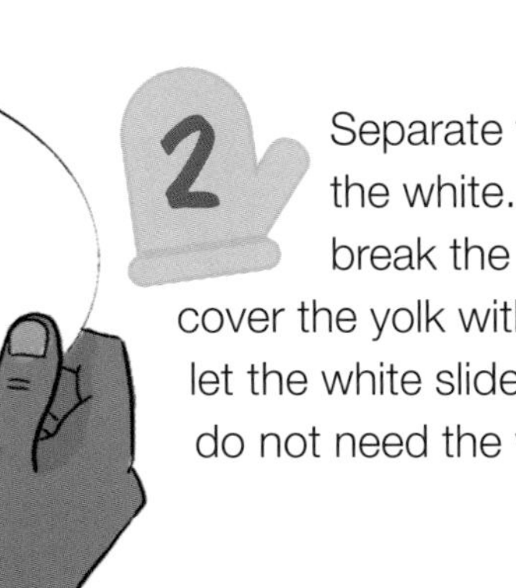

2 Separate the egg yolk from the white. To do this, carefully break the egg onto a plate, cover the yolk with an egg cup, and let the white slide off into a bowl. You do not need the white for this recipe.

3 Add the sugar, egg yolk, and water to the crumb mixture and stir with a round-bladed knife until the mixture comes together and you can form a ball with your hands. Wrap the dough in plastic wrap (clingfilm) and put it in the fridge for 30 minutes—this will make it easier to roll out.

4 Ask an adult to help you turn the oven on to 350ºF (180ºC) Gas 4. Put a little soft butter on a piece of paper towel and rub it around the inside of the muffin pans to grease them.

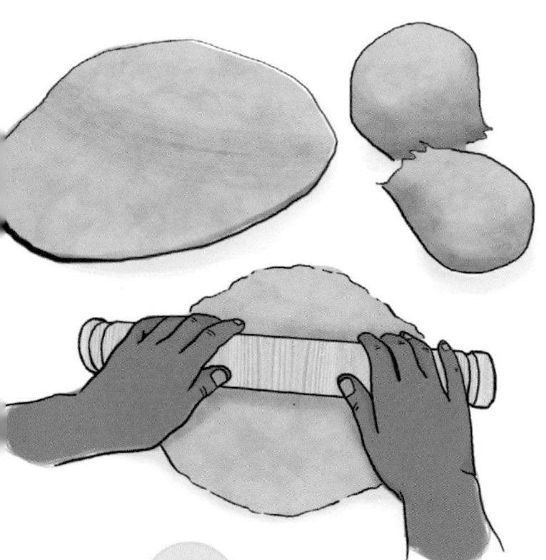

5 As it is easier to roll out smaller pieces of dough, break it into 4 pieces. Sprinkle a little flour on the work surface, then roll out the dough, one piece at a time, to about ¼ in. (5 mm) thick.

Sticky **TOFFEE APPLES** in a tart!

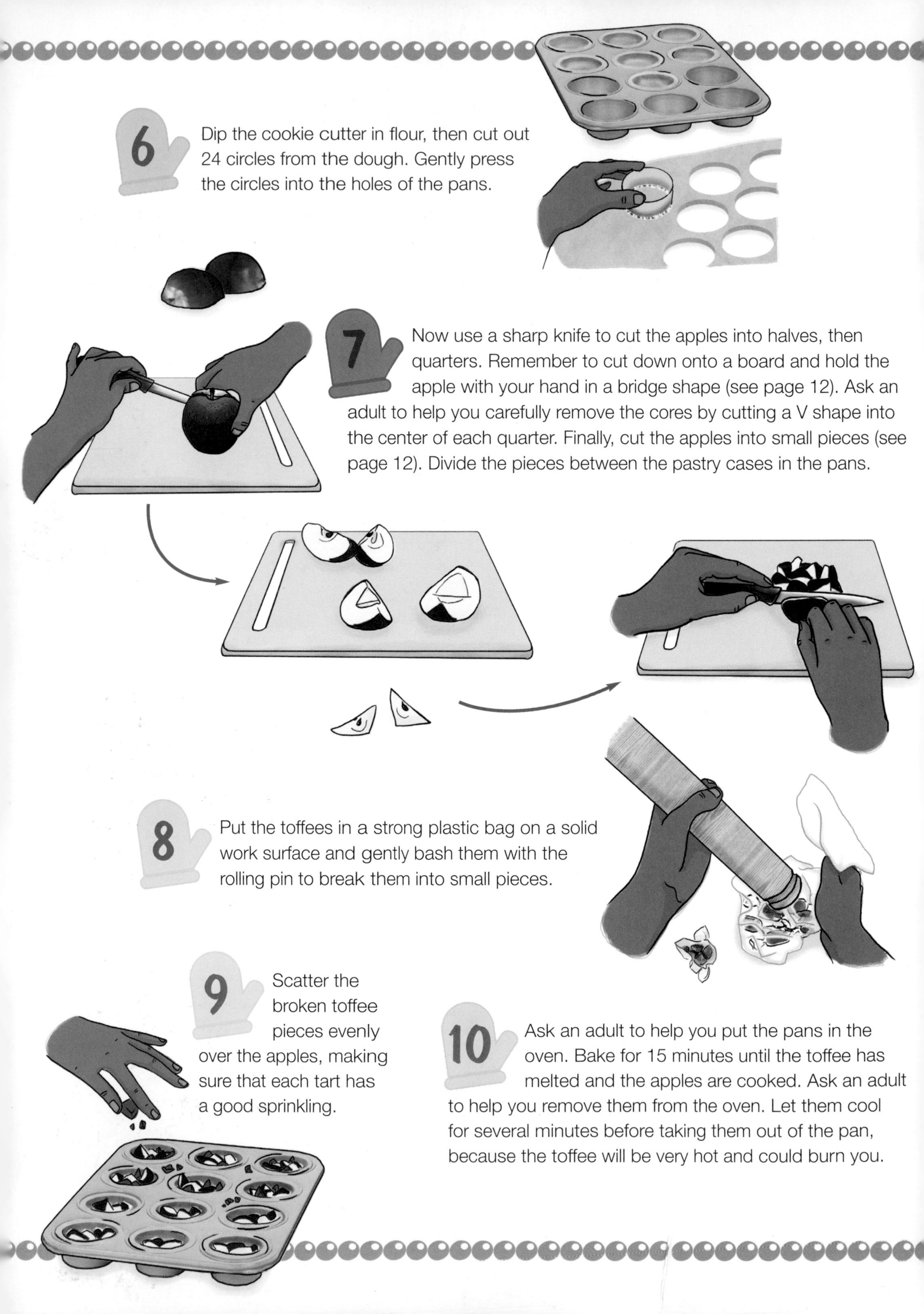

6 Dip the cookie cutter in flour, then cut out 24 circles from the dough. Gently press the circles into the holes of the pans.

7 Now use a sharp knife to cut the apples into halves, then quarters. Remember to cut down onto a board and hold the apple with your hand in a bridge shape (see page 12). Ask an adult to help you carefully remove the cores by cutting a V shape into the center of each quarter. Finally, cut the apples into small pieces (see page 12). Divide the pieces between the pastry cases in the pans.

8 Put the toffees in a strong plastic bag on a solid work surface and gently bash them with the rolling pin to break them into small pieces.

9 Scatter the broken toffee pieces evenly over the apples, making sure that each tart has a good sprinkling.

10 Ask an adult to help you put the pans in the oven. Bake for 15 minutes until the toffee has melted and the apples are cooked. Ask an adult to help you remove them from the oven. Let them cool for several minutes before taking them out of the pan, because the toffee will be very hot and could burn you.

Mini quiches

You can make the pastry for these yourself if you have the time or, if you want to make them quickly, use store-bought shortcrust pastry instead. You can try all sorts of different fillings—tuna and corn, chopped cooked bacon and cheese, broccoli and salmon. Or be a chef and invent your own filling!

You will need

1 lb (450 g) store-bought shortcrust pastry

1 small onion

1 small garlic clove (optional)

1 tablespoon olive oil

1 egg

⅓ cup (75 ml) heavy (double) cream

⅓ cup (75 ml) milk

2 skinless salmon fillets

Parmesan cheese

2 x 12-hole muffin pans

round cookie cutters to fit your muffin pan

(makes 18)

1 Ask an adult to turn the oven on to 400°F (200°C) Gas 6. Put a little butter on a paper towel and rub it around the inside of 18 holes in your muffin pans to grease them.

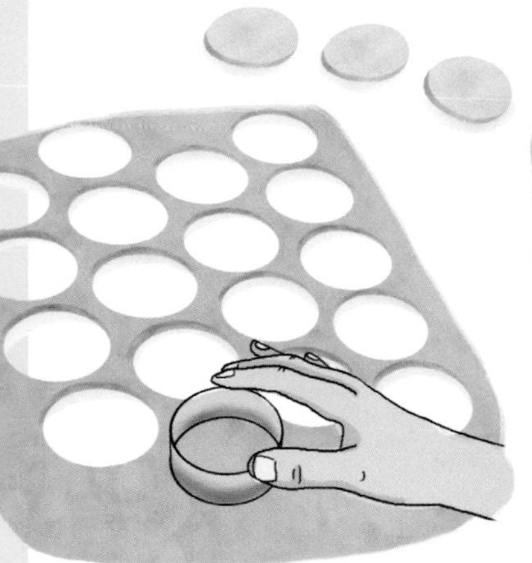

2 Sprinkle the work surface and your rolling pin with a little flour and roll the dough out to about ⅛ in. (3 mm) thick. Use the cookie cutter to cut out circles, cutting them as close together as possible. When you have cut as many as you can, gather the trimmings together and roll the dough out again. Make about 18 circles.

3 Lay the circles in the muffin pan holes and prick the bottom of each mini-quiche crust once with a fork. This will stop them from rising.

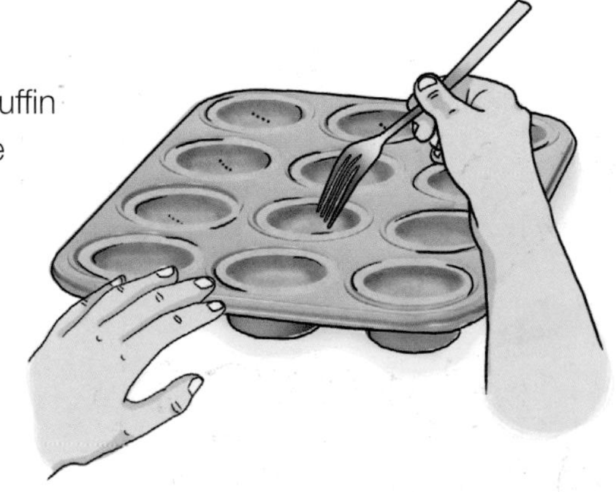

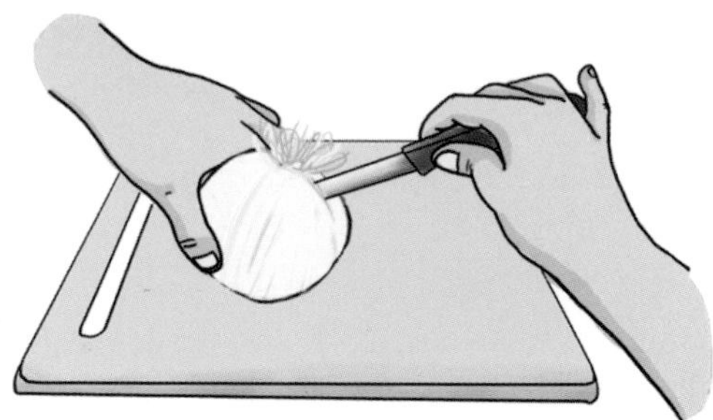

4 Ask an adult to put the pans in the preheated oven to bake for 5 minutes until the crust is a very pale golden color. Remove them from the oven and set them aside (don't take them out of the pan). Leave the oven on.

5 Now prepare everything you need for the filling. First the onion: peel off the papery outside skin of the onion and put the onion on a chopping board. Holding your hand in the bridge position (see page 12), cut the onion in half with a sharp knife (be very careful—onions are slippery and the knife can easily slip off). Lay each half flat on the board, trim off any hairy roots, and then cut into very small pieces.

6 If you are using garlic, peel the papery skin off a garlic clove and put the garlic into a garlic crusher, but don't it crush yet.

7 Ask an adult to put a skillet (frying pan) onto the stovetop (hob) on a medium heat. Add one tablespoon of olive oil and when it is hot, add the onion. Crush the garlic straight into the pan. Gently fry the onion and garlic for about 5 minutes, until the onion is soft. Take the pan off the heat and put it to one side to cool a little.

8 Put the salmon on the chopping board and use a sharp knife to cut it into small cubes. Grate the Parmesan cheese onto a plate using a fine grater—you will need a couple of handfuls.

9 Firmly tap the egg shell on the side of a measuring cup and pull the two halves apart with your fingertips. Pick out any pieces of shell. Add the cream and milk, and whisk together using a wire whisk.

10 Now fill the quiches: put a little salmon and a little cooled onion mixture in each pastry case, sharing it out equally. Pour in the egg mixture, until the cases are almost full. Sprinkle each with a little Parmesan cheese.

11 Ask an adult to put the pans into the oven and bake for 5–6 minutes until the quiches have puffed up, the top is slightly golden, and the egg mixture has set firm. Ask an adult to remove them from the oven and let them cool for a few minutes before taking them out of the pan.

PERFECT for a PICNIC!

CHAPTER TWO

SWEET TREATS

Choc-nut granola bars

You can pretend you are making something very healthy when you make these granola bars—there's lots of fruit, nuts, and oats in them—but they are also sweet, buttery, and covered in chocolate chips, making them perfect for a lunchbox treat!

You will need

¼ cup (30 g) whole almonds (optional)

1½ oz. (40 g) milk chocolate

candied (glacé) cherries (optional)

1 stick (125 g) unsalted butter

½ cup (100 g) light brown sugar

4 tablespoons light corn (golden) syrup

2 cups (190 g) rolled oats

½ cup (40 g) shredded (desiccated) unsweetened coconut

9-in (23-cm) square baking pan

baking parchment

(makes 12)

1 Ask an adult to turn the oven on to 350°F (180°C) Gas 4.

2 Prepare your pan. Put a little butter on a paper towel and rub it all over the inside of the baking pan to grease it. Then place the baking pan onto some baking parchment, draw around it, cut out the square, and fit it into the bottom of the pan.

3 If you are using almonds, carefully cut them into large chunks. Remember to use a sharp knife to cut down onto a board. Put them in a small bowl to use later. Now chop the chocolate into chunks and put that in a different bowl. If you are using them, cut the candied (glacé) cherries into small pieces and set aside.

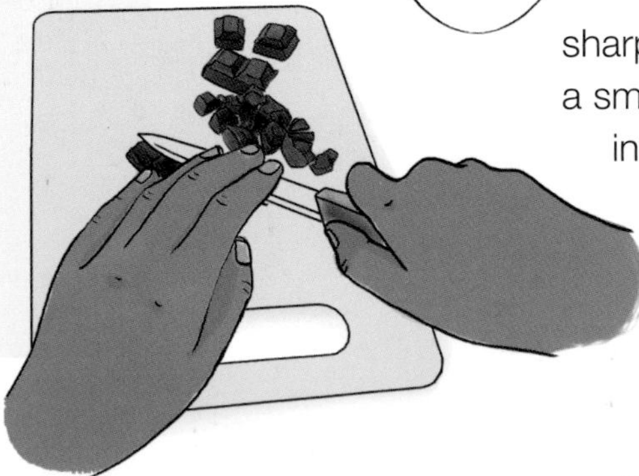

Chocolate, oats, AND MORE!

4

Put the butter, sugar, and corn (golden) syrup into a pan and ask an adult to help you place it on the stovetop (hob) over low heat and stir it until the butter has melted and the sugar has dissolved.

Remove the pan from the heat and stir the oats and coconut into the melted mixture.

Mix everything well, then spoon the oat mixture into the cake pan. Spread the mixture out and press it down evenly with the back of a spoon.

7 Scatter over the almonds and cherries (if you are using them), and press them lightly into the mixture with the back of a spoon.

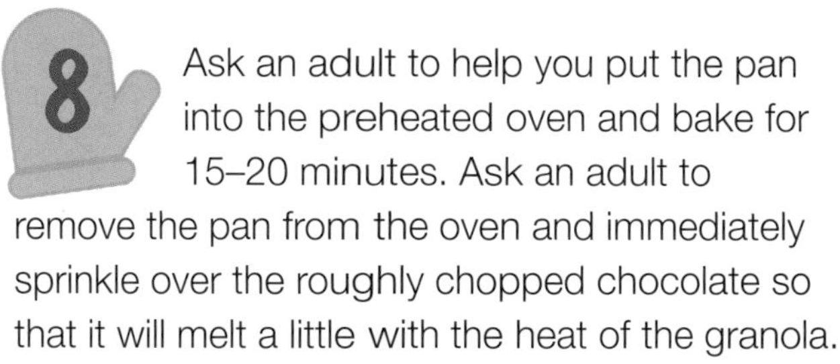

Ask an adult to help you put the pan into the preheated oven and bake for 15–20 minutes. Ask an adult to remove the pan from the oven and immediately sprinkle over the roughly chopped chocolate so that it will melt a little with the heat of the granola.

9 Mark the granola into bars or squares with a round-bladed knife while it is still warm, then let it cool before cutting through and removing the bars from the pan. These bars will last for 4 or 5 days in a sealed container.

Juicy fruit crisp

A meal always becomes special with a real homemade dessert. You can make your friends or relatives very happy with this one.

Ask an adult to turn the oven on to 375°F (190°C) Gas 5.

2 Put a little butter on a paper towel and rub it all over the inside of the baking dish to grease it.

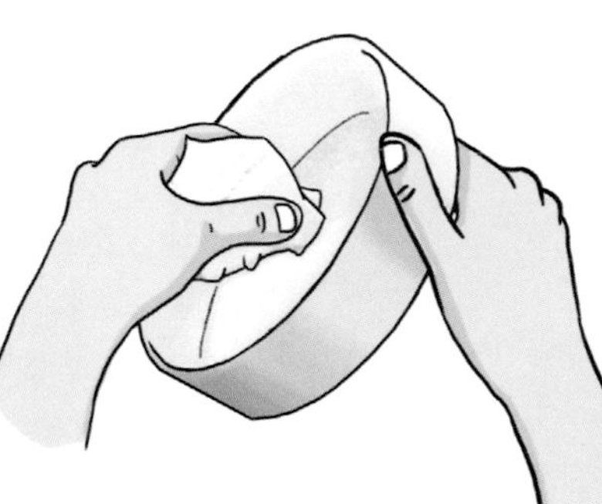

You will need

2 large Granny Smith apples or 2 medium pears

1⅔ cups (200 g) fresh or frozen raspberries, blueberries, or blackberries

2 tablespoons white or brown sugar

For the crisp topping:

1 cup (100 g) all-purpose (plain) flour

¾ stick (90 g) unsalted butter

⅓ cup (65 g) brown sugar

medium ovenproof baking dish

(serves 4)

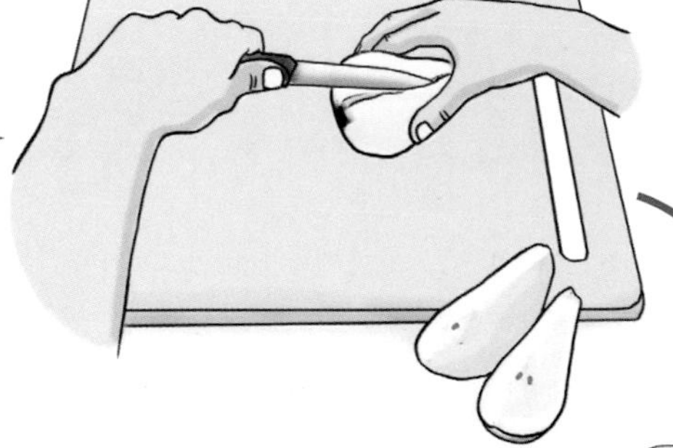

Prepare the apples or pears. Use a potato peeler to peel them all. Next, use a sharp knife to cut the fruit into halves, then quarters. Remember to cut down onto a board and hold the fruit with your hand in a bridge shape (see page 12). Ask an adult to help you carefully remove the cores by cutting a V shape into the center of each quarter. Finally, cut the fruit into small chunks (see page 12).

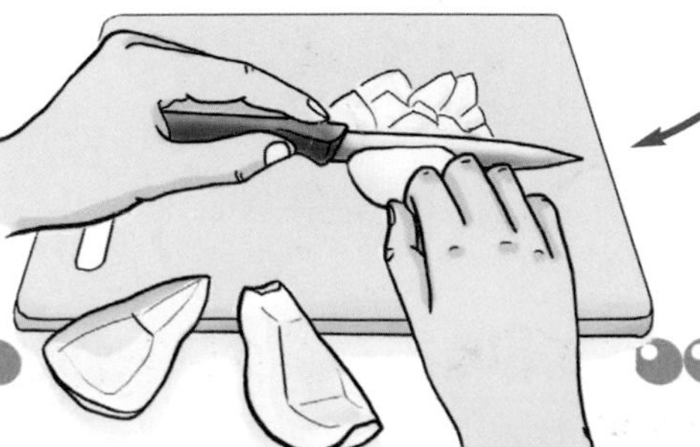

4 Put the fruit in the dish, then add the berries (you don't need to defrost them if they're frozen). Sprinkle with the sugar and toss gently until just mixed. You can use your fingers to do this. Spread the fruit evenly in the dish.

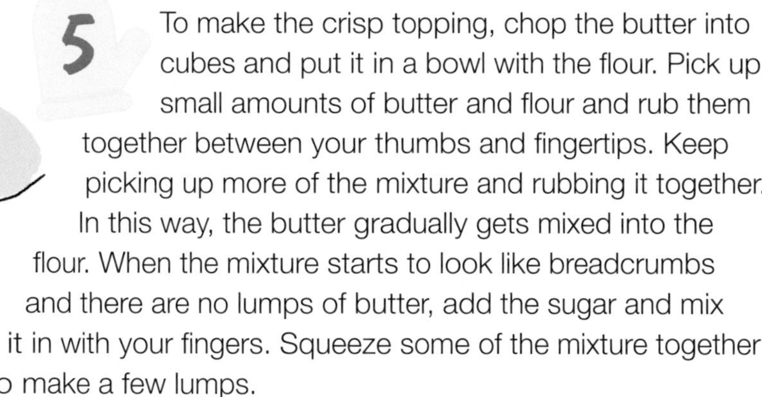

5 To make the crisp topping, chop the butter into cubes and put it in a bowl with the flour. Pick up small amounts of butter and flour and rub them together between your thumbs and fingertips. Keep picking up more of the mixture and rubbing it together. In this way, the butter gradually gets mixed into the flour. When the mixture starts to look like breadcrumbs and there are no lumps of butter, add the sugar and mix it in with your fingers. Squeeze some of the mixture together to make a few lumps.

6 Scatter the mixture over the fruit in the baking dish—don't press it down. Ask an adult to help you put the dish in the preheated oven and bake for 25 minutes, or until it is bubbling and golden on top.

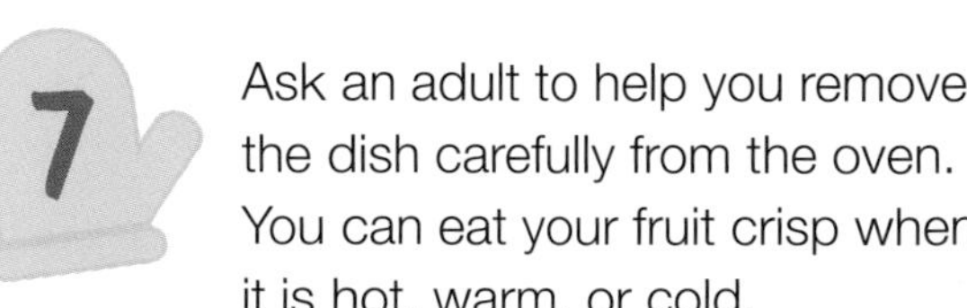

7 Ask an adult to help you remove the dish carefully from the oven. You can eat your fruit crisp when it is hot, warm, or cold.

Try this with a scoop of ICE CREAM!

Easter bunny cookies

These cute bunny cookies make wonderful gifts at Easter or can brighten up the tea table at a springtime birthday party. You can buy bunny cookie cutters from bakeware stores or online.

You will need

For the cookie dough:

2 cups (250 g) all-purpose (plain) flour

1¼ cups (140 g) self-rising (self-raising) flour

a pinch of salt

2 sticks (250 g) unsalted butter, at room temperature

⅔ cup (125 g) unrefined superfine (golden caster) sugar

1 egg

1 teaspoon vanilla extract

For the decoration:

1 lb (450 g) white fondant icing

confectioners' (icing) sugar, for dusting

pink and black writing icing

1 yd (1 m) each of blue and pink gingham ribbon

bunny cookie cutters (2 shapes if possible)

2 baking sheets

baking parchment

(makes 12)

1 Set a large strainer (sieve) over a mixing bowl. Pour the two flours and salt into the strainer and then sift them into the mixing bowl. Put the bowl to one side.

2 Put the soft butter and sugar in another large mixing bowl and beat them together with a wooden spoon until the mixture is soft, creamy, and pale. (If an adult is helping, you could use an electric beater.)

3 Carefully break the egg onto a plate and use an egg cup to separate the yolk from the white (see page 29). You do not need the white for this recipe.

4 Add the egg yolk and vanilla extract to the creamed butter mixture and mix all the ingredients together well.

5 Add the flour and stir everything together until all the flour is mixed in and the mixture forms a ball of dough. Stop mixing as soon as the flour is all mixed in.

6 Put the dough in a sealable plastic food bag, or wrap it in plastic wrap (clingfilm), and chill it in the refrigerator for 1–2 hours. When the dough is well chilled, cut some baking parchment to cover your baking sheets and ask an adult to turn the oven on to 400°F (200°C) Gas 6.

7 Sprinkle a clean work surface with flour and roll out the cookie dough until it is about ¼ in. (5 mm) thick.

8 Use your bunny cutters to cut out as many bunnies as you can, cutting them as close together as possible. When you have cut out the first batch, gather all the trimmings together, roll them out again, and cut out some more.

9 Lay all the cookies on the baking sheets and ask an adult to help you put them into the preheated oven for 12–16 minutes, until the cookies are golden. Ask an adult to take them out of the oven and let them cool on a wire rack.

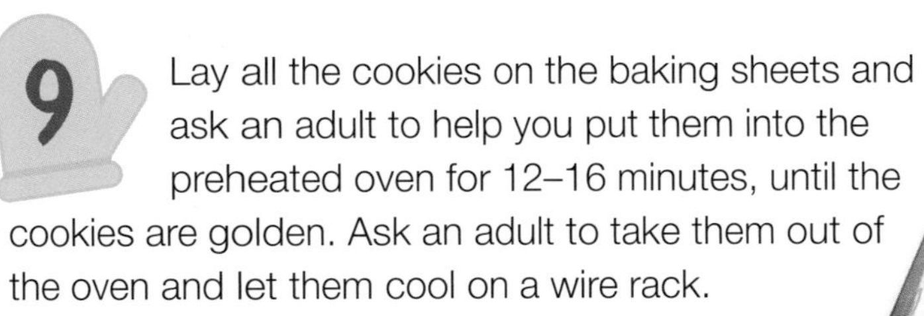

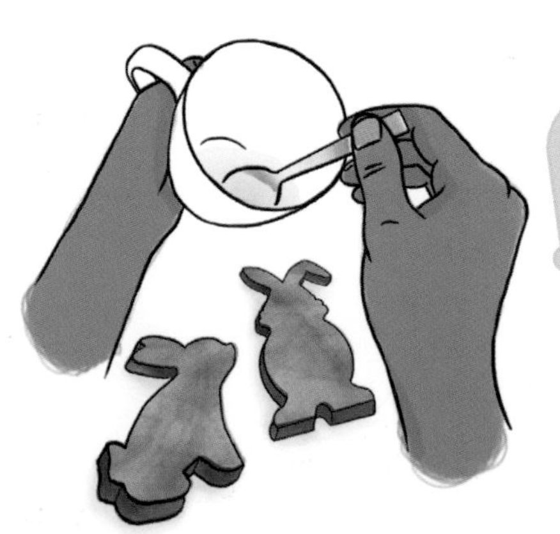

10 To decorate the bunnies, first make a little "edible glue" by putting two tablespoons of sugar in a cup and adding two tablespoons of warm water. Stir them together.

11 Sprinkle a little confectioners' (icing) sugar onto a clean work surface. Roll out the fondant icing until it is about ¼ in. (5 mm) thick. Each time you roll the icing, lift it, turn it a little, and sprinkle on a little more confectioners' sugar to stop it sticking to the work surface. Sprinkle a little confectioners' sugar onto the rolling pin too, if that sticks.

Cute BUNNIES for Easter!

12

Brush a little of your "sugar glue" onto the first cookie. Use the cookie cutter to cut out an icing shape to match the bunny and carefully stick it on. Do the same for the rest of the bunnies.

Use writing icing to draw on eyes, noses, tails, and whiskers. To make the fluffy tails, squeeze lots of dots close together. When the writing icing has set, loosely tie a piece of ribbon into a bow around each bunny's neck.

Yummy brownie squares

Scrumptious, deep chocolatey brownies! Top them with a delicious chocolate buttercream frosting and decorate them with colorful candies.

You will need

For the brownies:

⅔ cup (100 g) walnut or pecan pieces

1½ sticks (175 g) unsalted butter

8 oz. (250 g) bittersweet (dark) chocolate

1¼ cups (250 g) superfine (caster) sugar

3 eggs

1 teaspoon vanilla extract

1 cup plus 2 tablespoons (150 g) all-purpose (plain) flour

a pinch of salt

colorful candies and sprinkles

For the chocolate buttercream:

6 oz. (175 g) bittersweet (dark) chocolate

1 stick (125 g) unsalted butter

½ cup (125 ml) milk

1 teaspoon vanilla extract

1¾ cups (225 g) confectioners' (icing) sugar, sifted

9-in (23-cm) square baking pan

baking parchment

baking sheet

(makes 16)

1 Ask an adult to turn the oven on to 350ºF (180ºC) Gas 4.

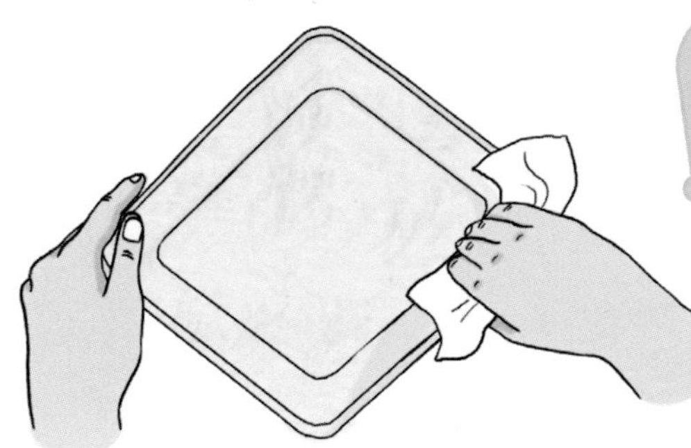

2 Prepare your pan. Put a little butter on a paper towel and rub it all over the inside of the baking dish to grease it. Then place the baking pan onto some baking parchment, draw round it, cut out the square, and fit it into the bottom of the pan.

3 Spread out the walnuts or pecans on a baking sheet and ask an adult to help you put them in the preheated oven. Toast them for 5 minutes and then ask an adult to help you remove them from the oven. Let them cool.

4 Break or cut the chocolate into small pieces. Cut the butter into small cubes. (Remember always to cut downward onto a board.)

5 Put the chocolate and butter in a heatproof bowl and ask an adult to help you set it over a saucepan of barely simmering water to melt. (You could melt the chocolate in a microwave instead—see page 11.) Stir until the butter and chocolate are smooth and mixed together. Let the mixture cool slightly.

6 Take another bowl and carefully break the eggs into it. Pick out any pieces of shell and then add the sugar and vanilla extract. Use a fork or a wire whisk to whisk them together for 2–3 minutes until they are light and foamy.

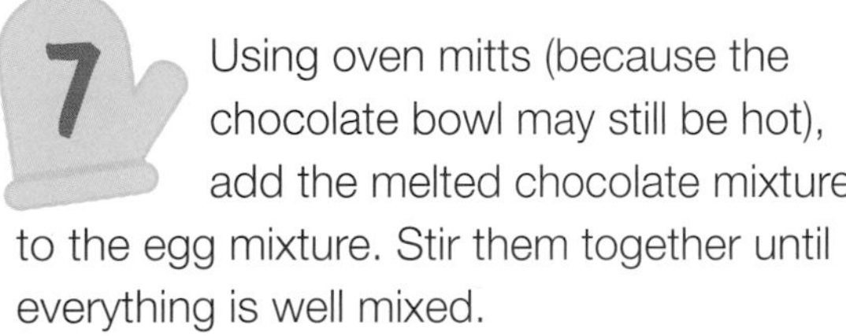

7 Using oven mitts (because the chocolate bowl may still be hot), add the melted chocolate mixture to the egg mixture. Stir them together until everything is well mixed.

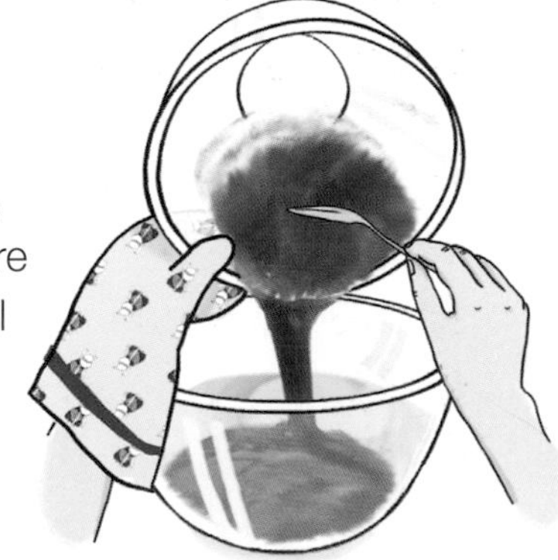

8 Set a strainer (sieve) over the bowl and sift the flour, baking powder, and salt into the mixture. Fold them in using a metal spoon (see page 10) and then stir in the nuts.

9 Pour the batter into the baking pan and spread it out evenly.

10 Ask an adult to help you put the pan on the middle shelf of the preheated oven. Bake for about 30 minutes. Ask an adult to help you remove the pan from the oven. Let it cool.

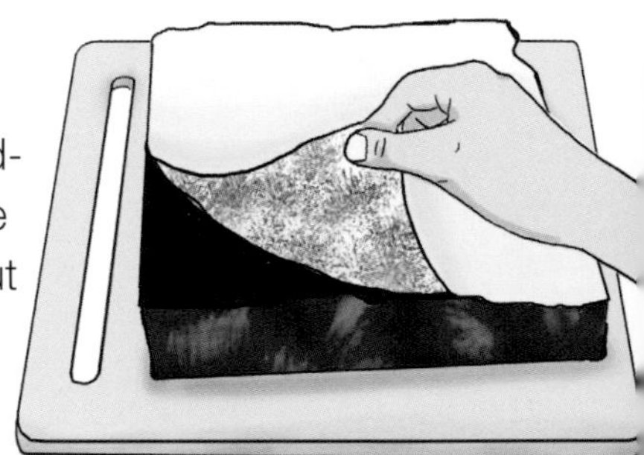

11 When the brownies are cool, slide a round-bladed knife around the inside edge of the pan to loosen the cake and then turn it out onto a board. Remove the parchment paper from the bottom and turn the cake the right side up.

12 Now make the chocolate buttercream frosting. Just like you did when you were making the brownies, break or cut the chocolate into small pieces and cut the butter into small cubes, and ask an adult to help you to melt them together (see steps 4 and 5 on the previous pages).

13 Put the milk, vanilla, and sugar into a mixing bowl and whisk them until they are smooth. Pour the melted chocolate mixture into the mixing bowl and stir until the mixture is smooth and thick. You may need to leave this somewhere cool for 30 minutes until it is thick enough to spread.

14 Spread the buttercream thickly over the brownies. Decorate with your favorite candies and sprinkles and then cut the brownies into squares.

Little peanut butter cakes

Chocolate and peanut butter go really well together, which makes these little cakes a big hit at any party. Remember to label them clearly so anyone who has an allergy to peanuts can avoid them.

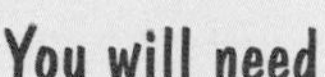

You will need

4 tablespoons smooth peanut butter

2 tablespoons (30 g) unsalted butter, very soft

⅔ cup (125 g) packed soft light brown sugar

2 US extra-large (UK large) eggs

½ teaspoon vanilla extract

1 cup (125 g) all-purpose (plain) flour

1 teaspoon baking powder

4 tablespoons milk

½ cup (100 g) bittersweet (dark) chocolate chips

confectioners' (icing) sugar, for dusting

12-hole muffin pan

paper muffin cups

heart stencil on page 126

paper

(makes 12)

1 Ask an adult to turn the oven on to 350°F (180°C) Gas 4. Put a paper muffin cup into each of the holes in the muffin pan.

2 Put the peanut butter and ordinary butter in a large mixing bowl. Add the sugar and beat with a wooden spoon. (You could ask an adult to help you do this in a food processor instead).

3 Break the eggs into a small bowl. Pick out any pieces of shell, then add the vanilla extract and mix it all up with a fork.

Add a little **STENCIL** magic!

4

Add a tablespoon of the egg mixture to the butter mixture in the mixing bowl and beat well. Keep adding it, one tablespoon at a time, beating well after each addition, until the egg mixture is all mixed in.

5

Set a strainer (sieve) over the mixing bowl. Pour the flour and baking powder into the strainer and sift onto the mixture.

Add the milk and then fold everything together with a metal spoon (see page 10). When they are well mixed, add the chocolate chips and fold them in, too.

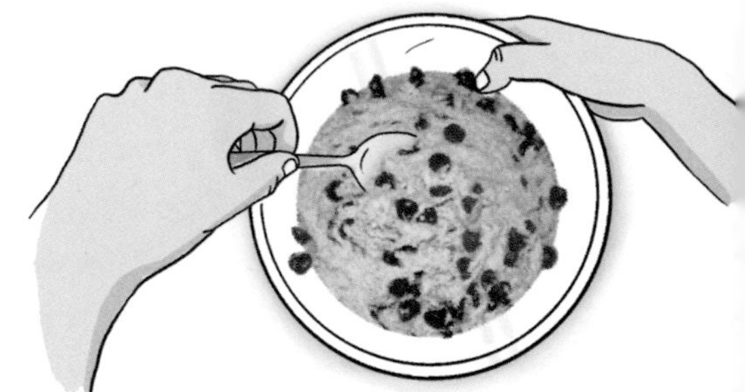

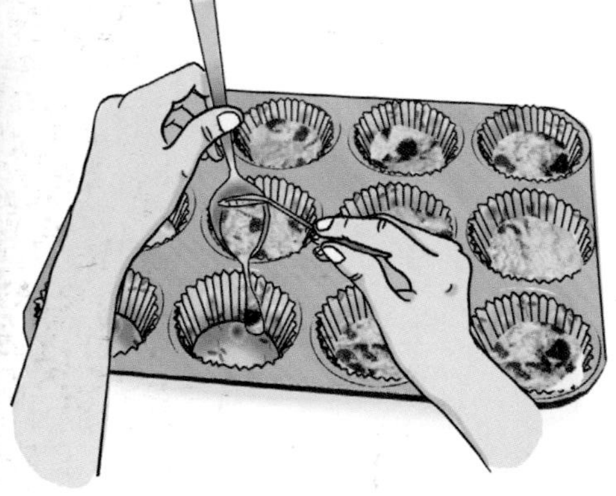

7

Spoon the mixture into the paper muffin cups until they are about one-third full. Ask an adult to help you put the cakes in the preheated oven to bake for 15–20 minutes, until they are a light golden color. Ask an adult to help you remove them from the oven and let them cool on a wire rack.

8

To stencil a decoration on your cake, trace the heart template on page 126 onto a piece of paper. Using a sharp pair of scissors, make a hole in the center of the heart and then cut out from here around the heart to leave a heart-shaped hole. Hold this stencil on top of each cake and use a pastry brush dipped in milk or water to brush inside the heart where you want the confectioners' (icing) sugar to stick. Be careful not to make it too wet.

9 Put some confectioners' (icing) sugar in a small strainer (sieve) and sift it over the cakes. Next, shake each cake and the sugar shape will appear. Magic! When completely cold, store your cakes in an airtight container and eat them within 4 days.

Carrot muffins

If you're always being told to eat up your vegetables, these are the cakes for you! You won't even notice the carrots in them because they taste so good.

You will need

8 oz. (250 g) carrots

3 eggs

⅔ cup (125 g) packed soft light brown sugar

7 tablespoons vegetable oil

1 cup plus 2 tablespoons (150 g) self-rising (self-raising) flour

1 teaspoon apple pie spice or a mixture of ground cinnamon and nutmeg

¾ cup (65 g) shredded (desiccated) coconut (if you don't like coconut add more dried fruit instead)

½ cup (75 g) mixed dried fruit, such as raisins, cranberries, and blueberries

12-hole muffin pan

12 paper or silicone muffin cups

(makes about 12)

1 Ask an adult to help you turn the oven on to 350°F (180°C) Gas 4. Put the muffin cups into the holes in the muffin pan.

2 Use a sharp knife to cut both ends off all the carrots. Remember to cut down onto a chopping board. Now peel the carrots with a potato peeler like this: hold a carrot at one end and rest the other end on the chopping board. Starting halfway down, run the potato peeler down the carrot, away from your body. Be careful—the peeler is sharp! Turn the carrot a little and peel the next strip. Keep turning and peeling until it is peeled all the way around. Now turn the carrot up the other way and hold the other end while you peel the other half.

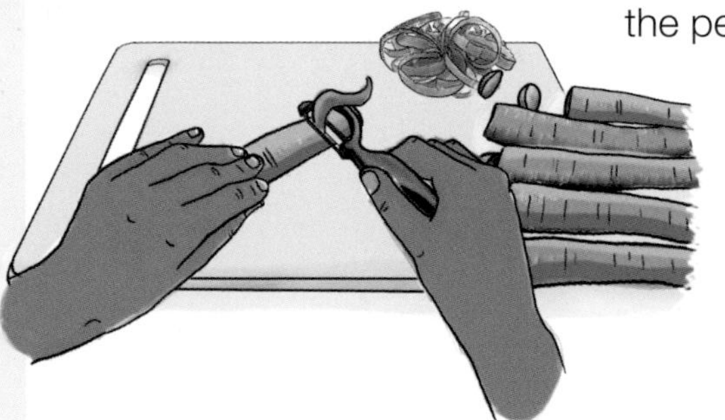

3 Grate the carrots using the smaller holes on the grater—you want the carrots to be grated finely so that they mix into the cake mixture easily.

The BEST WAY TO EAT carrots!

4 Break the eggs into a large mixing bowl, pick out any pieces of shell, and then beat them with a fork until they are mixed together and a little frothy.

5 Add the sugar to the mixing bowl and whisk together with a wire whisk until the mixture is thick and creamy. (You could ask an adult to help you do this with an electric beater.)

6 Keep whisking and add the oil, a little at a time, until it is all mixed in.

7 Add the flour, apple pie spice (or cinnamon and nutmeg), coconut, dried fruit, and grated carrot to the bowl, and stir with a wooden spoon until everything is mixed in.

8 Spoon the mixture into the paper cups in the muffin pan, so that they are about one third full, putting an equal amount into each one.

9 Ask an adult to help you put the muffin pan in the preheated oven and bake for 12–14 minutes, or until the muffins are baked and golden.

10 Ask an adult to help you take the muffin pan out of the oven and let it cool a little. Then take the muffins out of the pan and put them on a wire rack to cool down until you are ready to eat them.

Raspberry shortbread

This recipe is from Scotland and uses Scottish ingredients—shortcake, raspberries, and rolled oats. It builds up in layers into a heavenly sweet, sticky, crunchy bar.

You will need

For the base:

1½ cups (200 g) all-purpose (plain) flour

¼ cup (25 g) cornstarch (cornflour)

a pinch of salt

⅓ cup (60 g) superfine (caster) or granulated sugar

scant 1½ sticks (150 g) unsalted butter, chilled

For the filling:

1¼ cups (150 g) fresh raspberries

½ cup (125 g) raspberry jelly (jam)

For the topping:

½ cup (40 g) rolled oats (porridge oats)

3 tablespoons light brown muscovado sugar

7-in. (18-cm) square cake pan

(makes 9)

1 Ask an adult to help you turn the oven on to 350°F (180°C) Gas 4. Put a little soft butter on a piece of paper towel and rub it around the inside of the cake pan to grease it.

2 Put the flour, cornstarch (cornflour), salt, and sugar into a mixing bowl and mix together. Cut the butter into very small pieces and rub it into the flour using your fingers and thumbs until the mixture looks like fine crumbs (see page 9). (If an adult is helping, you can do this using a food processor.)

3 Take out one-third of the mixture and put it into another bowl to keep for the topping. Put the rest of the mixture into the greased pan. Spread it out evenly and then press it down with your hand to make a firm, even layer of shortbread. Use your fingers to press it down in the corners and at the edges. If it seems sticky, dip your fingers in a little flour.

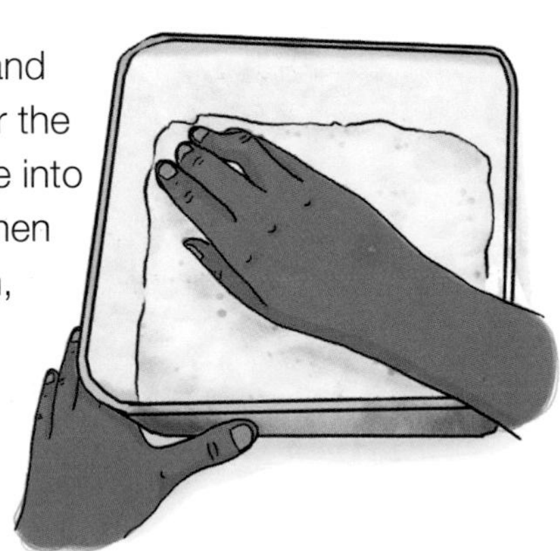

4 Ask an adult to help you put the shortbread base in the preheated oven to bake for 10 minutes, then remove it from the oven. Let it cool while you make the filling and topping. Leave the oven on.

5 Put the fresh raspberries and jelly (jam) into a bowl and mix gently so you don't break up the raspberries. Put to one side.

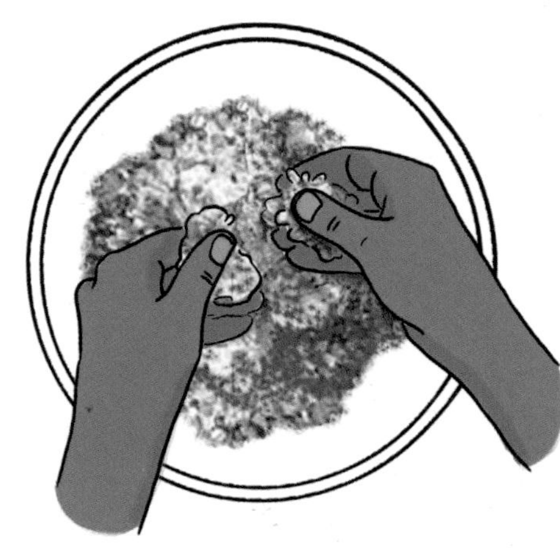

6 For the topping, put the rest of the shortbread crumbs back into the mixing bowl. Add the oats and brown sugar, mix well with your fingers, and then squeeze the mixture with your hands so it comes together into large crumbs.

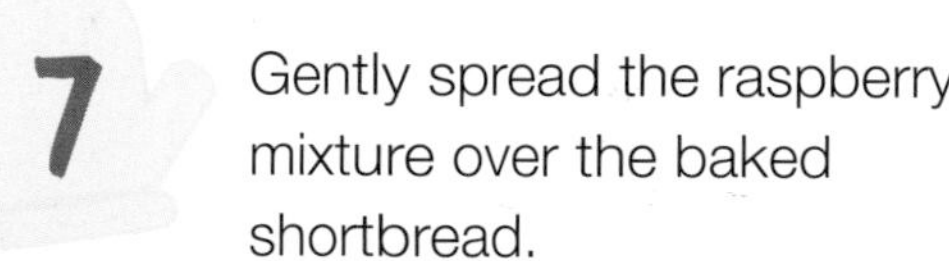

7 Gently spread the raspberry mixture over the baked shortbread.

8 Scatter the oat topping evenly over the raspberries.

9 Ask an adult to help you put the pan back into the oven and bake for another 15–20 minutes, until it is a light golden brown and bubbling around the edges. Ask an adult to help you remove the pan from the oven and let it cool on a wire rack.

10 When completely cold, run a round-bladed knife around the inside of the pan, then cut the shortbread into 9 squares. Lift each square out with a cake slice. Eat it as a snack or serve with custard as a dessert. You can store your shortbread in an airtight container, but eat it within 4 days.

A crunchy SCOTTISH TREAT!

Chocolate kisses

Who knows where these sweet little chocolate cookies got their name? With a delicious layer of raspberry cream sandwiched between them, little kisses are quick and easy to make and taste scrumptious.

You will need

For the chocolate kisses:

1¾ sticks (200 g) unsalted butter, softened

½ cup (100 g) natural cane sugar or granulated sugar

1 teaspoon vanilla extract

2 cups (250 g) self-rising (self-raising) flour

2 tablespoons cocoa powder

For the raspberry cream:

a few ripe raspberries (about 4–5)

scant stick (100 g) unsalted butter, softened

⅔ cup (100 g) confectioners' (icing) sugar

2 baking sheets

(makes 25)

1 Ask an adult to help you turn the oven on to 350°F (180°C) Gas 4. Put a little butter on a piece of paper towel and rub it all over the baking sheets to grease them.

2 Put the soft butter, sugar, and vanilla extract in a mixing bowl and mix well with a wooden spoon until the mixture becomes fluffy and paler in color.

3 Add the flour and cocoa powder to the bowl and mix well with your hands until it comes together into a dough.

Make chocolate kisses for SOMEONE YOU LOVE!

4 Pull off a small piece of dough and roll it into a ball about the size of a walnut. Then flatten it a little. Put it onto a baking sheet. Roll another one—make sure it is about the same size—and keep going until you have about 50 cookies (make sure you have an even number).

5 Ask an adult to help you put the baking sheets in the oven. Bake for 6–7 minutes and then ask an adult to help you take the sheets out of the oven. Let them cool.

6 For the raspberry cream, put the berries into a small bowl and mash them with a fork. Add the butter and sugar and mix them all together with the fork.

7 Spread a little cream onto a cookie and sandwich it together with another cookie. Keep going until you have 25 kisses.

Baked Alaska

A hot, meringue-topped cake with a freezing ice cream surprise inside—that's what a Baked Alaska is, and what could be more fun to make and eat! For a quicker way to make this, you could use a ready-made sponge cake for the base.

You will need

For the sponge cake:

¾ cup plus 2 tablespoons (115 g) all-purpose (plain) flour

1 teaspoon baking powder

½ cup plus 1 tablespoon (115 g) superfine (caster) sugar

1 stick (125 g) unsalted butter, very soft

½ teaspoon vanilla extract

2 US extra-large (UK large) eggs

1 tablespoon milk

To finish:

1 pint (500 ml) strawberry ice cream (or your favorite flavor)

4 eggs

1 cup plus 2 tablespoons (225 g) superfine (caster) sugar

1½ cups (150 g) raspberries

round cake pan, 8 in. (20 cm) diameter

baking parchment

baking sheet

(makes 1 large cake)

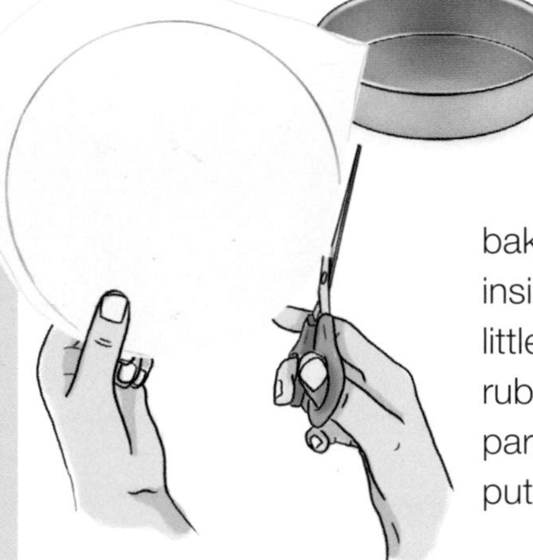

1 Ask an adult to help you turn the oven on to 350°F (180°C) Gas 4. Put the pan on the baking parchment and draw around it. Cut just inside the line to make a disk of paper. Put a little soft butter on a piece of paper towel and rub it around the inside of the cake pan. Fit the parchment disk into the base of the pan and put it to one side.

2 Put a strainer (sieve) over a mixing bowl and sift the flour and baking powder into the bowl. Stir in the sugar, then add the very soft butter and vanilla.

3 Break the eggs into a small bowl. Pick out any pieces of shell, then add the milk and lightly beat them with a fork to break them up. Pour the eggs into the mixing bowl. Beat all the ingredients with a wooden spoon (or ask an adult to help you use an electric hand-held beater), until the mixture is very smooth and light. Spoon the mixture into the prepared cake pan and spread it evenly around the pan.

4

Ask an adult to help you put the sponge cake in the preheated oven to bake for about 25 minutes, until it is a light golden brown. To test if the cake is baked, ask an adult to help you remove it from the oven and gently press it in the middle. If it springs back it is baked; if there is a dimple, then bake for 5 minutes more. Ask an adult to help you remove the sponge from the oven. Leave it for 2 minutes, then run a round-bladed knife around the inside of the pan and carefully turn out the cake onto a wire rack. Leave it to cool completely.

5

When the cake is cold, remove the ice cream from the freezer and leave it until it is soft enough to scoop out easily. Put the sponge cake onto a baking sheet, then scoop or spoon the ice cream on top and spread it out to make an even layer using a palette knife. Put the whole thing back into the freezer and leave it until the ice cream is very firm—at least 1 hour, but you can leave it in the freezer for up to 3 days.

6

When you are ready to finish the Alaska, ask an adult to help you turn the oven on to 425°F (220°C) Gas 7. Then separate the egg whites from the yolks. To do this, carefully break one egg at a time onto a plate, place an egg cup over the yolk, and let the white slide off into a very clean mixing bowl (see page 29). You do not need the yolks for this recipe, so put them into another bowl to use for something else.

7 Stand the bowl on a damp cloth to keep it from wobbling as you whisk the eggs. If you can, ask an adult to help you use an electric beater at this stage, it will be much quicker and easier, but you can whisk by hand. Whisk the egg whites until they turn into a stiff white foam. You'll know if you have whisked enough when you lift out the whisk and there are sharp little peaks of white standing up in the bowl.

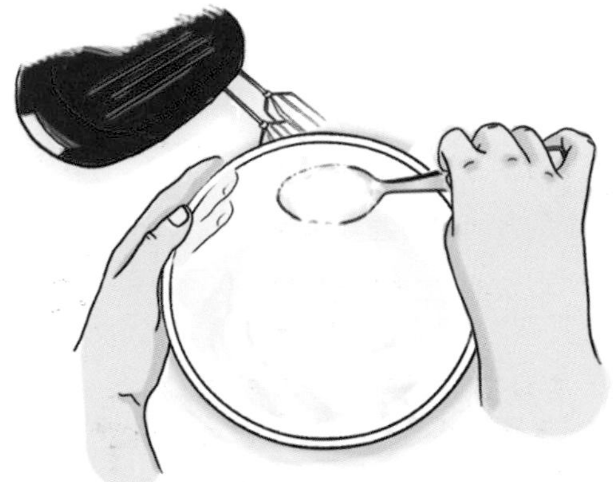

8 Now add 2 tablespoons of the superfine (caster) sugar and whisk it into the egg white, then add two more and whisk again. Keep going until you have whisked in all the sugar and have made a stiff, glossy meringue.

9 For the next stages you need to work really quickly so that the ice cream doesn't melt. First, check that the oven is really hot then remove the sponge and ice cream from the freezer. Quickly arrange the raspberries on top of the ice cream.

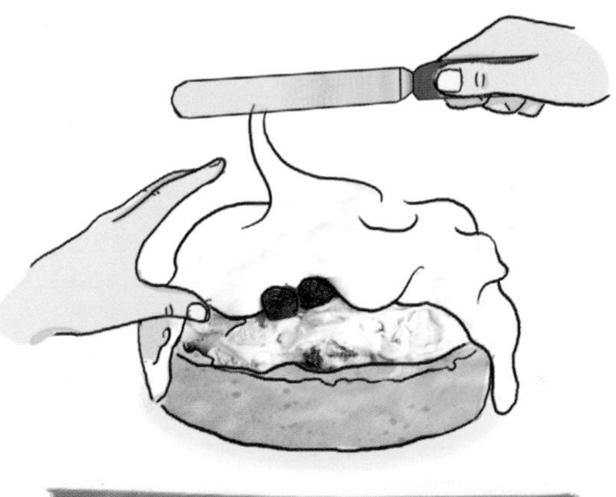

10 Now quickly cover the whole thing with the meringue, spreading it all over the top and sides of the cake, right down to the baking sheet. Make a few peaks in the topping. The meringue stops the ice cream from melting, so there must be no holes or gaps!

11 Ask an adult to help you put the Alaska in the oven to bake for just 4–5 minutes, until it is lightly browned. Any longer and the ice cream will melt. Serve immediately!

Chocolate swirl cake

For this cake, two different flavors and colors are swirled together to make lovely patterns. It is very pretty when you slice it, and you could always add a few drops of food coloring to the vanilla mix to make the colors even more dramatic!

You will need

2 oz. (50 g) bittersweet (dark) chocolate, chopped

1½ cups (175 g) all-purpose (plain) flour

1 rounded teaspoon baking powder

1½ sticks (175 g) unsalted butter, softened

1 cup (200 g) superfine (caster) sugar

4 eggs

2 teaspoons vanilla extract

2 tablespoons milk

1 quantity Chocolate Buttercream (see page 54)

chocolate chips and sprinkles

2-lb. (1-kg) loaf pan, or 2 x 1-lb. (500-g) loaf pans

Makes 1 large or 2 small loaf cakes

1 Ask an adult to turn the oven on to 350°F (180°C) Gas 4. Put a little butter on a piece of paper towel and wipe it around the inside of the pan to grease it. Put the loaf pan on the baking parchment and draw around the base. Take the pan off and make the rectangle longer at both ends so that, when you cut it out, the parchment is long enough to cover the base and stretch up both ends of the pan. Cut it out just inside the line and fit it into the pan (it should stick to the butter).

2 Ask an adult to help you put the chocolate in a heatproof bowl over a pan of barely simmering water, making sure the bottom of the bowl doesn't touch the water. Stir very carefully until melted or melt the chocolate in the microwave (see page 11).

3 Put a strainer (sieve) over a mixing bowl and sift in the flour and baking powder together.

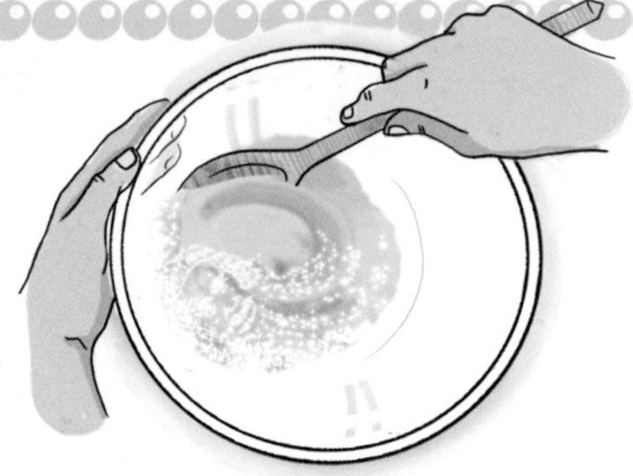

4 Put the butter and sugar in another bowl and beat them together with a wooden spoon until they are pale and fluffy. (If an adult is helping, this is quicker and easier to do with an electric beater.)

5 Firmly tap each egg on the side of a third bowl and pull the two halves apart with your fingertips. Pick out any pieces of shell. Whisk them up and then gradually add them, a tablespoonful at a time, to the butter and sugar. Each time you add some egg, mix it in really well before you add any more. Scrape down the side of the bowl with a rubber spatula from time to time, especially if you are using an electric beater. Add the vanilla and mix it in.

6 Tip the sifted flour and baking powder into the batter and mix until smooth. Stir in the milk.

7 Spoon half of this mixture into the melted chocolate and mix it in until smooth.

8 With a large spoon, drop alternate spoonfuls of vanilla and chocolate batter into the prepared loaf pan. When you have used up all the batter, give the pan a sharp tap on the work surface to level the mixture.

9

Now the really fun part! To create the swirly, marbled effect, drag the blade of a round-bladed knife through the mixture with a cutting action, going in different directions to create swirls. Don't do this too much or it will all just mix together without the pretty patterns.

10 Ask an adult to help you put the pan on the middle shelf of the preheated oven. Bake for about 40–45 minutes, or until a toothpick pushed into the middle of the cake comes out clean. Ask an adult to help you take the cake out of the oven. Let it cool for 15 minutes. Loosen the sides with a round-bladed knife, then carefully lift it out of the pan, by holding the ends of the paper. Put it onto a wire rack to cool completely.

11 Make some Chocolate Buttercream (see page 54) and spread it all over the top of the cold cake. Decorate it with assorted chocolate chips and sprinkles.

CHAPTER THREE

DELICIOUS DOUGH

Tomato pesto rolls

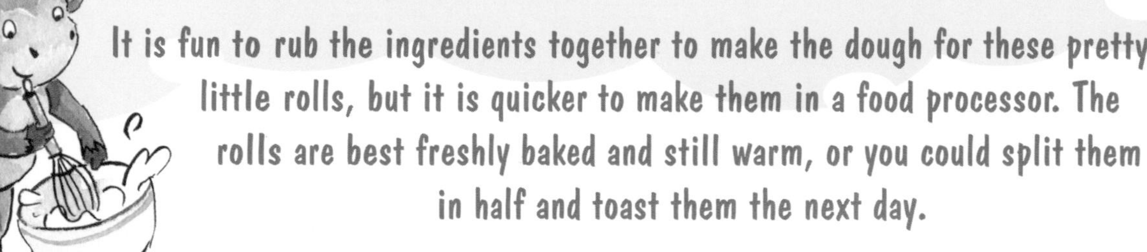

It is fun to rub the ingredients together to make the dough for these pretty little rolls, but it is quicker to make them in a food processor. The rolls are best freshly baked and still warm, or you could split them in half and toast them the next day.

You will need

4 cups (500 g) self-rising (self-raising) flour

½ teaspoon salt

1 cup (225 g) natural cottage cheese

a small handful of fresh basil leaves

1 US extra-large (UK large) egg

about ⅔ cup (150 ml) milk

5 cherry tomatoes

2 tablespoons pesto (or olive oil)

baking sheet

baking parchment

(makes 10 small rolls)

1 Ask an adult to turn the oven on to 375°F (190°C) Gas 5. Cut a piece of baking parchment to fit the baking sheet and sprinkle it with a little flour. Put it to one side.

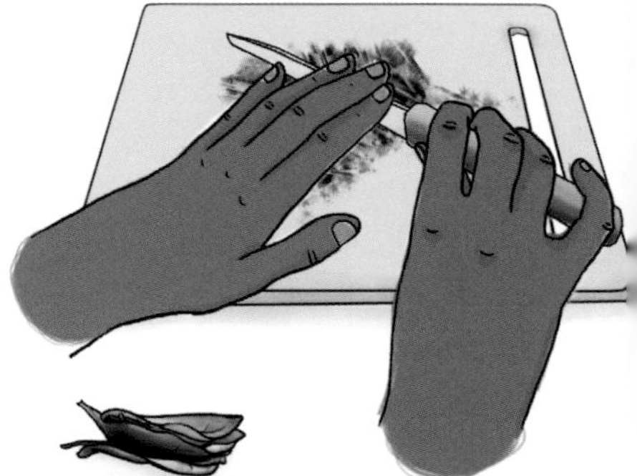

2 Count out ten basil leaves and put them to one side. If you are making the rolls by hand, tear or chop up the rest of the basil leaves, carefully using a sharp knife and remembering to cut down onto a board (see page 12). You won't need to chop the basil if you are using a food processor.

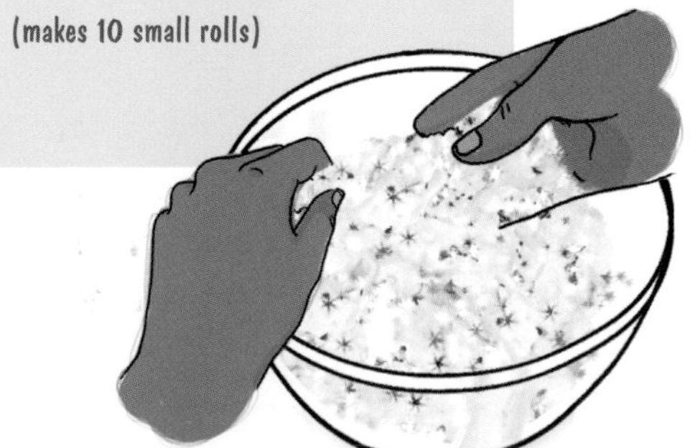

3 Put the flour, salt, cottage cheese, and basil into a mixing bowl and, using your fingers and thumbs (see page 9), rub the cheese into the flour until everything is mixed together and looks like crumbs (or ask an adult to help you do this in a food processor).

4 Break the egg into another bowl, pick out any pieces of shell, then add the milk and beat them together with a fork.

5 Add the egg mixture to the flour and cheese, stir it with a wooden spoon until it is mostly mixed in and then use your hands to gather it all together into a ball. If there are dry crumbs and the dough feels hard and dry, add a splash more milk.

(If you are using a food processor, ask an adult to help you run the machine and pour in the egg/milk mix through the feed tube. Stop the processor when the ingredients have come together to make a ball of soft dough. If there are dry crumbs and the dough feels hard and dry, add a little more milk.)

Will your tomatoes **POP** out of your rolls?

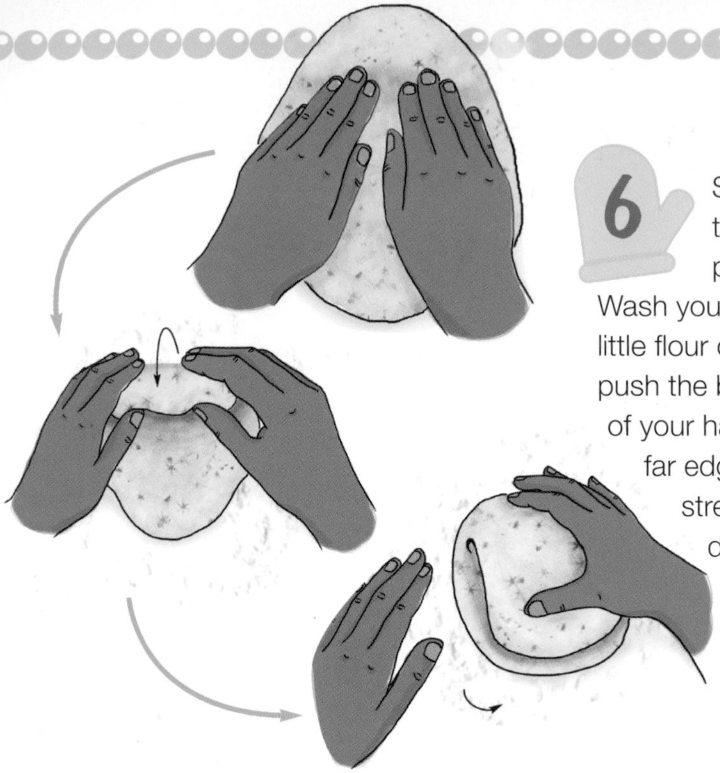

6 Sprinkle a little flour over the work surface and turn out the dough (ask an adult to help you remove the processor blade if you are using a food processor). Wash your hands if they are sticky, dry them, and then dust a little flour over them. Now gently knead the dough. To do this, push the ball of dough down and away from you with the heel of your hand, stretching and flattening it as you push. Fold the far edge toward you. Turn the ball around half a turn and stretch the dough out again. Fold and turn again. Keep doing this until the dough is silky smooth and stretchy.

7 Divide the dough into 10 equal pieces and roll each piece into a ball. Arrange the balls slightly apart on the baking sheet. Push a deep hole into the center of each one with your finger or thumb.

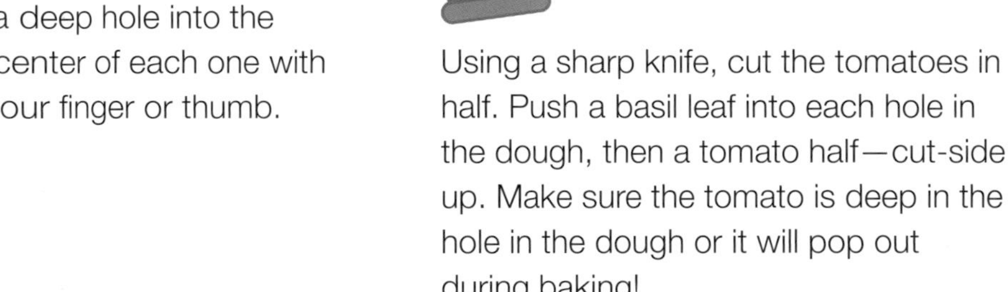

8 Using a sharp knife, cut the tomatoes in half. Push a basil leaf into each hole in the dough, then a tomato half—cut-side up. Make sure the tomato is deep in the hole in the dough or it will pop out during baking!

9 Use a pastry brush to brush the top of each roll with pesto or olive oil.

10 Ask an adult to help you put the rolls in the preheated oven and bake them for about 20 minutes, until they are golden brown. Ask an adult to help you take the baking sheet out of the oven and put it on a wire rack. Let the rolls cool for at least 10 minutes before you eat them.

Scandinavian buns

These buns are traditionally served on St Lucy's Day, December 13th, in Sweden, where they call them "lussekatter." They are normally made into a backward "S" shape, but you could make them into any shape you like—why not try simple animal shapes with raisins for eyes? Making dough with yeast is always magical because you can watch it rise and fill with bubbles as the yeast begins to work.

You will need

- 1 cup (250 ml) milk
- a good pinch of saffron strands
- 4–4¾ cups (500–600 g) strong (bread) flour
- 1 package (¼ oz./7 g) active dry yeast
- ½ teaspoon salt
- ¼ cup (50 g) sugar
- 3 tablespoons (45 g) unsalted butter, softened
- ⅓ cup (100 ml) sour cream, at room temperature
- 1 egg
- 24 raisins

2 baking sheets

baking parchment

(makes 12)

1. Cut pieces of baking parchment to fit the baking sheets.

2. Ask an adult to help you heat the milk in a small saucepan or in the microwave (see page 11), until it is hot but not boiling. Turn off the heat and drop the saffron strands in and let them soak in the hot milk for 10 minutes to flavor it and turn it yellow.

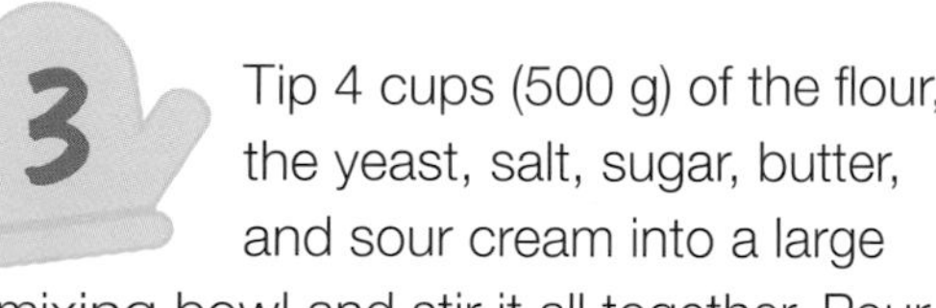

3. Tip 4 cups (500 g) of the flour, the yeast, salt, sugar, butter, and sour cream into a large mixing bowl and stir it all together. Pour in the warm milk and use your hands to mix it into the other ingredients until you get a dough. If the dough feels very dry and hard to mix, add a little more milk. If it is very sticky, add a little more flour.

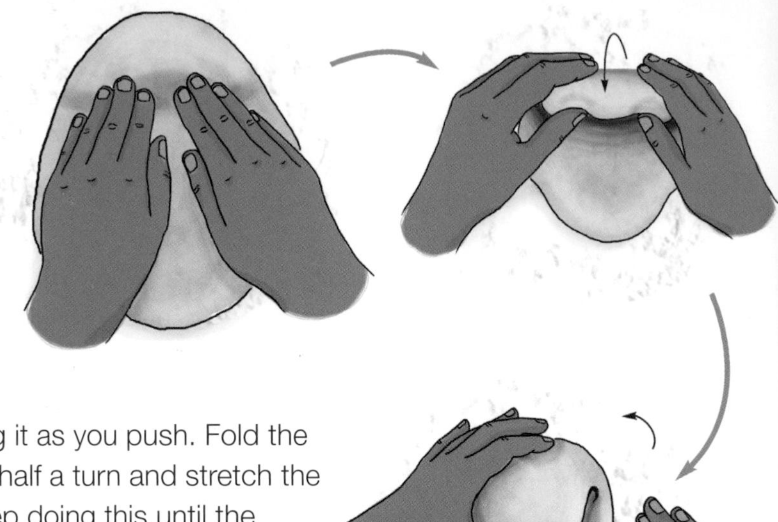

4 Sprinkle a little flour onto a clean work surface. Shape the dough into a ball, tip it out onto the work surface, and begin to knead it. To do this, push the ball of dough down and away from you with the heel of your hand, stretching and flattening it as you push. Fold the far edge toward you. Turn the ball around half a turn and stretch the dough out again. Fold and turn again. Keep doing this until the dough is silky smooth and stretchy—this will take up to 7 minutes and you may need to add more flour if the dough is too sticky.

5 Shape the dough into a neat ball again. Wash and dry the bowl and put the dough back into it. Cover the bowl tightly with plastic wrap (clingfilm) and put it in a warm place for the dough to rise. It needs to double in size, which will take about an hour or longer if you haven't got anywhere warm to leave it.

6 Tip the dough onto the floured work surface and knead it again for 1 minute. Divide it into 12 equal pieces. Roll each piece into an 8-in. (20-cm) long sausage and twist into a backward "S" shape. Place 6 of the buns on one of the baking sheets and the other 6 on the other sheet.

7 Pour a little oil onto a paper towel and use it to wipe over two large pieces of plastic wrap. Use the wrap to cover the baking sheets loosely (oiled-side down). Let the buns rise again for a further 30 minutes in a warm place.

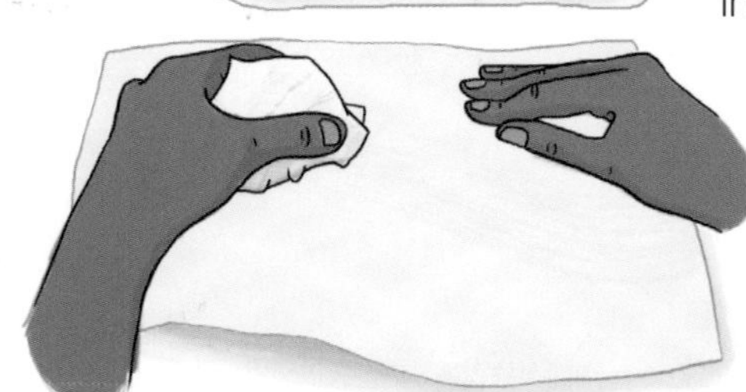

8 About 10 minutes before the buns are ready to be baked, ask an adult to turn the oven on to 375°F (190°C) Gas 5.

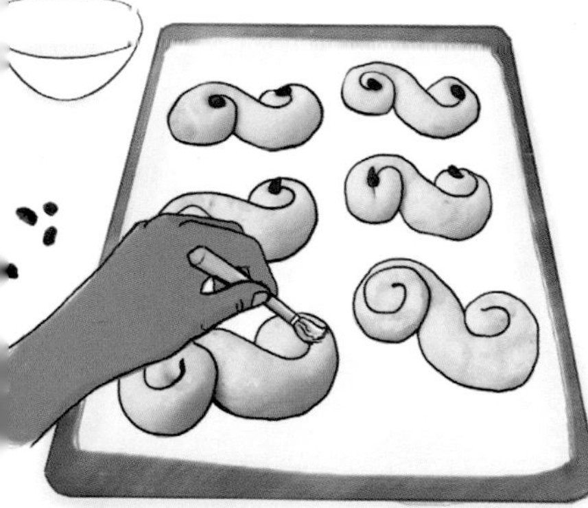

9 Break the egg into a small bowl, pick out any pieces of shell, and then beat it with a fork. Using a pastry brush, brush the buns lightly with the beaten egg and push a raisin into each end of the buns, in the center of the swirl.

10 Ask an adult to help you put the baking sheets on the middle shelf of the preheated oven. Bake for about 12–15 minutes, until well risen, shiny, and deep golden brown.

Saffron **BREAD** for a special feast!

Mini pizzas

If you've never made pizza, you've been missing out! It's lots of fun because you can make them any size or shape you like and choose all your favorite toppings.

1 Ask an adult to turn the oven on to 400ºF (200ºC) Gas 6. Pour a little olive oil onto a piece of paper towel and rub it over the baking sheets to stop the pizzas sticking.

2 To make the pizza bases, set a strainer (sieve) over a large mixing bowl. Tip the flour, sugar, baking soda, and salt into the strainer and sift into the bowl.

You will need

For the pizza bases:

3 cups (400 g) all-purpose (plain) flour

1 teaspoon sugar

1 teaspoon baking soda (bicarbonate of soda)

1 teaspoon salt

½ teaspoon dried oregano

1½ cups (350 ml) buttermilk (see page 10)

For the topping:

14-oz. (400-g) can chopped tomatoes

1 tablespoon tomato paste (purée)

1 tablespoon olive oil

1 teaspoon dried oregano

1 garlic clove

10 oz. (300 g) mozzarella cheese

choice of topping, such as pitted olives, slices of pepperoni or ham, sliced red or green bell pepper, or mushrooms

sea salt and freshly ground black pepper

2 large baking sheets

(makes 4 medium pizzas)

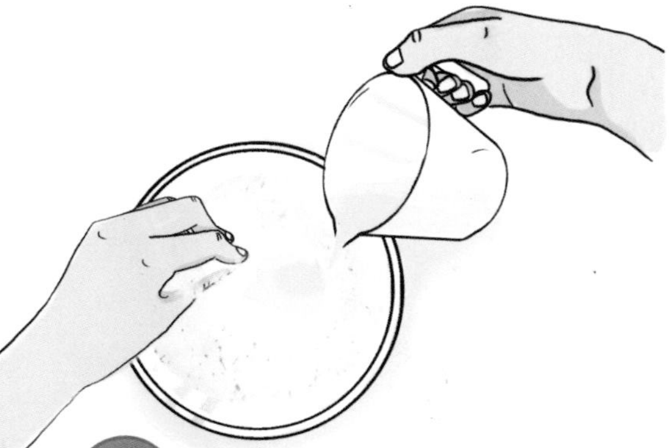

3 Stir in the oregano and then make a hole in the center of the flour and pour in the buttermilk. Using one hand, start to mix the flour into the liquid, then gradually work all the flour into the dough to make a soft and slightly sticky mixture. If there are dry crumbs, and it is hard to work all the flour into the dough, add 1 tablespoon of buttermilk or milk. If the dough is really sticky and feels wet, work in more flour, one tablespoon at a time.

4 Sprinkle a little flour over the work surface. When the dough comes together in a ball, tip it out of the bowl onto the work surface. Knead the ball of dough with both hands by squashing and squeezing it for 1 minute, or until it looks smooth.

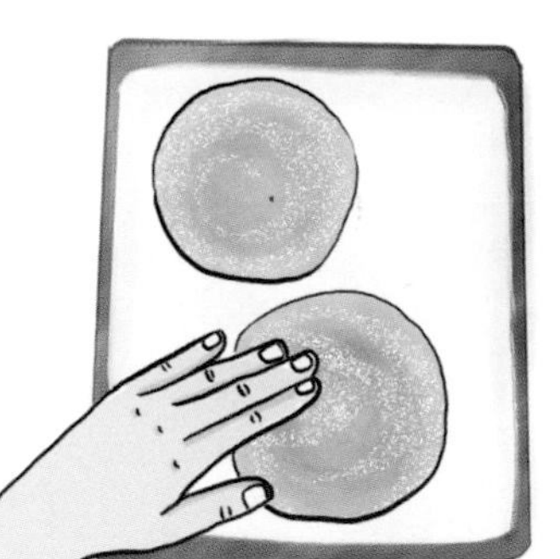

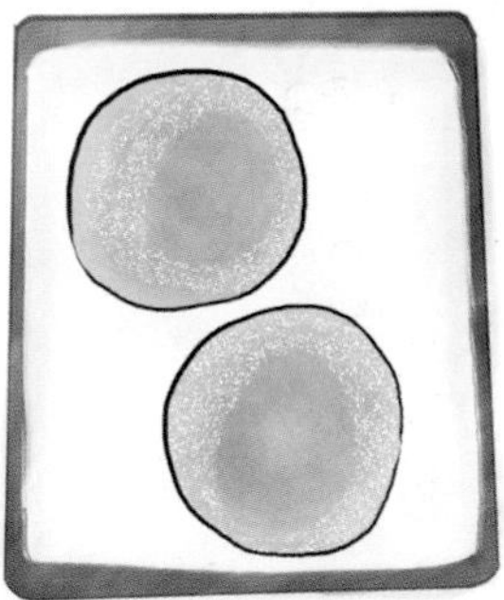

5 Divide the dough into 4 equal pieces and shape each piece into a ball. Rub flour onto your hands, then gently pat out each piece of the dough into a circle about 7 in. (13 cm) across. Set the circles slightly apart on the prepared baking sheets.

PERFECT pizzas for a PARTY!

6 To make the pizza topping, set a large strainer (sieve) over a bowl, then tip the can of tomatoes into the strainer and let them drain for a couple of minutes.

7 Ask an adult to help you use a food processor or blender for the next stage. First, peel the garlic clove, then tip the tomatoes into the food processor (the juice drained off can be saved for soups or sauces) and add the tomato paste, olive oil, oregano, garlic clove, and a pinch of salt and pepper. Blend the tomato mixture for just a few seconds to make a lumpy sauce. Tip the mixture into a bowl.

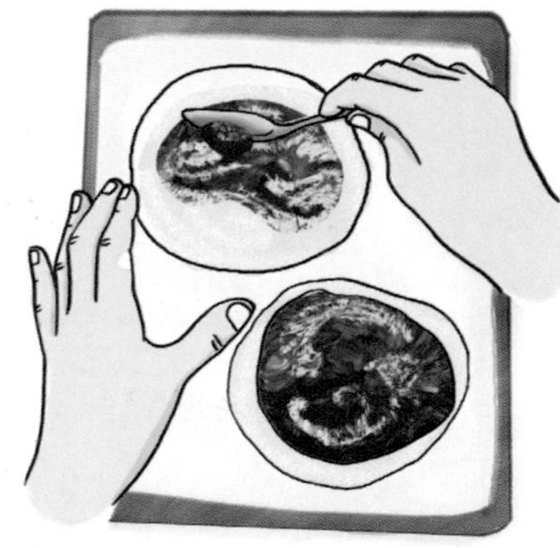

8 Spoon 2 tablespoons of the tomato topping onto the middle of each pizza base. Spread the tomato mixture over the base, leaving a 1-in. (2.5-cm) border of uncovered dough all around the edge.

Slice the mozzarella or pull it into long shreds. Arrange the pieces on top of the tomato sauce on the pizzas.

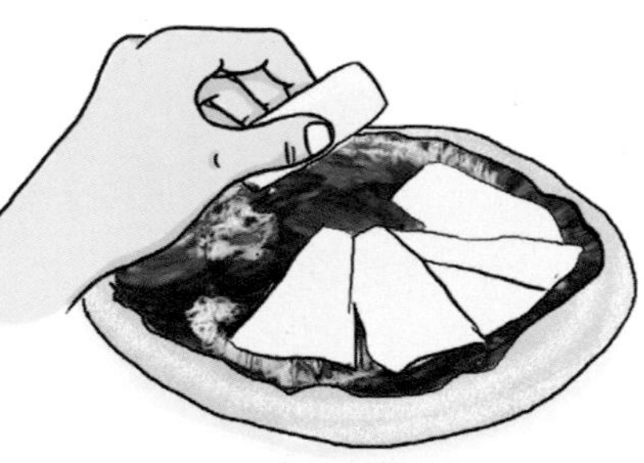

Finally, add as many extra toppings as you like.

11 Ask an adult to help you put the pizzas in the preheated oven and bake them until they are light golden and bubbling—about 15–18 minutes.

Ask an adult to help you carefully remove the pizzas from the oven, but let them cool for a couple of minutes before eating—the melted cheese can burn your mouth.

Sticky cinnamon buns

These buns use yeast to make a bread dough, but they are much richer than normal bread, because you add eggs and butter and milk. The dough is rolled up with sugar, cinnamon, and pecans or raisins then cut into slices—this makes pretty spiral buns. Eat them warm from the oven for a taste of perfection!

You will need

For the dough:

4 cups (500 g) unbleached white bread flour

1 package (¼ oz./7 g) or 2½ teaspoons active dry yeast

1 teaspoon salt

3 tablespoons superfine (caster) or granulated sugar

1⅓ cups (300 ml) milk

1 US extra-large (UK large) egg, at room temperature

3 tablespoons (45 g) unsalted butter, very soft

For the filling:

2 tablespoons (30 g) butter, very soft

1 teaspoon ground cinnamon

4 tablespoons soft light brown sugar

½ cup (60 g) pecan pieces or raisins

baking sheet

(makes 12)

1 Put the flour in a large mixing bowl. Add the yeast, salt, and sugar and mix everything together with your hand. Make a hole in the center of the flour mixture.

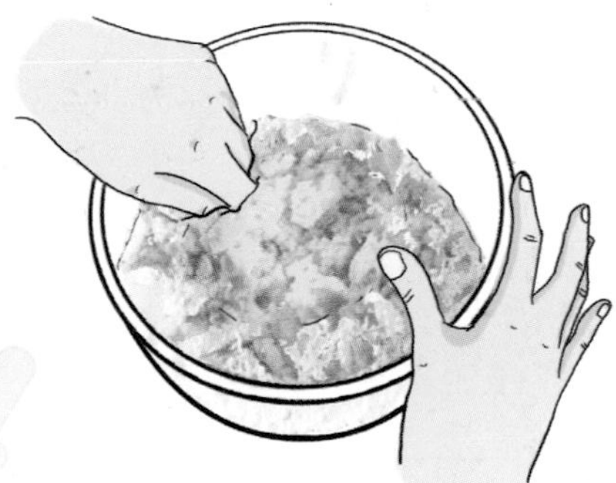

2 Ask an adult to help you warm the milk a little; either in a pan on the stove or in the microwave for about 30 seconds (see page 11). It should still be cool enough to put your finger in! Break the egg into a pitcher (jug), add the milk and beat them together with a fork. Pour the mixture into the hole in the flour and then add the butter.

3 Using your hand, slowly stir the flour into the liquid in the hollow, then work the mixture with your hand until all the flour has been mixed in. If there are dry crumbs in the bowl and the dough feels dry, add a little more milk, a tablespoonful at a time. If the dough is very sticky, add a little more flour.

Pretty **SPIRAL** buns!

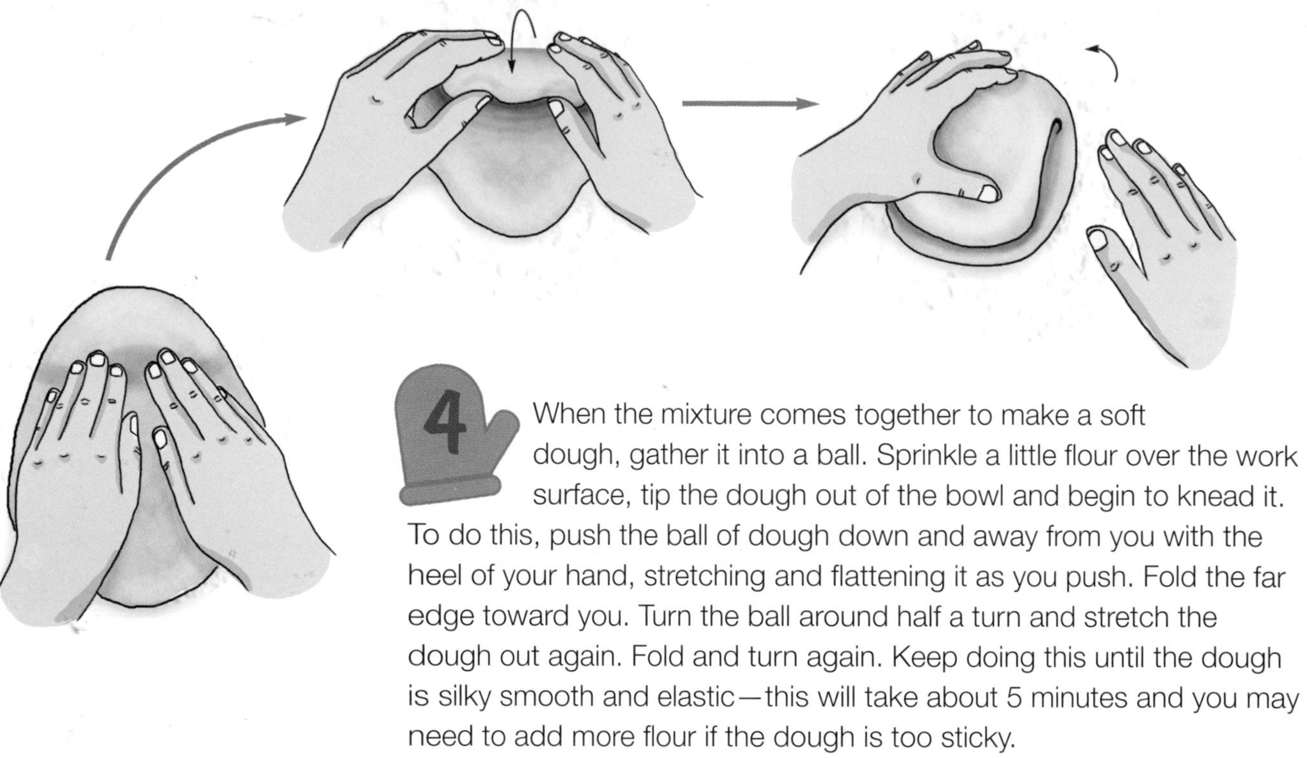

4 When the mixture comes together to make a soft dough, gather it into a ball. Sprinkle a little flour over the work surface, tip the dough out of the bowl and begin to knead it. To do this, push the ball of dough down and away from you with the heel of your hand, stretching and flattening it as you push. Fold the far edge toward you. Turn the ball around half a turn and stretch the dough out again. Fold and turn again. Keep doing this until the dough is silky smooth and elastic—this will take about 5 minutes and you may need to add more flour if the dough is too sticky.

5 Put the dough back into the mixing bowl and cover with plastic wrap (clingfilm). Leave the bowl in a warm place until it has doubled in size—about 1 hour. It will take longer at normal room temperature or on a cool day.

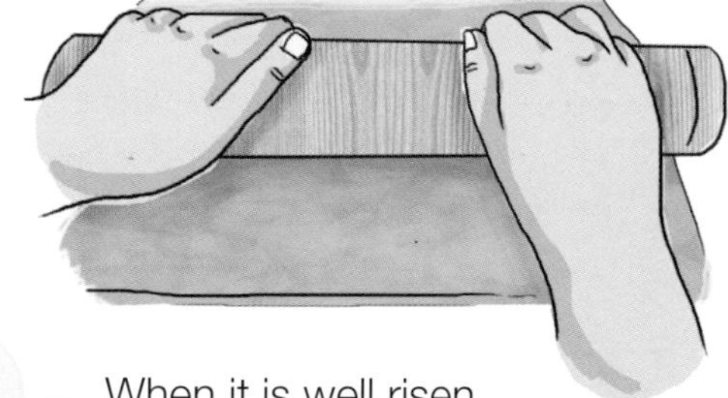

6 When it is well risen, uncover the bowl and gently punch down the dough with your fist. Sprinkle the work surface lightly with flour then tip the dough onto it. Using your hands or a rolling pin, press or roll the dough out to a rectangle about 10 x 14 in. (25 x 35 cm), with the long side toward you.

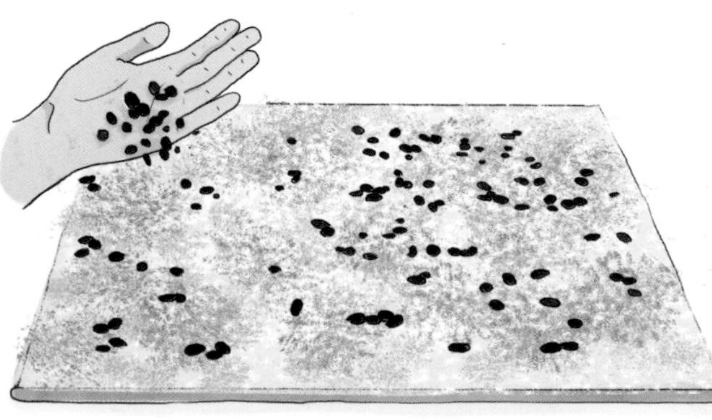

7 Spread the butter for the filling all over the dough. Mix the cinnamon and sugar together and sprinkle over the butter. Finally, scatter the nuts or raisins over the sugar and lightly press them down into the dough.

8 Roll up the dough from one of the long sides to make a long roll. Pinch the dough together all along the "seam" to seal it.

9 Put a little soft butter on a paper towel and rub it over the baking sheet to grease it.

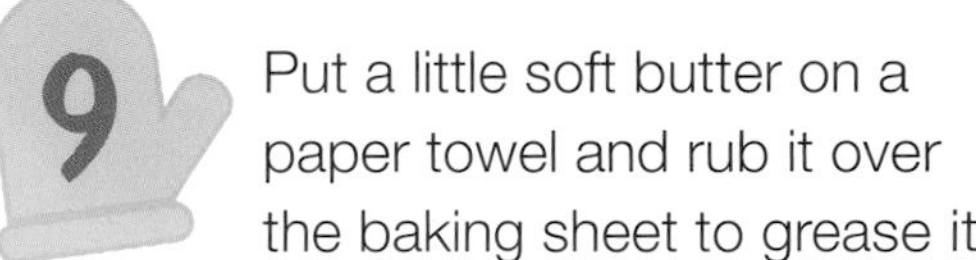

10 Place the long roll onto a cutting board and then, using a sharp knife, mark out 12 equal-sized slices. Carefully cut the slices one by one, and lay each one flat onto the baking sheet, spacing them slightly apart.

11 Cover the sheet with a clean, dry paper towel and leave to rise again for 20 minutes. Meanwhile, ask an adult to help you turn the oven on to 425°F (220°C) Gas 7.

12 Uncover the buns, then ask an adult to help you put the sheet in the preheated oven to bake for 20 minutes, until the buns are golden brown. Ask an adult to help you remove the sheet from the oven. Use a metal spatula to lift the buns onto a wire rack to cool. They are nicest when warm, but you can eat them cold. Once they are cold, you can keep them in an airtight container and eat them within 2 days or freeze them for up to 1 month.

Irish soda bread

Irish soda bread is bread made without yeast so it is much quicker to make than normal bread, but just as delicious, especially when warm from the oven with loads of butter and jelly (jam).

You will need

vegetable oil, for greasing

2 cups (250 g) all-purpose (plain) flour

2 cups (250 g) whole-wheat (wholemeal) flour

1¼ cups (125 g) rolled oats (porridge oats)

1 teaspoon baking soda (bicarbonate of soda)

1 teaspoon fine sea salt

2 tablespoons (30 g) butter

1⅔ cups (400 ml) buttermilk (see page 10)

1 tablespoon runny honey

baking sheet

baking parchment

(makes 1 loaf)

1. Ask an adult to turn the oven on to 400°F (200°C) Gas 6. Put a little vegetable oil on a paper towel and rub it over the baking sheet to grease it.

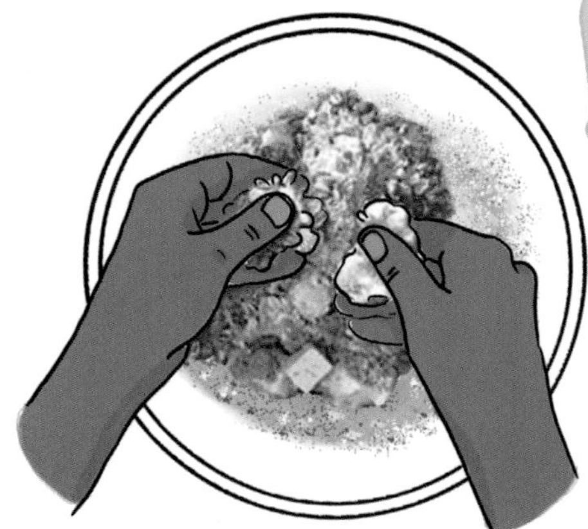

2. Put the flours, oats, baking soda, and salt in a mixing bowl and stir together well. Add the butter and rub it into the flour between your fingers and thumb. (see page 9).

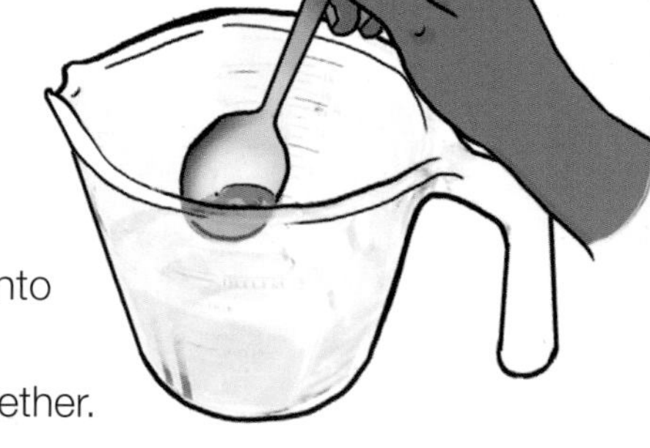

3. Measure the buttermilk into a pitcher (jug), add the honey, and stir them together.

Who doesn't like WARM BREAD and jelly?

4 Make a hole in the center of the flour mixture and pour in the buttermilk. Gradually stir the flour into the buttermilk until the mixture comes together into a ball of soft dough. If it feels a bit hard, add a little more milk (just add a tiny bit at a time, because you don't want the dough to go sloppy).

5 Sprinkle a little flour onto a clean work surface. Tip the dough onto the work surface and begin to knead it. To do this, push the ball of dough down and away from you with the heel of your hand, stretching and flattening it as you push. Fold the far edge toward you. Turn the ball around half a turn and stretch the dough out again. Fold and turn again. Keep kneading for 2–3 minutes until the dough is smooth and soft.

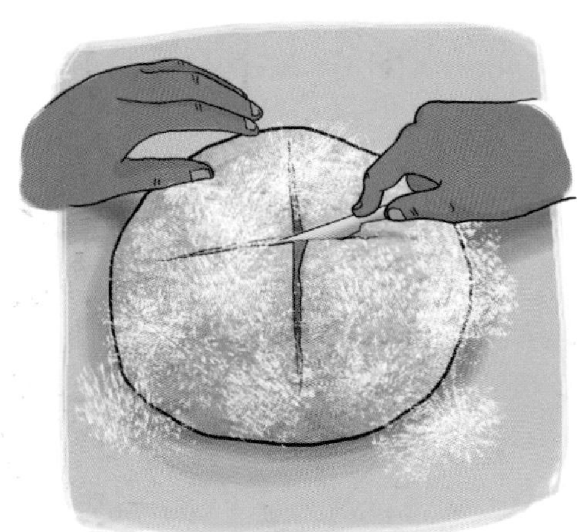

6 Shape the dough into a round loaf, sprinkle a little flour over the top, and then carefully make a large X-shaped slash in the top with a sharp knife.

7 Lift the loaf onto the baking sheet and ask an adult to help you put it in the preheated oven. Bake it for 50–55 minutes. After that time, ask an adult to take it out of the oven, then lift it up using oven mitts, and tap the bottom. Listen carefully! If it sounds hollow the bread is done. If it sounds solid it will need a little longer in the oven. When it is baked, let it cool on a wire rack.

Grandma's jelly buns

These jelly-filled cookies are sturdy enough to survive life in a lunchbox, and are easy to make—the only adult help you need is with using the oven at the end. They will keep for a week in an airtight container.

You will need

1⅔ cups (225 g) self-rising (self-raising) flour

scant ½ cup (90 g) sugar, plus extra for sprinkling

1 stick (125 g) unsalted butter, chilled

1 US extra-large (UK large) egg

1 tablespoon milk

about 1 tablespoon jelly (jam)—choose your favorite flavor

2 baking sheets

(makes 16)

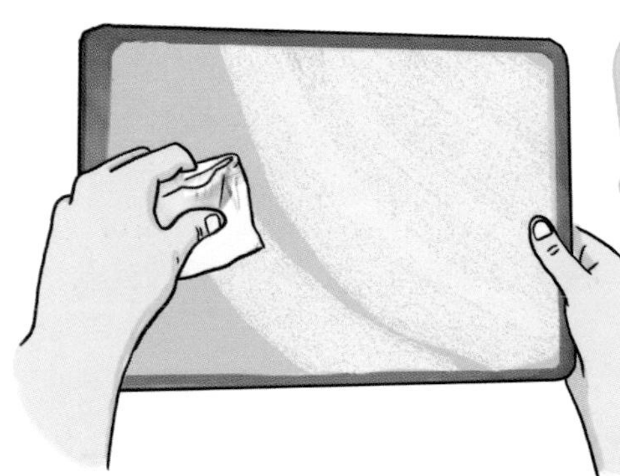

1. Ask an adult to help you turn the oven on to 400°F (200°C) Gas 6. Put a little butter on a piece of paper towel and rub it over each baking sheet to grease them.

2. Put the flour and sugar in a bowl and mix them well with your hands.

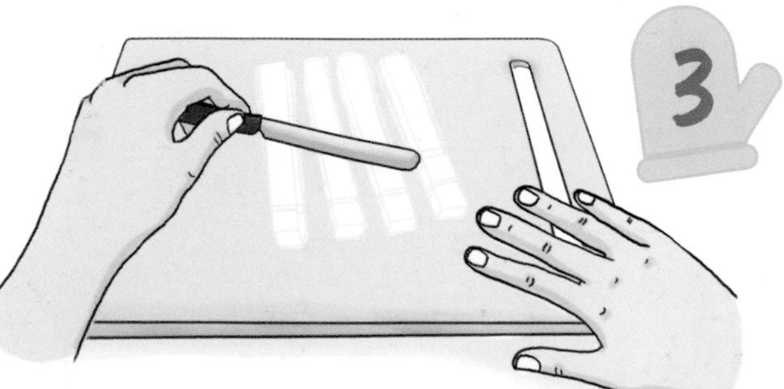

3. Cut the butter into small pieces with a round-bladed knife and add to the bowl.

Make yourself a LUNCHBOX TREAT!

4 Toss the pieces of butter in the flour so they are well coated then rub the butter into the flour, using your fingers and thumbs, until the mixture looks like fine crumbs (see page 9). Make a hole in the center of the crumby mixture.

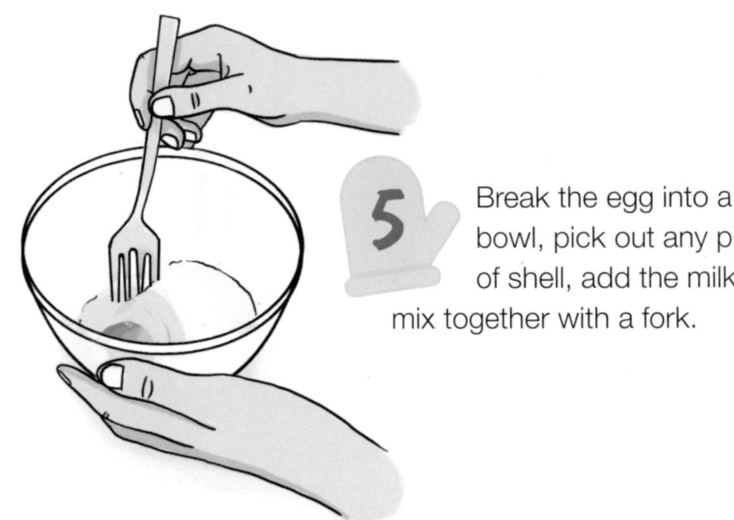

5 Break the egg into a small bowl, pick out any pieces of shell, add the milk, and mix together with a fork.

6 Tip the egg mixture into the hole in the crumb mixture and stir the crumbs into the liquid using a round-bladed knife. It will come together to make a soft dough. If the dough is too dry and the crumbs won't stick together, add extra milk, 1 tablespoon at a time. If the dough is too wet and sticky, add 1 tablespoon extra flour until it is right.

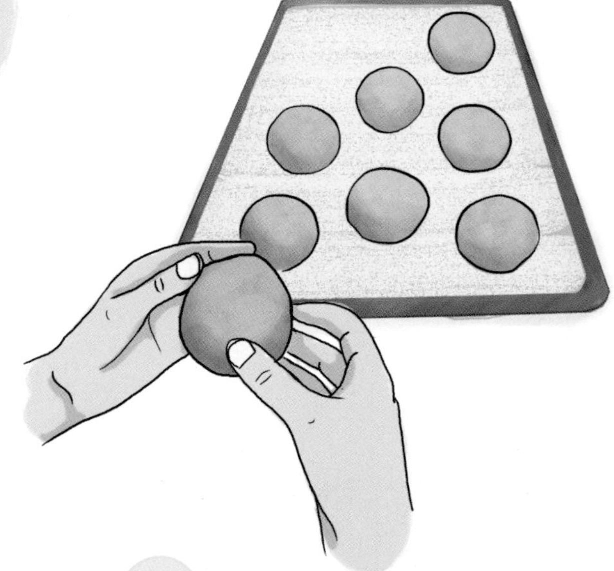

7 Divide the dough into 16 even pieces. Roll each piece into a ball with your hands and set the balls well apart on the baking sheets.

8 Stick your thumb or finger into the middle of each ball to make a small hole (don't go right down to the bottom).

9 Using a teaspoon, put a pea-size amount of the jelly (jam) in the hole, then pinch the dough back together to cover the hole (don't worry if it looks a bit messy at this point).

10 Now ask an adult to help you bake the buns. Bake for 10 minutes in the preheated oven, then turn down the heat to 350°F (180°C) Gas 4 and bake for 5 minutes more. Carefully remove the baking sheets from the oven, sprinkle the buns with a little sugar, and let them cool for 5 minutes (the jelly becomes very hot in the oven and can easily burn you). Using a spatula, transfer them to a wire cooling rack and let them cool completely.

Pick 'n' mix scones

Savory scones can be flavored with all kinds of different fillings—cheese, ham, olives, herbs, or sun-dried tomatoes. These scones make a delicious change from sandwiches to have for your lunch. You could even freeze some—take one out of the freezer in the morning, pop it in your lunchbox, and it will have thawed by lunch time.

You will need

1⅔ cups (225 g) self-rising (self-raising) flour, plus extra for kneading

1 teaspoon baking powder

3 tablespoons (45 g) butter, chilled

a handful each of only 2 of the following: cheese, fresh herbs, sun-dried tomatoes, pitted olives, or ham

½–⅔ cup (125–175 ml) milk, plus a little extra for glazing

round cookie cutter

baking sheet

(makes 8 large or 12 small scones)

1 Ask an adult to turn the oven on to 400°F (200°C) Gas 6. Put a little butter on a paper towel and rub it all over the baking sheet to grease it.

2 Decide on your two favorite fillings and prepare a handful of each. If you want cheese, you need to grate it (see page 13). If you want fresh herbs, you need to chop them carefully with a sharp knife (see page 12). Olives and sun-dried tomatoes will also need cutting carefully into small pieces with a sharp knife. You could snip up ham with a pair of kitchen shears (scissors). Put your fillings to one side.

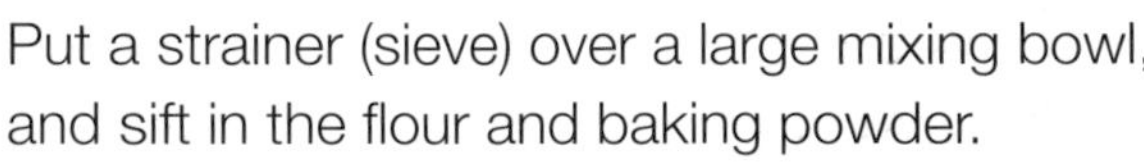

3 Put a strainer (sieve) over a large mixing bowl, and sift in the flour and baking powder.

4 Put the butter onto a chopping board and use a sharp knife to cut it into very small pieces, remembering always to cut down onto the board.

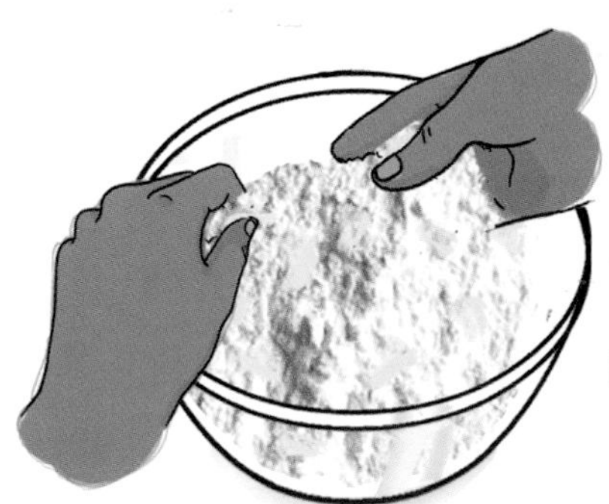

5 Add the butter to the bowl and rub it into the flour, using your fingers and thumbs (see page 9) until the mixture looks like fine breadcrumbs.

What are your **FAVORITE** fillings?

6 Stir in your two fillings, then use a round-bladed table knife to mix in the milk, one tablespoon at a time, until the mixture starts to come together into a dough. Be very careful not to add too much milk—your dough must be nice and firm and you may not need all the milk in your cup.

7 Sprinkle a little flour onto a clean work surface and then tip the dough out of the bowl. Put a little more flour on your hands and very lightly knead the mixture for about 30 seconds until it is smooth.

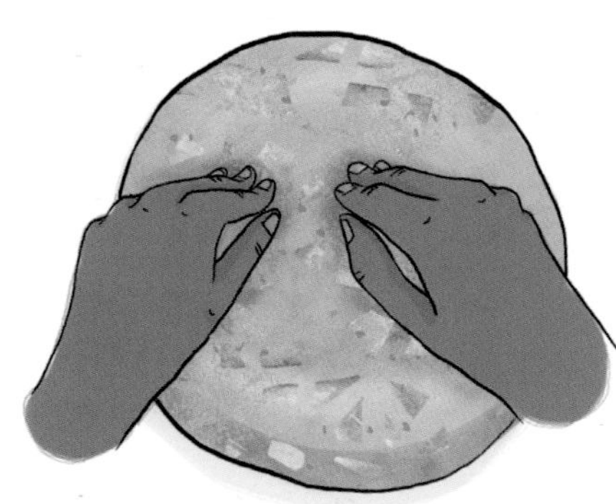

8 Make the mixture into a ball, and lightly pat it out until it is about 1¼ in. (3 cm) thick, which is quite thick.

9 Dip a round cookie cutter into a little flour and cut out the scones from the dough. Cut them as close together as you can. When you have cut as many as you can, gather up the trimmings, knead them lightly together, and pat them out—then cut some more scones. Put the scones onto the baking sheet, spaced a little apart. Use a pastry brush to brush the tops with a little milk.

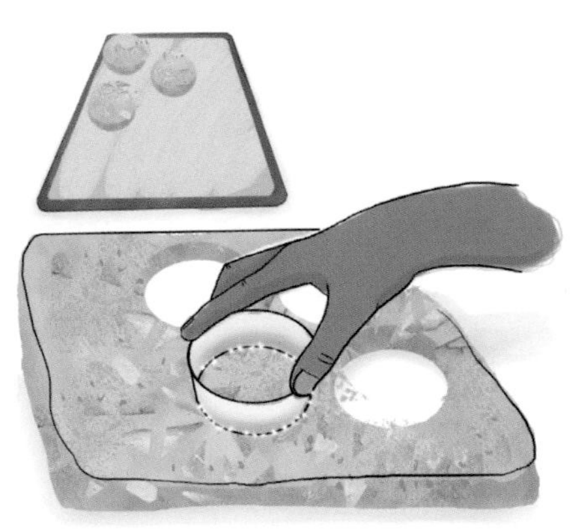

10 Ask an adult to put the scones into the preheated oven and bake for 8–10 minutes until they are risen and golden. Ask an adult to take them out of the oven and put them on a wire rack to cool. If you want to freeze some for later, wait till they are cold, pop a few into a freezer bag or box, seal it up, and put it in the freezer.

Mini focaccias with zucchini

This bread recipe is for savory focaccia, which are little Italian style rolls. These are flavored and decorated with grated zucchini (courgette) but you could have them plain or with a sprinkle of sea salt crystals instead.

You will need

3 cups (375 g) strong (bread) flour

1 package (¼ oz./7 g) fast-acting dried yeast

salt

3 tablespoons olive oil

about ¾ cup (180 ml) warm water

2 small zucchini (courgettes)

2 large baking sheets

(makes 8)

1. Dust the baking sheets with a little flour.

2. Put the flour, yeast, and 1 teaspoon salt into a bowl and stir well with your fingers. Add 2 tablespoons of the olive oil and 1–2 tablespoons warm water. Keep mixing with your fingers, adding more warm water a little at a time, until the mixture comes together into a soft but not sticky dough (if you add too much water, add a little more flour).

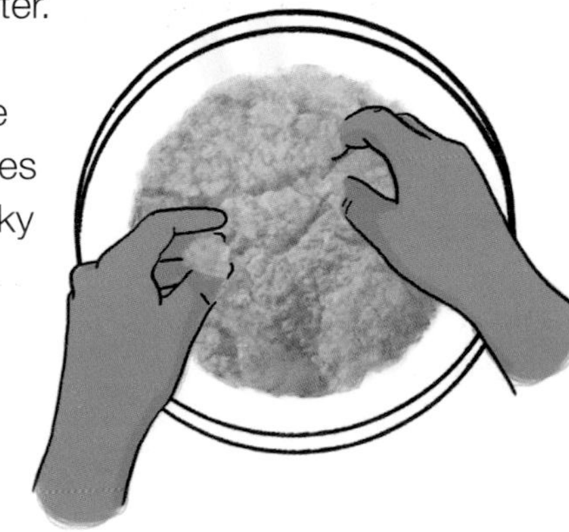

Easy FOCACCIA rolls!

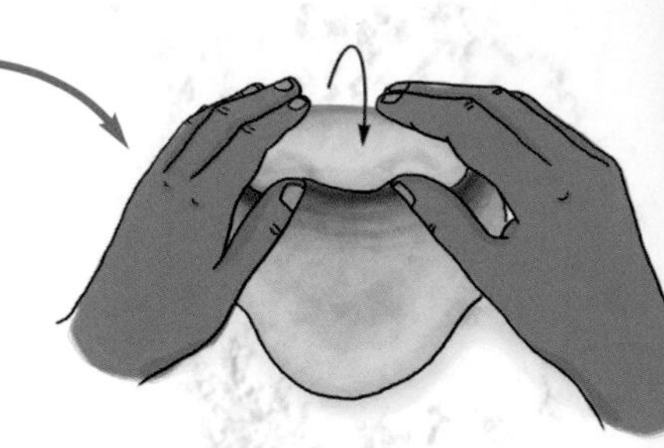

3 Sprinkle a little flour onto a clean work surface. Shape the dough into a ball, tip it out onto the work surface, and begin to knead it. To do this, push the ball of dough down and away from you with the heel of your hand, stretching and flattening it as you push. Fold the far edge toward you. Turn the ball around half a turn and stretch the dough out again. Fold and turn again. Keep doing this until the dough is silky smooth and stretchy—this will take 5–10 minutes and you may need to add more flour if the dough is too sticky.

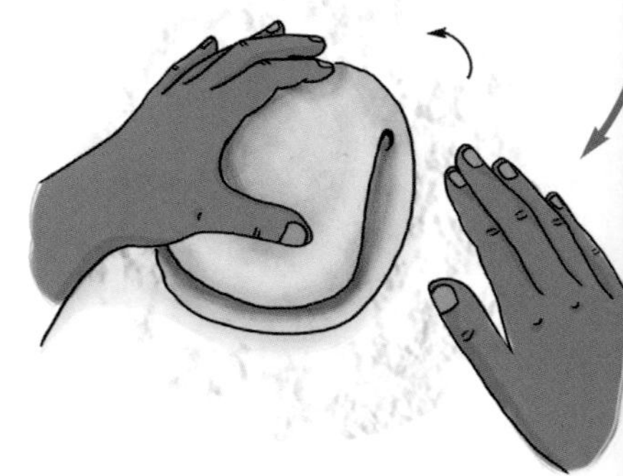

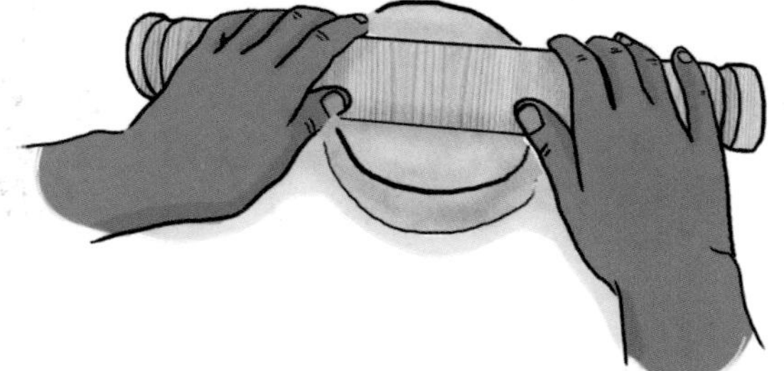

4 Divide the dough into 8 pieces and knead each piece again until it is smooth. Using a rolling pin, roll each piece into a small circle just over ½ in. (1.5 cm) thick. Lay the circles, spaced well apart, on the baking sheets and cover them with plastic wrap (clingfilm). Put them in a warm place to rise for about 40 minutes, until they have doubled in size. (They will take longer if you haven't got a warm place to put them.)

5 Ask an adult to help you turn the oven on to 425°F (220°C) Gas 7.

6 Wash the zucchini (courgettes) and then, using a sharp knife and cutting down onto a board, trim off both ends. Now grate them carefully onto a plate using a fine cheese grater (see page 13). Sprinkle on a little salt.

7 Add the remaining olive oil to the grated zucchini and mix up well with your hands. Scatter the grated zucchini over the mini-focaccias.

8 When the oven is hot, ask an adult to help you put in the mini-focaccias and bake them for about 10–15 minutes. Ask an adult to help you take them out and test them to see if they are baked—they should be firm and golden, and sound hollow when tapped on their bottoms! Serve them warm, or let them cool on a wire rack.

CHAPTER FOUR

SAVORY MEALS AND SNACKS

Tasty bread tartlets

Sometimes you want to do some cooking, but when you look in the fridge and the pantry, you find that there are none of the ingredients you need. These little tartlets use ingredients that almost everyone will find in their kitchen: bread, milk, eggs, and frozen peas. You can also make them with different fillings, like corn and tuna.

You will need

a little butter

6 slices of bread

3 eggs and 4 tablespoons milk (or 2 eggs and 6 tablespoons milk)

a handful of fresh mint leaves (optional)

2 handfuls of frozen peas (defrosted), fresh peas, or corn kernels

a small handful of grated Parmesan cheese

6-hole muffin pan

large, round cutter as wide as the slices of bread

(makes 6)

1 Ask an adult to help you turn the oven on to 375°F (190°C) Gas 5. Put a little butter on a piece of paper towel and rub it inside 6 of the holes in the muffin pan to grease it.

2 Lay a piece of bread on a chopping board and use the round cutter to cut out a circle of bread. Press it into the muffin pan. Do the same with the other slices of bread.

3 Ask an adult to help you put the muffin pan into the oven to bake for 5 minutes. Ask an adult to help you take the muffin pan out of the oven and let it cool.

EASY PEASY TARTLETS!

4

Break the eggs into a measuring cup (jug) and pick out any pieces of shell. Mix the eggs with a fork to break them up. Add the milk and keep mixing to blend them together.

5 If you are using mint, use scissors to snip it into small pieces and put a little into each tartlet. Now put a few peas on top—try to share them out evenly so that the tartlets have roughly the same amount.

6 Carefully pour the egg mixture into the tartlets, over the peas and mint—don't fill them too full as the tartlets will rise in the oven.

7 Sprinkle a little grated Parmesan over the tartlets.

Ask an adult to help you put the muffin pan back in the oven. Bake for 12 minutes, or until the filling has puffed up and the egg is cooked.

Oven risotto with tomatoes, peas, and tuna

This is an excellent one-pot meal to cook for a family supper. Try to be very organized when you make this and have everything prepared before you start cooking.

You will need

- 4 scallions (spring onions)
- 2 garlic cloves
- 2 x 6 oz. (175 g) cans tuna in oil or spring water
- 1 x 14 oz. (400 g) can chopped tomatoes with herbs
- vegetable or chicken stock cubes or powder
- ¾ cup (115 g) fresh or frozen peas (no need to thaw if frozen)
- 2 tablespoons olive oil
- 1 cup (200 g) arborio or other risotto rice
- salt and freshly ground black pepper
- Parmesan cheese
- a few fresh basil leaves, to garnish (optional)

medium-size heavy, flameproof, ovenproof casserole dish with lid

(serves 4–5)

1 Ask an adult to help you turn the oven on to 350°F (180°C) Gas 4.

2 Using a small sharp knife, trim off the hairy roots of the scallions (spring onions). Remember to cut down onto a board. Next, trim off the very dark green tops. Rinse the scallions in cold running water to get rid of any grit and mud. Finally cut them into thin rounds.

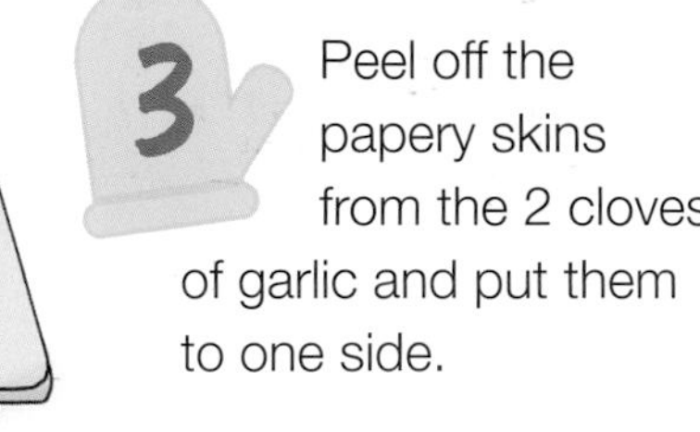

3 Peel off the papery skins from the 2 cloves of garlic and put them to one side.

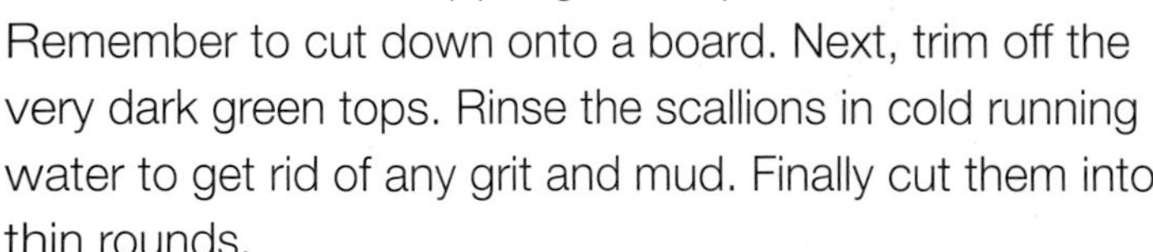

4

Carefully open the cans of tuna. Put a colander in the sink and tip in the tuna to drain off the liquid.

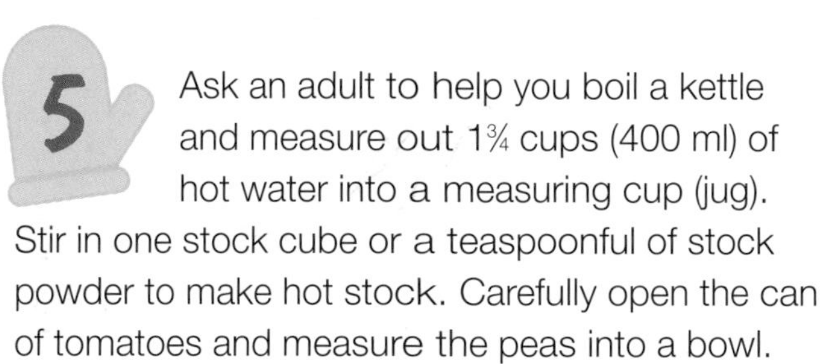

5

Ask an adult to help you boil a kettle and measure out 1¾ cups (400 ml) of hot water into a measuring cup (jug). Stir in one stock cube or a teaspoonful of stock powder to make hot stock. Carefully open the can of tomatoes and measure the peas into a bowl.

6

Now that everything is prepared you are ready to begin cooking. Spoon the olive oil into the casserole dish. Set the dish on the stove and ask an adult to help you gently heat it. Using a wooden spoon, stir in the scallions. Put the garlic into a garlic crusher and crush it into the dish. Cook very gently for 1 minute.

7

Add the rice to the casserole dish and stir well. Cook gently for 1 minute, then stir in the contents of the can of tomatoes, followed by the stock and tuna. Stir well, then add the peas and a little salt and black pepper. Stir once more, then put the lid on the dish. Ask an adult to help you put the dish in the preheated oven to bake for 35 minutes.

8 Just before the risotto is ready, grate about 3 tablespoons of Parmesan cheese onto a plate, using the finest holes, and tear up a few basil leaves, if you have some. Then, when the time is up, ask an adult to help you remove the casserole dish from the oven. Remove the lid, and check that the rice is soft—if not put it back for a little longer. If it is cooked, scatter over the Parmesan cheese and the basil leaves. Eat immediately.

A **ONE-POT** supper dish!

Chorizo and cheese muffins

These savory muffins are great for parties, picnics, and lunchboxes. If you eat them when they are still warm, you will find pockets of melted cheese as well as tasty bites of spicy sausage.

You will need

4 cups (500 g) all-purpose (plain) flour

2 teaspoons baking powder

a pinch of salt

freshly ground black pepper

8 oz. (225 g) Swiss cheese (such as Emmental)

4 oz. (115 g) thickly sliced chorizo sausage (or ham, or canned or frozen sweetcorn kernels)

2 US extra-large (UK large) eggs

scant stick (100 g) unsalted butter

1½ cups (350 ml) milk

12-hole muffin pan

paper muffin cases

(makes 12)

1. Line the muffin pan with the muffin cases. Ask an adult to turn the oven on to 400°F (200°C) Gas 6.

2. Set a large strainer (sieve) over a mixing bowl. Tip the flour into the strainer, then add the baking powder, salt, and a few grinds of pepper, and sift these ingredients into the bowl.

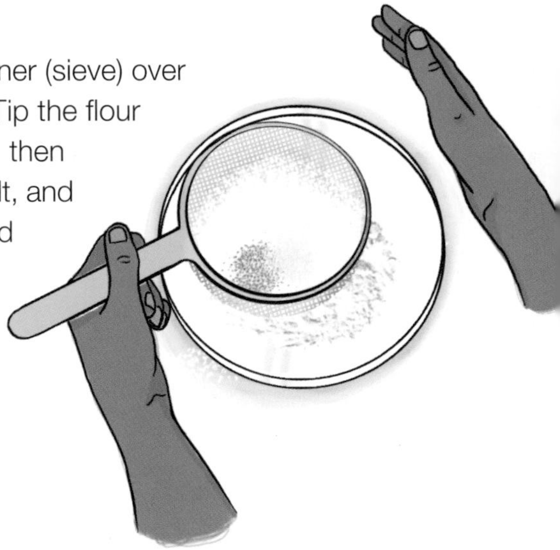

3. Using a sharp knife and cutting down onto a board, cut the cheese into small cubes. Use kitchen scissors to cut up the chorizo into pieces about the same size as the cheese.

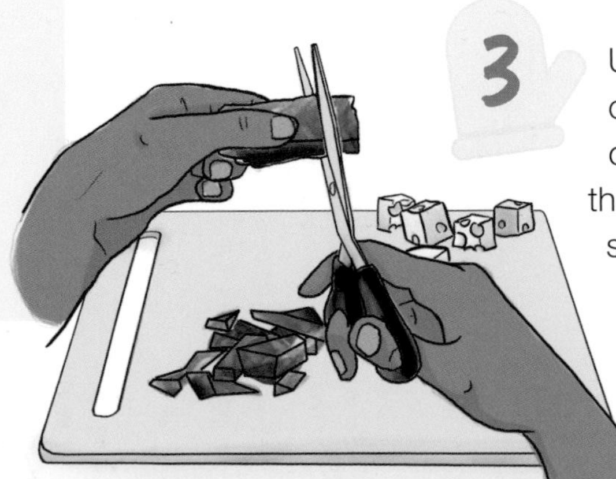

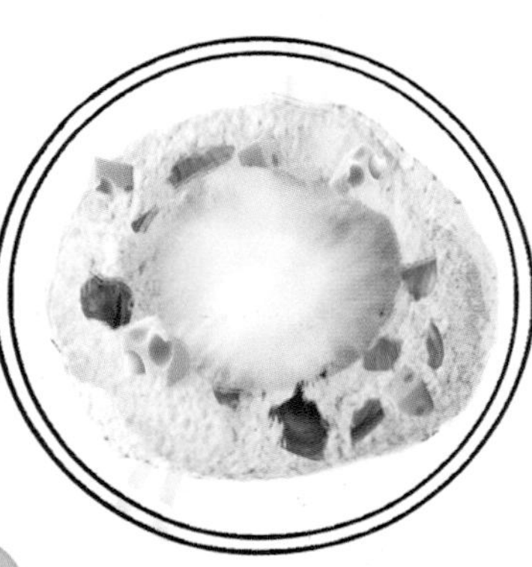

4 Add the cheese and chorizo to the bowl and mix well. Make a hole in the center of the mixture.

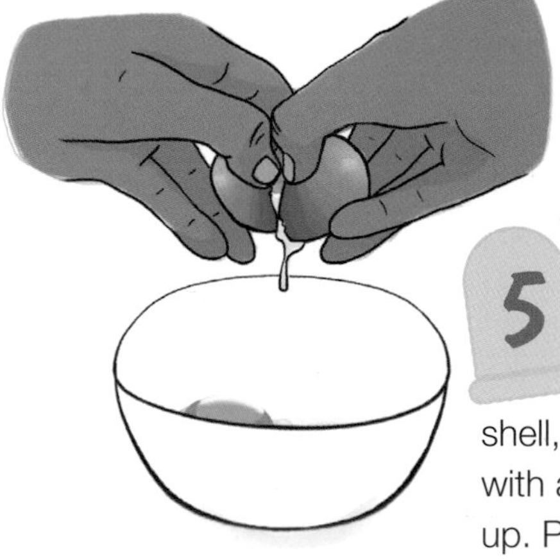

5 Break the eggs into a bowl. Pick out any pieces of shell, then beat the eggs with a fork until just broken up. Pour into the hole in the mixture in the mixing bowl.

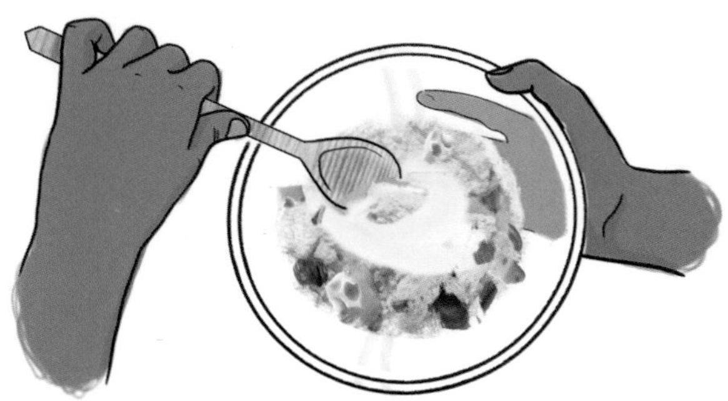

6 Put the butter in a small saucepan and ask an adult to help you melt the butter over very low heat. The butter can also be melted in a microwave (see page 11). Pour the butter into the hole in the mixture. Then pour in the milk.

7 Mix all the ingredients together with a wooden spoon, gradually mixing the dry ingredients into the well of liquids in the center. Keep stirring to make a rough-looking mixture.

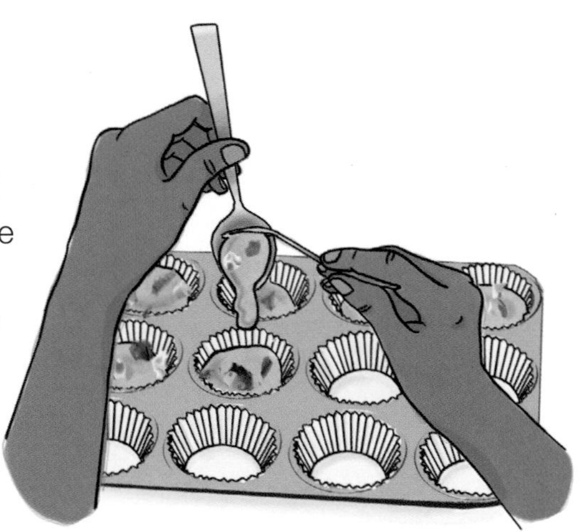

8 Spoon this mixture into the prepared muffin cases, making sure there is the same amount in each one. Ask an adult to help you put the muffins in the oven to bake for 30 minutes, until golden brown.

9 Ask an adult to help you remove the pan from the oven. Let it cool for a couple of minutes, then transfer the muffins to a wire rack. Eat warm or at room temperature. You can store them in an airtight container to eat the next day.

Cheese and chorizo SURPRISE!

Mini toads

Who likes eating toads? Yuk! What a thought—but you're sure to love this mini version of toad in the hole, which is a funny old-fashioned name for sausages in batter. You must work very carefully but quickly at the end of this recipe, because you need the oil to be really hot to make the batter puff up around the sausages.

You will need

¾ cup (75 g) all-purpose (plain) flour

a pinch of salt

a pinch of pepper

2 eggs

1 cup (250 ml) milk

a small bunch of fresh chives (optional)

12 breakfast link (chipolata) sausages (any type, including vegetarian)

¼ cup (60 ml) vegetable oil

large baking sheet or roasting pan

12-hole muffin pan

(makes 12)

1 Ask an adult to help you adjust the oven shelves—you will be using the middle one for the muffin pan, so make sure there is plenty of room for the batter to rise above the pan. Put a shelf under the middle one and put a large baking sheet or roasting pan on it to catch any drips. Ask an adult to help you turn the oven on to 425°F (220°C) Gas 7.

2 To make the batter, put the flour, salt, and pepper in a large bowl. Make a hole in the center.

3 Break the eggs into a bowl, pick out any pieces of shell, and add the milk. Whisk them together with a wire whisk then pour into the hole in the flour.

4 Still using the whisk, start to mix the flour into the milk and eggs, pulling in a little flour at a time. When all the flour has been mixed in, beat the batter well to get rid of any lumps.

5 Use kitchen shears (scissors) to snip the chives into the batter and stir them in. You can make the batter up to 3 hours before you start cooking.

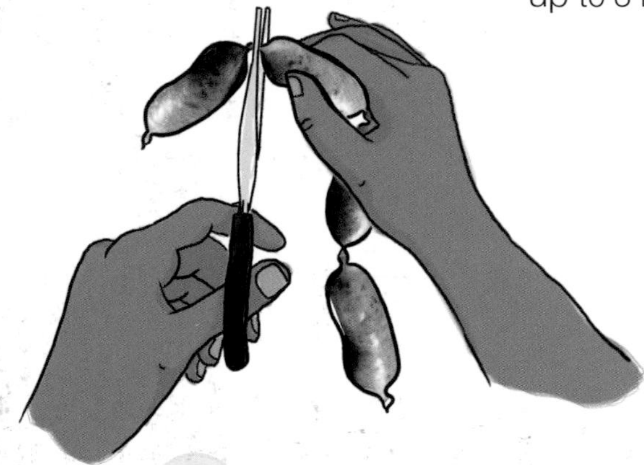

6 Using kitchen shears again, snip the links between the sausages to separate them. If your sausages are too long, then twist each one in the middle to make two small sausages and snip through the twist to separate them. Put them to one side. Wash your hands well after handling the sausages.

7 Put one teaspoon of oil into each hole of the muffin pan then ask an adult to help you put it in the oven to heat up. After 5 minutes, ask an adult to help you remove the pan—wear oven mitts as the pan and oil will be very, very hot—and put it onto a heatproof work surface. Carefully put one sausage into each hole, then ask an adult to help you put the pan back in the oven for another 5 minutes.

8 For the next stage you need to work quickly. Get ready by pouring or ladling the batter into a large measuring cup (jug) and stir it once or twice. Now, ask an adult to help you carefully remove the hot pan from the oven and put it onto the heatproof work surface again, then stand back (the oil can splutter), then ask an adult to help you quickly pour the batter into each hole so each one is half full.

9 Ask an adult to help you replace the pan in the oven and bake for 20 minutes until the batter is golden brown and crispy.

10 Ask an adult to help you remove the pan from the oven and lift each Mini Toad out of the pan with a round-bladed knife. Use an oven mitt to steady the pan. Eat straight away with salad, green vegetables, or baked beans.

Do you like EATING TOADS?

Cornmeal and sweetcorn fritters

These little fritters are made with a batter similar to that for Mini Toads (see page 111), but they are fried rather than baked. Although they don't really belong in a baking book, we've included them here as they taste so good and are such an easy supper for you to help make.

You will need

1 cup (160 g) cornmeal (or fine polenta)

¼ cup (40 g) all-purpose (plain) or whole-wheat (wholemeal) flour

2 teaspoons baking powder

¼ teaspoon paprika

½ teaspoon fine sea salt

¾ cup (200 ml) milk, plus more if needed

1 egg

2 cups (300 g) sweetcorn kernels, fresh, frozen, or canned

sunflower oil and butter

skillet (frying pan)

heatproof dish

(makes about 7)

1. In a large bowl, mix together the cornmeal, flour, baking powder, paprika, and salt.

2. Measure the milk into a measuring cup (jug), add the egg, and whisk until blended.

3. Pour the milk mixture into the cornmeal mixture and stir until it is well mixed together. Stir in the sweetcorn kernels.

Serve up a SIMPLE SUPPER!

4 Ask an adult to help you with all the next stages of cooking, as you will be using the stovetop (hob) and the oven. First, turn the oven on to low 225ºF (110ºC) Gas ¼ (just to keep the cooked fritters warm while you cook the others) and put a heatproof dish into the oven to warm up.

5 Put one tablespoon of oil and a small knob of butter into a large nonstick skillet (frying pan) and ask an adult to help you put it on the stove to heat up. When the oil is sizzling, ask an adult to help you pour a ladleful of the batter into the pan to make one fritter. Add one or two more ladles of batter to the pan, but space out the fritters so that they don't run into one other. Cooking fewer at a time is easier than having them too close.

6 Cook for 3–5 minutes on one side, until each fritter has bubbles all over and, when you lift the edge with a spatula, it is brown underneath. Using the spatula, turn each one over and cook the other side until, when you peep underneath, it is golden brown on that side too.

7 Ask an adult to help you remove the fritters from the pan, drain them on paper towels, then transfer them to the heatproof plate in the oven, to keep warm while you cook the rest. Serve immediately.

Baked polenta with cheese

Northern Italians often eat polenta rather than pasta. This dish is buttery, cheesy, and delicious. The polenta comes as tiny grains, which swell when you cook it and then you can cut it into shapes and bake it. A special Italian cheese called Taleggio is used for this recipe, but you could use any cheese that melts well, instead.

You will need

1½ cups (250 g) instant cornmeal (polenta)

vegetable stock cubes or powder

6 oz. (170 g) Parmesan cheese

2 handfuls of baby spinach

7 tablespoons (100 g) butter, softened

3½ oz. (100 g) Taleggio cheese (in one piece), or other melting cheese, such as Gruyère, Cheddar, Fontina, or Emmental

sunflower oil

salt and black pepper

baking sheet

cookie cutter

large ovenproof dish

(serves 4)

1. First prepare all your ingredients: grate the Parmesan onto a plate using the finest grater. Wash the spinach in a colander and tear the leaves into small pieces. Measure the polenta into a measuring cup or pitcher (jug). Measure the butter onto a plate. Have the salt and pepper handy.

2. You need an adult to help you with all of the next three stages as you will be working at the stove. Pour 4 cups (1 liter) of water into a large, heavy saucepan and then ask an adult to help you put it on the stovetop (hob) and turn on the heat. When it is nearly boiling, add a stock cube or some powder, according to the instructions on the packet, to make a vegetable stock.

A cheesy ITALIAN TREAT!

3 Give the stock a stir and, when it is bubbling nicely, pour in the polenta in a steady stream with one hand, while you stir quickly all the time with a large wire whisk. (It might be easier if the adult pours while you whisk.) Do it gently so that it doesn't splash. Cook the polenta for the time recommended on the package you are using.

4 When the polenta is cooked and thick, remove the pan from the heat and stand it on a heatproof work surface. Use an oven mitt to hold the saucepan handle. Swap the whisk for a wooden spoon and stir in the Parmesan, spinach, a little pepper, and half the butter. Try a little on a teaspoon (making sure it's not too hot first!) and see how it tastes. Add a little salt if you think it needs it.

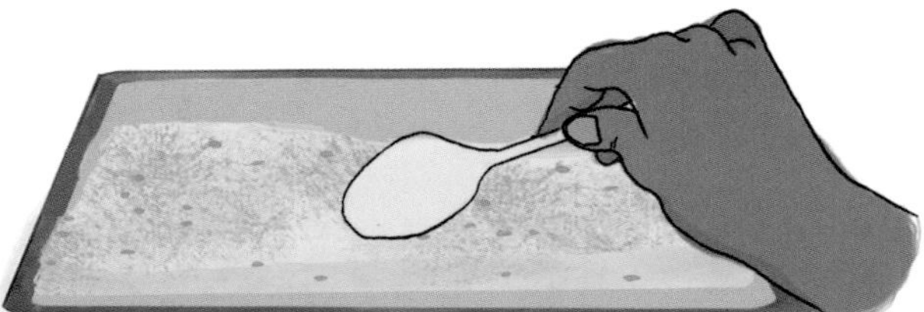

5 Put a little sunflower oil on a paper towel and wipe it over the baking sheet to grease it. Then ask an adult to help you pour the polenta mixture out onto the baking sheet. Smooth it over with the back of a spoon or a palette knife. Let it cool and set.

Ask an adult to help you turn the oven on to 400°F (200°C) Gas 6.

7 Cut the cooled polenta into circles using a cookie cutter—cut them as close together as possible—and lay them in the ovenproof dish. When you have cut as many as you can, push the trimmings together to cut some more.

8 Use a sharp knife to cut the cheese into little pieces; remember to cut down onto a chopping board. Dot the cheese evenly over the circles of polenta then dot over little pieces of the remaining butter.

9 Ask an adult to help you bake the polenta in the preheated oven for about 15–20 minutes, until the cheese is melted and bubbling.

Big pasta shells stuffed with herbs and ricotta

This is a really easy and unusual pasta dish for the whole family. It's just as tasty as lasagna, but much less trouble to make.

You will need

14 oz. (400 g) dried big pasta shells

a pinch of salt

3 ripe tomatoes

1 lb. (450 g) ricotta cheese

2 tablespoons mixed fresh herbs (such as chives, parsley, and basil)

3 tablespoons olive oil

Parmesan cheese

a crisp, green salad, to serve

ovenproof serving dish

(serves 4)

1 Ask an adult to help you turn the oven on to 350°F (180°C) Gas 4.

2 Ask an adult to help you cook the pasta. To do this, bring a big saucepan of water to a boil and add the salt. Drop in the pasta, give it a stir, and keep the heat high until the water boils again, then turn it down a little so the water doesn't boil over the top of the saucepan—but make sure it keeps boiling.

3 Cook the pasta for the amount of time it shows on the package. Use a slotted spoon to take out a piece to test when you think it is ready (be careful not to burn your tongue). The cooked shells should be "al dente," which means not quite soft. Ask an adult to help you drain them in a colander and let them cool.

4 While the pasta is cooking, start to prepare the filling. Carefully cut the tomatoes in half, holding your hand in the bridge position (see page 12) and using a sharp knife to cut down onto a board.

5

Use a teaspoon to scoop out the seeds and the center of the tomato. Squash the tomato halves flat on the board and chop them into small pieces. Put the pieces into a bowl.

6

Carefully, using a sharp knife, chop the herbs into very small pieces (see page 12).

7

Add the herbs and ricotta to the tomatoes and stir everything together.

8

When they are cool enough to hold, take a pasta shell, place a teaspoonful of the mixture inside and put it into the ovenproof serving dish. Fill all the shells in this way and arrange them in the dish—they can be packed quite tightly.

9

Sprinkle the olive oil over the pasta making sure each piece gets some. Grate about 3 tablespoons of Parmesan (see page 13) and sprinkle this on top. Ask an adult to help you put the dish into the oven and bake for 10 minutes, until it is hot. Serve with a nice crisp, green salad.

Leek frittata

A frittata is another Italian dish, a kind of super baked omelet that you can flavor with different ingredients. This one is filled with leeks and pancetta (Italian bacon), but you could try other vegetables—zucchini (courgette), onions, mushrooms, peas, or tomatoes—and perhaps top it with grated cheese. This is another great one-dish supper that you can help to make for your family.

You will need

3 leeks

3½ oz. (100 g) pancetta (or bacon)

2 tablespoons olive oil

8 US extra-large (UK large) eggs

a few fresh chives

salt and black pepper

a crisp, green salad, to serve

round ovenproof dish, about 9 in. (23 cm) diameter

(serves 4)

1 Ask an adult to help you turn the oven on to 400°F (200°C) Gas 6.

2 Using a sharp knife and cutting down carefully onto a board, trim off the bottom of the leeks where the roots are and cut off any thick, dark leaves at the top. Then, using the bridge position for your hand (see page 12), cut the leeks in half along their length and wash them very well under a running faucet (tap)—sometimes grit can get caught between the leaves.

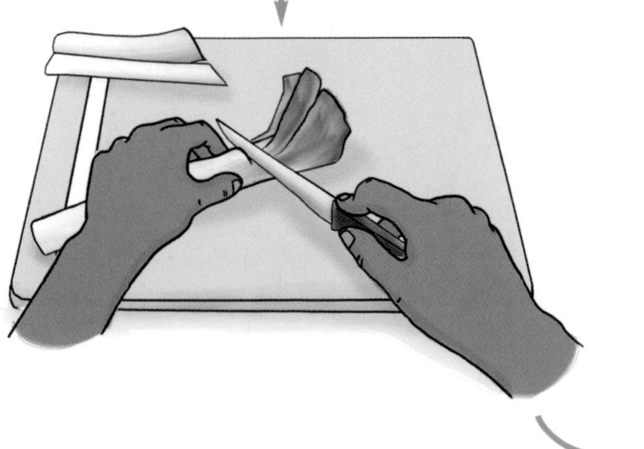

3 Lay the halved leeks on their flat sides on the cutting board and carefully cut them into fine slices. Scatter them over the base of the ovenproof dish.

4 Use a pair of kitchen shears (scissors) to cut the pancetta into very thin, matchstick-sized strips.

5 Scatter the pancetta pieces on top of the leeks and sprinkle the olive oil all over the dish.

6 Ask an adult to help you put the dish in the preheated oven and bake for about 15 minutes, until the pancetta is cooked and the leeks are softened.

7 In the meantime, firmly tap the eggs on the side of a bowl and pull the two halves apart with your fingertips. Pick out any pieces of shell, and beat with a wire whisk until they are very smooth. Sprinkle in a little salt and black pepper.

8 Ask an adult to help you remove the hot dish from the oven and put it on a heatproof surface. Carefully pour in the eggs, taking care not to touch the hot dish.

Snip the chives into pieces with kitchen shears and scatter over the frittata.

10 Ask an adult to help you return the dish to the oven and bake for about 20 minutes longer, until the eggs are set. Ask an adult to help you take the dish out of the oven. You can serve it warm or cold, if you prefer.

GET CRACKING on eight eggs!

Templates

You can use these templates to create stencils for the decorations on the Peanut Butter Cakes (see page 57). The recipe uses the heart stencil, but why not try pretty stars or Christmas trees instead?

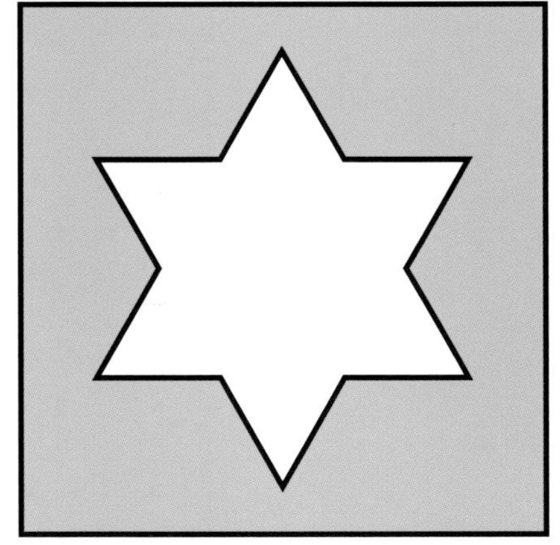

Suppliers

You will probably already have most of the equipment needed for these recipes in your kitchen, but for additional bakeware supplies and, in particular, child-friendly equipment, try the following stores.

US SUPPLIERS

Foodie Kids
www.kidscookingshop.com

Fancy Flours Inc
www.fancyflours.com

Growing Cooks
www.growingcooks.com

Kids Central Kitchen
www.kidscentralkitchen.com

Kitchen Krafts
www.kitchenkrafts.com

Michaels
www.michaels.com

Sugarcraft
www.sugarcraft.com

Wilton
www.wilton.com

UK SUPPLIERS

Cakes, Cookies & Crafts
www.cakescookiesandcraftsshop.co.uk

Hobbycraft
www.hobbycraft.co.uk

John Lewis
www.johnlewis.com

The Kids Baking Store
www.thekidsbakingstore.co.uk

Lakeland
www.lakeland.co.uk

Little Chef Big Chef
littlechef-bigchef.co.uk

Spotty Green Frog
www.spottygreenfrog.co.uk

Squires Kitchen
www.squires-shop.com

Index

Acknowledgments

Key: l = left, r = right, t = top, b = bottom, c=center

Recipes
Maxine Clark: 23; Chloe Coker: 50; Linda Collister: 26, 32, 47, 57, 63, 68, 76, 82, 85, 91, 105, 108, 111; Liz Franklin: 18, 97, 117, 120, 122; Amanda Grant: 16, 36, 39, 60, 66, 94, 102; Caroline Marson: 29, 44; Annie Rigg: 20, 54, 71, 79; Laura Washburn: 88, 114

Photography
Susan Bell: 5t, 13, 37, 42, 67, 103, 104; Martin Brigdale: 15, 25; Vanessa Davies: 5bc, 9, 27, 33, 49, 83, 93, 113; Tara Fisher: 1, 17, 41, 61, 95; Lisa Linder: 2, 4b, 5bl, 6, 14, 19, 21, 55, 73, 75, 79, 81, 97, 99, 117, 119, 121, 123; Martin Norris: 4t, 43, 51; Kate Whitaker: 5br, 74, 89, 100, 115, 116, 127; Polly Wreford: 3, 7, 31, 45, 57, 59, 65, 69, 77, 87, 101, 107, 109, 110, 126

Styling
Liz Belton: 2, 4b, 21, 55, 73, 75, 79, 81; Maxine Clark/Lindy Tubby/Helen Trent: 15, 25; Amanda Grant: 5t, 13, 17, 37, 42, 61, 67, 103, 104; Amanda Grant/Jacque Malouf/Liz Belton: 1, 41, 95; Rose Hammick: 31, 45; Joss Herd/Helen Trent: 3, 7, 57, 59, 65, 69, 77, 87, 101, 107, 109, 110, 126; Lucy McKelvie/Helen Trent: 5bc, 9, 27, 33, 49, 83, 93, 113; Luis Peral-Aranda: 4t, 43, 51; Joy Skipper/Liz Belton: 5bl, 6, 14, 19, 97, 99, 117, 119, 121, 123; Sunil Vijayakar/Liz Belton: 5br, 74, 89, 100, 115, 116, 127

Cover photography
Back cover tl/bl and cover spine: Susan Bell; back cover r: Lisa Linder; front cover tl/tc: Vanessa Davies; front cover tr: Martin Norris; front cover bc: Martin Brigdale; front cover bl/br and front inside flap: Polly Wreford

GLEIM®

21ST EDITION

AUDITING & SYSTEMS

EXAM QUESTIONS & EXPLANATIONS

by

Irvin N. Gleim, Ph.D., CPA, CIA, CMA, CFM

and

William A. Hillison, Ph.D., CPA, CMA

with the assistance of
Grady M. Irwin, J.D.

Gleim Publications, Inc.
PO Box 12848
University Station
Gainesville, Florida 32604
(800) 87-GLEIM or (800) 874-5346
(352) 375-0772
Website: www.gleim.com
Email: admin@gleim.com

For updates to the first printing of the twenty-first edition of ***Auditing & Systems Exam Questions and Explanations***

Go To: www.gleim.com/updates

Or: Email update@gleim.com with **AUD EQE 21-1** in the subject line. You will receive our current update as a reply.

Updates are available until the next edition is published.

ISSN: 1092-4159
ISBN: 978-1-61854-181-9

First Printing: July 2018

ACKNOWLEDGMENTS

Material from Uniform Certified Public Accountant Examination questions and unofficial answers, Copyright © 1972-2018 by the American Institute of Certified Public Accountants, Inc., is reprinted and/or adapted with permission.

The authors also appreciate and thank the Information Systems Audit and Control Association for permission to use sample CISA questions from *Study Guide - Certified Information Systems Auditor*.

The authors also appreciate and thank the Institute for Certification of Computing Professionals for permission to use sample CDP questions from the CDP *Instruction Manual*.

The authors also appreciate and thank The Institute of Internal Auditors, Inc., for permission to use the CIA Model Exam questions and The Institute's Certified Internal Auditor Examination questions, Copyright © 1978-2018 by The Institute of Internal Auditors, Inc.

The authors also appreciate and thank the Institute of Certified Management Accountants for permission to use problem materials from past CMA examinations, Copyright © 1977-2018 by the Institute of Management Accountants.

The authors appreciate questions contributed by the following individuals: Lynn M. Bailey, David Bradley, John Brooks, George Fiebelkorn, D. Finkbiner, Jim Heian, Kenneth M. Macur, D. Payne, Ken J. Plucinski, Nathan Schmukler, James Swearingen, and Don Wells.

Environmental Statement -- This book is printed on recyclable, environmentally friendly groundwood paper, sourced from certified sustainable forests and produced either TCF (totally chlorine-free) or ECF (elementally chlorine-free).

ABOUT THE AUTHORS

Irvin N. Gleim is Professor Emeritus in the Fisher School of Accounting at the University of Florida and is a member of the American Accounting Association, Academy of Legal Studies in Business, American Institute of Certified Public Accountants, Association of Government Accountants, Florida Institute of Certified Public Accountants, The Institute of Internal Auditors, and the Institute of Management Accountants. He has had articles published in the *Journal of Accountancy*, *The Accounting Review*, and *The American Business Law Journal* and is author/coauthor of numerous accounting books, aviation books, and CPE courses.

William A. Hillison is a Professor Emeritus of Accounting at Florida State University. His primary teaching duties included graduate and undergraduate auditing and systems courses. He is a member of the Florida Institute of Certified Public Accountants, American Accounting Association, and Institute of Certified Management Accountants. He has had articles published in many journals, including the *Journal of Accounting Research*, the *Journal of Accounting Literature*, the *Journal of Accounting Education*, *Cost and Management*, *The Internal Auditor*, *ABACUS*, the *Journal of Accountancy*, *The CPA Journal*, and *The Journal of Forecasting*.

REVIEWERS AND CONTRIBUTORS

Garrett W. Gleim, B.S., CGMA, received a Bachelor of Science degree from the University of Pennsylvania, The Wharton School. He also holds a CPA certificate issued by the State of Delaware. Mr. Gleim coordinated the production staff, reviewed the manuscript, and provided production assistance throughout the project.

Solomon E. Gonite, J.D., CPA, CIA, CRMA, CMA, CSCA, CFE, is a graduate of the Florida State University College of Law and the Fisher School of Accounting at the University of Florida. He has practiced as an auditor (in both the private and government sectors) and as a tax practitioner. Mr. Gonite provided substantial editorial assistance throughout the project.

Grady M. Irwin, J.D., is a graduate of the University of Florida College of Law, and he has taught in the University of Florida College of Business. Mr. Irwin provided substantial editorial assistance throughout the project.

Mark S. Modas, M.S.T., CPA, received a Bachelor of Arts in Accounting from Florida Atlantic University and a Master of Science in Taxation from Nova Southeastern University. He was the Sarbanes-Oxley project manager and internal audit department manager at Perry Ellis International, and the former Acting Director of Accounting and Financial Reporting for the School Board of Broward County, Florida. Mr. Modas provided substantial editorial assistance throughout the project.

A PERSONAL THANKS

This manual would not have been possible without the extraordinary effort and dedication of Jacob Bennett, Julie Cutlip, Ethan Good, Blaine Hatton, Kelsey Hughes, Fernanda Martinez, Bree Rodriguez, Teresa Soard, Justin Stephenson, Joanne Strong, Elmer Tucker, and Candace Van Doren, who typed the entire manuscript and all revisions and drafted and laid out the diagrams, illustrations, and cover for this book.

The authors also appreciate the production and editorial assistance of Sirene Dagher, Jessica Hatker, Kristen Hennen, Belea Keeney, Katie Larson, Diana León, Bryce Owen, Jake Pettifor, Shane Rapp, Drew Sheppard, and Alyssa Thomas.

The authors also appreciate the critical reading assistance of Matthew Blockus, Felix Chen, Corey Connell, Dean Kingston, Melissa Leonard, Monica Metz, Kelly Meyer, Timothy Murphy, Cristian Prieto, Crystal Quach, Martin Salazar, and Diana Weng.

Finally, we appreciate the encouragement, support, and tolerance of our families throughout this project.

IF YOU HAVE QUESTIONS

Gleim has an efficient and effective way for users to submit an inquiry and receive a response regarding Gleim materials directly through their Test Prep. This system also allows you to view your Q&A session in your Gleim Personal Classroom.

Questions regarding the information in the Introduction (study suggestions, studying plans, exam specifics) should be emailed to personalcounselor@gleim.com.

Questions concerning orders, prices, shipments, or payments should be sent via email to customerservice@gleim.com and will be promptly handled by our competent and courteous customer service staff.

For technical support, you may use our automated technical support service at www.gleim.com/support, email us at support@gleim.com, or call us at (800) 874-5346.

Returns of books purchased from bookstores and other resellers should be made to the respective bookstore or reseller. For more information regarding the Gleim Return Policy, please contact our offices at (800) 874-5346 or visit www.gleim.com/returnpolicy.

TABLE OF CONTENTS

ACRONYMS: See page 10 for definitions of AR-C, AS, AT-C, AU-C, BL, CS, FASB (ASC), PR, QC, SAS, SOX, and TS pronouncements. Pages 541-548 contain cross-references to these pronouncements.

DETAILED TABLE OF CONTENTS

PREFACE FOR ACCOUNTING STUDENTS

The purpose of this book is to help you learn and understand auditing and systems concepts and their application. In turn, these skills will enable you to perform better on your undergraduate exams, as well as look ahead to the CDP, CIA, CISA, CMA, and CPA exams.

One of the major benefits of this study manual is comprehensive coverage of auditing and systems topics. Accordingly, when you use this study manual to help prepare for auditing courses and exams, you are assured of covering virtually all topics that could reasonably be expected to be studied in typical college or university auditing courses. See Appendix A for a comprehensive list of cross-references.

The signature Gleim answer and explanation format is designed to facilitate effective study and learning. The Gleim EQE Test Prep is packed with features that allow you to customize quizzes to focus on the areas with the biggest opportunity for improvement and review detailed answer explanations for questions you missed.

The majority of the questions in this book are from past CDP, CIA, CISA, CMA, and CPA exams. Although a citation for the source of each question is provided, a substantial number have been modified to accommodate changes in professional pronouncements, to clarify questions, and/or to emphasize an auditing or systems concept or its application. In addition, hundreds of publisher-written questions test areas covered in current textbooks but not directly tested on accounting certification exams to help you better prepare for your accounting coursework.

Note that this study manual should not be relied upon exclusively to prepare for the professional exams. You should primarily use review systems specifically developed for each exam. The Gleim CIA, CMA, CPA, and EA Review Systems are up-to-date and comprehensively cover all material necessary for successful completion of these exams. Further descriptions of these exams and our review materials are provided in the Introduction. To obtain any of these materials, order online at www.gleim.com/students or call us at (800) 874-5346.

Thank you for your interest in this book. We deeply appreciate the many letters and suggestions received from accounting and auditing students and educators during the past years, as well as from CDP, CIA, CISA, CMA, CPA, and EA candidates. Please go to www.gleim.com/feedbackAUS to share your suggestions on how we can improve this edition.

Please read the Introduction carefully. It is short but very important.

Good Luck on Your Exams,

Irvin N. Gleim
William A. Hillison

July 2018

INTRODUCTION

This innovative accounting text provides students with a well-organized, extensive collection of multiple-choice questions covering the topics taught in typical auditing and information systems courses.

The Gleim *Exam Questions and Explanations* (EQE) series will help you to pretest yourself before class to determine whether you are strong or weak in the assigned area. Then test yourself after class to reinforce the concepts. The questions in these books cover **all** topics in your related courses, so you will encounter few questions on your exams for which you will not be well prepared.

The titles and organization of Study Units 1 through 22 are based on the current auditing and information systems textbooks listed in Appendix A, which contains a comprehensive cross-reference of your textbook to Gleim study units and subunits. If you are using a textbook that is not included in our list or if you have any suggestions on how we can improve these cross-references to make them more useful, please submit your request/feedback at www.gleim.com/crossreferences/AUS or email them to AUScrossreferences@gleim.com.

FEATURES

The Gleim EQE series will ensure your understanding of each topic you study in your courses with access to the largest bank of exam questions (including thousands from past certification exams) that is widely used by professors. This series provides immediate feedback on your study effort while you take your practice tests.

- Each book or EQE Test Prep question bank contains over 1,000 multiple-choice questions with correct and incorrect answer explanations and can be used in two or more classes.
- Exhaustive cross-references are presented for all related textbooks so that you can easily determine which group of questions pertains to a given chapter in your textbook.
- Questions taken directly from professional certification exams demonstrate the standards to which you will be held as a professional accountant and help prepare you for certification exams later.
- Titles include Auditing & Systems, Cost/Managerial Accounting, Financial Accounting, Federal Tax, and Business Law & Legal Studies. They thoroughly cover the topics you are presented with while pursuing your accounting degree. Go to www.gleim.com/eqe for more details.

After graduation, you will compete with graduates from schools across the country in the accounting job market. Make sure you measure up to standards that are as demanding as the standards of your counterparts at other schools. These standards will be tested on professional certification exams.

USE OF SUBUNITS

Each study unit of this book is divided into subunits to portion overwhelming topics into more manageable, bite-size learning components.

Topics and questions may overlap among subunits. The number of questions offers comprehensive coverage but does not present an insurmountable task. We define each subunit narrowly enough to cover a single topic but broadly enough to prevent questions from being repetitive.

QUESTION SOURCES

Past CDP, CIA, CISA, CMA, and CPA exams and sample questions are the primary sources of questions included in this study guide.

In addition, Gleim Exam Prep prepares questions (coded in this text as *Publisher, adapted*) based on the content of auditing and information systems textbooks, SASs, SSARSs, etc. Professionals and professors from schools around the country also have contributed to provide a more thorough and the largest bank of questions. See the Acknowledgments on page ii for a list of their names.

The source of each question appears in the first line of its answer explanation in the column to the right of the question. Summary of source codes:

CDP	*CDP* Instruction Manual	*CPA*	Uniform Certified Public Accountant Examination
CIA	Certified Internal Auditor Examination	*Publisher*	AUD EQE authors
CISA	Study Guide -- CISA	*Individual's name*	Name of professional or professor who contributed the question
CMA	Certified Management Accountant Examination		

If you, your professor, or your classmates wish to submit questions, we will consider using them in future editions. Please email questions you develop, complete with answers and explanations, to professor.relations@gleim.com.

Writing and analyzing multiple-choice questions is an excellent way to prepare yourself for your exams. We will make every effort to consider, edit, and use questions you submit. However, we ask that you send us only serious, complete, carefully considered efforts.

MULTIPLE-CHOICE QUESTIONS

The major advantage of multiple-choice questions is their ability to cover a large number of topics with little time and effort in comparison to essay questions and/or computational problems.

The advantage of multiple-choice questions over true/false questions is that they require more analysis and result in a lower score for those with little or no knowledge.

Students and professors both like multiple-choice questions. Students find them relatively easy to answer because only one of the answer choices needs to be selected. Professors like them because they are easy to grade and much more material can be tested in the same period of time. Most professors also will ask students to complete essays or computational questions.

Note that the detailed Gleim answer explanations also can help students prepare for the inevitable essay questions.

ANSWER EXPLANATIONS ALONGSIDE THE QUESTIONS

The format of our book presents multiple-choice questions side by side with their answer explanations. The example below is from the CPA exam.

Proper segregation of duties reduces the opportunities to allow persons to be in positions both to

A. Journalize entries and prepare financial statements.

B. Record cash receipts and cash disbursements.

C. Establish internal control and authorize transactions.

D. Perpetrate and conceal fraud and error.

Answer (D) is correct. *(CPA, adapted)*

REQUIRED: The effects of the segregation of duties.

DISCUSSION: Segregation of duties is a category of the control activities component of internal control. Segregating responsibilities for authorization, recording, and asset custody reduces an employee's opportunity to perpetrate fraud or error and subsequently conceal it in the normal course of his or her duties.

Answer (A) is incorrect. Accountants typically journalize entries and prepare financial statements. Answer (B) is incorrect. Accountants may record both cash receipts and cash disbursements as long as they do not have custody of cash. Answer (C) is incorrect. Management establishes internal control and ultimately has the responsibility to authorize transactions.

This format is designed to make studying more efficient by eliminating the need to turn pages back and forth from questions to answers.

Be careful, however. Do not misuse this format by consulting the answers before you have answered the questions. Misuse of the readily available answers will give you a false sense of security and will result in poor performance on your actual exams.

STUDY SUGGESTIONS

The emphasis in the next few pages is on developing strategies, approaches, and procedures to learn and retain the material in less time.

Using Tests to Study

Tests, especially quizzes and midterms, provide feedback on your study and test-taking procedures. It is extremely important to identify your opportunities for improvement on quizzes and tests at the beginning of the term so you can take corrective action on subsequent tests, including your final exam.

When your test is returned, determine how you did relative to the rest of your class and your professor's grading standards. Next, analyze your relative performance between types of questions (essay vs. multiple-choice) and types of subject matter (topics or study units). The objective is to identify the areas where you can improve.

Using Multiple-Choice Questions to Study

Experts on testing continue to favor multiple-choice questions as a valid means of evaluating various levels of knowledge. Using these questions to study for academic exams is an important tool not only for obtaining good grades, but also for long-range preparation for certification and professional exams. The following suggestions will help you study in conjunction with each Gleim *Exam Questions and Explanations* book and EQE Test Prep (visit www.gleim.com/students):

1. Locate the study unit that contains questions on the topic you are currently studying. Each *Exam Questions and Explanations* book and EQE Test Prep contains cross-references to the tables of contents of the most commonly used textbooks.
2. Work through a series of questions, selecting the answers you think are correct. Follow the Gleim multiple-choice question-answering technique outlined in the next section of this introduction.

3. **If you are using the Gleim book, do not consult the answer or answer explanations on the right side of the page until after you have chosen and written down an answer.**
   a. It is crucial that you cover the answer explanations and intellectually commit yourself to an answer. This method will help you understand the concept much better, even if you answered the question incorrectly. Our EQE Test Prep prevents you from consulting the answer, which allows you to study in an exam-like environment.
4. Study the explanations to the correct and incorrect answer choices for each question you answered incorrectly. In addition to learning and understanding the concept tested, analyze **why** you missed the question. Reasons for missing questions include
   - Misreading the requirement (stem)
   - Not understanding what is required
   - Making a math error
   - Applying the wrong rule or concept
   - Being distracted by one or more of the answers
   - Incorrectly eliminating answers from consideration
   - Not having any knowledge of the topic tested
   - Employing bad intuition when guessing

   Studying the important concepts that we provide in our answer explanations will help you understand the principles to the point that you can answer that question (or any other like it) successfully.
5. Identify your weaknesses in answering multiple-choice questions and take corrective action (before you take a test). The EQE Test Prep provides a detailed performance analysis.

   The analysis will show your weaknesses (areas needing more study) and also your strengths (areas of confidence). You can improve your performance on multiple-choice questions both by increasing your percentage of correct answers and by decreasing the time spent per question.

Multiple-Choice Question-Answering Technique

The following series of steps is suggested for answering multiple-choice questions. The important point is that you need to devote attention to and develop **the technique that works for you**. Personalize and practice your answering technique on questions in this study guide. Begin now to develop **your** control system.

1. **Budget your time.**
   a. We make this point with emphasis – **finish your exam before time expires**.
   b. Calculate the time allowed for each multiple-choice question after you have allocated time to the other questions (e.g., essays) on the exam. If 20 multiple-choice questions are allocated 40 minutes on your exam, you should spend a little under 2 minutes per question (always budget extra time for transferring answers to answer sheets, interruptions, etc.).
   c. Before beginning a series of multiple-choice questions, write the starting time on the exam near the first question.
   d. As you work through the questions, check your time. Assuming a time allocation of 120 minutes for 60 questions, you are fine if you worked 5 questions in 9 minutes. If you spent 11 minutes on 5 questions, you need to speed up. Remember that your goal is to answer all questions and achieve the maximum score possible.
2. **Answer the items in consecutive order.**
   a. Do **not** agonize over any one item. Stay within your time budget.
   b. Mark any questions you are unsure of and return to them later as time allows.
   c. Never leave a question unanswered **if** you will not be penalized for incorrect answers. Make your best guess in the time allowed.

3. **For each multiple-choice question,**
   a. **Ignore the answer choices.** Do not allow the answer choices to affect your reading of the question.
      1) If four answer choices are presented, three of them are incorrect. These incorrect choices are called **distractors** for good reason. Often, distractors are written to appear correct at first glance.
      2) In computational items, distractors are carefully calculated so they are the result of common mistakes. Be careful and double-check your computations if time permits.
   b. **Read the question carefully** to determine the precise requirement.
      1) Focusing on what is required enables you to ignore extraneous information and to proceed directly to determining the correct answer.
         a) Be especially careful to note when the requirement is an **exception**; e.g., "Which of the following payments is **not** an investing cash flow?"
   c. **Determine the correct answer** before looking at the answer choices.
   d. **Read the answer choices carefully.**
      1) Even if the first answer appears to be the correct choice, do **not** skip the remaining answer choices. Questions often ask for the "best" choice provided. Thus, each choice requires your consideration.
      2) Treat each answer choice as a true/false question as you analyze it.
   e. **Select the best answer.**
      1) If you are uncertain, guess intelligently (see "If You Don't Know the Answer" below). Improve on your 25% chance of getting the correct answer with blind guessing.
      2) For many multiple-choice questions, two answer choices can be eliminated with minimal effort, thereby increasing your educated guess to a 50-50 proposition.
4. **Transfer your answers to the answer sheet**, if one is provided.
   a. Make sure you are within your time budget so you will be able to perform this vital step in an unhurried manner.
   b. Do not wait to transfer answers until the very end of the exam session because you may run out of time.
   c. Double-check that you have transferred the answers correctly; e.g., recheck every 5th or 10th answer from your test paper to your answer sheet to ensure that you have not fallen out of sequence.

If You Don't Know the Answer

If the exam you are taking does not penalize incorrect answers, you should make an educated guess. First, rule out answers that you think are incorrect. Second, speculate on what the examiner is looking for and/or the rationale behind the question. Third, select the best answer or guess between equally appealing answers. Mark the question with a "?" in case you have time to return to it for further analysis.

If you cannot make an educated guess, read the stem and each answer, and pick the best or most intuitive answer. It's just a guess! Do **not** look at the previous answer to try to detect an answer. Answers are usually random, and it is possible to have four or more consecutive questions with the same answer letter, e.g., answer (B).

NOTE: Do not waste time beyond the amount you budgeted for each question. Move forward and stay on or ahead of schedule.

Examination Summary

	CPA (Certified Public Accountant)	CIA (Certified Internal Auditor)*	CMA (Certified Management Accountant)	EA (IRS Enrolled Agent)
Sponsoring Organization	American Institute of Certified Public Accountants	Institute of Internal Auditors	Institute of Certified Management Accountants	Internal Revenue Service
Contact Information	www.aicpa.org (888) 777-7077	www.theiia.org (407) 937-1111	www.imanet.org (800) 638-4427	www.irs.gov (313) 234-1280
Exam Parts	Auditing and Attestation (4 hrs.) Business Environment and Concepts (4 hrs.) Financial Accounting and Reporting (4 hrs.) Regulation (4 hrs.)	1 – Essentials of Internal Auditing (2.5 hrs.) 2 – Practice of Internal Auditing (2 hrs.) 3 – Business Knowledge for Internal Auditing (2 hrs.)	1 – Financial Reporting, Planning, Performance, and Control (4 hrs.) 2 – Financial Decision Making (4 hrs.)	1 – Individuals (3.5 hrs.) 2 – Businesses (3.5 hrs.) 3 – Representation, Practices, and Procedures (3.5 hrs.)
Exam Format	AUD: 72 multiple-choice questions 8 TBS BEC: 62 multiple-choice questions 4 TBS 3 written communications FAR: 66 multiple-choice questions 8 TBS REG: 76 multiple-choice questions 8 TBS	Part 1: 125 multiple-choice questions Parts 2 and 3: 100 multiple-choice questions	Parts 1 and 2: 100 multiple-choice questions 2 essays	Parts 1, 2, and 3: 100 multiple-choice questions
Avg. Pass Rate	AUD – 49% BEC – 53% FAR – 44% REG – 47%	Pass rates are not yet available for the reorganized exam.	1 – 40% 2 – 50%	1 – 61% 2 – 64% 3 – 86%
Testing Windows	January-March 10 April-June 10 July-September 10 October-December 10	On demand throughout the year	January-February May-June September-October	May-February (e.g., 5/01/2018-2/28/2019)
Resources	gleimcpa.com	gleimcia.com	gleimcma.com	gleimea.com
Available Prep Course Student Discounts	Up to 20%	Up to 20%	Up to 20%	Up to 10%

*Reflects the information for the reorganized 2019 exam.

ACCOUNTING CERTIFICATION PROGRAMS--OVERVIEW

The CPA (Certified Public Accountant) exam is the grandparent of all professional accounting exams. Its origin was in the 1896 public accounting legislation of New York. In 1917, the American Institute of CPAs (AICPA) began to prepare and grade a uniform CPA exam. It is currently used to measure the technical competence of those applying to be licensed as CPAs in all 50 states, Guam, Puerto Rico, the Virgin Islands, the District of Columbia, the Commonwealth of the Northern Mariana Islands, and an ever-expanding list of international locations.

The CIA (Certified Internal Auditor), CMA (Certified Management Accountant), and EA (IRS Enrolled Agent) exams are relatively new certification programs compared to the CPA. The CMA exam was first administered in 1972 and the first CIA exam in 1974. The EA exam dates back to 1959. Why were these other exams initially created? Generally, the requirements of the CPA designation instituted by the boards of accountancy (especially the necessity for public accounting experience) led to the development of the CIA and CMA programs, which allow for professionals to show proficiency in specific job functions. The EA designation is available for persons specializing in tax.

The table of selected CPA, CIA, CMA, and EA exam data on the preceding page provides an overview of these accounting exams.

ACCOUNTING CERTIFICATION PROGRAMS--PURPOSE

The primary purpose of professional exams is to measure the technical competence of candidates. Competence includes technical knowledge, the ability to apply such knowledge with good judgment, comprehension of professional responsibility, and ethical considerations. Additionally, the nature of these exams (low pass rate, broad and rigorous coverage, etc.) has several very important effects:

1. Candidates are forced to learn all of the material that should have been presented and learned in a good accounting education program.
2. Relatedly, candidates must integrate the topics and concepts that are presented in individual courses in accounting education programs.
3. The content of each exam provides direction to accounting education programs; i.e., what is tested on the exams will be taught to accounting students.

Certification is important to professional accountants because it provides

1. Participation in a recognized professional group
2. An improved professional training program arising out of the certification program
3. Recognition among peers for attaining the professional designation
4. An extra credential to enhance career opportunities
5. The personal satisfaction of attaining a recognized degree of competency

These reasons hold true in the accounting field due to wide recognition of the CPA designation. Accountants and accounting students are often asked whether they are CPAs when people learn they are accountants. Thus, there is considerable pressure for accountants to become **certified.**

A newer development is multiple certifications, which are important for the same reasons as initial certification. Accounting students and recent graduates should look ahead and obtain multiple certifications to broaden their career opportunities.

The CIA and CMA are now globally recognized certifications, making them appealing designations for multi-national companies.

When to Sit for the Certification Exams

Sit for all exams as soon as you can. Candidates are allowed to sit for the exam and then complete the requirements within a certain time period. The CIA program allows full-time students in their senior year to sit for the exam, and the CMA program offers a 7-year window for submission of educational credentials. The CIA and CMA exams are offered at a reduced fee for students. The requirements for the CPA vary by jurisdiction, but many state boards allow candidates to sit for the exam before they have completed the required hours. However, you will not be certified until you have met all requirements.

Register to take the parts of each exam that best match up to the courses you are currently taking. For example, if you are taking a Business Law course and a Federal Tax course this semester, schedule your CPA Regulation date for the week after classes end.

Dual certification can greatly enhance your career. Visit www.gleim.com/cmablog to find out why the CPA and CMA is an especially beneficial combination and to learn the steps on how to achieve dual certification.

Steps to Passing Certification Exams

1. Become knowledgeable about the exam you will be taking, and determine which part you will take first.
2. Purchase the complete Gleim Review System to thoroughly prepare yourself. Commit to systematic preparation for the exam as described in our review materials.
3. Communicate with your Personal Counselor to design a study plan that meets your needs. Call (800) 874-5346 or email personalcounselor@gleim.com.
4. Apply for membership in the exam's governing body and/or in the certification program as required.
5. Register online to take the desired part of the exam.
6. Schedule your test with the testing center in the location of your choice.
7. Work systematically through each study unit in the Gleim Review System.
8. Sit for and PASS the exam. Gleim guarantees success!
9. Email or call Gleim with your comments on our study materials and how well they prepared you for the exam.
10. Enjoy your career, pursue multiple certifications (CPA, CIA, CMA, EA, etc.), and recommend Gleim to others who are also taking these exams. Stay up-to-date on your Continuing Professional Education requirements with Gleim CPE.

CERTIFIED INFORMATION SYSTEMS AUDITOR PROGRAM

The Certified Information Systems Auditor (CISA) program, administered by the Information Systems Audit and Control Association (ISACA), is designed to assess and certify individuals in information systems auditing, control, and security. To earn the CISA designation, candidates must successfully complete the CISA examination, adhere to ISACA's Code of Professional Ethics and the Continuing Professional Education program, be in compliance with the Information Systems Auditing Standards as adopted by ISACA, and submit an application for certification. As part of the certification requirement, a candidate must submit evidence of a minimum of 5 years of professional information systems (IS) auditing, control, or security work experience. Substitutions and waivers of such experience, to a maximum of 3 years, may be obtained as follows:

- A maximum of 1 year of IS experience OR 1 year of non-IS auditing experience can be substituted for 1 year of experience.
- An A.A. or B.A. (the equivalent of 60 to 120 college semester credit hours) can be substituted for 1 or 2 years, respectively, of experience. This experience is not limited by the 10-year preceding restriction described below.
- A B.A. or M.A. from a university that enforces the ISACA-sponsored Model Curricula can be substituted for 1 year of experience.
- An M.A. in information security or information technology from an accredited university can be substituted for 1 year of experience.
- Two years of experience as a full-time university instructor in a related field can be substituted for 1 year of experience.

Candidates must have gained experience within the 10-year period preceding the date of the application for certification or within 5 years from the date of initially passing the exam. Experience is verified independently.

The CISA examination is offered during three testing windows per calendar year (February-May, June-September, and October-January) and can be taken at hundreds of PSI Testing Centers around the world. Candidates may take the exam in Chinese (Simplified and Traditional), English, French, German, Hebrew, Italian, Japanese, Korean, Spanish, or Turkish. The exam consists of 150 multiple-choice questions in 4 hours. Candidates may take the CISA exam prior to meeting the experience requirements.

Following is a summary of the content areas on the exam, with recommended percentages of questions for each subject.

- *The Process of Auditing Information Systems* (21%) – Provide audit services in accordance with IS audit standards to assist the organization in protecting and controlling information systems.
- *Governance and Management of IT* (16%) – Provide assurance that the necessary leadership and organizational structures and processes are in place to achieve objectives and to support the organization's strategy.
- *Information Systems Acquisition, Development, and Implementation* (18%) – Provide assurance that the practices for the acquisition, development, testing, and implementation of information systems meet the organization's strategies and objectives.
- *Information Systems Operations, Maintenance, and Service Management* (20%) – Provide assurance that the processes for information systems operations, maintenance, and service management meet the organization's strategies and objectives.
- *Protection of Information Assets* (25%) – Provide assurance that the organization's policies, standards, procedures, and controls ensure the confidentiality, integrity, and availability of information assets.

To assist candidates with the development of a successful study plan, ISACA offers a comprehensive study guide, question/answer/explanations manuals, and review courses. For additional information regarding the CISA certification program, visit www.isaca.org/CISA.

CITATION TO AUTHORITATIVE PRONOUNCEMENTS

This book cites authoritative pronouncements using the abbreviations in the following list.

AR-C	Statements on Standards for Accounting and Review Services (SSARS) are a series of AICPA pronouncements setting standards for engagements in connection with unaudited financial statements or other unaudited financial information of nonissuers.
AS	Auditing standards issued by the PCAOB are applicable to issuers (public companies).
AT-C	Statements on Standards for Attestation Engagements (SSAEs) are issued by the ASB, the Accounting and Review Services Committee, and the Management Consulting Services Executive Committee.
AU-C	SASs are codified in the professional standards volumes using the AU-C prefix.
BL	Bylaws of the AICPA are abbreviated as BL.
CS	Statements on Standards for Consulting Services are codified using the CS prefix.
FASB	The Financial Accounting Standards Board issues authoritative guidance [Accounting Standards Codification (ASC)] and nonauthoritative guidance (e.g., FASB Concepts Statements).
PR	Standards for Performing and Reporting on Peer Reviews are codified under the PR prefix. They apply to the parties involved in practice-monitoring programs.
QC	Statements on Quality Control Standards are codified using the QC prefix. These AICPA pronouncements set standards for quality control by CPA firms.
SAS	Statements on Auditing Standards issued by the AICPA Auditing Standards Board are codified using the SAS prefix. The *Code of Professional Conduct* requires compliance with the standards. See also AU-C above.
SOX	Sarbanes-Oxley Act of 2002.
TS	Statements on Standards for Tax Services (SSTS) set enforceable standards for responsibilities to the taxpayer (client), the public, the government, and the profession.

When a pronouncement is cited in the text, the pronouncement number follows the abbreviations. For example, AU-C 200 refers to Auditing Standards, Section 200.

STUDY UNIT ONE
ENGAGEMENT RESPONSIBILITIES

This study unit begins the consideration of engagement planning. For this purpose, an understanding of the types of services performed by CPAs is necessary. The differences among preparation, compilation, review, examination or audit, and agreed-upon procedures engagements are stressed.

The list below is an overview:

Preparation – Financial statements are prepared, but no assurance is provided and no report is issued.

Compilation – Financial statements are prepared, but a report disclaims any assurance.

Review – Financial statements are reviewed, and a report provides limited assurance.

Examination or audit – Evidence is obtained and positive assurance or an opinion is expressed in a report.

Agreed-upon procedures – The report describes the procedures applied and the findings but provides no assurance.

Additional professional services also are covered in this study unit. They represent an enlargement of the practice of CPAs. An understanding of how these services contrast with others provided by a CPA should be obtained.

Quality control standards apply to a CPA firm's responsibilities in its accounting and auditing practice. The candidate must learn the six specific quality control elements and what each includes. This topic is becoming more important.

QUESTIONS

1.1 Overview of Auditing Engagements

1.1.1. The primary reason for an audit by an independent, external audit firm is to

A. Satisfy governmental regulatory requirements.

B. Guarantee that there are no misstatements in the financial statements and ensure that any fraud will be discovered.

C. Relieve management of responsibility for the financial statements.

D. Provide increased assurance to users as to the fairness of the financial statements.

Answer (D) is correct. *(CMA, adapted)*

REQUIRED: The primary reason for an independent, external audit.

DISCUSSION: The overall objectives of the auditor include obtaining reasonable assurance about whether the financial statements as a whole are free of material misstatement, whether due to fraud or error. This determination permits an auditor to express an opinion on (attest to) whether the financial statements are presented fairly, in all material respects, in accordance with an applicable financial reporting framework (e.g., U.S. GAAP). An audit performed by an independent, external audit firm provides assurance of the objectivity of the auditor's opinion.

Answer (A) is incorrect. Although governmental regulation has increased (e.g., the requirements of the Sarbanes-Oxley Act regarding corporate governance), the primary objective of the audit continues to be an opinion on the fairness of the financial statements. Answer (B) is incorrect. The auditor is neither a guarantor nor an insurer. Answer (C) is incorrect. A precondition for an audit is management's agreement that it acknowledges and understands its responsibility for the preparation and fair presentation of the financial statements (AU-C 210).

1.1.2. Independent CPAs perform audits on the financial statements of issuers. This type of auditing can best be described as

A. An activity whose purpose is to search for fraud.

B. A discipline that attests to financial information presented by management.

C. A professional activity that measures and communicates financial and business data.

D. A regulatory function that prevents the issuance of improper financial information.

Answer (B) is correct. *(Publisher, adapted)*

REQUIRED: The statement that best describes independent auditing.

DISCUSSION: The overall objectives of the auditor include obtaining reasonable assurance about whether the financial statements as a whole are free of material misstatement, whether due to fraud or error. This determination permits an auditor to express an opinion on (attest to) whether the financial statements are presented fairly, in all material respects, in accordance with an applicable financial reporting framework (e.g., U.S. GAAP).

Answer (A) is incorrect. The auditor conducts an audit to obtain reasonable assurance of detecting material misstatements, whether caused by fraud or error. However, (s)he need not search for all instances of fraud, and the ultimate objective is to determine whether the statements are fairly presented. Answer (C) is incorrect. The accounting, not auditing, process is a professional activity that measures and communicates financial and business data. Answer (D) is incorrect. An auditor lacks regulatory authority.

1.1.3. Who establishes generally accepted auditing standards?

A. Auditing Standards Board and the Public Company Accounting Oversight Board.

B. Financial Accounting Standards Board and the Governmental Accounting Standards Board.

C. State Boards of Accountancy.

D. Securities and Exchange Commission.

Answer (A) is correct. *(Publisher, adapted)*

REQUIRED: The organization that issues generally accepted auditing standards (GAAS).

DISCUSSION: AICPA *Code of Professional Conduct* requires adherence to standards issued by bodies designated by the AICPA Council. The Auditing Standards Board (ASB) is the body designated to issue auditing standards for nonissuers. They are in the form of Statements on Auditing Standards (SASs). The Public Company Accounting Oversight Board (PCAOB) was created by the Sarbanes-Oxley Act of 2002. It establishes by rule auditing, quality control, ethics, independence, and other standards relating to the preparation of audit reports for issuers. The PCAOB is required to cooperate with the AICPA and other groups in setting auditing standards and may adopt their proposals. Nevertheless, the PCAOB is authorized to amend, modify, repeal, or reject any such standards. A number of auditing standards have been issued to date, the most significant requiring opinions on internal control for public companies.

Answer (B) is incorrect. The FASB and the GASB issue financial accounting pronouncements and interpretations. Answer (C) is incorrect. Boards of Accountancy in the states and territories regulate the practice of accounting. They typically grant CPA certificates and licenses. Answer (D) is incorrect. The SEC issues Financial Reporting Releases and Accounting and Auditing Enforcement Releases.

1.1.4. Users of an issuer's financial statements demand independent audits because

A. Users demand assurance that fraud does not exist.

B. Management may not be objective in reporting.

C. Users expect auditors to correct management errors.

D. Management relies on the auditor to improve internal control.

Answer (B) is correct. *(Publisher, adapted)*

REQUIRED: The reason for an independent audit.

DISCUSSION: Management and financial statement users may have an adversarial relationship because their interests in the firm are different. The independent auditor provides assurance that the financial statements are not biased for or against any interest.

Answer (A) is incorrect. The independent auditor is ultimately concerned with the fair presentation of the financial statements, not only the detection of fraud. However, the auditor should obtain reasonable assurance that material misstatements are detected. Answer (C) is incorrect. Management is responsible for error correction. Answer (D) is incorrect. Poorly designed internal control is not necessarily inconsistent with a fair presentation of the financial statements. However, AS 2201 issued by the Public Company Accounting Oversight Board (PCAOB) requires an auditor's opinion on internal control in conjunction with the opinion on the financial statements of issuers.

1.1.5. An audit of the financial statements of Camden Corporation is being conducted by an external auditor. The external auditor is expected to

A. Express an opinion as to the fairness of Camden's financial statements.

B. Express an opinion as to the attractiveness of Camden for investment purposes and critique the wisdom and legality of its business decisions.

C. Certify the correctness of Camden's financial statements.

D. Make a 100% examination of Camden's records.

Answer (A) is correct. *(CMA, adapted)*

REQUIRED: The responsibility of an external auditor for an audit of financial statements.

DISCUSSION: Auditing standards require the auditor to express an opinion regarding the financial statements as a whole or to assert that an opinion cannot be expressed. An opinion states whether the financial statements are presented fairly, in all material respects, in accordance with an applicable financial reporting framework.

Answer (B) is incorrect. The external auditor does not interpret the financial statement data for investment purposes or evaluate management decisions. Answer (C) is incorrect. The external audit normally cannot be so thorough as to permit a guarantee of correctness. Answer (D) is incorrect. A 100% examination is seldom, if ever, feasible.

1.1.6. Notes that are included with financial statements are the responsibility of the

A. Securities and Exchange Commission.

B. Company's management.

C. Independent auditor.

D. Internal auditor.

Answer (B) is correct. *(Publisher, adapted)*

REQUIRED: The person(s) primarily responsible for the accuracy of notes.

DISCUSSION: The notes are considered part of the basic financial statements. Because management has the primary responsibility for the financial statements, it also has the primary responsibility for the fairness of information included in notes.

Answer (A) is incorrect. The SEC is responsible for ensuring that firms comply with federal securities laws. Answer (C) is incorrect. The independent external auditor is responsible for expressing an opinion on the fairness of the financial statements. Answer (D) is incorrect. The internal auditor advises management.

1.1.7. Brandnew Company is going public, and its stock will be listed on a stock exchange. Audited financial statements are required to be filed with the Securities and Exchange Commission (SEC). Who is expected to be the primary user of the audited financial statements?

A. The stock exchange.

B. Brandnew Company's investors.

C. The SEC.

D. Brandnew Company's board of directors.

Answer (B) is correct. *(Publisher, adapted)*

REQUIRED: The primary user of audited financial statements of an issuer.

DISCUSSION: An audit's primary objective is to provide assurance to current and potential creditors and investors and other users of financial statements that the financial statements are presented fairly, in all material respects, in accordance with an applicable financial reporting framework.

Answer (A) is incorrect. A stock exchange can require disclosures suitable for its purposes. Investors may not have this power. Answer (C) is incorrect. The SEC can require whatever disclosures are desired. Answer (D) is incorrect. The board of directors can require whatever disclosures are desired.

1.1.8. The Committee of Sponsoring Organizations (COSO) of the Treadway Commission issued a document in 1992 that has been embraced by numerous organizations, including the AICPA and the GAO. That document is titled

A. The Yellow Book.

B. Internal Control--Integrated Framework.

C. Statements on Auditing Standards.

D. *Code of Professional Conduct.*

Answer (B) is correct. *(Publisher, adapted)*

REQUIRED: The document issued by the COSO.

DISCUSSION: Many professional and regulatory bodies, including the PCAOB, have recognized the COSO's internal control framework by incorporating its terms, definitions, and concepts into their policies, procedures, pronouncements, and other literature.

Answer (A) is incorrect. The Yellow Book, or *Government Auditing Standards*, is issued by the Government Accountability Office (GAO). Answer (C) is incorrect. Statements on Auditing Standards are issued by the Auditing Standards Board of the AICPA. Answer (D) is incorrect. The *Code of Professional Conduct* has been adopted by the members of the AICPA.

1.1.9. CPAs within each state have formed state societies or associations of CPAs. Which of the following statements about these associations is false?

A. Most associations have their own codes of professional ethics that closely parallel the AICPA *Code of Professional Conduct*.

B. The state societies are independent of the AICPA.

C. All CPAs in the state must be members of the state association or society.

D. Members of state associations may also be members of the AICPA.

Answer (C) is correct. *(Publisher, adapted)*

REQUIRED: The false statement about state associations or societies of CPAs.

DISCUSSION: Membership in state societies as well as the AICPA is voluntary. State societies typically function through small, full-time staffs or committees composed of their members. They promote the interests of the membership through communication and continuing education programs.

Answer (A) is incorrect. Many state societies have adopted codes of ethics that are similar to the AICPA *Code of Professional Conduct*. Answer (B) is incorrect. The state societies are independent of the AICPA, although they cooperate in promoting the mutual interests of CPAs. Answer (D) is incorrect. Members of state societies may also belong to the AICPA.

1.1.10. According to AU-C 200, *Overall Objectives of the Independent Auditor and the Conduct of an Audit in Accordance with Generally Accepted Auditing Standards*, "presumptively mandatory requirements" in the auditing standards use which word?

A. Must.

B. Can.

C. Should.

D. May.

Answer (C) is correct. *(Publisher, adapted)*

REQUIRED: The word to indicate a presumptively mandatory requirement.

DISCUSSION: The auditor must comply with a presumptively mandatory requirement in all cases in which the requirement is relevant except in rare cases. The standards use the word "should" to indicate this requirement.

Answer (A) is incorrect. "Must" is used for unconditional requirements whenever the requirement is relevant. Answer (B) is incorrect. The word "can" is not technically defined, but it is used when the auditor has alternatives. Answer (D) is incorrect. The word "may" is not technically defined, but it is used when the auditor has alternatives.

1.1.11. An auditor must obtain professional experience primarily to

A. Receive a positive employment evaluation.

B. Exercise professional judgment.

C. Receive a favorable peer review.

D. Earn a specialty designation by the AICPA.

Answer (B) is correct. *(CPA, adapted)*

REQUIRED: The purpose of requiring professional experience in the auditing profession.

DISCUSSION: Professional judgment is essential to perform an audit properly. An auditor must interpret relevant ethical requirements and GAAS and make informed decisions during the audit. Such interpretations and decisions require competencies developed through relevant training, knowledge, and experience (AU-C 200).

Answer (A) is incorrect. A positive employment evaluation is possible before significant professional experience has been obtained. Answer (C) is incorrect. A peer review is an external evaluation of a public accounting firm's practice. Answer (D) is incorrect. Although the AICPA may provide for specialty designations, professional experience will continue to be necessary for the development of the ability to exercise professional judgment.

1.1.12. Competence as an independent auditor includes all of the following except

A. Having the technical qualifications to perform an engagement.

B. Possessing the ability to supervise assistants.

C. Warranting the infallibility of the work performed.

D. Consulting others if additional technical information is needed.

Answer (C) is correct. *(CPA, adapted)*

REQUIRED: The statement not consistent with professional standards of competency.

DISCUSSION: The auditor is not a guarantor. The auditor's responsibility is to express (or disclaim) an opinion on whether the financial statements, taken as a whole, are presented fairly. The audit is planned and performed to provide reasonable, but not absolute, assurance that the financial statements are not materially misstated.

Answer (A) is incorrect. Competence means having the technical qualifications to perform an engagement and the ability to supervise and evaluate the work. Answer (B) is incorrect. Competence includes the ability to supervise and evaluate the work. Answer (D) is incorrect. Additional research and consultation is a normal part of performing services.

1.1.13. GAAS require the auditor to be independent. An auditor is independent if (s)he is

A. Competent.

B. Independent in fact and in appearance.

C. Consistent and independent in fact.

D. Logical and intellectually honest.

Answer (B) is correct. *(Publisher, adapted)*

REQUIRED: The true statement about auditor independence.

DISCUSSION: The auditor must be independent of the entity when performing an engagement in accordance with GAAS unless (1) GAAS provide otherwise or (2) the auditor is required by law to accept and report on the engagement. Barring one of the exceptions, an auditor who is not independent must not report under GAAS. Independence means independence in fact and appearance (AU-C 200 and AS 1005). This crucially important quality gives credibility to the auditor's opinion. If an auditor does not maintain the appearance of independence, however unbiased (s)he may be in fact, the public will be reluctant to believe that (s)he is unbiased.

Answer (A) is incorrect. Competence is not a dimension of auditor independence. Answer (C) is incorrect. Consistency is not a dimension of auditor independence. Answer (D) is incorrect. Logic is not a dimension of auditor independence.

1.1.14. Beth Babett, CPA, is associated with a client's financial statements but is not independent with respect to that client. If she is requested to perform an audit on the financial statements, she should

A. Recommend that the engagement be downgraded to a review.

B. Disclaim an opinion.

C. List the procedures performed in the audit report.

D. Express a piecemeal opinion.

Answer (B) is correct. *(Publisher, adapted)*

REQUIRED: The action taken by a CPA who lacks independence in connection with an audit.

DISCUSSION: The CPA may perform audit procedures according to an agreement with the client. However, a CPA who lacks independence is precluded from expressing an opinion on financial statements because any procedures (s)he performs are not in accordance with GAAS. Hence, the CPA should disclaim an opinion on the financial statements and state specifically that (s)he is not independent.

Answer (A) is incorrect. A review engagement is an attest service that requires the CPA to be independent. Answer (C) is incorrect. The public might be misled into believing that the CPA has performed an audit and is expressing an opinion on the statements if audit procedures are listed. Answer (D) is incorrect. A piecemeal opinion (expressing an opinion on only part of the financial statements) is not acceptable if the CPA has disclaimed an opinion or expressed an adverse opinion on the statements as a whole.

1.1.15. Audit committees have been identified as a major factor in promoting independence in both internal and external auditors. Which of the following is the most important limitation on the effectiveness of audit committees?

A. Audit committees are composed of independent directors. However, those directors may have close personal and professional friendships with management.

B. Audit committee members are compensated by the organization and thus favor a shareholder's view.

C. Audit committees devote most of their efforts to external audit concerns and do not pay much attention to internal auditing and the overall control environment.

D. Audit committee members do not normally have degrees in the accounting or auditing fields.

Answer (A) is correct. *(CIA, adapted)*

REQUIRED: The most important limitation on the effectiveness of audit committees.

DISCUSSION: The audit committee is a subcommittee of outside directors who are independent of corporate management. The Sarbanes-Oxley Act of 2002 requires members of audit committees of issuers to be independent. The act precludes audit committee members from (1) accepting any consulting, advisory, or other compensatory fee from the issuer or (2) being an affiliated person of the issuer or any subsidiary of it. The purpose of the audit committee is to help keep external and internal auditors independent of management and to ensure that the directors are exercising due care. However, if independence is impaired by personal and professional relationships, the effectiveness of the audit committee may be limited.

Answer (B) is incorrect. The compensation audit committee members receive is usually minimal. They should be independent and therefore not limited to a shareholder's perspective. Answer (C) is incorrect. Although audit committees are concerned with external audits, they also devote attention to the internal auditing function. Answer (D) is incorrect. Not all audit committee members need degrees or experience in accounting or auditing for the committee to function effectively. However, the Sarbanes-Oxley Act of 2002 requires at least one member of the audit committee of an issuer to be a financial expert.

1.1.16. Through legal precedent, generally accepted auditing standards established by the AICPA apply

A. Only to CPAs who belong to local CPA societies.

B. To all CPAs.

C. Only to those CPAs who choose to have quality reviews.

D. Only to CPAs conducting audits subject to AICPA jurisdiction.

Answer (B) is correct. *(Publisher, adapted)*

REQUIRED: The legally determined applicability of GAAS.

DISCUSSION: GAAS apply to all CPAs, whether or not they are members of the AICPA. GAAS are deemed to be standards of the profession (explicitly or implicitly) by state boards of accountancy, which issue, renew, suspend, or revoke licenses and otherwise regulate CPAs in all states. Furthermore, the courts in both civil and criminal cases involving independent accountants also treat GAAS as standards of the profession. However, the PCAOB standards explicitly apply to the audit of issuers.

Answer (A) is incorrect. GAAS are binding on all CPAs who perform independent, external audits. Answer (C) is incorrect. GAAS are binding on all CPAs who perform independent, external audits. Answer (D) is incorrect. AICPA jurisdiction concerns only membership in the AICPA. The right to perform the attest function is controlled by state boards of accountancy, all of which require compliance with GAAS.

1.1.17. Audit standards require that the engagement partner

A. Examine all available corroborating evidence.

B. Be responsible for the assignment of tasks to, and supervision of, assistants.

C. Review evidence and audit documentation once the report has been issued.

D. Design the audit to detect all instances of noncompliance with laws and regulations having direct effects on the determination of material financial statement amounts and disclosures.

Answer (B) is correct. *(CPA, adapted)*

REQUIRED: The responsibility of the engagement partner.

DISCUSSION: The engagement partner should take responsibility for the direction, supervision, and performance of the audit engagement in compliance with (1) professional standards, (2) applicable legal and regulatory requirements, and (3) the firm's policies and procedures (AU-C 220).

Answer (A) is incorrect. Cost-benefit considerations ordinarily require the auditor to examine evidence on a test basis. Answer (C) is incorrect. Evidence and audit documentation should be reviewed prior to the issuance of the report. Answer (D) is incorrect. The auditor is responsible for obtaining reasonable, not absolute, assurance that the statements as a whole are free of material misstatements, whether due to fraud or error.

1.1.18. Several sources of U.S. GAAP consulted by an auditor are in conflict as to the application of an accounting principle. Which of the following should the auditor consider the most authoritative?

A. FASB Accounting Standards Codification.

B. International Financial Reporting Standards (IFRS).

C. FASB Statements of Financial Accounting Concepts.

D. AICPA Issues Papers.

Answer (A) is correct. *(CPA, adapted)*

REQUIRED: The most authoritative source of GAAP.

DISCUSSION: The sources of authoritative U.S. GAAP recognized by the FASB as applicable by nongovernmental entities are (1) the FASB's Accounting Standards Codification and (2) (for SEC registrants only) pronouncements of the SEC. All guidance in the codification is equally authoritative. SEC pronouncements must be followed by registrants regardless of whether they are reflected in the codification. All other guidance is nonauthoritative.

Answer (B) is incorrect. IFRS issued by the IASB are GAAP but not U.S. GAAP. But they are authoritative for entities that are permitted to apply them. Answer (C) is incorrect. FASB Statements of Financial Accounting Concepts are nonauthoritative. Answer (D) is incorrect. AICPA Issues Papers are nonauthoritative.

1.2 Overview of Accounting and Review Engagements

1.2.1. Which of the following services, if any, may an accountant who is not independent provide?

A. Preparations and compilations but not reviews.

B. Reviews but not preparations.

C. Both compilations and reviews.

D. No services.

Answer (A) is correct. *(CPA, adapted)*

REQUIRED: The service(s), if any, that may be provided by an accountant who is not independent.

DISCUSSION: A compilation provides no assurance. Thus, the accountant need not be independent. The report describes the compilation service and disclaims an opinion or conclusion or any other form of assurance on the financial statements. The accountant discloses a lack of independence in the report. An accountant who prepares financial statements need not be, or determine whether (s)he is, independent. Also, no report is required.

Answer (B) is incorrect. A review requires independence. A preparation does not. Answer (C) is incorrect. A review requires independence. A compilation does not. Answer (D) is incorrect. A review, but not a preparation or compilation, requires independence.

1.2.2. Statements on Standards for Accounting and Review Services establish standards and procedures for which of the following engagements?

A. Assisting in adjusting the books of account for a partnership.

B. Reviewing interim financial information required to be filed by public companies with the SEC.

C. Processing financial data for clients of other accounting firms.

D. Compiling an individual's personal financial statement to be used to obtain a mortgage.

Answer (D) is correct. *(CPA, adapted)*

REQUIRED: The procedures covered under the SSARSs.

DISCUSSION: AR-C 80 describes the accountant's procedures and reporting responsibilities for compilations. The accountant should obtain an understanding of the applicable financial reporting framework. This framework may be a special purpose framework, e.g., (1) cash basis, (2) tax basis, (3) regulatory basis, (4) contractual basis, or (5) an other basis. An other basis uses a definite set of logical, reasonable criteria applied to all material items in the statements. The FASB's guidance (ASC 274-10) for presenting personal financial statements (a statement of financial condition and a statement of changes in net worth) apparently meet the criteria of an other basis of accounting.

Answer (A) is incorrect. SSARSs do not apply to assisting in adjusting the books of account. SSARSs apply to preparation, compilation, and review engagements performed for nonpublic entities. Answer (B) is incorrect. SSARSs apply only to nonissuers. Answer (C) is incorrect. SSARSs do not apply to processing financial data for clients of other accounting firms. SSARSs apply to preparation, compilation, and review engagements performed for nonpublic entities.

1.2.3. A CPA in public practice is required to comply with the provisions of the Statements on Standards for Accounting and Review Services when

	Advising a client regarding the selection of computer software	Advocating a client's position before the IRS
A.	Yes	Yes
B.	Yes	No
C.	No	Yes
D.	No	No

Answer (D) is correct. *(CPA, adapted)*

REQUIRED: The services, if any, requiring compliance with SSARSs.

DISCUSSION: SSARSs apply to services in connection with the unaudited statements or other unaudited information of a nonpublic entity. Advising a client regarding the selection of computer software is a consulting service (CS 100) and is outside the scope of SSARSs. Advocating a client's position before the IRS is subject to ethics requirements but also is a service outside the scope of SSARSs.

1.2.4. For the purposes of SSARSs, which of the following is a nonissuer?

A. One whose securities trade on a stock exchange or over the counter, including securities quoted only regionally or locally.

B. One that makes a filing with a regulatory agency in preparation for a sale of any class of securities to the public.

C. A subsidiary, corporate joint venture, or other entity controlled by an issuer.

D. A closely held corporation.

Answer (D) is correct. *(Publisher, adapted)*

REQUIRED: The entity considered a nonissuer for purposes of SSARSs.

DISCUSSION: A nonissuer (1) has shares that are not traded in a public market, (2) has not filed with a regulatory body preparatory to public sale of its securities, and (3) is not controlled by an issuer. For example, a proprietorship, partnership, or closely held corporation might be considered a nonissuer.

Answer (A) is incorrect. An entity whose shares are traded is considered to be an issuer for the purposes of SSARSs. Answer (B) is incorrect. An entity that makes a filing with a regulatory agency in preparation for a sale of any class of securities to the public is considered to be an issuer for the purposes of SSARSs. Answer (C) is incorrect. A subsidiary, corporate joint venture, or other entity controlled by an issuer are all considered to be issuers for the purposes of SSARSs.

1.3 Overview of Attestation Engagements

1.3.1. In performing an attest engagement, a CPA most likely

A. Supplies litigation support services.

B. Assesses the risks of material misstatement.

C. Expresses an opinion or conclusion about a written assertion.

D. Provides management consulting advice.

Answer (C) is correct. *(CPA, adapted)*

REQUIRED: The CPA's usual task in an attestation engagement.

DISCUSSION: A practitioner performs attest engagements in accordance with the clarified Statements on Standards for Attestation Engagements. In an attest engagement, a practitioner issues an examination, review, or agreed-upon procedures report on subject matter, or an assertion about the subject matter, that is the responsibility of another party. The report on an examination expresses an opinion on whether (1) the subject matter is in accordance with (or based on) the criteria or (2) the assertion is fairly stated in all material respects. The report on a review expresses a conclusion about whether material modifications should be made to (1) the subject matter for it to be in accordance with the criteria or (2) the assertion is fairly stated in all material respects. The report on an agreed-upon procedures engagement lists the procedures performed and the findings.

Answer (A) is incorrect. Litigation support services are consulting services. Answer (B) is incorrect. The CPA assesses the risks of material misstatement in an audit but not necessarily in all attest engagements. Answer (D) is incorrect. An attest engagement results in a report on subject matter or on an assertion about the subject matter.

1.3.2. Which of the following professional services is considered an attest engagement?

A. A consulting service engagement to provide computer advice to a client.

B. An engagement to report on compliance with statutory requirements.

C. An income tax engagement to prepare federal and state tax returns.

D. The compilation of an engagement to provide a peer review for another CPA firm.

Answer (B) is correct. *(CPA, adapted)*

REQUIRED: The attest service.

DISCUSSION: In an attest engagement, a practitioner issues an examination, a review, or an agreed-upon procedures report on subject matter (or an assertion about subject matter) that is the responsibility of another party (AT-C 105). Thus, attest engagements are not limited to traditional financial statement audits. For example, attest services may extend to management's compliance with specified requirements or the effectiveness of internal control over compliance.

Answer (A) is incorrect. The attestation standards explicitly do not apply to consulting services in which the practitioner provides advice or recommendations to a client. Answer (C) is incorrect. Tax return preparation is not an attest service according to the attestation standards. Answer (D) is incorrect. Peer reviews essentially are evaluations of quality control. They are performed to meet the practice-monitoring requirements applicable to public accounting firms. They are not attest engagements.

1.3.3. Which of the following is the authoritative body designated to promulgate attestation standards?

A. Auditing Standards Board.

B. Governmental Accounting Standards Board.

C. Financial Accounting Standards Board.

D. Government Accountability Office.

Answer (A) is correct. *(CPA, adapted)*

REQUIRED: The authoritative body designated to issue attestation standards.

DISCUSSION: Statements on Standards for Attestation Engagements are issued by the Auditing Standards Board, Accounting and Review Services Committee, and the Management Consulting Services Executive Committee. The Council of the AICPA granted these bodies, which issue SASs, SSARSs, and SSCSs, respectively, the authority to interpret the Compliance with Standards Rule. The attestation standards are issued under that authority.

Answer (B) is incorrect. The GASB issues accounting and reporting standards for local and state governments. Answer (C) is incorrect. The FASB establishes U.S. GAAP. Answer (D) is incorrect. The GAO issues *Government Auditing Standards.*

1.3.4. The practitioner's report on the examination of prospective financial statements should include all of the following except

A. An identification of the prospective financial statements presented and a statement that the examination was made in accordance with AICPA attestation standards.

B. A statement that the practitioner assumes no responsibility to update the report for events and circumstances after the report date.

C. The practitioner's opinion that the statements are in conformity with AICPA presentation guidelines and that the underlying assumptions provide a reasonable basis for the projection given the hypothetical assumptions or a reasonable basis for the forecast.

D. The practitioner's opinion that the prospective results will be attained.

Answer (D) is correct. *(Publisher, adapted)*

REQUIRED: The inappropriate element in a report on prospective financial statements.

DISCUSSION: Whenever a practitioner submits prospective financial statements that (s)he has assembled that reasonably might be expected to be used by a third party or reports on such statements, (s)he should examine, compile, or apply agreed-upon procedures to the statements. An examination is a professional service involving evaluation of the preparation of (1) the statements, (2) the support underlying the assumptions, and (3) the presentation of the statements in conformity with AICPA guidelines. It also requires issuance of a report. However, the practitioner should state that the prospective results may not be attained (AT-C 305).

1.4 Additional Professional Services

1.4.1. Assurance and advisory services are best described as

A. Services designed for the improvement of operations, resulting in better outcomes.

B. Independent professional services that improve the quality of information, or its context, for decision makers.

C. The assembly of financial statements based on information and assumptions of a responsible party.

D. Services designed to express an opinion on historical financial statements based on the results of an audit.

Answer (B) is correct. *(Publisher, adapted)*

REQUIRED: The description of assurance services.

DISCUSSION: The AICPA defines assurance services as independent professional services that improve the quality of information, or its context, for decision makers. Assurance services encompass audit and other attestation services but also include nonstandard services. Assurance services do not encompass consulting services.

Answer (A) is incorrect. Consulting services are services designed for the improvement of operations, resulting in better outcomes. Answer (C) is incorrect. Compilation services are the assembly of financial statements based on information and assumptions of a responsible party. Answer (D) is incorrect. The traditional audit consists of services designed to express an opinion on historical financial statements based on the results of an audit.

1.4.2. Assurance services differ from consulting services in that assurance services

	Focus on Providing Advice	Involve Monitoring of One Party by Another
A.	Yes	Yes
B.	Yes	No
C.	No	Yes
D.	No	No

Answer (C) is correct. *(Publisher, adapted)*

REQUIRED: The way(s) in which assurance services differ from consulting services.

DISCUSSION: Assurance services encompass attestation services but not consulting services. Assurance services differ from consulting services in two ways: (1) They focus on improving information rather than providing advice, and (2) they usually involve situations in which one party wants to monitor another rather than the two-party arrangements common in consulting engagements.

1.4.3. The objective of assurance services is to

A. Provide more timely information.

B. Enhance decision making.

C. Compare internal information and policies to those of other firms.

D. Improve the firm's outcomes.

Answer (B) is correct. *(Publisher, adapted)*

REQUIRED: The objective of assurance services.

DISCUSSION: The main objective of assurance services, as stated by the AICPA, is to provide information that assists in better decision making. Assurance services encompass audit and other attestation services but also include nonstandard services. Assurance services do not encompass consulting services.

Answer (A) is incorrect. Providing more timely information is not a stated objective. Answer (C) is incorrect. Assurance services do not involve analysis of other companies. Answer (D) is incorrect. Providing information that results in better outcomes is an objective of consulting services.

1.4.4. The guidance least likely to apply to personal financial planning (PFP) engagements is

A. Confidential Client Information Rule.

B. Independence Rule.

C. Statement on Standards for Consulting Services.

D. Statement on Standards for Attestation Engagements related to financial forecasts and projections.

Answer (B) is correct. *(Publisher, adapted)*

REQUIRED: The guidance least likely to apply to PFP engagements.

DISCUSSION: Personal financial planning is not a professional service that requires a CPA to be independent of the client. However, the CPA must follow the other pertinent Conduct Rules, including the Integrity and Objectivity Rule, the General Standards Rule, the Confidential Client Information Rule, and the Contingent Fees Rule.

Answer (A) is incorrect. PFP engagements require the CPA not to disclose confidential client information without the client's specific consent. Answer (C) is incorrect. The Statement on Standards for Consulting Services is relevant when a CPA values a business as part of a PFP engagement. Answer (D) is incorrect. A PFP engagement may involve preparation of financial forecasts or financial projections.

1.5 Quality Control

1.5.1. A CPA firm is reasonably assured of meeting its responsibility to provide services that conform with professional standards by

A. Adhering to generally accepted auditing standards.

B. Having an appropriate system of quality control.

C. Joining professional societies that enforce ethical conduct.

D. Maintaining an attitude of independence in its engagements.

Answer (B) is correct. *(CPA, adapted)*

REQUIRED: The means of reasonably assuring that a CPA firm's services meet professional standards.

DISCUSSION: A system of quality control should provide reasonable assurance that the firm's personnel comply with professional standards and applicable regulatory and legal requirements. However, deficiencies in individual engagements covered by the quality control standards do not, by themselves, signify that the firm's system of quality control is insufficient to provide it with reasonable assurance of compliance with the relevant standards. GAAS apply to individual audit engagements. Quality control standards apply to the firm's practice as a whole.

Answer (A) is incorrect. A firm must comply with all applicable standards, not merely GAAS. Answer (C) is incorrect. Adhering to ethical standards is only one aspect of quality control. Answer (D) is incorrect. Independence is one of many issues addressed by a system of quality control.

1.5.2. A firm of independent auditors must establish and follow quality control policies and procedures because these standards

A. Are necessary to meet increasing requirements of auditors' liability insurers.

B. Provide assurance that clients maintain quality reporting systems.

C. Include formal filing of records of such policies and procedures.

D. Give reasonable assurance that the firm as a whole will conform with applicable auditing standards.

Answer (D) is correct. *(Publisher, adapted)*

REQUIRED: The reason a firm of independent auditors establishes a quality control system.

DISCUSSION: The system of quality control includes the organizational structure and the policies adopted and procedures established to provide reasonable assurance that the firm as a whole will comply with auditing and other applicable professional standards. Policies and procedures should be established with respect to the following elements: (1) Leadership responsibilities for quality within the firm (the "tone at the top"), (2) relevant ethical requirements, (3) acceptance and continuance of client relationships and specific engagements, (4) human resources, (5) engagement performance, and (6) monitoring (QC 10).

Answer (A) is incorrect. Companies that insure CPAs against liability for malpractice establish their own requirements and insurance rates. Answer (B) is incorrect. Quality control standards apply to auditing firms, not their clients. Answer (C) is incorrect. Quality control standards do not require formal records to be filed with the AICPA or any other body.

1.5.3. Quality control for a CPA firm, as referred to in Statements on Quality Control Standards (SQCS), applies to

A. Auditing services only.

B. Auditing and consulting services.

C. Auditing and tax services.

D. Auditing and accounting and review services.

Answer (D) is correct. *(CPA, adapted)*

REQUIRED: The applicability of the quality control standards.

DISCUSSION: According to QC 10, quality control for a CPA firm applies to all audit, attest, accounting and review, and other services for which professional standards have been established by the ASB and the Accounting and Review Services Committee. The SQCS therefore do not apply to compliance with standards for consulting services and tax services, which are issued by different AICPA technical committees.

1.5.4. Which of the following are elements of a CPA firm's quality control that should be considered in establishing its quality control policies and procedures?

	Human Resources	Monitoring	Engagement Performance
A.	Yes	Yes	No
B.	Yes	Yes	Yes
C.	No	Yes	Yes
D.	Yes	No	Yes

Answer (B) is correct. *(CPA, adapted)*

REQUIRED: The elements that should be considered in establishing quality control policies and procedures.

DISCUSSION: The quality control element of human resources relates to providing reasonable assurance that the firm has sufficient personnel with the necessary capabilities, competence, and commitment to ethics. The quality control element of monitoring relates to providing reasonable assurance that the firm has a quality control system that is relevant, adequate, effective, and complied with. The quality control element of engagement performance relates to providing reasonable assurance that (1) engagements are consistently performed in accordance with applicable requirements and (2) issued reports are appropriate (QC 10).

1.5.5. The nature and extent of a CPA firm's quality control policies and procedures depend on

	The CPA Firm's Size	The Nature of the CPA Firm's Practice	Cost-Benefit Considerations
A.	Yes	Yes	Yes
B.	Yes	Yes	No
C.	Yes	No	Yes
D.	No	Yes	Yes

Answer (A) is correct. *(CPA, adapted)*

REQUIRED: The factors affecting a CPA firm's quality control policies and procedures.

DISCUSSION: The nature and extent of a firm's quality control policies and procedures depend on a number of factors, such as the firm's size, the degree of operating autonomy allowed, its human resources policies, the nature of its practice and organization, and appropriate cost-benefit considerations.

1.5.6. Which of the following is an element of a CPA firm's quality control system that should be considered in establishing its quality control policies and procedures?

A. Complying with laws and regulations.

B. Using statistical sampling techniques.

C. Managing human resources.

D. Considering audit risk and materiality.

Answer (C) is correct. *(CPA, adapted)*

REQUIRED: The element of quality control.

DISCUSSION: The quality control element of human resources requires establishment of policies and procedures to provide reasonable assurance that only qualified persons with the required technical training and proficiency perform the work.

Answer (A) is incorrect. The auditor considers compliance with laws and regulations. However, this consideration is not an element of quality control. Answer (B) is incorrect. An auditing firm may use statistical or nonstatistical sampling techniques in performing audits; a particular sampling technique is not an element of quality control. Answer (D) is incorrect. An auditor must consider audit risk and materiality in performing the audit, but this consideration is not an element of quality control.

1.5.7. One purpose of establishing quality control policies and procedures for deciding whether to accept a new client is to

A. Enable the CPA firm to attest to the reliability of the client.

B. Satisfy the CPA firm's duty to the public concerning the acceptance of new clients.

C. Provide reasonable assurance that the integrity of the client is considered.

D. Anticipate before performing any field work whether an unmodified opinion can be expressed.

Answer (C) is correct. *(CPA, adapted)*

REQUIRED: The purpose of establishing quality control policies and procedures for deciding whether to accept a new client.

DISCUSSION: CPA firms should have policies and procedures to determine whether to accept or continue a client or to perform a specific engagement. The firm's policies and procedures should provide reasonable assurance that it (1) has considered the integrity of the client and the risks involved, (2) is competent, (3) has the necessary capabilities and resources, and (4) is able to comply with applicable requirements (QC 10).

Answer (A) is incorrect. The CPA firm attests to the fairness of the financial statements, not to the reliability of the client. Answer (B) is incorrect. The CPA firm has a duty to the public with regard to its reporting responsibilities but not client acceptance. Answer (D) is incorrect. The field work will indicate whether an unmodified opinion can be expressed.

1.5.8. In connection with the element of human resources, a CPA firm's system of quality control should ordinarily provide that all personnel

A. Participate in professional development activities that enable them to fulfill responsibilities assigned.

B. Possess judgment and motivation.

C. Seek assistance from persons having appropriate levels of knowledge, judgment, and authority.

D. Demonstrate compliance with peer review directives.

Answer (A) is correct. *(CPA, adapted)*

REQUIRED: The requirement for all personnel.

DISCUSSION: The firm's policies and procedures should provide for all personnel to receive general and industry-specific CPE and engage in other professional development activities. The purpose is to enable personnel to carry out assigned responsibilities and satisfy CPE requirements of the AICPA and regulatory agencies, such as the GAO and state boards of accountancy (QC 10).

Answer (B) is incorrect. Motivation and judgment are often difficult to assess. Answer (C) is incorrect. Seeking assistance from persons having appropriate levels of knowledge, judgment, and authority relates to the element of engagement performance. Answer (D) is incorrect. Peer review directives may relate to any or all of the quality control elements.

1.5.9. Within the context of quality control, the primary purpose of continuing professional education (CPE) and training activities is to provide a CPA firm with reasonable assurance that personnel within the firm have

A. Technical training that ensures proficiency as an auditor.

B. Professional education that is required to perform with due professional care.

C. The ability to fulfill assigned responsibilities and the qualifications for advancement.

D. Knowledge required to perform a peer review.

Answer (C) is correct. *(CPA, adapted)*

REQUIRED: The primary purpose of CPE and training activities relative to a CPA firm's quality control.

DISCUSSION: According to QC 10, the firm should adopt policies and procedures to obtain reasonable assurance that personnel at all levels participate in general and industry-specific CPE and other professional development activities that enable them to fulfill responsibilities assigned and satisfy applicable CPE requirements of the AICPA and regulatory agencies. Furthermore, personnel chosen for advancement should "have the qualifications necessary for fulfillment of the responsibilities they will be called on to assume."

Answer (A) is incorrect. Technical training does not ensure proficiency as an auditor. Professional experience complements formal education to develop seasoned judgment. Answer (B) is incorrect. Professional education alone does not ensure performance with due professional care. Answer (D) is incorrect. CPE is important to all personnel, not just to peer reviewers.

1.5.10. In pursuing a CPA firm's quality control objectives, a CPA firm may maintain records indicating which partners or employees of the CPA firm were previously employed by the CPA firm's clients. Which quality control element is this procedure most likely to satisfy?

A. Professional relationship.

B. Experience requirements.

C. Relevant ethical requirements.

D. Advancement.

Answer (C) is correct. *(CPA, adapted)*

REQUIRED: The quality control element associated with records of employment of personnel by the firm's clients.

DISCUSSION: CPA firms should avoid situations in which third parties might question the firm's independence. Thus, they should adhere to the independence and other principles established by the AICPA *Code of Professional Conduct* and the requirements of regulators and other authorities (QC 10).

Answer (A) is incorrect. A professional relationship is not a quality control element. Answer (B) is incorrect. Experience requirements are not quality control elements. Answer (D) is incorrect. Advancement is an aspect of the element of human resources. It relates to ensuring that employees selected for advancement have the skills needed for their responsibilities.

1.5.11. Quality control policies and procedures should be relevant, adequate, effective, and complied with. This statement is most closely associated with the quality control element of

A. Review.

B. Supervision.

C. Relevant ethical requirements.

D. Monitoring.

Answer (D) is correct. *(Publisher, adapted)*

REQUIRED: The element related to effective application of quality control.

DISCUSSION: Monitoring is concerned with providing reasonable assurance that policies and procedures related to the system of quality control are relevant, adequate, operating effectively, and complied with. The objectives of monitoring these policies and procedures are to evaluate (1) compliance with professional standards and legal requirements, (2) the design and effectiveness of the quality control system, and (3) whether appropriate reports are issued (QC 10).

Answer (A) is incorrect. Policies and procedures for the element of engagement performance apply to review responsibilities. Answer (B) is incorrect. Supervision is an aspect of the element of engagement performance. Answer (C) is incorrect. The element of relevant ethical requirements provides reasonable assurance that personnel at all levels remain independent when required.

1.5.12. Williams & Co. is a medium-sized CPA firm enrolled in the Private Companies Practice Section (PCPS). The firm is to have a peer review under the AICPA Peer Review program. The review will most likely be performed by

A. Partners of Williams & Co. who are not associated with the particular audits being reviewed.

B. Audit review staff of the SEC.

C. Audit review staff of the AICPA.

D. Another CPA firm.

Answer (D) is correct. *(CPA, adapted)*

REQUIRED: The parties most likely to perform a peer review of a medium-sized CPA firm.

DISCUSSION: Peer review is a necessary part of the practice-monitoring requirement for AICPA membership. A peer review of a firm enrolled in the AICPA Peer Review program may be performed by a review team organized by (1) a firm engaged by the reviewed firm or (2) a state CPA society. Also, an association of firms may be authorized to aid its members by organizing review teams (PR 100). Furthermore, a PCPS firm need not perform the peer review of a PCPS firm, and the team captain need not be a PCPS member.

Answer (A) is incorrect. Partners of the firm being reviewed are not considered independent for the purpose of peer review. Answer (B) is incorrect. The SEC does not perform peer reviews. Answer (C) is incorrect. The AICPA does not have professional staff to perform peer reviews.

1.5.13. The requirement to promote a culture of quality is most closely associated with which of the following quality control elements?

A. Leadership responsibilities for quality within the firm.

B. Monitoring.

C. Engagement performance.

D. Relevant ethical requirements.

Answer (A) is correct. *(Publisher, adapted)*

REQUIRED: The quality control element relating to the culture of the firm.

DISCUSSION: A CPA firm should promote an internal culture based on the recognition that quality is essential in performing engagements and should establish policies and procedures to support that culture. Leadership responsibilities for quality within the firm relates to the tone at the top of the organization. It permeates the entire organization and is an important component in the establishment of quality within the firm (QC 10).

Answer (B) is incorrect. Monitoring relates to policies and procedures to provide reasonable assurance that the system of quality control is relevant, adequate, operating effectively, and complied with. Answer (C) is incorrect. Engagement performance relates to policies and procedures to provide reasonable assurance that engagements are consistently and effectively performed. Answer (D) is incorrect. The element of relevant ethical requirements relates to policies and procedures to provide reasonable assurance that the firm and its personnel comply with the AICPA *Code of Professional Conduct* and the requirements of regulators and other authorities.

1.5.14. In connection with the element of monitoring, a CPA firm's system of quality control ordinarily should provide for the maintenance of

A. A file of minutes of staff meetings.

B. Updated personnel files.

C. Documentation to demonstrate compliance with its policies and procedures.

D. Documentation to demonstrate compliance with peer review directives.

Answer (C) is correct. *(CPA, adapted)*

REQUIRED: The item maintained in connection with the quality control element of monitoring.

DISCUSSION: Monitoring relates to providing reasonable assurance that policies and procedures related to the system of quality control are relevant, adequate, operating effectively, and complied with. The objectives of monitoring these policies and procedures are to evaluate (1) compliance with professional standards and legal requirements, (2) the design and effectiveness of the quality control system, and (3) whether appropriate reports are issued. Documentation of monitoring includes procedures, evaluations, deficiencies, and the bases for taking or not taking further action. Documentation of all elements of quality control should be retained for a period of time sufficient to enable those performing monitoring procedures and a peer review to evaluate the extent of the firm's compliance with its quality control standards, or for a longer period if required by law or regulation (QC 10).

Answer (A) is incorrect. A file of minutes of staff meetings is an example of the documentation of engagement performance. Answer (B) is incorrect. Updated personnel files are examples of the documentation of human resources activities. Answer (D) is incorrect. Documentation to demonstrate compliance with peer review directives is an example of the documentation of compliance.

1.5.15. AICPA members in the practice of public accounting with a firm that is registered and inspected by the Public Company Accounting Oversight Board (PCAOB) may be associated with that firm only if it is enrolled in the AICPA Center for Public Company Audit Firms Peer Review Program (Center PRP). The purpose of the Center PRP is to

A. Act as a control over the PCAOB inspection process.

B. Review and evaluate those portions of a firm's practice that are not inspected by the PCAOB.

C. Substitute for the inspection process of the PCAOB.

D. Serve as part of the PCAOB inspection process.

Answer (B) is correct. *(Publisher, adapted)*

REQUIRED: The purpose of the Center PRP.

DISCUSSION: Inspections by the PCAOB entail evaluation of quality control related to the audits of public firms (issuers). The Center PRP provides an evaluation of quality control over other audit and attest engagements of the firm.

Answer (A) is incorrect. The PCAOB is responsible for controls over its inspections. Answer (C) is incorrect. The Center PRP complements the PCAOB inspection. Answer (D) is incorrect. The Center PRP is an AICPA program.

1.5.16. The AICPA peer review standards define three levels of peer review. The highest level is a(n)

A. System review.

B. Engagement review.

C. Report review.

D. Inspection review.

Answer (A) is correct. *(Publisher, adapted)*

REQUIRED: The highest level of AICPA peer review.

DISCUSSION: Under the AICPA peer review standards, a system review is the highest level of peer review. It includes visits to practice offices. The objective is to provide a reasonable basis for expressing an opinion on (1) the reviewed firm's design of its system of quality control and (2) compliance with quality control policies and procedures to provide reasonable assurance of conformity with professional standards.

Answer (B) is incorrect. An engagement review is for a firm not required to have a system review but not qualifying for a report review. It provides the reviewer with a reasonable basis for expressing limited assurance on whether the financial statements and accountant's reports materially conform to professional standards. Answer (C) is incorrect. A report review is for a firm that performs only compilations omitting substantially all disclosures. It consists of comments and recommendations after review of a sample of engagements. Answer (D) is incorrect. The PCAOB does inspections of CPA firms that perform audits of public companies (issuers).

1.5.17. Anyone inquiring about the professional reputation and standing of a CPA firm may contact the AICPA Division for CPA Firms and expect to receive

A. Copies of complaints against the CPA firm that are currently being adjudicated by the AICPA Joint Trial Board.

B. Copies of peer review reports on the CPA firm after the reports have been accepted.

C. Information regarding prima facie violations of the *Code of Professional Conduct* or AICPA bylaws not deemed of sufficient gravity to warrant further formal action.

D. Information regarding pending investigations of individuals within the CPA firm.

Answer (B) is correct. *(CPA, adapted)*

REQUIRED: The information obtainable from the Division for CPA Firms.

DISCUSSION: Anyone inquiring about the professional reputation and standing of a CPA firm may contact the Division for CPA Firms and receive information on the firm's enrollment in an AICPA-approved practice monitoring program. Also, if the firm is enrolled in either the Center for Public Company Audit Firms or Private Companies Practice Section (PCPS), anyone may obtain copies of the firm's most recent peer review report after the report has been accepted by the relevant report acceptance body. Moreover, the Division will provide information submitted by member firms on applications for membership and annual updates. There is no charge for this service.

Answer (A) is incorrect. Neither the Division for CPA Firms nor the Professional Ethics Division may respond to inquiries about complaints against CPA firms currently being adjudicated. Answer (C) is incorrect. The Division for CPA Firms will not provide information about violations not deemed of sufficient gravity to warrant further formal action. Answer (D) is incorrect. The Division for CPA Firms will not provide information about pending investigations of individuals within the CPA firm. However, the Professional Ethics Division may respond to inquiries about disciplinary action taken by the Joint Trial Board or one of its sub-boards and published in a membership periodical of the AICPA.

STUDY UNIT TWO
PROFESSIONAL RESPONSIBILITIES

Subunits 2.1 through 2.6 relate to the AICPA *Code of Professional Conduct*. Its Principles and Rules establish the profession's duties to the public and to clients. Subunit 2.7 applies to other standards that prescribe professional responsibilities for accountants, including the Sarbanes-Oxley Act, the PCAOB, the SEC, and the International Federation of Accountants. Subunit 2.8 covers the legal liability of CPAs. This liability may be civil or criminal and imposed by state or federal authorities. Subunit 2.9 addresses the AICPA Statements on Standards for Tax Services. SSTSs provide minimum standards of conduct in tax practice. Subunit 2.10 includes questions on the AICPA Statement on Standards for Consulting Services. It provides guidance for a broad range of services performed by CPAs that do not involve attesting to the assertions of others or providing assurance.

QUESTIONS

2.1 *Code of Professional Conduct*

2.1.1. Which AICPA Conduct Rule applies only to members in the practice of public accounting?

A. General Standards.

B. Accounting Principles.

C. Independence.

D. Compliance with Standards.

Answer (C) is correct. *(Publisher, adapted)*

REQUIRED: The AICPA Conduct Rule that applies only to members in public accounting.

DISCUSSION: The Independence Rule states, "A member in public practice shall be independent in the performance of professional services as required by standards promulgated by bodies designated by Council." The scope of services addressed is broader than the expression of opinions on financial statements. Thus, it applies to such professional services as reviews, reports on prospective financial information, and reports on other attestation engagements.

Answer (A) is incorrect. The General Standards Rule also applies to members in business. Answer (B) is incorrect. The Accounting Principles Rule also applies to members in business. Answer (D) is incorrect. The Compliance with Standards Rule also applies to members in business.

2.1.2. The AICPA *Code of Professional Conduct*

A. Prohibits encroachment on the practice of another CPA.

B. Prohibits offers of employment to employees of another CPA without notice.

C. Expects the CPA to honor the public trust.

D. Encourages but does not require CPAs to refrain from advertising or engaging in other forms of solicitation.

Answer (C) is correct. *(Publisher, adapted)*

REQUIRED: The true statement about the *Code of Professional Conduct.*

DISCUSSION: The nonbinding Principles state that members should act to benefit the public interest and honor the public trust.

Answer (A) is incorrect. No Conduct Rules currently govern responsibilities to colleagues. Answer (B) is incorrect. No Conduct Rules currently govern responsibilities to colleagues. Answer (D) is incorrect. CPAs are not encouraged or required to refrain from solicitation unless it is false, misleading, or deceptive.

2.1.3. Which of the following statements best explains why the CPA profession has found it essential to establish ethical standards and means for ensuring their observance?

A. A distinguishing mark of a profession is its acceptance of responsibility to the public.

B. A requirement for a profession is to establish ethical standards that stress primarily a responsibility to clients and colleagues.

C. Ethical standards that emphasize excellence in performance over material rewards establish a reputation for competence and character.

D. Vigorous enforcement of an established code of ethics is the best way to prevent unscrupulous acts.

Answer (A) is correct. *(CPA, adapted)*

REQUIRED: The best reason for issuing ethical standards.

DISCUSSION: According to the Principles section of the AICPA *Code of Professional Conduct*, "Members should accept the obligation to act in a way that will serve the public interest, honor the public trust, and demonstrate commitment to professionalism. A distinguishing mark of a profession is acceptance of its responsibility to the public."

Answer (B) is incorrect. The responsibility of CPAs is to a public that is not limited to clients and colleagues but includes all those who rely on their objectivity and integrity. Answer (C) is incorrect. Excellence in performance is but one of the effects of accepting responsibility to the public. Answer (D) is incorrect. Vigorous enforcement is significant but secondary to the creation of an environment in the profession that fosters voluntary adherence to ethical principles.

2.1.4. The AICPA *Code of Professional Conduct* contains both general ethical principles that are aspirational in character and also a

A. List of violations that would cause the automatic suspension of a member's license.

B. Set of specific, mandatory rules describing minimum levels of conduct a member must maintain.

C. Description of a member's procedures for responding to an inquiry from a trial board.

D. List of specific acts discreditable to the profession.

Answer (B) is correct. *(CPA, adapted)*

REQUIRED: The content of the *Code of Professional Conduct.*

DISCUSSION: The AICPA *Code* contains Principles and Rules. The principles are goal-oriented. The rules provide more specific guidance. The principles call for an unswerving commitment to honorable behavior but are not mandatory. The AICPA bylaws require members to adhere to the rules. Those who fail to comply with the rules may face disciplinary action.

Answer (A) is incorrect. The bylaws (BL 730), not the *Code*, list violations resulting in an automatic suspension. Answer (C) is incorrect. The bylaws (BL 740R) describe trial board procedures. Answer (D) is incorrect. The Acts Discreditable Rule simply prohibits discreditable acts. However, the related interpretations specify certain types of discreditable acts.

2.1.5. The AICPA *Code of Professional Conduct* does not include enforceable Rules of Conduct on which of the following?

A. Independence and integrity and objectivity.

B. Professional competence and due professional care.

C. Accounting principles.

D. Responsibilities to colleagues.

Answer (D) is correct. *(Publisher, adapted)*

REQUIRED: The subject on which the *Code* provides no enforceable Conduct Rules.

DISCUSSION: The *Code* previously included two rules regarding colleagues, but they were deleted after threats of antitrust actions against the profession by the Federal Trade Commission and the U.S. Justice Department. The principles express the profession's recognition of its responsibilities to colleagues as well as to the public and clients, but adherence to them is not mandatory.

Answer (A) is incorrect. Enforceable Rules of Conduct include (1) independence and (2) integrity and objectivity. Answer (B) is incorrect. Enforceable Rules of Conduct include (1) professional competence and (2) due professional care. Answer (C) is incorrect. Enforceable Rules of Conduct include accounting principles.

2.1.6. CPAs are required to complete engagements competently. Competence includes all of the following except

A. An unbiased mental attitude.

B. The technical qualifications of the CPA's staff.

C. The capacity to exercise judgment.

D. The ability to research subject matter and consult with others.

Answer (A) is correct. *(Publisher, adapted)*

REQUIRED: The item not associated with competence.

DISCUSSION: The *Code* requires the CPA to maintain an unbiased mental attitude. A member in public practice must be independent in the performance of professional services as required by standards issued by bodies designated by Council.

Answer (B) is incorrect. Competence relates both to knowledge of the profession's standards, techniques, and the technical subject matter involved, and to the ability to exercise sound judgment in applying such knowledge in the performance of professional services. Answer (C) is incorrect. Competence includes the ability to exercise sound judgment in applying knowledge in the performance of services. Answer (D) is incorrect. In some cases, additional research or consultation with others does not ordinarily represent a lack of competence, but rather is a normal part of the performance of professional services.

2.1.7. When management refuses to disclose material noncompliance with laws and regulations identified by the independent auditor, the independent auditor may be charged with violating the AICPA *Code of Professional Conduct* for

A. Disclaiming an opinion.

B. Withdrawing from the engagement.

C. Failing to uncover the illegal activities during prior audits.

D. Reporting these activities to those charged with governance.

Answer (A) is correct. *(CPA, adapted)*

REQUIRED: The inappropriate auditor action relative to disclosure of noncompliance with laws and regulations.

DISCUSSION: When the auditor concludes that noncompliance is material and has not been appropriately disclosed or accounted for, a normal disclaimer of opinion is not suitable. The auditor should disclose the problem in a report that includes either a qualified or an adverse opinion. If management or those charged with governance do not accept a modified opinion, the auditor may withdraw from the engagement. Moreover, the auditor may, in some circumstances, have a duty of disclosure outside the entity, e.g., in a report to the SEC on Form 8-K or in a response to a subpoena. The Private Securities Litigation Reform Act of 1995 also may apply.

Answer (B) is incorrect. Under AU-C 250, *Consideration of Laws and Regulations in an Audit of Financial Statements*, withdrawal may be warranted in certain cases. Answer (C) is incorrect. Audits in compliance with GAAS cannot ensure detection of all noncompliance. Answer (D) is incorrect. The auditor should notify those charged with governance about noncompliance.

2.2 Independence

2.2.1. Which of the following most completely describes how independence has been defined by the accounting profession?

A. Performing an audit from the viewpoint of the public.

B. Avoiding the appearance of significant interests in the affairs of an audit client.

C. Possessing the ability to act with integrity and objectivity.

D. Accepting responsibility to act professionally and in accordance with a professional code of ethics.

Answer (C) is correct. *(CPA, adapted)*

REQUIRED: The best description of the accounting profession's definition of independence.

DISCUSSION: Integrity, objectivity, and independence are overlapping concepts. Integrity requires honesty and candor within the limits of confidentiality. It also requires, among other things, observation of the Principle of objectivity and independence. Objectivity is impartiality, intellectual honesty, and freedom from conflicts of interest. Independence precludes relationships that "may appear to impair objectivity in rendering attestation services." Thus, in rendering services, a member in public practice should be independent in appearance as well as in fact.

Answer (A) is incorrect. Although his or her performance of the attest function serves the public interest, an auditor's adoption of any viewpoint other than strict impartiality is inconsistent with professional standards. Answer (B) is incorrect. The auditor must be independent in fact as well as in appearance. Answer (D) is incorrect. A person who accepts responsibility for acting in accordance with a set of professional standards need not necessarily be independent unless the standards require independence.

2.2.2. Jaye B. Honest, CPA, was offered the engagement to audit Wicket Corporation for the year ended June 30, Year 3. She had served as a director of Wicket Corporation until June 30, Year 1, and her spouse currently owns 600 of the 10,000 outstanding shares of Wicket Corporation. Jaye disassociated from Wicket prior to being offered the engagement. Moreover, the engagement does not cover any period that includes Jaye's association or employment with Wicket. Under the AICPA *Code of Professional Conduct*, she should

A. Accept the engagement.

B. Let a partner from the same office accept and conduct the engagement.

C. Refuse the engagement because she had served as a director.

D. Refuse the engagement because of her spouse's stock ownership.

Answer (D) is correct. *(Publisher, adapted)*

REQUIRED: The effect of a spouse's ownership of stock and the CPA's former position as a director.

DISCUSSION: According to the *Code*, independence is impaired if, during the period of the professional engagement, a covered member had or was committed to acquire any direct or material indirect financial interest in a client. With some exceptions, the immediate family (spouse, spousal equivalent, or dependent) of a covered member is subject to the *Code*. Thus, the CPA should refuse the engagement to audit the company because her spouse's stock ownership is a direct interest that is ascribed to her. Materiality is not an issue.

Answer (A) is incorrect. She is not independent and should not accept the engagement. Answer (B) is incorrect. The term "covered member" includes a partner in the office in which the lead attest engagement partner primarily practices in connection with the engagement. Answer (C) is incorrect. If she has not served as a director during the period covered by the financial statements or during the period of the professional engagement, independence is not impaired by reason of prior association with the client as a director.

2.2.3. The Conceptual Framework for AICPA Independence Standards

A. Adopts a risk-based approach to analysis of independence matters.

B. Defines independence of mind as avoiding circumstances in which reasonable persons would conclude that integrity or objectivity has been compromised.

C. Describes threats to independence as circumstances that impair independence.

D. States that safeguards must eliminate threats to independence to be considered effective.

Answer (A) is correct. *(Publisher, adapted)*

REQUIRED: The true statement about the AICPA's independence framework.

DISCUSSION: The risk-based approach evaluates the risk that a CPA is not independent or is perceived by a reasonable and informed third party with knowledge of all relevant information as not independent. That risk must be reduced to an acceptable level to establish independence. Risk is acceptable when threats are acceptable. They may be acceptable because of the types of threats and their potential effect. Moreover, threats may be sufficiently mitigated or eliminated by safeguards. Threats are acceptable when it is not reasonable to expect that they will compromise professional judgment.

Answer (B) is incorrect. Independence of mind "permits a member to perform an attest service without being affected by influences that compromise professional judgment, thereby allowing an individual to act with integrity and exercise objectivity and professional skepticism." Independence in appearance is the "avoidance of circumstances that would cause a reasonable and informed third party, having knowledge of all relevant information, including safeguards applied, to reasonably conclude that the integrity, objectivity, or professional skepticism of a firm or a member of the attest engagement team had been compromised." Answer (C) is incorrect. Threats to independence are circumstances that could cause impairment (an effective extinguishment of independence). Whether impairment occurs depends on (1) the nature of the threat, (2) whether it is reasonable to expect the threat to compromise professional judgment, and (3) the effectiveness of specific safeguards. Answer (D) is incorrect. Safeguards are controls that mitigate or eliminate threats to independence. They are effective if they eliminate the threat or reduce to an acceptable level the threat's potential to impair independence.

2.2.4. An auditor strives to achieve independence in appearance to

A. Maintain public confidence in the profession.

B. Become independent in fact.

C. Comply with the generally accepted accounting principles.

D. Maintain an unbiased mental attitude.

Answer (A) is correct. *(CPA, adapted)*

REQUIRED: The reason the auditor strives to achieve independence in appearance.

DISCUSSION: Third parties depend on the CPA's report because (s)he is viewed as possessing the necessary impartiality. Public confidence would be impaired if such objectivity even appeared to be lacking. The auditor must guard against the presumption of a loss of independence in addition to maintaining independence of mind.

Answer (B) is incorrect. An auditor must be independent both in fact (an unbiased mental attitude) and in appearance. Answer (C) is incorrect. Independence relates to auditing standards, not accounting principles. Answer (D) is incorrect. An auditor must be independent both in fact (an unbiased mental attitude) and in appearance.

2.2.5. The concept of materiality is least important to an auditor when considering the

A. Adequacy of disclosure of a client's illegal act.

B. Discovery of weaknesses in a client's internal control.

C. Effects of a direct financial interest in the client on the CPA's independence.

D. Decision whether to use positive or negative confirmations of accounts receivable.

Answer (C) is correct. *(CPA, adapted)*

REQUIRED: The item with respect to which materiality is least important.

DISCUSSION: Independence is impaired if a CPA has any direct financial interest in a client. Whether this direct financial interest is material is irrelevant. The test of materiality is applied, however, if the financial interest is indirect.

Answer (A) is incorrect. In considering the effect of an illegal act on the financial statements and its implications for other aspects of the audit, materiality is important. Answer (B) is incorrect. An auditor who is considering internal control in a financial statement audit must make materiality judgments. Answer (D) is incorrect. Materiality is one factor considered when deciding between positive or negative confirmations.

2.2.6. Dickins & Co., CPAs, offers to maintain on its computer certain routine accounting records for its audit client, Lake. If Lake accepts the offer and Dickins & Co. continues to function as independent auditor, Dickins & Co. is most likely to violate the rules relating to auditor's independence of which organization(s)?

	SEC	AICPA
A.	Yes	No
B.	Yes	Yes
C.	No	Yes
D.	No	No

Answer (A) is correct. *(Publisher, adapted)*

REQUIRED: The SEC and the AICPA positions on the independence of a CPA firm that provides computerized accounting services to its client.

DISCUSSION: Under federal law (Sarbanes-Oxley Act of 2002) as enforced by the SEC, performing nonaudit services for the audit client impairs the independence of the audit firm. The AICPA view, however, is that the firm may retain its independence while performing various bookkeeping and other nonattest services. Thus, certain "other services" may be allowed in some cases under the AICPA's *Code of Professional Conduct* but are prohibited by the SEC for issuer audit clients. Dickins & Co. has violated SEC rules, but not necessarily AICPA rules.

2.2.7. A CPA who has a direct financial interest in a nonclient having a material investment in the CPA's audit client

A. Lacks independence only if the CPA's investment in the nonclient is material.

B. Lacks independence only if the CPA can exercise significant influence over the nonclient.

C. Lacks independence.

D. Does not lack independence.

Answer (C) is correct. *(Publisher, adapted)*

REQUIRED: The effect of a direct financial interest in an entity having a material investment in an audit client.

DISCUSSION: If the investment by the nonclient in the client is material, any direct or material indirect financial interest a covered member has in the nonclient will impair independence. Thus, whenever the CPA has a direct financial interest, materiality is not an issue and the CPA lacks independence.

Answer (A) is incorrect. An immaterial direct interest impairs independence when the nonclient investor has a material interest in the client investee. Answer (B) is incorrect. The ability to exert significant influence is relevant only when the nonclient investor's interest in the client investee is immaterial. Answer (D) is incorrect. Independence is impaired.

2.2.8. Under the ethical standards of the profession, which of the following situations involving nondependent members of an auditor's family is most likely to impair the independence of an individual participating in an audit engagement?

A. A parent's immaterial investment in a client.

B. A first cousin's loan from a client.

C. A spouse's employment with a client.

D. A sibling's loan to a director of a client.

Answer (C) is correct. *(CPA, adapted)*

REQUIRED: The situation involving a nondependent family member that most likely impairs auditor independence.

DISCUSSION: The immediate family (spouse, spousal equivalent, or a dependent) of a covered member (such as an individual on the attest engagement team or who is able to influence the engagement) is subject to the Independence Rule. Under that Rule, independence is impaired if, during the period covered by the financial statements or during the engagement, a firm partner or professional employee (including an immediate family member of such an individual) was also associated with the client as an officer, director, employee, promoter, underwriter, voting trustee, or member of management. However, independence is not impaired solely because of an immediate family member's employment by the client in a nonkey position.

Answer (A) is incorrect. Independence is impaired if a close relative (parent, sibling, or nondependent child) holds a financial interest in the client that (1) is material to the close relative and is known to the covered member or (2) permits the close relative to exert significant influence over the client. A parent's immaterial financial interest does not impair the auditor's independence. Answer (B) is incorrect. A first cousin is not a member of the immediate family (unless dependent) or a close relative (parent, sibling, or nondependent child). Hence, the first cousin's position and financial interests are not attributed to the auditor. Answer (D) is incorrect. A loan by the auditor's sibling (a close relative) to a director of a client does not impair the auditor's independence. A loan to a director is not a financial interest in the client. However, a loan to a director by an immediate family member would be ascribed to the auditor.

2.2.9. Jordan is the executive partner of Cain & Jordan, CPAs. One of its clients is a large nonprofit charitable organization. The organization has asked Jordan to be on its board of directors, which consists of a large number of the community's leaders. For Jordan to be considered independent, which of the following requirements must be met?

	Board Participation Purely Honorary	Audit Participation by Jordan Prohibited
A.	Yes	Yes
B.	No	Yes
C.	No	No
D.	Yes	No

Answer (D) is correct. *(Publisher, adapted)*

REQUIRED: The best description of the effect of a CPA's position as a board member of a charitable organization.

DISCUSSION: According to an AICPA Interpretation, the member will be independent as long as the position is purely honorary, it is identified as such in all letterheads and externally circulated materials in which (s)he is named as a director or trustee, the member restricts participation to use of his or her name, and (s)he does not vote or participate in management functions. Jordan may directly participate in the audit even though (s)he serves as an honorary director.

2.2.10. A CPA purchased stock in an audit client corporation and placed it in a revocable educational trust for the CPA's dependent minor child. The trust securities were not material to the CPA but were material to the child's personal net worth. Is the independence of the CPA considered to be impaired with respect to the client?

A. Yes, because the stock is considered a direct financial interest and, consequently, materiality is not a factor.

B. Yes, because the stock is considered an indirect financial interest that is material to the CPA's child.

C. No, because the CPA is not considered to have a direct financial interest in the client.

D. No, because the CPA is not considered to have a material indirect financial interest in the client.

Answer (A) is correct. *(CPA, adapted)*

REQUIRED: The effect of a CPA's purchase of the client's stock and placing it in a revocable trust for a minor child.

DISCUSSION: Independence is impaired if, during the period of the professional engagement, a covered member had or was committed to acquire any direct or material indirect financial interest in the client. With some exceptions, the immediate family (spouse, spousal equivalent, or dependent) of a covered member is subject to the Independence Rule and its interpretations. Because the covered member is a grantor of a revocable trust, the trust and its underlying investments are direct financial interests. Given that the securities were stock in an audit client, independence is impaired.

Answer (B) is incorrect. A dependent person's interest is ascribed to the CPA. The CPA therefore has the same direct interest as the child. Answer (C) is incorrect. The CPA is deemed to have a direct interest. Answer (D) is incorrect. Materiality is irrelevant if the CPA is deemed to have a direct interest.

2.2.11. Under the *Code's* Independence Rule, which of the following must be independent in the performance of an audit?

A. Only the partners of the audit firm.

B. Only individuals on the attest engagement team.

C. All individuals on the attest engagement team, except those performing routine clerical functions.

D. All professional employees of the audit firm.

Answer (C) is correct. *(Publisher, adapted)*

REQUIRED: The personnel to whom the Independence Rule applies.

DISCUSSION: A covered member includes an individual on the attest engagement team. The attest engagement team consists of individuals participating in the engagement but excludes specialists and individuals who perform only routine clerical functions.

A covered member is (1) an individual on the attest engagement team, (2) an individual able to influence the engagement, (3) a partner or manager providing the client with nonattest services, (4) a partner in the same office as the lead engagement partner, (5) the firm (including its benefit plans), or (6) an entity that can be controlled (as defined by FASB ASC 810 Consolidation) by the foregoing. Moreover, partners and professional employees who own more than 5% of the client or who are associated with the client in certain capacities (director, officer, employee, promoter, underwriter, voting trustee, or trustee of a pension or profit-sharing trust) are also subject to the Independence Rule. In addition, a covered member's immediate family and close relatives may have relationships that impair the independence of a covered member.

2.2.12. The appearance of independence of a CPA, or that CPA's firm, is most likely to be impaired if the CPA

A. Provides appraisal, valuation, or actuarial services for an attest client.

B. Joins a trade association, which is an attest client, and serves in a nonmanagement capacity.

C. Accepts a token gift from an attest client.

D. Serves as an executor and trustee of the estate of an individual who owned the majority of the stock of a closely held client corporation.

Answer (D) is correct. *(CPA, adapted)*

REQUIRED: The basis for the impairment of the appearance of independence.

DISCUSSION: Independence is impaired with regard to the client if, during the period of the professional engagement, a covered member was a trustee of any trust or executor or administrator of any estate if such trust or estate had or was committed to acquire any direct or material indirect financial interest in the client, and the value of the estate's holdings in the client exceeded 10% of the estate's assets. Mere designation as a trustee or executor does not impair independence, but actual service does.

Answer (A) is incorrect. A member who performs other nonattest services for an attest client must meet certain conditions to be considered independent. Thus, a member who provides appraisal, valuation, or actuarial services for a nonissuer attest client should meet the general requirements, e.g., (1) not assuming management responsibilities and (2) documenting an understanding with the client. Furthermore, performing these services should not involve a significant degree of uncertainty. Accordingly, the member may perform such services if certain requirements are met. For example, an actuarial valuation of a pension liability does not impair independence because it ordinarily produces reasonably consistent results. Answer (B) is incorrect. Independence is not impaired, provided the CPA does not participate in management. Answer (C) is incorrect. A token gift does not impair independence. However, a CPA who accepts more than a token gift, even with the knowledge of the member's firm, appears to lack independence.

2.2.13. In which of the following circumstances would a CPA who audits XM Corporation lack independence?

A. The CPA is a director of, but does not control, YN Corporation, which has a loan from XM.

B. The CPA and XM's president each owns 25% of FOB Corporation, a closely held company.

C. The CPA has an automobile loan from XM, a financial institution. The loan is collateralized by the automobile.

D. The CPA reduced XM's usual audit fee by 40% prior to the audit because XM's financial condition was unfavorable.

Answer (B) is correct. *(CPA, adapted)*

REQUIRED: The circumstance in which a CPA lacks independence.

DISCUSSION: Independence is impaired if, during the period of the professional engagement, "a covered member had a joint, closely held investment that was material to the covered member." A joint, closely held investment by the member and the client (or its officers, directors, or an owner with significant influence) enables them to control the investee entity or property.

Answer (A) is incorrect. The CPA lacks independence only if (s)he controlled (as defined by the FASB) YN, and the loan was not a permitted type. However, a member who does not control such an entity but is an officer, director, or principal shareholder, must consider the conflict of interest. If the member believes the service can be performed with objectivity, and the relationship is disclosed to and consent is obtained from appropriate parties, the service may be performed. Answer (C) is incorrect. An automobile loan from a financial institution client is permitted. Four kinds of loans and leases are permitted even if the financial institution client is one for which independence is required, providing normal lending procedures are followed: (1) automobile loans and leases collateralized by the automobile, (2) loans of the cash surrender value under terms of an insurance policy, (3) borrowings fully collateralized by cash deposits at the same financial institution (e.g., passbook loans), and (4) credit cards and overdraft reserve accounts with an aggregate balance not paid currently of $10,000 or less. Answer (D) is incorrect. Contingent fees must not be charged for certain services (see the Contingent Fees Rule). Otherwise, fees may vary with many factors if they are related to services rendered and not to the CPA's findings or the results of findings. Thus, a CPA's fee might be charged on an ability-to-pay basis.

2.2.14. Under the AICPA *Code of Professional Conduct*, a covered member is most likely not permitted to

A. Have an immaterial indirect financial interest in an affiliate of an attest financial statement client.

B. Perform bookkeeping services for an audit client.

C. Perform tax preparation services for an audit client.

D. Have any joint closely held investment with a principal shareholder of an audit client during the period of the audit engagement.

Answer (D) is correct. *(Publisher, adapted)*

REQUIRED: The situation impairing independence.

DISCUSSION: According to an interpretation of the Independence Rule, during the period of the professional engagement, a covered member may not have a joint closely held investment that was material to the covered member. A joint closely held investment is an investment in an entity or property by the member and (1) the client, (2) its officers or directors, or (3) an owner with the ability to exercise significant influence over the client that enables the member and the other party(ies) to control (as defined by FASB ASC 810 Consolidation) the entity or property.

Answer (A) is incorrect. A covered member may have an immaterial indirect financial interest in an affiliate of a financial statement client. In general, the independence provisions of the *Code of Professional Conduct* that apply to the client also apply to the affiliates of the client. Answer (B) is incorrect. The member may perform such bookkeeping services as preparing financial statements from the trial balance, posting client-approved entries to the trial balance, proposing journal entries, providing data-processing services, posting coded transactions to the general ledger, and recording transactions if the client has approved the account classifications. However, auditors of issuers may not perform bookkeeping and related services. Answer (C) is incorrect. Tax preparation services do not impair independence. For an issuer client, tax preparation services are permitted if preapproved by the audit committee.

2.2.15. According to the profession's ethical standards, an auditor would be considered independent in which of the following instances?

A. The auditor's checking account, which is fully insured by a federal agency, is held at a client financial institution.

B. The auditor is also an attorney who advises the client as its general counsel.

C. A member donates service as CFO of a charitable organization that is a client during the period covered by the financial statements.

D. The client owes the auditor fees for two consecutive annual audits.

Answer (A) is correct. *(CPA, adapted)*

REQUIRED: The basis for considering whether an auditor is independent.

DISCUSSION: The independence of a member or a member's firm is not impaired if the member's depository relationship (checking, savings, certificates of deposit, money market accounts) is fully insured by a state or federal deposit insurance agency. Moreover, uninsured amounts do not impair independence if they are immaterial.

Answer (B) is incorrect. A member may perform other nonattest services in appropriate circumstances. However, certain general activities in the performance of these other services are deemed to impair independence, for example, serving the client as its stock transfer or escrow agent, registrar, general counsel, or the equivalent. Such service constitutes making management decisions or performing management functions. Answer (C) is incorrect. Independence is impaired if, during the period covered by the financial statements or during the period of the professional engagement, a partner or professional employee of the firm was simultaneously associated with the client as an officer, for example, as a CFO. Answer (D) is incorrect. Independence is impaired if fees for client services for previous audits remain unpaid when the current year's report is issued. This amount is viewed as a loan to the client.

2.2.16. A CPA audits the financial statements of a local bank. According to the AICPA *Code of Professional Conduct*, the appearance of independence ordinarily would not be impaired if the CPA

A. Serves on the bank's committee that approves loans.

B. Owns several shares of the bank's common stock.

C. Obtains a home mortgage from the bank.

D. Designs an information system for the bank that is unrelated to its accounting records.

Answer (D) is correct. *(CPA, adapted)*

REQUIRED: The situation in which the CPA firm retains the appearance of independence.

DISCUSSION: Independence is not impaired by designing, developing, installing, or integrating a client's information system that is unrelated to its financial statements or accounting records.

Answer (A) is incorrect. A CPA's independence is impaired if (s)he serves in any capacity equivalent to that of a member of management or of a decision-making employee. Answer (B) is incorrect. Even an immaterial direct financial interest impairs independence. Answer (C) is incorrect. A home mortgage impairs independence.

2.2.17. The *Code* prohibits loans to a covered member from a client financial institution except for certain permitted loans made under normal lending procedures, terms, and requirements. When making the comparison between the terms of the member's loan and those of other borrowers, which item(s) should be considered in the determination of normal lending procedures?

A. Repayment terms.

B. Interest rate, including points.

C. Closing costs.

D. All of the answers are correct.

Answer (D) is correct. *(Publisher, adapted)*

REQUIRED: The item(s) considered to determine whether normal lending procedures have been followed.

DISCUSSION: Covered members are permitted to obtain certain loans from client financial institutions for which independence is required if the loans are made under normal conditions. These conditions include (1) automobile loans and leases collateralized by the automobile, (2) loans fully collateralized by the cash surrender value of an insurance policy, (3) loans fully collateralized by cash deposits at the same lending institution (for example, passbook loans), and (4) aggregate outstanding balances from credit cards and overdraft reserve accounts that have a balance of $10,000 or less after payment of the most recent monthly statement made by the due date or within any available grace period.

Answer (A) is incorrect. The items to be considered include repayment terms. Answer (B) is incorrect. The items to be considered include the interest rate, including points. Answer (C) is incorrect. The items to be considered include closing costs.

2.2.18. In which of the following instances is the independence of the CPA most likely not considered to be impaired? The CPA has been retained as the auditor of a

A. Charitable organization in which the spouse of the CPA serves as treasurer.

B. Municipality in which the CPA owns $25,000 of the $2,500,000 indebtedness of the municipality.

C. Credit union of which the CPA is a member.

D. Company in which the CPA's participant-directed retirement plan owns a 10% interest.

Answer (C) is correct. *(CPA, adapted)*

REQUIRED: The service that does not impair the CPA's independence.

DISCUSSION: Membership in a credit union does not impair independence if (1) the member or his or her partners or employees individually qualify for the membership other than as a result of the services rendered; (2) the member has no significant influence over credit union policies; (3) any loans to the member meet the requirements of the relevant independence interpretation; and (4) any deposits are fully insured or, if uninsured, the amounts are not material.

Answer (A) is incorrect. The employment of the spouse is ascribed to the CPA. The treasurer is an officer and is therefore considered to be a member of management. Answer (B) is incorrect. Independence is impaired if a covered member has any loan to or from the client unless the loan is a "grandfathered loan" or an "other permitted loan" under the relevant independence interpretation. Answer (D) is incorrect. Ownership of stock in a client through a participant-directed retirement plan is a direct financial interest. It impairs independence regardless of materiality. A direct financial interest includes an interest in a retirement, savings, compensation, or similar plan that is a self-directed or participant-directed plan (e.g., the covered member selects plan investments).

2.2.19. A CPA who performs primary actuarial services for a nonissuer client normally is precluded from expressing an opinion on the financial statements of that client if the

A. Fees for the actuarial services have not been paid.

B. Actuarial services are a major determinant of the pension expense.

C. CPA prepared an actuarial report using assumptions not approved by the client.

D. Actuarial assumptions used are not in accordance with GAAS.

Answer (C) is correct. *(CPA, adapted)*

REQUIRED: The situation in which a CPA could not provide actuarial and auditing services.

DISCUSSION: A member must evaluate the effect on his or her independence of performing nonattest services. The member should not assume management responsibilities for the attest client. A nonattest service impairs independence if it involves the performance of an appraisal, valuation, or actuarial service using significant assumptions not determined or approved by the client.

Answer (A) is incorrect. Unless the fees have been unpaid for over a year at the date of the current year's report and might be deemed to be a loan to the client, the CPA may accept the audit engagement. Answer (B) is incorrect. Even if the results of the actuarial services are incorporated into the financial statements, the auditor's independence is not impaired if those results are not material to the statements, and the services do not involve significant subjectivity. But the auditor is precluded from performing actuarial services for an issuer. Answer (D) is incorrect. The assumptions should be in accordance with GAAP, not GAAS.

2.2.20. Which of the following legal situations would be considered to impair the auditor's independence?

A. An expressed intention by the current management to commence litigation against the auditor alleging deficiencies in audit work for the client, although the auditor considers that there is only a remote possibility that such a claim will be filed.

B. Actual litigation by the auditor against the client for an amount not material to the auditor or to the financial statements of the client arising out of disputes as to billings for consulting services.

C. Actual litigation by the auditor against the current management alleging management fraud or deceit.

D. Actual litigation by the client against the auditor for an amount not material to the auditor or to the financial statements of the client arising out of disputes as to billings for tax services.

Answer (C) is correct. *(CPA, adapted)*

REQUIRED: The actual or intended litigation that impairs the auditor's independence.

DISCUSSION: The following are situations in which actual or threatened litigation impairs independence: (1) litigation has begun alleging deficient audit work; (2) litigation has begun alleging fraud or deceit by current management; and (3) management has expressed an intention to commence litigation alleging deficient audit work, and the auditor concludes that it is probable that such a claim will be filed.

Answer (A) is incorrect. Independence is impaired if the auditor concludes that it is probable that such a claim will be filed. Answer (B) is incorrect. If the litigation is related to an engagement not requiring independence, such as consulting services, impairment does not necessarily result unless the amount in controversy is material to one of the litigants. Answer (D) is incorrect. If the litigation is related to an engagement not requiring independence, such as tax services, impairment does not necessarily result unless the amount in controversy is material to one of the litigants.

2.2.21. In which of the following situations would a covered member's independence be considered to be impaired?

I. The covered member maintains a checking account that is fully insured by a government deposit insurance agency at an audit-client financial institution.

II. The covered member has a direct financial interest in an audit client, but the interest is maintained in a blind trust.

III. The covered member owns a commercial building and leases it to an audit client. The lease is properly classified as a capital lease, and the rental income is material to the CPA.

A. I and II.

B. II and III.

C. I and III.

D. I, II, and III.

Answer (B) is correct. *(CPA, adapted)*

REQUIRED: The situations in which independence is impaired.

DISCUSSION: When a member leases property to or from a client, independence is not impaired if (1) the lease meets the criteria of an operating lease, (2) the terms and conditions of the agreement compare with those of similar leases, and (3) all amounts are paid in accordance with the lease. However, if the lease meets all the criteria of a capital lease, it impairs a covered member's independence. The reason is that a capital lease is considered a loan to or from the client. Moreover, independence is impaired if, during the period of the professional engagement, a covered member had (or was committed to acquire) any direct or any material indirect financial interest in the client. When a covered member is a trust beneficiary, the trust is deemed to be a direct financial interest, and the underlying investments are indirect financial interests. However, the beneficiary of a blind trust is also the grantor. The grantor normally can amend or revoke the trust, and the investments will finally revert to him or her. Thus, the blind trust and the investments are deemed to be direct financial interests of the covered member.

2.2.22. According to the profession's ethical standards, a CPA is considered independent in which of the following instances?

A. The CPA agrees to indemnify the client against losses from client acts.

B. The CPA has a material direct financial interest in a client but transfers the interest into a blind trust.

C. The CPA owns an office building, and the mortgage on the building is guaranteed by a client.

D. The CPA belongs to a country club client in which membership requires the acquisition of a pro rata share of equity.

Answer (D) is correct. *(CPA, adapted)*

REQUIRED: The circumstances in which a CPA is considered independent.

DISCUSSION: If membership is essentially social, independence is not impaired because the equity (or debt) ownership is not a direct financial interest. But the CPA should not serve on the governing board or participate in management.

Answer (A) is incorrect. This agreement violates the *Code*. Answer (B) is incorrect. Independence is impaired if a member has any direct financial interest in the client. Independence is impaired whether or not the financial interest is in a blind trust. Answer (C) is incorrect. Independence is impaired if the CPA has a loan from the client. A loan includes a guarantee of a loan.

2.2.23. An audit independence issue might be raised by the auditor's participation in consulting services engagements. Which of the following statements is most consistent with the profession's attitude toward this issue?

A. Information obtained as a result of a consulting engagement is confidential to that engagement and should not influence performance of the attest function.

B. The decision as to loss of independence must be made by the client based upon the facts of the particular case.

C. The auditor should not make management decisions for an audit client.

D. The auditor who is asked to review management decisions is also competent to make these decisions and can do so without loss of independence.

Answer (C) is correct. *(CPA, adapted)*

REQUIRED: The statement most consistent with the profession's attitude toward independence relative to consulting services.

DISCUSSION: A member must evaluate the effect on his or her independence of performing nonattest services. The member should not assume management responsibilities for the attest client.

Answer (A) is incorrect. The auditor should use all information available. Answer (B) is incorrect. The auditor, not the client, must determine whether (s)he is in a position in which independence might be questioned. Answer (D) is incorrect. The auditor may review management decisions and make suggestions, but (s)he may not actually make those decisions without losing independence.

2.2.24. Which of the following does not impair a CPA's independence?

A. The CPA performs the duties of a transfer agent or a registrar for a client.

B. The CPA participates as the treasurer of a charitable organization who is a client.

C. The client is in bankruptcy and has not paid fees related to the previous year's audit.

D. The CPA is a tenured university faculty member who audits the student senate fund.

Answer (C) is correct. *(Publisher, adapted)*

REQUIRED: The situation that does not impair a CPA's independence.

DISCUSSION: Independence is impaired if, when the current year's report is issued, billed or unbilled fees, or a note receivable resulting from such fees, remain unpaid for any professional services provided more than 1 year prior to the report date. These unpaid fees are equivalent to a loan. However, fees owed by a client in bankruptcy do not impair independence.

Answer (A) is incorrect. Serving as the attest client's stock transfer or escrow agent, general counsel, or its equivalent is deemed to impair independence. Answer (B) is incorrect. A CPA's independence is impaired by connection with the client as an officer or in another capacity equivalent to that of management. Answer (D) is incorrect. A part-time adjunct faculty member is independent as long as (s)he does not assume any management functions and does not participate on the audit engagement team or have the ability to influence the audit. However, the question states that the CPA audits the fund, so the CPA lacks independence because (s)he is a member of the audit engagement team.

2.2.25. Burrow & Co., CPAs, have provided annual audit and tax compliance services to Mare Corp. for several years. Mare has been unable to pay Burrow in full for services Burrow rendered 19 months ago. Burrow is ready to begin field work for the current year's audit. Under the ethical standards of the profession, which of the following arrangements will permit Burrow to begin the field work on Mare's audit?

A. Mare sets up a 2-year payment plan with Burrow to settle the unpaid fee balance.

B. Mare commits to pay the past due fee in full before the audit report is issued.

C. Mare gives Burrow an 18-month note payable for the full amount of the past due fees before Burrow begins the audit.

D. Mare engages another firm to perform the field work, and Burrow is limited to reviewing the working papers and issuing the audit report.

Answer (B) is correct. *(CPA, adapted)*

REQUIRED: The arrangement allowing the CPAs to conduct an audit of a client that has not paid for prior services.

DISCUSSION: Audit fees that are long past due have the characteristics of a loan. The *Code* considers independence to be impaired if billed or unbilled fees, or a note resulting from the fees, for client services rendered more than 1 year prior to the current year's report date remain unpaid when the current report is issued. However, independence is not impaired if the client is in bankruptcy. Moreover, long overdue fees do not preclude the CPA from performing services not requiring independence. Accordingly, payment in full prior to issuance of the report will satisfy the requirements of the *Code*.

Answer (A) is incorrect. Under a 2-year plan, some fees would still be unpaid at the date the report is issued. Answer (C) is incorrect. The note arising from the fees would still be unpaid at the date the report is issued. Answer (D) is incorrect. Reporting on the audit requires independence, which is impaired as a result of the overdue fees.

2.2.26. Under the ethical standards of the profession, which of the following investments by a CPA in a corporate client is an indirect financial interest?

A. An investment held in a retirement plan of which the CPA is a trustee.

B. An investment held in a blind trust.

C. An investment held through a regulated mutual fund.

D. An investment held through participation in an investment club.

Answer (C) is correct. *(CPA, adapted)*

REQUIRED: The indirect financial interest.

DISCUSSION: Independence is impaired if, during the period of the professional engagement, a covered member had a direct or material indirect financial interest in the client. Ownership of fund shares is a direct financial interest in the fund. Underlying investments in the fund are indirect interests.

Answer (A) is incorrect. Participation in a retirement plan constitutes a direct financial interest in the plan. Investments of a plan sponsored by the member's firm are direct interests of the firm. Investments of a plan controlled or supervised by the member (e.g., as a trustee) are the member's direct interests. Otherwise, they are indirect interests of the members. Answer (B) is incorrect. A blind trust and its investments are direct interests of the grantor. The investments will revert to the grantor. Answer (D) is incorrect. One kind of direct financial interest is a financial interest beneficially owned through an intermediary (e.g., an investment club) when the beneficiary has the authority to participate in the intermediary's investment decisions. In an investment club, the members make investment decisions.

2.2.27. Within the meaning of the Securities Act of 1933 and the Securities Exchange Act of 1934, an accountant deemed to be independent with regard to a specific entity must

I. Confirm in writing its independence from the audit client.

II. Have no relationships with the audit client.

III. Discuss its independence with the audit committee.

A. I and II only.

B. I and III only.

C. II and III only.

D. I, II, and III.

Answer (B) is correct. *(Publisher, adapted)*

REQUIRED: The requirements regarding independence discussions with the auditee.

DISCUSSION: An auditor who wishes to be deemed independent within the meaning of the Securities Act of 1933 and the Securities Exchange Act of 1934 must make an annual written disclosure to the audit committee of all relationships between the auditor and its related entities and the company and its related entities that may reasonably bear on independence. The auditor must confirm its independence in the letter and must discuss its independence with the audit committee. However, the standards do not require that auditors of issuers have no relationships with audit clients.

2.2.28. A CPA who is employed by a nonaccounting corporation performs services for the employer, including auditing the employer's financial statements. Reports issued with respect to such activities are distributed with the CPA's name and CPA designation appearing on the corporate letterhead. These reports should

A. Be restricted to internal use.

B. Make no reference to GAAS.

C. Be on plain paper (not on the corporate letterhead).

D. Refer to an audit.

Answer (B) is correct. *(Publisher, adapted)*

REQUIRED: The true statement about reports issued on the financial statements of a CPA's employer.

DISCUSSION: A CPA not in public practice who uses the CPA designation in a manner to imply that (s)he is independent of the employer has made a knowing misrepresentation of fact violating the *Code*. Thus, it is advisable that the employment title be clearly indicated. Moreover, an auditor who is not independent may not express an opinion. A reference to GAAS would imply independence.

Answer (A) is incorrect. If a report is made available to third parties, it may indicate the CPA's professional designation if no implication of independence is conveyed. Answer (C) is incorrect. If the report is to outsiders, it must be on the corporate letterhead. Answer (D) is incorrect. No reference should be made to GAAS, an audit, or a review. Such a reference might imply independence.

2.3 Integrity and Objectivity

2.3.1. Which of the following is prohibited by the AICPA *Code of Professional Conduct*?

A. Practice of public accounting in the form of a professional corporation that uses a firm name indicating specialization.

B. Use of the partnership name for a limited period by one of the partners in a public accounting firm after the death or withdrawal of all other partners.

C. Failing to provide working papers to the client after a request has been made.

D. Prematurely expressing an opinion based on an audit because of time pressures from the client.

Answer (D) is correct. *(Publisher, adapted)*

REQUIRED: The action considered a code violation.

DISCUSSION: The Integrity and Objectivity Rule prohibits a member from subordinating his or her judgment to others. The auditor must complete the audit prior to signing the report.

Answer (A) is incorrect. The *Code* does not prohibit the use of a fictitious name or the indication of a specialization. However, the name or indication of specialization may not be misleading. In addition, the AICPA permits CPAs to use trade names (e.g., "Suburban Tax Services") that are not false or deceptive. Answer (B) is incorrect. Names of one or more past owners may be included in the firm name of a successor organization as long as the name is not misleading. Answer (C) is incorrect. According to the AICPA standards, the audit documentation is deemed to be the property of the CPA. However, audit documentation containing client financial information not reflected in the client's books must be returned to the client upon request if the engagement is complete.

2.3.2. A CPA most likely does not violate the *Code's* Integrity and Objectivity Rule, if the CPA

A. Performs expert witness services for a nonissuer attest client that is one of many plaintiffs in a class action lawsuit.

B. Subordinates his or her judgment to that of client personnel when performing consulting services.

C. Knowingly makes materially misleading entries in an entity's financial records.

D. Accepts the judgment of a client instead of his or her own when performing tax services.

Answer (A) is correct. *(Publisher, adapted)*

REQUIRED: The situation in which the CPA most likely does not violate Conduct Rule 102.

DISCUSSION: Litigation services, a type of forensic accounting services, involve assisting in actual or potential legal or regulatory proceedings. They include expert witness services, that is, the expression of an opinion based on the member's expertise, not his or her knowledge of disputed facts. These services impair independence unless (1) they are rendered to a large group of parties, (2) no attest client is the lead plaintiff or defendant, and (3) other requirements related to the influence of attest clients on the proceedings are met. Thus, the attest client must be less than 20% of (1) the members of the group of plaintiffs (or defendants), (2) the voting interests of the group, and (3) the claim. Moreover, the client should not have sole power to select the expert witness. However, if expert services unrelated to the audit are provided to an audit client that is an issuer covered by the Securities Exchange Act of 1934, the CPA will lack independence (Sarbanes-Oxley Act of 2002).

Answer (B) is incorrect. In the performance of any professional service, a member must not subordinate his or her judgment to others, including the client. Answer (C) is incorrect. A member is deemed to have knowingly misrepresented facts in violation of the Rule when (s)he knowingly makes or permits or directs another to make, materially false and misleading entries in an entity's financial statements or records. Answer (D) is incorrect. In the performance of any professional service, a member must not subordinate his or her judgment to others, including the client.

2.3.3. Which of the following acts by a CPA who is not in public practice is most likely to be a violation of the ethical standards of the profession?

A. Using the CPA designation without disclosing employment status in connection with financial statements issued for external use by the CPA's employer.

B. Distributing business cards indicating the CPA designation and the CPA's title and employer.

C. Corresponding on the CPA's employer's letterhead, which contains the CPA designation and the CPA's employment status.

D. Compiling the CPA's employer's financial statements and referring to the CPA's lack of independence.

Answer (A) is correct. *(CPA, adapted)*

REQUIRED: The action violating ethical standards.

DISCUSSION: A member not in public practice who uses the CPA designation in a manner implying that (s)he is independent of the employer has committed a knowing misrepresentation of fact.

Answer (B) is incorrect. As long as the CPA's title and the employer's name are on the business cards, their use is permissible. Answer (C) is incorrect. As long as the CPA's title and the employer's name are on the letterhead, its use is permissible. Answer (D) is incorrect. An accountant may compile a nonissuer's financial statements if (s)he issues the appropriate report. The lack of independence should be disclosed. The accountant also may state the reason (s)he lacks independence (AR-C 80). If an accountant who is not independent is associated with the financial statements of an issuer (except a compilation report) but has not audited or reviewed them, (s)he must issue a disclaimer of opinion that states his or her lack of independence.

2.3.4. The AICPA *Code of Professional Conduct* states, in part, that a CPA should maintain integrity and objectivity. Objectivity in the *Code* refers to a CPA's ability

A. To maintain an impartial attitude on all matters that come under the CPA's review.

B. To independently distinguish between accounting practices that are acceptable and those that are not.

C. To be unyielding in all matters dealing with auditing procedures.

D. To independently choose between alternate accounting principles and auditing standards.

Answer (A) is correct. *(CPA, adapted)*

REQUIRED: The definition of objectivity in the *Code of Professional Conduct*.

DISCUSSION: According to the Principles, "Objectivity is a state of mind, a quality that lends itself to a member's services. It is a distinguishing feature of the profession. The principle of objectivity imposes the obligation to be impartial, intellectually honest, and free of conflicts of interest."

Answer (B) is incorrect. The CPA uses both judgment and GAAP to evaluate whether a client's accounting practices are acceptable. Answer (C) is incorrect. The CPA is expected to use professional judgment, which may include flexibility, in applying audit procedures. Answer (D) is incorrect. Auditing standards relate to the quality of the auditor's performance, but adherence to accounting principles by management is a prerequisite for fairly stated financial statements.

2.3.5. A violation of the profession's ethical standards would most likely have occurred when a CPA in public practice

A. Used a records-retention agency to store the CPA's working papers and client records.

B. Served as an expert witness in a damage suit and received compensation based on the amount awarded to the plaintiff.

C. Referred life insurance assignments to the CPA's spouse, who is a life insurance agent.

D. Serves on a municipal board of income tax appeals, discloses that status to concerned parties, participates as a board member in a tax appeal involving a client, but does not receive the client's consent for such action.

Answer (D) is correct. *(CPA, adapted)*

REQUIRED: The action most likely to be an ethics violation.

DISCUSSION: If the significant relationship creating a conflict of interest is disclosed to and consent is obtained from all appropriate parties, the Integrity and Objectivity Rule does not prohibit performance of the professional service. (But disclosure and consent do not eliminate an impairment of independence.) The failure to secure the client's consent therefore means that the arrangement could be viewed as impairing the CPA's objectivity.

Answer (A) is incorrect. Use of a third-party to assist in providing professional services must be disclosed to the client before confidential client information is disclosed to the provider. The third-party service provider may not be used if the client objects. But disclosure is not necessary if the services constitute administrative support (e.g., records storage). Answer (B) is incorrect. The AICPA does not prohibit contingent fees except in certain cases. Answer (C) is incorrect. The benefit (commission) received by the spouse as a result of the referral is ascribed to the CPA, but receipt of commissions is permissible in certain circumstances. The AICPA does not prohibit the acceptance of disclosed commissions for products or services supplied by third parties except in certain cases.

2.4 Professional Standards

2.4.1. Eagle Company's financial statements contain a departure from generally accepted accounting principles because, due to unusual circumstances, the statements would otherwise be misleading. The auditor should express an opinion that is

A. Qualified and describe the departure in a separate paragraph.

B. Unmodified but not mention the departure in the auditor's report.

C. Qualified or adverse, depending on materiality, and describe the departure in an other-matter paragraph.

D. Unmodified and describe the departure in an other-matter paragraph.

Answer (D) is correct. *(CPA, adapted)*

REQUIRED: The opinion expressed when a departure from GAAP results in a fair presentation.

DISCUSSION: A material departure from GAAP prohibits expression of an opinion that financial statements are in conformity with GAAP. However, an exception is permitted when the auditor can demonstrate that because of unusual circumstances the statements would otherwise have been misleading. Given these circumstances, and if no other basis for modifying the opinion exists, the auditor may express an unmodified opinion, provided that (s)he describes in an other-matter paragraph of the report the departure, its effects, and the reasons compliance with GAAP would have been misleading.

Answer (A) is incorrect. An adverse or qualified opinion is not expressed when the statements are fairly presented. Answer (B) is incorrect. An other-matter paragraph must be added even though the opinion is unmodified. Answer (C) is incorrect. An adverse or qualified opinion is not expressed when the statements are fairly presented.

2.4.2. The General Standards Rule does not require a member to

A. Complete all engagements with professional competence.

B. Plan and supervise adequately the performance of professional services.

C. Obtain sufficient relevant data to afford a reasonable basis for all conclusions.

D. Provide assurance about prospective financial statements.

Answer (D) is correct. *(Publisher, adapted)*

REQUIRED: The subject not encompassed by Rule 201.

DISCUSSION: Guidance for assurance on prospective statements is provided by AT-C 305, *Prospective Financial Information*.

Answer (A) is incorrect. The General Standards Rule requires compliance with the following standards: professional competence, due professional care, planning and supervision, and sufficient relevant data. A member should undertake only those professional services that can reasonably be expected to be completed with professional competence. Answer (B) is incorrect. The General Standards Rule requires that the performance of professional services be adequately planned and supervised. Answer (C) is incorrect. The General Standards Rule requires that a member obtain sufficient relevant data to afford a reasonable basis for all conclusions or recommendations related to any professional services performed.

2.4.3. Ann Covington, CPA, has been asked to perform a consulting services engagement concerning the analysis of a potential merger. She has little experience with the industry involved. What is her most appropriate action?

A. Accept the engagement and perform it in accordance with auditing standards.

B. Accept the engagement and perform additional research or consult with others to obtain sufficient competence.

C. Accept the engagement and issue a report vouching for the achievability of the results of the merger.

D. Decline the engagement because she lacks sufficient knowledge.

Answer (B) is correct. *(Publisher, adapted)*

REQUIRED: The appropriate action by a CPA who has been asked to provide consulting services regarding unfamiliar matters.

DISCUSSION: The CPA may accept the engagement but should conduct research or consult with others to obtain a sufficient level of knowledge about the subject of the engagement. An AICPA member should undertake only those professional services that the member or the member's firm can reasonably expect to be completed with professional competence.

Answer (A) is incorrect. Audits, not consulting services engagements, are performed in accordance with auditing standards. Answer (C) is incorrect. An accountant's report on prospective financial information must always contain a caveat that the prospective results may not be achieved. Answer (D) is incorrect. The CPA need not decline the engagement if she does the research necessary to complete the engagement with professional competence.

2.4.4. According to the standards of the profession, which of the following activities may be required in exercising due professional care?

	Consulting with Experts	Obtaining Specialty Accreditation
A.	Yes	Yes
B.	Yes	No
C.	No	Yes
D.	No	No

Answer (B) is correct. *(CPA, adapted)*

REQUIRED: The activity(ies) that may be required in exercising due care.

DISCUSSION: A CPA should undertake only those services that (s)he reasonably expects to complete with professional competence and should exercise due professional care in performing those services. Additional research or consultation with others may be necessary to gain sufficient competence to complete a service in accordance with professional standards. However, professional standards do not require specialty accreditation, although many CPAs choose to specialize in specific services.

2.4.5. When a CPA is associated with financial statements that do not comply with promulgated GAAP because the statements would be misleading without the departure, the CPA is not required to disclose

A. The departure.

B. The approximate effects of the departure in comparison to the application of GAAP.

C. The reason the departure does not have a material effect on the statements.

D. The reasons compliance would have been misleading.

Answer (C) is correct. *(Publisher, adapted)*

REQUIRED: The disclosure not required when application of promulgated GAAP would be misleading.

DISCUSSION: Under the Accounting Principles Rule, a CPA who performs services that require representations of conformity with promulgated GAAP is required to describe (1) the departure, (2) the approximate effects of the departure (if practicable), and (3) the reasons compliance would result in misleading financial statements. But this requirement applies only if the effect on the statements or data is material.

Answer (A) is incorrect. The CPA is required to disclose the departure. Answer (B) is incorrect. The CPA is required to disclose the approximate effects of the departure. Answer (D) is incorrect. The CPA is required to disclose the reasons compliance would have been misleading.

2.4.6. Under the AICPA *Code of Professional Conduct*, a CPA may express an unmodified opinion on financial statements that contain a departure from promulgated GAAP if (s)he can demonstrate that because of unusual circumstances the financial statements would be misleading if the departure were not made. Which of the following is an example of unusual circumstances that could justify such a departure?

A. New legislation.

B. An unusual degree of materiality.

C. Conflicting industry practices.

D. A theoretical disagreement with a standard promulgated by the FASB.

Answer (A) is correct. *(CPA, adapted)*

REQUIRED: The circumstance that could justify a departure from promulgated GAAP.

DISCUSSION: Examples of unusual circumstances that permit a departure from promulgated GAAP are (1) new legislation or (2) the evolution of a new form of business transaction. But determination of what constitutes unusual circumstances is normally a matter of professional judgment.

Answer (B) is incorrect. An unusual degree of materiality is an example of an event that is not so unusual as to justify departure from promulgated GAAP. Answer (C) is incorrect. The existence of conflicting industry practices is an example of an event that is not so unusual as to justify departure from promulgated GAAP. Answer (D) is incorrect. The client's or CPA's theoretical disagreement with a standard does not justify a departure.

2.5 Responsibilities to Clients

2.5.1. Which of the following statements concerning an accountant's disclosure of confidential client data is ordinarily true?

A. Disclosure may be made to any state agency without subpoena.

B. Disclosure may be made to any party on consent of the client.

C. Disclosure may be made to comply with an IRS audit request.

D. Disclosure may be made to comply with generally accepted accounting principles.

Answer (B) is correct. *(CPA, adapted)*

REQUIRED: The condition allowing disclosure of confidential client data.

DISCUSSION: Under the Confidential Client Information Rule, an accountant may disclose any confidential client information with the specific consent of the client.

Answer (A) is incorrect. Disclosure may be made to a state agency only in accordance with a subpoena or summons or with the client's consent. Answer (C) is incorrect. Without consent, an accountant may disclose confidential information to the IRS only in accordance with a subpoena or summons. Answer (D) is incorrect. Compliance with GAAP is a responsibility of clients who issue financial statements, not the accountants who report on them.

2.5.2. The Confidential Client Information Rule is violated when a member in public practice

A. Provides client profit and loss percentages to a trade association without the client's consent.

B. Uses outside computer services to process tax returns.

C. Performs consulting services for similar clients.

D. Advises potential consulting services clients about previous problems on similar engagements.

Answer (A) is correct. *(Publisher, adapted)*

REQUIRED: The activity that violates the Confidential Client Information Rule.

DISCUSSION: Prior to disclosing confidential client profit and loss percentages to a trade association, the CPA must have specific client consent.

Answer (B) is incorrect. Using outside computer services to process tax returns is permissible as long as client confidentiality is maintained. Answer (C) is incorrect. Most CPAs perform consulting services for clients in the same or related industries. Answer (D) is incorrect. CPAs must make full disclosure about any reservations concerning the usefulness of potential consulting services, especially those based on past experience with similar engagements. However, client confidentiality must be preserved or waived.

2.5.3. A CPA's retention of client-provided records as a means of enforcing payment of an overdue audit fee is an action that is

A. Not addressed by the AICPA *Code of Professional Conduct.*

B. Acceptable if sanctioned by state law.

C. Prohibited under the AICPA *Code of Professional Conduct.*

D. A violation of GAAS.

Answer (C) is correct. *(CPA, adapted)*

REQUIRED: The profession's policy concerning a CPA's retention of client records as a means of enforcing payment of an overdue fee.

DISCUSSION: The *Code* defines client-provided records as "accounting or other records belonging to the client that were provided to the member by or on behalf of the client." The retention (after a request is made for them) of client-provided records to enforce payment or for any other purpose is prohibited. Such an act is deemed to be discreditable to the profession.

Answer (A) is incorrect. Retention of client-provided records as a means of enforcing payment of an overdue audit fee is prohibited. Answer (B) is incorrect. The profession may require CPAs to adhere to standards beyond the legal minimum. Answer (D) is incorrect. Retention of client-provided records as a means of enforcing payment of an overdue audit fee is prohibited by the *Code of Professional Conduct*, not by GAAS.

2.5.4. A member of the AICPA may render which service under a contingent fee arrangement?

A. A CPA audits the financial statements of a company that intends to issue securities for sale to the public, with the fee contingent upon the proceeds from the sale of the securities.

B. A CPA compiles financial statements for a client seeking a loan, with the fee contingent upon the amount the client is able to borrow. The report does not disclose lack of independence.

C. A CPA examines prospective financial statements for a client who intends to sell limited partnerships, with the CPA's fee contingent upon the proceeds.

D. A CPA provides investment advisory services, with the fee based on a percentage of the client's investment portfolio.

Answer (D) is correct. *(Publisher, adapted)*

REQUIRED: The service that may be rendered under a contingent fee arrangement.

DISCUSSION: The member is not in violation of the *Code* if (1) the fee is based on a specified percentage of the portfolio, (2) the dollar amount of the portfolio on which the fee is based is determined at the beginning of each quarter (or longer period, if agreed) and is adjusted only for client additions or withdrawals, and (3) the fee arrangement is not renewed more often than quarterly.

Answer (A) is incorrect. A contingent fee is prohibited for an audit of financial statements. Answer (B) is incorrect. A contingent fee is prohibited for a compilation if the report does not disclose lack of independence and a third party is reasonably expected to use the financial statements. Answer (C) is incorrect. A contingent fee is prohibited for an examination of prospective financial statements.

2.5.5. An external auditor is not permitted to discuss confidential client information without the specific consent of the client. This ethical proscription

A. Is unenforceable.

B. Will prevent the auditor from engaging another auditing firm to conduct a peer review.

C. Will not preclude the auditor from complying with a validly issued court subpoena.

D. Is often used by a client to blunt the auditor's efforts to modify the standard auditor's report.

Answer (C) is correct. *(CMA, adapted)*

REQUIRED: The effect of prohibiting disclosure of confidential client information.

DISCUSSION: This prohibition does not prevent a CPA from disclosing confidential client information

1. In compliance with a validly issued and enforceable subpoena or summons;
2. In the proper discharge of his or her professional obligations under the Compliance with Standards Rule and the Accounting Principles Rule;
3. In a review of the CPA's professional practice under AICPA or state CPA society or board of accountancy authorization; or
4. During the initiation of a complaint with, or in response to any inquiry made by, the professional ethics division, trial board of the AICPA, or an investigative or disciplinary body of a state society or board of accountancy.

Answer (A) is incorrect. Conduct rules are enforceable through the AICPA and state CPA societies. Answer (B) is incorrect. An exception is made for peer reviews. Answer (D) is incorrect. The CPA is not independent if the client can dictate the content of the report. However, the auditor cannot ordinarily disclose, without the client's specific consent, information not required to be disclosed in financial statements to comply with the applicable standards.

2.5.6. To which of the following parties may a CPA partnership provide its audit documentation, without being lawfully subpoenaed or without the client's consent?

A. The IRS.

B. The FASB.

C. Any surviving partner(s) on the death of a partner.

D. A CPA before purchasing a partnership interest in the firm.

Answer (C) is correct. *(Publisher, adapted)*

REQUIRED: The true statement about records in the CPA's possession.

DISCUSSION: Audit documentation may be disclosed to another partner of the accounting firm without the client's consent because such information has not been communicated to outsiders. A partner of the CPA has a fiduciary obligation to the client not to disclose confidential information without consent.

Answer (A) is incorrect. The partnership may not provide the IRS with confidential client information without client permission, a subpoena, or a summons. Answer (B) is incorrect. The CPA or his or her firm may not disclose confidential information to the FASB without client consent. Answer (D) is incorrect. A CPA may not provide audit documentation to a prospective purchaser. However, an exception is made for a review of the practice in conjunction with a prospective purchase, sale, or merger.

2.5.7. Thorp, CPA, was engaged to audit Ivor Co.'s financial statements. During the audit, Thorp discovered that Ivor's inventory contained stolen goods. Ivor was indicted and Thorp was subpoenaed to testify at the criminal trial in state court. Ivor claimed accountant-client privilege to prevent Thorp from testifying. Which of the following statements is most likely true regarding Ivor's claim?

A. Ivor can claim an accountant-client privilege only in jurisdictions that have enacted a statute creating such a privilege.

B. Ivor could claim an accountant-client privilege if a criminal tax case were brought in federal court.

C. The accountant-client privilege can be claimed only in civil suits.

D. The accountant-client privilege can be claimed only to limit testimony to audit subject matter.

Answer (A) is correct. *(CPA, adapted)*

REQUIRED: The statement about accountant-client privilege most likely to be true.

DISCUSSION: Although communication between lawyers and clients is privileged, no common-law concept extends this privilege to the accountant-client relationship. A minority of states have enacted statutes recognizing as privileged the confidential communication between an accountant and a client.

Answer (B) is incorrect. Federal law does not recognize a broad privilege for accountant-client communications. However, the Internal Revenue Service Restructuring and Reform Act of 1998 extends a confidentiality privilege to most tax advice provided to a current or prospective client by any individual qualified under federal law to practice before the IRS. The federal law does not extend to (1) criminal tax matters, (2) private civil matters, (3) disclosures to other federal regulatory bodies, or (4) state and local tax matters. The privilege is available only in matters brought before the IRS or in proceedings in federal court in which the U.S. is a party and applies only to advice on legal issues. Answer (C) is incorrect. In jurisdictions where the privilege exists, it also applies to criminal actions. Answer (D) is incorrect. In jurisdictions where the privilege exists, it is not limited to audit matters.

2.5.8. The AICPA *Code of Professional Conduct* is violated if a CPA accepts a fee for services and the fee is

A. Fixed by a public authority.

B. Based on a price quotation submitted in competitive bidding.

C. Based on the results of judicial proceedings in a tax matter.

D. Payable after a specified finding is attained in a review of financial statements.

Answer (D) is correct. *(CPA, adapted)*

REQUIRED: The fee arrangement that violates the *Code of Professional Conduct*.

DISCUSSION: A contingent fee is dependent on a specified finding. The *Code* prohibits contingent fees (1) for the audit or review of a financial statement, (2) for a compilation if a third party is reasonably expected to use the financial statement and the report does not mention the member's lack of independence, (3) for an examination of prospective financial information, and (4) for the preparation of original or amended tax returns or claims for tax refunds. However, contingent fees may be accepted for other services.

Answer (A) is incorrect. The *Code* states that fees fixed by courts or other public authorities are not contingent. Answer (B) is incorrect. Competitive bidding is not prohibited. This change in the *Code* resulted from antitrust prosecution pressure on the accounting profession by the U.S. Department of Justice. Answer (C) is incorrect. In tax matters, fees determined based on the results of judicial proceedings or the findings of governmental agencies are not contingent.

2.5.9. With respect to records in a CPA's possession, the *Code of Professional Conduct* provides that

A. An auditor may retain client-provided records if fees due with respect to a completed engagement have not been paid.

B. Worksheets in lieu of a general ledger belong to the auditor and need not be furnished to the client upon request.

C. Extensive analyses of inventory prepared by the client at the auditor's request are working papers that belong to the auditor and need not be furnished to the client upon request.

D. The auditor who has provided records to a client must comply with any subsequent requests to again provide such information.

Answer (C) is correct. *(Publisher, adapted)*

REQUIRED: The true statement regarding records in the CPA's possession.

DISCUSSION: A member's working papers include, among other items, audit programs, analytical review schedules, statistical sampling results, analyses, and schedules prepared by the client at the request of the member. Working papers are the property of the member and need not be provided to the client unless required by (1) statute, (2) regulation, or (3) contract.

Answer (A) is incorrect. Client-provided records must be returned even if fees have not been paid. Answer (B) is incorrect. Client records prepared by the member must be returned to the client upon request if the engagement is complete and fees are paid. Answer (D) is incorrect. Once the member has complied with the requirements for the requested records, (s)he has no further obligation to provide such information.

2.5.10. An issuer client who disagrees with the independent auditor on a significant matter affecting its financial statements has several courses of action. Which of the following courses of action would be inappropriate?

A. Appeal to the FASB to review the significant matter.

B. Modify the financial statements by expressing in the notes its viewpoint with regard to the significant matter.

C. Ask the auditor to refer in the auditor's report to a client note in the financial statements that discusses the client point of view with regard to the significant matter.

D. Engage another independent auditor.

Answer (A) is correct. *(CPA, adapted)*

REQUIRED: The inappropriate action by an issuer when a disagreement arises with its auditor.

DISCUSSION: The FASB does not provide services for the settlement of disputes between clients and CPAs.

Answer (B) is incorrect. The viewpoint may be communicated in the notes. Answer (C) is incorrect. The viewpoint may be communicated in the notes. Answer (D) is incorrect. One alternative of the client is to engage a new auditor. However, the SEC requires issuers to disclose the reason for an auditor change by filing Form 8-K, and the AICPA requires predecessor-successor communication.

2.6 Other Responsibilities

2.6.1. Advertising or other forms of solicitation that are false, misleading, or deceptive are not in the public interest, and AICPA members in public practice shall not seek to obtain clients in such a manner. Such activities include all the following except those that

A. Indicate the CPA's educational and professional attainments.

B. Imply the ability to influence a court.

C. Claim to be able to save the taxpayer 20% of a determined tax liability.

D. Create unjustified expectations of favorable results.

Answer (A) is correct. *(Publisher, adapted)*

REQUIRED: The advertising activity not considered false, misleading, or deceptive.

DISCUSSION: Advertising and solicitation are acceptable if they do not involve falsehood or deception.

Answer (B) is incorrect. Advertisement of influence over courts, tribunals, regulatory agencies, or a similar body or official is deceptive. Answer (C) is incorrect. A correct amount of tax liability exists, and a claim to save a taxpayer part of that amount is deceptive. Answer (D) is incorrect. Creating false and unjustified expectations of favorable results is misleading.

2.6.2. The profession's ethical standards most likely are violated when a CPA represents that specific consulting services will be performed for a stated fee and it is apparent at the time of the representation that the

A. Actual fee would be substantially higher.

B. Actual fee would be substantially lower than the fees charged by other CPAs for comparable services.

C. CPA would not be independent.

D. Fee was a competitive bid.

Answer (A) is correct. *(CPA, adapted)*

REQUIRED: The action that violates ethical standards regarding fee representation.

DISCUSSION: The *Code* prohibits forms of solicitation that are false, misleading, or deceptive. A representation that specific services will be performed for a stated fee, when it is likely at the time that the actual fee will be substantially higher, is a prohibited form of solicitation.

Answer (B) is incorrect. A CPA is permitted to charge lower fees than other CPAs. Answer (C) is incorrect. Independence is required in an audit, but not for consulting services. Answer (D) is incorrect. Competitive bids for consulting services are allowed.

2.6.3. Ann Able, CPA, is considering forming a partnership with Ben Brown for the purpose of practicing public accounting. Which of the following is true?

A. The AICPA's *Code of Professional Conduct* requires Brown to be a CPA.

B. Brown need not be a CPA if the partnership does not represent itself as a partnership of CPAs.

C. If Brown is not a CPA, he need not conform to the AICPA *Code of Professional Conduct*.

D. If Brown is not a CPA, he may not participate in the management of the partnership.

Answer (B) is correct. *(Publisher, adapted)*

REQUIRED: The true statement about a partnership with a non-CPA.

DISCUSSION: The partnership may be created and public accounting services may be performed if the form of organization is permitted by law or regulation, provided that its characteristics conform to resolutions of the AICPA Council. Moreover, the firm may designate itself as "Members of the AICPA" if all CPA-owners are members. However, the partnership is not permitted to represent itself as a partnership of CPAs.

Answer (A) is incorrect. Some state boards and CPA societies have rules prohibiting mixed partnerships, but the *Code* does not prohibit a member from forming a partnership with non-CPAs. Answer (C) is incorrect. All partners must conform to the *Code*. Answer (D) is incorrect. The non-CPA is not precluded from participating in management.

2.6.4. Based on the *Code of Professional Conduct*, a CPA

A. May not, upon leaving a firm, take any of the firm's client files without permission.

B. Is not associated with unaudited interim reports issued by clients even if the CPA's name is listed in the report.

C. Cannot undertake the responsibility of supervising and evaluating the work of specialists.

D. May disclose currently used Uniform CPA Examination questions.

Answer (A) is correct. *(Publisher, adapted)*

REQUIRED: The true statement concerning a CPA's responsibilities.

DISCUSSION: When the relationship of a member of the AICPA with a firm is terminated, and the member was not an owner of the firm, unless permitted by contract, the member may not take or retain originals or copies from the firm's client files or proprietary information without permission. Such behavior is an act discreditable.

Answer (B) is incorrect. A member is associated with financial statements when (s)he has consented to the use of his or her name in a report, document, or written communication containing the statements. Answer (C) is incorrect. CPAs must be able to define the tasks to be performed by specialists and evaluate the results. Answer (D) is incorrect. Solicitation or knowing disclosure of currently used CPA examination questions is an act discreditable.

2.6.5. Inclusion of which of the following statements in a CPA's advertisement is not acceptable pursuant to the AICPA *Code of Professional Conduct*?

A. Paul Fall
Certified Public Accountant
Fluency in Spanish and French

B. Paul Fall
Certified Public Accountant
J.D., Evans Law School 2012

C. Paul Fall
Certified Public Accountant
Free Consultation

D. Paul Fall
Certified Public Accountant
Endorsed by AICPA

Answer (D) is correct. *(CPA, adapted)*

REQUIRED: The advertisement not in accordance with the AICPA *Code of Professional Conduct*.

DISCUSSION: Solicitation may not be false, misleading, or deceptive. Thus, a CPA may not claim to be endorsed by the Institute. The AICPA does not make endorsements. A member may, however, state that (s)he is a member.

Answer (A) is incorrect. An accurate statement about fluency in languages is acceptable. Answer (B) is incorrect. An accurate statement about educational attainments is acceptable. Answer (C) is incorrect. Advertising free consultation is acceptable.

2.6.6. Richard, CPA, performs compilation services for Norton Corporation, a nonpublic entity. The compilation reports issued by Richard disclose lack of independence and are not used by third parties. Richard has accepted a commission from a software company for recommending its products to Norton. The commission agreement was disclosed to Norton. Richard also refers Norton to Cruz, CPA, who is more competent with respect to engagements involving the industry in which Norton operates. Cruz performs an audit of Norton's financial statements and subsequently remits to Richard a portion of the fee collected. The referral fee agreement was likewise disclosed to Norton. Richard accepts the fee. Who, if anyone, has violated the *Code of Professional Conduct*?

A. Only Richard.

B. Both Richard and Cruz.

C. Only Cruz.

D. Neither Richard nor Cruz.

Answer (D) is correct. *(CPA, adapted)*

REQUIRED: The violator(s) of the *Code of Professional Conduct* when a CPA pays a referral fee to another CPA.

DISCUSSION: A commission is "compensation, except a referral fee, for recommending or referring any product or service to be supplied by another person" (FTC Order dated August 3, 1990). Receipt of a disclosed commission is prohibited only if the CPA performs for the client an audit, a review, a compilation when the report will be used by third parties and the report does not disclose the CPA's independence, or an examination of prospective financial information. A referral fee is "compensation for recommending or referring any service of a CPA to any person" (FTC Order cited above). Referral fees are allowed if they are disclosed to the client. Consequently, Richard has not violated the *Code* by accepting either the disclosed commission or the disclosed referral fee. Cruz has not violated the *Code* by paying the disclosed referral fee.

Answer (A) is incorrect. Richard has not violated the *Code*. Answer (B) is incorrect. Neither Richard nor Cruz has violated the *Code*. Answer (C) is incorrect. Cruz has not violated the *Code*.

2.6.7. A violation of the profession's ethical standards most likely occurs when a CPA

A. Purchases another CPA's accounting practice and bases the price on a percentage of the fees accruing from clients over a 3-year period.

B. Receives as a commission a percentage of the amounts invested by the CPA's audit clients in a tax shelter with the client's knowledge and approval.

C. Has a public accounting practice and also is the owner of a business that offers data processing services to the public.

D. Practices in a commercial corporation, a form of organization permitted by state law.

Answer (B) is correct. *(Publisher, adapted)*

REQUIRED: The most likely ethics violation.

DISCUSSION: The Commissions and Referral Fees Rule states that a member in public practice must not for a commission recommend or refer to a client any product or service, or for a commission recommend or refer any product or service to be supplied by a client, or receive a commission, when the member or the member's firm also performs for that client certain services. These include any attest services.

Answer (A) is incorrect. A sales price based on expected future cash flows is appropriate. Answer (C) is incorrect. A CPA may own a business offering services of a type performed by public accountants. However, (s)he is deemed to be in the practice of public accounting and must abide by the *Code*. Answer (D) is incorrect. The practice of public accounting may be any form permitted by law, provided the organization conforms to resolutions of the AICPA Council.

2.6.8. Under the Form of Organization and Name Rule, and the related resolution of the AICPA Council, which of the following is a characteristic of a form of organization in which a member may practice public accounting?

A. A CPA firm transfers all financial interests for attest services to another non-CPA firm through a leasing-of-employees arrangement.

B. The owners must be jointly and severally liable for the acts of the entity.

C. The entity must be a professional corporation.

D. A majority of the ownership of the firm must belong to CPAs.

Answer (D) is correct. *(Publisher, adapted)*

REQUIRED: The characteristic of an organization in which an AICPA member may practice public accounting.

DISCUSSION: A member may practice public accounting only in a form of organization permitted by law or regulation and only if such entity has specified characteristics.

1. CPAs own a majority of the firm.
2. A CPA must be responsible for all services.
3. A nonCPA owner must be active as a member of the firm or its affiliates.
4. NonCPA owners cannot hold themselves out as CPAs.
5. A member must not permit a person (s)he controls to do what is prohibited to the member by the *Code*. The member also may be responsible for the acts of such a person who is an associate in the practice of public accounting.
6. NonCPA owners are not eligible to be AICPA members unless they meet the requirements for membership.
7. Owners must, at all times, be the beneficial owners of the equity attributed to them. If an owner ceases to be actively engaged as a member of the firm or its affiliates, his or her ownership should be transferred to the firm or other qualified owners within a reasonable time.

Answer (A) is incorrect. Leasing arrangements may exist in alternative practice structures. However, the CPA-owners must remain financially responsible, under applicable laws or regulations, for the attest work performed. Answer (B) is incorrect. The relevant Council resolution does not address the question of liability. Answer (C) is incorrect. The entity may be in any form allowed under law or regulation.

2.6.9. Which of the following is required for a CPA firm to designate itself as "Members of the American Institute of Certified Public Accountants" on its letterhead?

A. All CPA owners must be members.

B. The owners whose names appear in the firm name must be members.

C. At least one of the owners must be a member.

D. The firm must be a dues-paying member.

Answer (A) is correct. *(CPA, adapted)*

REQUIRED: The requirement for a CPA firm to use the designation, "Members of the AICPA."

DISCUSSION: The Form of Organization and Name Rule states that a firm may not use the quoted designation unless all of its CPA owners are members of the AICPA.

Answer (B) is incorrect. All CPA owners, not just certain owners, must be AICPA members. Answer (C) is incorrect. All CPA owners must be members. Answer (D) is incorrect. The CPA owners, not the firm, must be members of the AICPA.

2.6.10. A violation of the profession's ethical standards most likely occurs when a CPA who

A. Has been admitted to the Bar represents on letterhead to be an attorney and a CPA.

B. Has not prepared a newsletter permits the publisher to attribute it to the CPA.

C. Is controller of a bank permits the bank to use the controller's CPA title in the listing of officers in its publications.

D. Maintains a separate, distinct practice but forms an association with other CPAs for joint advertising. The group practices public accounting under the association's name.

Answer (D) is correct. *(Publisher, adapted)*

REQUIRED: The most likely ethics violation.

DISCUSSION: The practice of public accounting under the name of an association or group is not permitted. The public is likely to be confused about the actual relationship of the parties. Accordingly, each firm should practice in its own firm name, but it may indicate the name of the association elsewhere on its stationery.

Answer (A) is incorrect. A single letterhead may be used. The *Code* does not prohibit the simultaneous practice of law and accounting. Answer (B) is incorrect. The *Code* permits attribution of a newsletter, tax booklet, or similar publication to a member if the member has a reasonable basis for concluding that information attributed to the member is not false, misleading, or deceptive. Answer (C) is incorrect. The *Code* permits the controller to be identified as a CPA in the listing of bank officers.

2.6.11. Which action is not considered a discreditable act under the *Code's* Acts Discreditable Rule?

A. A CPA-defendant has lost a final appeal of an adverse verdict in a sexual harassment suit in state court.

B. A CPA-defendant has lost a final appeal of an adverse verdict in a racial discrimination suit in federal court.

C. A CPA has a bank collect notes received from a client in payment of fees.

D. A CPA fails to follow standards and procedures established by governmental agencies in audits of grants by those agencies.

Answer (C) is correct. *(Publisher, adapted)*

REQUIRED: The action not a discreditable act.

DISCUSSION: The *Code* permits CPAs to assign client notes received in payment of fees to banks for collection.

Answer (A) is incorrect. A final adverse legal determination of culpability under antidiscrimination law creates a presumption that the member has committed an act discreditable. Answer (B) is incorrect. A final adverse legal determination of culpability under antidiscrimination law creates a presumption that the member has committed an act discreditable. Answer (D) is incorrect. A member must follow established governmental standards and procedures in addition to GAAS in auditing governmental agencies, grantees, etc. Thus, failing to follow standards and procedures established by governmental agencies in audits of grants by those agencies is a discreditable act.

2.6.12. According to the AICPA *Code of Professional Conduct*, which of the following records must a CPA return to the client when requested?

A. Client-provided records, even if fees are due to the CPA for the engagement and are unpaid.

B. Client-provided records requested for a second time because the client misplaced the first set of records.

C. Supporting records prepared by the CPA consisting of adjusting, closing, combining, or consolidating entries prior to the completion of the engagement.

D. The CPA's working papers consisting of analyses and schedules prepared by the client at the CPA's request.

Answer (A) is correct. *(CPA, adapted)*

REQUIRED: The records that must be returned to the client upon request.

DISCUSSION: Under the Acts Discreditable Rule, client-provided records must be returned after a client request without exception even if fees are due. Client-provided records are the client's accounting or other records, including hardcopy and electronic reproductions, that were provided to the member by, or for, the client.

Answer (B) is incorrect. A member who has complied with a requirement regarding a records request has no obligation to comply with a subsequent request. The sole exception is a client's loss due to a natural disaster or act of war. Answer (C) is incorrect. Member-prepared records (e.g., adjusting, closing, combining, or consolidating journal entries) may be withheld if fees are due. Answer (D) is incorrect. Working papers are the member's property and need not be made available to the client or others unless required by (1) statute, (2) regulation, or (3) contract.

2.6.13. Which is most likely a violation of the AICPA *Code of Professional Conduct*?

A. A member firm buys computer time at wholesale prices from another CPA firm and sells it at retail prices to clients.

B. A member begins a public accounting firm with the trade name "Pay Less Tax Service."

C. A member firm's name is imprinted on a tax booklet prepared by an outside author who is clearly identified.

D. A member forms a partnership for the practice of public accounting with non-CPAs.

Answer (B) is correct. *(Publisher, adapted)*

REQUIRED: The situation that is most likely a violation of the *Code*.

DISCUSSION: Members may use a trade name as long as it is not deceptive or misleading. "Pay Less" may be construed as misleading for a tax service.

Answer (A) is incorrect. A member is permitted to purchase a product and resell it to a client. Answer (C) is incorrect. The *Code* permits imprinting a member's name on a tax booklet if there is a reasonable basis for concluding that the content is not false, misleading, or deceptive. Answer (D) is incorrect. The partnership of a CPA with non-CPAs is not precluded by the *Code*.

2.7 Other Pronouncements on Professional Responsibilities

2.7.1. According to SEC independence regulations,

A. All audit partners must rotate every 5 years.

B. Preapproval of accountants' services may be in accord with detailed policies and procedures rather than explicit.

C. The issuer must disclose only those fees paid to the accountant for audit work.

D. No partner may sell nonaudit services to the client during the audit.

Answer (B) is correct. *(Publisher, adapted)*

REQUIRED: The true statement about SEC independence regulations.

DISCUSSION: Audit committees ordinarily must preapprove the services performed by accountants (permissible nonaudit services and all audit, review, and attest engagements). Approval must be either explicit or in accordance with detailed policies and procedures. If approval is based on detailed policies and procedures, the audit committee must be informed, and no delegation of its authority to management is allowed.

Answer (A) is incorrect. The lead and concurring (reviewing) audit partners must rotate every 5 years, with a 5-year time-out period. Other audit partners must rotate every 7 years, with a 2-year time-out. Answer (C) is incorrect. An issuer must disclose in its proxy statement or annual filing the fees paid to the accountant segregated into four categories: (1) audit, (2) audit-related, (3) tax, and (4) all other. Answer (D) is incorrect. An accountant is not independent if, during the audit and the period of the engagement, any audit partner (excluding specialty partners such as tax partners) earns or receives compensation for selling services (excluding audit, review, or attest services) to the client.

2.7.2. According to the PCAOB, an accounting firm's independence is least likely to be impaired if the firm

A. Provides a service to the audit client for a contingent fee.

B. Receives a commission from the audit client.

C. Has an audit client that employs a former firm professional.

D. Provides tax services to a person in a financial reporting oversight role at the audit client.

Answer (C) is correct. *(Publisher, adapted)*

REQUIRED: The circumstances least likely to impair an accounting firm's independence.

DISCUSSION: Firm independence is impaired by a client's employment of a former firm professional that could adversely affect the audit unless safeguards are established. Pre-change safeguards include removal from the audit of those negotiating with the client, and post-change safeguards include possibly modifying the audit plan.

Answer (A) is incorrect. A firm is not independent of its client if the firm or any affiliate, during the audit and engagement period, provides any service or product to the client for a contingent fee or a commission, or receives from the client a contingent fee or commission. Answer (B) is incorrect. A firm is not independent of its client if the firm or any affiliate, during the audit and engagement period, provides any service or product to the client for a contingent fee or a commission, or receives from the client a contingent fee or commission. Answer (D) is incorrect. A registered public accounting firm is not independent of its audit client if the firm or any affiliate, during the professional engagement period, provides any tax service to a person in a financial reporting oversight role at the audit client.

2.7.3. According to the PCAOB, an accounting firm is most likely to be independent of its audit client if

A. A reasonable investor would conclude that it is not objective and impartial.

B. The firm's audit professional is responsible for internal control over financial reporting.

C. The firm's audit professional implemented the client's internal control over financial reporting.

D. The firm recommended an aggressive tax position to the client that is more likely than not to be legally allowed.

Answer (D) is correct. *(Publisher, adapted)*

REQUIRED: The circumstances in which an accounting firm is most likely to be independent.

DISCUSSION: A firm is not independent of its audit client if, during the audit and engagement period, it provides any nonaudit service related to marketing, planning, or expressing an opinion in favor of the tax treatment of aggressive tax-position transactions for the purpose of tax avoidance. However, this Rule does not apply if the tax treatment is at least more likely than not to be allowable under tax law.

Answer (A) is incorrect. An auditor is not independent if (s)he is not, or a reasonable investor would conclude that (s)he is not, able to be objective and impartial. Answer (B) is incorrect. Guiding principles regarding independence include whether the auditor assumes a management role or audits his or her own work. Thus, an auditor is not independent if, for example, the auditor is responsible for internal control over financial reporting or had designed or implemented it. Answer (C) is incorrect. Designing or implementing internal control over financial reporting impairs independence.

2.7.4. Inspections performed by the PCAOB focus on quality control of registered CPA firms that perform audits of public companies (issuers). As required by the Sarbanes-Oxley Act, inspections determine all of the following except that

A. The lead partner of a client is rotated every 5 years.

B. A second partner review is performed.

C. Independence is maintained by audit staff.

D. Only staff with prior experience work on audits.

Answer (D) is correct. *(Publisher, adapted)*

REQUIRED: The issue not considered in a PCAOB inspection.

DISCUSSION: Staff members are required to be trained and supervised in accordance with auditing standards. However, there is no requirement that they have prior experience.

Answer (A) is incorrect. The lead partner must be rotated at least every 5 years. Answer (B) is incorrect. A second partner review is required for each audit engagement of an issuer. Answer (C) is incorrect. Registered firms must have "policies and procedures in place to comply" with applicable independence requirements.

2.7.5. The Sarbanes-Oxley Act of 2002 has strengthened auditor independence by requiring that management of a public company

A. Include only independent persons on the board of directors.

B. Report the nature of disagreements with former auditors.

C. Select auditors through audit committees.

D. Hire a different CPA firm from the one that performs the audit to perform the company's tax work.

Answer (C) is correct. *(CPA, adapted)*

REQUIRED: The Sarbanes-Oxley requirement that strengthened auditor independence.

DISCUSSION: The audit committee must hire and pay the external auditors. Such affiliation inhibits management from changing auditors to gain acceptance of a questionable accounting method. Also, a successor auditor must inquire of the predecessor before accepting an engagement.

Answer (A) is incorrect. The audit committee must include only independent members. Answer (B) is incorrect. Reporting disagreements with auditors is a long-time SEC requirement. Answer (D) is incorrect. The act does not restrict who may perform tax work. Other engagements, such as outsourcing internal auditing or certain consulting services, are limited.

2.7.6. When Congress passed the Sarbanes-Oxley Act of 2002, it imposed greater regulation on public companies and their auditors and required increased accountability. Which of the following is not a provision of the act?

A. Executives must certify the appropriateness of the financial statements.

B. The act provides criminal penalties for fraud.

C. Auditors may not provide specific nonaudit services for their audit clients.

D. Audit firms must be rotated on a periodic basis.

Answer (D) is correct. *(Publisher, adapted)*

REQUIRED: The provision not included in the Sarbanes-Oxley Act.

DISCUSSION: The act requires rotation of the lead audit or coordinating partner and the reviewing partner on audits of public clients every 5 years. However, the act does not require the rotation of audit firms.

Answer (A) is incorrect. The CEO and CFO of a public company must provide a statement to accompany the audit report. This statement certifies the appropriateness of the financial statements and disclosures. However, a violation of this requirement must be knowing and intentional. Answer (B) is incorrect. The act creates a new crime for securities fraud with penalties of fines and imprisonment, extends the statute of limitations on securities fraud claims, and makes it a felony to create or destroy documents to impede a federal investigation. Answer (C) is incorrect. The act makes it unlawful for a registered public accounting firm to perform certain nonaudit services for audit clients, for example, bookkeeping, systems design, management functions, or any other service the Public Company Accounting Oversight Board (PCAOB) determines by regulation to be impermissible.

2.7.7. Which of the following most likely is an allowable service that an auditor may provide to a public client?

A. Internal audit outsourcing.

B. Legal services.

C. Management consulting services.

D. Tax compliance services.

Answer (D) is correct. *(Publisher, adapted)*

REQUIRED: The type of service that an audit firm most likely may provide to an audit client.

DISCUSSION: The Sarbanes-Oxley Act prohibits audit firms from providing consulting, legal, and internal auditing services to public audit clients. However, the PCAOB may, on a case-by-case basis, create exemptions from the prohibition against providing certain nonaudit services at the time of the audit. Audit firms may provide conventional tax planning and compliance services to public audit clients.

Answer (A) is incorrect. Internal audit outsourcing is a service that may not be provided to public audit clients. Answer (B) is incorrect. Legal services are services that may not be provided to public audit clients. Answer (C) is incorrect. Management consulting services are services that may not be provided to public audit clients.

2.7.8. At least how often should the PCAOB inspect a registered public accounting firm that regularly issues audit reports to 50 issuers?

A. Annually.

B. Every 2 years.

C. Every 3 years.

D. As requested by the firm.

Answer (C) is correct. *(CPA, adapted)*

REQUIRED: The frequency of inspection of a registered public accounting firm that regularly issues audit reports to 50 issuers.

DISCUSSION: A registered public accounting firm is inspected at least once every 3 calendar years. This requirement must be met beginning with the 3-year period following the calendar year in which its application for registration with the PCAOB is approved. But the requirement does not apply unless the firm, during any of the 3 previous calendar years, (1) issued an audit report for at least 1, but no more than 100, issuers or (2) was substantially involved in preparing or providing an audit report for at least one issuer.

Answer (A) is incorrect. The PCAOB inspects audit firms every 3 years and every year if the firm audits 100 or more issuers. Answer (B) is incorrect. The PCAOB inspects audit firms every 3 years and every year if the firm audits 100 or more issuers. Answer (D) is incorrect. A firm is inspected by the PCAOB every 3 years and every year if the firm audits 100 or more issuers.

2.8 Legal Liability

2.8.1. The prevailing legal view is that an auditor's liability to third parties at common law may be based on

A. Fraud only when such parties were in privity of contract with the auditor.

B. Gross negligence only if the auditor knew such parties were intended beneficiaries of the audit.

C. Ordinary negligence and that any third party who relied on the auditor's work may recover.

D. Ordinary negligence if such parties belonged to a specifically foreseen class but were not specifically known.

Answer (D) is correct. *(Publisher, adapted)*

REQUIRED: The basis for an auditor's legal liability to a third party at common law.

DISCUSSION: An auditor has not contracted with third parties, so the potential responsibility to them is not as great as to the client. Auditors may be liable to any third parties for gross negligence and intentional acts of deceit (fraud). However, auditors may be liable at common law for ordinary negligence to third parties in certain circumstances. The majority of jurisdictions provide for liability when a third party, although not specifically known at the time of the audit, belonged to a limited and foreseen class of financial statement users. For example, banks would be included in the class if the audit report were intended to be used by the client to obtain a bank loan. Other creditors, however, would be excluded from the class of potential plaintiffs.

Answer (A) is incorrect. The auditor may be liable for fraud to all third parties. Answer (B) is incorrect. The auditor may be liable for gross negligence to all third parties. Answer (C) is incorrect. The majority view precludes recovery on the basis of ordinary negligence unless the plaintiff belonged to a specifically foreseen class of users (intended beneficiaries).

2.8.2. Contract law is the basis for the legal liability at common law of an auditor to his or her client. From which of the following may the auditor's liability arise?

A. Only fraudulent actions by the auditor.

B. Only gross negligence or fraudulent actions by the auditor.

C. Negligence, gross negligence, or fraudulent actions by the auditor.

D. Neither negligence nor fraudulent actions by the auditor.

Answer (C) is correct. *(Publisher, adapted)*

REQUIRED: The basis for an auditor's legal liability to a client at common law.

DISCUSSION: An auditor's liability to a client arises from their contract, which is documented in the audit engagement letter. The auditor is obligated to carry out the contract (perform the audit) by exercising reasonable care. (S)he will be liable to the client for any negligence or fraud.

Answer (A) is incorrect. The auditor will also be liable for negligence. Answer (B) is incorrect. The auditor will also be liable for failure to use reasonable care (ordinary negligence). Answer (D) is incorrect. Both negligence and fraud will create a contractual liability. The contract implies a duty to exercise reasonable care.

2.8.3. Under Section 11 of the Securities Act of 1933, which of the following standards may a CPA use as a defense?

	Generally Accepted Accounting Principles	Generally Accepted Fraud Detection Standards
A.	Yes	Yes
B.	Yes	No
C.	No	Yes
D.	No	No

Answer (B) is correct. *(CPA, adapted)*

REQUIRED: The standards a CPA may use as a defense under Section 11.

DISCUSSION: A CPA is strictly liable to investors under Section 11 but will not be liable if (s)he can prove due diligence. This defense requires proof that a reasonable investigation was conducted and that the CPA reasonably believed that the financial statements were accurate on the effective date of the registration statement. Proof of adherence to GAAP and GAAS is the usual basis for such a due diligence defense.

2.8.4. Which of the following best describes litigation involving CPAs?

A. The Racketeer Influenced and Corrupt Organizations Act was specifically passed by Congress to address illegitimate actions by CPAs.

B. A CPA may successfully assert as a defense that the CPA had no motive to be part of a fraud.

C. A CPA may be exposed to criminal as well as civil liability.

D. A CPA is primarily responsible for a client's notes in an annual report filed with the SEC.

Answer (C) is correct. *(Publisher, adapted)*

REQUIRED: The best description of litigation involving CPAs.

DISCUSSION: A CPA may be exposed to criminal as well as civil liability under the Securities Act of 1933, the Securities Exchange Act of 1934, and the Racketeer Influenced and Corrupt Organizations Act (RICO).

Answer (A) is incorrect. RICO was enacted to curtail inroads of organized crime into legitimate business. Answer (B) is incorrect. Although absence of intent is a defense to fraud, motive is not relevant. Answer (D) is incorrect. Management, not the CPA, is responsible for the financial statements, including the notes.

2.8.5. Under the antifraud provisions of Section 10(b) of the Securities Exchange Act of 1934, a CPA may be liable if the CPA acted

A. Negligently.

B. With independence.

C. Without due diligence.

D. Without good faith.

Answer (D) is correct. *(CPA, adapted)*

REQUIRED: The basis for a CPA's liability under Section 10(b).

DISCUSSION: The distinguishing element of fraud is scienter, the intent to deceive or defraud. Acting in good faith indicates lack of scienter. Accordingly, a CPA who acted without good faith cannot assert the good faith defense.

Answer (A) is incorrect. Fraud entails an intent to deceive or defraud, not mere negligence. Answer (B) is incorrect. A CPA who performs attest services must be independent. Answer (C) is incorrect. Lack of due diligence, per se, does not signify the existence of scienter.

2.8.6. Which is the true statement about an auditor's statutory legal liability?

A. The Securities Act of 1933 broadened the auditor's liability and the Securities Exchange Act of 1934 narrowed it.

B. The auditor has a greater burden of defense under the Securities Act of 1933 than the Securities Exchange Act of 1934.

C. Criminal liability only arises under state law.

D. The auditor may limit exposure to liability by destroying documents that might suggest an improper act.

Answer (B) is correct. *(Publisher, adapted)*

REQUIRED: The true statement about an auditor's statutory liability.

DISCUSSION: In general, the Securities Act of 1933 regulates initial sales of securities to the public. The Securities Exchange Act of 1934 regulates subsequent sales and exchanges of securities. Under the 1933 act, a purchaser need only prove damages resulting from the purchase of securities covered by a registration statement containing a false statement or omission in a section audited or prepared by the auditor. The auditor must then prove that (s)he was not negligent (or fraudulent), usually by showing that (s)he made a reasonable investigation (the "due diligence" defense). Under the 1934 act, the purchaser must prove that (s)he did not know the statement was false, that (s)he relied on it, and, under the antifraud provisions, that the auditor acted with intent or reckless disregard for the truth. Thus, gross negligence is the minimum basis for liability, and the auditor need not prove due diligence.

Answer (A) is incorrect. Both securities statutes imposed greater liability on auditors than had existed under the common law. However, the 1934 act places a greater burden of proof on the plaintiff than the 1933 act. Answer (C) is incorrect. Criminal liability can also arise under federal securities law. Answer (D) is incorrect. The Sarbanes-Oxley Act of 2002 makes it a felony to knowingly destroy or create documents to impede, obstruct, or influence any existing or contemplated federal investigation. The maximum prison term is 20 years. Moreover, a registered public accounting firm must retain audit working papers for at least 7 years. A nonregistered public accounting firm must retain working papers for at least 5 years. The documentation retained must be in sufficient detail to support the conclusions in the audit report.

2.8.7. Ocean and Associates, CPAs, audited the financial statements of Drain Corporation. As a result of Ocean's negligence in conducting the audit, the financial statements included material misstatements. Ocean was unaware of this fact. The financial statements and Ocean's unmodified opinion were included in a registration statement and prospectus for an original public offering of stock by Drain. Sharp purchased shares in the offering. Sharp received a copy of the prospectus prior to the purchase but did not read it. The shares declined in value as a result of the misstatements in Drain's financial statements becoming known. Under which of the following acts is Sharp most likely to prevail in a lawsuit against Ocean?

	Securities Exchange Act of 1934, Section 10(b), Rule 10b-5	Securities Act of 1933, Section 11
A.	Yes	Yes
B.	Yes	No
C.	No	Yes
D.	No	No

Answer (C) is correct. *(CPA, adapted)*

REQUIRED: The basis for recovery under securities law in a suit against negligent accountants.

DISCUSSION: Section 11 is the most frequently invoked basis for suit under the Securities Act of 1933. Under Sec. 11, the investor need prove only that (s)he suffered losses in a transaction involving the particular securities covered by the registration statement and that the registration statement contained a false statement or an omission of a material fact for which the CPAs were responsible, e.g., in the audited financial statements. Thus, under Sec. 11, Sharp need not prove reliance or negligence and will prevail if Ocean fails to prove due diligence. Sharp is unlikely to prevail under the antifraud provisions of the Securities Exchange Act of 1934 because of the absence of scienter.

2.8.8. DMO Enterprises, Inc., engaged the accounting firm of Martin, Seals, & Anderson to perform its annual audit. The firm performed the audit in a competent, nonnegligent manner and billed DMO for $16,000, the agreed fee. Shortly after delivery of the audited financial statements, Hightower, the assistant controller, disappeared, taking with him $28,000 of DMO's funds. It was then discovered that Hightower had been engaged in a highly sophisticated, novel defalcation scheme during the past year. He had previously embezzled $35,000 of DMO funds. DMO has refused to pay the accounting firm's fee and is seeking to recover the $63,000 that was stolen by Hightower. Which of the following is most likely true?

A. The accountants cannot recover their fee and are liable for $63,000.

B. The accountants are entitled to collect their fee and are not liable for $63,000.

C. DMO is entitled to rescind the audit contract and thus is not liable for the $16,000 fee, but it cannot recover damages.

D. DMO is entitled to recover the $28,000 defalcation and is not liable for the $16,000 fee.

Answer (B) is correct. *(CPA, adapted)*

REQUIRED: The true statement about the disputed fee of auditors who failed to uncover a sophisticated embezzlement scheme.

DISCUSSION: An audit cannot guarantee that fraud will be detected. The auditor's opinion reflects that the audit is intended to give only reasonable assurance that the financial statements are free of material misstatement. AU-C 200 states, "Reasonable assurance is a high, but not absolute, level of assurance." If the auditors planned and performed the audit in accordance with GAAS, the accounting firm fulfilled its contract with the client. The auditors should not be held liable for the loss and are entitled to their fee.

Answer (A) is incorrect. The accountants are entitled to the $16,000 in unpaid fees and are not liable for either the current embezzlement of $28,000 or the past embezzlement of $35,000. Answer (C) is incorrect. The client is liable for the $16,000 fee. Answer (D) is incorrect. The client is liable for the $16,000 fee and is not entitled to recover the $28,000 defalcation from the accountants.

2.8.9. How does the Securities Act of 1933, which imposes civil liability on auditors for misrepresentations or omissions of material facts in a registration statement, expand auditors' liability to purchasers of securities beyond that of common law?

A. Purchasers only have to prove loss caused by reliance on audited financial statements.

B. Privity with purchasers is not a necessary element of proof.

C. Purchasers have to prove either fraud or gross negligence as a basis for recovery.

D. Auditors are held to a standard of care described as professional skepticism.

Answer (B) is correct. *(CPA, adapted)*

REQUIRED: The expansion of auditor liability under the Securities Act of 1933.

DISCUSSION: Privity, i.e., being a party to the contract with the auditor, is not a required element of proof under Sect. 11, the most frequently invoked basis for recovery under the Securities Act of 1933. Privity is often the deciding factor in common law cases, however.

Answer (A) is incorrect. A plaintiff must simply prove that a loss occurred in a transaction involving the particular securities covered by the registration statement and that the registration statement contained a false statement or an omission of a material fact for which the auditors were responsible. If these elements are proven, the burden shifts to the auditors to prove that they exercised due diligence. Negligence, privity, and reliance are not elements of the plaintiff's case. Answer (C) is incorrect. The plaintiff need not prove fraud, gross negligence, negligence, privity, or reliance. Answer (D) is incorrect. Auditors are held to the standard of due diligence, which may be satisfied by following GAAS in the conduct of the audit.

2.8.10. Martin Corporation orally engages Dawson, CPA, to audit its year-end financial statements. The engagement is to be completed within 2 months after the close of Martin's fiscal year for a fixed fee of $2,500. Under these circumstances what obligation is assumed by Dawson?

A. None. The contract is unenforceable because it is not in writing.

B. An implied promise to exercise reasonable standards of competence and care.

C. An implied obligation to take extraordinary steps to discover all defalcations.

D. The obligation of an insurer of its work who is liable without fault.

Answer (B) is correct. *(CPA, adapted)*

REQUIRED: The obligation assumed by a CPA engaged to audit financial statements.

DISCUSSION: CPAs are required to adhere to reasonable standards of competence and care and perform an audit in accordance with GAAS. They are expected to complete the contract based upon the agreed terms.

Answer (A) is incorrect. An oral contract is enforceable (but subject to disagreement, which can be avoided with an engagement letter). Answer (C) is incorrect. An ordinary audit should be designed to provide reasonable assurance that material errors and fraud will be detected. Thus, it need not include extraordinary procedures to uncover all fraud, whether or not material. Answer (D) is incorrect. Auditors are not insurers. They do not undertake to guarantee the results of their work regardless of fault. Rather, they are required to use due professional care.

2.8.11. You are a CPA retained by the manager of a cooperative retirement village to do bookkeeping and a compilation of the financial statements. You are expected to prepare unaudited financial statements with each page marked "unaudited" and accompanied by a disclaimer of opinion stating no audit was made. In performing the work, you discover that there are no invoices to support $25,000 of the manager's claimed disbursements. The manager informs you that all the disbursements are proper. What should you do?

A. Submit the expected statements but omit the $25,000 of unsupported disbursements.

B. Include the unsupported disbursements in the statements because you are not expected to make an audit.

C. Obtain from the manager a written statement that you informed him or her of the missing invoices and that (s)he gave his or her assurance that the disbursements were proper.

D. Notify the owners that some of the claimed disbursements are unsupported and withdraw if the situation is not satisfactorily resolved.

Answer (D) is correct. *(CPA, adapted)*

REQUIRED: The appropriate action by a CPA who discovers a material irregularity while doing compilation work.

DISCUSSION: These facts are based on *1136 Tenants' Corp. v. Max Rothenburg & Co.* (1972), a case that imposed liability on a CPA doing compilation work for not pursuing an investigation of facts that appeared questionable on their face. Although the CPA need not audit the information, (s)he is responsible to take further action regarding information that is incorrect, incomplete, or otherwise unsatisfactory. Such action includes communication with the owners.

Answer (A) is incorrect. Submitting the statements but omitting the unsupported disbursements is an inappropriate action on the part of the CPA. Answer (B) is incorrect. Including the unsupported disbursements in the statements is an inappropriate action on the part of the CPA. Answer (C) is incorrect. Obtaining the manager's statement is insufficient.

2.9 Tax Services

2.9.1. Statements on Standards for Tax Services (SSTSs) have been issued by the Tax Executive Committee of the AICPA. The SSTSs

A. Also have been approved by the Council of the AICPA.

B. Are applicable to all CPAs, not just members of the AICPA.

C. Are enforceable under the AICPA *Code of Professional Conduct*.

D. Apply only to federal income tax engagements.

Answer (C) is correct. *(Publisher, adapted)*

REQUIRED: The true statement about SSTSs.

DISCUSSION: The *Code*'s General Standards Rule and Compliance with Standards Rule require members to comply with the SSTSs. Members who depart from the standards are required to justify those departures.

Answer (A) is incorrect. The SSTSs have been approved by at least two-thirds of the members of the Tax Executive Committee by formal vote. However, they have not been considered and acted upon by the Council of the Institute. Answer (B) is incorrect. The SSTSs (codified as TS 100 through TS 700) are specifically enforceable only against members of the AICPA. Answer (D) is incorrect. The SSTSs are applicable to all tax engagements, whether for preparing a federal income tax return or representing a client in a local sales tax appeal hearing.

2.9.2. A member of the AICPA who is engaged to prepare an income tax return has a duty to prepare it in such a manner that the tax is

A. The legal minimum.

B. Computed in conformity with generally accepted accounting principles.

C. Supported by the client's audited financial statements.

D. Not subject to change upon audit.

Answer (A) is correct. *(CPA, adapted)*

REQUIRED: The duty of a member of the AICPA in preparing a client's income tax return.

DISCUSSION: A member of the AICPA should serve to the best of his or her ability and with professional concern for the taxpayer's best interests, consistent with responsibilities to the tax system. According to TS 100, "It is well established that the taxpayer has no obligation to pay more taxes than are legally owed, and a member has a duty to the taxpayer to assist in achieving that result." Within the limits of the law and ethical practice, the member should strive for the legal minimum tax, not for tax evasion.

Answer (B) is incorrect. The tax is computed based on statutes and pronouncements of the taxing authority, not GAAP. Answer (C) is incorrect. The tax expense, according to the statements, is based on GAAP. Moreover, the tax preparer need not audit the client's statements. Answer (D) is incorrect. Discovery of errors may necessitate a change.

2.9.3. When a member of the AICPA prepares a taxpayer's federal income tax return, the member has the responsibility to

A. Be an advocate for the entity's position.

B. Verify the data to be used in preparing the return.

C. Take a position of independent neutrality.

D. Argue the position of the Internal Revenue Service.

Answer (A) is correct. *(CPA, adapted)*

REQUIRED: The responsibility of a member of the AICPA who prepares a federal income tax return.

DISCUSSION: A member of the AICPA engaged in tax practice has the right and responsibility to be an advocate for the client with regard to any tax return position that meets legal and professional standards. A taxpayer has no obligation to pay more taxes than legally owed (TS 100).

Answer (B) is incorrect. The data need not be verified unless the information seems incomplete, inconsistent, or incorrect. Answer (C) is incorrect. A member must be independent when performing attestation services, not for tax return preparation services. Answer (D) is incorrect. A member has the right and the responsibility to be an advocate of the client, not the IRS.

2.9.4. A CPA must sign the preparer's declaration on a federal income tax return

A. Only when the CPA prepares a tax return for compensation.

B. Only when the CPA can declare that a tax is based on information of which the CPA has personal knowledge.

C. Whenever the CPA prepares a tax return for others.

D. Only when the return is for an individual or corporation.

Answer (A) is correct. *(CPA, adapted)*

REQUIRED: The condition for signing the preparer's declaration on a federal income tax return.

DISCUSSION: Treasury Regulations require preparers to sign all the returns they prepare and to include their identification numbers. However, a preparer is defined as a person who prepares (or employs persons to prepare) for compensation any tax return, amended return, or claim for refund of tax imposed by Subtitle A of the Internal Revenue Code (which covers income taxes on all entities).

Answer (B) is incorrect. The CPA may prepare a return based on information provided by the taxpayer. Personal knowledge of the information is not required. Answer (C) is incorrect. The CPA must sign only when (s)he receives compensation. Answer (D) is incorrect. The signature requirement applies to returns and claims for refund by all income tax-paying entities.

2.9.5. The preparer of a federal income tax return signs a preparer's declaration that states,

> Under penalties of perjury, I declare that I have examined this return and accompanying schedules and statements, and to the best of my knowledge and belief, they are true, correct, and accurately list all amounts and sources of income I received during the tax year. Declaration of preparer (other than the taxpayer) is based on all information of which preparer has any knowledge.

A member of the AICPA who signs this declaration as preparer of a client's tax return warrants that

A. Information furnished by the client was relied upon in preparing the tax return unless it appeared incorrect, inconsistent, or incomplete.

B. Information furnished by the client was audited in accordance with GAAS.

C. All available evidence in support of material assertions in the tax return was audited in accordance with GAAS.

D. All available evidence in support of material assertions in the tax return was documented.

Answer (A) is correct. *(CPA, adapted)*

REQUIRED: The warranty given by a member of the AICPA who signs the tax preparer's declaration on a federal income tax return.

DISCUSSION: The preparer's declaration should be understood to relate to information known by the member of the AICPA or made available to him or her in connection with the preparation of a return. The declaration should not imply an investigation in support of material furnished by the client. The member may ordinarily rely on the information furnished by the client unless, in light of his or her knowledge, the information presented appears to be "incorrect, incomplete, or inconsistent either on its face or on the basis of other facts known to the member" (TS 300, *Certain Procedural Aspects of Preparing Returns*).

Answer (B) is incorrect. The member does not perform an audit in accordance with GAAS of the information furnished by the client. Answer (C) is incorrect. The member does not perform an audit in accordance with GAAS of all available evidence in support of material assertions in the tax return. Answer (D) is incorrect. The member need not examine or verify supporting data.

2.9.6. According to the AICPA Statements on Standards for Tax Services, why must a CPA be satisfied that a reasonable effort has been made to obtain information needed to provide appropriate answers to the questions on a tax return before signing the preparer's declaration?

A. The declaration requires the CPA to state that the return is true, correct, and complete based upon all information of which the preparer has knowledge.

B. Some information obtained may not be of use in determining taxable income but might help the CPA assess the long-term financial health of the taxpayer.

C. Making a reasonable effort to obtain information may prevent fraudulent responses by the taxpayer.

D. Evidence of the CPA's reasonable effort to obtain information could increase the likelihood of relief from tax preparer penalties.

Answer (A) is correct. *(CPA, adapted)*

REQUIRED: The reason a CPA must be satisfied that a reasonable effort has been made to obtain information needed to provide appropriate answers to tax return questions.

DISCUSSION: A member of the AICPA should be satisfied that a reasonable effort has been made to obtain information to provide answers to the questions on a tax return that apply to a taxpayer. Reasons include the following: (1) A question may be important in determining taxable income or loss, or tax liability, in which case an omission may detract from the quality of the return; (2) a request for information may require a disclosure necessary to complete the return or to avoid penalties; and (3) a member often must sign a declaration stating that the return is true, correct, and complete (TS 200).

Answer (B) is incorrect. The long-term financial health of the taxpayer is not relevant to preparation of the tax return. Answer (C) is incorrect. A tax return preparer may rely, without verification, on information provided by the taxpayer when the preparer is reasonably justified in relying upon the taxpayer's representations. However, a preparer must make a reasonable inquiry if the information appears to be incorrect or incomplete (TS 300). Answer (D) is incorrect. The omission of an answer, not the lack of a reasonable effort, may result in penalties.

2.9.7. In accordance with the AICPA's Statements on Standards for Tax Services, when reasonable grounds exist for omission of an answer to an applicable question on a tax return,

A. The member-preparer need not provide an explanation for the omission on the return.

B. A brief explanation of the reason for the omission must be provided on the return.

C. The question should be marked as nonapplicable.

D. A note on the return should state that the answer will be provided if the information is requested.

Answer (A) is correct. *(CPA, adapted)*

REQUIRED: The proper action when a reasonable basis exists for omission of an answer on a tax return.

DISCUSSION: According to TS 200, *Answers to Questions on Returns*, a member of the AICPA should sign the preparer's declaration when a question has not been answered only if the member has made "a reasonable effort to obtain from the taxpayer the information necessary to provide appropriate answers to all questions on a tax return." A possible disadvantage to the taxpayer does not justify omission of an answer. However, given reasonable grounds for the omission, the taxpayer is not required to provide an explanation on the return, although the member must consider whether the omission may cause the return to be incomplete.

Answer (B) is incorrect. Given reasonable grounds for the omission, the taxpayer is not required to provide an explanation on the return. Answer (C) is incorrect. An omission may be reasonable on grounds other than inapplicability. Answer (D) is incorrect. Given reasonable grounds for the omission, the taxpayer is not required to provide an explanation on the return.

2.9.8. As part of an annual audit of a client, a member of the AICPA prepares the federal income tax return. What modifications should be made to the preparer's declaration when signing the return?

	Modify to Conform to Audit Report	Modify to State That Information Was from Audited Financial Statements
A.	Yes	No
B.	No	No
C.	Yes	Yes
D.	No	Yes

Answer (B) is correct. *(Publisher, adapted)*

REQUIRED: The modifications that the member should make to the preparer's declaration.

DISCUSSION: The member should make no modification of the preparer's declaration on a federal income tax return. Modification will not affect the signer's responsibilities as preparer. Unusual circumstances may be disclosed in a rider not constituting a modification. Furthermore, the member neither audits the information in the tax return nor warrants by signing as preparer that an investigation has been made.

2.9.9. Jones, a member of the AICPA, prepared Smith's federal income tax return and appropriately signed the preparer's declaration. Several months later, Jones learned that Smith improperly altered several figures before mailing the tax return to the IRS. Jones should communicate disapproval of this action to Smith and

A. Take no further action with respect to the current year's tax return but consider the implications of Smith's actions for any future relationship.

B. Inform the IRS of the unauthorized alteration.

C. File an amended tax return.

D. Refund any fee collected, return all relevant documents, and refuse any further association with Smith.

Answer (A) is correct. *(CPA, adapted)*

REQUIRED: The proper action of a tax preparer-member after the taxpayer improperly altered the return.

DISCUSSION: When the member discovers an error, (s)he must inform the taxpayer and recommend the corrective measures to be taken. It is then the taxpayer's responsibility to correct the error. If the IRS is likely to bring criminal charges, the taxpayer should be advised to seek legal counsel. If the error is not corrected, "the member should consider whether to withdraw from preparing the return and whether to continue a professional or employment relationship with the taxpayer" (TS 600).

Answer (B) is incorrect. The member may not inform the IRS, except if required by law. Answer (C) is incorrect. The member may not file an amended return without the taxpayer's permission. Answer (D) is incorrect. TS 600 does not mention refunding fees and returning documents.

2.9.10. According to the AICPA's standards, which of the following actions should be taken by a member tax preparer who discovers an error in a taxpayer's previously filed tax return?

A. Advise the IRS.

B. Correct the error.

C. Advise the taxpayer.

D. End the relationship with the taxpayer.

Answer (C) is correct. *(CPA, adapted)*

REQUIRED: The proper action by a member of the AICPA who discovers an error in a previously filed tax return.

DISCUSSION: According to TS 600, *Knowledge of Error: Return Preparation and Administrative Proceedings*, a member should inform the taxpayer promptly upon becoming aware of an error in a previously filed return and "recommend the corrective measures to be taken." In the case of a material understatement, an amended return should be filed by the taxpayer. A claim for refund is appropriate for a material overstatement. The advice may be given to the taxpayer orally.

Answer (A) is incorrect. A member should not inform the IRS without the taxpayer's permission, except if required by law. Answer (B) is incorrect. A member is not responsible for correcting a discovered error unless requested to do so by the taxpayer. Answer (D) is incorrect. A member need not end the relationship with the taxpayer over the discovery of a previous error.

2.9.11. Kopel was engaged to prepare Riff Raff's Year 1 federal income tax return. During the tax preparation interview, Raff told Kopel that he paid $3,000 in property taxes in Year 1. Actually, Raff's property taxes amounted to only $600. Based on Raff's word, Kopel deducted the $3,000 on Raff's return, resulting in an understatement of Raff's tax liability. Kopel had no reason to believe that the information was incorrect. Kopel did not request underlying documentation and was reasonably satisfied by Raff's representation that Raff had adequate records to support the deduction. Which of the following statements is true?

A. To avoid the preparer penalty for willful understatement of tax liability, Kopel was obligated to examine the underlying documentation for the deduction.

B. To avoid the preparer penalty for willful understatement of tax liability, Kopel should obtain Raff's representation in writing.

C. Kopel is not subject to the preparer penalty for willful understatement of tax liability because the deduction that was claimed was more than 25% of the actual amount that should have been deducted.

D. Kopel is not subject to the preparer penalty for willful understatement of tax liability because Kopel was justified in relying on Raff's representation.

Answer (D) is correct. *(CPA, adapted)*

REQUIRED: The true statement about tax return preparer liability.

DISCUSSION: A tax return preparer may rely, without verification, on information provided by the taxpayer when the preparer is reasonably justified in relying upon the taxpayer's representations. However, a preparer must make a reasonable inquiry if the information appears to be incorrect or incomplete.

Answer (A) is incorrect. The preparer is not subject to preparer penalties for willful understatement. (S)he is justified in relying on the data furnished by the taxpayer. The preparer is not a guarantor of the accuracy of the return. Answer (B) is incorrect. A preparer is not required to obtain a written representation from the taxpayer prior to preparing a taxpayer's return. Answer (C) is incorrect. Preparer penalties are assessed only when the preparer has recommended a position that does not have a realistic possibility of success.

2.9.12. In accordance with Statements on Standards for Tax Services, which of the following is not considered a basis for a good faith belief that a tax return position may be recommended by a member of the AICPA?

A. A low probability that the return will be audited.

B. An administrative ruling of the taxing authority.

C. A well-reasoned interpretation of the relevant statute.

D. Well-reasoned articles by tax specialists.

Answer (A) is correct. *(Publisher, adapted)*

REQUIRED: The item not a basis for a good faith belief that a tax return position may be recommended.

DISCUSSION: A member of the AICPA may not recommend a tax return position or prepare or sign a tax return absent a good faith belief that the position "has a realistic possibility of being sustained administratively or judicially on its merits if challenged." But a member may, in appropriate cases, (1) recommend a position or (2) prepare or sign the return if this standard is not met. These exceptions apply if (1) the position is reasonable and (2) the member advises disclosure [when (s)he has recommended a position], or the position is properly disclosed [when (s)he has prepared or signed the return]. However, a member may never recommend a position that "exploits the audit selection process of a taxing authority" or serves solely as a bargaining position in negotiations with the taxing authority (TS 100).

NOTE: According to the Small Business and Work Opportunity Act of 2007 (as amended), an undisclosed, nonabusive position must be supported by substantial authority. But for tax shelters and reportable transactions, the preparer must have a reasonable belief that the position is more likely than not to be sustained on its merits. If the position is disclosed, its tax treatment must have a reasonable basis.

A member may conclude that a position meets the appropriate standard based on (1) a well-reasoned statutory interpretation (e.g., by an attorney), (2) well-reasoned articles or treatises, or (3) pronouncements of the taxing authority.

2.9.13. Elwyn, a member of the AICPA, is preparing a federal tax return for Emma, who stated that she had made about $150 of cash donations to charitable organizations for which she had no receipts. These donations had been given to solicitors at supermarkets, airports, and other similar settings. What should Elwyn do with this information when preparing the tax return?

A. Ignore it because the information cannot be verified.

B. Identify $150 as "Other miscellaneous contributions."

C. Request that Emma obtain receipts from the charitable organizations.

D. Increase one of the other specifically named contributions by $150.

Answer (B) is correct. *(Publisher, adapted)*

REQUIRED: The proper action by the CPA regarding the use of estimated tax data.

DISCUSSION: TS 400, *Use of Estimates*, permits a member of the AICPA to prepare tax returns involving the use of estimates if it is impracticable to obtain exact data and the amounts are reasonable. Estimates must not be presented so as to imply greater accuracy than exists. The member may therefore identify the approximate amount of the contribution as "Other miscellaneous contributions."

Answer (A) is incorrect. The use of estimates is not prohibited by the AICPA. Answer (C) is incorrect. The client is unable to obtain receipts. Answer (D) is incorrect. The information should not be presented in a manner implying greater accuracy than exists.

2.10 Consulting Services

2.10.1. Statements on Standards for Consulting Services are issued by the AICPA Management Consulting Services Executive Committee. Which statement concerning consulting services is false?

A. Consulting services differ fundamentally from the CPA's function of attesting to the assertions of other parties.

B. Consulting services ordinarily involve external reporting.

C. Most practitioners, including those who provide audit and tax services, also provide consulting services to their clients.

D. The performance of consulting services for attest clients does not necessarily impair independence.

Answer (B) is correct. *(Publisher, adapted)*

REQUIRED: The false statement about consulting services.

DISCUSSION: The nature and scope of a consulting service is determined solely by the agreement between the practitioner and the client. The work is usually performed for the sole use and benefit of the client.

Answer (A) is incorrect. In an attest service, the practitioner expresses a conclusion about the reliability of a written assertion that is the responsibility of another party. Answer (C) is incorrect. Consulting services have evolved from accounting-related matters to a broad array of services involving many technical disciplines, industry knowledge, and consulting skills. Answer (D) is incorrect. The CPA can maintain independence of mind and appearance for attestation clients while performing many consulting services. In the case of an issuer client, consulting services must be approved by the audit committee.

2.10.2. According to the profession's standards, which of the following are considered consulting services?

	Advisory Services	Implementation Services	Assurance Services
A.	Yes	Yes	Yes
B.	Yes	Yes	No
C.	Yes	No	Yes
D.	No	Yes	Yes

Answer (B) is correct. *(CPA, adapted)*

REQUIRED: The services that are considered to be consulting services.

DISCUSSION: Consulting services include advisory services, which are performed to develop findings, conclusions, and recommendations for the client's consideration. They also include implementation services, which are performed to put a plan into effect. Other consulting services include consultations, transaction services, and staff and other support services (CS 100). Assurance services differ from consulting services. They are independent professional services that improve the quality of information, or its context, for decision makers.

2.10.3. A pervasive characteristic of a CPA's role in a consulting services engagement is that of being a(n)

A. Objective advisor.

B. Independent practitioner.

C. Computer specialist.

D. Confidential reviewer.

Answer (A) is correct. *(CPA, adapted)*

REQUIRED: The pervasive characteristic of a CPA's role in a consulting services engagement.

DISCUSSION: A consulting services practitioner should serve the client's interest by seeking to accomplish the objectives established by the understanding with the client while maintaining integrity and objectivity.

Answer (B) is incorrect. Independence is not a requirement for consulting services. Answer (C) is incorrect. A consultant need not be a computer specialist to develop findings and provide recommendations. Answer (D) is incorrect. A review is an attestation service.

2.10.4. The form of communication with a client in a consulting service should be

A. Either oral or written.

B. Oral with appropriate documentation.

C. Written, and copies should be sent to both management and the board of directors.

D. Written, and a copy should be sent to management alone.

Answer (A) is correct. *(CPA, adapted)*

REQUIRED: The form of communication with a client in a consulting service.

DISCUSSION: In a consulting service, reports may be written or oral depending on the understanding with the client, the need for a formal record, the intended use of results, the significance or sensitivity of material covered, and the degree results are communicated during the engagement.

2.10.5. Which of the following general standards apply to consulting services?

	Due Professional Care	Independence in Mental Attitude	Planning and Supervision
A.	No	Yes	No
B.	No	Yes	Yes
C.	Yes	No	Yes
D.	Yes	No	No

Answer (C) is correct. *(CPA, adapted)*

REQUIRED: The general standard(s) applicable to consulting services.

DISCUSSION: The general standards for consulting services include the general standards for the profession given in the AICPA's General Standards Rule: (1) professional competence, (2) due professional care, (3) planning and supervision, and (4) sufficient relevant data. In addition, CS 100 requires the following general standards for all consulting services:

1. Serve the client interest by seeking to accomplish the objectives established by the understanding with the client while maintaining integrity and objectivity.
2. Establish with the client a written or oral understanding about the responsibilities of the parties and the nature, scope, and limitations of the services to be performed.
3. Inform the client of conflicts of interest, significant reservations concerning the scope or benefits of the engagement, and significant engagement findings or events.

Independence standards apply to attestation services, not to consulting services.

2.10.6. According to the standards of the profession, which of the following events will require a CPA performing a consulting services engagement for a nonaudit client to withdraw from the engagement?

I. The CPA has a conflict of interest that is disclosed to the client, and the client consents to the CPA's continuing the engagement.

II. The CPA fails to obtain a written understanding from the client concerning the scope of the engagement.

A. I only.

B. II only.

C. Both I and II.

D. Neither I nor II.

Answer (D) is correct. *(CPA, adapted)*

REQUIRED: The event(s) that will require a CPA to withdraw from a consulting engagement for a nonaudit client.

DISCUSSION: The additional general standards for consulting services require serving the client interest with integrity and objectivity. If a conflict of interest is disclosed and consented to, objectivity is not deemed to be impaired, and the professional service may be performed. In addition, an accountant may establish either a written or an oral understanding with the client regarding the scope of the engagement. Thus, an accountant need not withdraw from an engagement when the understanding of the scope of the engagement is not in writing.

2.10.7. Which of the following statements applies to consultation services engagements?

A. A practitioner should obtain an understanding of the internal control to assess control risk.

B. A practitioner is not permitted to compile a financial forecast.

C. A practitioner should obtain sufficient relevant data to complete the engagement.

D. A practitioner is to maintain an appearance of independence.

Answer (C) is correct. *(CPA, adapted)*

REQUIRED: The statement applicable to consultation services engagements.

DISCUSSION: Under the General Standards Rule, a member should obtain sufficient relevant data to afford a reasonable basis for conclusions or recommendations in relation to any professional services performed.

Answer (A) is incorrect. An assessment of control risk is irrelevant to many consulting services. Answer (B) is incorrect. A practitioner may perform a service regarding prospective financial information in conjunction with a consulting service. Answer (D) is incorrect. Consulting services require integrity and objectivity but not independence.

STUDY UNIT THREE
PLANNING AND RISK ASSESSMENT

This study unit addresses various fundamental questions about the conduct of audits. **Acceptance** of an engagement depends on issues such as (1) the evaluation of the client's integrity, (2) predecessor-successor communication, (3) determining whether the preconditions of an audit are present, and (4) reaching a common understanding of the terms. Audit planning involves establishing an overall strategy for the audit and developing an audit plan based on the strategy. **Audit risk** must be considered in every audit. The audit plan describes risk assessment procedures directed toward the **risks of material misstatement**. The RMM is the combined assessment of inherent risk and control risk. **Risk assessment procedures** include (1) inquiries within the entity, (2) inspection and observation, and (3) analytical procedures. **Materiality** is a matter of professional judgment about whether misstatements, individually or aggregated, could reasonably influence the economic decisions of users as a group. Obtaining an **understanding** of the entity and its environment, including its internal control, is an essential part of planning and performing an audit in accordance with GAAS. The auditor obtains the understanding to, for example, (1) identify and assess RMMs; (2) determine materiality for planning and performing the audit; (3) consider the appropriateness of accounting policies; (4) identify areas of audit emphasis; (5) set expectations for the results of analytical procedures; (6) respond to assessed risks, including performance of further procedures; and (7) evaluate audit evidence. **Fraud** is an intentional act involving deception that misstates the audited financial statements. The auditor should obtain reasonable assurance that the statements are free of material misstatements, whether caused by **fraud or error**. The auditor's responsibility for **noncompliance with laws and regulations** is to "obtain sufficient appropriate audit evidence regarding material amounts and disclosures in the financial statements that are determined by the provisions of those laws and regulations generally recognized to have a direct effect on their determination."

QUESTIONS

3.1 Pre-Engagement Acceptance Activities

3.1.1. An auditor is required to establish an understanding with a client regarding the services to be performed for each engagement. For an auditor of a nonissuer, this understanding generally includes

A. The auditor's responsibility for determining the preliminary judgments about materiality and audit risk factors.

B. Management's responsibility for identifying mitigating factors when the auditor has doubt about the entity's ability to continue as a going concern.

C. The auditor's responsibility for ensuring that management and those charged with governance are aware of any significant deficiencies or material weaknesses in control that come to the auditor's attention.

D. Management's responsibility for providing the auditor with an assessment of the risks of material misstatement due to fraud.

Answer (C) is correct. *(CPA, adapted)*

REQUIRED: The item required to be included in the understanding with the client.

DISCUSSION: An auditor should accept an engagement only when the basis for audit performance is agreed through (1) establishing whether the preconditions for an audit exist and (2) confirming that the auditor and management (and, possibly, those charged with governance) have a common understanding of the terms of engagement. The agreement typically is documented in an engagement letter (AU-C 210). An engagement letter for a nonissuer should indicate that a financial statement audit is not designed to provide assurance on internal control. However, the auditor is responsible for ensuring that management and those charged with governance are aware of any significant deficiencies or material weaknesses in control that come to his or her attention.

Answer (A) is incorrect. The auditor must make judgments about risk and materiality in planning the audit, but responsibility for these matters is not required to be shared with management. Answer (B) is incorrect. The understanding is ordinarily not established at a time when the auditor has such a doubt. Answer (D) is incorrect. The auditor should assess the risks of material misstatement.

3.1.2. An auditor's engagement letter most likely will include

A. Management's acknowledgment of its responsibility for maintaining effective internal control.

B. The auditor's preliminary assessment of the risk factors relating to misstatements arising from fraudulent financial reporting.

C. A reminder that management is responsible for illegal acts committed by employees.

D. A request for permission to contact the client's lawyer for assistance in identifying litigation, claims, and assessments.

Answer (A) is correct. *(CPA, adapted)*

REQUIRED: The item included in an auditor's engagement letter.

DISCUSSION: The auditor should agree with management on the terms of the engagement. The terms should be documented in an engagement letter. Among the matters addressed are management's responsibility for designing, implementing, and maintaining internal control relevant to preparing and fairly presenting financial statements that are free of material misstatement, whether due to fraud or error.

Answer (B) is incorrect. The auditor assesses risks relating to misstatements arising from fraudulent financial reporting during the engagement. Answer (C) is incorrect. Management is responsible for compliance with laws and regulations applicable to its activities. It is also responsible for acts of employees attributable to the entity. However, it is not responsible for other noncompliance by employees. Answer (D) is incorrect. A request for permission to contact the client's lawyer for assistance in identifying litigation, claims, and assessments is made during the audit.

3.1.3. Which of the following statements would least likely appear in an auditor's engagement letter?

A. Fees for our services are based on our regular per diem rates, plus travel and other out-of-pocket expenses.

B. Management is responsible for making all financial records and related information available to us.

C. Our engagement is subject to the risk that material fraud or errors, if they exist, will not be detected.

D. After performing our preliminary analytical procedures, we will discuss with you the other procedures we consider necessary to complete the engagement.

Answer (D) is correct. *(CPA, adapted)*

REQUIRED: The statement least likely to appear in an auditor's engagement letter.

DISCUSSION: The terms of the engagement should be documented in an engagement letter that states the (1) objective and scope of the audit, (2) responsibilities of the auditor and management, (3) inherent limitations of the audit and internal control, (4) applicable financial reporting framework, and (5) expected form and content of audit reports. But the engagement letter does not describe the specific evidence collection process to be completed by the auditor.

Answer (A) is incorrect. The engagement letter identifies the fees and the basis for those fees. Answer (B) is incorrect. Engagement letters include indicators of the understanding of management's responsibilities. Answer (C) is incorrect. The risk that material fraud or errors may exist and not be detected in the course of the audit should be addressed.

3.1.4. The scope and nature of an auditor's contractual obligation to a client is ordinarily set forth in the

A. Management representation letter.

B. Scope paragraph of the auditor's report.

C. Engagement letter.

D. Introductory paragraph of the auditor's report.

Answer (C) is correct. *(CPA, adapted)*

REQUIRED: The form of the contract with a client.

DISCUSSION: The terms of the engagement should be documented in an engagement letter that states the (1) objective and scope of the audit, (2) responsibilities of the auditor and management, (3) inherent limitations of the audit and internal control, (4) applicable financial reporting framework, and (5) expected form and content of audit reports. An engagement letter should be sent by the CPA to the prospective client on each engagement, audit or otherwise.

Answer (A) is incorrect. An auditor obtains a written management representation letter to complement other procedures, but it is not part of the engagement letter. Answer (B) is incorrect. The auditor's report contains an auditor's responsibility section, not a scope paragraph. The engagement letter should state the form and content of audit reports, not audit reports. Answer (D) is incorrect. The introductory paragraph (1) identifies the auditee, (2) states that the financial statements were audited, (3) identifies the title of each statement, and (4) specifies the date or period of each statement.

3.1.5. Which of the following factors would most likely cause an auditor not to accept a new audit engagement?

A. An inadequate understanding of the entity's internal controls.

B. The close proximity to the end of the entity's fiscal year.

C. Concluding that the entity's management probably lacks integrity.

D. An inability to perform preliminary analytical procedures before assessing control risk.

Answer (C) is correct. *(CPA, adapted)*

REQUIRED: The factor most likely to cause an auditor not to accept a new audit engagement.

DISCUSSION: CPA firms should have policies and procedures to determine whether to accept or continue a client or to perform a specific engagement. The firm's policies and procedures should provide reasonable assurance that it (1) has considered the integrity of the client and the risks involved, (2) is competent, (3) has the necessary capabilities and resources, and (4) is able to comply with applicable requirements (QC 10).

Answer (A) is incorrect. The understanding of the entity's internal controls is obtained subsequent to the acceptance of the engagement. Answer (B) is incorrect. Although early appointment is preferable, an independent auditor may accept an engagement near or after the close of the fiscal year. Answer (D) is incorrect. Analytical procedures are performed after the acceptance of the engagement.

3.1.6. In assessing whether to accept a client for an audit engagement, a CPA should consider the

	Client's Business Risk	CPA's Business Risk
A.	Yes	Yes
B.	Yes	No
C.	No	Yes
D.	No	No

Answer (A) is correct. *(CPA, adapted)*

REQUIRED: The issues related to client acceptance.

DISCUSSION: Before accepting an engagement, the CPA should consider the risks of being associated with the client. Auditor business risk relates to potential loss or injury to the auditor's professional practice from litigation and adverse publicity from the relationship with the client. The successful outcome of an audit and the ability to control auditor business risk often depends on the client's business risk. The auditor's understanding of the entity's business risks increases the likelihood of identifying risks of material misstatement. Thus, QC 10 states that policies and procedures should be established regarding acceptance and continuance of clients and specific engagements. They should provide reasonable assurance that the firm will undertake or continue relationships only when it does not have information leading to the conclusion that the client lacks integrity.

3.1.7. Which of the following conditions most likely would pose the greatest risk in accepting a new audit engagement?

A. Staff will need to be rescheduled to cover this new client.

B. There will be a client-imposed scope limitation.

C. The firm will have to hire a specialist in one audit area.

D. The client's financial reporting system has been in place for 10 years.

Answer (B) is correct. *(CPA, adapted)*

REQUIRED: The condition creating the greatest risk for client acceptance.

DISCUSSION: Matters to consider regarding integrity of management include indications of an inappropriate scope limitation (QC 10). It suggests that management will not be completely forthcoming with all necessary evidence to support the auditor's opinion.

Answer (A) is incorrect. New clients will often require rescheduling of staff to conduct the audit. Answer (C) is incorrect. Recognizing the need for the expertise of a specialist in one particular area prior to acceptance of a client does not create a significant risk to the auditor. Answer (D) is incorrect. Although the system may be dated, it may still meet the needs of the organization and be able to provide the evidence necessary to complete the audit.

3.1.8. Before accepting an engagement to audit a new client, an auditor is required to

A. Make inquiries of the predecessor auditor after obtaining the consent of the prospective client.

B. Obtain the prospective client's signature to the engagement letter.

C. Prepare a memorandum setting forth the staffing requirements and documenting the preliminary audit plan.

D. Discuss the management representation letter with the prospective client's audit committee.

Answer (A) is correct. *(CPA, adapted)*

REQUIRED: The step required of an auditor before accepting an engagement to audit a new client.

DISCUSSION: The auditor should request management to authorize the predecessor to respond fully to inquires. The auditor should inquire about (1) reasons for the change in auditors, (2) disagreements with management about accounting policies and auditing procedures, (3) facts about management's integrity, (4) communications to those charged with governance about fraud or noncompliance, and (5) communications to those charged with governance or management about internal control problems (AU-C 210, *Terms of Engagement*).

Answer (B) is incorrect. Although recommended, an engagement letter is not required for the auditor to accept an engagement. Answer (C) is incorrect. Planning the audit is not required to be performed prior to accepting an engagement. Answer (D) is incorrect. Discussion of the management representation letter is not required prior to accepting an engagement.

3.1.9. Ordinarily, the predecessor auditor permits the auditor to review the predecessor's audit documentation relating to

	Contingencies	Balance Sheet Accounts
A.	Yes	Yes
B.	Yes	No
C.	No	Yes
D.	No	No

Answer (A) is correct. *(CPA, adapted)*

REQUIRED: The item(s), if any, a successor auditor ordinarily requests for review.

DISCUSSION: The *Code of Professional Conduct* protects the confidentiality of client information. Accordingly, the predecessor auditor cannot permit the auditor to review the predecessor's audit documentation without management's specific consent. Moreover, the auditor and the predecessor auditor must keep in confidence information obtained from each other. However, the predecessor auditor ordinarily is expected to cooperate with the auditor and respond fully. Audit documentation records the audit procedures performed, relevant evidence obtained, and conclusions reached. The auditor ordinarily reviews audit documentation related to planning, internal control, audit results, and other matters of continuing accounting and auditing significance, such as the analysis of balance sheet accounts, and those relating to contingencies.

3.1.10. Which of the following circumstances would permit an independent auditor to accept an engagement after the close of the fiscal year?

A. Issuance of a disclaimer of opinion as a result of inability to conduct certain tests required by generally accepted auditing standards due to the timing of the acceptance of the engagement.

B. An expectation of the effectiveness of internal control.

C. Receipt of an assertion from the preceding auditor that the entity will be able to continue as a going concern.

D. Remedy of limitations resulting from accepting the engagement after the close of the end of the year, such as those relating to the existence of physical inventory.

Answer (D) is correct. *(CPA, adapted)*

REQUIRED: The circumstance permitting an auditor to accept an engagement after the close of the fiscal year.

DISCUSSION: The auditor may accept the engagement if (s)he can obtain sufficient appropriate evidence by performing alternative procedures, e.g., tests of prior transactions affecting inventory or reviews of the records of prior counts.

Answer (A) is incorrect. A disclaimer of opinion is necessary only if the auditor cannot resolve the issue by performing alternative procedures. Answer (B) is incorrect. Evidence permitting an expectation of the effectiveness of internal control should be available after year end. Answer (C) is incorrect. The auditor need not obtain representations from the predecessor auditor relative to the ability of the entity to continue as a going concern.

3.1.11. Upon discovering material misstatements in a client's financial statements that the client would not revise, a predecessor auditor withdrew from the engagement. If asked by the auditor about the termination of the engagement, the predecessor auditor should

A. State that (s)he found material misstatements that the client would not revise.

B. Suggest that the auditor ask the client.

C. Suggest that the auditor obtain the client's permission to discuss the reasons.

D. Indicate that a misunderstanding occurred.

Answer (C) is correct. *(Publisher, adapted)*

REQUIRED: The appropriate response by a predecessor auditor when asked about his or her relationship with the client.

DISCUSSION: The auditor must obtain the client's permission before the predecessor auditor may discuss the reasons for termination of the previous relationship (AU-C 210 and AU-C 510). Furthermore, a member of the AICPA in public practice must not disclose confidential client information without the specific consent of the client.

Answer (A) is incorrect. The predecessor auditor should not respond until client permission is obtained. Answer (B) is incorrect. The predecessor is usually expected to cooperate with the auditor, provided that the client consents. In unusual circumstances, such as pending litigation, the predecessor auditor may not respond fully to inquiries but should clearly state that his or her response is limited. The auditor should then consider the implications for acceptance of the engagement. Answer (D) is incorrect. The predecessor auditor should say nothing concerning the relationship until client permission is obtained.

3.2 Planning an Audit

3.2.1. Which of the following is required documentation in an audit in accordance with auditing standards?

A. A flowchart or narrative of the information system describing the recording and classification of transactions for financial reporting.

B. An audit plan documenting the procedures to be used to reduce audit risk.

C. A planning memorandum establishing the timing of the audit procedures and coordinating the assistance of entity personnel.

D. An internal control questionnaire identifying policies and procedures that assure specific objectives will be achieved.

Answer (B) is correct. *(CPA, adapted)*

REQUIRED: The required documentation in an audit.

DISCUSSION: An audit plan should be developed and documented based on the overall audit strategy. This strategy, the audit plan, significant changes in them, and the reasons for changes are documented. The audit plan records the nature, timing, and extent of risk assessment procedures and further procedures performed at the assertion level to respond to assessed risks. It also records other planned procedures required by GAAS. Thus, the audit plan is a record of the planning of the audit procedures that can be reviewed prior to their performance (AU-C 300 and AS 2101).

Answer (A) is incorrect. The auditor should document the understanding of internal control, but a flowchart or narrative of the information system for financial reporting is just one method. For example, the auditor may use a questionnaire to document the understanding. Answer (C) is incorrect. The auditor may request and receive assistance from entity personnel, but a planning memorandum establishing the timing is not required by auditing standards. Answer (D) is incorrect. The auditor should document the understanding of internal control, but a questionnaire is only one method of accomplishing this objective. For example, flowcharts and narratives are other methods.

3.2.2. Early appointment of the auditor enables preliminary work to be performed by the auditor. This benefits the client because it permits the audit to be performed in

A. A more efficient manner.

B. A more thorough manner.

C. Accordance with quality control standards.

D. Accordance with generally accepted auditing standards.

Answer (A) is correct. *(CPA, adapted)*

REQUIRED: The benefit of early appointment of the auditor.

DISCUSSION: Early appointment of the auditor is advantageous to both the auditor and the client. Early appointment aids the auditor in planning the work, especially that to be done before the end of the year. The client benefits from more efficient scheduling of the audit and an early completion of the work after the end of the fiscal year.

Answer (B) is incorrect. Thoroughness is directly related to the requirement to collect sufficient appropriate evidence, not to the time of appointment. Answer (C) is incorrect. Adherence to quality control standards is necessary regardless of the time of appointment. Answer (D) is incorrect. Adherence to GAAS is necessary regardless of the time of appointment.

3.2.3. With respect to the auditor's planning of a year-end audit, which of the following statements is always true?

A. An engagement should not be accepted after the fiscal year-end.

B. An inventory count must be observed at the balance sheet date.

C. Those charged with governance should not be told of the specific audit procedures that were performed.

D. It is an acceptable practice to carry out part of the audit at interim dates.

Answer (D) is correct. *(CPA, adapted)*

REQUIRED: The statement about the year-end audit that is always true.

DISCUSSION: Much of the audit planning, including obtaining a sufficient understanding of internal control, assessing control risk, and the application of substantive tests to transactions can be conducted prior to the balance sheet date.

Answer (A) is incorrect. An engagement may be accepted after year-end. Answer (B) is incorrect. If observation at year-end is not feasible, the auditor may observe inventory at another date. Answer (C) is incorrect. Those charged with governance sometimes may be told of specific audit procedures that have already been performed, e.g., how a major defalcation was discovered. However, specific procedures should not be discussed with the client prior to the audit.

3.2.4. The auditor should establish an overall audit strategy. Which one of the following statements is most consistent with this requirement?

A. The auditor should have appropriate proficiency to perform the audit.

B. The auditor must be independent of the client.

C. The auditor should communicate certain issues to those charged with governance.

D. The auditor should plan the audit so that it will be performed effectively.

Answer (D) is correct. *(Publisher, adapted)*

REQUIRED: The statement most closely related to the establishment of an overall audit strategy.

DISCUSSION: An audit plan is developed and documented based on the overall audit strategy. It is more detailed than the audit strategy because it includes the nature, timing, and extent of work to be performed. The plan includes (1) risk assessment procedures, (2) further audit procedures at the assertion level, and (3) other procedures to comply with GAAS.

Answer (A) is incorrect. The auditor should be proficient, but this requirement is not directly related to the audit strategy. Answer (B) is incorrect. The auditor must be independent regardless of the audit strategy. Answer (C) is incorrect. Communication to those charged with governance occurs during and after the audit.

3.2.5. In developing an audit plan, an auditor should

A. Determine whether the allowance for sampling risk exceeds the achieved upper precision limit.

B. Evaluate findings from substantive procedures performed at interim dates.

C. Consider whether the inquiry of the client's attorney identifies any litigation, claims, or assessments not disclosed in the financial statements.

D. Perform risk assessment procedures.

Answer (D) is correct. *(CPA, adapted)*

REQUIRED: The issue an auditor should consider when developing an overall audit plan.

DISCUSSION: The audit plan is based on the overall audit strategy. It describes (1) the nature and extent of risk assessment procedures; (2) the nature, timing, and extent of further audit procedures at the assertion level; and (3) other procedures required by GAAS. Risk assessment procedures are performed to obtain an understanding of the entity and its environment (including its internal control). Their purpose is to identify and assess the risks of material misstatement (whether due to fraud or error) at the financial statement and relevant assertion levels.

Answer (A) is incorrect. Sampling risk and upper precision limits are set subsequent to developing an overall audit strategy. Answer (B) is incorrect. Planning precedes performance of substantive procedures, including those performed at interim dates. Answer (C) is incorrect. The inquiry of the client's attorney occurs subsequent to developing an overall audit strategy.

3.2.6. Which of the following is an auditor least likely to perform in planning a financial statement audit?

A. Coordinating the assistance of entity personnel in data preparation.

B. Discussing matters that may affect the audit with firm personnel responsible for non-audit services to the entity.

C. Selecting a sample of vendors' invoices for comparison with receiving reports.

D. Reading the current year's interim financial statements.

Answer (C) is correct. *(CPA, adapted)*

REQUIRED: The procedure an auditor is least likely to perform in planning a financial statement audit.

DISCUSSION: Selecting a sample of vendors' invoices for comparison with receiving reports is a test of details (a substantive procedure). It is a further audit procedure performed to test relevant assertions.

Answer (A) is incorrect. Coordinating the assistance of entity personnel is a planning procedure. Answer (B) is incorrect. Discussing matters that may affect the audit with entity personnel is a planning procedure. Answer (D) is incorrect. Reading the current year's interim financial statements is a planning procedure.

3.2.7. In developing written audit plans, an auditor should design specific audit procedures that relate primarily to the

A. Timing of the audit.

B. Costs and benefits of gathering evidence.

C. Financial statements as a whole.

D. Financial statement assertions.

Answer (D) is correct. *(CPA, adapted)*

REQUIRED: The item to which specific audit procedures primarily relate.

DISCUSSION: Most audit work consists of obtaining and evaluating evidence about relevant financial statement assertions. They are management representations embodied in the financial statements that are used by the auditor to consider the types of possible material misstatements.

Answer (A) is incorrect. Timing is important in developing audit plans, but it is not the primary basis for determining the audit procedures to be performed. Answer (B) is incorrect. The costs and benefits of gathering evidence are important to the auditor but are not the primary basis for determining the audit procedures to be performed. Answer (C) is incorrect. Most audit procedures are performed at the assertion level.

3.2.8. In planning the audit engagement, the auditor should consider each of the following except

A. The auditor's independence.

B. Risks of material misstatement due to fraud.

C. Anticipated levels of audit risk and materiality.

D. The kind of opinion (unmodified, qualified, or adverse) that is likely to be expressed.

Answer (D) is correct. *(Publisher, adapted)*

REQUIRED: The factor not considered in planning the audit engagement.

DISCUSSION: Although the nature of the services expected to be rendered (e.g., a report on consolidated or consolidating financial statements or on compliance with contractual provisions) should be considered when establishing the understanding with the client, determining the kind of opinion to be expressed occurs after the completion of audit procedures.

Answer (A) is incorrect. The auditor's preliminary engagement activities include evaluating his or her compliance with ethical standards, such as independence. Answer (B) is incorrect. During planning, engagement personnel are required to discuss how and where the financial statements may be susceptible to material misstatements due to fraud. Answer (C) is incorrect. The anticipated levels of audit risk and materiality should be considered during audit planning.

3.2.9. Which of the following is an effective audit planning and control procedure that helps prevent misunderstandings and inefficient use of audit personnel?

A. Make copies of those client supporting documents examined by the auditor for inclusion in the audit documentation.

B. Provide the client with copies of the audit plans to be used during the audit.

C. Arrange a preliminary conference with the client to discuss audit objectives, fees, timing, and other information.

D. Arrange to have the auditor prepare and post any necessary adjusting or reclassification entries prior to final closing.

Answer (C) is correct. *(CPA, adapted)*

REQUIRED: The effective procedure to avoid misunderstandings and inefficient use of audit personnel.

DISCUSSION: A preliminary conference with the client to discuss various audit objectives, fees, timing, the reports to be prepared, the use of client personnel, etc., is an appropriate procedure to prevent misunderstandings during the audit. The arrangement should be documented in the engagement letter.

Answer (A) is incorrect. Copies of client supporting documents are made during the audit itself, not during the planning stages. Also, not all documents need to be copied. Answer (B) is incorrect. The client should not be told which audit procedures are going to be used. Such information might be misused to circumvent the audit. Answer (D) is incorrect. The client (not the auditor) must prepare and post adjusting or reclassification entries.

3.2.10. Audit planning for an initial audit most likely includes

A. Determining the opinion to be expressed.

B. Obtaining an engagement letter prepared by the auditee.

C. Performing procedures involving opening balances.

D. Selecting a sample of invoices for comparison with shipping reports.

Answer (C) is correct. *(Publisher, adapted)*

REQUIRED: The item most likely included in the planning for an initial audit.

DISCUSSION: First-year audits involve additional planning considerations. Examples are (1) communication with the predecessor auditor, (2) audit procedures regarding opening balances, (3) assignment of firm personnel with appropriate qualifications, and (4) procedures required by the firm's system of quality control for initial engagements.

Answer (A) is incorrect. Determining the kind of opinion to be expressed occurs after the completion of audit procedures. Answer (B) is incorrect. The auditor prepares the engagement letter. Answer (D) is incorrect. Comparing shipping reports with invoices is a substantive procedure.

3.2.11. Which of the following factors does a CPA ordinarily consider in the planning stage of an audit engagement?

I. Financial statement accounts likely to contain a misstatement.

II. Conditions that require extension of audit tests.

A. I only.

B. II only.

C. Both I and II.

D. Neither I nor II.

Answer (C) is correct. *(CPA, adapted)*

REQUIRED: The factor(s), if any, a CPA ordinarily considers in the planning stage of an audit engagement.

DISCUSSION: When planning an audit, the auditor should consider, among other things, the financial statement accounts likely to require adjustment and the conditions that require extension or modification of audit procedures (e.g., risk of material misstatement).

3.2.12. One of the primary roles of an engagement work program is to

A. Serve as a tool for planning and conducting engagement work.

B. Document an internal auditor's evaluations of controls.

C. Provide for a standardized approach to the engagement.

D. Assess the risks associated with the activity under review.

Answer (A) is correct. *(CIA, adapted)*

REQUIRED: The item that states one of the primary roles of an engagement work program.

DISCUSSION: Work programs (1) document procedures for collecting, analyzing, interpreting, and documenting information; (2) state engagement objectives; (3) identify technical requirements, risks, processes, and transactions to be examined; (4) state the nature and extent of testing required; and (5) are prepared before work begins, with appropriate modification during the engagement.

Answer (B) is incorrect. Engagement working papers include results of control evaluations. Answer (C) is incorrect. The work program may not be consistent from year to year given the changing conditions to which the engagement client must adapt. The work program reflects the current year's situation. Thus, standardization may not be appropriate. Answer (D) is incorrect. The risk assessment in the planning phase helps to identify objectives, a step that must be taken before the work program can be developed.

3.2.13. Which of the following ultimately determines the specific audit procedures necessary to provide an independent auditor with a reasonable basis for the expression of an opinion?

A. The audit plan.

B. The auditor's judgment.

C. Auditing standards.

D. The audit documentation.

Answer (B) is correct. *(CPA, adapted)*

REQUIRED: The factor determining specific procedures.

DISCUSSION: The auditor's professional judgment must determine the necessary audit plans and the specific audit procedures that will gather sufficient appropriate evidence to reduce audit risk to an acceptably low level and enable the auditor to draw reasonable conclusions on which to base the opinion.

Answer (A) is incorrect. Audit plans are usually modified during the engagement to adapt to audit evidence as it is gathered. Answer (C) is incorrect. Auditing standards, whether established by the AICPA's ASB or the PCAOB, are general objectives that are concerned with the quality of the auditor's performance. Answer (D) is incorrect. Audit documentation demonstrates that the auditor has carried out the procedures (s)he has deemed necessary. The documentation does not determine the procedures undertaken.

3.2.14. Financial statement audit plans usually should be developed

A. Prior to performing risk assessment procedures.

B. After the auditor has established the overall audit strategy.

C. After obtaining an understanding of the information and communication and control activities components of internal control.

D. When the engagement letter is prepared.

Answer (B) is correct. *(Publisher, adapted)*

REQUIRED: The time at which an audit plan should be developed.

DISCUSSION: Planning continues throughout the audit. It initially involves developing an overall audit strategy. The size and complexity of the entity, the auditor's experience with the entity, and the auditor's understanding of the entity and its environment (including internal control) affect planning. The auditor also should consider (1) characteristics of the engagement and reporting objectives; (2) appropriate materiality levels; (3) areas of high risk of material misstatement; (4) material client locations and the use of component auditors; (5) whether to seek evidence of the operating effectiveness of controls; (6) relevant entity-specific, industry, or financial developments; and (7) the audit resources required. The more detailed audit plan is developed after the formulation of the overall audit strategy.

Answer (A) is incorrect. The auditor cannot develop the audit plan, including planned risk assessment procedures, until (s)he has established the overall audit strategy. Answer (C) is incorrect. The auditor also must obtain an understanding of the entity and its environment, including its internal control, before planning the audit. Answer (D) is incorrect. The auditor must obtain an understanding of the entity and its environment, including its internal control, and assess the risks of material misstatement before preparing the audit plan. This process follows the preparation of the engagement letter.

3.2.15. Which of the following is an aspect of scheduling and controlling the audit engagement?

A. Include in the audit plan a column for estimated and actual time.

B. Perform audit work only after the client's books of account have been closed for the period under examination.

C. Write a conclusion in the audit documentation indicating how the results of the audit will affect the auditor's report.

D. Include in the engagement letter an estimate of the minimum and maximum audit fee.

Answer (A) is correct. *(CPA, adapted)*

REQUIRED: The aspect of scheduling and controlling the audit engagement.

DISCUSSION: The audit plan is a tool for scheduling and controlling the audit. It should contain a detailed set of procedures for accomplishing audit objectives, estimated times for each step, and the personnel required. Thus, it can be used to document the progress of the audit and the auditor's compliance with requirements for planning and supervision.

Answer (B) is incorrect. Audit work may be done throughout the year before the books have been closed. Answer (C) is incorrect. Writing a conclusion is an evaluation of the evidence rather than part of scheduling and controlling the audit. Answer (D) is incorrect. The engagement letter describing the contractual agreement between the auditor and client precedes the audit.

3.2.16. The auditor with final responsibility for an engagement and one of the assistants have a difference of opinion about the results of an auditing procedure. If the assistant believes it is necessary to be disassociated from the matter's resolution, the CPA firm's procedures should enable the assistant to

A. Refer the disagreement to the AICPA's Peer Review Board.

B. Document the details of the disagreement with the conclusion reached.

C. Discuss the disagreement with the entity's management or its audit committee.

D. Report the disagreement to an impartial peer review monitoring team.

Answer (B) is correct. *(CPA, adapted)*

REQUIRED: The action permitted to an assistant who disagrees with the auditor in charge.

DISCUSSION: According to AU-C 220 and QC 10, difference of opinion (1) within the engagement team, (2) with a consultant, or (3) between the engagement partner and the quality control reviewer should be resolved by following the firm's related policies and procedures. A member of the engagement team should be able to document his or her disagreement with the conclusions reached after appropriate consultation. Moreover, (1) conclusions should be documented and implemented, and (2) the report should be released only after resolution of the matter. According to AS 1201, in applying due professional care, each engagement team member has a responsibility to bring to the attention of appropriate persons any disagreements or concerns about accounting and auditing issues that (s)he believes are significant to the statements or the report regardless of how they may have arisen. The PCAOB's AS 1215 requires documentation of disagreements among members of the engagement team or with consultants about final conclusions on significant accounting or auditing matters.

Answer (A) is incorrect. The Peer Review Board issues standards for performing and reporting on peer reviews. Answer (C) is incorrect. The client need not be informed of the disagreement about the results of an auditing procedure. Answer (D) is incorrect. No peer review monitoring team exists.

3.2.17. The element of the audit-planning process most likely to be agreed upon with the client before implementation of the audit strategy is the determination of the

A. Evidence to be gathered to provide a sufficient basis for the auditor's opinion.

B. Procedures to be undertaken to discover litigation, claims, and assessments.

C. Pending legal matters to be included in the inquiry of the client's attorney.

D. Timing of inventory observation procedures to be performed.

Answer (D) is correct. *(CPA, adapted)*

REQUIRED: The element of audit planning most likely agreed upon with the client before implementation.

DISCUSSION: The client is responsible for taking the physical inventory. The auditor is responsible for observing this process and performing test counts. The audit procedures are dependent upon management's plans. Thus, the auditor must coordinate the collection of this evidence with management.

Answer (A) is incorrect. The evidence to be gathered is a matter of professional judgment to be determined solely by the auditor. Answer (B) is incorrect. The procedures performed to discover litigation, claims, and assessments are matters of professional judgment to be determined solely by the auditor. Answer (C) is incorrect. Pending legal matters to be included in the inquiry of the client's attorney are matters of professional judgment to be determined solely by the auditor.

3.2.18. Which of the following is an engagement attribute for an audit of an entity that processes most of its financial data in electronic form without any paper documentation?

A. Discrete phases of planning, interim, and year-end fieldwork.

B. Increased effort to search for evidence of management fraud.

C. Performance of audit tests on a continuous basis.

D. Increased emphasis on the completeness assertion.

Answer (C) is correct. *(CPA, adapted)*

REQUIRED: The engagement attribute for auditing in an electronic environment.

DISCUSSION: The audit trail for transactions processed in electronic form may be available for only a short period of time. The auditor may conclude that it is necessary to time audit procedures so that they correspond to the availability of the evidence. Thus, audit modules may be embedded in the client's software for this purpose.

Answer (A) is incorrect. This engagement attribute would be appropriate for any type of client. Answer (B) is incorrect. Processing transactions in electronic form does not inherently increase the risk of management fraud. Answer (D) is incorrect. No inherent additional concern arises about the completeness assertion as a result of processing transactions in electronic form.

3.2.19. The audit work performed by each assistant should be reviewed to determine whether it was adequately performed and to evaluate whether the

A. Auditor's system of quality control has been maintained at a high level.

B. Results are consistent with the conclusions to be presented in the auditor's report.

C. Audit procedures performed are approved in the professional standards.

D. Audit has been performed by persons having appropriate competence and capabilities.

Answer (B) is correct. *(CPA, adapted)*

REQUIRED: The reason for reviewing the audit work of each assistant.

DISCUSSION: According to AU-C 220, QC 10, and AS 1201, a review considers whether, for example, (1) the work supports the conclusions and is properly documented, (2) the evidence is sufficient and appropriate to support the auditor's report, and (3) the objectives of the procedures have been achieved.

Answer (A) is incorrect. The review of audit work is only a part of quality control. Answer (C) is incorrect. Determination of whether the procedures are in accordance with professional standards is necessary in the planning stage. Answer (D) is incorrect. Whether the audit has been performed by persons having appropriate competence and capabilities is a resource deployment, quality control, and ethical issue, not a matter of direction, supervision, or review.

3.2.20. The in-charge auditor for an audit of an issuer most likely has a supervisory responsibility to explain to the staff assistants

A. That immaterial fraud is not to be reported to the client's audit committee.

B. How the results of various auditing procedures performed by the assistants should be evaluated.

C. What benefits may be attained by the assistants' adherence to established time budgets.

D. Why certain documents are being transferred from the current file to the permanent file.

Answer (B) is correct. *(CPA, adapted)*

REQUIRED: The responsibility of the audit supervisor.

DISCUSSION: Assistants should be informed of their responsibilities and the objectives of the work they are to perform. They should be informed about the matters that affect the nature, timing, and extent of procedures, including how the results of tests should be evaluated (AS 1201).

Answer (A) is incorrect. Immaterial fraud may be reported to those charged with governance, e.g., the audit committee. Answer (C) is incorrect. Discussion of time budgets is not a responsibility under the auditing standards. Answer (D) is incorrect. At the end of the audit, supervisors determine which documents are to be transferred to the permanent file. These decisions need not be justified to staff assistants.

3.3 Audit Risk and Materiality

3.3.1. The audit risk against which the auditor and those who rely on his or her opinion require reasonable protection is a combination of two separate risks at the assertion level. The first risk (consisting of inherent risk and control risk) is that balances, classes of transactions, or disclosures contain material misstatements. The second is that

A. The auditor will reject a correct account balance as incorrect.

B. Material misstatements that occur will not be detected by the audit.

C. The auditor will apply an inappropriate audit procedure.

D. The auditor will apply an inappropriate measure of audit materiality.

Answer (B) is correct. *(Publisher, adapted)*

REQUIRED: The component of audit risk in addition to inherent risk and control risk.

DISCUSSION: Audit risk is a function of the risks of material misstatement and detection risk. Detection risk is the risk that the procedures performed to reduce audit risk to an acceptably low level will not detect a misstatement that exists and could be material individually or combined with other misstatements. The auditor assesses the risk of material misstatement after obtaining an understanding of the entity and its environment, including its internal control. It exists at the overall financial statement level and assertion level. The RMM at the assertion level consists of inherent risk and control risk. Some auditors use a mathematical model based on the relationships of the components of audit risk to arrive at an acceptable level of detection risk. For example, it reflects that the acceptable detection risk has an inverse relationship with the RMMs at the assertion level (AU-C 200 and AS 1101).

3.3.2. Some account balances, such as those for pensions or leases, are the results of complex calculations. The susceptibility to material misstatements in these types of accounts is defined as

A. Audit risk.

B. Detection risk.

C. Sampling risk.

D. Inherent risk.

Answer (D) is correct. *(CMA, adapted)*

REQUIRED: The susceptibility to material misstatements in account balances resulting from complex calculations.

DISCUSSION: Inherent risk is the susceptibility of an assertion about a transaction class, account balance, or disclosure that could be material, individually or in the aggregate, before consideration of any related controls. This risk is greater for some assertions and related balances, classes, or disclosures, than others. For example, complex calculations are more likely to be misstated than simple ones. Inherent risk exists independently of the audit (AU-C 200 and AS 1101).

Answer (A) is incorrect. Audit risk is the risk that the auditor expresses an inappropriate opinion on financial statements that are materially misstated. Answer (B) is incorrect. Detection risk is the risk that the procedures performed to reduce audit risk to an acceptably low level will not detect a misstatement that exists and could be material individually or in the aggregate. Answer (C) is incorrect. Sampling risk is the risk that the auditor's conclusion based on a sample differs from the conclusion if the entire population were subjected to the same audit procedure (AU-C 530).

3.3.3. As the acceptable level of detection risk decreases, an auditor may change the

A. Timing of substantive tests by performing them at an interim date rather than at year-end.

B. Nature of substantive procedures from a less effective to a more effective procedure.

C. Timing of tests of controls by performing them at several dates rather than at one time.

D. Assessed level of inherent risk to a higher amount.

Answer (B) is correct. *(CPA, adapted)*

REQUIRED: The change resulting from a decrease in the acceptable level of detection risk.

DISCUSSION: For a given audit risk, the acceptable detection risk is inversely related to the assessed risks of material misstatement. As the RMMs increase, the acceptable detection risk decreases, and the auditor requires more persuasive audit evidence. The auditor may (1) change the types of audit procedures and their combination, e.g., confirming the terms of a contract as well as inspecting it; (2) change the timing of substantive procedures, such as from an interim date to year end; or (3) change the extent of testing, such as by using a larger sample (AU-C 330 and AS 2301).

Answer (A) is incorrect. More assurance is provided by testing at year-end. Answer (C) is incorrect. The auditor tests controls when (s)he wishes to rely on them to reduce the risks of material misstatement (the combined inherent risk and control risk). The resulting assessment is then used to determine the acceptable level of detection risk. Answer (D) is incorrect. The assessed level of inherent risk affects the acceptable level of detection risk but not vice versa.

3.3.4. Which of the following would an auditor most likely use in determining the auditor's preliminary judgment about materiality for the financial statements as a whole?

A. The anticipated sample size of the planned substantive procedures.

B. The entity's year-to-date financial results and position.

C. The results of the internal control questionnaire.

D. The contents of the representation letter.

Answer (B) is correct. *(CPA, adapted)*

REQUIRED: The factor most likely used in determining the preliminary judgment about materiality for the financial statements as a whole.

DISCUSSION: The auditor's judgment about materiality for the financial statements as a whole might be based on benchmarks used as starting points. Examples are (1) categories of reported income (profit before tax, total revenue, gross profit, and total expenses), (2) total equity, and (3) net asset value. For profit-oriented entities, pretax profit from continuing operations is often used. The financial data for the benchmark usually includes (1) prior-period information, (2) period-to-date information, (3) budgets, or (4) forecasts. But recognition should be given to the effect of major changes in the entity's circumstances (for example, a significant merger) and relevant changes in the economy as a whole or the industry in which the entity operates (AU-C 320 and AS 2105).

Answer (A) is incorrect. The auditor's preliminary judgment about materiality is used to determine the sample sizes for substantive procedures. Sample sizes are calculated during evidence collection. Answer (C) is incorrect. Results of the internal control questionnaire are considered during the assessment of the risk of material misstatement. Answer (D) is incorrect. The contents of the representation letter are determined near the end of the audit.

3.3.5. Audit risk at the assertion level consists of inherent risk, control risk, and detection risk. Which of the following statements is true?

A. Cash has a greater inherent risk than an inventory of coal because it is more susceptible to theft.

B. The risk that material misstatement will not be timely prevented or detected by internal control can be reduced to zero by effective controls.

C. Detection risk is a function of the efficiency of an auditing procedure.

D. The existing levels of inherent risk, control risk, and detection risk can be changed at the discretion of the auditor.

Answer (A) is correct. *(Publisher, adapted)*

REQUIRED: The true statement about audit risk.

DISCUSSION: Inherent risk is the susceptibility of an assertion about a transaction class, account balance, or disclosure that could be material, individually or combined with other misstatements, before consideration of any related controls. Some assertions and related balances or classes of transactions have greater inherent risk. Thus, cash has a greater inherent risk than less liquid assets.

Answer (B) is incorrect. Some control risk will always exist. Internal control has inherent limitations. Answer (C) is incorrect. Detection risk is a function of auditing effectiveness (achieving results), not efficiency. Answer (D) is incorrect. The actual levels of inherent risk and control risk are independent of the audit process. Acceptable detection risk is a function of the desired level of audit risk and the assessed levels of inherent risk and control risk (risk of material misstatement at assertion level). Hence, detection risk can be changed at the discretion of the auditor, but inherent risk and control risk cannot. However, the auditor's preliminary judgments about inherent risk and control risk may change as the audit progresses.

3.3.6. The acceptable level of detection risk is inversely related to the

A. Assurance provided by substantive procedures.

B. Risk of misapplying auditing procedures.

C. Preliminary judgment about materiality levels.

D. Risk of failing to discover material misstatements.

Answer (A) is correct. *(CPA, adapted)*

REQUIRED: The concept to which acceptable detection risk is inversely related.

DISCUSSION: For a given audit risk, the acceptable detection risk is inversely related to the assessed risks of material misstatement. As the RMMs increase, the acceptable detection risk decreases, and the auditor requires more persuasive audit evidence. The auditor may (1) change the types of audit procedures and their combination, e.g., confirming the terms of a contract as well as inspecting it; (2) change the timing of substantive procedures, such as from an interim date to year end; or (3) change the extent of testing, such as by using a larger sample (AU-C 330 and AS 2301).

Answer (B) is incorrect. Detection risk, not the acceptable level of detection risk, relates directly to the risk of misapplying auditing procedures. As the effectiveness of audit procedures increases, e.g., because of adequate planning, proper assignment of personnel, and supervisory review, the risk of misapplication and detection risk decrease. Answer (C) is incorrect. Preliminary judgments about materiality levels are used by the auditor to determine the acceptable level of audit risk. Materiality and overall audit risk are inversely related. However, detection risk is just one component of audit risk. Answer (D) is incorrect. The lower the acceptable level of detection risk, the greater the required persuasiveness of audit evidence. Given this additional assurance, the risk of failing to detect material misstatements (detection risk) should be decreased. Accordingly, the relationship of acceptable detection risk and the risk of failing to detect material misstatements is direct.

3.3.7. Which of the following audit risk components may be assessed in nonquantitative terms?

	Control Risk	Detection Risk	Inherent Risk
A.	Yes	Yes	Yes
B.	No	Yes	Yes
C.	Yes	Yes	No
D.	Yes	No	Yes

Answer (A) is correct. *(CPA, adapted)*

REQUIRED: The audit risk components that may be assessed in nonquantitative terms.

DISCUSSION: The components of audit risk may be assessed in quantitative terms such as percentages or in nonquantitative terms that range, for example, from high to low.

3.3.8. The concepts of audit risk and materiality are interrelated and must be considered together by the auditor. Which of the following is true?

A. Audit risk is the risk that the auditor may unknowingly express a modified opinion when, in fact, the financial statements are fairly stated.

B. The phrase in the auditor's report "present fairly, in all material respects, in accordance with accounting principles generally accepted in the United States of America" indicates the auditor's belief that the financial statements as a whole are not materially misstated.

C. If misstatements are not important individually but are important in the aggregate, the concept of materiality does not apply.

D. Material fraud but not material errors cause financial statements to be materially misstated.

Answer (B) is correct. *(Publisher, adapted)*

REQUIRED: The true statement about the significance of audit risk and materiality.

DISCUSSION: The opinion paragraph of the auditor's report explicitly refers to materiality. Hence, financial statements that are presented fairly, in all material respects, in accordance with the applicable financial reporting framework are not materially misstated. Material misstatement can result from fraud or error.

Answer (A) is incorrect. Audit risk is the risk that the auditor expresses an inappropriate opinion on financial statements that are materially misstated. For the purposes of GAAS, audit risk does not include the ordinarily insignificant risk that the auditor may modify the opinion when the statements are not materially misstated. Answer (C) is incorrect. The concept of materiality recognizes that some misstatements, either individually or in the aggregate, are important for the fair presentation of financial statements. Qualitative as well as quantitative factors affect materiality judgments. This concept is consistent with an SEC Staff Accounting Bulletin, which also states, "A matter is 'material' if there is substantial likelihood that a reasonable person would consider it important" (SAB 99). Answer (D) is incorrect. Both material errors and material fraud cause financial statements to be materially misstated.

3.3.9. When expressing an unmodified opinion, the auditor who evaluates the audit findings should determine whether

A. The amount of identified misstatement is documented in the management representation letter.

B. Uncorrected misstatements are material.

C. The amount of identified misstatement is acknowledged and recorded by the client.

D. Estimates of total misstatement include the amounts of adjusting entries already recorded by the client.

Answer (B) is correct. *(Publisher, adapted)*

REQUIRED: The audit findings that support an unmodified opinion.

DISCUSSION: The evaluation of misstatements extends to (1) those identified during the audit and (2) those uncorrected. To evaluate misstatements accumulated during the audit, the auditor may classify them as (1) factual, (2) judgmental, and (3) projected. No doubt exists about factual misstatements. Judgmental misstatements result from management's (1) unreasonable accounting estimates or (2) application of inappropriate accounting policies. Projected misstatements are the auditor's best estimates of the misstatements in populations based on audit samples. Accordingly, when determining whether uncorrected misstatements are material, individually or combined with other misstatements, the auditor considers (1) uncorrected misstatements that are specifically identified and (2) undetected misstatements.

Answer (A) is incorrect. The auditor's judgment about whether the financial statements are fairly presented, in all material respects, relates to his or her evaluation of the materiality of (1) identified and (2) uncorrected misstatements, not identified misstatements documented in the management representation letter. Answer (C) is incorrect. The auditor's judgment regarding whether the financial statements are fairly presented, in all material respects, relates to his or her evaluation of uncorrected misstatements, not identified misstatements acknowledged and recorded by the client. Answer (D) is incorrect. Total misstatement excludes material misstatements eliminated by, for example, adjusting entries.

3.3.10. When planning an audit, an auditor should

A. Consider whether substantive procedures may be reduced based on the results of the internal control questionnaire.

B. Determine materiality for the financial statements as a whole.

C. Conclude whether changes in compliance with prescribed controls require a change in the reliance on controls.

D. Prepare a preliminary draft of the management representation letter.

Answer (B) is correct. *(CPA, adapted)*

REQUIRED: The matter included in audit planning.

DISCUSSION: Planning involves establishing an overall audit strategy. For this purpose, the auditor determines materiality for the financial statements as a whole. Circumstances also may indicate that misstatements of classes of transactions, balances, or disclosures of lesser amounts could influence the economic decisions of users. In those cases, the auditor also determines materiality for particular classes of transactions, balances, and disclosures.

Answer (A) is incorrect. Reducing substantive procedures requires a determination of the effectiveness of internal control, a step subsequent to audit planning. Answer (C) is incorrect. Procedures to determine whether changes in compliance with prescribed controls have occurred are performed subsequent to audit planning. Answer (D) is incorrect. The management representation letter is typically dated as of the date of the audit report.

3.3.11. A client decides not to correct misstatements communicated by the auditor that collectively are not material and wants the auditor to issue the report based on the uncorrected numbers. Which of the following statements is correct regarding the financial statement presentation?

A. The financial statements are free from material misstatement, and no disclosure is required in the notes to the financial statements.

B. The financial statements are not in accordance with the applicable financial reporting framework.

C. The financial statements contain uncorrected misstatements that should result in a qualified opinion.

D. The financial statements are free from material misstatement, but disclosure of the proposed adjustments is required in the notes to the financial statements.

Answer (A) is correct. *(CPA, adapted)*

REQUIRED: The action when a client decides not to correct misstatements communicated by the auditor that collectively are not material.

DISCUSSION: If the uncorrected misstatements are immaterial, by definition the financial statements are free from material misstatement, and an unmodified opinion may be expressed. However, the schedule of uncorrected misstatements must be included in the management representation letter, and management must assert that these uncorrected misstatements are individually and collectively immaterial.

Answer (B) is incorrect. The financial statements are free of material misstatements and are in accordance with the applicable financial reporting framework. Answer (C) is incorrect. An unmodified opinion is warranted. Answer (D) is incorrect. No disclosure in the notes is required.

3.3.12. Madison Corporation has a few large accounts receivable that total $1,000,000. Nassau Corporation has a great number of small accounts receivable that also total $1,000,000. The importance of a misstatement in any one account is therefore greater for Madison than for Nassau. This is an example of the auditor's concept of

A. Materiality.

B. Comparative analysis.

C. Reasonable assurance.

D. Audit risk.

Answer (A) is correct. *(CPA, adapted)*

REQUIRED: The concept applicable to the relative size of individual accounts receivable.

DISCUSSION: The concept of materiality requires the auditor to evaluate the relative importance of items to users of financial statements. In an entity with few but large accounts receivable, the individual accounts are relatively more important and the possibility of material misstatement is greater than in an entity with many small accounts.

Answer (B) is incorrect. Comparative analysis is a term that is associated with analytical procedures. Answer (C) is incorrect. In an audit of financial statements, reasonable assurance is a high, not absolute, level of assurance. The auditor must obtain reasonable assurance about whether the financial statements as a whole are free from material misstatement, whether due to fraud or error. Moreover, reasonable assurance is mentioned in the auditor's responsibility section in the report. Answer (D) is incorrect. Audit risk is the risk of expressing an inappropriate opinion on materially misstated financial statements.

3.3.13. Which of the following statements about materiality is most likely to be true?

A. Materiality requires that relatively more time be directed to those areas that are more susceptible to fraud.

B. Performance materiality is less than materiality for the financial statements as a whole.

C. Materiality at the assertion level is larger than for the financial statements as a whole.

D. Materiality is measured according to specific AICPA standards.

Answer (B) is correct. *(Publisher, adapted)*

REQUIRED: The statement about materiality most likely to be true.

DISCUSSION: Performance materiality is one or more amounts set by the auditor at less than the materiality for the statements as a whole. Performance materiality also refers to amounts set at less than materiality for particular classes of transactions, balances, or disclosures. Performance materiality is set to reduce to an appropriately low level the probability that the sum of uncorrected and undetected misstatements exceeds the applicable materiality. Accordingly, performance materiality is an adjustment for (1) individually immaterial misstatements and (2) possible undetected misstatements.

Answer (A) is incorrect. All fraud is considered to be significant. However, more time is not necessarily directed to those areas more susceptible to fraud if adequate controls are in place. Answer (C) is incorrect. Materiality at the financial statement level is not smaller than at the assertion level. Answer (D) is incorrect. The measurement of materiality is a matter of professional judgment.

3.4 Understanding the Entity and Its Environment

3.4.1. Which of the following statements is true concerning analytical procedures used as risk assessment procedures?

A. Analytical procedures usually involve comparisons of ratios developed from recorded amounts with assertions developed by management.

B. Analytical procedures used as risk assessment procedures ordinarily use data aggregated at a high level.

C. Analytical procedures can replace tests of controls in gathering evidence to support the assessed level of control risk.

D. Analytical procedures are more efficient, but not more effective, than tests of details and transactions.

Answer (B) is correct. *(CPA, adapted)*

REQUIRED: The true statement about analytical procedures.

DISCUSSION: Analytical procedures used as risk assessment procedures may use data aggregated at a high level.

Answer (A) is incorrect. Analytical procedures involve comparisons of recorded amounts, or ratios developed from recorded amounts, with expectations developed by the auditor. Answer (C) is incorrect. Tests of controls are required if controls will be relied on. Analytical procedures are used as substantive procedures but not as tests of controls. Answer (D) is incorrect. For many assertions, analytical procedures may not be as effective or efficient as tests of details in providing the desired level of assurance.

3.4.2. Which of the following procedures is the auditor most likely to perform after accepting an initial audit engagement?

A. Prepare a rough draft of the financial statement and of the auditor's report.

B. Assess control risk for the assertions embodied in the financial statements.

C. Tour the client's facilities.

D. Consult with and review the work of the predecessor auditor prior to discussing the engagement with the client management.

Answer (C) is correct. *(CPA, adapted)*

REQUIRED: The audit procedure performed after accepting an initial audit engagement.

DISCUSSION: The auditor performs risk assessment procedures to obtain an understanding of the entity and its environment, including internal control. They include (1) inquiries within the entity, (2) analytical procedures, and (3) observation and inspection. An example of observation and inspection is touring the client's facilities.

Answer (A) is incorrect. Preparing the report is one of the last steps performed in the engagement. Answer (B) is incorrect. The auditor must obtain an understanding of internal control before assessing control risk. Answer (D) is incorrect. Consulting with the predecessor auditor should be completed before accepting the engagement. The auditor should request permission from the client to make appropriate inquires (AU-C 210).

3.4.3. Analytical procedures used as risk assessment procedures should

A. Focus on forming an overall conclusion.

B. Provide a basis for the opinion.

C. Address the risk of material misstatement of revenue due to fraudulent financial reporting.

D. Assist in evaluating controls.

Answer (C) is correct. *(Publisher, adapted)*

REQUIRED: The use of analytical procedures as risk assessment procedures.

DISCUSSION: The audit plan includes a description of risk assessment procedures directed toward the risks of material misstatement (RMMs), whether due to fraud or error. The RMM is the combined assessment of inherent risk and control risk. Risk assessment procedures are performed to obtain an understanding of the entity and its environment, including its internal control, to assess the RMMs at the levels of (1) the financial statements as a whole and (2) relevant assertions about classes of transactions, account balances, and disclosures. They include (1) inquiries of management and others in the entity, (2) analytical procedures (also called analytical procedures used to plan the audit), and (3) observation and inspection (AU-C 315). The auditor specifically assesses the RMMs due to fraud at the financial statement and assertion levels. Moreover, the auditor should presume that risks of fraud exist in revenue recognition (AU-C 240).

Answer (A) is incorrect. Analytical procedures performed near the end of the audit assist in forming an overall conclusion about the consistency of the statements with the auditor's understanding of the entity. Answer (B) is incorrect. Risk assessment procedures do not by themselves provide a basis for the opinion. Answer (D) is incorrect. Analytical procedures are used as substantive procedures, not tests of the operating effectiveness of controls at the assertion level. They are designed to detect material misstatements at the assertion level.

3.4.4. Prior to beginning the field work on a new audit engagement in which a CPA does not possess expertise in the industry in which the client operates, the CPA should

A. Reduce audit risk by lowering initial levels of materiality.

B. Design special substantive procedures to compensate for the lack of industry expertise.

C. Engage financial experts familiar with the nature of the industry.

D. Perform risk assessment procedures.

Answer (D) is correct. *(CPA, adapted)*

REQUIRED: The action taken by an auditor who lacks experience with the client's industry.

DISCUSSION: The auditor should obtain an understanding of the entity and its environment, including its internal control. For this purpose, the auditor performs the following risk assessment procedures: (1) inquiries of management and others within the entity, (2) analytical procedures, and (3) observation and inspection.

Answer (A) is incorrect. The auditor cannot make judgments about materiality levels until (s)he has a sufficient understanding of the entity. Answer (B) is incorrect. The auditor cannot design substantive procedures until (s)he has a sufficient understanding of the entity. Answer (C) is incorrect. The use of experts does not relieve the auditor of the responsibility to obtain an understanding of the entity.

3.4.5. To obtain an understanding of a continuing client in planning an audit, an auditor most likely would

A. Perform tests of details of transactions and balances.

B. Read internal audit reports.

C. Read specialized industry journals.

D. Reevaluate the risks of material misstatement.

Answer (B) is correct. *(CPA, adapted)*

REQUIRED: The procedure used to obtain an understanding of a continuing client.

DISCUSSION: The auditor performs risk assessment procedures to obtain the understanding of the entity and its environment, including its internal control. These include, for example, reading (1) internal audit reports, (2) interim statements, (3) quarterly reports, and (4) minutes of board meetings.

Answer (A) is incorrect. Tests of details are used to collect sufficient, appropriate audit evidence to support the opinion. Answer (C) is incorrect. Reading specialized industry journals would provide information about the industry, but not necessarily about the specific client. Answer (D) is incorrect. The auditor reevaluates the RMMs after updating the understanding of a continuing client.

3.4.6. A CPA wishes to determine how various issuers have complied with the disclosure requirements of a new financial accounting standard. Which of the following information sources would the CPA most likely consult for this information?

A. AICPA Codification of Statements on Auditing Standards.

B. AICPA Accounting Trends and Techniques.

C. PCAOB Inspection Reports.

D. SEC Statement 10-K Guide.

Answer (B) is correct. *(CPA, adapted)*

REQUIRED: The most likely source of information about compliance with a new financial accounting standard.

DISCUSSION: Practical guidance for accounting and auditing engagements can be found in various nonauthoritative publications. An example is Accounting Trends and Techniques, which describes current practice regarding corporate financial accounting and disclosure policies. It is a useful source for practitioners in industry and public practice. This annual AICPA publication is based on a survey of the annual financial reports of over 600 public companies.

Answer (A) is incorrect. The AICPA Codification of Statements on Auditing Standards contains U.S. generally accepted auditing standards (GAAS). Answer (C) is incorrect. Although quality control extends to adherence to GAAP, the PCAOB Inspection Reports do not provide information about prevalent practice regarding compliance with particular disclosure requirements. Answer (D) is incorrect. The actual Form 10-K filings by public companies, which contain audited financial statements, are more useful than the guidance information provided by the SEC.

3.4.7. An auditor most likely obtains an understanding of a new client to

A. Make constructive suggestions concerning improvements to the client's internal control.

B. Develop an attitude of professional skepticism concerning management's financial statement assertions.

C. Evaluate whether the aggregation of known misstatements causes the financial statements taken as a whole to be materially misstated.

D. Identify areas of audit emphasis.

Answer (D) is correct. *(CPA, adapted)*

REQUIRED: The reason to obtain an understanding of a new client.

DISCUSSION: The understanding provides a basis for assessing risks of material misstatement and responding to them in the exercise of professional judgment. For example, the auditor needs to identify areas that need special audit consideration, such as complex or unusual transactions or related-party transactions.

Answer (A) is incorrect. Communication of internal control-related matters occurs during and after the audit. Obtaining the understanding occurs during audit planning. Answer (B) is incorrect. The auditor should adopt an attitude of professional skepticism in all phases of an engagement. Answer (C) is incorrect. Evaluating whether the financial statements are materially misstated is done after the collection of evidence.

3.4.8. The components of internal control include

A. Monitoring of controls that sets the tone of the organization.

B. A process of managing risks relevant to preparing financial statements.

C. A control environment consisting of policies and procedures to help ensure that management directives are carried out.

D. Control activities that identify, capture, and exchange information.

Answer (B) is correct. *(Publisher, adapted)*

REQUIRED: The components of internal control.

DISCUSSION: The risk assessment process is the entity's identification, analysis, and management of risks relevant to preparation of financial statements.

Answer (A) is incorrect. The control environment sets the tone of the organization, influencing the control consciousness of its people. Answer (C) is incorrect. Control activities are policies and procedures to help ensure that management directives are carried out. Answer (D) is incorrect. The information system, including related business processes, identifies, captures, and exchanges information in a form and time frame that enables people to carry out their responsibilities.

3.4.9. The objective of performing analytical procedures in planning an audit is to identify the existence of

A. Unusual transactions and events.

B. Noncompliance with laws and regulations that went undetected because of internal control deficiency.

C. Related party transactions.

D. Recorded transactions that were not properly authorized.

Answer (A) is correct. *(CPA, adapted)*

REQUIRED: The objective of performing analytical procedures as risk assessment procedures in an audit.

DISCUSSION: The objective of analytical procedures is to identify such things as the existence of unusual transactions and events, and amounts, ratios, and trends that might indicate matters that have financial statement and audit planning ramifications.

Answer (B) is incorrect. The objective of performing analytical procedures to plan the audit is to identify areas of specific risk, not specific noncompliance with laws and regulations. Answer (C) is incorrect. Although the auditor should evaluate disclosures about related party transactions, analytical procedures performed to plan the audit do not necessarily detect such transactions. Answer (D) is incorrect. Tests of controls are necessary to determine whether transactions were properly authorized.

3.4.10. When an auditor obtains an understanding of the entity and its environment, including its internal control, which of the following is the most likely order of performing the steps A through C below?

A = Tests of controls
B = Preparation of a flowchart documenting the understanding of the client's internal control
C = Substantive procedures

A. ABC.

B. ACB.

C. BAC.

D. BCA.

Answer (C) is correct. *(CPA, adapted)*

REQUIRED: The correct order of audit steps.

DISCUSSION: The auditor obtains an understanding of internal control. This understanding may include flowcharting the system. Next, the auditor must assess the risks of material misstatement, whether due to fraud or error. In response to this assessment, the auditor performs further audit procedures. These procedures ordinarily include tests of controls to evaluate their operating effectiveness when (1) the auditor intends to rely on the controls to determine substantive procedures or (2) substantive procedures alone are insufficient.

3.4.11. An auditor is planning an audit engagement for a new client in a business that is unfamiliar to the auditor. Which of the following would be the least useful source of information for the auditor during the preliminary planning stage, when the auditor is trying to obtain a general understanding of audit problems that might be encountered?

A. Textbooks and periodicals related to the industry.

B. AICPA Audit and Accounting Guides.

C. Financial statements of other entities in the industry.

D. Results of performing substantive procedures.

Answer (D) is correct. *(CPA, adapted)*

REQUIRED: The least useful source of information for early planning of the audit.

DISCUSSION: Substantive procedures are performed to detect material misstatements at the relevant assertion level. They include tests of details and substantive analytical procedures. They are performed after the auditor has obtained an understanding of the entity and its environment, including its internal control.

Answer (A) is incorrect. Textbooks and periodicals related to the industry are among the sources of information for planning the audit of a new client in a business that is unfamiliar to the auditor. Answer (B) is incorrect. AICPA Audit and Accounting Guides are useful sources of information. Answer (C) is incorrect. Financial statements of other entities in the industry are useful sources of information.

3.5 Analytical Procedures

3.5.1. Which of the following would be least likely to be comparable between similar corporations in the same industry line of business?

A. Earnings per share.

B. Return on total assets before interest and taxes.

C. Accounts receivable turnover.

D. Operating cycle.

Answer (A) is correct. *(CPA, adapted)*

REQUIRED: The measure least likely to be comparable between similar firms.

DISCUSSION: Similar companies in the same industry that are equally profitable may have quite different earnings per share because of differences in shares outstanding and in other aspects of their capital structures.

Answer (B) is incorrect. Similar firms should have comparable returns on total assets. Answer (C) is incorrect. Accounts receivable turnover is ordinarily comparable for firms in the same industry. Answer (D) is incorrect. Operating cycles are ordinarily comparable for firms in the same industry.

3.5.2. Analytical procedures can best be categorized as

A. Substantive procedures.
B. Tests of controls.
C. Qualitative tests.
D. Budget comparisons.

Answer (A) is correct. *(CIA, adapted)*

REQUIRED: The best classification of analytical procedures.

DISCUSSION: Substantive procedures are designed to detect material misstatements at the assertion level. According to AU-C 520, *Analytical Procedures*, analytical procedures consist of evaluations of financial information made by a study of plausible relationships among both financial and nonfinancial data. They involve comparisons of recorded amounts, or ratios developed from recorded amounts, to expectations developed by the auditor.

Answer (B) is incorrect. Tests of controls are used to evaluate the operating effectiveness of controls. Answer (C) is incorrect. Analytical procedures tend to be quantitative even when nonfinancial information is considered. Answer (D) is incorrect. Budget comparisons are only one of many types of analytical procedures.

3.5.3. Analytical procedures enable the auditor to predict the balance or quantity of an item under audit. Information to develop this estimate can be obtained from all of the following except

A. Tracing transactions through the system to determine whether procedures are being applied as prescribed.
B. Comparison of financial data with data for comparable prior periods, anticipated results (e.g., budgets and forecasts), and similar data for the industry in which the entity operates.
C. Study of the relationships of elements of financial data that would be expected to conform to a predictable pattern based upon the entity's experience.
D. Study of the relationships of financial data with relevant nonfinancial data.

Answer (A) is correct. *(Publisher, adapted)*

REQUIRED: The procedure that is not a source of information for analytical procedures.

DISCUSSION: Tracing transactions through the system is a test of controls directed toward the operating effectiveness of internal control, not an analytical procedure.

Answer (B) is incorrect. The basic premise of analytical procedures is that plausible relationships among data may be reasonably expected to exist and continue in the absence of known conditions to the contrary. Well-drafted budgets and forecasts prepared at the beginning of the year should therefore be compared with actual results, and client information should be compared with data for the industry in which the client operates. Answer (C) is incorrect. The auditor should expect financial ratios and relationships to exist and to remain relatively stable in the absence of reasons for variation. Answer (D) is incorrect. Financial information is related to nonfinancial information; e.g., salary expense should be related to the number of hours worked.

3.5.4. Which of the following nonfinancial information would an auditor most likely consider in performing analytical procedures during the planning phase of an audit?

A. Turnover of personnel in the accounting department.
B. Objectivity of audit committee members.
C. Square footage of selling space.
D. Management's plans to repurchase stock.

Answer (C) is correct. *(CPA, adapted)*

REQUIRED: The nonfinancial information considered in performing analytical procedures during audit planning.

DISCUSSION: Although analytical procedures used in planning the audit often use only financial data, sometimes relevant nonfinancial information is considered as well. For example, number of employees, square footage of selling space, volume of goods produced, and similar information may contribute to accomplishing the purpose of the procedures.

Answer (A) is incorrect. Turnover of personnel in the accounting department is not a measure related to analytical procedures. Answer (B) is incorrect. Objectivity of audit committee members is not a measure related to analytical procedures. Answer (D) is incorrect. Management's plans to repurchase stock is not a measure related to analytical procedures.

3.5.5. The objective of analytical procedures performed as risk assessment procedures is to

A. Evaluate the adequacy of evidence gathered in response to unusual balances identified during the audit.

B. Test individual account balances that depend on accounting estimates.

C. Enhance the auditor's understanding of the client's business.

D. Identify material weaknesses in internal control.

Answer (C) is correct. *(CPA, adapted)*

REQUIRED: The objective of analytical procedures performed as risk assessment procedures.

DISCUSSION: Analytical procedures applied as risk assessment procedures may (1) improve the understanding of the client's business and significant transactions and events and (2) identify unusual transactions or events and amounts, ratios, and trends that might indicate matters with audit ramifications (AU-C 315).

Answer (A) is incorrect. Analytical procedures used in forming an overall conclusion include reading the statements to evaluate the adequacy of evidence gathered in response to unusual balances identified during the audit. Answer (B) is incorrect. Analytical procedures are predictions or expectations of account balances or ratios. They are not tests of details of account balances or transactions. Answer (D) is incorrect. The auditor's understanding of internal control and tests of controls may identify material weaknesses.

3.5.6. Which of the following statements about analytical procedures is true?

A. Analytical procedures may be omitted entirely for some financial statement audits.

B. Analytical procedures used as risk assessment procedures should not use nonfinancial information.

C. Analytical procedures usually are effective and efficient for tests of controls.

D. Analytical procedures alone may provide the appropriate level of assurance for some assertions.

Answer (D) is correct. *(CPA, adapted)*

REQUIRED: The true statement about analytical procedures.

DISCUSSION: For some assertions, analytical procedures alone may suffice to reduce audit risk to an acceptably low level. For example, the auditor's risk assessment may be supported by audit evidence from tests of controls. Substantive analytical procedures generally are more applicable to large transaction volumes that are predictable over time (AU-C 330). The decision is based on the auditor's professional judgment about the expected effectiveness and efficiency of the available procedures.

Answer (A) is incorrect. Analytical procedures should be applied (1) as risk assessment procedures and (2) to help the auditor to form an overall conclusion near the end of the audit. They also may be used as substantive procedures. Answer (B) is incorrect. Analytical procedures used as risk assessment procedures often use financial data only, but relevant nonfinancial information may also be considered. Answer (C) is incorrect. Analytical procedures may be used as substantive procedures but not as tests of controls.

3.5.7. Analytical procedures performed to assist in forming an overall conclusion suggest that several accounts have unexpected relationships. The results of these procedures most likely indicate that

A. Misstatements exist in the relevant account balances.

B. Internal control activities are not operating effectively.

C. Additional audit procedures are required.

D. The communication with the audit committee should be revised.

Answer (C) is correct. *(CPA, adapted)*

REQUIRED: The implication when analytical procedures applied to form an overall conclusion have unexpected results.

DISCUSSION: Analytical procedures used to form an overall conclusion ordinarily include reading the financial statements and considering (1) the adequacy of evidence regarding unusual or unexpected balances detected during the audit and (2) such balances or relationships not detected previously. If analytical procedures detect a previously unrecognized risk of material misstatement, the auditor must revise the assessments of the RMMs and modify the further planned procedures. Inconsistent fluctuations or relationships or significant differences should result in (1) inquiries of management, (2) corroboration of responses with other audit evidence, and (3) performance of any necessary other procedures. Moreover, the RMM due to fraud should be considered.

Answer (A) is incorrect. Analytical procedures can identify unexpected relationships but not their causes. Answer (B) is incorrect. Tests of controls are conducted to determine the effectiveness of their design and operation. Answer (D) is incorrect. Until the auditor determines the cause of the unexpected relationships, the auditor does not know whether the communication with the audit committee should be revised.

3.5.8. Analytical procedures are most appropriate when testing which of the following types of transactions?

A. Payroll and benefit liabilities.

B. Acquisitions and disposals of fixed assets.

C. Operating expense transactions.

D. Noncurrent debt transactions.

Answer (C) is correct. *(CPA, adapted)*

REQUIRED: The most appropriate use of analytical procedures.

DISCUSSION: Relationships involving income statement accounts tend to be more predictable than relationships involving only balance sheet accounts. Income statement accounts represent transactions over a period of time, but balance sheet accounts represent an amount at a moment in time. Thus, operating expense transactions are likely to be more predictable than balance sheet accounts.

Answer (A) is incorrect. Payroll and benefit liabilities are balance sheet accounts and not as predictable as, for example, payroll expense. Answer (B) is incorrect. Acquisitions and disposals of fixed assets relate to balance sheet accounts, which are not typically as predictable as income statement accounts. Answer (D) is incorrect. Noncurrent debt transactions relate to balance sheet accounts, which are not typically as predictable as income statement accounts.

3.5.9. According to professional standards, analytical procedures are least likely to be applied to

A. Test disclosures about reportable operating segments.

B. Review financial statements or interim financial information.

C. Compile financial statements.

D. Assist in forming an overall conclusion.

Answer (C) is correct. *(Publisher, adapted)*

REQUIRED: The inappropriate use of analytical procedures.

DISCUSSION: AR-C 80, *Compilation of Financial Statements*, states that no audit procedures need be applied in a compilation of financial statements. The accountant is required only to read the financial statements to identify obvious material misstatements.

Answer (A) is incorrect. An auditor should consider applying analytical procedures consisting of comparisons of information about segments with comparable information for the prior year and with budgeted information. Answer (B) is incorrect. Analytical procedures ordinarily should be applied in a review of interim financial information (AU-C 930, *Interim Financial Information*) and in a review of financial statements of a nonissuer (AR-C 90). Answer (D) is incorrect. Analytical procedures should be applied as risk assessment procedures and to assist in forming an overall conclusion.

3.5.10. Which result of an analytical procedure suggests the existence of obsolete merchandise?

A. Decrease in the inventory turnover rate.

B. Decrease in the ratio of gross profit to sales.

C. Decrease in the ratio of inventory to accounts payable.

D. Decrease in the ratio of inventory to accounts receivable.

Answer (A) is correct. *(CIA, adapted)*

REQUIRED: The analytical procedure that might uncover obsolete merchandise.

DISCUSSION: Inventory turnover is equal to cost of sales divided by average inventory. If inventory is increasing at a faster rate than sales, the turnover rate decreases and suggests a buildup of unsalable inventory.

Answer (B) is incorrect. The ratio of gross profit to sales does not necessarily change when obsolete merchandise is on hand. Answer (C) is incorrect. The ratio of inventory to accounts payable does not necessarily change when obsolete merchandise is on hand. Answer (D) is incorrect. The ratio of inventory to accounts receivable does not necessarily change when obsolete merchandise is on hand.

3.5.11. A basic premise underlying analytical procedures is that

A. These procedures cannot replace tests of balances and transactions.

B. Statistical tests of financial information may lead to the discovery of material misstatements in the financial statements.

C. The study of financial ratios is an acceptable alternative to the investigation of unusual fluctuations.

D. Plausible relationships among data may reasonably be expected to exist and continue in the absence of known conditions to the contrary.

Answer (D) is correct. *(CPA, adapted)*

REQUIRED: The premise underlying analytical procedures.

DISCUSSION: A basic premise underlying the application of analytical procedures is that plausible relationships among data may reasonably be expected to exist and continue in the absence of known conditions to the contrary. Variability in these relationships can be explained by, for example, unusual events or transactions, business or accounting changes, misstatements, or random fluctuations.

Answer (A) is incorrect. For some assertions, analytical procedures alone may provide the auditor with the level of assurance (s)he desires. Answer (B) is incorrect. Analytical procedures, such as simple comparisons, do not necessarily require statistical testing. Answer (C) is incorrect. The objective of analytical procedures, such as ratio analysis, is to identify significant differences for evaluation and possible investigation.

3.5.12. For all audits of financial statements made in accordance with generally accepted auditing standards, the auditor should apply analytical procedures to some extent as

	Risk Assessment Procedures	Substantive Procedures	In the Review Stage
A.	Yes	No	Yes
B.	No	Yes	No
C.	No	No	Yes
D.	Yes	Yes	No

Answer (A) is correct. *(CPA, adapted)*

REQUIRED: The required use(s) of analytical procedures.

DISCUSSION: The auditor obtains an understanding of the entity and its environment, including its internal control, to identify and assess the risks of material misstatement of the financial statements, whether due to fraud or error. Risk assessment procedures are performed to obtain the understanding. They include (1) inquiries of management and others within the entity, (2) analytical procedures (analytical procedures used to plan the audit), and (3) observation and inspection. Substantive procedures are designed to detect material misstatements in assertions. They consist of tests of details and substantive analytical procedures. Analytical procedures are required to be used as risk assessment procedures (AU-C 315). However, the decision to use analytical procedures as substantive procedures is based on the auditor's judgment about their effectiveness and efficiency in reducing the risks of material misstatement to an acceptably low level (AU-C 520).

Answer (B) is incorrect. Analytical procedures are required to be performed as risk assessment procedures. The auditor has discretion whether to use analytical procedures as substantive procedures. Answer (C) is incorrect. Analytical procedures are required to be performed as risk assessment procedures. Answer (D) is incorrect. The auditor has discretion whether to use analytical procedures as substantive procedures.

3.5.13. Which of the following factors has the least influence on an auditor's consideration of the reliability of data for purposes of analytical procedures?

A. Whether the data were processed in a computer system or in a manual accounting system.

B. Whether sources within the entity were independent of those who are responsible for the amount being audited.

C. Whether the data were subjected to audit testing in the current or prior year.

D. Whether the data were obtained from independent sources outside the entity or from sources within the entity.

Answer (A) is correct. *(CPA, adapted)*

REQUIRED: The factor least likely to influence an auditor's consideration of the reliability of data for purposes of analytical procedures.

DISCUSSION: The consideration of the reliability of data should include sources of the data and the conditions under which the data were gathered. Whether (1) sources within the entity were independent of those who are responsible for the amount being audited, (2) the data were subjected to audit testing in the current or prior year, and (3) the data were obtained from independent sources outside the entity or from sources within the entity are more influential than the mode of processing. Other factors include whether the auditor's expectations were developed using data from a variety of sources and whether the data were developed under a reliable system with adequate controls.

3.5.14. Which of the following is the most reliable analytical approach to verification of the year-end financial statement balances of a wholesale business?

A. Verify depreciation expense by multiplying the depreciable asset balances by one divided by the depreciation rate.

B. Verify commission expense by multiplying sales revenue by the company's standard commission rate.

C. Verify interest expense, which includes imputed interest, by multiplying noncurrent debt balances by the year-end prevailing interest rate.

D. Verify FICA tax liability by multiplying total payroll costs by the FICA contribution rate in effect during the year.

Answer (B) is correct. *(CPA, adapted)*

REQUIRED: The reliable analytical procedure to verify balances of a wholesale business.

DISCUSSION: If the wholesaler uses a standard commission rate, commission expense should be related to sales revenue. The auditor should also compare actual with budgeted and prior year amounts.

Answer (A) is incorrect. One divided by the life of the asset is the formula for the straight-line depreciation rate per year. However, the client may use depreciation methods other than straight line. Answer (C) is incorrect. Interest expense is not related to the prevailing rate but to contracted and imputed rates. Answer (D) is incorrect. FICA tax is withheld from individual wages up to a ceiling amount. No tax liability exists for amounts above the ceiling, so the test will probably overstate the liability.

3.5.15. For the fiscal year ending December 31 of the previous year and for the current year, Justin Co. has net sales of $1,000,000 and $2,000,000; average gross receivables of $100,000 and $300,000; and an allowance for uncollectible accounts receivable of $30,000 and $50,000, respectively. If the accounts receivable turnover and the ratio of allowance for uncollectible accounts receivable to gross accounts receivable are calculated, which of the following best represents the conclusions to be drawn?

A. Accounts receivable turnovers are 10.0 and 6.6, and the ratios of uncollectible accounts receivable to gross accounts receivable are 0.30 and 0.16, respectively. Examine allowance for possible overstatement of the allowance.

B. Accounts receivable turnovers are 10.0 and 6.7, and the ratios of uncollectible accounts receivable to gross accounts receivable are 0.30 and 0.17, respectively. Examine allowance for possible understatement of the allowance.

C. Accounts receivable turnovers are 14.3 and 8.0, and the ratios of uncollectible accounts receivable to gross accounts receivable are 0.42 and 0.20, respectively. Examine allowance for possible overstatement of the allowance.

D. Accounts receivable turnovers are 14.3 and 8.0 and the ratios of uncollectible accounts receivable to gross accounts receivable are 0.42 and 0.20, respectively. Examine allowance for possible understatement of the allowance.

Answer (B) is correct. *(CPA, adapted)*

REQUIRED: The appropriate conclusions from the accounts receivable turnover and the ratio of allowance for uncollectible accounts receivable to gross acccunts receivable.

DISCUSSION: The accounts receivable turnover equals sales divided by average gross receivables. Thus, it equals 10.0 ($1,000,000 ÷ $100,000) and 6.7 ($2,000,000 ÷ $300,000) for the prior year and current year, respectively. The ratio of allowance for uncollectible accounts receivable to gross accounts receivable is .30 ($30,000 ÷ $100,000) for the prior year and .17 ($50,000 ÷ $300,000) for the current year. The gross accounts receivable tripled in the second year, yet the allowance for uncollectible accounts receivable increased by only 67%. This could be an indication that the allowance for uncollectible accounts receivable is understated.

Answer (A) is incorrect. The gross accounts receivable tripled in the second year, yet the allowance for uncollectible accounts receivable only went up by 67%. This could be an indication that the allowance for uncollectible accounts receivable is understated, not overstated. Answer (C) is incorrect. Net accounts receivable was used to calculate these ratios. Answer (D) is incorrect. Net accounts receivable was used to calculate these ratios.

3.5.16. An auditor's decision either to apply analytical procedures as substantive procedures or to perform tests of transactions and account balances usually is determined by the

A. Availability of data aggregated at a high level.

B. Auditor's determination about whether audit risk can be sufficiently reduced.

C. Timing of tests performed after the balance sheet date.

D. Auditor's familiarity with industry trends.

Answer (B) is correct. *(CPA, adapted)*

REQUIRED: The basis for choosing between analytical procedures and tests of details.

DISCUSSION: For some assertions, analytical procedures alone may suffice to reduce audit risk to an acceptably low level. For example, the auditor's risk assessment may be supported by audit evidence from tests of controls. Substantive analytical procedures generally are more applicable to large transaction volumes that are predictable over time (AU-C 330). The decision is based on the auditor's professional judgment about the expected effectiveness and efficiency of the available procedures.

Answer (A) is incorrect. Availability of data is among the factors in evaluating whether audit risk can be reduced to an acceptably low level. Answer (C) is incorrect. Timing of tests is among the factors in evaluating whether audit risk can be reduced to an acceptably low level. Answer (D) is incorrect. Familiarity with industry trends is among the factors in evaluating whether audit risk can be reduced to an acceptably low level.

3.5.17. An auditor's preliminary analysis of accounts receivable turnover revealed the following rates over these accounting periods:

Year 3	Year 2	Year 1
4.3	6.2	7.3

Which of the following is the most likely cause of the decrease in accounts receivable turnover?

A. Increase in the cash discount offered.

B. Liberalization of credit policy.

C. Shortening of due date terms.

D. Increased cash sales.

Answer (B) is correct. *(CIA, adapted)*

REQUIRED: The most likely cause of a decrease in accounts receivable turnover.

DISCUSSION: The accounts receivable turnover ratio equals net credit sales over average accounts receivable. Accounts receivable turnover will decrease if net credit sales decrease or average accounts receivable increase. Liberalization of credit policy will increase receivables.

Answer (A) is incorrect. An increase in cash sales that reduces credit sales as a result of an increased cash discount has an indeterminate effect on the turnover ratio. Both the numerator and denominator are decreased but not necessarily by the same amount. An increase in cash sales not affecting credit sales has no effect on the ratio. Answer (C) is incorrect. Shortening due dates decreases the average accounts receivable outstanding and increases the ratio if other factors are held constant. Answer (D) is incorrect. Increased cash sales have an indeterminate effect on the turnover ratio.

3.5.18. An auditor discovers that a client's accounts receivable turnover is substantially lower for the current year than for the prior year. This trend may indicate that

A. Fictitious credit sales have been recorded during the year.

B. Employees have stolen inventory just before year end.

C. The client recently tightened its credit-granting policies.

D. An employee has been lapping receivables in both years.

Answer (A) is correct. *(CPA, adapted)*

REQUIRED: The most likely cause of a decrease in accounts receivable turnover.

DISCUSSION: The accounts receivable turnover ratio equals net credit sales divided by average accounts receivable. Accounts receivable turnover will decrease if net credit sales decrease or average accounts receivable increases. Fictitious sales increase both the numerator and denominator. Adding an equal amount to both the numerator and denominator decreases a fraction greater than 1.0. For example, adding 1 to both parts of the fraction 3 ÷ 2 decreases it to 4 ÷ 3. The turnover ratio will decrease still more in the next period because fictitious items will continue to increase receivables (a real account) but not sales (a nominal account).

Answer (B) is incorrect. Stolen inventory has no effect on accounts receivable turnover. It affects inventory turnover. Answer (C) is incorrect. Tightening of credit-granting policies will decrease net credit sales and receivables. Subtracting an equal amount from the numerator and denominator increases a fraction greater than 1.0. Answer (D) is incorrect. Lapping is the delayed recording of cash receipts to cover a cash shortage. Current receipts are posted to accounts of customers who paid 1 or 2 days previously. If lapping occurs in both years, the turnover ratio is not affected.

3.5.19. Auditors sometimes use comparison of ratios as audit evidence. For example, an unexplained decrease in the ratio of gross profit to sales suggests which of the following possibilities?

A. Unrecorded purchases.

B. Unrecorded sales.

C. Merchandise purchases being charged to selling and general expense.

D. Fictitious sales.

Answer (B) is correct. *(CPA, adapted)*

REQUIRED: The reason for a decrease in the gross profit ratio.

DISCUSSION: Fraud or error that decreases gross profit relative to sales (or increases sales relative to gross profit) causes the ratio to decline. Unrecorded sales cause inventory to decrease and cost of sales to increase with no increase in sales, thereby decreasing gross profit relative to sales and lowering the ratio.

Answer (A) is incorrect. Unrecorded purchases result in a lower recorded cost of sales, a greater gross profit, and an increase in the ratio. Answer (C) is incorrect. Unrecorded purchases result in a lower recorded cost of sales, a greater gross profit, and an increase in the ratio. Answer (D) is incorrect. Fictitious sales increase sales with no associated cost, hence gross profit is inflated and the ratio increases.

3.5.20. Analytical procedures used to form an overall audit conclusion generally include

A. Considering unusual or unexpected account balances that were not previously identified.

B. Performing tests of transactions to corroborate management's financial statement assertions.

C. Gathering evidence concerning account balances that have not changed from the prior year.

D. Retesting controls that appeared to be ineffective during the assessment of control risk.

Answer (A) is correct. *(CPA, adapted)*

REQUIRED: The analytical procedures used to form an overall audit conclusion.

DISCUSSION: Analytical procedures should be applied near the end of the audit. The purpose is to form an overall audit conclusion about whether the statements are consistent with the auditor's understanding of the entity. Procedures ordinarily should include reading the statements and considering (1) the adequacy of evidence regarding previously identified unusual or unexpected balances and (2) unusual or unexpected balances or relationships not previously noted (AU-C 520).

Answer (B) is incorrect. Analytical procedures are not tests of details. Answer (C) is incorrect. The lack of change from the prior year may not be unusual or unexpected. Answer (D) is incorrect. Analytical procedures are substantive, not tests of controls.

3.5.21. The auditor is evaluating the effectiveness of a sales commission plan adopted 12 months earlier. An audit procedure likely to provide strong evidence of the plan's effectiveness is to

A. Calculate the percentage change in monthly sales by product line for the last 3 years.

B. Compare monthly selling costs of this year with those of the 2 preceding years.

C. Regress monthly indices of external economic conditions against sales for the 2 preceding years and compare predictions with reported sales.

D. Compare the ratio of selling costs per dollar of sales each month for the past year with that of other companies in the industry.

Answer (C) is correct. *(CIA, adapted)*

REQUIRED: The technique to determine the effectiveness of a newly installed sales commission plan.

DISCUSSION: The auditor requires evidence as to whether sales have increased more than could be expected from changes in external economic conditions. Regression analysis is a statistical tool to generate predictions based on projections of current economic conditions. It provides benchmarks whereby current sales may be compared with expected sales to evaluate the effect of the sales commission variable.

Answer (A) is incorrect. Simple comparison of month-to-month sales figures does not take into account changes in external economic factors. Answer (B) is incorrect. The effectiveness of the sales commission plan should be measured by the sales generated, not by costs. Answer (D) is incorrect. The effectiveness of the sales commission plan should be measured by the sales generated, not by costs.

3.6 Consideration of Fraud in a Financial Statement Audit

3.6.1. What is the definition of fraud in an audit of financial statements?

A. An intentional act that results in a material misstatement in financial statements that are the subject of an audit.

B. The unintentional misapplication of accounting principles relating to amounts, classification, manner of presentation, or disclosure.

C. An intentional act that results in a material weakness in financial statements that are the subject of an audit.

D. Management's inability to design and implement programs and controls to prevent, deter, and detect material misstatements.

Answer (A) is correct. *(CPA, adapted)*

REQUIRED: The definition of fraud.

DISCUSSION: Fraud is an "intentional act by one or more individuals among management, those charged with governance, employees, or third parties, involving the use of deception that results in a misstatement in financial statements that are the subject of an audit."

Answer (B) is incorrect. Fraud consists of an intentional act. An unintentional act would be considered an error rather than fraud. Answer (C) is incorrect. Fraud is an intentional misstatement, not a material weakness. Answer (D) is incorrect. Management's inability to design and implement programs is not fraud.

3.6.2. Which of the following is a true statement about an auditor's responsibility regarding consideration of fraud in a financial statement audit?

A. The auditor should consider the client's internal control and plan and perform the audit to provide absolute assurance of detecting all material misstatements.

B. The auditor should assess the risk that errors may cause the financial statements to contain any misstatements and determine whether the necessary controls are prescribed and are being followed satisfactorily.

C. The auditor should consider the types of misstatements that could occur and perform tests on 100% of the information subject to misstatement.

D. The auditor should assess the risks of material misstatement due to fraud.

Answer (D) is correct. *(Publisher, adapted)*

REQUIRED: The true statement about an auditor's responsibility regarding consideration of fraud in a financial statement audit.

DISCUSSION: The auditor assesses the identified risks of material misstatement due to fraud at the statement and assertion levels. The assessment is ongoing after the initial assessment. The assessed risks are treated as significant. Thus, to the extent not done previously, the auditor should obtain an understanding of the relevant controls. The understanding includes evaluating whether they are suitably designed, have been implemented, and reduce the risks.

Answer (A) is incorrect. Absolute assurance is impossible to achieve. Answer (B) is incorrect. The risks of material misstatement due to fraud must be assessed. Answer (C) is incorrect. The auditor should assess the risk of fraud but not test at a 100% level.

3.6.3. Which of the following is considered a fraudulent activity?

A. A mistake in gathering or processing accounting data from which financial statements are prepared.

B. An incorrect accounting estimate arising from oversight or misinterpretation of facts.

C. Misappropriation of assets.

D. A mistake in the application of accounting principles relating to amount, classification, manner of presentation, or disclosure.

Answer (C) is correct. *(Publisher, adapted)*

REQUIRED: The activity that is considered fraudulent.

DISCUSSION: Fraud is an intentional act involving the use of deception that results in misstatement of the financial statements. Two types of fraud that are relevant to the auditor are (1) misstatements arising from fraudulent financial reporting and (2) misstatements arising from misappropriation of assets.

Answer (A) is incorrect. A mistake is not intentional. Answer (B) is incorrect. An unintentionally incorrect accounting estimate is not fraud. Answer (D) is incorrect. Fraud is intentional. Mistakes are not.

3.6.4. Because of the risk of material misstatement due to fraud, an audit of financial statements in accordance with generally accepted auditing standards should be planned and performed with an attitude of

A. Objective judgment.

B. Integrity.

C. Professional skepticism.

D. Impartial conservatism.

Answer (C) is correct. *(CPA, adapted)*

REQUIRED: The attitude with which an audit in accordance with auditing standards should be planned and performed.

DISCUSSION: The auditor should maintain professional skepticism throughout the audit. Professional skepticism is an "attitude that includes a questioning mind, being alert to conditions that may indicate possible misstatement due to fraud or error, and critical assessment of audit evidence" (AU-C 200).

Answer (A) is incorrect. Although objective judgment is a quality appropriate for practitioners, it is not required to be applied specifically in an audit. Answer (B) is incorrect. Although independent integrity is a quality appropriate for practitioners, it is not required to be applied specifically in an audit. Answer (D) is incorrect. GAAS do not require conservatism.

3.6.5. Which of the following statements reflects an auditor's responsibility for detecting fraud and errors?

A. An auditor is responsible for detecting employee errors and simple fraud, but not for discovering fraudulent acts involving employee collusion or management override.

B. An auditor should plan the audit to detect errors and fraud that are caused by departures from the applicable financial reporting framework.

C. An auditor is not responsible for detecting fraud unless the application of GAAS would result in such detection.

D. An auditor should design the audit to provide reasonable assurance of detecting fraud and errors that are material to the financial statements.

Answer (D) is correct. *(CPA, adapted)*

REQUIRED: The statement reflecting the auditor's responsibility for detecting fraud and errors.

DISCUSSION: The auditor has a responsibility to plan and perform the audit to obtain reasonable assurance about whether the financial statements are free of material misstatements, whether caused by fraud or error. Thus, the auditor should (1) identify and assess the risks of material misstatement due to fraud at the financial statement and assertion levels, (2) obtain sufficient appropriate audit evidence regarding those risks through implementing responses, and (3) respond to identified fraud or suspected fraud. Moreover, the consideration of fraud should be logically integrated into the overall audit process in a manner consistent with other pronouncements, e.g., those on (1) planning and supervision, (2) audit risk and materiality, and (3) internal control.

3.6.6. Three conditions are generally present in the client's organization when fraud occurs. Those conditions include each of the following except a(n)

A. Incentive or pressure to commit fraud.

B. Professional skepticism about the likelihood of fraud.

C. Opportunity to commit fraud.

D. Attitude or rationalization about the act of fraud.

Answer (B) is correct. *(Publisher, adapted)*

REQUIRED: The condition not necessarily present when fraud occurs.

DISCUSSION: The auditor, not the client, should conduct the audit with professional skepticism. Professional skepticism is an "attitude that includes a questioning mind, being alert to conditions that may indicate possible misstatement due to fraud or error, and critical assessment of audit evidence" (AU-C 200).

Answer (A) is incorrect. Incentives for, or pressures on, management or others to commit fraud ordinarily exist (whether or not observable) when fraud occurs. Answer (C) is incorrect. The opportunity to commit fraud ordinarily exists (whether or not observable) when fraud occurs. Answer (D) is incorrect. An attitude or rationalization that justifies the fraud ordinarily exists (whether or not observable) when fraud occurs.

3.6.7. Certain individuals may have an attitude, character, or set of values that permit them to rationalize fraud. Moreover, individuals may have an incentive or be under pressure to commit fraud, or circumstances may provide an opportunity. The auditor's concern about the risk of material misstatements due to fraud is least likely to be increased if management

A. Consists of many individuals that make operating and financing decisions.

B. Commits to unduly aggressive forecasts.

C. Has an excessive interest in increasing the entity's stock price through use of unduly aggressive accounting practices.

D. Is interested in inappropriate means of minimizing reported earnings for tax-motivated reasons.

Answer (A) is correct. *(Publisher, adapted)*

REQUIRED: The circumstance least likely to indicate increased fraud risk.

DISCUSSION: Domination of the decision process by one individual or a small group (an opportunity to commit fraud) is a fraud risk factor. In that case, compensating controls, e.g., effective oversight by the audit committee, reduce risk (AU-C 240, *Appendix*).

Answer (B) is incorrect. A commitment to third parties to achieve unduly aggressive or clearly unrealistic forecasts is a fraud risk factor that reflects an attitude or rationalization permitting fraudulent financial reporting. Answer (C) is incorrect. An excessive interest in improving the entity's stock price or earnings trend is a fraud risk factor that reflects an attitude or rationalization permitting fraudulent financial reporting. Answer (D) is incorrect. An interest in inappropriate means of minimizing earnings for tax purposes is a fraud risk factor that reflects an attitude or rationalization permitting fraudulent financial reporting.

3.6.8. Which of the following circumstances most likely will cause an auditor to consider whether material misstatements due to fraud exist in an entity's financial statements?

A. Management places little emphasis on meeting earnings projections of external parties.

B. The board of directors oversees the financial reporting process and internal control.

C. Control deficiencies previously communicated to management are not corrected.

D. Transactions selected for testing are not supported by proper documentation.

Answer (D) is correct. *(CPA, adapted)*

REQUIRED: The circumstance most likely to cause an auditor to consider the existence of fraud risk.

DISCUSSION: Fraud risk factors relate to misstatements arising from (1) fraudulent financial reporting and (2) misappropriation of assets. Each of these categories may be further classified according to the three conditions that ordinarily exist when fraud occurs: (1) incentives/pressures, (2) opportunities, and (3) attitudes/rationalizations. For example, an opportunity for misappropriation of assets may arise because of inadequate control over assets. This fraud risk factor is reflected by a lack of timely and appropriate documentation of transactions, such as credit memos for returns of goods.

Answer (A) is incorrect. A risk factor exists when excessive pressure is placed on management to reach expectations of external parties. Answer (B) is incorrect. The involvement of those changed with governance reduces the likelihood of material misstatements due to fraud. Answer (C) is incorrect. Management may properly evaluate the costs and benefits in deciding whether to correct control deficiencies.

3.6.9. Which of the following characteristics most likely would heighten an auditor's concern about the risk of material misstatements arising from fraudulent financial reporting?

A. The entity's industry is experiencing declining customer demand.

B. Employees who handle cash receipts are not bonded.

C. Bank reconciliations usually include in-transit deposits.

D. Equipment is often sold at a loss before being fully depreciated.

Answer (A) is correct. *(CPA, adapted)*

REQUIRED: The characteristic that most likely increases concern about the risk of material misstatements from fraudulent financial reporting.

DISCUSSION: Certain risk factors are related to misstatements arising from fraudulent reporting. These factors may be grouped in three categories: (1) incentives or pressures, (2) opportunities, and (3) attitudes or rationalizations. One set of risk factors in the incentives or pressures category consists of threats to financial stability or profitability by economic, industry, or entity operating conditions. Examples are significant declines in customer demand and increasing business failures in either the industry or the overall economy (AU-C 240).

Answer (B) is incorrect. Failure to bond employees who handle cash receipts relates to misappropriation of assets, not fraudulent financial reporting. Answer (C) is incorrect. In-transit deposits are items requiring reconciliation. Answer (D) is incorrect. Equipment often is disposed of prior to being fully depreciated.

3.6.10. Which of the following circumstances most likely will cause an auditor to suspect that material misstatements exist in a client's financial statements?

A. The assumptions used in developing the prior year's accounting estimates have changed.

B. Differences between reconciliations of control accounts and subsidiary records are not investigated.

C. Negative confirmation requests yield fewer responses than in the prior year's audit.

D. Management consults with another CPA firm about complex accounting matters.

Answer (B) is correct. *(CPA, adapted)*

REQUIRED: The circumstances most likely causing an auditor to suspect that material misstatements exist in a client's financial statements.

DISCUSSION: A deficiency in internal control is one of the risk factors that provides an opportunity for misstatements arising from fraudulent financial reporting or misappropriation of assets. For example, inadequate internal control may increase susceptibility to misappropriation of assets because of a lack of complete and timely reconciliation of assets.

Answer (A) is incorrect. The assumptions used in developing the prior year's accounting estimates are expected to change. Answer (C) is incorrect. A negative confirmation requests the recipient to respond only if (s)he disagrees with the information stated. A lower yield from such requests may simply indicate that control has improved and fewer balances are misstated. Answer (D) is incorrect. Management's consultation with another CPA firm to obtain a second opinion about complex accounting matters is not necessarily an indicator of material misstatement. However, an auditor should communicate with those charged with governance to discuss his or her views about those matters.

3.6.11. Which of the following circumstances would an auditor most likely consider a risk factor relating to misstatements arising from fraudulent financial reporting?

A. Several members of management have recently purchased additional shares of the entity's stock.

B. Several members of the board of directors have recently sold shares of the entity's stock.

C. The entity distributes financial forecasts to financial analysts that predict conservative operating results.

D. Management is interested in maintaining the entity's earnings trend by using aggressive accounting practices.

Answer (D) is correct. *(CPA, adapted)*

REQUIRED: The most likely risk factor relating to misstatements arising from fraudulent financial reporting.

DISCUSSION: Fraud risk factors relate to misstatements arising from (1) fraudulent financial reporting and (2) misappropriation of assets. Each of these categories may be further classified according to the three conditions that ordinarily exist when fraud occurs: (1) incentives or pressures, (2) opportunities, and (3) attitudes or rationalizations. For example, excessive pressure may exist to meet the expectations of third parties (e.g., analysts, investors, and creditors) regarding profitability or trends (AU-C 240).

Answer (A) is incorrect. Managers routinely buy their company's stock. Answer (B) is incorrect. Sales of shares reduce the directors' financial interests in the entity. Answer (C) is incorrect. An unduly optimistic forecast is a fraud risk factor.

3.6.12. Which action regarding fraud is an activity related to performance of risk assessment procedures?

A. Discussions among the engagement team members regarding the risks of material misstatement due to fraud.

B. Document the results of procedures used to address the risk of fraud.

C. Consider the characteristics of journal entries, particularly those made near year end.

D. Consider whether estimates prepared and recorded by management could indicate a bias in reporting.

Answer (A) is correct. *(Publisher, adapted)*

REQUIRED: The procedure required during audit planning.

DISCUSSION: The key members of the engagement team should discuss the potential for material misstatement. The discussion should include an exchange of ideas (brainstorming) about (1) how and where the statements might be susceptible to material misstatement due to fraud ("fraud risk"), (2) how assets might be misappropriated or financial reports fraudulently misstated, (3) how management could conceal fraudulent reporting (including override of controls), (4) how to respond to fraud risk, (5) known factors reflecting pressures/incentives/ opportunities to commit fraud or an environment that permits rationalization of fraud, (6) an emphasis on the need to maintain professional skepticism, and (7) consideration of facts indicating manipulation of financial measures (e.g., earnings management).

Answer (B) is incorrect. The results of procedures are documented when evidence is collected. Answer (C) is incorrect. The auditor considers journal entries with characteristics indicative of fraud during evidence collection. Examples are entries (1) made to unrelated, unusual, or seldom-used accounts; (2) made by individuals who typically do not make journal entries; (3) recorded at the end of the period with no description; (4) made without account numbers during statement preparation; and (5) that include round numbers or a consistent ending number. Answer (D) is incorrect. Estimates made by management are considered during evidence collection.

3.6.13. Disclosure of possible fraud to parties other than the client's senior management and those charged with governance ordinarily is not part of an auditor's responsibility. However, to which of the following outside parties may a duty to disclose possible fraud exist?

I. To the SEC when the client reports an auditor change

II. To a successor auditor when the successor makes appropriate inquiries

III. To a government funding agency from which the client receives financial assistance

A. I and II.

B. I and III.

C. II and III.

D. I, II, and III.

Answer (D) is correct. *(CPA, adapted)*

REQUIRED: The outside parties to whom a duty to disclose fraud exists.

DISCUSSION: A duty of disclosure to parties other than the client is imposed by a subpoena. It also may exist when the entity reports an auditor change to the SEC on Form 8-K. For example, the auditor may have withdrawn because the client failed to take appropriate remedial action, and the failure may be a "reportable event" or the source of a "disagreement." These requirements also apply to reports on material noncompliance with laws and regulations that may be mandated by the Securities Exchange Act of 1934. Under AU-C 210, a predecessor auditor should respond promptly and fully, except in unusual circumstances, to inquiries by the auditor if the prospective client gives its specific permission. Under *Government Auditing Standards*, an auditor may have a duty to report fraud directly if it involves assistance received from a governmental agency. For example, when management has not taken remedial action, and the auditee does not report the fraud as soon as practicable to the entity that provided the assistance, the auditor must report the matter to that entity.

3.6.14. During the consideration of fraud in a financial statement audit, the auditor should identify and assess risks that may result in material misstatements due to fraud. This assessment

A. Must state an overall judgment about whether an identified risk is high, medium, or low.

B. Requires an observation that the three fraud conditions are present.

C. Follows the auditor's determination that the related controls are operating effectively.

D. Is based on evaluating whether the entity's related controls have been suitably designed and implemented.

Answer (D) is correct. *(Publisher, adapted)*

REQUIRED: The true statement about the assessment of identified fraud risks.

DISCUSSION: Identified and assessed fraud risks are treated as significant risks. Thus, the auditor obtains an understanding of the related controls relevant to the risks. This process includes evaluating whether the controls have been suitably designed and implemented to mitigate the fraud risks.

Answer (A) is incorrect. An overall judgment is too broad to be useful. Answer (B) is incorrect. An auditor must not assume that failing to observe all three conditions signifies that no fraud risk is present. Answer (C) is incorrect. The assessment is made after evaluating whether related controls have been suitably designed and implemented.

3.6.15. Which of the following statements describes why a properly planned and performed audit may not detect a material misstatement due to fraud?

A. Audit procedures that are effective for detecting an error may be ineffective for detecting fraud that is concealed through collusion.

B. An audit is designed to provide reasonable assurance of detecting material errors, but there is no similar responsibility concerning material fraud.

C. The factors considered in assessing the risk of material misstatement indicated an increased risk of intentional misstatements, but only a low risk of errors in the financial statements.

D. The auditor did not consider factors influencing audit risk for account balances that have effects pervasive to the financial statements as a whole.

Answer (A) is correct. *(CPA, adapted)*

REQUIRED: The reason a properly planned and performed audit may not detect a material fraud.

DISCUSSION: Absolute assurance is unattainable because of the characteristics of fraud and the limitations of audit evidence. Management may override controls in unpredictable ways or alter accounting records, and fraud may be concealed through collusion, falsifying documentation (including electronic approvals), or withholding evidence. Moreover, procedures that effectively detect an error (an unintentional misstatement) may not detect fraud (an intentional act that a perpetrator typically attempts to conceal).

Answer (B) is incorrect. The auditor's responsibility is the same for material misstatements due to fraud or error. Answer (C) is incorrect. A properly planned and performed audit will result in a response to fraud risks that have been identified and assessed. Answer (D) is incorrect. An audit that is properly planned and performed should consider audit risk factors for accounts having pervasive effects on the statements.

3.6.16. Which of the following situations represents a risk factor that relates to misstatements arising from misappropriation of assets?

A. A high turnover of senior management.

B. A lack of independent checks.

C. A strained relationship between management and the predecessor auditor.

D. An inability to generate cash flow from operations.

Answer (B) is correct. *(CPA, adapted)*

REQUIRED: The risk factor that relates to misstatements arising from misappropriation of assets.

DISCUSSION: Fraud in financial statements results from either fraudulent financial reporting by management or the misappropriation of assets by employees or others. Misappropriation of assets is mitigated by internal controls, including independent checks.

Answer (A) is incorrect. A high turnover of senior management represents a risk factor that relates to fraudulent financial reporting. Answer (C) is incorrect. A strained relationship between management and the predecessor auditor represents a risk factor that relates to fraudulent financial reporting. Answer (D) is incorrect. An inability to generate cash flow from operations represents a risk factor that relates to fraudulent financial reporting.

3.6.17. Which of the following procedures will an auditor most likely perform when evaluating audit evidence at the completion of the audit?

A. Obtain assurance from the entity's attorney that all material litigation has been disclosed in the financial statements.

B. Verify the clerical accuracy of the entity's proof of cash and its bank cutoff statement.

C. Determine whether inadequate provisions for the safeguarding of assets have been corrected.

D. Consider whether the results of audit procedures affect the assessment of the identified risks of material misstatement due to fraud.

Answer (D) is correct. *(CPA, adapted)*

REQUIRED: The procedure most likely performed when evaluating audit evidence at the completion of the audit.

DISCUSSION: AU-C 240 and AS 2110 state that the identified risks of material misstatement due to fraud should be assessed at the financial statement and assertion levels. This assessment is ongoing. Thus, at the audit's conclusion, the results of the audit procedures should be evaluated to determine whether they alter the assessments or indicate an unrecognized fraud risk. Furthermore, if not already performed to determine the overall conclusion, analytical procedures related to revenue should be performed through the end of the period.

Answer (A) is incorrect. Obtaining assurances from the client's attorney is a procedure performed during the audit and therefore prior to its completion. Answer (B) is incorrect. Testing cash is a procedure performed during the audit and therefore prior to its completion. Answer (C) is incorrect. Determining whether inadequate controls have been improved is a procedure performed during the audit and therefore prior to its completion.

3.6.18. Which of the following auditor concerns most likely could be so serious that the auditor concludes that a financial statement audit cannot be performed?

A. Management fails to modify prescribed internal controls for changes in information technology.

B. Internal control activities requiring segregation of duties are rarely monitored by management.

C. Management is dominated by one person who is also the majority shareholder.

D. There is a substantial risk of intentional misapplication of accounting principles.

Answer (D) is correct. *(CPA, adapted)*

REQUIRED: The auditor concern that is serious enough to lead the auditor to conclude that a financial statement audit cannot be performed.

DISCUSSION: According to AU-C 240, misstatements arising from fraudulent financial reporting are intentional misstatements or omissions to deceive financial statement users. The intentional misapplication of accounting principles relating to amounts, classification, manner of presentation, or disclosure is one such misstatement. The risk of material misstatement may be so significant that the auditor may be unable to continue the engagement. Because circumstances vary, for example, because of variations in the extent of fraud, the level of those involved in the fraud, and legal and regulatory requirements, the auditor's responses also vary.

Answer (A) is incorrect. A failure to modify prescribed internal controls does not necessarily indicate a lack of management integrity and require withdrawal from the engagement. However, the issue should be considered in assessing the risk of material misstatement. Answer (B) is incorrect. Depending on the nature of the duties, a lack of management monitoring does not necessarily indicate a lack of management integrity and require withdrawal from the engagement. However, the issue should be considered in assessing the risk of material misstatement. Answer (C) is incorrect. Domination of management by a single individual without compensating controls, such as oversight by an active board of directors or audit committee, is a weakness in the control environment. However, it is not serious enough for the auditor to conclude that a financial statement audit cannot be performed.

3.6.19. Which of the following circumstances is most likely to cause an auditor to change an assessment of the risk of material misstatement of the financial statements due to fraud?

A. Property and equipment are usually sold at a loss before being fully depreciated.

B. Unusual discrepancies between the entity's records and confirmation replies.

C. Monthly bank reconciliations usually include several in-transit items.

D. Clerical errors are listed on a computer-generated exception report.

Answer (B) is correct. *(CPA, adapted)*

REQUIRED: The circumstance most likely to change an assessment of the risk of material misstatement due to fraud.

DISCUSSION: An auditor's assessment of fraud risks must be ongoing. Conditions may be encountered during the field work that support or change the auditor's judgments. An example of such a condition is "unusual discrepancies between the entity's records and confirmation replies" (AU-C 240).

Answer (A) is incorrect. Sale at a loss before being fully depreciated suggests that the depreciation method is inadequate. Answer (C) is incorrect. In-transit items are normal. Answer (D) is incorrect. A listing of errors is an effective control.

3.6.20. Moor, CPA, discovers a likely fraud during an audit but concludes that its effects, if any, could not be so material as to affect the opinion. Moor most likely should

A. Perform additional audit procedures to establish that fraud has occurred.

B. Report the finding to the appropriate representatives of the client with the recommendation that it be pursued to a conclusion.

C. Confer with the client about the additional audit procedures necessary to establish that fraud has occurred.

D. Notify the proper external authorities.

Answer (B) is correct. *(Publisher, adapted)*

REQUIRED: The auditor's proper action when suspected fraud is not so material as to affect the opinion.

DISCUSSION: The auditor should refer the matter of an immaterial fraud to an appropriate level of management. The appropriate level of management ordinary is at least one level above the highest level involved. However, any fraud involving (1) management, (2) employees significantly involved in internal control, or (3) others when fraud materially misstates the financial statements, is reported to those charged with governance.

Answer (A) is incorrect. The auditor is not required to pursue immaterial errors. Answer (C) is incorrect. The auditor is not required to pursue fraud. Answer (D) is incorrect. The matter should be pursued with an appropriate level of management. But a statuary, regulatory, or other requirement may necessitate reporting to external authorities. For example, an auditor may be required to report misstatements to external authorities if management does not take corrective action.

3.6.21. An auditor's consideration of the risk of material misstatement due to fraud and the results of audit tests indicate a significant risk of fraud. The auditor should

A. Express either a qualified or an adverse opinion.

B. Consider withdrawing from the engagement and communicating the reasons for withdrawal to those charged with governance.

C. Express only an adverse opinion because of the strong possibility of fraud.

D. Inform proper authorities outside the entity.

Answer (B) is correct. *(Publisher, adapted)*

REQUIRED: The appropriate action by an auditor who has identified a significant risk of fraud.

DISCUSSION: If fraud risk is high, the auditor determines his or her responsibilities and considers withdrawing from the engagement. If the auditor withdraws, (s)he discusses the reasons with those charged with governance and determines whether reporting to others (e.g., regulators) is necessary.

Answer (A) is incorrect. A modified opinion is expressed only if (1) the financial statements are materially misstated, or (2) (a) the auditor cannot obtain sufficient appropriate evidence, and (b) the possible effects on the statements of undetected misstatements could be material and pervasive. Answer (C) is incorrect. An adverse opinion is appropriate only when the financial statements are not fairly presented. Answer (D) is incorrect. The auditor should inform proper authorities outside the entity only if required by law.

3.6.22. An auditor has withdrawn from an audit engagement of an issuer after finding fraud that may materially affect the financial statements. The auditor should set forth the reasons and findings in communication to the

A. PCAOB.

B. Client's legal counsel.

C. Stock exchanges where the company's stock is traded.

D. Board of directors.

Answer (D) is correct. *(CPA, adapted)*

REQUIRED: The party or parties to be notified when an auditor withdraws after finding fraud.

DISCUSSION: When the audit indicates the presence of error or fraud that requires a modification of the opinion, and the client refuses to accept the auditor's report as modified, the auditor should withdraw and communicate the reasons for withdrawal to the audit committee of the board. Withdrawal may or may not be appropriate in other circumstances, depending on the cooperation of management and the board.

Answer (A) is incorrect. The auditor is under no obligation to report fraud to outside parties, such as the PCAOB. The client firm, however, is required to disclose the reason for a change in auditors on SEC Form 8-K. In addition, the Private Securities Litigation Reform Act may require reports to the SEC about illegal acts. Answer (B) is incorrect. The auditor may wish to consult his or her legal counsel but not the client's counsel. Answer (C) is incorrect. The auditor is usually under no obligation to report fraud to outside parties.

3.6.23. Which of the following must an auditor document with respect to the consideration of fraud in a financial statement audit?

A. Reasons for not identifying management override as a fraud risk.

B. Reasons for not identifying collusion as a fraud risk.

C. Instances of the auditor's exercise of professional skepticism during the consideration of fraud.

D. Reasons for not identifying improper revenue recognition as a fraud risk.

Answer (D) is correct. *(Publisher, adapted)*

REQUIRED: The item that must be documented.

DISCUSSION: The auditor presumes the existence of a risk of material misstatement due to fraud related to revenue recognition. If the auditor concludes that the presumption is overcome in the circumstances of the engagement, the auditor should document the reasons for the conclusion (AU-C 240).

Answer (A) is incorrect. Management override is always a fraud risk because it is an inherent limitation of internal control. Thus, the results of procedures designed to address management override should be documented. Answer (B) is incorrect. The inherent limitations of an audit include the nature of auditing. For example, audit procedures for gathering evidence may not detect an intentional misstatement involving collusion. Thus, collusion is always a fraud risk. Answer (C) is incorrect. The auditor should approach every aspect of the audit with professional skepticism. Hence, specific, separate documentation of its exercise is not required.

3.7 Consideration of Laws and Regulations in an Audit of Financial Statements

3.7.1. Which of the following statements concerning noncompliance with laws and regulations by clients is correct?

A. An auditor has responsibility to detect noncompliance with laws and regulations that has a direct effect on the financial statements.

B. An audit in accordance with generally accepted auditing standards normally includes audit procedures specifically designed to detect noncompliance with laws and regulations having any effect on the financial statements.

C. Whether an act constitutes noncompliance with laws and regulations is a matter of auditor judgment.

D. An auditor has no responsibility to detect noncompliance with laws and regulations that has an effect on the financial statements.

Answer (A) is correct. *(Publisher, adapted)*

REQUIRED: The true statement concerning noncompliance with laws and regulations by clients.

DISCUSSION: According to AU-C 250, the auditor should obtain sufficient appropriate audit evidence regarding material amounts and disclosures in the financial statements that are determined by the provisions of those laws and regulations generally recognized to have a direct effect on their determination.

Answer (B) is incorrect. An audit in accordance with GAAS applies procedures to detect noncompliance having a direct effect in the determination of material amounts in the financial statements. Answer (C) is incorrect. Whether an act constitutes noncompliance with laws and regulations is a matter for legal determination. Answer (D) is incorrect. If illegal acts come to the auditor's attention, (s)he must undertake appropriate procedures.

3.7.2. The most likely reason the audit cannot reasonably be expected to bring all noncompliance with laws and regulations by the client to the auditor's attention is that

A. Noncompliance is perpetrated by management override of the information and communication component of internal control.

B. Noncompliance by clients often relates to operating aspects rather than accounting aspects.

C. The information and communication component of the client's internal control may be so effective that the auditor performs only minimal substantive testing.

D. Noncompliance may be attributed to the only person in the client's organization with access to both assets and the accounting records.

Answer (B) is correct. *(CPA, adapted)*

REQUIRED: The most likely reason an audit is not expected to detect all client noncompliance with laws and regulations.

DISCUSSION: Some noncompliance, such as violations of tax law, has a direct effect on the financial statements. Other noncompliance, such as violations of environmental protection laws, relates more to an entity's operating aspects than to its financial and accounting aspects, and their financial statement effect is indirect. An audit in accordance with GAAS usually does not include audit procedures specifically designed to detect noncompliance that has such indirect effects. Thus, no assurance is provided that such noncompliance will be detected or that resulting contingent liabilities will be disclosed. However, an audit should be designed to provide reasonable assurance that noncompliance having a direct and material effect on the financial statements will be detected.

Answer (A) is incorrect. Many acts of noncompliance are not subject to internal control; e.g., violations of insider trading rules may result from transactions that are recorded appropriately. Thus, no override of controls will be involved. Answer (C) is incorrect. Acts of noncompliance may involve matters outside the information and communication component, so even extensive substantive tests would not detect them. Answer (D) is incorrect. Noncompliance may not involve manipulation of records.

3.7.3. The auditor's responsibility for the detection of noncompliance with laws and regulations is greatest for laws and regulations that have

A. An indirect effect on financial statement amounts.

B. A direct effect on the financial statements that is either material or immaterial.

C. A direct effect on the determination of material amounts and disclosures in the financial statements.

D. All of the answers are correct.

Answer (C) is correct. *(Publisher, adapted)*

REQUIRED: The situation in which the auditor's responsibility to detect noncompliance with laws and regulations is the greatest.

DISCUSSION: An auditor is responsible for obtaining reasonable assurance that the financial statements are free of material misstatements, whether caused by fraud or error. This standard also applies to noncompliance with laws and regulations that are generally recognized to have a direct effect on the determination of material amounts and disclosures in the financial statements. Accordingly, the auditor should obtain sufficient appropriate audit evidence regarding material amounts and disclosures determined by such laws and regulations. However, other laws and regulations may have material but not direct effects on the financial statements. The auditor's responsibility is limited to performing specified audit procedures regarding these other laws and regulations.

Answer (A) is incorrect. The auditor performs only limited procedures regarding noncompliance with laws and regulations having indirect effects. Answer (B) is incorrect. The auditor provides no assurance about noncompliance having immaterial effects. Answer (D) is incorrect. The auditor's responsibility for laws and regulations that do not have direct effects is merely to perform certain specified procedures.

3.7.4. In a financial statement audit,

A. Regular audit procedures can reasonably be expected to detect all acts of noncompliance with laws and regulations.

B. The auditor should contact enforcement agencies when an act of noncompliance with laws and regulations is discovered.

C. The auditor should inquire of management about violations of laws and regulations as well as inspect correspondence with regulatory authorities.

D. Violations of laws having indirect effects on the financial statements are not of interest to the auditor.

Answer (C) is correct. *(Publisher, adapted)*

REQUIRED: The true statement about compliance.

DISCUSSION: Along with considering laws and regulations having a direct effect on the determination of material amounts and disclosures in the financial statements, the auditor should (1) inquire of management and, if appropriate, those charged with governance about compliance with other laws and regulations and (2) inspect correspondence from licensing and regulatory authorities.

Answer (A) is incorrect. The audit cannot be expected to detect all acts of noncompliance. Answer (B) is incorrect. The auditor is customarily not responsible for contacting outside agencies either in search of or to disclose acts of noncompliance. Answer (D) is incorrect. Acts of noncompliance relating to operating aspects of an entity are of interest to the auditor. They bear upon the integrity of management and may materially affect the financial statements.

3.7.5. When an auditor becomes aware of a possible act of noncompliance with laws or regulations, the auditor should obtain an understanding of the nature of the act to

A. Consider whether other similar acts have occurred.

B. Recommend remedial actions to those charged with governance.

C. Evaluate the effect on the financial statements.

D. Determine the reliability of management's representations.

Answer (C) is correct. *(CPA, adapted)*

REQUIRED: The reason the auditor obtains an understanding of the nature of a possible act of noncompliance with laws and regulations.

DISCUSSION: When the auditor becomes aware of information concerning possible noncompliance with laws or regulations, the auditor should obtain (1) an understanding of the nature of the act and the circumstances in which it occurred and (2) further information to evaluate the effect on the financial statements.

Answer (A) is incorrect. The auditor may consider whether other similar acts have occurred when applying any additional procedures necessary to obtain an understanding of the nature of the act. Answer (B) is incorrect. Recommending remedial actions to those charged with governance is a secondary objective of the audit. Answer (D) is incorrect. If the auditor determines that noncompliance has occurred, (s)he should assess the effects on the representations of management in other areas of the audit.

3.7.6. An audit in accordance with GAAS is most likely to include comprehensive audit procedures designed to detect material noncompliance by the client relating to

A. Environmental laws.

B. Tax laws.

C. Antitrust laws.

D. Insider trading rules.

Answer (B) is correct. *(Publisher, adapted)*

REQUIRED: The material illegal acts most likely to be detected by an audit in accordance with GAAS.

DISCUSSION: Some noncompliance, such as a violation of tax law, relates to laws and regulations that have a direct effect on the determination of material amounts and disclosures in the financial statements. Other noncompliance, such as a violation of environmental protection laws, relates to laws and regulations that do not have a direct effect. An audit usually includes only limited audit procedures specifically designed to detect noncompliance with laws and regulations of the second kind.

Answer (A) is incorrect. Environmental laws usually do not have direct effects. Answer (C) is incorrect. Antitrust laws usually do not have direct effects. Answer (D) is incorrect. Insider trading rules usually do not have direct effects.

3.7.7. During the annual audit of Ajax Corp., an issuer, Jones, CPA, a continuing auditor, determined that illegal political contributions had been made during each of the past 7 years, including the year under audit. Jones notified the board of directors about the illegal contributions, but they refused to take any action because the amounts involved were immaterial to the financial statements. Jones should reconsider the intended degree of reliance to be placed on the

A. Letter of audit inquiry to the client's attorney.

B. Prior years' audit plans.

C. Management representation letter.

D. Preliminary judgment about materiality levels.

Answer (C) is correct. *(CPA, adapted)*

REQUIRED: The effect on the auditor of the client's failure to take corrective action for noncompliance with laws and regulations.

DISCUSSION: If the client does not take the remedial action considered necessary by the auditor, the auditor should consider withdrawal from the engagement even when the violation is not material. (S)he should weigh the effects on his or her ability to rely on management's representations and the possible results of continued association with the client. The auditor may also wish to seek legal advice.

Answer (A) is incorrect. The letter of audit inquiry to the client's attorney will be responded to by the client's attorney, not the client. Answer (B) is incorrect. The prior years' audit plans will not be relied upon in the current audit. Answer (D) is incorrect. The results of the acts have been judged immaterial to the financial statements, and no reconsideration is necessary.

3.7.8. During the audit of a new client, the auditor determined that management had given illegal bribes to municipal officials during the year under audit and for several prior years. The auditor notified the client's board of directors, but the board decided to take no action because the amounts involved were immaterial to the financial statements. Under these circumstances, the auditor should

A. Add an explanatory paragraph emphasizing that certain matters, while not affecting the unmodified opinion, require disclosure.

B. Report the illegal bribes to the municipal official at least one level above those persons who received the bribes.

C. Consider withdrawing from the audit engagement and disassociating from future relationships with the client.

D. Issue an "except for" qualified opinion or an adverse opinion with a separate paragraph that explains the circumstances.

Answer (C) is correct. *(CPA, adapted)*

REQUIRED: The appropriate auditor action.

DISCUSSION: If the client does not take the remedial action the auditor deems necessary the auditor should consider withdrawal from the engagement even when the illegal bribes are not material. The auditor should determine (1) the effects on the ability to rely on management's representations and (2) the possible results of continued association with the client. The auditor may wish to seek legal advice (AU-C 250).

Answer (A) is incorrect. Illegal bribes may not require disclosure. However, remedial action is expected by the auditor. Answer (B) is incorrect. The auditor has no responsibility to report illegal bribes to the external organization associated with the bribes. Answer (D) is incorrect. Immaterial items do not affect the fairness of the financial statements. Thus, a modified opinion is not necessary.

3.7.9. If the auditor considers an act of noncompliance with laws and regulations to be sufficiently serious to warrant withdrawing from the engagement, the auditor would likely

A. Notify all parties who may rely upon the company's financial statements of the company's illegal act.

B. Consult with legal counsel as to what other action, if any, should be taken.

C. Return all incriminating evidence and working papers to the client's audit committee for follow-up.

D. Contact the successor auditor to make the successor aware of the possible consequences of relying on management's representations.

Answer (B) is correct. *(CPA, adapted)*

REQUIRED: The action by an auditor who withdraws as a result of noncompliance with laws and regulations.

DISCUSSION: According to AU-C 250, the auditor should consider consulting legal counsel in these circumstances. Such consultation may be necessary in determining the effects of continued association with the client or whether the auditor may have a duty to notify parties outside the client that overrides his or her duty of confidentiality to the client.

Answer (A) is incorrect. Notifying others is the responsibility of management. Answer (C) is incorrect. The auditor has no responsibility to return all incriminating evidence and working papers to the client's audit committee for follow-up. Answer (D) is incorrect. The successor auditor, with client approval, has the burden of initiating communication with the predecessor.

3.7.10. Under the Private Securities Litigation Reform Act of 1995, Baker, CPA, reported certain noncompliance with laws and regulations to Supermart's board of directors. Baker believed that failure to take remedial action would warrant a qualified audit opinion because the noncompliance had a material effect on Supermart's financial statements. Supermart failed to take appropriate remedial action, and the board of directors refused to inform the SEC that it had received such notification from Baker. Under these circumstances, Baker is required to

A. Resign from the audit engagement within 10 business days.

B. Deliver a report concerning the noncompliance to the SEC within 1 business day.

C. Notify the shareholders that the financial statements are materially misstated.

D. Withhold an audit opinion until Supermart takes appropriate remedial action.

Answer (B) is correct. *(CPA, adapted)*

REQUIRED: The requirements under the Private Securities Litigation Reform Act of 1995.

DISCUSSION: Disclosure of noncompliance with laws and regulations to outside parties is not normally the auditor's responsibility. However, under the Private Securities Litigation Reform Act of 1995, accountants must report noncompliance to the appropriate level of management and the audit committee unless it is clearly inconsequential. If senior management and the board fail to take action on reported material noncompliance, and this failure will result in a departure from a standard report or resignation from the audit, the accountants should report their conclusions to the board immediately. The board must then, within 1 business day, notify the SEC. If the accountants do not receive a copy of the notice within the 1-day period, they must furnish the SEC with a copy of their report within 1 business day.

Answer (A) is incorrect. The auditor is not required to resign from the engagement. Answer (C) is incorrect. A qualified audit opinion states that, except for the effects of the matter to which the qualification relates, the financial statements are presented fairly in all material respects. Any other notice to the shareholders is not required. Answer (D) is incorrect. The auditor should express a qualified opinion if it is justified by the lack of remedial action. GAAS do not provide for a delay in the report until remedial action is taken.

STUDY UNIT FOUR
STRATEGIC PLANNING ISSUES

This study unit considers issues that are fundamental to planning an audit. Moreover, most of the issues considered in this study unit affect other elements of the audit, including evidence collection and reporting.

QUESTIONS

4.1 Using the Work of Internal Auditors

4.1.1. The independent auditor should understand the internal audit function as it relates to internal control because

A. The audit programs, audit documentation, and reports of internal auditors may often be used as a substitute for the work of the independent auditor's staff.

B. The procedures performed by the internal audit staff may eliminate the independent auditor's need for considering internal control.

C. The work performed by internal auditors may be a factor in determining the nature, timing, and extent of the independent auditor's procedures.

D. The understanding of the internal audit function is an important substantive test to be performed by the independent auditor.

Answer (C) is correct. *(CPA, adapted)*

REQUIRED: The reason the independent auditor should understand the internal audit function.

DISCUSSION: The auditor should obtain an understanding of the internal audit function when obtaining an understanding of the client's internal control. The understanding should be sufficient to identify internal audit activities relevant to audit planning. Thus, an internal audit function is one of many factors to be considered in determining the nature, timing, and extent of audit procedures.

Answer (A) is incorrect. Programs, audit documentation, and reports of internal auditors may never be used to substitute for the work of the auditor's staff. Answer (B) is incorrect. AU-C 315 requires the auditor to obtain an understanding of internal control and to assess the risks of material misstatement. Answer (D) is incorrect. The understanding of the internal audit function is part of the auditor's consideration of internal control, not a substantive procedure.

4.1.2. Which of the following is a false statement about the relationship of the internal auditor and the scope of the external audit of a company's financial statements?

A. The nature, timing, and extent of the external auditor's substantive tests may be affected by the work of the internal auditors.

B. The internal auditors may assist the external auditor in performing substantive tests and tests of controls under certain circumstances.

C. The external auditor is not required to give consideration to the internal audit function beyond obtaining an understanding sufficient to identify activities relevant to planning the audit.

D. The internal auditors may determine the extent to which audit procedures should be employed by the external auditor.

Answer (D) is correct. *(CMA, adapted)*

REQUIRED: The false statement about the relationship between the internal auditor and external auditor.

DISCUSSION: If the external auditor plans to use the work of the internal auditors to obtain audit evidence or to provide direct assistance, the auditor should assess the competence and objectivity of the internal auditors. If they are sufficiently competent and objective, the auditor may then consider how (not whether) their work will affect the audit.

Answer (A) is incorrect. The work of the internal auditors may affect the substantive procedures performed by the external auditor. Answer (B) is incorrect. Internal auditors may directly assist in substantive procedures and tests of controls if their competence and objectivity are assessed and their work is properly supervised, reviewed, evaluated, and tested. Answer (C) is incorrect. The auditor must obtain an understanding of the internal audit function but may conclude that the activities of the internal auditors are not relevant to the audit. The auditor may also conclude that further consideration of their activities is not efficient or that they lack sufficient competence and objectivity.

4.1.3. In assessing the objectivity of internal auditors, the independent CPA who is auditing the entity's financial statements most likely considers the

A. Internal auditing standards developed by The Institute of Internal Auditors.

B. Tests of internal control activities that could detect errors and fraud.

C. Materiality of the accounts recently inspected by the internal auditors.

D. Results of the tests of transactions recently performed by the internal auditors.

Answer (A) is correct. *(Publisher, adapted)*

REQUIRED: The factor an independent CPA most likely considers when assessing the objectivity of an entity's internal auditors.

DISCUSSION: According to AU-C 610, the external auditor should obtain an understanding of the internal audit function (part of the entity's monitoring component) when obtaining the understanding of internal control. The purpose is to identify internal audit activities relevant to a financial statement audit. One inquiry customarily made is about the application of professional standards by the internal auditors. If the external auditor plans to use the work of the internal auditors to obtain evidence or to provide direct assistance, (s)he should assess the competence and objectivity of the internal auditors. Compliance with the internal auditing standards developed by The Institute of Internal Auditors or by the Government Accountability Office is one measure of the competence and objectivity of internal auditors. These standards require internal auditors to be objective in performing their work.

Answer (B) is incorrect. Tests of internal control activities that could detect errors and fraud concern the effects of the internal auditor's work on the audit. Answer (C) is incorrect. Materiality of the accounts recently inspected by the internal auditors concerns the effects of the internal auditor's work on the audit. Answer (D) is incorrect. Results of the tests of transactions recently performed by the internal auditors concern the effects of the internal auditor's work on the audit.

4.1.4. If the auditors plan to use the work of the internal auditors to obtain audit evidence or to provide direct assistance, they should assess the internal auditors'

A. Competence and objectivity.

B. Efficiency and experience.

C. Independence and review skills.

D. Training and supervisory skills.

Answer (A) is correct. *(CPA, adapted)*

REQUIRED: The internal auditors' traits that the independent auditors should consider.

DISCUSSION: If the external auditor decides to use the work of the internal auditors, the competence and objectivity of the internal auditors should be assessed. Assessing competence involves obtaining information about (1) education and experience; (2) professional certification and CPE; (3) audit policies, programs, and procedures; (4) practices regarding assignment of internal auditors; (5) supervision and review of their activities; (6) quality of audit documentation, reports, and recommendations; and (7) evaluation of internal auditors' performance. Assessing objectivity includes obtaining information about (1) organizational status (the level to which the internal auditors report, access to those charged with governance, and whether these individuals oversee employment decisions related to the internal auditors) and (2) policies to maintain internal auditors' objectivity concerning the areas audited (AU-C 610).

Answer (B) is incorrect. Competence encompasses the traits of efficiency and experience. Moreover, objectivity also must be assessed. Answer (C) is incorrect. Internal auditors are not independent in the sense intended by the *Code of Professional Conduct* and GAAS. Answer (D) is incorrect. Competence encompasses training and supervisory skills. Moreover, objectivity also must be assessed.

4.1.5. For which of the following judgments may an independent auditor share responsibility with an entity's internal auditor who is assessed to be both competent and objective?

	Materiality of Misstatements	Evaluation of Significant Accounting Estimates
A.	Yes	No
B.	No	Yes
C.	Yes	Yes
D.	No	No

Answer (D) is correct. *(CPA, adapted)*

REQUIRED: The judgment(s) for which an auditor may share responsibility with an internal auditor.

DISCUSSION: The responsibility to report on financial statements is solely the auditor's. It cannot be shared with internal auditors. Because the auditor has the ultimate responsibility to express an opinion on the financial statements, judgments about (1) assessments of RMMs, (2) materiality of misstatements, (3) sufficiency of tests performed, (4) evaluation of significant accounting estimates, and (5) other matters affecting the auditor's report always should be those of the auditor.

4.1.6. In assessing the competence and objectivity of an entity's internal auditor, an independent auditor would least likely consider information obtained from

A. Discussions with management personnel.

B. External quality reviews of the internal auditor's activities.

C. Previous experience with the internal auditor.

D. The results of analytical procedures.

Answer (D) is correct. *(CPA, adapted)*

REQUIRED: The least likely procedure in assessing the competence and objectivity of an entity's internal auditor.

DISCUSSION: Analytical procedures are evaluations of financial information made by a study of plausible relationships among both financial and nonfinancial data, using models that range from simple to complex. They are substantive procedures used by the auditor to gather evidence about the fairness of the financial statements.

4.1.7. Internal auditing can affect the scope of the external auditor's audit of financial statements by

A. Decreasing the external auditor's need to perform detailed tests.

B. Allowing the external auditor to limit his or her audit to substantive testing.

C. Limiting direct testing by the external auditor to assertions not directly tested by internal auditing.

D. Eliminating the need to be on hand during the physical count of inventory.

Answer (A) is correct. *(CIA, adapted)*

REQUIRED: The effect of internal auditing on the scope of the external audit.

DISCUSSION: The work of the internal auditors may affect the nature, timing, and extent of the audit procedures, which include those for understanding internal control, assessing the risk of material misstatement, and performing substantive procedures.

Answer (B) is incorrect. The external auditor always should obtain an understanding of internal control and assess the risk of material misstatement. Answer (C) is incorrect. The auditor should perform direct tests of assertions related to material financial statement amounts if the risk of material misstatement or the subjectivity involved in the evaluation of audit evidence is high. Answer (D) is incorrect. The external auditor should observe the client's physical inventory.

4.1.8. In assessing the competence of an internal auditor, an independent CPA most likely would obtain information about the

A. Quality of the internal auditor's documentation.

B. Organization's commitment to integrity and ethical values.

C. Influence of management on the scope of the internal auditor's duties.

D. Organizational levels to which the internal auditor reports.

Answer (A) is correct. *(CPA, adapted)*

REQUIRED: The information needed to assess the competence of an internal auditor.

DISCUSSION: In assessing the competence of an internal auditor the auditor should consider such factors as (1) educational level and professional experience; (2) professional certification and continuing education; (3) audit policies, programs, and procedures (4) supervision and review of the internal auditor's activities; (5) practices regarding assignments; (6) quality of documentation, reports, and recommendations; and (7) evaluation of the internal auditor's performance.

Answer (B) is incorrect. The organization's commitment to integrity and ethical values relates to objectivity rather than competence. Answer (C) is incorrect. The influence of management on the scope of the internal auditor's duties relates to objectivity rather than competence. Answer (D) is incorrect. The organizational levels to which the internal auditor reports relate to objectivity rather than competence.

4.1.9. During an audit, an internal auditor may provide direct assistance to an independent CPA in

	Obtaining an Understanding of Internal Control	Performing Tests of Controls	Performing Substantive Tests
A.	No	No	No
B.	Yes	No	No
C.	Yes	Yes	No
D.	Yes	Yes	Yes

Answer (D) is correct. *(CPA, adapted)*

REQUIRED: The types of direct assistance an internal auditor may provide to an independent CPA.

DISCUSSION: The auditor may request direct assistance from the internal auditor when performing the audit. Thus, the auditor may appropriately request the internal auditor's assistance in obtaining the understanding of internal control, performing tests of controls, or performing substantive procedures (AU-C 610). The internal auditor may provide assistance in all phases of the audit as long as (1) the internal auditor's competence and objectivity have been tested, and (2) the independent auditor supervises, reviews, evaluates, and tests the work performed by the internal auditor to the extent appropriate.

4.2 Using the Work of a Specialist

4.2.1. Which of the following statements is true about the use of the work of an auditor's specialist?

A. The specialist need not agree to the auditor's use of the specialist's findings.

B. The auditor is required to perform substantive procedures to verify the specialist's assumptions and findings.

C. The auditor must keep client information confidential, but the specialist is not obligated to do so.

D. The auditor should obtain an understanding of the methods and assumptions used by the specialist.

Answer (D) is correct. *(CPA, adapted)*

REQUIRED: The true statement about the auditor's use of the work of an auditor's specialist.

DISCUSSION: AU-C 620, *Using the Work of an Auditor's Specialist*, states that the auditor should evaluate the adequacy of the work of the auditor's specialist. This process includes (1) obtaining an understanding of any significant assumptions and methods used by the specialist and (2) evaluating the relevance and reasonableness of those assumptions and methods in the circumstances and in relation to the auditor's other findings and conclusions.

Answer (A) is incorrect. The auditor should agree with the specialist, in writing if appropriate, about various matters, such as their roles and responsibilities. These may include consent for the auditor to include details of the specialist's findings or conclusions in the basis for a modified opinion paragraph in the auditor's report. Answer (B) is incorrect. The auditor should understand the assumptions and methods and evaluate their relevance and reasonableness, not verify them. But the auditor may perform corroborative procedures on the specialist's findings and conclusions, e.g., reperformance of calculations and performance of detailed analytical procedures. Answer (C) is incorrect. The auditor should establish an agreement with the specialist to maintain confidentiality.

4.2.2. An auditor referred to the findings of an auditor's external specialist in the auditor's report. This may be an appropriate reporting practice if the

A. Auditor is not familiar with the professional certification, personal reputation, or particular competence of the specialist.

B. Auditor, as a result of the specialist's findings, adds a paragraph emphasizing a matter regarding the financial statements.

C. Auditor's report contains a qualified opinion.

D. Auditor, as a result of the specialist's findings, decides to indicate a division of responsibility with the specialist for the audit opinion.

Answer (C) is correct. *(CPA, adapted)*

REQUIRED: The instance in which an auditor may refer to an auditor's specialist's findings.

DISCUSSION: The auditor refers to the work of an auditor's external specialist because it is relevant to a modification of the opinion. In these circumstances, the report should indicate that the reference does not reduce the auditor's responsibility for the opinion. If the auditor's report contains an unmodified opinion, the auditor should not refer to the work of an auditor's specialist (AU-C 620). A modified opinion is a qualified opinion, an adverse opinion, or a disclaimer of opinion (AU-C 705).

Answer (A) is incorrect. The auditor should evaluate the auditor's specialist's competence, capabilities, and objectivity regardless of whether the auditor's report refers to the specialist. Answer (B) is incorrect. An emphasis-of-matter paragraph or an other-matter paragraph may be included in the auditor's report when the opinion is unmodified or modified. Thus, an emphasis-of-matter paragraph is not a basis for referring to a specialist. Answer (D) is incorrect. The auditor has sole responsibility for the audit opinion.

4.2.3. Which of the following is not considered an auditor's specialist?

A. Actuary.

B. Appraiser.

C. Internal auditor.

D. Tax attorney.

Answer (C) is correct. *(CPA, adapted)*

REQUIRED: The individual not considered an auditor's specialist.

DISCUSSION: For the purposes of AU-C 620, an auditor's specialist is an individual or organization possessing expertise in a field other than accounting or auditing. The external auditor should consider the work of internal auditors but should not deem them to be specialists in the sense contemplated by AU-C 620.

Answer (A) is incorrect. Expertise in a field other than accounting or auditing may include actuarial calculation of insurance or employee pension liabilities. Answer (B) is incorrect. Expertise in a field other than accounting or auditing may include valuation of nonfinancial assets, such as land and buildings, jewelry, or antiques. Answer (D) is incorrect. Expertise in a field other than accounting or auditing may include tax law. A tax attorney is a specialist for the purposes of AU-C 620 because the emphasis is on legal, not accounting or auditing, expertise.

4.2.4. In using the work of an auditor's external specialist, an agreement should exist between the auditor and the specialist as to the nature of the specialist's work. This agreement most likely should include

A. A statement that the specialist assumes no responsibility to update the specialist's report for future events or circumstances.

B. The conditions under which a division of responsibility may be necessary.

C. The applicability of the same confidentiality requirements to the auditor and the specialist.

D. The auditor's disclaimer as to whether the specialist's findings corroborate the representations in the financial statements.

Answer (C) is correct. *(CPA, adapted)*

REQUIRED: The matter covered in the agreement about the work of an auditor's external specialist.

DISCUSSION: The agreement should be documented and should cover (1) the nature, objectives, and scope of the work; (2) the roles of the auditor and specialist; (3) the nature, timing, and extent of communications between the auditor and specialist; and (4) the need for the specialist to observe confidentiality requirements. The agreement between the auditor and the auditor's external specialist generally is documented in an engagement letter. A matter that should be included is the need for the confidentiality provisions of the relevant ethical requirements that apply to the auditor also to apply to the specialist. For example, a member of the AICPA may use a third-party service provider to render professional services to clients. The member should have a contract with the third-party service provider to maintain the confidentiality of the information (Ethics Ruling). Other requirements may be imposed by law or regulation.

Answer (A) is incorrect. The agreement need not contain a disclaimer about the specialist's responsibility to update the report. Answer (B) is incorrect. The auditor may not divide responsibility with the specialist. Answer (D) is incorrect. The agreement need not contain a disclaimer about whether the findings corroborate the representations.

4.2.5. When a management's specialist has assumed full responsibility for taking the client's physical inventory, reliance on the specialist's work is acceptable if

A. The auditor is satisfied with the competence of the specialist.

B. Circumstances made it impracticable or impossible for the auditor to test the work done by the specialist.

C. The auditor conducted the same audit tests and procedures as would have been applicable if the client employees took the physical inventory.

D. The auditor's report contains a reference to the assumption of full responsibility by the specialist.

Answer (C) is correct. *(CPA, adapted)*

REQUIRED: The basis for relying on the work of an outside inventory specialist.

DISCUSSION: The auditor is responsible for the observation of inventories. The auditor performs this procedure whether the client or an external specialist takes the physical inventory. The auditor should (1) examine the specialist's program, (2) observe its procedures and controls, (3) make or observe some physical counts, (4) recompute calculations, and (5) test intervening transactions.

Answer (A) is incorrect. Although the auditor is concerned with the competence of the specialist, (s)he still should become satisfied as to the existence of the inventory. Answer (B) is incorrect. The auditor usually cannot express an unmodified opinion unless (s)he has made or observed some physical counts. Answer (D) is incorrect. The auditor cannot assign responsibility to a specialist.

4.3 Related Parties

4.3.1. Which of the following steps should an auditor perform first to determine the existence of related parties?

A. Examine invoices, contracts, and purchasing orders.

B. Inquire about the existence of related parties from management.

C. Review the company's business structure.

D. Review proxy and other materials filed with the SEC.

Answer (B) is correct. *(CPA, adapted)*

REQUIRED: The first step the auditor should perform to determine the existence of related parties.

DISCUSSION: When obtaining an understanding of the entity's related party relationships and transactions, the auditor should inquire of management regarding (1) the identity of the entity's related parties, including changes from the prior period; (2) the relationships of the entity with those parties; and (3) the types and purposes of transactions with them.

Answer (A) is incorrect. The auditor should be aware of the possibility of related parties when examining invoices, contracts, and purchasing orders. However, the first step should be to request a list from management. Answer (C) is incorrect. The business structure can provide the auditor with expectations about the likelihood of related parties. However, the auditor should first request a list from management. Answer (D) is incorrect. The auditor may review proxy and other materials filed with the SEC for possible related parties. However, the auditor should first request a list from management.

4.3.2. Which of the following would not necessarily be a related party transaction?

A. A sale to another corporation with a similar name.

B. A purchase from another corporation that is controlled by the corporation's chief shareholder.

C. Loan from the corporation to a major shareholder.

D. Sale of land to the corporation by the spouse of a director.

Answer (A) is correct. *(CPA, adapted)*

REQUIRED: The transaction not necessarily with a related party.

DISCUSSION: A related party is a party defined as such in the applicable financial reporting framework. For example, U.S. GAAP define related parties to include (1) affiliates; (2) equity-method investees or investees that would be equity-method investees if the fair value option had not been elected; (3) employee trusts; (4) management, principal owners, and their immediate families; (5) other parties with which the entity may deal if one party controls or can be significantly influenced by the other to the extent that a party may be prevented from pursuing its separate interests; and (6) other parties that can significantly influence the transacting parties to the extent that a party may be prevented from pursuing its separate interests. A corporation that merely has a similar name is not necessarily related.

Answer (B) is incorrect. A purchase from another corporation that is controlled by the corporation's chief shareholder is a related party transaction. Answer (C) is incorrect. A loan from the corporation to a major shareholder is a related party transaction. Answer (D) is incorrect. A sale of land to the corporation by the spouse of a director is a related party transaction.

4.3.3. Which of the following statements is true about related party transactions?

A. In the absence of evidence to the contrary, related party transactions should be assumed to be outside the ordinary course of business.

B. An auditor should determine whether a particular transaction would have occurred if the parties had not been related.

C. An auditor should substantiate that related party transactions were consummated on terms equivalent to those that prevail in arm's-length transactions.

D. The auditor should consider whether an identified related party transaction outside the normal course of business is appropriately accounted for and disclosed.

Answer (D) is correct. *(CPA, adapted)*

REQUIRED: The true statement about related party transactions.

DISCUSSION: The auditor should inspect any contracts or agreements to evaluate whether (1) the business purpose (or lack of a business purpose) implies that the transaction's intent was fraudulent, (2) the terms are consistent with management's explanations, and (3) the accounting and disclosure are appropriate. The auditor also should obtain evidence of appropriate authorization and approval.

Answer (A) is incorrect. In the absence of contrary evidence, related party transactions are assumed to be in the ordinary course of business. Answer (B) is incorrect. Determining whether a particular transaction would have occurred if the parties had not been related is ordinarily not an objective of the audit. Answer (C) is incorrect. The auditor should obtain sufficient appropriate evidence about a management assertion that related party transactions were conducted on terms equivalent to those that prevail in arm's-length transactions. Management is responsible for substantiating the assertion. The auditor evaluates management's support for the assertion.

4.3.4. After identifying a significant related party transaction outside the entity's normal course of business, an auditor should

A. Add an emphasis-of-matter paragraph to the auditor's report to explain the transaction.

B. Perform analytical procedures to identify similar transactions that were not recorded.

C. Evaluate the business purpose of the transaction.

D. Substantiate that the transaction was consummated on terms equivalent to those of an arm's-length transaction.

Answer (C) is correct. *(CPA, adapted)*

REQUIRED: The procedure performed after identifying a significant related party transaction outside the entity's normal course of business.

DISCUSSION: The auditor should inspect any contracts or agreements to evaluate whether (1) the business purpose (or lack of a business purpose) implies that the transaction's intent was fraudulent, (2) the terms are consistent with management's explanations, and (3) the accounting and disclosure are appropriate. The auditor also should obtain evidence of appropriate authorization and approval.

Answer (A) is incorrect. If (1) the transaction has been properly accounted for and disclosed, and (2) its effects do not prevent fair presentation of the statements, no modification of the opinion is required. But the auditor may wish to add a separate paragraph emphasizing that the entity has had a significant related party transaction (AU-C 706). Answer (B) is incorrect. Analytical procedures are not suitable for identifying particular unrecorded transactions. But the auditor should be alert when inspecting documents or records for indications of unidentified related party relationships or transactions. Answer (D) is incorrect. The auditor normally cannot determine whether a transaction was consummated on terms equivalent to those of an arm's-length transaction. Instead, management is responsible for substantiating the assertion about the transaction. Thus, the auditor should evaluate management's support for the assertion.

4.3.5. Ajax, Inc., is an affiliate of the audit client and is audited by another firm of auditors. Which of the following is most likely to be used by the auditor of the client to obtain assurance that all guarantees of the affiliate's indebtedness have been detected?

A. Send the standard bank confirmation request to all of the client's lender banks.

B. Review client minutes and obtain a representation letter.

C. Examine supporting documents for all entries in intercompany accounts.

D. Obtain written confirmation of indebtedness from the auditor of the affiliate.

Answer (B) is correct. *(CPA, adapted)*

REQUIRED: The procedure most likely to be used to obtain assurance that all guarantees of an affiliate's indebtedness have been identified.

DISCUSSION: The entity's auditor should review minutes of board of directors and relevant committee meetings and obtain a representation letter to obtain assurance that all guarantees of the affiliate's indebtedness have been identified.

Answer (A) is incorrect. Bank confirmations sent to the entity's lender banks would not detect guarantees of indebtedness to nonbank creditors. Answer (C) is incorrect. Guarantees are not reflected in the accounts. Answer (D) is incorrect. External confirmations, per se, are not typically obtained from other auditors.

4.3.6. In the absence of evidence to the contrary, transactions with related parties should not be assumed to be outside the normal course of business. The auditor should, however, be aware of the possibility that transactions with related parties may have been motivated solely or in large part by extraordinary conditions. Which of the following is not normally a condition motivating a transaction outside the normal course of business?

A. Lack of sufficient working capital or credit to continue business.

B. An overly optimistic earnings forecast.

C. Dependence on a single or relatively few product(s), customer(s), or transaction(s) for the ongoing success of the venture.

D. Mutual benefit to both parties.

Answer (D) is correct. *(Publisher, adapted)*

REQUIRED: The condition not considered a motive for a transaction outside the normal course of business.

DISCUSSION: Parties customarily execute transactions that are mutually beneficial. These are considered within the normal course of business. The absence of mutual benefit is an indication that the transaction is not at arm's-length and that special disclosure is required to prevent the statements from being misleading. Thus, related party transactions may indicate an increased risk of material misstatement of the statements.

Answer (A) is incorrect. Lack of sufficient working capital or credit to continue business is a condition motivating a transaction outside of the normal course of business. Other such conditions include (1) a declining industry characterized by a large number of business failures; (2) excess capacity; (3) significant litigation, especially litigation between shareholders and management; and (4) significant danger of obsolescence because the company is in a high-technology industry. Answer (B) is incorrect. An overly optimistic earnings forecast is a condition motivating a transaction outside of the normal course of business. Answer (C) is incorrect. Dependence on a single or relatively few product(s), customer(s), or transaction(s) for the ongoing success of the venture is a condition motivating a transaction outside of the normal course of business.

4.3.7. An auditor searching for related party transactions should obtain an understanding of each subsidiary's relationship to the total entity because

A. This may permit the audit of interentity account balances to be performed as of concurrent dates.

B. Interentity transactions may have been consummated on terms equivalent to arm's-length transactions.

C. This may reveal whether particular transactions would have taken place if the parties had not been related.

D. The business structure may be deliberately designed to obscure related party transactions.

Answer (D) is correct. *(CPA, adapted)*

REQUIRED: The reason for understanding parent-subsidiary relationships when searching for related party transactions.

DISCUSSION: The nature of related party relationships and transactions may result in greater risks of material misstatement than transactions with unrelated parties. Thus, related parties may operate through a complex set of relationships and structures, with increased complexity of related party transactions. For example, a transaction may involve multiple related parties in a consolidated group. Accordingly, in an audit of group statements, the group engagement team should request each component auditor to communicate with related parties not previously identified by group management or the group engagement team.

Answer (A) is incorrect. A concurrent audit is not required. Answer (B) is incorrect. The auditor's concern is that related party transactions were not at arm's length. Answer (C) is incorrect. Determining whether a transaction would have occurred and what the terms would have been if the parties were unrelated is not normally an objective of an audit.

4.3.8. An auditor would be most likely to consider modifying an otherwise unmodified opinion if the client's financial statements include a note on related party transactions

A. Representing without substantiation that certain related party transactions were consummated on terms equivalent to those obtainable in transactions with unrelated parties.

B. Presenting the dollar volume of related party transactions and the effects of any change in the method of establishing terms from that used in the prior period.

C. Explaining the business purpose of the sale of real property to a related party.

D. Disclosing compensating balance arrangements maintained for the benefit of related parties.

Answer (A) is correct. *(CPA, adapted)*

REQUIRED: The most likely basis for expressing a qualified opinion.

DISCUSSION: It is most often not possible to determine whether a particular transaction would have occurred if the parties had not been related or what the terms and manner of settlement would have been. Accordingly, assertions about such matters are difficult to substantiate. The auditor may (1) believe that the assertion is unsubstantiated or (2) not be able to obtain sufficient appropriate evidence. In these cases, the auditor considers the implications for the audit, including whether to modify the opinion (AU-C 550 and AS 2410). (S)he should consider including in the report a comment to that effect and expressing a qualified or adverse opinion.

Answer (B) is incorrect. The dollar volume of related party transactions and the effects of any change in the method of establishing terms are required disclosures. Answer (C) is incorrect. The business purpose of the sale of real property to a related party is a required disclosure. Answer (D) is incorrect. Compensating balance arrangements maintained for the benefit of related parties are required disclosures.

4.3.9. When auditing related party transactions, an auditor places primary emphasis on

A. Confirming the existence of the related parties.

B. Verifying the valuation of the related party transactions.

C. Assessing the risks of material misstatement of related party transactions.

D. Ascertaining the rights and obligations of the related parties.

Answer (C) is correct. *(Publisher, adapted)*

REQUIRED: The primary concern of the auditor about related party transactions.

DISCUSSION: The auditor has a responsibility to perform audit procedures to identify, assess, and respond to the risks of material misstatement arising from the entity's failure to appropriately account for or disclose related party relationships, transactions, or balances.

4.3.10. Which of the following is an unusual procedure that may be deemed necessary to discover the effect of a related party transaction?

A. Examine invoices and other pertinent documents such as receiving or shipping reports.

B. Confirm significant information with third parties other than banks or attorneys.

C. Determine whether the transaction has been approved by management, those charged with governance, or shareholders.

D. Inspect or confirm the transferability and value of collateral.

Answer (B) is correct. *(Publisher, adapted)*

REQUIRED: The unusual procedure to discover the effect of a related party transaction.

DISCUSSION: To understand fully a related party transaction, certain procedures not otherwise required to comply with auditing standards should be considered. Third-party confirmations (other than bank and legal confirmations) are unusual procedures that might be applied when necessary to understand a related party transaction.

4.3.11. U.S. GAAP ordinarily require material related party transactions to be

A. Accounted for differently from transactions between unrelated parties but not separately disclosed.

B. Accounted for on the same basis as transactions between unrelated parties and not separately disclosed.

C. Separately disclosed but not accounted for differently from transactions between unrelated parties.

D. Separately disclosed and accounted for differently from transactions between unrelated parties.

Answer (C) is correct. *(Publisher, adapted)*

REQUIRED: The accounting treatment of material related party transactions.

DISCUSSION: Certain accounting pronouncements prescribe accounting treatment when related parties are involved. However, U.S. GAAP ordinarily do not require transactions with related parties to be accounted for on a basis different from what would be appropriate if the parties were not related.

4.4 Accounting Estimates and Fair Value

4.4.1. When performing procedures to identify and assess the risks of material misstatement for accounting estimates, the auditor should

A. Review transactions occurring prior to the date of the auditor's report that indicate variations from expectations.

B. Compare independent expectations with recorded estimates to assess management's process.

C. Obtain an understanding of how management developed its estimates.

D. Analyze historical data used in developing assumptions to determine whether the process is consistent.

Answer (C) is correct. *(CPA, adapted)*

REQUIRED: The procedure performed to assess risks related to accounting estimates.

DISCUSSION: The auditor performs risk assessment procedures to provide a basis for identifying and assessing the RMMs for accounting estimates. Thus, the auditor obtains an understanding of the following: (1) the relevant requirements of the applicable financial reporting framework, (2) how management identifies factors that create a need for estimates, and (3) how management makes estimates and the data on which they are based (e.g., methods, models, controls, use of specialists, underlying assumptions, and whether and how the effects of estimation uncertainty are assessed).

Answer (A) is incorrect. The auditor should review transactions after obtaining an understanding of how management developed the estimates. Answer (B) is incorrect. The auditor should compare independent expectations and reported estimates after obtaining an understanding of how management developed the estimates. Answer (D) is incorrect. The auditor should analyze historical data after obtaining an understanding of how management developed the estimates.

4.4.2. Which of the following procedures will most likely assist an auditor in determining whether management has identified all accounting estimates that could be material to the financial statements?

A. Inquire about the existence of related party transactions.

B. Determine whether the outcomes of accounting estimates differ from the amounts originally recognized.

C. Confirm inventories at locations outside the entity.

D. Review the lawyer's letter for information about litigation.

Answer (D) is correct. *(CPA, adapted)*

REQUIRED: The procedure to determine whether management has identified all material accounting estimates.

DISCUSSION: The response to the letter of audit inquiry sent to the client's lawyer may help the auditor to determine whether material estimates have been identified concerning litigation, claims, and assessments.

Answer (A) is incorrect. A related party transaction may not involve an accounting estimate. Information about the outcome of pending litigation helps to estimate the amount of the recovery or liability. Answer (B) is incorrect. Differences between estimates and actual outcomes help to evaluate the reasonableness of accounting estimates, not their existence. Answer (C) is incorrect. Confirming inventories at locations outside the entity (e.g., public warehouses) tests the count of those inventories, not an estimate, such as the net realizable value.

4.4.3. As part of the audit of fair value estimates and disclosures, an auditor may need to test the entity's significant assumptions. In these circumstances, the auditor should

A. Verify that the entity has used its own assumptions, not those of marketplace participants.

B. Obtain sufficient evidence to express an opinion on the assumptions.

C. Evaluate whether the assumptions individually and as a whole form a reasonable basis for the fair value estimates.

D. Apply audit effort equally to all assumptions.

Answer (C) is correct. *(Publisher, adapted)*

REQUIRED: The necessary step in an audit of fair value estimates when the auditor tests significant assumptions.

DISCUSSION: Observable market prices are not always available for fair value estimates. In this case, the entity uses valuation methods based on the assumptions that the market would employ to estimate fair values, if obtainable without excessive cost. Accordingly, GAAS require the auditor to evaluate whether the significant assumptions form a reasonable basis for the estimates. Because assumptions often are interdependent and must be consistent with each other, the auditor should evaluate them independently and as a whole.

Answer (A) is incorrect. Valuation methods should be based on the assumptions that participants in the market would use to estimate fair value without undue cost and effort. Answer (B) is incorrect. The procedures applied to the entity's assumptions are required merely to evaluate whether, in the context of the audit of the financial statements as a whole, the assumptions form a reasonable basis for the estimates. Answer (D) is incorrect. The auditor considers the sensitivity of valuations to changes in assumptions. Accordingly, the auditor considers focusing on especially sensitive assumptions.

4.4.4. During the audit of fair value estimates and disclosures, the auditor most likely should

A. Understand the components of internal control but need not specifically obtain an understanding of the entity's process for determining fair value estimates.

B. Use the understanding of the audited entity's process for determining fair value estimates to assess the risks of material misstatement.

C. Determine that the entity has measured fair value estimates using discounted cash flows whenever feasible.

D. Focus primarily on the initial recording of transactions.

Answer (B) is correct. *(Publisher, adapted)*

REQUIRED: The necessary procedure in an audit of fair value estimates.

DISCUSSION: To meet its responsibility to make the fair value estimates included in the financial statements, management must adopt financial reporting processes that include (1) adequate internal control, (2) selecting appropriate accounting policies, (3) prescribing estimation processes (e.g., valuation methods, including models), (4) determining data and assumptions, (5) reviewing the circumstances requiring estimation, and (6) making necessary reestimates. The auditor should obtain an understanding of these processes and the relevant controls. It should be sufficient for an effective audit of fair value estimates. The understanding is used to assess the risks of material misstatement. Assessing these risks includes evaluating (1) estimation uncertainty (inherent lack of measurement precision) and (2) determining whether the risks are significant.

Answer (A) is incorrect. The auditor should obtain an understanding of the entity's process for determining fair value estimates. Answer (C) is incorrect. Accounting standards typically do not require a specific method for measuring fair value. However, use of observable market prices is preferable. In their absence, the measurement is based on the best available information, and the entity's process will be more complex. Answer (D) is incorrect. Measurements also are necessary for changes in fair value subsequent to initial recording, e.g., adjustments at the balance sheet date for holding gains or losses on trading and available-for-sale securities.

4.4.5. The client has equity securities classified as available for sale. The auditor is most concerned about controls related to

A. The determination of the fair value measurements of the securities.

B. The accrued interest receivable for the securities.

C. Why specific securities were purchased.

D. When the securities will be sold.

Answer (A) is correct. *(Publisher, adapted)*

REQUIRED: The auditor's control concern about available-for-sale securities.

DISCUSSION: The auditor should obtain an understanding of (1) the client's process for the determination of fair value measurements and disclosures and (2) the relevant controls. Available-for-sale and trading securities are required to be reported at fair value by U.S. GAAP.

Answer (B) is incorrect. Equity securities do not accrue interest. Answer (C) is incorrect. The reasons for the acquisition of specific securities and their uses are management's operating decisions. The auditor is only marginally interested in purchase decisions. Answer (D) is incorrect. The reasons for the acquisition of specific securities and their uses are management's operating decisions. The auditor is only marginally interested in these decisions.

4.4.6. An auditor is assessing the appropriateness of management's rationale for selecting a model to measure the fair value of debt securities. If, during the current year, an active trading market for the debt security was introduced, the auditor should validate each of the following criteria, except whether the valuation model is

A. Appropriate for the environment in which the entity operates.

B. Consistently applied from prior periods.

C. Evaluated and appropriately applied based on generally accepted accounting principles.

D. Appropriate for the debt security being valued.

Answer (B) is correct. *(CPA, adapted)*

REQUIRED: The item that is not used to validate a valuation model used to measure fair value.

DISCUSSION: The active trading market for the debt security was introduced in the current year. Therefore, a prior period cannot be used to validate the valuation model.

Answer (A) is incorrect. The valuation model used should be appropriate for the environment in which the entity operates. Answer (C) is incorrect. Valuation models should follow GAAP or the applicable financial reporting framework. Answer (D) is incorrect. The valuation model should be appropriate for the debt security being valued.

4.5 Consideration of Omitted Procedures after the Report Release Date

4.5.1. An auditor concludes that the omission of a substantive procedure considered necessary at the time of the audit may impair the auditor's current ability to support the previously expressed opinion. The auditor need not apply the omitted procedure if

A. The risk of adverse publicity or litigation is low.

B. The results of other procedures that were applied tend to compensate for the procedure omitted.

C. The auditor's opinion was qualified because of a material misstatement.

D. The results of the subsequent period's tests of controls make the omitted procedure less important.

Answer (B) is correct. *(CPA, adapted)*

REQUIRED: The circumstances in which an auditor need not apply an omitted procedure.

DISCUSSION: The results of other procedures applied or audit evidence obtained in a later audit (possibly at an interim date) may compensate for an omitted procedure. Furthermore, the auditor should assess the importance of the omitted procedure to his or her current ability to support the previously expressed audit opinion.

Answer (A) is incorrect. A low risk of adverse consequences to the auditor does not justify failing to apply the omitted procedure. Answer (C) is incorrect. The omission may have resulted in an inappropriate report or affected a matter not the basis for the qualification. Thus, the nature of the opinion does not justify failure to correct the omission. Answer (D) is incorrect. The results of the tests of controls in a subsequent period do not necessarily apply to the earlier period.

4.5.2. On March 15, Year 2, Kent, CPA, expressed an unmodified opinion on a client's audited financial statements for the year ended December 31, Year 1. On May 4, Year 2, Kent's internal inspection program disclosed that engagement personnel failed to observe the client's physical inventory. Omission of this procedure impairs Kent's present ability to support the unmodified opinion. If the shareholders are currently relying on the opinion, Kent should first

A. Advise management to disclose to the shareholders that Kent's unmodified opinion should not be relied on.

B. Undertake to apply alternative procedures that would provide a satisfactory basis for the unmodified opinion.

C. Reissue the auditor's report and add an additional paragraph describing the departure from generally accepted auditing standards.

D. Compensate for the omitted procedure by performing tests of controls to reduce audit risk to an acceptably low level.

Answer (B) is correct. *(CPA, adapted)*

REQUIRED: The appropriate action when an auditor discovers that a necessary audit procedure was not performed during the previous audit.

DISCUSSION: The auditor determines whether (1) the omission impairs his or her current ability to support the opinion, and (2) persons are currently relying or are likely to rely on the report. If these conditions currently exist, the auditor should promptly undertake to apply the omitted procedure or alternative procedures that would provide a satisfactory basis for the opinion (AU-C 585).

Answer (A) is incorrect. Notification of users is only necessary if the auditor could not become satisfied upon applying the procedure. Answer (C) is incorrect. The auditor has followed GAAS in becoming satisfied with the application of the procedure. Answer (D) is incorrect. Tests of controls do not substitute for required substantive procedures.

4.5.3. Which of the following circumstances most likely would require an auditor to apply an omitted procedure after the audit report issuance date?

A. The auditor's report is unsupported as a result of the omitted procedure.

B. Generally accepted accounting principles are violated.

C. The client has requested that the procedure be performed.

D. The engagement letter requires the procedure to be performed.

Answer (A) is correct. *(CPA, adapted)*

REQUIRED: The reason for applying an omitted procedure after the audit report issuance date.

DISCUSSION: When the auditor decides that a necessary procedure was omitted, (s)he should assess its importance to his or her current ability to support the previously expressed opinion. The results of other procedures applied or audit evidence obtained in a later audit (possibly at an interim date) may compensate for an omitted procedure. The auditor may determine that the omission impairs his or her current ability to support the opinion. If (s)he believes persons are currently relying, or are likely to rely, on the report, the auditor should promptly apply the omitted procedure or alternative procedures that provide a satisfactory basis for the opinion.

Answer (B) is incorrect. The misstatement may not (1) be material or (2) be reflected in the opinion expressed. Answer (C) is incorrect. Clients do not determine the procedures performed in an audit by an independent auditor. Answer (D) is incorrect. The engagement letter should state that the procedures selected depend on the auditor's judgment.

STUDY UNIT FIVE
INTERNAL CONTROL CONCEPTS AND INFORMATION TECHNOLOGY

AU-C 315, *Understanding the Entity and its Environment and Assessing Risks of Material Misstatement*, defines concepts and terminology relevant to internal control. It incorporates into the guidance on internal control (1) the management assertions model (described below) and (2) the audit risk model presented in the AICPA's Clarified Auditing Standards.

The PCAOB's auditing standards, which apply to issuers (entities reporting under the Securities Exchange Act of 1934), also require the auditor to obtain an understanding of internal control in a financial statement audit. They implement Section 404(b) of the Sarbanes-Oxley Act of 2002. Under PCAOB auditing standards, the auditor's objective in an audit of internal control over financial reporting is to express an opinion on the effectiveness of internal control over financial reporting. This issue is addressed in Study Unit 9.

Moreover, AICPA and PCAOB pronouncements adopt the concepts in the report on internal control issued by the Committee of Sponsoring Organizations (COSO). It defines internal control and the components of internal control.

The **premise** of an audit in accordance with GAAS is that management has certain responsibilities regarding (1) the presentation of the financial statements, (2) internal control, and (3) providing the auditor with (a) information and (b) access to persons with audit evidence. For example, management represents that the statements are in accordance with an applicable financial reporting framework. This representation includes implicit or explicit assertions about the recognition, measurement, presentation, and disclosure of the elements of the statements and related disclosures. The following **assertions** are used by auditors to consider the potential misstatements that may occur:

1. Assertions about classes of **transactions and events** for the period (the income statement and statement of cash flows)
   a. Occurrence – Recorded transactions and events actually occurred and pertain to the entity.
   b. Completeness – All transactions and events that should have been recorded were recorded.
   c. Accuracy – Amounts and other data were recorded appropriately.
   d. Cutoff – Transactions and events were recorded in the proper period.
   e. Classification – Transactions and events were recorded in the proper accounts.
2. Assertions about **account balances** at period end (the balance sheet)
   a. Existence – Assets, liabilities, and equity interests exist.
   b. Rights and obligations – The entity holds or controls the rights to assets, and liabilities are its obligations.
   c. Completeness – All assets, liabilities, and equity interests that should have been recorded were recorded.
   d. Valuation and allocation – Assets, liabilities, and equity interests are included at appropriate amounts, and adjustments are appropriately recorded.

3. Assertions about **presentation and disclosure** (notes to the financial statements)
   a. Occurrence and rights and obligations – Disclosed transactions and events have occurred and pertain to the entity.
   b. Completeness – All disclosures that should have been included were included.
   c. Classification and understandability – Financial information is appropriately presented and described, and disclosures are clearly expressed.
   d. Accuracy and valuation – Information is disclosed fairly and at appropriate amounts.
4. The PCAOB provides a less detailed (but substantially similar) assertions model with the following five categories:
   a. Existence or occurrence – Assets or liabilities exist at a given date, and recorded transactions have occurred during a given period.
   b. Completeness – All transactions and accounts that should be presented in the financial statements are so included.
   c. Valuation or allocation – Asset, liability, equity, revenue, and expense components have been included in the financial statements at appropriate amounts.
   d. Rights and obligations – The company holds or controls rights to the assets, and liabilities are obligations of the company at a given date.
   e. Presentation and disclosure – The components of the financial statements are properly classified, described, and disclosed.

QUESTIONS

5.1 Introduction to Internal Control

5.1.1. The PCAOB's AS 2201 states that internal controls may be preventive or detective. Which of the following controls is preventive?

A. Requiring two persons to open mail.
B. Reconciling the accounts receivable subsidiary file with the control account.
C. Using batch totals.
D. Preparing bank reconciliations.

Answer (A) is correct. *(Publisher, adapted)*

REQUIRED: The internal control that is preventive.

DISCUSSION: Preventive controls have the objective of preventing errors or fraud that could result in a misstatement of the financial statements. Detective controls have the objective of detecting errors and fraud that have already occurred that could misstate the financial statements. Assigning two individuals to open mail is an attempt to prevent misstatement of cash receipts.

Answer (B) is incorrect. Reconciling the subsidiary file with the master file may detect and lead to the correction of errors, but the control does not prevent errors. Answer (C) is incorrect. The use of batch totals may detect a missing or lost document but will not necessarily prevent a document from becoming lost. Answer (D) is incorrect. Bank reconciliations disclose errors in the accounts but have no preventive effect.

5.1.2. Internal control cannot be designed to provide reasonable assurance regarding the achievement of objectives concerning

A. Reducing the cost of an external audit.
B. Elimination of all fraud.
C. Availability of reliable data for decision-making purposes and protection of important documents and records.
D. Compliance with the Foreign Corrupt Practices Act of 1977.

Answer (B) is correct. *(Publisher, adapted)*

REQUIRED: The objective that internal control cannot achieve.

DISCUSSION: Internal control is a process designed to provide reasonable assurance regarding the achievement of the entity's objectives. It can provide reasonable assurance regarding (1) reliability of financial reporting, (2) compliance with applicable laws and regulations, and (3) effectiveness and efficiency of operations. Because of inherent limitations, however, no system can be designed to eliminate all fraud (AU-C 315).

Answer (A) is incorrect. More effective control permits the auditor to accept a higher level of detection risk and thus to reduce substantive testing. Answer (C) is incorrect. More effective internal control provides management with better data for decision-making purposes. The physical safety of important documents and records also is assured. Answer (D) is incorrect. More effective internal control provides some assurance of compliance with the FCPA provisions regarding recordkeeping, internal control, and prohibition of corrupt payments.

5.1.3. The organization chart is a graphic representation of the

A. Power structure.

B. Communications channels.

C. Locus of decision making.

D. Formal authority structure.

Answer (D) is correct. *(CDP, adapted)*

REQUIRED: The relationship graphically represented by an organization chart.

DISCUSSION: An organization chart represents pictorially the formal lines of authority within an organization. It depicts the organizational structure and the hierarchical relationships of the functional units in the organization.

Answer (A) is incorrect. The power structure concerns personalities more than assigned responsibilities. Answer (B) is incorrect. Although the organization chart customarily shows communication lines, it does not represent the informal channels that operate within an organization. Answer (C) is incorrect. The organization chart depicts responsibility and authority, which includes more than the loci of decision making.

5.1.4. Directors, management, external auditors, and internal auditors all play important roles in creating proper control processes. Senior management is primarily responsible for

A. Establishing risk management and control processes.

B. Reviewing the reliability and integrity of financial and operational information.

C. Ensuring that external and internal auditors oversee the administration of risk management and control processes.

D. Implementing and monitoring controls designed by the board of directors.

Answer (A) is correct. *(CIA, adapted)*

REQUIRED: The primary responsibility of senior management.

DISCUSSION: An organization establishes and maintains effective risk management and control processes. The purpose of control processes is to support the organization in the management of risks and the achievement of its established and communicated objectives. The control processes are expected to ensure, among other things, that (1) financial and operational information is reliable and possesses integrity; (2) operations are performed efficiently and achieve established objectives; (3) assets are safeguarded; and (4) actions and decisions of the organization are in compliance with laws, regulations, and contracts. Senior management's role is to oversee the establishment, administration, and assessment of the system of risk management and control processes. Among the responsibilities of the organization's line managers is the assessment of the control processes in their respective areas.

Answer (B) is incorrect. Internal auditors are responsible for evaluating the adequacy and effectiveness of controls, including those relating to the reliability and integrity of financial and operational information. Answer (C) is incorrect. Senior management's role also is to oversee the administration of the risk management and control processes. Answer (D) is incorrect. The board has oversight responsibilities but ordinarily does not become involved in the details of operations.

5.1.5. In an audit of financial statements, an auditor's primary consideration regarding an internal control is whether the control

A. Reflects management's philosophy and operating style.

B. Affects management's financial statement assertions.

C. Provides adequate safeguards over access to assets.

D. Relates to operational objectives.

Answer (B) is correct. *(CPA, adapted)*

REQUIRED: The auditor's primary consideration regarding an internal control.

DISCUSSION: Assertions are management representations embodied in the financial statements. They are used by the auditor to consider the different potential misstatements. A relevant assertion has a reasonable possibility of containing a misstatement that could cause a material misstatement(s) of the financial statements. Thus, a relevant assertion has a meaningful bearing on whether the account is fairly stated. Tests of controls are designed to evaluate the operating effectiveness of controls in preventing, or detecting and correcting, material misstatements at the assertion level. They should be performed when (1) the auditor's assessment of the RMMs at the relevant assertion level includes an expectation of the operating effectiveness of controls, or (2) substantive procedures alone do not provide sufficient appropriate evidence at the relevant assertion level. Thus, the auditor is primarily concerned with whether a control affects relevant financial statement assertions.

Answer (A) is incorrect. Management's philosophy and operating style is just one factor in one component (the control environment) of internal control. Answer (C) is incorrect. Restricting access to assets is only one of many physical controls, which constitute one element of one component (control activities) of internal control. Answer (D) is incorrect. Many controls relating to operational objectives are not relevant to an audit.

5.1.6. The primary reason to establish internal control is to

A. Safeguard the resources of the organization.

B. Provide reasonable assurance that the objectives of the organization are achieved.

C. Encourage compliance with organizational objectives

D. Ensure the accuracy, reliability, and timeliness of information.

Answer (B) is correct. *(Publisher, adapted)*

REQUIRED: The primary reason to establish internal control.

DISCUSSION: According to AU-C 315, internal control is a process, effected by those charged with governance, management, and other personnel, designed to provide reasonable assurance about the achievement of the entity's objectives. They include (1) reliability of financial reporting, (2) effectiveness and efficiency of operations, and (3) compliance with applicable laws and regulations.

Answer (A) is incorrect. Safeguarding resources is included in the overall purpose of providing reasonable assurance that the entity's objectives are achieved. Answer (C) is incorrect. Encouraging compliance with management's intentions is included in the overall purpose of providing reasonable assurance that the entity's objectives are achieved. Answer (D) is incorrect. Ensuring the accuracy, reliability, and timeliness of information is included in the overall purpose of providing reasonable assurance that the entity's objectives are achieved.

5.1.7. Effective internal control

A. Reduces the need for management to review exception reports on a day-to-day basis.

B. Eliminates risk and potential loss to the organization.

C. Cannot be circumvented by management.

D. Is unaffected by changing circumstances and conditions encountered by the organization.

Answer (A) is correct. *(CIA, adapted)*

REQUIRED: The service provided by effective control.

DISCUSSION: The need for management to spend time on a day-to-day basis reviewing exception reports is reduced when internal control is working effectively. Effective internal control should prevent as well as detect exceptions.

Answer (B) is incorrect. Some risks are unavoidable and others can be eliminated only at excessive costs. Answer (C) is incorrect. The potential for management override is a basic limitation of internal control. Answer (D) is incorrect. Controls should be modified as appropriate for changes in conditions.

5.1.8. Internal control is a function of management, and effective control is based upon the concept of charge and discharge of responsibility and duty. Which of the following is one of the overriding principles of internal control?

A. Responsibility for accounting and financial duties should be assigned to one responsible officer.

B. Responsibility for the performance of each duty must be fixed.

C. Responsibility for the accounting duties must be borne by the audit committee of the company.

D. Responsibility for accounting activities and duties must be assigned only to employees who are bonded.

Answer (B) is correct. *(CPA, adapted)*

REQUIRED: The identification of a principle of internal control.

DISCUSSION: Effective internal control may be obtained by decentralization of responsibilities and duties. Fixing the responsibility for each performance or duty makes it easier to trace problems to the person(s) responsible and hold them accountable for their actions.

Answer (A) is incorrect. Accounting (record keeping) should be separated from finance (asset custody). Answer (C) is incorrect. The audit committee is responsible for overseeing the internal and external audits, not for accounting duties. Answer (D) is incorrect. Bonding is not an overriding internal control principle. Employees having custodial, rather than accounting, responsibility are usually bonded.

5.1.9. Which of the following statements about internal control is true?

A. Properly maintained internal control reasonably ensures that collusion among employees cannot occur.

B. The establishment and maintenance of internal control are important responsibilities of the internal auditor.

C. Exceptionally effective internal control is enough for the auditor to eliminate substantive procedures on a significant account balance.

D. A limitation of internal control is that management makes judgments about the extent of controls it implements.

Answer (D) is correct. *(CPA, adapted)*

REQUIRED: The true statement about internal control.

DISCUSSION: Because of inherent limitations, internal control, no matter how effective, can provide only reasonable assurance about achieving the entity's objectives. For example, when management designs and implements controls, it makes judgments about the nature and extent of (1) controls it implements and (2) the risks it assumes (AU-C 315).

Answer (A) is incorrect. Collusion is an inherent limitation of internal control. Answer (B) is incorrect. Establishment and maintenance of internal control are responsibilities of management. Answer (C) is incorrect. Regardless of the assessed RMMs, substantive procedures should be performed for all relevant assertions about each material account balance, transaction class, and disclosure.

5.1.10. Internal controls are designed to provide reasonable assurance that

A. Material errors or fraud will be prevented, or detected and corrected, within a timely period by employees in the course of performing their assigned duties.

B. Management's plans have not been circumvented by worker collusion.

C. The internal auditing department's guidance and oversight of management's performance is accomplished economically and efficiently.

D. Management's planning, organizing, and directing processes are properly evaluated.

Answer (A) is correct. *(CIA, adapted)*

REQUIRED: The purpose of internal controls.

DISCUSSION: Cost-effective controls should restrict deviations to a tolerable rate. Thus, material errors and improper or illegal acts should be prevented, or detected and corrected, within a timely period by employees in the normal course of performing their assigned duties. Accordingly, the cost-benefit relationship is considered by management during the design of systems, and the potential loss associated with any exposure or risk is weighed against the cost to control it.

Answer (B) is incorrect. Collusion is an inherent limitation of internal control. Answer (C) is incorrect. The board of directors or a similar body is responsible for the guidance and oversight of management. Answer (D) is incorrect. The examination and evaluation of management processes is a function of the internal auditing department.

5.1.11. The design or operation of a control may not allow management or employees, in the normal course of performing their assigned functions, to prevent, or detect and correct, misstatements on a timely basis. According to AU-C 265, this circumstance is a

A. Material weakness.

B. Significant deficiency.

C. Control deficiency.

D. Critical deficiency.

Answer (C) is correct. *(Publisher, adapted)*

REQUIRED: The control term matching the given definition.

DISCUSSION: A control deficiency may arise either in the design or operation of a control. It is the lowest level of deficiency identified in the standards. A design deficiency results when (1) a necessary control is missing or (2) a control operating as designed does not meet the control objective. An operating deficiency results when (1) a properly designed control does not function as designed, or (2) the person performing the control does not have the authority or competence to perform it effectively.

Answer (A) is incorrect. A material weakness is a deficiency, or a combination of deficiencies, in internal control so that more than a remote chance exists that a material misstatement of the entity's financial statements will not be prevented, or detected and corrected, on a timely basis. Answer (B) is incorrect. A significant deficiency is a deficiency, or a combination of deficiencies, in internal control that is less severe than a material weakness but is important enough to merit attention by those charged with governance. Answer (D) is incorrect. The standards do not use the term "critical deficiency."

5.1.12. Which of the following most likely would not be considered an inherent limitation of the potential effectiveness of an entity's internal control?

A. Incompatible duties.

B. Management override.

C. Faulty judgment.

D. Collusion among employees.

Answer (A) is correct. *(CPA, adapted)*

REQUIRED: The item not considered an inherent limitation of internal control.

DISCUSSION: Internal control has inherent limitations. The performance of incompatible duties, however, is a failure to assign different people the functions of authorization, recording, and asset custody, not an inevitable limitation of internal control. Segregation of duties is a category of control activities.

Answer (B) is incorrect. Management establishes internal controls. Thus, it can override those controls. Answer (C) is incorrect. Human judgment in decision making may be faulty. Answer (D) is incorrect. Controls, whether manual or automated, may be circumvented by collusion among two or more people.

5.1.13. Internal control can provide only reasonable assurance of achieving an entity's control objectives. The likelihood of achieving those objectives is affected by which limitation inherent to internal control?

A. The auditor's primary responsibility is the detection of fraud.

B. The board of directors is active and independent.

C. The cost of internal control should not exceed its benefits.

D. Management monitors internal control.

Answer (C) is correct. *(Publisher, adapted)*

REQUIRED: The true statement about the limitation of internal control.

DISCUSSION: The cost of an entity's internal control should not exceed the benefits that are expected to be derived. Although the cost-benefit relationship is a primary criterion that should be considered in designing internal control, the precise measurement of costs and benefits usually is not possible.

Answer (A) is incorrect. The auditor's responsibility is to plan and perform the audit to obtain reasonable assurance about whether the financial statements are free of material misstatement, whether caused by fraud or error. Answer (B) is incorrect. An active and independent board strengthens the control environment. Answer (D) is incorrect. Monitoring strengthens internal control.

5.1.14. An entity should consider the cost of a control in relationship to the risk. Which of the following controls best reflects this philosophy for a large dollar investment in heavy machine tools?

A. Conducting a weekly physical inventory.

B. Placing security guards at every entrance 24 hours a day.

C. Imprinting a controlled identification number on each tool.

D. Having all dispositions approved by the vice president of sales.

Answer (C) is correct. *(Publisher, adapted)*

REQUIRED: The control appropriate for a large dollar investment in heavy machine tools.

DISCUSSION: A controlled identification number on each tool and periodic checking allow for an effective control at reasonable cost.

Answer (A) is incorrect. The cost of weekly inventories would likely outweigh the benefits derived. Answer (B) is incorrect. The cost of 24-hour guards would likely outweigh the benefits derived. Answer (D) is incorrect. Although the disposition of assets should be approved, the vice president of sales, who is not familiar with the heavy equipment, would not be the appropriate officer to provide the authorization.

5.2 Internal Control Components

5.2.1. Which of the following best describe the interrelated components of internal control?

A. Organizational structure, management philosophy, and planning.

B. Control environment; risk assessment process; control activities; the information system, including related business processes; and monitoring of controls.

C. Risk assessment process, backup facilities, responsibility accounting, and natural laws.

D. Assignment of authority and responsibility, management philosophy, and organizational structure.

Answer (B) is correct. *(CMA, adapted)*

REQUIRED: The components of internal control.

DISCUSSION: Internal control has five components: the control environment, risk assessment process, control activities, information systems, and monitoring of controls. The control environment sets the tone of an organization, influences control consciousness, and provides a foundation for the other components. The risk assessment process is the identification, analysis, and management of risks relevant to achievement of objectives. Control activities help ensure that management directives are executed. The information system, including the related business processes relevant to financial reporting and communication, consists of (1) physical and hardware components, (2) software, (3) people, (4) procedures, and (5) data. Monitoring assesses the performance of internal control over time (AU-C 315 and AS 2110).

Answer (A) is incorrect. Planning is not a component of internal control. Organizational structure and management philosophy are factors in the control environment component. Answer (C) is incorrect. The risk assessment process is the only control component listed. Answer (D) is incorrect. Assignment of authority and responsibility, management philosophy, and organizational structure are factors in the control environment component.

5.2.2. Which of the following are considered control environment factors?

	Detection Risk	Human Resources Policies and Practices
A.	Yes	Yes
B.	Yes	No
C.	No	Yes
D.	No	No

Answer (C) is correct. *(CPA, adapted)*

REQUIRED: The factor(s), if any, considered to be part of the control environment.

DISCUSSION: Human resource policies and practices are part of the control environment. These policies and practices relate to recruitment, orientation, training, evaluating, counseling, promoting, compensating, and remedial actions. The control environment is the component that sets the tone of an organization, influencing the control consciousness of its people. It is the foundation for the other components.

5.2.3. Control activities constitute one of the five components of internal control described in the COSO model. Control activities do not encompass

A. Performance reviews.

B. Information processing.

C. Physical controls.

D. An internal auditing function.

Answer (D) is correct. *(Publisher, adapted)*

REQUIRED: The item not belonging to the control activities component.

DISCUSSION: The COSO model describes control activities as policies and procedures that help ensure that management directives are carried out. They are intended to ensure that necessary actions are taken to address risks to achieve the entity's objectives. Control activities have various objectives and are applied at various organizational and functional levels. However, an internal auditing function is part of the monitoring component.

5.2.4. Monitoring of controls is an important component of internal control. Which of the following items is not an example of monitoring?

A. Management regularly compares divisional performance with budgets for the division.

B. Data processing management regularly generates exception reports for unusual transactions or volumes of transactions and follows up with investigation as to causes.

C. Data processing management regularly reconciles batch control totals for items processed with batch controls for items submitted.

D. Management has asked internal auditing to perform regular audits of the controls over cash processing.

Answer (C) is correct. *(CIA, adapted)*

REQUIRED: The item that is not an example of monitoring.

DISCUSSION: Monitoring assesses the quality of internal control over time. Management considers whether internal control is properly designed and operating as intended and modifies it to reflect changing conditions. Monitoring may be in the form of separate, periodic evaluations or of ongoing monitoring. Ongoing monitoring occurs as part of routine operations. It includes management and supervisory review, comparisons, reconciliations, and other actions by personnel as part of their regular activities. However, reconciling batch control totals is a processing control.

Answer (A) is incorrect. Budgetary comparison is a typical example of a monitoring control. Answer (B) is incorrect. Investigation of exceptions is a monitoring control used by lower-level management to determine when their operations may be out of control. Answer (D) is incorrect. Internal auditing is a form of monitoring. It serves to evaluate management's other controls.

5.2.5. Control activities include physical controls over access to and use of assets and records. A departure from the purpose of such procedures is that

A. Access to the safe-deposit box requires two officers.

B. Only storeroom personnel and line supervisors have access to the raw materials storeroom.

C. The mail clerk compiles a list of the checks received in the incoming mail.

D. Only salespersons and sales supervisors use sales department vehicles.

Answer (B) is correct. *(Publisher, adapted)*

REQUIRED: The departure from the purpose of control activities that limit access to assets.

DISCUSSION: Storeroom personnel have custody of assets, while supervisors are in charge of execution functions. To give supervisors access to the raw materials storeroom is a violation of the essential internal control principle of separation of functions.

Answer (A) is incorrect. It is appropriate for two officers to be required to open the safe-deposit box. One supervises the other. Answer (C) is incorrect. Mail room clerks typically compile a prelisting of cash. The list is sent to the accountant as a control for actual cash sent to the cashier. Answer (D) is incorrect. Use of sales department vehicles should be limited to sales personnel unless proper authorization is obtained.

5.2.6. Basic to a proper control environment are the quality and integrity of personnel who must perform the prescribed procedures. Which is not a factor in providing for competent personnel?

A. Segregation of duties.

B. Hiring practices.

C. Training programs.

D. Performance evaluations.

Answer (A) is correct. *(Publisher, adapted)*

REQUIRED: The factor not related to competence of personnel.

DISCUSSION: Human resource policies and practices are an element in the control environment component of internal control. They affect the entity's ability to employ sufficient competent personnel to accomplish its objectives. Policies and practices include those for recruitment, orientation, training, evaluation, promotion, compensation, and remedial actions. Although control activities based on the segregation of duties are important to internal control, they do not in themselves promote employee competence.

Answer (B) is incorrect. Effective hiring practices result in selection of competent employees. Answer (C) is incorrect. Effective training programs increase the competence of employees. Answer (D) is incorrect. Performance evaluations improve competence by identifying substandard work and by serving as a basis for rewarding exceptional efforts.

5.2.7. Proper segregation of duties reduces the opportunities to allow persons to be in positions both to

A. Journalize entries and prepare financial statements.

B. Record cash receipts and cash disbursements.

C. Establish internal control and authorize transactions.

D. Perpetrate and conceal fraud and error.

Answer (D) is correct. *(CPA, adapted)*

REQUIRED: The effects of the segregation of duties.

DISCUSSION: Segregation of duties is a category of the control activities component of internal control. Segregating responsibilities for authorization, recording, and asset custody reduces an employee's opportunity to perpetrate fraud or error and subsequently conceal it in the normal course of his or her duties.

Answer (A) is incorrect. Accountants typically journalize entries and prepare financial statements. Answer (B) is incorrect. Accountants may record both cash receipts and cash disbursements as long as they do not have custody of cash. Answer (C) is incorrect. Management establishes internal control and ultimately has the responsibility to authorize transactions.

5.2.8. Management's attitude toward aggressive financial reporting and its emphasis on meeting projected profit goals most likely will significantly increase opportunities for fraudulent financial reporting when

A. External policies established by parties outside the entity affect its accounting practices.

B. Management is dominated by one individual who is also a shareholder.

C. Internal auditors have direct access to the board of directors and the entity's management.

D. The audit committee is active in overseeing the entity's financial reporting policies.

Answer (B) is correct. *(CPA, adapted)*

REQUIRED: The factor that will most likely increase opportunities for fraudulent financial reporting.

DISCUSSION: One set of opportunity risk factors for misstatements arising from fraudulent financial reporting involves ineffective monitoring of management. One such risk factor is domination of management by a single person or small group (in a non-owner managed business) without compensating controls (Appendix to AU-C 240). A compensating control in that circumstance is effective oversight by the board or audit committee of the financial reporting process and internal control.

Answer (A) is incorrect. Establishment of policies by outside parties somewhat offsets the effect of an aggressive attitude toward financial reporting. Answer (C) is incorrect. Opportunities for fraudulent financial reporting are decreased when internal auditors have direct access to the board of directors. Answer (D) is incorrect. Opportunities for fraudulent financial reporting are decreased when the audit committee is active in overseeing policies.

5.2.9. It is important for the auditor to consider the competence of the audit client's employees, because their competence bears directly and importantly upon the

A. Relationship of the costs of internal control and its benefits.

B. Achievement of the objectives of internal control.

C. Comparison of recorded accountability with assets.

D. Timing of the tests to be performed.

Answer (B) is correct. *(CPA, adapted)*

REQUIRED: The reason an auditor must consider the competence of employees.

DISCUSSION: The control environment is the foundation of internal control. A commitment to competence is one of the factors in the control environment.

Answer (A) is incorrect. The cost-benefit relationship of internal control is a basic concept of internal control. Answer (C) is incorrect. Comparison of recorded accountability with assets is an essential characteristic of internal control, but not directly related to the competence of employees. Answer (D) is incorrect. The timing of particular tests is dependent on such factors as the convenience of the auditor and client and the need for applying certain tests concurrently.

5.2.10. Transaction authorization within an organization may be either specific or general. An example of specific transaction authorization is the

A. Setting of automatic reorder points for material or merchandise.

B. Approval of a detailed construction budget for a warehouse.

C. Establishment of requirements to be met in determining a customer's credit limits.

D. Establishment of sales prices for products to be sold to any customer.

Answer (B) is correct. *(CPA, adapted)*

REQUIRED: The example of a specific transaction authorization.

DISCUSSION: A specific transaction authorization is applicable to a unique decision. A general authorization establishes criteria and authorizes the routine making of decisions subject to the criteria. Approving a detailed construction budget for a warehouse is a one-time decision.

Answer (A) is incorrect. Setting of automatic reorder points for material or merchandise is a general transaction authorization. Answer (C) is incorrect. Establishment of requirements to be met in determining a customer's credit limits is a general transaction authorization. Answer (D) is incorrect. Establishment of sales prices for products to be sold to any customer is a general transaction authorization.

5.2.11. A proper segregation of duties requires that an individual

A. Authorizing a transaction records it.

B. Authorizing a transaction maintain custody of the asset that resulted from the transaction.

C. Maintaining custody of an asset be entitled to access the accounting records for the asset.

D. Recording a transaction not compare the accounting record of the asset with the asset itself.

Answer (D) is correct. *(CMA, adapted)*

REQUIRED: The item required for proper segregation of duties.

DISCUSSION: One person should not be responsible for all phases of a transaction, i.e., for authorization, recording, and custodianship of the related assets. These duties should be performed by separate individuals to reduce the opportunities for any person to be in a position of both perpetrating and concealing errors or fraud in the normal course of his or her duties. For instance, an employee who receives and lists cash receipts should not be responsible for comparing the recorded accountability for cash with existing amounts.

Answer (A) is incorrect. Authorization and recordkeeping should be separate. Answer (B) is incorrect. Authorization and asset custody should be separate. Answer (C) is incorrect. Recordkeeping and asset custody should be separate.

5.2.12. A small private entity may use less formal means to ensure that internal control objectives are achieved. For example, extensive accounting procedures, sophisticated accounting records, or formal controls are least likely to be needed if

A. Management is closely involved in operations.

B. The entity is involved in complex transactions.

C. The entity is subject to legal or regulatory requirements also found in larger entities.

D. Financial reporting objectives have been established.

Answer (A) is correct. *(Publisher, adapted)*

REQUIRED: The situation in which less formal means of achieving control objectives are appropriate.

DISCUSSION: Effective management involvement may eliminate the need for more formal means of ensuring that internal control objectives are met. Thus, a smaller entity may not have formal policies regarding credit approval, information security, or competitive bidding. It also may not have a written code of conduct. Instead, a smaller entity may develop a culture emphasizing integrity and ethical behavior through management example. Moreover, an effective control environment may not require outside members on the board. In a small entity, less detailed controls are possible when management retains authority for specific authorization of transactions and oversees employees performing incompatible tasks.

Answer (B) is incorrect. Complex transactions may necessitate the more formal arrangements found in larger entities. Answer (C) is incorrect. Legal or regulatory requirements may necessitate the more formal arrangements found in larger entities. Answer (D) is incorrect. All entities should establish financial reporting objectives. However, they may be recognized implicitly rather than explicitly in smaller entities. Management can assess the risks related to these objectives through direct personal involvement rather than a formal assessment process.

5.2.13. An auditor might consider the procedures performed by the internal auditors because

A. They are employees whose work must be reviewed during substantive testing.

B. They are employees whose work may affect the nature, timing, and extent of audit procedures.

C. Their work affects the cost-benefit trade-off.

D. Their degree of independence may be inferred from the nature of their work.

Answer (B) is correct. *(CPA, adapted)*

REQUIRED: The reason an independent auditor might consider the procedures performed by internal auditors.

DISCUSSION: The internal audit function is part of the monitoring component of internal control. Consequently, the auditor should obtain an understanding of the internal audit function sufficient to identify activities relevant to planning the audit. The external auditor may plan to use the work of the internal auditors to obtain audit evidence or to provide direct assistance. In this case, (s)he should assess their competence and objectivity. If that assessment is favorable, the auditor then considers how the internal auditors' work may affect the audit. If it significantly affects the audit procedures, the auditor should evaluate and test that work.

Answer (A) is incorrect. During the consideration of internal control, the auditor should obtain an understanding of the internal audit function sufficient to identify activities relevant to planning the audit. Answer (C) is incorrect. Management is responsible for evaluating the cost-benefit relationship. Answer (D) is incorrect. Internal auditors are not independent of the entity in the sense required by the AICPA *Code of Professional Conduct*. Hence, the auditor does not consider their independence but may, in appropriate circumstances, assess their competence and objectivity.

5.2.14. The frequency of the comparison of recorded accountability with assets (for the purpose of safeguarding assets) should be determined by

A. The amount of assets independent of the cost of the comparison.

B. The nature and amount of the asset and the cost of making the comparison.

C. The cost of the comparison and whether the susceptibility to loss results from errors or fraud.

D. The auditor in consultation with client management.

Answer (B) is correct. *(Publisher, adapted)*

REQUIRED: The factor(s) determining the frequency of comparing recorded accountability with assets.

DISCUSSION: Assets should be compared with the recorded accountability as frequently as the nature and amount of the assets require, within the limits of acceptable costs of comparison. The costs of safeguarding assets should not exceed the expected benefits.

Answer (A) is incorrect. The costs of controls should be considered when making the comparison. Answer (C) is incorrect. Whether the susceptibility to loss arises from errors or fraud should have little bearing on the frequency of the comparison. Answer (D) is incorrect. Management, not the auditor, has responsibility for internal control.

5.2.15. For which of the following transactions would the auditor ordinarily have the greatest difficulty in obtaining assurance that internal control objectives are met?

A. Collection of interest and dividends by a retailer.

B. Acquisition of production equipment by a manufacturer.

C. Collection of contributions from the public by a not-for-profit organization.

D. Collection of credit sales by a retailer.

Answer (C) is correct. *(Publisher, adapted)*

REQUIRED: The transaction for which the auditor would have the greatest difficulty in gaining assurance that control objectives are met.

DISCUSSION: Among other things, the information system component of internal control should (1) initiate, (2) authorize, (3) record, (4) process, (5) correct as needed, (6) transfer to the general ledger, and (7) report in the financial statements the entity's transactions. However, because corroborating documentation is often unavailable for contributions from the general public to a not-for-profit organization, determining that these donations were properly accounted for is difficult.

Answer (A) is incorrect. Collection of interest and dividends by a retailer is a transaction in the ordinary course of business for which corroborating evidence (documentation) should be available. Answer (B) is incorrect. Acquisition of production equipment by a manufacturer is a transaction in the ordinary course of business for which corroborating evidence (documentation) should be available. Answer (D) is incorrect. Collection of credit sales by a retailer is a transaction in the ordinary course of business for which corroborating evidence (documentation) should be available.

5.2.16. If internal control is properly designed, the same employee may be permitted to

A. Receive and deposit checks and also approve write-offs of customer accounts.

B. Approve vouchers for payment and also sign checks.

C. Reconcile the bank statements and also receive and deposit cash.

D. Sign checks and also cancel supporting documents.

Answer (D) is correct. *(CPA, adapted)*

REQUIRED: The duties that are not incompatible with effective control.

DISCUSSION: Checks for disbursements should be signed by an officer, normally the CFO, after necessary supporting evidence has been examined. The documentation typically consists of a voucher, purchase order, receiving report, and a vendor invoice. Canceling vouchers and supporting papers (with perforations, ink, etc.) upon payment of the voucher prevents the payment of a duplicate voucher. If the person signing the check cancels the documents, they cannot be recycled for duplicate payments. Securing the paid-voucher file from access by the accounts payable clerk is another effective control.

Answer (A) is incorrect. Authorization of transactions (write-offs of receivables) and custody of assets (checks) are incompatible duties. Answer (B) is incorrect. Authorization (voucher approval) and custody of assets (checks) are incompatible functions. Answer (C) is incorrect. Recordkeeping (reconciling the bank statements) and custody of cash are incompatible.

5.2.17. Audit evidence concerning undocumented monitoring controls ordinarily is best obtained by

A. Performing tests of transactions that corroborate management's financial statement assertions.

B. Observing the employees as they apply controls.

C. Obtaining a flowchart of activities performed by available personnel.

D. Developing audit objectives that reduce control risk.

Answer (B) is correct. *(CPA, adapted)*

REQUIRED: The best obtainable audit evidence about undocumented monitoring controls.

DISCUSSION: For some controls, documentation may not be available or relevant. For example, documentation of operation may not exist for (1) some factors in the control environment, such as assignment of authority and responsibility, or (2) some controls, such as computer controls. In such cases, evidence about effectiveness of operation may be obtained through inquiry combined with other procedures, e.g., observation or computer-assisted audit techniques.

Answer (A) is incorrect. Tests of transactions to corroborate assertions are substantive procedures, not tests of controls. They are procedures applied to account balances or classes of transactions to detect material misstatements in assertions. Answer (C) is incorrect. The question indicates that the controls are undocumented. Thus, a flowchart is not available. Answer (D) is incorrect. Audit objectives are not audit evidence.

5.2.18. Although substantive tests may support the accuracy of underlying information used in monitoring, these tests may provide no affirmative evidence of the effectiveness of monitoring controls because

A. Substantive tests rarely guarantee the accuracy of information used in monitoring if only a sample has been tested.

B. The information used in monitoring may be accurate even though it is subject to ineffective control.

C. Substantive tests relate to the entire period under audit, but tests of controls ordinarily are confined to the period during which the auditor is on the client's premises.

D. When procedures are computerized and leave no audit trail to indicate who performed them, substantive tests may necessarily be limited to inquiries and observation.

Answer (B) is correct. *(CPA, adapted)*

REQUIRED: The reason substantive procedures may provide no affirmative evidence of the effectiveness of monitoring controls.

DISCUSSION: When obtaining an understanding of each of the five components of internal control (including monitoring), the auditor must perform procedures to understand the design of relevant controls and must determine whether controls have been implemented. If (s)he intends to rely on the controls, (s)he must also determine their effectiveness. However, when controls based on monitoring leave no audit trail, for example, documentation of design or operation, evidence about effectiveness of design or operation may be obtained only by inquiries, observations, and computer-assisted audit methods. Moreover, substantive procedures likewise may provide no affirmative evidence of the effectiveness of monitoring controls because the information may be accurate even though controls over its creation are ineffective. Thus, the ineffectiveness of monitoring would not be revealed by substantive procedures unless the detection of material misstatements resulted in performance of additional audit procedures directed at the controls.

Answer (A) is incorrect. Properly applied sampling methods may provide reasonable assurance about the accuracy of information, including a quantification of the sampling risk. Answer (C) is incorrect. Tests of controls are concerned with the consistency of their application during the entire period under audit. Answer (D) is incorrect. Given computerized procedures, the auditor must use computer-assisted methods.

5.2.19. Organizational charts are useful to an independent external auditor because they

A. Depict all lines of organizational communication.

B. Provide a starting point for assessing the risk of material misstatement.

C. Ensure the proper division of responsibilities.

D. Are essential to effective internal control.

Answer (B) is correct. *(Publisher, adapted)*

REQUIRED: The reason organizational charts are useful.

DISCUSSION: AU-C 315 and AS 2110 identify the organizational structure as a control environment element to be considered in understanding internal control. An organizational chart depicts the assignment of authority and responsibility within an organization and is a consideration in evaluating the effectiveness of the organizational structure.

Answer (A) is incorrect. Only formal lines of communication are shown on an organizational chart. Answer (C) is incorrect. The organizational chart does not ensure a proper allocation and performance of responsibilities. Answer (D) is incorrect. An organizational chart pictorially describes an entity's purported organization, but it does not in itself provide internal control.

5.3 Understanding Internal Control

5.3.1. A secondary result of the auditor's understanding of internal control for a nonissuer is that the understanding may

A. Provide a basis for determining the nature, timing, and extent of audit tests.

B. Assure that management's procedures to detect fraud are properly functioning.

C. Bring to the auditor's attention possible control conditions required to be communicated to the client.

D. Develop evidence to support the assessed risks of material misstatement.

Answer (C) is correct. *(CPA, adapted)*

REQUIRED: The secondary result of understanding internal control.

DISCUSSION: The auditor is not required to search for significant deficiencies or material weaknesses in internal control. However, the auditor may identify these conditions during the audit. Significant deficiencies and material weaknesses should be communicated in writing to management and to those charged with governance (AU-C 265).

Answer (A) is incorrect. The auditor is required to understand the entity and its environment, including its internal control, to identify and assess the risks of material misstatement. The understanding provides a basis for responses to the assessed RMMs. Answer (B) is incorrect. Testing the effectiveness of controls is not required unless the auditor intends to rely on the controls. Answer (D) is incorrect. Gathering evidence to support the assessed RMMs is a primary result of understanding internal control.

5.3.2. The primary purpose of obtaining an understanding of the entity and its environment, including its internal control, is to provide an auditor with

A. Evidence to use in reducing detection risk.

B. A frame of reference within which to plan the audit.

C. A basis for modifying tests of controls.

D. Information necessary to prepare flowcharts.

Answer (B) is correct. *(CPA, adapted)*

REQUIRED: The primary purpose of obtaining an understanding of the entity.

DISCUSSION: Obtaining an understanding of the entity continues throughout the audit. The process of gathering, updating, and analyzing evidence provides a frame of reference within which to plan the audit and make judgments about many matters. For example, the understanding is a basis for (1) assessing RMMs at the financial statement level, (2) determining materiality, (3) evaluating the selection and application of accounting policies and the adequacy of disclosures, (4) identifying areas for special audit attention, (5) developing expectations for use in analytical procedures, (6) responding to assessed RMMs, and (7) evaluating audit evidence.

Answer (A) is incorrect. Detection risk relates to substantive procedures. It is managed by the auditor's response to the assessed RMMs. Answer (C) is incorrect. Understanding internal controls relevant to the audit involves evaluating the design of the controls and determining whether they have been implemented. The auditor of a nonissuer need not obtain an understanding about operating effectiveness as part of understanding internal control. Tests of controls evaluate their operating effectiveness. Answer (D) is incorrect. Flowcharts are but one part of the documentation of the understanding.

5.3.3. As part of understanding internal control relevant to the audit of a non issuer, an auditor does not need to

A. Consider factors that affect the risks of material misstatement.

B. Determine whether controls have been implemented.

C. Identify the risks of material misstatement.

D. Obtain knowledge about the operating effectiveness of internal control.

Answer (D) is correct. *(CPA, adapted)*

REQUIRED: The procedure not required in obtaining the understanding of internal control of a non issuer.

DISCUSSION: Understanding internal controls relevant to the audit involves evaluating the design of the controls and determining whether they have been implemented. The auditor of a nonissuer need not obtain an understanding about operating effectiveness as part of understanding internal control. However, (1) the auditor's assessment of the risks of material misstatement (RMMs) may include an expectation of the operating effectiveness of controls, or (2) substantive procedures may not provide sufficient appropriate evidence at the relevant assertion level about operating effectiveness. In these circumstances, the auditor should test controls (AU-C 330).

Answer (A) is incorrect. The auditor performs risk assessment procedures to obtain an understanding of the entity and its environment, including its internal control, to identify and assess the RMMs, whether due to fraud or error, at the financial statement and relevant assertion levels. Answer (B) is incorrect. The understanding of internal control provides assurance that controls have been implemented. Answer (C) is incorrect. The understanding of the entity and its environment, including its internal control, involves identifying and assessing RMMs.

5.3.4. Which of the following is not a medium that can normally be used by an auditor to record information concerning internal control?

A. Narrative memorandum.

B. Procedures manual.

C. Flowchart.

D. Decision table.

Answer (B) is correct. *(CPA, adapted)*

REQUIRED: The medium not used by an auditor to record information about a client's internal control.

DISCUSSION: A procedures manual is one source of information about the client's internal control. However, the auditor normally does not prepare this manual and record information in it. The accounting procedures manual is a client document that explains the client's accounting system and how to implement it.

Answer (A) is incorrect. Memoranda are means of documenting the understanding of internal control. Answer (C) is incorrect. Flowcharts are means of documenting the understanding of internal control. Answer (D) is incorrect. Decision tables are means of documenting the understanding of internal control.

5.3.5. A CPA's understanding of internal control in a financial statement audit of a nonissuer

A. Is usually more limited than that made in an audit of internal control integrated with an audit of financial statements.

B. Is usually more extensive than that made in an audit of internal control integrated with an audit of financial statements.

C. Will usually be identical to that made in an audit of internal control integrated with an audit of financial statements.

D. Will usually result in a report on the effectiveness of internal control.

Answer (A) is correct. *(CPA, adapted)*

REQUIRED: The scope of the understanding of internal control in a financial statement audit of a nonissuer.

DISCUSSION: The scope of the understanding of internal control in a financial statement audit of a nonissuer is usually less than that in an audit of internal control integrated with an audit of financial statements. In the integrated audit, the auditor tests controls to support the opinion on the effectiveness of internal control. To express an opinion on internal control, the auditor obtains evidence about the effectiveness of selected controls over all relevant assertions. When obtaining the understanding of internal control during a financial statement audit, the auditor need not test controls unless (1) the auditor's risk assessment is based on an expectation of the effectiveness of controls or (2) substantive procedures alone do not provide sufficient appropriate evidence.

Answer (B) is incorrect. In an integrated audit, the auditor tests controls ordinarily not tested when the engagement is solely to express an opinion on the statements of a nonissuer. Answer (C) is incorrect. In an integrated audit, the auditor tests controls ordinarily not tested when the engagement is solely to express an opinion on the statements of a nonissuer. Answer (D) is incorrect. An audit of the financial statements of a nonissuer does not result in a report on internal control unless the requirements for such an engagement are met.

5.3.6. The ultimate purpose of understanding the entity and its environment and assessing the risks of material misstatement is to contribute to the auditor's assessment of the risk that

A. Tests of controls may fail to identify procedures relevant to assertions.

B. Material misstatements may exist in the financial statements.

C. Specified controls requiring segregation of duties may be circumvented by collusion.

D. Entity policies may be inappropriately overridden by senior management.

Answer (B) is correct. *(CPA, adapted)*

REQUIRED: The purpose of understanding the entity and its environment and assessing the RMMs.

DISCUSSION: The auditor's objective is to identify and assess the RMMs, whether due to fraud or error, at the financial statement and relevant assertion levels. This objective is achieved through understanding the entity and its environment, including its internal control. The understanding provides a basis for designing and implementing responses to the assessed RMMs (AU-C 315 and AS 2110). Moreover, the auditor's overall objectives in an audit include obtaining reasonable assurance about whether the statements as a whole are free from material misstatement (AU-C 200).

Answer (A) is incorrect. An auditor should obtain an understanding of controls relevant to the audit. Thus, the auditor should evaluate their design and determine whether they have been implemented. The evaluation of design considers whether the controls can effectively prevent, or detect and correct, material misstatements (AU-C 315 and AS 2110). The auditor then tests relevant controls to obtain sufficient appropriate evidence about their operating effectiveness if (1) the auditor intends to rely on them in determining the nature, timing, and extent of substantive procedures or (2) substantive procedures alone cannot provide sufficient appropriate evidence at the relevant assertion level (AU-C 330 and AS 2301). Answer (C) is incorrect. Collusion is an inherent limitation of internal control. Answer (D) is incorrect. Inappropriate management override is an inherent limitation of internal control.

5.3.7. After obtaining an understanding of the entity and its environment, including its internal control, the auditor assesses

A. The need to apply auditing standards.

B. Detection risk to determine the acceptable level of inherent risk.

C. Detection risk and inherent risk to determine the acceptable level of control risk.

D. Control risk and inherent risk to determine the acceptable level of detection risk.

Answer (D) is correct. *(Publisher, adapted)*

REQUIRED: The procedure that follows obtaining the understanding of the entity.

DISCUSSION: The acceptable level of detection risk for a relevant assertion is a function of the assessed RMMs (the combined assessment of inherent risk and control risk) and the given level of audit risk. Thus, as the RMMs increase, the acceptable level of detection risk decreases.

Answer (A) is incorrect. Auditing standards must be applied in all financial statement audits. Answer (B) is incorrect. Inherent risk and control risk exist independently of the audit. Answer (C) is incorrect. Inherent risk and control risk exist independently of the audit.

5.3.8. In obtaining an understanding of an issuer's internal control, an auditor does all the following except

A. Inspect documents.

B. Observe employees.

C. Perform a walkthrough of the transaction process.

D. Send confirmations to customers.

Answer (D) is correct. *(Publisher, adapted)*

REQUIRED: The procedure least useful in obtaining an understanding of controls.

DISCUSSION: Confirmations to customers are substantive procedures used to test the existence assertion. They are not useful in obtaining an understanding of controls.

Answer (A) is incorrect. Inspection of documents provides insight into the application of internal controls, such as approvals and oversight. Answer (B) is incorrect. The auditor observes the application of specific controls by employees in gaining an understanding of the controls. Answer (C) is incorrect. A walkthrough of the system relevant to financial reporting allows the auditor to view the application of the controls in various stages of the process.

5.3.9. Which of the following statements indicates the wrong way to use an internal control questionnaire?

A. Clarifying all answers with written remarks and explanations.

B. Filling out the questionnaire during an interview with the person who has responsibility for the area that is being audited.

C. Constructing the questionnaire so that a no response requires attention.

D. Supplementing the completed questionnaire with a narrative description or flowchart.

Answer (A) is correct. *(CIA, adapted)*

REQUIRED: The statement indicating the wrong way to use an internal control questionnaire.

DISCUSSION: Only those answers that appear inappropriate should be pursued by means of the auditor's asking for clarification or explanation. In this way, problem areas may be pinpointed and either compensating controls identified or extensions to the audit procedures planned.

5.3.10. A financial statement auditor is considering internal control for a client with an information system that makes extensive use of information technology. Which of the following statements related to the understanding of internal control for this client is false?

A. A lack of control at a single user entry point might compromise the security of a single database.

B. The auditor may find it necessary to have an expectation of the operating effectiveness of controls for certain relevant assertions.

C. The auditor must possess all the information technology skills necessary to complete the engagement.

D. Because of the inherent consistency of computer processing, the auditor may be able to reduce the extent of testing an automated control.

Answer (C) is correct. *(Publisher, adapted)*

REQUIRED: The false statement about the understanding of internal control if extensive use is made of IT.

DISCUSSION: The auditor should consider whether specialized skills are needed to determine the effect of IT on the audit, to understand the IT controls, and to design and perform tests of IT controls or substantive procedures. A member of the auditor's staff or an auditor's external specialist with IT skills can be employed to provide technical guidance.

Answer (A) is incorrect. The concentration of processing and data storage make information systems vulnerable to weaknesses in access controls. Answer (B) is incorrect. Once a programmed control is tested and found to be effective, the auditor may conclude that the control will continue to operative effectively absent change in the system. Answer (D) is incorrect. Once a programmed control is tested and found to be effective, the auditor may conclude that the control will continue to operative effectively absent change in the system.

5.3.11. The following are steps in the financial statement audit process:

I. Prepare flowchart
II. Gather exhibits of all documents
III. Interview personnel

The most logical sequence of steps is

A. I, II, III.

B. I, III, II.

C. III, II, I.

D. II, I, III.

Answer (C) is correct. *(CPA, adapted)*

REQUIRED: The order of the steps in the consideration of internal control.

DISCUSSION: AU-C 315 and AS 2110 require the auditor to obtain an understanding of internal control and to document that understanding. For example, after making inquiries (interviewing client personnel) as part of performing risk assessment procedures, the auditor might gather client documents and then prepare a flowchart reflecting the information obtained about their flow.

5.3.12. In obtaining an understanding of internal control, the auditor may trace several transactions through the control process, including how the transactions interface with any service organizations whose services are part of the information system. The primary purpose of this task is to

A. Replace substantive procedures.

B. Determine whether the controls have been implemented.

C. Determine the effectiveness of the control procedures.

D. Detect fraud.

Answer (B) is correct. *(G. Fiebelkorn)*

REQUIRED: The reason an auditor traces several transactions through the control process.

DISCUSSION: The understanding should include information about the design of relevant controls and determining whether they have been implemented by the entity and by service organizations whose services are part of the entity's information system. Tracing a few transactions through the control process (a walkthrough) should provide that evidence. A walkthrough follows transactions from origination through the entity's processes, including IT systems, until they are reflected in the entity's financial records (AS 2110).

Answer (A) is incorrect. The auditor must perform at least some substantive procedures for all material financial statement assertions. Answer (C) is incorrect. In obtaining the understanding, the auditor need not consider operating effectiveness. If the auditor wishes to have an expectation of the operating effectiveness of controls, (s)he will test controls and evaluate their effectiveness. Answer (D) is incorrect. Tracing a few transactions is not likely to detect fraud.

5.3.13. When obtaining an understanding of an entity's internal control, an auditor should concentrate on their substance rather than their form because

A. The controls may be operating effectively but may not be documented.

B. Management may establish appropriate controls but not enforce compliance with them.

C. The controls may be so inappropriate that no reliance is expected by the auditor.

D. Management may implement controls whose costs exceed their benefits.

Answer (B) is correct. *(CPA, adapted)*

REQUIRED: The reason an auditor should concentrate on the substance of controls, not their form.

DISCUSSION: The auditor must concentrate on the substance rather than the form of controls because management may establish appropriate controls but not apply them. Whether controls have been implemented at a moment in time differs from their operating effectiveness over a period of time. Thus, operating effectiveness concerns not merely whether the entity is using controls but also how the controls (manual or automated) are applied, the consistency of their application, and by whom they are applied.

Answer (A) is incorrect. An auditor is concerned with the actual operating effectiveness of controls, not with a lack of evidence about form (documentation). Answer (C) is incorrect. If controls are so inappropriate that the auditor does not expect to rely on them, their substance is irrelevant. Answer (D) is incorrect. When considering internal control in a financial statement audit, the auditor is primarily concerned with the effectiveness of controls, not their cost-benefit relationship.

5.3.14. An auditor should obtain an understanding of an entity's information system, including

A. Safeguards used to limit access to computer facilities.

B. Process used to prepare significant accounting estimates.

C. Procedures used to ensure the proper supervision of staff.

D. Programs and controls intended to address the risks of fraud.

Answer (B) is correct. *(CPA, adapted)*

REQUIRED: The purpose of obtaining an understanding of an entity's information system.

DISCUSSION: The auditor should obtain an understanding of the information system, including (1) the classes of significant transactions; (2) the ways those transactions are initiated, authorized, recorded, processed, corrected, transferred to the general ledger, and reported; (3) the accounting records, whether electronic or manual; (4) how significant events and conditions other than transactions are captured; (5) the financial reporting process used to prepare the entity's financial statements, including significant accounting estimates and disclosures; and (6) controls over journal entries (AU-C 315 and AS No. 2110).

Answer (A) is incorrect. Limiting access to computer facilities involves activity outside the information system relevant to financial reporting. Answer (C) is incorrect. Ensuring the proper supervision of staff involves activity outside the information system relevant to financial reporting. Answer (D) is incorrect. Programs and controls intended to address the risks of fraud may be included in any of the components of internal control, not just the information system component (which encompasses the information system relevant to financial reporting).

5.3.15. According to AU-C 315, *Understanding the Entity and its Environment and Assessing the Risks of Material Misstatement*, not all controls are relevant to a financial statement audit. Which one of the following would most likely be considered in an audit?

A. Timely reporting and review of quality control results.

B. Maintenance of control over unused checks.

C. Marketing analysis of sales generated by advertising projects.

D. Maintenance of statistical production analyses.

Answer (B) is correct. *(Publisher, adapted)*

REQUIRED: The control most likely relevant to a financial statement audit.

DISCUSSION: Ordinarily, controls that are relevant to a financial statement audit pertain to the entity's objective of preparing financial statements that are fairly presented in accordance with the applicable reporting framework, including managing the risks of material misstatements. Maintenance of control over unused checks is an example of a relevant control because the objective is to provide assurance about the existence assertion for cash.

5.3.16. In obtaining an understanding of internal control in a financial statement audit, an auditor is not obligated to

A. Determine whether the controls have been implemented.

B. Perform procedures to understand the design of internal control.

C. Document the understanding of the entity's internal control components.

D. Search for significant deficiencies in the operation of internal control.

Answer (D) is correct. *(CPA, adapted)*

REQUIRED: The step an auditor need not take in obtaining an understanding of internal control.

DISCUSSION: In all audits, the auditor should obtain an understanding of each of the five components of internal control sufficient to plan the audit. An understanding is obtained by performing risk assessment procedures to evaluate the design of controls relevant to the audit and to determine whether they have been implemented. In addition, the auditor should obtain and document the understanding of the entity's internal control components. However, in an audit, the auditor is not obligated to search for significant deficiencies or material weaknesses (AU-C 265).

5.3.17. Which of the following statements regarding auditor documentation of the understanding of the client's internal control components obtained to plan the audit is correct?

A. Documentation must include flowcharts.

B. Documentation must include procedural write-ups.

C. No documentation is necessary although it is desirable.

D. No one particular form of documentation is necessary, and the extent of documentation may vary.

Answer (D) is correct. *(CPA, adapted)*

REQUIRED: The true statement about the auditor's documentation of the client's internal control.

DISCUSSION: In accordance with the documentation requirements in AU-C 315, the auditor should document such matters as (1) discussions among the engagement team; (2) the understanding of the entity and its environment, including each internal control component, sources of information, and the risk assessment procedures; (3) the risk assessments; and (4) risks requiring special audit consideration. The form and extent of documentation vary with (1) the nature, size, and complexity of the entity and its controls; (2) the availability of information; and (3) the audit methods and technology used (AU-C 315).

Answer (A) is incorrect. Flowcharts are not required. Answer (B) is incorrect. Procedural write-ups are not required. Answer (C) is incorrect. Documentation is required but not in any specific form.

5.3.18. A well-designed internal control questionnaire should

A. Elicit "yes" or "no" responses rather than narrative responses and be organized by department.

B. Be a sufficient source of data for assessment of control risk.

C. Help evaluate the effectiveness of internal control.

D. Be independent of the objectives of the audit.

Answer (C) is correct. *(CIA, adapted)*

REQUIRED: The function of a well-designed internal control questionnaire.

DISCUSSION: An internal control questionnaire consists of a series of questions about the firm's controls designed to prevent or detect errors or fraud. Answers to the questions help the auditor identify specific controls relevant to specific assertions and to design tests of controls to evaluate the effectiveness of their design and operation.

Answer (A) is incorrect. Yes/no question formats and question sequence by department may facilitate administering the questionnaire, but other formats and methods of question organization are possible. Answer (B) is incorrect. The questionnaire is a tool to help understand and document internal control but is not sufficient as the sole source of evidence to support the assessment of control risk. Answer (D) is incorrect. The internal control questionnaire must be designed to achieve the audit objectives.

5.3.19. The auditor's understanding of internal control is documented to substantiate

A. Conformity of the accounting records with generally accepted accounting principles.

B. Compliance with generally accepted auditing standards.

C. Adherence to procedures for effective and efficient management decision making.

D. The fairness of the financial statement presentation.

Answer (B) is correct. *(CPA, adapted)*

REQUIRED: The reason for the auditor's documentation of the understanding of internal control.

DISCUSSION: The auditor should prepare audit documentation that is sufficient to permit an experienced auditor to understand (1) the nature, timing, and extent of audit procedures performed to comply with GAAS and other requirements; (2) the results and evidence obtained; and (3) significant findings or issues, the conclusions reached, and judgments made (AU-C 230). Thus, the auditor should document, among other things, his or her understanding of the components of internal control and the assessed risks of material misstatement at the financial statement and assertion levels (AU-C 315).

Answer (A) is incorrect. A full audit, not just the understanding of internal control, is required to enable an auditor to obtain sufficient appropriate evidence to draw reasonable conclusions on which to base the opinion on the fairness of the financial statements in accordance with an applicable financial reporting framework. Answer (C) is incorrect. Adherence to procedures for certain decision-making processes, such as those relating to product pricing, may not be relevant to a financial statement audit. Answer (D) is incorrect. A full audit, not just the understanding of internal control, is required to enable an auditor to obtain sufficient appropriate evidence to draw reasonable conclusions on which to base the opinion on the fairness of the financial statements in accordance with an applicable financial reporting framework.

5.4 Flowcharting

5.4.1. When documenting internal control, the independent auditor sometimes uses a systems flowchart, which can best be described as a

A. Pictorial presentation of the flow of instructions in a client's internal computer system.

B. Diagram that clearly indicates an organization's internal reporting structure.

C. Graphic illustration of the flow of operations that is used to replace the auditor's internal control questionnaire.

D. Symbolic representation of a system or series of sequential processes.

Answer (D) is correct. *(CPA, adapted)*

REQUIRED: The best description of a systems flowchart.

DISCUSSION: A systems flowchart is a symbolic representation of the flow of documents and procedures through a series of steps in the accounting process of the client's organization.

Answer (A) is incorrect. A pictorial presentation of the flow of instructions in a client's internal computer system is a computer program flowchart. Answer (B) is incorrect. The organizational chart depicts the client's internal reporting structure. Answer (C) is incorrect. A flowchart does not necessarily replace the auditor's internal control questionnaire. Controls beyond those depicted on the systems flowchart must also be considered by the auditor, and information obtained from the questionnaire may be used to develop the flowchart.

5.4.2. An advantage of using systems flowcharts to document information about internal control instead of using internal control questionnaires is that systems flowcharts

A. Identify internal control deficiencies more prominently.

B. Provide a visual depiction of clients' activities.

C. Indicate whether controls are operating effectively.

D. Reduce the need to observe clients' employees performing routine tasks.

Answer (B) is correct. *(CPA, adapted)*

REQUIRED: The advantage of systems flowcharts over internal control questionnaires.

DISCUSSION: Systems flowcharts provide a visual representation of a series of sequential processes, that is, of a flow of documents, data, and operations. In many instances, a flowchart is preferable to a questionnaire because a picture is usually more easily comprehended.

Answer (A) is incorrect. A systems flowchart can present the flow of information and documents in a system, but it does not specifically identify the deficiencies. Answer (C) is incorrect. The flowchart does not provide evidence of how effectively controls are actually operating. Answer (D) is incorrect. The flowchart is useful in documenting the understanding of internal control, but it does not reduce the need for observation of employees performing tasks if those tests of controls are deemed necessary.

5.4.3. The normal sequence of documents and operations on a well-prepared systems flowchart is

A. Top to bottom and left to right.

B. Bottom to top and left to right.

C. Top to bottom and right to left.

D. Bottom to top and right to left.

Answer (A) is correct. *(CPA, adapted)*

REQUIRED: The normal sequence of documents and operations on a well-prepared systems flowchart.

DISCUSSION: The direction of flow in the normal sequence of documents and operations on a well-prepared systems flowchart is from top to bottom and from left to right.

Answer (B) is incorrect. The normal vertical movement is top to bottom. Answer (C) is incorrect. The normal horizontal movement is left to right. Answer (D) is incorrect. The normal sequence is top to bottom and left to right.

5.4.4. The diamond-shaped symbol is commonly used in flowcharting to show or represent a

A. Process or a single step in a procedure or program.

B. Terminal output display.

C. Decision point, conditional testing, or branching.

D. Predefined process.

Answer (C) is correct. *(CIA, adapted)*

REQUIRED: The meaning of the diamond-shaped symbol used in flowcharting.

DISCUSSION: Flowcharts illustrate in pictorial fashion the flow of data, documents, and/or operations in a system. Flowcharts may summarize a system or present great detail, e.g., as found in program flowcharts. According to the American National Standards Institute, the diamond-shaped symbol represents a decision point or test of a condition in a program flowchart, that is, the point at which a determination must be made as to which logic path (branch) to follow. The diamond is also sometimes used in systems flowcharts.

Answer (A) is incorrect. The rectangle is the appropriate symbol for a process or a single step in a procedure or program. Answer (B) is incorrect. A terminal display is signified by a symbol similar to the shape of a video screen. Answer (D) is incorrect. A predefined processing step is represented by a rectangle with double lines on either side.

5.4.5. In connection with the consideration of internal control, an auditor encounters the following flowcharting symbols:

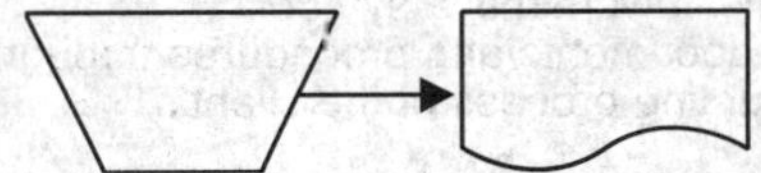

The auditor should conclude that a

A. Master file has been created by a manual operation.

B. Master file has been created by a computer operation.

C. Document has been generated by a computer operation.

D. Document has been generated by a manual operation.

Answer (D) is correct. *(CPA, adapted)*

REQUIRED: The meaning of the flowcharting symbols shown.

DISCUSSION: The symbol on the left represents a manual operation and the symbol on the right a document. The arrow's direction suggests that a document is prepared through a manual operation.

Answer (A) is incorrect. A master file is depicted by a parallelogram (input/output) or a symbol for the type of storage device used (e.g., magnetic tape or disk). Answer (B) is incorrect. A computer operation is depicted by a rectangle. Answer (C) is incorrect. A computer operation is depicted by a rectangle.

5.4.6. The correct labeling, in order, for the following flowchart symbols is

A. Document, display, online storage, and entry operation.

B. Manual operation, processing, offline storage, and input-output activity.

C. Display, document, online storage, and entry operation.

D. Manual operation, document, online storage, and entry operation.

Answer (D) is correct. *(CMA, adapted)*

REQUIRED: The correct sequence of labels of four flowchart symbols.

DISCUSSION: The first symbol indicates a manual operation, which is an offline process. The second symbol represents a document, and the third symbol indicates online storage (e.g., a disk drive). The final symbol represents an operation. An operation is defined as a process resulting in a change in the information or the flow direction. In other words, it can be an entry operation.

Answer (A) is incorrect. The first symbol, a trapezoid, is for a manual operation. Answer (B) is incorrect. The third symbol is for online storage. Answer (C) is incorrect. The first symbol does not represent display.

5.4.7. Which one of the following best reflects the basic elements of a data flow diagram?

A. Data sources, data flows, computer configurations, flowchart, and data storage.

B. Data source, data destination, data flows, transformation processes, and data storage.

C. Data flows, data storage, and program flowchart.

D. Data flows, program flowchart, and data destination.

Answer (B) is correct. *(CMA, adapted)*

REQUIRED: The best description of the basic elements of a data flow diagram.

DISCUSSION: Structured analysis is a graphical method of defining the inputs, processes, and outputs of a system and dividing it into subsystems. It is a top down approach that specifies the interfaces between modules and the transformations occurring within each. Data flow diagrams are used in structured analysis. The basic elements of a data flow diagram include data source, data destination, data flows, transformation processes, and data storage.

Answer (A) is incorrect. Computer configuration is not an element of a data flow diagram. Answer (C) is incorrect. A program flowchart is not an element of a data flow diagram. Answer (D) is incorrect. A program flowchart is not an element of a data flow diagram.

5.4.8. The symbol used to represent the file of hard-copy, computer-generated payroll reports kept for future reference is

A. 

B. 

C. 

D.

Answer (B) is correct. *(CMA, adapted)*

REQUIRED: The symbol used to represent the kept file of hard-copy, computer-generated payroll reports.

DISCUSSION: Hard-copy, computer-generated payroll reports are kept in offline storage, which is symbolized by a triangle with a mid-line parallel to its base.

Answer (A) is incorrect. A circle with a tangent at its base represents a magnetic tape. Answer (C) is incorrect. This symbol represents online storage. Answer (D) is incorrect. A parallelogram is the general symbol for input or output.

5.4.9. Decision tables differ from program flowcharts in that decision tables emphasize

A. Ease of manageability for complex programs.

B. Logical relationships among conditions and actions.

C. Cost-benefit factors justifying the program.

D. The sequence in which operations are performed.

Answer (B) is correct. *(CPA, adapted)*

REQUIRED: The distinction between decision tables and flowcharts.

DISCUSSION: A decision table identifies the contingencies considered in the description of a problem and the appropriate actions to be taken relative to those contingencies. Decision tables are logic diagrams presented in matrix form. Unlike flowcharts, they do not present the sequence of the actions described.

Answer (A) is incorrect. Neither flowcharts nor decision tables emphasize ease of manageability. Answer (C) is incorrect. Neither flowcharts nor decision tables emphasize cost-benefit factors. Answer (D) is incorrect. Unlike flowcharts, decision tables do not present the sequence of the actions described.

5.4.10. A document flowchart represents the

A. Sequence of logical operations performed during the execution of a computer program.

B. Possible combinations of alternative logic conditions and corresponding courses of action for each condition in a computer program.

C. Flow of data through a series of operations in an automated data processing system.

D. Flow of forms that relate to a particular transaction through an organization.

Answer (D) is correct. *(CMA, adapted)*

REQUIRED: The definition of a document flowchart.

DISCUSSION: A document flowchart graphically presents the flow of forms (documents) through a system that relate to a given transaction, e.g., the processing of a customer's order. It shows the source, flow, processing, and final disposition of the various copies of all related documents.

Answer (A) is incorrect. A program flowchart represents the sequence of logical operations performed during the execution of a computer program. Answer (B) is incorrect. A decision table consists of the possible combinations of alternative logic conditions and corresponding courses of action for each condition in a computer program. Answer (C) is incorrect. A system flowchart is used to represent the flow of data through an automated data processing system.

5.4.11. The following is a section of a system flowchart for a payroll application:

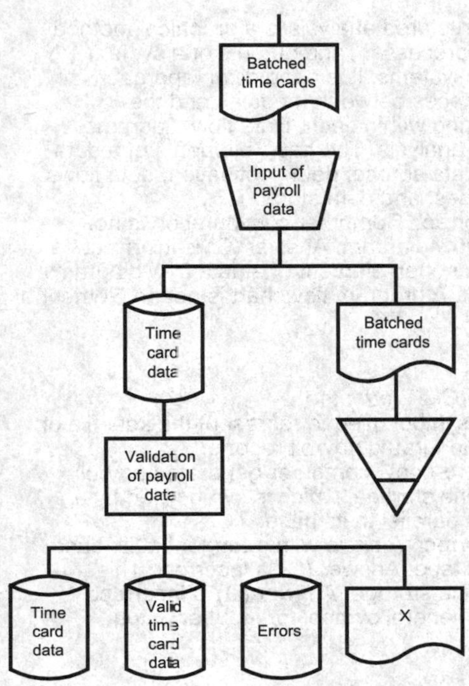

Symbol X could represent

A. Erroneous time cards.

B. An error report.

C. Batched time cards.

D. Unclaimed payroll checks.

Answer (B) is correct. *(CPA, adapted)*

REQUIRED: The item represented by Symbol X.

DISCUSSION: Symbol X is a document, that is, hard copy output of the validation routine shown. The time card data, the validated data, and the errors are recorded on magnetic disk after the validation process. Thus, either an error report or the valid time card information is represented by Symbol X.

Answer (A) is incorrect. Time cards were stored offline before the validation process. Answer (C) is incorrect. Time cards were stored offline before the validation process. Answer (D) is incorrect. No payroll checks are shown.

5.4.12. An internal auditor is reviewing the following computer logic diagram:

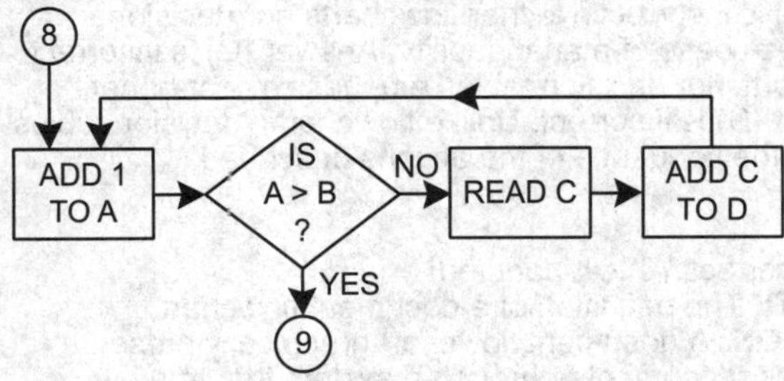

This diagram represents which of the following?

A. Program loop step.

B. Data validity check.

C. Balance test.

D. Limit test.

Answer (A) is correct. *(CIA, adapted)*

REQUIRED: The operation described by the computer logic diagram.

DISCUSSION: Variable A will be increased by 1 and C will be added to D repetitively until A exceeds B. The diagram illustrates a program loop, a technique for performing repeated iterations of an instruction a specified number of times.

Answer (B) is incorrect. A data validity check compares the bits of each transmitted character with the valid combinations of bits. Answer (C) is incorrect. A balance test compares a gross amount with its components. Answer (D) is incorrect. A limit test ascertains whether a number falls within a predetermined range of reasonable values.

5.4.13. The symbol employed to determine if an employee's wages are above or below the maximum limit for FICA taxes is

A.

B.

C.

D.

Answer (B) is correct. *(CMA, adapted)*

REQUIRED: The symbol to determine if an employee's wages are within a limit.

DISCUSSION: The question implies a decision, for which a diamond is the flowcharting symbol.

Answer (A) is incorrect. A rectangle is the general symbol for a process or operation. Answer (C) is incorrect. A trapezoid symbolizes a manual operation. Answer (D) is incorrect. A square represents an auxiliary operation performed by a machine other than a computer.

5.4.14. The graphic portrayal of the flow of data and the information processing of a system, including computer hardware, is best displayed in a

A. Data-flow diagram.

B. System flowchart.

C. Gantt chart.

D. Program flowchart.

Answer (B) is correct. *(CMA, adapted)*

REQUIRED: The best method of displaying the flow of data and the information processing of a system.

DISCUSSION: A system flowchart is a graphic analysis of a data processing application, usually prepared by a systems analyst. The system flowchart is general and stresses flows of data, not computer program logic. A program flowchart is a graphic representation of the detailed steps and logic of an individual computer program.

Answer (A) is incorrect. A data-flow diagram shows only the flow of data, not the total system. Answer (C) is incorrect. A Gantt chart is a bar chart used to monitor the progress of large projects. Answer (D) is incorrect. A program flowchart shows only the details of a single program, not the entire computer system.

5.4.15. The symbol employed to represent the printing of the employees' paychecks by the computer is

A.

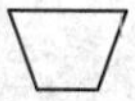

B.

C.

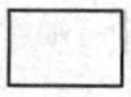

D.

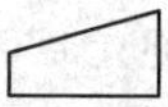

Answer (C) is correct. *(CMA, adapted)*

REQUIRED: The flowchart symbol for the printing of paychecks by a computer.

DISCUSSION: The printing of paychecks by the computer is an operation depicted by the general processing symbol, which is a rectangle.

Answer (A) is incorrect. A trapezoid depicts a manual operation. Answer (B) is incorrect. A square is an auxiliary operation performed by a machine other than a computer. Answer (D) is incorrect. This symbol indicates manual input, e.g., entry of a proper code through a computer console.

5.4.16. The symbol employed to represent the employees' checks printed by the computer is

A.

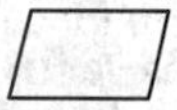

B.

C.

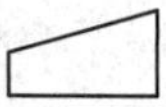

D.

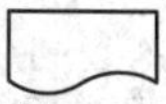

Answer (D) is correct. *(CMA, adapted)*

REQUIRED: The symbol used to represent employee checks printed by a computer.

DISCUSSION: Employee checks printed by the computer are depicted by the document symbol, which resembles the top of a grand piano.

Answer (A) is incorrect. A parallelogram is the general symbol for input or output. Answer (B) is incorrect. A trapezoid indicates a manual operation. Answer (C) is incorrect. This symbol indicates manual input.

Questions 5.4 17 through 5.4.21 are based on the following information. This flowchart depicts the processing of daily cash receipts for Rockmart Manufacturing. Please note that some procedures are not shown in this flowchart.

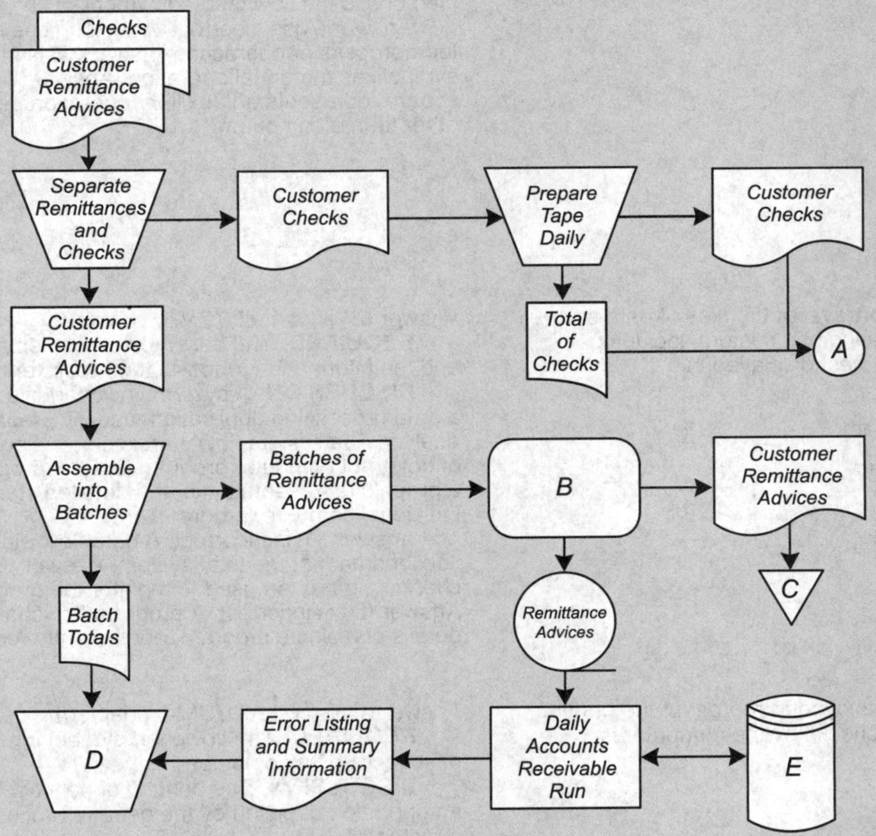

5.4.17. The customer checks accompanied by the control tape (refer to symbol A) should be

A. Forwarded daily to the billing department for deposit.

B. Taken by the mail clerk to the bank for deposit daily.

C. Forwarded to the CFO for deposit daily.

D. Accumulated for a week and then forwarded to the CFO for deposit weekly.

Answer (C) is correct. *(CMA, adapted)*

REQUIRED: The procedure for handling customer checks and the related control tape.

DISCUSSION: Symbol A is a connector between a point on this flowchart and another part of the flowchart not shown. The checks and the adding machine control tape should flow through symbol A to the CFO's office. The CFO is the custodian of funds and is responsible for deposit of daily receipts.

Answer (A) is incorrect. Record keepers perform functions that should be separate from custody of assets. Answer (B) is incorrect. The mail clerk should prepare a list of checks received before they are forwarded to the CFO for deposit. Answer (D) is incorrect. Daily receipts should be deposited intact daily and then reconciled with the bank deposit records.

5.4.18. The appropriate description that should be placed in symbol B is

A. Keying and verifying.

B. Error correction.

C. Collation of remittance advices.

D. Batch processing.

Answer (A) is correct. *(CMA, adapted)*

REQUIRED: The appropriate description for symbol B.

DISCUSSION: The figure below symbol B signifies magnetic tape, so the operation represented by symbol B must be keying the information onto the tape. Verifying the keyed data should also occur at this step.

Answer (B) is incorrect. Error correction other than for keying errors should occur subsequently. Answer (C) is incorrect. Collation has already occurred. Answer (D) is incorrect. Batch processing describes the entire system.

5.4.19. The next action to take with the customer remittance advices (refer to Symbol C) would be to

A. Discard them immediately.

B. File them daily by batch number.

C. Forward them to the internal audit department for internal review.

D. Forward them to the treasurer to compare with the monthly bank statement.

Answer (B) is correct. *(CMA, adapted)*

REQUIRED: The action taken at Symbol C.

DISCUSSION: All activity with respect to the paper documents most likely ceases at Symbol C. Thus, the batched documents must be filed.

Answer (A) is incorrect. The documents should be kept for reference and audit. Answer (C) is incorrect. Internal auditors cannot feasibly review all documents regarding transactions even in an audit. Answer (D) is incorrect. Comparison by the treasurer would be inappropriate. (S)he has custody of cash.

5.4.20. The appropriate description that should be placed in symbol D is

A. Attach batch total to report and file.

B. Reconcile cash balances.

C. Compare batch total and correct as necessary.

D. Proof report.

Answer (C) is correct. *(CMA, adapted)*

REQUIRED: The appropriate description for symbol D.

DISCUSSION: This flowcharting symbol indicates a manual operation or offline process. The input to this operation consists of an adding machine tape containing batch totals and a document containing summary information about the accounts receivable update and an error listing. Thus, the operation apparently involves comparing these items.

Answer (A) is incorrect. No filing symbol is given. Answer (B) is incorrect. The flowchart concerns daily receipts, not the reconciliation of cash balances. Answer (D) is incorrect. Symbol D indicates a comparison, not output in the form of a report.

5.4.21. The appropriate description that should be placed in symbol E is

A. Accounts receivable master file.

B. Bad debts master file.

C. Remittance advice master file.

D. Cash projection file.

Answer (A) is correct. *(CMA, adapted)*

REQUIRED: The appropriate description of symbol E.

DISCUSSION: The flowcharting figure at symbol E indicates magnetic disk storage. Given that it is an input and output for the daily computer processing of accounts receivable, it must be the accounts receivable master file.

Answer (B) is incorrect. Bad debts are not a part of processing daily receipts. Answer (C) is incorrect. The remittance advice master file was not used for the daily accounts receivable run. Answer (D) is incorrect. The cash projection file was not used for the daily accounts receivable run.

5.4.22. The symbol used to represent the physical act of collecting employees' time cards for processing is

A.

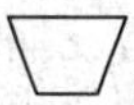

B.

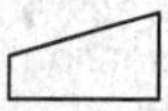

C.

D.

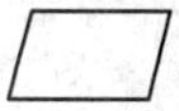

Answer (A) is correct. *(CMA, adapted)*

REQUIRED: The symbol used to represent the physical act of collecting employees' time cards for processing.

DISCUSSION: Collecting employees' time cards is a manual operation represented by a trapezoid with equal nonparallel sides.

Answer (B) is incorrect. This symbol represents manual input. Answer (C) is incorrect. A rectangle is the general symbol for processing. Answer (D) is incorrect. A parallelogram is the general symbol for input or output.

5.4.23. The symbol used to represent the employees' payroll records stored on magnetic tape is

A.

B.

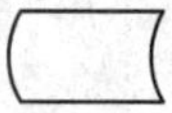

C.

D.

Answer (D) is correct. *(CMA, adapted)*

REQUIRED: The symbol representing employees' payroll records stored on magnetic tape.

DISCUSSION: The magnetic tape symbol (a circle with a tangent at its base) indicates storage on magnetic tape.

Answer (A) is incorrect. A triangle with a mid-line parallel to its base depicts offline storage. Answer (B) is incorrect. This symbol represents online storage. Answer (C) is incorrect. This symbol represents punched paper tape.

5.4.24. The symbol used to represent the weekly payroll register generated by the computer is

A. 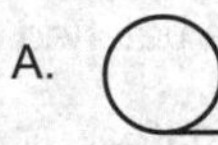

B. 

C. 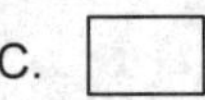

D. 

Answer (D) is correct. *(CMA, adapted)*

REQUIRED: The symbol used to represent a weekly payroll register printed by a computer.

DISCUSSION: The weekly payroll register on a computer printout is represented by a document symbol, which resembles the top of a grand piano.

Answer (A) is incorrect. A circle with a tangent at its base represents magnetic tape input-output or storage. Answer (B) is incorrect. A triangle with a mid-line parallel to its base depicts offline storage. Answer (C) is incorrect. A rectangle is the general symbol for a process.

5.4.25. Which of the following symbolic representations indicates that a sales invoice has been filed?

A. 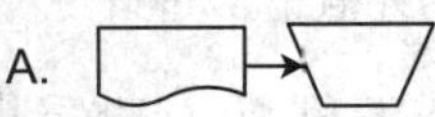

B. 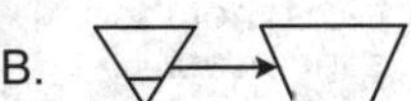

C. 

D. 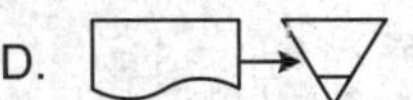

Answer (D) is correct. *(CPA, adapted)*

REQUIRED: The symbols indicating filing of a document.

DISCUSSION: The arrow from the document symbol to the triangle with the mid-line parallel to its base indicates that a document has been stored in an offline file.

Answer (A) is incorrect. The arrow from the document symbol to the trapezoid indicates manual (offline) processing of the document. Answer (B) is incorrect. The arrow from offline storage to the manual operation symbol signifies manual (offline) processing of an offline file. Answer (C) is incorrect. The arrow from the trapezoid to the triangle with a mid-line indicates that manual (offline) processing is followed by offline file storage of the result.

5.5 Internal Control and Information Technology

5.5.1. If a payroll system continues to pay employees who have been terminated, control weaknesses most likely exist because

A. Procedures were not implemented to verify and control the receipt by the computer processing department of all transactions prior to processing.

B. There were inadequate manual controls maintained outside the computer system.

C. Programmed controls such as limit checks should have been built into the system.

D. Input file label checking routines built into the programs were ignored by the operator.

Answer (B) is correct. *(CISA, adapted)*

REQUIRED: The control weakness allowing terminated employees to continue being paid.

DISCUSSION: The authorization to pay employees comes from outside the computer department. Thus, ineffective controls external to the computer processing department are most likely the cause of allowing the payments to terminated employees to continue without detection.

Answer (A) is incorrect. Batch totals are effective controls over properly authorized transactions but provide no control over unauthorized transactions. Answer (C) is incorrect. A limit check tests the reasonableness of a particular transaction but not whether it was authorized. Answer (D) is incorrect. Checking input file labels (header labels) will not detect unauthorized transactions.

5.5.2. Because of a power surge, a read-write head damaged the surface of the disk volume containing the savings account master file used by an online savings account update and inquiry program. At the time of the failure, there were 20 active teller terminals connected to the program. The disk damage was the only physical damage resulting from the power fluctuation. Possible recovery steps are

1. Restart the online update and inquiry program.
2. Restore the savings account master file from the good records on the original disk.
3. Restore the savings account master file from the most recent file backup.
4. Display each teller's last transaction and prompt each teller to reenter any subsequent transactions.
5. Apply transactions occurring since the last complete file backup to the master file.
6. Prompt tellers to reenter their last transaction.

The best recovery procedure consists of which sequence of steps?

A. 2, 5, 1, 6.
B. 2, 5, 1, 4.
C. 3, 5, 1, 4.
D. 3, 5, 1, 6.

Answer (C) is correct. *(CIA, adapted)*

REQUIRED: The sequence of steps in the best recovery procedure.

DISCUSSION: The use of restart and recovery procedures eliminates the need to reprocess all data in the event of a processing failure. If checkpoints are established during a processing run (e.g., by periodically copying necessary data and program indicators onto a storage medium), the run may be restarted from the checkpoint. Restart and recovery procedures can also be used in an online system. Accordingly, the recovery procedure should begin with updating the most recent copy of the damaged master file from the transactions log. The online update and inquiry program can then be activated and each teller told to reenter transactions after the last recorded transaction.

Answer (A) is incorrect. The original disk was damaged, thus preventing a full update from that source. Also, each teller should begin with the transaction following the last one logged before the power surge. Answer (B) is incorrect. The original disk was damaged, thus preventing a full update from that source. Answer (D) is incorrect. Each teller should begin with the transaction following the last one logged before the power surge.

5.5.3. So that the essential control features of a client's computer system can be identified and evaluated, the auditor of a nonissuer must, at a minimum, have

A. A basic familiarity with the computer's operating system.
B. A sufficient understanding of the entire computer system.
C. An expertise in computer systems analysis.
D. A background in programming procedures.

Answer (B) is correct. *(CPA, adapted)*

REQUIRED: The degree of understanding an auditor must have of a client's computer system.

DISCUSSION: The audit should be performed by a person having adequate technical training and proficiency as an auditor. That auditor is required to obtain a sufficient understanding of internal control to plan the audit and determine the nature, timing, and extent of tests to be performed. Hence, the auditor should have the training and proficiency that are necessary to understand controls relevant to the computer system.

Answer (A) is incorrect. Familiarity with the computer's operating system is less important than understanding the entire processing system. Answer (C) is incorrect. Auditors usually do not need to be experts in computer systems analysis, although certain audit procedures may require special expertise. Answer (D) is incorrect. Auditors usually do not need to be experts in computer programming, although certain audit procedures may require special expertise.

5.5.4. The two broad groupings of information systems control activities are general controls and application controls. General controls include controls

A. Designed to ensure that only authorized users receive output from processing.
B. For developing, modifying, and maintaining computer programs.
C. Relating to the correction and resubmission of faulty data.
D. Designed to ensure that all data submitted for processing have been properly authorized.

Answer (B) is correct. *(Publisher, adapted)*

REQUIRED: The general controls.

DISCUSSION: General controls are policies and procedures that relate to many information systems applications and support the effective functioning of application controls by helping to ensure the continued proper operation of information systems. General controls include controls over (1) data center and network operations; (2) systems software acquisition, change, and maintenance; (3) program change; (4) access security; and (5) application systems acquisition, development, and maintenance (AU-C 315).

Answer (A) is incorrect. Control over report distribution (output) is an application control. Answer (C) is incorrect. Correction of input errors is an application control. Answer (D) is incorrect. Authorization of input is an application control.

5.5.5. Which of the following statements most likely represents a disadvantage for an entity that keeps digital computer files rather than manually prepared files?

A. Attention is focused on the accuracy of the programming process rather than errors in individual transactions.

B. It is usually easier for unauthorized persons to access and alter the files.

C. Random error associated with processing similar transactions in different ways is usually greater.

D. It is usually more difficult to compare recorded accountability with physical count of assets.

Answer (B) is correct. *(CPA, adapted)*

REQUIRED: The disadvantage of digital computer files.

DISCUSSION: In a manual system, one individual is assigned responsibility for maintaining and safeguarding the records. However, in a computer environment, the data files may be subject to change by others without documentation or indication of who made the changes.

Answer (A) is incorrect. The focus on programming is an advantage of using the computer. A program allows transactions to be processed uniformly. Answer (C) is incorrect. An advantage of the computer is that it processes similar transactions in the same way. Answer (D) is incorrect. The method of maintaining the files is independent of the ability to compare this information in the file with the physical count of assets.

5.5.6. The significance of hardware controls is that they

A. Ensure correct programming of operating system functions.

B. Ensure the correct execution of machine instructions.

C. Reduce the incidence of user input errors in online systems.

D. Ensure that run-to-run totals in application systems are consistent.

Answer (B) is correct. *(CIA, adapted)*

REQUIRED: The significance of hardware controls.

DISCUSSION: Hardware controls are built into the equipment by the manufacturer to detect and control errors arising from the use of the equipment. Examples include parity checks, read-after-write checks, and echo checks.

Answer (A) is incorrect. Programmers and/or analysts must correct errors in computer programs. Answer (C) is incorrect. Use of input screens, limit tests, self-checking digits, and other input controls can reduce the incidence of input errors in online systems. Answer (D) is incorrect. Run-to-run totals ensure the completeness of update in an online system by accumulating separate totals for all transactions processed throughout a period. This total is compared with the total of items accepted for processing.

5.5.7. What type of computer processing system is characterized by data that are assembled from more than one location and records that are updated immediately?

A. Personal computer systems.

B. Data compression systems.

C. Batch processing systems.

D. Online, real-time systems.

Answer (D) is correct. *(CPA, adapted)*

REQUIRED: The system allowing data entry from multiple locations and immediate updating.

DISCUSSION: Real-time processing involves processing an input record and receiving the output soon enough to affect a current decision-making process. In a real-time system, the user interacts with the system to control an ongoing activity. Online indicates that the decision maker is in direct communication with the computer. Online, real-time systems usually permit access to the server computer system from multiple remote terminals.

Answer (A) is incorrect. Access from multiple locations is more typical of server computer systems than of personal computer systems. Answer (B) is incorrect. Data compression systems encode data to take up less storage space. Answer (C) is incorrect. Batching of transactions requires assembly of data at one place and a delay in updating.

5.5.8. Your firm has recently converted its purchasing cycle from a manual process to an online computer system. Which of the following is a probable result associated with conversion to the new automatic system?

A. Processing errors are increased.

B. The firm's risk exposures are reduced.

C. Processing time is increased.

D. Traditional duties are less separated.

Answer (D) is correct. *(CIA, adapted)*

REQUIRED: The probable result associated with conversion to the new automatic system.

DISCUSSION: In a manual system with appropriate internal control, separate individuals are responsible for authorizing transactions, recording transactions, and custody of assets. These checks and balances prevent fraud and detect inaccurate or incomplete transactions. In a computer environment, however, this segregation of duties is not always feasible. For example, a computer may print checks, record disbursements, and generate information for reconciling the account balance.

Answer (A) is incorrect. A computer system decreases processing errors. Answer (B) is incorrect. The conversion to a new system does not reduce the number of risk exposures. Answer (C) is incorrect. Processing time is decreased.

5.5.9. In a data center, many hardware controls ensure the accuracy of data processed. One hardware control used to evaluate stored data by counting the number of on bits in each character and then determining whether the total obtained is odd or even is a

A. Programmed check.

B. Header label check.

C. Check digit routine.

D. Parity check.

Answer (D) is correct. *(CIA, adapted)*

REQUIRED: The hardware control that counts on bits.

DISCUSSION: Hardware controls are built into the computer by the manufacturer. A parity check adds the on bits in a byte and determines whether the sum is odd or even, depending on whether the computer has odd or even parity, respectively. This check verifies that all data have been transferred without loss. For example, if the computer has even parity, the parity bit added to a byte will be turned on if the byte contains an odd number of on bits. The parity bit is turned off if the byte has an even number of on bits. Accordingly, if the number of on bits, including the parity bit, is not even, an error has occurred.

Answer (A) is incorrect. A programmed check is an edit test performed by a program (software). Answer (B) is incorrect. A header label identifies a file on a tape or disk. Software makes this check. Answer (C) is incorrect. A self-checking digit is a suffix digit related algorithmically to the preceding digits of an identification number. It is an application control to verify that the number has been transferred correctly from one medium or device to another.

5.5.10. Misstatements in a batch computer system caused by incorrect programs or data may not be detected immediately because

A. Errors in some transactions may cause rejection of other transactions in the batch.

B. The identification of errors in input data typically is not part of the program.

C. There are time delays in processing transactions in a batch system.

D. The processing of transactions in a batch system is not uniform.

Answer (C) is correct. *(CPA, adapted)*

REQUIRED: The reason errors may not be detected immediately in a batch computer system.

DISCUSSION: Transactions in a batch computer system are grouped together, or batched, prior to processing. Batches may be processed either daily, weekly, or even monthly. Thus, considerable time may elapse between the initiation of the transaction and the discovery of an error.

Answer (A) is incorrect. The transactions within the batch are typically not contingent upon one another. Answer (B) is incorrect. Edit checks can be incorporated into batch processing environments. However, the edit checks are used to test the transactions in batches. Answer (D) is incorrect. A batch of transactions is typically processed uniformly.

5.5.11. In the organization of the information systems function, the most important segregation of duties is

A. Not allowing the data librarian to assist in data processing operations.

B. Assuring that those responsible for programming the system do not have access to data processing operations.

C. Having a separate information officer at the top level of the organization outside of the accounting function.

D. Using different programming personnel to maintain utility programs from those who maintain the application programs.

Answer (B) is correct. *(CMA, adapted)*

REQUIRED: The most important segregation of duties in the information systems function.

DISCUSSION: Segregation of duties is a general control that is vital in a computerized environment. Some segregation of duties common in noncomputerized environments may not be feasible in a computer environment. However, certain tasks should not be combined. Systems analysts and programmers should be separate from computer operators. Both programmers and analysts may be able to modify programs, files, and controls, and should therefore have no access to those programs nor to computer equipment. Operators should not be assigned programming duties or responsibility for systems design, and should have no opportunity to make changes in programs and systems.

Answer (A) is incorrect. Librarians maintain control over documentation, programs, and data files; they should have no access to equipment, but they can assist in data processing operations. Answer (C) is incorrect. A separate information officer outside of the accounting function would not be as critical a segregation of duties as that between programmers and processors. Answer (D) is incorrect. Programmers usually handle all types of programs.

5.5.12. An auditor anticipates relying on the operating effectiveness of controls in a computerized environment. Under these circumstances, on which of the following activities would the auditor initially focus?

A. Programmed controls.

B. Application controls.

C. Output controls.

D. General controls.

Answer (D) is correct. *(CPA, adapted)*

REQUIRED: The initial focus when the auditor anticipates relying on controls in a computerized environment.

DISCUSSION: Relying on controls involves (1) identifying specific controls that are suitably designed to prevent, or detect and correct, material misstatements in relevant assertions; (2) performing tests of controls; and (3) assessing the RMMs. Some computer controls relate to all computer activities (general controls), and some relate to specific tasks (application controls). Because general controls have pervasive effects, they should be tested before application controls. If the general controls are ineffective, tests of the application controls over input, processing, and output are unlikely to permit the auditor to rely on controls.

Answer (A) is incorrect. Programmed activities relate to application controls, which should be tested for effectiveness if the general controls are effective. Answer (B) is incorrect. General controls are tested before application controls. Answer (C) is incorrect. Output controls are application controls, which are tested after general controls.

5.5.13. It is important to maintain proper segregation of duties in a computer environment. Which of the following access setups is appropriate?

	Update Access for Production Data		Update Access for Production Programs	
	Users Have?	Application Programmers Have?	Users Have?	Application Programmers Have?
A.	Yes	No	No	No
B.	Yes	No	No	Yes
C.	No	Yes	Yes	No
D.	No	Yes	Yes	Yes

Answer (A) is correct. *(CIA, adapted)*

REQUIRED: The appropriate access setup.

DISCUSSION: Incompatible duties should be separated for effective control. End users need access to applications data and functions but not to systems software, applications programs, and most computer equipment. Application programmers should be separated from computer operations, technical support staff, computer equipment, systems software, production versions of programs, and production data.

5.5.14. In which of the following circumstances would an auditor expect to find that an entity implemented automated controls to reduce risks of misstatement?

A. When errors are difficult to predict.

B. When misstatements are difficult to define.

C. When large, unusual, or nonrecurring transactions require judgment.

D. When transactions are high-volume and recurring.

Answer (D) is correct. *(CPA, adapted)*

REQUIRED: The circumstance in which an entity is most likely to implement automated controls.

DISCUSSION: Automated controls are cost effective when they are applied to high-volume, recurring transactions. For example, credit limit checks on customer orders could be automated to relieve management from evaluating each customer order as it is received.

Answer (A) is incorrect. When errors are difficult to predict, judgment may be required and it would be less likely that a control could be automated. Answer (B) is incorrect. When misstatements are difficult to define, designing automated controls to prevent, or detect and correct, them also is difficult. Answer (C) is incorrect. When judgment is required, automated controls are less likely to be effective.

5.5.15. The responsibilities of a data administrator (DA) include monitoring

A. The database industry.

B. The performance of the database.

C. Database security.

D. Backup of the system.

Answer (A) is correct. *(Publisher, adapted)*

REQUIRED: The responsibilities of a data administrator.

DISCUSSION: The DA handles administrative issues that arise regarding the database. The DA acts as an advocate by suggesting new applications and standards. One of the DA's responsibilities is to monitor the database industry for new developments. In contrast, the database administrator (DBA) deals with the technical aspects of the database.

5.5.16. For a specific computer application jobstream, an explanation of the purpose, identification of computer components used, identification of input-output forms and media, and identification of programmed terminations and prescribed restart instructions are found in the

A. Systems flowchart.

B. Program documentation.

C. Console log.

D. Computer run book.

Answer (D) is correct. *(CIA, adapted)*

REQUIRED: The document meeting the given definition.

DISCUSSION: Documentation is a general control. All programs, procedures, and operating instructions should be documented before final approval. The computer (or console) run book provides operations documentation regarding the matters described in the question.

Answer (A) is incorrect. A systems flowchart shows the flow of information through the system, not the detailed operating instructions found in the computer run book. Answer (B) is incorrect. Program documentation includes a statement of the purpose of the program, flowcharts and listings for the program, decision tables, controls, formats for records, inputs and outputs, program operating instructions, and program changes. It should be part of the computer run book. Answer (C) is incorrect. Computer console logs typically contain information about jobs processed, job start and stop times, and problems encountered.

5.5.17. One of the major problems in a computer system is that incompatible functions may be performed by the same individual. One compensating control is the use of

A. Echo checks.

B. A check digit system.

C. Computer-generated hash totals.

D. A computer access log.

Answer (D) is correct. *(CPA, adapted)*

REQUIRED: The control compensating for inadequate segregation of duties in a computer system.

DISCUSSION: A computer (console) access log is a record of computer and software usage usually produced by the operating system. Proper monitoring of the log is a compensating control for the lack of segregation of duties. For example, the log should list operator interventions.

Answer (A) is incorrect. Echo checks are hardware controls used to determine whether the correct message was received by an output device. Answer (B) is incorrect. A check digit system is an input control that tests identification numbers. Answer (C) is incorrect. Hash totals are control totals used to check for losses or inaccuracies arising during data processing or movement.

5.5.18. Which of the following represents an internal control weakness in a computer-based system?

A. Computer programmers write and revise programs designed by analysts.

B. The data control group is solely responsible for distributing reports and other output.

C. The computer librarian maintains custody and recordkeeping for computer application programs.

D. Computer operators have access to operator instructions and the authority to change programs.

Answer (D) is correct. *(CIA, adapted)*

REQUIRED: The control weakness in a computer-based system.

DISCUSSION: Computer operators need access to operator instructions. Otherwise, they could not perform their duties. Operators, however, should not have the authority to change computer programs.

Answer (A) is incorrect. Writing and revising computer programs are appropriate functions for programmers. Answer (B) is incorrect. Distributing computer reports is an appropriate function of the control group. Answer (C) is incorrect. Maintaining custody and related recordkeeping for computer programs is appropriate for a computer librarian.

5.5.19. In a large organization, the biggest risk in not having an adequately staffed information center help desk is

A. Increased difficulty in performing application audits.

B. Inadequate documentation for application systems.

C. Increased likelihood of use of unauthorized program code.

D. Persistent errors in user interaction with systems.

Answer (D) is correct. *(CIA, adapted)*

REQUIRED: The biggest risk in not having an adequately staffed information center help desk.

DISCUSSION: Help desk personnel should be properly trained to log problems, resolve minor problems, and forward more difficult problems to appropriate individuals. An effective help desk minimizes user frustration and delays in processing, continuation of errors in user interaction with the information systems, processing mistakes necessitating later correction or reruns, and failures to log errors and analysis of their causes.

Answer (A) is incorrect. Application audits are largely unaffected by help desk staffing. Answer (B) is incorrect. Preparation of documentation is a development function. Answer (C) is incorrect. Prevention of use of unauthorized program code is a function of change control.

5.5.20. In planning the physical location of a computer facility, the primary consideration for selecting a site is that it should

A. Maximize the visibility of the computer.

B. Minimize the distance that data control personnel must travel to deliver data and reports and be easily accessible by a majority of company personnel.

C. Be in the basement or on the ground floor.

D. Provide security.

Answer (D) is correct. *(J. Brooks)*

REQUIRED: The primary consideration in selecting a site for a computer.

DISCUSSION: The primary criterion for selecting a site should be the security of the environment of the computer. The computer must be protected from disasters such as fire, windstorm, sabotage, and improper access.

Answer (A) is incorrect. A highly visible site is usually not physically secure. Answer (B) is incorrect. Although minimizing travel distance is important, it is not the primary consideration. Additionally, only authorized personnel should be allowed in the computer site; thus, easy access by a majority of company personnel is not necessary. Answer (C) is incorrect. The basement or the ground floor is not always the best location. In certain geographic areas, these locations are subject to flooding.

5.5.21. Which of the following statements regarding security concerns for notebook computers is true?

A. The primary methods of control usually involve general controls.

B. Centralized control over the selection and acquisition of hardware and software is not a major concern.

C. Some traditional controls such as segregation of duties become more important.

D. As their use becomes more sophisticated, the degree of concern regarding physical security decreases.

Answer (A) is correct. *(CIA, adapted)*

REQUIRED: The true statement about security concerns for notebook computers.

DISCUSSION: General controls apply to all computer activities. General controls to prevent theft of equipment and data and to restrict access to the use of equipment and data are the primary consideration, given the nature of notebook computers.

Answer (B) is incorrect. To ensure compatibility with other computers, files, and databases, and to control expenditures, it is necessary to have centralized control over the selection and acquisition of hardware and software. Answer (C) is incorrect. Given the nature and uses of notebook computers, segregation of duties may not be feasible. Answer (D) is incorrect. As the use of notebook computers becomes more sophisticated, the degree of concern regarding physical security increases.

5.5.22. Which of the following should not be the responsibility of a database administrator?

A. Design the content and organization of the database.

B. Develop applications to access the database.

C. Protect the database and its software.

D. Monitor and improve the efficiency of the database.

Answer (B) is correct. *(CIA, adapted)*

REQUIRED: The item not the responsibility of a database administrator.

DISCUSSION: The database administrator (DBA) is the person who has overall responsibility for developing and maintaining the database. Some of the primary responsibilities of the DBA are to design the content of the database, protect and control the database, and monitor and improve the efficiency of the database. The responsibility of developing applications to access the database belongs to systems analysts and programmers.

Answer (A) is incorrect. Designing the content and organization of the database is a responsibility of the database administrator. Answer (C) is incorrect. Protecting the database and its software is a responsibility of the database administrator. Answer (D) is incorrect. Monitoring and improving the efficiency of the database is a responsibility of the database administrator.

5.5.23. The operational responsibility for the accuracy and completeness of computer-based information should be placed on which of the following groups?

A. Top management.

B. External auditors.

C. Internal auditors.

D. Users.

Answer (D) is correct. *(CIA, adapted)*

REQUIRED: The group operationally responsible for the accuracy and completeness of computer-based information.

DISCUSSION: The operational responsibility for the accuracy and completeness of computer-based information should be placed on users. Users are in the best position to review output in relation to the input provided and determine whether the results of processing are reasonable.

Answer (A) is incorrect. Top management is charged with the overall control of computer-based information systems. Operational control resides in the users. Answer (B) is incorrect. External auditing is an independent appraisal function. Its principal purpose is the expression of an opinion about financial statements. Answer (C) is incorrect. Internal auditing is an independent appraisal function. Internal auditors should not have operational responsibility.

5.5.24. Which of the following is most important when there is a lack of adequate fire detection and control equipment in the computer areas?

A. Adequate fire insurance.

B. Regular hardware maintenance.

C. Offsite storage of transaction and master files.

D. Fully tested backup processing facilities.

Answer (C) is correct. *(CISA, adapted)*

REQUIRED: The most important control given a lack of fire detection and control equipment.

DISCUSSION: One of the primary risks against which a computer operation must be protected is the loss of programs and files. Backup procedures, including offsite storage of backup copies, are necessary to protect against loss.

Answer (A) is incorrect. Although adequate fire insurance is an important element for recovery, offsite storage of transaction and master files is essential to recovery. Answer (B) is incorrect. Regular hardware maintenance does not relate to recovery. Answer (D) is incorrect. Although a fully tested backup processing facility is an important element for recovery, without offsite storage, recovery is ordinarily not feasible.

5.5.25. Contingency plans for information systems should include appropriate backup agreements. Which of the following arrangements is considered too vendor-dependent when vital operations require almost immediate availability of computer resources?

A. A “hot site” arrangement.

B. A “cold site” arrangement.

C. A “cold and hot site” combination arrangement.

D. Using excess capacity at another data center within the organization.

Answer (B) is correct. *(CIA, adapted)*

REQUIRED: The contingency plan that is too vendor-dependent.

DISCUSSION: Organizations should maintain contingency plans for operations in the case of a disaster. These plans usually include off-site storage of important backup data and an arrangement for the continuation of operations at another location. A “cold site” has all needed assets in place except the needed computer equipment and is vendor-dependent for timely delivery of equipment.

Answer (A) is incorrect. A “hot site” has all needed assets in place and is not vendor-dependent. Answer (C) is incorrect. A “cold and hot site” combination allows the “hot site” to be used until the “cold site” is prepared and is thus not too vendor-dependent. Answer (D) is incorrect. Excess capacity would ensure that needed assets are available and would not be vendor-dependent.

5.5.26. Which two of the following are part of a review to ensure that machine malfunctions, error recovery, and stop/restart procedures are clearly documented and periodically reviewed as a security precaution?

I. Reviewing for completeness the list of abnormal operations that require documented records

II. Reviewing the adequacy of procedures for processing on backup hardware

III. Interviewing management responsible for reviewing the records of abnormal operations and determining the adequacy of steps taken to assure the credibility and continuity of processing

IV. Interviewing the operations supervisor to determine the extent of rotation of personnel between shifts

A. I and III.

B. I and IV.

C. II and III.

D. II and IV.

Answer (A) is correct. *(CISA, adapted)*

REQUIRED: The two procedures that would be part of a review to ensure that machine malfunctions, error recovery, and stop/restart procedures are clearly documented and reviewed.

DISCUSSION: The auditor should review the completeness of the list of typical abnormal operations for which documented records are required. But the mere existence of documentation does not assure that the described procedures would be carried out. Thus, the auditor should interview management to determine the adequacy of the procedures employed in case of malfunctions.

Answer (B) is incorrect. Rotation of personnel is not a procedure to aid recovery from either a malfunction or an outright catastrophe. Answer (C) is incorrect. Auxiliary processing is part of a disaster (e.g., a flood, fire, or other interrupting regular operations) plan rather than a restart procedure (needed because of human errors or machine breakdowns). Answer (D) is incorrect. Rotation of personnel is not a procedure to aid recovery from either a malfunction or an outright catastrophe. Moreover, auxiliary processing is part of a disaster plan rather than a restart procedure.

5.5.27. At a remote computer center, management installed an automated scheduling system to load data files and execute programs at specific times during the day. The best approach for verifying that the scheduling system performs as intended is to

A. Analyze job activity with a queuing model to determine workload characteristics.

B. Simulate the resource usage and compare the results with actual results of operations.

C. Use library management software to track changes to successive versions of applications programs.

D. Audit job accounting data for file accesses and job initiation/termination messages.

Answer (D) is correct. *(CIA, adapted)*

REQUIRED: The best approach for verifying that the scheduling system performs as intended.

DISCUSSION: Job accounting data analysis permits programmatic examination of job initiation and termination, record counts, and processing times. Auditing job accounting data for file accesses and job initiation/termination messages will reveal whether the correct data files were loaded/dismounted at the correct times and the correct programs were initiated/terminated at the correct times.

Answer (A) is incorrect. Analyzing job activity with a queuing model to determine workload characteristics gives information about resource usage. Answer (B) is incorrect. A simulation helps management characterize the workload. Answer (C) is incorrect. Using library management software to track changes to successive versions of application programs permits control of production and test versions.

5.5.28. All of the following are examples of corrective controls except

A. Transaction trails.

B. Passwords.

C. Upstream resubmission.

D. Automatic error correction.

Answer (B) is correct. *(CISA, adapted)*

REQUIRED: The item that is not a corrective control.

DISCUSSION: Passwords are controls over unauthorized access to the computer or to data files. They are a preventive, not a corrective, control.

Answer (A) is incorrect. A transaction trail is primarily a corrective rather than a detective control in computer systems given the difficulty of manual review of a large volume of transactions. The transaction trail (an audit trail) is principally used to follow up and correct exceptions. Answer (C) is incorrect. Upstream resubmission is the input of error corrections under more stringent controls than those over the original transactions. Error corrections are especially error prone. Answer (D) is incorrect. Automatic error correction is a nonsense term.

5.5.29. A company updates its accounts receivable master file weekly and retains the master files and corresponding update transactions for the most recent 2-week period. The purpose of this practice is to

A. Verify run-to-run control totals for receivables.

B. Match internal labels to avoid writing on the wrong volume.

C. Permit reconstruction of the master file if needed.

D. Validate groups of update transactions for each version.

Answer (C) is correct. *(CIA, adapted)*

REQUIRED: The purpose of periodic retention of master files and transaction data.

DISCUSSION: The grandfather-father-son approach normally uses digital files to provide backup in a batch processing system. The procedure involves creation and retention of three generations of master files so that lost or destroyed data may be regenerated from the remaining master files and transaction data. In this case, a master file (the grandfather) and the first week's transactions are used to generate a second master file (the father). This file and the second week's transactions are the basis for the current master file (the son). Online systems use rollback and recovery procedures. Thus, the master file periodically is dumped onto a storage medium. Reconstruction is then possible using the backup copy and the transactions log.

Answer (A) is incorrect. Comparison of batch totals is a control over the completeness of processing, not a recovery procedure. Answer (B) is incorrect. Internal labels may avoid destruction of data but do not aid in recovery. Answer (D) is incorrect. Validation may avoid destruction of data but does not aid in recovery.

5.5.30. A company's management has expressed concern over the varied system architectures that the organization uses. Potential security and control concerns include all of the following except

A. Users may have different user ID codes and passwords to remember for the several systems that they use.

B. There are difficulties in developing uniform security standards for the various platforms.

C. Backup file storage administration is often decentralized.

D. Having data distributed across many computers throughout the organization increases the risk that a single disaster would destroy large portions of the organization's data.

Answer (D) is correct. *(CIA, adapted)*

REQUIRED: The item that is not a security and control risk resulting from use of varied system architectures.

DISCUSSION: The use of distributed systems with different architectures throughout the organization decreases the risk that a single disaster will destroy large portions of data. Centralization of data in a single mainframe environment would pose greater risk of data loss.

Answer (A) is incorrect. Password proliferation is a considerable security concern. Users may be tempted to record their passwords or make them overly simple. Answer (B) is incorrect. Consistent security across varied platforms is challenging as a result of the different features of various systems and the decentralization of security administration. Answer (C) is incorrect. Decentralization of backup file storage administration may lead to lack of consistency and difficulty in monitoring compliance.

5.5.31. Good planning will help an organization restore computer operations after a processing outage. Good recovery planning should ensure that

A. Backup/restart procedures have been built into job streams and programs.

B. Change control procedures cannot be bypassed by operating personnel.

C. Planned changes in equipment capacities are compatible with projected workloads.

D. Service level agreements with owners of applications are documented.

Answer (A) is correct. *(CIA, adapted)*

REQUIRED: The condition ensured by good recovery planning.

DISCUSSION: The disaster plan should embrace data center recovery, critical application recovery, and network recovery. It should be updated and current with regard to recent test results and new applications, equipment, and network configurations. The plan should also ensure that backup facilities are still able to process critical applications and that end-user responsibility is established. Another essential component of a disaster recovery plan is that backup/restart procedures have been anticipated and provided for in the application systems.

Answer (B) is incorrect. Whether change control procedures can be bypassed is not usually a consideration in disaster recovery planning. Answer (C) is incorrect. Planned rather than actual changes in equipment capacities are not relevant in disaster recovery planning. Answer (D) is incorrect. Ensuring that service level agreements with owners of critical applications are adequate is not a function of disaster recovery planning.

5.5.32. Each day, after all processing is finished, a bank performs a backup of its online deposit files and retains it for 7 days. Copies of each day's transaction files are not retained. This approach is

A. Valid, in that having a week's worth of backups permits recovery even if one backup is unreadable.

B. Risky, in that restoring from the most recent backup file would omit subsequent transactions.

C. Valid, in that it minimizes the complexity of backup/recovery procedures if the online file has to be restored.

D. Risky, in that no checkpoint/restart information is kept with the backup files.

Answer (B) is correct. *(CIA, adapted)*

REQUIRED: The true statement about retention of backup files but not each day's transaction files.

DISCUSSION: At appropriate intervals, the disk files should be copied on magnetic tape so that restart procedures can begin at those points if data are lost or destroyed. However, not retaining each day's transaction files is risky because information processed since the last backup file was created will be lost.

Answer (A) is incorrect. The practice of not retaining daily transaction data is unsound in that the bank loses a day's transactions for each backup that is unreadable. Answer (C) is incorrect. The practice of not retaining daily transaction data certainly minimizes complexity but at the expense of losing transaction data if the online file must be restored from the backup. Answer (D) is incorrect. Checkpoint/restart information is not needed. The backups are created after all processing is finished for the day.

5.5.33. An inexperienced computer operator loaded an incorrect version of the accounts receivable master file in a tape drive during processing. Because of this error, the entire processing run had to be repeated at a significant cost. Which of the following software controls is most effective in preventing this type of operator error from affecting the processing of files?

A. Data transmission check.

B. File header label check.

C. Memory isolation protection.

D. Unauthorized access protection.

Answer (B) is correct. *(CIA, adapted)*

REQUIRED: The software control for preventing use of an incorrect version of a master file.

DISCUSSION: The use of external, header, and trailer labels should be enforced to ensure the proper access and protection of files. A header label is a machine-readable record at the beginning of a file that identifies the file. Software makes this check. A trailer label is a machine-readable label at the end of a file containing record counts and control totals. An external label is a human-readable identifying label affixed to the outside of a file holder, such as a magnetic tape file.

Answer (A) is incorrect. A data transmission check verifies only the accuracy of the communication. Answer (C) is incorrect. Memory isolation protection (boundary protection) protects programs or data from interference (unauthorized reading and/or writing) caused by activity related to other programs or data stored on the same medium. Answer (D) is incorrect. Access controls (passwords, etc.) prevent unauthorized access from remote locations, not authorized use by an operator.

5.5.34. The use of external labels with rewritable computer data storage media is least likely to prevent which of the following?

A. Formatting media that was used for a backup of hard disk files.

B. Using a version of a file that has been subsequently revised.

C. Erasing an important file on media.

D. Spilling liquid on media and losing the files.

Answer (D) is correct. *(Publisher, adapted)*

REQUIRED: The error or problem not likely prevented by external labels on rewritable computer data storage media.

DISCUSSION: Proper handling of magnetic media requires safeguards from excessive heat, accidental magnetic contact, and physical abuse such as liquid spills. External labels do not prevent such occurrences.

Answer (A) is incorrect. All external file media, e.g., magnetic tapes and disks, should be properly labeled so that the user can determine the proper use of the files. Formatting the wrong media and thereby erasing its contents could therefore be prevented by use of external labels. Answer (B) is incorrect. Use of the wrong version of a file can be prevented by use of external labels. Answer (C) is incorrect. Erasing an important file on media can be prevented by use of external labels.

5.5.35. Data access security related to applications may be enforced through all the following except

A. User identification and authentication functions incorporated in the application.

B. Utility software functions.

C. User identification and authentication functions in access control software.

D. Security functions provided by a database management system.

Answer (B) is correct. *(CIA, adapted)*

REQUIRED: The functions through which data access security cannot be enforced.

DISCUSSION: Utility programs perform routine functions (e.g., sorting and copying), are available to all users, and are promptly available for many different applications. Utility programs can actually be a serious weakness in data access security because some can bypass normal access controls.

Answer (A) is incorrect. Although the trend is for this type of control function to be performed by other software, most such controls still reside in application software. Answer (C) is incorrect. Access control software has as one of its primary objectives improving data access security for all data on the system. Answer (D) is incorrect. Most database management systems provide for improved data access security while they are running.

Questions 5.5.36 through 5.5.38 are based on the following information. Baker Manufacturing Co. has the following 10 master files:

- Accounts payable
- Accounts receivable
- Bill of materials (material requirements for producing a product)
- Finished goods inventory
- Open production orders
- Open purchase orders
- Raw materials inventory
- Work-in-process inventory
- Production operations list (labor operations and machine requirements)
- Sales summary

5.5.36. Master files maintained as part of the sales order processing system are

A. Accounts receivable and bill of materials.

B. Accounts payable, accounts receivable, and finished goods inventory.

C. Accounts receivable, sales summary, and production operations list.

D. Accounts receivable and finished goods inventory.

Answer (D) is correct. *(Publisher, adapted)*

REQUIRED: The master files maintained as part of the sales order processing system.

DISCUSSION: A sales order processing cycle involves taking customers' orders and updating amounts owed by customers (accounts receivable) and the amount of inventory left after shipment (finished goods inventory).

Answer (A) is incorrect. The bill of materials file is used in production planning. Answer (B) is incorrect. The accounts payable files are used to process purchases. Answer (C) is incorrect. The production operations list file is used in production planning.

5.5.37. Master files maintained as part of the processing of purchase transactions are

A. Accounts payable, bill of materials, finished goods inventory, and open purchase orders.

B. Accounts payable, open purchase orders, raw materials inventory, and work-in-process inventory.

C. Accounts payable, bill of materials, and open purchase orders.

D. Accounts payable, open purchase orders, and raw materials inventory.

Answer (D) is correct. *(Publisher, adapted)*

REQUIRED: The master files maintained as part of the processing of purchases.

DISCUSSION: The processing of purchase transactions involves preparing purchase orders and updating raw materials inventory on order (raw materials inventory) and purchase orders not yet received (open purchase orders). Upon receipt of the purchased item, updating is required for the amount on hand (raw material inventory), open purchase orders since the item was received (open purchase orders), and the amount owed to the vendor (accounts payable).

Answer (A) is incorrect. The bill of materials file is used in production planning, and finished goods inventory is part of the sales order processing cycle. Answer (B) is incorrect. The work-in-process inventory file is used in production planning. Answer (C) is incorrect. The bill of materials file is used in production planning.

5.5.38. Master files used to plan and report on the resources required for the coming period include

A. Bill of materials, open production orders, work-in-process inventory, and production operations list.

B. Finished goods inventory, open production orders, open purchase orders, and work-in-process inventory.

C. Finished goods inventory, open purchase orders, raw materials inventory, and work-in-process.

D. Bill of materials, open production orders, accounts payable, and production operations list.

Answer (A) is correct. *(Publisher, adapted)*

REQUIRED: The master files used to plan and report on resources required for the coming period.

DISCUSSION: Production planning involves determining what needs to be produced (open production orders and finished goods inventory), what materials are required (bill of materials), what labor and machine operations are needed (production operations list), what resources are tied up in production (work-in-process), and what raw materials are available (raw materials inventory). Based on this evaluation, new production orders (open production orders) are issued.

Answer (B) is incorrect. The open purchase orders file is used in the processing of purchases. Answer (C) is incorrect. The open purchase orders file is used in the processing of purchases. Answer (D) is incorrect. The accounts payable file is used in the processing of purchases.

5.5.39. An auditor has just completed a physical security audit of a data center. Because the center engages in top-secret defense contract work, the auditor has chosen to recommend biometric authentication for workers entering the building. The recommendation might include devices that verify all of the following except

A. Fingerprints.

B. Retina patterns.

C. Speech patterns.

D. Password patterns.

Answer (D) is correct. *(CIA, adapted)*

REQUIRED: The method that does not provide biometric authentication.

DISCUSSION: Biometric technologies are automated methods of establishing an individual's identity using physiological or behavioral traits. These characteristics include fingerprints, retina patterns, hand geometry, signature dynamics, speech, and keystroke dynamics.

Answer (A) is incorrect. Verifying fingerprints is a biometric measure. Answer (B) is incorrect. Verifying retina patterns is a biometric measure. Answer (C) is incorrect. Verifying speech patterns is a biometric measure.

5.5.40. Data processing activities may be classified in terms of three stages or processes: input, processing, and output. An activity that is not normally associated with the input stage is

A. Batching.

B. Recording.

C. Verifying.

D. Reporting.

Answer (D) is correct. *(CMA, adapted)*

REQUIRED: The process not associated with input.

DISCUSSION: Reporting is normally associated with output, not input. Output is the processing result, e.g., account listings or displays, reports, magnetic files, invoices, or checks.

Answer (A) is incorrect. Batching is closely associated with input. Answer (B) is incorrect. Recording is closely associated with input. Answer (C) is incorrect. Verifying is closely associated with input.

5.5.41. A mail-order retailer of low-cost novelty items is receiving an increasing number of complaints from customers about the wrong merchandise being shipped. The order code for items has the format *wwxxyyzz*. The major category is *ww*, *xx* is the minor category, *yy* identifies the item, and *zz* identifies the catalog. In many cases, the wrong merchandise was sent because adjacent characters in the order code had been transposed. The best control for decreasing the number of orders with the wrong merchandise is to

A. Require customers to specify the name for each item they order.

B. Add check-digits to the order codes and verify them for each order.

C. Separate the parts of the order code with hyphens to make the characters easier to read.

D. Use a master file reference for all order codes to verify the existence of items.

Answer (B) is correct. *(CIA, adapted)*

REQUIRED: The control that prevents erroneous input.

DISCUSSION: Self-checking digits may be used to detect incorrect codes. The digit is generated by applying an algorithm to the code. During the input process, the check digit is recomputed by applying the same algorithm to the code actually entered.

Answer (A) is incorrect. Having customers specify the name for each item they order would let the company correct erroneous order codes once they had been detected, but would not, in general, detect erroneous codes. Answer (C) is incorrect. Separating the parts of the order code with hyphens would make the characters easier to read, but would not cure the problem of transposed characters. Answer (D) is incorrect. Using a master file reference for all order codes would verify the existence of items, but would not detect erroneous order codes in which transposed characters in an order code match other items.

5.5.42. The purpose of input controls is to ensure the

A. Authorization of access to data files.

B. Authorization of access to program files.

C. Completeness, accuracy, and validity of updating.

D. Completeness, accuracy, and validity of input.

Answer (D) is correct. *(CIA, adapted)*

REQUIRED: The purpose of input controls.

DISCUSSION: Input controls provide reasonable assurance that data received for computer processing have been properly authorized and are in a form suitable for processing, i.e., complete, accurate, and valid. Input controls also relate to rejection, correction, and resubmission of data that were initially incorrect.

Answer (A) is incorrect. Access controls authorize access to data files. Answer (B) is incorrect. Access controls authorize access to program files. Answer (C) is incorrect. Processing controls ensure the completeness, accuracy, and validity of updating.

5.5.43. Data conversion is the translation of data into a form the computer can accept. What method of data conversion is most difficult to audit?

A. Keying data to disk for online processing.

B. Keying data to disk for batch processing.

C. Keying data to source documents for magnetic-ink character recognition.

D. Reading source data using optical-character recognition.

Answer (A) is correct. *(CIA, adapted)*

REQUIRED: The type of data conversion that is most difficult to audit.

DISCUSSION: Data conversion in an online environment is difficult to audit because the audit trail is often invisible. Hard-copy source documents are often lacking.

Answer (B) is incorrect. Keying to disk creates records readily available for testing. Answer (C) is incorrect. Magnetic-ink character recognition provides batch control capability and hard-copy source documents. Answer (D) is incorrect. Optical-character recognition retains hard-copy source documents and reduces the risks associated with the manual data conversion process.

5.5.44. Which of the following computerized control procedures is most effective in ensuring that data uploaded from personal computers to a mainframe are complete and that no additional data are added?

A. Self-checking digits to ensure that only authorized part numbers are added to the database.

B. Batch control totals, including control totals and hash totals.

C. Passwords that effectively limit access to only those authorized to upload the data to the mainframe computer.

D. Field-level edit controls that test each field for alphanumerical integrity.

Answer (B) is correct. *(CIA, adapted)*

REQUIRED: The control over completeness of data uploaded from personal computers.

DISCUSSION: Batch control totals for the data transferred can be reconciled with the batch control totals in the existing file. This comparison provides information on the completion of the data transfer. Batch totals may include record counts, totals of certain critical amounts, or hash totals. A hash total is a control total without a defined meaning, such as the total of employee numbers or invoice numbers, that is used to verify the completeness of data. Thus, the hash total for the employee listing by the personnel department could be compared with the total generated during the payroll run.

Answer (A) is incorrect. Self-checking digits detect inaccurate identification numbers. They are an effective control to ensure that the appropriate part has been identified but not that data transfer is complete. Answer (C) is incorrect. Passwords help ensure that only authorized personnel make the transfer, not that data transfer is complete. Answer (D) is incorrect. Field checks are effective input controls, but they do not ensure completeness of data transfer.

5.5.45. If a control total were to be computed on each of the following data items, which would best be identified as a hash total for a payroll computer application?

A. Hours worked.

B. Total debits and total credits.

C. Net pay.

D. Department numbers.

Answer (D) is correct. *(CPA, adapted)*

REQUIRED: The example of a hash total.

DISCUSSION: The three types of control totals are record counts, financial (amount) totals, and hash totals. Record counts establish the number of source documents and reconcile it to the number of output records. Financial (amount) totals compute dollar or amount totals from source documents (e.g., the total dollar amount of invoices processed) and reconcile them with the output records. Hash totals add numbers on input documents that are not normally added (e.g., department numbers for payroll processing) and reconcile them with output records.

Answer (A) is incorrect. Hours worked is an example of a financial (amount) total. Answer (B) is incorrect. Total debits and total credits is a financial total. Answer (C) is incorrect. Net pay is a financial total.

5.5.46. An employee in the receiving department keyed in a shipment from a remote terminal and inadvertently omitted the purchase order number. The best systems control to detect this error is

A. Completeness test.

B. Sequence check.

C. Reasonableness test.

D. Compatibility test.

Answer (A) is correct. *(CMA, adapted)*

REQUIRED: The control to detect the omission of a purchase order number keyed in from a remote terminal.

DISCUSSION: A completeness test checks that all data elements are entered before processing. An interactive system can be programmed to notify the user to enter the number before accepting the receiving report.

Answer (B) is incorrect. A sequence check tests for the ordering, not omission, of records. Answer (C) is incorrect. A limit or reasonableness test checks the values of data items against established limits. Answer (D) is incorrect. A compatibility test (field check) determines whether characters are appropriate to a field.

5.5.47. Which one of the following input validation routines is not likely to be appropriate in a real-time operation?

A. Sign check.

B. Reasonableness check.

C. Sequence check.

D. Redundant data check.

Answer (C) is correct. *(CMA, adapted)*

REQUIRED: The input validation routine not appropriate in a real-time operation.

DISCUSSION: The program controls listed prescreen or edit data prior to processing, but the sequence check is most likely to be used only in batch processing. A sequence check tests to determine that records are in proper order. For example, a payroll input file can be sorted into Social Security number order. A sequence check can then be performed to verify record order. This control would not apply in a real-time operation because records are not processed sequentially.

Answer (A) is incorrect. Sign checks test data for the appropriate arithmetic sign. For instance, hours worked in a payroll should always be a positive number. Answer (B) is incorrect. Reasonableness tests verify that amounts fall within predetermined limits. Answer (D) is incorrect. A redundancy check requires sending additional data items to serve as a check on the other transmitted data; for example, part of a customer name can be matched against the name associated with the transmitted customer number.

5.5.48. In the accounting system of Apogee Company, the quantities counted by the receiving department and entered at a terminal are transmitted to the computer, which immediately transmits the amounts back to the terminal for display on the terminal screen. This display enables the operator to

A. Establish the validity of the account number.

B. Verify that the amount was entered accurately.

C. Verify the authorization of the disbursement.

D. Prevent the overpayment of the account.

Answer (B) is correct. *(CPA, adapted)*

REQUIRED: The effect of displaying the amounts entered at a terminal.

DISCUSSION: The display of the amounts entered is an input control that permits visual verification of the accuracy of the input by the operator. This is termed closed-loop verification.

Answer (A) is incorrect. Displaying the amounts entered at a terminal does not establish the validity of the account number. Answer (C) is incorrect. Displaying the amounts entered at a terminal does not verify the authorization of the disbursement. Answer (D) is incorrect. Displaying the amounts entered at a terminal does not prevent the overpayment of the account.

5.5.49. As part of an audit, the auditor was studying a computer flowchart containing the logic diagram shown below. Which of the following controls is represented by this diagram?

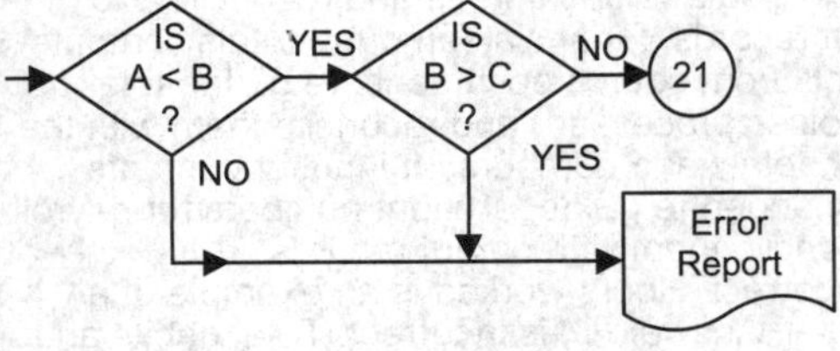

A. Field check.

B. Limit check.

C. Control total.

D. Password check.

Answer (B) is correct. *(CIA, adapted)*

REQUIRED: The control represented by the flowchart.

DISCUSSION: A limit check (often termed a reasonableness or range test) determines whether an amount is within a predetermined limit for given information. The first decision block asks if A, the lower limit, is less than B, the value of interest. The second decision block asks if B is greater than the upper limit C. The purpose of this test is to determine if B is within an acceptable or reasonable range. If it is not, an error report is generated.

Answer (A) is incorrect. A field check (valid character check) examines a field to test whether it contains an improper kind of character. Answer (C) is incorrect. A control total is used to control the completeness and accuracy of processing, not to evaluate the reasonableness of results. Answer (D) is incorrect. Passwords restrict unauthorized access to the computer.

5.5.50. When erroneous data are detected by computer program controls, such data may be excluded from processing and printed on an error report. This error report should be reviewed and followed up by the

A. Computer operator.

B. Systems analyst.

C. Data control group.

D. Computer programmer.

Answer (C) is correct. *(CPA, adapted)*

REQUIRED: The individual or group responsible.

DISCUSSION: Some entities use a data control group that acts as liaison between the users and the processing center. This group records input data in a control log, follows the progress of processing, distributes output, and establishes control totals. It is also responsible for following up error reports and assuring that erroneous records are reprocessed. The data control group must be organizationally independent of computer operations within the data processing function to allow for proper control.

Answer (A) is incorrect. Computer operators are not independent of the computer processing operation. Answer (B) is incorrect. Systems analysts are not independent of the computer processing operation. Answer (D) is incorrect. Computer programmers are not independent of the computer processing operation.

5.5.51. The key verification process associated with keying computer records for input to a computer system is

A. Effectively used to detect the erroneous recording of data on source documents.

B. Inexpensive and therefore widely used.

C. Used to detect errors introduced by the keying process.

D. Ordinarily used with a computer program written to check the data.

Answer (C) is correct. *(CIA, adapted)*

REQUIRED: The purpose of key verification.

DISCUSSION: Key verification is a procedure to determine if the keying process was performed properly. Information from source documents is rekeyed on a special keyboard by another operator and compared with that previously recorded.

Answer (A) is incorrect. Key verification does not detect errors in the source documents. Answer (B) is incorrect. Although widely used, key verification effectively doubles the work and therefore is expensive. Answer (D) is incorrect. Key verification is a manual process.

STUDY UNIT SIX
INTERNAL CONTROL --
SALES-RECEIVABLES-CASH RECEIPTS CYCLE

A standard approach to planning and performing the audit is to organize the auditee's transactions, balances, disclosures, and related controls into groups of related items. This cycle approach is consistent with how transactions are recorded in journals and ledgers. Among the accounts relevant to the sales-receivables-cash receipts cycle are cash, trade receivables, other receivables, the allowance for bad debts, sales, sales returns, and bad debt expense.

Understanding how information and documents flow through a cycle enables an auditor to determine what controls are in place and whether they are effective in safeguarding assets and preventing, or detecting and correcting, fraud and material misstatements. Auditors should obtain and document an understanding of internal control sufficient to plan the audit.

QUESTIONS

6.1 Responsibilities/Organizational Structure/Flowcharts

6.1.1. The internal control objectives of the revenue cycle include all of the following except

A. Revenue cycle transactions are properly executed.

B. Appropriate goods are ordered so that sales can be made.

C. Transactions relating to revenue are properly recorded.

D. Custody over assets resulting from the revenue cycle is properly maintained.

Answer (B) is correct. *(Publisher, adapted)*

REQUIRED: The internal control objective not directly related to the revenue cycle.

DISCUSSION: The revenue cycle consists of the activities involving exchanges with customers and the collection in cash of the amounts paid for the goods or services provided. Ordering appropriate goods, an objective of the purchases-payables cycle, is only indirectly related to the revenue cycle.

Answer (A) is incorrect. An internal control objective of the revenue cycle is that revenue-cycle transactions be properly executed. Answer (C) is incorrect. An internal control objective of the revenue cycle is that transactions relating to revenue be properly recorded. Answer (D) is incorrect. An internal control objective of the revenue cycle is that custody over assets resulting from the revenue cycle be properly maintained.

6.1.2. Which of the following are not directly involved in the revenue cycle?

A. Sales manager and the credit manager.

B. Chief financial officer and controller.

C. Billing clerk.

D. Receiving department clerk.

Answer (D) is correct. *(Publisher, adapted)*

REQUIRED: The person(s) not directly involved in the revenue cycle.

DISCUSSION: The receiving department clerk is involved in the purchases-payables cycle. The clerk counts the goods and prepares receiving reports that provide partial authorization for invoice payment.

Answer (A) is incorrect. The sales manager is responsible for executing sales transactions, and the credit manager authorizes sales. Answer (B) is incorrect. The CFO has custody of cash receipts from sales, and the controller maintains records for the sales and billing cycle. Answer (C) is incorrect. The billing clerk is responsible for the preparation of invoices and the billing process.

6.1.3. Which of the following employees should report to the chief financial officer?

A. Internal auditor.

B. Sales clerk.

C. Bookkeeper.

D. Credit manager.

Answer (D) is correct. *(Publisher, adapted)*

REQUIRED: The person who should report to the CFO.

DISCUSSION: The CFO's primary responsibility is to safeguard assets. Although credit approval is an authorization process, assets are lost if credit is improperly granted. Thus, the credit manager should be responsible to one who has no vested interest in the granting of credit.

Answer (A) is incorrect. The internal auditor is part of internal control and should report to the audit committee. Answer (B) is incorrect. The sales clerk is involved with the execution of sales transactions and would more appropriately report to the sales manager. Answer (C) is incorrect. Recordkeeping should be separated from authorization and asset custody.

6.1.4. An auditor tests an entity's policy of obtaining credit approval before shipping goods to customers in support of management's financial statement assertion of

A. Valuation.

B. Completeness.

C. Occurrence.

D. Rights and obligations.

Answer (A) is correct. *(CPA, adapted)*

REQUIRED: The assertion related to the policy of credit approval before shipping goods to customers.

DISCUSSION: The proper approval of credit provides assurance that the account receivable is collectible. Thus, it is related to the valuation assertion that balances are reported at appropriate amounts, e.g., accounts receivable at net realizable value.

Answer (B) is incorrect. The completeness assertion is that all transactions, events, and balances that should have been recorded have been recorded. Answer (C) is incorrect. The occurrence assertion is that recorded transactions and events have occurred and pertain to the entity. Answer (D) is incorrect. Rights and obligations assertions relate to whether assets are rights of the entity and liabilities are obligations of the entity.

6.1.5. Which of the following most likely would be the result of ineffective internal control in the revenue cycle?

A. Final authorization of credit memos by personnel in the sales department could permit an employee defalcation scheme.

B. Fictitious transactions could be recorded, causing an understatement of revenues and an overstatement of receivables.

C. Fraud in recording transactions in the subsidiary accounts could result in a delay in goods shipped.

D. Omission of shipping documents could go undetected, causing an understatement of inventory.

Answer (A) is correct. *(CPA, adapted)*

REQUIRED: The most likely result of ineffective internal controls in the revenue cycle.

DISCUSSION: Ineffective controls in the revenue cycle, such as inappropriate segregation of duties and responsibilities, inadequate supervision, or deficient authorization, may result in the ability of employees to perpetrate fraud. Thus, sales personnel should approve sales returns and allowances but not the related credit memos. Moreover, no authorization for the return of goods, defective or otherwise, should be considered complete until the goods are returned as evidenced by a receiving report.

Answer (B) is incorrect. Recording fictitious sales would overstate revenues. Answer (C) is incorrect. The customers' accounts are not posted until after goods are shipped. Answer (D) is incorrect. If shipping documents are omitted, shipments of goods may not be credited to inventory, thereby overstating the account.

6.1.6. Which of the following credit approval procedures would be the basis for developing a deficiency finding for a wholesaler?

A. Trade-credit standards are reviewed and approved by the finance committee of the board of directors.

B. Customers not meeting trade-credit standards are shipped merchandise on a cash-on-delivery (C.O.D.) basis only.

C. Salespeople are responsible for evaluating and monitoring the financial condition of prospective and continuing customers.

D. An authorized signature from the credit department denoting approval of the customer's credit is to appear on all credit-sales orders.

Answer (C) is correct. *(CIA, adapted)*

REQUIRED: The credit approval procedure justifying a deficiency finding.

DISCUSSION: Salespeople should be responsible for generating sales and providing service to customers. For effective control purposes, the credit department should be responsible for monitoring the financial condition of prospective and continuing customers in the credit approval process.

Answer (A) is incorrect. Trade-credit standards may be evaluated and approved by a committee of the board or delegated to management. Answer (B) is incorrect. Shipping merchandise on a cash-on-delivery (C.O.D.) basis only is customary if trade-credit standards are not met. Answer (D) is incorrect. The credit department should approve transactions based upon credit information before sales are processed.

6.1.7. Alpha Company uses its sales invoices for posting perpetual inventory records. Inadequate internal control over the invoicing function allows goods to be shipped that are not invoiced. The inadequate controls could cause an

A. Understatement of revenues, receivables, and inventory.

B. Overstatement of revenues and receivables and an understatement of inventory.

C. Understatement of revenues and receivables and an overstatement of inventory.

D. Overstatement of revenues, receivables, and inventory.

Answer (C) is correct. *(CPA, adapted)*

REQUIRED: The result of shipping goods that are not invoiced.

DISCUSSION: If goods are shipped before the sales are invoiced, inventory will not be credited for the shipments, thus overstating inventory. Moreover, if the accounting function does not receive copies of the invoices, sales and receivables will not be recorded, with the consequent understatement of those accounts.

Answer (A) is incorrect. Shipping goods that are not invoiced could cause an overstatement of inventory. Answer (B) is incorrect. Shipping goods that are not invoiced could cause an overstatement of inventory and an understatement of revenues and receivables. Answer (D) is incorrect. Shipping goods that are not invoiced could cause an understatement of revenues and receivables.

6.1.8. Which of the following controls most likely would help ensure that all credit sales transactions of an entity are recorded?

A. The billing department supervisor sends copies of approved sales orders to the credit department for comparison to authorized credit limits and current customer account balances.

B. The accounting department supervisor independently reconciles the accounts receivable subsidiary ledger to the accounts receivable control account monthly.

C. The accounting department supervisor controls the mailing of monthly statements to customers and investigates any differences they report.

D. The billing department supervisor matches prenumbered shipping documents with entries in the sales journal.

Answer (D) is correct. *(CPA, adapted)*

REQUIRED: The control to detect unrecorded sales.

DISCUSSION: The sequential numbering of documents provides a standard control over transactions. The numerical sequence should be accounted for by an independent party. A major objective is to detect unrecorded and unauthorized transactions. Moreover, comparing shipments with the sales journal also will detect unrecorded transactions.

Answer (A) is incorrect. Credit approval does not ensure that sales have been recorded. Answer (B) is incorrect. The reconciliation will not detect sales that were never recorded. Answer (C) is incorrect. Customers are unlikely to report understatement of their accounts.

6.1.9. An auditor observes the mailing of monthly statements to a client's customers and reviews evidence of follow-up on errors reported by the customers. This test of controls most likely is performed to support management's financial statement assertion(s) of

	Classification and Understandability	Existence
A.	Yes	Yes
B.	Yes	No
C.	No	Yes
D.	No	No

Answer (C) is correct. *(CPA, adapted)*

REQUIRED: The financial statement assertion(s) related to observing the client's follow-up on errors reported on monthly statements.

DISCUSSION: The existence assertion relates to whether the related balance exists at the balance sheet date. Observation of the mailing of monthly statements as well as observing the correction of reported errors provides evidence that controls may be effective in ensuring that client customers are genuine.

Answer (A) is incorrect. The observation of client activities related to customer statements provides little evidence about proper classification and understandability in the financial statements. Answer (B) is incorrect. The procedure provides little evidence about the classification and understandability assertion. Answer (D) is incorrect. The mailing and follow-up procedures provide evidence that controls may be effective in ensuring that client customers are genuine.

Questions 6.1.10 through 6.1.13 are based on the following information. Sales procedures that were encountered during the regular annual audit of Marvel Wholesale Distributing Company are described below.

Customer orders are received by the sales-order department. A clerk computes the dollar amount of the order and sends it to the credit department for approval. Credit approval is stamped on the order and returned to the sales-order department. An invoice is prepared in two copies, and the order is filed in the customer order file. The customer copy of the invoice is sent to the billing department and held in the pending file, awaiting notification that the order has been shipped. The shipping copy of the invoice is routed through the warehouse, and the shipping department has authority for the respective departments to release and ship the merchandise. Shipping department personnel pack the order and prepare a three-copy bill of lading: The original copy is mailed to the customer, the second copy is sent with the shipment, and the other is filed in sequence in the bill of lading file. The invoice shipping copy is sent to the billing department. The billing clerk matches the received shipping copy with the customer copy from the pending file. Both copies of the invoice are priced, extended, and footed. The customer copy is then mailed directly to the customer, and the shipping copy is sent to the accounts receivable clerk. The accounts receivable clerk enters the invoice data in a sales-accounts receivable journal, posts the customer's account in the subsidiary customers' accounts ledger, and files the shipping copy in the sales invoice file. The invoices are numbered and filed in sequence.

6.1.10. To gather audit evidence concerning the proper credit approval of sales at the Marvel Company, the auditor would select a sample of transaction documents from the population represented by the

A. Customer order file.

B. Bill of lading file.

C. Subsidiary customers' accounts ledger.

D. Sales invoice file.

Answer (A) is correct. *(CPA, adapted)*

REQUIRED: The file or ledger containing evidence of proper issuance of credit sale approvals.

DISCUSSION: The customer order is first sent to the credit department and credit approval is stamped on it. It is then returned to the sales department and filed. The customer order file thus contains the only documentation for credit approvals.

Answer (B) is incorrect. The bill of lading file contains no evidence of credit approvals. Answer (C) is incorrect. The subsidiary customers' accounts ledger contains no evidence of credit approvals. Answer (D) is incorrect. The sales invoice file contains no evidence of credit approvals.

6.1.11. To determine whether Marvel Company's internal control operated effectively to minimize errors of failure to post invoices to the customers' accounts ledger, the auditor should select a sample of transactions from the population represented by the

A. Customer order file.

B. Bill of lading file.

C. Subsidiary customers' accounts ledger.

D. Sales invoice file.

Answer (D) is correct. *(CPA, adapted)*

REQUIRED: The source of data to ascertain whether internal control minimized accounts receivable posting errors.

DISCUSSION: The auditor should trace sales according to the sales invoices to the accounts receivable subsidiary ledger. Sales invoices in the sales invoice file without corresponding entries in the subsidiary ledger represent transactions not posted.

Answer (A) is incorrect. The customer order file does not necessarily contain sales information. Customer orders may not be accepted or shipped. Answer (B) is incorrect. The bill of lading file does not necessarily contain sales information. All shipments do not necessarily pertain to customer orders. Answer (C) is incorrect. The items in the subsidiary ledger represent those transactions that have been posted. The direction of the testing should be from sales invoice to subsidiary ledger, not subsidiary ledger to sales invoice.

6.1.12. To gather audit evidence that uncollected items in Marvel Company's customers' accounts represented valid trade receivables, the auditor should select a sample of items from the population represented by the

A. Customer order file.

B. Bill of lading file.

C. Subsidiary customers' accounts ledger.

D. Sales invoice file.

Answer (C) is correct. *(CPA, adapted)*

REQUIRED: The test appropriate for determining the validity (existence) of accounts receivable.

DISCUSSION: The auditor should sample from records of open accounts receivable to determine if they represent valid assets. The open accounts receivable are maintained in the subsidiary customers' accounts ledger. Items would be confirmed directly with the debtors.

Answer (A) is incorrect. The customer order file is not updated for shipment or payment. Answer (B) is incorrect. The bill of lading file is not updated for shipment or payment. Answer (D) is incorrect. The sales invoice file is not updated for shipment or payment.

6.1.13. To determine whether Marvel Company's internal control operated effectively to minimize errors of failure to invoice a shipment, the auditor should select a sample of transactions from the population represented by the

A. Customer order file.

B. Bill of lading file.

C. Subsidiary customers' accounts ledger.

D. Sales invoice file.

Answer (B) is correct. *(CPA, adapted)*

REQUIRED: The appropriate test to ascertain whether internal control minimized failures to invoice shipments.

DISCUSSION: The auditor should match bill of lading file copies relating to customer shipments to sales invoices (or possibly to the accounts receivable subsidiary ledger) to determine whether shipments were not billed.

Answer (A) is incorrect. The customer order file may contain orders that were not approved and shipped. Answer (C) is incorrect. An inconsistency between a customer balance and an invoice may result from payment, not necessarily from failure to invoice a shipment. Answer (D) is incorrect. The direction of the testing is wrong. To test for failure to invoice, the auditor should not be sampling from a file containing only orders that have been invoiced.

6.1.14. One of two office clerks in a small company prepares a sales invoice for $4,300; however, the invoice is incorrectly entered by the bookkeeper in the general ledger and the accounts receivable subsidiary ledger as $3,400. The customer subsequently remits $3,400, the amount on the monthly statement. Assuming there are only three employees in the department, the most effective control to prevent this type of error is

A. Assigning the second office clerk to independently check the sales invoice prices, discounts, extensions, and footings and to account for the invoice serial number.

B. Requiring that monthly statements be prepared by the bookkeeper and verified by one of the other office clerks prior to mailing.

C. Using predetermined totals to control posting routines.

D. Requiring the bookkeeper to perform periodic reconciliations of the accounts receivable subsidiary ledger and the general ledger.

Answer (C) is correct. *(CIA, adapted)*

REQUIRED: The most effective control to prevent posting errors.

DISCUSSION: A control total should be generated for the transactions to be posted. It then should be compared with the total of items posted to the individual accounts.

Answer (A) is incorrect. The misposting was an error that occurred subsequent to assigning the second office clerk to independently check the sales invoice prices, discounts, extensions, and footings and to account for the invoice serial number. Answer (B) is incorrect. Requiring that monthly statements be prepared by the bookkeeper and verified by one of the other office clerks prior to mailing does not detect an initial misposting. The statements are based on the misposted records. Answer (D) is incorrect. Requiring the bookkeeper to perform periodic reconciliations of the accounts receivable subsidiary ledger and the general ledger does not detect an initial misposting. The reconciliations are based on the misposted records.

6.1.15. Cash receipts from sales on account have been misappropriated. Which of the following acts would conceal this defalcation and be least likely to be detected by an auditor?

A. Understating the sales journal.

B. Overstating the accounts receivable control account.

C. Overstating the accounts receivable subsidiary ledger.

D. Understating the cash receipts journal.

Answer (A) is correct. *(CPA, adapted)*

REQUIRED: The act that conceals misappropriation of cash.

DISCUSSION: Not recording sales on account in the books of original entry is the most effective way to conceal a subsequent theft of cash receipts. The accounts will be incomplete but balanced, and procedures applied to the accounting records will not detect the defalcation.

Answer (B) is incorrect. The discrepancy between the control account and the subsidiary ledger indicates a misstatement. Answer (C) is incorrect. The discrepancy between the control account and the subsidiary ledger indicates a misstatement. Answer (D) is incorrect. Cash receipts will not reconcile with the credits to accounts receivable. If accounts receivable are not credited, confirmation will detect the theft.

6.1.16. Which of the following would be the best protection for a company that wishes to prevent the lapping of trade accounts receivable?

A. Segregate duties so that the bookkeeper in charge of the general ledger has no access to incoming mail.

B. Segregate duties so that no employee has access to both checks from customers and currency from daily cash receipts.

C. Have customers send payments directly to the company's depository bank.

D. Request that customers' payment checks be made payable to the company and addressed to the CFO.

Answer (C) is correct. *(CPA, adapted)*

REQUIRED: The best protection against lapping of accounts receivable.

DISCUSSION: Lapping is the delayed recording of cash receipts to cover a cash shortage. Current receipts are posted to the accounts of customers who paid one or two days previously to avoid complaints (and discovery) when monthly statements are mailed. The best protection is for the customers to send payments directly to the company's depository bank. This procedure precludes client personnel from having access to the money.

Answer (A) is incorrect. Although physical custody should be segregated from recordkeeping, another answer provides better protection. Answer (B) is incorrect. All cash should be entrusted to the CFO for safekeeping. Answer (D) is incorrect. Although having checks made payable to the entity limits the ability of an individual to convert it to cash for his or her own use, it does not eliminate the risk.

6.1.17. Upon receipt of customers' checks in the mail room, a responsible employee should prepare a remittance listing that is forwarded to the cashier. A copy of the listing should be sent to the

A. Internal auditor to investigate the listing for unusual transactions.

B. CFO to compare the listing with the monthly bank statement.

C. Accounts receivable bookkeeper to update the subsidiary accounts receivable records.

D. Entity's bank to compare the listing with the cashier's deposit slip.

Answer (C) is correct. *(CPA, adapted)*

REQUIRED: The use of a copy of the client's remittance listing.

DISCUSSION: The individuals with recordkeeping responsibility should not have custody of cash. Hence, they should use either the remittance advices or a listing of the remittances to make entries to the cash and accounts receivable control account and to the subsidiary accounts receivable records. Indeed, having different people make entries in the control account and in the subsidiary records is an effective control.

Answer (A) is incorrect. The internal auditors should have no ongoing control responsibilities. The investigation of unusual transactions is first conducted in the CFO's department. Answer (B) is incorrect. The monthly bank statement should be reconciled by someone outside of the treasury function. Answer (D) is incorrect. The entity's bank supplies a validated deposit slip based on the deposit for the day. Company management outside the treasury function compares the validated deposit slip with the remittance listing.

6.1.18. Which of the following internal control activities most likely would deter lapping of collections from customers?

A. Independent internal verification of dates of entry in the cash receipts journal with dates of daily cash summaries.

B. Authorization of write-offs of uncollectible accounts by a supervisor independent of credit approval.

C. Separation of duties between receiving cash and posting the accounts receivable ledger.

D. Supervisory comparison of the daily cash summary with the sum of the cash receipts journal entries.

Answer (C) is correct. *(CPA, adapted)*

REQUIRED: The best protection from lapping of collections from customers.

DISCUSSION: Lapping is the delayed recording of cash receipts to cover a cash shortage. Current receipts are posted to the accounts of customers who paid one or two days previously to avoid complaints (and discovery) when monthly statements are mailed. The best protection is for the customers to send payments directly to the company's depository bank. The next best procedure is to ensure that the accounts receivable clerk has no access to cash received by the mail room. Thus, the duties of receiving cash and posting the accounts receivable ledger are separated.

Answer (A) is incorrect. Lapping delays recording cash receipts so that posting the cash receipts journal and recording in the cash summary occur on the same date and in the same amounts. Answer (B) is incorrect. Lapping involves delayed posting of cash payments, not bad debt write-offs. Moreover, the credit manager should initiate write-offs to be approved by the CFO. Answer (D) is incorrect. Lapping delays recording cash receipts so that posting the cash receipts journal and recording in the cash summary occur on the same date and in the same amounts.

6.1.19. For the purpose of effective internal control, postdated checks received from customers should be

A. Restrictively endorsed.

B. Returned to customer.

C. Recorded as a cash sale.

D. Placed in the joint custody of two officers.

Answer (A) is correct. *(CPA, adapted)*

REQUIRED: The appropriate procedure for handling postdated checks received from customers.

DISCUSSION: All checks received from customers should be restrictively endorsed with the phrase "For Deposit Only" in the company account regardless of their date. They should be physically safeguarded until deposit.

Answer (B) is incorrect. Acceptance of a postdated check may be the firm's best (only) chance to collect cash from the customer. Answer (C) is incorrect. A postdated check does not represent cash. Answer (D) is incorrect. The postdated check should be kept by the CFO and accounted for by the controller.

6.1.20. Cash receipts should be deposited on the day of receipt or the following business day. What is the most appropriate audit procedure to determine that cash is promptly deposited?

A. Review cash register tapes prepared for each sale.

B. Review the functions of cash handling and maintaining accounting records for proper segregation of duties.

C. Compare the daily cash receipts totals with the bank deposits.

D. Review the functions of cash receiving and disbursing for proper segregation of duties.

Answer (C) is correct. *(CIA, adapted)*

REQUIRED: The most appropriate audit procedure to determine that cash is promptly deposited.

DISCUSSION: A standard control over the cash receipts function is to require that daily cash receipts be deposited promptly and intact. Thus, the total of cash receipts for a day should equal the bank deposit because no cash disbursements are made from the daily receipts. To determine whether cash receipts are promptly deposited, the auditor should compare the daily cash receipts totals with bank deposits.

Answer (A) is incorrect. Reviewing the cash register tapes does not ensure that cash is deposited. Answer (B) is incorrect. Segregating functions does not ensure that cash is deposited. Answer (D) is incorrect. Segregating functions does not ensure that cash is deposited.

6.2 Controls in a Cash Sale Environment

6.2.1. At which point in an ordinary sales transaction of a wholesaling business is a lack of specific authorization of least concern to the auditor in the conduct of an audit?

A. Granting of credit.

B. Shipment of goods.

C. Determination of discounts.

D. Selling of goods for cash.

Answer (D) is correct. *(CPA, adapted)*

REQUIRED: The point in an ordinary sales transaction at which specific authorization is of least concern to an auditor.

DISCUSSION: Selling goods for cash is the consummation of a transaction that is likely to be covered by a general authorization. Thus, the risk of loss arising from lack of specific authorization of cash sales is minimal.

Answer (A) is incorrect. Granting of credit in a sales transaction may require specific authorization, i.e., special consideration before approval by the appropriate person. Answer (B) is incorrect. Shipment of goods in a sales transaction may require specific authorization. Answer (C) is incorrect. Determination of discounts in a sales transaction may require specific authorization.

6.2.2. In a retail cash sales environment, which of the following controls is often absent?

A. Competent personnel.

B. Separation of functions.

C. Supervision.

D. Asset access limited to authorized personnel.

Answer (B) is correct. *(Publisher, adapted)*

REQUIRED: The control often absent in a cash sales environment.

DISCUSSION: In the usual retail cash sales situation, the sales clerk authorizes and records the transactions and takes custody of assets. However, management ordinarily employs other compensating controls to minimize the effects of the failure to separate functions. The cash receipts function is closely supervised, cash registers provide limited access to assets, and an internal recording function maintains control over cash receipts.

Questions 6.2.3 and 6.2.4 are based on the following information. Management discovers that a supervisor at one of its restaurant locations removes excess cash and resets sales totals throughout the day on the point-of-sale (POS) system. At closing, the supervisor deposits cash equal to the recorded sales on the POS system and keeps the rest.

The supervisor forwards the close-of-day POS reports from the POS system along with a copy of the bank deposit slip to the company's revenue accounting department. The revenue accounting department records the sales and the cash for the location in the general ledger and verifies the deposit slip to the bank statement. Any differences between sales and deposits are recorded in an over/short account and, if necessary, followed up with the location supervisor. The customer food order checks are serially numbered, and it is the supervisor's responsibility to see that they are accounted for at the end of each day. Customer checks and the transaction journal tapes from the POS system are kept by the supervisor for 1 week at the location and then destroyed.

6.2.3. Which of the following controls allowed the fraud to occur?

A. The accounting for customer food checks by the supervisor.

B. The deposit of cash receipts by the supervisor.

C. The matching of the bank deposit slips to the bank statement by revenue accounting.

D. The forwarding of the close-of-day POS reports to revenue accounting.

Answer (A) is correct. *(CIA, adapted)*

REQUIRED: The control that allowed the fraud to occur.

DISCUSSION: An inappropriate segregation of duties existed because the supervisor was responsible for accounting for customer food checks and depositing receipts and had the ability to reset POS totals throughout the day.

Answer (B) is incorrect. The depositing of receipts by the supervisor is not the problem. The supervisor's access to cash and ability to reset POS totals throughout the day allowed the fraud. Answer (C) is incorrect. An independent verification of the deposits made by the supervisor is appropriate. Answer (D) is incorrect. The forwarding of the close-of-day POS reports to revenue accounting is a step in the process of independently verifying sales.

6.2.4. Which of the following audit procedures would have detected the fraud?

A. Flowcharting the controls over the verification of bank deposits.

B. Comparing a sample of the close-of-day POS reports to copies of the bank deposit slips.

C. On a test basis, verifying that the serial-numbered customer food checks are accounted for.

D. For selected days, reconciling the total of customer food checks to daily bank deposits.

Answer (D) is correct. *(CIA, adapted)*

REQUIRED: The audit procedure that would have detected the fraud.

DISCUSSION: Using the total of the customer food checks as a confirmation of sales would have detected the shortage in the bank deposit.

Answer (A) is incorrect. The fraud involved receipts, not deposits. Answer (B) is incorrect. The fraud involved altering the amounts on the close-of-day POS reports by resetting the POS system totals to zero. Answer (C) is incorrect. The accounting for individual customer food checks would not have detected the fraud. It did not involve manipulation of these documents.

6.2.5. To establish illegal "slush funds," corporations may divert cash received in normal business operations. An auditor would encounter the greatest difficulty in detecting the diversion of proceeds from

A. Scrap sales.

B. Dividends.

C. Purchase returns.

D. C.O.D. sales.

Answer (A) is correct. *(CPA, adapted)*

REQUIRED: The transaction from which the diversion of proceeds is most difficult to detect.

DISCUSSION: Because scrap sales often provide little documentary evidence to corroborate cash receipts, it is difficult to detect abstraction of proceeds from unrecorded sales.

Answer (B) is incorrect. The auditor can ordinarily reconcile the expected dividends from securities held with the actual amounts received. Answer (C) is incorrect. Purchase returns are usually well documented and controlled. Answer (D) is incorrect. C.O.D. sales are usually well documented and controlled.

6.2.6. Employers bond employees who handle cash receipts because fidelity bonds reduce the possibility of employing dishonest individuals and

A. Protect employees who make unintentional errors from possible monetary damages resulting from their errors.

B. Deter dishonesty by making employees aware that insurance companies may investigate and prosecute dishonest acts.

C. Facilitate an independent monitoring of the receiving and depositing of cash receipts.

D. Force employees in positions of trust to take periodic vacations and rotate their assigned duties.

Answer (B) is correct. *(CPA, adapted)*

REQUIRED: The purpose of bonding employees.

DISCUSSION: Effective internal control, including human resources practices that stress the hiring of trustworthy people, does not guarantee against losses from embezzlement and other fraudulent acts committed by employees. Accordingly, an employer may obtain a fidelity bond to insure against losses arising from fraud by the covered employees. Prior to issuing this form of insurance, the underwriters investigate the individuals to be covered. Also, employees should be informed that bonding companies are diligent in prosecuting bonded individuals who commit fraud.

Answer (A) is incorrect. Bonding insures employers against intentional wrongdoing. Answer (C) is incorrect. Bonding is irrelevant to monitoring the receipt and deposit of cash receipts. Answer (D) is incorrect. Bonding is irrelevant to periodic vacations and rotation of duties.

6.3 Other Sales-Receivables Related Transactions

6.3.1. Proper authorization of write-offs of uncollectible accounts should be approved in which of the following departments?

A. Accounts receivable.

B. Credit.

C. Accounts payable.

D. CFO.

Answer (D) is correct. *(CPA, adapted)*

REQUIRED: The department authorizing write-offs of applicable accounts.

DISCUSSION: The write-off of uncollectible accounts requires effective controls. The initiation of the write-off is performed by the credit manager. However, authorization should be by an independent party, typically the CFO. The credit manager is evaluated, in part, on the amount of bad debt written off and should require significant evidence before initiating a write-off.

Answer (A) is incorrect. Accounts receivable is a recording function and should not authorize transactions. Answer (B) is incorrect. The credit manager should not both initiate and approve the write-off. Answer (C) is incorrect. Accounts payable is a recording function and should not authorize transactions.

6.3.2. An auditor noted that the accounts receivable department is separate from other accounting activities. Credit is approved by a separate credit department. Control accounts and subsidiary ledgers are balanced monthly. Similarly, accounts are aged monthly. The accounts receivable manager writes off delinquent accounts after 1 year, or sooner if a bankruptcy or other unusual circumstances are involved. Credit memoranda are prenumbered and must correlate with receiving reports. Which of the following areas could be viewed as an internal control deficiency of the above organization?

A. Write-offs of delinquent accounts.

B. Credit approvals.

C. Monthly aging of receivables.

D. Handling of credit memos.

Answer (A) is correct. *(CIA, adapted)*

REQUIRED: The internal control deficiency.

DISCUSSION: The accounts receivable manager has the ability to perpetrate fraud because (s)he performs incompatible functions. Authorization and recording of transactions should be segregated. Thus, someone outside the accounts receivable department should authorize write-offs.

Answer (B) is incorrect. Credit approval is an authorization function that is properly segregated from the recordkeeping function. Answer (C) is incorrect. Monthly aging is appropriate. Answer (D) is incorrect. The procedures regarding credit memoranda are standard controls.

6.3.3. To conceal defalcations involving receivables, the auditor would expect an experienced bookkeeper to charge which of the following accounts?

A. Miscellaneous income.

B. Petty cash.

C. Miscellaneous expense.

D. Sales returns.

Answer (D) is correct. *(CPA, adapted)*

REQUIRED: The account an experienced bookkeeper charges to conceal embezzlement.

DISCUSSION: To conceal a theft of customer payments on account, a bookkeeper debits sales returns and credits accounts receivable. If accounts receivable are not credited, the customer will continue to be billed and will complain.

Answer (A) is incorrect. If miscellaneous income is debited with a corresponding credit to accounts receivable, the resulting unusual entry is more likely to be reviewed and discovered. Answer (B) is incorrect. If petty cash is debited with a corresponding credit to accounts receivable, the resulting unusual entry is more likely to be reviewed and discovered. Answer (C) is incorrect. If miscellaneous expense is debited with a corresponding credit to accounts receivable, the resulting unusual entry is more likely to be reviewed and discovered.

6.3.4. For effective internal control, employees maintaining the accounts receivable subsidiary ledger should not also approve

A. Employee overtime wages.

B. Credit granted to customers.

C. Write-offs of customer accounts.

D. Cash disbursements.

Answer (C) is correct. *(CPA, adapted)*

REQUIRED: The activity incompatible with maintaining the accounts receivable subsidiary ledger.

DISCUSSION: An employee who authorizes a transaction, such as the write-off of a receivable, ordinarily should not be responsible for recording the same transaction. Segregating the functions of authorization, recordkeeping, and custody of assets reduces the possibility that an employee may be able to perpetrate and conceal fraud or error in the normal course of his or her duties.

Answer (A) is incorrect. Authorization of cash disbursements, e.g., for overtime, is not related to receivables, which are reduced by cash receipts, not disbursements. Answer (B) is incorrect. An employee who approves credit and maintains the accounts receivable ledger should not be able to perpetrate and conceal a fraud. Answer (D) is incorrect. Authorization of cash disbursements is not related to receivables, which are reduced by cash receipts, not disbursements.

6.3.5. To safeguard the assets through effective internal control, accounts receivable that are written off should be transferred to

A. A separate ledger.

B. An attorney for evidence in collection proceedings.

C. A tax deductions file.

D. A credit manager, since customers may seek to reestablish credit by paying.

Answer (A) is correct. *(CPA, adapted)*

REQUIRED: The proper disposition of accounts receivable that are written off.

DISCUSSION: Accounts receivable that are written off should be transferred to a separate ledger. This ledger should be maintained by the accounting department and periodically reviewed to determine if any of the accounts have become collectible.

Answer (B) is incorrect. If collection proceedings are initiated, the expectation is that the accounts will be collected and therefore should not be written off. Answer (C) is incorrect. The tax effects of accounts receivable are reflected in bad debt expense. Answer (D) is incorrect. The credit manager should not control the accounts receivable. The credit manager's function is to authorize credit, not maintain custody of assets.

6.3.6. Sound internal control activities dictate that defective merchandise returned by customers be presented initially to the

A. Accounts receivable supervisor.

B. Receiving clerk.

C. Shipping department supervisor.

D. Sales clerk.

Answer (B) is correct. *(CPA, adapted)*

REQUIRED: The individual to whom customers should return defective merchandise.

DISCUSSION: For control purposes, all receipts of goods or materials should be handled by the receiving clerk. Receiving reports should be prepared for all items received.

6.3.7. When an office supply company is unable to fill an order completely, it marks the out-of-stock items as back ordered on the customer's order and enters these items in a back order file that management can view or print. Customers are becoming disgruntled with the company because it seems unable to keep track of and ship out-of-stock items as soon as they are available. The best approach for ensuring prompt delivery of out-of-stock items is to

A. Match the back order file to goods received daily.

B. Increase inventory levels to minimize the number of times that stockouts occur.

C. Implement electronic data interchange with supply vendors to decrease the time to replenish inventory.

D. Reconcile the sum of filled and back orders with the total of all orders placed daily.

Answer (A) is correct. *(CIA, adapted)*

REQUIRED: The best approach for ensuring prompt delivery of out-of-stock items.

DISCUSSION: Reconciling the back order file to shipments received daily would identify unfilled orders for appropriate action.

Answer (B) is incorrect. Increasing inventory levels might minimize the number of times that out-of-stock conditions occur but will not affect delivery of the items that are out of stock. Answer (C) is incorrect. Implementing electronic data interchange with supply vendors may decrease the time to replenish inventory but will not affect delivery of the items that are out of stock. Answer (D) is incorrect. Reconciling the sum of filled and back orders with the total of all orders placed daily ensures that orders are either filled or back ordered but will not affect delivery of the items that are out of stock.

6.4 Technology Considerations

6.4.1. When evaluating internal control of an entity that processes sales transactions on the Internet, an auditor would be most concerned about the

A. Lack of sales invoice documents as an audit trail.

B. Potential for computer disruptions in recording sales.

C. Inability to establish an integrated test facility.

D. Frequency of archiving and data retention.

Answer (B) is correct. *(CPA, adapted)*

REQUIRED: The greatest concern about Internet controls.

DISCUSSION: Processing sales on the Internet (often called e-commerce) creates new and additional risks for clients. The client should use effective controls to ensure proper acceptance, processing, and storage of sales transactions. Threats include not only attacks from hackers but also system overload and equipment failure.

Answer (A) is incorrect. E-commerce sales transactions would not typically result in sales invoice documents. Answer (C) is incorrect. An integrated test facility is just one of many techniques for testing sales processing controls and transactions. Answer (D) is incorrect. Although archival and data retention are disaster recovery concerns, the question relates to controls over sales processing.

6.4.2. A mail-order retailer has just modified its processing programs to charge each customer the appropriate sales tax. The best approach for detecting whether sales taxes are applied correctly is to

A. Move the program code that computes sales taxes to a single program and make this program part of the processing sequence.

B. Change the operator input screens to show the computation of sales taxes so the operator can verify the computation.

C. Modify the program code to prompt the operator to ask customers whether their areas have sales taxes and enter the appropriate rates.

D. Add the program code that will sort orders by area, compute taxes in the aggregate, and compare the amount with the sum of individual taxes charged for each area.

Answer (D) is correct. *(CIA, adapted)*

REQUIRED: The best approach for detecting whether sales taxes are applied correctly.

DISCUSSION: Sales taxes vary from one jurisdiction to another. Thus, the program should sort orders by area. Verification of the accuracy of the tax charges then can be obtained by calculating the total taxes for each area in two ways: applying the tax rate to total sales or adding the taxes charged on individual sales.

Answer (A) is incorrect. Moving the program code that computes sales taxes to a single program is a good system design approach, but it does not guarantee that sales tax processing is complete. Answer (B) is incorrect. Changing the operator input screens does not ensure correct application of sales taxes. The operator may not know what the appropriate computation is. Answer (C) is incorrect. Customers may not know the proper rates or may deny that their areas impose the taxes.

Questions 6.4.3 and 6.4.4 are based on the following information. A flowchart of a client's revenue cycle appears below.

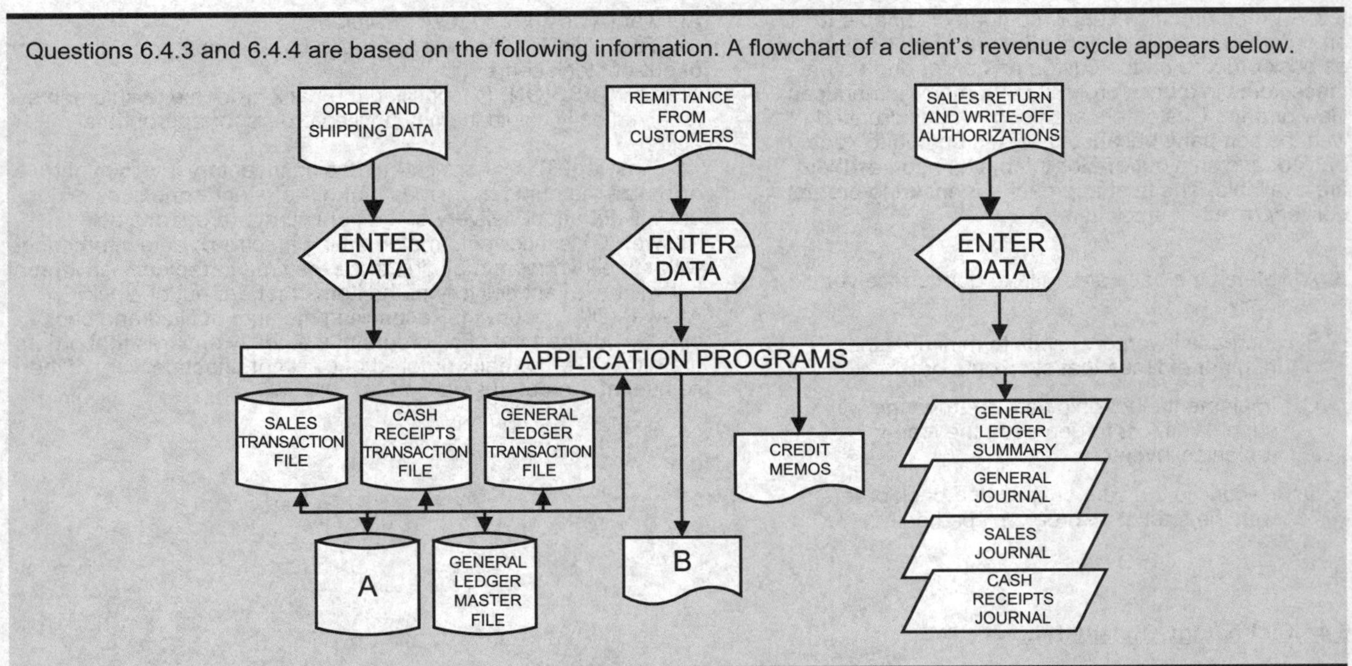

6.4.3. Symbol A most likely represents

A. Remittance advice file.
B. Receiving report file.
C. Accounts receivable master file.
D. Cash disbursements transaction file.

Answer (C) is correct. *(CPA, adapted)*

REQUIRED: The file accessed during the processing of a client's revenue transactions.

DISCUSSION: During the processing of sales orders and remittances from customers, as well as sales returns and write-off authorizations, the accounts receivable master file is accessed and updated. Thus, symbol A represents the accounts receivable master file.

Answer (A) is incorrect. The remittance advice file is represented by the cash receipts transaction file. Answer (B) is incorrect. The receiving report file relates to the purchasing cycle. Answer (D) is incorrect. The cash disbursements transaction file relates to the purchasing cycle.

6.4.4. Symbol B most likely represents

A. Customer orders.
B. Receiving reports.
C. Customer checks.
D. Sales invoices.

Answer (D) is correct. *(CPA, adapted)*

REQUIRED: The document represented by symbol B.

DISCUSSION: One output of the revenue cycle is the generation of sales invoices to be sent to customers.

Answer (A) is incorrect. Customer orders are entered online and not outputted from the system. Answer (B) is incorrect. Receiving reports are generated from the purchasing cycle, not the revenue cycle. Answer (C) is incorrect. Customer checks are represented by remittances from customers and entered online. However, the customer checks are safeguarded and deposited daily into the bank account.

STUDY UNIT SEVEN
INTERNAL CONTROL -- PURCHASES, PAYROLL, AND OTHER CYCLES

The first part of this study unit considers control concepts in a payment system. The focus is on a traditional manual voucher system that requires each payment to be vouched, or supported, prior to payment. This system has many variations, but the objectives and concepts of control are similar.

A computer system eliminates most of the paper flow from the manual system, but the objectives of internal control are the same.

The next part of this study unit relates to payroll. The questions provide a perspective on the document and information flow.

Controls related to other accounts are covered at the end of this study unit. Questions on internal control over other revenue and expense, production, inventory, investments, fixed assets, and other balance sheet accounts are included.

QUESTIONS

7.1 Purchases Responsibilities/Organizational Structure/Flowchart

7.1.1. The primary audit objective regarding the purchasing of materials by the client is to

A. Ascertain that materials paid for are on hand.

B. Observe the annual physical count.

C. Investigate the recording of unusual transactions regarding materials.

D. Determine the reliability of financial reporting by the purchasing function.

Answer (D) is correct. *(Publisher, adapted)*

REQUIRED: The auditor's primary objective in reviewing a client's materials purchasing cycle.

DISCUSSION: The auditor should obtain an understanding of internal control. The purpose of internal control is to address business risks that threaten the achievement of the following entity objectives: (1) reliability of financial reporting, (2) effectiveness and efficiency of operations, and (3) compliance with laws and regulations (AU-C 315).

Answer (A) is incorrect. Materials not on hand may have been sold or used in production. Answer (B) is incorrect. This question relates to purchasing, not the inventory function. Answer (C) is incorrect. Investigating the recording of unusual transactions is an audit procedure rather than an objective.

7.1.2. To minimize the risk that agents in the purchasing department will use their positions for personal gain, the organization should

A. Require competitive bidding.

B. Request internal auditors to confirm selected purchases and accounts payable.

C. Specify that all items purchased must pass value-per-unit-of-cost reviews.

D. Direct the purchasing department to maintain records on purchase prices paid, with review of such records required every 6 months.

Answer (A) is correct. *(CIA, adapted)*

REQUIRED: The control that will minimize the risk that purchasing agents will use their positions for personal gain.

DISCUSSION: The primary function of a purchasing department is to ensure the authorized acquisition of goods of a specified quality on a timely basis at an economical price. Competitive bidding procedures should reduce both costs and the likelihood that a purchasing agent will show favoritism to a vendor.

Answer (B) is incorrect. Confirmation establishes the existence of the liabilities but does not test the choice of vendor. Answer (C) is incorrect. Specifying that all items purchased must pass value-per-unit-of-cost reviews is essentially a detective, not a preventive, control. Answer (D) is incorrect. Directing the purchasing department to maintain records on purchase prices paid, with review of such records required every 6 months, is essentially a detective, not a preventive, control.

7.1.3. In a well-designed internal control system, employees in the same department most likely would approve purchase orders, and also

A. Reconcile the open invoice file.

B. Inspect goods upon receipt.

C. Authorize requisitions of goods.

D. Negotiate terms with vendors.

Answer (D) is correct. *(CPA, adapted)*

REQUIRED: The task appropriately performed by employees who approve purchase orders.

DISCUSSION: To prevent or detect fraud or error in the performance of assigned responsibilities, duties are often segregated. Approving purchase orders and negotiating terms with vendors are part of the authorization process performed by the purchasing department.

Answer (A) is incorrect. Reconciling the open invoice file is the accounting department's function. Answer (B) is incorrect. Inspection of goods upon receipt is the receiving department's function. Answer (C) is incorrect. Authorization of the requisition is inventory control's function.

7.1.4. A university does not have a centralized receiving function for departmental purchases of books, supplies, and equipment. Which of the following controls will most effectively prevent payment for goods not received, if performed prior to invoice payment?

A. Vendor invoices should be matched with department purchase orders.

B. Names and addresses on vendor invoices should be compared to a list of department-authorized vendors.

C. Vendor invoices should be approved by a departmental supervisor other than the employee ordering the goods.

D. Invoices over a specified amount should be approved by the vice president of finance.

Answer (C) is correct. *(CIA, adapted)*

REQUIRED: The control that most effectively prevents payment for goods not received, if performed prior to invoice payment.

DISCUSSION: The departmental supervisors are the most likely to be aware of the goods received by their departments. Moreover, separating ordering authority from payment authority will prevent unauthorized purchases.

Answer (A) is incorrect. Purchase orders do not provide evidence that the goods were received. Answer (B) is incorrect. Comparison with lists of authorized vendors does not provide evidence that goods were received. Answer (D) is incorrect. The vice president of finance is unlikely to have knowledge of goods received by the departments.

7.1.5. The principal function of a cash budget is to

A. Ensure that the accounting principles relevant to cash transactions are applied consistently from period to period.

B. Ensure that the accounting records are accurate.

C. Physically safeguard cash.

D. Implement asset and liability maturity matching.

Answer (D) is correct. *(Publisher, adapted)*

REQUIRED: The principal function of a cash budget.

DISCUSSION: Financial management customarily matches asset and liability maturities. Thus, noncurrent assets are usually financed with noncurrent debt and equity, and short-term financing is matched with temporary current assets. The purpose of maturity matching is to reduce the risk that the entity will be unable to pay its obligations as they become due.

Answer (A) is incorrect. The budget is ordinarily considered a financial tool, not an accounting check. Answer (B) is incorrect. The budget is ordinarily considered a financial tool, not an accounting check. Answer (C) is incorrect. The cash budget plans for the sources and uses of cash, whereas safes and bank accounts physically safeguard cash.

7.1.6. In a well-designed internal control system, the same employee may be permitted to

A. Mail signed checks and also cancel supporting documents.

B. Prepare receiving reports and also approve purchase orders.

C. Approve vouchers for payment and also have access to unused purchase orders.

D. Mail signed checks and also prepare bank reconciliations.

Answer (A) is correct. *(CPA, adapted)*

REQUIRED: The functions the same employee may be permitted to perform in a well-designed control system.

DISCUSSION: The cash disbursements department has an asset custody function. Consequently, this department is responsible for signing checks after verification of their accuracy by reference to the supporting documents. The supporting documents should then be canceled and the checks mailed. Cancelation prevents the documentation from being used to support duplicate payments. Moreover, having the party who signs the checks place them in the mail reduces the risk that they will be altered or diverted.

Answer (B) is incorrect. The receiving department should not know how many units have been ordered. Answer (C) is incorrect. Accounts payable is responsible for approving vouchers, and purchasing is the only department with access to the purchase orders. The same employee should not approve the purchase and approve payment. Answer (D) is incorrect. The bank reconciliation is performed by someone with no asset custody function.

7.1.7. Which of the following internal control activities is not usually performed in the vouchers payable department?

A. Matching the vendor's invoice with the related receiving report.

B. Approving vouchers for payment by having an authorized employee sign the vouchers.

C. Indicating the asset and expense accounts to be debited.

D. Accounting for unused prenumbered purchase orders and receiving reports.

Answer (D) is correct. *(CPA, adapted)*

REQUIRED: The control not usually performed in the vouchers payable department.

DISCUSSION: Employees in the vouchers payable department should have no responsibilities related to purchasing or receiving goods. The purchasing department accounts for unused prenumbered purchase orders. The receiving department accounts for unused prenumbered receiving reports.

7.1.8. Operating control of the check-signing machine normally should be the responsibility of the

A. General accounting function.

B. Treasury function.

C. Legal counsel.

D. Internal audit function.

Answer (B) is correct. *(CPA, adapted)*

REQUIRED: The department that should have operating control of the check-signing machine.

DISCUSSION: The operating control of a check-signing machine normally should be the responsibility of the CFO. (S)he maintains custody of the funds of the entity.

Answer (A) is incorrect. Cash custody responsibility should not be assigned to a function that maintains accounting records. Answer (C) is incorrect. Legal counsel should not have access to the check-signing machine. Legal counsel performs a staff function without operational authority. Answer (D) is incorrect. To maintain its organizational independence, the internal audit function should not have any responsibility for operations.

7.1.9. Which of the following questions is inappropriate on an internal control questionnaire concerning purchase transactions?

A. Are an approved purchase requisition and a signed purchase order required for each purchase?

B. Are prenumbered purchase orders and receiving reports used and accounted for?

C. Are all goods received in a centralized receiving department and counted, inspected, and compared with purchase orders on receipt?

D. Are intact cash receipts deposited daily in the bank?

Answer (D) is correct. *(Publisher, adapted)*

REQUIRED: The question not associated with purchase transactions.

DISCUSSION: The question about the daily deposit of intact cash receipts is related to the cash receipts cycle, not the purchases-payables-cash disbursements cycle.

Answer (A) is incorrect. A question about the requirement of an approved purchase requisition and a signed purchase order is relevant to internal control over purchase transactions. Answer (B) is incorrect. A question about the use of prenumbered purchase orders and receiving reports is relevant to internal control over purchase transactions. Answer (C) is incorrect. A question about activities of a centralized receiving department is relevant to internal control over purchase transactions.

7.1.10. In assessing risks of material misstatement for purchases, an auditor vouches a sample of entries in the voucher register to the supporting documents. Which assertion would this test of controls most likely support?

A. Completeness.

B. Occurrence.

C. Accuracy.

D. Classification.

Answer (B) is correct. *(CPA, adapted)*

REQUIRED: The assertion tested by vouching.

DISCUSSION: A voucher signifies a liability. Its issuance is recorded in the voucher register after comparison of the vendor's invoice with the purchase requisition, purchase order, and receiving report. The direction of testing is an important consideration in determining the relevant assertion. Selecting a sample of recorded entries in the voucher register and vouching them to the supporting documentation provides evidence that the transactions occurred.

Answer (A) is incorrect. Vouching entries in the voucher register to the supporting documents does not test for unrecorded transactions. Answer (C) is incorrect. Vouching entries in the voucher register to the supporting documents provides evidence about whether the amounts were recorded appropriately, but it most strongly supports the assertion about occurrence. Answer (D) is incorrect. Vouching entries in the voucher register to the supporting documents provides little evidence that the transactions have been recorded in the proper accounts.

7.1.11. Your objective is to determine that nonrecurring purchases, initiated by various user organizations, have been properly authorized. If all purchases are made through the purchasing department, to which of the following documents should you vouch purchases?

A. Purchase requisitions.

B. Purchase orders.

C. Invoices.

D. Receiving reports.

Answer (A) is correct. *(CIA, adapted)*

REQUIRED: The document to which purchases should be vouched.

DISCUSSION: When the auditor tests for unauthorized nonrecurring purchases, (s)he should vouch purchases to the purchase requisitions. The initiating authorization by the user department is embodied in a properly authorized purchase requisition.

Answer (B) is incorrect. The purchase order does not contain the crucial initiating authorization. Answer (C) is incorrect. The authorization for a purchase is not contained in the vendor's invoice. Answer (D) is incorrect. The authorization for a purchase is not contained in the receiving report.

7.1.12. Effective controls relevant to purchasing of raw materials should usually include all of the following except

A. Systematic reporting of product changes that will affect raw materials.

B. Determining the need for the raw materials prior to preparing the purchase order.

C. Obtaining third-party written quality and quantity reports prior to payment for the raw materials.

D. Obtaining financial approval prior to making a commitment.

Answer (C) is correct. *(CPA, adapted)*

REQUIRED: The procedure that is not an effective internal control over usual purchases.

DISCUSSION: Obtaining third-party written quality and quantity reports prior to payment for raw materials is unnecessary. Only in exceptional cases when client personnel are not sufficiently knowledgeable about the purchased goods would outside advice be necessary.

Answer (A) is incorrect. The latest product changes should be incorporated in the bill of materials records so that obsolete materials are not ordered. Answer (B) is incorrect. Only needed items should be ordered. Answer (D) is incorrect. Financial approval before making a commitment is important so that funds will be available when payment is required.

7.1.13. Based on observations made during an audit, the auditor should discuss with management the effectiveness of the company's controls that protect against the purchase of

A. Required supplies provided by a vendor who offers no trade or cash discounts.

B. Inventory items acquired based on an economic order quantity (EOQ) inventory management concept.

C. New equipment that is needed but does not qualify for an accelerated write-off under the class life rules.

D. Supplies individually ordered, without considering possible volume discounts.

Answer (D) is correct. *(CPA, adapted)*

REQUIRED: The potential weakness in internal control relevant to purchasing.

DISCUSSION: An auditor should communicate to management and those charged with governance significant deficiencies and material weaknesses observed during an audit (AU-C 265). (S)he should discuss procedures that permit the avoidable loss of assets. Thus, an auditor should determine whether the failure to consider possible volume discounts is due to fraud or error.

Answer (A) is incorrect. The entity may consider other factors such as quality and service, not just whether a discount is offered on the required supplies. Answer (B) is incorrect. Inventory management is appropriately based on economic order quantity (EOQ) concepts. It minimizes the sum of inventory ordering costs and inventory carrying costs. Answer (C) is incorrect. Equipment acquisition should be based on need for the equipment, not on whether the purchase qualifies for preferential tax treatment.

7.1.14. Effective controls relevant to the efficiency of purchases will result in proper evaluation of the time for ordering merchandise. When making this evaluation, the purchasing company should give primary consideration to

A. The price differences that exist among various vendors who can supply the merchandise at the required time.

B. The borrowing cost of money (interest) that the company must incur as a consequence of acquiring the merchandise.

C. The trade-off between the cost of owning and storing excess merchandise and the risk of loss by not having merchandise on hand.

D. The flow of funds within the company that indicates when money is available to pay for merchandise.

Answer (C) is correct. *(CPA, adapted)*

REQUIRED: The primary consideration regarding the timing of purchase orders.

DISCUSSION: Effective purchasing departments should use the basic economic order quantity (EOQ) calculation that minimizes both the cost of owning and storing excess merchandise and the cost of ordering merchandise (and thus the timing of ordering). This model assumes the demand is constant and does not consider the cost of stockouts. Probabilistic models have been developed to incorporate the risk of loss (cost) by not having merchandise on hand.

Answer (A) is incorrect. The price differences that exist among various vendors does not address the question of when to order. Answer (B) is incorrect. The borrowing cost of money (interest) that the company must incur as a consequence of acquiring the merchandise does not address the question of when to order. Answer (D) is incorrect. If the merchandise is needed, the CFO is responsible for assuring that financing, which may be external, is arranged.

7.1.15. Which of the following observations made during the preliminary survey of a local department store's disbursement cycle reflects a control strength?

A. Individual department managers use prenumbered forms to order merchandise from vendors.

B. The receiving department is given a copy of the purchase order complete with a description of goods, quantity ordered, and extended price for all merchandise ordered.

C. The CFO's office prepares checks for suppliers based on vouchers prepared by the accounts payable department.

D. Individual department managers are responsible for the movement of merchandise from the receiving dock to storage or sales areas as appropriate.

Answer (C) is correct. *(CIA, adapted)*

REQUIRED: The observation about the disbursement cycle indicative of a control strength.

DISCUSSION: Accounting for payables is a recording function. The matching of the supplier's invoice, the purchase order, and the receiving report (and usually the purchase requisition) should be the responsibility of the accounting department. These are the primary supporting documents for the payment voucher prepared by the accounts payable section that will be relied upon by the CFO in making payment.

Answer (A) is incorrect. The managers should submit purchase requisitions to the purchasing department. The purchasing function should be separate from operations. Answer (B) is incorrect. To encourage a fair count, the receiving department should receive a copy of the purchase order from which the quantity has been omitted. Answer (D) is incorrect. The receiving department should transfer goods directly to the storeroom to maintain security. A copy of the receiving report should accompany the goods to the storeroom so that the amount stored can be compared with the amount in the report.

7.1.16. An internal control narrative indicates that an approved voucher is required to support every check request for payment of merchandise. Which of the following procedures provides the greatest assurance that this control is operating effectively?

A. Select and examine vouchers and ascertain that the related canceled checks are dated no later than the vouchers.

B. Select and examine vouchers and ascertain that the related canceled checks are dated no earlier than the vouchers.

C. Select and examine canceled checks and ascertain that the related vouchers are dated no earlier than the checks.

D. Select and examine canceled checks and ascertain that the related vouchers are dated no later than the checks.

Answer (D) is correct. *(CPA, adapted)*

REQUIRED: The procedure giving the greatest assurance that approved vouchers support check requests.

DISCUSSION: Payment vouchers bearing the required approvals should be supported by a properly authorized purchase requisition, a purchase order executing the transaction, a receiving report indicating all goods ordered have been received in good condition, and a vendor invoice confirming the amount owed To determine that check requests are valid, the appropriate audit procedure is therefore to compare checks and the related vouchers. The direction of testing should be from a sample of checks to the approved vouchers. If the date of a voucher is later than the date of the related check, the inference is that a check was issued without proper support.

Answer (A) is incorrect. Tracing from vouchers to canceled checks does not give assurance that all checks are supported by approved vouchers. This test will not detect canceled checks unsupported by approved vouchers, although it will permit comparison of the dates of the respective documents. Answer (B) is incorrect. Tracing from vouchers to canceled checks does not give assurance that all checks are supported by approved vouchers. This test will not detect canceled checks unsupported by approved vouchers, although it will permit comparison of the dates of the respective documents. Answer (C) is incorrect. The checks should be dated no earlier than the vouchers. Each voucher should be dated earlier than (or have the same date as) the related check.

7.1.17. During the audit of a construction contract, it was discovered that the contractor was being paid for each ton of dirt removed. The contract called for payment based on cubic yards removed. Which internal control might have prevented this error?

A. Comparison of invoices with purchase orders or contracts.

B. Comparison of invoices with receiving reports.

C. Comparison of actual costs with budgeted costs.

D. Extension checks of invoice amounts.

Answer (A) is correct. *(CIA, adapted)*

REQUIRED: The internal control that might have prevented use of an incorrect measure of work done.

DISCUSSION: The contractor's invoice would have stated a unit of measure different from that in the contract. Thus, a comparison of the invoice with the original contract would have disclosed the error.

Answer (B) is incorrect. The dirt removed would not have been received by the company; hence, no receiving reports would have existed. Answer (C) is incorrect. This comparison would not have directly detected the specific reason for a variance. However, the cost comparison would have detected the variance and prompted an investigation of its cause. Answer (D) is incorrect. The problem was not a mathematical error but an erroneous basis for payment.

7.1.18. Which of the following questions should not appear in an internal control questionnaire relating to cash disbursements?

A. Are all disbursements except for petty cash made by check?

B. Are imprinted and prenumbered checks used and is a check protection device used in printing the check amount?

C. Is each check supported by an approved voucher?

D. Are prelistings made of all cash receipts?

Answer (D) is correct. *(Publisher, adapted)*

REQUIRED: The question not appearing in a questionnaire about cash disbursements.

DISCUSSION: Prelisting of cash receipts is performed in the mail room as part of the sales-receivables-cash receipts cycle. This question is inappropriate in a questionnaire relating to cash disbursements. The questionnaire should list inquiries as to whether (1) supporting documentation is mutilated upon signing, (2) issuing a check to cash or bearer is prohibited, (3) signing blank checks is prohibited, (4) unused checks are controlled, (5) voided checks are retained and accounted for, and (6) the check signer is responsible for mailing signed checks.

7.1.19. Propex Corporation uses a voucher register and does not record invoices in a subsidiary ledger. Propex will probably benefit most from the additional cost of maintaining an accounts payable subsidiary ledger if

A. There are usually invoices in an unmatched invoice file.

B. Vendors' requests for confirmation of receivables often go unanswered for several months until paid invoices can be reviewed.

C. Partial payments to vendors are continuously made in the ordinary course of business.

D. It is difficult to reconcile vendors' monthly statements.

Answer (C) is correct. *(CPA, adapted)*

REQUIRED: The situation in which an accounts payable subsidiary ledger is useful.

DISCUSSION: If a firm makes partial payments to vendors, tracking the amounts still due on vouchers may be difficult. An accounts payable subsidiary ledger provides a continuous record of amounts due to vendors.

Answer (A) is incorrect. Some unmatched invoices will usually be awaiting appropriate receiving reports in any organization. Answer (B) is incorrect. Propex will benefit only to the extent of good vendor relations if it promptly answers confirmation requests. Answer (D) is incorrect. Under a voucher system, reconciling vendors' monthly statements is unnecessary unless problems arise.

7.1.20. The procedure that best discourages the resubmission of vendor invoices after they have been paid is

A. A requirement for double endorsement of checks.

B. The cancelation of vouchers by accounting personnel.

C. The cancelation of vouchers by CFO personnel.

D. The mailing of payments directly to payees by accounting personnel.

Answer (C) is correct. *(CMA, adapted)*

REQUIRED: The procedure best discouraging resubmission of vendor invoices after payment.

DISCUSSION: Canceling vouchers and supporting papers (with perforations, ink, etc.) upon payment prevents the payment of a duplicate voucher. If the person signing the check does the canceling, the documents cannot be recycled for duplicate payments. Securing the paid-voucher file from access by the accounts payable clerk is another effective control.

Answer (A) is incorrect. A single endorsement is not a control weakness if the person who signs does not have incompatible functions and if proper documentation is required before signing. Answer (B) is incorrect. The vouchers should not be canceled before payment. Answer (D) is incorrect. Mailing payments directly to payees does not prevent a second use of invoices by unethical personnel. Also, record keepers should not have access to signed checks.

7.1.21. Which of the following items in a communication about control deficiencies in internal control over cash receipts and disbursements is least significant?

A. Cash receipts are not deposited intact daily.

B. CFO fails to verify the names and addresses of check payees.

C. Signed checks are distributed by the controller to approved payees.

D. Checks are signed by one person.

Answer (D) is correct. *(Publisher, adapted)*

REQUIRED: The control deficiency related to cash transactions that is least significant.

DISCUSSION: The auditor should be least concerned that the checks are signed by only one person if that person is not assigned other incompatible functions, and proper documentation is required before signing.

Answer (A) is incorrect. Cash receipts should be deposited intact daily. Answer (B) is incorrect. The CFO should sign checks based on proper documentation. The accounting function, which prepares the voucher (authorization for payment), should verify the payees' names and addresses. Answer (C) is incorrect. The controller, who is responsible for accounting for cash, should not have access to signed checks.

7.1.22. Which of the following questions would an auditor most likely include on an internal control questionnaire for notes payable?

A. Are assets that collateralize notes payable critically needed for the entity's continued existence?

B. Are two or more authorized signatures required on checks that repay notes payable?

C. Are the proceeds from notes payable used for the purchase of noncurrent assets?

D. Are direct borrowings on notes payable authorized by the board of directors?

Answer (D) is correct. *(CPA, adapted)*

REQUIRED: The question most likely included on an internal control questionnaire for notes payable.

DISCUSSION: Control is enhanced when different persons or departments authorize, record, and maintain custody of assets for a class of transactions. Authorization of notes payable transactions is best done by the board of directors.

Answer (A) is incorrect. The importance of specific assets to the entity is an operational matter and not a primary concern of an auditor when (s)he is considering internal control. Answer (B) is incorrect. Questions about the payment function are likely to be on the questionnaire relating to cash disbursements. Answer (C) is incorrect. The use of funds is an operating decision made by management and is not a primary concern of the auditor when considering internal control.

7.1.23. Fraudulent use of corporate credit cards will be minimized by which of the following controls?

A. Establishing a corporate policy on the issuance of credit cards to authorized employees.

B. Periodically reviewing the validity of the need for credit cards at executive and operating levels.

C. Reconciling the monthly statement from the credit card company with the submitted copies of the cardholders' charge slips.

D. Subjecting credit card charges to the same expense controls as those used on regular company expense forms.

Answer (D) is correct. *(CIA, adapted)*

REQUIRED: The control minimizing fraudulent use of corporate credit cards.

DISCUSSION: Credit card charges should be controlled in much the same manner as expense accounts and other expense reports, including use of limitations on specific kinds of expenditures. These charges should be compared with supporting documentation, such as receiving reports and invoices.

Answer (A) is incorrect. Establishing a corporate policy on the issuance of credit cards to authorized employees concerns the question of credit card availability, not credit card use. Answer (B) is incorrect. Periodically reviewing the validity of the need for credit cards at executive and operating levels concerns the question of credit card availability, not credit card use. Answer (C) is incorrect. Reconciling the monthly statement from the credit card company with the submitted copies of the cardholders' charge slips is a check on the billing of charges.

7.1.24. Which of the following is a standard control over cash disbursements?

A. Checks should be signed by the controller and at least one other employee of the company.

B. Checks should be sequentially numbered and the numerical sequence should be accounted for by the person preparing bank reconciliations.

C. Checks and supporting documents should be marked "Paid" immediately after the check is returned with the bank statement.

D. Checks should be sent directly to the payee by the employee who prepares documents that authorize check preparation.

Answer (B) is correct. *(CPA, adapted)*

REQUIRED: The standard control over cash disbursements.

DISCUSSION: The sequential numbering of checks provides a standard control over cash disbursements. The numerical sequence of canceled checks should be accounted for by the person preparing bank reconciliations. Physical control over blank checks should be maintained by the CFO. A major objective is to detect unrecorded and unauthorized checks.

Answer (A) is incorrect. To separate custody of and accounting for cash, the controller should not have the authority to sign checks. Answer (C) is incorrect. Supporting documents (but not the check) should be marked "Paid" immediately upon signing the check to preclude resubmission with a duplicate invoice. Answer (D) is incorrect. The check signer (not the check preparer) should oversee the mailing of the checks.

7.1.25. A purchasing agent places an order for inventory whenever a requisition is received from the warehouse. The warehouse clerk issues requisitions based on periodic physical counts because no perpetual records are maintained. Numerous duplicate orders have been placed for goods previously ordered but not received. To prevent this excess ordering, the firm should

A. Keep an adequate record of open purchase orders and review it before ordering.

B. Count goods in the warehouse less often.

C. Use prenumbered purchase orders.

D. Not use purchase requisitions.

Answer (A) is correct. *(Publisher, adapted)*

REQUIRED: The procedure by which a company using a monthly physical inventory as a basis for purchase orders can prevent excess ordering.

DISCUSSION: A well-kept open purchase order file will provide information on outstanding orders and, if reviewed prior to ordering, will prevent duplicate orders.

Answer (B) is incorrect. To requisition needed goods on a timely basis, goods must be counted often. Answer (C) is incorrect. Prenumbered purchase orders fail to provide information on purchase orders placed but not received. Answer (D) is incorrect. Purchase requisitions are authorizations for purchases and should be the basis for a purchase order.

7.1.26. Under which of the following circumstances would an auditor be most likely to intensify an audit of a $500 imprest petty cash fund?

A. Reimbursement vouchers are not prenumbered.

B. Reimbursement occurs twice each week.

C. The custodian occasionally uses the cash fund to cash employee checks.

D. The custodian endorses reimbursement checks.

Answer (B) is correct. *(CPA, adapted)*

REQUIRED: The circumstance in which the auditor would intensify an audit of a petty cash fund.

DISCUSSION: If the auditor determines that reimbursement occurs twice each week, (s)he should intensify the audit of the imprest cash fund. The frequent need for reimbursement suggests that the fund is not functioning as planned.

Answer (A) is incorrect. Although failure to prenumber vouchers is not a preferable practice, it does not suggest fraud or error. Answer (C) is incorrect. Use of the cash fund to cash employee checks is not a preferable practice, but it does not suggest fraud or error. Answer (D) is incorrect. The custodian's endorsement of reimbursement checks is an appropriate procedure to obtain reimbursement cash for the fund.

7.1.27. Which of the following control activities is not usually performed with regard to vouchers payable in the accounting department?

A. Determining the mathematical accuracy of the vendor's invoice.

B. Having an authorized person approve the voucher.

C. Controlling the mailing of the check and remittance advice.

D. Matching the receiving report with the purchase order.

Answer (C) is correct. *(CPA, adapted)*

REQUIRED: The procedure not usually performed with respect to vouchers by the accounting department.

DISCUSSION: The cash disbursements department, which is responsible to the CFO, has an asset custody function that should be segregated from the recording function of the accounting department. Consequently, checks for disbursements should be signed by a responsible person in that department after necessary supporting evidence has been examined. This individual also should be responsible for canceling the supporting documentation and mailing the signed checks and remittance advices. The documentation typically consists of a payment voucher, requisition, purchase order, receiving report, and vendor invoice.

Answer (A) is incorrect. The accounting department determines the mathematical accuracy of the vendor's invoice. Answer (B) is incorrect. The accounting department has an authorized person approve the voucher. Answer (D) is incorrect. The accounting department matches the receiving report with the purchase order.

7.1.28. A receiving department receives copies of purchase orders for use in identifying and recording inventory receipts. The purchase orders list the name of the vendor and the quantities of the materials ordered. A possible error that this system could allow is

A. Payment to unauthorized vendors.

B. Payment for unauthorized purchases.

C. Overpayment for partial deliveries.

D. Delay in recording purchases.

Answer (C) is correct. *(CIA, adapted)*

REQUIRED: The error that may occur in a purchasing system.

DISCUSSION: To ensure a fair count, the copy of the purchase order sent to the receiving clerk should not include quantities. The receiving clerk should count the items in the shipment and prepare a receiving report. Copies are sent to inventory control and accounts payable.

Answer (A) is incorrect. Comparing receipts with purchase orders will help detect unauthorized vendors. Answer (B) is incorrect. Comparing receipts with purchase orders will help detect unauthorized purchases. Answer (D) is incorrect. Using purchase orders to identify receipts will not delay recording purchases.

7.2 Purchases Technology Considerations

7.2.1. In the accounting system of Apogee Company, the quantities counted by the receiving department and entered at a terminal are transmitted to the computer, which immediately transmits the amounts back to the terminal for display on the terminal screen. This display enables the operator to

A. Establish the validity of the account number.

B. Verify that the amount was entered accurately.

C. Verify the authorization of the disbursement.

D. Prevent the overpayment of the account.

Answer (B) is correct. *(CPA, adapted)*

REQUIRED: The effect of displaying the amounts entered at a terminal.

DISCUSSION: The display of the amounts entered is an input control that permits visual verification of the accuracy of the input by the operator. This is termed closed-loop verification.

Answer (A) is incorrect. Displaying the amounts entered at a terminal does not establish the validity of the account number. Answer (C) is incorrect. Displaying the amounts entered at a terminal does not verify the authorization of the disbursement. Answer (D) is incorrect. Displaying the amounts entered at a terminal does not prevent the overpayment of the account.

7.2.2. A client's program that recorded receiving report information entered directly by the receiving department on vendor shipment receipt included a reasonableness or limit test. Which of the following errors would this test likely detect?

A. The receipt was for a shipment from an unauthorized vendor.

B. The vendor shipped the wrong item.

C. The receiving department clerk entered the quantity of the product received as 0.

D. The shipment received from the vendor was past due by 2 weeks.

Answer (C) is correct. *(Publisher, adapted)*

REQUIRED: The error likely to be detected by a reasonableness or limit test.

DISCUSSION: Reasonableness or limit tests are used to test quantities received to determine if they are within acceptable limits. Entry of a product number with 0 received is identified as probable error.

Answer (A) is incorrect. A validity test should be performed before order acceptance to determine whether the vendor is an authorized vendor. Answer (B) is incorrect. The received products should be compared with the product numbers ordered to determine whether they were ordered. Answer (D) is incorrect. The purchasing department should follow up on past due orders.

7.2.3. Which of the following is usually a benefit of using electronic funds transfer for international cash transactions?

A. Improvement of the audit trail for cash receipts and disbursements.

B. Creation of self-monitoring access controls.

C. Reduction of the frequency of data entry errors.

D. Off-site storage of source documents for cash transactions.

Answer (C) is correct. *(CPA, adapted)*

REQUIRED: The benefit of using EFT for international cash transactions.

DISCUSSION: The processing and transmission of electronic transactions, such as EFTs, virtually eliminates human interaction. This process not only helps eliminate errors but also allows for the rapid detection and recovery from errors when they do occur.

Answer (A) is incorrect. The audit trail is typically less apparent in an electronic environment than in a manual environment. Answer (B) is incorrect. A key control is management's establishment and monitoring of access controls. Answer (D) is incorrect. Source documents are often eliminated in EFT transactions.

7.3 Electronic Data Interchange (EDI)

7.3.1. A company using EDI made it a practice to track the functional acknowledgments from trading partners and to issue warning messages if acknowledgments did not occur within a reasonable length of time. What risk was the company attempting to address by this practice?

A. Transactions that have not originated from a legitimate trading partner may be inserted into the EDI network.

B. Transmission of EDI transactions to trading partners may sometimes fail.

C. There may be disagreement between the parties as to whether the EDI transactions form a legal contract.

D. EDI data may not be accurately and completely processed by the EDI software.

Answer (B) is correct. *(CIA, adapted)*

REQUIRED: The EDI risk addressed by tracking functional acknowledgments from trading partners.

DISCUSSION: Tracking of customers' functional acknowledgments, when required, will help to ensure successful transmission of EDI transactions. Some possible controls include (1) the provision of end-to-end acknowledgments, particularly when multiple, interconnected networks are involved, and (2) maintenance of a tickler file of outstanding functional acknowledgments, with issuance of warnings for those that are overdue.

Answer (A) is incorrect. Unauthorized access to the EDI system should be prevented by procedures that ensure the effective use of passwords, and data integrity and privacy should be maintained through the use of encryption and authentication measures. Answer (C) is incorrect. Contractual issues should be resolved by the company and its trading partners before EDI is implemented. Answer (D) is incorrect. The risk that EDI data may not be completely and accurately processed is minimized by system-based controls, not by acknowledgments from trading partners.

7.3.2. Which of the following statements is true concerning the security of messages in an electronic data interchange (EDI) system?

A. When confidentiality of data is the primary risk, message authentication is the preferred control rather than encryption.

B. Encryption performed by physically secure hardware devices is more secure than encryption performed by software.

C. Message authentication in EDI systems performs the same function as separation of duties in other information systems.

D. Security in the transaction phase in EDI systems is not necessary because problems at that level will usually be identified by the service provider.

Answer (B) is correct. *(CPA, adapted)*

REQUIRED: The true statement about the security of messages in an EDI system.

DISCUSSION: Physically secure hardware for performing encryption is under the direct control of the client. Software is not easily controlled because it is portable. More control is achieved with the hardware approach. However, in the business environment, most encryption applications rely on software.

Answer (A) is incorrect. When confidentiality is a concern, encryption and access controls should be used. Answer (C) is incorrect. Authentication relates to authorization, not security issues. Answer (D) is incorrect. Security in the EDI transaction phase is also an issue. The transmission of information to the service provider, such as a VAN, is subject to a variety of problems, for example, interception or alteration, that may not be detected by the service provider.

7.3.3. Which of the following are essential elements of the audit trail in an electronic data interchange (EDI) system?

A. Network and sender-recipient acknowledgments.

B. Message directories and header segments.

C. Contingency and disaster recovery plans.

D. Trading partner security and mailbox codes.

Answer (A) is correct. *(CPA, adapted)*

REQUIRED: The essential element in an EDI audit trail.

DISCUSSION: An audit trail allows for the tracing of a transaction from initiation to conclusion. Network and sender-recipient acknowledgments relate to the transaction flow and provide for the tracking of transactions.

Answer (B) is incorrect. Message directories and header segments provide information controlling the message, such as originating and destination stations and message type and priority level. Such information is part of the message and not the audit trail. Answer (C) is incorrect. Although contingency and disaster recovery plans are important controls, they do not relate to the audit trail. Answer (D) is incorrect. Although maintaining control over security and mailbox codes is an important control, it does not relate to the audit trail.

7.3.4. The best approach for minimizing the likelihood of software incompatibilities leading to unintelligible messages is for a company and its customers to

A. Acquire their software from the same software vendor.

B. Agree to synchronize their updating of EDI-related software.

C. Agree to use the same software in the same ways indefinitely.

D. Each write their own version of the EDI-related software.

Answer (B) is correct. *(CIA, adapted)*

REQUIRED: The best approach for minimizing the likelihood of software incompatibilities leading to unintelligible messages.

DISCUSSION: EDI entails the exchange of common business data converted into standard message formats. Thus, two crucial requirements are that the participants agree on transaction formats and that translation software be developed to convert messages into a form understandable by other companies. Thus, if one company changes its software, its trading partners must also do so.

Answer (A) is incorrect. The company and its customers may obtain their EDI-related software from the same vendor but still have software incompatibility problems if they do not synchronize their installation of updated versions. Answer (C) is incorrect. As business requirements change, it may not be possible to use the same software in the same ways indefinitely. Answer (D) is incorrect. Even if the company and its customers each write their own versions, synchronization problems will arise from updates.

7.3.5. The auditor plans to select a sample of transactions to assess the extent that purchase discounts may have been lost by the company. After assessing the risks associated with lost purchase discounts, the auditor was most likely to select a sample from which one of the following populations?

A. Open purchase orders.

B. Paid EDI invoices.

C. Paid non-EDI invoices.

D. Paid EDI and non-EDI invoices.

Answer (C) is correct. *(CIA, adapted)*

REQUIRED: The population sampled to assess the extent of lost purchase discounts.

DISCUSSION: Manual input and processing increase the risk of delayed payments and loss of purchase discounts. Furthermore, delays are less likely in an EDI system. Thus, the proper population from which to sample consists of paid invoices not processed through the EDI system.

Answer (A) is incorrect. Open purchase orders have not yet been invoiced or paid. Answer (B) is incorrect. Delays are less likely in an EDI system. Answer (D) is incorrect. Delays are less likely in an EDI system.

7.3.6. An audit of the electronic data interchange (EDI) area of a purchasing department revealed the facts listed below. Which one indicates the need for improved internal control?

A. Employees may access the computer system only via an ID and an encrypted password.

B. The system employs message sequencing as a way to monitor data transmissions.

C. Certain types of transactions may be made only at specific terminals.

D. Branch office employees may access the server with a single call via modem.

Answer (D) is correct. *(Publisher, adapted)*

REQUIRED: The condition that indicates the need for improved internal control.

DISCUSSION: The system should employ automatic dial-back to prevent intrusion by unauthorized parties. This procedure accepts an incoming modem call, disconnects, and automatically dials back a prearranged number to establish a permanent connection for data transfer or inquiry.

Answer (A) is incorrect. Employee access to the computer system via an ID and an encrypted password is considered acceptable. Encrypted passwords further decrease the likelihood of unauthorized access. Answer (B) is incorrect. Message sequencing detects unauthorized access by numbering each message and incrementing each message by one more than the last one sent. This procedure will detect a gap or duplicate. Answer (C) is incorrect. Allowing certain types of transactions to be made only at specific terminals minimizes the likelihood of unauthorized access.

7.3.7. Which of the following statements is correct concerning internal control in an electronic data interchange (EDI) system?

A. Preventive controls generally are more important than detective controls in EDI systems.

B. Control objectives for EDI systems generally are different from the objectives for other information systems.

C. Internal controls in EDI systems rarely permit the risks of material misstatement to be assessed at an acceptably low level.

D. Internal controls related to the segregation of duties generally are the most important controls in EDI systems.

Answer (A) is correct. *(CPA, adapted)*

REQUIRED: The true statement about EDI controls.

DISCUSSION: In general, preventive controls are more important than detective controls because the benefits typically outweigh the costs. In electronic processing, once a transaction is accepted, the opportunity to apply detective controls is often limited. Thus, preventing fraud or error is important.

Answer (B) is incorrect. The basic control objectives are the same regardless of the nature of the processing: to ensure the integrity of the information and to safeguard the assets. Answer (C) is incorrect. To gather sufficient evidence in a sophisticated computer system, testing controls is often necessary. The RMMs may be assessed at an acceptably low level if relevant controls are identified and tested and if the resulting evidence provides the degree of assurance desired regarding operating effectiveness. Answer (D) is incorrect. The level of segregation of duties achieved in a manual system is usually not feasible in a computer system.

7.3.8. Before sending or receiving EDI messages, a company should

A. Execute a trading partner agreement with each of its customers and suppliers.

B. Reduce inventory levels in anticipation of receiving shipments.

C. Demand that all its suppliers implement EDI capabilities.

D. Evaluate the effectiveness of its use of EDI transmissions.

Answer (A) is correct. *(CIA, adapted)*

REQUIRED: The process to be performed before sending or receiving EDI messages.

DISCUSSION: Before sending or receiving EDI messages, a company should execute a trading partner agreement with its customers and suppliers. For example, all parties should understand (1) their responsibilities, (2) the messages each will initiate, (3) how they will interpret messages, (4) the means of authenticating and verifying the completeness and accuracy of messages, (5) the moment when the contract between the parties is effective, and (6) the required level of security.

Answer (B) is incorrect. The company may intend to reduce inventory levels, but that intention is unrelated to the timing of its first EDI messages. Answer (C) is incorrect. The company may want to demand or encourage all its customers and suppliers to implement EDI capabilities, but that request is independent of sending and receiving messages. Answer (D) is incorrect. It is not possible to evaluate the effectiveness of EDI transmissions until after they occur.

7.3.9. A control that a company can use to detect forged EDI messages is to

A. Acknowledge all messages initiated externally with confirming messages.

B. Permit only authorized employees to have access to transmission facilities.

C. Delay action on orders until a second order is received for the same goods.

D. Write all incoming messages to a write-once/read-many device for archiving.

Answer (A) is correct. *(CIA, adapted)*

REQUIRED: The control to detect forged EDI messages.

DISCUSSION: If an entity acknowledges messages initiated externally, the alleged sender will have the opportunity to recognize that it had not sent the message and will then be able to notify the entity of the potential forgery. Then, corrective action can be taken.

Answer (B) is incorrect. Permitting only authorized employees to have access to transmission facilities controls for unauthorized access to the facilities but would not detect forged EDI messages. Answer (C) is incorrect. Delaying action on orders until a second order is received for the same goods defeats the purpose of using EDI, namely, rapid communication followed by rapid response. Answer (D) is incorrect. Writing all incoming messages to a write-once/read-many device is a good practice, but it will not detect forgeries.

7.3.10. In a review of an EDI application using a third-party service provider, the auditor should

I. Ensure encryption keys meet ISO standards

II. Determine whether an independent review of the service provider's operation has been conducted

III. Verify that only public-switched data networks are used by the service provider

IV. Verify that the service provider's contracts include necessary clauses, such as the right to audit

A. I and II.

B. I and IV.

C. II and III.

D. II and IV.

Answer (D) is correct. *(CIA, adapted)*

REQUIRED: The auditor's procedures in a review of an EDI application.

DISCUSSION: An auditor should review trading partner agreements and contracts with third-party service providers. These documents should contain necessary clauses and appropriately limit liabilities. Moreover, legal counsel should have reviewed the agreements or contracts. An auditor should also determine whether the third-party service provider's operations and controls have been independently reviewed (e.g., by public accountants).

Answer (A) is incorrect. Using a third-party service provider does not require encryption. Answer (B) is incorrect. Using a third-party service provider does not require encryption. Answer (C) is incorrect. Use of public-switched data networks is not a requirement of EDI.

7.3.11. Electronic data interchange (EDI) offers significant benefits to organizations, but it is not without certain major obstacles. Successful EDI implementation begins with which of the following?

A. Mapping the work processes and flows that support the organization's goals.

B. Purchasing new hardware for the EDI system.

C. Selecting reliable vendors for translation and communication software.

D. Standardizing transaction formats and data.

Answer (A) is correct. *(CIA, adapted)*

REQUIRED: The initial phase of EDI implementation.

DISCUSSION: Benefits result when EDI is combined with strategic efforts that alter previous practices. Applying EDI to an inefficient process results in continuing to do things the wrong way, only faster. Thus, the initial phase of EDI implementation includes understanding the organization's mission and an analysis of its activities as part of an integrated solution to the organization's needs.

Answer (B) is incorrect. The prerequisite for EDI success is an understanding of the mission of the business and the processes and flows that support its goals, followed by cooperation with external partners. Purchasing new hardware is a subsequent step. Answer (C) is incorrect. Before applying EDI technology to the business, EDI should be viewed as part of an overall integrated solution to organizational requirements. Answer (D) is incorrect. EDI is not a solution by itself. Instead of considering how to transmit and receive transactions, a company must first analyze the entire process.

7.3.12. Organizations that move to implement EDI often use value-added networks (VANs). Which of the following would not normally be performed by a VAN?

A. Store electronic purchase orders of one organization to be accessed by another organization.

B. Provide common interfaces across organizations thereby eliminating the need for one organization to establish direct computer communication with a trading partner.

C. Maintain a log of all transactions of an organization with its trading partner.

D. Provide translations from clients' computer applications to a standard protocol used for EDI communication.

Answer (D) is correct. *(CIA, adapted)*

REQUIRED: The function not performed by a VAN.

DISCUSSION: Companies must purchase their own software to translate their data to a national standard protocol for EDI purposes, either ANSI X.12 in the U.S. or EDIFACT in Europe and most of the rest of the world. Once the data are in the standard format, the VAN handles all aspects of the communication. VANs are privately owned telecommunications carriers that sell capacity to outside users. Among other things, a VAN provides a mailbox service permitting EDI messages to be sent, sorted, and held until needed in the recipient's computer system.

Answer (A) is incorrect. VANs normally provide mailbox services. Answer (B) is incorrect. VANs normally provide common communication interfaces. Answer (C) is incorrect. VANs normally provide logs of transactions.

7.3.13. Which of the following is usually a benefit of transmitting transactions in an electronic data interchange (EDI) environment?

A. A compressed business cycle with lower year-end receivables balances.

B. A reduced need to test computer controls related to sales and collections transactions.

C. An increased opportunity to apply statistical sampling techniques to account balances.

D. No need to rely on third-party service providers to ensure security.

Answer (A) is correct. *(CPA, adapted)*

REQUIRED: The benefit of EDI.

DISCUSSION: EDI transactions are typically transmitted and processed in real time. Thus, EDI compresses the business cycle by eliminating delays. The time required to receive and process an order, ship goods, and receive payment is greatly reduced compared with that of a typical manual system. Accordingly, more rapid receipt of payment minimizes receivables and improves cash flow.

Answer (B) is incorrect. Use of a sophisticated processing system increases the need to test computer controls. Answer (C) is incorrect. Computer technology allows all transactions to be tested rather than just a sample. Answer (D) is incorrect. EDI often uses a VAN (value-added network) as a third-party service provider, and reliance on controls provided by the VAN may be critical.

7.4 Payroll Responsibilities/Organizational Structure/Flowchart

7.4.1. Which of the following controls is most effective in providing reasonable assurance that salary, wage, and benefit expenses are incurred only for work performed?

A. All time cards and reports are reviewed and approved in writing by immediate line supervisors having no responsibilities for paycheck distribution.

B. The accuracy of extensions of hours worked and pay rates is rechecked by an independent party, and pay rate and other key payroll information is changed only upon the receipt of a written authorization from the human resources department.

C. Actual payroll amounts are regularly compared against budgeted amounts by management, with all material budget variances being investigated.

D. The payroll register is used as the source document for posting employment-related expenses to the general ledger.

Answer (A) is correct. *(CIA, adapted)*

REQUIRED: The most effective control providing reasonable assurance that salary, wage, and benefit expenses are incurred only for work performed.

DISCUSSION: Review and approval of time cards by line supervisors is appropriate because these supervisors should know whether work has been performed. Also, they do not distribute paychecks, so they are not able to divert falsely authorized checks.

Answer (B) is incorrect. An arithmetic check of payroll calculations provides no control over the actual hours reported, which is the basis for compensating work performed. Also, proper authority for pay rate changes controls the level of pay, not the reporting of hours of work performed. Answer (C) is incorrect. Comparisons between actual and budgeted labor expense may reveal overall inefficient labor use, but probably not particular improprieties. Answer (D) is incorrect. Posting to the general ledger from the payroll register controls recording of the expense, not the propriety of the labor hours reported.

7.4.2. The purpose of segregating the duties of hiring personnel and distributing payroll checks is to segregate the

A. Authorization of transactions from the custody of related assets.

B. Operational responsibility from the record-keeping responsibility.

C. Human resources function from the controllership function.

D. Administrative controls from the internal accounting controls.

Answer (A) is correct. *(CPA, adapted)*

REQUIRED: The purpose of segregating the duties of hiring personnel and distributing payroll checks.

DISCUSSION: In principle, the payroll function should be divided into its authorization, recording, and custody functions. Authorization of hiring, wage rates, and deductions is provided by human resources. Authorization of hours worked (executed by employees) is provided by production. Based upon these authorizations, accounting calculates and records the payroll. Based on the calculated amounts, the CFO prepares and distributes payroll checks.

Answer (B) is incorrect. Neither hiring personnel (authorization) nor distributing checks (asset custody) is a recordkeeping activity. Answer (C) is incorrect. Controllership is a recordkeeping activity. Neither the controller nor the human resources department should distribute checks. Answer (D) is incorrect. The professional standards no longer recognize the distinction between administrative controls and internal accounting controls.

7.4.3. Which of the following is an operating control over the staffing function?

A. Making background checks on all new hires.

B. Maintaining records of the department's accomplishments.

C. Encouraging new hires to participate in professional organizations.

D. Requiring personnel to participate in firm-sponsored external activities.

Answer (A) is correct. *(CIA, adapted)*

REQUIRED: The operating control over staffing.

DISCUSSION: Staffing provides the necessary personnel to achieve organizational objectives efficiently. Because honest and capable personnel also help create an environment that promotes effective internal control, hiring policies and procedures are crucial. Background checks, for example, may screen out potential hirees of questionable character.

Answer (B) is incorrect. Maintaining records is an accounting control. Answer (C) is incorrect. Professional development activities involve the directing function, that is, motivating people in an organization to contribute effectively to achieve goals. Answer (D) is incorrect. Professional development activities involve the directing function, that is, motivating people in an organization to contribute effectively to achieve goals.

7.4.4. Which of the following departments most likely would approve changes in pay rates and deductions from employee salaries?

A. Human resources.

B. CFO.

C. Controller.

D. Payroll.

Answer (A) is correct. *(CPA, adapted)*

REQUIRED: The department that most likely approves changes in pay rates and deductions.

DISCUSSION: The human resources department provides the authorization for payroll-related transactions, e.g., hiring, termination, and changes in pay rates and deductions.

Answer (B) is incorrect. The CFO performs a custody function for payroll-related transactions. Answer (C) is incorrect. The payroll department, which is overseen by the controller, has a recordkeeping function for payroll-related transactions. Answer (D) is incorrect. The payroll department, which is overseen by the controller, has a recordkeeping function for payroll-related transactions.

7.4.5. Organizational independence in the processing of payroll is achieved by functional segregations that are built into the system. Which one of the following functional segregations is not required for internal control purposes?

A. Segregation of timekeeping from payroll preparation.

B. Segregation of human resources function from payroll preparation.

C. Segregation of payroll preparation and paycheck distribution.

D. Segregation of payroll preparation and maintenance of year-to-date records.

Answer (D) is correct. *(CMA, adapted)*

REQUIRED: The functional segregation that is not required for internal control purposes.

DISCUSSION: Most companies have their payrolls prepared by the same individuals who maintain the year-to-date records. A functional segregation is not needed because both duties involve recordkeeping.

Answer (A) is incorrect. Segregating timekeeping and payroll preparation is an effective control. It prevents one person from claiming that an employee worked certain hours and then writing a check to that employee. Payment to an absent or fictitious employee therefore requires collusion between two employees. Answer (B) is incorrect. Human resources should be segregated from payroll. The first authorizes the calculation of the payroll by the second. Answer (C) is incorrect. Segregating paycheck preparation from distribution makes paying fictitious employees more difficult.

7.4.6. An auditor will ordinarily ascertain whether payroll checks are properly endorsed during the audit of

A. The payroll register.

B. The cost accounting system.

C. Cash in bank.

D. Accrued payroll.

Answer (A) is correct. *(CPA, adapted)*

REQUIRED: The phase in the audit when payroll check endorsements are audited.

DISCUSSION: Ordinarily, the auditor examines the endorsements on payroll checks while obtaining an understanding of and testing the payroll cycle, which includes consideration of the payroll register.

Answer (B) is incorrect. The cost accounting system relates primarily to the production cycle. Answer (C) is incorrect. Cash in bank is usually not integral to the payroll cycle. Answer (D) is incorrect. Accrued payroll implies that payroll checks were not issued, e.g., for a partial payroll period just prior to year end.

7.4.7. In the audit of which of the following types of profit-oriented enterprises is the auditor most likely to place special emphasis on testing the controls over proper classification of payroll transactions?

A. A manufacturing organization.

B. A retailing organization.

C. A wholesaling organization.

D. A service organization.

Answer (A) is correct. *(CPA, adapted)*

REQUIRED: The organization in which payroll transaction classifications are most important to the auditor.

DISCUSSION: A manufacturer is characteristically labor intensive with a high frequency and volume of payroll transactions requiring classification into direct labor and overhead. Payroll information is important in the costing of work-in-process, finished goods inventory, and cost of goods sold.

Answer (B) is incorrect. Retailers are normally not as labor intensive and do not require as many payroll transactions as a manufacturer. Furthermore, their labor costs are typically expensed rather than capitalized as part of inventory. Answer (C) is incorrect. Wholesalers are normally not as labor intensive and do not require as many payroll transactions as a manufacturer. Furthermore, their labor costs are typically expensed rather than capitalized as part of inventory. Answer (D) is incorrect. Service organizations are normally not as labor intensive and do not require as many payroll transactions as a manufacturer. Furthermore, their labor costs are typically expensed rather than capitalized as part of inventory.

7.4.8. Which of the following situations represents an internal control weakness in the payroll department?

A. Payroll department personnel are rotated in their duties.

B. Paychecks are distributed by the employees' immediate supervisors.

C. Payroll records are reconciled with quarterly tax reports.

D. The timekeeping function is independent of the payroll department.

Answer (B) is correct. *(CMA, adapted)*

REQUIRED: The internal control weakness in the payroll department.

DISCUSSION: A supervisor who distributes payroll checks can divert paychecks of fictitious employees if (s)he also has access to personnel records. This opportunity results from being assigned the incompatible functions of authorization, recordkeeping, and custodianship. A person unrelated to either payroll recordkeeping or the operating department should distribute checks. Many organizations use direct deposit programs to transfer pay directly to employees' bank accounts, eliminating the distribution process.

Answer (A) is incorrect. Periodic rotation of payroll personnel inhibits the perpetration and concealment of fraud. Answer (C) is incorrect. Reconciling payroll records with quarterly tax reports is an analytical procedure that may detect a discrepancy. Answer (D) is incorrect. Timekeeping should be independent of employee records.

7.4.9. Which of the following human resources department procedures reduces the risk of payroll fraud and represents an appropriate responsibility for the department?

A. Distributing paychecks.

B. Authorizing overtime hours.

C. Authorizing the addition or deletion of employees from the payroll.

D. Collection and retention of unclaimed paychecks.

Answer (C) is correct. *(CIA, adapted)*

REQUIRED: The procedure reducing the risk of fraud that is the responsibility of the human resources department.

DISCUSSION: The payroll department is responsible for assembling payroll information (recordkeeping). The human resources department is responsible for authorizing employee transactions such as hiring, firing, and changes in pay rates and deductions. Segregating the recording and authorization functions helps prevent fraud.

Answer (A) is incorrect. The CFO should perform the asset custody function regarding payroll. Answer (B) is incorrect. Authorizing overtime is a responsibility of operating management. Answer (D) is incorrect. Unclaimed checks should be in the custody of the CFO until they can be deposited in a special bank account.

7.4.10. Which of the following activities performed by a department supervisor most likely would help in the prevention or detection of a payroll fraud?

A. Distributing paychecks directly to department employees.

B. Setting the pay rate for departmental employees.

C. Hiring employees and authorizing them to be added to payroll.

D. Approving a summary of hours each employee worked during the pay period.

Answer (D) is correct. *(CPA, adapted)*

REQUIRED: The activity performed by a department supervisor to prevent or detect fraud.

DISCUSSION: The department supervisor is in the best position to determine that employees are present and performing the assigned functions.

Answer (A) is incorrect. Supervisors should not have a custody function. The paymaster (CFO's department) should be responsible for distribution of paychecks. Answer (B) is incorrect. Human resources should set the appropriate pay rates based on skills and needs. Answer (C) is incorrect. Human resources should identify and hire the appropriate employees and the payroll department (accounting) should add them to the payroll. Human resources may obtain input from supervisors, but the authorization comes from human resources.

7.4.11. A large retail enterprise has established a policy that requires the paymaster to deliver all unclaimed payroll checks to the internal audit department at the end of each payroll distribution day. This policy was most likely adopted to

A. Assure that employees who were absent on a payroll distribution day are not paid for that day.

B. To insure that the checks are voided immediately.

C. Prevent a bona fide employee's check from being claimed by another employee.

D. Detect any fictitious employee who may have been placed on the payroll.

Answer (D) is correct. *(CPA, adapted)*

REQUIRED: The reason for delivering unclaimed payroll checks to the internal auditing department.

DISCUSSION: A follow-up of unclaimed checks may result in identification of fictitious or terminated employees, thus eliminating an employee's opportunity to claim a paycheck belonging to a terminated employee. The unclaimed checks should then be turned over to a custodian so the internal audit function does not assume operating responsibilities.

Answer (A) is incorrect. Assuring that employees are not paid for absences is an operating responsibility, which should not be undertaken by the internal audit department. Answer (B) is incorrect. Checks should be held for a reasonable time so the employee may claim them when they return to work. Answer (C) is incorrect. Regardless of whether the paymaster distributes the checks or whether they are subsequently claimed by the employee, proper identification should be required to assure only bona fide employees receive a paycheck.

7.4.12. Effective internal control activities over the payroll function may include

A. Reconciliation of totals on job time tickets with job reports by employees responsible for those specific jobs.

B. Verification of agreement of job time tickets with employee time clock card hours by a timekeeping department employee.

C. Preparation of payroll transaction journal entries by an employee who reports to the supervisor of the human resources department.

D. Custody of rate authorization records by the supervisor of the payroll department.

Answer (B) is correct. *(CPA, adapted)*

REQUIRED: The effective control over payroll.

DISCUSSION: The total time spent on jobs should approximate the total time indicated on time clock cards. Timekeeping's comparison of these records should provide an independent check of the accuracy of time reported on the time clock cards.

Answer (A) is incorrect. An independent party should perform the review function. Employees should not review themselves. Answer (C) is incorrect. The payroll department should prepare the payroll transaction journal entries. If the human resources department performed this task, authorization and recordkeeping would be combined. Answer (D) is incorrect. Human resources authorizes the pay rates used in the payroll calculation.

7.4.13. In manufacturing environments, employees are often required to use time cards and job time tickets. Which is the false statement related to the use of these documents?

A. Job time tickets are completed by employees for each job worked on, and an employee may have one or many job time tickets in a day.

B. Only one time card should exist for each employee.

C. Time reported on job time tickets should be reconciled to time cards.

D. Payroll should be prepared from job time tickets.

Answer (D) is correct. *(Publisher, adapted)*

REQUIRED: The false statement about job time tickets and time cards.

DISCUSSION: The payroll should be prepared from the time cards, which are the official records of time worked. The allocation of direct labor to the various jobs and the identification of indirect labor that should be charged to overhead is determined from the job time tickets.

Answer (A) is incorrect. A different job time ticket should be prepared for each employee task, and an employee may work on one or many jobs in a day. Answer (B) is incorrect. Each employee should have only one time card, which is the official record of hours worked. Answer (C) is incorrect. The time reported on the time tickets should be reconciled to the time cards.

7.4.14. Which of the following internal control activities most likely would prevent direct labor hours from being charged to manufacturing overhead?

A. Periodic independent counts of work in process for comparison to recorded amounts.

B. Comparison of daily journal entries with approved production orders.

C. Use of time tickets to record actual labor worked on production orders.

D. Reconciliation of work-in-process inventory with periodic cost budgets.

Answer (C) is correct. *(CPA, adapted)*

REQUIRED: The control to prevent direct labor hours from being charged to manufacturing overhead.

DISCUSSION: Time tickets should specifically identify labor hours as direct or indirect.

Answer (A) is incorrect. Independent counts of work-in-process for comparison with recorded amounts provide assurance that all inventories are accounted for, but they do not ensure proper classification of the costs within the account. Answer (B) is incorrect. Comparison of daily journal entries with approved production orders only provides assurance that costs are being assigned to production orders. Answer (D) is incorrect. Reconciliation of work-in-process inventory with periodic cost budgets is an analytical procedure that might detect but would not prevent the problem.

7.4.15. Effective control over the cash payroll function would mandate which of the following?

A. The payroll clerk should fill the envelopes with cash and a computation of the net wages.

B. Unclaimed pay envelopes should be retained by the paymaster.

C. Each employee should be asked to sign a receipt.

D. A separate checking account for payroll should be maintained.

Answer (C) is correct. *(CPA, adapted)*

REQUIRED: The most appropriate control over cash payroll.

DISCUSSION: Under a cash payroll system, the receipt signed by the employee is the only document in support of payment. The signed receipt is essential to verify proper payment.

Answer (A) is incorrect. A person (e.g., a cashier) other than the one computing net wages should put the cash in the envelope. Answer (B) is incorrect. Unclaimed cash payroll should be deposited in a special bank account for safekeeping. Answer (D) is incorrect. Effective internal control does not require that a separate account be maintained. Only a limited number of checks is necessary for a cash payroll.

7.4.16. Each Friday afternoon, payroll checks are distributed by the shift superintendent. The plant is so large and the turnover is so great that the superintendent does not know many of the workers. Undelivered checks are returned to the payroll clerk, from whom the workers can obtain them at some later time. The payroll clerk routinely continues the payroll record for workers one week after their departure from the firm, ultimately cashes the unclaimed checks, and keeps the money. Which of the following is a control designed to prevent this misappropriation?

A. Require the shift superintendent to know all the workers by name.

B. Require the timekeeper to compute the weekly pay of each worker and to make distribution of the checks received from the CFO's office.

C. Require the CFO's office to prepare checks only on the basis of supporting documentation from both the timekeeper and payroll office.

D. Periodically rotate the shift superintendent.

Answer (C) is correct. *(CIA, adapted)*

REQUIRED: The control designed to prevent a misappropriation by a payroll clerk.

DISCUSSION: The payroll should be prepared from the time cards, which are the official records of time worked, and the authorized pay rates and deductions. After the payroll is prepared, it should be independently verified. Also, the payroll department has a recording function and should not be charged with custody of related assets (undelivered paychecks) even temporarily. Undelivered checks should be sent to the CFO for deposit in a bank account after a reasonable period of time.

Answer (A) is incorrect. Requiring the shift superintendent to know all workers by name is a control that would be difficult to execute. Answer (B) is incorrect. The timekeeper should not perform these incompatible functions. (S)he should neither compute weekly pay nor have custody of assets. Answer (D) is incorrect. The payroll clerk's fraud does not depend on the identity of the shift superintendent.

7.5 Payroll Technology Considerations

7.5.1. What information would the auditor expect to find in the data dictionary that would assist in a payroll application audit?

A. Programs that access the data.

B. Type of operating system.

C. Online user identification.

D. System network architecture and flowcharts.

Answer (A) is correct. *(CIA, adapted)*

REQUIRED: The information found in the data dictionary that would assist in the payroll audit.

DISCUSSION: The data dictionary is a file (possibly manual but usually computerized) in which the records relate to specified data items. It contains definitions of data records and files and the list of programs used to process them. Only certain persons or entities are permitted to retrieve data or to modify data items. Accordingly, these access limitations are also found in the data dictionary.

Answer (B) is incorrect. The type of operating system is not customarily part of the data dictionary. Answer (C) is incorrect. Online user identification is not customarily part of the data dictionary. Answer (D) is incorrect. System network architecture and flowcharts are not customarily part of the data dictionary.

7.5.2. Matthews Corp. has changed from a system of recording time worked on time clock cards to a computerized payroll system in which employees record time in and out with magnetic cards. The computer system automatically updates all payroll records. Because of this change

A. A generalized computer audit program must be used.

B. Part of the audit trail is altered.

C. The potential for payroll-related fraud is diminished.

D. Transactions must be processed in batches.

Answer (B) is correct. *(CPA, adapted)*

REQUIRED: The effect of computerization of a payroll system.

DISCUSSION: In a manual payroll system, a paper trail of documents would be created to provide audit evidence that controls over each step in processing were operating effectively. One element of a computer system that differentiates it from a manual system is that a transaction trail useful for auditing purposes might exist only for a brief time or only in computer-readable form.

Answer (A) is incorrect. Use of generalized audit software is only one of many ways of auditing through a computer. Answer (C) is incorrect. Conversion to a computer system may actually increase the chance of fraud by eliminating segregation of incompatible functions and other controls. Answer (D) is incorrect. Automatic updating indicates that processing is not in batch mode.

7.5.3. Which of the following activities most likely would detect whether payroll data were altered during processing?

A. Monitoring authorized distribution of data control sheets.

B. Using test data to verify the performance of edit routines.

C. Examining source documents for approval by supervisors.

D. Segregating duties between approval of hardware and software specifications.

Answer (B) is correct. *(CPA, adapted)*

REQUIRED: The activity most likely to detect alteration of payroll data during processing.

DISCUSSION: The test data approach uses the computer to test the processing logic and controls within the system and the records produced. The auditor prepares a set of dummy transactions specifically designed to test the control activities that management claims to have incorporated into the processing programs. The auditor can expect the controls to be applied to the transactions in the prescribed manner. Thus, the auditor is testing the effectiveness of the controls over the payroll data.

Answer (A) is incorrect. Monitoring authorized distribution of data control sheets detects alteration of data outside the computer, not during processing. Answer (C) is incorrect. Examining source documents for approval by supervisors detects alteration of data outside the computer, not during processing. Answer (D) is incorrect. Segregating duties between hardware and software approval does not affect data during processing.

7.6 Other Cycles

7.6.1. Each of the following is an appropriate control over securities and investments except

A. Proper authorization of transactions.

B. Custodian bonded and separate from investment records.

C. Storage in a safe-deposit box.

D. Custodian separate from treasury function.

Answer (D) is correct. *(Publisher, adapted)*

REQUIRED: The improper control over securities and investments.

DISCUSSION: The custody of cash and securities should be placed with the treasury function. Thus, the CFO should have custody of securities and investments.

Answer (A) is incorrect. Authorization of transactions is an appropriate control over securities and investments. Answer (B) is incorrect. The custodian should be bonded and should not have access to records. Answer (C) is incorrect. Storage in a safe-deposit box is an appropriate control over securities and investments.

7.6.2. A company operates its own truck fleet. Rising operating costs have caused the company to reassess its internal control. Which one of the following controls may help to lower operating costs?

A. Preventive maintenance is performed independently of driver-requested maintenance.

B. Each driver has a control card for fuel use at the self-service diesel fuel dock.

C. Maintenance and repair part orders are determined and placed by using an EOQ system.

D. Parts and hand tools must be requisitioned from the parts department.

Answer (B) is correct. *(CIA, adapted)*

REQUIRED: The best control to help lower operating costs.

DISCUSSION: Requiring each driver to use a control card will permit the matching of fuel used by each driver with the miles driven. This practice should lower or control fuel (operating) costs as well as create an audit trail as evidence of the incurrence of fuel costs.

Answer (A) is incorrect. A combination of preventive and driver-requested maintenance is more effective. Answer (C) is incorrect. Use of an EOQ system for parts orders is an effective control over maintenance rather than operating costs. Answer (D) is incorrect. Requiring requisitions for parts is an effective control over maintenance rather than operating costs.

7.6.3. An audit of a depository institution discloses the existence of a personal loan to the president of that institution. The loan is both sizable and below market rate. Which of the following is a cost-effective policy that will help prevent a recurrence of this questionable practice?

A. Loans above a nominal dollar level will not be extended to directors or to executives above a specified organizational level.

B. Loans above a nominal dollar level will not be extended to any director or employee.

C. Below-market-rate loans will not be extended to directors or to executives above a specified organizational level.

D. Below-market-rate loans will not be extended under any circumstances.

Answer (A) is correct. *(CIA, adapted)*

REQUIRED: The policy that will help prevent a recurrence of an improper loan to an officer of a company.

DISCUSSION: High-ranking officials of an organization may be in a position to exercise undue influence over lower-level employees, for example, by bargaining for a reduced-rate loan in a negotiation that is clearly not at arm's length. A direct prohibition of any loans to high-ranking persons is a simple, cost-effective way of increasing the obstacles to self-serving behavior.

Answer (B) is incorrect. Employees who are not in a position to bargain for below-market rates are appropriate institutional customers. Answer (C) is incorrect. Not extending below-market-rate loans to directors or to executives above a specified organizational level leaves open the possibility of making loans at marginal rates that are favorable to the executive. Answer (D) is incorrect. Not extending below-market-rate loans under any circumstances is neither cost effective nor prudent. Below-market-rate loans may be warranted, e.g., to prevent default.

7.6.4. Which of the following constitutes the best evidence of the transfer of accountability for incoming material from the receiving department to other departments or activities?

A. The physical evidence of that type of material in other departments.

B. Oral evidence from personnel in both receiving and other departments.

C. An authorized signature on the prescribed transfer form.

D. Documentary evidence in the form of entries in journals and ledgers.

Answer (C) is correct. *(CIA, adapted)*

REQUIRED: The best evidence of the transfer of accountability for incoming material.

DISCUSSION: Internal control should maintain effective accountability for assets. The signature on a prescribed form documents the transfer of accountability for assets and permits the recorded accountability to be compared with the existing assets when necessary.

Answer (A) is incorrect. The physical evidence of that type of material in other departments provides evidence of the physical transfer of material, not of accountability. Answer (B) is incorrect. A paper trail is preferable to oral evidence. Answer (D) is incorrect. The entries must be supported by documentation.

7.6.5. Which of the following internal control activities would an entity most likely use to assist in satisfying the completeness assertion related to long-term investments?

A. Senior management verifies that securities in the bank safe-deposit box are registered in the entity's name.

B. The internal auditor compares the securities in the bank safe-deposit box with recorded investments.

C. The CFO vouches the acquisition of securities by comparing brokers' advices with canceled checks.

D. The controller compares the current market prices of recorded investments with the brokers' advices on file.

Answer (B) is correct. *(CPA, adapted)*

REQUIRED: The control to test the completeness assertion for noncurrent investments.

DISCUSSION: The items being tested consist of the assets in the safe-deposit box. This population should be compared with the records of the investments to provide assurance that the balance is complete, that is, contains all long-term investments.

Answer (A) is incorrect. Verification that securities are registered in the entity's name relates to the rights assertion. Answer (C) is incorrect. Comparing canceled checks with brokers' advices pertains to the rights assertion. Answer (D) is incorrect. Comparing market prices with brokers' advices relates most directly to the valuation assertion.

7.6.6. Internal control over inventories is important for all of the following reasons except

A. Inventories are often the largest current asset.

B. Inventories directly affect the results of operations.

C. Inventories are the most liquid asset.

D. Inventories are a material component of total assets.

Answer (C) is correct. *(Publisher, adapted)*

REQUIRED: The statement not a reason internal control over inventories is important.

DISCUSSION: Cash is considered the most liquid asset and most subject to the risks of material misstatement.

Answer (A) is incorrect. Inventories typically represent an extremely large component of current assets. Answer (B) is incorrect. Inventories, once sold, become cost of goods sold and are an important component of the results of operations. Answer (D) is incorrect. Inventories typically are a large portion of the total assets of a firm.

7.6.7. Which of the following questions is not appropriate for an internal control questionnaire concerning securities?

A. Is there a periodic reconciliation of the detail of securities with the security control account?

B. Is there a record of all identification numbers of securities, and are securities held in the name of the company?

C. Do the internal auditors periodically test controls over securities?

D. All of the questions are appropriate.

Answer (D) is correct. *(Publisher, adapted)*

REQUIRED: The question not appropriate for a control questionnaire on securities.

DISCUSSION: Each item listed is an important control regarding securities.

Answer (A) is incorrect. Individual securities should be reconciled periodically with the control account in the general ledger. Answer (B) is incorrect. All aspects of the securities, including the identification numbers, should be recorded, and the securities should be in the name of the firm rather than held in bearer form or in the name of an individual. Answer (C) is incorrect. The internal auditors should periodically test the controls over securities.

7.6.8. An internal auditor is reviewing the company's policy regarding investing in financial derivatives. The auditor would normally expect to find all of the following in the policy except a

A. Statement indicating whether derivatives are to be used for hedging or speculative purposes.

B. Specific authorization limit for the amount and types of derivatives that can be used by the organization.

C. Specific limit on the amount authorized for any single trader.

D. Statement requiring board review of each transaction because of the risk involved in such transactions.

Answer (D) is correct. *(CIA, adapted)*

REQUIRED: The item not normally expected to be found in a policy regarding investing in financial derivatives.

DISCUSSION: Policies are general statements that guide managers' decision making. They are developed by the board of directors to provide guidelines for achieving objectives. Management is responsible for daily operations and should abide by the policies. Consequently, the board would not review each transaction.

7.6.9. When an entity uses a trust company as custodian of its trading securities, the possibility of concealing fraud most likely will be reduced if the

A. Trust company has no direct contact with the entity employees responsible for maintaining investment accounting records.

B. Securities are registered in the name of the trust company rather than the entity itself.

C. Interest and dividend checks are mailed directly to an entity employee who is authorized to sell securities.

D. Trust company places the securities in a bank safe-deposit vault under the custodian's exclusive control.

Answer (A) is correct. *(CPA, adapted)*

REQUIRED: The condition that most likely will reduce the possibility of the concealment of fraud.

DISCUSSION: To conceal fraud related to trading securities, collusion between those responsible for record keeping and custody is required. The possibility of collusion is reduced if no direct contact between responsible parties exists.

Answer (B) is incorrect. The securities should be registered in the name of the owner. Answer (C) is incorrect. Interest and dividends should be sent to the trust company custodian. Answer (D) is incorrect. Use of a bank safe-deposit vault under the custodian's exclusive control is an appropriate control but does not minimize the possibility of collusion.

7.6.10. What is a possible consequence of an employee's being able to visit the safe-deposit box unaccompanied?

A. The employee could pledge corporate investments as security for a short-term personal bank loan.

B. The employee could steal securities, and the theft would never be discovered.

C. It would be impossible to obtain a fidelity bond on the employee.

D. There would be no record of when company personnel visited the safe-deposit box.

Answer (A) is correct. *(CIA, adapted)*

REQUIRED: The possible result of an unaccompanied visit to the safe-deposit box.

DISCUSSION: The bank should maintain a record, which can be inspected by company personnel, of all safe-deposit box visits. Access should be limited to authorized officers. Firms typically require the presence of two authorized persons for access to the box. This precaution provides supervisory control over, for example, the temporary removal of the securities to serve as a pledge for a loan (hypothecation of securities).

Answer (B) is incorrect. An audit would eventually uncover an outright theft assuming no alteration of the asset records. Answer (C) is incorrect. Obtaining a fidelity bond is contingent upon the character of the employee, not the presence of a specific control. Answer (D) is incorrect. The bank maintains a record of visits.

7.6.11. Which control is most likely to give the greatest assurance that securities held as investments are safeguarded?

A. There is no access to securities between year-end and the date of the auditor's security count.

B. Proceeds from the sale of investments are received by an employee who does not have access to securities.

C. Investment acquisitions are authorized by a member of the board of directors before execution.

D. Access to securities requires the signatures and presence of two designated officials.

Answer (D) is correct. *(CPA, adapted)*

REQUIRED: The control procedure that best safeguards securities held as investments.

DISCUSSION: The presence of two authorized individuals is usually required for access to securities, especially those held in safe-deposit boxes. This precaution provides supervisory control.

Answer (A) is incorrect. Denying access to authorized officials is not consistent with successful financial management. Moreover, the control is effective for a short period only. Answer (B) is incorrect. Other employees may have improper access. Answer (C) is incorrect. The issue is the physical safety of assets already held, not authorization of acquisitions.

7.6.12. Which of the following questions is not appropriate for an internal control questionnaire about inventory?

A. Are goods stored in locked storage areas?

B. Are payment vouchers approved before payment?

C. Is access to the storeroom limited to authorized personnel?

D. Are independent, periodic comparisons made of inventory records with goods on hand?

Answer (B) is correct. *(Publisher, adapted)*

REQUIRED: The question inappropriate for an internal control questionnaire on inventory.

DISCUSSION: Payment vouchers should be prepared for all types of expenditures, not just inventory. Thus, a question about vouchers is more appropriately asked in the cash payments questionnaire.

Answer (A) is incorrect. Goods in locked storage areas relates directly to the internal controls over the inventory function. Answer (C) is incorrect. Limitation of access to the storeroom to authorized personnel relates directly to the internal controls over the inventory function. Answer (D) is incorrect. Independent, periodic comparisons of inventory records with goods on hand relates directly to the controls over the inventory function.

7.6.13. An essential procedural control to ensure the accuracy of the recorded inventory quantities is

A. Performing a gross profit test.

B. Testing inventory extensions.

C. Calculating unit costs and valuing obsolete or damaged inventory items in accordance with inventory policy.

D. Establishing a cutoff for goods received and shipped.

Answer (D) is correct. *(CIA, adapted)*

REQUIRED: The control over recorded inventory quantities.

DISCUSSION: A proper cutoff point for goods received and shipped assures that only goods owned by the client are included in inventory.

Answer (A) is incorrect. Performing a gross profit test primarily addresses the monetary valuation of inventory rather than the quantity of items in inventory. Answer (B) is incorrect. Testing inventory extensions primarily addresses the dollar monetary of inventory rather than the quantity of items in inventory. Answer (C) is incorrect. Calculating unit costs and measuring obsolete or damaged inventory items in accordance with inventory policy primarily addresses the monetary valuation of inventory rather than the quantity of items in inventory.

7.6.14. Apex Manufacturing Corporation mass produces eight different products. The controller who is interested in strengthening internal control over the accounting for materials used in production is most likely to implement a(n)

A. Economic order quantity (EOQ) system.

B. Job-order cost accounting system.

C. Perpetual inventory system.

D. Segregation of duties among production personnel.

Answer (C) is correct. *(CPA, adapted)*

REQUIRED: The best system to strengthen internal control over accounting for materials.

DISCUSSION: A perpetual inventory system provides for continuous updating of inventory records and thus accounts for materials used. Close and continuous attention must be paid to materials usage to keep a perpetual system up to date.

Answer (A) is incorrect. EOQ makes reordering more cost effective but does not strengthen the control over accounting for materials used. Answer (B) is incorrect. A job-order cost system determines the cost of special order products. Also, a process-cost system, not a job-order system, is applicable to mass production. Answer (D) is incorrect. Segregation of duties among production workers does not improve control over accounting for materials unless the functions of authorization, asset custody, and recording are also separated.

7.6.15. An internal auditor is examining inventory control in a merchandising division with annual sales of $3,000,000 and a 40% gross profit rate. Tests show that 2% of the dollar amount of purchases do not get into inventory because of breakage and employee theft. Adding certain controls costing $35,000 annually could reduce these losses to .5% of purchases. Should the controls be recommended?

A. Yes, because the projected saving exceeds the cost of the added controls.

B. No, because the cost of the added controls exceeds the projected savings.

C. Yes, because the ideal system of internal control is the most extensive one.

D. Yes, regardless of cost-benefit considerations, because the situation involves employee theft.

Answer (B) is correct. *(CIA, adapted)*

REQUIRED: The correct decision as to whether to add inventory controls and the reason.

DISCUSSION: Controls must be subject to the cost-benefit criterion. The annual cost of these inventory controls is $35,000, but the cost saving is only $27,000 {(2% – .5%) × [$3,000,000 sales × (100% – 40% gross profit rate)]}. Thus, the cost exceeds the benefit, and the controls should not be recommended.

Answer (A) is incorrect. Cost exceeds the benefit. Answer (C) is incorrect. The ideal system is likely to be too costly. Answer (D) is incorrect. Cost-benefit considerations apply even to employee theft.

7.6.16. The objectives of internal control for a production cycle are to provide assurance that transactions are properly executed and recorded, and that

A. Independent internal verification of activity reports is established.

B. Transfers to finished goods are documented by a completed production report and a quality control report.

C. Production orders are prenumbered and signed by a supervisor.

D. Custody of work-in-process and of finished goods is properly maintained.

Answer (D) is correct. *(CPA, adapted)*

REQUIRED: The objectives of internal control for a production cycle.

DISCUSSION: A principal objective of internal control is to safeguard assets. In the production cycle, control activities should be implemented to ensure that inventory is protected from misuse and theft. Accordingly, inventories should be in the custody of a storekeeper, and transfers should be properly documented and recorded to establish accountability.

Answer (A) is incorrect. Independent internal verification of activity reports is a control activity, not an objective. Answer (B) is incorrect. Documenting transfers to finished goods is a control activity, not an objective. Answer (C) is incorrect. The use of prenumbered production orders signed by a supervisor is a control activity, not an objective.

7.6.17. For several years a client's physical inventory count has been lower than what was shown on the books at the time of the count, and downward adjustments of the inventory account have been required. Contributing to the inventory problem could be material weaknesses in internal control that led to the failure to record some

A. Purchases returned to vendors.

B. Sales returns received.

C. Sales discounts allowed.

D. Cash purchases.

Answer (A) is correct. *(CPA, adapted)*

REQUIRED: The transaction that results in an overstatement of inventory.

DISCUSSION: Purchases returned to the vendor but not recorded overstate inventory records. The goods are reflected in inventory but are not on hand.

Answer (B) is incorrect. Unrecorded sales returns are included in the physical count but do not appear on the books, resulting in an understatement (not overstatement) of inventory. Answer (C) is incorrect. Failure to record sales discounts overstates sales but has no effect on the number of items in inventory or its carrying amount. Answer (D) is incorrect. Unrecorded cash purchases are included in the physical count but do not appear on the books, resulting in an understatement (not overstatement) of inventory.

7.6.18. A company uses an MRP (materials requirement planning) system to control inventory. One objective is to minimize raw material inventories while avoiding production shutdowns. One way to achieve this objective using MRP is to

A. Regularly update the authorized master production schedule.

B. Use an EOQ (economic order quantity) model.

C. Take a physical inventory monthly instead of annually.

D. Use a second-order exponential smoothing model with seasonality factors.

Answer (A) is correct. *(CIA, adapted)*

REQUIRED: The means of minimizing materials inventories.

DISCUSSION: MRP is a computer-based information system designed to plan and control materials used in production. It determines the quantity of finished goods that will be required and the point when they will be needed. The system requires prompt notice of changes in production schedules.

Answer (B) is incorrect. An EOQ system is a general inventory management model that attempts to balance ordering and carrying costs. Answer (C) is incorrect. Taking inventory does not reduce the amount on hand. Answer (D) is incorrect. An MRP system must address very short-term rather than seasonal variations in production requirements.

7.6.19. To determine whether an organization is purchasing excess raw materials, an internal auditor should

A. Be sure that standards are established for quality, quantity, and sourcing for raw materials.

B. Ascertain that production budgets and economic order quantities are integrated and have been used in determining quantities purchased.

C. Obtain assurance that purchasing agent assignments are rotated periodically.

D. Determine that the purchasing department has a written charter with a set of procedures and guidelines covering purchasing operations.

Answer (B) is correct. *(CIA, adapted)*

REQUIRED: The procedure to determine whether an organization is purchasing excess materials.

DISCUSSION: An economic order quantity (EOQ) model can be used to determine the order quantity (or production run) that minimizes the sum or order costs (or setup costs for production) and carrying costs, given annual demand. Production needs and the EOQ model should be coordinated to ascertain the optimal levels of materials purchases.

Answer (A) is incorrect. Standards are beneficial, but excess inventory will still result if production, EOQs, and purchasing are not coordinated. Answer (C) is incorrect. Rotation of purchasing agents is a control intended to prevent conflicts of interest, not excessive purchasing. Answer (D) is incorrect. The existence of procedures and guidelines is not proof that they are being followed.

7.6.20. A firm's inventory consisted of 1,000 different items, 20 of which accounted for 70% of the dollar value. The most recent regular quarterly manual count revealed an unnecessary 2 years' supply of several of the more expensive items. The control that would best help to correct this oversupply problem is

A. Use of a control total over the number of unique inventory items.

B. Limit check on the total dollar value of the inventory.

C. Use of authorizing signatures on requisitions for inventory requested by production.

D. Perpetual inventory of the larger dollar value items in the inventory.

Answer (D) is correct. *(CIA, adapted)*

REQUIRED: The control to prevent oversupply.

DISCUSSION: In a perpetual system, purchases (or transfers from work-in-process) are recorded directly in the inventory account when they are made. Inventory is correspondingly reduced as sales occur. Thus, a running total of inventory can be monitored throughout the period.

Answer (A) is incorrect. A control total should verify that no inventory records were lost or that no new ones were added. It does not help to solve the inventory acquisition problem. Answer (B) is incorrect. A limit test on the total inventory value provides information as to when the inventory dollar level reached a certain point but not on the composition of the inventory. Answer (C) is incorrect. Use of authorizing signatures provides control over requisitions but not over the rest of the inventory acquisition process.

7.6.21. EOQ formulas, ABC analysis, and two-bin systems are commonly used elements of the control cycle for the stores process. These controls primarily relate to what part of the cycle?

A. Determination of need.

B. Acceptance of materials.

C. Storage of materials.

D. Release of materials.

Answer (A) is correct. *(CIA, adapted)*

REQUIRED: The part of the control cycle for stores in which the listed techniques are used.

DISCUSSION: ABC analysis divides inventory into high-, medium-, and low-value items for purposes of frequency of review and reordering. EOQ models determine the economic order quantity that minimizes order and carrying costs. Once the reorder point is established, a two-bin system may be used to signal the time to reorder when perpetual records are not kept. An inventory item is divided into two groups; when the first is depleted, the order is placed, and the second protects against stockout until replenishment. Thus, each technique is concerned with determination of need.

7.6.22. Appropriate control over obsolete materials requires that they be

A. Carried at cost in the accounting records until the actual disposition takes place.

B. Sorted, treated, and packaged before disposition in order to obtain the best selling price.

C. Determined by an approved authority to be unusable for their normal purposes.

D. Retained within the regular storage area.

Answer (C) is correct. *(CIA, adapted)*

REQUIRED: The appropriate control over obsolete materials.

DISCUSSION: Because auditors, storekeepers, etc., may not have the expertise to determine whether materials are usable, that decision often is made by a designated independent authority. To provide effective control of materials, this determination, asset custody, and authorization for disposal are functions that should be segregated.

Answer (A) is incorrect. Obsolete materials should be carried at net realizable value. Answer (B) is incorrect. Costs of sorting, etc., may be greater than disposal value. Answer (D) is incorrect. Obsolete materials frequently should be segregated.

7.6.23. Which of the following organizational controls related to the processing of scrap would you recommend?

A. Segregate the responsibility for processing scrap materials from the operational activities that produce the scrap materials.

B. Define each manager's responsibility for processing scrap and authorize one person in each production department to perform this function.

C. Specify detailed procedures for each manager to follow in determining the quantity, grade, and packaging of scrap.

D. Give the managers the authority to obtain competitive bids for the disposal of scrap.

Answer (A) is correct. *(CIA, adapted)*

REQUIRED: The most appropriate organizational control relating to processing scrap.

DISCUSSION: Organizational controls address the segregation of functional responsibilities: custodianship, recordkeeping, authorization, and execution. Thus, those who generate the scrap should not subsequently process it.

7.6.24. Which of the following questions would an auditor least likely include on an internal control questionnaire concerning the initiation and execution of equipment transactions?

A. Are requests for major repairs approved at a higher level than the department initiating the request?

B. Are prenumbered purchase orders used for equipment and periodically accounted for?

C. Are competitive bids solicited for purchases of equipment?

D. Are procedures in place to monitor and properly restrict access to equipment?

Answer (D) is correct. *(CPA, adapted)*

REQUIRED: The question least likely to be included on an internal control questionnaire addressing initiation and execution of equipment transactions.

DISCUSSION: Although access to equipment should be restricted to authorized personnel only, the issue is the initiation and execution of equipment transactions, not custody of the assets.

Answer (A) is incorrect. Approval of major repairs is related to transaction initiation and execution. Answer (B) is incorrect. Use of prenumbered purchase orders is related to transaction initiation and execution. Answer (C) is incorrect. Competitive bidding is related to transaction initiation and execution.

7.6.25. Which control is not appropriate for property, plant, and equipment?

A. Disposal of fully depreciated assets.

B. Proper authority for acquisition and retirement of assets.

C. Detailed property records and physical controls over assets.

D. Written policies for capitalization and expenditure and review of application of depreciation methods.

Answer (A) is correct. *(Publisher, adapted)*

REQUIRED: The improper control over property, plant, and equipment.

DISCUSSION: No control should require disposal of fully depreciated assets. Such assets may still be productive and used in the business and should remain on the books until disposal.

Answer (B) is incorrect. Proper authority for acquisition and retirement of assets is a proper control over property, plant, and equipment. Answer (C) is incorrect. Detailed property records and physical controls over assets are proper controls over property, plant, and equipment. Answer (D) is incorrect. Written policies for capitalization and expenditure and review of application of depreciation methods are proper controls over property, plant, and equipment.

7.6.26. Equipment acquisitions that are misclassified as maintenance expense most likely would be detected by an internal control activity that provides for

A. Segregation of duties for employees in the accounts payable department.

B. Independent verification of invoices for disbursements recorded as equipment acquisitions.

C. Investigation of variances within a formal budgeting system.

D. Authorization by the board of directors of significant equipment acquisitions.

Answer (C) is correct. *(CPA, adapted)*

REQUIRED: The control to detect misclassification of equipment acquisitions as maintenance expense.

DISCUSSION: A formal planning and budgeting system that estimates maintenance expense at a certain level will report a significant variance if capital expenditures are charged to the account. Investigation of the variance is likely to disclose the misclassification.

Answer (A) is incorrect. Accounts payable assembles the required payment documentation but is unlikely to question the classification of the expenditure. Answer (B) is incorrect. Testing the population of recorded equipment acquisitions will not detect items misclassified as maintenance expense. Answer (D) is incorrect. The misclassification would occur subsequent to authorization.

7.6.27. Which of the following is an internal control weakness related to factory equipment?

A. Checks issued in payment of purchases of equipment are not signed by the controller.

B. All purchases of factory equipment are required to be made by the department in need of the equipment.

C. Factory equipment replacements are usually made when estimated useful lives, as indicated in depreciation schedules, have expired.

D. Proceeds from sales of fully depreciated equipment are credited to other income.

Answer (B) is correct. *(CPA, adapted)*

REQUIRED: The internal control weakness related to factory equipment.

DISCUSSION: Making purchases of factory equipment is a function incompatible with the production activities of user departments. Satisfactory internal control requires segregation of incompatible functions, so purchases of factory equipment should be made by a separate purchasing department.

Answer (A) is incorrect. Controllers who perform a recordkeeping function should not sign checks. Answer (C) is incorrect. If estimated useful lives are accurate, replacing equipment at the end of those lives is a reasonable policy, not a control weakness. Answer (D) is incorrect. Gains (all proceeds of fully depreciated equipment) from sales other than of inventory should be credited to other income or gain on sale of equipment.

7.6.28. One objective of internal control is to record property, plant, and equipment (PPE) additions correctly as to account, amount, and period. Which of the following environmental considerations indicates that the risks of material misstatement of these additions are high?

A. Most construction is performed in-house.

B. All material additions are required to be approved by the board of directors.

C. Recently acquired loans preclude further plant acquisition for 3 years.

D. Gross property, plant, and equipment increased 36% during the current period.

Answer (A) is correct. *(Publisher, adapted)*

REQUIRED: The environmental consideration indicating high risks of material misstatement.

DISCUSSION: The risks of material misstatement for in-house construction are high. For example, the entity must allocate overhead, allocate labor costs between regular and construction labor, and estimate the interest cost to be capitalized. An outside construction company would send an invoice, and determining the amount to record would be relatively easy.

Answer (B) is incorrect. Approval of all material additions by the board of directors is a control consideration relating to authorization, not recording. Answer (C) is incorrect. Reducing the amount of construction is most likely to decrease risk. Answer (D) is incorrect. The increase in PPE does not necessarily significantly increase the risks of misstatement, especially if valuation is based on vendors' prices rather than the entity's own estimates of the costs of in-house construction.

7.6.29. An auditor notes year-to-year increases of over $200,000 for small tool expense at a manufacturing facility that has produced the same amount of identical product for the last 3 years. Production inventory is kept in a controlled staging area adjacent to the receiving dock, but the supply of small tools is kept in an unsupervised area near the exit to the plant employees' parking lot. After determining that all of the following alternatives are equal in cost and are also feasible for local management, the auditor can best address the security issue by recommending that plant management

A. Move the small tools inventory to the custody of the production inventory staging superintendent and implement the use of a special requisition to issue small tools.

B. Initiate a full physical inventory of small tools on a monthly basis.

C. Place supply of small tools in a secured area, install a key-access card system for all employees, and record each key-access transaction on a report for the production superintendent.

D. Close the exit to the employee parking lot and require all plant employees to use a doorway by the receiving dock that also provides access to the plant employees' parking area.

Answer (A) is correct. *(CIA, adapted)*

REQUIRED: The best preventive control to reduce the risk of loss of small tools.

DISCUSSION: Physical control of assets is a preventive control that reduces the likelihood of theft or other loss. Giving responsibility for custody of small tools to one individual establishes accountability. Requiring that requisitions be submitted ensures that tool use is properly authorized.

Answer (B) is incorrect. A full physical inventory is a periodic, detective control that would only be effective in determining the amount of losses. Answer (C) is incorrect. Recording each key-access transaction is a preventive and detective control that does not record the number or type of tools removed from the inventory. Answer (D) is incorrect. Requiring all plant employees to use a doorway by the receiving dock is a preventive control that does not limit access to the small tools inventory.

7.6.30. Which of the following internal control activities most likely justifies reducing the assessment of the risks of material misstatement for plant and equipment acquisitions?

A. Periodic physical inspection of plant and equipment by the internal audit staff.

B. Comparison of current-year plant and equipment account balances with prior-year actual balances.

C. The review of prenumbered purchase orders to detect unrecorded trade-ins.

D. Approval of periodic depreciation entries by a supervisor independent of the accounting department.

Answer (A) is correct. *(CPA, adapted)*

REQUIRED: The control that justifies reducing an assessed risk of material misstatement.

DISCUSSION: A periodic physical inspection by the internal audit staff is the best activity for verifying the existence of plant and equipment. Direct observation by an independent, competent, and objective internal audit staff helps to reduce the potential for fictitious acquisitions or other fraudulent activities. The result is a lower assessment of the RMMs.

Answer (B) is incorrect. Comparing records of assets may not detect nonexistent assets. Answer (C) is incorrect. Reviewing purchase orders is less effective than direct verification. Answer (D) is incorrect. Depreciation is based on recorded amounts. If they are misstated, depreciation also is misstated.

7.6.31. Which of the following activities is most likely to prevent the improper disposition of equipment?

A. A segregation of duties between those authorized to dispose of equipment and those authorized to approve removal work orders.

B. The use of serial numbers to identify equipment that could be sold.

C. Periodic comparison of removal work orders with authorizing documentation.

D. A periodic analysis of the scrap sales and the repairs and maintenance accounts.

Answer (A) is correct. *(CPA, adapted)*

REQUIRED: The procedure most likely to prevent the improper disposition of equipment.

DISCUSSION: Segregation of duties reduces the opportunity for an individual both to perpetrate and to conceal fraud or error. Accordingly, the authorization, recording, and asset custody functions should be separated. Thus, the same individual should not approve removal work orders (authorization) and dispose of equipment (asset custody).

Answer (B) is incorrect. The use of serial numbers to identify equipment that could be sold may detect, but will not prevent, improper dispositions. Answer (C) is incorrect. Periodic comparison of removal work orders with authorizing documentation may detect, but will not prevent, improper dispositions. Answer (D) is incorrect. A periodic analysis of the scrap sales and the repairs and maintenance accounts may detect, but will not prevent, improper dispositions.

7.6.32. Which of the following controls will most likely allow for a reduction in the scope of the auditor's tests of depreciation expense?

A. Review and approval of the periodic equipment depreciation entry by a supervisor who does not actively participate in its preparation.

B. Comparison of equipment account balances for the current year with the current-year budget and prior-year actual balances.

C. Review of the miscellaneous income account for salvage credits and scrap sales of partially depreciated equipment.

D. Authorization of payment of vendors' invoices by a designated employee who is independent of the equipment receiving function.

Answer (A) is correct. *(CPA, adapted)*

REQUIRED: The control permitting reduction in tests of depreciation.

DISCUSSION: A reduction in control risk and the consequent increase in the acceptable level of detection risk may permit the auditor to alter the nature, timing, or extent of substantive tests. An independent check on the validity and accuracy of depreciation expense clearly enhances the effectiveness of internal control and is thus likely to reduce the external auditor's assessment of control risk.

Answer (B) is incorrect. Comparison of equipment account balances for the current year with the current-year budget and prior-year actual balances is an auditor's analytical procedure to test the completeness of the current-year equipment balance. Answer (C) is incorrect. Review of the miscellaneous income account for salvage credits and scrap sales of partially depreciated equipment is an audit procedure to detect unrecorded fixed asset disposals. Answer (D) is incorrect. Authorization of payment of invoices by a designated employee independent of the receiving function relates to authorization of cash disbursements.

STUDY UNIT EIGHT
RESPONSES TO ASSESSED RISKS

To respond to the assessed risks of material misstatement (RMMs), the auditor designs and implements overall responses at the financial statement level. The auditor also responds by designing and performing further audit procedures (tests of controls and substantive procedures) at the relevant assertion level.

QUESTIONS

8.1 Assessing Risks of Material Misstatement

8.1.1. The ultimate purpose of understanding internal control is to contribute to the auditor's evaluation of the risk that

A. Tests of controls may fail to identify controls relevant to assertions.

B. Material misstatements may exist in the financial statements.

C. Specified controls requiring segregation of duties may be circumvented by collusion.

D. Entity policies may be overridden by senior management.

Answer (B) is correct. *(CPA, adapted)*

REQUIRED: The purpose of understanding internal control.

DISCUSSION: The understanding of internal control assists the auditor to (1) identify types of potential misstatements; (2) consider factors that affect the RMMs; and (3) design the nature, timing, and extent of further audit procedures (AU-C 315 and AS 2110).

Answer (A) is incorrect. Tests of controls are performed when (1) the auditor's risk assessment is based on an expectation of the operating effectiveness of controls, or (2) substantive procedures alone cannot provide sufficient appropriate evidence at the relevant assertion level about operating effectiveness. An auditor must identify controls relevant to specific assertions before testing such controls. Answer (C) is incorrect. Collusion is an inherent limitation of internal control. Answer (D) is incorrect. Management override is an inherent limitation of internal control.

8.1.2. The risks of material misstatement (RMMs) should be assessed in terms of

A. Specific controls.

B. Types of potential fraud.

C. Financial statement assertions.

D. Control environment factors.

Answer (C) is correct. *(CPA, adapted)*

REQUIRED: The approach used in assessing the RMMs.

DISCUSSION: The auditor's objective is to identify and assess the RMMs, whether due to fraud or error, at the financial statement and relevant assertion levels. This objective is achieved through understanding the entity and its environment, including its internal control. The understanding provides a basis for designing and implementing responses to the assessed RMMs (AU-C 315 and AS 2110).

Answer (A) is incorrect. Relevant controls should relate to the identified RMMs, and the RMMs are identified and assessed at the financial statement and relevant assertion levels. Answer (B) is incorrect. The auditor should use information obtained from the understanding to identify types of potential misstatements. Answer (D) is incorrect. The auditor considers the control environment in assessing the RMMs but does not assess risk in terms of control environment factors.

8.1.3. When assessing the risks of material misstatement at a low level, an auditor is required to document the auditor's

	Understanding of the Entity's Control Environment	Overall Responses to Assessed Risks
A.	Yes	No
B.	No	Yes
C.	Yes	Yes
D.	No	No

Answer (C) is correct. *(CPA, adapted)*

REQUIRED: The item(s) that should be documented when assessing the RMMs at a low level.

DISCUSSION: The understanding of the components of internal control, including the control environment, should be documented regardless of the degree of risk (AU-C 315). The overall responses to the assessed RMMs at the financial statement level also should be documented (AU-C 330).

Answer (A) is incorrect. The overall responses to the assessed RMMs at the financial statement level also should be documented. Answer (B) is incorrect. The understanding of the components of internal control, including the control environment, should be documented. Answer (D) is incorrect. The understanding of the components of internal control, including the control environment, should be documented. The overall responses to the assessed RMMs at the financial statement level also should be documented.

8.1.4. Which of the following is a step in an auditor's decision to rely on internal controls?

A. Apply analytical procedures to both financial data and nonfinancial information to detect conditions that may indicate weak controls.

B. Perform tests of details of transactions and account balances to identify potential fraud and error.

C. Identify specific controls that are likely to prevent, or detect and correct, material misstatements and perform tests of controls.

D. Document that the additional audit effort to perform tests of controls exceeds the potential reduction in substantive testing.

Answer (C) is correct. *(CPA, adapted)*

REQUIRED: The step necessary to rely on internal controls.

DISCUSSION: An auditor should obtain an understanding of controls relevant to the audit. Thus, the auditor should evaluate their design and determine whether they have been implemented. The evaluation of design considers whether the controls can effectively prevent, or detect and correct, material misstatements (AU-C 315 and AS 2110). The auditor then tests relevant controls to obtain sufficient appropriate evidence about their operating effectiveness if (1) the auditor intends to rely on them in determining the nature, timing, and extent of substantive procedures, or (2) substantive procedures alone cannot provide sufficient appropriate evidence at the relevant assertion level (AU-C 330 and AS 2301).

Answer (A) is incorrect. Analytical procedures are substantive procedures. The auditor should perform tests of controls to rely on internal controls. Answer (B) is incorrect. Tests of details are substantive procedures. The auditor should perform tests of controls to rely on internal controls. Answer (D) is incorrect. If the effort to perform tests of controls exceeds the potential reduction in substantive testing, the auditor need not rely on controls.

8.2 Auditor's Response to Risks

8.2.1. Which of the following statements about the auditor's response to assessed risks of material misstatement in a financial statement audit is true?

A. Risk assessment procedures performed to obtain an understanding of an entity's internal control also may serve as tests of controls.

B. When the risks of material misstatement are high, an auditor should reduce the amount of substantive testing.

C. Reliance on internal control may be sufficient to allow the auditor to eliminate substantive testing for significant transaction classes.

D. When assessing the risks of material misstatement, an auditor should not consider evidence obtained in prior audits about the operation of controls.

Answer (A) is correct. *(CPA, adapted)*

REQUIRED: The true statement about the response to RMMs.

DISCUSSION: Performing risk assessment procedures to obtain an understanding of the entity and its environment involves, among other things, evaluating the design of controls and determining whether they have been implemented. Tests of controls evaluate their operating effectiveness in preventing, or detecting and correcting, material misstatements at the assertion level. Although risk assessment procedures and tests of controls differ, they may use the same types of procedures. Thus, the auditor may decide that it is efficient to test operating effectiveness and evaluate design and implementation at the same time. Furthermore, some risk assessment procedures may provide evidence about operating effectiveness. For example, the auditor may (1) inquire about the use of budgets, (2) observe comparison of budgets and actual results, and (3) inspect reports on the investigation of variances (AU-C 330 and AS 2301).

Answer (B) is incorrect. The auditor should increase the amount of substantive testing if the RMMs are high. Answer (C) is incorrect. Regardless of the assessed RMMs, some substantive procedures always should be performed on all relevant assertions about material account balances, classes of transactions, and disclosures. Answer (D) is incorrect. Evidence from previous audits may be considered subject to certain limitations, e.g., evidence obtained currently about changes in internal control.

8.2.2. Regardless of the assessed risks of material misstatement, an auditor should perform some

A. Tests of controls to determine their effectiveness.

B. Analytical procedures to verify the design of controls.

C. Substantive procedures to restrict detection risk for significant transaction classes.

D. Dual-purpose tests to evaluate both the risk of monetary misstatement and preliminary control risk.

Answer (C) is correct. *(CPA, adapted)*

REQUIRED: The procedures performed regardless of the assessed RMMs.

DISCUSSION: Regardless of the assessed RMMs (or the effectiveness of the relevant controls), the auditor should design and perform substantive procedures for all relevant assertions related to each material transaction class, account balance, and disclosure.

8.2.3. Based on an understanding of internal control completed at an interim date, the auditor assessed the risks of material misstatement at the relevant assertion level and performed interim substantive procedures. The records will most likely be tested again at year end if

A. Tests of controls were not performed by the internal auditor during the remaining period.

B. Internal control provides a basis for limiting the extent of substantive testing.

C. The auditor used nonstatistical sampling during the interim period testing of controls.

D. The remaining period is long.

Answer (D) is correct. *(CPA, adapted)*

REQUIRED: The reason for retesting records at year end.

DISCUSSION: The auditor should test controls throughout the period for which (s)he intends to rely on the controls. If the auditor obtains audit evidence about effectiveness during an interim period, (s)he should (1) obtain evidence about significant changes in the controls and (2) determine the other evidence needed for the remaining period. Relevant factors to consider in obtaining other evidence include (1) the significance of the assessed RMMs, (2) the controls tested and the results, (3) the length of the remaining period, (4) the extent of the intended reduction of further substantive procedures because of reliance on the controls, (5) the degree to which evidence about operating effectiveness was obtained, and (6) the effectiveness of the control environment.

Answer (A) is incorrect. By itself, the failure of the internal auditor to test controls during the remaining period does not require a change in audit strategy. Answer (B) is incorrect. Lower assessed RMMs increase the acceptable level of audit risk and decrease the necessary extent of substantive procedures. Answer (C) is incorrect. Use of nonstatistical methods at the interim date does not necessitate retesting if sufficient appropriate evidence has been obtained.

8.2.4. The auditor should perform tests of controls when the auditor's risk assessment includes an expectation

A. Of a low level of inherent risk.

B. Of the operating effectiveness of internal control.

C. That the controls are not suitably designed.

D. That the controls are not being applied.

Answer (B) is correct. *(Publisher, adapted)*

REQUIRED: The reason for testing controls.

DISCUSSION: The purpose of tests of controls is to evaluate the effectiveness of controls in preventing, or detecting and correcting, material misstatements. When the auditor intends to rely on the controls, tests of their effectiveness should be performed.

Answer (A) is incorrect. The auditor is more likely to test controls when inherent risk is high. Answer (C) is incorrect. The auditor cannot test controls if they are not suitably designed. Answer (D) is incorrect. The auditor cannot test controls if they are not being applied.

8.2.5. Which of the following procedures is not used in tests of controls over purchases?

A. Examine vouchers and supporting documents for authorization.

B. Trace vouchers to entries in the vouchers register.

C. Confirm inventory held in public warehouses.

D. Reperform calculations on some supporting documentation.

Answer (C) is correct. *(D. Wells)*

REQUIRED: The procedure that is not a test of controls over purchases.

DISCUSSION: The confirmation of inventory held in public warehouses is a substantive procedure performed on an account balance in the purchasing cycle.

8.2.6. Tests of controls are concerned primarily with each of the following questions except

A. How were the controls applied?

B. Were the controls approved by the board of directors?

C. Were the necessary controls consistently performed?

D. By whom were the controls applied?

Answer (B) is correct. *(CPA, adapted)*

REQUIRED: The question that is not directly relevant to tests of controls.

DISCUSSION: The purpose of tests of controls is to evaluate their effectiveness in preventing, or detecting and correcting, material misstatements at the assertion level. Thus, the auditor performs inquiry and other audit procedures to obtain evidence about such matters as the following: (1) how the controls were applied at relevant times, (2) the consistency of application, and (3) by whom and by what means they were applied. The auditor also should determine whether the controls depend on indirect controls and whether such controls should be tested. For example, when an auditor tests user review of exception reports, the controls over information in the reports are indirect controls (AU-C 330 and AS 2301).

8.2.7. The auditor should perform tests of controls when the auditor's assessment of the risks of material misstatement includes an expectation of the operating effectiveness of internal control or when

A. Substantive procedures alone cannot provide sufficient appropriate audit evidence at the relevant assertion level.

B. Tests of details and substantive analytical procedures provide sufficient appropriate audit evidence to support the assertion being evaluated.

C. The auditor is not able to obtain an understanding of internal controls.

D. The owner-manager performs virtually all the functions of internal control.

Answer (A) is correct. *(Publisher, adapted)*

REQUIRED: The reason to test controls.

DISCUSSION: For some RMMs, the auditor may determine that it is not feasible to obtain sufficient appropriate audit evidence only from substantive procedures. These RMMs may relate to routine, significant transactions subject to highly automated processing with no documentation except what is recorded in the IT system. In such circumstances, the controls over the RMMs are relevant to the audit. Thus, the auditor should obtain an understanding of, and test, the controls.

Answer (B) is incorrect. When evidence obtained from substantive procedures is sufficient and appropriate to support an assertion, the auditor need not test controls. Answer (C) is incorrect. The auditor should obtain an understanding of controls relevant to the audit. The understanding includes an evaluation of their design and a determination of whether they have been implemented. Answer (D) is incorrect. In small organizations, when the owner-manager performs many or most control activities, tests of controls ordinarily are not necessary.

8.2.8. The objective of tests of details of transactions performed as tests of controls is to

A. Monitor the design and use of entity documents such as prenumbered shipping forms.

B. Determine whether internal controls have been implemented.

C. Detect material misstatements in the account balances of the financial statements.

D. Evaluate whether internal controls operated effectively.

Answer (D) is correct. *(CPA, adapted)*

REQUIRED: The objective of tests of details of transactions performed as tests of controls.

DISCUSSION: The auditor may use tests of details of transactions concurrently as tests of controls (i.e., as dual-purpose tests). As substantive procedures, their objective is to support relevant assertions or detect material misstatements in the financial statements. As tests of controls, their objective is to evaluate whether a control operated effectively.

Answer (A) is incorrect. The client's controls should monitor the use of entity documents. Answer (B) is incorrect. Determination of whether controls have been implemented is made in conjunction with the auditor's understanding of internal control. Answer (C) is incorrect. The objective of substantive procedures is to support relevant assertions or detect material misstatements in the account balances.

8.2.9. To test the effectiveness of controls, an auditor ordinarily selects from a variety of techniques, including

A. Inquiry and analytical procedures.

B. Reperformance and observation.

C. Comparison and confirmation.

D. Inspection and verification.

Answer (C) is correct. *(CPA, adapted)*

REQUIRED: The procedures associated with tests of controls.

DISCUSSION: Comparison and confirmation are more closely associated with substantive procedures.

Answer (A) is incorrect. Analytical procedures are more closely associated with substantive procedures. Answer (B) is incorrect. Inquiry alone is not sufficient to test the operating effectiveness of controls. Other audit procedures performed in combination with inquiry may include inspection, recalculation, and reperformance of a control that pertains to an assertion. Answer (D) is incorrect. Verification is more closely associated with substantive procedures.

8.2.10. An auditor wishes to evaluate the design and perform tests of controls over a client's cash disbursements procedures. If the controls leave no audit trail of documentary evidence, the auditor most likely will test the procedures by

A. Confirmation and observation.

B. Observation and inquiry.

C. Analytical procedures and confirmation.

D. Inquiry and analytical procedures.

Answer (B) is correct. *(CPA, adapted)*

REQUIRED: The procedures performed to evaluate the design and perform tests of controls.

DISCUSSION: When the auditor obtains an understanding of controls relevant to the audit, (s)he performs risk assessment procedures to obtain evidence about their design and implementation. These procedures may include (1) inquiries, (2) observations of the application of the controls, (3) inspection of documents and reports, and (4) tracing transactions through the financial reporting system. Although risk assessment procedures and tests of controls differ, they may use the same types of procedures. Thus, the auditor may decide that it is efficient to test operating effectiveness and evaluate design and implementation at the same time. Furthermore, some risk assessment procedures may provide evidence about operating effectiveness. For example, the auditor may (1) inquire about the use of budgets, (2) observe comparison of budgets and actual results, and (3) inspect reports on the investigation of variances (AU-C 330 and AS 2301). In the absence of documentary evidence, the auditor performs observation and inquiry procedures and traces transactions through the system.

Answer (A) is incorrect. Confirmation and observation are substantive procedures, not tests of controls. Answer (C) is incorrect. Analytical procedures and confirmation are substantive procedures, not tests of controls. Answer (D) is incorrect. Inquiry and analytical procedures are substantive procedures, not tests of controls.

8.2.11. Which of the following procedures concerning accounts receivable is an auditor most likely to perform to obtain evidence in support of the effectiveness of controls?

A. Observing an entity's employee prepare the schedule of past due accounts receivable.

B. Sending confirmation requests to an entity's principal customers to verify the existence of accounts receivable.

C. Inspecting an entity's analysis of accounts receivable for unusual balances.

D. Comparing an entity's uncollectible accounts expense with actual uncollectible accounts receivable.

Answer (A) is correct. *(CPA, adapted)*

REQUIRED: The procedure performed to test the effectiveness of controls.

DISCUSSION: To test the effectiveness of controls, an auditor performs procedures such as inquiry, observation, inspection, recalculation, and reperformance of a control. Thus, observing an entity's employee prepare the schedule of past due accounts receivable provides evidence of the effectiveness of certain controls over accounts receivable.

Answer (B) is incorrect. Sending confirmation requests to verify the existence of accounts receivable is a test of the details of balances, a substantive procedure. Answer (C) is incorrect. Inspecting an entity's analysis of accounts receivable for unusual balances is a test of the details of balances, a substantive procedure. Answer (D) is incorrect. Comparing uncollectible accounts expense with actual uncollectible accounts receivable is a form of analytical procedure. It is used to determine whether the auditor's expectation is supported by client data.

8.2.12. In performing tests of controls, the auditor will normally find that

A. The level of inherent risk is directly proportional to the rate of error.

B. The rate of deviations in the sample exceeds the rate of error in the accounting records.

C. The rate of error in the sample exceeds the rate of deviations.

D. All unexamined items result in errors in the accounting records.

Answer (B) is correct. *(CPA, adapted)*

REQUIRED: The normal finding by an auditor during tests of controls.

DISCUSSION: When testing controls, the auditor is directly concerned with deviations from specific controls. Failure to comply with a control does not necessarily result in an error in the records. For example, the absence of an authorization signature does not necessarily mean that the transaction was improperly recorded. Accordingly, the rate of deviations from a control normally exceeds the error rate in the records.

Answer (A) is incorrect. Inherent risk and the rate of error are not necessarily correlated. Effective controls may minimize the error rate even though inherent risk is high. Answer (C) is incorrect. The sample error rate should approximate the rate of total deviations from the control tested. Answer (D) is incorrect. Unaudited items are not necessarily in error.

8.2.13. When an auditor plans to rely on controls that have changed since they were last tested, which of the following courses of action would be most appropriate?

A. Test the operating effectiveness of such controls in the current audit.

B. Document that reliance and proceed with the original audit strategy.

C. Inquire of management as to the effectiveness of the controls.

D. Report the reliance in the report on internal controls.

Answer (A) is correct. *(CPA, adapted)*

REQUIRED: The most appropriate action when an auditor plans to rely on controls that have changed.

DISCUSSION: Controls that have changed must be tested for operating effectiveness before they can be relied on.

Answer (B) is incorrect. The audit strategy may change once the new controls have been tested for effectiveness. Answer (C) is incorrect. The auditor should test controls, not just inquire of management as to effectiveness, to rely on controls. Answer (D) is incorrect. To rely on controls, the auditor should test their effectiveness, not just report on the controls.

8.2.14. Tests of controls in a financial statement audit are least likely to be omitted with regard to

A. Accounts believed to be subject to ineffective controls.

B. Accounts representing few transactions.

C. Accounts representing many transactions.

D. Subsequent events.

Answer (C) is correct. *(Publisher, adapted)*

REQUIRED: The circumstances in which tests of controls are least likely to be omitted.

DISCUSSION: For high-volume accounts, the auditor ordinarily tests controls because of efficiency considerations. The auditor tests suitably designed controls given an expectation that controls are operating with some degree of effectiveness.

Answer (A) is incorrect. The auditor tests controls when (1) (s)he has an expectation of their operating effectiveness or (2) substantive procedures alone cannot provide sufficient appropriate audit evidence at the relevant assertion level. Answer (B) is incorrect. Given few transactions, performing substantive procedures is more efficient than testing controls. Answer (D) is incorrect. Each subsequent event that requires consideration by management and evaluation by the independent auditor should be examined. Hence, tests of relevant controls are likely to be omitted.

8.2.15. A senior auditor conducted a dual-purpose test on a client's invoice to determine whether the invoice was approved and to ascertain the amount and other terms of the invoice. Which of the following lists two tests that the auditor performed?

A. Substantive procedures and analytical procedures.

B. Substantive analytical procedures and tests of controls.

C. Tests of controls and tests of details.

D. Tests of details and substantive procedures.

Answer (C) is correct. *(CPA, adapted)*

REQUIRED: The tests performed in a dual-purpose test.

DISCUSSION: Dual-purpose testing involves performing (1) a test of details and (2) a test of controls on the same transaction. Tests of controls are used to determine whether controls are operating effectively. Determining whether the invoice was approved verifies that the control was effective. Ascertaining the amount and terms of the invoice is used to detect material misstatements in financial statement assertions, which is a test of details.

Answer (A) is incorrect. Analytical procedures may be, but are not required to be, used as substantive procedures (along with tests of details) to provide sufficient appropriate evidence about specific financial statement assertions related to account balances or classes of transactions. Answer (B) is incorrect. Ascertaining the amount and terms of an invoice is a test of details, not an analytical procedure. Answer (D) is incorrect. Determining whether the invoice was approved is a test of control. Tests of details are substantive procedures performed to detect material misstatements in financial statements assertions.

8.3 Assessing Risk in a Computer Environment

8.3.1. Which of the following could the auditor examine only in online systems?

A. Results of test decks.

B. Resolution of errors.

C. Levels of terminal access.

D. Tests of transactions.

Answer (C) is correct. *(CIA, adapted)*

REQUIRED: The item an auditor could examine only in online systems.

DISCUSSION: Online operation implies direct communication with the CPU, and this typically requires computer terminals. Thus, only in online systems could the auditor examine levels of terminal access.

Answer (A) is incorrect. The auditor could examine results of test decks in offline systems. Answer (B) is incorrect. The auditor could examine resolution of errors in offline systems. Answer (D) is incorrect. The auditor could examine tests of transactions in offline systems.

8.3.2. Which of the following types of evidence should an auditor most likely examine to determine whether internal controls are operating as designed?

A. Gross margin information regarding the client's industry.

B. Confirmations of receivables verifying account balances.

C. Client records documenting the use of computer programs.

D. Anticipated results documented in budgets or forecasts.

Answer (C) is correct. *(CPA, adapted)*

REQUIRED: The items tested to determine the operating effectiveness of internal controls.

DISCUSSION: In testing controls over the computer processing function, the auditor should obtain evidence of proper authorization of access to computer programs and files.

Answer (A) is incorrect. Analytical procedures are applied as substantive procedures to gross margin information and anticipated results. Answer (B) is incorrect. Confirmations customarily request information regarding account balances and are substantive procedures, not tests of controls. Answer (D) is incorrect. Analytical procedures are applied as substantive procedures to gross margin information and anticipated results.

8.3.3. The major purpose of the auditor's study and evaluation of the company's computer processing operations is to

A. Evaluate the competence of computer processing operating personnel.

B. Ensure the exercise of due professional care.

C. Evaluate the reliability and integrity of financial information.

D. Become familiar with the company's means of identifying, measuring, classifying, and reporting information.

Answer (C) is correct. *(CIA, adapted)*

REQUIRED: The major purpose of the auditor's study and evaluation of the company's computer operations.

DISCUSSION: Information systems provide data for decision making, control, and compliance with external requirements. Thus, auditors should examine information systems and, as appropriate, determine (1) whether financial records and reports contain accurate, reliable, timely, complete, and useful information and (2) controls over recordkeeping and reporting are adequate and effective.

Answer (A) is incorrect. Determining the competence of computer processing operating personnel is not the major purpose of the evaluation. Answer (B) is incorrect. Due professional care should be exercised in all audits. Answer (D) is incorrect. Becoming familiar with the company's information system is a means to an end.

8.3.4. JP Industries conducts its business using IT, and the only documentation of transactions is produced through the IT system. The auditor has concluded that it is not possible to obtain sufficient appropriate audit evidence by performing only substantive procedures for a number of financial statement assertions. The auditor's alternative strategy is to

A. Increase the acceptable audit risk.

B. Focus audit tests on other assertions for which substantive procedures prove to be effective.

C. Require management to change its information system to provide appropriate evidence.

D. Perform tests of controls.

Answer (D) is correct. *(Publisher, adapted)*

REQUIRED: The appropriate audit strategy when the client processes significant information electronically.

DISCUSSION: The entity conducts its business using IT, and the only documentation of transactions is produced through the IT system. Because the auditor cannot obtain sufficient appropriate audit evidence by performing substantive procedures alone, the auditor should perform tests of controls. These procedures are designed to evaluate the operating effectiveness of controls in preventing, or detecting and correcting, material misstatements at the assertion level (AU-C 330 and AS 2301).

Answer (A) is incorrect. The auditor has already established an acceptable level of audit risk. Answer (B) is incorrect. The auditor cannot express an unmodified opinion if (s)he remains in substantial doubt about any material relevant assertion. Answer (C) is incorrect. The auditor should not expect management to change its information system solely to accommodate the audit.

8.3.5. After reviewing terminal security controls, the auditor has concluded that the controls are insufficient. Which of the following audit techniques could the auditor have used to reach this conclusion?

I. Observation
II. Generalized audit software
III. Internal control questionnaires
IV. Control flowcharting

A. I.

B. II and III.

C. I, III, and IV.

D. I, II, III, and IV.

Answer (C) is correct. *(CISA, adapted)*

REQUIRED: The audit procedures that could be the basis for concluding that security controls are insufficient.

DISCUSSION: An auditor reads documentation, observes the actions of employees, makes inquiries, prepares questionnaires, and develops flowcharts to gain an understanding of the controls. (S)he may then conclude that controls are inappropriate or insufficient, even without testing their effectiveness.

Answer (A) is incorrect. Observation alone will not provide sufficient evidence for an audit conclusion about terminal security. Answer (B) is incorrect. Generalized audit software is typically used to perform substantive tests but is not appropriate for testing terminal security. Answer (D) is incorrect. Generalized audit software is typically used to perform substantive tests but is not appropriate for testing terminal security.

8.3.6. Which of the following statements about the assessment of the risks of material misstatement in a client's computer environment is true?

A. The auditor's objectives with respect to the assessment of the risks of material misstatement are the same as in a manual system.

B. The auditor must obtain an understanding of internal control and test controls in computer environments.

C. If the general controls are ineffective, the auditor ordinarily can assess the risks of material misstatement at a low level if the application controls are effective.

D. The auditor usually can ignore the computer system if (s)he can obtain an understanding of the controls outside the computer system.

Answer (A) is correct. *(Publisher, adapted)*

REQUIRED: The true statement about the auditor's assessment of the RMMs in a computer environment.

DISCUSSION: The auditor is required to perform risk assessment procedures to obtain an understanding of the entity and its environment, including its internal control, to identify and assess the RMMs and to design further audit procedures. Whether the control system is manual or computerized does not affect this objective.

Answer (B) is incorrect. The auditor need not test the effectiveness of the controls if sufficient appropriate evidence can be obtained through substantive procedures. Answer (C) is incorrect. If general controls are weak, the auditor is unlikely to assess the RMMs at a low level, no matter how effective the application controls appear to be. Answer (D) is incorrect. When computer applications are significant, the auditor must consider the relevant control activities as an integral part of the assessment of the RMMs.

8.3.7. After gaining an understanding of a client's computer processing internal control, a financial statement auditor may decide not to test the effectiveness of the computer processing control procedures. Which of the following is not a valid reason for choosing to omit tests of controls?

A. The controls duplicate operative controls existing elsewhere in the system.

B. Risk assessment procedures have not identified relevant effective controls.

C. The time and dollar costs of testing exceed the time and dollar savings in substantive testing if the tests of controls show the controls to be effective.

D. The assessment of the risks of material misstatement permits the auditor to rely on the controls.

Answer (D) is correct. *(CPA, adapted)*

REQUIRED: The invalid reason for omitting tests of controls.

DISCUSSION: Although controls appear to be effective based on the understanding of internal control, the auditor should perform tests of controls when the assessment of the RMMs at the relevant assertion level includes an expectation of their operating effectiveness. This expectation reflects the auditor's intention to rely on the controls in determining the nature, timing, and extent of substantive procedures.

Answer (A) is incorrect. Compensating controls may appropriately limit the RMMs. Answer (B) is incorrect. Performing only substantive procedures is appropriate for certain assertions, e.g., when (1) testing controls is inefficient or (2) effective controls relevant to the assertions have not been identified. Answer (C) is incorrect. Difficulty, time, and cost do not justify (1) omitting an audit procedure for which no alternative exists or (2) being satisfied with less than persuasive audit evidence. But users of financial statements expect that the auditor will (1) form an opinion within a reasonable time and (2) balance benefit and cost (AU-C 200).

8.3.8. When an accounting application is processed by computer, an auditor cannot verify the reliable operation of automated controls by

A. Manually comparing detail transaction files used by an edit program with the program's generated error listings to determine that errors were properly identified by the edit program.

B. Constructing a processing system for accounting applications and processing actual data from throughout the period through both the client's program and the auditor's program.

C. Manually reperforming, as of a moment in time, the processing of input data and comparing the simulated results with the actual results.

D. Periodically submitting auditor-prepared test data to the same computer process and evaluating the results.

Answer (C) is correct. *(CPA, adapted)*

REQUIRED: The procedure that cannot verify the reliability of automated controls.

DISCUSSION: Manually reperforming, as of a moment in time, the processing of input data and comparing the simulated results with the actual results is auditing around the computer. The computer is treated as a black box, and only the inputs and outputs are evaluated. Because the actual controls may not be understood or tested, the technique is ordinarily inappropriate if the effectiveness of automated controls is important to the understanding of internal control and the assessment of control risk. Moreover, the auditor is concerned with the reliable operation of the controls throughout the audit period, not at a single moment in time.

Answer (A) is incorrect. A manual comparison of the computer-generated output of an auditor-controlled edit program with the error listings generated by the client's program provides evidence that the client's automated controls were operating as planned. Answer (B) is incorrect. Parallel simulation can be an effective method of testing the reliability of controls. Answer (D) is incorrect. Submitting auditor-prepared test data to the client's computer process is an effective method of assessing the reliability of controls.

8.3.9. The auditor's primary concern when an auditee's programmer writes a program to age inventory is

A. The auditor's programming expertise.

B. Loss of independence.

C. Saving valuable audit time.

D. The programmer's access to confidential information.

Answer (B) is correct. *(CIA, adapted)*

REQUIRED: The auditor's primary concern when an auditee's programmer writes a program to age inventory.

DISCUSSION: If the auditor uses a program written by the auditee's programmer to perform an audit function (aging receivables), the independence of the auditor may be questioned. The auditor must therefore take appropriate steps to evaluate the program and control its use.

Answer (A) is incorrect. The auditor is concerned with the programmer's expertise and integrity. The auditor does not necessarily need programming ability. Answer (C) is incorrect. Saving audit time is secondary to the need for objectivity in conducting the audit. Answer (D) is incorrect. The development of an inventory aging program typically does not involve access to confidential input information.

8.3.10. Which of the following is necessary to audit balances in an online computer system in an environment of destructive updating?

A. Periodic dumping of transaction files.

B. Year-end use of audit hooks.

C. An integrated test facility (ITF).

D. A well-documented audit trail.

Answer (D) is correct. *(CPA, adapted)*

REQUIRED: The condition necessary to audit balances in an online computer system.

DISCUSSION: The processing of input records in an online, real-time computer system typically destroys the previous master file entry in an environment of destructive updating. Thus, a well-documented audit trail is especially important for the auditor.

Answer (A) is incorrect. Periodic dumping of transaction files may be a way of monitoring transactions, but the auditor would not find it beneficial in the audit. Answer (B) is incorrect. An audit hook is a part of a program that allows for attachment of an audit module to allow continuous monitoring. However, given destructive updating, capturing values only at year end is much less useful than a well-documented audit trail. Answer (C) is incorrect. An ITF is a possible but unnecessary approach to auditing computer systems.

8.3.11. Which of the following strategies would a CPA most likely consider in auditing an entity that processes most of its financial data only in electronic form, such as a paperless system?

A. Continuous monitoring and analysis of transaction processing with an embedded audit module.

B. Increased reliance on internal control activities that emphasize the segregation of duties.

C. Verification of encrypted digital certificates used to monitor the authorization of transactions.

D. Extensive testing of firewall boundaries that restrict the recording of outside network traffic.

Answer (A) is correct. *(CPA, adapted)*

REQUIRED: The audit strategy for an electronic environment.

DISCUSSION: An audit module embedded in the client's software routinely selects and abstracts certain transactions. They may be tagged and traced through the information system. An alternative is recording in an audit log, that is, in a file accessible only by the auditor.

Answer (B) is incorrect. The same level of segregation of duties as in a manual system is not feasible in highly sophisticated computer systems. Answer (C) is incorrect. Encrypted digital signatures help ensure the authenticity of the sender of information, but verifying them is a less pervasive and significant procedure than continuous monitoring of transactions. Answer (D) is incorrect. Firewalls exclude unauthorized activity from entering a system; however, such activity would be independent of the internal processing of financial information.

8.3.12. Auditing through the computer is required when

A. Input transactions are batched and system logic is straightforward.

B. Processing primarily consists of sorting the input data and updating the master file sequentially.

C. Processing is primarily online and updating is real-time.

D. Generalized audit software is not available.

Answer (C) is correct. *(CIA, adapted)*

REQUIRED: The condition requiring auditing through the computer.

DISCUSSION: When the computer plays a significant role in processing, storing, and reporting the information being audited, the auditor should audit through the computer. When evidence of an entity's initiation, authorization, recording, processing, and reporting of financial data exists only in electronic form, the auditor's ability to obtain the desired assurance only from substantive procedures significantly diminishes.

Answer (A) is incorrect. In a straightforward batch system, printouts and other documentation may be sufficient for adequate testing outside the computer. Answer (B) is incorrect. When files are stored sequentially and processed in that manner, printouts and other documentation may be sufficient for adequate testing outside the computer. Answer (D) is incorrect. Whether or not generalized audit software is available, the auditor should consider the consequences of auditing around, rather than through, the computer.

8.3.13. A client maintains a large data center where access is limited to authorized employees. How may an auditor best determine the effectiveness of this control activity?

A. Inspect the policy manual establishing this control activity.

B. Ask the chief technology officer about known problems.

C. Observe whether the data center is monitored.

D. Obtain a list of current data center employees.

Answer (C) is correct. *(CPA, adapted)*

REQUIRED: The best procedure to determine the effectiveness of a control activity.

DISCUSSION: Physically observing that the data center is being monitored provides direct evidence that the control is in place and is being utilized effectively. The auditor will be able to see, first hand, if the control is preventing unauthorized access.

Answer (A) is incorrect. Inspecting the policy manual will ensure that a control has been established but will not test the effectiveness of this control. Answer (B) is incorrect. Inquiry will help the auditor understand the control but will not test its effectiveness. Answer (D) is incorrect. Obtaining a list of current employees does not provide evidence of who has been accessing the data center.

8.3.14. A primary reason auditors are reluctant to use an ITF (minicompany technique) is that it requires them to

A. Reserve specific master file records and process them at regular intervals.

B. Collect transaction and master file records in a separate file.

C. Notify user personnel so they can make manual adjustments to output.

D. Identify and reverse the fictitious entries to avoid contamination of control totals.

Answer (D) is correct. *(CIA, adapted)*

REQUIRED: The reason for not using an ITF.

DISCUSSION: An ITF permits dummy transactions to be processed with live transactions but requires additional programming to ensure that programs will recognize the specially coded test data. Also, dummy files must be established (the test facility or dummy entity). Nevertheless, output (for example, control totals) is affected by the existence of the ITF transactions. One way to avoid the problem is to use immaterial transactions. However, the resulting differences between control totals may be troublesome, and the inability to use large numbers may preclude auditing limit tests. An alternative is to submit reversing entries. However, reversals (1) threaten data integrity if they are inaccurate, (2) must be submitted in the same run, and (3) may allow users to obtain contaminated data before the entries are made.

Answer (A) is incorrect. Reserving specific master file records and processing them at regular intervals is typical of the base case system of evaluation. Answer (B) is incorrect. The embedded audit module technique involves selection of items of audit interest by the audit module included in an application program. These items are recorded in a separate audit log. Answer (C) is incorrect. Making manual adjustments to output does not reverse the fictitious entries in the master file.

8.3.15. The following flowchart depicts

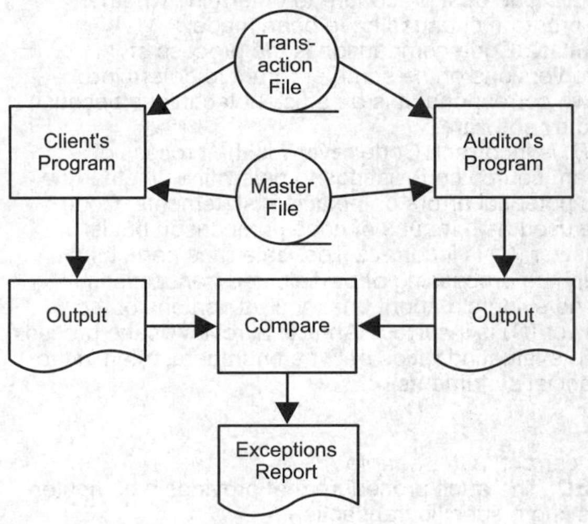

A. Program code checking.

B. Parallel simulation.

C. Integrated test facility.

D. Test data approach.

Answer (B) is correct. *(CPA, adapted)*

REQUIRED: The audit method depicted by the flowchart.

DISCUSSION: Parallel simulation is a test of the controls in a client's application program. An auditor-developed program is used to process actual client data and compare the output and the exceptions report with those of the client's application program. If the client's programmed controls are operating effectively, the two sets of results should be reconcilable.

Answer (A) is incorrect. Program code checking refers to checking the client's application program code to determine if it contains the appropriate controls. Answer (C) is incorrect. An ITF introduces dummy records into the client's files and then processes dummy transactions to update the records. The auditor can test the controls by including various types of transactions to be processed. Answer (D) is incorrect. Using the test data approach, the auditor prepares a set of dummy transactions specifically designed to test the control activities.

8.3.16. Tests of controls in an advanced computer system

A. Can be performed using only actual transactions because testing of simulated transactions is of no consequence.

B. Can be performed using actual transactions or simulated transactions.

C. Is impracticable because many procedures within the computer processing activity leave no visible evidence of having been performed.

D. Is inadvisable because they may distort the evidence in master files.

Answer (B) is correct. *(CPA, adapted)*

REQUIRED: The true statement about tests of controls in an advanced EDP system.

DISCUSSION: Tests of controls, that is, determining whether the prescribed controls are operating effectively at the assertion level, can be performed using either actual or simulated transactions. For example, the integrated test facility (ITF) method uses both actual and simulated transactions.

Answer (A) is incorrect. The auditor tests the effectiveness of a control, not the processing of a particular transaction. Answer (C) is incorrect. Many procedures that leave no visible evidence may leave machine-readable evidence. Answer (D) is incorrect. Master files can be protected during tests of controls. The integrated test facility method, for example, uses dummy records so that the test transactions will not contaminate actual data.

8.3.17. When an auditor tests a computerized accounting system, which of the following is true of the test data approach?

A. Several transactions of each type must be tested.

B. Test data are processed by the client's computer programs under the auditor's control.

C. Test data must consist of all possible valid and invalid conditions.

D. The program tested is different from the program used throughout the year by the client.

Answer (B) is correct. *(CPA, adapted)*

REQUIRED: The true statement about the test data approach.

DISCUSSION: In using the test data approach, the auditor prepares a set of dummy transactions specifically tailored to test the control procedures that management claims to have incorporated into the processing program. The auditor then processes these transactions using management's program and compares the expected results with the actual output of the program.

Answer (A) is incorrect. The computer processes each transaction in a consistent manner. Thus, only one type of transaction for each condition to be tested need be included. Answer (C) is incorrect. The test data should consist of those controls that the auditor desires to test. Answer (D) is incorrect. The auditor expects to test the program that the client has used throughout the year to gain assurance that the controls are in place and working.

8.3.18. To determine whether any unauthorized program changes have been made since the last authorized program update, the best computer audit technique is for the auditor to conduct a(n)

A. Code comparison.

B. Code review.

C. Test data run.

D. Analytical review.

Answer (A) is correct. *(CIA, adapted)*

REQUIRED: The best procedure to determine whether unauthorized program changes have been made.

DISCUSSION: Code comparison is the process of comparing two versions of the same program to determine whether the two correspond. It is an efficient technique because it is performed by software.

Answer (B) is incorrect. Code review is the process of reading program source code listings to determine whether the code contains potential errors or inefficient statements. Code review can be used as a means of code comparison but is inefficient. Answer (C) is incorrect. Test data runs permit the auditor to verify the processing of preselected transactions. They provide no evidence about unexecuted portions of the program. Answer (D) is incorrect. Analytical review is the process of creating and evaluating ratios between numbers, often in the context of financial statements.

8.3.19. In auditing an online perpetual inventory system, an auditor selected certain file-updating transactions for detailed testing. The audit technique that will provide a computer trail of all relevant processing steps applied to a specific transaction is described as

A. Simulation.

B. Snapshot.

C. Code comparison.

D. Tagging and tracing.

Answer (D) is correct. *(CIA, adapted)*

REQUIRED: The audit procedure that provides a computer trail for processing a specific transaction.

DISCUSSION: Tagging and tracing describes the selection of specific transactions to which an indicator is attached at input. A computer trail of all relevant processing steps of these tagged transactions in the application system can be printed or stored in a computer file for auditor evaluation.

Answer (A) is incorrect. Simulation permits comparisons of live data but does not produce a trail of all relevant processing steps. Answer (B) is incorrect. A snapshot is a technique for recording the content of computer memory to aid in verifying a decision process. Answer (C) is incorrect. A code comparison is used to verify that program changes and computer maintenance procedures are correctly followed.

8.3.20. Parallel simulation (the audit model technique) is an appropriate audit approach for

A. Testing for the presence of authorized signatures on documents.

B. Summarizing the results of accounts receivable confirmation work.

C. Calculating amounts for declining-balance depreciation charges.

D. Scanning the general ledger file for unusual transactions.

Answer (C) is correct. *(CIA, adapted)*

REQUIRED: The proper use of parallel simulation.

DISCUSSION: Parallel simulation involves duplicate processing of the client's data using a program developed by the auditor. The auditor's program simulates the logic of the client's application program. The auditor may thus enter data and compare simulated test results with those from the auditee's program. Parallel simulation is appropriate for auditing depreciation because controls such as limit or reasonableness tests can be tested by the auditor.

Answer (A) is incorrect. Testing for the presence of authorized signatures on documents is a test of controls that cannot be done by a program. Answer (B) is incorrect. Confirmations provide auditor-developed data from sources external to the auditee. Parallel simulation seeks to duplicate auditee processing. Answer (D) is incorrect. Scanning the general ledger file for unusual transactions does not replicate auditee processing.

8.3.21. To obtain evidence that online access controls are properly functioning, an auditor most likely will

A. Create checkpoints at periodic intervals after live data processing to test for unauthorized use of the system.

B. Examine the transaction log to discover whether any transactions were lost or entered twice because of a system malfunction.

C. Enter invalid identification numbers or passwords to ascertain whether the system rejects them.

D. Vouch a random sample of processed transactions to assure proper authorization.

Answer (C) is correct. *(CPA, adapted)*

REQUIRED: The procedure an auditor most likely performs to obtain evidence that user online access controls are functioning as designed.

DISCUSSION: Employees with access authority to process transactions that change records should not also have asset custody or program modification responsibilities. The auditor should determine that password authority is consistent with other assigned responsibilities. The auditor can directly test whether password controls are working by attempting entry into the system by using invalid identifications and passwords.

Answer (A) is incorrect. Checkpoints are used as a recovery procedure in batch processing applications. Answer (B) is incorrect. Testing for missing or duplicate transactions will not determine whether online access controls were functioning effectively. Answer (D) is incorrect. Unauthorized transactions may be entered by someone having knowledge of valid passwords, etc.

8.3.22. Which of the following computer-assisted auditing techniques allows fictitious and real transactions to be processed together without the knowledge of client operating personnel?

A. Integrated test facility (ITF).

B. Input controls matrix.

C. Parallel simulation.

D. Data entry monitor.

Answer (A) is correct. *(CPA, adapted)*

REQUIRED: The method that processes fictitious and actual transactions without the knowledge of client personnel.

DISCUSSION: The ITF or minicompany technique is a development of the test data method. It permits dummy transactions to be processed at the same time as live transactions but requires additional programming to ensure that programs will recognize the specially coded test data. The test transactions may be submitted without the computer operators' knowledge.

Answer (B) is incorrect. Input controls matrix is not a method typically used by auditors to test a client's computer systems. Answer (C) is incorrect. Parallel simulation reprocesses only real, not fictitious, transactions. Answer (D) is incorrect. Data entry monitor is not a method typically used by auditors to test a client's computer systems.

8.3.23. Which of the following is likely to be least important to an auditor who is considering internal control for the automated data processing function?

A. Ancillary program functions.

B. Disposition of source documents.

C. Operator competence.

D. Disk capacity.

Answer (D) is correct. *(CPA, adapted)*

REQUIRED: The least important item in the consideration of internal control.

DISCUSSION: Disk capacity relates to the number of characters the system can store. This is of little or no concern to an auditor considering internal control.

Answer (A) is incorrect. Ancillary or auxiliary program functions affect internal control. Answer (B) is incorrect. The auditor should inspect source documents. Answer (C) is incorrect. An entity must employ sufficient competent personnel to accomplish its goals and objectives. Thus, human resource policies and practices are a factor in the control environment that should be considered.

8.3.24. The audit effort most likely to yield relevant evidence in determining the adequacy of an organization's disaster-recovery plan should focus on

A. The completeness of the plan as to facilities, operations, communications, security, and data processing.

B. The sufficiency of the list of replacement equipment needed in the event of a disaster.

C. The question of whether the plan is in the planning or developmental stage.

D. The role of the internal auditing department in developing and testing the plan.

Answer (A) is correct. *(CIA, adapted)*

REQUIRED: The focus of the audit effort regarding a disaster recovery plan.

DISCUSSION: A computer center should have a comprehensive (complete) reconstruction and recovery plan that will allow it to regenerate important programs and data files and continue operations in the event of disasters, equipment failures, or errors. The center should create backup (duplicate) copies of data files, databases, programs, and documentation, store backup copies off-site, and plan for auxiliary processing at another site.

Answer (B) is incorrect. Consideration of the adequacy of the plan must extend to numerous factors other than the sufficiency of the list of replacement equipment. Answer (C) is incorrect. Consideration of the adequacy of the plan must extend to numerous factors other than the question of whether the plan is in the planning or development stage. Answer (D) is incorrect. The involvement of internal auditing does not ensure adequacy.

8.3.25. Auditors have learned that increased computerization has created more opportunities for computer fraud but has also led to the development of computer audit techniques to detect frauds. A type of fraud that has occurred in the banking industry is a programming fraud in which the programmer designs a program to calculate daily interest on savings accounts to four decimal points. The programmer then truncates the last two digits and adds it to his or her account balance. Which of the following computer audit techniques would be most effective in detecting this type of fraud?

A. Parallel simulation.

B. Generalized audit software that selects account balances for confirmation with the depositor.

C. Snapshot.

D. SCARF (Systems Control and Audit Review File).

Answer (A) is correct. *(CIA, adapted)*

REQUIRED: The audit technique most effective in detecting the programmer's fraud.

DISCUSSION: Parallel simulation uses specially prepared application-type programs to process transactions that have also been run in routine processing. This method is the most effective because the amounts credited to each account are compared with those calculated by the auditor's parallel program.

Answer (B) is incorrect. Confirmation of an account balance is unlikely to detect errors of less than one cent made on a daily basis. Answer (C) is incorrect. The snapshot technique captures data at a specific point in the processing of transactions through a system. It is not applicable here. Answer (D) is incorrect. SCARF includes an audit module in a program that captures unusual transactions (or transactions in excess of edit checks) that have been submitted for processing. The auditor can later evaluate the items. It is not applicable here.

8.3.26. Which of the following is the primary reason that many auditors hesitate to use embedded audit modules?

A. Embedded audit modules cannot be protected from computer viruses.

B. Auditors are required to monitor embedded audit modules continuously to obtain valid results.

C. Embedded audit modules can easily be modified through management tampering.

D. Auditors are required to be involved in the system design of the application to be monitored.

Answer (D) is correct. *(CPA, adapted)*

REQUIRED: The primary reason many auditors hesitate to use embedded audit modules.

DISCUSSION: Continuous monitoring and analysis of transaction processing can be achieved with an embedded audit module. For example, an auditor may establish an audit module that counts the number of times the credit manager overrides established credit limits. A disadvantage of an embedded audit module is that audit hooks must be programmed into the operating system and applications. An alternative is embedding code in the auditee's programs to routinely extract/select certain transactions or details to be recorded in a file accessible only by the auditors. These methods require that an auditor have a working understanding of the computer system and be involved in its design. Designing the system may impair independence unless the client makes all management decisions.

Answer (A) is incorrect. Embedded audit modules are protected from computer viruses. Answer (B) is incorrect. Auditors are not required to monitor audit modules continuously to obtain valid results. Answer (C) is incorrect. Embedded audit modules cannot be easily modified through management tampering.

STUDY UNIT NINE
INTERNAL CONTROL
COMMUNICATIONS AND REPORTS

This study unit concerns various auditor communications and reports, most involving internal control. During the conduct of an audit, the auditor may observe control deficiencies. If so, the auditor has a responsibility to communicate significant deficiencies and material weaknesses to management and those charged with governance (AU-C 265, *Communicating Internal Control Related Matters Identified in an Audit*, and AS 1305, *Communication about Control Deficiencies in an Audit of Financial Statements*). Other issues relating to the conduct of the audit also should be communicated to management and those charged with governance. Some of these issues are closely related to internal control, but others relate to the audit in general (AU-C 260, *The Auditor's Communication with Those Charged with Governance*, and AS 1301, *Communications with Audit Committees*). Public companies (issuers) are required by the Sarbanes-Oxley Act of 2002 to provide a management assessment of the effectiveness of internal control over financial reporting in annual reports. The auditor also expresses an opinion on the effectiveness of internal control. The PCAOB's Auditing Standard 2201, *An Audit of Internal Control over Financial Reporting That is Integrated with an Audit of Financial Statements*, provides guidance on the required process and reporting. For other entities (nonissuers), the auditor may be engaged to provide a report on the effectiveness of an entity's internal control over financial reporting. This service and the reports issued are governed by the AICPA's AU-C 940, *An Audit of an Entity's Internal Control over Financial Reporting That is Integrated with an Audit of Its Financial Statements*. A service auditor may prepare a report in accordance with AT-C 320, *Reporting on an Examination of Controls at a Service Organization Relevant to User Entities' Internal Control over Financial Reporting*, and the financial statement auditor may use a service auditor's report in accordance with AU-C 402, *Audit Considerations Relating to an Entity Using a Service Organization*. Such a report may affect the user auditor's assessment of a client's risks of material misstatement.

QUESTIONS

9.1 Communicating Internal Control Related Matters Identified in an Audit

9.1.1. A secondary result of the auditor's understanding of internal control for a nonissuer is that the understanding may

A. Provide a basis for determining the nature, timing, and extent of audit tests.

B. Assure that management's procedures to detect fraud are properly functioning.

C. Bring to the auditor's attention possible control conditions required to be communicated to the client.

D. Develop evidence to support the assessed risks of material misstatement.

Answer (C) is correct. *(CPA, adapted)*

REQUIRED: The secondary result of understanding internal control.

DISCUSSION: The auditor is not required to search for significant deficiencies or material weaknesses in internal control. However, the auditor may identify these conditions during the audit. Significant deficiencies and material weaknesses should be communicated in writing to management and to those charged with governance (AU-C 265).

Answer (A) is incorrect. The auditor is required to understand the entity and its environment, including its internal control, to identify and assess the risks of material misstatement. The understanding provides a basis for responses to the assessed RMMs. Answer (B) is incorrect. Testing the effectiveness of controls is not required unless the auditor intends to rely on the controls. Answer (D) is incorrect. Gathering evidence to support the assessed RMMs is a primary result of understanding internal control.

9.1.2. Which of the following issues related to internal control over financial reporting are required to be communicated in writing to management and those charged with governance?

I. Deficiencies in internal control
II. Significant deficiencies
III. Material weaknesses

A. I, II, and III.

B. II and III only.

C. III only.

D. None.

Answer (B) is correct. *(Publisher, adapted)*

REQUIRED: The control issues required to be communicated in writing to management and those charged with governance.

DISCUSSION: Only those control deficiencies considered to be significant deficiencies or material weaknesses are required to be communicated in writing to management and those charged with governance. (But certain deficiencies should not be reported directly to management.) Other control deficiencies that merit management's attention should be reported to management orally or in writing. A deficiency in internal control exists when the design or operation of a control does not allow management or employees, in the normal course of their assigned functions, to prevent misstatements or detect and correct them on a timely basis. A significant deficiency is a deficiency, or combination of deficiencies, in internal control that is less severe than a material weakness but merits attention by those charged with governance. A material weakness is a deficiency, or combination of deficiencies, in internal control that results in a reasonable possibility that a material misstatement of the financial statements will not be prevented, or detected and corrected, on a timely basis. A reasonable possibility means that the probability of the event is more than remote.

9.1.3. Which of the following best describes the responsibility of an auditor of a private entity with respect to significant deficiencies and material weaknesses under AU-C 265, *Communication of Internal Control Related Matters Identified in an Audit*?

A. The auditor need not report the conditions if those charged with governance know of them.

B. The auditor must exercise due diligence in searching for significant deficiencies and material weaknesses.

C. The communication by the auditor must be in writing.

D. The auditor's report is a general-use report and may be distributed to the shareholders.

Answer (C) is correct. *(D. Finkbiner)*

REQUIRED: The best description of the auditor's responsibility for significant deficiencies and material weaknesses.

DISCUSSION: The auditor communicates on a timely basis and in writing to those charged with governance significant deficiencies and material weaknesses identified during the audit. This communication includes those remediated during the audit. The auditor also communicates on a timely basis and in writing to the appropriate level of management significant deficiencies and material weaknesses communicated (or intended to be communicated) to those charged with governance. (But certain deficiencies should not be reported directly to management.)

Answer (A) is incorrect. The auditor should communicate significant deficiencies and material weaknesses even if they were previously reported. Answer (B) is incorrect. The auditor is required to obtain an understanding of internal control relevant to the audit but is not obligated to search for deficiencies. However, (s)he may identify deficiencies at any time during the audit. Answer (D) is incorrect. The report is a by-product of the engagement. It is intended solely for the information and use of those charged with governance, management, and others within the organization (or specified regulatory agency) and is not intended to be and should not be used by anyone other than the specified parties (AU-C 905). However, law or regulation may require the report to be given to governmental authorities.

9.1.4. When communicating significant deficiencies in internal control noted in a financial statement audit of a nonissuer, the communication should indicate that

A. Fraud or errors may occur and not be detected because of the inherent limitations of internal control.

B. The expression of an unmodified opinion on the financial statements may be dependent on corrective follow-up action.

C. The deficiencies noted were not detected within a timely period by employees in the normal course of performing their assigned functions.

D. The purpose of the audit was to report on the financial statements, not to provide assurance on internal control.

Answer (D) is correct. *(CPA, adapted)*

REQUIRED: The content of an auditor's communication issued on significant deficiencies.

DISCUSSION: According to an illustrative written communication in AU-C 265, the auditors state, "we considered the Company's internal control over financial reporting (internal control) as a basis for designing audit procedures that are appropriate in the circumstances for the purpose of expressing our opinion on the financial statements, but not for the purpose of expressing an opinion on the effectiveness of the Company's internal control. Accordingly, we do not express an opinion on the effectiveness of the Company's internal control."

Answer (A) is incorrect. The report identifies significant deficiencies and material weaknesses in the design or operation of internal control, not errors or fraud. Answer (B) is incorrect. The opinion on the financial statements should be supported by evidence collected by the auditor, not subsequent corrective actions by management. Answer (C) is incorrect. The report identifies significant deficiencies and material weaknesses in the design or operation of internal control, not fraud or errors.

9.1.5. Which of the following statements about an auditor's communication of internal control related matters identified in an audit of a nonissuer is true?

A. The auditor may issue a written report to management and those charged with governance that no significant deficiencies were noted.

B. Significant deficiencies or material weaknesses need not be recommunicated each year if the audit committee has acknowledged its understanding of such deficiencies.

C. Significant deficiencies or material weaknesses may not be communicated in a document that contains suggestions regarding activities that concern other topics such as business strategies or administrative efficiencies.

D. The auditor should communicate significant internal control related matters no later than 60 days after the report release date.

Answer (D) is correct. *(CPA, adapted)*

REQUIRED: The true statement about an auditor's communication of internal control related matters identified in an audit.

DISCUSSION: Timely communication of significant deficiencies or material weaknesses should be made no later than 60 days after the report release date. But the communication is best made by the report release date. However, early communication may be important because of the significance of the matters noted and the urgency of corrective action.

Answer (A) is incorrect. AU-C 265 prohibits issuance of a report declaring that no significant deficiencies were noted. However, a report can be issued stating that no material weaknesses were detected if it states that material weaknesses may exist and not be identified. Answer (B) is incorrect. Significant deficiencies and material weaknesses that previously were communicated and have not yet been remediated should continue to be communicated. Answer (C) is incorrect. Items beneficial to the client may be communicated even though they are not control related.

9.1.6. Under the AICPA's auditing standards, which of the following statements about an auditor's communication of significant control deficiencies is true?

A. A significant control deficiency previously communicated during the prior year's audit that remains uncorrected causes a scope limitation.

B. An auditor should perform tests of controls on significant control deficiencies before communicating them to the client.

C. An auditor's report on significant control deficiencies should include a restriction on the use of the report.

D. An auditor should communicate significant control deficiencies after tests of controls, but before commencing substantive tests.

Answer (C) is correct. *(CPA, adapted)*

REQUIRED: The true statement about the auditor's communication of significant control deficiencies.

DISCUSSION: A communication of significant control deficiencies should (1) state that the purpose of the audit was to report on the financial statements, not to provide assurance on internal control; (2) give the definition of significant control deficiencies and material weaknesses; and (3) state that the report is intended solely for the information and use of those charged with governance, management, and others within the organization (or specified regulatory agency) and is not intended to be, and should not be, used by anyone other than the specified parties.

Answer (A) is incorrect. Although a significant deficiency previously communicated requires continued communication in the following year, it does not necessarily cause a limitation of the scope of the audit (an inability to obtain sufficient appropriate audit evidence). Answer (B) is incorrect. Tests of controls are performed on internal control, not on significant deficiencies. Answer (D) is incorrect. Significant control deficiencies should be reported no later than 60 days from the report release date. However, they may be communicated orally during the audit if this information is significant or the need for corrective action is urgent.

9.1.7. Which of the following representations should not be included in a written report on internal control related matters identified in an audit under the AICPA's auditing standards?

A. Significant deficiencies related to the design of internal control exist, but none are deemed to be material weaknesses.

B. There are no significant deficiencies or material weaknesses in the design or operation of internal control.

C. Corrective action is recommended due to the relative significance of material weaknesses discovered during the audit.

D. The auditor's consideration of internal control would not necessarily disclose all significant deficiencies or material weaknesses that exist.

Answer (B) is correct. *(CPA, adapted)*

REQUIRED: The item not included in a written report on internal control related matters.

DISCUSSION: No report should be issued indicating that no significant deficiencies were noted. The potential for misinterpretation would exist if the auditor issued such a report (AU-C 265).

Answer (A) is incorrect. The report may state that the significant deficiencies noted are not material weaknesses. Answer (C) is incorrect. The communication may be the appropriate means for recommending corrective action on significant matters noted. Answer (D) is incorrect. The language in the report may state that the consideration of internal control might not disclose all significant deficiencies or material weaknesses that exist.

9.1.8. A CPA had previously communicated a significant control deficiency in connection with an audit of prior financial statements of a nonissuer. As of the current audit date, the deficiency has not been corrected. What communication should be made by the CPA?

A. None, because management has been previously put on notice and now has sole responsibility.

B. A new communication is required only if it involves an area in which the auditor has not relied on the controls.

C. A new communication is required only if the auditor has relied on the controls.

D. The condition should be reported.

Answer (D) is correct. *(Publisher, adapted)*

REQUIRED: The effect on the auditor of a previously communicated significant control deficiency.

DISCUSSION: AU-C 265 requires communication about significant deficiencies and material weaknesses and makes no exception solely for previous reporting of a condition. This can be accomplished by a written communication referring to the previously written communication and the date of that communication.

Answer (A) is incorrect. Even though internal control is the responsibility of management, the auditor has the responsibility to report the deficiency. Answer (B) is incorrect. The auditor should report the deficiency regardless of the reliance on control. Answer (C) is incorrect. The auditor should report the deficiency regardless of the reliance on control.

9.2 The Auditor's Communication with Those Charged with Governance

9.2.1. Which of the following matters is an auditor required to communicate to those in the entity charged with governance?

I. Disagreements with management about matters significant to the entity's financial statements that have been satisfactorily resolved

II. Initial selection of significant accounting policies in emerging areas that lack authoritative guidance

A. I only.

B. II only.

C. Both I and II.

D. Neither I nor II.

Answer (C) is correct. *(CPA, adapted)*

REQUIRED: The matter(s), if any, to be communicated to those charged with governance.

DISCUSSION: AU-C 260, *The Auditor's Communication with Those Charged with Governance*, states that the matters to be discussed include (1) an overview of the planned scope and timing of the audit; (2) the auditors' responsibilities regarding the audit, such as performing the audit to obtain reasonable, not absolute, assurance about whether the statements are fairly presented; (3) significant accounting policies; (4) sensitive accounting estimates; (5) uncorrected and corrected misstatements; (6) the qualitative aspects of the entity's accounting practices; (7) significant difficulties during the audit; (8) auditor disagreements with management, whether or not satisfactorily resolved; and (9) any other findings and issues judged to be significant and relevant to those charged with governance. Under the Sarbanes-Oxley Act of 2002, a registered audit firm must communicate (1) critical accounting policies, (2) all alternative treatments of information within GAAP discussed with management, (3) the ramifications of using such treatments, and (4) the treatment preferred by the firm.

9.2.2. During planning, an auditor of a nonissuer should communicate which of the following to those charged with governance at an entity?

A. The auditor is responsible for preparing financial statements in conformity with the applicable financial reporting framework.

B. The audit does not relieve management of its responsibilities for the financial statements.

C. The auditor will express an opinion on the effectiveness of internal controls over compliance with laws and regulations.

D. All audit findings will be communicated in writing to those charged with governance.

Answer (B) is correct. *(CPA, adapted)*

REQUIRED: The communication to those charged with governance by an auditor of a nonissuer.

DISCUSSION: Effective two-way communication, among other things, assists those charged with governance to fulfill their responsibility to oversee the financial reporting process. The result should be reduced risk of material misstatement. Communications with management should address its responsibility for the preparation and fair presentation of the financial statements.

Answer (A) is incorrect. A precondition of an audit is that the entity is responsible for preparing financial statements in conformity with the applicable financial reporting framework. Answer (C) is incorrect. If a governmental audit requirement mandates a report on internal control in a compliance audit, the auditor will express an opinion on the effectiveness of internal controls over compliance with laws and regulations. But the facts do not indicate that a compliance audit is to be performed. Also, an audit of financial statements does not result in an opinion on compliance controls. Answer (D) is incorrect. Significant and relevant findings and issues should be communicated.

9.2.3. Which of the following matters will an auditor most likely communicate to those charged with governance?

A. A list of negative trends that may lead to working capital deficiencies and adverse financial ratios.

B. The level of responsibility assumed by management for the preparation of the financial statements.

C. Difficulties encountered in achieving a satisfactory response rate from the entity's customers in confirming accounts receivables.

D. The effects of significant accounting policies adopted by management in emerging areas for which no authoritative guidance exists.

Answer (D) is correct. *(CPA, adapted)*

REQUIRED: The matter an auditor will most likely communicate to those charged with governance.

DISCUSSION: AU-C 260, *The Auditor's Communication with Those Charged with Governance*, requires the auditor to inform those charged with governance about his or her views on qualitative aspects of significant accounting practices. These include the initial selection of, and changes in, significant accounting policies or their application. The communication also extends to the effect of significant accounting policies in controversial or emerging areas for which authoritative guidance or consensus is lacking. An example of such an area is revenue recognition.

Answer (A) is incorrect. A list of negative trends that may lead to working capital deficiencies and adverse financial ratios is more likely to be communicated to management. Answer (B) is incorrect. The engagement letter should state that management is responsible for the financial statements. Moreover, those charged with governance presumably understand management's responsibilities. Answer (C) is incorrect. The difficulties encountered in performing the audit that are communicated to those charged with governance are more likely to involve dealings with management and other client personnel.

9.2.4. Which of the following matters should an auditor communicate to those charged with governance?

A. The basis for assessing the risks of material misstatement when the auditor intends to rely on controls.

B. The process used by management in formulating sensitive accounting estimates.

C. The auditor's preliminary judgments about materiality levels.

D. The justification for performing substantive procedures at interim dates.

Answer (B) is correct. *(CPA, adapted)*

REQUIRED: The required communication to those charged with governance.

DISCUSSION: Certain accounting estimates are particularly sensitive because they are significant to the financial statements, and future events affecting them may differ from current judgments. Those charged with governance should be informed about the process used in formulating sensitive estimates, including fair value estimates, and the basis for the auditor's conclusions about their reasonableness (AU-C 260).

9.2.5. Which of the following disagreements between the auditor and management do not have to be communicated by the auditor to those charged with governance?

A. Disagreements regarding management's judgment about accounting estimates for goodwill.

B. Disagreements about the scope of the audit.

C. Disagreements in the application of accounting principles relating to software development costs.

D. Disagreements of the amount of the LIFO inventory layer based on preliminary information.

Answer (D) is correct. *(CPA, adapted)*

REQUIRED: The disagreements that need not be communicated by the auditor to those charged with governance.

DISCUSSION: Auditor disagreements with management about significant matters, whether or not satisfactorily resolved, should be communicated to those charged with governance. However, disagreements do not include differences of opinion based on preliminary information or incomplete facts that are later resolved.

9.2.6. An auditor should communicate misstatements to those charged with governance

A. If they were not recorded before the end of the auditor's field work.

B. If they are uncorrected.

C. If they are immaterial and corrected but frequently recurring.

D. Even if they are clearly trivial.

Answer (B) is correct. *(CPA, adapted)*

REQUIRED: The circumstances in which misstatements should be communicated.

DISCUSSION: The auditor communicates uncorrected misstatements and the effect they may have, individually or aggregated, on the opinion. Furthermore, material uncorrected misstatements should be identified individually. Also, the auditor should communicate to those charged with governance the effect of uncorrected misstatements related to prior periods (AU-C 260).

Answer (A) is incorrect. The entries affecting the year-end financial statement balances may be made subsequent to year end. Answer (C) is incorrect. The auditor may, but is not required to, communicate immaterial corrected misstatements, such as those that frequently recur and may indicate a bias in statement preparation. Answer (D) is incorrect. The auditor need not communicate misstatements if they are clearly trivial. Clearly trivial items are not merely immaterial but are clearly inconsequential (1) individually and in the aggregate and (2) when judged by any criteria.

9.2.7. In an audit engagement, should an auditor communicate the following matters to those charged with governance?

	Auditor's Judgments About the Quality of the Client's Accounting Principles	Issues Discussed with Management Prior to the Auditor's Retention
A.	Yes	Yes
B.	Yes	No
C.	No	Yes
D.	No	No

Answer (A) is correct. *(CPA, adapted)*

REQUIRED: The matter(s), if any, to be communicated to those charged with governance.

DISCUSSION: The matters to be discussed with those charged with governance include the quality of the accounting principles used by management. Management is normally a participant in the discussion. Matters covered may include the auditor's views on the entity's significant accounting practices, e.g., policies, estimates, and disclosures. Furthermore, in any audit engagement, the auditor and those charged with governance should discuss any major issues discussed with management in connection with the initial or recurring retention of the auditors, for example, issues concerning the application of accounting principles and auditing standards.

9.2.8. An auditor s most likely to communicate to those charged with governance that

A. The turnover in the accounting department was unusually high.

B. The auditor encountered significant difficulties during the audit.

C. The auditor discovered subsequent events.

D. Management agreed with the auditor's assessed risks of material misstatement.

Answer (B) is correct. *(CPA, adapted)*

REQUIRED: The matter communicated to those charged with governance.

DISCUSSION: Significant difficulties encountered during the audit may result in a scope limitation. Accordingly, the auditor communicates such matters as (1) delays in receiving required information from management, (2) an unnecessarily brief time to perform the audit, (3) extensive and unexpected effort to obtain audit evidence, (4) unavailability of expected information, (5) restrictions placed on the auditor by management, and (6) management's unwillingness to provide information about its plans to respond to going concern issues (AU-C 260).

Answer (A) is incorrect. A high turnover of employees may increase the assessed RMMs but does not require communication with those charged with governance. Answer (C) is incorrect. The subsequent events discovered by the auditor need not be communicated to those charged with governance. Answer (D) is incorrect. The assessment of RMMs is a matter of auditor judgment and is not negotiated with the client.

9.3 Reporting on an Entity's Internal Control

9.3.1. Firms subject to the reporting requirements of the Securities Exchange Act of 1934 are required by the Foreign Corrupt Practices Act of 1977 to maintain satisfactory internal control. Moreover, the Sarbanes-Oxley Act of 2002 requires that annual reports include (1) a statement of management's responsibility for establishing and maintaining adequate internal control and procedures for financial reporting, and (2) management's assessment of their effectiveness. The role of the registered auditor relative to the assessment made by management is to

A. Express an opinion on the assessment.

B. Report clients with unsatisfactory internal control to the SEC.

C. Express an opinion on whether the client is subject to the Securities Exchange Act of 1934.

D. Determine whether management's report is complete and properly presented.

Answer (D) is correct. *(Publisher, adapted)*

REQUIRED: The role of the auditor relative to the assessment by management of internal control.

DISCUSSION: According to PCAOB AS 2201, the auditor must express (or disclaim) an opinion on the effectiveness of internal control. Moreover, if the auditor determines that elements of management's annual report on internal control over financial reporting are incomplete or improperly presented, the auditor should modify his or her report to describe the reasons for this determination.

Answer (A) is incorrect. According to PCAOB AS 2201, the auditor must express (or disclaim) an opinion on internal control but not necessarily on management's assessment. Answer (B) is incorrect. The auditor's report on internal control is issued with the audit report on the financial statements. Answer (C) is incorrect. Issuers must report to the SEC, but the auditor need not express an opinion on whether the client is subject to the Securities Exchange Act of 1934.

9.3.2. The Sarbanes-Oxley Act of 2002 requires management to include a report on internal control in the firm's annual report. It also requires auditors to evaluate management's internal control report. Which of the following statements concerning these requirements is false?

A. The auditors should provide recommendations for improving internal control in their assessment.

B. Management should identify significant deficiencies and material weaknesses in its report.

C. Management's report should state its responsibility for establishing and maintaining an adequate internal control system.

D. The auditors should evaluate whether internal controls are effective in accurately and fairly reflecting the firm's transactions.

Answer (A) is correct. *(Publisher, adapted)*

REQUIRED: The false statement about the Sarbanes-Oxley Act.

DISCUSSION: The auditors may provide management with recommendations for improving controls, but the Sarbanes-Oxley Act does not require such a communication in their report.

Answer (B) is incorrect. Management's report should include any significant deficiencies and material weaknesses as well as any corrective action taken. Answer (C) is incorrect. Management's report should state that it is responsible for establishing and maintaining internal controls. Answer (D) is incorrect. The auditors should evaluate and express an opinion on the effectiveness of internal control over financial reporting.

9.3.3. Which of the following best describes a CPA's engagement to report on an entity's internal control over financial reporting?

A. An audit engagement that results in issuance of a report relating to the effectiveness of internal control.

B. An audit of the financial statements that results in communicating significant deficiencies in internal control.

C. A prospective engagement to project, for a period of time not to exceed one year, and report on the expected benefits of the entity's internal control.

D. A consulting engagement to provide constructive advice to the entity on its internal control.

Answer (A) is correct. *(CPA, adapted)*

REQUIRED: The best description of an engagement to report on an entity's internal control over financial reporting.

DISCUSSION: In such an attest engagement, the auditor issues a report relating to the effectiveness of the entity's internal control over financial reporting. The practitioner, as part of engagement performance, obtains from management a written assessment about such effectiveness. AU-C 940 and AS 2201 define the objective of the engagement to express an opinion on the effectiveness of internal control over financial reporting similarly.

Answer (B) is incorrect. An engagement to report on internal control is a service in addition to the traditional financial statement audit. Answer (C) is incorrect. The opinion expressed should not extend into the future. Answer (D) is incorrect. Consulting engagements do not result in the expression of an opinion.

9.3.4. A CPA's understanding of internal control in a financial statement audit of a nonissuer

A. Is usually more limited than that made in an audit of internal control integrated with an audit of financial statements.

B. Is usually more extensive than that made in an audit of internal control integrated with an audit of financial statements.

C. Will usually be identical to that made in an audit of internal control integrated with an audit of financial statements.

D. Will usually result in a report on the effectiveness of internal control.

Answer (A) is correct. *(CPA, adapted)*

REQUIRED: The scope of the understanding of internal control in a financial statement audit of a nonissuer.

DISCUSSION: The scope of the understanding of internal control in a financial statement audit of a nonissuer is usually less than that in an audit of internal control integrated with an audit of financial statements. In the integrated audit, the auditor tests controls to support the opinion on the effectiveness of internal control. To express an opinion on internal control, the auditor obtains evidence about the effectiveness of selected controls over all relevant assertions. When obtaining the understanding of internal control during a financial statement audit, the auditor need not test controls unless (1) the auditor's risk assessment is based on an expectation of the effectiveness of controls or (2) substantive procedures alone do not provide sufficient appropriate evidence.

Answer (B) is incorrect. In an integrated audit, the auditor tests controls ordinarily not tested when the engagement is solely to express an opinion on the statements of a nonissuer. Answer (C) is incorrect. In an integrated audit, the auditor tests controls ordinarily not tested when the engagement is solely to express an opinion on the statements of a nonissuer. Answer (D) is incorrect. An audit of the financial statements of a nonissuer does not result in a report on internal control unless the requirements for such an engagement are met.

9.3.5. Snow, CPA, was engaged by Master Co., a nonissuer, to audit the effectiveness of Master's internal control over financial reporting as part of an integrated audit. Snow's report should state that

A. Because of inherent limitations, internal control may not prevent, or detect and correct, misstatements.

B. Management's evaluation of the effectiveness of internal control is based on criteria established by the American Institute of Certified Public Accountants.

C. The results of Snow's tests will form the basis for Snow's opinion on the fairness of Master's financial statements in accordance with U.S. GAAP.

D. The purpose of the engagement is to enable Snow to plan an audit and determine the nature, timing, and extent of tests to be performed.

Answer (A) is correct. *(CPA, adapted)*

REQUIRED: The statement in an auditor's report on an audit of the effectiveness of internal control over financial reporting.

DISCUSSION: The auditor's report states that because of its inherent limitations, internal control over financial reporting may not prevent, or detect and correct, misstatements. Also, projections of any evaluation of effectiveness to future periods are subject to the risks that (1) controls may become inadequate because of changes in conditions or (2) the degree of compliance with the policies or procedures may deteriorate (AU-C 940).

Answer (B) is incorrect. The audit is based on auditing standards established by the AICPA. Answer (C) is incorrect. The audit of internal control is the basis for an opinion on the effectiveness of internal control. Answer (D) is incorrect. The auditor's objective in an audit of the internal control of a nonissuer is to express an opinion on its effectiveness. Thus, the auditor plans and performs the audit to obtain sufficient appropriate evidence to obtain reasonable assurance about the existence of material weaknesses.

9.3.6. An issuer who is an accelerated filer subject to the Securities Exchange Act of 1934 is required to include in its annual report an auditor's opinion on whether internal control over financial reporting was

A. Sufficient to meet the needs of the shareholders.

B. Properly designed and operated effectively.

C. Adequate to eliminate fraud.

D. Complete and fair.

Answer (B) is correct. *(Publisher, adapted)*

REQUIRED: The purpose of an auditor's opinion on internal control.

DISCUSSION: According to PCAOB's AS 2201, the report states the auditor's opinion on whether the entity maintained, in all material respects, effective internal control over financial reporting as of the specified date based on the control criteria.

Answer (A) is incorrect. Internal control should meet the needs of the entity, including the requirements of external financial reporting, not merely the needs of shareholders. Answer (C) is incorrect. No system of internal control can be expected to eliminate all fraud. Answer (D) is incorrect. The terms "complete" and "fair" are more closely associated with the financial statements than internal control.

9.3.7. The Sarbanes-Oxley Act of 2002 (SOX) requires management of issuers to do all of the following except

A. Establish and document internal control procedures and to include in their annual reports a report on the company's internal control over financial reporting.

B. Provide a report to include a statement of management's responsibility for and assessment of internal control.

C. Provide an identification of the framework used to evaluate the effectiveness of internal control.

D. Provide a statement that the board approves changes in internal control procedures.

Answer (D) is correct. *(Publisher, adapted)*

REQUIRED: The false statement about management's responsibilities under SOX.

DISCUSSION: SOX imposes many requirements on management, boards of directors, and auditors. Section 404 applies to internal controls and reports on them. Section 404 requires management to establish and document internal control procedures and to include in their annual reports a report on the entity's internal control over financial reporting. The report is to include (1) a statement of management's responsibility for internal control, (2) management's assessment of the effectiveness of internal control as of the end of the most recent fiscal year, and (3) identification of the framework used to evaluate the effectiveness of internal control (such as the COSO report). Because of this requirement, PCAOB AS 2201 states that audit opinions are to be expressed on the effectiveness of those controls and on the financial statements. Section 301 addresses activities of the board but does not require the board to approve changes in controls.

9.3.8. Cain Company's management engaged Bell, CPA, to audit the effectiveness of Cain's internal control over financial reporting. Bell's report, which was accompanied by management's separate report presenting its written assessment about the effectiveness of internal control, described several material weaknesses and potential errors and fraudulent activities that could occur. Subsequently, management included Bell's report in its annual report to the board of directors with a statement that the cost of correcting the weaknesses would exceed the benefits. Bell should

A. Disclaim an opinion as to management's cost-benefit statement.

B. Advise the board that Bell either agrees or disagrees with management's statement.

C. Express an adverse opinion as to management's cost-benefit statement.

D. Advise both management and the board that Bell is withdrawing the opinion.

Answer (A) is correct. *(CPA, adapted)*

REQUIRED: The auditor's action when the report is included in the client's annual report with a statement that the cost of corrective action exceeds the benefits.

DISCUSSION: If the assessment accompanying the auditor's report includes a statement that the cost of corrective action exceeds the benefits of implementing new controls, the auditor should include language that disclaims an opinion on the cost-benefit statements as the last paragraph of the report. Also, given material weaknesses, the auditor should express an adverse opinion on the effectiveness of internal control.

Answer (B) is incorrect. The auditor should discuss the matter with management if (s)he believes that the statement is a material misstatement of fact. Answer (C) is incorrect. An adverse opinion should be expressed when the auditor believes that the internal control is not effective. Answer (D) is incorrect. Even assuming that the auditor believes that the statement is a material misstatement, withdrawal of the opinion is not a necessary immediate action.

9.3.9. Management of an issuer subject to SEC requirements requests the auditor to report on whether a previously reported material weakness in internal control continues to exist. The request comes 3 months after the annual audited financial statements and report on internal control were released.

A. No report may be issued on subsequent information.

B. The auditor may accept the engagement if (s)he withdraws the original report.

C. The auditor may accept the engagement if management provides a statement that the identified material weakness no longer exists.

D. The auditor may accept the engagement but must wait until the next year's audit to report the remediation of the internal control weakness.

Answer (C) is correct. *(Publisher, adapted)*

REQUIRED: The circumstances in which an auditor of an issuer may report on whether a material weakness still exists.

DISCUSSION: PCAOB AS 6115 applies to engagements solely to report on whether a previously reported material weakness continues to exist. Such an engagement is voluntary and may be performed as of any reasonable date selected by management. To perform such an engagement, the auditor should receive a written report from management that the identified material weakness no longer exists as of the date specified. The auditor then applies appropriate procedures to assess whether remediation has been accomplished.

Answer (A) is incorrect. The auditor may perform the engagement. Answer (B) is incorrect. The previous reports are not withdrawn. Answer (D) is incorrect. The report may be issued as soon as the auditor has concluded whether the material weakness has been remedied.

9.3.10. A practitioner has been engaged to examine the effectiveness of a nonissuer's internal control. The practitioner has obtained from the responsible party a written assertion about the effectiveness of internal control. The assertion is contained in a separate report that will accompany the practitioner's report and is based on control criteria issued by experts that follow due process procedures. What restrictions, if any, should the practitioner place on the use of this report?

A. This report should be restricted for use by management.

B. This report should be restricted for use by the audit committee.

C. This report should be restricted for use by a specified regulatory agency.

D. The practitioner does not need to place any restrictions on the use of this report.

Answer (D) is correct. *(CPA, adapted)*

REQUIRED: The restrictions, if any, on the use of a report on an examination of the effectiveness of internal control.

DISCUSSION: An examination of the effectiveness of internal control over financial reporting may be performed if management accepts responsibility for the effectiveness of internal control, the responsible party evaluates effectiveness using suitable criteria, and sufficient evidence exists or can be developed to support the evaluation. As part of engagement performance, the practitioner must obtain from the responsible party a written assertion about effectiveness, contained either in a separate report to accompany the practitioner's report or in a representation letter. Criteria issued by groups of experts that follow due process procedures, such as COSO, are usually suitable. Accordingly, no basis for restricting use of the report is presented.

9.3.11. Issuers are required by the PCAOB to obtain an auditor's report attesting to the effectiveness of internal control over financial reporting (AS 2201). Likewise, nonissuers may retain an auditor to issue a report on internal control in accordance with the AICPA's auditing standards (AU-C 940). Which of the following statements best characterizes the relation between these two standards?

A. The two standards have different purposes: The AICPA standards address only controls relating to the safeguarding of assets, while the PCAOB's standards relate more broadly to financial statements.

B. The AICPA standards recognize that the internal controls are the responsibility of the auditor, while the PCAOB standards recognize that the internal controls are the responsibility of management.

C. The AICPA standards accept COSO's *Internal Control – Integrated Framework* as suitable and available framework for control, while the PCAOB standards do not.

D. Both the AICPA standards and the PCAOB standards require management to provide a written assessment or assertion concerning the effectiveness of controls.

Answer (D) is correct. *(Publisher, adapted)*

REQUIRED: The representative statement about the AICPA and PCAOB standards on reporting on internal control.

DISCUSSION: Both standards require management to assess internal controls over financial reporting and provide a written assessment of the effectiveness of those controls.

Answer (A) is incorrect. Both standards define internal control over financial reporting to include the process necessary to properly record the transactions to permit the preparation of financial statements in accordance with GAAP and to detect unauthorized acquisition, use, or disposition of assets that could have a material effect on the financial statements. Answer (B) is incorrect. Both standards recognize that management is responsible for internal control over financial reporting. Answer (C) is incorrect. COSO is recognized as a suitable and available framework for both AU-C 940 and AS 2201.

9.3.12. During the audit of internal controls integrated with the audit of the financial statements, the auditor discovered a material weakness in internal control. The auditor most likely will express a(n)

A. Adverse opinion on internal control.

B. Qualified opinion on internal control.

C. Unmodified opinion on internal control.

D. Disclaimer of opinion on internal control.

Answer (A) is correct. *(Publisher, adapted)*

REQUIRED: The type of opinion expressed because of discovery of a material weakness.

DISCUSSION: Material weaknesses are significant control deficiencies that result in more than a remote chance that a material misstatement will result in the financial statements. A material weakness requires the auditor to express an adverse opinion on the effectiveness of internal control.

Answer (B) is incorrect. A qualified opinion (or disclaimer of opinion) is expressed if there is a scope limitation. Answer (C) is incorrect. An unmodified opinion is not expressed if a material weakness exists. Answer (D) is incorrect. Disclaimer of opinion (or qualified opinion) is expressed if there is a scope limitation.

9.3.13. Which of the following is a true statement concerning an engagement to examine the effectiveness of an entity's internal control over financial reporting?

A. The practitioner relies on management's assessment about the effectiveness of internal control.

B. The management evaluates the effectiveness of internal control.

C. Management relies on the practitioner's audit in making the assessment about the effectiveness of internal control.

D. Management agrees not to include the practitioner's report in a general-use document.

Answer (B) is correct. *(CPA, adapted)*

REQUIRED: The true statement concerning an engagement to examine and report on an entity's internal control.

DISCUSSION: As part of engagement performance for both AU-C 940 and AS 2201, the auditor should obtain from management a written assessment about internal control effectiveness.

Answer (A) is incorrect. The practitioner gathers evidence to test management's assessment that internal control is effective. Answer (C) is incorrect. The practitioner gathers evidence to test management's assessment that internal control is effective. Answer (D) is incorrect. The report is for general use.

9.3.14. For a nonissuer, how do the scope, procedures, and purpose of an engagement to examine the effectiveness of an entity's internal control compare with those for the consideration of internal control in a financial statement audit?

	Scope	Procedures	Purpose
A.	Similar	Different	Similar
B.	Different	Similar	Similar
C.	Different	Different	Different
D.	Different	Similar	Different

Answer (D) is correct. *(CPA, adapted)*

REQUIRED: The comparison of an engagement to examine a nonissuer's internal control and the understanding of internal control in an audit.

DISCUSSION: The purpose of an examination of internal control is to express an opinion on the effectiveness of internal control (AU-C 940). The purpose of the consideration of internal control in a financial statement audit is to enable the auditor to plan the audit. The two engagements also differ in scope. In the latter, the auditor is only required to obtain an understanding of internal control and assess the risk of material misstatement. Accordingly, the consideration in an audit is usually more limited than that undertaken to express an opinion. However, the types of procedures typically performed are similar.

9.3.15. King Corp. has received a local government grant and asked you, as a CPA, to examine the effectiveness of internal control that is required by the terms of the grant. The governmental agency responsible for the grant has prepared written criteria for such a report. During your consideration of internal control to prepare the report, you find what you consider to be a material weakness in accounting for the grant. This weakness was not covered by the criteria established by the governmental agency. What action should you take in your report to the governmental agency?

A. Include the weakness in the report even though it is not covered by the agency's criteria.

B. Do not include the weakness in the report because it is outside the criteria established by the agency.

C. Advise King Corp.'s audit committee but do not include the weakness in the report.

D. Include a comment in the report that you do not believe the criteria established by the agency are comprehensive but do not include the weakness in the report.

Answer (A) is correct. *(CPA, adapted)*

REQUIRED: The proper action when a material weakness is discovered that was not covered by the applicable criteria established by a governmental agency.

DISCUSSION: A material weakness in this context is a condition in which the design or operation of one or more of the specific internal control components does not reduce to a relatively low level the risk that misstatements due to error or fraud in amounts that would be material in relation to the applicable grant or program might occur and not be detected on a timely basis by employees in the normal course of performing their assigned functions. A material weakness is also a condition in which the lack of conformity with the regulatory agency's criteria is material in accordance with any guidelines for determining materiality that are included in such criteria. A practitioner who identifies material weaknesses in internal control that are not covered by the criteria set by the agency should include these material weaknesses in the report. (S)he does not, however, assume responsibility for the comprehensiveness of the agency's criteria.

Answer (B) is incorrect. Professional standards require that this weakness be included. Answer (C) is incorrect. Although the CPA should advise King's audit committee about the problem, (s)he should also include it in the report. Answer (D) is incorrect. It is inappropriate to comment about the criteria established by the agency.

9.3.16. An auditor reports on an examination of the effectiveness of an entity's internal control over financial reporting. If the control criteria used are established by a regulatory agency, the report should

A. State that the practitioner assumes responsibility for the comprehensiveness of the criteria if they have not been subjected to due process procedures.

B. Modify the inherent limitations paragraph.

C. Contain a statement of restriction on use if the criteria are appropriate only for a limited number of users.

D. List the control criteria.

Answer (C) is correct. *(Publisher, adapted)*

REQUIRED: The true statement about a report on internal control based on established criteria.

DISCUSSION: If the criteria were established by a regulatory agency are available and useful to users, a standard form of reporting may be used. If the control criteria are appropriate only for a limited group of users (e.g., those who participated in their establishment), the appropriate form of the report should be modified to include an alert restricting use stated in a paragraph following the opinion paragraph (AT-C 205).

Answer (A) is incorrect. The auditor assumes no responsibility for the control criteria in these circumstances. Answer (B) is incorrect. Omission or amendment of the inherent limitations paragraph should not be made. Answer (D) is incorrect. The control criteria are identified but not listed in the report.

9.4 Service Organizations

9.4.1. Which of the following is a requirement for accepting an attestation engagement to report on the controls at a service organization?

A. The description of the controls is completed prior to the signing of the engagement letter.

B. The service auditor has the competence and capability to perform the engagement.

C. The suitability of the evaluation criteria is reviewed by a third party.

D. Management agrees that the service auditor will be responsible for documenting the controls.

Answer (B) is correct. *(CPA, adapted)*

REQUIRED: The requirement for accepting an attestation engagement to report on the controls at a service organization.

DISCUSSION: A requirement for accepting or continuing an attestation engagement to report on the controls at a service organization is satisfaction of the preconditions of the engagement. A precondition common to all attestation engagements is that the engagement team and any of its external specialists collectively have the necessary competence (including knowledge of the subject matter) and capabilities. They should be able to perform the engagement in accordance with the relevant standards and legal and regulatory requirements. They also should be able to issue an appropriate practitioner's report.

Answer (A) is incorrect. One precondition of acceptance (continuation) of the engagement applies to management's description of the service organization's system (including control objectives and controls). The service auditor's preliminary knowledge of the engagement should indicate that the description will not be so limited that it is not useful. Management also must acknowledge its responsibility for the description. Answer (C) is incorrect. The criteria to be applied should be suitable and available to users. The responsible (or engaging) party selects the criteria, and the engaging party (not a third party) determines their appropriateness. Answer (D) is incorrect. Management is responsible for documenting the service organization's system.

9.4.2. AU-C 402, *Audit Considerations Relating to an Entity Using a Service Organization*, applies to a financial statement audit of an entity that uses services of another organization as part of its information system. For this purpose, the user auditor may need to obtain a service auditor's report. Which of the following is a true statement about a service auditor's report?

A. It provides the user auditor with assurance regarding whether control procedures have been implemented at the user organization.

B. It should include an opinion.

C. If it proves to be inappropriate for the user auditor's purposes, (s)he must personally perform procedures at the service organization.

D. A user auditor need not be concerned about the service auditor's professional competence.

Answer (B) is correct. *(Publisher, adapted)*

REQUIRED: The true statement about a service auditor's report regarding internal control.

DISCUSSION: A service auditor's report should be helpful in providing a sufficient understanding to plan the audit of the user organization. The service auditor's report may express an opinion on the fairness of the description of the controls implemented at the service organization and whether they were suitably designed. If the service auditor also has tested controls, the report may express an opinion on the operating effectiveness of the controls.

Answer (A) is incorrect. A service auditor's report is helpful to the user auditor in obtaining an understanding of internal control at the service organization, but it does not provide assurance regarding conditions at the user organization. Answer (C) is incorrect. Audit procedures at the service organization may be applied by the service auditor at the request of (and under the direction of) the user auditor. Answer (D) is incorrect. The user auditor should be satisfied about the service auditor's independence and professional competence.

9.4.3. A service organization processes payroll data having a material effect on the financial statements of an audit client. The client has established certain internal controls over input and output data. If the user auditor intends to rely on the operating effectiveness of the service organization's controls, which of the following statements is false?

A. The user auditor may decide that obtaining evidence of the operating effectiveness of the service organization's controls is not necessary or efficient.

B. The user auditor may need to perform tests of the service organization's controls to provide a basis for relying on the controls.

C. If certain relevant controls exist only at the service organization, the user auditor must evaluate the operating effectiveness of those controls to place reliance on the controls.

D. If certain relevant controls exist only at the service organization and a service auditor issues a report only on the design of the controls, the user auditor may use the report as a basis for reliance on the controls.

Answer (D) is correct. *(Publisher, adapted)*

REQUIRED: The false statement about reliance on the controls of a service organization that processes transactions for an audit client.

DISCUSSION: The evaluation of operating effectiveness should be based on (1) the user auditor's tests of controls at the service organization, (2) the work of another auditor that tests the controls on the user auditor's behalf, or (3) an appropriate type 2 service auditor's report. The service auditor may provide two types of reports. A type 1 report expresses an opinion on (1) the fair presentation of the management's description of the system that was designed and implemented and (2) whether the controls are suitably designed. Suitable design means the controls can attain the control objectives if they operate effectively. A type 2 report expresses not only the type 1 opinions but also an opinion on whether the controls were operating effectively (meeting the control objectives). Management must give the service auditor a written assertion about (1) the fair presentation of the system description and (2) the suitability of the design of controls (type 1) and their operating effectiveness (type 2). The system description and the opinion on it address the period covered by the tests of operating effectiveness (type 2). Accordingly, a type 1 service auditor's report is not a basis for the user auditor's reliance on the effectiveness of the service organization's controls.

Answer (A) is incorrect. The user auditor must still obtain an understanding of the controls in assessing risk. An engagement resulting in a type 1 or type 2 report provides this understanding. Answer (B) is incorrect. If the relevant controls are at the service organization and an appropriate service auditor's type 2 report is not available or is not used, the user auditor should test controls at the service organization or use another auditor to do so. Answer (C) is incorrect. The evaluation of operating effectiveness should be based on (1) the user auditor's tests of controls at the service organization, (2) the work of another auditor that tests the controls on the user auditor's behalf, or (3) an appropriate type 2 service auditor's report.

9.4.4. The activities of the user entity and the service organization have a high degree of interaction. The user auditor

A. Is not required to evaluate the service organization's controls.

B. Should obtain absolute assurance that the service organization's internal control will prevent or detect fraud or error.

C. Should not consider weaknesses in the service organization's internal control to be weaknesses in the user entity's system.

D. Need not test the service organization's internal control if the user entity has effective controls related to service organization processing.

Answer (D) is correct. *(Publisher, adapted)*

REQUIRED: The true statement about the interaction of controls at the service and user organizations.

DISCUSSION: The significance of controls at the service organization depends on the degree of interaction between its activities and those of the user entity. The degree of interaction is the extent to which the user entity can, and chooses to, implement effective controls over service organization processing. In these circumstances, the user auditor may be able to obtain an understanding from the user entity of the service organization's services that suffices to assess the RMMs. Accordingly, the user auditor need not obtain a type 1 or type 2 report.

Answer (A) is incorrect. When controls of both the user and the service organization interact, the service organization's controls should be evaluated in conjunction with the user's. Answer (B) is incorrect. Reasonable, not absolute, assurance should be obtained that the service organization's controls will prevent or detect fraud or error. Answer (C) is incorrect. The user auditor should consider the combination of controls at the user entity and service organization.

9.4.5. Green, CPA, is auditing the financial statements of Ajax Co. Ajax uses the DP Service Center to process its payroll. DP's financial statements are audited by Blue, CPA, who recently issued a report on DP's policies and procedures regarding the processing of other entities' transactions. In considering whether Blue's report is satisfactory for Green's purposes, Green should

A. Make inquiries about Blue's professional reputation.

B. Not rely on DP's controls.

C. Review the audit plan followed by Blue.

D. Perform tests of controls at the DP Service Center.

Answer (A) is correct. *(CPA, adapted)*

REQUIRED: The procedure to determine whether a service auditor's report is satisfactory for the user auditor's purposes.

DISCUSSION: The user auditor should be satisfied about (1) the service auditor's professional competence and (2) the adequacy of the standards governing the type 1 or type 2 report.

Answer (B) is incorrect. If the service auditor issues a type 2 report, the user auditor may be able to rely on DP's controls. Answer (C) is incorrect. The user auditor need not review the audit plan of the service auditor. Answer (D) is incorrect. If the user auditor determines that the service auditor's report is satisfactory for the user auditor's purposes, no tests of controls need be performed at the service organization.

9.4.6. Payroll Data Co. (PDC) processes payroll transactions for a retailer. Cook, CPA, is engaged to issue a report on PDC's internal controls implemented as of a specific date. These controls are relevant to the retailer's internal control, so Cook's report may be useful in providing the retailer's independent auditor with information necessary to plan a financial statement audit. Cook's report should

A. Contain a disclaimer of opinion on the operating effectiveness of PDC's controls.

B. State whether PDC's controls were suitably designed to achieve the retailer's objectives.

C. Identify PDC's controls relevant to specific financial statement assertions.

D. Disclose Cook's assessed risks of material misstatement for PDC.

Answer (A) is correct. *(CPA, adapted)*

REQUIRED: The components of a service auditor's report.

DISCUSSION: Service auditors may report (1) on the fairness of management's description of the controls and whether the controls have been implemented and are suitably designed (type 1 report) or (2) additionally on operating effectiveness (type 2 report). The type 1 report should include a disclaimer of opinion related to operating effectiveness of the controls.

Answer (B) is incorrect. The report should state whether PDC's controls were suitably designed to provide reasonable assurance of achieving the specified control objectives of the service organization. Answer (C) is incorrect. Specific controls relevant to specific financial statement assertions need not be identified in the service auditor's report. Answer (D) is incorrect. The assessed RMMs are not disclosed.

STUDY UNIT TEN
EVIDENCE -- OBJECTIVES AND NATURE

The auditor should design and perform audit procedures to obtain sufficient appropriate audit evidence. The objective is to be able to draw reasonable conclusions as a basis for the auditor's opinion. Thus, most audit work involves obtaining and evaluating audit evidence. Audit evidence is obtained by performing (1) risk assessment procedures and (2) further audit procedures. **Risk assessment procedures** are performed to obtain an understanding of the entity and its environment, including internal control, to assess the risks of material misstatement (RMMs) at the statement and relevant assertion levels. **Further audit procedures** consist of (1) tests of the operating effectiveness of controls and (2) substantive procedures (tests of details) and substantive analytical procedures designed to detect material misstatements at the assertion level. Audit procedures include (1) inquiry, (2) inspection, (3) observation, (4) confirmation, (5) recalculation, (6) reperformance, and (7) analytical procedures.

GAAS require the auditor to obtain **reasonable assurance** about whether the statements as a whole are free from material misstatement. It is obtained when sufficient appropriate evidence reduces audit risk to an acceptable low level.

Sufficiency measures the quantity of evidence. It is affected by (1) the assessment of the RMMs and (2) the quality of evidence. **Appropriateness** measures the quality of evidence. Quality depends on relevance and reliability in supporting the auditor's conclusions. **Relevance** is the logical connection of information with the purpose of the audit procedure and any assertion considered. The **reliability** of information used as audit evidence is affected by (1) its source, (2) its nature, and (3) how it is obtained. These circumstances include controls over its preparation and maintenance.

QUESTIONS

10.1 Nature, Sufficiency, and Appropriateness

10.1.1. Which of the following is a false statement about the relationship of financial statement assertions and audit procedures?

A. The relationship between financial statement assertions and audit procedures should be one-to-one.

B. Audit procedures should be developed in light of financial statement assertions about the financial statement components.

C. Selection of tests of financial statement assertions should depend upon the understanding of internal control.

D. The auditor should resolve any substantial doubt about any of management's relevant financial statement assertions.

Answer (A) is correct. *(Publisher, adapted)*

REQUIRED: The false statement about financial statement assertions and audit procedures.

DISCUSSION: Some auditing procedures may relate to more than one assertion. But a combination of auditing procedures may be needed to test a single relevant assertion because audit evidence from different sources or of a different nature may be relevant to the same assertion. For example, when relating controls to assertions, the auditor may determine that multiple controls are needed to address a risk and the related assertion.

Answer (B) is incorrect. Financial statement assertions should be considered when the auditor develops audit procedures. Answer (C) is incorrect. The understanding of internal control and the assessed RMMs affect the nature, timing, and extent of the auditor's substantive procedures (AU-C 315 and AS 2110). Answer (D) is incorrect. A relevant assertion has a reasonable possibility of containing misstatements that could materially misstate the financial statements. All substantial doubts about relevant financial statement assertions should be resolved before an opinion is formed. Otherwise, the auditor should modify the opinion or disclaim an opinion.

10.1.2. Most of the auditor's work in forming an opinion on financial statements consists of

A. Understanding internal control.

B. Obtaining and evaluating audit evidence.

C. Examining cash transactions.

D. Comparing recorded accountability with assets.

Answer (B) is correct. *(CPA, adapted)*

REQUIRED: The principal activity of an auditor in forming an opinion.

DISCUSSION: According to AU-C 500, *Audit Evidence*, most of the auditor's work in forming an opinion on financial statements consists of obtaining and evaluating audit evidence. Audit evidence is the information used by the auditor in drawing the conclusions on which the auditor's opinion is based. It includes the information contained in the accounting records and sources of information other than accounting records.

Answer (A) is incorrect. Understanding internal control is an example of obtaining and evaluating audit evidence. Answer (C) is incorrect. Examining cash transactions is an example of obtaining and evaluating audit evidence. Answer (D) is incorrect. Comparing recorded accountability with assets is an example of obtaining and evaluating audit evidence.

10.1.3. Which of the following statements about audit evidence is true?

A. To be appropriate, audit evidence should be either persuasive or relevant but need not be both.

B. The sufficiency and appropriateness of audit evidence is a matter of professional judgment.

C. The difficulty and expense of obtaining audit evidence about an account balance is a valid basis for omitting the test.

D. A client's accounting records can be sufficient audit evidence to support the financial statements.

Answer (B) is correct. *(CPA, adapted)*

REQUIRED: The true statement about audit evidence.

DISCUSSION: The auditor exercises professional judgment when forming a conclusion about whether sufficient appropriate audit evidence has been obtained to reduce audit risk to an acceptably low level. Sufficiency measures the quantity of audit evidence. Appropriateness measures its quality (relevance and reliability). To form this conclusion, the auditor considers all relevant evidence, regardless of whether it corroborates or contradicts the assertions in the statements.

Answer (A) is incorrect. To be appropriate, audit evidence should be relevant and reliable. Also, because of the inherent limitations of the audit, most audit evidence is persuasive rather than conclusive. Answer (C) is incorrect. Although the cost of obtaining evidence and its usefulness should be rationally related, the matter of difficulty, time, or cost is not in itself a valid basis for (1) omitting a procedure when no alternative exists or (2) being satisfied with less than persuasive evidence. Answer (D) is incorrect. Accounting records should be supported by corroborating information.

10.1.4. The primary difference between an audit of the balance sheet and an audit of the income statement is that the audit of the income statement deals with the verification of

A. Transactions.

B. Authorizations.

C. Costs.

D. Cutoffs.

Answer (A) is correct. *(CPA, adapted)*

REQUIRED: The difference between the audit of the income statement and the balance sheet.

DISCUSSION: The audit of the income statement focuses on the propriety of handling transactions because most income statement accounts represent large volumes of transactions. The audit of the balance sheet concentrates on verification of account balances.

Answer (B) is incorrect. All transactions must be authorized. Answer (C) is incorrect. The auditor is equally concerned with the costs reflected in the income statement and the balance sheet. Answer (D) is incorrect. Cutoffs to verify that only current period transactions are reflected apply to both statements.

10.1.5. The appropriateness of evidence available to an auditor is least likely to be affected by the

A. Relevance of such evidence to the financial statement assertion being investigated.

B. Relationship of the preparer of such evidence to the entity being audited.

C. Timeliness of such audit evidence.

D. Sampling method employed by the auditor to obtain a sample of such evidence.

Answer (D) is correct. *(Publisher, adapted)*

REQUIRED: The factor that does not affect the appropriateness of audit evidence.

DISCUSSION: Appropriate audit evidence is relevant and reliable. Evidence is usually more reliable when it (1) is obtained from independent sources; (2) is generated internally under effective internal control; (3) is obtained directly by the auditor; (4) is in documentary form, whether paper, electronic, or other medium; and (5) consists of original documents. The sample selection method does not affect the appropriateness of evidence as long as the sample is representative of the population.

Answer (A) is incorrect. Appropriate evidence should be reliable and relevant. Answer (B) is incorrect. The independence of the source (or preparer) of the evidence from the auditee provides greater assurance of its reliability. Answer (C) is incorrect. The relevance and value of information is reduced by the passage of time. Appropriate evidence must be relevant.

10.1.6. In gathering evidence in the performance of substantive procedures, the auditor most likely

A. Uses the test month approach.

B. Relies on persuasive rather than conclusive evidence in the majority of cases.

C. Considers the client's documentary evidence less reliable than evidence gathered orally by inquiry of management.

D. Expresses an adverse opinion if (s)he has substantial doubt as to any assertion of material significance.

Answer (B) is correct. *(Publisher, adapted)*

REQUIRED: The correct assumption about the performance of substantive procedures.

DISCUSSION: To be appropriate, audit evidence should be relevant and reliable. Also, because of the inherent limitations of the audit, most audit evidence is persuasive rather than conclusive. However, although the cost of obtaining evidence and its usefulness should be rationally related, the matter of difficulty, time, or cost is not in itself a valid basis for (1) omitting a procedure when no alternative exists or (2) being satisfied with less than persuasive evidence.

Answer (A) is incorrect. Selecting specific months for detail testing is not required. "Test month approach" is a nonsense term. Answer (C) is incorrect. Documentary evidence is more reliable than evidence obtained orally. For example, a written record of a meeting made when the meeting occurred is more reliable than a subsequent oral statement of the matters discussed. Answer (D) is incorrect. The auditor must be convinced that the financial statements as a whole are not presented fairly before (s)he expresses an adverse opinion.

10.1.7. AU-C 500 describes five generalizations about the reliability of evidence. The situations given below indicate the relative degrees of assurance provided by two types of evidence obtained in different situations. Which describes an exception to one of the generalizations?

A. The auditor has obtained greater assurance about the balance of sales at Plant A, where (s)he has made limited tests of details because of effective internal control, than at Plant B, where (s)he has made extensive tests of details because of ineffective internal control.

B. The auditor's computation of interest payable on outstanding bonds provides greater assurance than reliance on the client's calculation.

C. The report of an auditor's specialist regarding the valuation of a collection of paintings held as an investment provides greater assurance than the auditor's physical observation of the paintings.

D. The schedule of insurance coverage obtained from the company's insurance agent provides greater assurance than one prepared by the internal audit staff.

Answer (C) is correct. *(Publisher, adapted)*

REQUIRED: The exception to the generalizations about reliability of audit evidence.

DISCUSSION: Appropriate audit evidence is relevant and reliable. Evidence is usually more reliable when it (1) is obtained from independent sources; (2) is generated internally under effective internal control; (3) is obtained directly by the auditor; (4) is in documentary form, whether paper, electronic, or another medium; and (5) consists of original documents. Preference for the report of an auditor's specialist over the auditor's physical observation of works of art is acceptable because the auditor is not expected to have such expertise. Physical observation provides evidence of the existence of assets but often does not verify their value, ownership, cost, or condition. Consequently, the generalization in favor of the auditor's direct knowledge is overcome in this case.

Answer (A) is incorrect. The RMMs should be lower when control is effective. The lower the assessed RMMs, the less audit evidence is likely to be required. Answer (B) is incorrect. The auditor's direct knowledge should be preferred to indirect knowledge. Answer (D) is incorrect. Information obtained from independent sources is more reliable than that prepared by the client's staff.

10.1.8. Which of the following statements about evidence is true?

A. Appropriate evidence supporting management's assertions should be conclusive rather than merely persuasive.

B. Effective internal control contributes little to the reliability of the evidence created within the entity.

C. The cost of obtaining evidence is not an important consideration to an auditor in deciding what evidence should be obtained.

D. A client's accounting records cannot be considered sufficient appropriate audit evidence on which to base the auditor's opinion.

Answer (D) is correct. *(CPA, adapted)*

REQUIRED: The true statement about evidence.

DISCUSSION: Audit evidence consists of accounting records (initial entries and supporting records, such as ledgers, worksheets, and spreadsheets) and other information (minutes of meetings, confirmations, information obtained by inquiry, etc.). But accounting records alone do not provide sufficient appropriate evidence as a basis for an opinion on the financial statements.

Answer (A) is incorrect. The auditor must usually rely on evidence that is merely persuasive. Answer (B) is incorrect. The more effective internal control, the more assurance it provides about the reliability of the accounting data and financial statements. Answer (C) is incorrect. The auditor considers the cost of evidence relative to its usefulness. However, although the cost of obtaining evidence and its usefulness should be rationally related, the matter of difficulty, time, or cost is not in itself a valid basis for (1) omitting a procedure when no alternative exists or (2) being satisfied with less than persuasive evidence.

10.1.9. The most reliable forms of documentary evidence are those documents that are

A. Prenumbered.

B. Internally generated.

C. Easily duplicated.

D. Authorized by a responsible official.

Answer (D) is correct. *(CMA, adapted)*

REQUIRED: The most reliable forms of documentary evidence.

DISCUSSION: Documents generated externally by independent sources are more reliable than those produced by the auditee. However, the reliability of internal evidence is enhanced if it is subject to effective control. Accordingly, authorization by an appropriate party lends credibility to a document because it increases the probability that the underlying transaction is valid.

Answer (A) is incorrect. The use of prenumbered and sequentially issued documents is an effective control, but such documents may be accessible to an employee who is perpetrating fraud. Answer (B) is incorrect. Internally generated documents are readily available to those attempting to commit fraud. Answer (C) is incorrect. Easily duplicated documents are readily available to those attempting to commit fraud.

10.1.10. Which of the following procedures would provide the most reliable audit evidence?

A. Inquiries of the client's internal audit staff held in private.

B. Inspection of prenumbered client purchase orders filed in the vouchers payable department.

C. Analytical procedures performed by the auditor on the entity's trial balance.

D. Inspection of bank statements obtained directly from the client's financial institution.

Answer (D) is correct. *(CPA, adapted)*

REQUIRED: The procedure that provides the most reliable audit evidence.

DISCUSSION: When documentation is prepared solely by client personnel, its reliability is less than that prepared by the auditor or an independent party. Ordinarily, the most reliable documentation is created outside the entity and has never been within the client's control, e.g., statements obtained from the bank, letters from attorneys, and letters from insurance brokers.

Answer (A) is incorrect. The internal audit staff is not independent. Answer (B) is incorrect. The purchase orders are internally generated. Answer (C) is incorrect. Analytical procedures are based on the entity's internal records.

10.1.11. Observation is considered a reliable audit procedure but one that is limited in usefulness. However, it is used in a number of different audit situations. Which of the following statements is true regarding observation as an audit technique?

A. It is the most effective audit methodology to use in filling out internal control questionnaires.

B. It is the most persuasive methodology to learn how transactions are really processed during the period under audit.

C. It is most persuasive about the performance of a process but is limited to the moment in time at which the observation takes place.

D. It is the most persuasive audit technique for determining if fraud has occurred.

Answer (C) is correct. *(CIA, adapted)*

REQUIRED: The true statement about the audit procedure of observation.

DISCUSSION: Observation consists of looking at a process or procedure being performed by others. It provides audit evidence about the process or procedure but is limited to that moment in time by the fact that the act of being observed may affect how the process or procedure is performed.

Answer (A) is incorrect. Interviews are the most effective method to fill out questionnaires. The interview results should be supplemented with observations. Answer (B) is incorrect. Observation provides information on how transactions are processed at one moment in time, not how they are processed throughout the period under audit investigation. Answer (D) is incorrect. The auditor very seldom is able to observe a fraud.

10.1.12. Assuming a low assessed risk of material misstatement, which of the following audit procedures would be least likely to be performed?

A. Physical inspection of a sample of inventory.

B. Search for unrecorded cash receipts.

C. Obtaining a client representation letter.

D. Confirmation of accounts receivable.

Answer (B) is correct. *(CPA, adapted)*

REQUIRED: The procedure least necessary when the RMM is low.

DISCUSSION: GAAS do not specifically require a search for unrecorded cash receipts. Given a low assessed RMM, the auditor might decide to reduce the audit effort devoted to substantive tests of assertions about cash and omit the procedure.

Answer (A) is incorrect. Observation of inventories is generally required. An auditor who expresses an opinion when inventories have not been observed should justify the opinion expressed. Answer (C) is incorrect. AU-C 580, *Written Representations*, requires written representations from management. Answer (D) is incorrect. According to AU-C 505, *External Confirmations*, confirmation of accounts receivable is generally required. A low RMM might allow the auditor to send negative (instead of positive) confirmations.

10.1.13. Which of the following presumptions is least likely to relate to the reliability of audit evidence?

A. The more effective internal control is, the more assurance it provides about the accounting data and financial statements.

B. An auditor's opinion is formed within a reasonable time to achieve a balance between benefit and cost.

C. Evidence obtained from independent sources outside the entity is more reliable than evidence secured solely within the entity.

D. The auditor's direct personal knowledge obtained through observation and inspection is more persuasive than information obtained indirectly.

Answer (B) is correct. *(CPA, adapted)*

REQUIRED: The presumption not relating to the reliability of audit evidence.

DISCUSSION: Appropriate audit evidence is relevant and reliable. Evidence is usually more reliable when it (1) is obtained from independent sources; (2) is generated internally under effective internal control; (3) is obtained directly by the auditor; (4) is in documentary form, whether paper, electronic, or other medium; and (5) consists of original documents. However, the need for (1) reporting to be timely and (2) maintaining a balance between benefit and cost are inherent limitations of the audit. Thus, for the opinion to be relevant, it must be formed within a reasonable period of time.

Answer (A) is incorrect. The more effective internal control is, the more assurance it provides about the reliability of the accounting data and financial statements. Answer (C) is incorrect. Evidence obtained from independent sources outside an entity provides greater assurance of reliability than evidence secured solely within the entity. Answer (D) is incorrect. The auditor's direct personal knowledge obtained through physical examination, observation, computation, and inspection is more persuasive than information obtained indirectly.

10.1.14. Which of the following elements ultimately determines the specific auditing procedures that are necessary in the circumstances to provide a reasonable basis for an opinion?

A. Auditor judgment.

B. Materiality.

C. Audit risk.

D. Reasonable assurance.

Answer (A) is correct. *(CPA, adapted)*

REQUIRED: The ultimate determinant of specific auditing procedures.

DISCUSSION: Professional judgment involves applying relevant knowledge and experience to the facts and circumstances of an audit. The auditor exercises judgment to (1) interpret ethical requirements and GAAS and (2) make informed decisions, for example, about the sufficiency and appropriateness of audit evidence. The auditor also plans and performs the audit with professional skepticism. This is an attitude that includes (1) a questioning mind, (2) being alert to possible misstatements, and (3) a critical assessment of audit evidence (AU-C 500). Thus, judgment is required to select the specific auditing procedures needed to obtain that evidence.

Answer (B) is incorrect. Materiality is among the considerations in exercising professional judgment. Answer (C) is incorrect. Audit risk is among the considerations in exercising professional judgment. Answer (D) is incorrect. The audit objective is to obtain reasonable assurance about whether the financial statements are free of material misstatement, whether due to fraud or error, to enable the auditor to express an opinion. However, whether such assurance has been obtained is ultimately a matter of auditor judgment.

10.1.15. You have been assigned to audit the maintenance department of an organization. Which of the following is likely to produce the least reliable audit evidence?

A. Notes on discussions with mechanics in the maintenance operation.

B. A schedule comparing actual maintenance expenses with budgeted expenses and those of the prior period and disclosing important differences.

C. A narrative covering review of user reports on maintenance service.

D. An analysis of changes in certain maintenance department ratios.

Answer (A) is correct. *(CIA, adapted)*

REQUIRED: The procedure that is likely to produce the least reliable evidence in an audit of a maintenance department.

DISCUSSION: Although representations by personnel of the auditee are evidence, auditor observation and analysis of documents provide more reliable evidence.

Answer (B) is incorrect. The comparison provides more reliable evidence relative to the maintenance department's operations. Such documentary evidence is presumably prepared independently of the audited department. Answer (C) is incorrect. Reports by users of maintenance services are likewise independent evidence. They are of interest to internal auditors because they bear on the quality of performance. Answer (D) is incorrect. Analytical procedures are typically considered more reliable than representations by client personnel.

10.1.16. If an auditor conducts an audit of financial statements in accordance with applicable auditing standards, which of the following will the auditor most likely detect?

A. Misposting of recorded transactions.

B. Unrecorded transactions.

C. Forgery.

D. Collusive fraud.

Answer (A) is correct. *(Publisher, adapted)*

REQUIRED: The fraud or error most likely to be detected.

DISCUSSION: Until a transaction is recorded, leaving an audit trail, standard audit procedures are often ineffective. A misposting of previously recorded transactions is therefore the most likely item to be detected.

Answer (B) is incorrect. Unrecorded transactions leave no audit trail. Answer (C) is incorrect. Auditors usually are not qualified to detect forgery. Answer (D) is incorrect. The possibility of collusion is an inherent limitation of internal control. The purpose of segregation of duties can be circumvented if two or more persons agree to commit fraud.

10.1.17. Each of the following might, by itself, form a valid basis for an auditor to decide to omit a procedure except for the

A. Difficulty and cost involved in testing a particular item.

B. Assessment of the risks of material misstatement at a low level.

C. Inherent risk involved.

D. Relationship between the cost of obtaining evidence and its usefulness.

Answer (A) is correct. *(CPA, adapted)*

REQUIRED: The consideration not a valid reason for omission of an audit procedure.

DISCUSSION: The costs and benefits of obtaining evidence should have a rational relationship. However, the difficulty, time, or cost required to perform a procedure is not in itself a valid reason for its omission if no alternative is available. Such matters also do not justify being satisfied with audit evidence that is less than persuasive (AU-C 500).

Answer (B) is incorrect. The lower the RMMs, the higher the acceptable audit risk and the greater the justification for omitting a substantive procedure. Answer (C) is incorrect. A procedure might be omitted if the susceptibility to material misstatement of an assertion before consideration of related controls is slight. Answer (D) is incorrect. The cost of obtaining evidence and its usefulness should have a rational relationship.

10.1.18. Before performing substantive analytical procedures at an interim date prior to the balance sheet date, an auditor should

A. Obtain audit evidence about the operating effectiveness of controls.

B. Determine that the accounts selected for interim testing are not material to the financial statements taken as a whole.

C. Consider whether the amounts of the year-end balances selected for interim testing are reasonably predictable.

D. Obtain written representations from management that all financial records and related data will be made available.

Answer (C) is correct. *(CPA, adapted)*

REQUIRED: The auditor action prior to applying analytical procedures at an interim date.

DISCUSSION: Among the auditor's considerations is whether the year-end balances of accounts on which substantive analytical procedures are performed at an interim date are reasonably predictable as to amount, relative significance, and composition.

Answer (A) is incorrect. Relying on controls is not required. Answer (B) is incorrect. The accounts selected for interim testing are likely to be material. Answer (D) is incorrect. Written representations will be obtained from the client regardless of when testing is done.

10.1.19. A client uses a suspense account for unresolved questions whose final accounting has not been determined. If a balance remains in the suspense account at year-end, the auditor would be most concerned about

A. Suspense debits that management believes will benefit future operations.

B. Suspense debits that the auditor verifies will have realizable value to the client.

C. Suspense credits that management believes should be classified as "current liability."

D. Suspense credits that the auditor determines to be customer deposits.

Answer (A) is correct. *(CPA, adapted)*

REQUIRED: The accounting disposition of year-end suspense items most troublesome for an auditor.

DISCUSSION: Although the auditor must evaluate relevant assertions about all accounts, the greatest risks are overstated assets and understated liabilities. The unverified suspense debits represent assets that may not exist.

Answer (B) is incorrect. The auditor has verified that the debits (assets) have future value. Thus, they are properly classified as assets. Answer (C) is incorrect. For each suspense credit, a liability is reflected. Consequently, liabilities are not understated. Answer (D) is incorrect. For each suspense credit, a liability is reflected. Consequently, liabilities are not understated.

10.2 External Confirmations

10.2.1. The negative request form of accounts receivable confirmation may be used when the

	Risk of Material Misstatement is	Number of Small Balances is	Consideration by the Recipient is
A.	Low	Many	Likely
B.	Low	Few	Unlikely
C.	High	Few	Likely
D.	High	Many	Likely

Answer (A) is correct. *(CPA, adapted)*

REQUIRED: The conditions appropriate for use of negative accounts receivable confirmation.

DISCUSSION: AU-C 505 states, "Negative confirmations provide less persuasive audit evidence than positive confirmations. Accordingly, the auditor should not use negative confirmation requests as the sole substantive audit procedure to address an assessed risk of material misstatement at the assertion level unless all of the following are present: (1) the auditor has assessed the risk of material misstatement as low and has obtained sufficient appropriate audit evidence regarding the operating effectiveness of controls relevant to the assertion; (2) the population of items subject to negative confirmation procedures comprises a large number of small, homogeneous account balances, transactions, or conditions; (3) a very low exception rate is expected; and (4) the auditor is not aware of circumstances or conditions that would cause recipients of negative confirmation requests to disregard such requests." Returned negative confirmations provide evidence about assertions in the financial statements, but unreturned negative confirmation requests rarely provide significant evidence about assertions other than some aspects of existence. Unreturned requests provide no explicit evidence that the intended parties received them and verified the correctness of the information stated.

10.2.2. In confirming accounts receivable, an auditor decided to confirm customers' account balances rather than individual invoices. Which of the following most likely will be included with the client's confirmation letter?

A. An auditor-prepared letter explaining that a nonresponse may cause an inference that the account balance is correct.

B. A client-prepared letter reminding the customer that a nonresponse will cause a second request to be sent.

C. An auditor-prepared letter requesting the customer to supply missing and incorrect information directly to the client.

D. A client-prepared statement of account showing the details of the customer's account balance.

Answer (D) is correct. *(CPA, adapted)*

REQUIRED: The nature of a confirmation request regarding an accounts receivable balance.

DISCUSSION: A confirmation request should contain management's authorization to the confirming party to respond. Also, an external confirmation should be requested by the client because the receiving party has no relationship with the client's auditor. In confirming the customer's account balance, display of the details of the balance will likely help the customer in reconciling the amount and may increase response rates. The auditor, however, will send the request directly to the customer, who will be requested to send the response directly to the auditor.

Answer (A) is incorrect. The request should come from the client. Answer (B) is incorrect. No threats should be included in a confirmation. Answer (C) is incorrect. The response should go directly to the auditor.

10.2.3. Which of the following statements is an auditor most likely to add to the negative form of confirmation of accounts receivable to encourage timely consideration by the recipient?

A. "This is not a request for payment; remittances should not be sent to our auditors in the enclosed envelope."

B. "Report any differences on the enclosed statement directly to our auditors; no reply is necessary if this amount agrees with your records."

C. "If you do not report any differences within 15 days, it will be assumed that this statement is correct."

D. "The following invoices have been selected for confirmation and represent amounts that are overdue."

Answer (C) is correct. *(CPA, adapted)*

REQUIRED: The statement to encourage timely consideration of a negative form of receivables confirmation.

DISCUSSION: An issue with respect to negative confirmation requests is whether recipients are likely to disregard them (AU-C 505). Providing a time limit encourages a recipient to respond in a timely manner.

Answer (A) is incorrect. Although the statement is appropriate for a confirmation, it does not encourage a timely response. Answer (B) is incorrect. Although the statement is appropriate for a confirmation, it does not encourage a timely response. Answer (D) is incorrect. Noting that an amount is overdue could discourage a customer from replying in a timely manner.

10.2.4. Two assertions for which confirmation of accounts receivable balances provides primary evidence are

A. Completeness and valuation.

B. Valuation and rights and obligations.

C. Rights and obligations and existence.

D. Existence and completeness.

Answer (C) is correct. *(CPA, adapted)*

REQUIRED: The assertions tested by confirming accounts receivable.

DISCUSSION: An external confirmation is audit evidence obtained as a direct, written response from a third party (the confirming party). External confirmation of accounts receivable is required unless (1) the overall account balance is not material; (2) the procedure would be ineffective; or (3) the assessed RMM at the assertion level is low, and other planned substantive procedures address the assessed risk. External confirmations are frequently relevant to assertions about account balances. Assertions about account balances at period end include (1) existence, (2) rights and obligations, (3) completeness, and (4) valuation and allocation. Assertions about existence address whether assets, liabilities, or equity interests of the entity exist. Assertions about rights and obligations address whether (1) the entity holds or controls the rights to assets, and (2) liabilities are the obligations of the entity. Thus, external confirmation provides relevant evidence that receivables exist and that the client has the right of collection. The valuation and allocation assertion states whether items have been included in the financial statements at appropriate amounts, and any valuation or allocation adjustments are recorded appropriately. However, external confirmation provides less relevant evidence for the valuation of gross accounts receivable balances than for the valuation of the related allowance accounts. The completeness assertion states whether all items that should be recorded are recorded, for example, all receivables. Unrecorded receivables are usually not discovered by confirmation. Thus, confirmation provides less relevant evidence about the valuation assertion and the completeness assertion than about the existence and rights and obligations assertions.

10.2.5. Auditors may use positive or negative forms of confirmation requests. An auditor most likely will use

A. The positive form to confirm all balances regardless of size.

B. The negative form for small balances.

C. A combination of the two forms, with the positive form used for trade balances and the negative form for other balances.

D. The positive form when the assessed risk of material misstatement is acceptably low and the negative form when it is unacceptably high.

Answer (B) is correct. *(CPA, adapted)*

REQUIRED: The true statement about the use of positive and negative confirmations.

DISCUSSION: Negative confirmation requests may be used to reduce audit risk to an acceptably low level when (1) the assessed risk of material misstatement is low, (2) a large number of small homogeneous balances is involved, (3) a very low exception rate is expected, (4) the auditor has no reason to believe that the recipients of the requests are unlikely to consider them, and (5) the auditor has obtained sufficient appropriate evidence about the effectiveness of relevant controls (AU-C 505). A combination of the two forms is often used.

Answer (A) is incorrect. The negative form is often used, e.g., when many small balances are involved. Answer (C) is incorrect. The nature of the balances does not dictate the form used. Answer (D) is incorrect. The positive form is used when the assessed risk of material misstatement is high.

10.2.6. In the confirmation of accounts receivable, the auditor would most likely

A. Request confirmation of a sample of the inactive accounts.

B. Seek to obtain positive confirmations for at least 50% of the total dollar amount of the receivables.

C. Require confirmation of all receivables from agencies of the federal government.

D. Require that confirmation requests be sent within 1 month of the fiscal year end.

Answer (A) is correct. *(CPA, adapted)*

REQUIRED: The most likely auditor action regarding confirmation of receivables.

DISCUSSION: When the risk of material misstatement at the relevant assertion level is at an acceptably low level, the auditor will confirm only a sample of receivables. The sample should include inactive or past due accounts. If such accounts are to be regarded as assets, acknowledgment of the debts must be obtained. Confirming inactive accounts may also detect lapping or establish what amounts are in dispute.

Answer (B) is incorrect. GAAS do not establish a percentage dollar amount to be confirmed. Confirming all large balances, however, may account for a substantial dollar value of the receivables. Answer (C) is incorrect. The record systems and operating procedures of governmental agencies may not permit confirmation. Answer (D) is incorrect. When internal control is effective, confirmations may be sent more than 1 month before year end.

10.2.7. Negative confirmation of accounts receivable is less effective than positive confirmation of accounts receivable because

A. A majority of recipients usually lack the willingness to respond objectively.

B. Some recipients may report incorrect balances that require extensive follow-up.

C. The auditor cannot infer that all nonrespondents have verified their account information.

D. Negative confirmations do not produce evidence that is statistically quantifiable.

Answer (C) is correct. *(CPA, adapted)*

REQUIRED: The reason negative confirmations are less effective than positive confirmations.

DISCUSSION: A failure to reply is assumed to indicate the debtor's agreement when negative confirmations are used. Thus, no auditor follow-up occurs, and no explicit evidence is provided that the intended parties received their requests and verified the information. Thus, unreturned negative confirmation requests rarely provide significant evidence about assertions other than existence. Positive confirmations require a reply, whether or not the debtor agrees with the balance. Alternative procedures are applied to the nonresponses to obtain the evidence necessary to reduce audit risk to an acceptable level (AU-C 505).

Answer (A) is incorrect. The assumed lack of objectivity to which this answer refers would affect both forms of confirmation. Answer (B) is incorrect. Inaccurate reporting would affect positive and negative confirmations. Answer (D) is incorrect. Both forms of confirmation produce evidence that is quantifiable.

10.2.8. Confirmation of accounts receivable is a generally accepted auditing procedure. The presumption is that an auditor will request confirmation of accounts receivable. Confirmation is necessary when

A. Based on prior years' audit experience, response rates will be inadequate.

B. Based on experience with similar engagements, responses are expected to be unreliable.

C. The combined assessed level of inherent and control risk is high.

D. The accounts receivable are immaterial.

Answer (C) is correct. *(Publisher, adapted)*

REQUIRED: The condition not sufficient to overcome the presumption that an auditor will confirm accounts receivable.

DISCUSSION: The presumption may be overcome if (1) the risk of material misstatement (the combined assessed inherent risk and control risk) is low and (2) other procedures address the assessed risk for the relevant assertions. An auditor who has decided not to request confirmations must document how the presumption was overcome.

Answer (A) is incorrect. The presumption may be overcome if confirmations would be ineffective. Answer (B) is incorrect. The presumption may be overcome if confirmations would be ineffective. Answer (D) is incorrect. Confirmations are not required if accounts receivable are not material to the financial statements.

10.2.9. To reduce the risks associated with accepting fax responses to requests for confirmations of accounts receivable, an auditor most likely would

A. Examine the shipping documents that provide evidence for the existence assertion.

B. Verify the sources and contents of the faxes in telephone calls to the senders.

C. Consider the faxes to be nonresponses and evaluate them as unadjusted differences.

D. Inspect the faxes for forgeries or alterations and consider them to be acceptable if none are noted.

Answer (B) is correct. *(CPA, adapted)*

REQUIRED: The procedure to reduce the risk of accepting false confirmations by fax.

DISCUSSION: Because establishing the source of a fax is often difficult, the auditor should ensure that the confirmations returned by fax are genuine. One way is to verify the sources by following up with telephone calls to the senders.

Answer (A) is incorrect. The purpose of the confirmation is to test the existence of the receivable by direct communication with the debtor. Answer (C) is incorrect. A fax is considered a valid response if the source can be verified. Answer (D) is incorrect. Faxes may not be signed. Furthermore, the auditor is unlikely to be qualified to recognize forgeries.

10.2.10. During the process of confirming receivables as of December 31, Year 1, a positive confirmation was returned indicating the "balance owed as of December 31 was paid on January 9, Year 2." The auditor would most likely

A. Determine whether any changes in the account occurred between January 1 and January 9, Year 2.

B. Determine whether a customary trade discount was taken by the customer.

C. Reconfirm the zero balance as of January 10, Year 2.

D. Verify that the amount was received.

Answer (D) is correct. *(CPA, adapted)*

REQUIRED: The auditor action when a confirmation response states that the year-end balance was paid.

DISCUSSION: Responses to confirmation requests that involve significant differences are investigated by the auditor. Others are delegated to client employees with a request that explanations be given to the auditor. Such differences often arise because of recent cash payments. In that event, the auditor should trace remittances to verify that stated amounts were received.

Answer (A) is incorrect. The auditor wishes to confirm a year-end balance, not transactions in the subsequent period. Also, the reply does not suggest a discrepancy in the account. Answer (B) is incorrect. The auditor is more concerned with confirming the balance due at year end than with whether a customer took a discount. Answer (C) is incorrect. Reconfirmation is not required.

10.2.11. An auditor confirms a representative number of open accounts receivable as of December 31 and investigates respondents' exceptions and comments. By this procedure, the auditor would be most likely to learn of which of the following?

A. One of the cashiers has been covering a personal embezzlement by lapping.

B. One of the sales clerks has not been preparing charge slips for credit sales to family and friends.

C. One of the computer control clerks has been removing all sales invoices applicable to his account from the data file.

D. The credit manager has misappropriated remittances from customers whose accounts have been written off.

Answer (A) is correct. *(CPA, adapted)*

REQUIRED: The fraud most likely to be detected by confirming receivables.

DISCUSSION: Lapping is the theft of a cash payment from one customer concealed by crediting that customer's account when a second customer makes a payment. When lapping exists at the balance sheet date, the confirmation of customer balances will probably detect the fraud because the customers' and entity's records of lapped accounts will differ.

Answer (B) is incorrect. If a charge slip has not been prepared, no accounts receivable balance will exist to be confirmed. Answer (C) is incorrect. If a sales invoice is not processed, no account balance will appear in the records. Answer (D) is incorrect. Once the account has been written off, the account is no longer open.

10.3 Audit Documentation

10.3.1. Audit documentation that records the procedures used by the auditor to gather evidence should be

A. Considered the primary support for the financial statements being audited.

B. Viewed as the connecting link between the books of account and the financial statements.

C. Designed to meet the circumstances of the particular engagement.

D. Destroyed when the audited entity ceases to be a client.

Answer (C) is correct. *(CPA, adapted)*

REQUIRED: The true statement about audit documentation.

DISCUSSION: Audit documentation should be designed to meet the circumstances of a particular engagement. Audit documentation should provide (1) a sufficient and appropriate record of the basis for the auditor's report and (2) evidence that the audit was planned and performed in accordance with GAAS (AU-C 230).

Answer (A) is incorrect. The financial statements are primarily supported by the client's accounting records. Answer (B) is incorrect. Audit documentation is not a part of, or substitute for, the client's accounting records. Answer (D) is incorrect. The auditor should retain audit documentation for a period sufficient to meet the needs of his or her practice and to satisfy any applicable legal or regulatory requirements of records retention. For issuers, audit documentation should be maintained for at least 7 years from the date of the release of the audit report.

10.3.2. An auditor's audit documentation will least likely show how the

A. Client's schedules were prepared.

B. Engagement was planned.

C. Understanding of the client's internal control was obtained and the risks of material misstatement were assessed.

D. Significant issues were resolved.

Answer (A) is correct. *(CPA, adapted)*

REQUIRED: The item least likely to be documented in the auditor's working papers.

DISCUSSION: The objectives of audit documentation are to provide (1) a sufficient and appropriate record of the basis of the auditor's report and (2) evidence that the audit was performed in accordance with GAAS and other requirements. Audit documentation is the record of (1) the audit procedures performed, (2) relevant evidence obtained, and (3) conclusions reached. But how the client's schedules were prepared may not be relevant to the audit.

Answer (B) is incorrect. AU-C 300 and AS 2101 require the audit plan to be documented. Answer (C) is incorrect. The audit documentation should provide evidence that the audit was planned and performed in accordance with GAAS. GAAS require the auditor to obtain an understanding of internal control and to assess the RMMs. Answer (D) is incorrect. The audit documentation records significant audit findings or issues, the conclusions reached, and significant professional judgments made.

10.3.3. Which of the following documentation is not required for an audit in accordance with auditing standards?

A. A written audit plan setting forth the procedures necessary to accomplish the audit's objectives.

B. An indication that the accounting records agree or reconcile with the financial statements.

C. A client letter that details the auditor's planned field work.

D. The basis for the auditor's conclusions about the assessed risks of material misstatement.

Answer (C) is correct. *(CPA, adapted)*

REQUIRED: The documentation not required for an audit.

DISCUSSION: The auditor should not provide the client with a detailed description of the audit procedures to be performed.

Answer (A) is incorrect. AU-C 300 and AS 2101 require the audit plan to be documented. Answer (B) is incorrect. The audit documentation should demonstrate that the accounting records agree or reconcile with the financial statements (AS 1215). Audit documentation includes the results of audit procedures performed and the audit evidence obtained (AU-C 230). Some audit evidence is obtained by testing accounting records to determine whether they agree with the financial statements (AU-C 500). Answer (D) is incorrect. AU-C 230 requires the auditor to document the assessment of the RMMs at the financial statement and assertion levels.

10.3.4. The PCAOB's AS 1215, *Audit Documentation*, requires that a complete and final set of audit documentation be assembled for retention as of a date not more than 45 days after the audit report release date. After that date, audit documentation may

A. Be deleted or discarded, but no information may be added.

B. Be added, but no audit documentation may be deleted or discarded.

C. Not be deleted, discarded, or added.

D. Be deleted, discarded, or added as necessary.

Answer (B) is correct. *(Publisher, adapted)*

REQUIRED: The responsibility for audit documentation retention after the finalization date.

DISCUSSION: Circumstances may require additions to audit documentation after the report release date, for example, discovery of an audit issue after the financial statements have been issued. Any documentation added must indicate the date the information was added, the person who added it, and the reason for adding it. However, no audit documentation may be deleted or discarded after the document finalization date.

10.3.5. Standardized working papers are often used, chiefly because they allow audit documentation to be prepared more

A. Efficiently.

B. Professionally.

C. Neatly.

D. Accurately.

Answer (A) is correct. *(CIA, adapted)*

REQUIRED: The reason for standardized working papers.

DISCUSSION: Use of standardized (pro forma) working papers improves audit efficiency by diminishing the time spent in their preparation. For example, standard forms may be developed for the audit plan, records of the results of interviews, and worksheets.

Answer (B) is incorrect. Standard forms do not necessarily result in greater professionalism. Answer (C) is incorrect. Standard forms clearly reduce time spent in working paper preparation but do not necessarily result in greater neatness. Answer (D) is incorrect. Standard forms do not necessarily result in greater accuracy.

10.3.6. Which of the following is usually included or shown in the audit documentation?

A. The procedures used by the auditor to verify the personal financial status of members of the client's management team.

B. Analyses that are designed to be a part of, or a substitute for, the client's accounting records.

C. Excerpts from authoritative pronouncements that support the underlying generally accepted accounting principles used in preparing the financial statements.

D. A summary of how significant findings were addressed.

Answer (D) is correct. *(CPA, adapted)*

REQUIRED: The component of audit documentation.

DISCUSSION: Auditors may document a summary, or completion memorandum, describing the significant findings or issues identified and how they were addressed. This summary facilitates (1) reviews of the audit documentation, (2) the auditor's consideration of significant findings and issues, and (3) determination of whether any individual audit objective cannot be achieved that will prevent achievement of the overall audit objectives.

Answer (A) is incorrect. Although the auditor should consider incentives or pressures for the client's management to commit fraud, the personal financial status of managers is normally not verified. Answer (B) is incorrect. Audit documentation is not to be regarded as a part of, or a substitute for, the client's accounting records (AU-C 230). Answer (C) is incorrect. Management, not the auditor, must document and support the general acceptability of the accounting principles used by the client.

10.3.7. Although the quantity and content of audit documentation vary with each engagement, an auditor's permanent files most likely include

A. Schedules that support the current year's adjusting entries.

B. Prior years' accounts receivable confirmations that were classified as exceptions.

C. Documentation indicating that the audit work was adequately planned and supervised.

D. Analyses of capital stock and other owners' equity accounts.

Answer (D) is correct. *(CPA, adapted)*

REQUIRED: The component of the permanent section of audit documentation.

DISCUSSION: The permanent section of audit documentation usually contains copies of important client documents. They may include (1) the articles of incorporation, stock options, contracts, and bylaws; (2) the engagement letter, the contract between the auditor and the client; (3) analyses from previous audits of accounts of special importance to the auditor, such as noncurrent debt, PP&E, and equity; and (4) information concerning internal control, e.g., flowcharts, organization charts, and questionnaires.

Answer (A) is incorrect. Schedules that support the current year's adjusting entries are not carried forward in the permanent file. They are unlikely to have continuing significance. Answer (B) is incorrect. Prior years' accounts receivable confirmations that were classified as exceptions are not carried forward in the permanent file. They are unlikely to have continuing significance. Answer (C) is incorrect. Documentation indicating that the audit work was adequately planned and supervised is always included in the current files.

10.3.8. Audit working papers are indexed by means of reference numbers. The primary purpose of indexing is to

A. Permit cross-referencing and simplify supervisory review.

B. Support the audit report.

C. Eliminate the need for follow-up reviews.

D. Determine that working papers adequately support findings, conclusions, and reports.

Answer (A) is correct. *(CIA, adapted)*

REQUIRED: The primary purpose of indexing.

DISCUSSION: Indexing permits cross-referencing, which is important because it simplifies supervisory review either during the audit or subsequently by creating an audit trail of related items through the working papers. Thus, it facilitates preparation of the final report, later audits of the same auditee, and peer review.

Answer (B) is incorrect. The working papers as a whole should support the audit report. Answer (C) is incorrect. Follow-up is necessitated by the auditee conditions, not the state of working papers. Answer (D) is incorrect. Determining that working papers adequately support findings, conclusions, and reports is the purpose of supervisory review.

10.3.9. The audit working paper that reflects the major components of an amount reported in the financial statements is the

A. Interbank transfer schedule.

B. Carryforward schedule.

C. Supporting schedule.

D. Lead schedule.

Answer (D) is correct. *(CPA, adapted)*

REQUIRED: The working paper that reflects the major components of a reported amount.

DISCUSSION: Lead schedules help to eliminate detail from the auditor's working trial balance by classifying and summarizing similar or related items that are contained on the supporting schedules. A lead schedule contains the detailed accounts from the general ledger making up the line item total in the financial statements; e.g., the cash account in the financial statements might consist of petty cash, cash-general, cash-payroll, etc.

Answer (A) is incorrect. An interbank transfer schedule is a working paper prepared for several days before and after the end of the period to determine that both parts of these transactions are recorded in the same period. Answer (B) is incorrect. A carryforward schedule is a continuing schedule of an account with a balance carried forward for several years. Answer (C) is incorrect. Supporting schedules provide details aggregated in the lead schedule.

10.3.10. An auditor ordinarily uses a working trial balance resembling the financial statements without notes, but containing columns for

A. Cash flow increases and decreases.

B. Risk assessments and assertions.

C. Reclassifications and adjustments.

D. Reconciliations and tick marks.

Answer (C) is correct. *(CPA, adapted)*

REQUIRED: The columns contained on a working trial balance in the audit documentation.

DISCUSSION: A working trial balance is ordinarily used to record the year-end ledger balances prior to audit in the audit documentation. Reclassifications and adjustments are accumulated on the trial balance to reflect the final audited balances.

Answer (A) is incorrect. Cash flow increases or decreases are reflected on the client's statement of cash flows. Answer (B) is incorrect. Risk assessments and relevant assertions are determined in the planning stage of the audit and reflected in the audit documentation. Answer (D) is incorrect. The working trial balance has no column for either reconciliations or tick marks.

10.3.11. In the course of the audit of financial statements for the purpose of expressing an opinion, the auditor will normally prepare a schedule of uncorrected misstatements. The primary purpose served by this schedule is to

A. Point out to the responsible entity officials the errors made by various entity personnel.

B. Summarize the corrections that must be made before the entity can prepare and submit its federal tax return.

C. Identify the potential financial statement effects of misstatements that were not considered clearly trivial when discovered.

D. Summarize the misstatements made by the entity so that corrections can be made after the audited financial statements are released.

Answer (C) is correct. *(CPA, adapted)*

REQUIRED: The purpose of the schedule of uncorrected misstatements for which the auditor did not propose correction.

DISCUSSION: The schedule of uncorrected misstatements identifies for management and the auditor the potential cumulative financial statement effect of misstatements. A misstatement arises from fraud or error. It is a difference between the amount, classification, presentation, or disclosure of a reported item and the amount, etc., required for the item to be presented fairly. Misstatements also include adjustments of amounts, etc., the auditor judges to be needed for the statements to be fairly presented. The auditor accumulates misstatements that are not clearly trivial. ("Clearly trivial" is not the same as immaterial. Clearly trivial matters are clearly inconsequential individually and combined with other misstatements. Given any uncertainty about whether a matter is clearly trivial, it is considered not clearly trivial.) The auditor should communicate to appropriate management on a timely basis the accumulated misstatements and evaluate the effect of material uncorrected misstatements.

Answer (A) is incorrect. Detection of errors by specific employees is not the primary purpose of the schedule. Answer (B) is incorrect. The uncorrected misstatements normally are not corrected for tax purposes. Answer (D) is incorrect. If corrections are necessary, i.e., if the misstatements are material, the corrections should be made before the financial statements are released.

10.3.12. Using personal computers in auditing may affect the methods used to review the work of staff assistants because

A. Supervisory personnel may not have an understanding of the capabilities and limitations of personal computers.

B. Audit documentation may not contain readily observable details of calculations.

C. The audit standards for supervision may differ.

D. Documenting the supervisory review may require assistance of consulting services personnel.

Answer (B) is correct. *(CPA, adapted)*

REQUIRED: The reason using personal computers may affect the review of the work of staff assistants.

DISCUSSION: With the introduction of computers, accountants have been able to perform fewer manual calculations. Usually, the necessary numbers are entered into computer spreadsheets, and the answer is produced. Thus, the use of computers makes the review of a staff assistant's work different from that needed when the calculations are done manually.

Answer (A) is incorrect. Supervisors of the audit staff typically have the skills to evaluate the appropriate use of personal computers. Answer (C) is incorrect. The audit standards for supervision are the same whether or not a computer is used. Answer (D) is incorrect. Audit staff typically have skills appropriate for the use of personal computers in documenting the work product of the audit.

10.3.13. A difference of opinion concerning accounting and auditing matters relative to a particular phase of the audit arises between an assistant auditor and the auditor responsible for the engagement. After appropriate consultation, the assistant auditor asks to be dissociated from the resolution of the matter. The audit documentation would probably be

A. Silent on the matter because it is an internal matter of the auditing firm.

B. Expanded to note that the assistant auditor is completely dissociated from responsibility for the auditor's opinion.

C. Expanded to record the additional work required because all disagreements of this type will require expanded substantive testing.

D. Expanded to detail the assistant auditor's position and how the difference of opinion was resolved.

Answer (D) is correct. *(CPA, adapted)*

REQUIRED: The proper action when the auditor and an assistant have a difference of opinion.

DISCUSSION: A public accounting firm should have policies and procedures that address differences of opinion. They should enable an engagement team member to document his or her disagreement with the conclusions reached after proper consultation. The policies and procedures should require that (1) conclusions be documented and implemented and (2) the report not be released until the matter is resolved (QC 10). For an audit of an issuer, AS 1215, *Audit Documentation*, requires working papers to document significant findings issues. They include "disagreements among members of the engagement team or with others consulted on the engagement about final conclusions reached on significant accounting or auditing matters."

Answer (A) is incorrect. The dispute and its resolution should be documented. Answer (B) is incorrect. The audit documentation should describe the assistant's position. Answer (C) is incorrect. Not all disagreements require expanded testing.

10.3.14. A CPA is conducting the first audit of a nonissuer's financial statements. The CPA hopes to reduce the audit work by consulting with the predecessor auditor and reviewing the predecessor's audit documentation. This procedure is

A. Acceptable if the client and the predecessor auditor agree to it.

B. Acceptable if the CPA refers in the audit report to reliance upon the predecessor auditor's work as part of the basis for the CPA's own opinion.

C. Required if the CPA is to express an unmodified opinion.

D. Unacceptable because the CPA should bring an independent viewpoint to a new engagement.

Answer (A) is correct. *(CPA, adapted)*

REQUIRED: The appropriate action in an initial audit regarding cooperation with the predecessor auditor.

DISCUSSION: In an initial audit, the auditor should ask management to permit the predecessor auditor to (1) respond fully to inquiries and (2) allow a review of his or her audit documentation. In accordance with the ethical requirement for AICPA members to cooperate with each other, the predecessor auditor ordinarily agrees to these requests (AU-C 510).

Answer (B) is incorrect. In reporting on the audit, the auditor should not refer to the report or work of the predecessor auditor as the basis, in part, for the auditor's own opinion. These circumstances should be distinguished from the case in which an auditor refers to the audit of a component auditor. For example, the component auditor may have audited the financial statements of a subsidiary of the auditee not audited by the group auditor. Such a reference is a decision not to assume responsibility for the work of the component auditor (AU-C 600). Answer (C) is incorrect. The auditor is required only to request that management authorize the predecessor auditor to (1) respond fully to inquiries and (2) allow a review of his or her audit documentation. Answer (D) is incorrect. Reviewing the predecessor auditor's audit documentation does not affect the auditor's independence.

10.3.15. Which of the following in a predecessor's audit documentation is the auditor least likely to be interested in reviewing?

A. Analysis of noncurrent balance sheet accounts.

B. Analysis of current balance sheet accounts.

C. Analysis of contingencies.

D. Analysis of income statement accounts.

Answer (D) is correct. *(CPA, adapted)*

REQUIRED: The analysis in a predecessor's audit documentation that is least interesting to auditor.

DISCUSSION: The predecessor auditor ordinarily should allow the auditor to review audit documentation of matters of continuing accounting and auditing significance, such as the schedule of uncorrected misstatements and analyses of balance sheet accounts and contingencies. The auditor should obtain sufficient appropriate evidence about whether (1) the opening balances of the current-year statements are materially misstated and (2) accounting policies are consistently applied (or changes are appropriate) (AU-C 510). However, analyses of income statement accounts have less significance for an initial audit because they have no beginning balances.

Answer (A) is incorrect. The predecessor's analysis of balance sheet accounts provides evidence about the impact of opening balances on the current-year statements and the consistent application of accounting principles. Answer (B) is incorrect. The predecessor's analysis of balance sheet accounts provides evidence about the impact of opening balances on the current-year statements and the consistent application of accounting principles. Answer (C) is incorrect. Analysis of contingencies provides evidence about matters of continuing accounting and auditing significance.

10.3.16. After audit procedures are completed, a partner of the CPA firm who has not been involved in the audit performs a second or wrap-up audit documentation review. This second review usually focuses on

A. Whether the financial statements are consistent with the auditor's understanding of the entity.

B. Fraud involving the client's management and its employees.

C. The materiality of the adjusting entries proposed by the audit staff.

D. The communication of internal control weaknesses to those charged with governance.

Answer (A) is correct. *(CPA, adapted)*

REQUIRED: The purpose of a second review by an audit partner.

DISCUSSION: Analytical procedures should be used to assist the auditor to form an overall conclusion. The purpose of those procedures is to determine whether the statements are consistent with the auditor's understanding of the entity (AU-C 520).

Answer (B) is incorrect. Forming an overall conclusion has a broader focus than fraud involving the client's management and its employees. Answer (C) is incorrect. Forming an overall conclusion has a broader focus than the materiality of the adjusting entries proposed by the audit staff. Answer (D) is incorrect. Communication of significant deficiencies and material weaknesses in control is performed by the supervisor in charge of the audit.

10.3.17. Which of the following statements is most accurate regarding sufficient and appropriate documentation?

A. Accounting estimates are not considered sufficient and appropriate documentation.

B. Sufficient and appropriate documentation should include evidence that it has been reviewed.

C. If additional evidence is required to document significant findings or issues, the original evidence is not considered sufficient and appropriate and therefore should be deleted from the working papers.

D. Audit documentation is the property of the client, and sufficient and appropriate copies should be retained by the auditor for at least 5 years.

Answer (B) is correct. *(CPA, adapted)*

REQUIRED: The most accurate statement about sufficient and appropriate documentation.

DISCUSSION: On or before the date of the auditor's report, the engagement partner should review the audit documentation and have discussions with the engagement team. The purpose is to be satisfied that sufficient and appropriate evidence supports the conclusions and the report (AU-C 220). The requirement to document (1) who reviewed the audit work and (2) the extent of the review does not require each working paper to bear evidence of review. But it does mean documenting (1) what work was reviewed, (2) who reviewed the work, and (3) when it was reviewed (AU-C 230).

Answer (A) is incorrect. Accounting estimates are part of the financial statements, not audit documentation. However, the auditor should evaluate management's estimates and document the conclusions. Answer (C) is incorrect. Relevant and reliable (appropriate) evidence, although not sufficient by itself, should not be deleted. Answer (D) is incorrect. Audit documentation is the property of the auditor.

10.4 The Computer as an Audit Tool

10.4.1. Smith Corporation has numerous customers. A customer file is kept on disk storage. Each customer record contains the name, address, credit limit, and account balance. The auditor wishes to test this file to determine whether credit limits are being exceeded. The best procedure for the auditor to follow is to

A. Develop test data that would cause some account balances to exceed the credit limit and determine if the system properly detects such situations.

B. Develop a program to compare credit limits with account balances and print out the details of any account with a balance exceeding its credit limit.

C. Request a printout of all account balances so they can be manually checked against the credit limits.

D. Request a printout of a sample of account balances so they can be individually checked against the credit limits.

Answer (B) is correct. *(CPA, adapted)*

REQUIRED: The method of testing a customer computer file to determine whether credit limits are being exceeded.

DISCUSSION: The auditor should consider developing a program to compare the balances with the credit limits and to print out the exceptions. The auditor can then focus on those customers whose credit limits may have been exceeded.

Answer (A) is incorrect. The auditor needs only to use information already available in the client's files. Answer (C) is incorrect. Requesting a printout of all account balances so they can be manually checked against the credit limits involves extensive manual work that could be done far more quickly and accurately by the computer. Answer (D) is incorrect. Although a sample may be useful, the information is available and the speed and power of the computer allows the auditor to identify all customers exceeding the credit limit.

10.4.2. Computer technology makes it possible to perform paperless audits. For example, in an audit of computer-processed customer accounts receivable balances, an auditor might use a personal computer to access the accounts receivable files directly and copy selected customer records into the computer for audit analysis. Which of the following is an advantage of this type of paperless audit of accounts receivable balances?

A. It reduces the amount of substantive testing required.

B. It allows immediate processing of audit data on a spreadsheet working paper.

C. It increases the amount of technical skill required of the auditor.

D. It allows direct confirmation of customer account balances.

Answer (B) is correct. *(CIA, adapted)*

REQUIRED: The advantage of a paperless audit of accounts receivable balances.

DISCUSSION: Electronic spreadsheets are software packages that display multicolumn worksheets, which may be used as automated audit working papers. A major advantage of this type of auditing is the ability to process data immediately using personal computer software without first having to enter the data manually into the computer.

Answer (A) is incorrect. Audit technology has no direct effect on the amount of substantive testing required. Answer (C) is incorrect. The need for increased expertise is not an advantage. Answer (D) is incorrect. Processing computer files does not in itself provide confirmation of customer account balances, although software may assist in preparing confirmation requests.

10.4.3. An auditor would least likely use computer software to

A. Construct parallel simulations.

B. Access data files.

C. Prepare spreadsheets.

D. Assess risk.

Answer (D) is correct. *(CPA, adapted)*

REQUIRED: The task least likely to be done with computer software.

DISCUSSION: The auditor is required to obtain an understanding of the entity and its environment, including its internal control, and to assess the risk of material misstatement to plan the audit. This assessment is a matter of professional judgment that cannot be accomplished with a computer.

Answer (A) is incorrect. Parallel simulation involves using an auditor's program to reproduce the logic of the client's program. Answer (B) is incorrect. Computer software makes accessing client files much faster and easier. Answer (C) is incorrect. Many audit spreadsheet programs are available.

10.4.4. A primary advantage of using generalized audit software packages to audit the financial statements of a client that uses a computer system is that the auditor may

A. Consider increasing the use of substantive tests of transactions in place of analytical procedures.

B. Substantiate the accuracy of data through self-checking digits and hash totals.

C. Reduce the level of required tests of controls to a relatively small amount.

D. Access information stored on computer files while having a limited understanding of the client's hardware and software features.

Answer (D) is correct. *(CPA, adapted)*

REQUIRED: The advantage of using generalized audit software (GAS).

DISCUSSION: These packages permit the auditor to audit through the computer; e.g., to extract, compare, analyze, and summarize data; and to generate output for use in the audit. Although generalized audit software requires the auditor to provide certain specifications about the client's records, computer equipment, and file formats, a detailed knowledge of the client's system may be unnecessary because the audit package is designed to be used in many environments.

Answer (A) is incorrect. The auditor is required to apply analytical procedures in the planning and overall review phases of the audit. Answer (B) is incorrect. Self-checking digits and hash totals are application controls used by clients. Answer (C) is incorrect. Audit software may permit far more comprehensive tests of controls than a manual audit.

10.4.5. Specialized audit software

A. Is written to interface with many different client systems.

B. May be written while its purposes and users are being defined.

C. Requires the auditor to have less computer expertise than generalized audit software.

D. May be written in a procedure-oriented language.

Answer (D) is correct. *(Publisher, adapted)*

REQUIRED: The true statement regarding specialized audit software.

DISCUSSION: Specialized audit software is written to fulfill a specific set of audit tasks. The purposes and users of the software are well defined before the software is written. Auditors develop specialized audit software for the following reasons:

1. Unavailability of alternative software
2. Functional limitations of alternative software
3. Efficiency considerations
4. Increased understanding of systems
5. Opportunity for easy implementation
6. Increased auditor independence and prestige

Answer (A) is incorrect. Generalized audit software is written to interface with many different client systems. Answer (B) is incorrect. The purposes and users of this software must be defined before it is written. Answer (C) is incorrect. Generalized audit software purchased "off the shelf" requires less computer expertise than specialized software created by the auditor.

10.4.6. Which of the following represents a limitation on the use of generalized audit software (GAS)?

A. It requires lengthy detailed instructions in order to accomplish specific tasks.

B. It has limited application without significant modification.

C. It requires significant programming knowledge to be used effectively.

D. It can only be used on hardware with compatible operating systems.

Answer (D) is correct. *(CIA, adapted)*

REQUIRED: The disadvantage of using GAS.

DISCUSSION: Diversity of programming languages, computers, systems designs, and differing data structures makes generalized audit software impossible to apply in some situations.

Answer (A) is incorrect. The use of GAS is normally more efficient. Less time is required to write instructions to accomplish a function than to manually select and examine items. Answer (B) is incorrect. The program is generalized, i.e., designed to be used on a variety of systems without significant modifications. Answer (C) is incorrect. An advantage is that GAS requires minimal knowledge of computer technology.

10.4.7. The two requirements crucial to achieving audit efficiency and effectiveness with a personal computer are selecting

A. The appropriate audit tasks for personal computer applications and the appropriate software to perform the selected audit tasks.

B. The appropriate software to perform the selected audit tasks and audit procedures that are generally applicable to several clients in a specific industry.

C. Client data that can be accessed by the auditor's personal computer and audit procedures that are generally applicable to several clients in a specific industry.

D. Audit procedures that are generally applicable to several clients in a specific industry and the appropriate audit tasks for personal computer applications.

Answer (A) is correct. *(CPA, adapted)*

REQUIRED: The two requirements necessary to achieve audit efficiency and effectiveness using a personal computer.

DISCUSSION: The question relates to using the computer as an audit tool. To use a personal computer for this purpose effectively and efficiently, the auditor must have the appropriate hardware and software.

Answer (B) is incorrect. Selection of standardized procedures for the industry does not relate directly to the efficient and effective use of a personal computer. Answer (C) is incorrect. Access to the client's records and selection of standardized audit procedures pertain more to the use of generalized audit software to perform substantive tests than to using the personal computer as an audit tool. Answer (D) is incorrect. Selection of standardized procedures for the industry does not relate directly to the efficient and effective use of a personal computer.

10.4.8. Which of the following concepts distinguishes the retention of computerized audit documentation from the traditional hard copy form?

A. Analyses, conclusions, and recommendations are filed on electronic media and are therefore subject to computer system controls and security procedures.

B. Evidential support for all findings is copied and provided to local management during the closing conference and to each person receiving the final report.

C. Computerized data files can be used in computer audit procedures.

D. Audit programs can be standardized to eliminate the need for a preliminary survey at each location.

Answer (A) is correct. *(CIA, adapted)*

REQUIRED: The distinction between computerized audit documentation and the traditional hard copy.

DISCUSSION: The only difference between the computerized audit documentation and hard copy form is how the working papers are stored. Electronic audit documentation is saved either on hard drives, magnetic tape, or flash drives, whereas hard copy is stored in a file cabinet. Unlike computerized audit documentation, hard copies are not subject to computer controls and security procedures.

Answer (B) is incorrect. Evidential support would be retained and provided on the basis of the nature of the finding and not the media used for storing audit documentation. Answer (C) is incorrect. This capability is not an exclusive function of computerized audit documentation. Answer (D) is incorrect. Though the nature of the preliminary survey may change in some cases, the requirement for this phase of the audit is not eliminated by computerized audit documentation.

10.4.9. Which of the following tasks can be achieved using generalized audit software?

A. Determining acceptable risk levels for substantive testing of account balances.

B. Filtering data based on accounts receivable data recording.

C. Detecting transactions that may be suspicious due to alteration of data input.

D. Assessing likelihood of fraud based on input of fraud risk factors.

Answer (B) is correct. *(CPA, adapted)*

REQUIRED: The audit task achieved using generalized audit software.

DISCUSSION: Generalized audit software is used to analyze data to identify anomalies, errors, and omissions. It improves efficiency by automating manual procedures. It can sort and filter data based on various criteria.

Answer (A) is incorrect. Generalized audit software is not able to determine an acceptable risk level. The auditor must establish the level of acceptable audit risk. Answer (C) is incorrect. Generalized audit software cannot detect suspicious data input due to intentional data alteration. Answer (D) is incorrect. The auditor should assess the likelihood of misstatement due to fraud.

10.4.10. Auditors often make use of computer programs that perform routine processing functions, such as sorting and merging. These programs are made available by computer companies and others and are specifically referred to as

A. Compiler programs.

B. Supervisory programs.

C. Utility programs.

D. User programs.

Answer (C) is correct. *(CPA, adapted)*

REQUIRED: The term for programs used to perform routine functions.

DISCUSSION: Utility programs are provided by manufacturers of equipment to perform routine processing tasks required by both clients and auditors, such as extracting data, sorting, merging, and copying. Utility programs are pretested, are independent of the client's own programming efforts, and furnish useful information without the trouble of writing special programs for the engagement.

Answer (A) is incorrect. Compiler programs convert source programs written in a higher-level language into computer-readable object programs, i.e., into machine language. Answer (B) is incorrect. Supervisory programs, also termed operating systems, are master programs responsible for controlling operations within a computer system. Answer (D) is incorrect. User programs are those prepared for a particular application.

10.4.11. An auditor using audit software probably would be least interested in which of the following fields in a computerized perpetual inventory file?

A. Economic order quantity.

B. Warehouse location.

C. Date of last purchase.

D. Quantity sold.

Answer (A) is correct. *(CPA, adapted)*

REQUIRED: The field from an inventory record that is least interesting to an auditor.

DISCUSSION: The economic order quantity, which is based on the most cost effective combination of ordering and carrying costs, is a management decision with little effect on the fairness of the inventory balance on the financial statements.

Answer (B) is incorrect. The auditor is interested in the storage location of the inventory item for test-count purposes. Answer (C) is incorrect. The auditor is interested in the date of last purchase for various reasons. For example, if the date is not relatively recent, the item may be slow-moving or obsolete, with consequent implications for its lower-of-cost-or-market valuation. But a date of purchase near year end suggests the need for cutoff tests. Answer (D) is incorrect. The quantity sold is obviously significant for determining the accuracy of the inventory balance, sales, cost of sales, and related accounts.

STUDY UNIT ELEVEN
EVIDENCE -- THE SALES-RECEIVABLES-CASH CYCLE

The primary purpose of the collection of evidence is to test relevant assertions about the transaction classes, balances, and disclosures in the financial statements. The auditor uses these assertions as a basis for assessing risks of material misstatement (RMMs) and designing and performing further audit procedures. Many audit procedures performed in accordance with the risk assessment are intended to detect overstatement of sales, receivables, and cash. They should be performed as part of a comprehensive audit plan for the sales-receivables-cash cycle. This plan includes the customary procedures assuming no unusual risks. But some questions apply to significant risks that require modification of the audit plan.

QUESTIONS

11.1 Substantive Testing of Sales and Receivables

11.1.1. Which of the following is not a principal objective of the auditor in the audit of revenues?

A. To verify cash deposited during the year.

B. To obtain an understanding of internal control and assess the risks of material misstatement, with particular emphasis on the use of accrual accounting to record revenue.

C. To verify that earned revenue has been recorded and recorded revenue has been earned.

D. To identify and interpret significant trends and variations in the amounts of various categories of revenue.

Answer (A) is correct. *(CPA, adapted)*
REQUIRED: The statement not a principal objective of an auditor when auditing revenues.
DISCUSSION: The verification of cash deposits during the year is not part of the audit of revenues. Verification of cash and marketable securities is undertaken as a separate part of the audit program.
Answer (B) is incorrect. The auditor should obtain an understanding of the entity and its environment, including its internal control, to assess the risks of material misstatement at the financial statement and relevant assertion levels. The understanding is a basis for responses to the assessed RMMs.
Answer (C) is incorrect. Proper verification of accrual method application is an important objective of the audit of revenues.
Answer (D) is incorrect. The heavy volume of transactions in revenue accounts may result in substantial audit risk, which may be reduced through the application of analytical procedures.

11.1.2. A company's sales cutoff is December 31. All goods sold are shipped FOB destination, and the company records sales 3 days after shipment. The following sales were recorded as indicated:

Date Shipped	Month Recorded	(In Thousands) Selling Price	Cost
December 28	December	$182	$190
December 29	December	60	50
December 30	January	144	145
January 2	December	230	215
January 5	January	182	174

Ignoring tax effects, the net effect on income for the month ended December 31 of any failures to observe a proper cutoff was

A. $(1,000)

B. $15,000

C. $24,000

D. $25,000

Answer (D) is correct. *(Publisher, adapted)*
REQUIRED: The net effect on income of the failure to observe a proper cutoff.
DISCUSSION: FOB destination means that title and risk of loss do not pass to the buyer until the goods are tendered at the specified place. The December 29 shipment (which resulted in a $10,000 gain) should have been recorded in January because the company records sales 3 days after shipment. Because the selling price of this shipment was greater than its cost, the effect of the error was to overstate income for December by the $10,000 difference. The January 2 shipment (which resulted in a $15,000 gain) was also erroneously recorded in December. Because its selling price was more than cost, the effect of the error was to overstate income for December by the $15,000 gain. The net effect of these errors is that income for the month ended December 31 was overstated by $25,000.

11.1.3. Auditors are often concerned with the possibility of overstatement of sales and receivables. However, management may also have reasons for understating these balances. Which of the following would explain understatement of sales and receivables?

A. To window-dress the financial statements.

B. To avoid paying taxes.

C. To meet budgets and forecasts.

D. All of the answers are correct.

Answer (B) is correct. *(Publisher, adapted)*

REQUIRED: The reason(s) for understating sales and receivables.

DISCUSSION: State sales taxes and federal and state income taxes are based upon sales or profits, respectively. Management may attempt to reduce or avoid tax liability by not recording and reporting all sales and receivables.

Answer (A) is incorrect. Sales and receivables would be overstated to window-dress the statements. Answer (C) is incorrect. Management may attempt to overstate sales to achieve forecasts or to meet budgets. Answer (D) is incorrect. Only one of the choices is correct.

11.1.4. An auditor most likely would review an entity's periodic accounting for the numerical sequence of shipping documents and invoices to support management's financial statement assertion of

A. Occurrence.

B. Rights and obligations.

C. Valuation and allocation.

D. Completeness.

Answer (D) is correct. *(CPA, adapted)*

REQUIRED: The assertion supported by reviewing the numerical sequence of shipping documents and invoices.

DISCUSSION: The completeness assertion concerns whether all transactions (or assets, liabilities, and equity interests) that should be recorded are recorded. Testing the numerical sequence of shipping documents and invoices is a means of detecting omitted items.

Answer (A) is incorrect. The occurrence assertion addresses whether recorded transactions have occurred and pertain to the entity. Answer (B) is incorrect. The rights and obligations assertion concerns whether assets are the rights of the entity and liabilities are obligations at a given date. Answer (C) is incorrect. The valuation and allocation assertion concerns whether assets, liabilities, and equity interests have been included at appropriate amounts.

11.1.5. An auditor observed that a client mails monthly statements to customers. Subsequently, the auditor reviewed evidence of follow-up on the errors reported by the customers. This test of controls was most likely performed to support management's financial statement assertion(s) of

	Classification and Understandability	Rights and Obligations
A.	Yes	Yes
B.	Yes	No
C.	No	Yes
D.	No	No

Answer (C) is correct. *(CPA, adapted)*

REQUIRED: The financial statement assertion(s) related to observing the client's follow-up on errors reported in monthly statements.

DISCUSSION: The rights and obligations assertion applies to account balances. It relates to whether (1) the related assets are the rights of the entity and (2) the related liabilities are the obligations of the entity at the balance sheet date. Observation of the mailing of monthly statements and the correction of reported errors provides evidence that controls may be effective in ensuring that receivables are genuine. However, the test of controls performed provide little or no evidence about whether particular financial statement components are properly presented and described, and disclosures are clear.

Answer (A) is incorrect. The observation of client activities related to customer statements provides little or no evidence concerning presentation or disclosure in the financial statements. Answer (B) is incorrect. The observation of client activities related to customer statements provides little or no evidence concerning presentation or disclosure in the financial statements. Answer (D) is incorrect. The mailing and follow-up procedures provide evidence that controls may be effective in ensuring that receivables are genuine.

11.1.6. Which of the following might be detected by an auditor's review of the client's sales cutoff?

A. Excessive goods returned for credit.

B. Unrecorded sales discounts.

C. Lapping of year-end accounts receivable.

D. Inflated sales for the year.

Answer (D) is correct. *(CPA, adapted)*

REQUIRED: The condition that might be detected by review of the client's sales cutoff.

DISCUSSION: Sales cutoff tests are designed to detect the client's manipulation of sales. By examining recorded sales for several days before and after the balance sheet date and comparing them with sales invoices and shipping documents, the auditor may detect the recording of a sale in a period other than that in which title passed.

Answer (A) is incorrect. Sales returns are not examined in the sales cutoff test. Answer (B) is incorrect. Examination of cash receipts would reveal unrecorded discounts. Answer (C) is incorrect. Lapping may be detected by the confirmation of customer balances and tracing amounts received according to duplicate deposit slips to the accounts receivable subsidiary ledger.

11.1.7. Material misstatements due to fraudulent financial reporting often result from an overstatement of revenues (for example, through premature revenue recognition or recording of fictitious revenues) or an understatement of revenues (for example, through improperly shifting revenues to a later period). To address the risk of improper revenue recognition, the auditor most likely should

A. Increase the assessment of the risks of material misstatement.

B. Assume the existence of risks of material misstatement due to fraud relating to revenue recognition.

C. Focus testing of journal entries on those made during the reporting period rather than at the end of the reporting period.

D. Focus testing on the actions of the client's staff-level employees.

Answer (B) is correct. *(Publisher, adapted)*

REQUIRED: The auditor response to the risk of misstated revenues.

DISCUSSION: Management may be subject to incentives or pressures to misstate revenues. Given management's opportunity to override controls, the auditor ordinarily should assume the existence of fraud risks relating to revenue recognition (AU-C 240 and AS 2110).

Answer (A) is incorrect. The auditor assesses the RMMs based on the audit evidence regarding inherent risk and the effectiveness of the client's controls, not on the need to adjust for an unspecified risk of improper revenue recognition. Answer (C) is incorrect. Focus of testing should be on the end of the reporting period, when it is most likely that fraudulent adjustments to revenue will be made. Answer (D) is incorrect. The focus should be on management-level employees or those with both the incentive pressure and opportunity to commit frauds related to revenue.

11.1.8. An audit client sells 15 to 20 units of product annually. A large portion of the annual sales occur in the last month of the fiscal year. Annual sales have not materially changed over the past 5 years. Which of the following approaches would be most effective concerning the timing of audit procedures for revenue?

A. The auditor should perform analytical procedures at an interim date and discuss any changes in the level of sales with senior management.

B. The auditor should inspect transactions occurring in the last month of the fiscal year and review the related sale contracts to determine that revenue was posted in the proper period.

C. The auditor should perform tests of controls at an interim date to obtain audit evidence about the operational effectiveness of internal controls over sales.

D. The auditor should review period-end compensation to determine if bonuses were paid to meet earnings goals.

Answer (B) is correct. *(CPA, adapted)*

REQUIRED: The most effective audit procedure given the timing of revenue.

DISCUSSION: Tests of the details of transactions at year end are most effective given that total sales consist mostly of a few transactions. Also, because most occur in the last month of the year, the auditor should establish that management made a proper cutoff.

Answer (A) is incorrect. Because most sales occur at year end, interim analytical procedures are not likely to be effective. Answer (C) is incorrect. Although internal controls are important, given the small number of transactions, substantive procedures are most effective. Answer (D) is incorrect. Firms often pay bonuses as incentives to meet objectives.

11.1.9. A CPA is engaged in the annual audit of a calendar year client. The client took a complete physical inventory under the CPA's observation on December 15 and adjusted its inventory account and detailed perpetual inventory records to agree with the physical inventory. The client considers a sale to be made in the period that goods are shipped. Listed below are four items taken from the CPA's sales cutoff test worksheet. Which item does not require an adjusting entry on the client's books?

	Shipped	Recorded as Sale	Credited to Inventory
A.	12/10	12/19	12/12
B.	12/14	12/16	12/16
C.	12/31	1/2	12/31
D.	1/2	12/31	12/31

Answer (A) is correct. *(CPA, adapted)*

REQUIRED: The item not requiring an adjusting entry.

DISCUSSION: Goods shipped on 12/10 would have been properly recorded as a sale on 12/19, a date within the same accounting period. Moreover, the credit to inventory on 12/12 preceded the physical count on 12/15. No adjustment is necessary.

Answer (B) is incorrect. Items shipped on 12/14 would have been properly excluded from the 12/15 inventory, and no credit should have been made on 12/16. Answer (C) is incorrect. The 12/31 shipment should have been recorded as a sale in the same period or year. Answer (D) is incorrect. The 1/2 shipment should have been recorded as a sale in the same period or year that the goods were shipped.

11.1.10. The auditor finds a situation in which one person has the ability to collect receivables, make deposits, issue credit memos, and record receipt of payments. The auditor suspects the individual may be stealing from cash receipts. Which of the following audit procedures will be most effective in discovering fraud in this scenario?

A. Send positive confirmations to a random selection of customers.

B. Send negative confirmations to all outstanding accounts receivable customers.

C. Perform a detailed review of debits to customer discounts, sales returns, or other debit accounts, excluding cash posted to the cash receipts journal.

D. Take a sample of bank deposits and trace the detail in each bank deposit back to the entry in the cash receipts journal.

Answer (C) is correct. *(CIA, adapted)*

REQUIRED: The audit procedure most effective in detecting theft from cash receipts.

DISCUSSION: The most effective procedure is to perform a detailed review of debits to customer discounts, sales returns, and other debit accounts. These accounts could be used to conceal a theft of cash payments without alerting customers.

Answer (A) is incorrect. An employee who performs asset custody, authorization, and recording functions can conceal the theft by debiting customer discounts or sales returns. Customers would be unaware of the activity because their balances would reflect their expectations. Answer (B) is incorrect. An employee who performs asset custody, authorization, and recording functions can conceal the theft by debiting customer discounts or sales returns. Customers would be unaware of the activity because their balances would reflect their expectations. Answer (D) is incorrect. Bank deposits will agree with journal entries. The stolen amounts are never recorded.

11.1.11. In the audit of which of the following general ledger accounts will tests of controls be particularly appropriate?

A. Equipment.

B. Bonds payable.

C. Bank charges.

D. Sales.

Answer (D) is correct. *(CPA, adapted)*

REQUIRED: The account for which tests of controls are most appropriate.

DISCUSSION: In auditing the sales or revenue account, tests of controls are particularly appropriate, provided the auditor believes that the risks of material misstatement at the relevant assertion level can be assessed at a low level. Because of the large volume of transactions, examining all items will seldom be cost-effective.

Answer (A) is incorrect. The ease of verifying the physical existence of equipment and computing depreciation may make it inefficient to evaluate the effectiveness of controls. Answer (B) is incorrect. The ready availability of evidence in the contractual agreements and the infrequency of transactions make tests of controls less necessary for bonds payable. Answer (C) is incorrect. Evidence of bank charges is easily obtainable from an independent source. Bank charges are usually reported as a single amount on each monthly bank statement.

11.1.12. A large university has relatively ineffective internal control. The university's auditor seeks assurance that all tuition revenue has been recorded. The auditor could best obtain the desired assurance by

A. Confirming a sample of tuition payments with the students.

B. Observing tuition payment procedures on a surprise basis.

C. Comparing business office revenue records with registrar's office records of students enrolled.

D. Preparing a year-end bank reconciliation.

Answer (C) is correct. *(CIA, adapted)*

REQUIRED: The best procedure for testing whether all tuition revenue has been recorded.

DISCUSSION: To be assured that all tuition revenue is being recorded, the auditor must perform substantive procedures, which are tests of details and substantive analytical procedures to detect material misstatements in an account balance, transaction class, or disclosure component. Comparing business office revenue records with registrar's office records of students enrolled provides analytical evidence based on independently generated records.

Answer (A) is incorrect. Confirmations of payments do not detect unrecorded receipts. Answer (B) is incorrect. Observation is a test of controls, not a substantive test of the completeness assertion for the revenue balance. Answer (D) is incorrect. Preparing a year-end bank reconciliation would only detect an unrecorded deposit or other cash accounting error.

11.1.13. If the objective of an auditor's test of details is to detect a possible understatement of sales, the auditor most likely would trace transactions from the

A. Sales invoices to the shipping documents.

B. Cash receipts journal to the sales journal.

C. Shipping documents to the sales invoices.

D. Sales journal to the cash receipts journal.

Answer (C) is correct. *(CPA, adapted)*

REQUIRED: The procedure that tests for understatement of sales.

DISCUSSION: If a shipment occurred, matching shipping documents to recorded sales would disclose the understatement if no recorded sale could be found.

Answer (A) is incorrect. Tracing sales invoices to the shipping documents detects a possible overstatement of sales. Answer (B) is incorrect. If sales are not recorded, there will not likely be a cash receipt. Answer (D) is incorrect. If sales were not recorded, there would be no record in the sales journal.

11.1.14. A CPA auditing an electric utility wishes to determine whether all customers are being billed. The CPA's best direction of test is from the

A. Meter department records to the billing (sales) register.

B. Billing (sales) register to the meter department records.

C. Accounts receivable ledger to the billing (sales) register.

D. Billing (sales) register to the accounts receivable ledger.

Answer (A) is correct. *(CPA, adapted)*

REQUIRED: The best direction of testing to determine whether all customers are being billed.

DISCUSSION: The best direction of testing is to proceed from the meter department records, which indicate those customers who have received service, to the billing (sales) register. Comparing services rendered with billings is the best way to detect omitted billings.

Answer (B) is incorrect. Comparing the sales register with the meter records is useful for verifying the amounts billed for which service was not provided. Answer (C) is incorrect. Comparisons between the accounts receivable ledger and the sales register are useful for verifying the accuracy of the posting of accounts receivable. Answer (D) is incorrect. Comparisons between the accounts receivable ledger and the sales register are useful for verifying the accuracy of the posting of the accounts receivable.

11.1.15. If the objective of a test of details is to detect overstatements of sales, the auditor should compare transactions in the

A. Cash receipts journal with the sales journal.

B. Sales journal with the cash receipts journal.

C. Source documents with the accounting records.

D. Accounting records with the source documents.

Answer (D) is correct. *(CPA, adapted)*

REQUIRED: The appropriate test to detect overstatement of sales.

DISCUSSION: Overstatements of sales likely result from entries with no supporting documentation. The proper direction of testing is to sample entries in the sales account and vouch them to the shipping documents. The source documents represent the valid sales.

Answer (A) is incorrect. The cash receipts journal and the sales journal are books of original entry, not source documents. Answer (B) is incorrect. The cash receipts journal and the sales journal are books of original entry, not source documents. Answer (C) is incorrect. The proper direction of testing is from the accounting records to the source documents.

11.1.16. An inappropriate audit procedure relative to accounts receivable is to determine that the

A. Accounts exist and are properly valued.

B. Accounts represent the complete transaction process.

C. Accounts are collected by the balance sheet date.

D. Client has rights in the accounts receivable.

Answer (C) is correct. *(Publisher, adapted)*

REQUIRED: The determination that is not an audit objective relative to accounts receivable.

DISCUSSION: Accounts receivable represent the amounts due the client at the balance sheet date. The auditor should not expect the accounts to be collected at the balance sheet date.

Answer (A) is incorrect. The determination that accounts exist and are properly valued is an appropriate audit procedure relating to assertions about (existence and valuation) made in financial statements. The auditor's responsibility is to obtain and evaluate evidence concerning the assertions made by management. Answer (B) is incorrect. An audit procedure may appropriately relate to the completeness assertion. Answer (D) is incorrect. An audit procedure may be performed to test an assertion about rights.

11.1.17. Which of the following most likely would give the most assurance concerning the valuation assertion about accounts receivable?

A. Vouching amounts in the subsidiary ledger to details on shipping documents.

B. Comparing receivable turnover ratios with industry statistics for reasonableness.

C. Inquiring about receivables pledged under loan agreements.

D. Assessing the allowance for uncollectible accounts for reasonableness.

Answer (D) is correct. *(CPA, adapted)*

REQUIRED: The procedure providing the most assurance about the valuation of accounts receivable.

DISCUSSION: Assertions about valuation concern whether balance sheet components have been included at appropriate amounts. One such assertion is that trade accounts receivable are stated at net realizable value (gross accounts receivable minus allowance for uncollectible accounts). Hence, assessing the allowance provides assurance about the valuation of the account.

Answer (A) is incorrect. Vouching amounts in the subsidiary ledger to details on shipping documents provides evidence about the occurrence assertion for transactions. Answer (B) is incorrect. Comparing receivable turnover ratios with industry statistics for reasonableness provides evidence about completeness. Answer (C) is incorrect. Inquiring about receivables pledged under loan agreements pertains to presentation and disclosure assertions.

11.1.18. A company has computerized sales and cash receipts journals. The computer programs for these journals have been properly debugged. The auditor discovered that the total of the accounts receivable subsidiary accounts differs materially from the accounts receivable control account. This discrepancy could indicate

A. Credit memoranda being improperly recorded.

B. Lapping of receivables.

C. Receivables not being properly aged.

D. Statements being intercepted prior to mailing.

Answer (A) is correct. *(CIA, adapted)*

REQUIRED: The reason the accounts receivable subsidiary ledger may differ from the control account.

DISCUSSION: Sales returns and allowances require the crediting of accounts receivable. The recording of unauthorized credit memoranda is one explanation for the discrepancy if sales and cash receipts are properly recorded.

Answer (B) is incorrect. Lapping entails the theft of cash receipts and the use of subsequent receipts to conceal the theft. The effect is to overstate receivables, but no difference between the control total and the total of subsidiary accounts would arise. Answer (C) is incorrect. Aging does not involve accounting entries. Answer (D) is incorrect. Interception of customer statements might indicate fraudulent receivables but would not cause the subsidiary ledger discrepancy.

11.1.19. An auditor learns that collections of accounts receivable during the last 10 days of December were not recorded. The effect will be to

A. Leave both working capital and the current ratio unchanged at December 31.

B. Overstate both working capital and the current ratio at December 31.

C. Overstate working capital with no effect on the current ratio at December 31.

D. Overstate the current ratio with no effect on working capital at December 31.

Answer (A) is correct. *(Publisher, adapted)*

REQUIRED: The effect of failing to record year-end collections.

DISCUSSION: Working capital is equal to current assets minus current liabilities, and the current ratio is equal to current assets divided by current liabilities. Because cash and accounts receivable are both current assets, the error has no effect on working capital and the current ratio at December 31 because it did not change total current assets.

Answer (B) is incorrect. Neither working capital nor the current ratio is affected by failing to record cash collections. The only effects are that cash is understated and accounts receivable overstated. Answer (C) is incorrect. Working capital is not affected. Answer (D) is incorrect. The current ratio is not affected.

11.1.20. Which of the following procedures would an auditor most likely perform for year-end accounts receivable confirmations when the auditor did not receive replies to second requests?

A. Review the cash receipts journal for the month prior to year end.

B. Intensify the study of internal control concerning the revenue cycle.

C. Increase the assessed level of detection risk for the existence assertion.

D. Inspect the shipping records documenting the merchandise sold to the debtors.

Answer (D) is correct. *(CPA, adapted)*

REQUIRED: The most appropriate audit procedure when customers fail to reply to second request forms.

DISCUSSION: When customers fail to answer a second request for a positive confirmation, the accounts may be in dispute, uncollectible, or fictitious. The auditor should then apply alternative procedures (examination of subsequent cash receipts, shipping documents, and other client documentation of existence) to obtain evidence about the validity of nonresponding accounts.

Answer (A) is incorrect. Previous collections cannot substantiate year-end balances. Answer (B) is incorrect. Nonresponse to a confirmation request is not proof of ineffective controls. Nonresponses do occur and are expected. Answer (C) is incorrect. RMMs are assessed, but detection risk is not. However, the acceptable level of detection risk may be decreased if the assessment of RMMs is increased as a result of nonresponses to confirmation requests.

11.1.21. Which of the following is the greatest drawback of using subsequent collections evidenced only by a deposit slip as an alternative procedure when responses to positive accounts receivable confirmations are not received?

A. Checking of subsequent collections can never be used as an alternative auditing procedure.

B. By examining a deposit slip only, the auditor does not know whether the payment is for the receivable at the balance sheet date or a subsequent transaction.

C. A deposit slip is not received directly by the auditor.

D. A customer may not have made a payment on a timely basis.

Answer (B) is correct. *(Publisher, adapted)*

REQUIRED: The greatest drawback of using subsequent collections as an alternative to confirmation.

DISCUSSION: The deposit slip does not indicate which receivables are being paid. The deposits may not be from the collection of accounts receivable, or the receipts may be for sales made after year end.

Answer (A) is incorrect. The auditor may use alternative procedures. Indeed, the alternative procedures may be omitted when no unusual qualitative factors or systematic characteristics are related to the nonresponses and when treating the nonresponses as 100% misstatements does not affect the auditor's decision about whether the financial statements are materially misstated. If an account receivable is paid, an account receivable presumably existed. Answer (C) is incorrect. Copies of the deposit slips can be provided to the auditor by the bank. Also, the bank proofs the original of the deposit slip when received. Answer (D) is incorrect. Although late payment may cause a problem, the auditor typically performs field work 45 to 60 days after year end.

11.1.22. The most effective audit procedure for determining the collectibility of an account receivable is the

A. Confirmation of the account.

B. Examination of the related sales invoice(s).

C. Review of the subsequent cash collections.

D. Review of authorization of credit sales to the customer and the previous history of collections.

Answer (C) is correct. *(CMA, adapted)*

REQUIRED: The most effective audit procedure for determining collectibility.

DISCUSSION: Collectibility pertains to the assertion of valuation. It is the principal issue with regard to the adequacy of the allowance for doubtful accounts. The best way to determine collectibility is to learn whether the receivable was subsequently collected. A confirmation provides evidence that a contract exists and that the debtor acknowledges the debt, but the subsequent collection of the receivable is the only means of gaining complete assurance that the amount will be paid.

Answer (A) is incorrect. Confirmation tends to be more effective in providing evidence about the existence than the valuation (collectibility) assertion. Answer (B) is incorrect. Examination of the related sales invoice(s) is a test of the validity, not the collectibility, of a receivable. Answer (D) is incorrect. Experience is a good indicator of collectibility but is not as good as collection.

11.1.23. An auditor suspects that a client's customer, whose accounts receivable balance represents a material proportion of the client's total receivables, is fictitious. The evidence that provides the strongest proof that the auditor's suspicion is unfounded, given the existence of weaknesses in the client's internal control over accounts receivable, is

A. Receipt of a positive confirmation response.

B. Subsequent posting of the collection of the account balance.

C. Nonresponse to a negative confirmation request.

D. Location of the customer's name and address in a published industry directory.

Answer (D) is correct. *(Publisher, adapted)*

REQUIRED: The best evidence that a client's customer is not fictitious.

DISCUSSION: Verifying that the debtor exists and has the same address as appears in the client's records provides evidence that the customer is not fictitious. A published industry directory is an independent source of evidence of the customer's existence. Taken together with the return of a positive confirmation, the industry directory provides strong proof of the validity of the account.

Answer (A) is incorrect. Confirmation responses can be falsified to conceal fraud. A false address may be given at which the confirmation request will be intercepted by a participant in the fraud. Answer (B) is incorrect. The payment may be either entirely fictitious or the posting of another customer's payment (lapping). Answer (C) is incorrect. A negative confirmation request may be intercepted by a party to fraud.

11.1.24. An auditor who has confirmed accounts receivable may discover that the sales journal was held open past year end if

A. Positive confirmation requests sent to debtors are not returned.

B. Negative confirmation requests sent to debtors are not returned.

C. Most of the returned negative confirmation requests indicate that the debtor owes a larger balance than the amount being confirmed.

D. Most of the returned positive confirmation requests indicate that the debtor owes a smaller balance than the amount being confirmed.

Answer (D) is correct. *(Publisher, adapted)*

REQUIRED: The result of confirmations indicating that the sales journal was held open past year end.

DISCUSSION: When the majority of the returned positive confirmation requests indicate smaller balances at year end than those in the client's records, the client may have held open the sales journal after year end. Thus, the client debited customers' accounts for the period under audit rather than for the subsequent period. The effect is to overstate sales and receivables.

Answer (A) is incorrect. The failure to receive replies to positive confirmation requests may cause the auditor concern about the existence assertion. Answer (B) is incorrect. Nonresponses to negative confirmation requests provide some evidence about the existence assertion. Answer (C) is incorrect. Replies indicating balances larger than those confirmed suggest that the sales journal was closed prior to year end.

11.1.25. All of the following are examples of substantive tests to verify the valuation of net accounts receivable except the

A. Recomputation of the allowance for bad debts.

B. Inspection of accounts for current versus noncurrent status in the statement of financial position.

C. Inspection of the aging schedule and credit records of past due accounts.

D. Comparison of the allowance for bad debts with past records.

Answer (B) is correct. *(CMA, adapted)*

REQUIRED: The item that is not an example of a test of valuation.

DISCUSSION: The inspection of accounts for current versus noncurrent status is a test of management's assertion relating to statement presentation and disclosure. It is not a test of valuation.

Answer (A) is incorrect. Recomputation of the allowance for bad debts tests the valuation of the account balance. Answer (C) is incorrect. Inspection of the aging schedule and credit records of past due accounts tests the valuation of the account balance. Answer (D) is incorrect. Comparison of the allowance for bad debts with past records tests the valuation of the account balance.

11.1.26. Once a CPA has determined that accounts receivable have increased because of slow collections in a tight money environment, the CPA is likely to

A. Increase the balance in the allowance for bad debts account.

B. Review the going concern ramifications.

C. Review the credit and collection policy.

D. Expand tests of collectibility.

Answer (D) is correct. *(CPA, adapted)*

REQUIRED: The appropriate audit response when receivables have increased because of slow collections.

DISCUSSION: Whenever collections of receivables have slowed, the auditor should determine the effects on the allowance for doubtful accounts. (S)he should therefore expand tests of collectibility, e.g., with a review of collections subsequent to the balance sheet date and investigation of credit ratings. The verification of the allowance for doubtful accounts ensures that receivables are fairly presented at their net realizable value in the balance sheet and that bad debt expense is fairly stated in the income statement.

Answer (A) is incorrect. An increase in the allowance account may not be required if the accounts are collectible as in the past. Answer (B) is incorrect. Questioning whether the client is a going concern is necessary only if the client is on the verge of bankruptcy or some other form of cessation. Answer (C) is incorrect. A review of credit and collection policy is only one part of the expansion of tests of collectibility.

11.1.27. An auditor reconciles the total of the accounts receivable subsidiary ledger to the general ledger control account, as of October 31. By this procedure, the auditor would be most likely to learn of which of the following?

A. An October invoice was improperly computed.

B. An October check from a customer was posted in error to the account of another customer with a similar name.

C. An opening balance in a subsidiary ledger account was improperly carried forward from the previous accounting period.

D. An account balance is past due and should be written off.

Answer (C) is correct. *(CPA, adapted)*

REQUIRED: The misstatement most likely to be detected by reconciling the total of the subsidiary ledger to the general ledger.

DISCUSSION: By reconciling the accounts receivable ledger to the general ledger control account, transfer misstatements will be identified.

Answer (A) is incorrect. Reconciliation of the subsidiary ledger and control account will not detect a misstatement if entries to both are based on the same document. Only recalculation of invoices will detect this misstatement. Answer (B) is incorrect. Posting to the wrong account would most likely be detected by confirmation. The trial balance total and the control account are not affected by such a misstatement. Answer (D) is incorrect. Uncollectibility would most probably be detected through aging receivables.

11.2 Substantive Testing of Cash

11.2.1. Which of the following is not a financial statement assertion about cash?

A. Reported cash exists.

B. The client has rights to the reported cash.

C. Compensating cash balances are classified as other current assets.

D. The reported cash balance includes all cash transactions that should have been recorded.

Answer (C) is correct. *(Publisher, adapted)*

REQUIRED: The item not a financial statement assertion about cash.

DISCUSSION: Normally, cash should be identified as a current asset. When compensating balances exist, however, any cash balances legally restricted under loan or line of credit agreements should be segregated on the balance sheet and classified according to the appropriate classification of the related debt, either current or noncurrent.

Answer (A) is incorrect. One objective is to verify management's assertion that cash exists. Answer (B) is incorrect. The auditor should establish that the client has rights to the cash balances. Answer (D) is incorrect. The completeness assertion requires the auditor to gather evidence that the reported cash balance includes all cash transactions that should have been recorded.

11.2.2. The standard AICPA form directed to financial institutions requests all of the following except

A. Due date of a direct liability.

B. The principal amount paid on a direct liability.

C. Description of collateral for a direct liability.

D. The interest rate of a direct liability.

Answer (B) is correct. *(Publisher, adapted)*

REQUIRED: The item not requested on a standard financial institution confirmation form.

DISCUSSION: The principal amount paid on a direct liability is not listed on the Standard Form to Confirm Account Balance Information with Financial Institutions. The auditor is not concerned with the amount of a liability already paid. The form confirms account number/description, balance, due date, interest rate, date through which interest is paid, and description of collateral.

11.2.3. Normally, the financial statement assertion about valuation is of minimum concern during the audit of cash. However, the auditor's concern about the valuation assertion will most likely increase when

A. Both currency and negotiable securities are on hand.

B. The client uses a demand deposit account.

C. The proof of cash cannot be reconciled.

D. The client has foreign currency accounts.

Answer (D) is correct. *(Publisher, adapted)*

REQUIRED: The most likely reason for the auditor to be concerned about the valuation of cash.

DISCUSSION: Foreign currency accounts must be converted to U.S. dollars based upon the current exchange rate. Changes in the conversion rate and restrictions on the movement of foreign currency create problems of valuation for the auditor.

Answer (A) is incorrect. The auditor is more concerned about the existence than the valuation of cash. The latter is ordinarily easily determined once the former is established. Thus, currency can usually be valued at its face amount, and negotiable securities normally have readily ascertainable market values. Answer (B) is incorrect. A demand deposit account, which is simply a checking account, is used by most organizations for cash disbursements. Answer (C) is incorrect. The inability to reconcile a proof of cash affects the auditor's concern about the existence, not the valuation, of cash.

11.2.4. An auditor ordinarily sends a standard confirmation request to all banks with which the client has done business during the year under audit, regardless of the year-end balance. A purpose of this procedure is to

A. Provide the data necessary to prepare a proof of cash.

B. Request that a cutoff bank statement and related checks be sent to the auditor.

C. Detect kiting activities that may otherwise not be discovered.

D. Seek information about other deposit and loan amounts that come to the attention of the institution in the process of completing the confirmation.

Answer (D) is correct. *(CPA, adapted)*

REQUIRED: The reason confirmations are sent to all banks used by the client.

DISCUSSION: The AICPA *Standard Form to Confirm Account Balance Information with Financial Institutions* is used to confirm specifically listed deposit and loan balances. Nevertheless, the standard confirmation form contains this language: "Although we do not request or expect you to conduct a comprehensive, detailed search of your records, if, during the process of completing this confirmation, additional information about other deposit and loan accounts we may have with you comes to your attention, please include such information below."

Answer (A) is incorrect. The information for a proof of cash is in the month-end bank statement. Answer (B) is incorrect. A cutoff bank statement is for some period subsequent to the balance sheet date. Answer (C) is incorrect. The auditor should compare the returned checks in the cutoff bank statement with those listed as outstanding on the bank reconciliation, as well as prepare a bank transfer schedule for a few days before and after the balance sheet date.

11.2.5. A bank cutoff statement is least likely to detect

A. Inclusion of a nonexistent deposit in transit on the bank reconciliation.

B. Omission of checks that were written prior to year end from the outstanding check list on the bank reconciliation.

C. Dating of checks prior to year end that are not issued until after year end.

D. Application of cash receipts from one customer to another customer's account (lapping).

Answer (D) is correct. *(D. Wells)*

REQUIRED: The purpose not served by a bank cutoff statement.

DISCUSSION: Lapping is detected through confirmation of accounts receivable and comparing information on remittance advices and deposit slips with the cash receipts journal.

Answer (A) is incorrect. The cutoff bank statement would not show the nonexistent deposit. Answer (B) is incorrect. Some checks returned with the cutoff bank statement dated prior to year end would not appear on the year-end bank reconciliation. Answer (C) is incorrect. Few, if any, of the checks that appear as outstanding on the bank reconciliation at year end would have cleared the bank and be included in the cutoff bank statement.

11.2.6. When counting cash on hand, the auditor must exercise control over all cash and other negotiable assets to prevent

A. Theft.

B. Irregular endorsement.

C. Substitution.

D. Deposits in transit.

Answer (C) is correct. *(CPA, adapted)*

REQUIRED: The reason for controlling cash and negotiable assets.

DISCUSSION: Simultaneous verification of cash and cash equivalents, such as negotiable securities, is common practice to avoid the possibility of conversion of negotiable assets to cash to conceal a cash shortage. The auditor should control and verify all liquid assets at one time.

Answer (A) is incorrect. Simultaneous verification does not directly prevent theft except during the time the auditor controls the assets. Rather, it helps to uncover an irregularity that has already occurred by making its concealment more difficult. Answer (B) is incorrect. Simultaneous verification does not directly prevent irregular endorsement except during the time the auditor controls the assets. Answer (D) is incorrect. Deposits in transit (those recorded on the client's but not the bank's books) are a normal result of business activity.

11.2.7. Bank teller supervisors might manipulate accounts using their privileged computer access codes. They could withdraw money for their own use and move money among accounts when depositors complain to the bank about errors. The audit procedure most likely to detect this is

A. Reviewing transactions on privileged access codes.

B. Reviewing transactions for employees' accounts.

C. Verifying proof records for teller access codes.

D. Testing the accuracy of account posting programs.

Answer (A) is correct. *(CIA, adapted)*

REQUIRED: The audit procedure most likely to detect fraud by bank teller supervisors.

DISCUSSION: A basic control problem in a computer system is the absence of the separation of functions found in manual systems. Thus, the supervisors' possession of privileged codes allows access to both deposits and related records. Controls must be implemented to compensate for this lack of separation. Reviewing the system access log for transactions involving the supervisors' codes is one such control.

Answer (B) is incorrect. Reviewing transactions for employees' accounts will not detect transfers to accounts not in the employees' names. Answer (C) is incorrect. Verifying proof records for teller access codes determines whether daily transactions balance. Answer (D) is incorrect. The issue is whether transactions are authorized, not whether the postings are accurate.

11.2.8. During the examination of a cutoff bank statement, an auditor noticed that the majority of checks listed as outstanding at the preceding December 31 had not cleared the bank. Which of the following is not a likely explanation of this finding?

A. Checks were written prior to year end but were not mailed on a timely basis.

B. Kiting was used to cover a shortage of cash.

C. The cash disbursements journal had been held open past year end.

D. The cutoff bank statement was requested too soon after year end.

Answer (B) is correct. *(Publisher, adapted)*

REQUIRED: The unwarranted conclusion when the majority of checks outstanding at year end have not cleared.

DISCUSSION: Kiting is an attempt to conceal a cash shortage by recording a deposit in the current period from an interbank transfer but failing to record the disbursement until the following period. The check is returned in the cutoff bank statement with no record in the cash disbursements journal or on the bank reconciliation.

Answer (A) is incorrect. If the checks were held after year end, they would not likely have cleared the bank prior to receipt of the cutoff bank statement. Answer (C) is incorrect. The cash disbursements journal could have been held open, thus permitting disbursements actually made in the subsequent period to be predated and recorded in the period under audit. Answer (D) is incorrect. If the cutoff bank statement is requested too soon after year end, the checks mailed at year end may not have had time to clear the bank and be returned.

11.2.9. Which of the following cash transfers results in a misstatement of cash at December 31, Year 1?

Bank Transfer Schedule

	Disbursement		Receipt	
	Recorded in Books	Paid by Bank	Recorded in Books	Received by Bank
A.	12/31/Yr 1	1/4/Yr 2	12/31/Yr 1	12/31/Yr 1
B.	1/4/Yr 2	1/5/Yr 2	12/31/Yr 1	1/4/Yr 2
C.	12/31/Yr 1	1/5/Yr 2	12/31/Yr 1	1/4/Yr 2
D.	1/4/Yr 2	1/11/Yr 2	1/4/Yr 2	1/4/Yr 2

Answer (B) is correct. *(CPA, adapted)*

REQUIRED: The interbank cash transfer that indicates an error in cash cutoff.

DISCUSSION: An error in cash cutoff occurs if one half of the transaction is recorded in the current period and one half in the subsequent period. Inspection of the Recorded in Books columns indicates the transfer was recorded as a receipt on 12/31/Yr 1 but not as a disbursement until 1/4/Yr 2. This discrepancy is an error in cutoff called a kite, and it overstates the cash balance.

11.2.10. Which of the following characteristics is most likely indicative of check kiting?

A. High turnover of employees who have access to cash.

B. Many large checks that are recorded on Mondays.

C. Low average balance compared with high level of deposits.

D. Frequent ATM checking account withdrawals.

Answer (C) is correct. *(CPA, adapted)*

REQUIRED: The item most likely to indicate check kiting.

DISCUSSION: Kiting is the recording of a deposit from an interbank transfer in the current period, while failing to record the related disbursement until the next period. It overstates the cash balance because the amount of the transfer is included in both bank accounts at year end. A low average balance compared with a high level of deposits is an indication of check kiting.

Answer (A) is incorrect. High turnover of employees who have access to cash indicates susceptibility to theft. Answer (B) is incorrect. Recording of large checks on Mondays has no necessary connection with check kiting. Answer (D) is incorrect. The frequency of ATM checking account withdrawals has no necessary connection with check kiting.

11.2.11. On receiving a client's bank cutoff statement, an auditor most likely will trace

A. Prior-year checks listed in the cutoff statement to the year-end outstanding checklist.

B. Deposits in transit listed in the cutoff statement to the year-end bank reconciliation.

C. Checks dated after year end listed in the cutoff statement to the year-end outstanding checklist

D. Deposits recorded in the cash receipts journal after year end to the cutoff statement.

Answer (A) is correct. *(CPA, adapted)*

REQUIRED: The search an auditor most likely performs after receiving a client's bank cutoff statement.

DISCUSSION: A cutoff bank statement should be used to test reconciling items on the year-end bank reconciliation, e.g., deposits in transit and outstanding checks. Analysis of a cutoff bank statement is a procedure that entails consideration of a bank statement for part of a month that includes canceled checks and other debit/credit memos. The cutoff bank statement covers at least 7 business days following the client's year end, thus permitting the auditor to verify that deposits in transit and checks outstanding listed on the client's year-end bank reconciliation have been recorded by the bank. Tracing prior-year checks listed in the cutoff statement to the year-end outstanding checklist in the bank reconciliation helps the auditor to detect outstanding but unrecorded checks at year end (an overstatement of cash).

Answer (B) is incorrect. The auditor is more likely to vouch the deposits in transit on the reconciliation of the cutoff statement to determine that the recorded amount was actually deposited. Overstatement is a greater risk than the understatement of cash resulting from an unrecorded deposit in transit. Answer (C) is incorrect. Checks dated after year end are not listed in the year-end checklist. Answer (D) is incorrect. The auditor's primary concern with regard to the deposits is that amounts recorded as in transit at year end were not actually received by the bank.

11.2.12. A proof of cash used by an auditor

A. Proves that the client's year-end balance of cash is fairly stated.

B. Confirms that the client has properly separated the custody function from the recording function with respect to cash.

C. Validates that the client's bank did not make an error during the period being examined.

D. Determines whether any unauthorized disbursements or unrecorded deposits were made for the given time period.

Answer (D) is correct. *(CMA, adapted)*

REQUIRED: The purpose of a proof of cash.

DISCUSSION: A proof of cash consists of a four-column worksheet with bank reconciliations in the first and fourth columns for the beginning and end of the period and reconciliations of cash receipts and disbursements in the middle columns. The amounts per books and per bank should reconcile both horizontally and vertically. The proof of cash thus detects unauthorized disbursements or unrecorded deposits for the period. It is useful when internal control over cash transactions is ineffective.

Answer (A) is incorrect. A proof of cash only reconciles one bank account. Other procedures are necessary to provide evidence concerning the fairness of the cash balance, e.g., examination of cash on hand and cash in foreign countries. Answer (B) is incorrect. The auditor must obtain an understanding of internal control relevant to cash to determine whether the custody function is properly separated from the recording function. Answer (C) is incorrect. A proof of cash may detect an error made by the client's bank, but that is not the reason the auditor performs the proof.

11.2.13. On the last day of the fiscal year, the cash disbursements clerk drew a company check on bank A and deposited the check in the company account bank B to cover a previous theft of cash. The disbursement has not been recorded. The auditor will best detect this form of kiting by

A. Comparing the detail of cash receipts as shown by the cash receipts records with the detail on the confirmed duplicate deposit tickets for three days prior to and subsequent to year end.

B. Preparing from the cash disbursements book a summary of bank transfers for one week prior to and subsequent to year end.

C. Examining the composition of deposits in both bank A and B subsequent to year end.

D. Examining paid checks returned with the bank statement of the next accounting period after year end.

Answer (D) is correct. *(CPA, adapted)*

REQUIRED: The best audit procedure to detect kiting.

DISCUSSION: Because the check used to make the bank transfer is not recorded in the current period, the check is not listed as outstanding on the reconciliation of the bank account on which it was drawn. The auditor detects kiting by comparing paid checks, returned in the next period and dated prior to year end, with the checks listed as outstanding on the related bank reconciliation. In other words, the auditor searches for checks that should have been listed as outstanding but were not.

Answer (A) is incorrect. The deposits and receipts records are accounted for correctly in kiting. Answer (B) is incorrect. The cash disbursements book would not contain this disbursement at year end. Answer (C) is incorrect. The deposit records are accounted for correctly in kiting.

Questions 11.2.14 and 11.2.15 are based on the following information. The following was taken from the bank transfer schedule prepared during the audit of Fox Co.'s financial statements for the year ended December 31, Year 1. Assume all checks are dated and issued on December 30, Year 1.

Check	Bank Accounts		Disbursement Date		Receipt Date	
No.	From	To	Per Books	Per Bank	Per Books	Per Bank
101	National	Federal	Dec. 30	Jan. 4	Dec. 30	Jan. 3
202	County	State	Jan. 3	Jan. 2	Dec. 30	Dec. 31
303	Federal	American	Dec. 31	Jan. 3	Jan. 2	Jan. 2
404	State	Republic	Jan. 2	Jan. 2	Dec. 31	Jan. 2

11.2.14. Which of the following checks might indicate kiting?

A. #101 and #303.

B. #202 and #404.

C. #101 and #404.

D. #202 and #303.

Answer (B) is correct. *(CPA, adapted)*

REQUIRED: The checks that might indicate kiting.

DISCUSSION: Kiting is the recording of a deposit from an interbank transfer in the current period while failing to record the related disbursement until the next period. It is a fraud that exploits the lag (float period) between the deposit of a check in one account and the time it clears the bank on which it is drawn. Checks #202 and #404 may indicate kiting. They were recorded as receipts on the books in the current period. However, they were recorded as disbursements on the books in the next year.

11.2.15. Which of the following checks illustrate deposits or transfers in transit at December 31, Year 1?

A. #101 and #202.

B. #101 and #303.

C. #202 and #404.

D. #303 and #404.

Answer (B) is correct. *(CPA, adapted)*

REQUIRED: The checks indicating deposits or transfers in transit.

DISCUSSION: A deposit or transfer in transit is one recorded in the entity's books as a receipt by the balance sheet date but not recorded as a deposit by the bank until the next period. Check #101 is a deposit or transfer in transit because the check was recorded in the books before the end of the year but not recorded by either bank until January. Check #303 is also a deposit or transfer in transit because the check was deducted from Federal's balance in December but was not added to American's balance until January.

11.2.16. Which of the following procedures would an auditor most likely perform in auditing the statement of cash flows?

A. Reconcile the amounts included in the statement of cash flows to the other financial statements' amounts.

B. Vouch a sample of cash receipts and disbursements for the last few days of the current year.

C. Reconcile the cutoff bank statement to the proof of cash to verify the accuracy of the year-end cash balance.

D. Confirm the amounts included in the statement of cash flows with the entity's financial institution.

Answer (A) is correct. *(CPA, adapted)*

REQUIRED: The procedure performed in auditing the statement of cash flows.

DISCUSSION: The information presented on a statement of cash flows is taken from the income statement and balance sheet. Indeed, a reconciliation of net income and net operating cash flow is required to be presented. Thus, reconciliation of amounts in the statement of cash flows with other financial statements' balances and amounts is an important procedure in the audit of the statement of cash flows.

Answer (B) is incorrect. Vouching a sample of cash receipts and disbursements for the last few days of the year is effective for detecting cutoff misstatements but not for auditing the statement of cash flows. Answer (C) is incorrect. Reconciling the cutoff bank statement to the proof of cash to verify the accuracy of the year-end cash balance is an appropriate procedure to audit the cash account but not necessarily the statement of cash flows. Answer (D) is incorrect. Confirmation of the amounts included in the statement of cash flows is a procedure for cash that is not effective for auditing the statement of cash flows.

Questions 11.2.17 and 11.2.18 are based on the following information.

Miles Company
Bank Transfer Schedule
December 31

	Bank Accounts			Date Disbursed per		Date Deposited per	
Check	From	To	Amount	Books	Bank	Books	Bank
#2020	1st Natl.	Suburban	$32,000	12/31	1/5þ	12/31	1/3Ø
#2021	1st Natl.	Capital	21,000	12/31	1/4þ	12/31	1/3Ø
#3217	2nd State	Suburban	6,700	1/3	1/5	1/3	1/6
#0659	Midtown	Suburban	5,500	12/30	1/5þ	12/30	1/3Ø

11.2.17. The tick mark þ likely indicates that the amount was traced to the

A. December cash disbursements journal.

B. Outstanding check list of the applicable bank reconciliation.

C. January cash disbursements journal.

D. Year-end bank confirmations.

Answer (B) is correct. *(CPA, adapted)*

REQUIRED: The meaning of the tick mark þ in the bank transfer schedule.

DISCUSSION: The tick marks indicate the dates amounts were disbursed according to the bank. In each case, the amount was recorded in the books at the end of the preceding period. Because the checks traced had not cleared at December 31, they would not have been included in the December bank statement. Thus, these outstanding checks are reconciling items (differences between the books and the December bank statements for the respective drawee banks).

Answer (A) is incorrect. The transfer schedule already indicates that the marked transactions were recorded in the December cash disbursements journal. Tracing to the bank reconciliation serves the more useful purpose of determining whether these checks were included as reconciling items. Answer (C) is incorrect. The marked disbursements were recorded in December. Answer (D) is incorrect. The bank confirmation requests information about the year-end balance, which would not include the outstanding checks.

11.2.18. The tick mark Ø most likely indicates that the amount was traced to the

A. Deposits in transit of the applicable bank reconciliation.

B. December cash receipts journal.

C. January cash receipts journal.

D. Year-end bank confirmations.

Answer (A) is correct. *(CPA, adapted)*

REQUIRED: The meaning of the tick mark Ø in the bank transfer schedule.

DISCUSSION: The tick marks indicate transfers recorded by the depository banks in January that were recorded in the books in December. Accordingly, these transactions were deposits in transit at December 31 and should have been included in the appropriate bank reconciliations.

Answer (B) is incorrect. The marked amounts were known to be recorded in the books. Answer (C) is incorrect. The December cash receipts journal includes the marked transactions. Answer (D) is incorrect. The bank confirmation at year end would not include items recorded by the bank in January.

11.2.19. An auditor is concerned about the possibility of fraud if

A. Cash receipts, net of the amounts used to pay petty cash-type expenditures, are deposited in the bank daily.

B. The monthly bank statement reconciliation is performed by the same employee who maintains the perpetual inventory records.

C. The accounts receivable subsidiary ledger and accounts payable subsidiary ledger are maintained by the same person.

D. One person, acting alone, has sole access to the petty cash fund (except for a provision for occasional surprise counts by a supervisor or auditor).

Answer (A) is correct. *(CIA, adapted)*

REQUIRED: The reason an auditor is concerned about the possibility of fraud.

DISCUSSION: Paying petty cash expenditures from cash receipts facilitates the unauthorized removal of cash before deposit. All cash receipts should be deposited intact daily. Petty cash expenditures should be handled through an impress fund.

Answer (B) is incorrect. The monthly bank reconciliation should not be performed by a person who makes deposits or writes checks, but the inventory clerk does not have these responsibilities. Answer (C) is incorrect. There is no direct relationship between the transactions posted to the accounts receivable and accounts payable subsidiary ledgers. Having the same person maintain both ledgers does not create a control weakness. Answer (D) is incorrect. To establish accountability for petty cash, only one person should have access to the fund.

11.2.20. Using a wide variety of solicitation techniques, a large public charity raises funds for medical research from the general public. In an audit of donations, the internal auditor is least likely to use which of the following audit procedures?

A. Written confirmation of a sample of direct mail pledges.

B. Reconciliation of depository bank accounts.

C. Surprise observation of door-to-door solicitation teams.

D. Reconciliation of raffle tickets sold to amounts deposited in the bank.

Answer (C) is correct. *(CIA, adapted)*

REQUIRED: The least likely audit procedure in an audit of donations.

DISCUSSION: An analysis of the instructions given to door-to-door solicitation teams is more appropriate than a surprise observation. The lack of materiality of individual donations, the presence of other controls, and the inability to sample enough teams all make direct observation an inefficient audit procedure.

Answer (A) is incorrect. Written confirmation of mail pledges provides evidence of existence. Answer (B) is incorrect. Reconciliation of depository bank accounts provides evidence of the completeness of cash. Answer (D) is incorrect. Reconciliation of raffle tickets sold to amounts deposited in the bank tests completeness of the raffle revenues.

11.2.21. When auditing a client's statement of cash flows, an auditor will rely primarily upon

A. Determination of the amount of cash at year-end.

B. Cross-referencing to balances and transactions considered in connection with the audit of the other financial statements.

C. Analysis of significant ratios of prior years as compared to the current year.

D. The standard bank confirmation.

Answer (B) is correct. *(CPA, adapted)*

REQUIRED: The evidence on which the auditor will primarily rely when auditing a statement of cash flows.

DISCUSSION: The statement of cash flows represents balances taken from the other statements as well as analysis of changes in those balances. Consequently, this statement is audited in conjunction with the balance sheet and income statement accounts.

Answer (A) is incorrect. The statement reflects the changes in the cash balance rather than the balance in the account at year-end. Answer (C) is incorrect. Analysis of ratios (an analytical procedure) used as a substantive test may be effective and efficient for testing some assertions but not all of those encompassed by a statement of cash flows. Answer (D) is incorrect. The standard bank confirmation provides evidence only to the ending balance in cash.

11.2.22. An auditor is reviewing a corporate client's statement of cash flows. The auditor should expect the cash flows to be classified according to

A. Fund inflows and fund outflows.

B. Cash inflows and cash outflows.

C. Operating activities, sources, and uses.

D. Investing, financing, and operating activities.

Answer (D) is correct. *(Publisher, adapted)*

REQUIRED: The activities into which cash receipts and cash payments should be classified.

DISCUSSION: To provide the most useful information about cash receipts and cash payments to investors, creditors, and others, a statement of cash flows should report the cash effects of an entity's operations, its investing transactions, and its financing transactions during the period. In addition, the related disclosures should report the effects of investing and financing transactions that do not directly affect cash.

Answer (A) is incorrect. A statement of cash flows is based on cash. Answer (B) is incorrect. The cash flows must be classified according to investing, financing, and operating activities. Answer (C) is incorrect. Sources and uses were used in the now-superseded statement of changes in financial position.

11.2.23. Many of the Granada Corporation's convertible bondholders have converted their bonds into stock during the year under audit. The independent auditor should review the Granada Corporation's statement of cash flows and related disclosures to ascertain that they show

A. Only the cash used to reduce the convertible debt.

B. Only the cash provided by the issuance of stock.

C. The issuance of the stock and reduction in convertible debt.

D. Nothing relating to the conversion because it does not affect cash.

Answer (C) is correct. *(CPA, adapted)*

REQUIRED: The proper reporting of the conversion of bonds to stock.

DISCUSSION: Information about noncash financing and investing activities must be reported in related disclosures but not on the face of the statement of cash flows. Exclusion of such transactions from the statement avoids complicating it and emphasizes the entity's cash receipts and payments. The issuance of stock and the reduction of convertible debt should therefore be disclosed in a related but separate schedule. All financing (and investing) activities during the period should be reported, including those that do not directly affect cash.

Answer (A) is incorrect. Although this part of the financing activity should be reported, it does not involve a cash flow. Answer (B) is incorrect. Although both parts of the financing activity should be reported, neither involves a cash flow. Answer (D) is incorrect. All financing and investing activities should be reported.

STUDY UNIT TWELVE EVIDENCE -- PURCHASES, INVENTORY, PAYROLL, AND OTHER CYCLES

In general, most testing of the inventory-acquisition process is applied to accounts payable and inventory. The emphasis is on the likelihood of understatement of accounts payable and overstatement of inventory. Evidençe about the debit in the payables transaction (inventory in a perpetual system and purchases in a periodic system) is gathered when the credit (accounts payable) is tested. The interrelationship also is apparent in the opposite direction. As the debit is tested, evidence about the credit is produced.

This study unit also contains questions based on comprehensive audit plans for other specific accounts. Separate subunits are not included for income statement items, but questions on revenues and expenses are assigned to subunits for the related balance sheet accounts. For example, questions on depreciation expense are included in Subunit 12.3, Substantive Testing of Property, Plant, and Equipment (PPE).

QUESTIONS

12.1 Substantive Testing of Accounts Payable and Purchases

12.1.1. An audit assistant found a purchase order for a regular supplier in the amount of $5,500. The purchase order was dated after receipt of the goods. The purchasing agent had forgotten to issue the purchase order. Also, a disbursement of $450 for materials did not have a receiving report. The assistant wanted to select additional purchase orders for investigation but was unconcerned about the lack of a receiving report. The audit director should

A. Agree with the assistant because the amount of the purchase order exception was considerably larger than the receiving report exception.

B. Agree with the assistant because the cash disbursement clerk had been assured by the receiving clerk that the failure to fill out a report did not happen very often.

C. Disagree with the assistant because the two problems have an equal risk of loss associated with them.

D. Disagree with the assistant because the lack of a receiving report has a greater risk of loss associated with it.

Answer (D) is correct. *(CIA, adapted)*

REQUIRED: The implications of a missing purchase order and a missing receiving report.

DISCUSSION: The risk of a material fraud is greater for the missing receiving report than for the postdated purchase order. In the latter case, the goods were received, and the company has obtained what it paid for. Because the goods come from a regular supplier, the likelihood is that the purchase was actually authorized. However, the lack of a receiving report in support of a disbursement is a much more serious matter. It suggests potential fraud because an approved payment voucher should be accompanied by a purchase order, supplier's invoice, and a receiving report. One possibility is that duplicate payments are being made.

Answer (A) is incorrect. The potential for fraud and heightened control risk made the absence of a receiving report a material matter despite its dollar amount. Answer (B) is incorrect. The hearsay testimony of the cash disbursement clerk has very little evidentiary value. Answer (C) is incorrect. The missing receiving report indicates a much greater risk than the postdated purchase order.

12.1.2. In auditing accounts payable, an auditor's procedures most likely will focus primarily on the relevant assertion about

A. Existence.

B. Classification and understandability.

C. Completeness.

D. Valuation and allocation.

Answer (C) is correct. *(CPA, adapted)*

REQUIRED: The assertion that is the focus of an audit of accounts payable.

DISCUSSION: The primary audit risk for accounts payable is understatement of the liability. Thus, the auditor will most likely focus on the completeness assertion.

Answer (A) is incorrect. The existence assertion concerns whether liabilities exist at a given date. The audit risk for accounts payable is not great for that assertion. Answer (B) is incorrect. The risk of inappropriate classification and understandability on the financial statements is not as great as the risk that some items are not included. Answer (D) is incorrect. The risk that accounts payable are not measured in accordance with the applicable reporting framework is lower than the risk that the balance may not be complete.

12.1.3. An auditor performs a test to determine whether all merchandise for which the client was billed was received. The population for this test consists of all

A. Merchandise received.

B. Vendors' invoices.

C. Canceled checks.

D. Receiving reports.

Answer (B) is correct. *(CPA, adapted)*

REQUIRED: The population for a test to determine whether all merchandise for which the client was billed was received.

DISCUSSION: Vendors' invoices are the billing documents received by the client. They describe the items purchased, the amounts due, and the payment terms. The auditor should trace these invoices to the related receiving reports.

Answer (A) is incorrect. Testing merchandise received will not detect merchandise billed but not received. Answer (C) is incorrect. Tracing canceled checks to the related receiving reports tests whether goods paid for, not goods billed, were received. Answer (D) is incorrect. Tracing receiving reports to vendors' invoices tests whether all goods received were billed.

12.1.4. The primary audit procedure to determine whether accounts payable are measured properly is

A. A confirmation of accounts payable.

B. Vouching accounts payable to supporting documentation.

C. An analytical procedure.

D. Verification that accounts payable are reported as a current liability in the balance sheet.

Answer (B) is correct. *(Publisher, adapted)*

REQUIRED: The audit procedure to determine whether accounts payable are properly measured.

DISCUSSION: Relatively few problems are encountered by the auditor in meeting the objective of determining the proper measurement of accounts payable. The auditor vouches the recorded accounts payable to the supporting documentation, the invoice and purchase order, to determine whether the balances are accurately measured.

Answer (A) is incorrect. The confirmation of accounts payable cannot be relied on to reveal unrecorded liabilities. Answer (C) is incorrect. Analytical procedures provide an overall review of the payables, but they are not specifically directed at valuation of individual accounts. Answer (D) is incorrect. Whether accounts payable are reported as a current liability is related to the audit objective for statement presentation and disclosure rather than proper measurement.

12.1.5. Which of the following procedures is least likely to be performed before the balance sheet date?

A. Observation of inventory.

B. Testing internal control over cash.

C. Search for unrecorded liabilities.

D. Confirmation of receivables.

Answer (C) is correct. *(CPA, adapted)*

REQUIRED: The procedure least likely to be performed before the balance sheet date.

DISCUSSION: A significant risk is that all payables may not be reflected in the year-end balance. The auditor will review cash disbursements made subsequent to year end to determine whether payments are for previously unrecorded liabilities. Other procedures that would not be performed prior to the balance sheet date include reviewing subsequent events, requesting the lawyer's letter, and obtaining management representations.

Answer (A) is incorrect. If controls are effective, the risk of material misstatement is low, and the client maintains reliable perpetual records, the auditor's observation procedures usually can be performed prior to year end. Answer (B) is incorrect. The understanding of internal control is customarily obtained prior to the balance sheet date to permit the auditor to assess the risk of material misstatement and design the nature, timing, and extent of further procedures. Answer (D) is incorrect. Receivables confirmation may be made either during (if controls are effective), at the end of, or after the period under audit.

12.1.6. Which of the following tests of details most likely would help an auditor determine whether accounts payable have been misstated?

A. Examining reported purchase returns that appear too low.

B. Examining vendor statements for amounts not reported as purchases.

C. Searching for customer-returned goods that were not reported as returns.

D. Reviewing bank transfers recorded as cash received from customers.

Answer (B) is correct. *(CPA, adapted)*

REQUIRED: The tests of details most likely to detect a misstatement in accounts payable.

DISCUSSION: Vendor statements should reflect currently recorded accounts payable. Examining statements at year end and matching line items to recorded payables will detect unrecorded payables.

Answer (A) is incorrect. Examining purchase returns that appear too low could result in the discovery of the overstatement of accounts payable. Although a possibility, it would not be as likely as conditions that would understate payables. Answer (C) is incorrect. Customer-returned goods would affect the recording of receivables, not payables. Answer (D) is incorrect. Bank transfers affect the recording of cash, not accounts payable.

12.1.7. When using confirmations to provide evidence about the completeness assertion for accounts payable, the appropriate population most likely is

A. Vendors with whom the entity has previously done business.

B. Amounts recorded in the accounts payable subsidiary ledger.

C. Payees of checks drawn in the month after the year end.

D. Invoices filed in the entity's open invoice file.

Answer (A) is correct. *(CPA, adapted)*

REQUIRED: The appropriate population when confirmations of accounts payable are used to test the completeness assertion.

DISCUSSION: When sending confirmations for accounts payable, the population of accounts should include small and zero balances as well as large balances. The auditor should use the activity in the account as a gauge for sample selection. That is, if orders are placed with a vendor on a consistent basis, a confirmation should be sent to that vendor regardless of the recorded balance due.

Answer (B) is incorrect. The auditor, in testing the completeness assertion, is concerned with balances that have not been recorded or invoices that have not been filed. Answer (C) is incorrect. The payees of checks are not an appropriate population for the confirmation process. Payments in the month after year end do not necessarily reflect year-end liabilities. Answer (D) is incorrect. The auditor, in testing the completeness assertion, is concerned with balances that have not been recorded or invoices that have not been filed.

12.1.8. Which of the following is a substantive procedure that an auditor most likely would perform to verify the existence and valuation assertions about recorded accounts payable?

A. Investigating the open purchase order file to ascertain that prenumbered purchase orders are used and accounted for.

B. Receiving the client's mail, unopened, for a reasonable period of time after year end to search for unrecorded vendor's invoices.

C. Vouching selected entries in the accounts payable subsidiary ledger to purchase orders and receiving reports.

D. Confirming accounts payable balances with known suppliers who have zero balances.

Answer (C) is correct. *(CPA, adapted)*

REQUIRED: The substantive procedure for the existence and valuation assertions about recorded accounts payable.

DISCUSSION: Vouching a sample of recorded accounts payable to purchase orders and receiving reports provides evidence that the obligations exist at a given date. The purchase orders evidence the initiation of the transactions, and the receiving reports indicate that goods were received and that liabilities were thereby incurred. Thus, these documents provide evidence that amounts are owed to others, that the transactions occurred, and that the liabilities have been included at appropriate amounts.

Answer (A) is incorrect. Ascertaining that prenumbered documents are used and accounted for relates most directly to the completeness assertion. Answer (B) is incorrect. Searching for unrecorded liabilities relates most directly to completeness. Answer (D) is incorrect. Confirming payables with known suppliers having zero balances is a procedure for detecting unrecorded liabilities. Thus, it relates most directly to completeness.

12.1.9. Audit procedures applied to purchase transactions at year end address the cutoff assertion. An entity should include goods in its inventory if it

A. Has sold the goods.

B. Holds legal title to the goods.

C. Has physical possession of the goods.

D. Has paid for the goods.

Answer (B) is correct. *(Publisher, adapted)*

REQUIRED: The purpose of testing cutoff.

DISCUSSION: In general, cutoff procedures determine that transactions are recorded in the appropriate period. A proper purchase cutoff is intended to assure inclusion of the goods in inventory and the recognition of a liability in the period in which the client acquired title to the goods.

Answer (A) is incorrect. Sold goods should be removed from inventory. Answer (C) is incorrect. Title can pass without actual possession (e.g., shipments to the client FOB shipping point). Answer (D) is incorrect. The goods may be purchased on credit and need not be paid for by the cutoff date.

12.1.10. When title to merchandise in transit has passed to the audit client, the auditor engaged in the performance of a purchase cutoff will encounter the greatest difficulty in gaining assurance with respect to the

A. Quantity.

B. Quality.

C. Price.

D. Terms.

Answer (B) is correct. *(CPA, adapted)*

REQUIRED: The greatest difficulty in performing a purchase cutoff when title to merchandise in transit passes to the client.

DISCUSSION: The purpose of the cutoff is to ensure that the asset and related liability are recognized in the correct period. Accordingly, merchandise included in ending inventory but not yet arrived may not be available for inspection. The quality of such merchandise cannot be assured until the inspection has been conducted after the goods are received.

12.1.11. Confirmation of accounts payable with creditors is most appropriate when

A. The majority of accounts payable balances are owed to related parties.

B. Creditor statements are not available, and internal control over accounts payable is unsatisfactory.

C. Accounts payable balances are immaterial.

D. Internal control over accounts payable is effective, and sufficient evidence exists to minimize the risk of a material misstatement.

Answer (B) is correct. *(Publisher, adapted)*

REQUIRED: The reason for confirming accounts payable.

DISCUSSION: When internal control relevant to assertions about accounts payable is ineffective, the risk of material misstatement is increased. The auditor may need to change the nature, timing, or extent of substantive procedures and consider the use of external confirmations. The auditor also should confirm accounts payable when (1) documentary evidence is lacking, (2) individual creditors have relatively large balances, (3) the client has made a major purchase from the creditor regardless of the size of the balance, (4) unusual transactions are involved, or (5) the account is secured.

Answer (A) is incorrect. The auditor only needs to give particular consideration to confirming the accounts with related parties in the presence of other indications that the payables should be confirmed. Answer (C) is incorrect. Confirmation of accounts payable is usually unnecessary when the payables are immaterial. Answer (D) is incorrect. The confirmation of accounts payable is usually not considered when internal control is effective.

12.1.12. Which of the following procedures would best detect a liability omission by management?

A. Inquiry of senior support staff and recently departed employees.

B. Review and check mathematical accuracy of financial statements.

C. Review articles of incorporation and corporate bylaws.

D. Review purchase contracts and other legal documents.

Answer (D) is correct. *(CPA, adapted)*

REQUIRED: The procedure to detect a liability omission by management.

DISCUSSION: The auditor's search for unrecorded liabilities should include reading contracts, loan agreements, leases, correspondence from governmental agencies, and any legal documents in the client's possession.

Answer (A) is incorrect. The support staff and departed employees do not likely have knowledge about devious actions of management. Answer (B) is incorrect. The omitted liabilities would not be included in the financial statements. Answer (C) is incorrect. The articles of incorporation and the bylaws will not address litigation or liabilities.

12.1.13. A firm has recently converted its purchasing cycle from a manual system to an online computer system. The internal auditor in charge of the first post-implementation audit of the new system has access to a generalized audit software package. One audit objective is to determine whether all material liabilities for trade accounts payable have been recorded. Which of the following is most useful in achieving this objective?

A. A listing of all purchase transactions processed after the cutoff date.

B. A listing of all accounts payable ledger accounts with a post office box given as the vendor mailing address.

C. A listing of all duplicate purchase orders, receiving reports, and vendor invoices.

D. A listing of all vendors with a debit balance in the accounts payable ledgers.

Answer (A) is correct. *(CIA, adapted)*

REQUIRED: The procedure for determining whether all liabilities for trade accounts payable have been recorded.

DISCUSSION: Examining a listing of all purchase transactions processed after the cutoff date tests the completeness of accounts payable. It investigates the possibility that accounts payable have been recorded in the wrong period.

Answer (B) is incorrect. Listing payables with post office boxes is useful in the detection of fraud, but has little efficacy in the determination of the completeness of accounts payable. Answer (C) is incorrect. Listing duplicate documents is not helpful in the search for all legitimate accounts payable. Answer (D) is incorrect. Liability accounts typically have a credit balance. An account payable with a debit balance is often the result of the misclassification of a receivable. The result of such an error is the overstatement of accounts payable. The internal auditor is testing for an understatement of accounts payable.

12.1.14. Unrecorded liabilities are most likely to be found during the review of which of the following documents?

A. Unpaid bills.

B. Shipping records.

C. Bills of lading.

D. Unmatched sales invoices.

Answer (A) is correct. *(CPA, adapted)*

REQUIRED: The documents that should be reviewed to detect unrecorded liabilities.

DISCUSSION: The auditor examines the accounts payable vouchers prepared during the subsequent period to determine whether they were for amounts recorded as liabilities at year end. (S)he also examines unvouchered invoices (unpaid bills) because they could represent payables that should have been recorded prior to year end. This procedure should be performed through the date of the auditor's report.

Answer (B) is incorrect. Shipping records relate to the entity's sales. Answer (C) is incorrect. Bills of lading relate to the entity's sales. Answer (D) is incorrect. Unmatched sales invoices relate to the entity's sales.

12.1.15. In a payables application, checks are authorized and paid based on matching purchase orders, receiving reports, and vendor invoices. Partial payments are common. An appropriate audit procedure for verifying that a purchase order has not been paid twice is to sort the

A. Receiving report file by purchase order, compute total amounts received by purchase order, compare total amounts received with purchase order amounts, and investigate any discrepancies between the total amounts received and purchase order amounts.

B. Vendor invoice file by purchase order, compute total amounts invoiced by purchase order, compare total amounts invoiced with purchase order amounts, and investigate any discrepancies between the total amounts invoiced and purchase order amounts.

C. Receiving report file by vendor invoice amounts and investigate any discrepancies between the total amounts received and vendor invoice amounts.

D. Check register file by purchase order, compute total amounts paid by purchase order, compare total amounts paid with purchase order amounts, and investigate any discrepancies between the total amounts paid and purchase order amounts.

Answer (D) is correct. *(CIA, adapted)*

REQUIRED: The appropriate audit procedure for verifying that a purchase order has not been paid twice.

DISCUSSION: The audit objectives for payables include the discovery of unrecorded liabilities and overpayments. Effective internal control over payments avoids these problems by (1) matching supporting documents, (2) using proper check preparation methods, and (3) providing for strict authorization procedures. The audit process described tests the effectiveness of internal control over payments in a way that merely tracing a sample of checks to purchase orders could not.

Answer (A) is incorrect. The procedure described compares goods received with goods ordered. Answer (B) is incorrect. The procedure described compares goods invoiced by the vendor and goods ordered. Answer (C) is incorrect. The procedure described compares goods received and goods invoiced.

12.1.16. Which of the following audit procedures is best for identifying unrecorded trade accounts payable?

A. Reviewing cash disbursements recorded subsequent to the balance sheet date to determine whether the related payables apply to the prior period.

B. Investigating payables recorded just prior to and just subsequent to the balance sheet date to determine whether they are supported by receiving reports.

C. Examining unusual relationships between monthly accounts payable balances and recorded cash payments.

D. Reconciling vendors' statements to the file of receiving reports to identify items received just prior to the balance sheet date.

Answer (A) is correct. *(CPA, adapted)*

REQUIRED: The procedure most likely to reveal unrecorded liabilities.

DISCUSSION: The greatest risk in the audit of payables is that unrecorded liabilities exist. Omission of an entry to record a payable is a misstatement that is more difficult to detect than an inaccurate or false entry. The search for unrecorded payables should (1) include examining cash payments made after the balance sheet date and comparing them with the accounts payable trial balance, (2) sending confirmations to vendors with small and zero balances, and (3) reconciling payable balances with vendors' documentation.

Answer (B) is incorrect. Investigating recorded payables to determine whether they are supported by receiving reports tests only the amounts recorded. Answer (C) is incorrect. Examining unusual relationships between monthly accounts payable balances and recorded cash payments tests only the amounts that have been recorded. Answer (D) is incorrect. Reconciling vendors' statements to the file of receiving reports to identify items received just prior to the balance sheet date does not determine whether those items are recorded.

12.1.17. One objective of an audit of the purchasing function is to determine the cost of late payment of invoices containing trade discounts. The appropriate population from which a sample would be drawn is the file of

A. Receiving reports.

B. Purchase orders.

C. Canceled checks.

D. Paid vendor invoices.

Answer (D) is correct. *(CIA, adapted)*

REQUIRED: The sample to determine the cost of late payment of invoices containing trade discounts.

DISCUSSION: A vendor invoice shows both the amount and terms of payment for purchase. Failure to pay within the discount period is normally not advantageous. Thus, lost discounts may signify inefficiency in the purchases-payables-cash disbursements function or a shortage of cash.

Answer (A) is incorrect. Receiving reports indicate the date and quantity received but not whether discounts were offered or taken. Answer (B) is incorrect. Purchase orders show only the quantity and expected price of a purchase. Answer (C) is incorrect. Canceled checks show only the total paid, not whether a discount was offered or taken.

12.1.18. When auditing a public warehouse, which of the following is the most important audit procedure with respect to disclosing unrecorded liabilities?

A. Confirmation of negotiable receipts with holders.

B. Review of outstanding receipts.

C. Inspection of receiving and issuing procedures.

D. Observation of inventory.

Answer (C) is correct. *(CPA, adapted)*

REQUIRED: The most important audit procedure to disclose unrecorded liabilities when auditing a public warehouse.

DISCUSSION: When auditing a public warehouse, the inspection of receiving and issuing procedures is the most important procedure for disclosing unrecorded liabilities. Shipping orders and receiving reports that are not reflected in the records suggest that transactions are not being properly recorded.

Answer (A) is incorrect. The auditor is not likely to know the names of the holders when receipts are negotiable. Answer (B) is incorrect. A review of outstanding receipts only provides audit evidence about those known to be outstanding, i.e., recorded. Answer (D) is incorrect. Observation of inventory provides evidence that the inventory exists but not that the related liabilities are unrecorded.

12.1.19. In an audit of a purchasing department, which of the following usually is considered a risk factor?

A. Purchase specifications are developed by the department requesting the material.

B. Purchases are made against blanket or open purchase orders for certain types of items.

C. Purchases are made from parties related to buyers or other company officials.

D. Purchases are not rotated among suppliers included on an approved vendor list.

Answer (C) is correct. *(CIA, adapted)*

REQUIRED: The item considered to be a risk factor.

DISCUSSION: Purchasing from parties related to buyers or other entity officials is a risk factor because it suggests the possibility of fraud. Such conflicts of interest may result in transactions unfavorable to the company.

Answer (A) is incorrect. The requesting department normally develops specifications. Answer (B) is incorrect. Open purchase orders are customary for high-use items. Answer (D) is incorrect. An approved vendor list is often maintained as a control to help ensure that purchases are made only from reliable vendors. However, rotation is not usually appropriate.

12.1.20. In verifying debits to perpetual inventory records of a nonmanufacturing firm, the auditor would be most interested in examining the purchase

A. Journal.

B. Requisitions.

C. Orders.

D. Invoices.

Answer (D) is correct. *(CPA, adapted)*

REQUIRED: The document(s) most useful to the auditor when verifying debits to perpetual inventory records.

DISCUSSION: Vendor invoices, which state the items purchased, the amount due, and the payment terms, document inventory cost when compared with purchase orders and receiving reports.

Answer (A) is incorrect. The purchase journal is created from the information on the vendor invoices. Answer (B) is incorrect. Purchase requisitions, which are requests by authorized personnel to order goods, other assets, or services, do not authoritatively state vendor prices. Answer (C) is incorrect. Although the purchase order is a formal written offer to buy specified goods and serves as a purchase authorization, it may not state the price the vendor ultimately charges.

12.1.21. Which of the following procedures relating to the examination of accounts payable could the auditor delegate entirely to the client's employees?

A. Test footings in the accounts payable ledger.

B. Reconcile unpaid invoices to vendors' statements.

C. Prepare a schedule of accounts payable.

D. Mail confirmations for selected account balances.

Answer (C) is correct. *(CPA, adapted)*

REQUIRED: The procedure that could be delegated entirely to the entity's employees.

DISCUSSION: Preparation of schedules is usually delegated to the entity's employees. The auditor should review and test the schedules prepared by them.

Answer (A) is incorrect. The auditor should perform test footings in the accounts payable ledger to assure proper addition. Answer (B) is incorrect. Reconciliation of unpaid invoices to vendors' statements might disclose unrecorded liabilities and should be performed by the auditor. Answer (D) is incorrect. The auditor should mail all confirmations to the creditors.

12.2 Substantive Testing of Inventory

12.2.1. When auditing inventories, an auditor would least likely verify that

A. All inventory owned by the client is on hand at the time of the count.

B. The client has used proper inventory pricing.

C. The financial statement presentation of inventories is appropriate.

D. Damaged goods and obsolete items have been properly accounted for.

Answer (A) is correct. *(CPA, adapted)*

REQUIRED: The procedure not performed in an audit of inventories.

DISCUSSION: An auditor does not expect all inventory to which the auditee has title to be on hand at the date of the count. Some purchased goods may still be in transit at that time. Also, some inventory may be on consignment or in public warehouses although properly included in the count.

Answer (B) is incorrect. The auditor should test relevant assertions about valuation of inventory. Answer (C) is incorrect. The auditor should test relevant assertions about presentation in the financial statements. Answer (D) is incorrect. The auditor should test relevant assertions about valuation of inventory.

12.2.2. Observation of inventories is a generally accepted auditing procedure. Which of the following statements about this accepted auditing procedure is false?

A. Regardless of the inventory system maintained by the client, an annual physical count must be made of each item in the inventory, and test counts must be made by the auditor.

B. The auditor, when asked to audit financial statements covering the current period and one or more periods for which (s)he had not observed or made some physical counts, may be able to become satisfied as to such prior inventories through appropriate alternative procedures.

C. When the well-kept perpetual inventory records are checked by the client periodically by comparisons with physical counts, the auditor's observation procedures usually can be performed either during or after the end of the period under audit.

D. Material inventories, which are physically located in public warehouses in the ordinary course of business, should be verified by direct confirmation in writing from the custodians, by performing other procedures as appropriate, or both.

Answer (A) is correct. *(Publisher, adapted)*

REQUIRED: The false statement about observation of inventory.

DISCUSSION: The auditor should attend physical inventory counting, if practicable, to (1) evaluate management's instructions and procedures for recording and controlling the results of the count, (2) observe management's count procedures, (3) inspect the inventory, and (4) perform test counts. The auditor also should test final inventory records to determine whether they reflect the actual counts. However, management may not conduct an annual physical count. Instead, it may use a perpetual inventory system. When a perpetual inventory system is used, management may perform physical counts or other tests of the reliability of inventory quantity information. In such cases, the auditor should perform procedures to determine whether changes in amounts between the count date(s) and the final records are properly recorded (AU-C 501).

Answer (B) is incorrect. If the auditor is able to become satisfied as to the fairness of the current year's inventory, (s)he may be able to apply tests of prior transactions, review records of prior counts, and employ other procedures to become satisfied as to the prior year's inventory. Answer (C) is incorrect. If the client's controls are effective, the physical count and audit work may take place before, at, or after year end. Answer (D) is incorrect. Direct confirmation of goods held by third parties may be appropriate. However, other procedures also may be applied. These may include (1) obtaining another auditor's report on the third party's controls, (2) attending physical counts whenever practicable, (3) securing confirmations from other parties when inventory has been pledged as collateral, and (4) inspecting documents regarding inventory held by third parties (e.g., warehouse receipts).

12.2.3. Which of the following audit procedures probably would provide the most reliable evidence concerning the entity's assertion of rights and obligations related to inventories?

A. Trace test counts noted during the entity's physical count to the entity's summarization of quantities.

B. Inspect agreements to determine whether any inventory is pledged as collateral or subject to any liens.

C. Select the last few shipping advices used before the physical count and determine whether the shipments were recorded as sales.

D. Inspect the open purchase order file for significant commitments that should be considered for disclosure.

Answer (B) is correct. *(CPA, adapted)*

REQUIRED: The procedure providing the most reliable evidence of rights and obligations related to inventories.

DISCUSSION: Testing the assertion of rights and obligations for inventories determines that the entity has legal title or similar rights to the inventories. Typically, the auditor examines paid vendors' invoices, consignment agreements, and contracts.

Answer (A) is incorrect. Tracing test counts to the summary of quantities tests the assertion of completeness. Answer (C) is incorrect. Examining purchase transactions at year end tests the assertion of cutoff. Answer (D) is incorrect. Determining whether commitments should be disclosed tests the assertions about statement classification and understandability.

12.2.4. An auditor most likely would inspect loan agreements under which an entity's inventories are pledged to support management's financial statement assertion of

A. Existence.

B. Accuracy.

C. Classification and understandability.

D. Valuation and allocation.

Answer (C) is correct. *(CPA, adapted)*

REQUIRED: The assertion tested by inspection of loan agreements under which inventories are pledged.

DISCUSSION: Assertions about presentation and disclosure address whether particular components of the financial statements are properly classified, described, and disclosed. Determining that the pledge or assignment of inventories is appropriately disclosed is an audit objective related to the classification and understandability assertion.

Answer (A) is incorrect. Inspection of loan agreements does not determine whether inventories physically exist. Answer (B) is incorrect. Inspection of loan agreements does not determine whether the inventory is accurately recorded. Answer (D) is incorrect. Inspection of loan agreements does not determine whether inventory is included at proper amounts.

12.2.5. An auditor selected items for test counts while observing a client's physical inventory. The auditor then traced the test counts to the client's inventory listing. Tracing test counts most likely obtained evidence concerning the relevant assertion about

A. Rights and obligations.

B. Completeness.

C. Existence.

D. Valuation.

Answer (B) is correct. *(CPA, adapted)*

REQUIRED: The assertion relevant to tracing test counts to the client's inventory listing.

DISCUSSION: Tracing the details of test counts to the final inventory schedule assures the auditor that items in the observed physical inventory are included in the inventory records. The auditor should compare the inventory tag sequence numbers in the final inventory schedule with those in the records of his or her test counts made during the client's physical inventory.

Answer (A) is incorrect. The reconciliation of the test counts with the inventory listing does not provide assurance that the inventory is owned by the client. Answer (C) is incorrect. Although the observation of inventory provides evidence as to existence, specifically tracing test counts to the inventory listing provides evidence of completeness. Answer (D) is incorrect. The valuation assertion is tested by determining whether inventory items are included in inventory at lower of cost or market.

12.2.6. If the perpetual inventory records show lower quantities of inventory than the physical count, an explanation of the difference might be unrecorded

A. Sales.

B. Sales discounts.

C. Purchases.

D. Purchase discounts.

Answer (C) is correct. *(CPA, adapted)*

REQUIRED: The reason the physical count might exceed the perpetual inventory amount.

DISCUSSION: In a perpetual system, purchases are debited directly to inventory at the time of the transaction rather than to a purchases account. A sale requires an immediate credit to inventory. Thus, failure to record a purchase would understate inventory.

Answer (A) is incorrect. An unrecorded sale overstates inventory. Answer (B) is incorrect. Sales discounts affect neither the quantity nor the valuation of inventory. Answer (D) is incorrect. Unrecorded purchase discounts affect the valuation but not the quantity of inventory.

12.2.7. A client maintains perpetual inventory records in both quantities and dollars. If the assessment of the risks of material misstatement is high, an auditor will probably

A. Apply gross profit tests to ascertain the reasonableness of the physical counts.

B. Increase the extent of tests of controls relevant to the inventory cycle.

C. Request the client to schedule the physical inventory count at the end of the year.

D. Insist that the client perform physical counts of inventory items several times during the year.

Answer (C) is correct. *(CPA, adapted)*

REQUIRED: The auditor's action if the assessment of the RMMs for inventory is high.

DISCUSSION: If the assessment of the RMMs is high, the acceptable detection risk for a given level of audit risk decreases. The auditor should change the nature, timing, or extent of substantive procedures to increase the reliability and relevance of the evidence they provide. Thus, extending work done at an interim date to year end might be inappropriate. Observation of inventory at year end provides more reliable and relevant evidence.

Answer (A) is incorrect. Comparing the gross profit test results with those of the prior year provides evidence about sales and cost of goods sold but not inventory. Answer (B) is incorrect. If the auditor believes controls are unlikely to be effective, e.g., because the assessment of the RMMs is high, tests of controls may not be performed. However, the auditor needs to be satisfied that performing only substantive procedures will reduce audit risk to an acceptably low level. Answer (D) is incorrect. The risk is that year-end inventory is misstated.

12.2.8. Periodic or cycle counts of selected inventory items are made at various times during the year rather than a single inventory count at year end. Which of the following is necessary if the auditor plans to observe inventories at interim dates?

A. Complete recounts by independent teams are performed.

B. Perpetual inventory records are maintained.

C. Unit cost records are integrated with production accounting records.

D. Inventory balances are rarely at low levels.

Answer (B) is correct. *(CPA, adapted)*

REQUIRED: The situation in which inventory counts prior to year end are acceptable.

DISCUSSION: If the risk of material misstatement is acceptable and reliable perpetual inventory records are subject to effective internal control, the auditor's observation procedures usually can be performed either during or after the end of the period under audit. If substantive procedures are performed at an interim date, the risk of material misstatement at the balance sheet date is increased. The incremental risk may be reduced if substantive procedures can be designed to cover the remaining period.

Answer (A) is incorrect. Complete recounts of inventory by independent teams are rarely necessary. Answer (C) is incorrect. Although integrating cost records into the production records may provide for increased coordination, the process is not necessary to rely on cycle counts of inventory. Answer (D) is incorrect. Cycle inventory counts can be accomplished regardless of inventory levels.

12.2.9. When outside firms of nonaccountants specializing in the taking of physical inventories are used to count, list, price, and subsequently compute the total dollar amount of inventory on hand at the date of the physical count, the auditor will ordinarily

A. Consider the report of the outside inventory-taking firm to be an acceptable alternative procedure to the observation of physical inventories.

B. Make or observe some physical counts of the inventory, recompute certain inventory calculations, and test certain inventory transactions.

C. Not reduce the extent of work on the physical count of inventory.

D. Consider the reduced audit effort with respect to the physical count of inventory as a scope limitation.

Answer (B) is correct. *(CPA, adapted)*

REQUIRED: The auditor's responsibility when an outside firm has taken the inventory.

DISCUSSION: The taking of inventory by an outside firm of nonaccountants (use of a management's specialist) does not substitute for the auditor's own observation or performance of some test counts. The auditor may, as a result, be able to reduce the extent of his or her procedures but only after an evaluation of the work of management's specialist. For example, the auditor may (1) examine its program, (2) observe its procedures and controls, (3) make or observe some physical counts, (4) recompute calculations, and (5) apply tests to post-count transactions.

Answer (A) is incorrect. The use of a management's specialist to count the inventory may reduce the extent of the auditor's other work on the inventory, but it cannot be a complete substitute. Answer (C) is incorrect. The auditor may be able to reduce the extent of his or her procedures but only after a proper evaluation of the management's specialist's work. Answer (D) is incorrect. A scope limitation should not be reported unless management limits the CPA's involvement in the observation and review of the inventory count.

12.2.10. After accounting for a sequence of inventory tags, an auditor traces a sample of tags to the physical inventory listing to obtain evidence that all items

A. Included in the listing have been counted.

B. Represented by inventory tags are included in the listing

C. Included in the listing are represented by inventory tags.

D. Represented by inventory tags are bona fide.

Answer (B) is correct. *(CPA, adapted)*

REQUIRED: The reason for tracing a sample to the physical inventory listing.

DISCUSSION: The auditor should observe the counting process, determine that proper procedures are followed, and make selected test counts. Because the auditor does not make a complete count, not every misstatement will be detected, but (s)he should be able to determine that no large block of inventory has been omitted. Having accounted for a sequence of inventory tags, the auditor should trace a sample of the tags to the physical inventory sheets. The purpose is to test the completeness assertion that all inventory listed on a tag is reflected in the inventory listing.

Answer (A) is incorrect. The direction of testing should be from the listing to the tags to obtain evidence that all items included in the listing have been counted. Answer (C) is incorrect. The direction of testing should be from the listing to the tags to obtain evidence that all items included in the listing are represented by inventory tags. Answer (D) is incorrect. The validity of the tags is determined by examining the inventory itself.

12.2.11. The physical count of inventory of a retailer was higher than shown by the perpetual records. Which of the following could explain the difference?

A. Inventory items had been counted but the tags placed on the items had not been taken off the items and added to the inventory accumulation sheets.

B. Credit memos for several items returned by customers had not been recorded.

C. No journal entry had been made on the retailer's books for several items returned to its suppliers.

D. An item purchased "FOB shipping point" had not arrived at the date of the inventory count and had not been reflected in the perpetual records.

Answer (B) is correct. *(CPA, adapted)*

REQUIRED: The reason that the physical count exceeded the amount in the perpetual records.

DISCUSSION: If credit memos for items returned by customers have not been prepared and recorded, the returned items will be reflected in the physical inventory but not in the perpetual records.

Answer (A) is incorrect. Items counted but not added to the inventory accumulation sheets will understate the physical count. Answer (C) is incorrect. If no journal entry has been made for items returned to vendors, the perpetual records will be overstated. Answer (D) is incorrect. If an entry has not been made in the perpetual records and the item has not been received, both the records and physical inventory are understated by the same amount. FOB shipping point means that title and risk of loss pass when the items are shipped, and they should be included in both inventory and accounts payable at that time.

12.2.12. An auditor would be most likely to learn of slow-moving inventory through

A. Inquiry of sales personnel.

B. Inquiry of stores personnel.

C. Physical observation of inventory.

D. Review of perpetual inventory records.

Answer (D) is correct. *(CPA, adapted)*

REQUIRED: The procedure most likely to detect slow-moving inventory.

DISCUSSION: To identify slow-moving inventory, the auditor should review perpetual inventory records. In a perpetual system, receipts and issuances of goods are recorded as the transactions occur, both as to quantities and prices. By comparing the dates of receipt and issuance, the auditor is able to readily identify slow-moving and possibly obsolete inventory.

Answer (A) is incorrect. Inquiry of sales personnel is less reliable and less comprehensive than another answer. Answer (B) is incorrect. Inquiry of stores personnel is less reliable and less comprehensive than another answer. Answer (C) is incorrect. Observation would prove useful in this regard only if the appearance of the items suggested the length of time they had been held.

12.2.13. For the week before Moore Company's physical count, all receiving reports include a notation that they have been prepared prior to the count. For the week after the physical count, all receiving reports indicate that they have been prepared after the count. The receiving department continues to receive goods after the cutoff time while the physical count is in process. To determine the accuracy of the cutoff, the auditor should

A. Trace a sample of receiving reports issued after the last receiving report to the physical items to see that they have been included in the physical count.

B. Trace a sample of receiving reports issued before the last receiving report to the physical items to see that they have not been included in the physical count.

C. Observe that the receiving clerk is stamping the receiving reports properly.

D. List the number of the last receiving report for items included in the physical count.

Answer (D) is correct. *(Publisher, adapted)*

REQUIRED: The procedure for testing the inventory cutoff.

DISCUSSION: The numbers of the last receiving and shipping reports should be recorded so that the auditor may determine whether an accurate cutoff was made. For example, merchandise represented by receiving reports numbered after the cutoff should not be included in inventory.

Answer (A) is incorrect. Receiving reports prepared after the cutoff should be traced on a test basis to the inventory records to determine that the items have not been included. Answer (B) is incorrect. Receiving reports prepared before the cutoff should be traced on a test basis to the inventory records to determine that the items have been included. Answer (C) is incorrect. The least effective method of checking the accuracy of the cutoff of inventory is to observe that the receiving clerk is stamping the receiving reports properly. The auditor is primarily concerned with the dates on the receiving reports in order to verify that goods received or shipped near year end are accounted for in the proper reporting period.

12.2.14. Which of the following procedures will best detect the theft of valuable items from an inventory that consists of hundreds of different items selling for $1 to $10 and a few items selling for hundreds of dollars?

A. Maintain a perpetual inventory of only the more valuable items with frequent periodic verification of the validity of the perpetual inventory record.

B. Have an independent auditing firm examine and report on management's assertion about the design and operating effectiveness of the control activities relevant to inventory.

C. Have separate warehouse space for the more valuable items with sequentially numbered tags.

D. Require an authorized officer's signature on all requisitions for the more valuable items.

Answer (A) is correct. *(CPA, adapted)*

REQUIRED: The best procedure to detect the theft of valuable items from an inventory.

DISCUSSION: The costs of maintaining perpetual records for a large volume of inexpensive items are likely to exceed the benefits of more accurate and timely information and better safeguards against theft. For high value items, maintaining such records, with frequent reconciliations to physical counts, may prove cost beneficial.

Answer (B) is incorrect. The engagement would not necessarily result in detection of theft, although it might identify control deficiencies that encourage theft. Answer (C) is incorrect. Separate warehouse space for the more valuable items with sequentially numbered tags is helpful but not as effective in detecting (as opposed to preventing) theft as a system whereby the quantity that should be on hand is known with reasonable accuracy at all times. Answer (D) is incorrect. Requiring an authorized officer's signature on all requisitions for the more valuable items is useful but less effective than maintaining perpetual inventory records.

12.2.15. Which of the following is the best audit test to evaluate the accuracy of the inventory records for materials inventory in a production operation?

A. Trace selected inventory receipts to perpetual inventory records.

B. Vouch selected postings in the perpetual inventory records to source documents.

C. Perform turnover tests for materials inventory.

D. Reconcile quantities on hand per physical counts of selected items with perpetual inventory records and verify pricing.

Answer (D) is correct. *(CIA, adapted)*

REQUIRED: The best audit test for evaluating the accuracy of records for materials inventory.

DISCUSSION: The objectives in designing an audit test should be to verify both the quantity on hand and the dollar value of inventory. By reconciling the quantities on hand determined by the physical count with the perpetual inventory records and verifying pricing, both objectives are met. The auditor's observation of the physical count is an indispensable audit procedure.

Answer (A) is incorrect. Tracing selected inventory receipts to perpetual inventory records provides less reliable evidence than observation of the physical count. Answer (B) is incorrect. Vouching selected postings in the perpetual inventory records to source documents provides less reliable evidence than observation of the physical count. Answer (C) is incorrect. Analytical procedures do not provide direct evidence of inventory amounts.

12.2.16. Purchase cutoff procedures should be designed to test whether all inventory

A. Purchased and received before year end was paid for.

B. Ordered before year end was received.

C. Purchased and whose title has passed before year end was recorded.

D. Owned by the company is in the possession of the company at year end.

Answer (C) is correct. *(CPA, adapted)*

REQUIRED: The purpose of purchase cutoff procedures.

DISCUSSION: Evaluations of purchase transactions at year end are performed to test the cutoff assertion about inventories. Tests are performed to obtain evidence that all goods owned by the client at the balance sheet date are included in inventory and that the related liability is recorded. Legal title to goods in transit is determined by whether the shipping terms are FOB shipping point or destination.

Answer (A) is incorrect. Items may be included in inventory although not yet paid for. Answer (B) is incorrect. The company may not have title to goods on order. Answer (D) is incorrect. The company may have title to goods in transit or held on consignment.

12.2.17. The audit of year-end physical inventories should include steps to verify that the client's purchases and sales cutoffs were adequate. The audit steps should be designed to detect whether merchandise included in the physical count at year end was not recorded as a

A. Sale in the subsequent period.

B. Purchase in the current period.

C. Sale in the current period.

D. Purchase return in the subsequent period.

Answer (C) is correct. *(CPA, adapted)*

REQUIRED: The error that the audit of purchases and sales cutoffs should detect.

DISCUSSION: Goods on hand and counted in the year-end inventory also should not have been recorded as sold during the current audit period. If they were sold, they could not have been owned by the client at year end. The auditor should perform cutoff tests to assure the proper recording of year-end inventory. These tests include comparison of the records of sales and purchases for several days before and after the balance sheet date with duplicate sales invoices and shipping records. Items purchased and items not yet sold should be in inventory. Items sold or not yet purchased should not be in inventory.

Answer (A) is incorrect. Year-end inventory is likely to be sold in the subsequent period. Answer (B) is incorrect. Year-end inventory is likely to have been purchased in the current period. Answer (D) is incorrect. Unreturned items are owned by the client and should be in ending inventory.

12.2.18. An auditor's observation of physical inventories at the main plant at year end provides direct evidence to support which of the following objectives?

A. Accuracy of the priced-out inventory.

B. Evaluation of lower of cost or market test.

C. Identification of obsolete or damaged merchandise to evaluate allowance (reserve) for obsolescence.

D. Determination of goods on consignment at another location.

Answer (C) is correct. *(CIA, adapted)*

REQUIRED: The objective supported by observation of inventory.

DISCUSSION: One way to discover damaged or obsolete merchandise is to observe the client's physical inventory count and inspect the merchandise during the inventory process. The auditor should check for dusty packages, rusted metal, physical damage to the merchandise, etc. The auditor may also need to consult a specialist regarding the quality or condition of merchandise.

Answer (A) is incorrect. Observation verifies physical existence and condition, not price accuracy. Answer (B) is incorrect. Observation verifies physical existence and condition, not cost accuracy. Answer (D) is incorrect. Observation at the main plant is not evidence of the existence of goods at another site.

12.2.19. Some firms that dispose of only a small part of their total output by consignment shipments fail to make any distinction between consignment shipments and regular sales. Which of the following would suggest to the auditor that the client's goods have been shipped on consignment?

A. Numerous shipments of small quantities.

B. Numerous shipments of large quantities and few returns.

C. Large debits to accounts receivable and small periodic credits.

D. Large debits to accounts receivable and large periodic credits.

Answer (C) is correct. *(CPA, adapted)*

REQUIRED: The condition indicative of goods shipped on consignment.

DISCUSSION: A consignment is a shipment of inventory by the owner to a sales agent (the consignee), who sells the goods and then pays the consignor. Goods on consignment are owned by the consignor. If the entity does not distinguish between consignments and sales, large debits to accounts receivable and small periodic credits suggest that large quantities have been consigned, and smaller quantities have been sold. Typically, consignment payments are remitted periodically as the consignee makes sales. Failing to distinguish sales and consignments overstates net income and understates inventory.

Answer (A) is incorrect. Fewer but larger shipments with many returns indicate consignments. Answer (B) is incorrect. Fewer but larger shipments with many returns indicate consignments. Answer (D) is incorrect. Consigned goods are normally paid for in small amounts as the consignee makes sales.

12.2.20. An auditor concluded that no excessive costs for an idle plant were charged to inventory. This conclusion most likely related to the auditor's objective to obtain evidence about the relevant assertions regarding inventory, including presentation and disclosure and

A. Valuation and allocation.

B. Completeness.

C. Occurrence.

D. Rights and obligations.

Answer (A) is correct. *(CPA, adapted)*

REQUIRED: The assertion related to the conclusion that no excessive costs for an idle plant were inventoried.

DISCUSSION: Inventory should properly include the costs of direct labor, direct materials, and manufacturing overhead. Thus, to be properly measured, an appropriate amount of manufacturing overhead should be charged to inventory. Costs of an idle plant should not be included in manufacturing overhead.

12.2.21. During an investigation of unexplained inventory shrinkage, an internal auditor is testing inventory additions as recorded in the perpetual inventory records. Because of internal control weaknesses, the information recorded on receiving reports may not be reliable. Under these circumstances, which of the following documents provides the best evidence of additions to inventory?

A. Purchase orders.

B. Purchase requisitions.

C. Vendors' invoices.

D. Vendors' statements.

Answer (C) is correct. *(CIA, adapted)*

REQUIRED: The best evidence of additions to inventory when receiving reports are unreliable.

DISCUSSION: Vendors' invoices state the quantities and costs of goods shipped. Thus, they provide an external source of evidence of additions to inventory. However, an adjustment must be made for purchase returns.

Answer (A) is incorrect. The quantity ordered may not equal the quantity shipped by the vendor. Answer (B) is incorrect. The quantity requested in a purchase requisition may not equal the quantity actually ordered or the quantity shipped by the vendor. Answer (D) is incorrect. Vendors' statements normally list only the invoice number, date, and total. They do not list invoice detail such as quantities shipped.

12.2.22. To obtain evidence as to the reasonableness and completeness of inventory balances, auditors often perform analytical procedures. Which of the following quantitative relationships is not applicable to inventory balances?

A. The gross profit percentage.

B. Debt-to-equity ratio.

C. Inventory turnover ratios.

D. Number of days' sales in inventory.

Answer (B) is correct. *(Publisher, adapted)*

REQUIRED: The quantitative relationship not applicable to inventory balances.

DISCUSSION: The debt-to-equity ratio, a measure of leverage, relates to corporate financing, not inventory. It equals total debt divided by total equity.

Answer (A) is incorrect. The gross profit percentage (gross profit ÷ net sales) provides information about inventories. Gross profit is equal to net sales minus cost of goods sold, and inventories affect cost of goods sold. Any significant unexplained variance in the percentage may be the result of an inventory misstatement. Answer (C) is incorrect. Inventory ratios, such as cost of goods sold divided by average inventory, should remain relatively constant in the absence of known conditions to the contrary. Answer (D) is incorrect. The number of days' sales in inventory (360 ÷ inventory turnover) is a measure that can be monitored by the auditor. The number of days' sales in inventories should be relatively constant.

12.2.23. During the preliminary survey phase of an audit of the organization's production cycle, management stated that the sale of scrap was well controlled. Evidence to verify that assertion can best be gained by

A. Comparing current revenue from scrap sales with that of prior periods.

B. Interviewing persons responsible for collecting and storing the scrap.

C. Comparing the quantities of scrap expected from the production process with the quantities sold.

D. Comparing the results of a physical inventory of scrap on hand with perpetual inventory records.

Answer (C) is correct. *(CIA, adapted)*

REQUIRED: The best procedure to verify the assertion that the sale of scrap is well controlled.

DISCUSSION: If the sale of scrap is well controlled, a large amount will not be on hand. Most scrap will be sold when produced. Hence, if the quantities sold are approximately the same as those expected, an auditor can assume that the controls over the sale of scrap are effective.

Answer (A) is incorrect. Comparing current revenue from scrap sales with that of prior periods presumes that prior periods' amounts were correct and that no change has occurred in quantity produced. Answer (B) is incorrect. The persons responsible for collecting and storing the scrap can only describe the safeguards in place to handle scrap before its sale. Answer (D) is incorrect. Comparing the physical count with perpetual inventory records verifies only the accuracy of perpetual inventory records.

12.3 Substantive Testing of Property, Plant, and Equipment (PPE)

12.3.1. Property, plant, and equipment (PPE) is typically judged to be one of the accounts least susceptible to fraud because

A. The amounts recorded on the balance sheet for most companies are immaterial.

B. The inherent risk is usually low.

C. The depreciated values are always smaller than cost.

D. Internal control is inherently effective regarding this account.

Answer (B) is correct. *(Publisher, adapted)*

REQUIRED: The reason PPE is not susceptible to fraud.

DISCUSSION: Property, plant, and equipment is one of the accounts least susceptible to material misstatement in the absence of related controls. Inherent risk is low because of the infrequency of transactions in the account, the relative ease with which the existence of these assets can be verified, the slow turnover, and the simplicity of cutoff procedures.

Answer (A) is incorrect. PPE amounts are often quite large. Answer (C) is incorrect. Some PPE items (e.g., land) are not depreciated. Answer (D) is incorrect. The susceptibility to misstatement is a matter of inherent risk, not control risk.

12.3.2. Which is the best audit procedure to obtain evidence to support the legal ownership of real property?

A. Examination of corporate minutes and board resolutions with regard to approvals to acquire real property.

B. Examination of closing documents, deeds, and ownership documents registered and on file at the county courthouse.

C. Discussion with corporate legal counsel concerning the acquisition of a specific piece of property.

D. Confirmation with the title company that handled the escrow account and disbursement of proceeds for the closing of the property.

Answer (B) is correct. *(CIA, adapted)*

REQUIRED: The best audit procedure for obtaining evidence to support the legal ownership of real property.

DISCUSSION: Examination of title documents, the deed, and any other supporting documents, such as closing documents, will be helpful in verifying ownership. But these are not conclusive. An inspection of public records will determine if there are any interests in the property (e.g., mortgages, judgment liens, or claims to the title) that do not appear in the auditee's records.

Answer (A) is incorrect. An examination of corporate minutes and board resolutions will not provide evidence of actual ownership, only approval to acquire the property. Answer (C) is incorrect. The testimony of corporate legal counsel provides only corroborating evidence. Answer (D) is incorrect. Confirmation with an escrow agent is evidence only of the closing. It does not provide evidence regarding subsequent transactions, such as a mortgage liability not recorded in the company books.

12.3.3. In the audit of property, plant, and equipment, the auditor tries to do all of the following except to

A. Obtain an understanding of the relevant internal controls.

B. Determine the extent of property abandoned during the year.

C. Assess the adequacy of replacement funds.

D. Judge the reasonableness of the depreciation.

Answer (C) is correct. *(CPA, adapted)*

REQUIRED: The determination not made during an audit of property, plant, and equipment.

DISCUSSION: In performing the attest function, the external auditor does not directly evaluate the soundness of the client's business practices or financial prospects. Whether replacement funds are adequate is not relevant to whether the financial statements are fairly presented in accordance with the applicable reporting framework.

Answer (A) is incorrect. In all audits, GAAS require the auditor to obtain an understanding of the entity and its environment, including its internal control. Answer (B) is incorrect. The auditor should determine whether abandonments of property were properly recorded so as to avoid overstatement of assets. Answer (D) is incorrect. Depreciation affects asset valuation and income.

12.3.4. If an auditor tours a production facility, which of the misstatements or questionable practices is most likely to be detected?

A. Depreciation expense on fully depreciated machinery has been recognized.

B. Overhead has been overapplied.

C. Necessary facility maintenance has not been performed.

D. Insurance coverage on the facility has lapsed.

Answer (C) is correct. *(CIA, adapted)*

REQUIRED: The misstatement or questionable practice uncovered by touring the client's plant.

DISCUSSION: The auditor is likely to discover that necessary plant maintenance was not performed during the year through direct observation of asset condition.

Answer (A) is incorrect. Only inspection of depreciation records will reveal depreciation recorded for fully depreciated machines. Answer (B) is incorrect. The auditor compares actual overhead incurred with overhead applied to determine whether overhead was underapplied. Answer (D) is incorrect. The auditor inspects the insurance contracts to detect lapsed insurance coverage.

12.3.5. Which of the following combinations of procedures would an auditor most likely perform to obtain evidence about fixed asset additions?

A. Inspecting documents and physically examining assets.

B. Recomputing calculations and obtaining written management representations.

C. Observing operating activities and comparing balances with prior-period balances.

D. Confirming ownership and corroborating transactions through inquiries of client personnel.

Answer (A) is correct. *(CPA, adapted)*

REQUIRED: The combination of procedures most likely to obtain evidence about fixed asset additions.

DISCUSSION: The auditor's direct observation of fixed assets is one means of determining whether additions have been made. Tracing to the detailed records determines whether additions have been recorded. Inspection of deeds, lease agreements, insurance policies, invoices, canceled checks, and tax notices may also reveal additions.

Answer (B) is incorrect. Recomputations are based on recorded amounts and will not reveal unrecorded additions. Answer (C) is incorrect. Analytical procedures may not detect additions offset by disposals. Answer (D) is incorrect. The auditor must become aware of additions before confirming ownership or corroborating transactions.

12.3.6. When few property and equipment transactions occur during the year, the continuing auditor usually obtains an understanding of the related internal controls and performs

A. Tests of controls.

B. Analytical procedures to verify current year additions to property and equipment.

C. A thorough examination of the balances at the beginning of the year.

D. Extensive tests of current year property and equipment transactions.

Answer (D) is correct. *(CPA, adapted)*

REQUIRED: The procedures performed by a continuing auditor when few property and equipment transactions occur during the year.

DISCUSSION: Testing the details of transactions is the preferable procedure for property, plant, and equipment. The beginning balance has been audited, and subsequent transactions in the account ordinarily are few. The auditor also may not rely on controls after obtaining an understanding of internal control because (s)he believes that (1) no effective controls are relevant to the assertion or (2) testing controls would be inefficient.

Answer (A) is incorrect. Tests of controls are unnecessary if the auditor does not rely on internal controls. Answer (B) is incorrect. The auditor also should perform tests of details. Answer (C) is incorrect. A continuing auditor already should have examined the beginning balances.

12.3.7. Treetop Corporation acquired a building and arranged mortgage financing during the year. Verification of the related mortgage acquisition costs would be least likely to include an examination of the related

A. Deed.

B. Canceled checks.

C. Closing statement.

D. Interest expense.

Answer (A) is correct. *(CPA, adapted)*

REQUIRED: The item that the auditor is least likely to inspect to verify mortgage acquisition costs.

DISCUSSION: A deed provides evidence of ownership rights and obligations relative to mortgaged property. However, it typically does not contain information about costs of mortgages.

Answer (B) is incorrect. Canceled checks provide evidence of the cost of a mortgage. Answer (C) is incorrect. A closing statement provides evidence of the cost of a mortgage. Answer (D) is incorrect. Interest expense provides evidence of the cost of a mortgage.

12.3.8. In testing for unrecorded retirements of equipment, an auditor most likely would

A. Select items of equipment from the accounting records and then locate them during the plant tour.

B. Compare depreciation journal entries with similar prior-year entries in search of fully depreciated equipment.

C. Inspect items of equipment observed during the plant tour and then trace them to the equipment subsidiary ledger.

D. Scan the general journal for unusual equipment additions and excessive debits to repairs and maintenance expense.

Answer (A) is correct. *(CPA, adapted)*

REQUIRED: The procedure most useful in detecting unrecorded retirements of equipment.

DISCUSSION: The existence assertion about account balances is that assets (and liabilities and equity interests) exist. To test for unrecorded retirements, the auditor inspects selected items chosen from the records. However, unlike external confirmation of receivables or observation of inventories, inspection of equipment, especially a complete physical inventory, is not a required auditing procedure. However, a high assessed risk of material misstatement may require the auditor to inspect a sample of items.

Answer (B) is incorrect. Fully depreciated equipment may still be in service. Answer (C) is incorrect. To detect unrecorded retirements, the direction of testing should be from the records to the physical assets. Answer (D) is incorrect. The audit is testing retirements of equipment, not additions.

12.3.9. One audit procedure for an audit of facilities and equipment is to test the accuracy of recorded depreciation. Which of the following is the best source of evidence that the equipment in question is in service?

A. A review of depreciation policies and procedures.

B. A comparison of depreciation schedules with a listing of insurance appraisals for the same equipment.

C. A comparison of depreciation schedules with the maintenance and repair logs for the same equipment.

D. A review of inventory documentation for the equipment.

Answer (C) is correct. *(CIA, adapted)*

REQUIRED: The best source of evidence that the equipment in question is in service.

DISCUSSION: The maintenance and repair records provide evidence that equipment exists and is in use. Equipment in service is more likely to require maintenance than retired equipment. However, the best evidence is the auditor's direct observation.

Answer (A) is incorrect. A review of policies and procedures provides no evidence about the existence assertion for specific assets. Answer (B) is incorrect. A comparison with current insurance records would be inconclusive. Retired equipment could still be insured. Answer (D) is incorrect. Retired equipment could still be in the inventory.

12.3.10. Determining that proper amounts of depreciation are expensed provides assurance about management's assertions of valuation and allocation and

A. Classification and understandability.

B. Completeness.

C. Rights and obligations.

D. Occurrence.

Answer (A) is correct. *(CPA, adapted)*

REQUIRED: The assertions tested by consideration of the amounts of depreciation that are expensed.

DISCUSSION: The classification and understandability assertion states whether particular components of the financial statements are properly presented, described, and disclosed. For example, if cost of sales includes depreciation, the auditor should determine that this classification is appropriate and that it is properly disclosed.

Answer (B) is incorrect. The completeness assertion addresses whether all transactions, accounts, and disclosures that should be presented are included. Answer (C) is incorrect. The rights and obligations assertion addresses whether assets are rights, and obligations are liabilities, of the entity at a specified time. Answer (D) is incorrect. The occurrence assertion addresses whether recorded transactions and events occurred during the period.

12.3.11. The auditor is least likely to learn of retirements of equipment through which of the following?

A. Review of the purchase return and allowance account.

B. Review of depreciation.

C. Analysis of the debits to the accumulated depreciation account.

D. Review of insurance policy riders.

Answer (A) is correct. *(CPA, adapted)*

REQUIRED: The procedure least likely to provide evidence about retirements of equipment.

DISCUSSION: Review of the purchase return and allowance account provides no audit evidence about the retirement of equipment. This account records the return of purchased inventory and is unaffected by the entries to record the acquisition, depreciation, and disposition of fixed assets. To detect unrecorded retirements, the auditor should determine whether (1) the entity uses special sequentially numbered forms to authorize and record such transactions and (2) regular physical inventories of equipment are taken. Inquiry of appropriate personnel should be made. Major additions should be investigated to determine the fate of old equipment. Reduction in insurance coverage also may indicate a retirement of equipment. Finally, miscellaneous revenue accounts may furnish clues of otherwise unrecorded dispositions.

Answer (B) is incorrect. Review of depreciation may reveal equipment retirement. Retirements decrease depreciation expense and result in debits to accumulated depreciation and credits to equipment. Answer (C) is incorrect. Analysis of debits to accumulated depreciation may reveal equipment retirement. Retirements decrease depreciation expense and result in debits to accumulated depreciation and credits to equipment. Answer (D) is incorrect. Reduction in insurance coverage may indicate a retirement of equipment.

12.3.12. The auditor may conclude that depreciation charges are insufficient by noting

A. Insured values greatly in excess of carrying amounts.

B. Large numbers of fully depreciated assets.

C. Continuous trade-ins of relatively new assets.

D. Excessive recurring losses on assets retired.

Answer (D) is correct. *(CPA, adapted)*

REQUIRED: The condition indicating insufficient depreciation charges.

DISCUSSION: Excessive recurring losses on assets retired indicate excess carrying amounts at the dates of disposition. The implication is that the method of cost allocation has not been sufficient. The effect of understating depreciation in prior periods would have been to overstate income in those periods and understate income in the period of retirement.

Answer (A) is incorrect. The insured values of assets should reflect fair values. Carrying amounts reflect historical cost. Answer (B) is incorrect. Large numbers of fully depreciated assets indicate excessive, not insufficient, depreciation charges. Answer (C) is incorrect. Trade-ins of relatively new assets suggest rapid technological change in the entity's industry.

12.3.13. Which of the following costs should not be capitalized?

A. Major reconditioning of a delivery truck.

B. Machine operator's wages during a period of testing and adjusting new machinery.

C. Fencing the plant parking lot.

D. Maintenance of an unused standby plant.

Answer (D) is correct. *(Publisher, adapted)*

REQUIRED: The cost that should not be capitalized.

DISCUSSION: Keeping an unused plant on stand-by for current operations suggests that maintenance on the plant should be reflected in current costs. The plant, even though unused, is not the same as a nonproductive asset. If the idle plant is not expected to be used, however, it should be written down to net realizable value and excluded from the fixed assets accounts. Maintenance costs might then be considered as costs of disposal.

Answer (A) is incorrect. The costs of a major reconditioning of a delivery truck should be capitalized. Improvements, additions, and replacements benefit several periods by extending the useful life of an asset or by increasing future service potential. Answer (B) is incorrect. Costs of putting a capital asset into service are capitalized according to GAAP. Answer (C) is incorrect. The costs of fencing the plant parking lot should be capitalized and depreciated as land improvements.

12.3.14. The most appropriate reason for a decrease in accumulated depreciation is that

A. Depreciation for prior periods was understated.

B. Major repairs have lengthened the life of an asset.

C. A depreciable asset has been recorded at current cost.

D. Retained earnings have been appropriated for a possible loss on retirement.

Answer (B) is correct. *(Publisher, adapted)*

REQUIRED: The reason for a decrease in accumulated depreciation.

DISCUSSION: If major repairs have lengthened the life of an asset, the company should reduce the amount of accumulated depreciation to increase the carrying amount of the asset. This practice is acceptable for representing the increased life of an asset.

Answer (A) is incorrect. An adjustment for understated depreciation requires a credit, not a debit, to accumulated depreciation. Answer (C) is incorrect. Depreciable assets ordinarily should be recorded at historical cost. Answer (D) is incorrect. An appropriation affects retained earnings accounts only.

12.3.15. An auditor analyzes repairs and maintenance accounts primarily to obtain evidence in support of the relevant assertion that all

A. Noncapitalizable expenditures for repairs and maintenance have been recorded in the proper period.

B. Expenditures for property and equipment have been recorded in the proper period.

C. Noncapitalizable expenditures for repairs and maintenance have been properly charged to expense.

D. Expenditures for property and equipment have not been charged to expense.

Answer (D) is correct. *(CPA, adapted)*

REQUIRED: The reason an auditor analyzes repairs and maintenance expense.

DISCUSSION: The auditor should vouch significant debits from the repairs and maintenance expense account to determine whether any should have been capitalized.

Answer (A) is incorrect. An improper cutoff of repairs and maintenance expenses is not typically a major risk. Answer (B) is incorrect. The repairs and maintenance expense accounts are not the appropriate sources of evidence regarding the cutoff of expenditures for property and equipment. Answer (C) is incorrect. Vouching additions to plant, property, and equipment provides evidence of whether any expense has been inappropriately charged as a capital item.

12.3.16. In violation of a company policy, Lowell Company erroneously capitalized the cost of painting its warehouse. The auditor examining Lowell's financial statements would most likely detect this error when

A. Discussing capitalization policies with Lowell's controller.

B. Examining maintenance expense accounts.

C. Observing, during the physical inventory observation, that the warehouse had been painted.

D. Examining the construction work orders supporting items capitalized during the year.

Answer (D) is correct. *(CPA, adapted)*

REQUIRED: The procedure to detect the error of capitalizing a maintenance expense.

DISCUSSION: The audit plan for property, plant, and equipment includes verification of additions by vouching them to the original documents. The entries are traced from the journals back to authorizations, vendors' invoices, contracts, deeds, and construction work orders. Inspection of the work order for painting the warehouse should alert the auditor to the capitalization of an expense.

Answer (A) is incorrect. Given that the policy of the entity is to expense painting costs, discussion with the controller would not detect the misstatement. Answer (B) is incorrect. Items capitalized are not recorded in maintenance accounts. Answer (C) is incorrect. Observing the painted warehouse is not relevant to accounting for the cost.

12.3.17. An audit client has leased an asset and appropriately recorded a capital lease. Because of the existence of a bargain purchase option, the auditor should determine

A. Whether the sum of the minimum lease payments equals the fair value of the property.

B. That the leased property is being depreciated over the life of the lease.

C. Whether the interest rate used in discounting the minimum lease payments is the client's incremental borrowing rate or the lessor's implicit rate.

D. That the cost of the property to the lessor is the cost recorded by the client.

Answer (C) is correct. *(Publisher, adapted)*

REQUIRED: The audit procedure applied to the recorded amount of a capital lease with a bargain purchase option.

DISCUSSION: A leased asset should be capitalized at the sum of the discounted minimum lease payments. Thus, the interest rate used in the discounting process is an important consideration in determining whether the asset is fairly presented in the balance sheet. The interest rate is the client's incremental borrowing rate, unless the lessor's implicit rate is known and is less than the client's incremental rate.

Answer (A) is incorrect. The total amount of lease payments equals the cost of the asset plus interest expense. Answer (B) is incorrect. The asset should be depreciated over its estimated life, which is not necessarily the life of the lease (given that the lease is capitalized as a result of a bargain purchase option). Answer (D) is incorrect. The lessee does not capitalize the asset at the cost to the lessor.

12.4 Substantive Testing of Investments and Derivatives

12.4.1. The auditor observes the count of marketable securities on December 31. (S)he records the serial number of each security and checks the serial number and number of shares (or principal) against company records. Which error or bad practice has the best chance of being detected by this procedure?

A. The CFO misappropriated interest receipts by clipping coupons from company-owned bonds and redeeming them in his or her own name.

B. The CFO misappropriated and sold securities on April 4. (S)he speculated successfully with the proceeds and replaced the misappropriated securities on December 29.

C. The CFO borrowed securities on May 15 to use as collateral for a personal loan. (S)he repaid the loan and replaced the securities on December 2.

D. The no par stock of Sure-Shot Mines split two for one on November 19. The stock certificate for the additional shares was received directly by the CFO who made no record of the receipt and misappropriated the shares.

Answer (B) is correct. *(CPA, adapted)*

REQUIRED: The fraud likely to be detected by reconciling the serial numbers of securities and the number of shares (or principal) with company records.

DISCUSSION: The auditor is most likely to detect a misappropriation and replacement of securities by comparing information for the securities counted with the entity's records. The records would indicate that the recorded serial numbers differ from those of securities counted by the auditor.

Answer (A) is incorrect. Tests of interest income accounts, not serial numbers of securities, show whether interest has been misappropriated. Answer (C) is incorrect. A surprise interim count or joint control of securities would be necessary to detect or prevent the temporary misappropriation of the securities. Answer (D) is incorrect. Information about stock splits, stock dividends, and cash dividends from publications such as *The Wall Street Journal* or other similar sources would have to be consulted to determine the client's holdings.

12.4.2. In an audit of other assets, all of the following are done except

A. Determining that the asset is written off on a periodic basis.

B. Confirming that the asset exists.

C. Determining the basis of the carrying amount of the asset.

D. Determining whether the asset is fairly presented in the financial statements.

Answer (A) is correct. *(Publisher, adapted)*

REQUIRED: The procedure not performed in an audit of other assets.

DISCUSSION: The auditor should be concerned that each asset is presented fairly in accordance with the applicable financial reporting framework. If it requires periodic allocation of costs, determining that the asset is written off on a periodic basis is an appropriate audit objective. However, for nondepreciable assets, e.g., land, verification of the write-off is not necessary.

Answer (B) is incorrect. Externally confirming the asset's existence is an appropriate test of an assertion about other assets. Answer (C) is incorrect. Determining the basis of the carrying amount of the asset is in an audit of other assets. It addresses the valuation and allocation assertion. Answer (D) is incorrect. Determining whether the asset is fairly presented in the financial statements is an overall objective of an audit of other assets.

12.4.3. A client has a large and active investment portfolio that is kept in a bank safe-deposit box. If the auditor is unable to count the securities at the balance sheet date, the auditor most likely will

A. Request the bank to confirm to the auditor the contents of the safe-deposit box at the balance sheet date.

B. Examine supporting evidence for transactions occurring during the year.

C. Count the securities at a subsequent date and confirm with the bank whether securities were added or removed since the balance sheet date.

D. Request the client to have the bank seal the safe-deposit box until the auditor can count the securities at a subsequent date.

Answer (D) is correct. *(CPA, adapted)*

REQUIRED: The procedure most likely performed when the auditor cannot count securities at the balance sheet date.

DISCUSSION: Securities should be inspected simultaneously with the verification of cash and the count of other liquid assets to prevent transfers among asset categories for the purpose of concealing a shortage. If this procedure is not possible but the securities are kept by a custodian in a bank safe-deposit box, the client may instruct the custodian that no one is to have access to the securities unless in the presence of the auditor. Thus, when the auditor finally inspects the securities, (s)he may conclude that they represent what was on hand at the balance sheet date.

Answer (A) is incorrect. The bank does not have access to the contents of the client's safe-deposit box. Answer (B) is incorrect. Supporting evidence for transactions occurring during the year is not a substitute for inspection of the securities. Answer (C) is incorrect. The bank does not have access to the contents of the client's safe-deposit box.

12.4.4. The auditor's primary objectives in an audit of an investment in securities do not include determining whether the securities are

A. Authentic.

B. The property of the client.

C. In existence.

D. Properly classified on the balance sheet.

Answer (A) is correct. *(CPA, adapted)*

REQUIRED: The item that is not one of the auditor's primary objectives in examining an investment in securities.

DISCUSSION: The objectives of the auditor's audit of an investment in securities include determining whether it is accounted for in accordance with the applicable financial reporting framework. Thus, most of the auditor's work involves obtaining and evaluating evidence about financial statement assertions, for example, whether (1) the securities actually exist, and the entity has the rights to them, and (2) they are reported at appropriate amounts and appropriately classified (presented and described) in the statements. The auditor is not expected, however, to be able to evaluate the authenticity of securities. If forgery is suspected, (s)he should engage an auditor's specialist.

Answer (B) is incorrect. A primary objective of the audit is to test the rights and obligations (ownership) assertions. Answer (C) is incorrect. A primary objective of the audit is to test the existence of assertions. Answer (D) is incorrect. A primary objective of the audit is to test the presentation and disclosure assertions.

12.4.5. Which of the following statements regarding the audit of negotiable notes receivable in bearer form is not correct?

A. Confirmation by the debtor is an acceptable alternative to inspection.

B. Materiality of the amount involved is a factor considered when selecting the accounts to be confirmed.

C. Physical inspection of a note by the auditor does not provide conclusive evidence.

D. Notes receivable discounted with recourse need to be confirmed.

Answer (A) is correct. *(CPA, adapted)*

REQUIRED: The false statement about the audit of negotiable notes receivable.

DISCUSSION: Negotiable notes in bearer form are highly liquid assets because they are negotiable by transfer of possession alone. Thus, they should be inspected to determine whether the entity has custody. External confirmation also does not establish collectibility. For this purpose, the auditor should examine cash receipts records to determine promptness of interest and principal payments.

Answer (B) is incorrect. The auditor usually should externally confirm a substantial amount of the dollar value of receivables. Answer (C) is incorrect. Inspection by auditors may not detect forgery or establish ownership. Answer (D) is incorrect. Receivables discounted with recourse should be confirmed. Those discounted without recourse need not be because the client has no contingent liability.

12.4.6. Which of the following is the least effective audit procedure regarding the existence assertion for the securities held by the auditee?

A. Examination of paid checks issued in payment of securities purchased.

B. Vouching all changes during the year to supporting documents.

C. Simultaneous count of liquid assets.

D. Confirmation from the custodian.

Answer (A) is correct. *(Publisher, adapted)*

REQUIRED: The audit procedure giving the least assurance of the existence of securities.

DISCUSSION: Paid checks issued in payment for securities do not assure that the investments are in existence and still owned by the client at the balance sheet date.

Answer (B) is incorrect. Vouching changes in the account to supporting documents provides evidence of both purchases and sales. Answer (C) is incorrect. A simultaneous count of securities, cash, and other liquid assets is the ideal way to verify the investment balance. Answer (D) is incorrect. An external confirmation request sent by the auditor directly to a bank, broker, or other holder is a means of independently identifying which securities are in existence and owned by the client.

12.4.7. A company makes a practice of investing excess short-term cash in trading securities that are traded regularly on national exchanges. A reliable test of the valuation of these securities is

A. Consideration of current market quotations.

B. Confirmation of securities held by the broker.

C. Recalculation of investment value using a valuation model.

D. Calculation of premium or discount amortization.

Answer (A) is correct. *(CIA, adapted)*

REQUIRED: The reliable test of the valuation of trading securities.

DISCUSSION: Trading and available-for-sale securities should be measured on the statement of financial position at fair value. If market quotations are based on sufficient market activity, they usually provide sufficient appropriate evidence regarding valuation.

Answer (B) is incorrect. Although confirmation of securities held by the broker addresses the existence and rights and obligations assertions, it does not determine the valuation of the securities. Answer (C) is incorrect. Valuation models may be used for certain securities when no quoted market prices exist. In that case, the auditor should assess the reasonableness and appropriateness of the model. Answer (D) is incorrect. Any discount or premium on trading securities is not amortized.

12.4.8. Auditors may need to plan and perform auditing procedures for financial statement assertions about derivatives and hedging activities. Which of the following substantive procedures most clearly tests the completeness assertion about derivatives?

A. Assessing the reasonableness of the use of an option-pricing model.

B. Determining whether changes in the fair value of derivatives designated and qualifying as hedging instruments have been reported in earnings or in other comprehensive income.

C. Requesting counterparties to provide information about them, such as whether side agreements have been made.

D. Physically inspecting the derivative contract.

Answer (C) is correct. *(Publisher, adapted)*

REQUIRED: The substantive procedure that most clearly tests the completeness assertion about derivatives.

DISCUSSION: An audit of the completeness assertion addresses whether balances and transactions related to derivatives and hedging activities that should be recorded are recorded. A substantive procedure for the completeness assertion about derivatives and hedging activities is a request to the counterparty to a derivative for information about it, for example, whether an agreement exists to repurchase securities sold or whether side agreements have been made.

Answer (A) is incorrect. Assessing the reasonableness of the use of an option-pricing model tests the valuation assertion. Answer (B) is incorrect. Determining whether changes in the fair value of derivatives designated and qualifying as hedging instruments have been reported in earnings or in other comprehensive income tests the classification and understandability assertion. Answer (D) is incorrect. Physically inspecting the derivative contract tests the existence assertion.

12.4.9. An auditor's analytical procedures indicate a lower than expected return on an equity method investment. This situation most likely could have been caused by

A. An error in recording amortization of the excess of the investor's cost over the investment's underlying carrying amount.

B. The investee's decision to reduce cash dividends declared per share of its common stock.

C. An unrealized loss from an increase in the fair value of available-for-sale debt securities was recorded by crediting equity securities and debiting earnings.

D. A substantial fluctuation in the price of the investee's common stock on a national stock exchange.

Answer (A) is correct. *(CPA, adapted)*

REQUIRED: The potential cause of a lower than expected return on an equity method investment.

DISCUSSION: The transaction to record the amortization is a recurring entry that, if miscalculated, could result in a lower return than expected.

Answer (B) is incorrect. Cash dividends do not affect the return on investments accounted for under the equity method. Answer (C) is incorrect. An unrealized loss from a decrease in the fair value of available-for-sale debt securities should be recorded by debiting other comprehensive income, not earnings. The error understates the return on equity method investments. Answer (D) is incorrect. The change in price in the fair value of stock does not affect the return on an equity method investment.

12.4.10. In establishing the existence and ownership of an investment held by a corporation in the form of publicly traded stock, an auditor should inspect the securities or

A. Obtain written representations from management confirming that the securities are properly classified as trading securities.

B. Inspect the audited financial statements of the investee company.

C. Confirm the number of shares owned that are held by an independent custodian.

D. Determine that the investment is carried at the lower of cost or market.

Answer (C) is correct. *(CPA, adapted)*

REQUIRED: The procedure to establish the existence and ownership of an investment in stock.

DISCUSSION: To test the existence assertion and the rights and obligations (ownership) assertion, the auditor should perform one or more of the following procedures, depending on the nature of the investments and the assessment of audit risk: (1) inspection; (2) external confirmation by the issuer, custodian, or counterparty; (3) external confirmation of unsettled transactions by the broker-dealer; or (4) reading partnership or similar agreements. Thus, brokers, banks, agents, or others holding securities for the client should be requested by the client to respond directly in writing to the auditor's confirmation requests.

Answer (A) is incorrect. The classification of securities relates to the presentation and disclosure assertions. Furthermore, equity securities held for long-term investment purposes are classified as available-for-sale, not trading. Answer (B) is incorrect. An investment accounted for using the equity method might require the auditor to inspect audited financial statements of the investee to test the assertion about valuation. Answer (D) is incorrect. Determining the carrying amount does not test the existence and rights and obligations assertions.

12.4.11. A client is holding securities as collateral for an outstanding account receivable. During the course of the audit engagement, the CPA should

A. Verify that title to the securities rests with the client.

B. Determine that the amount recorded in the investment account is equal to the fair market value of the securities at the date of receipt.

C. Examine the securities and determine their fair value.

D. Refer to independent sources to determine that recorded dividend income is proper.

Answer (C) is correct. *(CPA, adapted)*

REQUIRED: The audit procedure for securities held as collateral.

DISCUSSION: When an entity holds an asset of another entity as security for an outstanding debt, the auditor should examine the collateral and estimate its fair value to determine the reasonableness of the arrangement. The auditor may refer to published data such as current market quotations to determine the value of securities.

Answer (A) is incorrect. The client will take title from the debtor only if the account receivable is not paid. Answer (B) is incorrect. The securities are not recorded as a client investment until the debtor defaults and the client obtains title. Answer (D) is incorrect. The entity (creditor) has no dividend income from the collateral. The debtor still owns the securities and earns the income, although the entity may apply cash dividends to reduce the debt.

12.4.12. In connection with an audit of the prepaid insurance account, which of the following procedures is usually not performed by the auditor?

A. Recompute the portion of the premium that expired during the year.

B. Prepare excerpts of insurance policies for audit documentation.

C. Confirm premium rates with an independent insurance broker.

D. Examine support for premium payments.

Answer (C) is correct. *(CPA, adapted)*

REQUIRED: The procedure not usually performed in an audit of prepaid insurance.

DISCUSSION: An audit of prepayments includes determining that amounts shown reflect all prepayments and that they (1) are properly valued according to the applicable reporting framework, (2) apply to future periods, (3) are expected to be realized (to provide future benefits), and (4) are accurately classified. Determining that a prepayment is properly valued involves verifying the amount of the expenditure by examining invoices from insurers, canceled checks, and the insurance policy. But the auditor does not confirm premium rates with an independent insurance broker. Paid checks and other documents are sufficient appropriate evidence of the amounts paid by the client.

Answer (A) is incorrect. Recomputing the portion of the premium that expired during the year is an appropriate procedure. Answer (B) is incorrect. Preparing excerpts of insurance policies for audit working papers is an appropriate procedure. Answer (D) is incorrect. Examining support for premium payments is an appropriate procedure.

12.4.13. When auditing prepaid insurance, an auditor discovers that the original insurance policy on plant equipment is not available for inspection. The policy's absence most likely indicates the possibility of a(n)

A. Insurance premium due but not recorded.

B. Deficiency in the coinsurance provision.

C. Lien on the plant equipment.

D. Understatement of insurance expense.

Answer (C) is correct. *(CPA, adapted)*

REQUIRED: The likely reason an insurance policy is not available for inspection.

DISCUSSION: When liens are placed on equipment or property, the lienholder often requires that the assets be insured and that the lienholder be named as the beneficiary. Hence, the policy is likely to be held by the lienholder even though the client is required to pay the premiums.

Answer (A) is incorrect. The premium has been paid and recorded as prepaid insurance. Answer (B) is incorrect. Coinsurance provisions require that the policy holder maintain coverage of a certain percentage of the value of the property (often 80-90%). Answer (D) is incorrect. The issue is not the recording of insurance, but the physical existence of the policy.

12.4.14. An auditor would most likely verify the interest earned on bond investments by

A. Verifying the receipt and deposit of interest checks.

B. Confirming the bond interest rate with the issuer of the bonds.

C. Recomputing the interest earned on the basis of face amount, interest rate, and period held.

D. Testing internal controls relevant to cash receipts.

Answer (C) is correct. *(CPA, adapted)*

REQUIRED: The method most likely used to verify bond interest earned.

DISCUSSION: The audit plan for investments includes making an independent computation of revenue (such as dividends and interest). For example, the auditor may use information from bond certificates (interest rates, payment dates, issue date, and face amount) to recalculate bond interest earned. This amount includes uncollected accruals.

Answer (A) is incorrect. Verifying the receipt and deposit of interest checks does not consider accrued interest. Answer (B) is incorrect. Confirming the rate would not, by itself, verify interest earned, which must be recomputed. Answer (D) is incorrect. Verification of interest earned requires substantive testing, not tests of controls.

12.4.15. The auditor, in determining whether the client has adopted the appropriate accounting method for an investment in the voting stock of an investee that is not consolidated, should obtain evidence primarily by

A. Inquiries to the client as to whether the client can exercise significant influence over the investee.

B. Direct confirmation with the investee concerning the control or influence that can be exercised by the client.

C. Comparison of the number of shares held by the investor with the investee's number of shares outstanding according to the written confirmation.

D. An independent, third party's opinion concerning the potential influence or control that can be exercised by the client over the investee.

Answer (A) is correct. *(Publisher, adapted)*

REQUIRED: The procedure to determine whether an investment in an unconsolidated investee is properly accounted for.

DISCUSSION: An entity that is not required to consolidate an investee may nevertheless exercise significant influence over it. Significant influence, which is rebuttably presumed if the investor holds 20% to 50% of the voting interests, requires the entity to account for the investee using the equity method. Thus, the auditor should inquire of the investor's management about the client's ability to exercise significant influence over the investee. The auditor should also inquire as to the circumstances serving as a basis for management's conclusions.

Answer (B) is incorrect. Inquiry should be made of the client. The investee might not want to disclose that the client has such influence. Answer (C) is incorrect. Significant influence may depend more upon the diversity of ownership of the investee than the number of shares held by the client. Answer (D) is incorrect. The auditor normally considers management's responses to inquiries in conjunction with the attendant circumstances as a basis for the conclusion.

12.4.16. A company owns a 30% voting interest in another entity. Assuming the investor did not elect the fair value option, which of the following provides the best form of audit evidence pertaining to the annual measurement of the investment?

A. Market quotations of the investee's stock.

B. Current fair value of the investee's assets.

C. Historical cost of the investee's assets.

D. Audited financial statements of the investee.

Answer (D) is correct. *(CPA, adapted)*

REQUIRED: The best evidence for measurement of a 30% voting interest in an investee.

DISCUSSION: A 30% voting interest creates a presumption that the investor is able to exercise significant influence over the investee. Thus, the equity method of accounting for the investment must be used if the FVO has not been elected. This method requires the investor to recognize the appropriate percentage of the investee's earnings as a debit to the investment and a credit to income. Dividends reduce the investment. Audited financial statements of the investee are usually sufficient appropriate evidence regarding the investor's equity. However, the auditor should satisfy the requirements either for (1) referring to the component auditor in the auditor's report or (2) assuming responsibility for the work of the component auditor (AU-C 600).

Answer (A) is incorrect. Market quotations may provide evidence regarding the current fair value of the securities but not the equity in net assets and results of operations of the investee. Answer (B) is incorrect. The relevant measurement is of the equity in net assets and results of operations. Answer (C) is incorrect. An equity method investment is not carried at historical cost.

12.4.17. In verifying the amount of goodwill recorded by a client in the current period, the most convincing evidence an auditor can obtain is by comparing the recorded amounts of assets acquired and liabilities assumed with the

A. Assessed values as evidenced by tax bills.

B. Seller's carrying amounts as evidenced by financial statements.

C. Insured values as evidenced by insurance policies.

D. Fair values as evidenced by independent appraisals.

Answer (D) is correct. *(CPA, adapted)*

REQUIRED: The most convincing evidence about goodwill recorded by a client.

DISCUSSION: Goodwill is recorded in a business combination when the fair value of (1) the consideration transferred, (2) any noncontrolling interest, and (3) any previously held equity interest exceeds the fair value of the net assets acquired. If the carrying amount of an investment reflects (1) factors such as goodwill not recognized by the investee or (2) fair values materially different from the investee's carrying amounts, the auditor should consider obtaining current appraisals of these amounts. Evaluations by persons independent of the investor and investee usually provide greater assurance of reliability than those by persons associated with those entities, although evaluations by associated parties may be acceptable. The acquiring entity should subsequently test goodwill for impairment at least annually.

Answer (A) is incorrect. A tax bill is an assessment on physical asset value only, not on the entity's going concern value. Answer (B) is incorrect. The seller's financial statements reflect the historical cost to the acquired company, not current fair value. Answer (C) is incorrect. The client may not even have insured the full fair value of the physical assets, much less the presumably greater going concern value of the business.

12.4.18. Deferred charges, such as the costs of direct-response advertising, usually should be

A. Disallowed by the auditor.

B. Reported on the balance sheet as a noncurrent asset.

C. Written off immediately as a current operating expense.

D. Converted to deferred credits by periodic transactions.

Answer (B) is correct. *(Publisher, adapted)*

REQUIRED: The proper disposition of deferred charges.

DISCUSSION: Deferred charges that are allocable to the operations of several years should be classified separately as noncurrent assets. The auditor's objective in examining deferred charges is to determine that they are proper charges to future operations and that their amounts and allocation are reported fairly in accordance with the applicable financial reporting framework. NOTE: The Accounting Standards Codification does not use the term "deferred charges." The relevant section is ASC 340, *Other Assets and Deferred Costs*.

Answer (A) is incorrect. Deferred charges are proper assets and may be presented in the balance sheet. Answer (C) is incorrect. Deferred charges are assets. They provide probable future economic benefits controllable by the entity that arise from past transactions or events. Answer (D) is incorrect. Deferred charges cannot be converted into deferred credits.

12.4.19. A corporate balance sheet indicates that one of the corporate assets is a patent. An auditor will most likely obtain evidence regarding the continuing validity and existence of this patent by obtaining a written representation from

A. A patent attorney.

B. A regional state patent office.

C. The patent inventor.

D. The patent owner.

Answer (A) is correct. *(CPA, adapted)*

REQUIRED: The appropriate source of evidence of the validity and existence of a patent.

DISCUSSION: A patent is an intangible asset representing a governmental grant of rights to an invention for a specified time. The lack of physical substance makes verifying its existence and ownership difficult. To obtain evidence of the continuing validity and existence of a patent, the auditor should obtain a written representation from an auditor's specialist. A patent attorney is an auditor's external specialist who has expertise not normally possessed by auditors. The attorney can perform the necessary research and express an opinion on which the auditor may reasonably rely.

Answer (B) is incorrect. Patents are obtained from the Patent and Trademark Office of the Department of Commerce. Answer (C) is incorrect. The inventor may have no current knowledge of the status of the patent. Answer (D) is incorrect. The owner is usually the client. The auditor needs independent evidence to corroborate client representations.

12.4.20. The auditor can best verify a client's bond sinking-fund transactions and year-end balance by

A. Confirmation with individual holders of retired bonds.

B. Confirmation with the bond trustee.

C. Recomputation of interest expense, interest payable, and amortization of bond discount or premium.

D. Examination and count of the bonds retired during the year.

Answer (B) is correct. *(CPA, adapted)*

REQUIRED: The best way to verify a client's bond sinking fund transactions.

DISCUSSION: The bond trustee is an outside, independent agent responsible for maintaining subsidiary ledgers and paying dividends. (S)he also often keeps the sinking-fund accounts. Consequently, the auditor should verify bond sinking-fund transactions with this trustee.

Answer (A) is incorrect. External confirmation with individual holders of retired bonds provides some evidence about the retirement process, not about the balance in the sinking fund or the transactions during the year. Answer (C) is incorrect. Recomputation of interest expense, interest payable, and amortization of bond discount or premium is only part of the overall procedure, of which trustee confirmation is the most important step. Answer (D) is incorrect. Examination and count of the bonds retired during the year provides some evidence about the retirement process, not about the balance in the sinking fund or the transactions during the year.

12.4.21. The best audit procedure for determining the existence of open commodity futures contracts at year end is the review of

A. Canceled checks in the subsequent period.

B. Available broker trade advices.

C. The replies to the standard confirmation requests sent to financial institutions.

D. Direct confirmations with the client's commodity traders.

Answer (D) is correct. *(CPA, adapted)*

REQUIRED: The best audit procedure for determining the existence of open commodity futures contracts.

DISCUSSION: Direct external confirmation by the client's commodity traders provides independent verification of open commodity futures contracts and may reveal undisclosed liabilities.

Answer (A) is incorrect. Payment for futures would have been made when the contract was made. Answer (B) is incorrect. Trade advices may be lost or destroyed. Answer (C) is incorrect. The standard form inquires specifically about deposit balances and direct liabilities to the financial institution. The client's bank or other financial institution would not likely have information relative to open commodity futures contracts.

12.5 Substantive Testing of Noncurrent Debt

12.5.1. An audit plan for noncurrent debt should include steps that require

A. Examining bond trust indentures.

B. Inspecting the accounts payable subsidiary ledger.

C. Investigating credits to the bond interest income account.

D. Verifying the existence of the bondholders.

Answer (A) is correct. *(CPA, adapted)*

REQUIRED: The procedure to be included in the audit plan for noncurrent debt.

DISCUSSION: The bond trust indenture contains information about contractual arrangements made with bondholders, such as (1) the face amount of the bonds, (2) interest rates, (3) payment dates, (4) descriptions of collateral, (5) provisions for conversion or retirement, (6) trustee duties, and (7) sinking fund requirements. The auditor should examine any bond trust indenture to determine that the client is meeting the conditions of the contract and is in compliance with the law.

Answer (B) is incorrect. Accounts payable are current liabilities, not noncurrent debt. Answer (C) is incorrect. Credits to bond interest income do not pertain to noncurrent debt (income relates to investments, not debt). Answer (D) is incorrect. The existence of bondholders is implied by the reporting of bonded debt.

12.5.2. In an audit of bonds payable, an auditor expects the trust indenture to include the

A. Auditee's debt-to-equity ratio at the time of issuance.

B. Effective yield of the bonds issued.

C. Subscription list.

D. Description of the collateral.

Answer (D) is correct. *(Publisher, adapted)*

REQUIRED: The information in a bond trust indenture.

DISCUSSION: A bond trust indenture is the contract between the bondholders and the bond issuer. It contains (1) the dates of issue and maturity of the bond issue, (2) the amount of the bonds, (3) interest rates, (4) payment dates, (5) descriptions of collateral, (6) provisions for conversion or retirement, (7) trustee duties, (8) sinking-fund requirements, and (9) restrictions on the borrower.

Answer (A) is incorrect. Current financial ratios are usually not included, but restrictive ratios may be; e.g., the debt-to-equity ratio might not be permitted to exceed 2 to 1. Answer (B) is incorrect. The effective yield to maturity of the bonds issued may be calculated from the premium or discount and the stated interest rate, but is not included in the trust indenture. Answer (C) is incorrect. The subscriptions list contains the names of the original subscribers, but these names are not normally included in the trust indenture.

12.5.3. An auditor's purpose in reviewing the renewal of a note payable shortly after the balance sheet date most likely is to obtain evidence concerning relevant assertions about

A. Existence.

B. Classification and understandability.

C. Completeness.

D. Valuation and allocation.

Answer (B) is correct. *(CPA, adapted)*

REQUIRED: The auditor's purpose in reviewing the renewal of a note payable shortly after year end.

DISCUSSION: Events such as the renewal of the note payable do not require adjustment of the financial statements but may require disclosure. Accordingly, the auditor should determine that the renewal had essentially the same terms and conditions as the recorded debt at year end. A significant change may affect the classification of notes payable (e.g., as current or noncurrent), the understandability of the statements, and the required disclosures.

Answer (A) is incorrect. The renewal does not raise an issue as to whether the note existed. Answer (C) is incorrect. The renewal does not raise an issue as to whether all notes were reported. Answer (D) is incorrect. The renewal does not affect the valuation of notes payable.

12.5.4. During an audit of an issuer of bonds, the auditor should obtain written confirmation regarding debenture transactions from the

A. Debenture holders.

B. Client's attorney.

C. Internal auditors.

D. Trustee.

Answer (D) is correct. *(CPA, adapted)*

REQUIRED: The source of confirmation of debenture transactions.

DISCUSSION: Debentures are bonds backed by the general credit of the issuer and not secured by specific assets. A bond issuer normally employs the services of an independent financial institution as trustee. The bond trustee is responsible for executing bond transactions, e.g., distributing or paying interest, and protecting the interests of bondholders. Accordingly, the auditor should confirm transactions with the trustee.

Answer (A) is incorrect. Direct communication with bondholders is unnecessary when a trustee is used. Answer (B) is incorrect. The entity's attorney does not have the information necessary to provide independent evidence about bond transactions. Answer (C) is incorrect. Internal auditors cannot provide independent evidence about bond transactions. They are neither independent nor knowledgeable about bond transaction details.

12.5.5. During its fiscal year, a company issued, at a discount, a substantial amount of first-mortgage bonds. When performing audit work in connection with the bond issue, the independent auditor should

A. Confirm the existence of the bondholders.

B. Review the minutes for authorization.

C. Trace the net cash received from the issuance to the bonds payable account.

D. Inspect the records maintained by the bond trustee.

Answer (B) is correct. *(CPA, adapted)*

REQUIRED: The audit procedure for a new issue of bonds.

DISCUSSION: Bonds issued during the year under audit should be traced to the minutes of the shareholders' or board of directors' meetings to check for proper authorization. The amount sold should be no greater than the amount authorized in the minutes.

Answer (A) is incorrect. Bondholder rights exist on the basis of the sale of bonds. A liability for interest and principal exists irrespective of who and where the bondholders are. Answer (C) is incorrect. The credit to bonds payable should be for the face amount of the bonds. The debit to cash ordinarily does not equal face amount because bonds are usually issued at a premium or a discount. Answer (D) is incorrect. An auditor ordinarily can rely on the confirmation of information with the bond trustee (who is an independent third party).

12.5.6. With respect to bonds issued during the period under audit, the auditor should

A. Review proper presentation and disclosure in the financial statements.

B. Consider whether the bond issue complied with applicable laws and regulations.

C. Calculate the effective interest rate to see if it is substantially the same as the rates for similar issues.

D. Determine that bonds are not owned by directors or officers of the company.

Answer (A) is correct. *(Publisher, adapted)*

REQUIRED: The audit procedure relevant to the audit of bonds payable currently being issued.

DISCUSSION: The objectives of the audit of noncurrent debt include (1) determining that all noncurrent debt has been recorded and constitutes bona fide liabilities; (2) verifying that federal and state laws relative to financial reporting have been complied with; (3) determining that premium, discount, interest payable, and interest expense are accurately recorded; (4) monitoring compliance with debt contracts; and (5) reviewing proper presentation and disclosure in the financial statements.

Answer (B) is incorrect. The opinion of counsel on the legality of the issue should address these matters. Answer (C) is incorrect. The effective interest rate for similar issues changes with the overall interest rate. Answer (D) is incorrect. Directors or officers of a company may invest in company bonds.

12.5.7. During an audit, Mr. Wick learns that the audit client was granted a 3-month waiver of the repayment of principal on the installment loan with Blank Bank without an extension of the maturity date. With respect to this loan, the audit program used by Mr. Wick is least likely to include a verification of the

A. Interest expense for the year.

B. Balloon payment.

C. Total liability at year end.

D. Installment loan payments.

Answer (B) is correct. *(CPA, adapted)*

REQUIRED: The item least likely to be verified in the audit of an installment loan.

DISCUSSION: The auditor's primary concern is that the liability is reported correctly at the balance sheet date. The balloon payment pertains to the next period's results of operations, financial position, and cash flows.

Answer (A) is incorrect. The auditor should verify interest expense to determine that it is recorded properly. Answer (C) is incorrect. Becoming satisfied as to the total liability at year end is a primary objective of the auditor. Answer (D) is incorrect. The amount of installment loan payments determines the amount of the current liability at year end.

12.5.8. During the year under audit, a client issued a substantial amount of bonds to an insurance company (a private placement). Which of the following is the most important step in the auditor's plan for the audit of bonds payable?

A. Confirming the amount issued with the SEC.

B. Tracing the cash received from the issue to the accounting records.

C. Examining the bond records maintained by a third party such as a transfer agent.

D. Recomputing the annual interest cost and the effective yield.

Answer (B) is correct. *(CPA, adapted)*

REQUIRED: The most important procedure in an audit of a private placement of bonds.

DISCUSSION: In a private placement of bonds, one not involving the use of an independent trustee, the auditor is most concerned that the cash received from the issue is accurately recorded. The auditor also is concerned that the cash is adequately safeguarded by the CFO's department. Failure to employ a trustee substantially increases the risks of material misstatement for all aspects of bond issues.

Answer (A) is incorrect. The SEC does not confirm transactions. Answer (C) is incorrect. A transfer agent is not likely to be used by the issuer if the bonds are privately placed. Even if a third party exists, the auditor confirms the information instead of examining the records. Answer (D) is incorrect. The mathematical check of the accuracy of the annual interest cost and the effective yield is not as important as the auditor's verification that cash received is properly accounted for.

12.5.9. Several years ago, Conway, Inc., secured a conventional real estate mortgage loan. Which of the following audit procedures would be least likely to be performed by an auditor auditing the mortgage balance?

A. Examine the current year's canceled checks.

B. Review the mortgage amortization schedule.

C. Inspect public records of lien balances.

D. Recompute mortgage interest expense.

Answer (C) is correct. *(CPA, adapted)*

REQUIRED: The audit procedure least likely to be performed regarding a mortgage loan.

DISCUSSION: Public real estate records do not disclose current balances. They disclose only the original amounts of mortgages. Other evidence is normally available, such as receipts for payments to the mortgagee and confirmations from payees.

Answer (A) is incorrect. Canceled checks represent the decrease in the mortgage balance and should be inspected by the auditor. Answer (B) is incorrect. The mortgage amortization schedule is evidence of the amount that should have been paid during the period as well as the principal balance at year end. Answer (D) is incorrect. The recomputation of interest expense and interest payable is an important means of verifying the amount of outstanding liabilities.

12.5.10. In auditing for unrecorded noncurrent bonds payable, an auditor most likely will

A. Perform analytical procedures on the bond premium and discount accounts.

B. Examine documentation of assets purchased with bond proceeds for liens.

C. Compare interest expense with the bond payable amount for reasonableness.

D. Confirm the existence of individual bondholders at year end.

Answer (C) is correct. *(CPA, adapted)*

REQUIRED: The appropriate procedure for testing noncurrent bonds payable.

DISCUSSION: The recorded interest expense should reconcile with the outstanding bonds payable. If interest expense appears excessive relative to the recorded bonds payable, unrecorded noncurrent liabilities may exist.

Answer (A) is incorrect. Performing analytical procedures on bond premium and discount are not likely to uncover unrecorded payables. Answer (B) is incorrect. The examination of documentation related to asset additions is considered in the audit of assets, not bonds payable. Answer (D) is incorrect. The greatest risk is that the bonds payable balance is not complete.

12.5.11. The audit procedures used to verify accrued liabilities differ from those employed for the verification of accounts payable because

A. Accrued liabilities usually pertain to services of a continuing nature whereas accounts payable are the result of completed transactions.

B. Accrued liability balances are less material than accounts payable balances.

C. Evidence supporting accrued liabilities is nonexistent, whereas evidence supporting accounts payable is readily available.

D. Accrued liabilities at year end will become accounts payable during the following year.

Answer (A) is correct. *(CPA, adapted)*

REQUIRED: The reason audit procedures used to verify accrued liabilities differ from those applied to accounts payable.

DISCUSSION: The procedures differ because the balances result from different transactional processes. Liabilities are accrued for such continuing transactions as rent, salaries, and interest. Accounts payable are short-term obligations arising from the purchase of goods and services in the ordinary course of business.

Answer (B) is incorrect. One balance is not inherently more or less material than the other. Answer (C) is incorrect. Supporting documentary evidence exists for both. Answer (D) is incorrect. Once accrued liabilities become accounts payable (not necessarily at year end), the audit procedures do not differ.

12.5.12. The auditor is most likely to verify accrued commissions payable in conjunction with the

A. Sales cutoff test.

B. Verification of contingent liabilities.

C. Review of post balance sheet date disbursements.

D. Examination of trade accounts payable.

Answer (A) is correct. *(CPA, adapted)*

REQUIRED: The audit procedures performed when verifying accrued commissions payable.

DISCUSSION: Sales commissions and accrued sales commissions payable are based upon sales of the period. The auditor verifies accrued commissions payable in conjunction with procedures applied to the sales cutoff test. The purpose is to obtain reasonable assurance that revenues and related liabilities are recorded in the same period in accordance with the matching principle.

Answer (B) is incorrect. The auditor would review the minutes of board meetings, send an inquiry letter to the client's legal counsel, send bank confirmations, obtain a representation letter from the client, and review correspondence with financial institutions to verify and/or uncover contingent liabilities. Answer (C) is incorrect. The review of disbursements in the subsequent period is performed to identify unrecorded liabilities. Answer (D) is incorrect. The examination of trade accounts payable is performed in conjunction with the audit of inventories, purchases, and cash disbursements.

12.5.13. A loss contingency may require recognition in the financial statements. An accrual is not normally made as a result of

A. Guarantees of indebtedness incurred by others.

B. Repurchase commitments.

C. Pending litigation or threats of expropriation.

D. General business risks.

Answer (D) is correct. *(Publisher, adapted)*

REQUIRED: The inappropriate basis for accruing a contingent liability and recognizing a loss.

DISCUSSION: General business risks are not a permissible basis for accrual of a contingent liability. Not all uncertainties inherent in the accounting process result in contingencies. General or unspecified business risks cannot meet the conditions for accrual: (1) The loss is probable at the balance-sheet date, and (2) it can be reasonably estimated.

Answer (A) is incorrect. Guarantees of indebtedness incurred by others are considered loss contingencies. Furthermore, if the conditions for accrual of a loss contingency are not met, the guarantor still must record a liability (a noncontingent obligation) for the fair value of the guarantee. If the conditions are met, the greater of the amount of the contingent liability or the fair value of the guarantee is recorded. Answer (B) is incorrect. Repurchase commitments are considered loss contingencies. Answer (C) is incorrect. Pending litigation or threats of expropriation are considered loss contingencies.

12.5.14. In an audit for the fiscal year ended on December 31, Year 1, the auditor discovered that a debit had been made on January 15, Year 2, to a notes receivable account from the cash payments journal. This entry may indicate that a

A. Receivable has been established from a party for whom the client has guaranteed a debt.

B. Provision for contingencies is required.

C. Contingent liability was created in Year 2.

D. Contingent asset has been recognized.

Answer (A) is correct. *(Publisher, adapted)*

REQUIRED: The implication of a debit to notes receivable from the cash payments journal.

DISCUSSION: The entry suggests that a contingent liability has become noncontingent and has been settled. The payment of the debt upon default of the party is recognized in the accounts by a debit to notes receivable and a credit to cash.

Answer (B) is incorrect. No provision for contingencies is needed if the liability has been paid. Answer (C) is incorrect. The entry suggests that a contingent liability became an actual liability and has been paid. Answer (D) is incorrect. Contingent assets are never recognized in the accounts until realized. Contingent liabilities are recognized when they are probable and they are subject to reasonable estimation.

12.6 Substantive Testing of Equity

12.6.1. In an audit of equity, an auditor is most concerned that

A. Capital stock transactions are properly authorized.

B. Stock splits are capitalized at par or stated value on the dividend declaration date.

C. Dividends during the year under audit were approved by the shareholders.

D. Changes in the accounts are verified by a bank serving as a registrar and stock transfer agent.

Answer (A) is correct. *(Publisher, adapted)*

REQUIRED: The most important consideration in an audit of equity.

DISCUSSION: A primary concern of the auditor is that all capital stock transactions are properly authorized. Accordingly, all entries in the capital stock account should be vouched to the minutes of the board of directors' meetings. The articles of incorporation, by-laws, and minutes of shareholders' meetings should also be reviewed. The auditor requires information about the number and rights of shares authorized and issued, the par or stated value, conversion and call features, stock dividends, and stock splits. The auditor also determines whether transactions are properly accounted for and equity items are presented in accordance with the applicable financial reporting framework.

Answer (B) is incorrect. Stock splits require no transfer from retained earnings. Answer (C) is incorrect. The board of directors usually approves dividends. Answer (D) is incorrect. The registrar and transfer agent, who is responsible for increases and exchanges of stock, is not responsible for monitoring all changes in the accounts.

12.6.2. In the audit of a medium-sized manufacturing company, which one of the following areas would be expected to require the least amount of audit time?

A. Owners' equity.

B. Revenue.

C. Assets.

D. Liabilities.

Answer (A) is correct. *(CPA, adapted)*

REQUIRED: The area requiring the least audit time for a medium-sized manufacturer.

DISCUSSION: Transactions affecting owners' equity are usually few even though they may be significant in amount. Consequently, the audit time required is probably small compared with that needed for active accounts. Shareholders' equity ordinarily is affected only by stock issuance, treasury stock transactions, dividends, and closing entries.

Answer (B) is incorrect. The auditor usually spends significant audit time on revenues. Answer (C) is incorrect. The auditor usually spends significant audit time on assets. Answer (D) is incorrect. The auditor usually spends significant audit time on liabilities.

12.6.3. The auditor does not expect the client to debit retained earnings for which of the following transactions?

A. A 10% stock dividend.

B. A 60% stock dividend.

C. A four-for-one stock split.

D. An appropriation of retained earnings for treasury stock.

Answer (C) is correct. *(Publisher, adapted)*

REQUIRED: The transaction not requiring a debit to retained earnings.

DISCUSSION: A four-for-one stock split results in an increase in the number of shares and a proportionate decrease in the par or stated value per share. No entry is recorded for a stock split. A memo entry, however, is made indicating that the par value has been changed.

Answer (A) is incorrect. A small stock dividend should be capitalized at fair value. Answer (B) is incorrect. A large stock dividend is normally capitalized at par value. Answer (D) is incorrect. Crediting appropriations for treasury stock and debiting retained earnings is a necessary entry.

12.6.4. Mayer, CPA, is auditing equity. Tests typically include all the following except

A. Reviewing the bank reconciliation for the imprest dividend account.

B. Tracing individual dividend payments to the capital stock records.

C. Verifying the authorization of dividends by inspecting the directors' minutes.

D. Determining that dividend declarations comply with debt agreements.

Answer (B) is correct. *(Publisher, adapted)*

REQUIRED: The procedure not normally performed in an audit of equity.

DISCUSSION: An auditor does not normally trace individual dividend payments to the capital stock records. (S)he may test certain large dividend payments but, because the amount of each dividend is usually small, detail checking is minimal. The need for extensive checking is reduced when the client uses an independent financial institution as its agent for dividend payments. The stock transfer agent often performs this function because it maintains detailed records of shareholders.

Answer (A) is incorrect. Reviewing the bank reconciliation for the imprest dividend account is an appropriate auditing procedure. Answer (C) is incorrect. Verifying the authorization of dividends is an appropriate auditing procedure. Answer (D) is incorrect. Determining that dividend declarations comply with debt agreements is an appropriate auditing procedure.

12.6.5. When a corporate client maintains its own stock records, the auditor primarily will rely upon

A. Confirmation with the company secretary of shares outstanding at year end.

B. Review of the corporate minutes for data as to shares outstanding.

C. Confirmation of the number of shares outstanding at year end with the appropriate state official.

D. Inspection of the stock book at year end and accounting for all certificate numbers.

Answer (D) is correct. *(Publisher, adapted)*

REQUIRED: The appropriate procedure when a company is its own registrar and transfer agent.

DISCUSSION: When an independent registrar and a stock transfer agent are employed by the client, the auditor may simply confirm the shares issued and outstanding at year end. But when the client acts as its own registrar and transfer agent, the auditor should perform procedures equivalent to external confirmations. (S)he should account for stock certificate numbers, examine all canceled certificates, and reconcile the subsidiary shareholder ledger with the general ledger.

Answer (A) is incorrect. Confirmations are usually sent to independent parties. Answer (B) is incorrect. The minutes indicate the number of shares authorized, not the number outstanding. Answer (C) is incorrect. State officials and officers do not maintain records as to the number of a corporation's outstanding shares.

12.6.6. When a client's company does not maintain its own stock records, the auditor should obtain written confirmation from the transfer agent and registrar concerning

A. Restrictions on the payment of dividends.

B. The number of shares issued and outstanding.

C. Guarantees of preferred stock liquidation value.

D. The number of shares subject to agreements to repurchase.

Answer (B) is correct. *(CPA, adapted)*

REQUIRED: The information confirmed by the transfer agent and registrar.

DISCUSSION: The independent stock registrar is a financial institution employed to prevent improper issuances of stock, especially over-issuances. The transfer agent maintains detailed shareholder records and facilitates transfer of shares. Both are independent and reliable sources of evidence concerning total shares issued and outstanding.

Answer (A) is incorrect. The payment of dividends is confirmed, but dividend restrictions are found in the articles of incorporation, bylaws, and minutes of directors' and shareholders' meetings. Answer (C) is incorrect. Guarantees of preferred stock liquidation value are not made by the transfer agent and registrar. Answer (D) is incorrect. The number of shares subject to agreements to repurchase is not the concern of the transfer agent and registrar.

12.6.7. A company declared and paid a stock dividend. Its independent external auditor should determine that

A. The officers authorized the issuance of the stock dividend.

B. The stock dividend was properly recorded by means of a memorandum entry only.

C. Shareholders received their additional shares by confirming year-end holdings with them.

D. Appropriate amounts were transferred from retained earnings to capital stock and additional paid-in capital.

Answer (D) is correct. *(Publisher, adapted)*

REQUIRED: The appropriate audit procedure for a stock dividend.

DISCUSSION: The auditor should gather evidence that the stock dividend was properly authorized by the board of directors and does not result in the issuance of shares in excess of the number permitted by the articles of incorporation. The auditor must also verify the amounts transferred from retained earnings to capital stock and additional paid-in capital.

Answer (A) is incorrect. Usually, only the board of directors authorizes stock and cash dividends. Answer (B) is incorrect. Issuances in excess of 20-25% of the shares outstanding are capitalized at an amount specified by the applicable state statute, which is usually the par value. Other stock dividends are recorded at fair value. Answer (C) is incorrect. The auditor usually does not confirm holdings with shareholders. Instead, the auditor confirms the total shares issued and outstanding with the independent registrar and stock transfer agent.

12.6.8. The auditor is concerned with establishing that dividends are paid to client corporation shareholders who hold stock as of the

A. Issue date.

B. Declaration date.

C. Record date.

D. Payment date.

Answer (C) is correct. *(CPA, adapted)*

REQUIRED: The date that establishes the right to receive a declared dividend.

DISCUSSION: Persons who hold stock in the corporation as of the record date are entitled to payment of the dividend. The auditor should test the dividend payment list to gather evidence that dividends were paid to the appropriate shareholders. The integrity of the dividend payment process is enhanced when an independent agent (usually a financial institution) is used to pay dividends.

Answer (A) is incorrect. The issue date is the date the stock was issued. Answer (B) is incorrect. The declaration date is the date the entity declares the amount of a dividend and specifies the date of record. Answer (D) is incorrect. On the payment date, the dividends are paid to those shareholders who owned stock as of the record date.

12.6.9. An audit program for the retained earnings account should include a step that requires verification of the

A. Market value used to charge retained earnings to account for a two-for-one stock split.

B. Approval of the adjustment to the beginning balance as a result of a write-down of an account receivable.

C. Authorization for both cash and stock dividends.

D. Gain or loss resulting from disposition of treasury shares.

Answer (C) is correct. *(CPA, adapted)*

REQUIRED: The procedure performed in the audit of retained earnings.

DISCUSSION: The auditor should determine from the minutes of the board of directors' meetings that proper authorization has been made for both cash and stock dividends. All dividends require transfers from (debits to) retained earnings. Thus, dividends should be audited in conjunction with retained earnings.

Answer (A) is incorrect. No change is made in retained earnings for stock splits. Answer (B) is incorrect. A write-down of accounts receivable is taken through the income statement, not directly to retained earnings. Answer (D) is incorrect. Only losses on treasury stock transactions can be charged to retained earnings. Gains and some losses are taken to paid-in-capital accounts.

12.6.10. During an audit of a company's equity accounts, the auditor determines whether restrictions have been imposed on retained earnings resulting from loans, agreements, or state law. This audit procedure most likely is intended to verify relevant assertion about

A. Existence or occurrence.

B. Completeness.

C. Valuation and allocation.

D. Classification and understandability.

Answer (D) is correct. *(CPA, adapted)*

REQUIRED: The assertion that the auditor tests relative to restrictions on retained earnings.

DISCUSSION: The presentation and disclosure assertions include assertions about classification and understandability. Financial information should be properly presented and disclosed, and disclosures should be clear (AU-C 315 and AS 1105). Thus, when restrictions have been placed on retained earnings, the auditor should determine that they are properly disclosed in the notes to the financial statements.

Answer (A) is incorrect. Restrictions on retained earnings have little relevance to the existence or occurrence assertion. Answer (B) is incorrect. Restrictions on retained earnings have little relevance to the completeness assertion. Answer (C) is incorrect. Restrictions on retained earnings have little relevance to the valuation assertion.

12.6.11. With respect to treasury stock, the auditor should not object to which of the following?

A. Restrictions on retained earnings have not been met.

B. Dividends have been paid on treasury stock.

C. The treasury stock certificates have been destroyed.

D. Treasury stock is recorded at cost rather than par value.

Answer (D) is correct. *(Publisher, adapted)*

REQUIRED: The appropriate treatment of treasury stock.

DISCUSSION: Treasury stock may be measured at cost or at par value according to U.S. GAAP.

Answer (A) is incorrect. Certain states restrict retained earnings relative to treasury stock. The auditor should take exception to the failure to comply with the restriction. Answer (B) is incorrect. Dividends are paid only on shares issued and outstanding. Answer (C) is incorrect. The auditor should inspect the treasury stock or confirm the stock with the custodian or registrar. Even after retirement, the certificates should be kept to provide evidence that they have not been reissued.

12.6.12. If the auditee has a material amount of treasury stock on hand at year end, the auditor should

A. Count the certificates at the same time other securities are counted.

B. Count the certificates only if the company had treasury stock transactions during the year.

C. Not count the certificates if treasury stock is a deduction from equity.

D. Count the certificates only if the company classifies treasury stock with other assets.

Answer (A) is correct. *(Publisher, adapted)*

REQUIRED: The true statement about the audit of treasury stock.

DISCUSSION: All capital transactions should be verified. Thus, the auditor must count the certificates of treasury stock on hand at year end at the same time the other securities are counted. This procedure provides direct evidence that the treasury stock exists and is in the possession of the client. Any treasury stock certificates not on hand are confirmed with the holders.

Answer (B) is incorrect. The auditor should inspect treasury stock certificates at year end. Answer (C) is incorrect. The auditor should inspect treasury stock certificates at year end. Answer (D) is incorrect. Treasury stock is never classified as an asset.

12.6.13. In performing tests concerning the granting of stock options, an auditor should

A. Confirm the transaction with the Secretary of State in the state of incorporation.

B. Verify the existence of option holders in the entity's payroll records or stock ledgers.

C. Determine that sufficient treasury stock is available to cover any new stock issued.

D. Trace the authorization for the transaction to a vote of the board of directors.

Answer (D) is correct. *(CPA, adapted)*

REQUIRED: The tests performed by the auditor on the granting of stock options.

DISCUSSION: Shareholders' equity transactions, for example, issuances of stock, purchases of treasury stock, declarations of dividends, and the issuance of share options to employees or others require authorization by the board of directors. Thus, the auditor should inspect minutes of board meetings to verify that share options were authorized.

Answer (A) is incorrect. The Secretary of State is not likely to have knowledge of the granting of options within a particular entity. Answer (B) is incorrect. The existence of option holders is not a major risk in an audit of options. Answer (C) is incorrect. The entity need not hold treasury stock at the time of granting options if the shares are publicly traded and can be acquired as needed or if the entity has the ability to issue new shares.

12.6.14. In an examination of equity, the auditor should determine that the entity reports accumulated other comprehensive income in the balance sheet in the

A. Liabilities section.

B. Equity section as a component separate from retained earnings and additional paid-in capital.

C. Retained earnings section.

D. Other assets section.

Answer (B) is correct. *(Publisher, adapted)*

REQUIRED: The treatment of accumulated other comprehensive income.

DISCUSSION: If an entity that reports a full set of financial statements has items of other comprehensive income, it must report comprehensive income in one continuous statement or in two separate but consecutive statements. The total of other comprehensive income for a period must be transferred to a component of equity in the balance sheet that is presented separately from retained earnings and additional paid-in capital. A descriptive title, such as accumulated other comprehensive income, must be used for that component.

12.7 Substantive Testing of Payroll

12.7.1. In auditing payroll when control risk is assessed as low, an auditor most likely will

A. Verify that checks representing unclaimed wages are mailed.

B. Trace individual employee deductions to entity journal entries.

C. Observe entity employees during a payroll distribution.

D. Compare payroll costs with entity standards or budgets.

Answer (D) is correct. *(CPA, adapted)*

REQUIRED: The procedure most likely performed during the audit of payroll.

DISCUSSION: Comparing payroll costs with budgeted amounts is a standard analytical procedure that is performed in most audits of payroll.

Answer (A) is incorrect. Checks representing unclaimed wages should be maintained by the CFO until claimed by the appropriate employees. Answer (B) is incorrect. The individual employee deductions do not result in entity journal entries, but cumulative journal entries record the sum of the payroll. Answer (C) is incorrect. Observation of payroll distribution may not be necessary when the RMMs are low.

12.7.2. In an audit of payroll, an auditor is primarily concerned about

A. Excess FICA and income tax withholding.

B. Errors in employee time records.

C. Misposted payroll amounts.

D. Errors or fraud in the amount of payments.

Answer (D) is correct. *(Publisher, adapted)*

REQUIRED: The auditor's primary concern in an audit of payroll.

DISCUSSION: The auditor is primarily concerned about the possibility of errors or fraud in the amount of payment when auditing payroll transactions. Employee compensation is a major item of expense and is especially susceptible to fraud unless internal control is effective. The inherent risk for payroll transactions is increased by the need for rapid processing of a large amount of information.

Answer (A) is incorrect. Excess FICA and income tax withholding is an important, but secondary, consideration. Answer (B) is incorrect. Errors in employee time records is an important, but secondary, consideration. Answer (C) is incorrect. Misposted payroll amounts is an important, but secondary, consideration.

12.7.3. Which of the following audit procedures provides the least relevant evidence in determining that payroll payments were made to bona fide employees?

A. Reconcile time cards in use to employees on the job.

B. Examine canceled checks for proper endorsement and compare with human resources records.

C. Test for separation of the authorization for payment from the hire/fire authorization.

D. Test the payroll account bank reconciliation by tracing outstanding checks to the payroll register.

Answer (D) is correct. *(CIA, adapted)*

REQUIRED: The procedure that provides the least relevant evidence that payroll payments were made to bona fide employees.

DISCUSSION: A payroll account proof tests for completeness of the recorded transactions, not for their validity.

Answer (A) is incorrect. Verification that an employee is actually working is a common procedure to test for nonexistent employees. Answer (B) is incorrect. Examining for proper endorsements and comparing with records may detect improper payments. Answer (C) is incorrect. Separation of payroll authorization from employment decisions helps to eliminate the conditions in which one person can arrange payment to fictitious employees.

12.7.4. An auditor most likely would perform substantive tests of details on payroll transactions and balances when

A. Cutoff tests indicate a substantial amount of accrued payroll expense.

B. The assessed risk of material misstatement relative to payroll transactions is low.

C. Analytical procedures indicate unusual fluctuations in recurring payroll entries.

D. Accrued payroll expense consists primarily of unpaid commissions.

Answer (C) is correct. *(CPA, adapted)*

REQUIRED: The reason an auditor most likely tests details of payroll transactions and balances.

DISCUSSION: The auditor should evaluate significant unexpected differences revealed by analytical procedures. The first step is to reconsider the methods and factors used in developing the expectations and to make inquiries of management. If a suitable explanation is not received, additional procedures to investigate the differences are necessary.

Answer (A) is incorrect. A substantial amount of accrued payroll expense is not an abnormal condition. Answer (B) is incorrect. A low assessed RMM may permit the auditor to devote less effort to substantive tests. Answer (D) is incorrect. The existence of unpaid earned commissions provides no indication of a misstatement.

12.7.5. To check the accuracy of hours worked, an auditor would ordinarily compare clock cards with

A. Personnel records.

B. Shop job time tickets.

C. Labor variance reports.

D. Time recorded in the payroll register.

Answer (B) is correct. *(CPA, adapted)*

REQUIRED: The item with which the auditor compares clock cards to verify hours worked.

DISCUSSION: The auditor should compare shop job time tickets with the clock cards to determine the accuracy of the hours worked. The job tickets, which contain the total hours worked on each job, should not vary significantly from the employee time cards used to compute payroll.

Answer (A) is incorrect. The human resources department is responsible for authorizing employment, pay rates, and employee reclassifications. The timekeeping function should be performed separately. Answer (C) is incorrect. Labor variance reports only show the difference between the time budgeted and the time charged to certain jobs. Answer (D) is incorrect. The time recorded in the payroll register is taken from clock time cards.

12.7.6. Analytical procedures may be applied to payroll to detect unusual items. Which of the following is an appropriate analytical procedure for payroll?

A. Compare the relationship of hours worked to payroll with that of the preceding year.

B. Inspect authorizations on time cards.

C. Compare rates authorized under a union contract with payroll records.

D. Review payroll bank account reconciliation.

Answer (A) is correct. *(Publisher, adapted)*

REQUIRED: The analytical procedure for payroll.

DISCUSSION: When designing and performing analytical procedures, the auditor should develop expectations of recorded amounts or ratios. Sources of information for developing these expectations include (1) financial information for comparable prior periods; (2) anticipated results, e.g., budgets and forecasts; (3) relationships of elements of financial information; (4) industry information; and (5) relationships of financial information with relevant nonfinancial information (AU-C 520). Evaluating the relationship of hours worked and payroll for the current and preceding years involves comparing financial information with relevant nonfinancial information in the light of an expectation developed based on data from a comparable prior period.

Answer (B) is incorrect. Inspecting authorizations on time cards is a test of controls. Answer (C) is incorrect. Comparing rates authorized under a union contract with payroll records directly tests the validity of payroll. Answer (D) is incorrect. Reviewing the payroll bank account reconciliation directly tests the validity of payroll.

12.7.7. An internal auditor wishes to determine whether salaried employees in the division being audited are taking more paid vacation time than they have earned. Which of the following audit procedures will be most effective?

A. Observing which employees were absent because of vacations and tracing those absences through the payroll records to subtractions from accumulated vacation time.

B. Comparing total vacation time taken by selected employees in the most recent 12 months per payroll records to the time taken by the same employees in the preceding 12 months.

C. Sending confirmations to selected employees, asking them to verify the accuracy of the number of days of vacation used during the year and the number of remaining unused days as obtained from the payroll records.

D. Comparing the accrued vacation pay liability as computed for the firm's most recent balance sheet with the corresponding amount for 1 year earlier and investigating any significant change.

Answer (A) is correct. *(CIA, adapted)*

REQUIRED: The audit procedure to test for excessive vacation time.

DISCUSSION: Salaried employees do not punch a clock to create a record of their presence, so observation by the auditor may be necessary to determine whether they are present. The time such an employee is absent may be compared with vacation pay and the payroll charged to vacation time to determine whether an excessive amount is being taken.

Answer (B) is incorrect. Many reasons may justify the year-to-year change; for example, increased employee seniority or use of time accumulated from the previous year. Also, comparison of payroll records tests recorded amounts only. Answer (C) is incorrect. A confirmation sent to a wrongdoer is not likely to elicit an incriminating reply. Answer (D) is incorrect. Comparing the accrued vacation pay liability with the corresponding amount for 1 year earlier tests recorded amounts only.

12.7.8. An auditor found that employee time cards in one department are not properly approved by the supervisor. Which of the following could result?

A. Duplicate paychecks might be issued.

B. The wrong hourly rate could be used to calculate gross pay.

C. Employees might be paid for unworked hours.

D. Payroll checks might not be distributed to the appropriate payees.

Answer (C) is correct. *(CIA, adapted)*

REQUIRED: The misstatement that could occur if time cards are not approved by a supervisor.

DISCUSSION: The time cards report the number of hours worked. Failure to approve the time worked could result in an amount of pay inconsistent with actual hours worked.

Answer (A) is incorrect. Each employee would have one time card and be issued one check based on the time card. Answer (B) is incorrect. The authorized pay rates should be provided by the human resources department. Answer (D) is incorrect. The paymaster should ensure that only authorized employees receive a paycheck.

12.7.9. One payroll audit objective is to determine whether the employees received pay in amounts recorded in the payroll journal. To satisfy this objective, the auditor should

A. Reconcile the payroll bank account.

B. Request that a company official distribute all paychecks.

C. Determine whether a proper segregation of duties exists between recording payroll and reconciling the payroll bank account.

D. Compare canceled payroll checks with the payroll journal.

Answer (D) is correct. *(CIA, adapted)*

REQUIRED: The procedure to verify that employees received pay in amounts recorded in the payroll journal.

DISCUSSION: To test the accuracy of the payroll journal, the auditor should vouch a sample of the entries to supporting documents, i.e., the canceled checks, timekeeping information, and records of wage rates and authorized deductions.

Answer (A) is incorrect. Reconciling the payroll bank account should be part of the audit plan for payroll, but it does not test the agreement of amounts received by employees with the payroll journal entries. Answer (B) is incorrect. A company official should distribute all paychecks, but this procedure does not ensure the agreement of amounts received by employees with the payroll journal entries. Answer (C) is incorrect. Determining whether a proper segregation of duties exists between recording payroll and reconciling the payroll bank account should be part of the audit plan for payroll, but it does not test the agreement of amounts received by employees with the payroll journal entries.

12.7.10. The client's bookkeeper perpetrated a theft by preparing erroneous W-2 forms. The bookkeeper's FICA withheld was overstated by $2,000 and the FICA withheld from all other employees was understated by the same amount. Which of the following is an audit procedure that would detect such a fraud?

A. Multiplication of the applicable FICA rate by each individual's gross annual taxable earnings.

B. Utilizing Form W-4 and withholding charts to determine whether deductions authorized per pay period agree with amounts deducted per pay period.

C. Footing and crossfooting of the payroll register followed by tracing postings to the general ledger.

D. Vouching canceled checks to the appropriate federal tax form.

Answer (A) is correct. *(CPA, adapted)*

REQUIRED: The audit procedure to detect a manipulation of withholding taxes.

DISCUSSION: One objective of the audit of payroll is to verify the client's compliance with various legal requirements, e.g., income tax withholding, Social Security taxes, workers' compensation, unemployment insurance, and wages and hours laws. The auditor should perform tests of controls by sampling payroll transactions. The deductions authorized by employees or required by law should be compared with those actually made. By comparing the recorded amounts withheld on individual employees' W-2 forms with those independently calculated by the auditor, (s)he should detect any misstatement of FICA withholding.

Answer (B) is incorrect. The fraud was not in the records for each pay period but in the year-end summaries of withholding (W-2). Answer (C) is incorrect. The total amount of FICA taxes is correct, so the records foot and crossfoot correctly. Answer (D) is incorrect. The total amount of FICA taxes remitted with the appropriate form is correct.

12.7.11. An auditor reviews the reconciliation of payroll tax forms that a client is responsible for filing to

A. Verify that payroll taxes are deducted from employees' gross pay.

B. Determine whether internal control activities are operating effectively.

C. Uncover fictitious employees who are receiving payroll checks.

D. Identify potential liabilities for unpaid payroll taxes.

Answer (D) is correct. *(CPA, adapted)*

REQUIRED: The reason an auditor reviews the reconciliation of payroll tax forms.

DISCUSSION: To satisfy the completeness assertion, payroll tax expense should be reconciled with payroll tax returns (income tax, FICA, and unemployment taxes). Moreover, to satisfy the rights and obligations assertion, the auditor must determine whether the assets, expenses, and payables (liabilities) are the client's. Thus, the review of the reconciliation of payroll tax forms identifies the client's potential liabilities for unpaid payroll taxes. Detection of unrecorded amounts is a primary objective of an audit of liabilities.

Answer (A) is incorrect. Payroll records indicate whether deductions have been made. Answer (B) is incorrect. The reconciliation is just one control. Answer (C) is incorrect. Examination of payroll records and a surprise observation of payroll distribution are typical procedures for detecting fictitious employees.

STUDY UNIT THIRTEEN
EVIDENCE -- KEY CONSIDERATIONS

This study unit presents various topics related to the collection of evidence. Inquiry of the client's lawyer, an entity's ability to continue as a going concern, and client representations have received the most attention. Reporting issues related to uncertainties and the entity's ability to continue as a going concern are covered in Study Unit 16.

QUESTIONS

13.1 Consideration of Litigation, Claims, and Assessments

13.1.1. The primary reason an auditor requests letters of inquiry be sent to a client's legal counsel is to provide the auditor with

A. The probable outcome of asserted claims and pending or threatened litigation.

B. Corroboration of the information furnished by management about litigation, claims, and assessments.

C. Legal counsel's opinion of the client's historical experiences in recent similar litigation.

D. A description and evaluation of litigation, claims, and assessments that existed at the balance sheet date.

Answer (B) is correct. *(CPA, adapted)*

REQUIRED: The primary reason that letters of audit inquiry are sent to a client's legal counsel.

DISCUSSION: A letter of inquiry to a client's external legal counsel is the auditor's primary means of corroborating information furnished by management about litigation, claims, and assessments. If in-house legal counsel is primarily responsible for the entity's litigation, claims, and assessments, the auditor should send a similar letter of inquiry to in-house legal counsel. But the letter to in-house legal counsel is not a substitute for direct communication with external legal counsel.

Answer (A) is incorrect. Management provides information about the probable outcome of asserted claims and impending or threatened litigation. Answer (C) is incorrect. The auditor is concerned with current litigation, not recent similar litigation. Answer (D) is incorrect. Management provides a description and evaluation of litigation, claims, and assessments that existed at the balance sheet date. The letter of inquiry corroborates that information.

13.1.2. Which of the following is not an audit procedure that the auditor performs with respect to litigation, claims, and assessments?

A. Inquire of and discuss with management the policies and procedures adopted for litigation, claims, and assessments.

B. Obtain from management a description and evaluation of litigation, claims, and assessments that existed at the balance sheet date.

C. Obtain assurance from management that it has disclosed all unasserted claims that legal counsel has advised are probable of assertion and must be disclosed.

D. Confirm directly with the client's legal counsel that all claims have been recorded in the financial statements.

Answer (D) is correct. *(CPA, adapted)*

REQUIRED: The procedure not performed regarding legal matters.

DISCUSSION: Legal counsel's expertise does not extend to accounting matters. Legal counsel evaluates whether claims may be asserted and the likelihood and magnitude of the outcomes. These evaluations bear upon accounting and reporting decisions, for example, whether disclosure only or recognition of a contingent liability is required. But all claims do not necessarily require recognition, and legal counsel does not have information about the content of financial statements that have not been issued.

Answer (A) is incorrect. Inquiring of and discussing with management the policies and procedures adopted for litigation, claims, and assessments is a procedure required by AU-C 501. Answer (B) is incorrect. Obtaining from management a description and evaluation of litigation, claims, and assessments that existed at the balance sheet date is a procedure required by AU-C 501. Answer (C) is incorrect. Obtaining assurance from management that it has disclosed all unasserted claims and assessments that legal counsel has advised are probable of assertion is a procedure required by AU-C 501.

13.1.3. The primary source of information to be reported about litigation, claims, and assessments is the

A. Client's legal counsel.

B. Court records.

C. Client's management.

D. Independent auditor.

Answer (C) is correct. *(CPA, adapted)*

REQUIRED: The primary source of information to be reported about litigation, claims, and assessments.

DISCUSSION: According to AU-C 501, "Management is responsible for adopting policies and procedures to identify, evaluate, and account for litigation, claims, and assessments as a basis for the preparation of financial statements in accordance with the requirements of the applicable financial reporting framework." The auditor should discuss with management its policies and procedures for identifying and evaluating these matters.

Answer (A) is incorrect. The client's legal counsel is the auditor's primary source of evidence to corroborate the information furnished by management. Answer (B) is incorrect. The auditor does not ordinarily examine court records. Answer (D) is incorrect. The auditor collects evidence to support management's assertions about litigation, claims, and assessments.

13.1.4. The letter of audit inquiry addressed to the client's external legal counsel will not ordinarily be

A. Sent to legal counsel who was engaged by the audit client during the year and soon thereafter resigned the engagement.

B. Used to corroborate the information originally obtained from management concerning litigation, claims, and assessments.

C. Limited to references concerning only pending or threatened litigation in connection with which the legal counsel has been engaged.

D. Needed during the audit of clients whose securities are not registered with the SEC.

Answer (C) is correct. *(CPA, adapted)*

REQUIRED: The false statement about the letter of audit inquiry to the client's external legal counsel.

DISCUSSION: A letter of audit inquiry to a client's external legal counsel includes, but is not limited to, management-prepared lists of unasserted claims and assessments as well as pending or threatened litigation, claims, and assessments in connection with which legal counsel has been engaged. Legal counsel is expected to respond appropriately (within the limits of materiality) if (s)he has given substantive attention to any of these matters on behalf of the entity in the form of legal consultation or representation.

Answer (A) is incorrect. If deemed necessary, the auditor would communicate with all legal counsel engaged by the client during the year. Answer (B) is incorrect. Management is the auditor's primary source of information about litigation, claims, and assessments. The inquiry letter is the primary means of corroboration. Answer (D) is incorrect. External legal counsel's letter is often obtained in other audits.

13.1.5. Legal counsel's response to an auditor's inquiry about litigation, claims, and assessments may be limited to matters that are considered individually or collectively material to the client's financial statements. Which parties may reach an understanding on the limits of materiality for this purpose that are stated in the letter of inquiry?

A. The auditor and the client's management.

B. The client's audit committee and legal counsel.

C. The client's management and legal counsel.

D. Legal counsel and the auditor.

Answer (A) is correct. *(CPA, adapted)*

REQUIRED: The parties responsible for materiality limits stated in the letter of inquiry to legal counsel.

DISCUSSION: The letter of inquiry is prepared by management and sent by the auditor to the entity's legal counsel. Among other things, the letter requests a statement about the nature of, and reasons for, any limitation on legal counsel's response. Legal counsel may limit the response to matters to which (s)he has given substantive attention in the form of legal consultation or representation. Furthermore, legal counsel's response may be limited to those matters that are considered individually or collectively material to the financial statements, such as when the entity and the auditor have agreed on materiality limits, and management has stated the limits in the letter of inquiry (AU-C 501). NOTE: According to the American Bar Association's statement of policy, the lawyer may wish to reach an understanding with the auditor about the test of materiality. However, the lawyer need not do so if (s)he assumes responsibility for the criteria.

Answer (B) is incorrect. Legal counsel and the audit committee do not draft the letter of inquiry or agree on its terms. Answer (C) is incorrect. Legal counsel may reach an understanding with the auditor about materiality but does not draft the letter of inquiry. Moreover, the auditor ultimately must make materiality judgments relevant to the audit. Answer (D) is incorrect. Legal counsel does not determine the content of the letter of inquiry.

13.1.6. A CPA has received legal counsel's letter in which no significant disagreements with the client's assessments of contingent liabilities were noted. The resignation of the client's legal counsel shortly after receipt of the letter should alert the auditor that

A. Undisclosed unasserted claims may have arisen.

B. Legal counsel was unable to form a conclusion with respect to the significance of litigation, claims, and assessments.

C. The auditor must begin a completely new examination of contingent liabilities.

D. An adverse opinion will be necessary.

Answer (A) is correct. *(CPA, adapted)*

REQUIRED: The implication of the resignation of the client's legal counsel soon after responding to the inquiry letter.

DISCUSSION: Legal counsel may be required to resign from an engagement (under his or her Code of Professional Responsibility) if the client disregards advice about financial accounting and reporting for litigation, claims, and assessments. Because the response to the letter of inquiry stated that the client's assessment of contingent liabilities was satisfactory, the source of disagreement may be undisclosed, unasserted claims.

Answer (B) is incorrect. Inability to form a legal conclusion does not ordinarily cause an ethical conflict with the client sufficient to cause legal counsel's resignation. Answer (C) is incorrect. Much of the auditor's work, particularly that performed on client records, may still be valid. Answer (D) is incorrect. An adverse opinion is expressed only when the financial statements or related disclosures (including omissions) are not presented fairly.

13.1.7. Which of the following statements about litigation, claims, and assessments extracted from a letter from a client's legal counsel is most likely to cause the auditor to request clarification?

A. "I believe that the possible liability to the company is nominal in amount."

B. "I believe that the action can be settled for less than the damages claimed."

C. "I believe that the plaintiff's case against the company is without merit."

D. "I believe that the company will be able to defend this action successfully."

Answer (B) is correct. *(CPA, adapted)*

REQUIRED: The statement by legal counsel most likely causing an auditor's request for clarification.

DISCUSSION: The letter of inquiry requests, among other things, that legal counsel evaluate the likelihood of pending or threatened litigation, claims, and assessments. It also requests that legal counsel estimate, if possible, the amount or range of potential loss. Thus, the auditor is concerned about the amount of the expected settlement as well as the likelihood of the outcome. The statement that the action can be settled for less than the damages claimed is an example given in AU-C 501 of an evaluation that is unclear about the likelihood of an unfavorable outcome.

Answer (A) is incorrect. Legal counsel's statement that the amount of possible liability will not be material states an amount or range of loss. Answer (C) is incorrect. Legal counsel has stated that no liability is expected. Answer (D) is incorrect. Legal counsel has stated that no liability is expected.

13.1.8. The appropriate date for the client to specify as the effective date in the audit inquiry to legal counsel is

A. The balance-sheet date.

B. Seven working days after the request is received by legal counsel.

C. The date of the audit inquiry itself.

D. As close to the date of the auditor's report as possible.

Answer (D) is correct. *(Publisher, adapted)*

REQUIRED: The appropriate effective date of the response to the letter of inquiry to legal counsel.

DISCUSSION: The date of legal counsel's response should be as close to the date of the auditor's report as practicable. The auditor is concerned with events occurring through the date of the report that may require adjustment to, or disclosure in, the financial statements. The date of the report is the date on which the auditor obtained sufficient appropriate audit evidence on which to base the opinion. Moreover, the auditor should specify the earliest acceptable effective date of the response and the latest date by which it is to be sent to the auditor. A 2-week period between these dates generally suffices.

Answer (A) is incorrect. The balance-sheet date is not ordinarily as close as practicable to the completion of field work. Answer (B) is incorrect. Seven working days after the request is received by legal counsel is not ordinarily as close as practicable to the completion of field work. Answer (C) is incorrect. The date of the audit inquiry itself is not ordinarily as close as practicable to the completion of field work.

13.1.9. The refusal of a client's legal counsel to provide a representation on the legality of a particular act committed by the client is ordinarily

A. Sufficient reason to express a "subject to" opinion.

B. A scope limitation.

C. Insufficient reason to modify the auditor's report because of the legal counsel's obligation of confidentiality.

D. Proper grounds to withdraw from the engagement.

Answer (B) is correct. *(CPA, adapted)*

REQUIRED: The auditor's response when legal counsel refuses to address the legality of a client act.

DISCUSSION: Legal counsel's refusal either orally or in writing to provide the requested information may be a scope limitation sufficient to preclude an unmodified opinion. The reason is that the letter of inquiry to the client's legal counsel is the primary means of corroborating management's representations about litigation, claims, and assessments. However, a statement in the letter such as, "It would be inappropriate for this firm to respond to a general inquiry relating to the existence of unasserted possible claims and assessments," is not considered a scope limitation. The quoted language is based on the preamble of the American Bar Association's statement of policy regarding lawyers' responses to auditors' requests for information.

Answer (A) is incorrect. "Subject to" is an unacceptable phrase in an audit opinion. Answer (C) is incorrect. An unmodified opinion cannot be expressed when a material scope limitation has been imposed. Answer (D) is incorrect. The failure could preclude an unmodified opinion but would not likely be grounds for withdrawal.

13.1.10. A CPA had the management of Paper Plate Corp. prepare a letter requesting Paper Plate's external counsel to identify any pending and/or unasserted claims against Paper Plate. The CPA received a letter from the external counsel with the following response:

> "We are only aware of the following: Paper Plate was named as the defendant in a class action lawsuit for an alleged defective product manufactured 2 years ago. There is a remote possibility that Paper Plate will suffer any damages, because this firm has successfully defended similar cases in the past. However, similar cases that have been brought against competitors were settled between $1.5 and $2 million."

Should the CPA accept the letter from the external counsel?

A. No, because the CPA allowed Paper Plate to prepare the letter.

B. Yes, even though the CPA did not get a specific amount of loss.

C. No, because the CPA did not consult a specialist in class action suits.

D. Yes, if the CPA discusses the prior lawsuits with the competitors' lawyers.

Answer (B) is correct. *(CPA, adapted)*

REQUIRED: The appropriate acceptance and use of an external counsel letter.

DISCUSSION: No specific amount of loss is required. The external counsel believes the possibility is remote that the company will suffer any damages.

Answer (A) is incorrect. The auditor should contact the legal counsel through a letter of inquiry prepared by management and sent by the auditor requesting the entity's external legal counsel to communicate directly with the auditor. Answer (C) is incorrect. The external counsel of the company is considered a specialist in class action lawsuits. Answer (D) is incorrect. It is not necessary for the auditor to contact the competitor's lawyers.

13.2 Subsequent Events and Subsequently Discovered Facts

13.2.1. Which of the following procedures will an auditor most likely perform to obtain evidence about the occurrence of subsequent events?

A. Confirming a sample of material accounts receivable established after year end.

B. Comparing the financial statements being reported on with those of the prior period.

C. Investigating personnel changes in the accounting department occurring after year end.

D. Inquiring as to whether any unusual adjustments were made after year end.

Answer (D) is correct. *(CPA, adapted)*

REQUIRED: The subsequent events procedure.

DISCUSSION: Subsequent events procedures include inquiring of management as to whether (1) subsequent events occurred that might affect the statements; (2) new commitments, borrowings, or guarantees were made; (3) sales or acquisitions of assets occurred or were planned; (4) capital increased or debt was issued; (5) developments regarding contingencies occurred; (6) any events occurred (a) casting doubt on the appropriateness of accounting policies or (b) that are relevant to the measurement of estimates or the recovery of assets; (7) any unusual accounting adjustments were made or considered; and (8) changes occurred in the current status of items that were accounted for on the basis of preliminary or inconclusive data.

Answer (A) is incorrect. The auditor confirms receivables before year end. Answer (B) is incorrect. Comparing the financial statements being reported on with those of the prior period is an analytical procedure performed at the beginning of the audit. Answer (C) is ncorrect. Personnel changes after year end do not typically relate to the recording of subsequent events.

13.2.2. Which of the following statements best expresses the auditor's responsibility with respect to events occurring after the balance-sheet date?

A. The auditor has no responsibility for events occurring in the subsequent period unless these events affect transactions recorded on or before the balance-sheet date.

B. The auditor's responsibility is to determine that transactions recorded on or before the balance-sheet date actually occurred.

C. The auditor is fully responsible for subsequent events and should extend all detailed procedures through the last day of field work.

D. The auditor is responsible for identifying subsequent events affecting the financial statements.

Answer (D) is correct. *(Publisher, adapted)*

REQUIRED: The best description of the auditor's responsibility for subsequent events.

DISCUSSION: Events that have a material effect on the financial statements sometimes occur subsequent to the balance-sheet date but prior to the auditor's report date and, therefore, require adjustment of, or disclosure in, the statements. Certain specif c procedures, such as the determination that proper cutoffs have been made and the examination of data to aid in evaluating assets and liabilities as of the balance-sheet date, are normally applied in this period. Other phases of the audit, however, will have been substantially completed by year end. The auditor is responsible for obtaining sufficient appropriate evidence about subsequent events that require adjustment of, or disclosure in, the statements. This responsibility extends to determining whether subsequent events are appropriately reflected in those statements.

Answer (A) is incorrect. The auditor is responsible for conditions not existing at year end that must be disclosed to prevent the statements from being misleading. Answer (B) is incorrect. Transactions occurring prior to year end are not subsequent events. Answer (C) is incorrect. The auditor is only expected to apply the subsequent events procedures described in AU-C 560.

13.2.3. Which of the following procedures can be performed only after the date of the financial statements?

A. Examination of data to determine that a proper cutoff has been made.

B. Tests of the details of balances.

C. Tests of the details of transactions.

D. Reading of the minutes of the board of directors' meetings.

Answer (A) is correct. *(Publisher, adapted)*

REQUIRED: The procedure that can be performed only in the subsequent period.

DISCUSSION: The objective of a cutoff test is to determine that transactions are reported in the correct period. A cutoff test can be performed only after year end when all transactions for the year can be identified.

Answer (B) is incorrect. The tests of the details of balances and most other audit procedures can be performed during the year. Answer (C) is incorrect. The tests of the details of transactions and most other audit procedures can be performed during the year. Answer (D) is incorrect. Minutes of meetings of owners, management, and those charged with governance held after the date of the financial statements should be considered.

13.2.4. An auditor is concerned with completing various phases of the audit after the balance sheet date. This subsequent period extends to the date of the

A. Auditor's report.

B. Final review of the audit documentation.

C. Public issuance of the financial statements.

D. Delivery of the auditor's report to the client.

Answer (A) is correct. *(CPA, adapted)*

REQUIRED: The date to which subsequent events work should be extended.

DISCUSSION: Subsequent events procedures should be performed to cover the period from the date of the financial statements to the date of the auditor's report (or as near as practicable to it) (AU-C 560).

Answer (B) is incorrect. Subsequent events work should be extended to the date of the report. Answer (C) is incorrect. The date of the public issuance of the financial statements is later than the date of the report. Answer (D) is incorrect. The delivery of the auditor's report to the client occurs after the date of the report.

13.2.5. A major customer of an audit client suffers a fire just prior to completion of year-end field work. The audit client believes that this event could have a significant direct effect on the financial statements. The auditor should

A. Advise management to disclose the event in notes to the financial statements.

B. Disclose the event in the auditor's report.

C. Withhold submission of the auditor's report until the extent of the direct effect on the financial statements is known.

D. Advise management to adjust the financial statements.

Answer (A) is correct. *(CPA, adapted)*

REQUIRED: The appropriate action by the auditor regarding a subsequent event.

DISCUSSION: Subsequent events, such as a fire or other casualty, that provide evidence of conditions that did not exist at the balance sheet date should not result in adjustment of the financial statements. But some of these subsequent events should be disclosed if required by the applicable financial reporting framework. For example, U.S. GAAP require disclosure to keep the statements from being misleading.

Answer (B) is incorrect. Subsequent events, such as a fire or other casualty, that provide evidence of conditions that did not exist at the balance sheet date are rarely disclosed in the audit report. Answer (C) is incorrect. An unreasonable amount of time may elapse before all the effects are known. Answer (D) is incorrect. Adjustment of the financial statements is inappropriate. The fire damage did not exist at the balance sheet date.

13.2.6. Which of the following procedures should an auditor ordinarily perform regarding subsequent events?

A. Read the latest subsequent interim financial statements.

B. Send second requests to the client's customers who failed to respond to initial accounts receivable confirmation requests.

C. Communicate material weaknesses in internal control to the client's audit committee.

D. Review the cutoff bank statements for several months after the year end.

Answer (A) is correct. *(CPA, adapted)*

REQUIRED: The subsequent events procedure.

DISCUSSION: Subsequent events procedures include (1) reading the latest subsequent interim statements, if any; (2) inquiring of management and those charged with governance about the occurrence of subsequent events and various financial and accounting matters; (3) reading the minutes of meetings of owners, management, and those charged with governance; (4) obtaining a letter of representations from management; (5) inquiring of client's legal counsel; and (6) obtaining an understanding of management's procedures for identifying subsequent events.

Answer (B) is incorrect. Second confirmation requests do not disclose subsequent events. Answer (C) is incorrect. Communication of material weaknesses is not a subsequent events procedure. Answer (D) is incorrect. Cutoff bank statements are requested from banks 7 to 10 days after year end. They are used to verify the client's bank reconciliations and detect kiting.

13.2.7. On January 15, Year 2, before the Mapleview Co. released its financial statements for the year ended December 31, Year 1, it settled a long-standing lawsuit. A material loss resulted and no prior liability had been recorded. How should this loss be disclosed or recognized?

A. The loss should be disclosed in notes to the financial statements, but the financial statements themselves need not be adjusted.

B. The loss should be disclosed in an explanatory paragraph in the auditor's report.

C. No disclosure or recognition is required.

D. The financial statements should be adjusted to recognize the loss.

Answer (D) is correct. *(Publisher, adapted)*

REQUIRED: The proper disclosure or recognition of a material loss on an existing lawsuit after year end.

DISCUSSION: Subsequent events that provide evidence of conditions that existed at the balance sheet date and that require adjustment of the financial statements should be reflected in those statements in accordance with the applicable financial reporting framework. For example, U.S. GAAP require recognition in the statements of the effects of a subsequent event providing additional evidence about conditions at the balance sheet date, including accounting estimates. Settlement of a lawsuit is indicative of conditions existing at year end and calls for adjustment of the statements.

Answer (A) is incorrect. The financial statements should be adjusted to reflect the loss. Answer (B) is incorrect. The audit report need not be modified. Answer (C) is incorrect. Failure to adjust the statements for a material loss on an asset that existed at year end would be misleading.

13.2.8. Subsequent events that provide evidence of conditions that arose subsequent to the date of the financial statements

A. Require adjustment of the financial statements.

B. Should not be considered for any purposes.

C. Should ordinarily be disclosed in the auditor's report.

D. May require disclosure in notes to the financial statements.

Answer (D) is correct. *(Publisher, adapted)*

REQUIRED: The response to subsequent events.

DISCUSSION: According to U.S. GAAP, subsequent events that provide evidence of conditions arising after the balance sheet date but before the statements are issued or available to be issued are not recognized. However, a nonrecognized subsequent event may be of such a nature that it must be disclosed to keep the statements from being misleading.

Answer (A) is incorrect. Only the subsequent events that provide evidence of conditions existing at year end should result in adjustment. Answer (B) is incorrect. Subsequent events that provide evidence of conditions that did not exist at the balance sheet date should be disclosed. Answer (C) is incorrect. Subsequent events that provide evidence of conditions that did not exist at the balance sheet date should be disclosed but are rarely included in the auditor's report.

13.2.9. Subsequent events are defined as events that occur subsequent to the

A. Release of the financial statements.

B. Date of the auditor's report.

C. Balance sheet date but prior to the auditor's report date.

D. Date of the auditor's report and concern contingencies that are not reflected in the financial statements.

Answer (C) is correct. *(CPA, adapted)*

REQUIRED: The definition of subsequent events.

DISCUSSION: Subsequent events occur between the date of the financial statements and the date of the auditor's report. The auditor should perform procedures to determine whether subsequent events that require adjustment of, or disclosure in, the statements are appropriately reflected in the statements in accordance with the applicable financial reporting framework (AU-C 560).

13.2.10. Zero Corp. suffered a loss having a material effect on its financial statements as a result of a customer's bankruptcy that rendered a trade receivable uncollectible. This bankruptcy occurred suddenly because of a natural disaster 10 days after Zero's balance sheet date but 1 month before the issuance of the financial statements and the auditor's report. Under these circumstances, the

	Financial Statements Should Be Adjusted	Event Requires Financial Statement Disclosure, but No Adjustment	Auditor's Report Should Be Modified for a Lack of Consistency
A.	Yes	No	No
B.	Yes	No	Yes
C.	No	Yes	Yes
D.	No	Yes	No

Answer (D) is correct. *(CPA, adapted)*

REQUIRED: The effect on the financial statements and the auditor's report of a subsequent event.

DISCUSSION: Certain subsequent events may provide evidence about conditions at the date of the balance sheet and require adjustment of the statements in accordance with the applicable financial reporting framework. For example, U.S. GAAP require recognition in the statements of the effects of a subsequent event providing additional evidence about conditions at the balance sheet date, including accounting estimates. Other subsequent events provide evidence about conditions not existing at the date of the balance sheet but arising subsequent to that date. These events may require disclosure but do not require adjustment of financial statement balances. In this case, the financial statements should not be adjusted, but disclosure should be made. The report is unaffected if disclosure is made.

13.2.11. When a contingency is resolved immediately subsequent to the issuance of financial statements with a report that included a paragraph emphasizing the contingency, the auditor should

A. Insist that the client issue revised financial statements.

B. Inform the audit committee that the report cannot be relied upon.

C. Take no action regarding the event.

D. Inform the appropriate authorities that the report cannot be relied upon.

Answer (C) is correct. *(CPA, adapted)*

REQUIRED: The auditor's response to resolution of a contingency after the date of the report.

DISCUSSION: AU-C 560 states, "The auditor is not required to perform any audit procedures regarding the financial statements after the date of the auditor's report." But the auditor has responsibilities for subsequently discovered facts. The resolution of a contingency is not deemed to be a subsequently discovered fact for this purpose.

13.2.12. Some subsequent events provide evidence of conditions not in existence at the balance sheet date. Under U.S. GAAP, some of these events are of such a nature that disclosure is required to keep the financial statements from being misleading. Adequate disclosure of these events may include

A. Adjustment of the financial statements.

B. Pro forma financial statement presentation.

C. Notes to the auditor's report.

D. Restatement of prior-period financial statements.

Answer (B) is correct. *(Publisher, adapted)*

REQUIRED: The disclosure of a subsequent event related to a condition not existing at year end.

DISCUSSION: Under U.S. GAAP, subsequent events related to conditions that did not exist at the date of the balance sheet should not result in adjustments of (recognition in) the financial statements. These events are disclosed, if necessary, to keep the financial statements from being misleading. Occasionally, such an event may be so significant that disclosure can best be made by means of pro forma financial data. Such data make the event seem as if it had occurred on the date of the balance sheet. In some cases, U.S. GAAP suggest presentation of pro forma statements, usually a balance sheet only, in columnar form on the face of the historical statements. But firms usually incorporate the pro forma balance sheets in notes.

Answer (A) is incorrect. Only subsequent events that relate to conditions existing at the balance sheet date require recognition in the financial statements. Answer (C) is incorrect. Notes are attached to financial statements, not auditors' reports. Answer (D) is incorrect. Only subsequent events that relate to conditions existing at the balance sheet date require recognition in the financial statements.

13.2.13. Which of the following procedures will an auditor most likely perform to obtain evidence about the occurrence of subsequent events?

A. Recomputing a sample of large-dollar transactions occurring after year end for arithmetic accuracy.

B. Investigating changes in equity occurring after year end.

C. Inquiring of the entity's legal counsel concerning litigation, claims, and assessments arising after year end.

D. Confirming bank accounts established after year end.

Answer (C) is correct. *(CPA, adapted)*

REQUIRED: The auditing procedure for the subsequent events period.

DISCUSSION: Subsequent events procedures include (1) reading the latest subsequent interim statements, if any; (2) inquiring of management and those charged with governance about the occurrence of subsequent events and various financial and accounting matters; (3) reading the minutes of meetings of owners, management, and those charged with governance; (4) obtaining a letter of representations from management; (5) inquiring of client's legal counsel; and (6) obtaining an understanding of management's procedures for identifying subsequent events.

Answer (A) is incorrect. Testing the arithmetic accuracy of known events does not obtain evidence about the occurrence of a subsequent event. Answer (B) is incorrect. The auditor should inquire of officers and other executives as to significant changes in equity, but an investigation of such changes is less likely than the inquiry of legal counsel. Answer (D) is incorrect. A bank account established after year end is not an asset that existed at the balance sheet date.

13.2.14. Subsequent events affecting the realization of assets ordinarily will require adjustment of the financial statements under audit because such events typically represent the

A. Culmination of conditions that existed at the balance sheet date.

B. Final estimates of losses relating to casualties occurring in the subsequent events period.

C. Discovery of new conditions occurring in the subsequent events period.

D. Preliminary estimate of losses relating to new events that occurred subsequent to the balance sheet date.

Answer (A) is correct. *(CPA, adapted)*

REQUIRED: The reason subsequent events affecting asset realization require adjustment of the statements.

DISCUSSION: Subsequent events that provide evidence of conditions that existed at the balance sheet date and that require adjustment of the financial statements should be reflected in those statements in accordance with the applicable financial reporting framework. For example, U.S. GAAP require recognition in the statements of the effects of a subsequent event providing additional evidence about conditions at the balance sheet date, including accounting estimates. Subsequent events affecting the realization of assets typically represent the culmination of conditions that existed at year end.

13.2.15. Wilson, CPA, obtained sufficient appropriate audit evidence on which to base the opinion on Abco's December 31, Year 1, financial statements on March 6, Year 2, the date of the auditor's report. A subsequently discovered fact requiring revision of the Year 1 financial statements occurred on April 10, Year 2, and came to Wilson's attention on April 24, Year 2. If the fact became known prior to the report release date, and the revision is made, Wilson's report ordinarily should be dated

A. March 6, Year 2.

B. April 10, Year 2.

C. April 24, Year 2.

D. Using dual dating.

Answer (D) is correct. *(CPA, adapted)*

REQUIRED: The date of the report if the statements are adjusted for a subsequently discovered fact.

DISCUSSION: A subsequently discovered fact (1) becomes known to the auditor after the report date and (2) may cause the auditor to revise the report. The report date is no earlier than the date when sufficient appropriate evidence is obtained. If such a fact becomes known to the auditor before the report release date, the auditor should (1) discuss the matter with management and (2) determine whether the statements need revision (adjustment or disclosure). If management revises the statements, the auditor should perform the necessary procedures on the revision. The auditor also (1) dates the report as of a later date or (2) dual-dates the report. Dual-dating indicates that the procedures performed subsequent to the original date are limited to the revision. Unless the auditor extends subsequent events procedures to a new date (one presumably later than April 24, Year 2, the date when the subsequently discovered fact became known), the auditor should dual-date the report.

Answer (A) is incorrect. March 6, Year 2, is the original report date. Answer (B) is incorrect. April 10, Year 2, is inappropriate because the discovery of a fact requiring revision of the report did not occur until later. Answer (C) is incorrect. The new (or additional) date is presumably later than April 24, Year 2, the date when the subsequently discovered fact became known.

13.2.16. Which of the following material events occurring subsequent to the December 31, Year 1, balance sheet date will not ordinarily result in an adjustment of the financial statements before they are issued on March 2, Year 2?

A. Write-off of a receivable from a debtor who had suffered from a deteriorating financial condition for the past 6 years. The debtor filed for bankruptcy on January 23, Year 2.

B. Acquisition of a subsidiary on January 23, Year 2. Negotiations had begun in December of Year 1.

C. Settlement of extended litigation on January 23, Year 2, in excess of the recorded year-end liability.

D. A 3-for-5 reverse stock split consummated on January 23, Year 2.

Answer (B) is correct. *(CPA, adapted)*

REQUIRED: The material subsequent event not requiring adjustment of the statements.

DISCUSSION: Under U.S. GAAP, an entity recognizes in the financial statements the effects of all subsequent events that provide additional evidence about conditions existing at the balance sheet date. The acquisition of the subsidiary did not occur until after year end. Thus, the purchase required at most disclosure, not adjustment of (recognition in) the statements.

Answer (A) is incorrect. The poor financial condition of the debtor existed at year end. Answer (C) is incorrect. The litigation was pending at year end. Answer (D) is incorrect. Retroactive effect should be given to stock splits according to U.S. GAAP.

13.2.17. Creditor Co. had a large account receivable that was considered fully collectible at its year end. However, the debtor's plant was destroyed during the subsequent events period. Because the debtor was uninsured, it is unlikely that the account will be paid. What is the effect of this event on the year-end statements?

A. Disclosure by means of supplemental, pro forma financial data.

B. Adjustment of the financial statements.

C. Disclosure in a note to the financial statements.

D. No financial statement disclosure necessary.

Answer (C) is correct. *(Publisher, adapted)*

REQUIRED: The creditor's treatment of a debtor's major casualty subsequent to year end.

DISCUSSION: A debtor's major casualty subsequent to year end rendering a major receivable uncollectible is not indicative of conditions existing at the balance sheet date, so adjustment of (recognition in) the financial statements is not appropriate. But disclosure should be made to keep the statements from being misleading.

Answer (A) is incorrect. Disclosure by means of supplemental, pro forma financial data is only occasionally necessary because of the significance of the event. Answer (B) is incorrect. Recognition in the financial statements would be inappropriate. Answer (D) is incorrect. Financial statement disclosure is necessary to keep the statements from being misleading.

13.2.18. Advertiser Co.'s directors voted immediately after year end to double the advertising budget for the coming year and authorized a change in advertising agencies. What is the effect of this event on the year-end statements?

A. Disclosure by means of supplemental, pro forma financial data.

B. Adjustment of the financial statements.

C. Disclosure in a note to the financial statements.

D. No financial statement revision.

Answer (D) is correct. *(Publisher, adapted)*

REQUIRED: The proper treatment of an increase in the advertising budget subsequent to the balance sheet date.

DISCUSSION: Changing of budgets and other managerial decisions made by the directors or management are not significant subsequent events. Hence, no financial statement revision (disclosure or adjustment) is necessary.

Answer (A) is incorrect. Disclosure by means of supplemental, pro forma financial data is inappropriate. Answer (B) is incorrect. Adjustment of the financial statements is inappropriate. Answer (C) is incorrect. Disclosure in the financial statements is inappropriate.

13.2.19. An auditor has found that the notes to the financial statements do not mention that, 15 days after the balance sheet date, the company issued a substantial amount of debentures. According to the company's attorney, the debenture agreement restricts the payment of future cash dividends. The client has declined to include the matter of the debentures in the notes because the issuance occurred after the balance sheet date. The auditor should

A. Add the note to the financial statements.

B. Provide the missing information in the report and express an adverse opinion.

C. Provide the missing information in the report and express a qualified opinion.

D. Provide the missing information in the report and disclaim an opinion.

Answer (C) is correct. *(Publisher, adapted)*

REQUIRED: The auditor's response to the client's refusal to disclose a material subsequent event.

DISCUSSION: A subsequent event not providing evidence as to conditions existing at the balance sheet date does not result in adjustment of the statements. However, it may require disclosure to keep the statements from being misleading. The sale of a bond issue is an example of a subsequent event requiring disclosure but not adjustment. When such an event occurs between the report date and the date of the related financial statements, it should be disclosed in a note, or the auditor should modify the opinion.

Answer (A) is incorrect. The auditor has no authority to add a note to the financial statements. All assertions in the statements are the representations of management. Answer (B) is incorrect. The auditor should usually express a qualified opinion if the client refuses to make a necessary disclosure about subsequent events. However, an adverse opinion may be justified in some cases. Answer (D) is incorrect. The auditor should usually express a qualified opinion if the client refuses to make a necessary disclosure about subsequent events. However, an adverse opinion may be justified in some cases.

13.2.20. After issuing an auditor's report, an auditor has no obligation to make continuing inquiries about audited financial statements unless

A. Information about a material transaction that occurred just after the auditor's report was issued is deemed to be reliable.

B. A final resolution is made of a contingent liability that had been disclosed in the financial statements.

C. Information that existed at the report date and may affect the report comes to the auditor's attention.

D. An event occurs just after the auditor's report was issued that affects the entity's ability to continue as a going concern.

Answer (C) is correct. *(CPA, adapted)*

REQUIRED: The auditor's responsibility after the issuance of the auditor's report.

DISCUSSION: Although the auditor may need to extend subsequent events procedures when issuers make filings under the Securities Act of 1933 (AU-C 925, *Filings with the U.S. Securities and Exchange Commission Under the Securities Act of 1933*), (s)he ordinarily need not apply any procedures after the date of the report. However, facts may be discovered by the auditor after the report release date that, if known at that date, might have caused the auditor to revise the report. In this case, the auditor should (1) discuss the matter with management and (2) determine whether the statements should be revised and, if so, how management intends to address the matter in the statements (AU-C 560).

Answer (A) is incorrect. A material subsequent event must have occurred prior to the date of the auditor's report for the auditor to have additional responsibilities. Answer (B) is incorrect. The auditor has no continuing responsibility to monitor disclosed contingencies. Answer (D) is incorrect. An event occurring after the date of the report need not be considered by the auditor if it does not affect the report.

13.2.21. Under which of the following circumstances may audited financial statements contain a note that is labeled "unaudited," disclosing an event occurring after the balance sheet date?

A. When the subsequent event requires adjustment of the financial statements.

B. When the event occurs after the date of the related financial statements.

C. When audit procedures with respect to the event were not performed by the auditor.

D. When the event occurs after the date of the auditor's original report.

Answer (D) is correct. *(CPA, adapted)*

REQUIRED: The basis for including a note disclosing an unaudited event.

DISCUSSION: To prevent the financial statements from being misleading, management may disclose an event that arose after the date of the auditor's report. If the event is included in a separate note labeled as unaudited [e.g., a note captioned as "Event (Unaudited) Subsequent to the Date of the Independent Auditor's Report"], the auditor need not perform any procedures on the note. Moreover, the auditor's report should have the same date as the original report (AU-C 560).

Answer (A) is incorrect. An unaudited note may only pertain to an event that does not require adjustment. Answer (B) is incorrect. The auditor's report must cover events occurring prior to its date. Answer (C) is incorrect. The note is not appropriate for any unaudited event occurring after the balance sheet date.

13.2.22. Which of the following events occurring after the date of the report most likely will cause the auditor to make further inquiries about the previously issued financial statements?

A. A technological development that could affect the entity's future ability to continue as a going concern.

B. The discovery of information regarding a contingency that existed before the financial statements were issued.

C. The entity's sale of a subsidiary that accounts for 30% of the entity's consolidated sales.

D. The final resolution of a lawsuit explained in a separate paragraph of the auditor's report.

Answer (B) is correct. *(CPA, adapted)*

REQUIRED: The event after the date of the report most likely resulting in further inquiries.

DISCUSSION: Facts may be discovered by the auditor after the date of the report that, if known at that date, might have caused the auditor to revise the report. In this case, the auditor should (1) discuss the matter with management and (2) determine whether the statements should be revised and, if so, how management intends to address the matter in the statements (AU-C 560).

Answer (A) is incorrect. An event occurring after the date of the report need not be considered by the auditor if it would not affect the report. Answer (C) is incorrect. An event occurring after the date of the report need not be considered by the auditor if it would not affect the report. Answer (D) is incorrect. The auditor need not consider final determinations or resolutions of contingencies that were disclosed in the financial statements or that resulted in a modification of the auditor's report.

13.2.23. On February 25, financial statements were released with an auditor's report expressing an unmodified opinion on the statements for the year ended January 31. On March 2, the CPA learned that on February 11, the entity incurred a material loss on an uncollectible trade receivable as a result of the deteriorating financial condition of the entity's principal customer that led to the customer's bankruptcy. Management then refused to adjust the financial statements for this subsequent event. The CPA determined that the information is reliable and that creditors are currently relying on the financial statements. The CPA's next course of action most likely is to

A. Notify the entity's creditors that the financial statements and the related auditor's report should no longer be relied on.

B. Notify management and those charged with governance that the auditor will seek to prevent future reliance on the auditor's report.

C. Issue revised financial statements and distribute them to each creditor known to be relying on the financial statements.

D. Issue a revised auditor's report and distribute it to each creditor known to be relying on the financial statements.

Answer (B) is correct. *(CPA, adapted)*

REQUIRED: The actions of an auditor related to an event discovered subsequent to the release of the financial statements.

DISCUSSION: If management does not take the necessary steps to revise the financial statements and ensure that anyone in receipt of the audited financial statements is informed of the situation, the auditor should notify management and those charged with governance that the auditor will seek to prevent future reliance on the auditor's report. If, despite such notice, management or those charged with governance do not take the necessary steps, the auditor should take appropriate action to prevent reliance on the auditor's report (AU-C 560).

Answer (A) is incorrect. Management and those charged with governance should be notified first. Answer (C) is incorrect. The auditor has no authority to revise management's financial statements. Answer (D) is incorrect. The auditor should not revise the report but should notify those relying on the report that it is no longer valid.

13.2.24. The auditor learned of the following situations after issuing the audit report on February 6. Each is important to users of the financial statements. For which one does the auditor have responsibility for disclosure of the newly discovered facts?

A. A major lawsuit against the company, which was the basis for a modified report, was settled on unfavorable terms on March 1.

B. The client undertook merger negotiations on March 16 and concluded a merger agreement on April 1.

C. On February 16, a fire destroyed the principal manufacturing plant.

D. A conflict of interest involving credit officers and a principal company supplier that existed during the audit year was discovered on March 3.

Answer (D) is correct. *(CPA, adapted)*

REQUIRED: The situation for which the auditor has a responsibility for disclosure of newly discovered facts.

DISCUSSION: The auditor has a responsibility after the date of the report for events that come to his or her attention that may have caused revision of the report. A conflict of interest situation would have been examined by the auditor had (s)he known about it during the audit.

Answer (A) is incorrect. The auditor has no responsibility to update the report for resolutions of contingencies that were properly disclosed. Answer (B) is incorrect. The auditor need not apply any other audit procedures or update the report for occurrences after the date of the report if they do not affect the report. Answer (C) is incorrect. The auditor need not apply any other audit procedures or update the report for occurrences after the date of the report if they do not affect the report.

13.2.25. Subsequent to the date of the auditor's report, the auditor became aware of facts existing at the report date that would have affected the report had the auditor then been aware of such facts. The auditor should

A. Notify the board of directors that the auditor's report must no longer be associated with the financial statements.

B. Determine whether the financial statements need revision.

C. Request that management disclose the effects of the newly discovered information by adding a note to subsequently issued financial statements.

D. Issue revised pro forma financial statements taking into consideration the newly discovered information.

Answer (B) is correct. *(CPA, adapted)*

REQUIRED: The response to discovery of facts existing at the report date that would have affected the report.

DISCUSSION: When new information that existed at the report date has been discovered, the auditor should (1) discuss the matter with management and, when appropriate, those charged with governance and (2) determine whether the financial statements need revision and, if so, inquire how management intends to address the matter in the financial statements.

Answer (A) is incorrect. Notifying the board of directors that the auditor's report must no longer be associated with the financial statements is only necessary when the client refuses to make necessary revisions. Answer (C) is incorrect. The appropriate action will depend on the effects of the new information. Answer (D) is incorrect. The appropriate action will depend on the effects of the new information.

13.2.26. After an audit report containing an unmodified opinion on a nonissuer's financial statements was dated and the financial statements issued, the client decided to sell the shares of a subsidiary that accounts for 30% of its revenue and 25% of its net income. The auditor should

A. Determine whether the information is reliable and, if determined to be reliable, request that revised financial statements be issued.

B. Notify the entity that the auditor's report may no longer be associated with the financial statements.

C. Describe the effects of this subsequently discovered information in a communication with persons known to be relying on the financial statements.

D. Take no action because the auditor has no obligation to make any further inquiries.

Answer (D) is correct. *(CPA, adapted)*

REQUIRED: The auditor's responsibility after the report date when the client sells shares of its subsidiary.

DISCUSSION: AU-C 560 states, "The auditor is not required to perform any audit procedures regarding the financial statements after the date of the auditor's report."

13.3 Written Representations

13.3.1. For which of the following matters should an auditor obtain written management representations?

A. Management's cost-benefit justifications for not correcting internal control weaknesses.

B. Management's knowledge of future plans that may affect the price of the entity's stock.

C. Management's compliance with contractual agreements that may affect the financial statements.

D. Management's acknowledgment of its responsibility for employees' violations of laws.

Answer (C) is correct. *(CPA, adapted)*

REQUIRED: The item included in written management representations.

DISCUSSION: The auditor should obtain written representations in the form of a management representation letter to complement other auditing procedures. In addition to certain required written representations, the auditor may decide that requesting certain other representations is necessary. These may include aspects of contracts that may affect the statements, including noncompliance (AU-C 580).

Answer (A) is incorrect. The auditor need not obtain written representations of the cost and benefit justifications of internal controls. Answer (B) is incorrect. Management's knowledge of future plans that may affect the price of the entity's stock does not directly affect the fairness of the financial statements. It might, however, be addressed in management's discussion and analysis. Thus, a practitioner who examines or reviews an MD&A presentation might obtain written representations about such forward-looking information. Answer (D) is incorrect. The entity is not necessarily responsible for the violations of laws by its employees. But it should provide representations about noncompliance or suspected noncompliance with laws or regulations that should be considered when preparing the financial statements.

13.3.2. A purpose of a management representation letter is to reduce

A. Audit risk to an aggregate level of misstatement that could be considered material.

B. An auditor's responsibility to detect material misstatements only to the extent that the letter is relied on.

C. The possibility of a misunderstanding concerning management's responsibility for the financial statements.

D. The scope of an auditor's procedures concerning related party transactions and subsequent events.

Answer (C) is correct. *(CPA, adapted)*

REQUIRED: The purpose of a management representation letter.

DISCUSSION: Management's written representations should be in the form of a representation letter addressed to the auditor. The auditor should have possession of the letter before release of the auditor's report. Among other things, the auditor should request that management provide a written representation that it has met its responsibilities stated in the terms of the audit engagement. These responsibilities include those for (1) the preparation and fair presentation of the statements in accordance with the applicable reporting framework and (2) the design, implementation, and maintenance of the relevant internal control.

13.3.3. When an audit is made in accordance with auditing standards, the auditor should always

A. Document the understanding of the entity's internal control but not the bases for the conclusions about the assessed risks of material misstatement.

B. Employ analytical procedures as substantive procedures to obtain evidence about specific assertions related to account balances.

C. Obtain certain written representations from management.

D. Observe the taking of physical inventory on the balance sheet date.

Answer (C) is correct. *(CPA, adapted)*

REQUIRED: The requirement of an audit made in accordance with auditing standards.

DISCUSSION: Written representations are written statements by management provided to confirm certain matters or to support other audit evidence. They do not include financial statements, the assertions in them, or supporting books and records (AU-C 580).

Answer (A) is incorrect. The auditor should document the support for the risk assessments. Answer (B) is incorrect. Analytical procedures assist in forming an overall audit conclusion and also are used as substantive procedures. They are not a substitute for tests of details. Answer (D) is incorrect. Physical inventory counting may occur at a date other than the date of the financial statements. The auditor also may be unable to attend the physical counting. In the first case, the auditor may be able to obtain evidence about whether changes between the count date and the date of the financial statements are properly recorded. In the second case, the auditor should make or observe some physical counts on another date and perform procedures on intervening transactions.

13.3.4. Which of the following matters will an auditor most likely include in a management representation letter?

A. Communications with the audit committee concerning weaknesses in internal control.

B. All concentrations of credit risk not expected to change materially within the next year.

C. Plans to acquire or merge with other entities in the subsequent year.

D. Management's acknowledgment of its responsibility to detect employee fraud.

Answer (D) is correct. *(CPA, adapted)*

REQUIRED: The item included in a management representation letter.

DISCUSSION: Management should make specific representations about (1) acknowledgment of its responsibility for designing, implementing, and maintaining internal control to prevent and detect fraud; (2) knowledge of fraud or suspected fraud affecting the entity involving management, employees with significant roles in internal control, or others if the fraud could materially affect the financial statements; and (3) knowledge of allegations of fraud or suspected fraud affecting the entity obtained in communications from employees or others.

Answer (A) is incorrect. Communication with those charged with governance is the responsibility of the auditor, not a responsibility of management that is fundamental to an audit in accordance with GAAS. Answer (B) is incorrect. The representation letter may state that the entity has properly disclosed significant concentrations of credit risk from all financial instruments. Answer (C) is incorrect. Plans to acquire or merge with other entities in the subsequent year affects the following year but not the current year.

13.3.5. When considering the use of management's written representations as audit evidence about the completeness assertion, an auditor should understand that such representations

A. Complement, but do not replace, substantive procedures designed to support the assertion.

B. Constitute sufficient appropriate evidence to support the assertion when considered in combination with sufficiently low assessed risks of material misstatement.

C. Are not part of the evidence considered to support the assertion.

D. Replace low assessed risks of material misstatement as evidence to support the assertion.

Answer (A) is correct. *(CPA, adapted)*

REQUIRED: The use of written representations as audit evidence of the completeness assertion.

DISCUSSION: AU-C 580 states that written representations provide necessary audit evidence that complements other audit procedures. However, they do not, by themselves, provide sufficient appropriate evidence about the matters to which they are relevant. Moreover, obtaining reliable written representations has no effect on the nature and extent of other procedures applied regarding (1) fulfillment of management's responsibilities or (2) specific assertions.

Answer (B) is incorrect. Regardless of the assessed RMMs, some substantive testing of significant account balances, transaction classes, and disclosure components of financial statements is required. Written representations do not substitute for such testing, even in combination with low RMMs. Answer (C) is incorrect. Written representations are audit evidence. Answer (D) is incorrect. Although substantive procedures may vary with the assessed RMMs, representations cannot substitute for them.

13.3.6. To which of the following matters would an auditor not apply materiality limits when obtaining specific written management representations?

A. Disclosure of compensating balance arrangements involving restrictions on cash balances.

B. Information concerning related party transactions and related amounts receivable or payable.

C. The absence of errors and unrecorded transactions in the financial statements.

D. Fraud involving employees with significant roles in internal control.

Answer (D) is correct. *(CPA, adapted)*

REQUIRED: The matter to which an auditor does not apply materiality limits.

DISCUSSION: Management's representations may be limited to matters that are considered individually or collectively material if management and the auditor have reached an understanding about materiality for this purpose. Materiality considerations do not apply to certain representations not directly related to amounts in the financial statements, for example, representations about the premise of the audit (i.e., acknowledgment of responsibility for fair presentation, internal control, and auditor access to information and people). Materiality also does not apply to knowledge of fraud or suspected fraud affecting the entity involving (1) management, (2) employees with significant roles in internal control, or (3) others if the fraud could materially affect the statements (AU-C 580).

Answer (A) is incorrect. Materiality considerations apply to disclosure of compensating balance arrangements involving restrictions on cash balances. Answer (B) is incorrect. Materiality considerations apply to information about related party transactions and related amounts receivable or payable. Answer (C) is incorrect. Materiality considerations apply to the absence of errors and unrecorded transactions in the financial statements.

13.3.7. Key Co. plans to present comparative financial statements for the years ended December 31, Year 1 and Year 2, respectively. Smith, CPA, audited Key's financial statements for both years and plans to report on the comparative financial statements on May 1, Year 3. Key's current management team was not present until January 1, Year 2. What period of time should be covered by Key's management representation letter?

A. January 1, Year 1, through December 31, Year 2.

B. January 1, Year 1, through May 1, Year 3.

C. January 1, Year 2, through December 31, Year 2.

D. January 1, Year 2, through May 1, Year 3.

Answer (B) is correct. *(CPA, adapted)*

REQUIRED: The dates to be covered by a management representation letter.

DISCUSSION: The auditor is concerned with events occurring through the date of his or her report that may require adjustment of, or disclosure in, the financial statements. Thus, the representations should be made (1) as of a date no earlier than the date of the auditor's report and (2) for all periods referred to in the report. Moreover, if current management was not present during all periods covered by the auditor's report, the auditor should nevertheless obtain written representations from current management for all such periods (AU-C 580).

13.3.8. An auditor finds several misstatements in the financial statements that the client prefers not to correct. The auditor determines that the misstatements are not material in the aggregate. Which of the following actions by the auditor is most appropriate?

A. Document all misstatements accumulated during the audit and the conclusion about whether uncorrected misstatements are material.

B. Document the conclusion that the misstatements do not cause the financial statements to be misstated, but do not accumulate uncorrected misstatements in the audit documentation.

C. Accumulate the uncorrected misstatements in the working papers, but do not document whether they cause the financial statements to be misstated.

D. Do not accumulate the uncorrected misstatements in the audit documentation, and do not document a conclusion about whether the uncorrected misstatements cause the financial statements to be misstated.

Answer (A) is correct. *(CPA, adapted)*

REQUIRED: The most appropriate auditor action when uncorrected misstatements are not material in the aggregate.

DISCUSSION: The auditor should document (1) the amount below which misstatements are clearly trivial; (2) all misstatements accumulated during the audit and whether they were corrected; and (3) the conclusion about whether uncorrected misstatements are material, individually or aggregated, and the basis for the conclusion (AU-C 450). Furthermore, the representation letter should have an accompanying list of uncorrected misstatements. The letter should include a sentence stating, "The effects of the uncorrected misstatements are immaterial, both individually and in the aggregate, to the financial statements as a whole."

Answer (B) is incorrect. The auditor should accumulate all misstatements that are not clearly trivial. Answer (C) is incorrect. The auditor should document the conclusion about whether uncorrected misstatements are material. Answer (D) is incorrect. The auditor should accumulate all misstatements that are not clearly trivial, and the auditor should document the conclusion about whether uncorrected misstatements are material.

13.3.9. A written management representation letter is most likely to be an auditor's best source of corroborative information of a client's intention to

A. Terminate an employee pension plan.

B. Make a public offering of its common stock.

C. Settle an outstanding lawsuit for an amount less than the accrued loss contingency.

D. Discontinue a line of business.

Answer (D) is correct. *(CPA, adapted)*

REQUIRED: The client's intent best corroborated by a management representation letter.

DISCUSSION: Written management representations complement, but do not substitute for, other auditing procedures. However, the plan for discontinuing a line of business is an example of a matter about which other procedures may provide little evidence. Accordingly, the written representation may be necessary as confirmation of management's intent.

Answer (A) is incorrect. Minutes of directors' meetings document the intention to terminate an employee pension plan. Answer (B) is incorrect. Minutes of directors' meetings document the intention to make a public offering of common stock. Answer (C) is incorrect. An inquiry of legal counsel provides better evidence about settlement of litigation.

13.3.10. A written representation from a client's management that, among other matters, acknowledges responsibility for the fair presentation of financial statements, should normally be signed by the

A. Chief executive officer and the chief financial officer.

B. Chief financial officer and the chair of the board of directors.

C. Chair of the audit committee of the board of directors.

D. Chief executive officer, the chair of the board of directors, and the client's legal counsel.

Answer (A) is correct. *(CPA, adapted)*

REQUIRED: The persons who normally should sign the management representation letter.

DISCUSSION: The management representation letter should be signed by members of management who are responsible for and knowledgeable about the areas covered in the representations. AU-C 580 indicates that these members are normally the chief executive officer and the chief financial officer.

13.3.11. An auditor frequently asks the client's personnel questions about the accounts under audit. Although this evidence may be useful, it is weak and should be corroborated by the auditor. Which of the following replies is most useful to the auditor?

A. "Yes, that's how we record that item."

B. "No, I always perform that procedure."

C. "No, we don't always require authorization."

D. "Yes, all inventory is counted."

Answer (C) is correct. *(Publisher, adapted)*

REQUIRED: The oral response by client personnel most likely to be useful.

DISCUSSION: Although oral evidence furnished by client personnel should not be relied upon exclusively, the results of inquiries may help the auditor to identify matters that require additional audit attention. For example, the reply to the question about authorization indicates that the client may not be complying with authorization requirements. Assurances by client personnel that procedures have been performed provide audit evidence of limited value.

13.3.12. If management refuses to provide certain written representations that the auditor believes are essential, which of the following is appropriate?

A. The auditor can rely on oral evidence relating to the matter as a basis for an unmodified opinion.

B. The client's refusal does not constitute a scope limitation that may lead to a modification of the opinion.

C. The client's refusal may have an effect on the auditor's ability to rely on other representations of management.

D. The auditor should express an adverse opinion because of management's refusal.

Answer (C) is correct. *(CPA, adapted)*

REQUIRED: The effect of management's refusal to provide essential written representations.

DISCUSSION: The refusal constitutes a scope limitation that is often sufficient to preclude an unmodified opinion and may cause the auditor to disclaim an opinion or withdraw from the engagement. The auditor should also consider the effects of the refusal on his or her ability to rely on management's other representations (AU-C 580).

Answer (A) is incorrect. Oral representations should be confirmed in writing. Answer (B) is incorrect. The auditor should modify the opinion, disclaim an opinion, or withdraw. Answer (D) is incorrect. A qualified opinion or a disclaimer is more appropriate than an adverse opinion unless the auditor knows that the financial statements are not fairly presented.

13.3.13. An auditor should obtain written representations from management about litigation, claims, and assessments. These representations may be limited to matters that are considered either individually or collectively material provided an understanding on the limits of materiality for this purpose has been reached by

A. The auditor and the client's legal counsel.

B. Management and the auditor.

C. Management, the client's legal counsel, and the auditor.

D. The auditor independently of management.

Answer (B) is correct. *(CPA, adapted)*

REQUIRED: The materiality limitation on the scope of management's representations.

DISCUSSION: Management's representations may be limited to matters that are considered individually or collectively material if management and the auditor have reached an understanding about materiality. Such limitations do not apply to certain representations not directly related to amounts in the financial statements, e.g., acknowledgment of responsibility for fair presentation, availability of records, and fraud involving management and persons with significant roles in internal control.

Answer (A) is incorrect. Client legal counsel does not determine materiality. Answer (C) is incorrect. Client legal counsel does not determine materiality. Answer (D) is incorrect. The auditor and management must reach an understanding.

13.3.14. A client requests that a predecessor auditor reissue the report on financial statements of a prior period to be presented comparatively with the financial statements of a subsequent period. If no filings with the SEC are contemplated, the auditor

A. May reissue the report without performing additional procedures.

B. Should obtain management representation letter before reissuing the report.

C. Should refuse to reissue the report because (s)he is not a continuing auditor.

D. May reissue the report only if it refers to the auditor's work.

Answer (B) is correct. *(Publisher, adapted)*

REQUIRED: The true statement about reissuance of an audit report by a predecessor auditor given no SEC filings.

DISCUSSION: A predecessor auditor may be requested to reissue the report on prior-period financial statements to be presented comparatively with the audited statements of a subsequent period. In these circumstances, (s)he must obtain, among other things, a representation letter from the former client's management. This requirement applies even if no SEC filings are necessary. The letter should state whether (1) any information has come to management's attention requiring modification of prior representations and (2) subsequent events have occurred that necessitate adjustment of, or disclosure in, the current financial statements. The predecessor auditor also should obtain a representation letter from the successor auditor stating whether his or her audit revealed any material matters affecting the statements reported on by the predecessor (AU-C 560).

Answer (A) is incorrect. Various procedures must be performed (AU-C 700). For example, updating representations must be obtained. Answer (C) is incorrect. A predecessor auditor may reissue a report. Answer (D) is incorrect. No reference should be made to the auditor's report or work (AU-C 700).

13.4 Auditor's Consideration of an Entity's Ability to Continue as a Going Concern

13.4.1. Which of the following conditions or events is most likely to cause an auditor to have substantial doubt about an entity's ability to continue as a going concern?

A. Cash flows from operating activities are negative.

B. Research and development projects are postponed.

C. Significant related party transactions are pervasive.

D. Stock dividends replace annual cash dividends.

Answer (A) is correct. *(CPA, adapted)*

REQUIRED: The most likely basis for substantial doubt about the going concern assumption.

DISCUSSION: The significance of conditions or events depends on circumstances, and some conditions or events may be significant only in conjunction with others. Such conditions and events include negative trends, financial difficulties, internal matters, and external matters. Negative cash flows from operating activities provide evidence of negative trends and financial difficulties.

Answer (B) is incorrect. An entity may postpone R&D and not raise doubts about its ability to continue as a going concern. Answer (C) is incorrect. The audit issue is the adequacy of disclosure for related party transactions. Answer (D) is incorrect. Stock dividends preserve cash and do not indicate going concern problems.

13.4.2. An auditor believes that there is substantial doubt about an entity's ability to continue as a going concern for a reasonable period of time. In evaluating the entity's plans for dealing with the adverse effects of future conditions and events, the auditor most likely would consider, as a mitigating factor, the entity's plans to

A. Extend the due dates of existing loans.

B. Operate at increased levels of production.

C. Accelerate expenditures for research and development projects.

D. Issue stock options to key executives.

Answer (A) is correct. *(CPA, adapted)*

REQUIRED: The entity plan that is most likely a mitigating factor.

DISCUSSION: When an auditor has substantial doubt about the entity's ability to continue as a going concern, (s)he should consider management's plans for mitigating the adverse effects of the future conditions and events. Mitigating factors include plans to (1) dispose of assets, (2) borrow money or restructure debt, (3) reduce or delay expenditures (e.g., by leasing, not purchasing), or (4) increase equity ownership (AU-C 570).

Answer (B) is incorrect. Increasing production could either increase operating losses or produce excess inventory that cannot be sold. Answer (C) is incorrect. Management more likely should decrease or postpone excess expenditures. Answer (D) is incorrect. Stock options raise little or no additional capital currently.

13.4.3. An auditor has substantial doubt about the entity's ability to continue as a going concern for a reasonable period of time because of negative cash flows and working capital deficiencies. Under these circumstances, the auditor would be most concerned about the

A. Control environment factors that affect the organizational structure.

B. Correlation of detection risk and inherent risk.

C. Effectiveness of the entity's internal control activities.

D. Possible effects on the entity's financial statements.

Answer (D) is correct. *(CPA, adapted)*

REQUIRED: The auditor's priority given substantial doubt about the entity's ability to continue as a going concern for a reasonable period of time.

DISCUSSION: If an auditor has substantial doubt about the entity's ability to continue as a going concern for a reasonable period of time, (s)he should assess the possible effects on the entity's financial statements, including the adequacy of disclosure of uncertainties related to the going-concern issue. The auditor also should include in the auditor's report an additional paragraph.

Answer (A) is incorrect. The control environment factors that affect the organizational structure have a lower audit priority than a substantial doubt about the entity's ability to continue as a going concern for a reasonable period of time. Answer (B) is incorrect. The correlation of detection risk and inherent risk is considered in every audit. For a given audit risk, the acceptable detection risk is inversely related to the assessed risks of material misstatement (combined inherent risks and control risks). Answer (C) is incorrect. The auditor sometimes may obtain sufficient appropriate evidence without testing controls.

13.4.4. Which of the following auditing procedures most likely would assist an auditor in identifying conditions and events that may indicate substantial doubt about an entity's ability to continue as a going concern?

A. Inspecting title documents to verify whether any assets are pledged as collateral.

B. Confirming with third parties the details of arrangements to maintain financial support.

C. Reconciling the cash balance per books with the cutoff bank statement and the bank confirmation.

D. Comparing the entity's depreciation and asset capitalization policies to other entities in the industry.

Answer (B) is correct. *(CPA, adapted)*

REQUIRED: The audit procedure that may identify conditions indicating substantial doubt about an entity's continuation as a going concern.

DISCUSSION: The procedures typically employed to identify going-concern issues include (1) analytical procedures, (2) review of subsequent events, (3) review of compliance with debt and loan agreements, (4) reading minutes of meetings, (5) inquiry of legal counsel, and (6) confirmation with related and third parties of arrangements for financial support.

Answer (A) is incorrect. Searching for pledged assets is related to disclosure issues. Answer (C) is incorrect. Reconciling the cash balance with cutoff bank statements and the bank confirmation tests the existence of cash. Answer (D) is incorrect. This comparison might identify conditions needing additional consideration but would not provide evidence about going-concern issues.

13.4.5. Cooper, CPA, believes there is substantial doubt about the ability of Zero Corp. to continue as a going concern for a reasonable period of time. In evaluating Zero's plans for dealing with the adverse effects of future conditions and events, Cooper most likely will consider, as a mitigating factor, Zero's plans to

A. Discuss with lenders the terms of all debt and loan agreements.

B. Strengthen internal controls over cash disbursements.

C. Purchase production facilities currently being leased from a related party.

D. Postpone expenditures for research and development projects.

Answer (D) is correct. *(CPA, adapted)*

REQUIRED: The managerial action that mitigates adverse effects of future conditions and events.

DISCUSSION: Once an auditor has identified conditions and events indicating that substantial doubt exists about an entity's ability to continue as a going concern, the auditor should first obtain written representations and then consider management's plans to mitigate their adverse effects. The auditor should consider plans to dispose of assets, borrow money or restructure debt, reduce or delay expenditures, and increase equity.

Answer (A) is incorrect. Discussion with lenders is not a sufficient action to mitigate the circumstances. Answer (B) is incorrect. Internal control improvements do not increase cash flows or postpone expenditures. Answer (C) is incorrect. The purchase of facilities may worsen the company's problems.

STUDY UNIT FOURTEEN
EVIDENCE -- SAMPLING

Audit sampling permits an auditor to obtain and evaluate evidence about a characteristic of the sampled items for the purpose of reaching a conclusion about the underlying population. This study unit primarily covers statistical sampling applications for auditing. **Statistical sampling** uses (1) random selection of sample items and (2) a statistical method of evaluating results, including measurement of sampling risk. Any approach not having these two characteristics is nonstatistical. **Sampling risk** is the risk that the conclusion based on a sample may differ from the conclusion based on applying the same audit procedure to all items in the population.

The following are considered in **designing a sample**:

1. The purpose to be achieved and the combination of procedures likely to achieve it
2. An understanding of the nature of the evidence sought and deviation or misstatement conditions so that only conditions relevant to assertions are included in the evaluation of results

The following are considered in determining **sample size**:

1. The lower the acceptable sampling risk, the greater the sample size.
2. **Tests of controls:**
   a. The tolerable rate of deviation set by the auditor
   b. The auditor's assessment of the expected rate of deviation based on an understanding of relevant controls
   c. The desired assurance (1.0 – risk of overreliance) that the actual rate in the population does not exceed the tolerable rate
      1) The desired assurance may be based on the extent to which the risk assessment considers relevant controls.
   d. If the population is very small, the number of sampling units (physical items or monetary units)
3. **Tests of details:**
   a. The desired assurance (1.0 – risk of incorrect acceptance) that the actual misstatement in the population does not exceed tolerable misstatement. The following may affect the desired assurance:
      1) The assessed risk of material misstatement (RMM)
      2) The assurance provided by other substantive procedures related to the assertion
      3) Tolerable misstatement
      4) Expected misstatement in the population
      5) Any stratification of the population and the sampling units in each stratum

Selection of the sample should provide a reasonable expectation that the sample (1) represents the population and (2) is a reasonable basis for conclusions. Random selection methods include (1) simple random sampling, (2) systematic random sampling, and (3) probability-weighted sampling (including monetary-unit sampling).

The auditor should **project the results** of the sample to the population.

1. **Tests of controls**
   a. The sample deviation rate is the projected deviation rate for the population.
   b. If the auditor detects control deviations, (s)he should make inquiries and determine whether
      1) Tests of controls provide a basis for reliance,
      2) More tests of controls are needed, or
      3) Substantive procedures should be applied to address the possible risks of material misstatement.
2. **Tests of details**
   a. The auditor should project the observed misstatements to obtain likely misstatement. Projected misstatement is the best estimate of population misstatement. However, because of sampling risk, the projected misstatement may not suffice to determine the amount to be recorded.

The auditor should **evaluate the results** of the sample, including sampling risk, and whether a reasonable basis exists for conclusions about the population.

1. **Tests of controls.** An increase in the assessed RMMs may result from an unexpectedly high deviation rate.
2. **Tests of details.** An unexpectedly high misstatement amount may result in a belief that a class of transactions or account balance is materially misstated.
3. If the sample does not provide a reasonable basis for conclusions, the auditor may (a) request that management investigate and make needed adjustments or (b) revise the nature, timing, and extent of further audit procedures.

Textbooks, firm literature, professional exams, and auditing standards often use different vocabulary for the same concept. However, if you study the questions and answer explanations in this study unit, you should be able to cope effectively with differences among the terms you encounter. The two terms defined below cause considerable misunderstanding.

Confidence level or reliability is the estimated percentage of repeated simple random samples of size *n* that will adequately represent a normally distributed population. Thus, a confidence level of 90% indicates that samples should adequately represent the population about 90% of the time. Confidence level is related to audit risk. When an auditor accepts a confidence level of 90%, (s)he accepts a risk of 10% (100% – 90%) that the sample will not represent the population.

In sampling for variables (substantive testing), the primary concern is the risk of incorrect acceptance. In sampling for attributes (tests of controls), the primary concern is the risk of overreliance. The risk of overreliance is that internal control is actually less effective than indicated by the sample. These wrong conclusions relate to effectiveness issues.

Precision or confidence interval (allowance for sampling risk) is an interval around the sample statistic (for example, the mean) that is expected to contain the true value of the population. In principle, given repeated sampling and a normally distributed population, the confidence level is the percentage of all the precision intervals that may be constructed from simple random samples of size *n* that will include the population value. In practice, the confidence level is regarded as the probability that a precision interval will contain the population value.

In sampling for attributes (tests of controls), precision may be estimated by subtracting the expected deviation rate from the tolerable rate in the population.

In sampling for variables (substantive testing), planned precision is determined by considering tolerable misstatement in conjunction with the risks of incorrect acceptance and incorrect rejection. Tolerable misstatement should not exceed performance materiality. The risk of incorrect rejection relates to efficiency issues because the auditor will likely continue auditing until the balance is finally supported. A table is typically consulted to determine the appropriate precision as a percentage of tolerable misstatement.

The following symbols and abbreviations are used in this study unit:

P	-- required precision interval	N	-- population size
C	-- confidence coefficient	μ	-- (mu) population mean or average
σ	-- (sigma) population standard deviation	x	-- an observed value
s	-- sample standard deviation	$\bar{x}$	-- mean of a sample
p	-- deviation rate	FPC	-- finite population correction factor
q	-- 100% minus p	Σ	-- (Sigma) summation symbol
n	-- sample size		

QUESTIONS

14.1 Sampling Fundamentals

14.1.1. AU-C 530, *Audit Sampling*, identifies two general approaches to audit sampling. They are

A. Random and nonrandom.

B. Statistical and nonstatistical.

C. Precision and reliability.

D. Risk and nonrisk.

Answer (B) is correct. *(Publisher, adapted)*

REQUIRED: The two approaches to audit sampling.

DISCUSSION: Statistical sampling has two characteristics: (1) random selection of sample items and (2) use of an appropriate statistical method to evaluate results, including measurement of sampling risk. A sampling method that does not have (1) and (2) is nonstatistical (AU-C 530).

Answer (A) is incorrect. Random selection is necessary in statistical sampling so that the sample will represent the population. Answer (C) is incorrect. Precision is the allowance for sampling risk, and reliability is the degree to which the sample is expected to be representative. Answer (D) is incorrect. All sampling involves risk.

14.1.2. In a sampling application, the group of items about which the auditor wants to estimate some characteristic is called the

A. Population.

B. Attribute of interest.

C. Sample.

D. Sampling unit.

Answer (A) is correct. *(CIA, adapted)*

REQUIRED: The group of items about which an auditor wants to draw conclusions.

DISCUSSION: The population is the group of items about which an auditor wishes to draw conclusions. However, the difference between the targeted population (the population about which information is desired) and the sampled population (the population from which the sample is actually drawn) should be understood.

Answer (B) is incorrect. The attribute is the characteristic of the population the auditor wants to estimate. Answer (C) is incorrect. The sample is a subset of the population used to estimate the characteristic. Answer (D) is incorrect. A sampling unit is the item that is actually selected for examination. It is a subset of the population.

14.1.3. An advantage of statistical sampling over nonstatistical sampling is that statistical sampling helps an auditor to

A. Minimize the failure to detect errors and fraud.

B. Eliminate the risk of nonsampling errors.

C. Reduce the level of audit risk and materiality to a relatively low amount.

D. Measure the sufficiency of the evidence obtained.

Answer (D) is correct. *(CPA, adapted)*

REQUIRED: The advantage of statistical sampling over nonstatistical sampling.

DISCUSSION: Statistical sampling helps the auditor to design an efficient sample, to measure the sufficiency of the evidence obtained, and to evaluate the sample results. Auditors are required to obtain sufficient appropriate evidence. Sufficiency is the measure of the quantity of evidence. It relates to the design and size of the sample.

Answer (A) is incorrect. In some circumstances, professional judgment may indicate that nonstatistical methods are preferable to minimize the failure to detect errors and fraud. Answer (B) is incorrect. Statistical sampling is irrelevant to nonsampling errors. Answer (C) is incorrect. Statistical sampling is irrelevant to materiality. Moreover, nonstatistical methods may be used to reduce audit risk.

14.1.4. When using sampling for substantive tests of details, the auditor is required to do all but which of the following?

A. Determine the tolerable misstatement.

B. Project sample misstatement results to the population.

C. Compute the sample standard deviation.

D. Select a representative sample.

Answer (C) is correct. *(J. Swearingen)*

REQUIRED: The procedure not required in sampling.

DISCUSSION: AU-C 530 does not require that the sample standard deviation be calculated. The computation would be necessary if parametric statistical sampling were used, but statistical sampling is not required by AU-C 530.

Answer (A) is incorrect. Evaluation in monetary terms of the sample results is related to the auditor's judgments. Tolerable misstatement is a monetary amount set by the auditor. The auditor seeks to obtain appropriate assurance that this amount is not exceeded by the actual misstatement in the population. An estimate of tolerable misstatement is vital to planning the audit. Answer (B) is incorrect. AU-C 530 requires that misstatement projected from the sample be compared with tolerable misstatement, with appropriate consideration given to sampling risk. Projected misstatement is the best estimate of population misstatement. Answer (D) is incorrect. AU-C 530 also requires that samples be representative. Thus, all population items should have an opportunity to be chosen.

14.1.5. An auditor suspects that the invoices from a small number of vendors contain serious misstatements and therefore limits the sample to those vendors only. A major disadvantage of selecting such a directed sample of items to examine is the

A. Difficulty in obtaining sample items.

B. Inability to quantify the sampling error related to the total population of vendor invoices.

C. Absence of a normal distribution.

D. Tendency to sample a greater number of units.

Answer (B) is correct. *(CIA, adapted)*

REQUIRED: The disadvantage of a directed sample.

DISCUSSION: Judgment sampling uses the auditor's subjective judgment to determine the sample size (number of items examined) and sample selection (which items to examine). This subjectivity is not always a weakness. The auditor, based on other audit work, may be able to test the most material and risky transactions and to emphasize the types of transactions subject to high control risk. Probability (random) sampling provides an objective method of determining sample size and selecting the items to be examined. Unlike judgment sampling, it also provides a means of quantitatively assessing precision and reliability.

Answer (A) is incorrect. Obtaining invoices for a small number of vendors should be simple. Answer (C) is incorrect. The sampling distribution is expected to be normal even if the population distribution is not. Answer (D) is incorrect. Judgment sampling provides no objective means for determining the appropriate sample size. Thus, it has no tendency to sample a greater number of units.

14.1.6. If the size of the sample to be used in a particular test of attributes has not been determined by using statistical concepts, but the sample has been chosen in accordance with random selection procedures,

A. No inferences can be drawn from the sample.

B. The auditor has caused nonsampling risk to increase.

C. The auditor may or may not achieve desired precision at the desired level of confidence.

D. The auditor will have to evaluate the results by reference to the principles of discovery sampling.

Answer (C) is correct. *(CPA, adapted)*

REQUIRED: The significance of choosing sample size without regard to statistical concepts.

DISCUSSION: The determination of sample size for a test of attributes is a function of (1) the allowable risk of overreliance, (2) the tolerable deviation rate, (3) the expected population deviation rate, and (4) the size of the population. When the auditor does not use these criteria to determine sample size, (s)he risks not meeting the audit objectives.

Answer (A) is incorrect. Inferences can be drawn from both statistical and nonstatistical samples. Answer (B) is incorrect. Nonsampling risk includes all aspects of audit risk not arising from sampling, e.g., misapplying a procedure or choosing an inappropriate procedure. Answer (D) is incorrect. Discovery sampling is a statistical sampling method. It is a form of attribute sampling that emphasizes the discovery of critical errors.

14.1.7. To quantify the risk that sample evidence leads to erroneous conclusions about the sampled population,

A. Each item in the sampled population must have an equal chance of being selected.

B. Each item in the sampled population must have a chance of being selected that is proportional to its carrying amount.

C. Each item in the sampled population must have an equal or known probability of being selected.

D. The precise number of items in the population must be known.

Answer (C) is correct. *(CIA, adapted)*

REQUIRED: The requirement for quantifying sampling risk.

DISCUSSION: Probability (random) sampling is used in any sampling plan in which every item in the population has an equal (or known) and nonzero probability of being chosen. A probability sample permits the use of statistical methods based on the laws of probability to quantify an estimate of sampling risk.

Answer (A) is incorrect. Sampling risk can be quantified when purely random sampling is not used if the probability of selection is known and nonzero. Stratified random sampling is an example. Answer (B) is incorrect. Each item in the sampled population must have a chance of being selected that is proportional to its carrying amount in monetary-unit sampling, but this characteristic does not apply to other methods. Answer (D) is incorrect. Sampling risk for an infinite population is quantifiable.

14.1.8. Each time an auditor draws a conclusion based on evidence from a sample, an additional risk, i.e., sampling risk, is introduced. An example of sampling risk is

A. Projecting the results of sampling beyond the population tested.

B. Properly applying an improper audit procedure to sample data.

C. Improperly applying a proper audit procedure to sample data.

D. Drawing an erroneous conclusion from sample data.

Answer (D) is correct. *(CIA, adapted)*

REQUIRED: The example of sampling risk.

DISCUSSION: Sampling risk is the risk that the auditor's conclusion based on a sample may differ from the conclusion if the same audit procedure were applied to every item in the population. Sampling risk can result in two types of erroneous conclusions: those affecting effectiveness or those affecting efficiency (AU-C 530).

Answer (A) is incorrect. Sample results are relevant only to the population tested. Improper projection of results is a nonsampling risk. Answer (B) is incorrect. Sampling risk arises even though the proper procedure is correctly applied and the results are evaluated appropriately. Thus, choice of the wrong procedure is a nonsampling risk. Answer (C) is incorrect. Sampling risk arises even though the proper procedure is correctly applied and the results are evaluated appropriately. Thus, improper application of the right procedure is a nonsampling risk.

14.1.9. A confidence level of 90% means that

A. The expected deviation rate is equal to 10%.

B. The point estimate obtained is within 10% of the true population value.

C. The probability is 90% that the sample results will not vary from the true characteristics of the population by more than a specified amount.

D. A larger sample size is required than if the desired confidence level were equal to 95%.

Answer (C) is correct. *(CIA, adapted)*

REQUIRED: The meaning of a 90% confidence level.

DISCUSSION: A 90% confidence level signifies that, in repeated sampling from a normally distributed population, the precision intervals constructed around the results of simple random samples of size *n* will contain the true population value approximately 90% of the time.

Answer (A) is incorrect. The confidence level is a probability, not a deviation rate or a range of values. For attribute sampling (used in tests of controls), the complement of a 90% confidence level is a 10% risk of assessing control risk too low. For variables sampling (used in substantive testing), the complement of a 90% confidence level is a 10% risk of incorrect rejection. Answer (B) is incorrect. The confidence level is a probability, not a deviation rate or a range of values. For attribute sampling (used in tests of controls), the complement of a 90% confidence level is a 10% risk of assessing control risk too low. For variables sampling (used in substantive testing), the complement of a 90% confidence level is a 10% risk of incorrect rejection. Answer (D) is incorrect. A smaller sample is required if the desired confidence level is 90% rather than 95%.

14.1.10. When planning a sample for a substantive test of details, an auditor should consider tolerable misstatement for the sample. This consideration should

A. Be related to the auditor's business risk.

B. Not be adjusted for qualitative factors.

C. Be related to preliminary judgments about materiality levels.

D. Not be changed during the audit process.

Answer (C) is correct. *(CPA, adapted)*

REQUIRED: The true statement about the consideration of tolerable misstatement.

DISCUSSION: When planning a sample for a test of details, the auditor should consider how much monetary misstatement in the related account balance or class of transactions may exist without causing the financial statements to be materially misstated. This maximum misstatement is the tolerable misstatement for the sample. It is used in audit planning to determine the necessary precision and sample size. Tolerable misstatement, combined for the entire audit plan, should not exceed the auditor's preliminary judgments about materiality.

Answer (A) is incorrect. The auditor's business risk is irrelevant. Answer (B) is incorrect. Qualitative factors should be considered, for example, the nature and cause of misstatements and their relationship to other phases of the audit. Answer (D) is incorrect. If sample results suggest that planning assumptions were incorrect, the auditor should take appropriate action.

14.1.11. As lower acceptable levels of the risk of incorrect acceptance and performance materiality are established, the auditor should plan more work on individual accounts to

A. Find smaller misstatements.

B. Find larger misstatements.

C. Increase the tolerable misstatement in the accounts.

D. Decrease the risk of overreliance.

Answer (A) is correct. *(CPA, adapted)*

REQUIRED: The result of lowering the risk of incorrect acceptance and performance materiality.

DISCUSSION: A lower performance materiality means that the tolerable misstatement in an account is smaller. As a result, the auditor must plan for a larger sample size and more audit work on the accounts to discover smaller misstatements. For substantive tests of details, the sample size depends on the auditor's desired assurance (1.0 – the risk of incorrect acceptance) that tolerable misstatement is not less than actual misstatement in the population. The desired assurance may be based on, among other things, the following: (1) the assessed risk of material misstatement, (2) the assurance provided by other substantive procedures related to the same assertion, (3) tolerable misstatement, and (4) expected misstatement for the population. Accordingly, as the acceptable risk of incorrect acceptance decreases, the desired assurance increases, and the auditor decreases the tolerable misstatement.

Answer (B) is incorrect. The auditor should plan to find smaller misstatements. Answer (C) is incorrect. As the size of performance materiality decreases, tolerable misstatement decreases. Answer (D) is incorrect. During substantive testing of an account balance, the auditor is ultimately concerned with decreasing the risk of incorrectly accepting the balance. Tests of controls, not substantive tests, are designed to decrease the risk of overreliance.

14.1.12. An auditor's statistical sample drawn from a population of invoices indicates a mean value of $150 and sampling precision of ± $30 at a 95% confidence level. Which of the following statements correctly interprets these sample data?

A. In repeated sampling, the point estimate of the true population mean will be $150 about 95% of the time.

B. The probability is 95% that the true population mean is $150.

C. In repeated sampling, intervals with precision ± $30 around the sample mean will always contain the true population mean.

D. The probability is 95% that the range $120 to $180 contains the true population mean.

Answer (D) is correct. *(CIA, adapted)*

REQUIRED: The interpretation of the sample data.

DISCUSSION: The relationship between the estimated mean, the precision interval, and the confidence level is that the auditor can state, at the desired confidence level given a simple random sample of size *n* taken from a normally distributed population, that the precision interval (the sample mean ± the precision amount) contains the true population mean. Here, the auditor is 95% confident that the interval $120 to $180 ($150 ± $30) contains the true population mean.

Answer (A) is incorrect. Repeated samples will result in many different point estimates. Answer (B) is incorrect. The probability is 95% that the range $120 to $180 contains the true population value, not that this value is equal to the point estimate of $150. Answer (C) is incorrect. The probability is 95%, not 100%.

14.1.13. Which one of the following statements is true regarding two random samples drawn in the same way from the same population, one of size 30 and one of size 300?

A. The two samples would have the same expected value.

B. The larger sample is more likely to produce a large sample mean.

C. The smaller sample will have a smaller 95% confidence interval for the mean.

D. The smaller sample will, on the average, produce a lower estimate of the variance of the population.

Answer (A) is correct. *(CIA, adapted)*

REQUIRED: The true statement about random samples of different size.

DISCUSSION: The expected value of a random sample of any size is equal to the population mean.

Answer (B) is incorrect. The larger sample is more reliable, but both samples will produce an unbiased estimate of the population mean. Answer (C) is incorrect. The smaller sample is less reliable and, therefore, will have a wider 95% confidence interval. Answer (D) is incorrect. The variance is also a population parameter, and the expected value of the sample variance does not change with sample size.

14.1.14. In statistical sampling for variables, setting the appropriate confidence level and desired sample precision are decisions made by the auditor that will affect sample size for a substantive test. Which of the following should not be a factor in the choice of desired precision?

A. The sampling risk.

B. The size of an account balance misstatement considered material.

C. The audit resources available for execution of the sampling plan.

D. The objective of the audit test being conducted.

Answer (C) is correct. *(CIA, adapted)*

REQUIRED: The factor not considered when selecting desired precision.

DISCUSSION: The basic sample size equation for variables sampling is

$$n = \frac{C^2\sigma^2}{P^2}$$

In this equation, *P* is the average precision (per item in the population), *C* is the confidence coefficient, σ is the population standard deviation, and *n* is the sample size. The confidence coefficient, *C*, is the number of standard deviations in the standard normal distribution that corresponds to the specified confidence level. Thus, it controls sampling risk. The tolerable misstatement is related to materiality judgments. It determines the estimated precision. A table is ordinarily consulted to determine precision as a percentage of tolerable misstatement. The objective of the audit sample affects both sampling risk and precision. The audit resources available determine whether the test will be undertaken but should not affect the process once the audit procedure is undertaken.

Answer (A) is incorrect. Sampling risk is a factor in calculating desired precision. Answer (B) is incorrect. Materiality is a factor in calculating desired precision. Answer (D) is incorrect. The objective of the audit test is a factor in calculating desired precision.

14.1.15. The accounting department reports the accounts payable balance as $175,000. You are willing to accept that balance if it is within $15,000 of the actual balance. Using a variables sampling plan, you compute a 95% confidence interval of $173,000 to $190,000. You would therefore

A. Find it impossible to determine the acceptability of the balance.

B. Accept the balance but with a lower level of confidence.

C. Take a larger sample before totally rejecting the balance and requiring adjustments.

D. Accept the $175,000 balance because the confidence interval is within the materiality limits.

Answer (D) is correct. *(CIA, adapted)*

REQUIRED: The conclusion regarding a balance that is within the computed confidence interval.

DISCUSSION: The auditor is willing to accept the carrying amount if it is within $15,000 (the tolerable misstatement) of the population value. The sample mean used to estimate the population value must be $181,500 [($173,000 + $190,000) ÷ 2] because it is at the midpoint of the computed (achieved) confidence interval (precision). This interval is based on a precision (± $8,500) that is well within the tolerable misstatement (materiality limits) of ± $15,000. Thus, the auditor should accept the $175,000 value. The interval based on tolerable misstatement and the narrower achieved precision limits contain this value.

Answer (A) is incorrect. The achieved confidence interval ($173,000 to $190,000) contains the accounts payable balance at the 95% confidence level. Answer (B) is incorrect. The achieved confidence interval ($173,000 to $190,000) contains the accounts payable balance at the 95% confidence level. Answer (C) is incorrect. The auditor does not need to take a larger sample. The carrying amount is acceptable based on the initial sample.

14.1.16. The measure of variability of a statistical sample that serves as an estimate of the population variability is the

A. Basic precision.

B. Range.

C. Standard deviation.

D. Confidence interval.

Answer (C) is correct. *(CIA, adapted)*

REQUIRED: The measure of population variability.

DISCUSSION: Variability (dispersion) is measured by the variance, standard deviation, quartile deviations, range, etc., of a sample or population. The population standard deviation (σ) is a measure of the degree of compactness of values. It is used to determine appropriate sample sizes. Given that *N* equals population size, μ is the population mean, and x_i is an observed value of a population item, the formula is

$$\sigma = \sqrt{\frac{\sum (x_i - \mu)^2}{N}}$$

Answer (A) is incorrect. Basic precision is the range around the sample value that is expected to contain the true population value. Answer (B) is incorrect. The range is the difference between the largest and smallest values in a sample. It is a crude measure of variability but is not used to estimate population variability. Answer (D) is incorrect. Confidence interval is a synonym for precision.

14.1.17. The concept of standard deviation is significant in statistical sampling because

A. The central limit theorem states that repeated samples from a population will produce sample standard deviations that cluster around the actual standard deviation of the population.

B. The sample size for variables estimation is directly related to the magnitude of the population standard deviation.

C. The magnitude of the finite population correction factor is directly related to the magnitude of the standard deviation of the population.

D. Statistical sampling is inappropriate if the standard deviation is very small relative to the mean of the population.

Answer (B) is correct. *(CIA, adapted)*

REQUIRED: The significance of the standard deviation.

DISCUSSION: The standard deviation is used to calculate sample size in variables sampling applications. The formula is

$$n = \frac{C^2\sigma^2}{P^2}$$

The variable *n* is the sample size, *C* is the confidence coefficient, σ is the standard deviation of the population, and *P* is the average precision (per item in the population) specified by the auditor. As the population dispersion increases, so does the required sample size.

Answer (A) is incorrect. The central limit theorem relates to means, not standard deviations, of samples. Answer (C) is incorrect. The finite population correction factor is used to adjust the sample size for small populations. Answer (D) is incorrect. If the standard deviation of the population is small, the result is very accurate estimation.

14.1.18. The variability of a population, as measured by the standard deviation, is the

A. Extent to which the individual values of the items in the population are spread about the mean.

B. Degree of asymmetry of a distribution.

C. Tendency of the means of large samples (at least 30 items) to be normally distributed.

D. Measure of the closeness of a sample estimate to a corresponding population characteristic.

Answer (A) is correct. *(CIA, adapted)*

REQUIRED: The definition of standard deviation.

DISCUSSION: Standard deviation is a mathematical measure (denoted by σ) of the dispersion of items in a population about its mean.

Answer (B) is incorrect. Skewness or asymmetry means that extreme values at one end of the distribution are not balanced by large values at the other end. Answer (C) is incorrect. The central limit theorem states that the distribution of sample means for large samples should be normally distributed even if the underlying population is not. Answer (D) is incorrect. Precision is the interval about the sample value that is expected to contain the true value of the population.

14.1.19. The standard deviation of the population is required in the sample size determination formula. However, the true value for the standard deviation of the population is not likely to be known. The auditor usually employs an estimate of this value based upon all the following except

A. A pre-sample.

B. The prior year's audit.

C. The available carrying amounts.

D. Inquiries of management.

Answer (D) is correct. *(Publisher, adapted)*

REQUIRED: The item not involved in estimating the standard deviation of the population.

DISCUSSION: Although inquiries of management are important, management is unlikely to be able to estimate the standard deviation of the population under audit.

Answer (A) is incorrect. One acceptable approach is to determine an estimated population standard deviation from testing a pre-sample of 30-50 items. Once the total sample required is calculated, the pre-sample items can be included as part of the sample. Answer (B) is incorrect. The prior year's audit may provide evidence that might be used as an estimate for the current period. Answer (C) is incorrect. The available carrying amounts (e.g., the accounts receivable balances) may be used to determine the standard deviation of the carrying amounts, which in turn may be employed as a surrogate for the actual but unknown population standard deviation.

14.1.20. An auditor has taken a large sample from an audit population that is skewed in the sense that it contains a large number of small monetary balances and a small number of large monetary balances. The auditor can conclude

A. The sampling distribution is not normal. Thus, monetary-unit sampling based on the Poisson distribution more accurately defines the nature of the population.

B. The sampling distribution is normal. Thus, the *Z* value can be used in evaluating the sample results.

C. The sampling distribution is not normal. Thus, attribute sampling is the only alternative statistical tool that can appropriately be used.

D. None of the answers are correct.

Answer (B) is correct. *(CIA, adapted)*

REQUIRED: The auditor's conclusion about a skewed population.

DISCUSSION: The central limit theorem states that, regardless of the distribution of the population from which random samples are taken, the shape of the sampling distribution of the means approaches the normal distribution as the sample size increases. Hence, *Z* values (the number of standard deviations in the standard normal distribution needed to provide specified levels of confidence) can be used. *Z* (sometimes designated as *C* in the sample-size formula) values represent areas under the curve for the standard normal distribution.

Answer (A) is incorrect. The sampling distribution is deemed to be normal (a continuous distribution). The Poisson distribution approaches the binomial distribution (a discrete distribution) for large samples and thus is related to attribute sampling. Answer (C) is incorrect. The sampling distribution can be normally distributed if a large enough sample size is taken. Moreover, attribute sampling is not appropriate for estimating population values. Answer (D) is incorrect. The sampling distribution is normal.

14.1.21. Using the following results from a variables sample, compute the standard error of the mean.

Population size = 10,000
Sample size = 144
Sample standard deviation = $24.00
Confidence level = 90% (C = 1.65)
Mean = $84.00

A. $60.00

B. $7.00

C. $3.30

D. $2.00

Answer (D) is correct. *(CIA, adapted)*

REQUIRED: The standard error of the mean, given results from a variables sample.

DISCUSSION: The standard error of the mean equals the population standard deviation divided by the square root of the sample size. To determine achieved precision, the standard error of the mean is multiplied by the confidence coefficient. If the sample standard deviation is used as an estimate of the population standard deviation, the standard error of the mean is

$$\frac{\$24.00}{\sqrt{144}} = \$2.00$$

Answer (A) is incorrect. The amount of $60.00 is a nonsensical number in this context. Answer (B) is incorrect. The amount of $7.00 equals the mean ($84) divided by the square root of the sample size (square root of 144). Answer (C) is incorrect. The amount of $3.30 is the estimated precision $[(1.65 \times \$24) \div \sqrt{144}\,]$.

14.1.22. While performing a test of details during an audit, the auditor determined that the sample results supported the conclusion that the recorded account balance was materially misstated. It was, in fact, not materially misstated. This situation illustrates the risk of

A. Incorrect rejection.

B. Incorrect acceptance.

C. Overreliance.

D. Underreliance.

Answer (A) is correct. *(CPA, adapted)*

REQUIRED: The risk of erroneously concluding that a balance is materially misstated.

DISCUSSION: An auditor is concerned with two aspects of sampling risk in performing substantive tests of details: the risk of incorrect acceptance and the risk of incorrect rejection. The second is the risk that the sample supports the conclusion that the recorded account balance is materially misstated when it is not materially misstated.

Answer (B) is incorrect. The risk of incorrect acceptance is the risk that an auditor will erroneously conclude that a balance is not materially misstated. Answer (C) is incorrect. The risk of overreliance is an aspect of sampling risk for tests of controls. Answer (D) is incorrect. The risk of underreliance is an aspect of sampling risk for tests of controls.

14.1.23. The auditor failed to recognize a deviation included in a sample intended to test controls related to a transaction process. This failure best reflects

A. Statistical risk.

B. Sampling risk.

C. Audit risk.

D. Nonsampling risk.

Answer (D) is correct. *(Publisher, adapted)*

REQUIRED: The term for the failure to recognize a control deviation.

DISCUSSION: Nonsampling risk is the risk that the auditor may draw an erroneous conclusion for any reason not related to sampling risk. Examples include the use of inappropriate audit procedures or misinterpretation of audit evidence and failure to recognize a misstatement or deviation. Nonsampling risk may be reduced to an acceptable level through such factors as adequate planning and proper conduct of a firm's audit practice in accordance with the quality control standards (AU-C 530).

Answer (A) is incorrect. Without examining every item, the exact population parameter cannot be determined, and statistical risk results. Answer (B) is incorrect. Without examining every item, the exact population parameter cannot be determined, and sampling risk results. Answer (C) is incorrect. Audit risk is the risk of expressing an inappropriate audit opinion when the financial statements are materially misstated.

14.1.24. The auditor uses variables and attribute sampling to make accounting estimates. These methods estimate, respectively,

A. Deviation rate and quantities.

B. Quantities and deviation rate.

C. Constants and dollars.

D. Dollars and constants.

Answer (B) is correct. *(Publisher, adapted)*

REQUIRED: The use of variables and attribute sampling.

DISCUSSION: Variables sampling is used by auditors to estimate quantities or dollar amounts in substantive testing. Attribute sampling applies to tests of controls and is used to estimate a deviation rate (occurrence rate) for a population.

14.1.25. An auditor of a manufacturing company analyzes cost variances incurred in the manufacturing process to determine their statistical significance. Which of the following techniques is most likely to be used for this purpose?

A. Markov chains.

B. Monte Carlo method.

C. Application of probability theory.

D. Sensitivity analysis.

Answer (C) is correct. *(CIA, adapted)*

REQUIRED: The technique used to determine the statistical significance of cost variances.

DISCUSSION: An auditor may use statistical control charts to determine the significance of variances in a cost accounting system. Control limits are established using probability theory to determine the likelihood that an observed variance indicates the system is out of control. If an observation falls outside the limits, an investigation should be made to determine the cause of the deviation.

Answer (A) is incorrect. Markov chains relate to a decision process. Answer (B) is incorrect. The Monte Carlo method is used in simulation models. Answer (D) is incorrect. Sensitivity analysis studies the effect of changing a variable or parameter in a decision process.

14.1.26. In appraising the results of a statistical sample, the finite population correction (FPC) factor

A. Can be greater than one.

B. Has less effect as the sample becomes a larger proportion of the population.

C. Is needed when sampling is performed with replacement.

D. Is applied to reduce the size of the sample.

Answer (D) is correct. *(CIA, adapted)*

REQUIRED: The use of the FPC factor.

DISCUSSION: The FPC factor reduces the sample size when it is large relative to the population size (*N*). The larger the sample size, the greater the probability that extreme values (which greatly affect the sample result) will be included in the sample. Thus, a somewhat smaller sample size is needed than if the population were infinite. An approximation of the FPC formula is

$$\sqrt{\frac{N - n}{N}}$$

Answer (A) is incorrect. The FPC factor cannot be greater than one. Answer (B) is incorrect. The FPC factor has a greater effect as the sample becomes larger. Answer (C) is incorrect. Using the FPC factor is independent of whether sampling is performed with replacement.

14.1.27. Which of the following sampling methods is used to estimate a numerical measurement of a population, such as a dollar value?

A. Attribute sampling.

B. Stop-or-go sampling.

C. Variables sampling.

D. Random-number sampling.

Answer (C) is correct. *(CPA, adapted)*

REQUIRED: The sampling method used to estimate a numerical measurement of a population.

DISCUSSION: Variables sampling samples dollar amounts or other quantities. The purpose of variables sampling is to estimate a measure of a population.

Answer (A) is incorrect. Attribute sampling is a method to test internal control. Answer (B) is incorrect. Stop-or-go sampling is a method to test internal control. Answer (D) is incorrect. Random number sampling is a generic term relating to the selection of the sampling units.

14.1.28. The appropriate sampling plan to use to identify at least one deviation, assuming some number of such deviations exist in a population, and then to discontinue sampling when one irregularity is observed is

A. Stop-or-go sampling.

B. Discovery sampling.

C. Variables sampling.

D. Attribute sampling.

Answer (B) is correct. *(CIA, adapted)*

REQUIRED: The sampling plan that should be used.

DISCUSSION: Discovery sampling is a form of attribute sampling applied when a control is critical and a single deviation is important, for example, commission of a material fraud. The expected deviation rate should be at or near zero, and the sample size is calculated so that the sample will include at least one example of a deviation if it occurs in the population at a given rate.

Answer (A) is incorrect. Stop-or-go sampling is a variant of attribute sampling intended to reduce sample sizes when the population is relatively deviation free. It allows for discontinuing sampling when few or no deviations are found or for expanding the sample if the initial sample does not provide sufficient assurance. Answer (C) is incorrect. Variables sampling estimates the value of a population. Answer (D) is incorrect. Most attribute sampling applications are not discontinued when a single deviation is found.

14.1.29. In performing tests of controls over authorization of cash disbursements, which of the following statistical sampling methods would be most appropriate?

A. Variables.

B. Stratified.

C. Ratio.

D. Attributes.

Answer (D) is correct. *(CPA, adapted)*

REQUIRED: The sampling method most appropriate for tests of controls.

DISCUSSION: The auditor uses attribute sampling to test the effectiveness of controls. The auditor should consider the occurrence rate of deviations in the population. Attribute sampling enables the auditor to estimate these occurrence rates and to determine whether the estimated rates are within an acceptable range.

Answer (A) is incorrect. Variables sampling relates to quantities and dollar values (population totals). Answer (B) is incorrect. Stratified sampling relates to variables estimation. Answer (C) is incorrect. Ratio estimation is a method of variables sampling.

14.1.30. When would difference estimation or ratio estimation sampling methods be inappropriate?

A. If differences between the carrying amounts and audit amounts of a population are rare.

B. If the average difference between the audit amount and carrying amount of a population is small.

C. If differences between the carrying amount and audit amount of a population are numerous.

D. If the average difference between the audit amount and carrying amount of a population is large.

Answer (A) is correct. *(CIA, adapted)*

REQUIRED: The circumstances in which difference or ratio estimation is inappropriate.

DISCUSSION: Difference estimation approximates total misstatement in the population by calculating the mean difference between the audited and carrying amounts in the sample and then multiplying by the number of population items. Ratio estimation approximates the total population misstatement by multiplying the proportion of the sample misstatement times the population carrying amount. These methods are not reliable when misstatements are few or tend to be in one direction.

Answer (B) is incorrect. The frequency and direction of misstatements rather than their size determine whether difference and ratio estimation are reliable. However, difference estimation is preferable when the size of misstatements is independent of the recorded values. Answer (C) is incorrect. Difference and ratio estimation are more reliable when misstatement rates are high. Answer (D) is incorrect. The frequency and direction of misstatements rather than their size determine whether difference and ratio estimation are reliable. However, difference estimation is preferable when the size of misstatements is independent of the recorded amounts.

14.1.31. Which sampling method is most appropriate for the audit of the parts inventory of a wholesale electronic supply house when many small over- and understatements are expected?

A. Monetary-unit sampling.

B. Ratio or difference estimation.

C. Mean-per-unit sampling.

D. Stratified mean-per-unit sampling.

Answer (B) is correct. *(J. Heian)*

REQUIRED: The appropriate sampling method when many small over- and understatements are expected.

DISCUSSION: Difference estimation of population misstatement entails determining the differences between the audit and carrying amounts for items in the sample, adding the differences, calculating the mean difference, and multiplying the mean by the number of items in the population. An allowance for sampling risk is also calculated. Ratio estimation is similar except that it estimates the population misstatement by multiplying the carrying amount of the population by the ratio of the total audit value of the sample items to their total carrying amount. Both methods are reliable and efficient when misstatements are relatively frequent, small misstatements predominate, and they do not tend to be in one direction (they are not skewed).

Answer (A) is incorrect. Monetary-unit sampling is not appropriate when many misstatements are expected or the population contains understatements. Answer (C) is incorrect. MPU is considered less efficient than either ratio or difference estimation when many misstatements are present. Answer (D) is incorrect. MPU is considered less efficient than either ratio or difference estimation when many misstatements are present.

14.1.32. The major reason that the difference and ratio estimation methods are expected to produce audit efficiency is that the

A. Number of members of the populations of differences or ratios is smaller than the number of members of the population of carrying amounts.

B. The risk of incorrect acceptance may be completely ignored.

C. Calculations required in using difference or ratio estimation are less arduous and fewer than those required when using direct estimation.

D. Variability of the populations of differences or ratios is less than that of the populations of carrying amounts or audited values.

Answer (D) is correct. *(CPA, adapted)*

REQUIRED: The reason for increased audit efficiency.

DISCUSSION: Difference estimation approximates total misstatement in the population by calculating the mean difference between the audited and carrying amounts in the sample and then multiplying by the number of population items. Ratio estimation approximates the total population misstatement by multiplying the proportion of the sample misstatement times the population carrying amount. The variability in both of these estimates is likely to be smaller than the variability within the population. Because the sample size varies directly with the variability of the population, the use of differences or ratios will usually allow for smaller sample sizes and greater efficiency in sampling.

Answer (A) is incorrect. The number of sampling units (items) in the population does not change if the sampling method changes. Answer (B) is incorrect. The risk of accepting the carrying amount when it is materially misstated is present in any sampling method. Answer (C) is incorrect. The sample size must be calculated using basically the same formula for any sampling method employed.

14.1.33. Which of the following best describes an inherent limitation of the monetary-unit sampling (MUS) method?

A. It can only be used for substantive testing of asset accounts.

B. It is complicated and always requires the use of a computer system to perform the calculations.

C. Misstatement rates must be large, and the misstatements must be overstatements.

D. Misstatement rates must be small, and the misstatements must be overstatements.

Answer (D) is correct. *(CIA, adapted)*

REQUIRED: The inherent limitation of MUS.

DISCUSSION: MUS combines attribute sampling and variables sampling concepts to estimate dollar amounts instead of deviation rates. Efficient use of MUS requires misstatement rates to be small. The monetary-unit sample size increases with the expected misstatement. Hence, the monetary-unit sample size may be greater than that for classical variables sampling. Moreover, MUS is not designed to address understatements or negative values without special modifications. Another disadvantage of MUS sampling is that misstatement estimates may be overly conservative, thereby increasing the risk of incorrect rejection.

Answer (A) is incorrect. MUS is appropriate for substantive testing of most accounts when overstatement is of concern. Answer (B) is incorrect. MUS is relatively simple and can be used with a table of the Poisson distribution. Answer (C) is incorrect. Misstatement rates should be small.

14.1.34. An auditor is preparing to sample accounts receivable for overstatement. A statistical sampling method that automatically provides stratification when using systematic selection is

A. Attribute sampling.

B. Ratio-estimation sampling.

C. Monetary-unit sampling (MUS).

D. Mean-per-unit (MPU) sampling.

Answer (C) is correct. *(CIA, adapted)*

REQUIRED: The sampling method that automatically stratifies accounts receivable.

DISCUSSION: Monetary-unit or probability-proportional-to-size (PPS) sampling combines attribute sampling and variables sampling concepts to estimate dollar amounts instead of deviation rates. It is a procedure for selecting items from a population using each dollar as a sampling unit. The procedure is applied by selecting every *n*th dollar in the population (the population consists of dollars in ascending value from $1 to the total value of the population). The item that contains the dollar selected is included in the sample. It effectively stratifies the population because the larger the account balance, the greater the chance of selection. Moreover, MUS is not designed to address understatements or negative values without special modifications.

Answer (A) is incorrect. Attribute sampling estimates deviation rates, not dollar amounts. Answer (B) is incorrect. Ratio-estimation sampling uses the ratio of audited amounts to recorded amounts and does not automatically stratify. Answer (D) is incorrect. MPU averages the audit values of sample items and multiplies by the number in the population to estimate the population value. It does not automatically stratify.

14.1.35. An auditor for the state highway and safety department needs to estimate the average highway weight of tractor-trailer trucks using the state's highway system. Which estimation method must be used?

A. Mean-per-unit (MPU).

B. Difference.

C. Ratio.

D. Monetary-unit.

Answer (A) is correct. *(CIA, adapted)*

REQUIRED: The best sampling estimation method to estimate an average weight.

DISCUSSION: MPU estimation estimates the average value of population items. MPU averages the audit values of the sample items and multiplies the result by the number of items in the population.

Answer (B) is incorrect. Difference is a technique that compares book with audit values. Answer (C) is incorrect. Ratio estimation is a technique that compares book with audit values. Answer (D) is incorrect. Monetary-unit sampling selects items denominated in monetary units using individual units as sampling units.

14.1.36. Using statistical sampling to assist in verifying the year-end accounts payable balance, an auditor has accumulated the following data:

	Number of Accounts	Book Balance	Balance Determined by the Auditor
Population	4,100	$5,000,000	?
Sample	200	250,000	$300,000

Using the ratio estimation technique, the auditor's estimate of the year-end accounts payable balance would be

A. $6,150,000

B. $6,000,000

C. $5,125,000

D. $5,050,000

Answer (B) is correct. *(CPA, adapted)*

REQUIRED: The year-end accounts payable balance using ratio estimation.

DISCUSSION: Ratio estimation estimates the total population misstatement by multiplying the proportion of the sample misstatement by the population carrying amount. If the proportion of the sample misstatement is 20% [($300,000 – $250,000) ÷ $250,000], the estimated population misstatement is $1,000,000 ($5,000,000 × 20%). The estimated year-end balance is therefore $6,000,000 ($5,000,000 carrying amount + $1,000,000 estimated misstatement).

Answer (A) is incorrect. The amount of $6,150,000 results from the assumption that the ratio is 23% [($6,150,000 – $5,000,000) ÷ $5,000,000]. Answer (C) is incorrect. The amount of $5,125,000 results from the assumption that the ratio is 2.5% [($5,125,000 – $5,000,000) ÷ $5,000,000]. Answer (D) is incorrect. The amount of $5,050,000 equals the carrying amount of the population ($5,000,000) plus the understatement in the sample ($50,000).

14.1.37. In which sampling method is the probability of selection of an item proportional to the size or the value of the item (e.g., a $1,000 item is 10 times more likely to be selected than a $100 item)?

A. Discovery sampling.

B. Ratio estimation.

C. Dollar-unit sampling.

D. Stratified sampling.

Answer (C) is correct. *(Publisher, adapted)*

REQUIRED: The sampling method in which the probability of selection of an item is proportional to its size.

DISCUSSION: Dollar-unit, monetary-unit, or probability-proportional-to-size sampling defines an individual monetary unit within an item or balance as the sampling unit. Thus, an item containing 1,000 sampling units ($1,000) has a 10 times greater chance of being selected for audit than a balance with 100 sampling units ($100).

Answer (A) is incorrect. Discovery sampling is a sampling plan to search for critical deviations. Answer (B) is incorrect. Ratio estimation estimates the population misstatement by multiplying the proportion of sample misstatement times the population carrying amount. Answer (D) is incorrect. Stratification divides a population into subpopulations so that variability can be minimized and a more efficient sample can be drawn.

14.1.38. An internal auditor plans to test the accuracy of recorded quantities-on-hand in an inventory file against the actual quantities-on-hand. Under which of the following conditions is the auditor least likely to use a stop-or-go sampling plan?

A. The population to be sampled is very large.

B. The auditor expects the population to contain a high rate of deviations.

C. The auditor plans to draw a relatively small sample size.

D. The auditor plans to determine an upper precision limit for the estimated percentage of deviations contained in the population.

Answer (B) is correct. *(CIA, adapted)*

REQUIRED: The condition in which stop-or-go sampling is least likely to be used.

DISCUSSION: Stop-or-go sampling is an attribute sampling model that helps prevent oversampling by allowing the auditor to halt an audit test at the earliest possible moment. It is used when the auditor believes that the population contains relatively few deviations.

Answer (A) is incorrect. Stop-or-go sampling is appropriate for populations of any size. Answer (C) is incorrect. Stop-or-go sampling is designed to reduce sample size. Answer (D) is incorrect. The purpose of stop-or-go sampling is to state that a deviation rate is below a prespecified rate (upper precision limit) with a prespecified level of confidence.

14.1.39. A statistical sampling technique that will minimize sample size whenever a low deviation rate is expected is

A. Ratio-estimation sampling.

B. Difference-estimation sampling.

C. Stratified mean-per-unit sampling.

D. Stop-or-go sampling.

Answer (D) is correct. *(CIA, adapted)*

REQUIRED: The technique that minimizes sample size.

DISCUSSION: Stop-or-go sampling is typically used when a low deviation rate is expected. It is a version of acceptance sampling that, like other attribute sampling methods, is used to test the effectiveness of controls. Stop-or-go sampling is unlike acceptance sampling in that it does not rely on a fixed sample size. Thus, it may reduce the sample size because sample items are examined only until enough evidence has been gathered to reach the desired conclusion.

Answer (A) is incorrect. Deviation rate is irrelevant to variables sampling methods such as ratio-estimation sampling. Answer (B) is incorrect. Deviation rate is irrelevant to variables sampling methods such as difference estimation. Answer (C) is incorrect. Deviation rate is irrelevant to variables sampling methods such as MPU.

14.1.40. A distinguishing characteristic of random number sample selection is that

A. Each item is selected from a stratum having minimum variability.

B. Each item's chance for selection is proportional to its dollar value.

C. Each item in the population has a known and nonzero chance of being selected.

D. Each stratum in the population has an equal number of items selected.

Answer (C) is correct. *(CIA, adapted)*

REQUIRED: The distinguishing characteristic of random number sample selection.

DISCUSSION: Probability sampling is possible if every item in the population has a known and nonzero chance of being drawn. Simple random sampling is a special case of probability sampling in which every possible sample of a given size has the same probability of being chosen, and every item in the population has an equal probability of being chosen. Random selection can be used for stratified and other samples in which items do not have an equal chance of being selected.

Answer (A) is incorrect. Stratifying the population is not required for random selection. Answer (B) is incorrect. Dollar values are not used in random selection. Answer (D) is incorrect. Stratifying the population is not required for random selection.

14.1.41. Which of the following sample planning factors would influence the sample size for a substantive test of details for a specific account?

	Expected Amount of Misstatements	Measure of Tolerable Misstatement
A.	No	No
B.	Yes	Yes
C.	No	Yes
D.	Yes	No

Answer (B) is correct. *(CPA, adapted)*

REQUIRED: The factors that would influence the sample size for a substantive test of details.

DISCUSSION: Certain variables sampling plans (e.g., monetary-unit sampling) specifically consider the expected amount of misstatement and the measure of tolerable misstatement or performance materiality in the determination of sample size.

14.1.42. An auditor wishes to sample 200 sales receipts from a population of 5,000 receipts issued during the last year. The receipts have preprinted serial numbers and are arranged in chronological (and thus serial number) order. The auditor randomly chooses a receipt from the first 25 receipts and then selects every 25th receipt thereafter. The sampling procedure described here is called

A. Systematic random sampling.

B. Monetary-unit sampling.

C. Judgment interval sampling.

D. Variables sampling.

Answer (A) is correct. *(CIA, adapted)*

REQUIRED: The sampling plan that selects a random start and then chooses each *n*th item.

DISCUSSION: Systematic (interval) sampling is accomplished by selecting a random start and taking every *n*th item in the population. The value of *n* is computed by dividing the population by the size of the sample. The random start should be in the first interval. An advantage of systematic sampling is its relative ease. It requires merely counting items in the population, not assigning a random number to each item. However, a systematic sampling plan assumes the items are arranged randomly in the population. If the auditor discovers that this condition does not exist, a random selection method should be used.

Answer (B) is incorrect. Monetary-unit sampling selects individual dollars within an item or balance as the sampling units. Answer (C) is incorrect. Judgment sampling uses the auditor's subjective judgment to determine the sample size (number of items examined) and sample selection (which items to examine). Answer (D) is incorrect. The sampling procedure described can be used for attribute as well as variables sampling.

14.1.43. To test compliance with a policy regarding sales returns recorded during the most recent year, an auditor systematically selected 5% of the actual returns recorded in March and April. Returns during these 2 busiest months of the year represented about 25% of total annual returns. Projections of deviation rates from this sample have limited usefulness because

A. The small size of the sample relative to the population makes sampling risk unacceptable.

B. The failure to stratify the population according to sales volume results in bias.

C. The systematic selection of returns during the 2 months is not sufficiently random.

D. The deviation rates during the 2 busiest months may not be representative of the whole year.

Answer (D) is correct. *(CIA, adapted)*

REQUIRED: The reason for the limited usefulness of projections of deviation rates.

DISCUSSION: By selecting a sample from only 2 months, the auditor may be able to draw conclusions about the overall deviation rate during those months, but the sample does not provide sufficient information to draw conclusions about the overall rate for the year.

Answer (A) is incorrect. Although sampling risk is related to sample size, it is not related to the ratio of sample size to the population size. In addition, this problem does not contain sufficient information to evaluate the acceptability of sampling risk. Answer (B) is incorrect. The objective of stratifying a population is to decrease the sampling risk, not bias. This problem does not give enough information to decide whether stratification might have enabled the auditor to use a smaller sample. Answer (C) is incorrect. Systematic selection with a random start is unbiased if the population is randomly organized.

14.1.44. Internal auditing is conducting an operational audit of the organization's mailroom activities to determine whether the use of express mail service is limited to cases of necessity. To test cost-effectiveness, the auditor selects the 100 most recent express-mail transactions for review. A major limitation of such a sampling technique is that it

A. Does not allow a statistical generalization about all express-mail transactions.

B. Results in a sample size that is too small to project to the population.

C. Does not evaluate existing controls in this area.

D. Does not describe the population from which it was drawn.

Answer (A) is correct. *(CIA, adapted)*

REQUIRED: The major limitation of selecting a sample of the most recent transactions for review.

DISCUSSION: The last 100 express-mail transactions may not be representative of all express-mail transactions. The sample is a judgment rather than a statistical (probability or random) sample. Every item in the population (all express-mail transactions of the organization) does not have an equal (or known) and nonzero probability of being chosen. Thus, sampling risk cannot be quantified.

Answer (B) is incorrect. A sample of 100 may be sufficient. Answer (C) is incorrect. The auditor is testing for cost effectiveness. Answer (D) is incorrect. The last 100 transactions may describe the population from which they were drawn.

14.1.45. A CPA's client wishes to determine inventory shrinkage by weighing a sample of inventory items. If a stratified random sample is to be drawn, the strata should be identified in such a way that

A. The overall population is divided into subpopulations of equal size so that each subpopulation can be given equal weight when estimates are made.

B. Each stratum differs as much as possible with respect to expected shrinkage, but the shrinkages expected for items within each stratum are as close as possible.

C. The sample means and standard deviation of each individual stratum will be equal to the means and standard deviations of all other strata.

D. The items in each stratum will follow a normal distribution so that probability theory can be used in making inferences from the sample data.

Answer (B) is correct. *(CPA, adapted)*

REQUIRED: The proper way to stratify a population of inventory items.

DISCUSSION: When the items in a population are heterogeneous, it may be advantageous to stratify the population into homogeneous subpopulations. Each stratum should differ from the others, but the items within each stratum should be similar.

Answer (A) is incorrect. The purpose of stratification is to divide the population so that homogeneous items are grouped together, not to create subpopulations of equal size. Answer (C) is incorrect. The individual strata should be as different from each other as possible. Thus, the means and standard deviations of the strata should differ. Answer (D) is incorrect. Whether an item should be included in a stratum is based upon the characteristic used for stratifying, not upon the distribution of the items within the stratum.

14.1.46. An auditor is conducting a survey of perceptions and beliefs of employees concerning an organization health care plan. The best approach to selecting a sample is to

A. Focus on people who are likely to respond so that a larger sample can be obtained.

B. Focus on managers and supervisors because they can also reflect the opinions of the people in their departments.

C. Use stratified sampling when the strata are defined by marital and family status, age, and salaried/hourly status.

D. Use monetary-unit sampling according to employee salaries.

Answer (C) is correct. *(CIA, adapted)*

REQUIRED: The best way to sample employee beliefs.

DISCUSSION: Stratified sampling divides a population into subpopulations, thereby permitting the application of different techniques to each stratum. This approach reduces the effect of high variability if the strata are selected so that variability among the strata is greater than variability within each stratum. For example, one expects to find greater similarities among married people than between married people and unmarried people.

Answer (A) is incorrect. This convenience sample is likely to emphasize people with the time to respond. It tends to omit employees who are too busy to respond. Answer (B) is incorrect. Managers and supervisors often do not have the same needs and perceptions as their subordinates and also often misperceive the views of employees. Answer (D) is incorrect. The survey tests perceptions and beliefs, not monetary amounts.

14.1.47. To use stratified sampling to evaluate a large, heterogeneous inventory, which of the following is least likely to be used as a criterion to classify inventory items into strata?

A. Fair value.

B. Number of items.

C. Turnover volume.

D. Storage locations.

Answer (B) is correct. *(CIA, adapted)*

REQUIRED: The least likely criterion to classify inventory items into strata.

DISCUSSION: Stratifying a population means dividing it into subpopulations, which permits application of different sampling techniques to each subpopulation or stratum. Stratifying allows for greater emphasis on larger or more important items. When the items in a population are heterogeneous, stratifying the population into homogeneous subpopulations may be advantageous. Each stratum should differ from the others, but the items within each stratum should be similar. Number of items is not usually associated with the risk of misstatement.

Answer (A) is incorrect. The risk of misstatement is correlated with fair value. Answer (C) is incorrect. The risk of misstatement is correlated with turnover. Answer (D) is incorrect. The risk of misstatement is correlated with location.

14.1.48. Stratified mean-per-unit (MPU) sampling is a statistical technique that may be more efficient than unstratified MPU because it usually

A. May be applied to populations in which many monetary misstatements are expected to occur.

B. Produces an estimate having a desired level of precision with a smaller sample size.

C. Increases the variability among items in a stratum by grouping sampling units with similar characteristics.

D. Yields a weighted sum of the strata standard deviations that is greater than the standard deviation of the population.

Answer (B) is correct. *(CPA, adapted)*

REQUIRED: The reason for using stratification.

DISCUSSION: The primary objective of stratification is to reduce the effect of high variability by dividing the population into subpopulations. Reducing the variance within each subpopulation allows the auditor to sample a smaller number of items while holding precision and confidence level constant.

Answer (A) is incorrect. The number of misstatements in the population is independent of the advantages of stratification. Answer (C) is incorrect. Stratification is used to decrease the effects of variation within the strata. Answer (D) is incorrect. The standard deviation, which measures variation, should be less within the strata than for the population as a whole.

14.1.49. Which of the following is not a criterion for a good, stratified random sampling plan?

A. Every item must belong to one and only one stratum.

B. The original population of items must be normally distributed.

C. An identifiable means of subdividing a heterogeneous population into groups with more homogeneous characteristics must be available.

D. The number of items in each group must be known or determinable.

Answer (B) is correct. *(CIA, adapted)*

REQUIRED: The condition not a criterion for stratified sampling.

DISCUSSION: The population need not be normally distributed. Indeed, the purpose of stratification is to overcome skewness of distribution in the original population by defining subpopulations that are as nearly homogeneous as possible.

Answer (A) is incorrect. A necessary condition for stratification is that every item belong to one and only one stratum. Answer (C) is incorrect. A necessary condition for stratification is that an identifiable means of subdividing a heterogeneous population into groups with more homogeneous characteristics be available. Answer (D) is incorrect. A necessary condition for stratification is that the number of items in each group be known or determinable.

14.1.50. An accounts receivable aging schedule was prepared on 300 pages with each page containing the aging data for 50 accounts. The pages were numbered from 1 to 300 and the accounts listed on each were numbered from 1 to 50. An auditor selected accounts receivable for confirmation using a table of numbers as illustrated:

Select Column from Table of Numbers	Separate Five Digits: First Three Digits Last Two Digits
02011	020-11[x]
85393	853-93*
97265	972-65*
61680	616-80*
16656	166-56*
42751	427-51*
69994	699-94*
07942	079-42[y]
10231	102-31[z]
53988	539-88*

x Mailed confirmation to account 11 listed on p. 20.
y Mailed confirmation to account 42 listed on p. 79.
z Mailed confirmation to account 31 listed on p. 102.
* Rejected.

This is an example of which of the following sampling methods?

A. Acceptance sampling.

B. Systematic sampling.

C. Sequential sampling.

D. Random sampling.

Answer (D) is correct. *(CPA, adapted)*

REQUIRED: The appropriate term associated with the sampling method illustrated.

DISCUSSION: This sampling method is random. When random sampling is used, each item in the population has an equal or known and nonzero chance of being selected for inclusion in the sample. The auditor selected a random sample using a random number table. Before this approach can be used, a correspondence between the random numbers and the items in the population must be established. The relationship was established by designating the first three digits from the random number table as corresponding to the page number and the last two digits as corresponding to the item number. The number 85393 is rejected because (1) the page number (853) does not lie between 1 and 300, and (2) the item number (93) does not lie between 1 and 50. If either of these conditions occurs, the random number is rejected. If the random number falls within both ranges (e.g., 02011), the item corresponding to the random number is included in the sample. The eleventh item on page 20 is therefore chosen for confirmation.

Answer (A) is incorrect. Acceptance sampling is a form of attribute sampling. The described plan tests the balance of the account and is therefore an example of variables sampling. Answer (B) is incorrect. Systematic sampling is a special type of random sampling that needs no correspondence between random numbers and items in the population. Answer (C) is incorrect. Sequential (stop-or-go) sampling needs no correspondence between random numbers and items in the population.

14.1.51. In a regional survey of suburban households to obtain data on television viewing habits, a statistical sample of suburban areas is first selected. Within the chosen areas, statistical samples of whole blocks are selected, and, within the selected blocks, random samples of households are selected. This type of sample selection can best be described as

A. Attribute sampling.

B. Stratified sampling.

C. Cluster sampling.

D. Interval sampling.

Answer (C) is correct. *(CIA, adapted)*

REQUIRED: The sampling method used to select random samples from statistically selected groups.

DISCUSSION: Block (cluster) sampling selects groups of items rather than individual items. For this plan to be effective, dispersion within clusters should be greater than dispersion among clusters. If blocks of homogeneous items are selected, the sample will be biased. Cluster sampling is most appropriate when each group is representative of the entire population.

Answer (A) is incorrect. Attribute sampling is not a selection technique. Answer (B) is incorrect. Stratified sampling separates the population into several strata, with the elements in each stratum possessing some common attribute. The sample is then chosen using a statistical sampling approach. Answer (D) is incorrect. Interval sampling selects every *n*th item for sampling with a randomized starting point.

14.1.52. Which of the following is a false statement about cluster sample selection?

A. Every item in the sample must correspond to a random number.

B. Sample groups of items rather than individual items are selected.

C. Cluster sampling is normally used when the sampling units (documents) are filed sequentially.

D. Dispersion within clusters should be greater than between clusters.

Answer (A) is correct. *(Publisher, adapted)*

REQUIRED: The false statement about cluster sampling.

DISCUSSION: Because cluster sampling entails selection of groups rather than individual items from a population, random numbers are not assigned to individual items within the population. Rather, clusters or blocks are randomly selected for audit.

Answer (B) is incorrect. Cluster sampling selects blocks or clusters of items rather than individual items for audit. Answer (C) is incorrect. When documents are sequentially filed, time can be saved by selecting blocks rather than individual items from the population. Answer (D) is incorrect. Dispersion within the clusters should be large, and dispersion among the clusters should be small.

14.1.53. An auditor is designing a sampling plan to test the accuracy of daily production reports over the past 3 years. All of the reports contain the same information except that Friday reports also contain weekly totals and are prepared by managers rather than by supervisors. Production normally peaks near the end of a month. If the auditor wants to select two reports per month using an interval sampling plan, which of the following techniques reduces the likelihood of bias in the sample?

A. Estimating the rate of misstatements in the population.

B. Using multiple random starts.

C. Increasing the confidence level.

D. Increasing the precision.

Answer (B) is correct. *(CIA, adapted)*

REQUIRED: The technique that reduces the chance of bias in the sample.

DISCUSSION: Systematic (interval) sampling entails choosing a random start and then selecting subsequent items at fixed intervals. However, if the population is not random, for example, because it exhibits cyclical variation, the results will be biased. This bias may be overcome by taking repeated systematic samples, each with a random start. In effect, each possible systematic sample in the population is a cluster. Thus, the repeated systematic samples, each with a random start, constitute a random sample of clusters.

Answer (A) is incorrect. Estimating the rate of misstatements in the population has no effect on bias. Bias is related to the selection method. Answer (C) is incorrect. Increasing the confidence level has no effect on bias. Answer (D) is incorrect. Increasing the precision has no effect on bias.

14.1.54. An auditor desires to use a table of random digits to select a sample from a population of documents that have the following broken number sequences: 0001-1000, 2000-5000, and 8000-11000. Which of the following is the most efficient approach to overcome the problem of the broken number sequences?

A. Deduct four-digit constant values from the second and third sequences, choose the appropriate random numbers, and add the constants back to the individual numbers.

B. Skip through the entire random number tables until large blocks of digits appear that will fit within the three different number sequences.

C. Choose appropriate random numbers from the tables without modifying the approach and recognize that a large selection of unusable numbers will occur.

D. Select three different starting points in the random tables and vary the selection pattern to obtain needed numbers in the three different sequences.

Answer (A) is correct. *(CIA, adapted)*

REQUIRED: The most efficient approach to overcoming the problem of broken number sequences when using a random digits table.

DISCUSSION: Efficient use of random digits tables often requires that constants be subtracted from the items in the population so that it more closely matches the numbers in the table. After an acceptable number is found in the table, the constant is added back to determine which item is selected. Randomness of selection is not impaired by this technique.

Answer (B) is incorrect. Random digits tables do not contain large blocks of usable numbers. Answer (C) is incorrect. Selecting many unusable numbers is inefficient. Answer (D) is incorrect. Use of random digits tables requires a single starting point and a consistent selection pattern.

14.1.55. The size of a sample designed for dual-purpose testing should be

A. The larger of the samples that would otherwise have been designed for the two separate purposes.

B. The smaller of the samples that would otherwise have been designed for the two separate purposes.

C. The combined total of the samples that would otherwise have been designed for the two separate purposes.

D. More than the larger of the samples that would otherwise have been designated for the two separate purposes, but less than the combined total of the samples that would otherwise have been designed for the two separate purposes.

Answer (A) is correct. *(CPA, adapted)*

REQUIRED: The true statement about sample size for dual-purpose testing.

DISCUSSION: Dual-purpose testing is the use of a sample for both tests of controls and substantive testing. It is customarily used when the auditor believes that the rate of deviations from the prescribed control in the population is acceptable. Thus, a related substantive procedure might be planned at a level of risk that anticipates a low assessed risk of material misstatement. The sample size should be the larger of the samples that would otherwise have been designed for the two separate purposes.

14.1.56. The advantage of selecting a sample by cluster is that this method

A. Increases the precision and confidence level of the sample.

B. Reduces the time required to locate the individual items chosen for examination.

C. Decreases the standard deviation of the sample.

D. Decreases sample size.

Answer (B) is correct. *(Publisher, adapted)*

REQUIRED: The advantage of cluster sampling.

DISCUSSION: The use of cluster or block sampling may allow the auditor to select on a random basis a large set of data (a block) to be examined. Because the auditor need not establish a correspondence between random numbers and items in the population, time may be saved.

Answer (A) is incorrect. The precision and confidence level of the sample are independent of the sample selection method. Answer (C) is incorrect. The standard deviation of the sample is independent of the sample selection method. Answer (D) is incorrect. Sample size is independent of the sample selection method.

14.1.57. A number of factors influence the sample size for a substantive test of details of an account balance. All other factors being equal, which of the following would lead to a larger sample size?

A. A lower assessed risk of material misstatement.

B. Increased use of analytical procedures to obtain evidence about particular assertions.

C. Smaller expected frequency of deviations.

D. Smaller measure of tolerable misstatement.

Answer (D) is correct. *(CPA, adapted)*

REQUIRED: The factor leading to a larger sample.

DISCUSSION: Holding the risk of incorrect acceptance constant, a reduction in acceptable tolerable misstatement would require the auditor to select a larger sample. The larger sample would reduce the allowance for sampling risk.

Answer (A) is incorrect. As the assessed RMM decreases, the acceptable level of detection risk for a given audit risk increases. Substantive procedures are applied to reduce detection risk to the acceptable level. As that level rises, the assurance that must be provided by substantive procedures declines. Smaller samples may therefore be appropriate when acceptable detection risk increases. Answer (B) is incorrect. The auditor's substantive procedures to achieve an audit objective related to a particular assertion may include tests of details, analytical procedures, or a combination. Thus, use of analytical procedures might reduce the need for tests of details. Answer (C) is incorrect. Frequency of deviations relates sampling for attributes, not for variables.

14.1.58. An auditor initially planned to use unrestricted random sampling with replacement in the audit of accounts receivable. Later, the auditor decided to use unrestricted random sampling without replacement. As a result of this decision, the sample size should

A. Increase.

B. Remain the same.

C. Decrease.

D. Either increase or decrease, but the direction cannot be determined.

Answer (C) is correct. *(CPA, adapted)*

REQUIRED: The effect of sampling without replacement on the sample size.

DISCUSSION: Unrestricted random sampling means that each item in the population has an equal and nonzero chance of being selected. Sampling with replacement means that an item may be included more than once in the sample. Sampling without replacement removes an item from the population after selection. Thus, sampling without replacement uses information about the population more efficiently. It results in a smaller sample, if other things are held constant, because the sample size formula for sampling with replacement is multiplied by the finite population correction factor (always less than 1.0).

14.1.59. What effect does an increase in the standard deviation have on the required sample size of mean-per-unit estimation and monetary-unit sampling? Assume no change in any of the other characteristics of the population and no change in desired precision and confidence.

	Mean-per-Unit Estimation	Monetary-Unit Sampling
A.	Decrease in sample size	No change in sample size
B.	No change in sample size	Decrease in sample size
C.	Increase in sample size	No change in sample size
D.	No change in sample size	Increase in sample size

Answer (C) is correct. *(CIA, adapted)*

REQUIRED: The effect of an increase in the standard deviation on the required sample size.

DISCUSSION: An increase in the standard deviation represents an increase in the variability of the population. It therefore requires increasing the sample size when MPU is used. A sample for an MPU application is determined from the standard variables sampling sample size formula. The MUS sample size formula does not include the population standard deviation or other measure of variability. The sampling units consist of individual monetary units. Hence, they are homogeneous, and no measure of their variability is necessary.

14.2 Statistical Sampling in Tests of Controls (Attribute Sampling)

14.2.1. Statistical sampling may be used to test the effectiveness of controls. The auditor's procedures should result in a statistical conclusion about

A. Population characteristics occurring at least once in the population.

B. The population value not being misstated by more than a fixed amount.

C. Monetary precision exceeding a certain predetermined amount.

D. The relation of the population deviation rate to the tolerable rate.

Answer (D) is correct. *(Publisher, adapted)*

REQUIRED: The conclusion that can be drawn from statistical tests of controls.

DISCUSSION: The auditor uses attribute sampling to test the effectiveness of controls. The auditor is concerned with the occurrence rate of procedural deviations in the population. Attribute sampling enables the auditor to estimate the occurrence rate of deviations and to determine the relation of the estimated rate to the tolerable rate.

Answer (A) is incorrect. The only way to be certain that a characteristic occurs at least once is to examine items until one is located. Answer (B) is incorrect. Variables sampling is concerned with quantities (e.g., population totals). Answer (C) is incorrect. Variables sampling is concerned with dollar values (e.g., monetary precision), whereas attribute sampling is concerned with deviation rates.

14.2.2. An auditor plans to examine a sample of 20 purchase orders for proper approvals as prescribed by the client's internal control. One of the purchase orders in the chosen sample of 20 cannot be found, and the auditor is unable to use alternative procedures to test whether that purchase order was properly approved. The auditor should

A. Choose another purchase order to replace the missing purchase order in the sample.

B. Consider this test of controls invalid and proceed with substantive procedures because internal control is ineffective.

C. Treat the missing purchase order as a deviation for the purpose of evaluating the sample.

D. Select a completely new set of 20 purchase orders.

Answer (C) is correct. *(CPA, adapted)*

REQUIRED: The effect of failure to locate a sample item.

DISCUSSION: If the auditor is not able to apply the planned audit procedures or appropriate alternative procedures to selected items, (s)he should consider the reasons for this limitation. Furthermore, the auditor ordinarily should consider those selected items to be deviations from the procedures for the purpose of evaluating the sample.

Answer (A) is incorrect. The auditor should choose another purchase order only if an item in the sample is not used, e.g., if it is properly voided. Answer (B) is incorrect. The sampling plan could be completed by counting the missing purchase order as a deviation. Answer (D) is incorrect. Selecting a new sample is unnecessary.

14.2.3. An auditor planning an attribute sample from a large number of invoices intends to estimate the actual rate of deviations. Which factor below is the most important for the auditor to consider?

A. Audit objective.

B. Population size.

C. Desired confidence level.

D. Population variance.

Answer (A) is correct. *(CIA, adapted)*

REQUIRED: The most important factor in planning an attribute sample.

DISCUSSION: Attribute sampling enables the auditor to estimate the occurrence rate in a population and to determine the relation of the estimated rate to the tolerable rate. However, the audit objective must be known before audit procedures can be designed and their results evaluated.

Answer (B) is incorrect. Knowing the population is large is sufficient. Answer (C) is incorrect. The desired confidence level is a function of the purposes to be served by the audit. Answer (D) is incorrect. The variance is calculated in variables, not attribute, sampling applications.

14.2.4. Statistical sampling usually may be applied in tests of controls when the client's internal controls

A. Depend primarily on appropriate segregation of duties.

B. Are carefully reduced to writing and are included in client accounting manuals.

C. Leave an audit trail in the form of documentary evidence of their effectiveness.

D. Enable the detection of material fraud in the accounting records.

Answer (C) is correct. *(CPA, adapted)*

REQUIRED: The condition permitting use of statistical sampling in tests of controls.

DISCUSSION: Sampling is useful when a population can be identified from which to sample. When attribute sampling is applied in tests of controls, an audit trail of documents and notations on them (such as signatures) should exist to provide evidence of the effectiveness of the control.

Answer (A) is incorrect. Segregation of duties is tested through inquiry and observation rather than through sampling. Answer (B) is incorrect. The auditor is more concerned with the existence and effectiveness of controls than their documentation. Answer (D) is incorrect. Controls, if appropriate, always are expected to detect material fraud.

14.2.5. For which of the following audit tests would an auditor most likely use attribute sampling?

A. Making an independent estimate of the amount of a LIFO inventory.

B. Examining invoices in support of the measurement of fixed asset additions.

C. Selecting accounts receivable for confirmation of account balances.

D. Inspecting employee time cards for proper approval by supervisors.

Answer (D) is correct. *(CPA, adapted)*

REQUIRED: The appropriate use of attribute sampling.

DISCUSSION: The auditor uses attribute sampling to test the effectiveness of controls. Attribute sampling enables the auditor to estimate the occurrence rate of deviations and to determine its relation to the tolerable deviation rate. Thus, a control, such as proper approval of time cards by supervisors, can be tested for effectiveness using attribute sampling.

Answer (A) is incorrect. Variables sampling is useful in estimating the amount of inventory. Answer (B) is incorrect. Examining invoices in support of the measurement of fixed asset additions is a substantive test for which variables sampling is appropriate. Answer (C) is incorrect. The selection of accounts receivable for confirmation is a substantive test.

14.2.6. In testing payroll transactions, an auditor discovers that 4 out of a statistical sample of 100 selected time cards were not signed by the appropriate supervisor. To evaluate the materiality or significance of this control deficiency, the auditor should

A. Compare the tolerable deviation rate with the expected deviation rate.

B. Compute an upper precision limit and compare with the tolerable deviation rate.

C. Evaluate the dollar amount of the four time cards in relation to the financial statements.

D. Report the deviations and let management assess the significance because they are in the best position to know.

Answer (B) is correct. *(CIA, adapted)*

REQUIRED: The procedure applied to evaluate the materiality of the control deficiency.

DISCUSSION: After specifying the confidence level and tolerable rate of deviations, the auditor determines the sample size and precision. The tolerable rate is the rate the auditor is willing to accept without altering the assessed level of control risk. The achieved precision is the range of values constructed based on a statistic derived from a random sample. At the stated confidence level, the auditor expects this range to contain the true population value. In this attribute sampling application, the upper, but not the lower, precision limit is of interest. This limit should be compared with the maximum tolerable rate.

Answer (A) is incorrect. Both the expected deviation rate and the tolerable rate are known before sampling. Answer (C) is incorrect. Any monetary misstatement in the sample must first be extrapolated to the population before the significance can be assessed. Answer (D) is incorrect. The auditor should determine the significance of detected deviations.

14.2.7. In addition to evaluating the frequency of deviations in tests of controls, an auditor should also consider certain qualitative aspects of the deviations. The auditor most likely would give broader consideration to the implications of a deviation if it was

A. The only deviation discovered in the sample.

B. Identical to a deviation discovered during the prior year's audit.

C. Caused by an employee's misunderstanding of instructions.

D. Initially concealed by a forged document.

Answer (D) is correct. *(CPA, adapted)*

REQUIRED: The aspect of a control deviation requiring broader consideration.

DISCUSSION: The discovery of a fraud ordinarily requires broader consideration than the discovery of an error. The discovery of an initially concealed forged document indicates that the integrity of employees may be in doubt.

Answer (A) is incorrect. A single deviation discovered in a sample may not cause major concern. Answer (B) is incorrect. Deviations are often repetitive. Discovery of an identical deviation in a subsequent year is not unusual. Answer (C) is incorrect. A misunderstanding is an error rather than fraud and does not necessarily arouse concern.

14.2.8. The tolerable deviation rate for a test of controls depends primarily on which of the following?

A. The cause of the deviations.

B. The effect on substantive procedures of the auditor's assessment of the risks of material misstatement.

C. The amount of any substantive misstatement.

D. The limit used in audits of similar clients.

Answer (B) is correct. *(L.M. Bailey)*

REQUIRED: The determinant of the tolerable rate.

DISCUSSION: The auditor seeks to obtain an appropriate level of assurance (complement of the risk of overreliance) that the actual deviation rate in the population is not greater than the rate set by the auditor (tolerable deviation rate). The auditor decides the desired level of assurance based on the extent to which the auditor's risk assessment considers relevant internal controls (AU-C 530). The auditor tests controls if (1) substantive procedures alone do not provide sufficient appropriate evidence at the assertion level or (2) the auditor's assessed RMMs at the assertion level include an expectation of the operating effectiveness of the controls. In the second case, the auditor intends to rely on the effectiveness of controls to determine the nature, timing, and extent of further audit procedures (AU-C 530).

Answer (A) is incorrect. The cause of the deviations is unknown prior to testing. The auditor sets the tolerable rate prior to such tests. Answer (C) is incorrect. The misstatement is unknown prior to testing. Answer (D) is incorrect. Audit clients are unlikely to be so similar that the same tolerable rate can be used.

14.2.9. The diagram below depicts the auditor's estimated maximum deviation rate compared with the tolerable deviation rate and also depicts the true population deviation rate compared with the tolerable deviation rate.

Auditor's Estimate Based on Sample Results	True State of Population: Deviation rate is less than tolerable rate.	Deviation rate exceeds tolerable rate.
Maximum deviation rate is less than tolerable rate.	I. Correct	III. Incorrect
Maximum deviation rate exceeds tolerable rate.	II. Incorrect	IV. Correct

As a result of testing controls, the auditor underrelies on the controls and increases substantive testing. This is illustrated by situation

A. I.

B. II.

C. III.

D. IV.

Answer (B) is correct. *(CPA, adapted)*

REQUIRED: The situation that involves underreliance.

DISCUSSION: The risk of underreliance (situation II) is one aspect of sampling risk in testing controls. It is the risk that the controls are more effective than indicated by the sample. Like the risk of incorrect rejection in substantive testing, the risk of underreliance relates to the efficiency, not effectiveness, of the audit. It ordinarily leads to application of further audit procedures and ultimate arrival at the correct conclusion.

Answer (A) is incorrect. In situation I, the auditor properly should rely on the controls. Answer (C) is incorrect. In situation III, the sample might lead to overreliance. Answer (D) is incorrect. In situation IV, the auditor properly should not rely on the controls.

14.2.10. Which of the following statements is true concerning statistical sampling in tests of controls?

A. As the population size increases, the sample size should increase proportionately.

B. Deviations from specific control activities increase the likelihood of misstatements but do not always cause misstatements.

C. There is an inverse relationship between the expected population deviation rate and the sample size.

D. In determining the tolerable deviation rate, an auditor considers detection risk and the sample size.

Answer (B) is correct. *(CPA, adapted)*

REQUIRED: The true statement about statistical sampling in tests of controls.

DISCUSSION: Deviations from a specific control increase the risk of misstatements in the accounting records but do not always result in misstatements. Thus, deviations from a specific control at a given rate ordinarily result in misstatements at the financial statement level at a lower rate.

Answer (A) is incorrect. As population size increases, the required sample size increases at a decreasing rate. Answer (C) is incorrect. The relationship between the expected population deviation rate and the required sample size is direct. Answer (D) is incorrect. The tolerable rate depends on the planned assessed risk of material misstatement and the assurance to be provided by the evidence in the sample.

14.2.11. As a result of sampling procedures applied as tests of controls, an auditor incorrectly assesses the risk of overreliance too low. The most likely explanation for this situation is that

A. The deviation rates of both the auditor's sample and the population exceed the tolerable rate.

B. The deviation rates of both the auditor's sample and the population are less than the tolerable rate.

C. The deviation rate in the auditor's sample is less than the tolerable rate, but the deviation rate in the population exceeds the tolerable rate.

D. The deviation rate in the auditor's sample exceeds the tolerable rate, but the deviation rate in the population is less than the tolerable rate.

Answer (C) is correct. *(CPA, adapted)*

REQUIRED: The most likely explanation for assessing the risk of overreliance too low.

DISCUSSION: When the deviation rate in the sample is less than the tolerable rate, the auditor concludes that the controls tested are effective. If, in fact, the true deviation rate in the population is greater than the tolerable rate, control is less effective than indicated by the sample.

Answer (A) is incorrect. If the sample rate and the population rate are both greater than the tolerable rate, the auditor's conclusion should be accurate. Answer (B) is incorrect. If the sample rate and the population rate are both less than the tolerable rate, the auditor's conclusion should be accurate. Answer (D) is incorrect. If the sample rate exceeds the population rate, the auditor is likely to assess the risk of overreliance too high.

Questions 14.2.12 through 14.2.15 are based on the following information.

Confidence Level	Deviation Rate	Field Size	Sample Sizes for Precision of +1%	+2%	+3%	+4%	+5%	+6%	+8%	+10%
95%	10%	200					82	65		
		400			196	140	103	77		
		500			217	151	108	81		
		1,000		464	278	178	121	88	51	50
		2,000		604	322	195	129	92	53	51
99%	10%	200						91	64	
		400				193	149	117	76	52
		500				214	162	124	79	53
		1,000			399	272	193	142	85	56
		2,000		854	498	314	213	153	89	58

14.2.12. You are using attribute sampling to test the effectiveness of a control over a file of 1,000 purchase orders. You expect a 10% deviation rate in the population and would like to select a sample sufficiently large to provide a precision of 10% with a 99% level of confidence. What sample size is needed?

A. 50

B. 56

C. 121

D. 193

Answer (B) is correct. *(CIA, adapted)*

REQUIRED: The determined sample size.

DISCUSSION: For a population of 1,000, an expected deviation rate of 10%, a confidence level of 99%, and a precision of 10%, the attribute sampling table specifies a minimum sample size of 56.

Answer (A) is incorrect. The minimum sample size for a confidence level of 95% is 50. Answer (C) is incorrect. The minimum sample size for a confidence level of 95% and a precision of 5% is 121. Answer (D) is incorrect. The minimum sample size for a population of 400 and a precision of 4% is 193.

14.2.13. You are using attribute sampling to test the effectiveness of a control over a file of 1,000 purchase orders. You expect a 10% deviation rate in the population and would like your sample results to vary by no more than 40 purchase orders. If you selected a sample size of 178, how reliable will you conclude your sample results to be?

A. 90%

B. 95%

C. 96%

D. 99%

Answer (B) is correct. *(CIA, adapted)*

REQUIRED: The determined reliability.

DISCUSSION: For a population of 1,000, an expected deviation rate of 10%, a precision of 4% (40 ÷ 1,000), and a sample size of 178, the attribute sampling table specifies a 95% confidence level or reliability.

Answer (A) is incorrect. The table gives no values for a confidence level of 90%. Answer (C) is incorrect. The table gives no values for a confidence level of 96%. Answer (D) is incorrect. The sample size for a population of 1,000, precision of 4%, and a 10% deviation rate is 272.

14.2.14. You used attribute sampling to test a population of 1,000 purchase orders, and the results showed a deviation rate of 9%. If your sample size was 85 and your confidence level was 99%, what was the upper occurrence limit?

A. 17%

B. 9%

C. 8%

D. 1%

Answer (A) is correct. *(CIA, adapted)*

REQUIRED: The determined upper occurrence limit.

DISCUSSION: For a population size of 1,000, a confidence level of 99%, and a sample size of 85, the precision is +8%. Given the deviation rate of 9%, the upper occurrence limit is 17% (8% + 9%).

Answer (B) is incorrect. The deviation rate is 9%. Answer (C) is incorrect. The precision is 8%. Answer (D) is incorrect. The difference between the precision and the deviation rate is 1%, which has no relevance.

14.2.15. You used attribute sampling to test a population of 2,000 purchase orders. Using a reliability level of 99%, an expected deviation rate of 10%, and a sample size of 195, the precision is

A. More than 5%.

B. More than 3% but less than 5%.

C. More than 6% but less than 8%.

D. Indeterminable from the data given.

Answer (A) is correct. *(CIA, adapted)*

REQUIRED: The determined precision.

DISCUSSION: At the 99% confidence level and population size of 2,000, the attribute sampling table shows that a sample size of 195 has a precision of between 5% and 6%.

Answer (B) is incorrect. At the 95% confidence level and a population size of 2,000, a sample size of 195 has a precision of 4%. Answer (C) is incorrect. A sample of 195 has a precision of less than 6% for all values in the table. Answer (D) is incorrect. The precision is determinable from the data given.

14.2.16. A test of 200 invoices randomly selected by the auditor revealed that 35 had not been approved for payment. At the 95% confidence level, what precision can be assigned?

A. 6.9%

B. 5.3%

C. 9.1%

D. 3.5%

Answer (B) is correct. *(CIA, adapted)*

REQUIRED: The achieved precision.

DISCUSSION: The following sample size formula for an attribute sampling application can be solved for precision:

$$n = \frac{C^2pq}{P^2}$$

C is the confidence coefficient, *p* is the expected deviation rate, *q* is 1 – *p*, *P* is the specified precision rate, and *n* is the sample size.

$$P^2 = \frac{(1.96)^2 \times (35 \div 200) \times [1 - (35 \div 200)]}{200}$$

$$P^2 = .0028$$

$$P = .053 \text{ or } 5.3\%$$

14.2.17. What is an auditor's evaluation of a statistical sample for attributes when a test of 50 documents results in 3 deviations if the tolerable rate is 7%, the expected population deviation rate is 5%, and the allowance for sampling risk is 2%?

A. Modify the planned assessed risk of material misstatement because the tolerable deviation rate plus the allowance for sampling risk exceeds the expected population deviation rate.

B. Accept the sample results as support for the assessed risk of material misstatement because the sample deviation rate plus the allowance for sampling risk exceeds the tolerable deviation rate.

C. Accept the sample results as support for the assessed risk of material misstatement because the tolerable deviation rate minus the allowance for sampling risk equals the expected population deviation rate.

D. Modify the assessed risk of material misstatement because the sample deviation rate plus the allowance for sampling risk exceeds the tolerable deviation rate.

Answer (D) is correct. *(CPA, adapted)*

REQUIRED: The evaluation of an attribute sample given the deviations in the sample, sampling risk, tolerable rate, and expected rate.

DISCUSSION: The sample has a 6% (3 ÷ 50) deviation rate. The auditor's achieved upper deviation limit is 8% (6% + the 2% allowance for sampling risk). The allowance for sampling risk may be calculated from a standard table as the difference between the upper deviation limit and the sample rate. However, the allowance is given. Thus, the true deviation rate could be as large as 8% and exceed the tolerable rate. Accordingly, the auditor should revise the assessed risk of material misstatement for the relevant assertions and possibly alter the nature, timing, and extent of substantive procedures.

Answer (A) is incorrect. The precision interval is constructed around the sample rate, not the tolerable deviation rate. Answer (B) is incorrect. A deviation rate that may be as large as 8% is a reason for revising the assessed risk of material misstatement. Answer (C) is incorrect. The sample deviation rate, which is the best estimate of the true rate, must not be ignored.

14.2.18. In evaluating an attribute sample, the estimated range that is expected to contain the population characteristic is the

A. Confidence level.

B. Precision.

C. Upper deviation limit.

D. Expected deviation rate.

Answer (B) is correct. *(CIA, adapted)*

REQUIRED: The range within which the estimate of the population characteristic is expected to fall.

DISCUSSION: Precision, or the confidence interval, is an interval around the sample statistic that is expected to contain the true population value. Precision for an attribute sample is based upon the tolerable rate of deviation. The upper limit of the interval is of greatest interest in attribute sampling applications.

Answer (A) is incorrect. The confidence level is the specified measure of how reliable the auditor wants the sample results to be. Answer (C) is incorrect. Precision is the range between the lower and upper deviation limits. Answer (D) is incorrect. The expected deviation rate is a measure of how frequently the auditor expects the characteristic of interest to exist in the population prior to selecting and evaluating the sample.

14.2.19. Which of the following combinations results in a decrease in sample size in an attribute sample?

	Allowable Risk of Overreliance	Tolerable Rate	Expected Population Deviation Rate
A.	Increase	Decrease	Increase
B.	Decrease	Increase	Decrease
C.	Increase	Increase	Decrease
D.	Increase	Increase	Increase

Answer (C) is correct. *(CPA, adapted)*

REQUIRED: The combination that results in a decrease in size in an attribute sample.

DISCUSSION: To determine the sample size for a test of controls, the auditor considers (1) the tolerable rate of deviations from the control being tested, (2) the expected actual rate of deviations, and (3) the allowable risk of overreliance. An increase in the allowable risk of overreliance, an increase in the tolerable rate, and a decrease in the expected rate each has the effect of reducing the required sample size.

14.2.20. An auditor should consider the tolerable rate of deviation when determining the number of check requests to select for a test to obtain assurance that all check requests have been properly authorized. The auditor should also consider

	The Average Dollar Value of the Check Requests	The Allowable Risk of Overreliance
A.	Yes	Yes
B.	Yes	No
C.	No	Yes
D.	No	No

Answer (C) is correct. *(CPA, adapted)*

REQUIRED: The issue(s), if any, to consider in determining the size of a sample in a test of controls.

DISCUSSION: Tests of controls, such as tests whether check requests have been properly authorized, are binary in nature. The auditor determines whether the control has been applied. Dollar amounts are irrelevant in this form of testing. However, in sampling, the auditor must consider the acceptable risk of overreliance to determine sample size. The auditor also must estimate a population deviation rate.

14.2.21. In an audit of a governmental agency, you are searching for expenditures that are improperly classified. Assuming a statistical sampling plan is adopted, which of the factors listed below most directly affects the number of items that you seek to review?

A. Magnitude of the budget for the agency.

B. Number of items you found misclassified in last year's audit.

C. Quality of internal control.

D. Estimated deviation rate.

Answer (D) is correct. *(CIA, adapted)*

REQUIRED: The most significant factor used in determining the size of the sample.

DISCUSSION: In the attribute sample size formula, the estimated deviation rate, its complement, and the square of the confidence coefficient are factors appearing in the numerator. The square of the precision is in the denominator.

Answer (A) is incorrect. Attribute sampling is concerned with deviation rates, not quantities or monetary amounts. Answer (B) is incorrect. Although the number of items misclassified in the previous period may be helpful, the auditor still must calculate the estimated deviation rate for the current period. Answer (C) is incorrect. The quality of internal control is not explicitly recognized in the sample size formula. However, the estimation of the deviation rate may be influenced by the auditor's understanding of internal control.

14.2.22. In attribute sampling, a 10% change in which of the following factors normally will have the least effect on the size of a statistical sample?

A. Population size.

B. Precision (confidence interval).

C. Reliability (confidence level).

D. Standard deviation.

Answer (A) is correct. *(CPA, adapted)*

REQUIRED: The factor having the least effect on sample sizes in attribute sampling.

DISCUSSION: A change in the size of the population has a very small effect on the required sample size when the population is large. This conclusion can be shown by analyzing the finite population correction factor sometimes applied to the standard sample size formula. An approximation of the FPC formula is

$$n = n'\sqrt{\frac{N - n'}{N}}$$

In this formula, *n'* equals the preliminary sample size, *n* equals the determined sample size, and *N* is the population size. Changes in *N* cause very little change in the expression; e.g., a reduction in the population such that the former sample size now constitutes about 20% of the reduced population only decreases the required sample size by about 10%.

Answer (B) is incorrect. Precision (confidence interval) has a major effect on sample size. Answer (C) is incorrect. Reliability (confidence level) has a major effect on sample size. Answer (D) is incorrect. Standard deviation has a major effect on sample size.

14.2.23. In testing a control, an auditor established an upper precision limit of 6% and a confidence level of 95%. The expected deviation rate was 4%. If the auditor expects a deviation rate of only 2% but wishes to retain the same upper precision limit and confidence level, the sample size should approximate

A. 518

B. 412

C. 369

D. 47

Answer (D) is correct. *(Publisher, adapted)*

REQUIRED: The effect of a change in occurrence rate on sample size.

DISCUSSION: In attribute sampling, the expected deviation rate varies directly with sample size. Thus, a reduction in the deviation rate should cause a reduction in the required sample size. Based on the attribute sampling formula below, the sample size should be the number calculated with the formula for sample size.

$$n = \frac{C^2pq}{P^2} = \frac{1.96^2 \times .02 \times .98}{.04^2} = 47$$

The variable *C* is the confidence coefficient, *p* is the deviation rate, *q* is 100% minus *p*, *P* is the specified precision interval (tolerable rate minus the expected occurrence rate), and *n* is the sample size. The specified precision is equal to the desired upper precision limit minus the occurrence rate. In this example, *P* increases from 2% to 4%.

14.2.24. If all other sample size planning factors were exactly the same in attribute sampling, changing the confidence level from 95% to 90% and changing the desired precision from 2% to 5% would result in a revised sample size that is

A. Larger.

B. Smaller.

C. Unchanged.

D. Indeterminate.

Answer (B) is correct. *(CIA, adapted)*

REQUIRED: The sample size effect of decreasing the confidence level and widening the desired precision interval.

DISCUSSION: If *C* is the confidence coefficient, *p* is the expected deviation rate, *q* is 100% minus *p*, and *P* is the desired precision, the basic sample-size formula for attribute sampling is

$$n = \frac{C^2pq}{P^2}$$

Thus, if the confidence level is reduced (the numerator item *C* is lower) and precision is widened (the denominator item *P* is greater), sample size will be smaller.

Answer (A) is incorrect. Increasing *C* and narrowing *P* would result in a larger sample size. Answer (C) is incorrect. Decreasing *C* and widening *P* decreases the sample size. Answer (D) is incorrect. Decreasing *C* and widening *P* decreases the sample size.

Questions 14.2.25 and 14.2.26 are based on the following information.

Determination of Sample Size
RISK LEVEL -- 10% (90% RELIABILITY)

Sample Size	Occurrence Rate (%)				
	1.0	2.0	3.0	4.0	5.0
	Upper Precision Limit (%)				
100	3.3	5.2	6.6	7.8	9.1
200	2.6	4.0	5.2	6.4	7.6
300	2.2	3.5	4.7	5.9	7.0
350		3.3		5.7	
400	2.0	3.2	4.4	5.6	6.7
450		3.1		5.5	
500	1.8	3.1	4.2	5.4	6.5
550		3.0		5.3	
600	1.7	2.9	4.1	5.2	6.3
700	1.7	2.9	4.0	5.1	6.2

14.2.25. If 10% risk (90% reliability) is acceptable with an expected occurrence rate of 3% and an upper precision limit (tolerable rate) of 5%, the minimum sample size should be

A. 117

B. 240

C. 300

D. 550

Answer (B) is correct. *(CIA, adapted)*

REQUIRED: The minimum sample size given risk, expected occurrence rate, and an upper precision limit.

DISCUSSION: At an occurrence rate of 3%, the sample size for an upper precision limit of 5.2% is 200. For a limit of 4.7%, the sample size is 300. For a limit of 5%, interpolation yields a sample size of 240.

$$\left[\frac{(5.2 - 5.0)}{(5.2 - 4.7)} \times (300 - 200)\right] + 200 = 240$$

Answer (A) is incorrect. A sample size of 117 signifies an upper precision limit between 6.6% and 5.2%. Answer (C) is incorrect. A sample size of 300 corresponds to an upper precision limit of 4.7%. Answer (D) is incorrect. A sample size of 550 relates to an upper precision limit between 4.2% and 4.1%.

14.2.26. At 10% risk (90% reliability), a sample of 200 items has been drawn and tested. The upper precision limit (tolerable rate) is 3%. Which of the following statements is true?

A. If four deviations were found, the population would be acceptable.

B. If two deviations were found, the population would be acceptable.

C. A tolerable rate of 3% indicates a high planned assessed level of control risk for the control tested.

D. The auditor should assume that each deviation results in a misstatement in the accounting records.

Answer (B) is correct. *(CIA, adapted)*

REQUIRED: The true statement given risk, sample size, and the tolerable rate.

DISCUSSION: If the sample consists of 200 items and two deviations are found, the occurrence rate is 1%. At 90% reliability, the upper precision limit for an occurrence rate of 1% is 2.6%. The population is acceptable because one can state with 90% reliability that the true occurrence rate is 2.6% or less, which is less than the tolerable rate of 3%.

Answer (A) is incorrect. At an occurrence rate of 2% (four deviations in a sample of 200), the upper precision limit (4%) exceeds the tolerable rate (3%). Answer (C) is incorrect. A low tolerable rate suggests that the planned assessed level of control risk is low. Answer (D) is incorrect. A deviation does not signify a misstatement in the records.

14.3 Classical Variables Sampling (Mean-per-Unit)

14.3.1. Very small random samples (fewer than 30) should normally be avoided when using a variables sampling plan because

A. The estimated standard deviation of the population will increase disproportionately.

B. The skew of the distribution of sample means cannot be determined.

C. The estimated population mean value will increase disproportionately.

D. The size of the sampling risk will increase disproportionately.

Answer (D) is correct. *(CIA, adapted)*

REQUIRED: The reason to avoid small sample sizes.

DISCUSSION: When small samples are selected from a population, the chance is greater that the sample will not adequately represent the population. Small samples (fewer than 30) should therefore be avoided because of the increase in sampling risk.

Answer (A) is incorrect. If the sample is too small and is therefore not representative, the misstatement may lie in either direction, depending on the sample. Answer (B) is incorrect. The results of a small sample can be statistically evaluated, but they are usually not as precise or reliable as those achieved when the sample is larger. Thus, the mean, standard error, skewness, etc., are less useful for very small samples. Answer (C) is incorrect. If the sample is too small and is therefore not representative, the misstatement may lie in either direction, depending on the sample.

14.3.2. In applying variables sampling, an auditor attempts to

A. Estimate a qualitative characteristic of interest.

B. Determine various rates of occurrence for specified attributes.

C. Discover at least one instance of a critical deviation.

D. Predict a monetary population value within a range of precision.

Answer (D) is correct. *(CIA, adapted)*

REQUIRED: The purpose of variables sampling.

DISCUSSION: Variables sampling is used to estimate the value of a population. In auditing, this process entails estimating the monetary value of an account balance or other accounting total. The result is often stated in terms of a point estimate plus or minus a stated dollar value (the range of precision at the desired level of confidence).

Answer (A) is incorrect. The estimate is quantitative. Answer (B) is incorrect. Determining various rates of occurrence for specified attributes applies to attribute sampling. Answer (C) is incorrect. Discovering at least one instance of a critical deviation is the purpose of discovery sampling.

14.3.3. In estimation sampling for variables, which of the following must be known in order to estimate the appropriate sample size required to meet the auditor's needs in a given situation?

A. The qualitative aspects of misstatements.

B. The total dollar amount of the population.

C. The acceptable level of risk.

D. The estimated deviation rate in the population.

Answer (C) is correct. *(CPA, adapted)*

REQUIRED: The factor that must be known to estimate sample size.

DISCUSSION: Variables sampling is used in tests of details because it may be used to (1) estimate the amount of a variable, such as an account balance, and (2) quantify the risk that the estimate may not approximate the true value. For substantive tests of details, the sample size depends on the auditor's desired assurance (1.0 – the risk of incorrect acceptance) that tolerable misstatement is not less than actual misstatement in the population. The desired assurance may be based on, among other things, the following: (1) the assessed risk of material misstatement, (2) the assurance provided by other substantive procedures related to the same assertion, (3) tolerable misstatement, and (4) expected misstatement for the population. Accordingly, as the acceptable risk of incorrect acceptance decreases, the desired assurance increases, and the auditor decreases the tolerable misstatement.

Answer (A) is incorrect. Qualitative aspects of misstatements are a matter for sample evaluation, not sample size selection. Answer (B) is incorrect. Estimating the population value is the objective of the sample. Also, some sampling methods ignore the carrying amounts of individual sample items (such as MPU, or mean-per-unit sampling). Answer (D) is incorrect. Attribute sampling is concerned with deviation rates.

14.3.4. An auditor selected a random sample of 100 items from a population of 2,000 items. The total dollars in the sample were $10,000, and the standard deviation was $10. If the achieved precision based on this sample was plus or minus $4,000, the minimum acceptable value of the population would be

A. $204,000

B. $196,000

C. $199,000

D. $199,800

Answer (B) is correct. *(CIA, adapted)*

REQUIRED: The minimum acceptable value of the population.

DISCUSSION: The mean value of a sample item is $100 ($10,000 ÷ 100), so the estimated population value is $200,000. Given achieved precision of $4,000, the minimum acceptable value of the population is $196,000 ($200,000 – $4,000).

Answer (A) is incorrect. The amount of $204,000 results from adding $4,000. Answer (C) is incorrect. The amount of $199,000 subtracts the total standard deviation of the sample, assuming $10 is the standard deviation per sample item. Answer (D) is incorrect. The amount of $199,800 subtracts the standard deviation of the population, assuming $10 is the total standard deviation of the 100-item sample.

14.3.5. An auditor used a mean-per-unit sampling plan to estimate the average cost of repairing photocopy machines. The sample size was 50, and population size was 2,000. The mean of the sample was $75. The standard deviation was $14, and the standard error of the mean was $2. What is the achieved confidence interval at a 95% confidence level (Z = 2)?

A. $47 to $103.

B. $71 to $79.

C. $61 to $89.

D. $73 to $75.

Answer (B) is correct. *(CIA, adapted)*

REQUIRED: The achieved confidence interval for a given confidence level.

DISCUSSION: If *C* is the confidence coefficient, *n* is the sample size, and σ is the standard deviation, the following is the basic variables sampling formula solved for precision (P):

$$P = \frac{C\sigma}{\sqrt{n}}$$

If C is given as 2 (Z = 2), the confidence interval equals the mean plus or minus two times the standard error of the mean (σ ÷ √n = $2). Thus, the achieved confidence interval equals $75 ± $4, or $71 to $79.

Answer (A) is incorrect. The range of $47 to $103 equals two standard deviations above and below the mean. Answer (C) is incorrect. The range of $61 to $89 equals one standard deviation above and below the mean. Answer (D) is incorrect. The range of $73 to $75 equals one standard error below the mean.

14.3.6. In a variables sampling application, an auditor draws random samples from two equal-sized groups of inventory items. The mean value of the inventory in the first group was calculated to be $3,000, with a standard deviation of $500. The mean value of inventory in the second group was estimated to be $1,000, with a standard deviation of $90. If the auditor had drawn an unstratified sample from the entire population, the expected mean value of inventory would be $2,000, and the expected standard deviation would be

A. Between $90 and $500, but not $295.

B. Less than $90.

C. Greater than $500.

D. $295.

Answer (C) is correct. *(Publisher, adapted)*

REQUIRED: The standard deviation given an unstratified sample.

DISCUSSION: The standard deviation is a measure of variability within a population. The fact that the population was stratified indicates that each stratum has a smaller standard deviation than the population as a whole. If the two diverse populations are combined, the resulting standard deviation is likely to be larger than that of either of the separate strata. Because the standard deviations of the two strata were $500 and $90, the expected standard deviation is likely to be greater than $500.

Answer (A) is incorrect. The resulting standard deviation is likely to be larger than that of either of the separate strata. Answer (B) is incorrect. The resulting standard deviation is likely to be larger than that of either of the separate strata. Answer (D) is incorrect. The simple average of the standard deviations of the two strata is $295. The resulting standard deviation is likely to be larger than that of either of the separate strata.

14.3.7. An auditor's finding was stated as follows: "Twenty of one hundred randomly selected items tested revealed that $200 of cash discounts on purchases were lost."

This variables sampling finding is deficient because the

A. Recommendation specifies no action.

B. Sampling methodology is not defined.

C. Amount is not material.

D. Probable effect on the entire population is not provided.

Answer (D) is correct. *(CIA, adapted)*

REQUIRED: The reason the variables sampling finding is deficient.

DISCUSSION: The finding states the number of population items selected and the total amount of purchase discounts lost but does not extend the sample results to the population.

Answer (A) is incorrect. No action may be necessary if there is a reason for the loss of purchase discounts or if the amount is immaterial. Answer (B) is incorrect. The methodology was stated to be random sampling. Answer (C) is incorrect. The amount may or may not be material.

14.3.8. In an application of mean-per-unit sampling, the following information has been obtained:

Reported carrying amount	$600,000
Point estimate (estimated total value)	591,000
Allowance for sampling risk (precision)	± 22,000
Tolerable misstatement	± 45,000

The appropriate conclusion is that the reported carrying amount is

A. Acceptable only if the risk of incorrect rejection is at least twice the risk of incorrect acceptance.

B. Acceptable.

C. Not acceptable.

D. Acceptable only if the risk of incorrect acceptance is at least twice the risk of incorrect rejection.

Answer (B) is correct. *(CIA, adapted)*

REQUIRED: The correct conclusion given an application of mean-per-unit sampling.

DISCUSSION: In mean-per-unit sampling, the audit estimate of the population value is obtained by multiplying the number of items in the population by the average value of the audited sample items. The precision interval is constructed around the audited value of the sample items. When the point estimate of the audited population value is $591,000 with a precision interval of plus or minus $22,000, a carrying amount of $600,000 is acceptable because it falls within the allowance for sampling risk (precision). The precision is determined by considering the tolerable misstatement in conjunction with the allowable risk of incorrect acceptance (an issue related to audit effectiveness) and allowable risk of incorrect rejection (an efficiency issue). A table is typically consulted that gives the ratio of the precision to tolerable misstatement for the specified risks of incorrect rejection and incorrect acceptance. For example, the table sets precision at 50% of tolerable misstatement, or approximately $22,000, when the specified risk of incorrect acceptance is 50% of the risk of incorrect rejection.

Answer (A) is incorrect. The allowable risk of incorrect rejection is separately determined by the auditor based on professional judgment. Answer (C) is incorrect. The reported value is acceptable. Answer (D) is incorrect. The allowable risk of incorrect acceptance is separately determined by the auditor and based on professional judgment.

14.3.9. An auditor seeks to determine the misstatements made in recording sales invoices. Which of the following factors will usually be most significant in determining the number of sales invoices to select for testing?

A. The total number of invoices for the period.

B. The estimated loss being incurred by the division.

C. The amount of sales revenue considered to be material.

D. The precision desired.

Answer (D) is correct. *(CIA, adapted)*

REQUIRED: The factor most significant in determining the required sample size.

DISCUSSION: The auditor's precision is usually the most important factor in determining the number of sales invoices to be selected. The precision is squared before it is used in the sample size formula. Accordingly, relatively small changes in the desired precision have a great effect on the required sample size.

Answer (A) is incorrect. The population size has a relatively small effect on the required sample size. The finite population correction factor reduces the required sample size for samples that are large relative to the population. Answer (B) is incorrect. The estimated loss being incurred by the division is not a factor used in calculating sample size. Answer (C) is incorrect. The amount of sales considered to be material is not a factor used in calculating sample size.

14.3.10. An auditor is considering a sample size of 50 to estimate the average amount per invoice in a large trucking company. How will the precision of the sample results be affected if the sample size is increased to 200?

A. The larger sample will be about two times as precise as the smaller sample.

B. The larger sample will be about four times as precise as the smaller sample.

C. Although precision will not be increased that much, a possible downward bias in the estimate of the average per invoice would be corrected.

D. Both sample sizes are larger than 30, so the increase will not have that much of an effect on precision.

Answer (A) is correct. *(CIA, adapted)*

REQUIRED: The effect on precision of increasing the sample size.

DISCUSSION: In variables sampling, the precision of the sample results is inversely proportional to the square root of the sample size. Thus, increasing the sample by a factor of four decreases (tightens) the precision by a factor of two.

Answer (B) is incorrect. The precision of sample results does not increase at the same rate as sample size. Answer (C) is incorrect. The expected value of the sample mean is the same, regardless of sample size. Answer (D) is incorrect. Precision will tighten by a factor of two.

Questions 14.3.11 through 14.3.15 are based on the following information. The following table shows comparative population characteristics and audit specifications of two populations:

	Characteristics of Population 1 Relative to Population 2		Audit Specifications as to a Sample from Population 1 Relative to a Sample from Population 2	
	Size	Variability	Specified Precision	Specified Confidence Level
Case 1	Equal	Equal	Equal	Higher
Case 2	Equal	Larger	Wider	Equal
Case 3	Larger	Equal	Tighter	Lower
Case 4	Smaller	Smaller	Equal	Lower
Case 5	Larger	Equal	Equal	Higher

For this question (this case), you are to indicate the required sample size to be selected from Population 1 relative to the sample from Population 2.

The effects on sample size of changing the characteristics and specifications of two populations result from four factors in a variables sampling application: (1) population size, (2) variability of the population, (3) specified precision (allowance for sampling risk), and (4) specified confidence level (reliability). Increases in population size, variability, and specified confidence level cause sample sizes to become larger. Increases in specified precision cause sample sizes to become smaller.

14.3.11. In Case 1, the required sample size from Population 1 is

A. Larger than the required sample size from Population 2.

B. Equal to the required sample size from Population 2.

C. Smaller than the required sample size from Population 2.

D. Indeterminate relative to the required sample size from Population 2.

Answer (A) is correct. *(CPA, adapted)*

REQUIRED: The effects on sample size of changing the characteristics and specifications of two populations.

DISCUSSION: In Case 1, all other characteristics are the same except that Population 1 will have a higher specified confidence level. A higher confidence level has a higher confidence coefficient, which varies directly with sample size. Thus, the auditor must take a larger sample size from Population 1 than from Population 2.

14.3.12. In Case 2, the required sample size from Population 1 is

A. Larger than the required sample size from Population 2.

B. Equal to the required sample size from Population 2.

C. Smaller than the required sample size from Population 2.

D. Indeterminate relative to the required sample size from Population 2.

Answer (D) is correct. *(CPA, adapted)*

REQUIRED: The effects on sample size of changing the characteristics and specifications of two populations.

DISCUSSION: In Case 2, variability in Population 1 is larger, and the specified precision is wider. Larger variability (a larger σ) requires a larger sample size, but the wider precision decreases the sample size. The magnitudes are unknown, so the relative required sample size is not determinable.

14.3.13. In Case 3, the required sample size from Population 1 is

A. Larger than the required sample size from Population 2.

B. Equal to the required sample size from Population 2.

C. Smaller than the required sample size from Population 2.

D. Indeterminate relative to the required sample size from Population 2.

Answer (D) is correct. *(CPA, adapted)*

REQUIRED: The effects on sample size of changing the characteristics and specifications of two populations.

DISCUSSION: Case 3 specifies a larger population size, a tighter specified precision, and a lower confidence level. The larger size of Population 1 and the tighter precision require a larger sample size; however, the lower specified confidence level requires a smaller sample size. Because the magnitudes are unknown, the effect on sample size is not determinable.

14.3.14. In Case 4, the required sample size from Population 1 is

A. Larger than the required sample size from Population 2.

B. Equal to the required sample size from Population 2.

C. Smaller than the required sample size from Population 2.

D. Indeterminate relative to the required sample size from Population 2.

Answer (C) is correct. *(CPA, adapted)*

REQUIRED: The effects on sample size of changing the characteristics and specifications of two populations.

DISCUSSION: In Case 4, Population 1 is smaller than Population 2, the variability is smaller, and the required specified confidence level is lower. Smaller population size indicates a smaller sample size. The smaller variability and lower confidence level also decrease the sample size. Thus, the sample required from Population 1 is smaller than that from Population 2.

14.3.15. In Case 5, the required sample size from Population 1 is

A. Larger than the required sample size from Population 2.

B. Equal to the required sample size from Population 2.

C. Smaller than the required sample size from Population 2.

D. Indeterminate relative to the required sample size from Population 2.

Answer (A) is correct. *(CPA, adapted)*

REQUIRED: The effects on sample size of changing the characteristics and specifications of two populations.

DISCUSSION: In Case 5, Population 1 is larger and has a higher specified confidence level. Both attributes are directly related to sample size. Thus, the sample from Population 1 will be larger than that from Population 2.

14.3.16. An auditor is determining the sample size for an inventory observation using mean-per-unit estimation, which is a variables sampling plan. To calculate the required sample size, the auditor usually determines the

	Variability in the Dollar Amounts of Inventory Items	Risk of Incorrect Rejection
A.	Yes	Yes
B.	Yes	No
C.	No	Yes
D.	No	No

Answer (A) is correct. *(CPA, adapted)*

REQUIRED: The factor(s), if any, used to determine a mean-per-unit sample size.

DISCUSSION: Four factors are considered in determining the sample size for mean-per-unit estimation. Those factors include (1) the population size, (2) an estimate of population variation (the standard deviation), (3) the risk of incorrect rejection (its complement is the confidence level), and (4) the tolerable misstatement (the desired allowance for sampling risk is a percentage thereof, and this percentage is a function of the risk of incorrect rejection and the allowable risk of incorrect acceptance).

Questions 14.3.17 through 14.3.21 are based on the following information. Robert Lambert is a CPA of Rainbow Manufacturing Corporation. Rainbow manufactures two products, Product A and Product B. Product A requires raw materials that have a very low per-item cost, and Product B requires raw materials that have a very high per-item cost. Raw materials for both products are stored in a single warehouse. In Year 1, Rainbow established the total value of raw materials stored in the warehouse by physically inventorying an unrestricted random sample of items selected without replacement. Mr. Lambert is evaluating the statistical validity of alternative sampling plans Rainbow is considering for Year 2. Lambert knows the size of the Year 1 sample and that Rainbow did not use stratified sampling in Year 1. Assumptions about the population, variability, specified precision (confidence interval), and specified reliability (confidence level) for a possible Year 2 sample are given in individual cases. You are to indicate in each case the effect upon the size of the Year 2 sample as compared to the Year 1 sample. Each case is independent of cases presented in other questions relating to this fact pattern.

14.3.17. Rainbow wants to use stratified sampling in Year 2 (the total population will be divided into two strata, one each for the raw materials for Product A and Product B). Compared with Year 1, the population size of the raw materials inventory is approximately the same, and the variability of the items in the inventory is approximately the same. The specified precision and specified reliability are to remain the same. Under these assumptions, the required sample size for Year 2 should be

A. Larger than the Year 1 sample size.

B. Equal to the Year 1 sample size.

C. Smaller than the Year 1 sample size.

D. Of a size that is indeterminate based upon the information given.

Answer (C) is correct. *(CPA, adapted)*

REQUIRED: The effects of changing population size, variability of population, specified precision, specified reliability, and sample selection methods on sample size.

DISCUSSION: In this case, all factors are held constant except that the population is to be stratified. One subpopulation will contain materials with a very low per-item cost, while the other subpopulation will include raw materials that have a high per-item cost. By dividing the population into two strata, the variability within each subpopulation will probably be greatly reduced compared to that of the single population sampled in Year 1. Because the variability is less, the sample sizes will be smaller. The sum of the two samples will likely be less than the prior year's sample size.

14.3.18. Rainbow wants to use stratified sampling in Year 2. Compared with Year 1, the population size of the raw materials inventory is approximately the same, and the variability of the items in the inventory is approximately the same. Rainbow specified the same precision but desires to change the specified reliability from 90% to 95%. Under these assumptions, the required sample size for Year 2 should be

A. Larger than the Year 1 sample size.

B. Equal to the Year 1 sample size.

C. Smaller than the Year 1 sample size.

D. Of a size that is indeterminate based upon the information given.

Answer (D) is correct. *(CPA, adapted)*

REQUIRED: The effects of changing population size, variability of population, specified precision, specified reliability, and sample selection methods on sample size.

DISCUSSION: Stratification allows smaller sample sizes when the total population contains a high amount of variability. The purpose of stratification is to create strata, each of which has less variability than the total population. However, the effect of increasing the specified reliability from 90% to 95% is to increase sample size. Because the magnitude of the variability change is unknown, the effect on the sample size is not determinable.

14.3.19. Rainbow wants to use unrestricted random sampling without replacement in Year 2. Compared with Year 1, the population size of the raw materials inventory is approximately the same, and the variability of the items in the inventory is approximately the same. Rainbow specifies the same precision but desires to change the specified reliability from 90% to 95%. Under these assumptions, the required sample size for Year 2 should be

A. Larger than the Year 1 sample size.

B. Equal to the Year 1 sample size.

C. Smaller than the Year 1 sample size.

D. Of a size that is indeterminate based upon the information given.

Answer (A) is correct. *(CPA, adapted)*

REQUIRED: The effects of changing population size, variability of population, specified precision, specified reliability, and sample selection methods on sample size.

DISCUSSION: The only change from Year 1 to Year 2 is that the specified reliability (confidence level) will increase from 90% to 95%. Because reliability varies directly with sample size, a larger sample will be required for Year 2.

14.3.20. Rainbow wants to use unrestricted random sampling without replacement in Year 2. Compared with Year 1, the population size of the raw materials inventory has increased, and the variability of the items in the inventory has increased. The specified precision and specified reliability are to remain the same. Under these assumptions, the required sample size for Year 2 should be

A. Larger than the Year 1 sample size.

B. Equal to the Year 1 sample size.

C. Smaller than the Year 1 sample size.

D. Of a size that is indeterminate based upon the information given.

Answer (A) is correct. *(CPA, adapted)*

REQUIRED: The effects of changing population size, variability of population, specified precision, specified reliability, and sample selection methods on sample size.

DISCUSSION: The increase in population size and in variability are directly related to sample size. Because both changes increase the necessary sample size, the sample for Year 2 will be larger than that for Year 1.

14.3.21. Rainbow wants to use unrestricted random sampling without replacement in Year 2. Compared with Year 1, the population size of the raw materials inventory has increased, but the variability of the items in the inventory has decreased. The specified precision and specified reliability are to remain the same. Under these assumptions, the required sample size for Year 2 should be

A. Larger than the Year 1 sample size.

B. Equal to the Year 1 sample size.

C. Smaller than the Year 1 sample size.

D. Of a size that is indeterminate based upon the information given.

Answer (D) is correct. *(CPA, adapted)*

REQUIRED: The effects of changing population size, variability of population, specified precision, specified reliability, and sample selection methods on sample size.

DISCUSSION: Population size and variability are directly related to sample size. The increase in population dictates an increase in sample size, while the decrease in variability requires a decrease in sample size. Because the magnitudes of the changes are not given, the change in the size of the sample is indeterminate.

14.4 Monetary-Unit Sampling (MUS)

14.4.1. An auditor is planning to use monetary-unit sampling for testing the dollar value of a large accounts receivable population. The advantages of using monetary-unit sampling (MUS) include all of the following except

A. It is an efficient model for establishing that a low error rate population is not materially misstated.

B. It does not require the normal distribution approximation required by variables sampling.

C. It can be applied to a group of accounts because the sampling units are homogeneous.

D. It results in a smaller sample size than classical variables sampling for larger numbers of misstatements.

Answer (D) is correct. *(CIA, adapted)*

REQUIRED: The item not an advantage of MUS.

DISCUSSION: MUS is also known as probability-proportional-to-size (PPS) sampling or dollar-unit sampling. It is a combination of attribute sampling and variables sampling that arrives at a result stated as a dollar amount instead of a deviation rate. It uses the dollar as the sampling unit. MUS is appropriate for testing account balances, such as those for inventory and receivables, in which some items may be far larger than others in the population. In effect, it stratifies the population because the larger account balances have a greater chance of being selected. MUS is most useful if few misstatements are expected. Moreover, it is designed to detect overstatements. It is not effective for estimating understatements because, the greater the understatement, the less likely the item will be selected. Furthermore, as the number of expected misstatements increases, MUS requires a larger sample size than classical variables sampling.

Answer (A) is incorrect. MUS is efficient when few misstatements are expected. Answer (B) is incorrect. MUS does not assume normally distributed populations. Answer (C) is incorrect. MUS uses dollars as sampling units.

14.4.2. When an auditor uses monetary-unit sampling to examine the total value of invoices, each invoice

A. Has an equal probability of being selected.

B. Can be represented by no more than one monetary unit.

C. Has an unknown probability of being selected.

D. Has a probability proportional to its monetary value of being selected.

Answer (D) is correct. *(CIA, adapted)*

REQUIRED: The effect of using monetary-unit sampling to examine invoices.

DISCUSSION: Monetary-unit sampling results in the selection of every *n*th monetary unit. Thus, a $1,000 item is 1,000 times more likely to be selected than a $1 item. The probability of selection of a sampled item is directly proportional to the size of the item.

Answer (A) is incorrect. Each monetary unit, but not each invoice, has an equal probability of being selected unless all invoices are for the same amount. Answer (B) is incorrect. It is possible for two or more monetary units to be selected from the same item; e.g., a $4,500 item will be represented by $4 if every 1,000th dollar is selected. Answer (C) is incorrect. The probability of selection can be calculated using the monetary values of the item and the population.

14.4.3. Monetary-unit sampling (MUS) is most useful when the auditor

A. Is testing the accounts payable balance.

B. Cannot cumulatively arrange the population items.

C. Expects to find several material misstatements in the sample.

D. Is concerned with overstatements.

Answer (D) is correct. *(CIA, adapted)*

REQUIRED: The best use of MUS.

DISCUSSION: MUS is also known as probability-proportional-to-size (PPS) sampling or dollar-unit sampling. It combines attribute sampling and variables sampling to arrive at a monetary amount instead of a deviation rate. It uses the dollar as the sampling unit. MUS sampling is appropriate for testing account balances, such as those for inventory and receivables, in which some items may be far larger than others in the population. In effect, it stratifies the population because the larger account balances have a greater chance of being selected. MUS is most useful if few misstatements are expected. Moreover, it is designed to detect overstatements. It is not effective for estimating understatements because, the greater the understatement, the less likely the item will be selected. Special design considerations are required if the auditor anticipates understatements or zero or negative balances.

Answer (A) is incorrect. An audit of accounts payable is primarily concerned with understatements. Answer (B) is incorrect. The items in the population must be arranged by cumulative monetary total. The first monetary unit is chosen randomly, the second equals the random start plus the sample interval in dollars, etc. Answer (C) is incorrect. As the expected amount of misstatement increases, the MUS sample size increases. MUS may also overstate the upper misstatement limit when misstatements are found. The result might be rejection of an acceptable balance.

14.4.4. Which of the following most likely would be an advantage in using classical variables sampling rather than monetary-unit sampling?

A. An estimate of the standard deviation of the population's recorded amounts is not required.

B. The auditor rarely needs the assistance of a computer program to design an efficient sample.

C. Inclusion of zero and negative balances usually does not require special design considerations.

D. Any amount that is individually significant is automatically identified and selected.

Answer (C) is correct. *(CPA, adapted)*

REQUIRED: The advantage of using classical variables sampling rather than MUS.

DISCUSSION: MUS is most useful if few misstatements are expected, and overstatement is the most likely kind of misstatement. One disadvantage of MUS is that it is designed to detect overstatements. It is not effective for estimating understatements. The smaller the item, the less likely it will be selected in the sample, but the more likely the item is understated.

Answer (A) is incorrect. The sample size formula for estimation of variables includes the standard deviation of the population. Answer (B) is incorrect. A computer program is helpful in many sampling applications. Answer (D) is incorrect. In classical variables sampling, every item has an equal and nonzero probability of selection.

14.4.5. Which of the following is an improper technique when using monetary-unit statistical sampling in an audit of accounts receivable?

A. Combining negative and positive monetary misstatements in the appraisal of a sample.

B. Using a sampling technique in which the same account balance could be selected more than once.

C. Selecting a random starting point and then sampling every *n*th monetary unit (systematic sampling).

D. Defining the sampling unit in the population as an individual monetary unit and not as an individual account balance.

Answer (A) is correct. *(CIA, adapted)*

REQUIRED: The improper technique when using monetary-unit sampling in an audit of receivables.

DISCUSSION: When using monetary-unit sampling, the auditor may calculate the gross projected likely misstatement (GPLM) and the gross upper misstatement limit (GUML) for overstatements, ignoring understatements. (S)he then calculates these values for understatements, ignoring overstatements. The net upper misstatement limits are then determined by subtracting the GPLM for one kind of misstatement from the GUML for the other. The resulting net upper misstatement limits for overstatements and understatements define the precision interval. However, more complicated computations may be appropriate in certain extreme cases. The GUMLs may not be netted, and individual positive and negative misstatements also cannot be netted.

Answer (B) is incorrect. Two or more monetary units may be selected from the same item; e.g., a $10,000 item will be represented twice if every 5,000th dollar is selected. Answer (C) is incorrect. Monetary-unit sampling consists of selecting a random start and then sampling every *n*th unit. Answer (D) is incorrect. Monetary-unit sampling defines the sampling unit in the population as an individual monetary unit and not as an individual account balance.

14.4.6. The use of monetary-unit sampling (MUS) is inefficient if

A. Bank accounts are being audited.

B. Statistical inferences are to be made.

C. Each account is of equal importance.

D. The number of sampling units is large.

Answer (C) is correct. *(CIA, adapted)*

REQUIRED: The inefficient use of MUS.

DISCUSSION: MUS gives greater weight to larger, more significant items. If all items are of the same importance, MUS is inappropriate.

Answer (A) is incorrect. MUS could be appropriate in an audit of bank accounts if larger items are more important than smaller items (which is usually true in variables sampling). Answer (B) is incorrect. MUS permits statistical inferences to be made. Answer (D) is incorrect. MUS could be appropriate with a large number of sampling units if larger items are more important than smaller items.

14.4.7. In selecting a sample using monetary-unit sampling, the dollar is the sampling unit. For example, if the 300th dollar of invoices is selected,

A. Only that dollar is audited.

B. Only an invoice with exactly $300 is audited.

C. An invoice of less than $300 cannot be selected.

D. The invoice containing the 300th dollar is audited.

Answer (D) is correct. *(Publisher, adapted)*

REQUIRED: The item sampled.

DISCUSSION: The monetary unit selected is a basis for choosing the sales invoice to be audited. Thus, the 300th dollar identifies an invoice on which all dollars will be audited.

Answer (A) is incorrect. Not only is the 300th dollar audited, but also all other monetary units on the invoice selected. Answer (B) is incorrect. An invoice with any amount may be selected by the technique, not just those for exactly $300. Answer (C) is incorrect. An invoice with any amount may be selected by the technique, not just those for $300 or more.

14.4.8. In a monetary-unit sample with a sampling interval of $5,000, an auditor discovered that a selected account receivable with a recorded amount of $10,000 had an audit amount of $8,000. If this were the only error discovered by the auditor, the projected misstatement of this sample would be

A. $1,000

B. $2,000

C. $4,000

D. $5,000

Answer (B) is correct. *(CPA, adapted)*

REQUIRED: The total projected misstatement of the MUS sample.

DISCUSSION: Monetary-unit sampling is a commonly used method of statistical sampling for tests of details of balances because it provides a simple statistical result expressed in dollars. The projected misstatement in this sampling method equals the actual misstatement of the sampled item when the recorded amount of the item ($10,000) exceeds the sampling interval ($5,000). Thus, the projected misstatement is $2,000 ($10,000 recorded amount – $8,000 audit amount).

Answer (A) is incorrect. The amount of $1,000 equals the amount of the misstatement divided by the recorded amount, times the sampling interval. Answer (C) is incorrect. The amount of $4,000 transposes the sampling interval and the audit value in the tainting formula. Answer (D) is incorrect. The amount of $5,000 is the sampling interval.

Questions 14.4.9 through 14.4.12 are based on the following information. Edwards has decided to use probability-proportional-to-size (PPS), also called monetary-unit, sampling in the audit of a client's accounts receivable balance. Few, if any, account balance overstatements are expected. Edwards plans to use the following PPS sampling table:

Reliability Factors for Overstatements

Number of Overstatements	Risk of Incorrect Acceptance				
	1%	5%	10%	15%	20%
0	4.61	3.00	2.31	1.90	1.61
1	6.64	4.75	3.89	3.38	3.00
2	8.41	6.30	5.33	4.72	4.28

The following information was also available:

Tolerable misstatement	$15,000
Risk of incorrect acceptance	5%
Recorded amount of accounts receivable	$300,000

Three overstatements were discovered in a PPS sample:

	Recorded Amount	Audit Amount
1st	$ 400	$ 320
2nd	500	0
3rd	3,000	2,500

14.4.9. Edwards should use a sampling interval of

A. $20,000

B. $15,000

C. $10,000

D. $5,000

Answer (D) is correct. *(Publisher, adapted)*

REQUIRED: The sampling interval for a PPS sample.

DISCUSSION: Because the dollar amount of anticipated misstatement is not given, it must be assumed to be zero. In that case, the PPS sample size formula is

$$n = \frac{RM \times RF}{TM}$$

The variable *n* is the sample size, RM the recorded or carrying amount of the population, RF the reliability factor (always from the zero line of the table), and TM the tolerable misstatement. The sampling interval equals RM divided by *n*. Solving the formula for this value establishes that the interval also equals TM divided by RF, or $5,000 ($15,000 ÷ 3.00 at 5% risk of incorrect acceptance and zero overstatements).

Answer (A) is incorrect. The amount of $20,000 equals the $15,000 TM divided into the $300,000 BV. Answer (B) is incorrect. The amount of $15,000 is the tolerable misstatement. Answer (C) is incorrect. The derivation of $10,000 cannot be readily determined.

14.4.10. Given a sampling interval of $5,000, Edwards should use a sample size of

A. 60

B. 50

C. 40

D. 30

Answer (A) is correct. *(Publisher, adapted)*

REQUIRED: The sample size for a PPS sample.

DISCUSSION: The sample size equals the recorded amount of the population divided by the sampling interval, or 60 ($300,000 ÷ $5,000).

Answer (B) is incorrect. A sample size of 50 assumes an interval of $6,000, not $5,000. Answer (C) is incorrect. A sample size of 40 assumes an interval of $7,500. Answer (D) is incorrect. A sample size of 30 assumes an interval of $10,000.

14.4.11. Assume that the sampling interval is $1,000. What is the total projected misstatement given the three misstatements discovered?

A. $1,750

B. $1,700

C. $1,200

D. $1,000

Answer (B) is correct. *(Publisher, adapted)*

REQUIRED: The total projected misstatement.

DISCUSSION: The total projected misstatement is the sum of the misstatements projected based on the respective logical sampling units (accounts receivable) containing misstatements. If a logical unit has a recorded amount less than the sampling interval, a tainting percentage [(recorded amount – audit amount) ÷ recorded amount] is calculated for that misstatement and then multiplied by the sampling interval. The percentage taint in the logical unit is extended to all dollars in the sampling interval it represents. If the recorded amount is equal to or greater than the sampling interval, the misstatement in the logical unit is the projected misstatement.

Recorded Amount	Audit Amount	Tainting %	Sampling Interval	Projected Misstatement
$ 400	$ 320	20%	$1,000	$ 200
500	0	100%	1,000	1,000
3,000	2,500	--	--	500
				$1,700

Answer (A) is incorrect. The derivation of $1,750 cannot be readily determined. Answer (C) is incorrect. The total projected misstatement for the first two items is $1,200. Answer (D) is incorrect. The projected misstatement for item two is $1,000.

14.4.12. Assuming a sampling interval of $1,000, what is the upper misstatement limit (UML) based on this sample?

A. $1,700

B. $3,000

C. $5,560

D. $5,790

Answer (C) is correct. *(Publisher, adapted)*

REQUIRED: The upper misstatement limit (UML).

DISCUSSION: The first component of the UML is basic precision: the product of the sampling interval ($1,000) and the reliability factor (3.00) for zero misstatements at the specified risk of incorrect acceptance (5%). The second is the total projected misstatement ($1,700). The third is an allowance for widening the precision gap as a result of finding more than zero misstatements. This allowance is determined only with respect to logical sampling units with recorded amounts less than the sampling interval. If a sample item is equal to or greater than the sampling interval, the taint for that interval is certain, and no further allowance is necessary. Calculating this allowance requires determining the adjusted incremental changes in the reliability factors (these factors increase, and precision widens, as the number of misstatements increases). The factors are from the 5% column in the table. To prevent double counting of amounts included in basic precision, in projected misstatement, and in the adjustments for higher-ranked misstatements, the preceding reliability factor plus 1.0 is subtracted from each factor. The projected misstatements are then ranked from highest to lowest, each adjusted incremental reliability factor is multiplied by the related projected misstatement, and the products are summed.

Basic precision ($1,000 × 3.00)		$3,000
Total projected misstatement		1,700
Allowance for precision gap widening:		
(4.75 – 3.00 – 1.00) × $1,000 =	$750	
(6.30 – 4.75 – 1.00) × $ 200 =	110	860
UML		$5,560

Answer (A) is incorrect. The amount of $1,700 is the total projected misstatement given the misstatements found. Answer (B) is incorrect. The amount of $3,000 is basic precision. Answer (D) is incorrect. The amount of $5,790 {$5,560 + [(7.76 – 6.30 – 1.00) × $500]} includes an allowance for precision gap widening for a third misstatement.

Questions 14.4.13 and 14.4.14 are based on the following information.

An auditor has been assigned to take a monetary-unit sample of a population of vouchers in the purchasing department. The population has a total recorded amount of $300,000. The auditor believes that a maximum misstatement of $900 is acceptable and would like to have 95% confidence in the results. (The confidence factor at 95% and zero misstatements = 3.00.) Additional information is provided in the opposite column.

Table of First 10 Vouchers in Population

Voucher #	Balance	Cumulative Balance
1	$100	$ 100
2	150	250
3	40	290
4	200	490
5	10	500
6	290	790
7	50	840
8	190	1,030
9	20	1,050
10	180	1,230

14.4.13. Given a random start of $50 as the first dollar amount, what is the number of the fourth voucher to be selected, assuming that the sample size will be 1,000?

A. 4

B. 6

C. 7

D. 8

Answer (D) is correct. *(CIA, adapted)*

REQUIRED: The number of the fourth voucher selected using MUS.

DISCUSSION: The vouchers have a recorded amount of $300,000, and 1,000 items are to be sampled, so every 300th dollar will be chosen. Given a random start of $50, the vouchers containing the 50th, 350th, 650th, and 950th dollars will be selected. The cumulative amount of the first eight vouchers is $1,030. Accordingly, voucher 8 should be the fourth voucher audited because it contains the 950th dollar.

Answer (A) is incorrect. Voucher 4 contains the 350th dollar and should be the second voucher selected. Answer (B) is incorrect. Voucher 6 contains the 650th dollar and should be the third voucher selected. Answer (C) is incorrect. Voucher 7 should not be selected.

14.4.14. In examining the sample, one overstatement was detected causing an extension of $270 to the tolerable misstatement. Assuming a sample size of 1,000 and assuming that the maximum dollar amount of overstatement, if no misstatements were found, was established to be $900 before the sampling analysis, what conclusion can the auditor now make from the sampling evidence?

A. (S)he is 95% confident that the dollar amount of overstatement in the population of vouchers is between $900 and $1,170.

B. (S)he is 95% confident that the dollar amount of overstatement in the population of vouchers exceeds $1,170.

C. (S)he is 95% confident that the dollar amount of overstatement in the population of vouchers is less than $1,170.

D. An insufficient number of misstatements were detected to warrant a conclusion.

Answer (C) is correct. *(CIA, adapted)*

REQUIRED: The conclusion from the audit evidence given an extension of tolerable misstatement.

DISCUSSION: Had the auditor detected no misstatements in the sample, (s)he could have been 95% confident that the dollar amount of overstatement in the balance was less than $900. Given discovery of an overstatement causing an extension to the tolerable misstatement of $270, the auditor can conclude with 95% confidence that the overstatement is less than $1,170 ($900 + $270).

Answer (A) is incorrect. The auditor is 95% confident that the overstatement is less than $1,170. Answer (B) is incorrect. The auditor is 95% confident that the overstatement is less than $1,170. Answer (D) is incorrect. A conclusion is warranted even if no misstatements were found.

14.4.15. Hill has decided to use monetary-unit sampling (MUS), sometimes called dollar-unit sampling, in the audit of a client's accounts receivable balances. Hill plans to use the following MUS sampling table:

TABLE 1
Reliability Factors for Overstatements

Number of Overstatements	Risk of Incorrect Acceptance 1%	5%	10%	15%	20%
0	4.61	3.00	2.31	1.90	1.61
1	6.64	4.75	3.89	3.38	3.00
2	8.41	6.30	5.33	4.72	4.28

TABLE 2
Expansion Factors for Expected Errors

	Risk of Incorrect Acceptance 1%	5%	10%	15%	20%
Factor	1.9	1.6	1.5	1.4	1.3

Additional Information	
Tolerable misstatement	$ 24,000
Anticipated misstatement	$ 5,000
Risk on incorrect acceptance	5%
Recorded amount of accounts receivable	$240,000
Number of accounts	360

What sample size should Hill use?

A. 120
B. 108
C. 45
D. 30

Answer (C) is correct. *(Publisher, adapted)*

REQUIRED: The size of the MUS sample.

DISCUSSION: MUS sampling is appropriate for account balances that may include a few overstated items, such as inventory and receivables. MUS sampling relies on an attribute sampling approach (Poisson distribution) to reach a conclusion regarding the probability of overstating an account balance by a specified amount of dollars. The MUS sample size formula is

$$n = \frac{RM \times RF}{TM - (AM \times EF)}$$

The variable *n* equals sample size, RM is the recorded or carrying amount of the account, RF is the appropriate reliability factor (always from the zero line of Table 1), TM is tolerable misstatement, AM is the anticipated misstatement, and EF is the expansion factor (from Table 2).

$$n = \frac{\$240,000 \times 3.00}{\$24,000 - (\$5,000 \times 1.6)} = 45$$

14.4.16. Which of the following statements is true concerning monetary-unit sampling (MUS), also known as probability-proportional-to-size sampling?

A. The sampling distribution should approximate the normal distribution.
B. Overstated units have a lower probability of sample selection than units that are understated.
C. The auditor controls the risk of incorrect acceptance by specifying that risk level for the sampling plan.
D. The sampling interval is calculated by dividing the number of physical units in the population by the sample size.

Answer (C) is correct. *(CPA, adapted)*

REQUIRED: The true statement about MUS.

DISCUSSION: MUS is one technique whereby the auditor can measure and control the risks associated with observing less than 100% of the population. The auditor can quantify and measure the risk of accepting a client's recorded amount as fair when it is materially misstated.

Answer (A) is incorrect. MUS is most closely associated with the Poisson distribution. Answer (B) is incorrect. As the size of the units in the population increases, so does the probability of selection. Answer (D) is incorrect. The sampling interval is calculated by dividing the total dollars, not units, in the population by the sample size. Every *n*th dollar is then selected after a random start.

STUDY UNIT FIFTEEN REPORTS -- OPINIONS AND DISCLAIMERS

This study unit presents interrelated reporting issues, beginning with the auditor's responsibilities. The overall objectives of an audit include reporting on the financial statements, and communicating as required by GAAS or the PCAOB standards, in accordance with the audit findings. Subunit 15.2 should be studied carefully because it addresses reporting when no basis exists for modifying the opinion or other elements of the auditor's report. The last three subunits and all of Study Unit 16 outline the requirements for modifications of the auditor's report. Many matters considered in Study Unit 17 relate to standard reporting issues. Study Units 18 and 19 apply to the reporting requirements for (1) preparation, compilation, and review services and (2) attestation engagements. Governmental audit reports, covered in Study Unit 20, are variations of the auditor's report.

In this study unit, Subunits 15.1, 15.2, and 15.3 relate to the auditor's report and reporting in general. Subunits 15.4, 15.5, and 15.6 address modifications of the opinion in the auditor's report. These modifications are summarized in the table below. Pervasive effects are the (1) effects of misstatements of the financial statements or (2) the possible effects of any misstatements that are undetected due to an inability to obtain sufficient appropriate audit evidence. Pervasive effects (1) are not confined to specific elements, accounts, or items of the financial statements; (2) represent or could represent a substantial proportion of the financial statements, even if confined; or (3), with regard to disclosures, are fundamental to users' understanding of the financial statements.

Nature of Matter Resulting in a Modification	Auditor's Professional Judgment about the Pervasiveness of the Effects or Possible Effects on the Financial Statements	
	Material but Not Pervasive	Material and Pervasive
Financial statements are materially misstated	Qualified opinion	Adverse opinion
Inability to obtain sufficient appropriate audit evidence	Qualified opinion	Disclaimer of opinion

QUESTIONS

15.1 The Auditor's Reporting Responsibility

15.1.1. The objective of the audit of GAAP-based financial statements is to

A. Make suggestions as to the form or content of the financial statements or to draft them in whole or in part.

B. Express an opinion on the fairness with which the statements present financial position, results of operations, and cash flows in accordance with generally accepted accounting principles.

C. Ensure adoption of sound accounting policies and the establishment and maintenance of internal control.

D. Express an opinion on the accuracy with which the statements present financial position, results of operations, and cash flows in accordance with generally accepted accounting principles.

Answer (B) is correct. *(Publisher, adapted)*

REQUIRED: The objective of an audit.

DISCUSSION: Based on an audit, the auditor expresses an opinion (or a disclaimer of opinion) on the fairness, in all material respects, of the presentation of financial statements, i.e., on whether they will be misleading to users.

Answer (A) is incorrect. The auditor may make suggestions about the statements or help prepare them, but (s)he is responsible only for expressing an opinion as to their fairness. The statements remain the representations of management. Answer (C) is incorrect. Management is responsible for adopting sound accounting policies and establishing and maintaining internal control. Answer (D) is incorrect. The auditor expresses an opinion on the fairness of financial statements, not their accuracy.

15.1.2. Which of the following statements best describes the distinction between the auditor's responsibilities and management's responsibilities?

A. Management has responsibility for maintaining and adopting sound accounting policies, and the auditor has responsibility for internal control.

B. Management has responsibility for the basic data underlying financial statements, and the auditor has responsibility for drafting the financial statements.

C. The auditor's responsibility is confined to the audited portion of the financial statements, and management's responsibility is confined to the unaudited portions.

D. The auditor's responsibility is confined to expressing an opinion, but the financial statements remain the responsibility of management.

Answer (D) is correct. *(Publisher, adapted)*

REQUIRED: The statement that best distinguishes between the auditor's and management's responsibilities for audited financial statements.

DISCUSSION: The auditor is responsible for the opinion on financial statements, but management is responsible for the representations made in the financial statements.

Answer (A) is incorrect. Management has responsibility for establishing and maintaining internal control. Answer (B) is incorrect. Management is responsible for preparing the financial statements. Answer (C) is incorrect. The auditor expresses an opinion on the financial statements as a whole, and management is responsible for all the assertions in the financial statements.

15.1.3. The evaluation of fairness in determining the appropriate opinion to express should include consideration of the qualitative aspects of the entity's accounting practices, including whether

A. Indicators of possible bias exist in management's judgments.

B. The accounting principles used are the most conservative available.

C. Management and those charged with governance agree with all the standards used in the reporting process.

D. The auditor and management agree with all the standards used in the reporting process.

Answer (A) is correct. *(Publisher, adapted)*

REQUIRED: The auditor's conclusion about a qualitative aspect of the entity's accounting practices.

DISCUSSION: The auditor should be aware of the potential for management bias. For example, management's judgments may indicate a lack of neutrality that results in selective correction of identified misstatements and bias in making accounting estimates.

Answer (B) is incorrect. The accounting principles need to be in accordance with the framework and appropriate, not the most conservative. Answer (C) is incorrect. Fair presentation depends on the qualities of information in the statements, not whether management and those charged with governance agree with all the standards used in the reporting process. Answer (D) is incorrect. Fair presentation depends on the qualities of information in the statements, not whether the auditor and management agree with all the standards used in the reporting process.

15.1.4. Which of the following best describes why an independent auditor is asked to express an opinion on the fair presentation of financial statements?

A. It is difficult to prepare financial statements that fairly present a company's financial position, results of operations, and cash flows without the expertise of an independent auditor.

B. It is management's responsibility to seek available independent aid in the appraisal of the financial information shown in its financial statements.

C. The opinion of an independent party is needed because a company may not be objective with respect to its own financial statements.

D. It is a customary courtesy that all shareholders of a company receive an independent report on management's stewardship in managing the affairs of the business.

Answer (C) is correct. *(CPA, adapted)*

REQUIRED: The best reason for an independent auditor's opinion.

DISCUSSION: The opinion of a suitably qualified, independent, outside party lends credibility to the financial statements and provides some protection to third parties who may rely upon them when making investment decisions. The opinion contained in the audit report, which accompanies audited financial statements, is the result of the auditor's performance of the attest function, that is, the gathering of evidence during the audit and the issuance of an opinion on the fairness of the presentation of the statements.

Answer (A) is incorrect. The auditor's independence is vital to the performance of the attest function, not his or her preparation of financial statements. Indeed, for purposes of SEC reporting, preparing the financial statements may be considered an impairment of independence. Also, the assertions in the statements are the sole responsibility of management. Answer (B) is incorrect. Management does not seek an appraisal of the financial statements, only an opinion as to whether they are presented fairly. Answer (D) is incorrect. Although the distribution of information to shareholders is customary, it is not the primary reason for an auditor's report.

15.1.5. If a company's external auditor expresses an unmodified opinion as a result of the audit of the company's financial statements, readers of the audit report can assume that

A. The external auditor found no fraud.

B. The company is financially sound and the financial statements are accurate.

C. Internal control is effective.

D. Material issues about the application of accounting principles were resolved to the satisfaction of the external auditor.

Answer (D) is correct. *(CMA, adapted)*

REQUIRED: The assumption made about an external auditor's unmodified opinion.

DISCUSSION: When the statements are materially misstated, the auditor should express a qualified or adverse opinion (AU-C 700).

Answer (A) is incorrect. The reader may only assume that any fraud found did not, in the auditor's opinion, prevent the statements from being fairly presented. Answer (B) is incorrect. The auditor is not an appraiser of the company, and an opinion offers no prediction about the performance of the auditee. Also, an unmodified opinion provides reasonable assurance that the statements are not materially misstated, not that they are accurate. Answer (C) is incorrect. An unmodified opinion on the financial statements does not provide assurance about controls.

15.1.6. A major purpose of the auditor's report on financial statements is to

A. Assure investors of the complete accuracy of the financial statements.

B. Clarify for the public the nature of the auditor's responsibility and performance.

C. Deter creditors from extending loans in high-risk situations.

D. Describe the specific auditing procedures undertaken to gather evidence for the opinion.

Answer (B) is correct. *(N. Schmukler)*

REQUIRED: The purpose of the auditor's report.

DISCUSSION: One of the highest priorities of the AICPA has been to reduce the gap between the nature of the auditor's responsibility and performance and the public's perception of the audit function. The auditor's report issued in accordance with auditing standards clarifies the role of the auditor with the intention of diminishing the gap.

Answer (A) is incorrect. An auditor's opinion provides no assurance of complete accuracy. The report explicitly states that an audit provides "reasonable assurance."Answer (C) is incorrect. The sole purpose of the auditor's report is to express an opinion on the fairness of presentation of the financial statements. The report provides some of the information upon which users of the statements may make informed decisions, but it does not substitute for the judgment of users or accept responsibility for the assertions contained in the statements. Answer (D) is incorrect. The auditor's responsibility section provides only a brief, general explanation of what an audit involves.

15.1.7. The securities of Donley Corporation are listed on a regional stock exchange and registered with the SEC. The management of Donley engages a CPA to perform an independent audit of Donley's financial statements. The primary objective of this audit is to provide assurance to the

A. Regional stock exchange.

B. Investors in Donley securities.

C. Securities and Exchange Commission.

D. Board of directors of Donley.

Answer (B) is correct. *(CPA, adapted)*

REQUIRED: The persons assured by an audit of a publicly held corporation.

DISCUSSION: An audit's primary objective is to provide assurance to the external users of financial statements that they present fairly, in all material respects, the financial position, results of operations, and cash flows of the company. Users include creditors, investors, and potential investors.

15.1.8. The auditor's judgment concerning the overall fairness of the presentation of financial position, results of operations, and cash flows is applied within the framework of

A. Quality control.

B. Generally accepted auditing standards, which include the concept of materiality.

C. The auditor's assessment of the risk of material misstatement.

D. Generally accepted accounting principles.

Answer (D) is correct. *(CPA, adapted)*

REQUIRED: The framework within which the auditor judges the financial statements.

DISCUSSION: Reporting standards require the auditor to state whether the audited entity's financial statements are presented in conformity with GAAP. Without an applicable reporting framework, the auditor would have no uniform standard for judging fairness of presentation.

Answer (A) is incorrect. Quality control standards relate to the conduct of a CPA firm's audit practice as a whole. Adequate quality control provides reasonable assurance of the independent auditor's compliance with GAAS. Answer (B) is incorrect. Although the auditor must comply with GAAS, (s)he must specifically judge whether the statements are presented fairly. Answer (C) is incorrect. The assessment of the RMM is but one step in an audit, the ultimate purpose of which is to express an opinion on the fair presentation of the statements.

15.1.9. To which of the following material asset balances should an auditor object as not in accordance with U.S. GAAP?

A. Franchise fees paid.

B. Increase in goodwill resulting from annual testing.

C. Acquisition cost of an Internet domain name.

D. Research and development costs that will be billed to a customer at a subsequent date.

Answer (B) is correct. *(CPA, adapted)*

REQUIRED: The material asset balance that is not in accordance with U.S. GAAP.

DISCUSSION: Goodwill should be tested for impairment at the reporting-unit level at least annually. If goodwill is impaired, the asset should be written down to fair value. However, goodwill should not be increased or amortized. Goodwill is recognized only in a business combination.

Answer (A) is incorrect. The cost of a franchise should be capitalized and accounted for subsequently depending whether the asset has a finite or indefinite life. Answer (C) is incorrect. Acquisition cost of an Internet domain name is an intangible asset that meets the contractual-legal criterion for recognition. Answer (D) is incorrect. Costs incurred in conducting R&D activities under contractual arrangements may be capitalized.

15.1.10. A closely held manufacturing company must disclose all of the following information in audited financial statements except

A. Replacement cost of inventory.

B. Pledged inventory.

C. LIFO reserves.

D. Changes in methods of accounting for inventory.

Answer (A) is correct. *(CPA, adapted)*

REQUIRED: The disclosure not required of a closely held manufacturing company.

DISCUSSION: A U.S. manufacturer should report inventory at full absorption cost unless the fair value is less than cost. Neither closely nor publicly held companies must report replacement cost of inventory.

Answer (B) is incorrect. Pledged inventory is a disclosure required of all U.S. companies. Answer (C) is incorrect. LIFO reserves are disclosures required of all U.S. companies. Answer (D) is incorrect. Changes in methods of accounting for inventory are disclosures required of all U.S. companies.

15.1.11. Patentex developed a new secret formula that is of great value because it resulted in a virtual monopoly. Patentex has capitalized all research and development costs associated with this formula. Greene, CPA, who is auditing this account, will probably

A. Confer with management regarding transfer of the amount from the balance sheet to the income statement.

B. Confirm that the secret formula is registered and on file with the county clerk's office.

C. Confer with management regarding a change in the title of the account to goodwill.

D. Confer with management regarding ownership of the secret formula.

Answer (A) is correct. *(CPA, adapted)*

REQUIRED: The auditor's proper response after discovering the capitalization of R&D costs.

DISCUSSION: U.S. GAAP require that R&D costs be expensed as incurred. The auditor should confer with management about this material misstatement. If management refuses to correct the misstatement, the auditor should express a qualified or an adverse opinion if the misstatement is material. The required restatement is to expense the amounts capitalized, i.e., to transfer the amounts from the balance sheet to the income statement.

Answer (B) is incorrect. Confirming registration of the formula (an intangible asset) is appropriate for assessing its existence, ownership, and value. But this procedure is not relevant to determining the accounting principle to apply. Answer (C) is incorrect. Reclassifying R&D costs as goodwill is misleading to financial statement users. The costs must be expensed. Answer (D) is incorrect. Although appropriate for assessing the rights assertion, ownership is not relevant to determining the proper accounting principle.

15.1.12. A client owning 18% of the voting stock of an investee has accounted for the investment under the equity method. The effect of using the equity method rather than the fair value method is material. In this instance,

A. The financial statements are not fairly presented.

B. A decision as to whether an 18% interest provides an ability to exercise significant influence rests with management, and the auditor should consider the equity method to be the appropriate valuation method.

C. Because an interest of less than 20% implies that the investor cannot exercise significant influence over the investee, the auditor will need to obtain evidence to support a claim to the contrary.

D. If the equity method is used in the published financial statements, and the auditor agrees that this method is appropriate, no disclosure that the 20% presumption was set aside is required.

Answer (C) is correct. *(Publisher, adapted)*

REQUIRED: The true statement about accounting for an 18% ownership interest under the equity method.

DISCUSSION: Accounting for a less than 20% investment under the equity method misstates the financial statements unless the client can exercise significant influence over the investee. The rebuttable presumption is that no significant influence exists when less than 20% of the investee's voting stock is held. If the client cannot demonstrate significant influence, given the material effect of using the equity rather than the fair value method, the auditor should express a qualified or an adverse opinion.

Answer (A) is incorrect. The equity method is appropriate if the client exercises significant influence over the investee. Answer (B) is incorrect. The auditor is responsible for determining whether the client has demonstrated that it exercises significant influence. Answer (D) is incorrect. The accounting method used and, in this case, the reason the equity method was chosen are disclosed.

15.1.13. If financial statements are to meet the requirements of adequate disclosure,

A. All information pertaining to the company must be disclosed in the statements or related notes, even though some of the disclosures are potentially detrimental to the company or its shareholders.

B. All information believed by the auditor to be essential to the fair presentation of the financial statements must be disclosed, no matter how confidential management believes the data to be.

C. Statement notes should be written in very technical language to avoid misinterpretation by the reader.

D. A statement note must clearly detail any deficiencies contained in the financial statements themselves.

Answer (B) is correct. *(Publisher, adapted)*

REQUIRED: The true statement about the requirements of adequate disclosure.

DISCUSSION: In considering the adequacy of disclosure, the auditor necessarily uses confidential client information. Otherwise, forming an opinion on the statements would be difficult. To the extent required by GAAP or an other appropriate financial reporting framework, such information must be disclosed. But beyond these requirements, the auditor who discloses confidential information without specific consent violates the *Code of Professional Conduct*.

Answer (A) is incorrect. Only the information required by the applicable financial reporting framework must be disclosed. Answer (C) is incorrect. Notes need only be written so that the informative disclosures are reasonably adequate. Answer (D) is incorrect. Notes do not list deficiencies contained in the financial statements. The financial statements must conform with the appropriate financial reporting framework.

15.1.14. Adequate disclosure means that sufficient information is presented so that financial statements are not misleading. The decisions about adequate disclosure should reflect the needs of

A. Users with a reasonable knowledge of business.

B. All readers of the financial statements.

C. Experts in accounting and finance.

D. Governmental regulatory agencies.

Answer (A) is correct. *(Publisher, adapted)*

REQUIRED: The parties toward whom the adequate disclosure requirement is directed.

DISCUSSION: The auditor considers the needs of users of the financial statements. However, it is reasonable for the auditor to assume that users (1) have reasonable knowledge of business and accounting, (2) are willing to study financial information with reasonable diligence, (3) understand the materiality limits of audited statements, (4) recognize that many amounts in the statements are based on estimates and judgments, and (5) make reasonable decisions based on the statements.

Answer (B) is incorrect. Even if financial statements are general-purpose, they are not expected to meet the needs of all readers. Answer (C) is incorrect. The disclosure should be such that expertise in accounting or finance is not required to interpret the statements. Answer (D) is incorrect. Regulatory bodies exist to protect the public, who are the ultimate beneficiaries of the disclosure requirements.

15.1.15. The financial statements of a nonissuer include a separate statement of changes in equity. This statement should

A. Not be identified in the introductory paragraph but should be reported on separately in the opinion paragraph.

B. Be excluded from both the introductory and opinion paragraphs.

C. Be identified in the introductory paragraph of the report but need not be reported on separately in the opinion paragraph.

D. Be identified in the introductory paragraph of the report and must be reported on separately in the opinion paragraph.

Answer (C) is correct. *(CPA, adapted)*

REQUIRED: The recognition in the report of the statement of changes in equity.

DISCUSSION: The balance sheet, statement of income, statement of changes in equity, and statement of cash flows are the financial statements upon which the auditor customarily reports. The introductory paragraph of the auditor report for an audit of a nonissuer identifies the titles of the entity's financial statements. However, the statement of changes in equity and a separate statement of comprehensive income are not separately reported on the opinion paragraph. The reason is that changes in equity and comprehensive income are included in financial position, results of operations, and cash flows.

15.1.16. Which of the following statements is false regarding disclosure in a client's GAAP-based financial statements?

A. Information essential for a fair presentation should be set forth in the financial statements.

B. Omission of a statement of cash flows is considered inadequate disclosure.

C. Inadequate disclosure normally results in the auditor including the required information in the report.

D. The auditor should never disclose information in the report that the client has not shown in the financial statements.

Answer (D) is correct. *(Publisher, adapted)*

REQUIRED: The false statement about disclosure in the financial statements.

DISCUSSION: Omission from the financial statements, including the notes, of material information required by the applicable financial reporting framework results in expression of a qualified or an adverse opinion. The auditor also should provide the information in the report, if practicable.

Answer (A) is incorrect. Information essential for a fair presentation should be set forth in the financial statements. Answer (B) is incorrect. Omission of a statement of cash flows is considered inadequate disclosure. Answer (C) is incorrect. Inadequate disclosure normally results in the auditor's including the required information in the report.

15.1.17. Notes to financial statements may be used to

A. Describe the nature and type of auditing procedures applied to the financial statements.

B. Make an unsubstantiated claim that related party transactions were consummated on terms equivalent to those that prevail in arm's-length transactions.

C. Correct an improper financial statement presentation.

D. Indicate bases for measuring assets.

Answer (D) is correct. *(Publisher, adapted)*

REQUIRED: The purpose of notes.

DISCUSSION: Notes should be used to describe the measurement bases of the assets on the balance sheet. For example, property, plant, and equipment is recorded at historical cost and systematically allocated to appropriate accounting periods.

Answer (A) is incorrect. The financial statements should not refer to the audit or the work of the auditor. Answer (B) is incorrect. Disclosures should not imply that related party transactions were consummated on terms equivalent to those that prevail in arm's-length transactions unless such representations can be substantiated. Answer (C) is incorrect. Notes are not a substitute for recognition in financial statements of items that meet recognition criteria.

15.1.18. If the auditor discovers that the fair value of a client's investments in trading securities has increased, the auditor of the GAAP-based financial statements should insist that the

A. Investments be reported at lower of cost or market.

B. Investments be classified as long-term for balance sheet purposes with full disclosure in the notes.

C. Holding gain be recognized in the financial statements of the client.

D. Equity section of the balance sheet separately show a credit equal to the amount of the gain.

Answer (C) is correct. *(Publisher, adapted)*

REQUIRED: The auditor's action when (s)he discovers that the fair value of trading securities has increased.

DISCUSSION: Unrealized holding gains and losses on trading securities are included in earnings. If material, failure to do so is a misstatement that requires a qualified or adverse opinion.

Answer (A) is incorrect. The gain must be recognized in the income statement and the investment reported at fair value. Answer (B) is incorrect. No reclassification is necessary for a change in fair value of an investment. Answer (D) is incorrect. Under U.S. GAAP, an unrealized gain or loss on available-for-sale securities is reported in accumulated other comprehensive income (an equity account) until realized.

15.1.19. Late in December, Tech Products Company sold available-for-sale securities that had appreciated in value and then repurchased them the same day. The sale and purchase transactions resulted in a large gain. Without the gain, the company would have reported a loss for the year. Which statement with respect to the auditor is true?

A. If the sale and repurchase are disclosed, an unmodified opinion should be expressed.

B. The repurchase transaction is a sham and the auditor should insist upon a reversal or express an adverse opinion.

C. The auditor should withdraw from the engagement and refuse to be associated with the company.

D. A disclaimer of opinion should be expressed.

Answer (A) is correct. *(CPA, adapted)*

REQUIRED: The auditor's proper reaction to a sale and repurchase of appreciated securities.

DISCUSSION: Unrealized holding gains and losses on available-for-sale securities are recorded in other comprehensive income. Thus, to include the appreciation in the determination of net income, the company had to sell the securities. Because a transaction occurred, the proper accounting is to record the gain realized on the sale. Although management has indulged in obvious window-dressing, an unmodified opinion may still be expressed if disclosure is adequate to prevent the financial statements from being misleading.

Answer (B) is incorrect. The transactions should be recorded. Answer (C) is incorrect. No legal or ethical principle requires the auditor to withdraw. Answer (D) is incorrect. The transactions do not preclude forming an opinion on the statements and accompanying notes.

15.2 The Auditor's Report

15.2.1. The auditor's report refers to the U.S. GAAP-based financial statements, which are customarily considered to include the balance sheet and the statements of

A. Income and cash flows.

B. Income, changes in retained earnings, and cash flows.

C. Income, changes in equity, and cash flows.

D. Income and changes in equity.

Answer (C) is correct. *(CPA, adapted)*

REQUIRED: The basic financial statements upon which the auditor reports.

DISCUSSION: The balance sheet, statement of income, statement of changes in equity, and statement of cash flows are the financial statements upon which the auditor customarily reports. Furthermore, provided that the entity has items of other comprehensive income, U.S. GAAP require that comprehensive income be reported in a financial statement that is displayed with the same prominence as other financial statements that constitute a full set of financial statements. The format may be (1) one continuous statement consisting of net income and other comprehensive income (OCI) or (2) two separate but consecutive statements. The introductory paragraph identifies the titles of the entity's financial statements. However, the statement of changes in equity and a separate statement of comprehensive income are not separately reported on the opinion paragraph. The reason is that changes in equity and comprehensive income are included in financial position, results of operations, and cash flows.

15.2.2. An auditor's client is a nonprofit organization. U.S. GAAP for this type of nonprofit organization have been clearly defined, and the client has followed such practices. The preferred method of reporting on the client's adherence to such practices is to

A. Use the phrase "In accordance with accounting principles generally accepted in the United States of America" in the opinion paragraph.

B. Use the phrase "In conformity with generally accepted accounting practices for a nonprofit organization in the . . . field" in the opinion paragraph.

C. Describe the accounting practices in a separate paragraph, with appropriate reference thereto in the opinion paragraph.

D. Make no reference because accounting practices differ for each nonprofit organization.

Answer (A) is correct. *(Publisher, adapted)*

REQUIRED: The preferred method of stating that a nonprofit organization uses U.S. GAAP.

DISCUSSION: Because the auditee uses U.S. GAAP, the following example language is appropriate: "In our opinion, the consolidated financial statements referred to above present fairly, in all material respects, the financial position of ABC Company and its subsidiaries as of December 31, 20X1 and 20X0, and the results of their operations and their cash flows for the years then ended in accordance with accounting principles generally accepted in the United States of America."

Answer (B) is incorrect. The opinion paragraph does not require modification for the type of organization being reported on. Answer (C) is incorrect. The client should describe the accounting principles employed in a summary of significant accounting policies preceding the notes or as the first note to the statements. Answer (D) is incorrect. GAAS must be adhered to when an auditor reports on any statement. The auditor must therefore indicate whether the statements are presented in conformity with U.S. GAAP.

15.2.3. Without affecting the CPA's willingness to express an unmodified opinion on the client's U.S.-GAAP-based financial statements, corporate management may refuse a request to

A. Authorize its attorney to confirm that a list of pending or threatened litigation prepared by management includes all items known to the attorney.

B. Change its basis of accounting for inventories from FIFO to LIFO because, in the opinion of the CPA, the FIFO method fails to give adequate recognition to the extraordinary increases in prices of merchandise acquired and held by the company.

C. Write down to salvage value certain equipment that is no longer useful.

D. Allow the CPA to examine tax returns for years prior to that of the financial statements being audited.

Answer (B) is correct. *(CMA, adapted)*

REQUIRED: The request from an auditor that the client can refuse without jeopardizing an unmodified opinion.

DISCUSSION: FIFO (first-in, first-out) and LIFO (last-in, first-out) are both methods of accounting for inventories that are generally accepted in the U.S. LIFO has the advantage during periods of inflation of matching current costs with current revenues. An independent auditor who has requested a change from FIFO to LIFO is likely to express an unmodified opinion even if management refuses to do so because the financial statements would still conform with U.S. GAAP.

Answer (A) is incorrect. A lawyer's refusal to furnish the information requested in the inquiry letter is a scope limitation sufficient to preclude an unmodified opinion. Answer (C) is incorrect. Refusal to write down obsolete equipment is a misstatement that will result in modification of the opinion if it is material. Answer (D) is incorrect. An inability to obtain sufficient appropriate audit evidence concerning tax liabilities may require qualifying or disclaiming an opinion depending on the importance of the omitted procedures to the auditor's ability to form an opinion.

15.2.4. Green, CPA, was engaged to audit the financial statements of Essex Co. after its fiscal year had ended. The timing of Green's appointment as auditor and the start of field work made confirmation of accounts receivable by direct communication with the debtors ineffective. However, Green applied other procedures and was satisfied as to the reasonableness of the account balances. Green's auditor's report most likely contained a(n)

A. Unmodified opinion.

B. Unmodified opinion with an emphasis-of-matter paragraph.

C. Qualified opinion because of a scope limitation.

D. Qualified opinion because of a departure from auditing standards.

Answer (A) is correct. *(CPA, adapted)*

REQUIRED: The opinion expressed when an auditor becomes satisfied as to receivables by using alternate procedures.

DISCUSSION: Because the CPA is satisfied as to the amounts of receivables, no scope limitation exists. Accordingly, the report need not refer to the omission of the procedures or the use of alternative procedures, and the CPA may express an unmodified opinion.

Answer (B) is incorrect. No basis is given for including an emphasis-of-matter paragraph. Answer (C) is incorrect. No scope limitation exists. Answer (D) is incorrect. The auditor has not departed from auditing standards. The presumption that confirmation requests will be made is overcome if (1) the use of confirmations would be ineffective; (2) overall balance is immaterial; or (3) the assessed RMM is low, and other procedures address the risk.

15.2.5. A United States auditor of a nonissuer is aware that the report on the financial statements will be available on the Internet to parties outside the United States. In the auditor's report, how should the auditor refer to the country of origin of the accounting principles used to prepare the financial statements?

A. In the auditor's responsibility section and opinion paragraph.

B. In the auditor's responsibility section and management's responsibility for the financial statements paragraph.

C. In the opinion paragraph only.

D. In the management's responsibility for the financial statements and opinion paragraphs.

Answer (D) is correct. *(Publisher, adapted)*

REQUIRED: The standard report's reference to the country of origin of the accounting principles.

DISCUSSION: If the applicable financial reporting framework is U.S. GAAP, the management's responsibility section of the report states that management is responsible for the preparation and fair presentation of the financial statements in accordance with accounting principles generally accepted in the U.S. The opinion paragraph also contains this reference (AU-C 700).

15.2.6. A client makes test counts on the basis of a statistical plan. The auditor observes such counts as are deemed necessary and is able to become satisfied as to the reliability of the client's procedures. In reporting on the results of the audit, the auditor

A. Can express an unmodified opinion.

B. Must comment in the auditor's responsibility section as to the inability to observe year-end inventories.

C. Is required to disclaim an opinion if the inventories were material.

D. Must qualify the opinion if the inventories were material.

Answer (A) is correct. *(Publisher, adapted)*

REQUIRED: The report when a client uses statistical sampling to count inventory.

DISCUSSION: When the client uses statistical sampling to determine inventory quantities, the auditor must become satisfied that the procedures are reliable. The auditor must observe at least some counts and must be satisfied that the sampling plan is reasonable and statistically valid, that it has been properly applied, and that its results are reasonable. Given no significant scope limitation, the report need not refer to failure to observe a year-end physical count or to the alternative procedures employed. The auditor may express an unmodified opinion.

Answer (B) is incorrect. Comment in the auditor's responsibility section on the omission of a procedure is unnecessary if the auditor has become satisfied by applying alternative procedures. Answer (C) is incorrect. No significant scope limitation existed. Answer (D) is incorrect. The auditor need not qualify the opinion if the financial statements are fairly stated.

15.2.7. A note to the financial statements of the First Security Bank indicates that all of the records relating to the bank's business operations are stored on magnetic disks and that no emergency backup systems or duplicate disks are stored because the bank and its auditors consider the occurrence of a catastrophe to be remote. Based upon this note, the auditor's report on the financial statements should express

A. A "subject to" opinion.

B. A qualified opinion.

C. An unmodified opinion.

D. An adverse opinion.

Answer (C) is correct. *(CPA, adapted)*

REQUIRED: The opinion the auditor should express when a client fails to provide for backup records.

DISCUSSION: Failure to provide for backup records does not affect the fairness of the financial statements, regardless of the negative implications for the client's internal control. The auditor should therefore express an unmodified opinion in the absence of other indications to the contrary.

Answer (A) is incorrect. The wording "subject to" is not acceptable in any report. Answer (B) is incorrect. The absence of backup records is not a basis for expressing a qualified opinion if the financial statements are fairly presented in accordance with the applicable reporting framework. Answer (D) is incorrect. The absence of backup records is not a basis for expressing an adverse opinion if the financial statements are fairly presented in accordance with the applicable reporting framework.

15.2.8. If the auditor obtains satisfaction with respect to the accounts receivable balance by alternative procedures because it is impracticable to confirm accounts receivable, the auditor's report should be unmodified and could be expected to

A. Disclose that alternative procedures were used because of a management-imposed scope limitation.

B. Disclose in the opinion paragraph that confirmation of accounts receivable was impracticable.

C. Not mention the alternative procedures.

D. Refer to a note that discloses the alternative procedures.

Answer (C) is correct. *(CPA, adapted)*

REQUIRED: The reporting on alternative procedures performed to obtain evidence relevant to receivables.

DISCUSSION: External confirmation of receivables is required except when (1) they are immaterial, (2) confirmation would be ineffective, or (3) the assessed risk of material misstatement is low; other substantive procedures address the assessed risk (AU-C 505). Thus, if the auditor is able to obtain sufficient appropriate audit evidence without external confirmation, the opinion is unmodified, and the report should not refer to the omission of the procedures or the use of alternative procedures.

Answer (A) is incorrect. The report need not refer to the alternative procedures. Answer (B) is incorrect. Reference to the omitted procedure is not necessary. Answer (D) is incorrect. Reference to a note that discloses the alternative procedures is not appropriate.

15.2.9. An external auditor discovers that a payroll supervisor of the firm being audited has misappropriated $10,000. The firm's total assets and before-tax net income are $14 million and $3 million, respectively. Assuming no other issues affect the report, the external auditor's report will most likely contain a(n)

A. Disclaimer of opinion.

B. Adverse opinion.

C. Scope qualification.

D. Unmodified opinion.

Answer (D) is correct. *(CMA, adapted)*

REQUIRED: The audit report issued after detection of a misappropriation.

DISCUSSION: The auditor is likely to express an unmodified opinion for two reasons. First, the misappropriated amount is immaterial relative to assets and income. Second, as long as the misappropriation is accounted for properly, the financial statements will be fairly presented.

Answer (A) is incorrect. A disclaimer is appropriate when the audit is insufficient to permit formation of an opinion. Answer (B) is incorrect. An adverse opinion states that the statements are not fairly presented. An immaterial item, properly accounted for, does not impair the fairness of presentation. Answer (C) is incorrect. The audit scope has not been limited.

15.2.10. A critical audit matter (CAM) was included in the auditor's report on an audit under the PCAOB's auditing standards. The users of the report can conclude all of the following except that

A. The audit opinion was modified because of the critical matter.

B. The matter addressed was communicated or required to be communicated to those charged with governance.

C. The matter relates to accounts or disclosures that are material to the financial statements.

D. The matter involved especially challenging, subjective, or complex judgments by the auditor.

Answer (A) is correct. *(Publisher, adapted)*

REQUIRED: The false statement about a CAM.

DISCUSSION: Critical audit matters result from the current-period audit of the financial statements. They (1) were communicated or required to be communicated to the audit committee; (2) relate to material accounts or disclosures; and (3) involve especially challenging, subjective, or complex judgments. A CAM does not necessarily result in a modified opinion (qualified opinion, adverse opinion, or disclaimer of opinion).

Answer (B) is incorrect. A CAM results from the current-period audit of the financial statements and was communicated or required to be communicated to those charged with governance (the audit committee). Answer (C) is incorrect. CAMs relate to issues that are material to the financial statements. Answer (D) is incorrect. CAMs relate to issues that involve especially challenging, subjective, or complex judgments by the auditor.

15.2.11. An auditor of the financial statements of an issuer has determined that a critical audit matter exists. This matter

A. Must be of a kind required by PCAOB standards to be communicated to the audit committee.

B. May substitute for qualification of the opinion if described in the Critical Audit Matters section of the report.

C. May substitute for an explanatory paragraph if the matter itself requires an explanatory paragraph.

D. Involves especially challenging, subjective, or complex auditor judgment.

Answer (D) is correct. *(Publisher, adapted)*

REQUIRED: The nature of a critical audit matter in an audit of an issuer.

DISCUSSION: A critical audit matter results from the audit of the financial statements. It must (1) have been communicated or (2) be required to be communicated to the audit committee. It (1) relates to accounts or disclosures material to the financial statements and (2) involves especially challenging, subjective, or complex auditor judgment.

Answer (A) is incorrect. A critical audit matter results from the audit. Among other things, it must (1) have been communicated to the audit committee or (2) be required to be communicated to the audit committee. Answer (B) is incorrect. A critical audit matter does not replace an auditor's departure from an unqualified opinion (i.e., qualified opinion, adverse opinion, or disclaimer of opinion). Answer (C) is incorrect. The matter does not substitute for required explanatory language. If it also requires an explanatory paragraph (e.g., for a change in reporting entity), the auditor may include the required information regarding the matter in the explanatory paragraph. A cross-reference to the paragraph then should be made in the Critical Audit Matters section of the report. An alternative is to include the explanatory paragraph and the critical audit matter communication separately in the report with a cross-reference between the sections.

15.3 Addressing and Dating the Report

15.3.1. The auditor's report in an audit of an issuer may be addressed to

A. The chief operating officer.

B. Whom it may concern.

C. The board of directors and shareholders.

D. The chief financial officer.

Answer (C) is correct. *(CPA, adapted)*

REQUIRED: The correct addressee of the auditor's report.

DISCUSSION: The PCAOB standards (AS 3101) require the audit report to be addressed to the board of directors and shareholders.

15.3.2. An auditor has been engaged by the State Bank to audit the XYZ Corporation, a nonissuer, in conjunction with a loan commitment. The report would most likely be addressed to

A. The shareholders, XYZ Corporation.

B. The State Bank.

C. The board of directors, XYZ Corporation.

D. Whom it may concern.

Answer (B) is correct. *(Publisher, adapted)*

REQUIRED: The proper addressee of the report when the auditee is not the client.

DISCUSSION: Occasionally, an auditor is retained to audit the financial statements of an entity that is not his or her client. According to AICPA standards, the report customarily is addressed to the client and not to those charged with governance of the entity whose financial statements are being audited.

Answer (A) is incorrect. The State Bank is the CPA's client, and the report should be addressed to it. Answer (C) is incorrect. The State Bank is the CPA's client, and the report should be addressed to it. Answer (D) is incorrect. An audit report should not be addressed to whom it may concern.

15.3.3. An auditor's report on comparative financial statements should be dated as of the date of the

A. Issuance of the report.

B. No earlier than completion of the auditor's most recent audit.

C. Latest financial statements being reported on.

D. Last subsequent event disclosed in the statements.

Answer (B) is correct. *(CPA, adapted)*

REQUIRED: The date of the report on comparative financial statements.

DISCUSSION: The auditor's report on comparative financial statements should be dated no earlier than the date the auditor obtained sufficient appropriate evidence for the opinion on the most recent audit.

Answer (A) is incorrect. Using the date of issuance implies that the auditor performed audit procedures up to that date. Answer (C) is incorrect. The report should be dated as of the end of the audit so as to encompass the subsequent events period. Answer (D) is incorrect. If an event requiring disclosure occurs after the audit report date, the auditor may dual date the report, i.e., date the report as of the original report date except for the note disclosing the subsequent event, which would be dated as of its occurrence.

15.3.4. On February 13, Year 2, Fox, CPA, met with the audit committee of the Gem Corporation to review the draft of Fox's report on the company's financial statements as of and for the year ended December 31, Year 1. On February 16, Year 2, Fox completed all remaining field work and obtained sufficient appropriate evidence to support the opinion on the financial statements. On February 28, Year 2, the final report was mailed to Gem's audit committee. What date most likely would be used on Fox's report?

A. December 31, Year 1.

B. February 13, Year 2.

C. February 16, Year 2.

D. February 28, Year 2.

Answer (C) is correct. *(CPA, adapted)*

REQUIRED: The date most likely used on the auditor's report.

DISCUSSION: The report should be dated no earlier than the date on which the auditor has obtained sufficient appropriate audit evidence. February 16, Year 2, is the date that Fox obtained sufficient appropriate evidence to support the opinion on the financial statements. The auditor is not responsible for making any inquiries or carrying out any audit procedures for the period after the date of the report (but see AU-C 925).

15.3.5. The date of the audit report is important because

A. The auditor cannot date the report earlier than the date on which sufficient appropriate evidence to support the opinion has been obtained.

B. The auditor bills time to the client up to and including the audit report date, and the statement to the client should reflect this date.

C. Auditing standards require all audits to be performed on a timely basis.

D. It should coincide with the date of the financial statements.

Answer (A) is correct. *(Publisher, adapted)*

REQUIRED: The importance of the audit report date.

DISCUSSION: The auditor cannot date the report until sufficient appropriate evidence has been obtained. This date informs users that the auditor has considered the effects of events and transactions occurring up to that date of which the auditor became aware.

Answer (B) is incorrect. The auditor may bill the client for services after the report date. Answer (C) is incorrect. The auditor must use due care, but no standard requires the audit to be performed on a timely basis. Answer (D) is incorrect. The report should usually be dated when all necessary evidence has been obtained.

15.3.6. On September 30, Year 2, Miller was asked to reissue an auditor's report dated March 31, Year 2, on a client's financial statements for the year ended December 31, Year 1. Miller will submit the reissued report to the client in a document that contains information in addition to the client's basic financial statements. However, Miller discovered that the client suffered substantial losses on receivables resulting from conditions that occurred since March 31, Year 2. Miller should

A. Request the client to disclose the event in a separate, appropriately labeled note to the financial statements and reissue the original report with its original date.

B. Request the client to restate the financial statements and reissue the original report with a dual date.

C. Reissue the original report with its original date without regard to whether the event is disclosed in a separate note to the financial statements.

D. Not reissue the original report but express a subject to qualified opinion that discloses the event in a separate explanatory paragraph.

Answer (A) is correct. *(CPA, adapted)*

REQUIRED: The auditor action regarding reissuance of a report.

DISCUSSION: To prevent the financial statements from being misleading, management may disclose an event that arose after the date of the auditor's report. If the event is included in a separate note labeled as unaudited [e.g., a note captioned as "Event (Unaudited) Subsequent to the Date of the Independent Auditor's Report"], the auditor need not perform any procedures on the note. Moreover, the auditor's report should have the same date as the original report (AU-C 560).

Answer (B) is incorrect. Restatement is not necessary. The conditions arose after the balance sheet date. Also, the auditor is not assuming responsibility for the event and thus should not dual-date the report. The event is not a subsequent event or a subsequently discovered fact. Answer (C) is incorrect. When financial statements are reissued, management may revise them by including disclosures about events occurring after the original report date to prevent the statements from being misleading. Answer (D) is incorrect. A "subject to" opinion is never permissible.

15.3.7. An auditor released an audit report that was dual-dated for a subsequently discovered fact occurring after the date of the auditor's report but before issuance of the related financial statements. The auditor's responsibility for events occurring subsequent to the original report date was

A. Limited to the specific event referenced.

B. Limited to include only events occurring before the date of the last subsequent event referenced.

C. Extended to subsequent events occurring through the date of issuance of the related financial statements.

D. Extended to include all events occurring since the original report date.

Answer (A) is correct. *(CPA, adapted)*

REQUIRED: The auditor's responsibility for events occurring subsequent to the original report date when the report is dual-dated.

DISCUSSION: Subsequent to the original report date, the auditor is responsible only for the specific subsequently discovered fact for which the report was dual-dated. (S)he is responsible for other events only up to the original report date.

15.3.8. In May Year 3, an auditor reissues the auditor's report on the Year 1 financial statements at a former client's request. The Year 1 financial statements are to be presented comparatively with subsequent audited statements. They are not restated, and the auditor does not revise the wording of the report. The auditor should

A. Dual-date the reissued report.

B. Use the release date of the reissued report.

C. Use the original report date on the reissued report.

D. Use the current-period auditor's report date on the reissued report.

Answer (C) is correct. *(CPA, adapted)*

REQUIRED: The date of a reissued report.

DISCUSSION: Use of the original date in a reissued report removes any implication that records, transactions, or events after such date have been audited or reviewed. However, the predecessor auditor should perform the following procedures to determine whether the report is still appropriate: (1) read the statements of the subsequent period, (2) compare the prior statements with the current statements, and (3) obtain written representations from management and the successor auditor about information obtained or events that occurred subsequent to the original date of the report.

Answer (A) is incorrect. The report is dual-dated only if it has been revised since the original reissue date. Answer (B) is incorrect. The release date of the reissued report implies that additional audit procedures have been applied. Answer (D) is incorrect. Use of the current report date implies that the report has been updated for additional audit procedures applied between the original issue date and the current auditor's report date.

15.3.9. An auditor's decision concerning whether to dual date the audit report is based upon the auditor's willingness to

A. Extend auditing procedures.

B. Accept responsibility for subsequent events.

C. Permit inclusion of a note captioned "event (unaudited) subsequent to the date of the auditor's report."

D. Assume responsibility for events subsequent to the issuance of the auditor's report.

Answer (A) is correct. *(CPA, adapted)*

REQUIRED: The factor upon which the decision to dual date the audit report is based.

DISCUSSION: When a subsequent event disclosed in the financial statements occurs after the date of the auditor's report but before the release of the auditor's report, the auditor may use dual dating. (S)he may date the report as of the original report date except for the matters affected by the subsequent event, which would be assigned the appropriate later date. In that case, the auditor's responsibility for events after the original report date would be limited to the specific event. If the auditor is willing to accept responsibility to the later date and accordingly extends subsequent events procedures to that date, the auditor may choose the later date as the date for the entire report.

Answer (B) is incorrect. The auditor must assume responsibility for subsequent events occurring between the balance sheet date and the date of the report. Answer (C) is incorrect. A caption regarding an unaudited event subsequent to the date of the auditor's report is appropriate for a reissuance of an auditor's report, not for the original report. Answer (D) is incorrect. The auditor does not assume responsibility for events subsequent to the date of the report (but see AU-C 925 regarding filings under the Securities Act of 1933).

15.3.10. Normally, an independent accountant's responsibility for subsequent events work ends at the date of the report. However, when registration filings with the SEC contain audited financial statements, the accountant must extend subsequent events work to the

A. Prospectus date.

B. Filing date.

C. Effective date.

D. Date the final security is sold.

Answer (C) is correct. *(Publisher, adapted)*

REQUIRED: The date to which the auditor should extend subsequent events work for a registration statement.

DISCUSSION: The auditor should extend procedures to the effective date or as close to it as reasonable and practicable. In addition to the subsequent-events procedures outlined in AU-C 560, the accountant also should (1) read the entire prospectus and other pertinent portions of the registration statement and (2) inquire of and obtain written representations from officers and other executives responsible for financial and accounting matters about whether any significant events have occurred other than those reflected or disclosed in the registration statement (AU-C 925). The registration statement speaks as of the effective date, which differs from the prospectus date (the date the document is prepared for first submission to the SEC), the filing date (the date the prospectus and other documents are submitted to the SEC), and the date the last security is sold.

15.3.11. If a subsequently discovered fact becomes known to the auditor before the release of the audit report, the auditor should

A. Modify the opinion and dual date the audit report. No additional audit procedures are required.

B. Date the audit report as of the original date of the auditor's report and caption the note disclosing the subsequent event as being subsequent to the completion of the audit procedures.

C. Not modify the audit opinion if the event is properly disclosed and date the audit report as of the original date of the auditor's report.

D. Either dual date the audit report or date the audit report as of the time of the completion of the extended audit procedures.

Answer (D) is correct. *(Publisher, adapted)*

REQUIRED: The action when a subsequently discovered fact occurs after the date of the report but prior to its release.

DISCUSSION: The auditor may use dual dating or date the entire report as of the date of the subsequently discovered fact occurring after the date of the auditor's report. If the report is dual dated, the auditor's responsibility is limited to the specific event. If the date of the report is the date of that event, responsibility extends to that date. Accordingly, the auditor should perform the necessary additional procedures through the new date of the report.

Answer (A) is incorrect. If the client properly notes or otherwise discloses the item, no opinion modification is necessary. Answer (B) is incorrect. Captioning the note is insufficient. Answer (C) is incorrect. The subsequently discovered fact must be acknowledged in dating the report.

15.3.12. An auditor dated the audit report for a client on February 15. The related financial statements were issued on March 10. On April 8, the client suffered the loss of a significant portion of its plant facilities by fire. The client requested additional copies of the previously issued report on May 5. Assuming no additional audit work has been or will be performed, the auditor should

A. Disregard the casualty and reissue the original report with no change in date.

B. Have the client disclose the event in a separate note to the statements identified as "Event (Unaudited) Subsequent to the Date of the Report of the Independent Auditor."

C. Use dual dating.

D. Either have the client disclose the event in a separate note to the statements identified as "Event (Unaudited) Subsequent to the Date of the Report of the Independent Auditor" or use dual dating.

Answer (B) is correct. *(Publisher, adapted)*

REQUIRED: The treatment in a reissued report of a material event that occurred after the original report date.

DISCUSSION: A major casualty occurring after the date of the original report requires disclosure in the financial statements covered by the reissued report. The reissuance of a report includes furnishing additional copies of a previously issued report. If the auditor performs procedures with respect to the casualty, (s)he may use dual dating. If no audit work is performed relative to this event, it should be marked unaudited in a note to the financial statements captioned as described.

Answer (A) is incorrect. The auditor cannot disregard the casualty. It must be disclosed in the financial statements. Answer (C) is incorrect. Dual dating is inappropriate when the subsequently discovered fact is unaudited. Answer (D) is incorrect. Dual dating is inappropriate when the subsequently discovered fact is unaudited.

15.3.13. Karr has audited the financial statements of Lurch Corporation for the year ended December 31, Year 1. Although Karr completed all audit procedures necessary to support the opinion on February 17, Year 2, Karr's report was dated February 28, Year 2, and was received by the management of Lurch on March 5, Year 2. On April 4, Year 2, the management of Lurch asked that Karr approve inclusion of this report in its annual report to shareholders that will include unaudited financial statements for the first quarter ended March 31, Year 2. Karr approved the inclusion. Under the circumstances, Karr is responsible for inquiring as to events occurring through

A. February 17, Year 2.

B. February 28, Year 2.

C. March 31, Year 2.

D. April 4, Year 2.

Answer (B) is correct. *(CPA, adapted)*

REQUIRED: The date through which the auditor assumes responsibility.

DISCUSSION: The audit report can be dated no earlier than the date that the auditor obtained sufficient appropriate evidence. The auditor has no responsibility to make any inquiry or carry out any procedures for the period after the date of the report. An independent auditor also may reissue the report. Use of the original report date in the reissued report removes any implication that records, transactions, or events after that date have been audited or reviewed. The auditor has no responsibility in such cases to make further investigation or inquiry as to events after the original report date.

Answer (A) is incorrect. In this situation, the auditor assumed responsibility up to 2/28/Yr 2, not the date of completion of the audit procedures, 2/17/Yr 2. Answer (C) is incorrect. The auditor assumed responsibility for events only up to the date of the report. Answer (D) is incorrect. The auditor assumed responsibility for events only up to the date of the report.

15.4 Qualified Opinions

15.4.1. When financial statements are materially but not pervasively misstated, an auditor may express a

	Qualified Opinion	Disclaimer of an Opinion
A.	Yes	No
B.	Yes	Yes
C.	No	Yes
D.	No	No

Answer (A) is correct. *(CPA, adapted)*

REQUIRED: The proper report when statements are materially misstated.

DISCUSSION: A material misstatement results in either a qualified or an adverse opinion. The auditor must exercise judgment as to whether the misstatement is pervasive. If the misstatement is not pervasive, the auditor should express a qualified opinion.

Answer (B) is incorrect. A disclaimer of opinion is expressed when (1) the auditor cannot obtain sufficient appropriate audit evidence and (2) the possible effects of any undetected misstatements could be material and pervasive. Answer (C) is incorrect. A material but not pervasive misstatement requires expression of a qualified opinion. A disclaimer of opinion cannot be expressed when the statements are materially misstated. Answer (D) is incorrect. A material but not pervasive misstatement requires expression of a qualified opinion. A disclaimer of opinion is expressed when (1) the auditor cannot obtain sufficient appropriate audit evidence and (2) the possible effects of any undetected misstatements could be material and pervasive.

15.4.2. A CPA engaged to audit financial statements observes that the accounting for a certain material but not pervasive item is not in conformity with the applicable financial reporting framework, although the matter is prominently disclosed in a note to the financial statements. The CPA should

A. Express an unmodified opinion but insert an emphasis-of-matter paragraph with a reference to the note.

B. Disclaim an opinion.

C. Not allow the accounting treatment for this item to affect the type of opinion because the misstatement was disclosed.

D. Qualify the opinion because of the misstatement.

Answer (D) is correct. *(CPA, adapted)*

REQUIRED: The effect on the audit opinion of a material but not pervasive misstatement.

DISCUSSION: When financial statements are materially misstated, but the effects are not pervasive, the auditor should express a qualified opinion if the audit has been in accordance with GAAS. The cause of the qualified opinion should be described in the report even if full and prominent note disclosure has been made.

Answer (A) is incorrect. An unmodified opinion cannot be expressed when the statements are materially misstated. Answer (B) is incorrect. A disclaimer is appropriate when the auditor is unable to obtain sufficient appropriate audit evidence. Answer (C) is incorrect. Note disclosure does not overcome the need for a modified opinion.

15.4.3. When the financial statements of a nonissuer contain a misstatement, the effect of which is material but not pervasive, the auditor should

A. Qualify the opinion and include a basis for qualified opinion paragraph that describes the matter resulting in the qualification.

B. Qualify the opinion and describe the misstatement within the opinion paragraph.

C. Disclaim an opinion and explain the effect of the misstatement in a disclaimer of opinion paragraph.

D. Disclaim an opinion and describe the misstatement within the opinion paragraph.

Answer (A) is correct. *(CPA, adapted)*

REQUIRED: The auditor's report when the statements of a nonissuer contain a material but not pervasive misstatement.

DISCUSSION: When the financial statements are materially misstated, but the effects are not pervasive, the auditor should express a qualified opinion. The report should contain a basis for qualified opinion paragraph preceding the opinion paragraph. If the material misstatement relates to specific amounts, the basis paragraph should describe and quantify the financial effects, if practicable. If the misstatement relates to narrative disclosures, the auditor should include an explanation. If the misstatement relates to an omission of required information, the auditor should describe the nature of the information and, if practicable, include the information. The opinion paragraph should refer to the basis paragraph.

Answer (B) is incorrect. A basis for qualified opinion paragraph is required. Answer (C) is incorrect. A material misstatement requires a qualified or adverse opinion. A disclaimer of opinion is appropriate when the auditor is unable to obtain sufficient appropriate audit evidence. Answer (D) is incorrect. A material misstatement requires a qualified or adverse opinion. A disclaimer of opinion is appropriate when the auditor is unable to obtain sufficient appropriate audit evidence.

15.4.4. On January 2, Year 2, the Retail Auto Parts Co. received a notice from its primary suppliers that effective immediately all wholesale prices would be increased 10%. On the basis of the notice, Retail Auto Parts Co. revalued its December 31, Year 1, inventory to reflect the higher costs. The inventory constituted a material proportion of total assets. However, the effect of the revaluation was material to current assets but not to total assets or net income. In reporting on the company's financial statements for the year ended December 31, Year 1, in which inventory is valued at the adjusted amounts, the auditor would most likely

A. Express an unmodified opinion provided the nature of the adjustment and the amounts involved are disclosed in notes.

B. Express a qualified opinion.

C. Disclaim an opinion.

D. Express an adverse opinion.

Answer (B) is correct. *(CPA, adapted)*

REQUIRED: The effect on the opinion of the client's revaluation of inventory.

DISCUSSION: The auditor should express a qualified opinion when the financial statements are materially misstated, but the effects are not pervasive. Inventory is misstated because it should be recorded at lower of cost or market. Holding gains should not be recognized until realized, i.e., when inventory is sold. Furthermore, the effect on current assets is material. However, it (1) is confined to specific elements, accounts, or items and (2) is not a substantial proportion of the financial statements.

Answer (A) is incorrect. The *Code of Professional Conduct* prohibits expression of an unmodified opinion in these circumstances even though full disclosure is made. Answer (C) is incorrect. A disclaimer is proper only when the auditor is unable to obtain sufficient appropriate audit evidence. Answer (D) is incorrect. An adverse opinion is probably not appropriate. The effect of revaluation was not pervasive.

15.4.5. The client includes in the determination of net income certain material items properly classifiable as other comprehensive income (OCI). In this situation, the auditor must express a(n)

A. Unmodified opinion.

B. Qualified opinion.

C. Adverse opinion.

D. Qualified or adverse opinion.

Answer (D) is correct. *(Publisher, adapted)*

REQUIRED: The opinion when a client includes items of OCI in the determination of net income.

DISCUSSION: Items of OCI (for example, foreign currency translation adjustments; unrealized gains and losses on available-for-sale securities; and net gain or loss on derivatives designated, qualifying, and effective as cash flow hedges) are excluded from the determination of net income. The total of other comprehensive income for a period is transferred to a component of equity that is displayed separately from retained earnings and paid-in capital in the balance sheet. Given that the misstatement is material, the auditor should express either a qualified or an adverse opinion.

Answer (A) is incorrect. The report must be modified for a material misstatement. Answer (B) is incorrect. If the auditor concludes that the misstatement is material and its effects are pervasive, an adverse opinion is expressed. Answer (C) is incorrect. The auditor may conclude that the effects of the material misstatement are not pervasive. In that case, a qualified opinion is expressed.

15.4.6. When an auditor qualifies an opinion in an audit of a nonissuer because of the omission of information required to be disclosed, the auditor should describe the nature of the omission in the basis for qualified opinion paragraph and modify the

	Introductory Paragraph	Auditor's Responsibility Section	Opinion Paragraph
A.	Yes	No	No
B.	Yes	Yes	No
C.	No	Yes	Yes
D.	No	No	Yes

Answer (C) is correct. *(CPA, adapted)*

REQUIRED: The effect(s) on the report if disclosures are omitted.

DISCUSSION: If the material misstatement relates to specific amounts, the basis paragraph should describe and quantify the financial effects, if practicable. If the misstatement relates to narrative disclosures, the auditor should include an explanation. If the misstatement relates to an omission of required information, the auditor should describe the nature of the information and, if practicable, include the information. If the opinion is qualified, (1) the introductory paragraph and management's responsibility for the financial statements paragraph are unchanged, (2) the auditor's responsibility section mentions that the audit opinion is qualified, and (3) the opinion paragraph includes the language ". . ., except for the effects of the matter(s) described in the basis for qualified opinion paragraph, . . ."

Answer (A) is incorrect. The opinion paragraph and the auditor's responsibility section are modified. Answer (B) is incorrect. The opinion paragraph is modified but the introductory paragraph is not. Answer (D) is incorrect. The auditor's responsibility section mentions that the audit opinion is qualified.

15.4.7. An auditor expresses a qualified opinion because of a material misstatement related to specific amounts in the financial statements. Which of the following phrases should be included in the opinion paragraph?

	"When Read in Conjunction with Note X"	"With the Foregoing Explanation"
A.	Yes	No
B.	No	Yes
C.	Yes	Yes
D.	No	No

Answer (D) is correct. *(CPA, adapted)*

REQUIRED: The phrase(s) used in an opinion qualified because of a material misstatement related to specific amounts in the financial statements.

DISCUSSION: The auditor should use the phrase "except for" to qualify an opinion, and include a reference to a paragraph that describes the deficiency. Given a qualification because of a material misstatement related to specific amounts in the financial statements, the reference should describe the matter resulting in the qualification. It also should include (1) a description and quantification of the financial effects, if practicable; (2) an explanation of how narrative disclosures are misstated; or (3) omitted information, if practicable, and a description of its nature. However, if financial-effects disclosures are made in a note to the statements, the report may refer to it. Furthermore, the notes are part of the financial statements, and a phrase such as "when read in conjunction with Note X" in the opinion paragraph is likely to be misunderstood. Also, wording such as "with the foregoing explanation" is neither clear nor forceful enough.

15.4.8. If an issuer releases financial statements that purport to present its financial position and results of operations but omits the statement of cash flows, the auditor ordinarily will express a(n)

A. Disclaimer of opinion.

B. Qualified opinion.

C. Review report.

D. Unmodified opinion with a separate emphasis-of-matter paragraph.

Answer (B) is correct. *(CPA, adapted)*

REQUIRED: The opinion expressed when a client fails to present a statement of cash flows.

DISCUSSION: An entity that reports financial position and results of operations should provide a statement of cash flows. Thus, the omission of the cash flow statement is normally a basis for modifying the opinion. If the statements fail to disclose required information, the auditor should provide the information in the report, if practicable. However, the auditor is not required to prepare a basic financial statement. Accordingly, (s)he should qualify the opinion and explain the reason in a basis for qualified opinion paragraph.

Answer (A) is incorrect. The question concerns disclosure rather than an inability to obtain sufficient appropriate audit evidence. Answer (C) is incorrect. The engagement is an audit. Answer (D) is incorrect. A material omission of disclosures normally requires modification of the opinion.

15.4.9. Which of the following phrases will an auditor most likely include in the auditor's report on an engagement for a nonissuer when expressing a qualified opinion because of inadequate disclosure?

A. Subject to the departure from generally accepted accounting principles, as described above.

B. With the foregoing explanation of these omitted disclosures.

C. Except for the omission of the information.

D. Does not present fairly in all material respects.

Answer (C) is correct. *(CPA, adapted)*

REQUIRED: The phrase included when the opinion is qualified because of inadequate disclosure.

DISCUSSION: A report qualified for inadequate disclosure includes a basis for qualified opinion paragraph preceding the opinion paragraph. The opinion paragraph states, "In our opinion, except for the omission of information described in the Basis for Qualified Opinion paragraph, the financial statements referred to above present fairly . . ."

Answer (A) is incorrect. A "subject to" opinion should not be expressed in any circumstance. Answer (B) is incorrect. The phrase "with the foregoing explanation" is not forceful enough, lacks clarity, and should not be used. Answer (D) is incorrect. The phrase "does not present fairly" indicates an adverse opinion.

15.4.10. An auditor most likely modifies the opinion if the entity's financial statements include a note on related party transactions

A. Disclosing loans to related parties at interest rates significantly below prevailing market rates.

B. Describing an exchange of real estate for similar property in a nonmonetary related party transaction.

C. Stating without substantiation that a particular related party transaction occurred on terms equivalent to those that would have prevailed in an arm's-length transaction.

D. Presenting the dollar volume of related party transactions and the effects of any change from prior periods in the method of establishing terms.

Answer (C) is correct. *(CPA, adapted)*

REQUIRED: The modification to an opinion when an entity's financial statements include a note on related party transactions.

DISCUSSION: The auditor should obtain sufficient appropriate evidence about a management assertion that related party transactions were conducted on terms equivalent to those that prevail in arm's-length transactions. Management is responsible for substantiating the assertion. The auditor evaluates management's support for the assertion.

Answer (A) is incorrect. An opinion modification is unnecessary, but the auditor may wish to include these matters in an emphasis-of-matter paragraph. Answer (B) is incorrect. An opinion modification is unnecessary, but the auditor may wish to include these matters in an emphasis-of-matter paragraph. Answer (D) is incorrect. An opinion modification is unnecessary, but the auditor may wish to include these matters in an emphasis-of-matter paragraph.

15.4.11. An auditor may reasonably express a "subject to" qualified opinion for

	Lack of Consistency	Departure from an Applicable Financial Reporting Framework
A.	Yes	Yes
B.	Yes	No
C.	No	Yes
D.	No	No

Answer (D) is correct. *(CPA, adapted)*

REQUIRED: The type of opinion that uses the phrase "subject to."

DISCUSSION: The phrase "subject to" should not be used in any report. It is not clear or forceful enough (AU-C 705).

15.4.12. When an issuer refuses to include in its audited financial statements the segment disclosures that the auditor believes are required, the auditor should express a(n)

A. Unmodified opinion with an emphasis-of-matter paragraph.

B. Qualified opinion because of inadequate disclosure.

C. Adverse opinion because of a significant uncertainty.

D. Disclaimer of opinion because of the significant scope limitation.

Answer (B) is correct. *(CPA, adapted)*

REQUIRED: The effect on the report when an issuer refuses to include in its audited financial statements any of the segment disclosures that the auditor believes are required.

DISCUSSION: If the statements are materially misstated because of the omission of required information, the auditor should modify the opinion for inadequate disclosure and describe the information omitted. The auditor also should include this information in the report, if practicable. But the auditor is not expected to prepare segment information. (S)he need not assume the position of a preparer of financial information.

Answer (A) is incorrect. Inadequate disclosure requires an opinion modification if it is material. Answer (C) is incorrect. The issue is disclosure, not uncertainty. Moreover, by itself, an uncertainty does not result in a required report modification. Answer (D) is incorrect. Inadequate disclosure is a misstatement, that is, a difference between the disclosure of the reported item and the disclosure required for the item to be in accordance with the applicable financial reporting framework.

15.4.13. An auditor may not express a qualified opinion when

A. A scope limitation prevents the auditor from completing an important audit procedure.

B. The auditor's report refers to the work of a specialist.

C. An accounting principle at variance with the applicable financial reporting framework is used.

D. The auditor lacks independence with respect to the audited entity.

Answer (D) is correct. *(CPA, adapted)*

REQUIRED: The situation in which an auditor may not express a qualified opinion.

DISCUSSION: An auditor must be independent of the entity when performing an audit in accordance with GAAS unless (1) GAAS provide otherwise or (2) a law or regulation requires the auditor to report on the statements (AU-C 200).

Answer (A) is incorrect. An auditor may express a qualified opinion due to an inability to obtain sufficient appropriate audit evidence if the possible effects are material but not pervasive (AU-C 705). Answer (B) is incorrect. The report may refer to and identify an auditor's external specialist if the auditor modifies the opinion (AU-C 620, *Using the Work of an Auditor's Specialist*). Answer (C) is incorrect. If a material misstatement does not have pervasive effects, the auditor may express a qualified opinion.

15.4.14. An auditor may express a qualified opinion for which of the following reasons?

	Circumstances Related to the Work	Limitations Imposed by Management
A.	Yes	Yes
B.	Yes	No
C.	No	Yes
D.	No	No

Answer (A) is correct. *(CPA, adapted)*

REQUIRED: The reasons for which the auditor may express a qualified opinion.

DISCUSSION: An auditor may express a qualified opinion due to an inability to obtain sufficient appropriate audit evidence if the possible effects are material but not pervasive. The inability to obtain sufficient audit evidence (also called a scope limitation) may result from (1) circumstances not controlled by the entity, such as destruction or government seizure of accounting records; (2) circumstances related to the nature or timing of the work, such as not being able to (a) observe inventory due to the late appointment of the auditor, (b) obtain an investee's financial information, or (c) determine that controls are ineffective; or (3) limitations imposed by management, such as preventing the auditor from observing inventory or confirming receivables (AU-C 705).

15.4.15. When qualifying an opinion because of an insufficiency of appropriate audit evidence, an auditor of a nonissuer client should refer to the situation in the

	Auditor's Responsibility Section	Notes to the Financial Statements
A.	Yes	Yes
B.	Yes	No
C.	No	Yes
D.	No	No

Answer (B) is correct. *(CPA, adapted)*

REQUIRED: The effect on the auditor's report when the opinion is qualified because of an insufficiency of appropriate audit evidence.

DISCUSSION: An auditor may express a qualified opinion due to an inability to obtain sufficient appropriate audit evidence if the possible effects are material but not pervasive. But the notes to the financial statements are unchanged because they were not drafted by the auditor. Moreover, a sentence in the auditor's responsibility section states, "We believe that the audit evidence we have obtained is sufficient and appropriate to provide a basis for our qualified audit opinion."

Answer (A) is incorrect. The notes to the financial statements are unchanged. Answer (C) is incorrect. The notes to the financial statements are unchanged, but the auditor's responsibility section is modified. Answer (D) is incorrect. The auditor's responsibility section is modified.

15.4.16. If the independent auditor has not become satisfied by means of other auditing procedures with respect to opening inventories, (s)he should

A. Disclaim an opinion or qualify the opinion on the statements as a whole.

B. Either disclaim an opinion on the statement of income or qualify the opinion, depending on materiality and the pervasiveness of the possible effects.

C. Either disclaim an opinion or qualify the opinion on the statement of income, regardless of the degree of materiality of the amounts involved.

D. Express an adverse opinion on the statements as a whole when the amount in question is material.

Answer (B) is correct. *(Publisher, adapted)*

REQUIRED: The opinion expressed when the auditor is not satisfied as to opening inventories.

DISCUSSION: An inability to perform a specific procedure is not a limitation on the audit scope if the auditor can obtain sufficient appropriate audit evidence by performing alternative procedures. If the auditor cannot, (s)he expresses (1) a qualified opinion if the possible effects are material but not pervasive and (2) a disclaimer opinion if they are material and pervasive. Because cost of goods sold is dependent on opening inventories, an unmodified opinion on the income statement is not possible.

Answer (A) is incorrect. The scope limitation may apply only to the income statement. Answer (C) is incorrect. The materiality of the amounts involved determines the opinion expressed. Answer (D) is incorrect. An adverse opinion is expressed for a material misstatement with pervasive effects. It is inappropriate for an inability to obtain sufficient appropriate audit evidence.

Questions 15.4.17 through 15.4.22 are based on the following information. An audit was performed by Leo Scott, CPA, of the financial statements of Lectronic Leasing Company, a nonissuer, for the year ended December 31. A cash advance to Computer Credit Corporation is material to the presentation of Lectronic's financial position. Computer Credit's unaudited financial statements show negative working capital, negative equity, and losses in each of the 5 preceding years. Mr. Scott has suggested an allowance for the uncollectibility of the advance to Computer Credit. All of the stock of both Lectronic and Computer Credit is owned by Paul McRae and his family. Mr. McRae adamantly refuses to consider an allowance for uncollectibility. He insists that Computer Credit eventually will be profitable and be able to repay the advance. Mr. McRae proposes the following note to Lectronic's statements:

Note 1 to Financial Statements

At December 31, the Company had advanced $500,000 to Computer Credit Corporation. We obtained written confirmation of this debt from Computer Credit Corporation and reviewed unaudited financial statements of Computer Credit Corporation. Computer Credit Corporation is not in a position to repay this advance at this time, but the Company has informed us that it is optimistic as to the future of Computer Credit Corporation. Computer Credit Corporation's stock is wholly owned by Lectronic Leasing Company's common shareholders.

15.4.17. Assume that Mr. Scott concludes, based upon appropriate audit procedures, that Mr. McRae's optimism concerning Computer Credit can be neither substantiated nor disproved and that evidence to form an opinion is not available because of the auditee's record retention policies. His report will include a(n)

A. Disclaimer of opinion.

B. Qualified opinion for the failure to follow GAAP.

C. Other-matter paragraph based on the uncertainty or an adverse opinion.

D. Adverse opinion only.

Answer (A) is correct. *(CPA, adapted)*

REQUIRED: The report issued given an uncertainty.

DISCUSSION: If the auditor has not obtained sufficient appropriate audit evidence to support management's assertions about an uncertainty, an unmodified opinion is not expressed. A qualification or disclaimer of opinion is appropriate when sufficient appropriate audit evidence related to an uncertainty does or did exist but was not available for reasons such as management's record retention policies or a restriction imposed by management.

Answer (B) is incorrect. No misstatement is described. Answer (C) is incorrect. An adverse opinion is expressed only when the auditor believes the statements are not fairly presented. Answer (D) is incorrect. An adverse opinion is expressed only when the auditor believes the statements are not fairly presented.

15.4.18. With respect to Lectronic's advance to Computer Credit, Mr. Scott

A. Needs no disclosure in his auditor's report because the common ownership of the two companies has been adequately disclosed.

B. Needs no disclosure in his auditor's report because the auditor is not expected to be an expert appraiser of property values.

C. Should be concerned in formulating his auditor's opinion primarily with the issue of collectibility from Lectronic's viewpoint.

D. Should be concerned in formulating his auditor's opinion primarily with the consolidated financial position of the two companies.

Answer (C) is correct. *(CPA, adapted)*

REQUIRED: The treatment in the report of a material advance to a related party that may be uncollectible.

DISCUSSION: The auditor has apparently concluded that a material receivable is uncollectible. Management refuses to create an allowance for the bad debt. Thus, the auditor may conclude that Lectronic's statements are materially misstated, requiring a modification of the opinion. The debt also represents a material transaction with a related party. The auditor will expect the client to summarize and present the facts and circumstances of the related party relationships and transactions so that disclosures are understandable.

Answer (A) is incorrect. Both the related party transaction and uncollectibility of the receivable should be mentioned in the audit report. The basis for the modification of the opinion should be explained. Answer (B) is incorrect. Although not expected to be an appraiser of property values, the auditor should modify the opinion unless convinced that the financial statements are fairly presented. Answer (D) is incorrect. The scope of the engagement extends only to Lectronic's statements.

15.4.19. A deficiency in the given note is that it

A. Does not identify the auditor.

B. Is worded as a representation of the auditor.

C. Does not state the auditor's conclusion or opinion.

D. Includes the client's representation as to collectibility.

Answer (B) is correct. *(CPA, adapted)*

REQUIRED: The deficiency in the given note.

DISCUSSION: The financial statements and notes are the representations of management. The assertions of the auditor are made in the audit report, although the report may refer to the notes in certain cases.

Answer (A) is incorrect. Notes should not identify the auditor. Answer (C) is incorrect. Notes should not restate the auditor's conclusions. Answer (D) is incorrect. The client may properly include a representation as to the collectibility of a debt in the notes.

15.4.20. Assume that Mr. Scott introduces the opinion paragraph of his report as follows: "With the explanation given in Note 1, in our opinion the aforementioned financial statements present fairly . . ." This is a(n)

A. Unmodified opinion.

B. Adverse opinion.

C. Qualified opinion.

D. Improper type of reporting.

Answer (D) is correct. *(CPA, adapted)*

REQUIRED: The proper characterization of the phrase "With the explanation given in Note 1."

DISCUSSION: Because the notes are part of the financial statements, reporting that those statements are fairly presented when read in conjunction with a cited note is likely to be misunderstood and accordingly should not be done.

Answer (A) is incorrect. The quoted phrase is not used in any report. Answer (B) is incorrect. The quoted phrase is not used in any report. Answer (C) is incorrect. The quoted phrase is not used in any report.

15.4.21. Assume that Mr. Scott concludes, based upon appropriate audit procedures, that the advance to Computer Credit will not be repaid. His report will include a

A. Disclaimer of opinion.

B. Qualified opinion or disclaimer of opinion.

C. "Subject to" opinion or adverse opinion.

D. Qualified opinion or adverse opinion.

Answer (D) is correct. *(CPA, adapted)*

REQUIRED: The type of report if the auditor concludes that the advance will not be repaid.

DISCUSSION: If the advance is treated as uncollectible, the financial statements are materially misstated because management has refused to establish an allowance account. The auditor should express a qualified opinion or an adverse opinion depending on the pervasiveness of the effects of the misstatement.

Answer (A) is incorrect. A disclaimer of opinion is appropriate only when the auditor is unable to form an opinion. Answer (B) is incorrect. A disclaimer of opinion is appropriate only when the auditor is unable to form an opinion. Answer (C) is incorrect. A "subject to" opinion is not an acceptable form of reporting.

15.4.22. Assume that subsequent to the date of the auditor's report (but prior to its release) Mr. McRae and his family sell all of their stock in Computer Credit and the new owners repay the advance from Lectronic. Mr. Scott's opinion as to Lectronic's financial statements will be

A. Unaffected because the sale of Computer Credit stock occurred subsequent to the audit date.

B. Unaffected because the sale of Computer Credit stock occurred subsequent to the date of the auditor's report.

C. Qualified unless the repayment of the advance is recorded by Lectronic as a December 31 transaction.

D. Unmodified because the issue of collectibility is now settled.

Answer (D) is correct. *(CPA, adapted)*

REQUIRED: The effect on the report of a subsequent event.

DISCUSSION: The subsequent event provides additional evidence with respect to conditions existing at the balance sheet date. Such an event may require adjustment of the financial statements and consequently may affect the audit report (AU-C 560). Here, the auditor can now express an unmodified opinion, assuming no other basis exists for modifying the opinion. The subsequent event has eliminated the issue of collectibility of the receivable.

Answer (A) is incorrect. The auditor is responsible for subsequent events occurring prior to the issuance of the related financial statements. Answer (B) is incorrect. The auditor is responsible for a subsequently discovered fact prior to the report release date. Answer (C) is incorrect. No qualification as to collectibility of the receivable is necessary. The best evidence of collectibility is payment.

15.4.23. In which circumstance does the auditor not consider the need to modify the wording in the report?

A. The client's legal counsel is requested to advise whether a material act constitutes noncompliance with tax law but refuses to do so.

B. The auditor concludes that the effect of noncompliance with pension regulations creates substantial doubt about the entity's ability to continue as a going concern.

C. The auditor concludes that the effect of noncompliance, taken alone or with similar acts, is material in amount and has not been properly accounted for or disclosed in the financial statements.

D. All of the circumstances require modification of the auditor's report.

Answer (D) is correct. *(Publisher, adapted)*

REQUIRED: The circumstance in which the auditor does not consider modifying the wording in the report.

DISCUSSION: All of the answer choices given describe circumstances in which the report should be modified.

Answer (A) is incorrect. The auditor may be unable to determine noncompliance or the amounts associated with it as a result of an inability to gather sufficient appropriate evidence. For example, the client's legal counsel may have refused to give advice. In these circumstances, the scope limitation may require a qualified opinion or a disclaimer depending on the materiality and pervasiveness of the possible effects. Answer (B) is incorrect. If the effects of noncompliance create substantial doubt about the entity's ability to continue as a going concern, an emphasis-of-matter (explanatory) paragraph is required. Answer (C) is incorrect. If the effects of noncompliance are material but have not been properly accounted for or disclosed, the misstatement may result in a qualified or an adverse opinion depending on the pervasiveness of the possible effects (AU-C 250).

15.4.24. During the course of an audit of the financial statements of Excellent Corporation, a nonissuer, Smart, CPA, discovered that the company vice-president had misrepresented one of the company's products before the Food and Drug Administration by falsifying test results. Unasserted claims, material in amount, loom in the near future. Management refuses to permit the inclusion of a liability for such claims even though it is probable that they will be asserted and the amount of loss can be reasonably estimated. Smart should issue a report with a(n)

A. Adverse opinion or a qualified opinion.

B. Qualified opinion but should not consider expressing an adverse opinion.

C. Disclaimer.

D. Unmodified opinion and an other-matter paragraph.

Answer (A) is correct. *(Publisher, adapted)*

REQUIRED: The opinion that should be expressed when the client improperly refuses to provide for a material loss contingency.

DISCUSSION: According to U.S. GAAP, a loss contingency should be recognized in the accounts if its occurrence is probable and its amount can be reasonably estimated. The client's refusal to do so is a misstatement. Given that the amount involved is material, depending on pervasiveness of the effects, the auditor should express a qualified opinion or an adverse opinion.

Answer (B) is incorrect. The matter may be sufficiently pervasive to require an adverse rather than a qualified opinion. Answer (C) is incorrect. A disclaimer is not appropriate when financial statements are materially misstated. Answer (D) is incorrect. A material misstatement requires a qualified or an adverse opinion.

15.4.25. When financial statements audited by the independent auditor contain notes that are captioned "unaudited" or "not covered by the auditor's report," the auditor

A. May refer to these notes in the auditor's report.

B. Has no responsibility with respect to information contained in these notes.

C. Must refer to these notes in the auditor's report.

D. Is precluded from referring to these notes in the auditor's report.

Answer (A) is correct. *(CPA, adapted)*

REQUIRED: The auditor's responsibility when financial statements include notes labeled "unaudited."

DISCUSSION: If information included in the basic statements is (1) not required by the applicable reporting framework, (2) not necessary for fair presentation, and (3) clearly differentiated from the statements, the information may be identified as "unaudited" or "not covered by the auditor's report" (AU-C 700). If the auditor wishes to draw attention to such a matter that is appropriately presented or disclosed, (s)he may include an emphasis-of-matter paragraph in the auditor's report (AU-C 705). If (1) the information constitutes other information, (2) the information is materially inconsistent with the audited statements, and (3) management has not revised the information after a request by the auditor, the auditor should (1) include an other-matter paragraph in the report, (2) withhold the report, or (3) withdraw from the engagement. If the information contains a material misstatement of fact that management refuses to correct, the auditor should take further appropriate action (AU-C 720).

Answer (B) is incorrect. The auditor should consider whether the information is materially inconsistent or materially misstated. Answer (C) is incorrect. The auditor is not required to refer to unaudited notes in the report if the information is not materially misstated or inconsistent. Answer (D) is incorrect. The auditor is not precluded from referring to unaudited notes in the auditor's report.

15.4.26. An auditor decides to express a qualified opinion on an entity's financial statements because a major inadequacy in its computerized accounting records prevents the auditor from applying necessary procedures. The opinion paragraph of the auditor's report should state that the qualification pertains to

A. A client-imposed scope limitation.

B. A departure from generally accepted auditing standards.

C. The possible effects on the financial statements.

D. Inadequate disclosure of necessary information.

Answer (C) is correct. *(CPA, adapted)*

REQUIRED: The wording in the opinion paragraph when the opinion is qualified because of a scope limitation.

DISCUSSION: When an auditor qualifies his or her opinion because of a scope limitation, the wording in the opinion paragraph should indicate that the qualification pertains to the possible effects on the financial statements and not to the scope limitation itself.

Answer (A) is incorrect. The qualification should not pertain to the scope limitation. Answer (B) is incorrect. The auditor apparently has followed GAAS in the conduct of the audit. Answer (D) is incorrect. Inadequate disclosure is a misstatement, not a lack of sufficient appropriate evidence.

15.4.27. Which of the following actions should be taken by a CPA who has been asked to audit the financial statements of a company whose fiscal year has ended?

A. Discuss with the client the possibility of an adverse opinion because of the late engagement date.

B. Ascertain whether circumstances are likely to permit the auditor to obtain sufficient appropriate evidence and express an unmodified opinion.

C. Inform the client of the need to express a qualified opinion if the physical inventory has already been taken.

D. Ascertain whether an understanding of internal control can be obtained and the risks of material misstatement can be assessed after completion of the audit.

Answer (B) is correct. *(CPA, adapted)*

REQUIRED: The proper action when the CPA is engaged after the end of the fiscal year.

DISCUSSION: Before acceptance of an engagement near or after the close of the fiscal year, an independent auditor should determine whether circumstances permit him or her to obtain sufficient appropriate audit evidence to reduce audit risk to an acceptably low level and to express an unmodified opinion. If they do not, the auditor and client should discuss the possibility of a qualified opinion or a disclaimer of opinion. In some cases, the auditor may be able to remedy the audit limitations, for example, by observation of another physical inventory.

Answer (A) is incorrect. A scope limitation, by itself, cannot result in an adverse opinion. Answer (C) is incorrect. A qualified opinion is not inevitable. The auditor may consider the application of alternative procedures if it is impracticable to observe the taking of the physical inventory. Answer (D) is incorrect. The consideration of internal control should precede other aspects of the audit.

15.4.28. An auditor refers to significant related party transactions in a separate emphasis-of-matter paragraph of the report. If the ensuing opinion paragraph contains the words "when considered with the following emphasis-of-matter," the auditor is considered to have

A. Expressed an unmodified opinion with appropriate reference to the separate paragraph.

B. Expressed an adverse opinion.

C. Expressed a negative assurance opinion.

D. Reported inappropriately.

Answer (D) is correct. *(CPA, adapted)*

REQUIRED: The correct statement about usage of the phrase.

DISCUSSION: A separate paragraph may be used to emphasize a matter regarding the statements. The phrase "when considered with the following emphasis-of-matter" should not be used because it may be misunderstood as an attempt to qualify the opinion or, when a qualified opinion is expressed, because it is not clear or forceful enough.

15.4.29. An auditor's opinion reads as follows: "In our opinion, except for the above-mentioned limitation on the scope of our audit..." This is an example of an

A. Acceptable review opinion.

B. Acceptable emphasis of a matter.

C. Acceptable qualified opinion.

D. Unacceptable reporting practice.

Answer (D) is correct. *(CPA, adapted)*

REQUIRED: The true statement about combining the phrases "except for" and "limitation on the scope."

DISCUSSION: When an opinion is qualified because of a scope limitation, the opinion paragraph should indicate that the qualification pertains to the possible effects on the statements of undetected misstatements (AU-C 705 and AS 3105). The language given in the question bases the qualification on the restriction itself and is unacceptable.

Answer (A) is incorrect. A review report states that no opinion is expressed. Answer (B) is incorrect. A matter is emphasized in a paragraph separate from the opinion paragraph. Emphasis of a matter also is consistent with an unmodified opinion. Answer (C) is incorrect. A qualified opinion should include language similar to the following: "In our opinion, except for the possible effects of the matter described . . ."

15.5 Adverse Opinions

15.5.1. Tread Corp., an issuer, accounts for the effect of a material change in an accounting principle prospectively when period-specific adjustments are required for prior periods presented in comparison with the current year. The auditor would choose between expressing a(n)

A. Qualified opinion and a disclaimer of opinion.

B. Disclaimer of opinion and an unqualified opinion with an explanatory paragraph.

C. Unqualified opinion with an explanatory paragraph and an adverse opinion.

D. Adverse opinion and a qualified opinion.

Answer (D) is correct. *(CPA, adapted)*

REQUIRED: The auditor's reporting options given a material misstatements.

DISCUSSION: The applicable reporting framework defines accounting changes and the treatment for reporting them. When the financial statements contain a material misstatement, for example, because of an inappropriate selection or application of an accounting principle, the auditor should express a qualified or adverse opinion. A misstatement is a difference between the amount, classification, presentation, or disclosure of a reported item and the amount, etc., required for it to be in accordance with the applicable framework. Misstatements also include adjustments needed for amounts, etc., to be presented fairly. Assuming the principle selected was appropriate, the application of the principle was the basis for the misstatement. A change in principle is accounted for retrospectively, not prospectively. Given that the change was material, the misstatement of financial statement amounts required (1) modification of the opinion and (2) a description and quantification of the financial effects of the misstatement.

Answer (A) is incorrect. A disclaimer is expressed only when the auditor cannot obtain sufficient appropriate evidence. Answer (B) is incorrect. A disclaimer or unqualified opinion would be inappropriate for a material misstatement. Answer (C) is incorrect. An unqualified opinion can be expressed only if the financial statements contain no material misstatement.

15.5.2. In which of the following situations would an auditor ordinarily choose between expressing a qualified opinion and an adverse opinion?

A. The auditor did not observe the entity's physical inventory and is unable to become satisfied as to its balance by other auditing procedures.

B. The financial statements fail to disclose information that is required by the applicable reporting framework.

C. The auditor is asked to report only on the entity's balance sheet and not on the other basic financial statements.

D. Events disclosed in the financial statements cause the auditor to have substantial doubt about the entity's ability to continue as a going concern.

Answer (B) is correct. *(CPA, adapted)*

REQUIRED: The situation in which an auditor chooses between expressing a qualified opinion and an adverse opinion.

DISCUSSION: Misstatements, including inadequate disclosures, may result in either a qualified or an adverse opinion. The auditor should exercise judgment about materiality by considering such factors as (1) benchmarks for dollar amounts, (2) significance to the statements and the entity, and (3) pervasiveness. If the misstatement is not pervasive, the auditor should express a qualified opinion.

Answer (A) is incorrect. A scope limitation is not a basis for an adverse opinion. Answer (C) is incorrect. A limited reporting engagement may result in the expression of an unmodified opinion. Answer (D) is incorrect. Substantial doubt about the entity's ability to continue as a going concern normally results in the addition of an emphasis-of-matter paragraph to the report.

15.5.3. An auditor expresses an adverse opinion if

A. A severe scope limitation has been imposed by management.

B. A misstatement is material and pervasive.

C. A qualified opinion cannot be expressed because the auditor lacks independence.

D. The company's ability to continue as a going concern is subject to substantial doubt.

Answer (B) is correct. *(K.J. Plucinski)*

REQUIRED: The circumstances in which the auditor expresses an adverse opinion.

DISCUSSION: When the effects on the financial statements of a material misstatement are pervasive, the auditor expresses an adverse opinion. Pervasive effects are not confined to specific elements, accounts, or items of the financial statements. If they are confined, they represent a substantial proportion of the statements.

Answer (A) is incorrect. A severe management-imposed scope limitation results in a disclaimer of opinion. Answer (C) is incorrect. If the auditor is not independent, (s)he ordinarily cannot report on an engagement performed in accordance with GAAS. Answer (D) is incorrect. Such a doubt results in a separate explanatory paragraph or a disclaimer of opinion.

15.5.4. When an auditor expresses an adverse opinion, the opinion paragraph should include

A. The effects of the material misstatement.

B. A direct reference to a separate paragraph disclosing the basis for the opinion.

C. The financial effects of the misstatement.

D. A description of the uncertainty or scope limitation that prevents an unmodified opinion.

Answer (B) is correct. *(CPA, adapted)*

REQUIRED: The matter included in the opinion paragraph when an adverse opinion is expressed.

DISCUSSION: An adverse opinion states that the financial statements are not fairly presented in accordance with the applicable financial reporting framework. When an adverse opinion is expressed, the opinion paragraph should directly refer to a basis for adverse opinion paragraph that discloses the basis for the adverse opinion.

Answer (A) is incorrect. The effects of the material misstatement, if practicable, should be stated in the basis for adverse opinion paragraph. Answer (C) is incorrect. The financial effects of the misstatement should be stated in the basis paragraph. Answer (D) is incorrect. An adverse opinion is not expressed as a result of an uncertainty or scope limitation.

15.5.5. During the year ended December 31, Price Corporation reported its fixed assets at lower of cost or market (LCM) because their fair value had declined. The loss has been included in the income statement and the adjustment has been fully disclosed in the notes. If a CPA believes that the amounts reported in the financial statements are reasonable, what opinion is most appropriate?

A. An unmodified opinion.

B. A "subject to" qualified opinion.

C. An adverse opinion.

D. A disclaimer of opinion.

Answer (C) is correct. *(Publisher, adapted)*

REQUIRED: The opinion expressed when fixed assets are reported at LCM.

DISCUSSION: Fixed assets should be recorded at historical cost minus accumulated depreciation. Recording them at LCM is therefore a misstatement. The CPA should express either a qualified opinion or an adverse opinion, assuming that the effects of the misstatement are material (AU-C 705).

Answer (A) is incorrect. A material misstatement precludes an unmodified opinion. Answer (B) is incorrect. A "subject to" qualified opinion is an unacceptable form of reporting. Answer (D) is incorrect. A disclaimer is proper when an inability to obtain sufficient appropriate audit evidence is material and its possible effects are pervasive.

15.5.6. During the year, the research staff of Dermoplex, a nonissuer, devoted its entire efforts toward developing a skin cancer ointment. All costs that could be attributed directly to the project were accounted for as deferred charges and classified on the balance sheet as an asset. If the amounts involved are material, the auditor should

A. Express an unmodified opinion with an other-matter paragraph explaining the uncertainty of cost recovery.

B. Disclaim an opinion.

C. Express an adverse opinion.

D. Express an unmodified opinion provided that the uncertainty about ultimate realization of the deferred charges is disclosed in the notes.

Answer (C) is correct. *(Publisher, adapted)*

REQUIRED: The appropriate opinion when the client has capitalized R&D costs.

DISCUSSION: Capitalizing R&D costs is not permitted. Ordinarily, they must be expensed in the period in which they were incurred. Because capitalizing R&D costs is a misstatement and the amounts involved are material, the auditor should express an adverse opinion if the effects are pervasive. A qualified opinion might be appropriate, however, depending on the materiality and pervasiveness of the exception.

Answer (A) is incorrect. The issue is not uncertainty but the material misstatement. Answer (B) is incorrect. The auditor has sufficient appropriate evidence to express an opinion that the financial statements are materially misstated. Answer (D) is incorrect. The issue is not uncertainty but the misstatement.

15.5.7. In which of the following instances would it be appropriate for the auditor to refer to the work of an appraiser in the auditor's report?

A. An unmodified opinion is expressed and no additional paragraph is added, but the auditor wishes to disclose the use of an auditor's specialist.

B. A qualified opinion is expressed because of a matter unrelated to the work of the auditor's external specialist.

C. An adverse opinion is expressed based on a difference of opinion between the client and the auditor's external specialist about the value of certain assets.

D. A disclaimer of opinion is expressed owing to a scope limitation imposed on the auditor by the auditor's external specialist.

Answer (C) is correct. *(CPA, adapted)*

REQUIRED: The basis for reference to an appraiser in the audit report.

DISCUSSION: An auditor's external specialist has expertise in a field other than accounting or auditing. Expertise in a field other than accounting or auditing may include valuation of nonfinancial assets, such as land and buildings, jewelry, or antiques. If, after considering the work of the auditor's external specialist, the auditor concludes that managements' assertions are materially misstated, a qualified or adverse opinion should be expressed. When the opinion is modified, the auditor may report the work of the external specialist when it is relevant to understanding the opinion modification (AU-C 620).

Answer (A) is incorrect. The auditor should not refer to an auditor's specialist when an unmodified opinion is expressed. Answer (B) is incorrect. The qualification must be related to the work of the auditor's external specialist. Answer (D) is incorrect. It is unlikely that an appraiser could impose a scope limitation on the auditor. The auditor could simply consult another appraiser.

15.6 Disclaimers of Opinion

15.6.1. When a scope limitation has precluded the auditor from obtaining sufficient appropriate evidence to determine whether certain client acts are illegal, (s)he would most likely express

A. An unmodified opinion with a separate explanatory paragraph.

B. Either a qualified opinion or an adverse opinion.

C. Either a disclaimer of opinion or a qualified opinion.

D. Either an adverse opinion or a disclaimer of opinion.

Answer (C) is correct. *(CPA, adapted)*

REQUIRED: The report issued when evidence about illegal client acts is insufficient.

DISCUSSION: The auditor may be unable to determine the legality of certain acts or the amounts associated with them because of an inability to gather sufficient appropriate evidence; e.g., the internal control may have been circumvented, resulting in failure to record or properly document the acts, or client's legal counsel may have refused to give advice. In these circumstances, the scope limitation requires a qualified opinion or a disclaimer, although a client-imposed scope limitation ordinarily results in a disclaimer.

Answer (A) is incorrect. A material scope limitation results in a qualified opinion or a disclaimer. Answer (B) is incorrect. An adverse opinion is only appropriate when the auditor is able to conclude that the statements as a whole are not fairly presented. Answer (D) is incorrect. An adverse opinion is only appropriate when the auditor is able to conclude that the statements as a whole are not fairly presented.

15.6.2. A disclaimer of opinion on the financial statements that was issued because of a scope limitation on an audit differs from a compilation report on the unaudited statements of a nonissuer in that

A. A compilation report offers some assurances. A disclaimer offers none.

B. A compilation relates only to income statements and balance sheets. A disclaimer pertains to all financial statements presented.

C. Any procedures applied in a compilation should be described in the report, but procedures applied when a disclaimer is issued should not be described.

D. A compilation report states what service was performed. A disclaimer states what service was to be performed.

Answer (D) is correct. *(Publisher, adapted)*

REQUIRED: The difference between a disclaimer and a compilation report.

DISCUSSION: The disclaimer of opinion issued because of a scope limitation on an audit begins, "We were engaged to audit the accompanying" financial statements (AU-C 705). A compilation report states, "I (we) have performed compilation engagements" (AR-C 80).

Answer (A) is incorrect. Neither report offers any form of assurance. Answer (B) is incorrect. Both reports refer to all financial statements presented. Answer (C) is incorrect. The procedures performed should not be described in either report.

15.6.3. In which of the following circumstances would an auditor usually choose between expressing a qualified opinion or disclaiming an opinion?

A. Material misstatement.

B. Inadequate disclosure of accounting policies.

C. Inability to obtain sufficient appropriate audit evidence.

D. Unreasonable justification for a change in accounting principle.

Answer (C) is correct. *(CPA, adapted)*

REQUIRED: The circumstance in which the auditor chooses between a disclaimer and a qualified opinion.

DISCUSSION: Scope limitations may require a qualification of the opinion or a disclaimer. The choice depends on whether the possible effects of undetected misstatements are material and pervasive.

Answer (A) is incorrect. A material misstatement usually requires a choice between a qualified or an adverse opinion. Answer (B) is incorrect. Inadequate disclosure that constitutes a material misstatement usually requires a choice between a qualified or an adverse opinion. Answer (D) is incorrect. An unjustified change in accounting principle usually requires a choice between a qualified or an adverse opinion.

15.6.4. Under which of the following circumstances might an auditor disclaim an opinion?

A. The financial statements contain a material misstatement.

B. Material related party transactions are disclosed in the financial statements.

C. There has been a material change between periods in the method of application of accounting principles.

D. The auditor is unable to obtain sufficient appropriate evidence to support management's assertions concerning an uncertainty.

Answer (D) is correct. *(CPA, adapted)*

REQUIRED: The reason for a disclaimer.

DISCUSSION: Based on the audit evidence that is, or should be, available, the auditor assesses whether the audit evidence is sufficient to support managements' assertions about an uncertainty. When the auditor cannot obtain sufficient appropriate evidence, (s)he expresses a qualified opinion if the possible effects are material but not pervasive. If the possible effects are material and pervasive, (s)he disclaims an opinion.

Answer (A) is incorrect. The auditor should express a qualified or an adverse opinion when the statements contain a material misstatement. Answer (B) is incorrect. It is appropriate to disclose related party transactions. Answer (C) is incorrect. If the auditor concurs in the change, lack of consistency requires only an emphasis-of-matter paragraph.

15.6.5. A CPA is concerned about a relationship with unaudited financial statements of an issuer because

A. Users may be misled regarding the degree of responsibility the CPA is accepting.

B. A fee cannot be charged unless the CPA is associated with financial statements.

C. Association is necessary for compliance with the requirement of due professional care.

D. An audit must be performed if the CPA is in any way related to the financial statements.

Answer (A) is correct. *(Publisher, adapted)*

REQUIRED: The reason for concern about a relationship with unaudited financial statements.

DISCUSSION: A relationship of a CPA with financial statements may lead users to attribute undeserved credibility to them. When the statements are unaudited or unreviewed, the CPA should make clear the degree of responsibility assumed by including a disclaimer of opinion in the report.

Answer (B) is incorrect. Fees should be based on the extent and degree of difficulty of the services performed, not on whether the CPA is associated with statements. Answer (C) is incorrect. A member of the AICPA must perform all services with due care. Answer (D) is incorrect. A CPA may be related to financial statements without auditing or reviewing them if (s)he disclaims an opinion.

15.6.6. Under which of the following circumstances would a disclaimer of opinion not be appropriate?

A. The auditor is engaged after fiscal year-end and is unable to observe physical inventories or apply alternative procedures to verify their balances.

B. The auditor is unable to determine the amounts associated with fraud committed by the client's management.

C. The financial statements fail to contain adequate disclosure concerning related party transactions.

D. The client refuses to permit its attorney to furnish information requested in a letter of audit inquiry.

Answer (C) is correct. *(CPA, adapted)*

REQUIRED: The circumstances in which a disclaimer is inappropriate.

DISCUSSION: A disclaimer is inappropriate when the financial statements contain material departures from the applicable financial reporting framework. Inadequacy of the disclosures required by the applicable financial reporting framework is such a departure. Because U.S. GAAP require certain disclosures about related party transactions, the inadequacy of such disclosures is a basis for expressing a qualified or an adverse opinion.

Answer (A) is incorrect. A significant scope limitation, such as a failure to perform a generally accepted auditing procedure (observing inventory) and not becoming satisfied by alternative procedures, may result in a qualified opinion or in a disclaimer. Answer (B) is incorrect. A disclaimer or qualified opinion (and communication with the audit committee or the board) should be expressed in these circumstances if the auditor (1) is precluded from applying necessary procedures or (2) has applied extended procedures and is still unable to conclude whether fraud materially affects the statements. Answer (D) is incorrect. A client-imposed scope limitation ordinarily results in a disclaimer.

15.6.7. Harris, CPA, performed the audit of the Year 2 financial statements of Lanco, Inc., an issuer. The unaudited Year 1 financial statements were to be presented with the Year 2 financial statements for comparative purposes. Harris prepared a report to accompany both sets of financial statements. The statements are not to be presented in documents filed with the SEC. The presentation should not include

A. Marking the Year 1 columns as unaudited.

B. A separate paragraph.

C. The language "except for."

D. A statement in the report that the Year 1 financial statements were not audited by Harris.

Answer (C) is correct. *(L.M. Bailey)*

REQUIRED: The improper aspect of a report on audited and unaudited statements of an issuer presented in comparative form.

DISCUSSION: The phrase "except for" is used to qualify an opinion on audited financial statements.

Answer (A) is incorrect. The unaudited statements should be clearly marked to identify their status according to PCAOB standards. Answer (B) is incorrect. The prior period's report should be reissued, or the current period's report should include a separate paragraph describing the responsibility assumed for the prior period's statements. However, when unaudited statements are presented in comparative form with audited statements in an SEC filing, the unaudited statements need not be referred to in the auditor's report. Answer (D) is incorrect. If the Year 1 report is reissued, it should contain a statement that the Year 1 financial statements were not audited by Harris.

15.6.8. Due to a scope limitation, an auditor disclaimed an opinion on the financial statements as a whole, but the auditor's report included a statement that the current asset portion of the entity's balance sheet was fairly stated. The inclusion of this statement is

A. Not appropriate because it may tend to overshadow the auditor's disclaimer of opinion.

B. Not appropriate because the auditor is prohibited from reporting on only one basic financial statement.

C. Appropriate, provided the auditor's responsibility section adequately describes the scope limitation.

D. Appropriate, provided the statement is in the basis for disclaimer of opinion paragraph preceding the disclaimer of opinion paragraph.

Answer (A) is correct. *(CPA, adapted)*

REQUIRED: The suitability of a statement in an auditor's disclaimer about whether an element was stated fairly.

DISCUSSION: A piecemeal opinion is an expression of an opinion on a specific element of a financial statement when the auditor has disclaimed an opinion or expressed an adverse opinion on the financial statements as a whole. This type of assurance is inappropriate because it would contradict a disclaimer of opinion or an adverse opinion (AU-C 705).

Answer (B) is incorrect. The auditor may report on one basic financial statement and not on the others. Such a limited reporting engagement is acceptable. Answer (C) is incorrect. A piecemeal opinion is inappropriate in this circumstance. Answer (D) is incorrect. A piecemeal opinion is inappropriate in this circumstance.

15.6.9. If an accountant concludes that unaudited financial statements of an issuer on which the accountant is disclaiming an opinion also lack adequate disclosure, the accountant should suggest appropriate revision. If the client does not accept the accountant's suggestion, the accountant should

A. Express an adverse opinion and describe the appropriate revision in the report.

B. Refer to the appropriate revision and issue a modified report expressing limited assurance.

C. Describe the appropriate revision to the financial statements in the accountant's disclaimer of opinion.

D. Accept the client's inaction because the statements are unaudited and the accountant has disclaimed an opinion.

Answer (C) is correct. *(CPA, adapted)*

REQUIRED: The action when the client refuses to revise unaudited statements to provide adequate disclosure.

DISCUSSION: PCAOB auditing standards apply to engagements involving issuers. Under these standards, inadequate disclosure is a departure from U.S. GAAP. When an accountant who is associated with the unaudited statements of an issuer suggests revision because of such a departure and the client declines to provide the necessary disclosures, the disclaimer should be modified to describe the departure. The description should refer specifically to the nature of the departure and, if practicable, state the effects on the financial statements or include the necessary information for adequate disclosure (PCAOB AS 3320).

Answer (A) is incorrect. An opinion may be expressed only if an audit has been performed. Answer (B) is incorrect. A disclaimer expresses no assurance. Answer (D) is incorrect. The accountant should modify the disclaimer if the client does not act.

15.6.10. A CPA concludes that the unaudited financial statements of an issuer on which the CPA is disclaiming an opinion are not in conformity with generally accepted accounting principles (GAAP) because management has failed to capitalize leases. The CPA suggests appropriate revisions to the financial statements, but management refuses to accept the CPA's suggestions. Under these circumstances, the CPA ordinarily would

A. Express limited assurance that no other material modifications should be made to the financial statements.

B. Restrict the distribution of the CPA's report to management and the entity's board of directors.

C. Issue a qualified opinion or adverse opinion depending on the materiality of the departure from GAAP.

D. Describe the nature of the departure from GAAP in the CPA's report and state the effects on the financial statements, if practicable.

Answer (D) is correct. *(CPA, adapted)*

REQUIRED: The appropriate action when the CPA suggests revisions to the financial statements but management refuses to accept them.

DISCUSSION: An accountant planning to disclaim an opinion on an issuer's financial statements may discover a material departure from GAAP. Under PCAOB standards, the accountant should disclose the departure in the disclaimer, including its effects if they have been determined by management or by the accountant's procedures.

Answer (A) is incorrect. A disclaimer should provide no assurance. Answer (B) is incorrect. The disclaimer should not be restricted in use. Answer (C) is incorrect. A disclaimer of opinion is necessary when the CPA has not audited the statements.

15.6.11. Park, CPA, was engaged to audit the financial statements of Tech Co., a new client, for the year ended December 31, Year 1. Park obtained sufficient appropriate audit evidence for all of Tech's financial statement items except Tech's opening inventory. Due to inadequate financial records, Park could not verify Tech's January 1, Year 1, inventory balances. Park's opinion on Tech's Year 1 financial statements most likely will be

	Balance Sheet	Income Statement
A.	Disclaimer	Disclaimer
B.	Unmodified	Disclaimer
C.	Disclaimer	Adverse
D.	Unmodified	Adverse

Answer (B) is correct. *(CPA, adapted)*

REQUIRED: The appropriate opinion on each financial statement when the auditor cannot verify opening inventory.

DISCUSSION: The auditor may report on one basic financial statement and not on the others. Because the balance sheet presents information at a specific moment in time, the auditor should be able to become satisfied regarding the balances presented at year end. However, beginning inventory is included in the determination of the results of operations and cash flows. Thus, the auditor will probably not be able to form an opinion as to the fairness of these statements and should disclaim an opinion on them.

15.6.12. A limitation on the scope of an audit sufficient to preclude an unmodified opinion is most likely to result when management

A. Engages the auditor after the year-end physical inventory count is completed.

B. Fails to correct a material internal control weakness that had been identified during the prior year's audit.

C. Refuses to furnish a management representation letter to the auditor.

D. Prevents the auditor from reviewing the audit documentation of the predecessor auditor.

Answer (C) is correct. *(CPA, adapted)*

REQUIRED: The scope limitation that is most likely to preclude an unmodified opinion.

DISCUSSION: According to AU-C 580, *Written Representations*, management's refusal to furnish written representations constitutes a limitation on the scope of the audit. The refusal is often sufficient to preclude an unmodified opinion. Moreover, it may cause an auditor to disclaim an opinion or withdraw from the engagement, especially with regard to representations about (1) fraud, (2) noncompliance, (3) uncorrected misstatements, (4) litigation and claims, (5) estimates, (6) related party transactions, and (7) subsequent events. However, the circumstances may permit a qualified opinion. Furthermore, the auditor should consider the effects of management's refusal on his or her ability to rely on other management representations.

Answer (A) is incorrect. A limitation sufficient to preclude an unmodified opinion does not arise if the auditor becomes satisfied as to inventory by other procedures. Answer (B) is incorrect. Failure to correct a previously identified material internal control weakness is not a limitation on the auditor's ability to obtain sufficient appropriate evidence. Answer (D) is incorrect. Review of the predecessor's audit documentation may not be necessary to the audit.

15.6.13. Morris, CPA, suspects that a pervasive scheme of illegal bribes exists throughout the operations of Worldwide Import-Export, Inc., a new audit client. Morris notified the audit committee and Worldwide's legal counsel, but neither would assist Morris in determining whether the amounts involved were material to the financial statements or whether senior management was involved in the scheme. Under these circumstances, Morris most likely should

A. Express an unmodified opinion with an other-matter paragraph.

B. Disclaim an opinion on the financial statements.

C. Express an adverse opinion on the financial statements.

D. Issue a special report regarding the illegal bribes.

Answer (B) is correct. *(CPA, adapted)*

REQUIRED: The auditor action when (s)he cannot determine the amounts involved in material noncompliance with laws or regulations or the extent of management's involvement.

DISCUSSION: Bribery is a violation of laws or governmental regulations. If the auditor is precluded by management or those charged with governance (e.g., the audit committee) from obtaining sufficient appropriate evidence to evaluate whether material noncompliance with laws or regulations has (or is likely to have) occurred, the auditor should disclaim an opinion or express a qualified opinion.

Answer (A) is incorrect. An unmodified opinion is not justified. Answer (C) is incorrect. An adverse opinion is expressed only when the financial statements are not presented fairly. Answer (D) is incorrect. Special reports as defined in AU-C 805 are not issued on such topics.

15.6.14. A limitation on the scope of an audit sufficient to preclude an unmodified opinion will usually result when management

A. Presents financial statements that are prepared in accordance with the cash receipts and disbursements basis of accounting.

B. States that the financial statements are not intended to be presented in accordance with generally accepted accounting principles.

C. Does not make the minutes of the board of directors' meetings available to the auditor.

D. Asks the auditor to report on the balance sheet and not on the other basic financial statements.

Answer (C) is correct. *(CPA, adapted)*

REQUIRED: The basis for a scope limitation sufficient to preclude an unmodified opinion.

DISCUSSION: An inability to obtain sufficient appropriate evidence may result from limitations imposed by management. Failing to make the minutes of board meetings available is such a limitation. It also raises a question about management's compliance with the preconditions for an audit, e.g., providing access to relevant information and persons within the entity.

Answer (A) is incorrect. An auditor's report on financial statements prepared using a special purpose framework, for example, the cash basis, may express an unmodified opinion if the statements are fairly presented in accordance with that framework. Answer (B) is incorrect. Stating that the financial statements are not intended to be presented in accordance with GAAP does not constitute a scope limitation. Answer (D) is incorrect. A limitation on the reporting engagement is not a scope limitation if the auditor is able to apply necessary procedures and his or her access to information is not limited.

15.6.15. The auditor is most likely to disclaim an opinion because of

A. Management's failure to present supplementary information required by the FASB.

B. Inadequate disclosure of material information.

C. A management-imposed limitation.

D. A significant number of changes in accounting principles.

Answer (C) is correct. *(CPA, adapted)*

REQUIRED: The most likely basis for a disclaimer.

DISCUSSION: An inability to obtain sufficient appropriate evidence may result from (1) circumstances beyond the control of the entity, (2) circumstances related to the nature or the timing of the work, or (3) a management-imposed limitation. They result in either a qualified opinion or a disclaimer (AU-C 705).

Answer (A) is incorrect. The omission does not affect the opinion. The required information does not change accounting and reporting standards for preparing basic financial statements. But the auditor should include an other-matter paragraph. Answer (B) is incorrect. Inadequate disclosure of material matters is a misstatement requiring a qualified or an adverse opinion. Answer (D) is incorrect. Changes in accounting principles may be justified. If they are justified and material, the auditor should describe them in an emphasis-of-matter paragraph.

15.6.16. A limitation on the scope of the audit sufficient to preclude an unmodified opinion is most likely to result when management

A. Asks the auditor to report on the balance sheet and not on the other basic financial statements.

B. Refuses to permit its lawyer to respond to the letter of audit inquiry.

C. Discloses material related party transactions in the notes to the financial statements.

D. Knows that confirmation of accounts receivable is not feasible.

Answer (B) is correct. *(CPA, adapted)*

REQUIRED: The limitation on the scope of the audit sufficient to preclude an unmodified opinion.

DISCUSSION: Direct communication with the entity's external legal counsel should be made if actual or potential litigation, claims, or assessments may result in a risk of material misstatement. If management refuses to permit this communication, the auditor should modify the opinion.

Answer (A) is incorrect. A limitation on the reporting engagement is not a scope limitation if the auditor's ability to obtain sufficient appropriate evidence is not limited. Answer (C) is incorrect. Disclosure of material related party transactions is required. Answer (D) is incorrect. When circumstances other than a management-imposed limitation preclude confirmation of receivables, the auditor need not qualify the opinion or disclaim an opinion if (s)he can become satisfied about receivables by applying alternative procedures.

15.6.17. A limitation on the scope of an audit sufficient to preclude an unmodified opinion is most likely to result when management

A. Is unable to obtain audited financial statements supporting the entity's investment in a foreign subsidiary.

B. Refuses to disclose in the notes to the financial statements related party transactions authorized by the board of directors.

C. Does not attend discussions held among the audit team about the susceptibility of the financial statements to material misstatements.

D. Fails to correct a significant deficiency in internal control communicated to the audit committee after the prior year's audit.

Answer (A) is correct. *(CPA, adapted)*

REQUIRED: The scope limitation sufficient to preclude an unmodified opinion.

DISCUSSION: An auditor's inability to obtain sufficient appropriate evidence may arise from, among other things, circumstances related to the nature or timing of the auditor's work. An example is an inability, not resulting from a management-imposed limitation, to obtain audited financial statements of a long-term investee. If the possible effects are material, the auditor expresses a qualified opinion or disclaims an opinion, depending on pervasiveness.

Answer (B) is incorrect. Refusal to make related party disclosures is a misstatement, not a scope limitation. Answer (C) is incorrect. Management should not attend these required audit team discussions. Answer (D) is incorrect. Failure to correct a significant deficiency in internal control is not a limitation of scope.

15.6.18. Green, CPA, is aware that Green's name is to be included in the interim report of National Company, a publicly held entity. National's quarterly financial statements are contained in the interim report. Green has not audited or reviewed these interim financial statements. Green should request that

I. Green's name not be included in the communication.

II. The financial statements be marked as unaudited, with a notation that no opinion is expressed on them.

A. I only.

B. II only.

C. Neither I nor II.

D. Either I or II.

Answer (D) is correct. *(CPA, adapted)*

REQUIRED: The request(s) that an accountant should make when (s)he is associated with financial statements of an issuer that (s)he has not audited or reviewed.

DISCUSSION: The accountant may become aware that his or her name is to be included in a client-prepared written communication of an issuer containing financial statements that have not been audited or reviewed. Under PCAOB standards, which apply to engagements involving issuers, (s)he should request either that (1) his or her name not be included in the communication or (2) the financial statements be marked as unaudited, with a notation included to the effect that (s)he does not express an opinion on them.

STUDY UNIT SIXTEEN
REPORTS -- OTHER MODIFICATIONS

This study unit covers additional language modifying the auditor's report. These modifications normally do not affect the auditor's opinion on the financial statements. They permit the users of the financial statements and readers of the auditor's report to better understand the responsibility assumed by the auditor. They also provide information about the client's financial statements that the auditor considers important.

In reports for nonissuers (AICPA standards), the information addressed in Subunits 16.2, 16.3, and 16.4 is contained in an additional paragraph with a heading "Emphasis-of-Matter" if the information relates to the financial statements or in an additional paragraph with a heading "Other Matter" if the information relates to some other issue.

In reports for issuers (PCAOB standards), the information addressed in Subunits 16.2, 16.3, and 16.4 is contained in an additional "explanatory paragraph" with an appropriately labeled heading (e.g., "Depreciation Method Change").

QUESTIONS

16.1 Group Audits and Component Auditors

16.1.1. Thomas, CPA, has audited the consolidated financial statements of Kass Corporation. Jones, CPA, has audited the financial statements of its sole subsidiary, which is significant in relation to the total audited by Thomas. It would be appropriate for Thomas to serve as the group auditor, but it is impracticable for Thomas to review the work of Jones. Assuming an unmodified opinion is expressed by Jones, Thomas should

A. Refuse to express an opinion on the consolidated financial statements.

B. Express an unmodified opinion on the consolidated financial statements and not refer to the work of Jones.

C. Express an unmodified opinion on the consolidated financial statements and refer to the work of Jones.

D. Express a qualified opinion on the consolidated financial statements as a result of referring to the work of Jones.

Answer (C) is correct. *(CPA, adapted)*

REQUIRED: The reporting by the group auditor when (s)he cannot review the work of a component auditor.

DISCUSSION: The group engagement team should obtain an understanding of the component auditor, a process that includes determining the extent, if any, to which the team will be able to be involved in the component auditor's work. The group engagement partner then may decide to refer to the component auditor if (1) the component auditor meets relevant independence requirements for the group audit, (2) the group engagement team has no serious concerns about his or her professional competence or other ethical issues, (3) the component's statements are prepared using the same reporting framework as that of the group statements (or responsibility is taken for adjustments to the group framework), (4) the component auditor's report is not use-restricted, and (5) the component auditor has performed an audit in accordance with PCAOB standards (if required by law or regulation) or GAAS. If these requirements are met, the group engagement partner may decide (1) not to assume responsibility for the audit of the component auditor and (2) to refer to that audit. Moreover, the reference to the component auditor does not prohibit an unmodified opinion.

Answer (A) is incorrect. The group auditor should not refuse to express an opinion. Part of an audit may be made by other independent auditors. Answer (B) is incorrect. When the group auditor assumes responsibility for the component auditor's audit, the group engagement team should be involved in the component auditor's work (e.g., reviewing documentation of identified risks of material misstatement). If this cannot be done, but the component auditor meets ethical and competence requirements, reference should be made to the component auditor. Answer (D) is incorrect. The reference to a component auditor is not a qualification.

16.1.2. William Halsey is auditing the consolidated financial statements of Rex, Inc. Abbey Lincoln is the auditor who has audited and reported on the financial statements of a wholly owned subsidiary of Rex, Inc. Halsey's first concern with respect to the Rex financial statements is to decide whether he

A. May serve as the group auditor and report as such on the consolidated financial statements of Rex, Inc.

B. May refer to the work of Lincoln in his report on the consolidated financial statements.

C. Obtain an understanding of Lincoln's professional competence.

D. Should resign from the engagement because an unmodified opinion cannot be expressed on the consolidated financial statements.

Answer (A) is correct. *(CPA, adapted)*

REQUIRED: The first concern of an auditor when a subsidiary has been audited by another auditor.

DISCUSSION: The first objective of the group engagement partner is to determine whether to serve as the auditor of the group statements. If so, the objectives are to (1) determine whether to refer to the component auditor's report, (2) communicate clearly with the component auditor or auditors, and (3) obtain sufficient appropriate evidence about the financial information of the components and the consolidation process. Thus, the group engagement partner should evaluate whether sufficient appropriate evidence can be obtained to serve as the auditor of the group statements. Factors relevant to the decision to act as the group auditor also include (1) the financial significance of individual components for which responsibility will be assumed, (2) the significant risks of material misstatement of the group statements from assuming responsibility for components, and (3) the group engagement team's knowledge of the overall financial statements.

Answer (B) is incorrect. The decision whether to refer to the component auditor is made only after the decision to serve as the group auditor. Answer (C) is incorrect. Obtaining an understanding of a component auditor's professional competence is done after the decision to serve as group auditor. Answer (D) is incorrect. Performance of part of the audit by another auditor does not preclude expressing an unmodified opinion.

16.1.3. The opinion paragraph of an independent auditor's report includes, "In our opinion, based on our audit and the report of the other auditors, the consolidated financial statements present fairly, in all material respects, the financial position . . ." This language states a(n)

A. Disclaimer of opinion.

B. Unmodified opinion.

C. "Except for" opinion.

D. Qualified opinion.

Answer (B) is correct. *(Publisher, adapted)*

REQUIRED: The opinion expressed when the report refers to the report of other auditors.

DISCUSSION: When the group engagement partner decides to refer to the report of a component auditor, the report on the group statements should clearly indicate that the component was not audited by the group auditor. It also should state (1) that the component was audited by the component auditor and (2) the magnitude of the portion of the statements audited. This reference is not a modification of the opinion. Accordingly, the report expresses an unmodified opinion despite the reference to the other auditors.

Answer (A) is incorrect. An opinion is expressed. Answer (C) is incorrect. The quotation contains no qualifying language. Answer (D) is incorrect. The quotation contains no qualifying language.

16.1.4. A group auditor has decided to assume responsibility and not make reference to a component auditor. The report of the component auditor expressed a qualified opinion, but the group auditor believes the qualification to be immaterial in regard to the consolidated financial statements. Accordingly, the group auditor

A. May express an unmodified opinion but must include a separate paragraph describing the component auditor's report.

B. Must express a qualified opinion but need not refer to the audit of the component auditor.

C. Must express a qualified opinion and refer to the audit of the component auditor.

D. Need not refer to the audit of the component auditor.

Answer (D) is correct. *(Publisher, adapted)*

REQUIRED: The recognition given by the group auditor to an immaterial qualification by a component auditor.

DISCUSSION: The group auditor need not refer to the audit of the component auditor if (s)he is willing to assume responsibility for the component auditor's work. Because the qualification stated by the component auditor is immaterial to the group financial statements, it need not cause a qualification of the opinion. For example, the component may not (1) be financially significant to the group or (2) be likely to include significant risks of material misstatement of the group statements.

Answer (A) is incorrect. Given that the component auditor's qualification is not material to the consolidated statements, the group auditor need not refer to the component auditor's audit. Answer (B) is incorrect. Given that the component auditor's qualification is not material to the consolidated statements, the group auditor need not qualify the opinion. Answer (C) is incorrect. Given that the component auditor's qualification is not material to the consolidated statements, the group auditor need not refer to the component auditor's audit or qualify the opinion.

16.1.5. Regarding the magnitude of financial statements audited by the component auditor relative to the overall statements upon which the group auditor expresses an opinion,

A. The dollar amounts or percentages of total assets, total revenues, or other appropriate criteria should be disclosed in the group auditor's report.

B. The general amounts (e.g., significant amount or insignificant amount) of total revenues and total assets must be disclosed in the group auditor's report.

C. No mention is necessary unless approximately 50% or more of the assets or revenues are audited by the component auditor. Disclosure, if necessary, should be according to the appropriate criteria and reveal the portion of the financial statements audited by the component auditor.

D. No mention is necessary unless the audit report of the component auditor is not presented. Disclosure, if necessary, should be according to the appropriate criteria and reveal the portion of the financial statements audited by the component auditor.

Answer (A) is correct. *(Publisher, adapted)*

REQUIRED: The true statement about disclosure of the portion of the statements audited by a component auditor.

DISCUSSION: When the group engagement partner decides to refer to the report of a component auditor, the report on the group statements should clearly indicate that the component was not audited by the group auditor. It also should state (1) that the component was audited by the component auditors and (2) the magnitude of the portion of the statements audited. This language is included in the auditor's responsibility section of an AICPA report and in the opinion section of a PCAOB report.

Answer (B) is incorrect. The magnitude of the component auditor's work may be stated either in dollar amounts or in percentages of total assets, total revenues, or other appropriate criteria. Answer (C) is incorrect. A group auditor who refers to the audit of a component auditor must disclose the magnitude of the portion of the statements audited by the component auditor. Answer (D) is incorrect. A group auditor who refers to the audit of a component auditor must disclose the magnitude of the portion of the statements audited by the component auditor.

16.1.6. When a group auditor decides to refer to a component auditor's audit, the group auditor's report should indicate clearly, in the auditor's responsibility section, the

A. Magnitude of the portion of the financial statements audited by the component auditor.

B. Disclaimer of responsibility concerning the portion of the financial statements examined by the other auditor.

C. Name of the other auditor.

D. Qualification of the report.

Answer (A) is correct. *(CPA, adapted)*

REQUIRED: The disclosure requirement when referring to a component auditor.

DISCUSSION: When the group engagement partner decides to refer to the report of a component auditor, the report on the group statements should clearly indicate that the component was not audited by the group auditor. It also should state (1) that the component was audited by the component auditor and (2) the magnitude of the portion of the statements audited. This language is included in the auditor's responsibility section of the report.

Answer (B) is incorrect. Referring to a component auditor is not a disclaimer. Whether or not a component auditor is referred to, the group auditor is responsible for the group audit opinion. Answer (C) is incorrect. Naming the component auditor is not required. (S)he may be named only if (1) (s)he gives express permission and (2) his or her report is presented together with that of the group auditor. Answer (D) is incorrect. Referring to a component auditor is not a qualification of the report.

16.1.7. If the group auditor decides to refer in the report to the audit made by a component auditor, the

A. Group auditor assumes responsibility for the report of the component auditor.

B. Component auditor is relieved of responsibility for his or her report but not his or her work.

C. Component auditor is responsible for both his or her report and his or her work.

D. Component auditor is relieved of responsibility for his or her work but not his or her report.

Answer (C) is correct. *(Publisher, adapted)*

REQUIRED: The effect of referring to a component auditor's audit.

DISCUSSION: Whether or not the group auditor refers in the report to the audit of the component auditor, the component auditor remains responsible for his or her overall findings, conclusions, or opinions.

Answer (A) is incorrect. The group auditor assumes responsibility for the component auditor's work to the extent it relates to the group auditor's opinion on the group financial statements only when (s)he does not refer to the audit of the component auditor. Answer (B) is incorrect. The component auditor is not relieved of the responsibility for his or her work. Answer (D) is incorrect. The component auditor is not relieved of the responsibility for his or her report.

16.1.8. Pell, CPA, is the group engagement partner in the audit of the financial statements of Tech Consolidated, Inc. Smith, CPA, audits one of Tech's subsidiaries. In which situation(s) should Pell refer to Smith's audit?

I. Pell reviews Smith's audit documentation and assumes responsibility for Smith's work but expresses a qualified opinion on Tech's financial statements.

II. Pell is unable to review Smith's audit documentation but reads the financial statements and gains an understanding that Smith has an excellent reputation for professional competence and integrity.

A. I only.

B. II only.

C. Both I and II.

D. Neither I nor II.

Answer (B) is correct. *(CPA, adapted)*

REQUIRED: The situation, if any, in which a group auditor should refer to a component auditor's audit.

DISCUSSION: Regardless of the decision to make reference, the group engagement team should obtain an understanding of the component auditor's professional competence and compliance with ethical requirements (especially independence). The understanding also addresses (1) the extent of the team's involvement in the component auditor's work, (2) whether (s)he operates under regulatory oversight, and (3) whether the team will be able to obtain information about the consolidation process from the component auditor. Serious concerns about (1) compliance with ethical requirements or (2) lack of competence preclude a reference to the audit of the component auditor. Moreover, the group engagement partner's assumption of responsibility for the component auditor's audit indicates a decision not to refer to the audit of the component auditor.

Answer (A) is incorrect. Assumption of responsibility reflects a decision not to refer. Answer (C) is incorrect. Assumption of responsibility reflects a decision not to refer. Answer (D) is incorrect. The component auditor's (1) compliance with ethical requirements and (2) professional competence generally permit a reference.

16.1.9. An auditor's report contains the following: "We did not audit the financial statements of JK Co., a wholly owned subsidiary whose statements reflect total assets and revenues constituting 17% and 19%, respectively, of the related consolidated totals. Those statements were audited by other auditors whose report has been furnished to us, and our opinion, insofar as it relates to the amounts included for JK Company, is based solely on the report of the other auditors." These sentences

A. Disclaim an opinion.

B. Qualify the opinion.

C. Assume no responsibility for the audit of JK Co.

D. Are an improper form of reporting.

Answer (C) is correct. *(CPA, adapted)*

REQUIRED: The effect of the quoted language in an auditor's report.

DISCUSSION: The decision to refer to the work of a component auditor in the report signifies that the group engagement partner does not assume responsibility for the audit of the component auditor.

Answer (A) is incorrect. The last sentence refers to the expression of an opinion. Answer (B) is incorrect. The language cited does not preclude an unmodified or an adverse opinion. Answer (D) is incorrect. The wording is appropriate.

16.1.10. The group engagement partner has identified a significant component of the group that is being audited by a component auditor. The group auditor intends to assume responsibility for the work of the component auditor. Accordingly,

A. A qualified opinion should be expressed on that component.

B. The component auditor should become a member of the group engagement team.

C. The group engagement team should either audit the component directly or have the component auditor audit the information on its behalf.

D. The group engagement team should obtain a representation letter from component management.

Answer (C) is correct. *(Publisher, adapted)*

REQUIRED: The requirement when a significant component is identified in a group audit with no reference to the component auditor.

DISCUSSION: A significant component is one that is (1) of individual financial significance to the group or (2) likely to include significant risks of material misstatement of the group financial statements. When the group engagement partner assumes responsibility for the audit of the component, the audit report does not refer to the audit of the component auditor. Thus, the group engagement team should (1) audit the financial information directly or (2) have the component auditor audit the information on its behalf, using appropriate component materiality.

Answer (A) is incorrect. The opinion is based on the evidence obtained, not on how it is audited. Answer (B) is incorrect. The component auditor may or may not become part of the group engagement team. Answer (D) is incorrect. The communication requested from the component auditor should include exceptions in the written representations that (s)he requested from component management. Thus, the group engagement team's involvement in the work of the component auditor does not necessarily require obtaining a representation letter from component management.

16.1.11. An auditor may issue an unmodified audit report when the

A. Auditor refers to the findings of an auditor's specialist.

B. Financial statements are derived from audited financial statements but contain less detail.

C. Financial statements are prepared on the cash receipts and disbursements basis of accounting chosen by management.

D. Group engagement partner assumes responsibility for the work of a component auditor.

Answer (D) is correct. *(CPA, adapted)*

REQUIRED: The situation in which an auditor's report may be unmodified.

DISCUSSION: If the group engagement partner assumes responsibility for the work of the component auditor, the component auditor is not referred to in the report on the group financial statements.

Answer (A) is incorrect. The auditor does not refer to an auditor's specialist unless (s)he departs from an unmodified opinion. Answer (B) is incorrect. The report on summary financial statements varies in many respects, e.g., it identifies the summary financial statements and the audited financial statements. Answer (C) is incorrect. A modification of the report is appropriate to describe the special purpose framework.

16.1.12. In which of the following situations will a group auditor be most likely to refer to a component auditor who audited a subsidiary of the entity?

A. The component auditor performed an audit in accordance with PCAOB standards.

B. The component auditor issued a restricted use report.

C. The financial statements audited by the component auditor are prepared using a financial reporting framework different from that used in the group statements.

D. The component auditor is not independent.

Answer (A) is correct. *(CPA, adapted)*

REQUIRED: The situation in which a group auditor is most likely to refer to a component auditor.

DISCUSSION: The group engagement partner may not refer to the audit of the component auditor unless the component auditor performed an audit in accordance with (1) GAAS or (2), if required by law or regulation, PCAOB auditing standards.

Answer (B) is incorrect. Reference to the audit of the component auditor is not made unless the component auditor has issued an unrestricted report. Answer (C) is incorrect. When the reporting frameworks differ, no reference is made unless certain conditions are met. Moreover, the group auditor's report should disclose that responsibility is taken for evaluating the adjustments needed to convert from one framework to the other. Answer (D) is incorrect. When the component auditor is not independent or the group engagement team has serious concerns about other ethical issues or professional competence, no reference is made.

16.1.13. If a group engagement partner refers to a component auditor in an audit that would otherwise result in an unmodified opinion, the type of audit report issued should express a(n)

A. Unmodified opinion.

B. Qualified opinion.

C. Adverse opinion.

D. Disclaimer of opinion.

Answer (A) is correct. *(CMA, adapted)*

REQUIRED: The audit opinion expressed when the group engagement partner refers to the work of a component auditor.

DISCUSSION: When the group engagement partner decides to refer to the report of a component auditor, the report on the group statements should clearly indicate that the component was not audited by the group auditor. It also should state (1) that the component was audited by the component auditor and (2) the magnitude of the portion of the statements audited. This reference is not a modification of the opinion. Accordingly, the report expresses an unmodified opinion despite the reference to the other auditors.

Answer (B) is incorrect. If the statements are fairly presented, an unmodified opinion is indicated. Answer (C) is incorrect. If the statements are fairly presented, an unmodified opinion is indicated. Answer (D) is incorrect. If sufficient appropriate audit evidence can be obtained, an opinion should be expressed.

16.1.14. Which of the following is not a responsibility of a group engagement team?

A. Choose one member to be the group engagement partner.

B. Develop a group audit plan.

C. Establish an overall audit strategy.

D. Determine materiality for the group as a whole.

Answer (A) is correct. *(Publisher, adapted)*

REQUIRED: The responsibility not assigned to the group engagement team.

DISCUSSION: The audit firm chooses the group engagement partner. This individual is responsible for (1) the group engagement, (2) its performance, and (3) the report on the group statements.

Answer (B) is incorrect. The group engagement team, subject to approval by the group engagement partner, should develop a group audit plan. Answer (C) is incorrect. The group engagement team, subject to approval by the group engagement partner, should establish an overall group audit strategy. Answer (D) is incorrect. It is the responsibility of the group engagement team to determine materiality for the group financial statements as a whole.

16.1.15. When the report of a group auditor refers to the audit by a component auditor, the component auditor may be named if express permission to do so is given and if the

A. Report of the group auditor names the component auditor in both the introductory and opinion paragraphs.

B. Group auditor accepts responsibility for the work of the component auditor.

C. Report of the component auditor is presented together with the report of the group auditor.

D. Component auditor is not a member of the group engagement team whose work is done at the request of the group engagement team.

Answer (C) is correct. *(CPA, adapted)*

REQUIRED: The circumstances in which a group auditor may name the component auditor.

DISCUSSION: The component auditor may be named but only with his or her express permission and provided his or her report is presented together with that of the group auditor.

Answer (A) is incorrect. The group auditor may refer to a component auditor in the auditor's responsibility section and the opinion paragraph of an AICPA report and in the opinion and basis for opinion section of a PCAOB report. But the other auditor is not named unless certain conditions are met. Answer (B) is incorrect. If the group auditor accepts responsibility for the work of the component auditor, no mention should be made of the component auditor. Answer (D) is incorrect. The component auditor may be part of the group engagement team. However, the group auditor is more likely not to refer to the component auditor in such a case.

16.2 Consistency of Financial Statements

16.2.1. Below are lists of accounting changes affecting consistency and comparability for a nonissuer. All items are material. Which list does not contain a change requiring recognition in the audit report?

A. Correction of an error in an accounting principle; change in accounting estimate; reclassification.

B. A change in accounting estimate; a substantially different transaction; an accounting change having no material effect on the financial statements in the current year but having a substantial effect in subsequent years.

C. Substantially different transactions; correction of a misstatement in previously issued statements; a change in reporting entity not resulting from a transaction or event.

D. Correction of a misstatement in previously issued statements; change in accounting estimate; a change in reporting entity not resulting from a transaction or event.

Answer (B) is correct. *(Publisher, adapted)*

REQUIRED: The set of items requiring no reference in the auditor's report as to consistency for a nonissuer.

DISCUSSION: Various material accounting changes affect consistency and require an additional paragraph in the auditor's report: (1) changes in accounting principle, (2) changes in the reporting entity not resulting from a transaction or event, (3) correction of an error in principle, (4) adjustments to correct misstatements in previously issued financial statements, (5) changes in principle inseparable from a change in estimate, and (6) certain reclassifications. Other changes affect comparability but not consistency and require no modification of the report: (1) changes in accounting estimate, (2) changes in classification that do not represent a material misstatement or a change in principle, (3) substantially different transactions or events, and (4) changes having no material effect in the current year but expected to have a material future effect.

Answer (A) is incorrect. A correction of an error in an accounting principle and certain reclassifications require modification of the report. Answer (C) is incorrect. A correction of a misstatement in previously issued statements and a change in the reporting entity not resulting from a transaction or event require modification of the report. Answer (D) is incorrect. A correction of a misstatement in previously issued statements and a change in the reporting entity not resulting from a transaction or event require modification of the report.

16.2.2. The objective of the auditor's evaluation of the consistency of financial statements is to determine whether

A. Changes in classification have occurred.

B. Substantially different transactions and events are not accounted for on an identical basis.

C. The auditor should be consulted before material changes are made in the application of accounting principles.

D. The comparability of financial statements between periods has been materially affected by a change in accounting principle.

Answer (D) is correct. *(CPA, adapted)*

REQUIRED: The objective of the evaluation of consistency.

DISCUSSION: The objective of the evaluation of consistency for the periods presented is to communicate in the report when the comparability of financial statements between periods has been materially affected by (1) a change in accounting principle or (2) adjustments to correct a material misstatement in previous statements.

Answer (A) is incorrect. Changes in classification are not considered to be changes affecting consistency unless such changes also are changes in principle or adjustments to correct material misstatements. Answer (B) is incorrect. The auditor reports on whether accounting practices were consistent, not identical. Answer (C) is incorrect. Consultation with the auditor is not required.

16.2.3. Seripak Corporation, a nonissuer, made a material change in accounting principle with which the auditor concurs. The auditor should express

A. An unmodified opinion with an emphasis-of-matter paragraph.

B. A qualified opinion with an emphasis-of-matter paragraph.

C. An adverse opinion with an emphasis-of-matter paragraph.

D. An "except for" opinion without an emphasis-of-matter paragraph.

Answer (A) is correct. *(K.J. Plucinski)*

REQUIRED: The appropriate report when the auditor concurs with a change in accounting principle.

DISCUSSION: An auditor includes an emphasis-of-matter paragraph in the audit report when a material change in accounting principle has occurred. If (1) the new principle and the method of accounting for the effect of the change are in accordance with the applicable reporting framework, (2) disclosures are adequate, and (3) the entity has justified that the principle is preferable, the opinion is unmodified.

Answer (B) is incorrect. A qualified opinion is expressed when the client's financial statements are materially but not pervasively misstated. However, given that the auditor concurs with this change in accounting principle, no modification of the opinion is needed. Answer (C) is incorrect. An adverse opinion is expressed when the client's financial statements are materially and pervasively misstated. However, given that the auditor concurs with the client's change in accounting principle, no modification of the opinion is needed. Answer (D) is incorrect. The report should contain an emphasis-of-matter paragraph but no qualification.

16.2.4. Which of the following is a change in the reporting entity of a nonissuer that does not require an emphasis-of-matter paragraph about consistency to be added to the audit report?

A. Presenting consolidated statements in place of statements of individual companies.

B. Changing specific subsidiaries included in the group of companies for which consolidated financial statements are presented.

C. Purchase of a subsidiary.

D. Changing the companies included in combined financial statements.

Answer (C) is correct. *(Publisher, adapted)*

REQUIRED: The change in reporting entity not requiring a consistency reference.

DISCUSSION: The users of financial statements have a right to expect that changes in account balances are the results of transactions or events. If changes in account balances arise from changes in accounting principles, including certain changes in the reporting entity other than from transactions or events, the auditor has a responsibility to report accordingly. However, a change in the reporting entity caused by the creation, cessation, purchase, or disposition of a subsidiary or other business unit is a change in the reporting entity resulting from a transaction or event. This kind of change in the reporting entity does not require the auditor to include in the report an emphasis-of-matter paragraph about consistency (AU-C 708).

Answer (A) is incorrect. Presenting consolidated or combined statements in place of statements of individual companies does not result from a transaction or event. Answer (B) is incorrect. Changing specific subsidiaries included in the group of companies for which consolidated financial statements are presented does not result from a transaction or event. Answer (D) is incorrect. Changing the companies included in combined financial statements does not result from a transaction or event.

16.2.5. The ABC Manufacturing Co. in Year 1 and Year 2 included certain manufacturing administrative expenses in the general and administrative expense category. For the year ended December 31, Year 3, ABC has decided that these expenses should be allocated to units produced as part of manufacturing overhead. The amount involved is material. The auditor should regard this change as a

A. Classification change that does not require special treatment or comment.

B. Change in an accounting principle that requires management justification.

C. Change in an accounting estimate that requires note explanation.

D. Change from the absorption costing inventory method to the direct costing inventory method.

Answer (B) is correct. *(Publisher, adapted)*

REQUIRED: The auditor's treatment of a change in accounting for certain expenses.

DISCUSSION: The change in the treatment of manufacturing administrative expenses is a change in accounting principle. A change in accounting principle requires justification by the client and a separate paragraph in the auditor's report ("emphasis-of-matter" paragraph in an AICPA report or "explanatory" paragraph in a PCAOB report). The auditor also must determine that the new principle is in accordance with the applicable financial reporting framework.

Answer (A) is incorrect. Classification changes may result from changes in principle or correction of material misstatements. Answer (C) is incorrect. Changes in estimates require no modification of the auditor's report unless they are inseparable from a change in principle. However, a material change in estimate may require note disclosure. Answer (D) is incorrect. A change to direct costing involves treating fixed manufacturing costs as period costs (immediate expenses), not as product (inventoriable) costs.

16.2.6. The following additional paragraph was included in an auditor's report of a nonissuer to indicate a lack of consistency:

> "As discussed in note T to the financial statements, the company changed its method of computing depreciation in Year 1."

How should the auditor report on this matter if the auditor concurred with the change?

	Type of Opinion	Location of Additional Paragraph
A.	Unmodified	Before Opinion paragraph
B.	Unmodified	After Opinion paragraph
C.	Qualified	Before Opinion paragraph
D.	Qualified	After Opinion paragraph

Answer (B) is correct. *(CPA, adapted)*

REQUIRED: The reporting of a lack of consistency.

DISCUSSION: A change in accounting principle meeting certain criteria and having a material effect on the financial statements of a nonissuer requires the auditor to refer to the change in an emphasis-of-matter paragraph of the report. This paragraph should follow the opinion paragraph, describe the change, and refer to the entity's disclosure. If the report is for an issuer, the wording of the paragraph is unchanged. But it is included in explanatory language (or an explanatory paragraph). It is not included in an emphasis paragraph.

Answer (A) is incorrect. The emphasis-of-matter paragraph should follow the opinion paragraph. Answer (C) is incorrect. The opinion should be unmodified, and the emphasis-of-matter paragraph should follow the opinion paragraph. Answer (D) is incorrect. The opinion should be unmodified.

16.2.7. If management of a nonissuer fails to justify a material change in accounting principle, the auditor should

A. Add a basis for modified opinion paragraph to the report and express a qualified or an adverse opinion.

B. Disclaim an opinion because of uncertainty.

C. Disclose the matter in a separate emphasis-of-matter paragraph but not modify the opinion paragraph.

D. Neither modify the opinion nor disclose the matter because both principles are generally accepted.

Answer (A) is correct. *(Publisher, adapted)*

REQUIRED: The effect of management's failure to justify a change in accounting principle.

DISCUSSION: If (1) the new principle and the method of accounting for the effect of the change are in accordance with the applicable reporting framework, (2) disclosures are adequate, and (3) the entity has justified that the principle is preferable, the auditor expresses an unmodified opinion. Otherwise, if the change is material, the misstatement results in expression of a qualified or an adverse opinion in the report for the year of change. A basis for modified opinion paragraph is added preceding the opinion paragraph.

Answer (B) is incorrect. A disclaimer may be issued for a scope limitation but not for failure to justify a change in principle. Answer (C) is incorrect. A modified opinion must be expressed. Answer (D) is incorrect. A modified opinion must be expressed.

16.2.8. When there has been a change in accounting principle but the effect of the change on the comparability of the financial statements is not material, the auditor should

A. Not refer to the change in the auditor's report.

B. Refer to the note in the financial statements that discusses the change.

C. Refer to the change in an additional paragraph.

D. Explicitly state whether the change conforms with GAAP.

Answer (A) is correct. *(CPA, adapted)*

REQUIRED: The effect on the auditor's report of a change in accounting principle that is not material.

DISCUSSION: An auditor should evaluate whether the comparability of the financial statements has been materially affected by (1) a change in accounting principle, (2) adjustments to correct a material misstatement in previously issued financial statements, or (3) a change in entity not resulting from a transaction or event. If the auditor's report does not state otherwise, it implies that comparability has not been materially affected by such changes or corrections.

Answer (B) is incorrect. An auditor should not refer to the note in the financial statements that discusses the change. Answer (C) is incorrect. An additional paragraph is used in the auditor's report to draw users' attention to a matter appropriately presented or disclosed in the financial statements that is of such importance that it is fundamental to users' understanding of the financial statements. An additional paragraph is used only in certain circumstances. An immaterial change in accounting principle is not one of them. Answer (D) is incorrect. An auditor should not explicitly state whether the change in accounting principle conforms with GAAP.

16.2.9. A nonissuer company has made a material change in its method of inventory measurement from an unacceptable one to one in accordance with the applicable financial reporting framework. The auditor's report on the financial statements of the year of the change should include

A. No reference to consistency.

B. A reference to the entity's disclosure of the correction.

C. A note explaining the change.

D. Justification for the change and the effect of the change on reported net income.

Answer (B) is correct. *(CPA, adapted)*

REQUIRED: The effect on the report when a change is made from an unacceptable to an acceptable principle.

DISCUSSION: The auditor's report should include an emphasis-of-matter paragraph to describe the correction of a material misstatement in previous statements. The paragraph should (1) state that the previous statements have been restated and (2) refer to the entity's disclosure of the correction.

Answer (A) is incorrect. A reference should be made in a separate emphasis-of-matter paragraph following the opinion paragraph. Answer (C) is incorrect. An auditor's report should not contain notes. Answer (D) is incorrect. Justification for the change in principle is the responsibility of management, and the effect of those changes should be reflected in management's financial statements.

16.2.10. A change in accounting principle made by a nonissuer has no material effect on the financial statements in the current year but is expected to have a material effect in later years. Accordingly, the change should be

A. Treated as a consistency modification of the opinion in the auditor's report for the current year.

B. Disclosed in the notes to the financial statements of the current year.

C. Disclosed in the notes to the financial statements and referred to in the auditor's report for the current year.

D. Treated as a subsequent event.

Answer (B) is correct. *(CPA, adapted)*

REQUIRED: The treatment of a change in accounting principle with no material current effect.

DISCUSSION: The accounting change has no material effect on the financial statements in the current year but is expected to have a material effect in later years. The applicable financial reporting framework may require that the change be disclosed in the notes to the financial statements. But the independent auditor need not recognize the change in the current period's report.

Answer (A) is incorrect. The auditor should consider modifying the opinion for lack of adequate disclosure if the change is not included in the notes by the client. By itself, however, lack of consistency does not necessitate modification of the opinion. Answer (C) is incorrect. The auditor need not recognize the change in the current period's audit report. Answer (D) is incorrect. Changes in accounting principles are not subsequent events.

16.2.11. Which of the following situations concerning consistency should the auditor not recognize in the report of an issuer?

A. A change in the specific subsidiaries included in the group of companies for which consolidated statements are presented.

B. A change from an accounting principle that is not generally accepted to one that is generally accepted.

C. A change in the percentage used to calculate the provision for warranty expense.

D. The correction of a mistake in the application of an accounting principle required by the applicable financial reporting framework.

Answer (C) is correct. *(CPA, adapted)*

REQUIRED: The situation in which the auditor's report is not modified.

DISCUSSION: A change in the calculation of warranty expense is a change in accounting estimate. Changes that affect comparability but not the consistent application of accounting principles do not require recognition in the auditor's report.

Answer (A) is incorrect. This change in the reporting entity affects consistency. It does not result from a transaction or event and therefore requires an explanatory paragraph. Answer (B) is incorrect. A change from an accounting principle that is not generally accepted to one that is generally accepted is a correction of a misstatement and requires recognition in the report. Answer (D) is incorrect. Correction of a mistake in the application of an accounting principle is a correction of a misstatement requiring recognition in the report.

16.2.12. An auditor is reporting on several periods of a nonissuer, and a change in accounting principle occurred in the earliest period reported upon. If the new principle is applied in all periods presented, the auditor should

A. Refer to the change in the report even though there is no inconsistency subsequent to the change.

B. Qualify the opinion for the first year reported on but express an unmodified opinion for the subsequent years.

C. Not refer to the change.

D. Refer to the change in a note to the audit report.

Answer (C) is correct. *(Publisher, adapted)*

REQUIRED: The effect on the report when a change in principle occurs in the earliest period reported upon.

DISCUSSION: In the period of the change, the auditor must add an emphasis-of-matter paragraph following the opinion paragraph to reflect the inconsistency. This paragraph is required in reports on financial statements in the period of change and in subsequent periods until the new principle is applied in all periods presented.

Answer (A) is incorrect. The emphasis-of-matter paragraph is no longer needed when the new principle is applied in all periods presented. Answer (B) is incorrect. A justified change in principle does not require modification of the opinion. Answer (D) is incorrect. An emphasis-of-matter paragraph is used to describe a justified change in principle until the new principle is applied in all periods presented.

16.2.13. If a material change in estimate is inseparable from a change in accounting principle, this event should be evaluated by the auditor as a change in

A. Estimate, and the auditor should report on consistency.

B. Principle, and the auditor should report on consistency.

C. Estimate, and the auditor should not recognize the change in the report.

D. Principle, and the auditor should not recognize the change in the report.

Answer (B) is correct. *(CPA, adapted)*

REQUIRED: The true statement about a change in estimate effected by a change in principle.

DISCUSSION: When a material change in estimate is inseparable from a change in accounting principle, the FASB requires the change to be accounted for prospectively as a change in estimate. However, an auditor should evaluate and report on the change as a change in principle. This type of change requires recognition in the auditor's report as to consistency. An example is a change in a method of depreciation of an asset to reflect a change in benefits or in their pattern of consumption (AU-C 708).

Answer (A) is incorrect. The auditor evaluates and reports on the change as a change in principle. Answer (C) is incorrect. The auditor evaluates and reports on the change as a change in principle accounted for as an estimate, and the auditor should refer to the change in the report. Answer (D) is incorrect. The auditor should refer to the change in the report.

16.2.14. A nonissuer changed from the straight-line method to the declining-balance method of depreciation for all newly acquired assets. This change has no material effect on the current year's financial statements but is reasonably certain to have a material effect in later years. If the change is disclosed in the notes to the financial statements, the auditor should issue a report with a(n)

A. Qualified opinion.

B. Emphasis-of-matter paragraph.

C. Unmodified opinion.

D. Consistency modification.

Answer (C) is correct. *(CPA, adapted)*

REQUIRED: The report issued when a change in accounting principle has no current material effect.

DISCUSSION: If a change in accounting principle has no material effect on the current financial statements but is expected to have a material effect in future years, the change should be disclosed by the client if required by the applicable financial reporting framework. But it need not be recognized in the report.

Answer (A) is incorrect. A justified change in accounting principle does not result in an opinion qualified because of the change. Answer (B) is incorrect. If an accounting change has no material effect on the current financial statements, the auditor need not modify the current-period report. Answer (D) is incorrect. If an accounting change has no material effect on the current financial statements but is likely to affect future financial statements, the auditor need not modify the current-period report.

16.2.15. Green Company, an issuer, uses the first-in, first-out method of costing for its international subsidiary's inventory and the last-in, first-out method of costing for its domestic inventory. The different costing methods will cause Green's auditor to issue a report with a(n)

A. Explanatory paragraph as to consistency.

B. Qualified opinion.

C. Opinion modified as to consistency.

D. Unqualified opinion.

Answer (D) is correct. *(CPA, adapted)*

REQUIRED: The audit report when two business segments use different inventory methods.

DISCUSSION: The objective of the evaluation of consistency for the periods presented is to communicate in the report when the comparability of financial statements between periods has been materially affected by a change in accounting principles or by adjustments to correct a material misstatement in previous statements. Thus, the use of two different cost flow assumptions does not, by itself, affect the comparability of the entity's financial statements between periods if no accounting changes have occurred.

Answer (A) is incorrect. No explanatory paragraph is necessary if (1) no change in principle, (2) correction of a material misstatement in previous statements, or (3) change in reporting entity not from a transaction or event has occurred. Answer (B) is incorrect. An unqualified opinion is possible even when the comparability of financial statements between periods has been materially affected. Answer (C) is incorrect. The use of different principles does not require modification of the opinion.

16.3 Uncertainties and Going Concern

16.3.1. Green, CPA, is auditing JKL Co., a nonissuer. Green concludes that there is substantial doubt about JKL Co.'s ability to continue as a going concern. If JKL's financial statements adequately disclose its financial difficulties, Green's auditor's report should

	Include a Paragraph Following the Opinion Paragraph	Specifically Use the Words "Going Concern"	Specifically Use the Words "Substantial Doubt"
A.	Yes	Yes	Yes
B.	Yes	Yes	No
C.	Yes	No	Yes
D.	No	Yes	Yes

Answer (A) is correct. *(CPA, adapted)*

REQUIRED: The effect of a substantial doubt about the going-concern assumption.

DISCUSSION: An evaluation should be made as to whether substantial doubt exists about the entity's ability to continue as a going concern for a reasonable period of time (U.S. GAAP is 1 year from the date the statements are released or available to be released). If the auditor reaches this conclusion after identifying conditions and events that create such doubt and after evaluating management's plans to reduce their effects, (s)he should consider the possible effects on the statements and the adequacy of disclosure. (S)he also should include an emphasis-of-matter paragraph (after the opinion paragraph) in the report. The auditor should use language in the emphasis-of-matter paragraph that includes the phrases "substantial doubt" and "going concern." Also, the emphasis-of-matter paragraph should not use conditional language in expressing its conclusion about the existence of a substantial doubt. The substantial doubt is not a basis for a qualified or an adverse opinion, but a disclaimer is not precluded in the case of such a material uncertainty.

16.3.2. Grant Company's financial statements adequately disclose uncertainties that concern future events, the outcome of which are not susceptible to reasonable estimation. The auditor's report should include a(n)

A. Unmodified opinion.

B. "Subject to" qualified opinion.

C. "Except for" qualified opinion.

D. Adverse opinion.

Answer (A) is correct. *(CPA, adapted)*

REQUIRED: The opinion when financial statements adequately disclose uncertainties.

DISCUSSION: An auditor assesses whether management's assertions about uncertainties are supported by sufficient appropriate audit evidence. This judgment is based on the evidence that is, or should be, available. Thus, in the absence of (1) an inability to obtain sufficient appropriate evidence or (2) a material misstatement, an uncertainty does not require modification of the report.

Answer (B) is incorrect. A "subject to" qualified opinion is never permissible. Answer (C) is incorrect. A qualified opinion related to an uncertainty is appropriate given (1) a scope limitation with possible effects that are material but not pervasive or (2) a misstatement with effects that are material but not pervasive. Answer (D) is incorrect. Absent a material misstatement, an uncertainty does not result in an adverse opinion.

16.3.3. In which of the following circumstances would an auditor most likely add an emphasis-of-matter paragraph of a nonissuer to the auditor's report while expressing an unmodified opinion?

A. The auditor is asked to report on the balance sheet but not on the other basic financial statements.

B. There is substantial doubt about the entity's ability to continue as a going concern.

C. Management's estimates of the effects of future events are unreasonable.

D. Certain material transactions cannot be tested because of management's records retention policy.

Answer (B) is correct. *(CPA, adapted)*

REQUIRED: The reason for including an emphasis-of-matter paragraph when expressing an unmodified opinion.

DISCUSSION: An auditor may have a substantial doubt about the entity's ability to continue as a going concern after (1) identifying conditions and events that create such doubt and (2) evaluating management's plans to mitigate their effects. In this circumstance, (s)he should (1) consider the adequacy of disclosure and (2) include an emphasis-of-matter paragraph (after the opinion paragraph) in the report. The auditor must use language in the emphasis-of-matter paragraph that includes the words "substantial doubt" and "going concern." By itself, however, the substantial doubt is not a basis for modifying the opinion.

Answer (A) is incorrect. An auditor may be asked to report on one financial statement. In that event, (s)he may appropriately express an unmodified opinion without adding an additional paragraph. Answer (C) is incorrect. The statements are not fairly presented if material estimates included in them are unreasonable. An unmodified opinion could not then be expressed. Answer (D) is incorrect. A qualification or disclaimer of opinion is appropriate when the scope of the audit is limited.

16.3.4. A separate paragraph of an auditor's report of a nonissuer describes an uncertainty as follows:

> As discussed in Note X to the financial statements, the Company is a defendant in a lawsuit alleging infringement of certain patent rights and claiming damages. Discovery proceedings are in progress.

What type of opinion should the auditor express under these circumstances?

A. Unmodified.

B. "Subject to" qualified.

C. "Except for" qualified.

D. Disclaimer.

Answer (A) is correct. *(CPA, adapted)*

REQUIRED: The opinion that should be expressed because of an uncertainty.

DISCUSSION: Audit standards do not require the addition of an uncertainties paragraph. However, standards provide the auditor with the option of emphasizing a matter regarding the financial statements by adding an emphasis-of-matter paragraph (an emphasis paragraph for an issuer). This paragraph does not affect the opinion expressed on the financial statements.

Answer (B) is incorrect. The phrase "subject to" is not permitted in any report. Answer (C) is incorrect. By itself, an uncertainty does not result in an opinion modification. Answer (D) is incorrect. A disclaimer is less likely than an unmodified opinion on these facts. Moreover, an auditor's report containing a disclaimer includes a basis-for-disclaimer paragraph stating the reasons for the inability to obtain sufficient appropriate evidence.

16.3.5. If an auditor of a nonissuer is satisfied that sufficient appropriate evidence supports management's assertions about an uncertainty, the auditor should

A. Express an unmodified opinion.

B. Express an unmodified opinion with a separate emphasis-of-matter paragraph.

C. Disclaim an opinion.

D. Express a qualified opinion or disclaim an opinion, depending upon the materiality of the loss.

Answer (A) is correct. *(CPA, adapted)*

REQUIRED: The opinion expressed when sufficient appropriate evidence supports assertions about an uncertainty.

DISCUSSION: If sufficient appropriate evidence supports management's assertions about an uncertainty and its presentation or disclosure, the opinion ordinarily is unmodified (AU-C 705).

Answer (B) is incorrect. An emphasis-of-matter paragraph is not required. Answer (C) is incorrect. A disclaimer is appropriate only when the possible effects of an inability to obtain sufficient appropriate evidence are pervasive. Answer (D) is incorrect. A disclaimer is appropriate only when the possible effects of an inability to obtain sufficient appropriate evidence are pervasive. Moreover, an uncertainty does not, by itself, require any report modification.

16.3.6. Toni Hooper, CPA, had drafted an unmodified opinion on the audit of Chem Waste Disposal when she received a letter from the client's independent counsel. The letter indicated that the state Department of Environmental Protection may prohibit Chem Waste from accepting any further waste for processing because of irregularities in its operating practices. Counsel intends to take all appropriate action to keep the firm in business, but the outcome is highly uncertain, and Hooper has substantial doubt about the company's continued existence. Based on this information, Hooper should

A. Express an unmodified opinion with disclosure of the event in a separate paragraph of her report.

B. Issue an unmodified report because the event happened after year end.

C. Express an adverse opinion on the financial statements and disclose the reasons.

D. Add a note to the audit report explaining the event.

Answer (A) is correct. *(Publisher, adapted)*

REQUIRED: The appropriate report when a CPA has substantial doubt about the company's continued existence.

DISCUSSION: An auditor may have a substantial doubt about the entity's ability to continue as a going concern after (1) addressing management's evaluation, (2) identifying conditions and events that create doubt, and (3) performing additional procedures that include evaluating management's plans to mitigate the relevant conditions or events. In this circumstance, (s)he should (1) consider the adequacy of disclosure and (2) include a separate paragraph (titled "Emphasis-of-Matter" in an AICPA report or one with an appropriate title, e.g., "Going-Concern Issue" in a PCAOB report) in the report. Under U.S. GAAP, the auditor must use language in the separate paragraph that includes the words "substantial doubt" and "going concern." By itself, however, the substantial doubt is not a basis for modifying the opinion.

Answer (B) is incorrect. If a material uncertainty exists as to whether the client is a going concern, the report should be modified. Answer (C) is incorrect. No basis exists for an opinion that the statements are not fairly presented. Answer (D) is incorrect. A note is not an appropriate form of audit reporting.

16.3.7. If a company is experiencing financial difficulty that raises substantial doubt about its ability to continue as a going concern, auditing standards require the auditor to

A. Withdraw from the engagement.

B. Value the assets on a liquidation basis.

C. Plan to conduct a complete audit rather than perform procedures on a test basis.

D. Include in the report a paragraph describing the nature of the difficulties.

Answer (D) is correct. *(N. Schmukler)*

REQUIRED: The auditor's responsibility when the entity may not be able to continue as a going concern.

DISCUSSION: Auditing standards require the auditor to alert financial statement users to the existence of doubt about the ability of an auditee to continue in existence. The requirement is intended to reduce the instances when, shortly after the expression of an unmodified opinion, the auditee becomes bankrupt. Thus, the auditor's substantial doubt requires inclusion of an emphasis-of-matter paragraph in the report for a nonissuer or an explanatory paragraph in the report of an issuer. This paragraph should include the words "substantial doubt" and "going concern."

Answer (A) is incorrect. The auditor need not withdraw. Answer (B) is incorrect. The existence of a substantial doubt does not require that assets be presented on a liquidation basis. They may continue to be presented on a going concern basis unless liquidation is imminent. Answer (C) is incorrect. Even when the entity may not be able to continue as a going concern, the audit will normally be performed on a test basis.

16.3.8. The federal government alleges that your client has overcharged on certain contracts and is demanding a material refund. If the client is compelled to return this sum, the current ratio of 2:1 in the present financial statements would be reduced to 1.2:1, and a substantial reduction in retained earnings would occur. No decision has been reached at the end of field work, and a note adequately describing the event and negotiations has been written by the client. The auditor should most likely

A. Express an adverse opinion because of the material uncertainty.

B. Issue an unmodified report because adequate disclosure of the uncertainty has been made in the notes.

C. Express a qualified opinion because of the material uncertainty.

D. Express a piecemeal opinion.

Answer (B) is correct. *(Publisher, adapted)*

REQUIRED: The appropriate report when a properly disclosed loss contingency exists.

DISCUSSION: When a material uncertainty exists, the auditor need only modify the report when a scope limitation exists or the financial statements are materially misstated. Given that (1) disclosure is adequate and (2) no indication is given of a scope limitation, the auditor need not modify the report.

Answer (A) is incorrect. An adverse opinion is not appropriate if the financial statements are presented fairly. Answer (C) is incorrect. A qualified opinion is not expressed solely on the basis of an uncertainty. Answer (D) is incorrect. A piecemeal opinion is never appropriate.

16.3.9. An auditor concludes that there is substantial doubt about an issuer entity's ability to continue as a going concern for a reasonable period of time. The entity's financial statements adequately disclose its financial difficulties. Under these circumstances, the auditor's report is required to include an explanatory paragraph that specifically uses the phrase(s)

	"Except for the effects of such adjustments"	"Possible discontinuance of the entity's operations"
A.	Yes	Yes
B.	Yes	No
C.	No	Yes
D.	No	No

Answer (D) is correct. *(CPA, adapted)*

REQUIRED: The phrase(s), if any, required to be included in a paragraph describing a substantial doubt about a firm's ability to continue as a going concern.

DISCUSSION: The auditor has a substantial doubt about the firm's ability to continue as a going concern for a reasonable period of time. Accordingly, the auditor should include explanatory language or an explanatory paragraph in the report. This language or paragraph should include the terms "substantial doubt" and "going concern." The specific phrases included in the question are not required.

Answer (A) is incorrect. The terms "Except for the effects of such adjustments" and "Possible discontinuance of the entity's operations" are not required. Answer (B) is incorrect. The term "Except for the effects of such adjustments" is not required. Answer (C) is incorrect. The term "Possible discontinuance of the entity's operations" is not required.

16.3.10. A continuing auditor should update the report on prior financial statements by issuing a report modified for the

A. Resolution of an uncertainty related to and discovered in the current period.

B. Removal in the current period of doubt about the entity's ability to continue as a going concern.

C. Determination in the current period that a substantial doubt exists about the entity's ability to continue as a going concern for a reasonable time.

D. Purchase and consolidation of a new company by the client.

Answer (B) is correct. *(Publisher, adapted)*

REQUIRED: The reason a continuing auditor should update the report on prior statements.

DISCUSSION: A continuing auditor should update the report on prior-period statements presented comparatively with those of the current period. If the auditor determines that a substantial doubt about the reporting entity's ability to continue as a going concern for a reasonable period has been removed in the current period, the related separate paragraph in the report on the prior-period statements need not be repeated.

Answer (A) is incorrect. Resolution of an uncertainty discovered in the current period does not affect prior-period statements. Answer (C) is incorrect. Determination that a going concern issue exists in the current period typically does not affect prior-period statements. Answer (D) is incorrect. Transactions in the current period do not affect the auditor's report in the prior period.

16.4 Comparative Financial Statements

16.4.1. Which of the following is a true statement about the auditor's report on comparative financial statements?

A. A continuing auditor may under certain circumstances express an opinion different from the previous opinion.

B. The report should not express an opinion different from that previously expressed on the statements of a prior period because the differences would lessen the public's confidence in the integrity of the auditor's report.

C. A predecessor auditor may reissue the report on the financial statements of a prior period provided (s)he performs certain procedures, including obtaining representation letters from the successor auditor and from management, and provided (s)he refers in the reissued report to the work of the successor auditor.

D. If the financial statements of the prior period have been audited but those of the current period have not, the auditor should update the report on the prior period and include as a separate paragraph in the report a disclaimer of opinion on the unaudited financial statements.

Answer (A) is correct. *(Publisher, adapted)*

REQUIRED: The true statement about reports on comparative financial statements.

DISCUSSION: A continuing auditor should update the report on the statements of one or more prior periods presented comparatively with the statements of the current period. An updated report is distinguishable from the reissuance of a prior report because the continuing auditor considers information acquired during the audit of the current period's statements and issues the updated report in conjunction with the report on the current period statements. An updated report may contain an opinion different from that expressed in the previous report because, during the current audit, the auditor may have become aware of circumstances or events affecting a prior period's statements, e.g., restatement in the current period to correct a material misstatement.

Answer (B) is incorrect. The auditor is required to be alert during the current audit for circumstances and events that materially affect the prior period statements. Answer (C) is incorrect. The predecessor auditor should perform certain procedures, including obtaining representation letters from the successor auditor and from management, but should not refer to the report or work of the successor auditor. Answer (D) is incorrect. Updating implies that the auditor has considered information obtained during the current year's audit.

16.4.2. The predecessor auditor, who is satisfied after properly communicating with the current auditor, has reissued a report because the audit client desires comparative financial statements. The predecessor auditor's report should

A. Refer to the report of the current auditor only in the auditor's responsibility section.

B. Refer to the work of the current auditor in the opinion paragraph.

C. Refer to both the work and the report of the current auditor only in the opinion paragraph.

D. Not refer to the report or the work of the current auditor.

Answer (D) is correct. *(CPA, adapted)*

REQUIRED: The true statement about a reference to the current auditor in a reissued report.

DISCUSSION: A predecessor auditor who has been asked to reissue his or her report should (1) read the current-period statements, (2) compare the statements (s)he reported on with other statements to be presented comparatively, (3) obtain a representation letter from the auditor, and (4) obtain a representation letter from management of the former client. However, the reissued report should not refer to the report or work of the auditor.

16.4.3. When financial statements of a prior period are presented on a comparative basis with financial statements of the current period, the continuing auditor is responsible for

A. Expressing dual-dated opinions.

B. Updating the report on the previous financial statements only if there has not been a change in the opinion.

C. Updating the report on the previous financial statements only if the previous opinion was qualified and the reasons for the qualification no longer exist.

D. Updating the report on the previous financial statements regardless of the opinion previously expressed.

Answer (D) is correct. *(CPA, adapted)*

REQUIRED: The responsibility of a continuing auditor relative to comparative statements.

DISCUSSION: A continuing auditor should update the report on the individual statements of one or more prior periods presented on a comparative basis. An updated report considers information of which the continuing auditor is aware as a result of the current audit. Furthermore, the updated report is issued in conjunction with the report on the current statements. For example, if the opinion was modified because of a material misstatement, and management revises the statements, the updated report expresses an unmodified opinion.

Answer (A) is incorrect. Dual-dated reports relate to events that occur between the original date of the auditor's report and the additional date of a revision of the statements for subsequently discovered facts. Answer (B) is incorrect. The report should be updated regardless of whether the opinion has changed. Answer (C) is incorrect. The report should be updated regardless of whether the opinion on the previous financial statements was unmodified, qualified, adverse, or disclaimed.

16.4.4. When reporting on comparative financial statements, which of the following circumstances ordinarily should cause the auditor to change the previously expressed opinion on the prior year's financial statements?

A. The prior year's financial statements are restated to reflect a change in an account title from "Trade Receivables" to "Accounts Receivable."

B. A material misstatement caused an adverse opinion on the prior year's financial statements, and those statements have been properly restated.

C. A change in accounting principle caused the auditor to make a consistency modification in the current year's auditor's report.

D. A scope limitation caused a qualified opinion on the prior year's financial statements, but the current year's opinion was properly unmodified.

Answer (B) is correct. *(CPA, adapted)*

REQUIRED: The event that causes an auditor to change a previously expressed opinion.

DISCUSSION: If an opinion in an updated report is different from the one previously expressed, the auditor should disclose the following in an additional paragraph: (1) the date of the auditor's previous report, (2) the type of opinion previously expressed, (3) the substantive reasons for the different opinion, and (4) a statement that the auditor's updated opinion on the statements of the prior period is different from the previous opinion.

Answer (A) is incorrect. This change in classification most likely has no effect on the auditor's opinion. Answer (C) is incorrect. A change in accounting principle in the current period has no effect on the opinion on the prior year's statements. The auditor should add to the current report an additional paragraph relating to the change. Answer (D) is incorrect. The scope limitation from the prior year requires the auditor to express a qualified opinion on the prior year's financial statements.

16.4.5. An auditor expressed a qualified opinion on the prior year's financial statements for a nonissuer because of a lack of adequate disclosure. These financial statements are properly restated in the current year and presented in comparative form with the current year's financial statements. The auditor's updated report on the prior year's financial statements should

A. Be accompanied by the auditor's original report on the prior year's financial statements.

B. Continue to express a qualified opinion on the prior year's financial statements.

C. Not refer to the type of opinion expressed on the prior year's financial statements.

D. Express an unmodified opinion on the restated financial statements of the prior year.

Answer (D) is correct. *(CPA, adapted)*

REQUIRED: The effect on the auditor's updated report when the opinion has changed from the previous year.

DISCUSSION: During the audit, an auditor may become aware of information affecting the statements of a prior period and should consider them when updating the report. For example, if the opinion was modified because of a material misstatement, and the statements are restated in the current period, the updated report should express an unmodified opinion. The report should contain an emphasis-of-matter or other-matter paragraph following the opinion paragraph to disclose (1) the date of the auditor's previous report, (2) the type of opinion previously expressed, (3) the substantive reasons for the different opinion, and (4) a statement that the auditor's updated opinion on the statements of the prior period is different from the previous opinion.

Answer (A) is incorrect. The original report should not be reissued. Answer (B) is incorrect. The opinion has changed and the auditor should not continue to express the previous opinion. Answer (C) is incorrect. An other-matter paragraph should be added to the current audit report explaining the reason for the change and the type of opinion previously expressed.

16.4.6. Which of the following portions of a continuing auditor's report on comparative financial statements of a nonissuer is incorrect?

A. "In our opinion, the financial statements referred to above present fairly, in all material respects, the financial position . . . "

B. "Of XYZ Company as of December 31, Year 2 and Year 1 and the results of its operations and its cash flows."

C. "For the years then ended in accordance with accounting principles generally accepted in the United States of America."

D. "Applied on a basis consistent with that of the preceding year."

Answer (D) is correct. *(CPA, adapted)*

REQUIRED: The incorrect portion of a continuing auditor's standard report on comparative statements.

DISCUSSION: The auditor's report is silent as to consistency unless the comparability of the financial statements has been materially affected by a change in accounting principle or by correction of a material misstatement in previous statements. The change should be referred to in an emphasis-of-matter paragraph following the opinion paragraph. Agreement with the change is implied unless the auditor takes exception to it.

Answer (A) is incorrect. The opinion paragraph in a report on comparative statements states an opinion. Answer (B) is incorrect. The opinion paragraph in a report on comparative statements identifies the auditee. Answer (C) is incorrect. The opinion paragraph in a report on comparative statements mentions the applicable reporting framework.

16.4.7. When single-year financial statements are presented, an auditor ordinarily expresses an unmodified opinion if the

A. Auditor is unable to obtain audited financial statements supporting the entity's investment in a foreign affiliate.

B. Entity declines to present a statement of cash flows with its balance sheet and related statements of income and retained earnings.

C. Auditor is not independent but judges that an unmodified opinion is appropriate.

D. Prior year's financial statements were audited by another CPA whose report, which expressed an unmodified opinion, is not presented.

Answer (D) is correct. *(CPA, adapted)*

REQUIRED: The condition for expressing an unmodified opinion on single-year financial statements.

DISCUSSION: When single-year financial statements are presented, the auditor's reporting responsibility is limited to those statements. If the prior year's financial statements are not presented for comparative purposes, the current-year auditor should not refer to the prior year's statements and the report thereon. Furthermore, the failure to present comparative statements is not a basis for modifying the opinion.

Answer (A) is incorrect. An inability to obtain audited financial statements supporting an entity's material investment in a foreign affiliate is a scope limitation requiring either a qualified opinion or a disclaimer of opinion. Answer (B) is incorrect. If the entity declines to present a statement of cash flows, the auditor should express a qualified opinion. Answer (C) is incorrect. The auditor should not express an opinion if (s)he is not independent.

16.4.8. Audited financial statements of the prior period are presented comparatively with unaudited statements of the current period in a document not filed with the SEC, and the report on the current period is to contain a separate paragraph describing the responsibility assumed for the financial statements of the prior period. In accordance with PCAOB auditing standards, the report on the current period should not indicate

A. That the prior-period financial statements were audited and no auditing procedures were performed after the previous report date.

B. The date of the previous report and the type of opinion expressed previously.

C. The substantive reasons for any modification of the opinion on the prior-period statements.

D. That nothing has come to the auditor's attention to lead him or her to believe that material changes have taken place since that date.

Answer (D) is correct. *(Publisher, adapted)*

REQUIRED: The disclosure not required in the report.

DISCUSSION: When unaudited financial statements are presented in comparative form with audited financial statements, the financial statements that have not been audited should be clearly marked to indicate their status. In an SEC filing, the unaudited statements should not be referred to in the auditor's report. But in any other document, either (1) the report on the prior period should be reissued or (2) the report on the current period should include a separate paragraph describing the responsibility assumed for the financial statements of the prior period. When the statements of the prior period have been audited and the report on the current period is to contain a separate paragraph, it should state that the prior-period financial statements were audited, and no auditing procedures were performed after the previous report date. It should also state the substantive reasons for any modification of the opinion on the prior-period statements, the date of that report, and the type of opinion expressed.

Answer (A) is incorrect. The report should state that the prior-period financial statements were audited and no auditing procedures were performed after the previous report date. Answer (B) is incorrect. The report should state the date of the previous report and the type of opinion expressed. Answer (C) is incorrect. The report should state the substantive reasons for any modification of the opinion on the prior-period statements.

16.4.9. A nonissuer's unaudited financial statements for the prior period are presented in comparative form with audited financial statements for the subsequent year. If the prior-period statements were reviewed,

I. The report on the unaudited financial statements should be reissued.

II. The report on the audited financial statements should include an other-matter paragraph.

A. I only.

B. II only.

C. Neither I nor II.

D. Either I or II.

Answer (D) is correct. *(CPA, adapted)*

REQUIRED: The appropriate reporting when the prior-period's unaudited financial statements of a nonissuer are presented in comparative form with current-period audited financial statements.

DISCUSSION: A nonissuer's audited statements for the current period may be presented comparatively with the prior period's reviewed or compiled statements. If the prior period's report is not reissued, the auditor's current-period report should include an other-matter paragraph that states (1) the service performed in the prior period, (2) the date of the service, (3) a description of material modifications noted in the report, and (4) that the service was not an audit and did not provide a basis for an opinion (AU-C 700).

16.4.10. When management does not provide reasonable justification for a change in accounting principle, and it presents comparative financial statements, the auditor should express a qualified opinion

A. Only in the year of the accounting principle change.

B. Each year that the financial statements initially reflecting the change are presented.

C. Each year until management changes back to the accounting principle formerly used.

D. Only if the change is to an accounting principle that is not generally accepted.

Answer (B) is correct. *(CPA, adapted)*

REQUIRED: The year(s) or circumstance in which an unjustified accounting change requires a qualified opinion.

DISCUSSION: If (1) the new principle and the method of accounting for the effect of the change are in accordance with the applicable reporting framework, (2) disclosures are adequate, and (3) the entity has justified that the principle is preferable, the auditor expresses an unmodified opinion. Otherwise, if the change is material, the misstatement results in expression of a qualified or an adverse opinion in the report for the year of change. The basis for the modified opinion is included in the report. In the period of the change, the auditor also must add an additional paragraph following the opinion paragraph to reflect the inconsistency. This paragraph is required in reports on financial statements in the period of change and in subsequent periods until the new principle is applied in all periods presented.

Answer (A) is incorrect. The qualified opinion should be expressed each year the statements for the year of change are presented and reported on. Answer (C) is incorrect. The qualified opinion should be expressed each year the statements for the year of change are presented and reported on. Answer (D) is incorrect. A qualified opinion may be appropriate if the auditor determines that the change to an acceptable principle is unjustified.

16.4.11. Comparative financial statements include the prior year's statements that were audited by a predecessor auditor whose report is not presented. If the predecessor's opinion was unmodified, the auditor should

A. Express an opinion on the current year's statements alone and not refer to the prior year's statements.

B. Indicate in the auditor's report that the predecessor auditor expressed an unmodified opinion.

C. Obtain a letter of representations from the predecessor concerning any matters that might affect the auditor's opinion.

D. Request the predecessor auditor to reissue the prior year's report.

Answer (B) is correct. *(CPA, adapted)*

REQUIRED: The auditor's disclosure about the report of a predecessor that is not presented.

DISCUSSION: The auditor should state in a separate paragraph following the opinion paragraph that the prior year's financial statements were audited by another auditor. (S)he should give the date and the type of opinion and, if the report was modified, the reasons for modification. If the predecessor auditor expressed an unmodified opinion but included an additional paragraph (i.e., an emphasis-of-matter or other-matter paragraph for a nonissuer or an explanatory paragraph for an issuer), the nature of such a paragraph should be described.

Answer (A) is incorrect. The prior year's financial statements presented comparatively should be considered in an auditor's report. Answer (C) is incorrect. The auditor should communicate with the predecessor prior to accepting the engagement. Answer (D) is incorrect. The predecessor's report may be reissued, and the auditor's report would then not refer to the predecessor. However, the question indicates that the predecessor's report is not presented.

16.4.12. Comparative financial statements include the financial statements of the prior year that were audited by a predecessor auditor whose opinion is not presented. If the predecessor's opinion was qualified, the auditor should

A. Indicate the reasons for the qualification in the predecessor auditor's opinion.

B. Request the client to reissue the predecessor's report on the prior year's statements.

C. Issue an updated comparative audit report indicating the division of responsibility.

D. Express an opinion only on the current year's statements and make no reference to the prior year's statements.

Answer (A) is correct. *(CPA, adapted)*

REQUIRED: The auditor's action if the predecessor's report expressing a qualified opinion is not present.

DISCUSSION: When the predecessor's report is not presented, the auditor's report should include an additional paragraph titled "other matter" if for a nonissuer or with no title if for an issuer. The statement also includes (1) a statement that the financial statements of the prior period were audited by another auditor, (2) the date of the report, (3) the opinion expressed, (4) the reasons if the opinion was modified, and (5) the nature of any additional paragraphs.

Answer (B) is incorrect. Although the report may be reissued, the question states that the report is not presented. Answer (C) is incorrect. Division of responsibility is only appropriate when component auditors have audited a portion of the current statements being reported on. Answer (D) is incorrect. The statements presented in comparative form must be reported on, or a disclaimer must be presented.

16.4.13. Unaudited financial statements are presented in comparative form with audited financial statements in a document filed with the Securities and Exchange Commission. In accordance with the PCAOB's Auditing Standards, such statements should be

	Marked as "Unaudited"	Withheld until Audited	Referred to in the Auditor's Report
A.	Yes	No	No
B.	Yes	No	Yes
C.	No	Yes	Yes
D.	No	Yes	No

Answer (A) is correct. *(CPA, adapted)*

REQUIRED: The treatment of unaudited statements presented comparatively with audited statements in a document filed with the SEC.

DISCUSSION: According to the PCAOB's Auditing Standards, when unaudited financial statements are presented in comparative form with audited statements in documents filed with the SEC, such statements should be clearly marked as "unaudited." They should not be referred to in the auditor's report or withheld until audited. NOTE: The source of authoritative guidance is the PCAOB's Auditing Standards, not the clarified SASs published by the AICPA. The PCAOB Standards apply to services for issuers.

16.4.14. When a predecessor auditor reissues the report on the prior period's financial statements at the request of the former client, the predecessor should

A. Indicate in the introductory paragraph of the reissued report that the financial statements of the subsequent period were audited by another CPA.

B. Obtain a representation letter from the auditor but not from management.

C. Compare the prior period's financial statements that the predecessor reported on with the financial statements to be presented for comparative purposes.

D. Add an additional paragraph to the reissued report stating that the predecessor has not performed additional auditing procedures on the prior period's financial statements.

Answer (C) is correct. *(CPA, adapted)*

REQUIRED: The procedure performed by the predecessor auditor before reissuing a report.

DISCUSSION: The predecessor auditor should perform certain procedures before reissuing a report on prior-period financial statements. (S)he should (1) read the current period's financial statements, (2) compare the prior and current financial statements, (3) obtain a representation letter from the auditor stating whether (s)he has discovered matters having a material effect on (or requiring disclosure in) the statements reported on by the predecessor auditor, and (4) obtain a representation letter from management confirming past representations and stating whether post-balance-sheet events require adjustment of or disclosure in the financial statements.

Answer (A) is incorrect. The reissued report should not refer to another auditor. Answer (B) is incorrect. The predecessor auditor should obtain a representation letter from the auditor and from management. Answer (D) is incorrect. The report should not be modified unless the auditor's previous conclusions have changed.

16.5 Emphasis-of-Matter and Other-Matter Paragraphs

16.5.1. An auditor judges that additional communication in the report of a nonissuer is needed to draw users' attention to an important matter. If the matter is appropriately presented and disclosed in the statements, the matter is referred to

A. Only in the management's responsibility for the financial statements paragraph.

B. Only in an emphasis-of-matter paragraph.

C. In the introductory paragraph and the opinion paragraph.

D. In the opinion paragraph and the basis for modification paragraph.

Answer (B) is correct. *(Publisher, adapted)*

REQUIRED: The treatment in the audit report of additional communication about a matter appropriately presented and disclosed in the statements.

DISCUSSION: An auditor may wish to emphasize a matter affecting the statements even though (s)he intends to express an unmodified opinion. This information should be contained in an emphasis-of-matter paragraph and not referred to in any other part of the report. An emphasis-of-matter paragraph is used when (1) the matter is fundamental to users' understanding of the statements, (2) the auditor considers that drawing users' attention to the matter is necessary, and (3) the matter is appropriately presented and disclosed in the statements.

Answer (A) is incorrect. The management's responsibility for the financial statements paragraph should remain unchanged. Answer (C) is incorrect. The introductory and opinion paragraphs should remain unchanged. Answer (D) is incorrect. The opinion paragraph should remain unchanged.

16.5.2. An auditor's report expresses an unmodified opinion and includes an emphasis-of-matter paragraph for a nonissuer. The auditor's report is deficient if the emphasis-of-matter paragraph states that the entity

A. Is significantly affected by a major catastrophe.

B. Has omitted a statement of cash flows.

C. Has had an unusually important subsequent event.

D. Has significant related party transactions.

Answer (B) is correct. *(CPA, adapted)*

REQUIRED: The statement in an emphasis-of-matter paragraph indicating a deficiency in the report.

DISCUSSION: The statement of cash flows is a basic financial statement. Its omission when financial position and results of operations are presented is a material misstatement that requires the auditor to modify the opinion. An emphasis-of-matter paragraph is used when (1) the matter is fundamental to users' understanding of the statements, (2) the auditor considers that drawing users' attention to the matter is necessary, and (3) the matter is appropriately presented and disclosed in the statements.

Answer (A) is incorrect. A major catastrophe may be emphasized when the auditor expresses an unmodified opinion. Answer (C) is incorrect. An unusually important subsequent event may be emphasized when the auditor expresses an unmodified opinion. Answer (D) is incorrect. Significant related party transactions may be emphasized when the auditor expresses an unmodified opinion.

16.5.3. In which situation is the auditor most likely not to include an emphasis-of-matter paragraph in the auditor's report of a nonissuer?

A. An important audit procedure was performed.

B. The client suffered a major catastrophe.

C. Significant transactions with related parties were recorded.

D. Unusually important subsequent events occurred.

Answer (A) is correct. *(Publisher, adapted)*

REQUIRED: The situation in which an emphasis-of-matter paragraph is not included in the auditor's report.

DISCUSSION: An emphasis-of-matter paragraph is not used to describe an audit procedure. It is used to draw attention to a matter appropriately presented or disclosed in the financial statements that is fundamental to users' understanding. The following are examples of circumstances in which the auditor may need to include an emphasis-of-matter paragraph: (1) an uncertainty relating to the future outcome of unusually important litigation or regulatory action; (2) a major catastrophe that has had, or continues to have, a significant effect on the entity's financial position; (3) significant transactions with related parties; and (4) unusually important subsequent events.

Answer (B) is incorrect. The auditor may need to include an emphasis-of-matter paragraph because of a major catastrophe. Answer (C) is incorrect. The auditor may need to include an emphasis-of-matter paragraph because of significant transactions with related parties. Answer (D) is incorrect. The auditor may need to include an emphasis-of-matter paragraph because of unusually important subsequent events

16.5.4. An auditor includes an emphasis-of-matter paragraph in an otherwise unmodified report when the entity being reported on had significant transactions with related parties. The inclusion of this paragraph

A. Is considered a qualification of the opinion.

B. Violates auditing standards if this information is already disclosed in notes to the financial statements.

C. Necessitates a revision of the opinion paragraph to include the phrase "with the foregoing explanation."

D. Is appropriate and would not negate the unmodified opinion.

Answer (D) is correct. *(CPA, adapted)*

REQUIRED: The effect of an emphasis-of-matter paragraph in an otherwise unmodified report.

DISCUSSION: An auditor may emphasize a matter in a separate paragraph and express an unmodified opinion. Matters to be emphasized might include that the entity has had significant related party transactions. Subsequent events and accounting matters affecting comparability (e.g., a change in the reporting entity) are other matters suitable for this treatment.

Answer (A) is incorrect. Emphasis of a matter is not inconsistent with an unmodified opinion. Answer (B) is incorrect. The auditor may emphasize a matter without violating GAAS or the PCAOB standards. Answer (C) is incorrect. The phrase "with the foregoing explanation" creates doubt as to whether the report was intended to be qualified.

16.5.5. An emphasis-of-matter paragraph is used in the auditor's report to draw users' attention to

A. A material misstatement.

B. A matter that is not presented or disclosed in the financial statements that is relevant to users' understanding of the audit.

C. A matter that management wishes to highlight.

D. A matter appropriately presented or disclosed in the financial statements.

Answer (D) is correct. *(Publisher, adapted)*

REQUIRED: The use of an emphasis-of-matter paragraph.

DISCUSSION: An emphasis-of-matter paragraph is used in the auditor's report to draw users' attention to a matter appropriately presented or disclosed in the financial statements that is fundamental to users' understanding of the financial statements.

Answer (A) is incorrect. A material misstatement requires a qualified or adverse opinion. Answer (B) is incorrect. An other-matter paragraph draws attention to a matter not required to be presented or disclosed in the financial statements that is relevant to users' understanding of the auditor's audit, responsibilities, or report. Answer (C) is incorrect. The auditor, not management, determines the content of the auditor's report.

16.5.6. An other-matter paragraph is included in the auditor's report of a nonissuer except when

A. The opinion on the prior-period statements has changed.

B. Required supplementary information is presented.

C. A predecessor auditor's report is not reissued.

D. The client has materially restated the prior year's comparative financial statements.

Answer (D) is correct. *(Publisher, adapted)*

REQUIRED: The purpose for which an other-matter paragraph is inappropriate.

DISCUSSION: An other-matter paragraph draws attention to a matter not required to be presented or disclosed in the financial statements that is relevant to users' understanding of the auditor's audit, responsibilities, or report. A correction of a material misstatement in previously issued financial statements requires the auditor to include an emphasis-of-matter paragraph. This matter is appropriately presented or disclosed in the financial statements and is fundamental to users' understanding.

Answer (A) is incorrect. An auditor's opinion on prior-period statements reported on in connection with the current audit may have changed. If so, the auditor should make certain disclosures in an emphasis-of-matter or other-matter paragraph. Answer (B) is incorrect. An auditor should include an other-matter paragraph in the auditor's report to refer to the presentation of required supplementary information. Answer (C) is incorrect. The auditor should include an other-matter paragraph in the auditor's report when prior-period statements presented comparatively with the current period's statements were audited by a predecessor auditor whose report is not reissued.

STUDY UNIT SEVENTEEN
RELATED REPORTING TOPICS

This study unit addresses miscellaneous reporting issues. Subunit 17.1 applies the relevant standards to a review of interim (e.g., quarterly) financial information. The procedures and the report are similar to those of a review of annual statements of nonissuers (see Study Unit 18). Subunits 17.2 and 17.3 relate to SEC engagements. The next four subunits (17.4 through 17.7) apply to information outside the basic financial statements. Subunit 17.8 addresses the auditor's responsibilities for financial statements prepared for use in other countries. Subunit 17.9 includes questions about the accountant's responsibility when requested to provide an evaluation of, or a conclusion on, how accounting principles will be applied to specific transactions of a particular entity. Subunits 17.10 and 17.11 relate respectively to audits of (1) statements prepared in accordance with a special purpose framework and (2) single statements, specific elements, or accounts.

QUESTIONS

17.1 Interim Financial Information

17.1.1. The objective of a review of interim financial information (IFI) of a nonissuer is to provide an auditor with a basis for reporting whether

A. Material modifications should be made to conform with the applicable financial reporting framework.

B. A reasonable basis exists for expressing an updated opinion regarding the financial statements that were previously audited.

C. Condensed financial statements or pro forma financial information should be included in a registration statement.

D. The financial statements are presented fairly in accordance with the applicable financial reporting framework.

Answer (A) is correct. *(CPA, adapted)*

REQUIRED: The objective of a review of IFI.

DISCUSSION: The objective of a review of IFI is to provide the auditor with a basis for reporting on whether material modifications should be made for such information to conform with the applicable financial reporting framework, that is, to provide negative assurance.

Answer (B) is incorrect. A review does not provide a basis for expressing an opinion. Answer (C) is incorrect. The SEC, not an auditor, determines whether certain information should be included in a registration statement. Moreover, an opinion may be expressed on condensed information and pro forma statements. Answer (D) is incorrect. A review does not provide a basis for expressing an opinion.

17.1.2. Which procedure ordinarily is not performed during a review of interim financial information?

A. Vouching items in the accounts and tracing source documents.

B. Applying analytical procedures.

C. Directing inquiries to management about internal control.

D. Reading the minutes of meetings of shareholders, directors, and committees.

Answer (A) is correct. *(Publisher, adapted)*

REQUIRED: The procedure not performed in a review of interim financial information.

DISCUSSION: Timeliness is an important element of interim reporting. The development of documentation and information underlying the report is necessarily less extensive at interim dates than at year end. A review consists principally of analytical procedures and inquiries of persons responsible for financial and accounting matters. But the auditor should obtain an understanding of the entity and its environment, including its internal control. A review ordinarily does not involve (1) tests of accounting records, (2) tests of the effectiveness of controls, (3) obtaining corroboration of responses to inquiries, or (4) other procedures normally performed in an audit. Vouching and tracing are tests of details of accounting records. Thus, they are not customarily performed in a review.

Answer (B) is incorrect. Analytical procedures are required to be performed in a review of interim financial information. Answer (C) is incorrect. The auditor should inquire about significant deficiencies, including material weaknesses, in the design or operation of internal controls. Answer (D) is incorrect. The auditor should read the available minutes of meetings of shareholders, directors, and appropriate committees. Inquiries should also be made about matters addressed in meetings for which minutes are unavailable.

17.1.3. Which of the following statements is not included in an auditor's report on interim financial statements?

A. "Our responsibility is to conduct our review in accordance with generally accepted SEC standards."

B. "A review of interim financial information consists principally of applying analytical procedures and making inquiries of persons responsible for financial and accounting matters."

C. "Based on our review, we are not aware of any material modifications that should be made to the accompanying interim financial information (statements) for it (them) to be in conformity with accounting principles generally accepted in the United States of America."

D. "The Company's management is responsible for the preparation and fair presentation of the interim financial information."

Answer (A) is correct. *(Publisher, adapted)*

REQUIRED: The statement not in a report on interim financial information.

DISCUSSION: A review is conducted in accordance with auditing standards applicable to reviews of interim financial information.

Answer (B) is incorrect. A description of the procedures is a proper element of the report. Answer (C) is incorrect. A statement about whether the auditor is aware of any material modifications that should be made is a proper element of the report. Answer (D) is incorrect. A statement that the financial statements are the responsibility of management is a proper element of the report.

17.1.4. The auditor should establish a clear understanding with the entity about the services to be performed in a review of interim financial information. Accordingly, the auditor should document the understanding in writing. Thus, an engagement letter includes all of the following except

A. A statement that a review is not designed to identify significant deficiencies in internal control.

B. An explanation that such procedures are substantially less in scope than an audit made in accordance with auditing standards.

C. A statement that management is responsible for correcting material misstatements.

D. The form and content of the documentation that will be maintained by the accountant.

Answer (D) is correct. *(Publisher, adapted)*

REQUIRED: The topic not included in the understanding about a review of interim financial information.

DISCUSSION: The form and content of the documentation are the responsibility of the auditor and are inappropriate for discussion in an engagement letter. The form or content of the documentation that the auditor should prepare cannot be specified because circumstances differ from one engagement to another. The documentation includes significant findings, facilitates supervision and review, and identifies evidence supporting the conclusion that the IFI reconciled with the accounting records (AU-C 930).

Answer (A) is incorrect. A review is not designed to provide assurance on internal control. However, any significant deficiencies or material weaknesses found should be communicated to those charged with governance. Answer (B) is incorrect. The auditor should communicate that the scope of the review is less than that of an audit. Answer (C) is incorrect. Management is responsible for adjusting the IFI to correct material misstatements and for stating in the representation letter that uncorrected misstatements are not material.

17.1.5. The extent to which the procedures for a review of interim financial information are to be applied depends on each of the following considerations except

A. The auditor's time budget allotted for the tests.

B. Conditions indicating the possible inability of the entity to continue as a going concern.

C. Litigation, claims, and assessments.

D. Questions raised in performing other procedures.

Answer (A) is correct. *(Publisher, adapted)*

REQUIRED: The matter not considered in determining the extent of procedures applied.

DISCUSSION: The procedures in a review of IFI include (1) analytical procedures; (2) reading the minutes of meetings; (3) reading the IFI to consider whether it is in accordance with the applicable reporting framework; (4) obtaining reports of other auditors who have reviewed interim information of components of the entity; (5) inquiries of management; (6) reconciling the IFI with the accounting records; (7) obtaining written representations from management; (8) reading other information accompanying the IFI; and (9) obtaining an understanding of the entity and its environment, including its internal control (AU-C 930). The matter of the difficulty, time, or cost involved in performing such procedures is not in itself a valid basis to omit a procedure for which no alternative exists (AU-C 200).

Answer (B) is incorrect. A review is not intended to identify conditions indicating the possible inability of the entity to continue as a going concern. However, if they existed at the date of the previous statements or if the auditor becomes aware of them, (s)he should (1) inquire of management about its plans to deal with the conditions and (2) consider the adequacy of disclosure. Answer (C) is incorrect. Information about litigation, claims, and assessments that raises questions about whether the IFI is in accordance with the framework may come to the auditor's attention. In these circumstances, the auditor should inquire of legal counsel. Answer (D) is incorrect. A matter that calls into question whether the IFI is in accordance with the framework may come to the auditor's attention. In this case, the auditor should make additional inquiries or perform other procedures.

17.1.6. A modification of the auditor's report on a review of interim financial information is necessitated by which of the following?

A. A substantial doubt about the entity's ability to continue as a going concern.

B. Lack of consistency.

C. Use of another auditor's report.

D. Inadequate disclosure.

Answer (D) is correct. *(CPA, adapted)*

REQUIRED: The reason for modifying a review report on interim financial information.

DISCUSSION: Modification of the report on a review of IFI is necessary if it is not, in all material respects, in accordance with the applicable reporting framework. If the departure is due to inadequate disclosure, the auditor should, if feasible, include the information in the report. But many circumstances that preclude the issuance of an unmodified report on audited statements do not cause a modification of a review report (AU-C 930).

Answer (A) is incorrect. AU-C 930 specifically states that a substantial doubt about the entity's ability to continue as a going concern is not a cause for modification if appropriately disclosed. Answer (B) is incorrect. AU-C 930 specifically states that lack of consistency is not a cause for modification if appropriately disclosed. Answer (C) is incorrect. The use of the report of another auditor may result in, but does not require, modification of the report. After considering the guidance in AU-C 600 relating to component auditors, the auditor may be able to assume responsibility for the component auditor's work.

17.1.7. An entity includes selected interim financial information in the notes to its annual financial statements. The auditor has made a review of the information and is satisfied with its presentation. The note containing the information is marked as unaudited. Under these circumstances, the auditor's report on the annual financial statements

A. Should be modified to refer to the review and the selected interim financial information.

B. Need not be modified to refer to the review but should be modified to refer to the selected financial information.

C. Should be modified to refer to the review but not the selected interim financial information.

D. Need not be modified to refer to the review or the selected interim financial information.

Answer (D) is correct. *(CPA, adapted)*

REQUIRED: The effect on the audit report of including IFI in a note.

DISCUSSION: An auditor normally is not required to modify the report on the audited financial statements to indicate that (s)he had previously performed a review if the IFI is marked as unaudited (AU-C 930). If the note is not appropriately marked, the audit report should include a disclaimer on the IFI. The IFI is not necessary for the fair presentation of the statements in accordance with the applicable financial reporting framework.

17.1.8. The SEC requires a registrant to obtain a review by its independent auditors of interim financial statements to be filed on SEC Form 10-Q. In performing this review, the auditor should determine whether matters that should be communicated to those charged with governance, as they relate to the interim statements, have been identified. Accordingly, the auditor

A. Rather than management must communicate the process used by management to make sensitive accounting estimates directly to those charged with governance.

B. Must communicate such matters prior to the entity's filing or refuse to be associated with the interim financial statements.

C. Should discuss with those charged with governance the quality of the entity's accounting principles; the consistency of their application; the clarity and completeness of the statements; and matters affecting the representational faithfulness, verifiability, and neutrality of the information.

D. Ordinarily should limit the discussion of the quality of the entity's accounting principles to the effect of significant events, transactions, and changes in estimates considered in performing the review.

Answer (D) is correct. *(Publisher, adapted)*

REQUIRED: The communication with the audit committee in connection with a review of interim financial statements of an SEC client.

DISCUSSION: Auditors of SEC clients should attempt to discuss with those charged with governance the matters listed in the standards (i.e., AU-C 260, *The Auditor's Communication with those Charged with Governance*, or AS 1301, *Communications with Audit Committees*) prior to the filing of Form 10-Q. However, the discussion of judgments about the quality of the accounting principles applied in the entity's interim reporting ordinarily is limited to the effects of (1) significant events, (2) transactions, and (3) changes in estimates considered while performing the review procedures described in AU-C 930 or AS 4105. Such procedures do not provide as much assurance as an audit.

Answer (A) is incorrect. The auditor should communicate the matters described in the standards to those charged with governance or be satisfied through discussions with those charged with governance that management has done so. However, material fraud, fraud involving senior management, and significant control deficiencies must be communicated directly to those charged with governance. Answer (B) is incorrect. The auditor should attempt to communicate the identified matters to those charged with governance, or at least its chair, and management prior to the filing. If the communication cannot be made at that time, the auditor should make it as soon as practicable. Answer (C) is incorrect. Responsibilities for the communication of judgments about the quality of accounting principles are imposed on practitioners in SEC engagements who have performed audits, not reviews.

17.2 Letters for Underwriters and Certain Other Requesting Parties

17.2.1. Auditors are often called upon to confer with clients, underwriters, and their respective counsel concerning the accounting and auditing requirements of the Securities Act of 1933 and of the SEC. A service often requested is the issuance of letters for underwriters and certain other requesting parties, commonly called comfort letters. Which of the following statements is true?

A. Comfort letters by the accountant are required under the Securities Act of 1933.

B. Comfort letters should not state that the accountant carried out procedures that (s)he considered necessary in the circumstances.

C. Copies of comfort letters should be filed with the SEC.

D. All of the answers are correct.

Answer (B) is correct. *(Publisher, adapted)*

REQUIRED: The true statement about comfort letters.

DISCUSSION: Much of the uncertainty and consequent risk of misunderstanding with regard to the nature and scope of comfort letters has arisen from the necessary limitations on the comments that accountants are permitted to make with respect to financial information in a registration statement that has not been audited. What constitutes a reasonable investigation of unaudited financial information sufficient for the purposes of an underwriter or other requesting party has never been authoritatively established. Consequently, the underwriter or other party should establish those procedures necessary for his or her purposes. However, the auditors cannot provide any assurance about the sufficiency of those procedures, and they should avoid any implication that they are carrying out such procedures as they consider necessary (AU-C 920).

Answer (A) is incorrect. Comfort letters are not required by the SEC. They are requested by underwriters and certain others. Answer (C) is incorrect. Comfort letters need not be filed with the SEC. Answer (D) is incorrect. Two statements are false.

17.2.2. Comfort letters most likely are

	Addressed to the	Signed by the
A.	Audit committee	Independent auditor
B.	Underwriters of securities	Senior management
C.	Audit committee	Senior management
D.	Underwriters of securities	Independent auditor

Answer (D) is correct. *(CPA, adapted)*

REQUIRED: The addressee and signor of a comfort letter.

DISCUSSION: The letter should be addressed only to the requesting party (or that party and the entity) and should not be given to anyone else. A requesting party is a specified party that has negotiated an agreement with the entity. Requesting parties may include (1) underwriters (purchasers of securities for public distribution) and (2) others who are conducting a review process consistent with the due diligence process performed when a securities offering is registered. Thus, a comfort letter signed by an independent auditor assists the requesting party in developing a record of a reasonable investigation.

17.2.3. A comfort letter ordinarily is addressed to the

A. Requesting party and dated on, or shortly after, the date the underwriting agreement is signed.

B. SEC and dated as of the filing date of the securities.

C. Intermediary with whom the auditor will deal in discussions about the letter and dated as of the end of field work.

D. SEC and dated as of the effective date of the securities.

Answer (A) is correct. *(Publisher, adapted)*

REQUIRED: The addressee of a comfort letter.

DISCUSSION: The letter should be addressed only to the requesting party (or that party and the entity). It should not be given to anyone else. The letter ordinarily is dated on, or shortly after, the date the underwriting agreement is signed. The letter also states that the procedures described in the letter did not cover the period from the cut-off date to the date of the letter.

Answer (B) is incorrect. The comfort letter should be addressed only to the requesting party and the entity, not to the SEC. Answer (C) is incorrect. The letter ordinarily is dated on, or shortly after, the date the underwriting agreement is signed. Answer (D) is incorrect. The comfort letter should be addressed only to the requesting party and the entity, not to the SEC, and ordinarily is dated on, or shortly after, the date the underwriting agreement is signed.

17.2.4. Underwriters or other requesting parties occasionally request the auditor to repeat in a comfort letter the report on the audited financial statements included in the securities offering. They also may request negative assurance regarding the auditor's report. When these requests are made, the auditor should

A. Honor both requests.

B. Not honor either request.

C. Honor the request to repeat the report but not provide negative assurance.

D. Provide negative assurance but not repeat the report.

Answer (B) is correct. *(Publisher, adapted)*

REQUIRED: The appropriate response to a request to repeat the audit report or to provide negative assurance about the report.

DISCUSSION: Because of the significance of the date of the auditor's report, the auditor must not repeat the report. Also, the auditor must not provide negative assurance regarding the report. Auditors have a statutory responsibility for their opinion as of the effective date of the securities offering. Moreover, the significance of negative assurance is unclear, and such assurance might result in misunderstanding.

Answer (A) is incorrect. Neither request should be honored. Answer (C) is incorrect. The auditor must not repeat the report on the audited statements in the comfort letter. Answer (D) is incorrect. The auditor must not provide negative assurance on the audited statements in the comfort letter.

17.2.5. When an auditor issues to an underwriter a comfort letter containing comments on data that have not been audited, the underwriter most likely will receive

A. Positive assurance on supplementary disclosures.

B. Negative assurance on capsule information.

C. A disclaimer on prospective financial statements.

D. A limited opinion on pro forma financial statements.

Answer (B) is correct. *(CPA, adapted)*

REQUIRED: The most likely assurance, if any, provided in a comfort letter commenting on unaudited data.

DISCUSSION: Capsule information is (1) unaudited summarized interim information for periods subsequent to the periods covered by the audited financial statements or (2) unaudited interim financial information in the securities offering. The auditor may provide negative assurance on whether the capsule information is in accordance with the applicable financial reporting framework. The auditor must review the underlying statements in accordance with GAAS, and the capsule information must meet the framework's disclosure requirements.

Answer (A) is incorrect. A comfort letter does not express positive assurance. Answer (C) is incorrect. Prospective statements do not appear in a registration statement. Answer (D) is incorrect. A limited opinion is not a permissible form of reporting.

17.2.6. In a comfort letter, an auditor may provide negative assurance about

A. The absence of any significant deficiencies in internal control.

B. Whether the entity's unaudited interim financial information complies as to form with the accounting requirements of the Securities Act of 1933.

C. The results of procedures performed in compiling the entity's financial forecast.

D. The compliance of the entity's registration statement with the requirements of the Securities Act of 1933.

Answer (B) is correct. *(CPA, adapted)*

REQUIRED: The negative assurance provided by a comfort letter.

DISCUSSION: A typical comfort letter includes negative assurance on whether the unaudited interim financial information included in the registration statement complies as to form, in all material respects, with the applicable accounting requirements of the Securities Act of 1933 and rules and regulations of the SEC.

Answer (A) is incorrect. The auditor should have knowledge of the client's internal controls but does not comment on them in the comfort letter. Answer (C) is incorrect. Practitioners do not provide limited assurance on forecasts. Answer (D) is incorrect. Auditors can comment only on matters to which their expertise is relevant. Compliance with aspects of the law is beyond that expertise.

17.2.7. A typical comfort letter

A. Need not include a statement about the auditor's independence.

B. Contains an opinion on whether audited financial statements comply as to form with applicable accounting requirements of the Securities Act of 1933.

C. Contains an opinion about subsequent changes in capital stock or long-term debt.

D. Contains an opinion as to whether unaudited interim financial information is in conformity with the applicable financial reporting framework.

Answer (B) is correct. *(Publisher, adapted)*

REQUIRED: The item in a typical comfort letter.

DISCUSSION: A typical comfort letter expresses, if applicable, an opinion on whether the audited financial statements included in the securities offering comply as to form, in all material respects, with the applicable accounting requirements of the Securities Act of 1933 and the related rules and regulations adopted by the SEC. However, the comfort letter does not repeat an opinion about the fairness of presentation of the statements.

Answer (A) is incorrect. The letter should include a statement about the auditor's independence. Answer (C) is incorrect. A comfort letter includes only negative assurance about subsequent changes. Answer (D) is incorrect. In a comfort letter, the auditor provides only negative assurance on unaudited interim financial information.

17.2.8. A comfort letter to underwriters or other requesting parties provided by a CPA may use which of the following terms to describe the work performed?

	Audited	Read	Made General Review
A.	Yes	Yes	Yes
B.	No	No	No
C.	Yes	No	Yes
D.	Yes	Yes	No

Answer (D) is correct. *(Publisher, adapted)*

REQUIRED: The terms an auditor may use in a letter for underwriters or other requesting parties.

DISCUSSION: The auditor performs a reasonable investigation to provide negative assurance in a comfort letter. Terms of uncertain meaning (such as "general review," "limited review," "reconcile," "check," or "test") should not be used in describing the work unless the procedures encompassed by these terms are described in the comfort letter (AU-C 920).

17.2.9. Whenever negative assurance is provided by a CPA, it is based upon

A. An absence of nullifying evidence.

B. A presence of substantiating evidence.

C. An objective audit in accordance with generally accepted auditing standards.

D. A judgmental determination in accordance with guidelines promulgated by the SEC.

Answer (A) is correct. *(CPA, adapted)*

REQUIRED: The basis upon which a CPA provides negative assurance.

DISCUSSION: Negative assurance consists of a statement by the auditor that, as a result of the procedures performed, nothing came to the auditor's attention that caused the auditor to believe that specified matters do not meet specified criteria (AU-C 920). Procedures performed for reviews provide a basis for this limited assurance.

Answer (B) is incorrect. Substantiating evidence is the basis for positive assurance. Answer (C) is incorrect. Negative assurance is provided by the application of procedures substantially more limited than those in an audit in accordance with GAAS. Answer (D) is incorrect. The SEC does not provide guidance on negative assurance.

17.2.10. An item typically included in a comfort letter is

A. The independence of the CPA.

B. Permission to distribute the letter to interested parties.

C. Positive assurance about whether the financial statements are fairly presented in conformity with GAAP.

D. Negative assurance about information included in management's discussion and analysis (MD&A).

Answer (A) is correct. *(Publisher, adapted)*

REQUIRED: The item to which a CPA typically refers in a comfort letter.

DISCUSSION: The independence of the CPA is a matter customarily addressed in comfort letters. The following example of a statement about independence is given in AU-C 920: "We are independent certified public accountants with respect to the company within the meaning of the 1933 Act and the applicable rules and regulations thereunder adopted by the SEC." The reference is to the Securities Act of 1933.

Answer (B) is incorrect. The letter should include a statement that the "letter is solely for the information of the addressees and to assist the underwriters." Answer (C) is incorrect. The auditor should not repeat the audit opinion in the comfort letter. Answer (D) is incorrect. Although the auditor may refer to an examination or review of MD&A information, no assurance should be included in the comfort letter. Furthermore, the auditor should not refer to any restricted use report, such as a report on agreed-upon procedures.

17.2.11. Which of the following is a true statement about the auditor's responsibility for letters to underwriters and certain other requesting parties?

A. An auditor who states in the letter that (s)he is independent may have an interest of the type requiring disclosure in the prospectus or registration statement.

B. An auditor may comment in the letter on compliance as to form in regard to any information contained in a registration statement.

C. An auditor may issue a draft comfort letter regarding a single shelf registration statement filed to cover delayed offerings of securities over an extended period.

D. Certain reports previously issued by an accountant may be repeated in the letter if they are not included in the registration statement.

Answer (C) is correct. *(Publisher, adapted)*

REQUIRED: The auditor's responsibility for letters to underwriters and certain other parties.

DISCUSSION: A shelf registration statement permits a company to register a designated amount of securities for continuous or delayed offerings during an extended period. At the date of the registration, an underwriter may not have been chosen, but the client or legal counsel for the underwriting group may request a comfort letter. Because only the underwriter can determine the procedures necessary for its purposes, the auditors should not issue a letter addressed to the client, legal counsel, or a nonspecific addressee. But the auditor may issue a draft describing procedures performed and comments based on them with a statement that the final letter will depend on procedures requested by the underwriter.

Answer (A) is incorrect. Regulation S-X lists the interests that must be disclosed. An auditor with one or more of these interests cannot be independent. Answer (B) is incorrect. An auditor should comment on compliance with SEC rules and regulations as to form only with respect to those requirements that apply to the form and content of financial statements and schedules. Answer (D) is incorrect. Certain reports previously issued by an auditor may be attached to, but not repeated in, a letter for underwriters if they are not included in the statement.

17.3 Filings with the SEC under the Securities Act of 1933

17.3.1. A registration statement filed with the Securities and Exchange Commission may contain the reports of two or more independent auditors on their audits of the financial statements for different periods. What responsibility does the auditor who has not audited the most recent financial statements have relative to events occurring after the date of his or her report that may affect the financial statements on which (s)he reported?

A. The auditor has responsibility for events up to the subsequent fiscal year end.

B. The auditor has responsibility for events up to the date of the subsequent audit report.

C. The auditor has responsibility for events up to the effective date of the registration statement.

D. The auditor has no responsibility beyond the date of the original report.

Answer (C) is correct. *(CPA, adapted)*

REQUIRED: The responsibility of the predecessor auditor when comparative statements are provided to the SEC.

DISCUSSION: An auditor who has audited the financial statements for a prior period but not for the most recent audited period has a responsibility for events occurring after the date of the prior-period financial statements through a date at or shortly before the effective date of the registration statement. The predecessor auditor should (1) read the statements for the subsequent period and compare them with the statements the predecessor reported on, (2) obtain management representations, and (3) obtain a letter of representations from the auditor regarding whether the audit revealed any matters that might have a material effect on the financial statements reported on by the predecessor.

Answer (A) is incorrect. Although the auditor ordinarily has no responsibility beyond the date of the original report, the filing of a registration statement extends the responsibility to the effective date of the registration statement. Answer (B) is incorrect. The filing of a registration statement extends the responsibility to the effective date of the registration statement. Answer (D) is incorrect. The filing of a registration statement extends the responsibility to the effective date of the registration statement.

17.3.2. When an auditor's report is incorporated by reference in an SEC registration statement, a prospectus that includes a statement about the auditor's involvement should refer to the auditor as

A. Auditor of the prospectus.

B. Management's representative before the SEC.

C. Certified preparer of the report.

D. Expert in auditing and accounting.

Answer (D) is correct. *(CPA, adapted)*

REQUIRED: The appropriate reference in a registration statement to an auditor's involvement.

DISCUSSION: In filings under the Securities Act of 1933, the prospectus often states that certain information is included in the registration statement in reliance on the report of a named expert. Accordingly, the prospectus may state that the report of the auditor is relied on because of his or her authority as an expert in auditing and accounting (AU-C 925).

17.3.3. The Securities and Exchange Commission has authority to

A. Prescribe specific auditing procedures to detect fraud concerning inventories and accounts receivable of companies engaged in interstate commerce.

B. Deny lack of privity as a defense in third-party actions for gross negligence against the auditors of issuers.

C. Determine accounting principles for the purpose of financial reporting by companies offering securities to the public.

D. Require a change of auditors of governmental entities after a given period of years as a means of ensuring independence.

Answer (C) is correct. *(CPA, adapted)*

REQUIRED: The authority of the SEC.

DISCUSSION: The SEC has the authority to regulate the form and content of all financial statements, notes, and schedules filed with the SEC and also the financial reports to shareholders if the company is subject to the Securities Exchange Act of 1934. The SEC has stated that financial statements conforming to FASB standards will be presumed to be in accordance with U.S. GAAP. However, the SEC reserves the right to substitute its principles for those of the accounting profession and to require any additional disclosures it deems necessary. The Sarbanes-Oxley Act of 2002 authorized the SEC to recognize as generally accepted any accounting principles established by a standards-setting body that meets the act's criteria.

Answer (A) is incorrect. The SEC may not prescribe specific auditing procedures. The Public Company Accounting Oversight Board (PCAOB), established by the Sarbanes-Oxley Act, adopts auditing standards related to preparation of audit reports for issuers. Answer (B) is incorrect. The SEC may not deny lack of privity as a defense. Answer (D) is incorrect. The SEC may not require a change of auditors of governmental entities.

17.3.4. An independent auditor's report is based on a review of interim financial information. If this report is presented in a registration statement, a prospectus should include a statement clarifying that the

A. Auditor's review report is not a part of the registration statement within the meaning of the Securities Act of 1933.

B. Auditor assumes no responsibility for subsequent events.

C. Auditor's review was performed in accordance with rules and regulations adopted by the Securities and Exchange Commission.

D. Auditor obtained corroborating evidence to determine whether material modifications are needed for such information to be in accordance with GAAP.

Answer (A) is correct. *(CPA, adapted)*

REQUIRED: The statement in a review report on IFI included in a registration statement.

DISCUSSION: The auditor has reviewed interim information, and his or her report is presented or incorporated by reference in a registration statement. In these circumstances, the SEC requires that a prospectus containing a statement about the auditor's involvement clarify that the report is not a report on, or a part of, the registration statement within the meaning of sections 7 and 11 of the Securities Act of 1933. The prospectus should state that reliance on the report should be restricted given the limited procedures applied and that the auditor is not subject to the liability provisions of section 11.

Answer (B) is incorrect. The registration statement contains audited financial statements. Thus, procedures should be extended from the date of the audit report to the effective date of the filing. Answer (C) is incorrect. The report might state that the independent public accountants have reported that they have applied limited procedures in accordance with professional standards for a review of such information. Answer (D) is incorrect. The auditor makes inquiries and applies analytical procedures to determine whether modifications are needed for financial information to be in accordance with the applicable framework. The auditor does not collect corroborating evidence in a review.

17.3.5. Form 8-K must be filed within

A. 90 days after the end of the fiscal year covered by the report.

B. 45 days after the end of each of the first 3 quarters of each fiscal year.

C. 90 days after the end of an employee stock purchase plan fiscal year.

D. 4 business days after significant events.

Answer (D) is correct. *(CMA, adapted)*

REQUIRED: The filing deadline for Form 8-K.

DISCUSSION: Current reports must be promptly filed on Form 8-K. It describes certain material events that must be disclosed within 4 business days. They include (1) changes in control of the registrant, (2) the acquisition or disposition of a significant amount of assets other than in the ordinary course of business, (3) bankruptcy or receivership, (4) resignation of a director, and (5) a change in the registrant's certifying accountant. Reporting of material other events involving changes in financial condition or operations is optional. Thus, no mandatory time for filing is established. Nevertheless, registrants are encouraged to file promptly and with due regard for the accuracy, completeness, and currency of the information.

17.3.6. SEC Form S-3 is an optional, short-form registration statement that relies on the incorporation by reference of periodic reports required by the Securities Exchange Act of 1934. Form S-3 offers substantial savings in filing costs over other forms because minimal disclosures are required in the prospectus. The SEC permits the use of Form S-3 by an issuer that

A. Does not have stock held by nonaffiliates.

B. Does not qualify for Form S-1.

C. Is a seasoned issuer or a well-known seasoned issuer.

D. Has not had to file Form 8-K during the most recent 2-year period.

Answer (C) is correct. *(CMA, adapted)*

REQUIRED: The issuer(s) that may use Form S-3.

DISCUSSION: Under the SEC's integrated disclosure system, four categories of issuers are recognized. A nonreporting issuer (one who need not file reports under the 1934 act) must use detailed Form S-1. An unseasoned issuer has reported for at least 3 consecutive years under the 1934 act. It must use Form S-1 but provides less detailed information and may include some information by reference to other 1934 act reports. A seasoned issuer has filed for at least 1 year and has a market capitalization of at least $75 million. It may use Form S-3 to report even less detail and may include even more information by reference. A well-known seasoned issuer has filed for at least 1 year and (1) has a worldwide market capitalization of at least $700 million or (2) has issued for cash in a registered offering at least $1 billion of debt or preferred stock in the past 3 years. Such an issuer also may use Form S-3.

Answer (A) is incorrect. Form S-3 may not be used unless nonaffiliates hold the company's stock. Answer (B) is incorrect. Form S-1 is used for original filings. Answer (D) is incorrect. Not having to file Form 8-K during the most recent 2-year period is not a requirement for use of Form S-3.

17.3.7. An audit of the financial statements included in Form 10-Q is not required. However, an external auditor's involvement with a Form 10-Q that is being prepared for filing with the SEC most likely consists of a(n)

A. Compilation report on the financial statements included in Form 10-Q.

B. Comfort letter that covers stub-period financial data.

C. Opinion on internal controls under which the Form 10-Q data were developed.

D. Review of the interim financial statements included in Form 10-Q.

Answer (D) is correct. *(CMA, adapted)*

REQUIRED: The external auditor's most likely involvement with Form 10-Q.

DISCUSSION: Form 10-Q is the quarterly report to the SEC. It must be filed by accelerated filers and large accelerated filers within 40 days of the last day of the first 3 quarters of the year (within 45 days by nonaccelerated filers). It need not contain audited financial statements, but it should be prepared in accordance with GAAP. Moreover, the SEC requires a registrant to obtain a review by its independent auditors of interim financial statements reported on Form 10-Q. The independent accountant who has audited the annual financial statements for the periods for which such data are presented should review the selected quarterly data. A review by an accountant permits an expression of limited assurance that no material modifications need to be made to the statements for them to be in conformity with the applicable financial reporting framework. A review helps satisfy the SEC requirement of adequate and accurate disclosure of material facts.

Answer (A) is incorrect. A compilation provides no assurance and would thus not satisfy the SEC requirement stated above. Answer (B) is incorrect. Comfort letters are addressed to underwriters, not the SEC. Answer (C) is incorrect. The SEC does not require an external auditor's opinion on internal control.

17.3.8. Form 10-K is filed with the SEC to update the information a company supplied when filing a registration statement under the Securities Exchange Act of 1934. A large accelerated filer must submit Form 10-K within

A. 60 days of the end of the company's fiscal year.

B. 45 days of the end of each quarter.

C. 2 weeks of the end of each month.

D. 15 days of significant events.

Answer (A) is correct. *(CMA, adapted)*

REQUIRED: The true statement about filing Form 10-K.

DISCUSSION: Form 10-K is the annual report to the SEC. A large accelerated filer must submit Form 10-K within 60 days after the corporation's year end. A large accelerated filer has $700 million or more of publicly held voting and nonvoting stock. Form 10-K must contain audited financial statements and be signed by the principal executive, financial, and accounting officers and by a majority of the board. The content is essentially that in the Basic Information Package.

17.4 Other Information in Documents Containing Audited Financial Statements

17.4.1. Which of the following best describes other information in documents containing audited financial statements?

A. Required supplementary information.

B. Summary financial statements.

C. Information presented in addition to the audited financial statements, such as a report by management on operations.

D. Notes to the financial statements.

Answer (C) is correct. *(Publisher, adapted)*

REQUIRED: The best description of other information.

DISCUSSION: Other information is financial or nonfinancial information (other than the financial statements and the auditor's report) that is included in a document containing audited statements and the auditor's report (excluding RSI). An example of such a document is an annual report to owners. Examples of other information are (1) a management report on operations, (2) selected quarterly data, and (3) financial summaries (AU-C 720).

Answer (A) is incorrect. Other information is not required by the designated accounting standards setter. By definition, other information excludes RSI. Answer (B) is incorrect. Summary financial statements are not other information. They consist of historical information derived from statements in accordance with GAAS audited by the same auditor. Answer (D) is incorrect. The notes are part of the basic statements.

17.4.2. The other information in a document containing audited financial statements and the auditor's report on them may be relevant to an independent auditor. With respect to other information, the

A. Auditor's responsibility is to read the other information to identify any material inconsistencies with the statements.

B. Auditor is obligated to perform auditing procedures to corroborate other information contained in a document.

C. Auditor need not be concerned with the other information.

D. Auditor must include the other information in the report if it needs revision.

Answer (A) is correct. *(Publisher, adapted)*

REQUIRED: The auditor's responsibility for other information.

DISCUSSION: The auditor's responsibility is to respond appropriately when the other information may undermine the credibility of the statements and the auditor's report. Thus, the auditor should read the other information to determine whether it is materially inconsistent with the audited statements. The auditor also must respond when (s)he becomes aware of a material misstatement of fact in the other information.

Answer (B) is incorrect. The auditor need not perform auditing procedures to corroborate other information. Answer (C) is incorrect. The auditor should read the other information and consider whether it is materially inconsistent with the audited financial statements. Answer (D) is incorrect. When the other information is materially inconsistent with the audited statements and needs revision, the auditor should request that management revise it. If revision is not made, (s)he should communicate the matter to those charged with governance and (1) modify the report to include an other-matter paragraph, (2) withhold use of the report, or (3) withdraw from the engagement.

17.4.3. When audited financial statements are presented in a document containing other information, the auditor

A. Has an obligation to perform auditing procedures to corroborate the other information.

B. Should express a qualified opinion if the other information is materially inconsistent with the statements.

C. Should be aware of whether the other information contains a material misstatement of fact.

D. Has no responsibility for the other information because it is not part of the basic financial statements.

Answer (C) is correct. *(CPA, adapted)*

REQUIRED: The auditor's responsibility for other information.

DISCUSSION: A misstatement of fact is other information that is unrelated to matters in the audited statements and is incorrectly stated or presented. If material, it may undermine the credibility of the document containing the audited statements. When management refuses to correct a material misstatement of fact, the auditor should notify those charged with governance.

Answer (A) is incorrect. The auditor should read, but need not corroborate, the other information. Answer (B) is incorrect. If the audited information is presented fairly, the opinion should be unmodified. However, if the other information needs revision, the auditor should request that management revise it. If revision is not made, (s)he should communicate the matter to those charged with governance and (1) modify the report to include an other-matter paragraph, (2) withhold use of the report, or (3) withdraw from the engagement. Answer (D) is incorrect. The auditor should read the other information to consider whether it is inconsistent with the audited financial statements.

17.4.4. An auditor concludes prior to the release date of the report that a material inconsistency exists in the other information in an annual report to shareholders. The report contains audited financial statements. If the auditor concludes that the financial statements do not require revision, but management refuses to revise or eliminate the material inconsistency, the auditor may

A. Revise the auditor's report to include a separate other-matter paragraph describing the material inconsistency.

B. Express a qualified opinion after discussing the matter with the client's directors.

C. Consider the matter closed because the other information is not in the audited statements.

D. Disclaim an opinion on the financial statements after explaining the material inconsistency in a separate other-matter paragraph.

Answer (A) is correct. *(CPA, adapted)*

REQUIRED: The auditor's response when management presents other information with a material inconsistency.

DISCUSSION: If the other information contains a material inconsistency that requires revision, and management refuses to make the revision, the auditor should communicate the matter to those charged with governance. The auditor also should (1) revise the report to include an other-matter paragraph, (2) withhold use of the report, or (3) withdraw from the engagement.

Answer (B) is incorrect. The opinion is expressed on the financial statements only. The inconsistency in the other information does not affect that opinion. Answer (C) is incorrect. The auditor may not ignore a material inconsistency in other information. Answer (D) is incorrect. The auditor's decision to disclaim an opinion is not affected by the other information.

17.5 Required Supplementary Information (RSI)

17.5.1. The auditor's inquiries of management regarding required supplementary information (RSI) should be directed to the judgments made concerning

A. Relevance and validity.

B. Measurement and presentation.

C. Accuracy and objectivity.

D. Rights and obligations.

Answer (B) is correct. *(CPA, adapted)*

REQUIRED: The direction of auditor inquiries about RSI.

DISCUSSION: RSI is information that the designated accounting standards setter has determined must accompany the basic financial statements. Thus, authoritative guidelines for its measurement and presentation have been prescribed. The auditor should inquire about whether the RSI is within the guidelines, (2) whether methods of measurement or presentation have changed and the reasons for any change, and (3) any significant assumptions or interpretations (AU-C 730).

Answer (A) is incorrect. The appropriateness of audit evidence (its relevance and reliability) is a professional judgment made by an auditor when performing an audit. The auditor does not audit the RSI. Answer (C) is incorrect. AU-C 730 specifically refers to measurement and presentation rather than accuracy and objectivity. Answer (D) is incorrect. An auditor's judgments about rights and obligations assertions are made in an audit of the basic financial statements.

17.5.2. If management declines to present required supplementary information, the auditor should express a(n)

A. Adverse opinion.

B. Qualified opinion with an additional paragraph.

C. Unmodified opinion without an additional paragraph.

D. Unmodified opinion with an other-matter paragraph.

Answer (D) is correct. *(CPA, adapted)*

REQUIRED: The effect on the auditor's report of management's failure to disclose RSI.

DISCUSSION: Omission of RSI does not affect the auditor's opinion because such information is not part of the basic financial statements. Instead, the auditor should express an unmodified opinion on the basic financial statements (assuming it is otherwise justified). In the other-matter paragraph, the auditor should (1) state that management omitted the RSI; (2) describe the missing RSI; (3) describe the applicable financial reporting framework that requires the RSI to be presented to supplement the basic statements; (4) identify the designated accounting standards setter; (5) state that the RSI is considered to be essential by the designated accounting standards setter, although it is not a part of the basic financial statements; and (6) state that the audit opinion is unaffected by the omission. The information itself need not be presented by the auditor (AU-C 730).

Answer (A) is incorrect. The auditor should modify the other-matter paragraph but not the opinion. Answer (B) is incorrect. The auditor should not modify the opinion. Answer (C) is incorrect. The report should include an other-matter paragraph.

17.5.3. What is an auditor's responsibility for required supplementary information (RSI)?

A. Include a disclaimer on the information only if the auditor is unable to apply limited procedures to it.

B. Add an emphasis-of-matter paragraph to the auditor's report before the opinion paragraph.

C. Apply limited procedures to the information and report its omission or the need for material modifications.

D. Audit the RSI in accordance with applicable auditing standards.

Answer (C) is correct. *(CPA, adapted)*

REQUIRED: The auditor's responsibility for RSI.

DISCUSSION: RSI differs from other information outside the basic statements because the designated accounting standard setter considers it to be an essential part of financial reporting for placing the basic financial statements in context. The auditor at minimum should apply limited procedures and report on the RSI in an other-matter paragraph that follows the opinion paragraph.

Answer (A) is incorrect. The other-matter paragraph referring to RSI (by definition, not part of the basic statements) contains a disclaimer even if limited procedures are completed. Answer (B) is incorrect. An other-matter paragraph is added after the opinion paragraph. Answer (D) is incorrect. RSI need not be audited.

17.6 Supplementary Information in Relation to the Financial Statements as a Whole

17.6.1. The auditor is engaged to report on whether supplementary information is fairly stated in relation to the audited financial statements as a whole. Which of the following best describes the auditor's responsibility for this information if it is outside the basic financial statements and not deemed necessary to their fair presentation?

A. The auditor has no reporting responsibility concerning information accompanying the basic financial statements.

B. The auditor should report on the supplementary information only if the auditor participated in its preparation.

C. The auditor must disclaim an opinion on the information if it is supplementary information required by the applicable financial reporting framework.

D. The auditor should not express an opinion on the supplementary information if (s)he disclaimed an opinion on the financial statements.

Answer (D) is correct. *(CPA, adapted)*

REQUIRED: The auditor's reporting responsibility.

DISCUSSION: Supplementary information is presented outside the basic statements and is not deemed necessary for their fair presentation in accordance with the applicable financial reporting framework. For example, it includes (1) additional details or explanations of items in or related to the statements, (2) consolidating information, (3) statistical data, and (4) historical summaries. The auditor should not express an opinion on the supplementary information if (s)he expressed an adverse opinion or disclaimed an opinion on the audited financial statements. Moreover, the auditor should have served as the group auditor of those statements.

Answer (A) is incorrect. The auditor was engaged to report on the supplementary information. Answer (B) is incorrect. Management is responsible for preparing the supplementary information. Answer (C) is incorrect. The auditor is not precluded from performing an engagement to express an opinion on RSI. But the opinion on the audited financial statements does not cover RSI, absent a specific requirement in the agreement with the client.

17.6.2. Investment and property schedules are presented for purposes of additional analysis in a document outside the basic financial statements. The schedules are not required supplementary information. When the auditor is engaged to report on whether the supplementary information is fairly stated in relation to the audited financial statements as a whole, the measurement of materiality is the

A. Same as that used in forming an opinion on the basic financial statements as a whole.

B. Lesser of the individual schedule of investments or schedule of property by itself.

C. Greater of the individual schedule of investments or schedule of property by itself.

D. Combined total of both the individual schedules of investments and property as a whole.

Answer (A) is correct. *(CPA, adapted)*

REQUIRED: The measure of materiality.

DISCUSSION: When reporting on whether supplementary information is fairly stated in relation to the statements as a whole, the measurement of materiality is the same as that used in forming an opinion on the basic financial statements taken as a whole. Accordingly, the auditor need not apply procedures as extensive as would be necessary to express an opinion on the information by itself.

17.7 Engagements to Report on Summary Financial Statements

17.7.1. An auditor is reporting on summary financial statements for an annual period. The auditor's unmodified opinion should indicate whether the information in the summary financial statements is consistent, in all material respects, with

A. Accounting principles generally accepted in the United States of America.

B. The audited financial statements.

C. A special purpose framework.

D. Supplementary filings under federal security statutes.

Answer (B) is correct. *(CPA, adapted)*

REQUIRED: The auditor's opinion on summary financial statements.

DISCUSSION: If an unmodified opinion is appropriate, the auditor states that the summary statements are consistent, in all material respects, with the audited statements from which they are derived, in accordance with the applied criteria.

Answer (A) is incorrect. The opinion paragraph of a report on the audited, not the summary, statements identifies the applicable financial reporting framework and its origin. Answer (C) is incorrect. The summary statements should provide a structured representation that is consistent with, but contains less detail than, the audited statements. Answer (D) is incorrect. Summary statements should be consistent, in all material respects, with the audited statements from which they are derived.

17.7.2. The report on summary financial statements should indicate that the

A. Summary financial statements are prepared in conformity with a special purpose framework.

B. Procedures performed included evaluating whether they are prepared in accordance with the applied criteria.

C. Summary financial statements are fairly presented in all material respects.

D. The auditor expresses limited assurance that the financial statements conform with GAAP.

Answer (B) is correct. *(CPA, adapted)*

REQUIRED: The indication in a report on summary financial statements.

DISCUSSION: The report on the summary statements describes, among other things, the procedures performed. They primarily include (1) comparing the summary statements with the related information in the audited statements and (2) evaluating whether the summary statements are prepared in accordance with the criteria applied by management.

Answer (A) is incorrect. Summary financial statements are prepared on the same basis as the audited financial statements. Answer (C) is incorrect. Summary financial statements are to be presented consistently with the audited financial statements. Answer (D) is incorrect. The auditor expresses an opinion.

17.7.3. The auditor should not accept an engagement to report on summary statements unless

A. The auditor has been engaged to audit the financial statements from which the summary statements are derived.

B. The auditor issued an unmodified report on the statements from which the summary statements are derived.

C. The auditor takes responsibility for the summary financial statements.

D. A complete audit can be completed on the summary statements.

Answer (A) is correct. *(Publisher, adapted)*

REQUIRED: The requirement to report on summary financial statements.

DISCUSSION: Summary financial statements consist of historical information derived from financial statements audited in accordance with GAAS by the same auditor. The auditor should not accept an engagement to report on summary statements unless (s)he has been engaged to audit the statements from which they are derived. The report expresses an opinion on whether the summary statements are consistent, in all material respects, with the audited statements, in accordance with the applied criteria.

Answer (B) is incorrect. The auditor may have expressed a qualified opinion on the audited statements or included an emphasis-of-matter or other-matter paragraph in the report. But the auditor should not report on the summary statements if an adverse opinion or disclaimer of opinion has been expressed on the audited statements. Answer (C) is incorrect. Management is responsible for the summary financial statements. Answer (D) is incorrect. An auditor applies procedures to determine whether the summary statements are consistent with the audited statements.

17.8 Financial Statements Prepared in Accordance with a Financial Reporting Framework Generally Accepted in Another Country

17.8.1. An auditor practicing in the U.S. has been engaged to report on the financial statements of a U.S. entity that have been prepared in accordance with a financial reporting framework generally accepted in another country. The auditor should

A. Understand the framework.

B. Be certified by the appropriate auditing or accountancy board of the other country.

C. Notify management that the auditor is required to disclaim an opinion on the financial statements.

D. Receive a waiver from the auditor's state board of accountancy to perform the engagement.

Answer (A) is correct. *(CPA, adapted)*

REQUIRED: The requirement for reporting on financial statements prepared in accordance with a financial reporting framework generally accepted in another country.

DISCUSSION: An auditor practicing in the U.S. may report on financial statements prepared in accordance with a financial reporting framework generally accepted in another country. Such a framework is not one adopted by a standards setter designated by the AICPA Council to establish GAAP (e.g., the FASB for U.S. GAAP and the IASB for IFRS). In these circumstances, because of the requirement to understand the entity's selection and application of accounting policies (AU-C 315), the auditor should obtain an understanding of the framework. The auditor's report should identify the country of origin of the accounting standards used to prepare the statements. It also should identify the auditing standards followed in performing the audit.

Answer (B) is incorrect. The auditor needs to be a CPA in the U.S. Answer (C) is incorrect. The auditor can express an opinion on the fairness of the financial statements. Answer (D) is incorrect. No waiver is required to perform this service.

17.9 Reports on Application of Requirements of an Applicable Financial Reporting Framework

17.9.1. AU-C 915, *Reports on Application of Requirements of an Applicable Financial Reporting Framework*, provides guidance to a reporting accountant who

A. Has been engaged to report on financial statements.

B. Is preparing a written report on the application of an applicable financial reporting framework to a specific transaction.

C. Intends to give oral advice in the form of a position paper not related to a specific transaction.

D. Is requested to provide expert testimony in litigation involving accounting matters.

Answer (B) is correct. *(Publisher, adapted)*

REQUIRED: The applicability of AU-C 915.

DISCUSSION: AU-C 915 guides the reporting accountant when (s)he prepares a written report or gives oral advice on (1) the application of the requirements of a financial reporting framework to a specific transaction (completed or proposed) involving facts and circumstances of a particular entity or (2) the type of report that may be issued on a specific entity's financial statements. The accountant should not issue a written report on a hypothetical transaction.

Answer (A) is incorrect. AU-C 915 does not apply to (1) a continuing accountant who has been engaged to report on the entity's statements, (2) engagements to assist in litigation or provide expert testimony, or (3) advice to other public accountants. Answer (C) is incorrect. AU-C 915 does not apply to position papers, e.g., articles or speeches, unless they are intended to provide guidance on the application of the requirements of a financial reporting framework to a specific transaction. Answer (D) is incorrect. AU-C 915 does not apply to engagements to assist in litigation or provide expert testimony.

17.9.2. Blue, CPA, has been asked to report on the application of a financial reporting framework to a specific transaction by an entity that is audited by another CPA. Blue may accept this engagement but should

A. Consult with the continuing accountant to obtain information relevant to the transaction.

B. Report the engagement's findings to the entity's audit committee, the continuing accountant, and management.

C. Disclaim any opinion on the application of the financial reporting framework to the hypothetical transaction.

D. Be independent of the client.

Answer (A) is correct. *(CPA, adapted)*

REQUIRED: The responsibility of an accountant who is reporting on the application of a financial reporting framework to a specific transaction if (s)he is not the continuing accountant.

DISCUSSION: The reporting accountant should consult with the continuing accountant to determine the available facts relevant to a professional judgment. The continuing accountant may provide information not otherwise available to the reporting accountant. (S)he should (1) explain to the entity's management the need to consult with the continuing accountant, (2) request permission to do so, and (3) request authorization for the continuing accountant to respond fully.

Answer (B) is incorrect. The accountant's written report should be addressed to the requesting entity. Answer (C) is incorrect. The report should describe (1) the appropriate application of the financial reporting framework to the specific transaction and (2), if appropriate, the reasons for the conclusion, not an opinion or a disclaimer. Also, the engagement may not involve reporting on the application of the financial reporting framework to a hypothetical transaction. Answer (D) is incorrect. The accountant need not be independent. But if (s)he is not, the report should state the lack of independence.

17.9.3. In connection with a proposal to obtain a new client, an accountant in public practice is asked to prepare a written report on the requirements of an applicable financial reporting framework to a specific transaction. The accountant's report should include a statement that

A. Any difference in the facts, circumstances, or assumptions presented may change the report.

B. The engagement was performed in accordance with Statements on Standards for Consulting Services.

C. The guidance provided is for general use.

D. Nothing came to the accountant's attention that caused the accountant to believe that the application of the financial reporting framework to the facts is inappropriate.

Answer (A) is correct. *(CPA, adapted)*

REQUIRED: The statement in a report on the application of a financial reporting framework to a specific transaction.

DISCUSSION: The accountant's report is addressed to the requesting party. The report should contain (1) a description of the engagement and a statement that it was performed in accordance with AU-C 915; (2) a description of the transaction and identification of the entity; (3) a description of the financial reporting framework applied (including its country of origin), the type of report that may be issued, and the reasons for the conclusion; (4) a statement that the responsibility for proper accounting is with the preparers of the financial statements; (5) statements of the facts, circumstances, and assumptions and their sources; (6) a statement that any difference in the facts, etc., may change the report; (7) an alert restricting the use of the report to specified parties; and (8), if the accountant is not independent, a statement of the lack of independence.

Answer (B) is incorrect. The accountant's report should state that the engagement is conducted in accordance with AU-C 915. Answer (C) is incorrect. The use of the report is restricted to specified parties. Answer (D) is incorrect. The report does not provide for limited assurance.

17.10 Audits of Financial Statements Prepared in Accordance with Special Purpose Frameworks

17.10.1. The following appeared in an auditor's report: "We draw attention to Note X of the financial statements, which describes the basis of accounting. The financial statements are prepared on the cash basis of accounting, which is a basis of accounting other than accounting principles generally accepted in the United States of America. Our opinion is not modified with respect to this matter." This paragraph is

A. Unacceptable in any audit report.

B. Acceptable in a report.

C. An indication that the partnership is in liquidation.

D. In a report that must be approved by the IRS.

Answer (B) is correct. *(Publisher, adapted)*

REQUIRED: The true statement about the quoted language.

DISCUSSION: When financial statements are prepared using a special purpose framework (the cash, tax, regulatory, contractual, or other basis), a paragraph should be included in the auditor's report referring to a note describing the framework. The auditor's opinion should indicate whether the statements are presented fairly in accordance with the framework described (AU-C 800).

Answer (A) is incorrect. The quoted wording for a report on statements prepared using the cash basis is from an illustration in AU-C 800. Answer (C) is incorrect. An entity in liquidation is likely to record assets at net realizable value. Answer (D) is incorrect. The IRS need not be consulted about auditors' reports.

17.10.2. An auditor expresses an opinion stating that financial statements of a nonissuer client intended for general use are in accordance with prescribed accounting regulations of a regulatory authority. The auditor

A. Is expressing a piecemeal opinion.

B. Should not modify the report except for substitution of "prescribed accounting regulations of . . . regulatory body" in place of GAAP.

C. Also should express an opinion as to whether the financial statements are presented fairly in accordance with GAAP.

D. Should add an other-matter paragraph to restrict the use of the report.

Answer (C) is correct. *(Publisher, adapted)*

REQUIRED: The reporting when statements intended for general use are prepared on the regulatory basis.

DISCUSSION: Even though the statements are prepared in accordance with a special purpose framework, they are for general use and should be evaluated for fairness relative to GAAP. Consequently, the auditor should modify the opinion if the statements are not presented fairly in accordance with GAAP. In a separate paragraph, the auditor also expresses an opinion about whether the statements are prepared in accordance with the special purpose framework. But if the use of the auditor's report is restricted solely to those within the entity and the regulatory agency, an other-matter paragraph should be included in the report. In that case, only one opinion is expressed. NOTE: GAAP are accounting principles issued by bodies designated by the AICPA Council under the *Code of Professional Conduct* (e.g., the FASB for U.S. GAAP and the IASB for IFRS).

Answer (A) is incorrect. Piecemeal opinions are prohibited. A piecemeal opinion is the expression of an unmodified opinion on a specific element of the financial statements when the auditor has expressed an adverse opinion or disclaimed an opinion on the statements as a whole. Answer (B) is incorrect. If financial statements are prepared in accordance with a regulatory basis of accounting and are intended for general use, the auditor should express two opinions. Answer (D) is incorrect. The statements are for general use, so the report cannot be restricted.

17.10.3. The client's general use financial statements do not reflect a provision for a deferred income tax liability because this accounting procedure is not required by the regulatory commission that prescribes uniform accounting procedures for the industry in which this company operates. A note accompanying the financial statements correctly discloses the amount of the deferred tax liability at the statement date as $2,200,000, an amount material to the financial statements as a whole. What is the effect of these circumstances on the auditor's opinion?

A. They will not affect the auditor's opinion because the client's accounting procedures conform to the uniform accounting procedures applicable to the industry of which the client is a part.

B. The auditor should modify the opinion as to whether the financial statements are presented fairly in accordance with GAAP.

C. They will not affect the auditor's opinion because the note disclosure provides the reader with the information necessary for a proper interpretation of the client's financial position and results of operations.

D. They will affect the auditor's opinion only if (s)he believes the content of the note is insufficient to meet the requirements of adequate disclosure.

Answer (B) is correct. *(Publisher, adapted)*

REQUIRED: The effect of a material misstatement resulting from the application of a regulatory basis of accounting.

DISCUSSION: Even though the statements are prepared in accordance with a special purpose framework, they are for general use and should be evaluated for fairness relative to GAAP. Consequently, the auditor should modify the opinion if the statements are not presented fairly in accordance with GAAP. In a separate paragraph, the auditor also expresses an opinion about whether the statements are prepared in accordance with the special purpose framework. But if the use of the auditor's report is restricted solely to those within the entity and the regulatory agency, an additional paragraph should be included in the report. In that case, only one opinion is expressed.

NOTE: GAAP are accounting principles issued by bodies designated by the AICPA Council under the *Code of Professional Conduct* (e.g., the FASB for U.S. GAAP and the IASB for IFRS).

Answer (A) is incorrect. Given that a general-use report is to be issued, the auditor may not express an opinion solely on fair presentation in accordance with the special purpose reporting framework. Answer (C) is incorrect. A material misstatement is not remedied by note disclosure. Answer (D) is incorrect. A material misstatement is not remedied by note disclosure.

17.10.4. Auditors' reports issued in connection with which of the following are not considered to be on financial statements based on a special purpose framework?

A. Financial statements prepared in accordance with the cash basis of accounting.

B. Financial statements prepared in accordance with a contractual agreement between the entity and a third party.

C. Financial statements prepared in accordance with the tax basis of accounting.

D. Compiled financial statements prepared in accordance with appraised liquidation values.

Answer (D) is correct. *(CPA, adapted)*

REQUIRED: The statements not prepared using a special purpose framework.

DISCUSSION: AU-C 800 identifies special purpose frameworks for financial statements as frameworks other than GAAP. They are (1) the cash basis, (2) the tax basis, (3) a regulatory basis, (4) a contractual basis, and (5) a definite set of logical and reasonable criteria applied to all natural items in the statements. Compiled statements are not audited, and appraised value is not a special purpose framework.

17.10.5. An auditor's report on financial statements prepared in accordance with the income tax basis of accounting should include all of the following except

A. Reference to the note to the financial statements that describes the basis of accounting.

B. A statement that the basis of accounting is other than GAAP.

C. An opinion as to whether the basis of accounting used is appropriate under the circumstances.

D. An opinion as to whether the financial statements are presented fairly, in all material respects, in accordance with the basis of accounting used for income tax purposes.

Answer (C) is correct. *(CPA, adapted)*

REQUIRED: The item not in a report on statements prepared in accordance with a special purpose framework.

DISCUSSION: The auditor's report should include paragraphs or sections that (1) describe the financial statements; (2) state management's responsibility for the financial statements; (3) describe the auditor's responsibilities; (4) express an opinion on fair presentation in accordance with the income tax basis; and (5) identify in an emphasis-of-matter paragraph the basis of accounting, state that the basis is other than GAAP, and refer to the note that describes that basis. The auditor's responsibilities include evaluating the appropriateness of the accounting policies used. They do not include expression of an opinion on whether the basis of accounting used is appropriate under the circumstances.

Answer (A) is incorrect. The report should refer to the note describing the basis of accounting. Answer (B) is incorrect. The report should state that the basis of accounting is other than GAAP. Answer (D) is incorrect. The report should express an opinion.

17.10.6. When an auditor reports on financial statements prepared on an entity's income tax basis, the auditor's report should

A. Disclaim an opinion on whether the statements were examined in accordance with generally accepted auditing standards.

B. Not express an opinion on whether the statements are presented in conformity with income tax basis.

C. Include an explanation of how the results of operations differ from the cash receipts and disbursements basis of accounting.

D. State that the special purpose framework is a basis of accounting other than GAAP.

Answer (D) is correct. *(CPA, adapted)*

REQUIRED: The content of a report on financial statements prepared on the income tax basis.

DISCUSSION: An emphasis-of-matter paragraph in an auditor's report on financial statements prepared in accordance with a special purpose framework, e.g., the income tax basis, should (1) state that the statements are prepared in accordance with the applicable framework, (2) refer to the note describing the framework, and (3) state that the special purpose framework is a basis other than GAAP. The special purpose framework may be (1) the tax basis, (2) the cash basis, (3) a regulatory basis, (4) a contractual basis, or (5) a definite set of logical and reasonable criteria applied to all material items in the statements.

Answer (A) is incorrect. The auditor applies GAAS in the engagement. Answer (B) is incorrect. The auditor expresses an opinion on whether the statements are presented in conformity with the income tax basis. Answer (C) is incorrect. A note in the financial statements should describe the special purpose framework, but the report need only refer to that note.

17.10.7. Delta Life Insurance Co. prepares its financial statements on an accounting basis insurance companies use pursuant to the rules of a state insurance commission. If Wall, CPA, Delta's auditor, discovers that the statements are not suitably titled, Wall should

A. Disclose any reservations in a basis for qualified opinion paragraph and qualify the opinion.

B. Apply to the state insurance commission for an advisory opinion.

C. Issue a special statutory-basis report that clearly disclaims any opinion.

D. Explain in the notes to the financial statements the terminology used.

Answer (A) is correct. *(CPA, adapted)*

REQUIRED: The proper action when statements prepared using a special purpose framework are not suitably titled.

DISCUSSION: Terms such as "balance sheet," "statement of income," or other unmodified titles are ordinarily understood to apply to statements presented in accordance with GAAP. Consequently, the auditor of statements prepared under a special purpose framework should consider whether the statements are suitably titled. If (s)he believes they are not, the auditor should disclose his or her reservations in a basis for qualified opinion paragraph (AU-C 800).

Answer (B) is incorrect. AU-C 800 does not require the auditor to apply to the state insurance commission for an advisory opinion. Answer (C) is incorrect. The opinion should be qualified. Answer (D) is incorrect. The notes are the responsibility of management, not the auditor.

17.10.8. Whenever a report filed on a printed form designed by authorities calls upon the independent auditor to make an assertion that the auditor believes is not justified, the auditor should

A. Reword the form.

B. Submit an unmodified report with explanations.

C. Submit the form with questionable items clearly omitted.

D. Withdraw from the engagement.

Answer (A) is correct. *(CPA, adapted)*

REQUIRED: The auditor's action when asked to make an unjustified assertion in a prescribed form.

DISCUSSION: The auditor may be required by law or regulation to use a specific layout, form, or wording of the auditor's report. For example, printed forms designed by the agencies or other authorities that they will be filed with often prescribe the wording of the auditor's report. Many are unacceptable to auditors because they conflict with GAAS. When a report form calls for an unjustified assertion, an auditor should reword the form. If rewording the form would not (1) be permitted or (2) mitigate the risk that users will misunderstand the report, the auditor should not accept the audit unless required by law or regulation. In this case, the auditor's report should not refer to performing an audit in accordance with GAAS (AU-C 210).

Answer (B) is incorrect. An unmodified report with explanations is not appropriate for a special purpose reporting situation. Answer (C) is incorrect. Omission of questionable items does not meet the auditor's reporting responsibility. These items should be resolved. Answer (D) is incorrect. Withdrawal from the engagement is an extreme measure unnecessary in most circumstances and may not be permitted.

17.10.9. An auditor is reporting on cash-basis financial statements. These statements are best referred to in the opinion by which of the following descriptions?

A. "Financial position" and "results of operations arising from cash transactions."

B. "Assets and liabilities arising from cash transactions" and "revenue collected and expenses paid."

C. "Balance sheet" and "income statement resulting from cash transactions."

D. "Cash balance sheet" and "statement of cash flows."

Answer (B) is correct. *(CPA, adapted)*

REQUIRED: The best description of cash-basis financial statements in an auditor's report.

DISCUSSION: Terms such as "balance sheet," "statement of financial position," "statement of operations," "income statement," "statement of cash flows," and similar unmodified titles suggest that the statements were prepared in accordance with GAAP. Appropriate titles for comparable cash-basis statements include "statement of assets and liabilities arising from cash transactions" and "statement of revenue collected and expenses paid."

Answer (A) is incorrect. Terms such as "financial position" and "results of operations" imply that the statements were prepared in accordance with GAAP. Answer (C) is incorrect. Terms such as "balance sheet" and "income statement" imply that the statements were prepared in accordance with GAAP. Answer (D) is incorrect. Terms such as "balance sheet" and "statement of cash flows" imply that the statements were prepared in accordance with GAAP.

17.11 Audits of Single Financial Statements and Specific Elements, Accounts, or Items of a Financial Statement

17.11.1. For reporting purposes, the auditor should consider each of the following types of financial presentation to be a financial statement except the statement of

A. Retained earnings.

B. Operations by product lines.

C. Changes in the elements of working capital.

D. Revenue and expenses.

Answer (C) is correct. *(CPA, adapted)*

REQUIRED: The presentation not a financial statement.

DISCUSSION: AU-C 805 defines financial statements as a structured representation of historical financial information, including related notes, intended to communicate an entity's economic resources and obligations at a point in time or the changes therein for a period of time in accordance with a financial reporting framework. The related notes ordinarily comprise a summary of significant accounting policies and other explanatory information. AU-C 805 lists various types of financial statements but excludes the statement of changes in working capital.

Answer (A) is incorrect. Statements of retained earnings are financial statements. Answer (B) is incorrect. Statements of operations by product lines are financial statements. Answer (D) is incorrect. Statements of revenue and expenses are financial statements.

17.11.2. An auditor may express an opinion on an entity's accounts receivable balance even if the auditor has disclaimed an opinion on the financial statements as a whole, provided that the

A. Report on the accounts receivable discloses the reason for the disclaimer of opinion on the financial statements.

B. Distribution of the report on the accounts receivable is restricted to internal use only.

C. Auditor also reports on the current asset portion of the entity's balance sheet.

D. Report on the accounts receivable is presented separately from the disclaimer of opinion on the financial statements.

Answer (D) is correct. *(CPA, adapted)*

REQUIRED: The condition for expressing an opinion on an account balance despite disclaiming an opinion on the financial statements as a whole.

DISCUSSION: An auditor may be requested to express an opinion on one or more specified elements, accounts, or items of a financial statement. However, the auditor may not express such an opinion after disclaiming an opinion on the financial statements if such reporting is tantamount to a piecemeal opinion on the financial statements. Nevertheless, an auditor may be able to express an opinion in these circumstances if a major portion of the financial statements is not involved. For example, an auditor who has disclaimed an opinion on the financial statements may be able to express an opinion on the accounts receivable balance. Moreover, the report should be presented separately.

Answer (A) is incorrect. The report on accounts receivable should disclose the modification of the report on the financial statements if it is considered relevant, but any reasons for the modification need not be described. Answer (B) is incorrect. The report need not be restricted to internal use. Answer (C) is incorrect. A report may be presented on one or more specified elements, accounts, or items of a financial statement.

17.11.3. Which of the following statements is true with respect to an auditor's report expressing an opinion on a specific item on a financial statement?

A. Materiality must be related to the specified item rather than to the financial statements as a whole.

B. Such a report can only be issued if the auditor is also engaged to audit the entire set of financial statements.

C. The attention devoted to the specified item is usually less than it would be if the financial statements as a whole were being audited.

D. The auditor who has expressed an adverse opinion on the financial statements as a whole can never express an opinion on a specified item in these financial statements.

Answer (A) is correct. *(CPA, adapted)*

REQUIRED: The true statement about expressing an opinion on specified elements of financial statements.

DISCUSSION: In an engagement to express an opinion on one or more specific elements, accounts, or items of a financial statement, materiality must be measured in relation to each element, account, or item reported on rather than in relation to their aggregate or to the financial statements as a whole (AU-C 805).

Answer (B) is incorrect. Reporting on a specific element does not require a complete audit. Answer (C) is incorrect. The attention devoted to the specified item is usually greater (not less). Answer (D) is incorrect. Although piecemeal opinions are prohibited, the auditor is allowed to express an opinion on specific items after expressing an adverse opinion if the specified items do not constitute a major portion of the financial statements.

17.11.4. An auditor is reporting on a single financial statement. How should materiality be determined?

A. The same as for the complete set of financial statements.

B. Based on directives from management.

C. Based on the single financial statement being reported on.

D. Materiality need not be considered for audits of single financial statements.

Answer (C) is correct. *(Publisher, adapted)*

REQUIRED: The determination of materiality if the auditor is reporting on a single financial statement.

DISCUSSION: The auditor should determine materiality for the single financial statement being reported on, not for the complete set of financial statements. The auditor will express an opinion on the fairness of the single financial statement.

Answer (A) is incorrect. The single financial statement should be considered individually. Answer (B) is incorrect. The auditor determines the appropriate materiality levels in an audit. Answer (D) is incorrect. An auditor should consider materiality in every audit.

17.11.5. A client has requested an auditor to audit and report on the single element of net income. The auditor should obtain audit evidence relating to the fairness of

A. Only the net income element.

B. The net income element and its related notes but not financial position.

C. The net income element, the associated notes, and internal control over net income.

D. Financial position and results of operations.

Answer (D) is correct. *(Publisher, adapted)*

REQUIRED: The audit evidence obtained by an auditor reporting on the single element of net income.

DISCUSSION: If the specific element reported on is the entity's net income, the auditor should perform procedures necessary to obtain sufficient appropriate audit evidence to permit the expression of an opinion on the financial position and results of operations. The reason is that net income affects the balance sheet and the income statement.

Answer (A) is incorrect. The auditor also should perform procedures necessary to obtain sufficient appropriate audit evidence to express an opinion on financial position. Answer (B) is incorrect. A specific element includes the related notes. The notes do not constitute a separate element. Moreover, the auditor also must perform procedures sufficient to express an opinion on financial position. Answer (C) is incorrect. The auditor should perform procedures necessary to obtain sufficient appropriate audit evidence to enable the auditor to express an opinion only on financial position and results of operations.

STUDY UNIT EIGHTEEN
PREPARATION, COMPILATION, AND REVIEW ENGAGEMENTS

This study unit is based on Statements on Standards for Accounting and Review Services (SSARSs). They apply to engagements performed for nonissuers (nonpublic entities) and provide guidance for an accountant's services to **prepare**, **compile**, or **review** financial statements.

Regardless of the service provided, the accountant should document the **terms** of the engagement in a suitable form of written agreement. Common terms include (1) the objectives and limitations of the engagement; (2) the responsibilities of management and the accountant; (3) an identification of the reporting framework; and (4) a statement that the engagement cannot be relied on to disclose fraud, error, or noncompliance with laws or regulations.

The following table compares the preparation, compilation, and review services with an audit:

Issue	Preparation	Compilation	Review	Audit
Is assurance provided?	No	No	Limited	Positive
Is an engagement letter required?	Yes	Yes	Yes	Yes
Is independence required?	No[1]	No[2]	Yes	Yes
Is a report required?	No	Yes	Yes	Yes
May the financial statements be released to users other than management?	Yes	Yes	Yes	Yes
May the financial statements omit disclosures (notes)?	Yes	Yes	No	No

[1] No determination of independence is required.

[2] A determination of independence is required. The report is modified if the accountant is not independent.

QUESTIONS

18.1 General Principles for SSARSs Engagements (AR-C 60)

18.1.1. May an accountant accept an engagement to compile or review the financial statements of a not-for-profit entity if the accountant is unfamiliar with the specialized industry accounting principles but plans to obtain the required level of knowledge before compiling or reviewing the financial statements?

	Compilation	Review
A.	No	No
B.	Yes	No
C.	No	Yes
D.	Yes	Yes

Answer (D) is correct. *(CPA, adapted)*

REQUIRED: The ability of an accountant to accept an engagement without the required level of knowledge.

DISCUSSION: The accountant may accept a compilation or review engagement for an entity in an industry with which the accountant has no previous experience. However, (s)he has a responsibility to obtain the required level of knowledge prior to completing the engagement.

18.1.2. Statements on Standards for Accounting and Review Services (SSARSs) require an accountant to report when the accountant has

A. Photocopied client-prepared financial statements, without modification, as an accommodation to the client.

B. Provided a client with a financial statement format that does not include monetary amounts, to be used by the client in preparing financial statements.

C. Proposed correcting journal entries to be recorded by the client that change client-prepared financial statements.

D. Compiled, through the use of computer software, financial statements to be used by third parties.

Answer (D) is correct. *(CPA, adapted)*

REQUIRED: The situation in which an accountant must issue a report.

DISCUSSION: Unlike a preparation, compilations and reviews require an accountant's report.

Answer (A) is incorrect. Typing or reproducing client-prepared financial statements, without modification, as an accommodation to a client does not constitute a SSARSs service. Answer (B) is incorrect. Without monetary amounts, the presentation is not a financial statement. Answer (C) is incorrect. Journal entries are not a financial statement.

18.1.3. An accountant is required to comply with the provisions of Statements on Standards for Accounting and Review Services when

I. Reproducing client-prepared financial statements, without modification, as an accommodation to a client

II. Preparing standard monthly journal entries for depreciation and expiration of prepaid expenses

A. I only.

B. II only.

C. Both I and II.

D. Neither I nor II.

Answer (D) is correct. *(CPA, adapted)*

REQUIRED: The services that require compliance with SSARSs.

DISCUSSION: An accountant performs a preparation, compilation, or review in accordance with SSARSs. A preparation is a service to prepare a client's financial statements without attaching a report or considering the accountant's independence. A compilation is a service to assist management in presenting financial statements without providing any assurance. The accountant reports on the statements and determines whether (s)he is independent. But need not be independent. A review is a service to obtain limited assurance that no material modifications need to be made to the statements for them to be in accordance with the applicable reporting framework. Thus, reproducing client-prepared financial statements, without modification, as an accommodation to a client or preparing standard monthly journal entries is not a preparation, compilation, or review of financial statements.

Answer (A) is incorrect. Reproducing client-prepared financial statements, without modification, as an accommodation to a client is not a compilation or review of financial statements. Answer (B) is incorrect. Preparing standard monthly journal entries for depreciation and expiration of prepaid expenses is not a compilation or review of financial statements. Answer (C) is incorrect. Reproducing client-prepared financial statements, without modification, as an accommodation to a client or preparing standard monthly journal entries for depreciation and expiration of prepaid expenses is not a compilation or review of financial statements.

18.1.4. An accountant is required to comply with the provisions of the Statements on Standards for Accounting and Review Services when performing which of the following tasks?

A. Preparing monthly journal entries.

B. Providing the client with software to generate financial statements.

C. Generating financial statements of a nonissuer.

D. Providing a blank financial statement format or template.

Answer (C) is correct. *(CPA, adapted)*

REQUIRED: The task that requires compliance with SSARSs.

DISCUSSION: An accountant performs a preparation, compilation, or review engagement for a nonissuer in accordance with Statements on Standards for Accounting and Review Services (SSARS). A preparation is a service to prepare financial statements without attaching a report or determining whether the accountant is independent. A compilation is a service to assist management in presenting financial statements with a report attached. A review is a service to obtain limited assurance that no material modifications need to be made to the statements for them to be in accordance with the applicable reporting framework.

Answer (A) is incorrect. Preparing monthly journal entries is not a SSARSs engagement. Answer (B) is incorrect. Providing the client with software to generate financial statements is not a SSARSs engagement. Answer (D) is incorrect. Providing a blank financial statement format or template is not a SSARSs engagement.

18.1.5. Which of the following describes how the objective of a review of financial statements differs from the objective of a compilation engagement?

A. The primary objective of a review engagement is to test the completeness of the financial statements prepared, but a compilation tests for reasonableness.

B. The primary objective of a review engagement is to provide positive assurance that the financial statements are fairly presented, but a compilation provides no such assurance.

C. In a review engagement, accountants provide limited assurance, but a compilation expresses no assurance.

D. In a review engagement, accountants provide reasonable or positive assurance that the financial statements are fairly presented, but a compilation provides limited assurance.

Answer (C) is correct. *(CPA, adapted)*

REQUIRED: The difference between a review of financial statements and a compilation engagement.

DISCUSSION: The principal difference between a review and a compilation is the level of assurance provided. In a compilation of financial statements, the accountant expresses no assurance regarding the fairness of the information provided. In a review, the accountant performs inquiries and analytical procedures to provide him or her with a reasonable basis for expressing limited assurance that no material modifications are necessary for the financial statement to be in conformity with the applicable reporting framework (AR-C 90).

Answer (A) is incorrect. The inquiries and analytical procedures performed in a review engagement do not address the completeness assertion. Answer (B) is incorrect. A review engagement does not provide positive assurance. Answer (D) is incorrect. A compilation engagement provides no assurance, and a review does not provide positive assurance.

18.1.6. Which of the following circumstances would generally require an accountant to decline to perform a compilation of financial statements under Statements on Standards for Accounting and Review Services?

A. A substantial portion of generally accepted accounting principles disclosures was omitted.

B. There was a lack of independence between the accountant and client.

C. The accountant had no prior experience with similar organizations within the industry.

D. The accountant was not able to come to an understanding with representatives of the organization for services to be performed.

Answer (D) is correct. *(CPA, adapted)*

REQUIRED: The basis for declining a compilation of financial statements under SSARSs.

DISCUSSION: The accountant should establish an understanding with management about the services to be performed for compilation engagements and should document the understanding through a written communication with management (e.g., an engagement letter). The understanding reduces the risk that the accountant or management might misinterpret the other party's expectations.

Answer (A) is incorrect. If the omission of disclosures is not done to mislead users of the statements, the accountant may accept an engagement for a compilation of financial statements. Answer (B) is incorrect. An accountant need not be independent of the client to perform a compilation. However, the lack of independence should be indicated in the final paragraph of the report. The accountant also may disclose the basis for lack of independence. Answer (C) is incorrect. Lack of knowledge does not prevent the accountant from accepting a compilation engagement for an entity in an industry with which the accountant has no previous experience. It does, however, place upon the accountant a responsibility to obtain the required level of knowledge.

18.1.7. An accountant is engaged to perform compilation services for a new client in an industry with which the accountant has no previous experience. How should the accountant obtain sufficient knowledge of the industry to perform the compilation service?

A. By obtaining the most recent letter of credit from the entity's primary financial institution.

B. By consulting AICPA guides, industry publications, or individuals knowledgeable about the industry.

C. By researching the entity's Internet site and searching for current press releases.

D. By reviewing the predecessor accountant's workpapers without the knowledge of the entity.

Answer (B) is correct. *(CPA, adapted)*

REQUIRED: The means of obtaining sufficient knowledge of the industry to perform a compilation service.

DISCUSSION: Lack of previous experience in the entity's industry does not preclude acceptance of a compilation engagement. The accountant may obtain the necessary understanding of the applicable reporting framework by consulting, for example, (1) financial statements of other entities in the industry, (2) textbooks and periodicals, (3) appropriate CPE, (4) individuals knowledgeable about the industry, (5) AICPA guides, and (6) industry publications.

Answer (A) is incorrect. A letter of credit does not provide an understanding of the applicable reporting framework. Moreover, obtaining such financial documents is not a compilation procedure. Answer (C) is incorrect. The entity's Internet site and current press releases are unlikely to contain information about the entity's financial reporting framework. Answer (D) is incorrect. Before accepting an audit engagement, the auditor should make inquiries of the predecessor auditor. No corresponding requirement applies in a compilation engagement.

18.1.8. Before accepting an engagement to compile or review the financial statements of a nonissuer, which of the following specific inquiries should a successor accountant consider making to the predecessor accountant?

A. How cooperative was the owner's lawyer in providing a legal opinion?

B. How did you assess inherent risk and control risk?

C. How would you describe the integrity of the owner?

D. What evaluation did you make of any accounting estimates?

Answer (C) is correct. *(CPA, adapted)*

REQUIRED: The specific inquiries a successor accountant should consider making to the predecessor in a compilation or review engagement.

DISCUSSION: Statements on Standards for Accounting and Review Services (SSARSs) apply to engagements to perform preparation, compilation, or review services for nonissuers. An accountant should not accept an engagement in accordance with SSARSs if (s)he has (1) reason to believe that ethical requirements will not be satisfied or (2) cause to doubt management's integrity such that engagement performance is likely to be affected.

Answer (A) is incorrect. An accountant who performs a compilation or review is not required to seek a legal opinion. Answer (B) is incorrect. An accountant who performs a compilation or review is not required to assess inherent risk and control risk. Answer (D) is incorrect. An accountant who performs a compilation or review is not required to evaluate accounting estimates.

18.1.9. To obtain an understanding of the applicable financial reporting framework and the significant accounting policies adopted by management, the accountant who performs a compilation service does not

A. Consult Audit and Accounting Guides.

B. Read industry publications and consult textbooks and periodicals.

C. Obtain an understanding of internal control and assess fraud risks.

D. Make inquiries of individuals knowledgeable about the industry.

Answer (C) is correct. *(Publisher, adapted)*

REQUIRED: The procedure not normally performed.

DISCUSSION: An accountant performing a preparation, compilation, or review service does not (1) obtain an understanding of internal control, (2) assess fraud risks, (3) test accounting records, (4) examine source documents, or (5) perform other audit procedures.

Answer (A) is incorrect. AICPA Audit and Accounting Guides are appropriate sources of the understanding of the reporting framework and significant accounting policies. Answer (B) is incorrect. Industry publications, textbooks, and periodicals are appropriate sources of the understanding of the reporting framework and significant accounting policies. Answer (D) is incorrect. Inquiries of individuals knowledgeable about the industry are appropriate sources of the understanding of the reporting framework and significant accounting policies.

18.1.10. When engaged to compile the financial statements of a nonissuer, an accountant should possess a level of knowledge of the entity's accounting principles and practices. This most likely will include obtaining a general understanding of the

A. Significant accounting policies adopted by management.

B. Design of the entity's internal controls that have been implemented.

C. Risk factors relating to misstatements arising from illegal acts.

D. Internal control awareness of the entity's senior management.

Answer (A) is correct. *(CPA, adapted)*

REQUIRED: The knowledge required to perform a compilation.

DISCUSSION: To perform a compilation, the accountant should obtain an understanding of (1) the applicable financial reporting framework and (2) the significant accounting policies adopted by management.

Answer (B) is incorrect. The consideration of internal control is not necessary to perform compilation services. Answer (C) is incorrect. No assessment of risk or application of auditing procedures is required in a compilation. Answer (D) is incorrect. The consideration of internal control is not necessary to perform compilation services.

18.2 Preparation of Financial Statements (AR-C 70)

18.2.1. Which of the following is a true statement about preparing financial statements in accordance with SSARSs?

A. The accountant must be independent.

B. The accountant's name must appear on the financial statements.

C. The financial framework must be GAAP.

D. Management must accept responsibility for the financial statements.

Answer (D) is correct. *(Publisher, adapted)*

REQUIRED: The true statement about preparing financial statements under SSARSs.

DISCUSSION: Management is responsible for (1) selection of the reporting framework, (2) internal control over financial reporting, (3) prevention and detection of fraud, (4) ensuring compliance with laws and regulations, and (5) maintaining accurate and complete information. Thus, management must accept responsibility for the financial statements.

Answer (A) is incorrect. The accountant need not be independent of the entity, and no disclosure is made if independence is lacking. Answer (B) is incorrect. AR-C 70 does not require an accountant's name to be identified or associated with the financial statements. But it also does not prohibit the identification of the accountant if a disclaimer is included with the financial statements. Answer (C) is incorrect. The statements may be prepared using any acceptable financial reporting framework.

18.2.2. In accordance with SSARSs, which of the following is an accurate comparison of a preparation service with a compilation service?

A. Both services require a full set of notes to be presented with the financial statements.

B. Only a compilation service requires an engagement letter.

C. Both services allow the financial statements to be released to outside users.

D. Both services require a report to be presented by the accountant.

Answer (C) is correct. *(Publisher, adapted)*

REQUIRED: The accurate comparison of a preparation service with a compilation service.

DISCUSSION: SSARSs allows release of financial statements for a preparation, compilation, or review service.

Answer (A) is incorrect. Neither a preparation nor a compilation requires management to present appropriate note disclosures. Answer (B) is incorrect. All SSARSs engagements require the accountant to obtain an engagement letter or other suitable form of written agreement. Answer (D) is incorrect. The preparation service does not require the accountant to present a report.

18.2.3. An accountant may complete an engagement to prepare financial statements under SSARSs even if

A. The accountant lacks professional competence.

B. Management uses an unacceptable financial reporting framework.

C. Management does not accept responsibility for the financial statements.

D. The accountant is not independent.

Answer (D) is correct. *(Publisher, adapted)*

REQUIRED: The item not a condition for accepting a preparation engagement.

DISCUSSION: The accountant need not (1) be independent or (2) determine whether (s)he is independent to prepare financial statements under SSARSs.

Answer (A) is incorrect. The accountant must have or be able to obtain professional competence to complete the engagement. Answer (B) is incorrect. The accountant must determine whether management has selected an acceptable financial reporting framework. Answer (C) is incorrect. The accountant must obtain management's agreement that it acknowledges and understands its responsibilities for the financial statements.

18.2.4. A potential client has requested that an accountant prepare financial statements. The accountant has no understanding of the client's industry. The accountant should

A. Not accept the engagement because of the lack of understanding of the industry.

B. Accept the engagement only after (s)he has obtained an understanding in the industry.

C. Accept the engagement with the expectation of obtaining an understanding in the industry.

D. Accept the engagement and use an understanding of other industries to complete the engagement.

Answer (C) is correct. *(Publisher, adapted)*

REQUIRED: The decision whether to accept a preparation engagement when the accountant has no understanding of the industry.

DISCUSSION: The accountant is required to obtain an understanding of the financial reporting framework and the entity's significant accounting policies. An accountant is not prevented from accepting an engagement to prepare financial statements for an entity in an industry in which the accountant has no previous experience. The accountant may obtain such an understanding, for example, by consulting AICPA guides, industry publications, etc.

Answer (A) is incorrect. The accountant may obtain such an understanding, for example, by consulting AICPA guides, industry publications, etc. Answer (B) is incorrect. The accountant may accept the engagement before obtaining the understanding if it is expected that (s)he will do so. Answer (D) is incorrect. The accountant is required to obtain an understanding of the financial reporting framework and the entity's significant accounting policies.

18.2.5. Which of the following is a true statement about a report on a preparation of financial statements under SSARSs?

A. The report must state whether the accountant is independent.

B. The report must state whether any material fraud was detected.

C. The report must state any reservations the accountant experienced during the engagement.

D. No report is presented for a preparation engagement.

Answer (D) is correct. *(Publisher, adapted)*

REQUIRED: The true statement about reporting on a preparation service.

DISCUSSION: An engagement to compile, review, or audit financial statements requires a report by the accountant or auditor. A preparation engagement does not result in a report presented by the accountant.

Answer (A) is incorrect. A preparation engagement does not require even a determination of independence. Answer (B) is incorrect. A preparation engagement does not result in a report. Answer (C) is incorrect. A preparation engagement does not result in a report presented by the accountant.

18.2.6. An accountant may prepare financial statements that exclude substantially all disclosures unless

A. The notes are important to understanding the financial statements.

B. The purpose is to mislead users.

C. The notes describe significant related party transactions.

D. The accountant believes that the notes help the users interpret the financial statements.

Answer (B) is correct. *(Publisher, adapted)*

REQUIRED: The reason for not performing a preparation service when the financial statements omit all disclosures.

DISCUSSION: Disclosures may be excluded unless the purpose is to mislead users. But the accountant still must disclose the omission in the financial statements.

Answer (A) is incorrect. Disclosures almost always are important to understanding financial statements. However, they may be excluded unless the purpose is to mislead users. Answer (C) is incorrect. Disclosures almost always are important to understanding financial statements, including transactions with related parties. However, notes may be excluded unless the purpose is to mislead users. Answer (D) is incorrect. Disclosures may be excluded unless the purpose is to mislead users.

18.2.7. Which phrase is included in an engagement letter for a preparation of financial statements?

A. "We will not express an opinion or a conclusion . . ."

B. "We are required to verify the accuracy . . ."

C. "Our engagement can be relied upon to identify fraud or error . . ."

D. "Our report will accompany the prepared financial statements . . ."

Answer (A) is correct. *(Publisher, adapted)*

REQUIRED: The phrase in an engagement letter for a preparation service.

DISCUSSION: The engagement letter for a preparation service states that the accountants will not gather evidence for the purpose of expressing an opinion or conclusion. Accordingly, an opinion or conclusion will not be expressed, and the accountants will not provide any assurance on the statements.

Answer (B) is incorrect. The engagement letter states that the accountants are not required to, and will not, verify the accuracy or completeness of the information provided for the engagement. Answer (C) is incorrect. The engagement letter states that the engagement cannot be relied on to identify or disclose misstatements, including those caused by fraud or error. Answer (D) is incorrect. No report is presented in a preparation engagement.

18.3 Compilation of Financial Statements (AR-C 80)

18.3.1. When an accountant is not independent with respect to an entity, which of the following types of compilation reports may be issued?

A. The standard compilation report may be issued, regardless of independence.

B. A compilation report with negative assurance may be issued.

C. A compilation report with special wording that notes the accountant's lack of independence may be issued.

D. A compilation report may be issued if the engagement is upgraded to a review.

Answer (C) is correct. *(CPA, adapted)*

REQUIRED: The type of compilation report that may be issued when an accountant is not independent.

DISCUSSION: A report may be issued, but it should state that the accountant is not independent. The accountant is permitted, but not required, to include the reason for the lack of independence.

Answer (A) is incorrect. The report should state the accountant's lack of independence. Answer (B) is incorrect. A compilation provides no assurance. Answer (D) is incorrect. A review report must not be issued if the accountant lacks independence.

18.3.2. Which of the following representations may an accountant make implicitly when issuing a report on the compilation of a nonissuer's financial statements?

A. The accountant is independent with respect to the entity.

B. The financial statements have not been audited.

C. A compilation consists principally of inquiries and analytical procedures.

D. The accountant does not express any assurance on the financial statements.

Answer (A) is correct. *(CPA, adapted)*

REQUIRED: The implicit representation in a compilation report.

DISCUSSION: The compilation report does not refer to independence unless the accountant determines that (s)he is not independent. The accountant then is ethically obligated to state his or her lack of independence in a final paragraph of the report.

Answer (B) is incorrect. A compilation report explicitly states that the financial statements have not been audited. Answer (C) is incorrect. A review, not a compilation, primarily includes application of inquiry and analytical procedures. Thus, a compilation report does not make this representation explicitly or implicitly. Answer (D) is incorrect. A compilation report explicitly states that a compilation does not provide any assurance.

18.3.3. An accountant's compilation report should be dated as of the date of

A. Completion of field work.

B. Completion of the compilation.

C. Transmittal of the compilation report.

D. The latest subsequent event referred to in the notes to the financial statements.

Answer (B) is correct. *(CPA, adapted)*

REQUIRED: The date of an accountant's compilation report.

DISCUSSION: When an accountant has performed a compilation for a nonissuer, the date of the report should be the date of the completion of the compilation (AR-C 80).

Answer (A) is incorrect. Field work is performed in attestation engagements, such as a financial statement audit or a review, not a compilation. Answer (C) is incorrect. The transmittal of the compilation report, which refers to the time of its communication to the user, is not an appropriate date. Answer (D) is incorrect. The dates of subsequent events may be significant for an audit but not a compilation.

18.3.4. An accountant has compiled the financial statements of a nonissuer in accordance with Statements on Standards for Accounting and Review Services (SSARSs). Do the SSARSs require that the compilation report be printed on the accountant's letterhead and that the report be manually signed by the accountant?

	Printed on the Accountant's Letterhead	Manually Signed by the Accountant
A.	Yes	Yes
B.	Yes	No
C.	No	Yes
D.	No	No

Answer (D) is correct. *(CPA, adapted)*

REQUIRED: The requirements of a compilation report.

DISCUSSION: The compilation report need not be printed on the accountant's letterhead or manually signed by the accountant. However, the report must be signed by the accounting firm or the accountant as appropriate. Thus, the signature may be manual, printed, or digital.

18.3.5. Which of the following should not be included in an accountant's report based upon the compilation of an entity's financial statements?

A. A statement that management is responsible for the financial statements.

B. A statement that the compilation was performed in accordance with Statements on Standards for Accounting and Review Services issued by the AICPA.

C. A statement that the accountant has not audited or reviewed the statements.

D. A statement that the accountant does not express an opinion but provides only limited assurance on the statements.

Answer (D) is correct. *(CPA, adapted)*

REQUIRED: The statement not made in the compilation report.

DISCUSSION: A compilation report does not express an opinion or any other form of assurance (AR-C 80). A review report may provide limited (negative) assurance.

Answer (A) is incorrect. The report should include a statement that management is responsible for the financial statements. Answer (B) is incorrect. The report should include a statement that the compilation was performed in accordance with the SSARSs. Answer (C) is incorrect. The report should include a statement that the accountant has not audited or reviewed the statements.

18.3.6. Each page of the financial statements compiled and reported on by an accountant may include a reference such as

A. See Accompanying Accountant's Notes.

B. Unaudited, See Accountant's Disclaimer.

C. See Accountant's Compilation Report.

D. Subject to Compilation Restrictions.

Answer (C) is correct. *(CPA, adapted)*

REQUIRED: The reference that may be on each page of a compilation report.

DISCUSSION: The accountant's report may become unattached from the statements. Thus, (s)he may request that management refer to the report on each page of the statements. An appropriate reference is "See Accountant's Compilation Report" (AR-C 80).

18.3.7. In performing a compilation of financial statements of a nonissuer, the accountant decides that modification of the standard report is not adequate to indicate deficiencies in the financial statements as a whole, and the client is not willing to correct the deficiencies. The accountant should therefore

A. Perform a review of the financial statements.

B. Issue a special purpose report.

C. Withdraw from the engagement.

D. Express an adverse audit opinion.

Answer (C) is correct. *(CPA, adapted)*

REQUIRED: The appropriate action when modification of the compilation report is inadequate.

DISCUSSION: If the accountant believes that modification of the report is not adequate to indicate the deficiencies in the financial statements as a whole, the accountant should withdraw from the compilation engagement. (S)he should provide no further services with respect to those financial statements. The accountant may wish to consult with his or her legal counsel upon withdrawal.

Answer (A) is incorrect. The accountant has no obligation to upgrade his or her service to a review. Answer (B) is incorrect. The accountant should withdraw from the engagement. Answer (D) is incorrect. An opinion may be expressed only after an audit has been performed.

18.3.8. Miller, CPA, is engaged to compile the financial statements of Web Co., a nonissuer, in conformity with the income tax basis of accounting. If Web's financial statements do not disclose the basis of accounting used, Miller should

A. Disclose the special purpose framework in the accountant's compilation report.

B. Clearly label each page "Distribution Restricted--Material Modifications Required."

C. Issue a special report describing the effect of the incomplete presentation.

D. Withdraw from the engagement and provide no further services to Web.

Answer (A) is correct. *(CPA, adapted)*

REQUIRED: The effect on a compilation report of failure to disclose the basis of accounting used.

DISCUSSION: The report should include a separate paragraph that (1) indicates that the statements are prepared in accordance with the special purpose framework (e.g., the income tax basis of accounting), (2) refers to the note to the statements that describes the framework (if applicable), and (3) states that the framework is a basis of accounting other than GAAP.

Answer (B) is incorrect. Each page of the financial statements may contain the statement, "See Accountant's Compilation Report." Answer (C) is incorrect. The term "special report" is no longer used in SASs. Answer (D) is incorrect. The accountant need not withdraw from the engagement.

18.3.9. In the course of an engagement to compile unaudited financial statements, the client requests that the accountant perform normal accounts receivable audit confirmation procedures. (S)he agrees and performs such procedures. The confirmation procedures

A. Are part of an auditing service and change the scope of the engagement to that of an audit in accordance with GAAS.

B. Are part of an accounting service and are not performed for the purpose of conducting an audit in accordance with GAAS.

C. Are not permitted when the purpose of the engagement is to prepare unaudited financial statements and the work to be performed is not in accordance with GAAS.

D. Would require the accountant to issue a report indicating that the audit was conducted in accordance with GAAS but was limited in scope.

Answer (B) is correct. *(CPA, adapted)*

REQUIRED: The true statement about audit procedures performed during an engagement to compile unaudited statements.

DISCUSSION: Accountants may perform other accounting services either in connection with a preparation, compilation, or review of unaudited financial statements of a nonissuer or separately.

Answer (A) is incorrect. Confirming accounts receivable does not convert the engagement to an audit. An audit is an engagement that involves performing procedures to obtain reasonable assurance about whether the financial statements are free from material misstatement. Answer (C) is incorrect. The accountant is allowed to perform accounts receivable confirmations when compiling unaudited statements, but such procedures must not be disclosed in the report. Answer (D) is incorrect. The accountant should prepare a report stating that the statements have not been audited or reviewed.

18.3.10. An accountant has been asked to compile and report on the financial statements of a nonissuer on a prescribed form that omits substantially all the disclosures required by generally accepted accounting principles. The prescribed form is a standard preprinted form adopted by the entity's industry trade association and is to be transmitted only to the association. The accountant

A. Should revise the report.

B. Should disclose the details of the omissions in separate paragraphs of the compilation report.

C. Is precluded from issuing a compilation report when all disclosures are omitted.

D. Should express limited assurance that the financial statements are free of material misstatements.

Answer (A) is correct. *(Publisher, adapted)*

REQUIRED: The accountant's responsibility.

DISCUSSION: If the omission is not (to the accountant's knowledge) intended to mislead users, the accountant may issue a compilation report. It should state that (1) management has elected to omit substantially all disclosures required by the framework, (2) the omissions might influence users' conclusions, and (3) the statements are not designed for those not informed about such matters. The accountant also modifies the report if the prescribed form meets the criteria for a special purpose framework.

Answer (B) is incorrect. Disclosure of the omissions is unnecessary. Answer (C) is incorrect. The report may be issued in these circumstances. Answer (D) is incorrect. A compilation report expresses no assurance.

18.3.11. When an accountant compiles a nonissuer's financial statements that omit substantially all disclosures required by U.S. GAAP, the accountant should indicate in the compilation report that the financial statements are

A. Restricted for internal use only by the entity's management.

B. Not to be given to financial institutions for the purpose of obtaining credit.

C. Compiled in conformity with a special purpose framework other than U.S. GAAP.

D. Not designed for those who are uninformed about such matters.

Answer (D) is correct. *(CPA, adapted)*

REQUIRED: The language in the report when compiled statements omit most disclosures required by the applicable reporting framework.

DISCUSSION: The accountant may not accept the engagement unless (1) (s)he modifies the standard compilation report to indicate that substantially all disclosures required by the applicable reporting framework have been omitted and (2) the omission is not, to the accountant's knowledge, made to mislead users of the statements. The language given is appropriate for a compilation report when substantially all disclosures are omitted.

Answer (A) is incorrect. The accountant need not indicate in the compilation report that the financial statements are restricted for internal use only. Answer (B) is incorrect. The statements may be given to financial institutions for the purpose of obtaining credit. Answer (C) is incorrect. The omission of disclosures required by the applicable reporting framework does not result in conformity with a special purpose framework (OCBOA).

18.4 Review of Financial Statements (AR-C 90)

18.4.1. Which of the following would not be included in an accountant's report based upon a review of the financial statements of a nonissuer?

A. A statement that the review was in accordance with GAAS.

B. A statement that management is responsible for the financial statements.

C. A statement describing the primary procedures performed.

D. A statement describing the results of the review.

Answer (A) is correct. *(CPA, adapted)*

REQUIRED: The statement not included in an accountant's report based upon a review.

DISCUSSION: The report should include a statement that the review is substantially less in scope than an audit. GAAS apply to audits, not reviews. A review is in accordance with SSARSs issued by the AICPA. It consists primarily of inquiries of entity personnel (including requests to management for written representations) and analytical procedures applied to financial data (AR-C 90).

Answer (B) is incorrect. The standard report states that management is responsible for preparing and fairly presenting the statements in accordance with the applicable reporting framework. Answer (C) is incorrect. According to the standard review report, a review primarily includes applying analytical procedures and making inquiries. Answer (D) is incorrect. The standard review report states the results of the review. This unmodified report states that the accountant is not aware of any material modifications that should be made to the statement for them to conform to the applicable reporting framework.

18.4.2. An accountant's standard report on a review of the financial statements of a nonissuer should state that the accountant

A. Does not express an opinion or any form of limited assurance on the financial statements.

B. Is not aware of any material modifications that should be made to the financial statements for them to conform with GAAP.

C. Obtained reasonable assurance about whether the financial statements are free of material misstatement.

D. Examined evidence, on a test basis, supporting the amounts and disclosures in the financial statements.

Answer (B) is correct. *(CPA, adapted)*

REQUIRED: The statement in a review report.

DISCUSSION: The review report states, "Based on my review, I am not aware of any material modifications that should be made to the accompanying financial statements in order for them to be in accordance with accounting principles generally accepted in the United States of America" (AR-C 90).

Answer (A) is incorrect. A review provides limited assurance. Answer (C) is incorrect. An audit provides reasonable assurance about whether the financial statements are free of material misstatement. Answer (D) is incorrect. An audit involves gathering sufficient appropriate evidence to support the amounts and disclosures in the financial statements.

18.4.3. Baker, CPA, was engaged to review the financial statements of Hall Company, a nonissuer. Evidence came to Baker's attention that indicated substantial doubt as to Hall's ability to continue as a going concern. The principal conditions and events that caused the substantial doubt have been fully disclosed in the notes to Hall's financial statements. Which of the following statements best describes Baker's reporting responsibility concerning this matter?

A. Baker is not required to modify the accountant's review report.

B. Baker is not permitted to modify the accountant's review report.

C. Baker should issue an accountant's compilation report instead of a review report.

D. Baker should express a qualified opinion in the accountant's review report.

Answer (A) is correct. *(CPA, adapted)*

REQUIRED: The accountant's reporting responsibility in a review engagement if (s)he concludes that a substantial doubt exists as to whether the entity is a going concern.

DISCUSSION: AR-C 90 states that, normally, neither an uncertainty about an entity's ability to continue as a going concern nor an inconsistency in the application of accounting principles should cause the accountant to modify the report, provided the financial statements appropriately disclose such matters. Nothing in this statement, however, is intended to preclude an accountant from including an emphasis-of-matter paragraph in the report describing a matter regarding the financial statements. Nevertheless, if management's conclusions about a going-concern issue are unreasonable, or if disclosure is inadequate, the accountant must follow the guidance for departures from the applicable reporting framework.

Answer (B) is incorrect. The accountant may emphasize a matter. Answer (C) is incorrect. If appropriate procedures have been applied and the accountant has formed a conclusion, a review report may be issued. Answer (D) is incorrect. Unless an audit has been conducted, an opinion may not be expressed.

18.4.4. Which of the following is required of an accountant in reviewing a company's financial statements under Statements on Standards for Accounting and Review Services (SSARSs)?

A. Obtain an understanding of the client's industry.

B. Send bank confirmations.

C. Perform risk assessment procedures.

D. Observe client's physical inventory.

Answer (A) is correct. *(CPA, adapted)*

REQUIRED: The required procedure in a review engagement.

DISCUSSION: The accountant should obtain an understanding of the industry and knowledge of the entity in a review engagement. Review procedures primarily include inquiries of management and analytical procedures. The accountant also obtains written representations from management.

18.4.5. Which of the following procedures would a CPA ordinarily perform when reviewing the financial statements of a nonissuer in accordance with Statements on Standards for Accounting and Review Services (SSARSs)?

A. Apply year-end cutoff tests for the sales and purchasing functions.

B. Compare the financial statements with budgets or forecasts.

C. Obtain an understanding of the entity's internal control components.

D. Document whether control risk is assessed at or below the maximum level.

Answer (B) is correct. *(CPA, adapted)*

REQUIRED: The procedure ordinarily performed in a review engagement.

DISCUSSION: Review procedures include inquiries of management, analytical procedures, and obtaining a representation letter. Comparing the financial statements with budgets or forecasts is an analytical procedure.

Answer (A) is incorrect. The accountant does not normally perform substantive procedures in a review engagement. Answer (C) is incorrect. The accountant need not obtain an understanding of internal control or assess risks in a review engagement. Answer (D) is incorrect. The accountant need not obtain an understanding of internal control or assess risks in a review engagement.

18.4.6. Which of the following situations would preclude an accountant from issuing a review report on a company's financial statements in accordance with Statements on Standards for Accounting and Review Services (SSARSs)?

A. The owner of a company is the accountant's father.

B. The accountant was engaged to review only the balance sheet.

C. Land has been recorded at appraisal value instead of historical cost.

D. Finished-goods inventory does not include any overhead amounts.

Answer (A) is correct. *(CPA, adapted)*

REQUIRED: The situation that precludes issuance of a review report.

DISCUSSION: The accountant should be independent to perform review services. The relationship of the accountant with the owner of the firm (the accountant's father) impairs independence because a close relative has a key position with the client.

Answer (B) is incorrect. An engagement to report on the balance sheet only is a permitted engagement if the scope of the procedures is not restricted. Answer (C) is incorrect. The accountant may be able to issue a modified review report indicating that land was reported at appraisal value instead of cost. Answer (D) is incorrect. The accountant may be able to issue a modified review report indicating that inventory was reported at prime cost rather than at full cost.

18.4.7. In a review engagement, if the accountant becomes aware that information coming to his or her attention is incorrect, incomplete, or otherwise unsatisfactory, (s)he should

A. Withdraw immediately from the engagement.

B. Perform the additional procedures necessary to obtain limited assurance.

C. Perform a complete audit and issue a standard audit report with appropriate qualifications.

D. Downgrade the engagement to a compilation and issue the appropriate report.

Answer (B) is correct. *(Publisher, adapted)*

REQUIRED: The accountant's response to unsatisfactory information in a review.

DISCUSSION: In a review, the accountant primarily makes inquiries, applies analytical procedures, and obtains a management representation letter. If information appears unsatisfactory, (s)he should perform the additional procedures necessary to obtain limited assurance that no material modifications need be made to the statements for them to conform with the reporting framework (AR-C 90).

Answer (A) is incorrect. The accountant should withdraw only after (s)he has concluded that (1) the financial statements are not in conformity with the reporting framework and (2) modification of the report is inadequate. Answer (C) is incorrect. The accountant cannot decide to perform a complete audit. (S)he must be engaged to do so by the client. Answer (D) is incorrect. Unsatisfactory information is not a basis for changing the engagement if the accountant can perform necessary procedures.

18.4.8. Each page of a nonissuer's financial statements reviewed by an accountant may include the following reference:

A. See Accountant's Review Report.

B. Reviewed, No Accountant's Assurance Expressed.

C. See Accompanying Accountant's Notes.

D. Reviewed, No Material Modifications Required.

Answer (A) is correct. *(CPA, adapted)*

REQUIRED: The reference that may be on each page of financial statements reviewed by an accountant.

DISCUSSION: The reviewed statements may become unattached from the review report. Thus, the accountant may consider including a reference to the report on each page of the statements. An example is "See Accountant's Review Report" (AR-C 90).

Answer (B) is incorrect. A review report ordinarily expresses limited assurance. Answer (C) is incorrect. Notes are part of the financial statements, not the accountant's report. Answer (D) is incorrect. The review report states that the accountant is not aware of any modifications that should be made other than those indicated in the report.

18.4.9. An accountant has been asked to issue a review report on the balance sheet of a nonissuer but not to report on the other basic financial statements. The accountant may not do so

A. Because compliance with this request would result in a violation of the ethical standards of the profession.

B. Because compliance with this request would result in an incomplete review.

C. If the review of the balance sheet discloses material departures from U.S. GAAP.

D. If the scope of the inquiry and analytical procedures has been restricted.

Answer (D) is correct. *(CPA, adapted)*

REQUIRED: The circumstance preventing an accountant from issuing a review report on the balance sheet of a nonissuer.

DISCUSSION: Financial statements are a structured representation of historical information, including notes, intended to communicate an entity's economic resources and obligations at a moment in time, or their changes for a period of time, in accordance with a financial reporting framework. The term ordinarily means a complete set but also may refer to (1) a single statement or (2) statements without notes (AR-C 60). Thus, an accountant may be asked to issue a review report on one financial statement, such as the balance sheet, and not the other related financial statements, such as the statements of income, changes in shareholders' equity, and cash flows. The accountant may do so if the review is complete, that is, if it provides an adequate basis for a report. The review is complete if the accountant is able to perform the inquiry and analytical procedures necessary to obtain limited assurance and the client provides the requested representation.

Answer (A) is incorrect. The accountant may accept an engagement to report on one but not the other financial statements. Answer (B) is incorrect. A review report expressing negative assurance could be issued for the balance sheet. Answer (C) is incorrect. The accountant may issue a modified review report on the balance sheet if it materially departs from the applicable reporting framework.

18.4.10. An accountant has been engaged to review a nonissuer's financial statements that contain several departures from GAAP. If the financial statements are not revised, and modification of the standard review report is not adequate to indicate the deficiencies, the accountant should

A. Withdraw from the engagement and provide no further services concerning these financial statements.

B. Inform management that the engagement can proceed only if distribution of the report is restricted to internal use.

C. Determine the effects of the departures from GAAP and issue a special report on the financial statements.

D. Issue a modified review report provided the entity agrees that the financial statements will not be used to obtain credit.

Answer (A) is correct. *(CPA, adapted)*

REQUIRED: The effect of uncorrected departures from the applicable reporting framework when modifying the review report is not adequate.

DISCUSSION: The statements may contain a material departure from the applicable reporting framework. If the statements are not revised, the accountant considers whether modification of the report is adequate to disclose the departure. If the accountant believes that modification of the report is not adequate, (s)he should withdraw from the engagement and provide no further services with respect to the statements. The accountant may wish to consult legal counsel in such circumstances (AR-C 90).

Answer (B) is incorrect. No report should be issued in this situation. Answer (C) is incorrect. Special purpose financial statements are prepared in accordance with a special purpose framework. A special purpose framework is one of the following: (1) cash basis; (2) tax basis; (3) regulatory basis; (4) contractual basis; or (5) a definite set of logical, reasonable criteria applied to all material items in the statements. Thus, GAAP is not a special purpose framework, and GAAP-based statements are not special purpose statements. Answer (D) is incorrect. No report should be issued in this situation.

18.4.11. During an engagement to review the financial statements of a nonissuer, an accountant becomes aware of a material departure from GAAP. If the accountant decides to modify the standard review report because management will not revise the financial statements, the accountant should

A. Express negative assurance on the accounting principles that conform with GAAP.

B. Disclose the departure from GAAP in a separate paragraph of the report.

C. Express an adverse or a qualified opinion, depending on materiality.

D. Express positive assurance on the accounting principles that conform with GAAP.

Answer (B) is correct. *(CPA, adapted)*

REQUIRED: The accountant's reporting responsibility in a review engagement given a material departure from the applicable reporting framework and management's refusal to revise the statements.

DISCUSSION: If the accountant concludes that a modified report is adequate to disclose a departure from the applicable reporting framework, the report should contain a separate paragraph disclosing the departure. The paragraph should have the heading, "Known Departure From Accounting Principles Generally Accepted in the United States of America (or other applicable framework)." It should include the effects on the financial statements if they have been determined by management or are known as the result of the accountant's procedures (AR-C 90).

Answer (A) is incorrect. The accountant provides negative assurance when departures from the applicable reporting framework exist. Answer (C) is incorrect. A review does not result in the expression of any form of positive assurance, including an opinion. Answer (D) is incorrect. A review does not result in the expression of any form of positive assurance, including an opinion.

18.4.12. Davis, CPA, accepted an engagement to audit the financial statements of Tech Resources, a nonissuer. Before the completion of the audit, Tech requested Davis to change the engagement to a review of financial statements. Before Davis agrees to change the engagement, Davis is required to consider the

	Additional Audit Effort Necessary to Complete the Audit	Reason Given for Tech's Request
A.	No	No
B.	Yes	Yes
C.	Yes	No
D.	No	Yes

Answer (B) is correct. *(CPA, adapted)*

REQUIRED: The matter(s) considered before changing an engagement from an audit to a review.

DISCUSSION: Before an accountant who was engaged to perform an audit in accordance with GAAS agrees to change the engagement to a review, at least the following should be considered: (1) the reason given for the client's request, particularly the implications of a restriction on the scope of the audit, whether imposed by the client or by circumstances; (2) the additional audit effort required to complete the audit; and (3) the estimated additional cost to complete the audit.

18.4.13. An accountant began an audit of the financial statements of a nonissuer and was asked to change the engagement to a review because of a restriction on the scope of the audit. If there is reasonable justification for the change, the review report should include reference to the

	Original Engagement That Was Agreed To	Scope Limitation That Caused the Changed Engagement
A.	Yes	Yes
B.	Yes	No
C.	No	Yes
D.	No	No

Answer (D) is correct. *(CPA, adapted)*

REQUIRED: The item(s), if any, that should be referred to in the accountant's review report.

DISCUSSION: An accountant may be asked to change the engagement from a higher to a lower level of service. If the accountant (1) concludes that the change is reasonably justified and (2) complies with the standards applicable to the changed engagement, the accountant may issue the appropriate compilation or review report. The report on the changed engagement should not mention (1) the original engagement, (2) any auditing procedures performed, or (3) scope limitations that led to the changed engagement.

18.4.14. If comparative statements have been reviewed, a continuing accountant should

A. Update his or her report on the financial statements of a prior period.

B. Disclaim any assurance on the prior periods' statements.

C. Issue a report on the statements of a prior period separately from the current-period report.

D. Express an adverse opinion with respect to the prior period's financial statements.

Answer (A) is correct. *(Publisher, adapted)*

REQUIRED: The report by a continuing accountant if comparative statements have been reviewed.

DISCUSSION: A continuing accountant should update the report on one or more prior periods presented comparatively with those of the current period. An updated report considers information obtained during the current engagement and (1) expresses the previous conclusions or (2) expresses different conclusions on the statements of a prior period as of the date of the current report, depending on the circumstances.

Answer (B) is incorrect. The previous conclusions should be reexpressed unless circumstances require otherwise. Answer (C) is incorrect. The updated report should be issued in conjunction with the report on the current-period statements. Answer (D) is incorrect. Opinions do not result from compilations and reviews.

18.5 Compilation of Pro Forma Financial Information (PFFI) (AR-C 120)

18.5.1. Which of the following presents what the effects on historical financial data might have been if a consummated transaction had occurred at an earlier date?

A. Prospective financial statements.

B. Pro forma financial information.

C. Interim financial information.

D. A financial projection.

Answer (B) is correct. *(Publisher, adapted)*

REQUIRED: The financial presentation showing what the effects of a consummated transaction might have been if it had occurred at an earlier date.

DISCUSSION: PFFI shows what the significant effects on historical financial information might have been had a consummated or proposed transaction (or event) occurred at an earlier date. Examples of these transactions include a business combination, disposal of a segment, a change in the form or status of an entity, and a change in capitalization.

Answer (A) is incorrect. PFSs do not cover periods that have completely expired. Thus, they are not historical statements. Answer (C) is incorrect. Interim financial information states actual results. Answer (D) is incorrect. A financial projection is a prospective statement and therefore is not a presentation of historical information.

18.5.2. An accountant has been engaged to compile pro forma financial statements. During the accountant's acceptance procedures, it is discovered that the accountant is not independent with respect to the company. What action should the accountant take with regard to the compilation?

A. The accountant should discuss the lack of independence with legal counsel to determine whether it is appropriate to accept the engagement.

B. The accountant should disclose the lack of independence in the accountant's compilation report.

C. The accountant should withdraw from the engagement.

D. The accountant should compile the pro forma financial statements but should not provide a compilation report.

Answer (B) is correct. *(CPA, adapted)*

REQUIRED: The action of an accountant who has been engaged to compile pro forma financial statements but is not independent.

DISCUSSION: Pro forma financial information is intended to show the significant effects on historical financial information if an underlying transaction or event had occurred earlier. Example transactions are business combinations and dispositions of a significant part of a business. If an accountant is not independent, (s)he nevertheless may report on a compilation of pro forma financial information. But the lack of independence requires modification of the report (AR-C 120).

Answer (A) is incorrect. The accountant may perform the engagement if the report is modified for the lack of independence. Answer (C) is incorrect. The accountant may perform the engagement if the report is modified for the lack of independence. Answer (D) is incorrect. The accountant may issue a report if it is modified for the lack of independence.

STUDY UNIT NINETEEN
SSAEs – EXAMINATION, REVIEW, AND AGREED-UPON PROCEDURES ENGAGEMENTS

The eight subunits in this study unit are based on Statements on Standards for Attestation Engagements (SSAEs). They provide guidance for attest services to which other specific standards (e.g., SASs and SSARSs) do not apply. Subunit 19.1 addresses general concepts of attest engagements. The next three subunits cover the three general types of engagements: examination, review, and agreed-upon procedures. Subunit 19.5 applies to examination and agreed-upon procedures engagements to report on prospective financial information (forecasts and projections). Subunit 19.6 addresses examinations and reviews of pro forma information based on the SSAEs. (Compilations of pro forma financial information are covered in Study Unit 18, Subunit 5, and are subject to the guidance in the SSARSs.) Subunit 19.7 applies to examination and agreed-upon procedures engagements related to compliance. Subunit 19.8 covers examinations and reviews of MD&A.

QUESTIONS

19.1 Concepts Common to All Attestation Engagements (AT-C 105)

19.1.1. Preconditions for all attestation engagements include all of the following except

A. Be satisfied that the practitioner can be considered the responsible party.

B. Determine that the subject matter is appropriate.

C. Expect to prepare a written report.

D. Have unrestricted access to information the practitioner considers necessary.

Answer (A) is correct. *(Publisher, adapted)*

REQUIRED: The response not a precondition of an attest engagement.

DISCUSSION: The responsible party is responsible for the subject matter. The practitioner cannot be the responsible party.

Answer (B) is incorrect. The practitioner should determine that the subject matter is appropriate. Answer (C) is incorrect. All successful attestation engagements should result in a written report. Answer (D) is incorrect. The practitioner must have access to all persons and information considered necessary for the engagement.

19.1.2. All attestation engagements require the practitioner to

A. Be independent.

B. Express a conclusion.

C. Consider financial information.

D. Collect audit evidence.

Answer (A) is correct. *(Publisher, adapted)*

REQUIRED: The item required for all attestation engagements.

DISCUSSION: All attestation engagements require the practitioner to be independent.

Answer (B) is incorrect. Only a review results in the expression of a conclusion. Agreed-upon procedures engagements result in a report on procedures and findings. An examination results in the expression of an opinion. Answer (C) is incorrect. Attestation engagements can entail other than financial information. Answer (D) is incorrect. Audit evidence is collected in an audit, not necessarily an attest engagement.

19.1.3. According to the AICPA Statements on Standards for Attestation Engagements, a public accounting firm should establish quality control policies to provide assurance about which of the following matters related to agreed-upon procedures engagements?

A. Use of the report is not restricted.

B. The public accounting firm takes responsibility for the sufficiency of procedures.

C. The practitioner is independent from the client and other specified parties.

D. The practitioner sets the criteria to be used in the determination of findings.

Answer (C) is correct. *(CPA, adapted)*

REQUIRED: The subject of quality control policies for agreed-upon procedures engagements.

DISCUSSION: A practitioner must be independent of the client and other specified parties to perform an agreed-upon procedures engagement. The practitioner assists specified parties in evaluating subject matter or an assertion as a result of the needs of the specified parties. The practitioner's services are obtained because the specified parties require that findings be independently derived.

Answer (A) is incorrect. Use of the report is restricted to specified parties. Answer (B) is incorrect. The specified parties are responsible for the sufficiency of the procedures. Answer (D) is incorrect. The practitioner and specified parties agree to the criteria to be used.

19.1.4. A practitioner is engaged to express an opinion on management's assertion that the square footage of a warehouse offered for sale is 150,000 square feet. The practitioner should refer to which of the following sources for professional guidance?

A. Statements on Auditing Standards.

B. Statements on Standards for Attestation Engagements.

C. Statements on Standards for Accounting and Review Services.

D. Statements on Standards for Consulting Services.

Answer (B) is correct. *(CPA, adapted)*

REQUIRED: The guidance applicable to services outside of financial reporting.

DISCUSSION: SSAEs relate to services that practitioners provide beyond those on traditional historical financial statements. Thus, an engagement to express an opinion on management's assertion that the square footage of a warehouse offered for sale is 150,000 square feet is a service beyond those on traditional historical financial statements.

Answer (A) is incorrect. Statements on Auditing Standards do not provide guidance for a practitioner performing other than a traditional audit. Answer (C) is incorrect. Statements on Standards for Accounting and Review Services are the basic pronouncements on compilations and reviews. They apply to unaudited financial statements, not assertions about square footage of buildings available for sale. Answer (D) is incorrect. Statements on Standards for Consulting Services provide guidance for various consulting services, such as tax planning, not relevant to management assertions about square footage of buildings available for sale.

19.1.5. Which of the following professional services would be considered an attestation engagement?

A. Advocating on behalf of a client about trust tax matters under review by the Internal Revenue Service.

B. Providing financial analysis, planning, and capital acquisition services as a part-time, in-house controller.

C. Advising management in the selection of a computer system to meet business needs.

D. Examining the financial statements for one year in the future based on client expectations and predictions.

Answer (D) is correct. *(CPA, adapted)*

REQUIRED: The attestation engagement.

DISCUSSION: Statements on Standards for Attestation Engagements (SSAEs) apply generally to performance of an examination, review, or agreed-upon procedures attestation engagement to report on subject matter, or an assertion about it, that is the responsibility of another party. The subject matter may be prospective financial statements (PFSs). PFSs include financial forecasts and projections. A forecast is based on the responsible party's assumptions reflecting the conditions it expects to exist and the course of action it expects to take. Furthermore, a review is not permitted to be performed with regard to a forecast or projection. However, a practitioner may examine or apply agreed-upon procedures to PFSs.

Answer (A) is incorrect. Advocacy of a client's position is not a service within the scope of the SSAEs. Answer (B) is incorrect. An engagement in which the practitioner's only purpose is to assist the client is not a service within the scope of the SSAEs. Answer (C) is incorrect. Advisory services are consulting services and therefore not within the scope of the SSAEs.

19.2 Examination Engagements (AT-C 205)

19.2.1. An attestation examination engagement most likely results in which of the following?

A. Limited assurance on subject matter that is the responsibility of others.

B. An opinion on the subject matter.

C. A conclusion about whether criteria are appropriate for specific subject matter.

D. The results of a set of procedures provided by the responsible party.

Answer (B) is correct. *(Publisher, adapted)*

REQUIRED: The result of an examination attestation engagement.

DISCUSSION: Examination attestation engagements result in an opinion on whether the subject matter is presented in accordance with the specified criteria.

Answer (A) is incorrect. Reviews result in limited assurance provided by the practitioner. Answer (C) is incorrect. Examinations result in conclusions about subject matter, not criteria. Answer (D) is incorrect. Agreed-upon procedures engagements result in findings from performing specified procedures.

19.2.2. A qualified opinion in an attestation examination engagement most likely is expressed when

A. Misstatements are material but not pervasive to the subject matter.

B. Evidence to support an opinion is not available.

C. Misstatements are material and pervasive to the subject matter.

D. Evidence to support an opinion is available but the practitioner is precluded from acquiring it.

Answer (A) is correct. *(Publisher, adapted)*

REQUIRED: The most likely basis for expressing a qualified opinion in an attestation examination engagement.

DISCUSSION: A qualified opinion is expressed when, having collected sufficient appropriate evidence, the practitioner concludes that misstatements, individually or in the aggregate, are material, but not pervasive, to the subject matter.

Answer (B) is incorrect. A disclaimer should be expressed if sufficient appropriate evidence is not available. Answer (C) is incorrect. An adverse opinion should be expressed if misstatements are material and pervasive. Answer (D) is incorrect. A disclaimer should be expressed if sufficient appropriate evidence is not available to the practitioner.

19.3 Review Engagements (AT-C 210)

19.3.1. In an attestation review engagement, the practitioner should request from the responsible party

A. A written assertion.

B. A disclaimer.

C. A hold-harmless agreement.

D. Permission to communicate with the responsible party's attorney.

Answer (A) is correct. *(Publisher, adapted)*

REQUIRED: The item that the practitioner should request from the responsible party.

DISCUSSION: The practitioner must request a written assertion from the responsible party in attestation examination or review engagements.

Answer (B) is incorrect. Auditors disclaim an opinion when sufficient appropriate evidence is unavailable. Answer (C) is incorrect. A practitioner is responsible for his or her work. Answer (D) is incorrect. Evidence for a review is primarily a combination of inquiries and analytical procedures. No communication with the responsible party's attorney is required.

19.3.2. In an attestation review engagement, the objectives of the practitioner are to

A. Form an opinion about whether the subject matter is in accordance with the criteria.

B. Express a conclusion about the fairness of financial statements.

C. Offer assurance that the practitioner's subject matter is appropriately presented.

D. Obtain limited assurance about whether any material modifications should be made to the subject matter in order for it be in accordance with the criteria.

Answer (D) is correct. *(Publisher, adapted)*

REQUIRED: The objective of an attestation review engagement.

DISCUSSION: The objective of a review is to provide limited assurance about whether the subject matter requires material modifications.

Answer (A) is incorrect. Examinations, not reviews, result in an opinion on the subject matter. Answer (B) is incorrect. Attestation reviews are on subject matter other than financial statements. Answer (C) is incorrect. The responsible party, not the practitioner, is accountable for the subject matter.

19.3.3. In an attestation review engagement, the practitioner concludes that misstatements are material and pervasive. The practitioner therefore should

A. Express an adverse conclusion.

B. Express a qualified conclusion.

C. Withdraw from the engagement.

D. Request additional management representations.

Answer (C) is correct. *(Publisher, adapted)*

REQUIRED: The review report appropriate, if any, when the practitioner concludes that misstatements to the subject matter are material and pervasive.

DISCUSSION: When misstatements are material and pervasive, the practitioner should withdraw from the engagement.

Answer (A) is incorrect. An adverse review conclusion must not be expressed. Answer (B) is incorrect. A qualified conclusion is inappropriate when misstatements are material and pervasive. Answer (D) is incorrect. The practitioner has already concluded that the misstatements are material and pervasive. No additional information is necessary.

19.4 Agreed-Upon Procedures Engagements (AT-C 215)

19.4.1. An accountant may accept an engagement to apply agreed-upon procedures to prospective financial statements provided the

A. Provisions of Statements on Standards for Accounting and Review Services (SSARSs) are followed.

B. Accountant also examines the prospective financial statements.

C. Use of the report is restricted to the specified users.

D. The accountant takes responsibility for the adequacy of the procedures performed.

Answer (C) is correct. *(CPA, adapted)*

REQUIRED: The requirement to apply agreed-upon procedures on prospective financial statements.

DISCUSSION: The following conditions should be met to accept an engagement: (1) The specified parties agree to the procedures and take responsibility for their sufficiency, (2) an alert restricts report use to those parties, and (3) the statements include a summary of significant assumptions.

Answer (A) is incorrect. SSARSs apply only to the unaudited financial statements of nonissuers. Answer (B) is incorrect. An examination of the prospective financial statements is not required unless it is one of the agreed-upon procedures. Answer (D) is incorrect. The specified party takes responsibility for the sufficiency of the procedures.

19.4.2. Which of the following statements should be included in a practitioner's report on the application of agreed-upon procedures?

A. A statement that the practitioner performed an examination of prospective financial statements.

B. A statement of scope limitation that will qualify the practitioner's opinion.

C. A statement referring to standards established by the AICPA.

D. A statement of negative assurance based on procedures performed.

Answer (C) is correct. *(CPA, adapted)*

REQUIRED: The statement in a report on an agreed-upon procedures engagement.

DISCUSSION: An agreed-upon procedures engagement is an attestation engagement in which a practitioner is engaged by a client to issue a report of findings based on specific procedures performed on subject matter. A statement referring to the standards established by the AICPA is included in all practitioner reports on attestation engagements. Thus, it should be included in a practitioner's report on the application of agreed-upon procedures.

Answer (A) is incorrect. A practitioner may examine or apply agreed-upon procedures on PFSs. Accordingly, agreed-upon procedures are not performed in an examination. Answer (B) is incorrect. A practitioner does not express an opinion based on the application of agreed-upon procedures. Answer (D) is incorrect. The practitioner's report is in the form of procedures and findings, and neither an opinion nor negative assurance should be provided.

19.4.3. Which of the following components is appropriate in a practitioner's report on the results of applying agreed-upon procedures?

A. A list of the procedures performed, as agreed to by the specified parties identified in the report.

B. A statement that management is responsible for expressing an opinion.

C. A title that includes the phrase "independent audit."

D. A statement that the report is unrestricted in its use.

Answer (A) is correct. *(CPA, adapted)*

REQUIRED: The component appropriate for an agreed-upon procedures report.

DISCUSSION: In an agreed-upon procedures engagement, the practitioner is engaged to report on the results of performing specific procedures agreed upon with specified parties. The report lists the procedures performed and provides the results of those procedures but provides no form of positive or negative assurance.

Answer (B) is incorrect. No opinion is expressed in an agreed-upon procedures report. Answer (C) is incorrect. The report does not refer to an audit. Answer (D) is incorrect. An agreed-upon procedures report should have a statement restricting its use to the specified parties who agreed upon the procedures to be performed.

19.4.4. A nonissuer engaged a practitioner to perform agreed-upon procedures on specified matters. The date of the practitioner's report would ordinarily be determined by the occurrence of which of the following events?

A. The receipt of the signed engagement letter from the client.

B. The completion of the agreed-upon procedures.

C. The client's review and approval of the contents of a draft report.

D. The delivery of the final report to the client.

Answer (B) is correct. *(CPA, adapted)*

REQUIRED: The report date for an engagement to perform agreed-upon procedures on specified matters.

DISCUSSION: The date of the report is no earlier than when the practitioner completed the agreed-upon engagement procedures and determined the findings. Completion includes (1) review of documentation, (2) preparation of the written presentation of the subject matter (if applicable), and (3) the receipt of the responsible party's written assertion (unless that party has refused).

Answer (A) is incorrect. The agreed-upon terms should be documented prior to the beginning of the engagement. Answer (C) is incorrect. The specified parties agree to the procedures. Moreover, the client may see a draft report. However, the client must not have the power to approve the final report. Otherwise, the practitioner violates the objectivity and independence principle. Answer (D) is incorrect. The practitioner's findings are valid only as of the completion of the engagement. They do not address the period between completion of the engagement and delivery of the final report to the client.

19.4.5. Limited assurance may be expressed when a practitioner is requested to apply agreed-upon procedures to specified

	Elements of a Financial Statement	Accounts of a Financial Statement
A.	Yes	Yes
B.	Yes	No
C.	No	No
D.	No	Yes

Answer (C) is correct. *(Publisher, adapted)*

REQUIRED: The report in which limited assurance may be expressed.

DISCUSSION: The practitioner does not express an opinion or limited assurance when engaged to apply agreed-upon procedures. Instead, the practitioner's report on agreed-upon procedures should be in the form of procedures and findings.

19.5 Prospective Financial Information (AT-C 305)

19.5.1. A financial forecast

A. Is based on the most conservative estimates.

B. Present estimates given one or more hypothetical assumptions.

C. Unlike a projection, may contain a range.

D. Presents expected financial position, results of operations, and cash flows.

Answer (D) is correct. *(Publisher, adapted)*

REQUIRED: The true statement about a financial forecast.

DISCUSSION: According to AT-C 305, a financial forecast consists of prospective financial statements that present, to the best of the responsible party's knowledge and belief, an entity's expected financial position, results of operations, and cash flows. A forecast is based on the responsible party's assumptions reflecting conditions it expects to exist and the course of action it expects to take.

Answer (A) is incorrect. The information presented is based on expected (most likely) conditions and course of action, not the most conservative estimates. Answer (B) is incorrect. A financial projection (not a forecast) is based on assumptions by the responsible party reflecting expected conditions and course of action, given one or more hypothetical assumptions (a condition or action not necessarily expected to occur). Answer (C) is incorrect. Both forecasts and projections may be stated either as point estimates or ranges.

19.5.2. Which of the following examination reports on prospective financial statements is (are) appropriate for general use?

	Financial forecast	Financial projection
A.	Yes	Yes
B.	Yes	No
C.	No	Yes
D.	No	No

Answer (B) is correct. *(CPA, adapted)*

REQUIRED: The prospective financial statement appropriate for general use.

DISCUSSION: A financial forecast is based on conditions the responsible party expects to exist and the course of action it expects to take. A projection is sometimes prepared to present one or more hypothetical courses of action for evaluation, as in response to a question such as "What would happen if . . .?" Only an examination report on a forecast is appropriate for general use. All other engagement services are for limited use.

Answer (A) is incorrect. Any engagement service for a financial projection is not appropriate for general use. Answer (C) is incorrect. An examination report on a financial forecast is appropriate for general use. An examination report on a financial projection is not. Answer (D) is incorrect. An examination report on a financial forecast is appropriate for general use.

19.5.3. The AICPA recommends that the format of prospective financial statements be similar to

A. Historical financial statements, such as income statements, balance sheets, and statements of cash flows.

B. Worksheet formats so that adjustments can be readily made.

C. Specialized schedules that do not resemble financial statements.

D. Computer printouts so that the sophisticated nature of forecasting can be demonstrated.

Answer (A) is correct. *(Publisher, adapted)*

REQUIRED: The recommended format appropriate for PFSs.

DISCUSSION: Information in PFSs should be communicated by using the format of historical financial statements issued for the period(s) covered, unless the responsible party and potential users agree on another format. Thus, this information may be in the form of income statements, balance sheets, and statements of cash flows to facilitate comparisons with (1) prior periods and (2) the actual statements for the prospective period (AT-C 305).

Answer (B) is incorrect. Worksheet formats are inappropriate for prospective financial statements. Answer (C) is incorrect. Specialized schedules are inappropriate for prospective financial statements. Answer (D) is incorrect. Computer printouts are inappropriate for prospective financial statements.

19.5.4. Which of the following statements concerning prospective financial statements is true?

A. Only a financial forecast would normally be appropriate for limited use.

B. Only a financial projection would normally be appropriate for general use.

C. Any type of prospective financial statements would normally be appropriate for limited use.

D. Any type of prospective financial statements would normally be appropriate for general use.

Answer (C) is correct. *(CPA, adapted)*

REQUIRED: The true statement about PFSs.

DISCUSSION: Limited use of PFSs means use by the responsible party and those with whom that party is negotiating directly, e.g., in a submission to a regulatory body or in negotiations for a bank loan. These third parties can communicate directly with the responsible party. Consequently, any PFSs useful in the circumstances are appropriate for limited use.

Answer (A) is incorrect. Projections are appropriate for limited use. Answer (B) is incorrect. Only a forecast is appropriate for general use. Answer (D) is incorrect. Only a forecast is appropriate for general use.

19.5.5. When a practitioner examines a financial forecast that fails to disclose several significant assumptions used to prepare the forecast, the practitioner should describe the assumptions in the practitioner's report and express

A. An "except for" qualified opinion.

B. A "subject to" qualified opinion.

C. An unmodified opinion with a separate explanatory paragraph.

D. An adverse opinion.

Answer (D) is correct. *(CPA, adapted)*

REQUIRED: The appropriate opinion if a forecast fails to disclose several significant assumptions.

DISCUSSION: An examination results in issuance of a report stating the practitioner's opinion on whether (1) the presentation conforms with AICPA guidelines and (2) the underlying assumptions are suitably supported and provide a reasonable basis for the forecast. If significant assumptions are not disclosed in the presentation, including the summary of assumptions, the practitioner must express an adverse opinion. Moreover, a practitioner should not examine a presentation that omits all such disclosures.

Answer (A) is incorrect. Omission of significant assumptions requires an adverse opinion. Other departures from the presentation guidelines, however, may justify a qualified opinion. Answer (B) is incorrect. The language "subject to" is never permissible. Answer (C) is incorrect. An explanatory paragraph is insufficient when significant assumptions are omitted.

19.5.6. The party responsible for assumptions identified in the preparation of prospective financial statements is usually

A. A third-party lending institution.

B. The client's management.

C. The reporting accountant.

D. The client's independent CPA.

Answer (B) is correct. *(CPA, adapted)*

REQUIRED: The party usually responsible for assumptions identified in the preparation of PFSs.

DISCUSSION: Management is usually the responsible party, that is, the person(s) responsible for the assumptions underlying PFSs. However, the responsible party may be a party outside the entity, such as a possible acquirer.

19.5.7. When a CPA examines a client's projected financial statements, the CPA's report on these statements should

A. Explain the principal differences between historical and projected financial statements.

B. State that the CPA performed procedures to evaluate management's assumptions.

C. Refer to the CPA's auditor's report on the historical financial statements.

D. Include the CPA's opinion on the client's ability to continue as a going concern.

Answer (B) is correct. *(CPA, adapted)*

REQUIRED: The true statement about a report on the examination of a projection.

DISCUSSION: In an examination of PFSs, the objectives of the practitioner are to (1) obtain reasonable assurance about whether, in all material respects, (a) the PFSs conform with AICPA guidelines and (b) the assumptions provide a reasonable basis for the responsible party's forecast (or the responsible party's projection, given the hypothetical assumptions), and (2) express an opinion in a written report on such matters. Accordingly, examination procedures should be based, among other things, on a consideration of whether the responsible party's assumptions (1) are suitably supported, individually and in the aggregate, and (2) provide a reasonable basis for the forecast (or the projection, given the hypothetical assumptions). Thus, an unmodified opinion on an examination of a forecast states that the underlying assumptions are suitably supported and provide a reasonable basis for management's forecast.

19.5.8. Given one or more hypothetical assumptions, a responsible party may prepare, to the best of its knowledge and belief, an entity's expected financial position, results of operations, and cash flows. Such prospective financial statements are known as

A. Pro forma financial statements.

B. Financial projections.

C. Partial presentations.

D. Financial forecasts.

Answer (B) is correct. *(CPA, adapted)*

REQUIRED: The PFSs based on one or more hypothetical assumptions.

DISCUSSION: PFSs include forecasts and projections. The difference between a forecast and a projection is that only the projection is based on one or more hypothetical assumptions, which are conditions or actions not necessarily expected to occur.

Answer (A) is incorrect. Pro forma statements are essentially historical, not prospective, statements. Answer (C) is incorrect. Partial presentations are not PFSs. They do not meet the minimum presentation guidelines. Answer (D) is incorrect. A financial projection, not a financial forecast, contains one or more hypothetical assumptions.

19.5.9. Accepting an engagement to examine an entity's financial projection most likely would be appropriate if the projection were to be distributed to

A. All employees who work for the entity.

B. Potential shareholders who request a prospectus or a registration statement.

C. A bank with which the entity is negotiating for a loan.

D. All shareholders of record as of the report date.

Answer (C) is correct. *(CPA, adapted)*

REQUIRED: The situation in which acceptance of an engagement to examine a projection is appropriate.

DISCUSSION: A projection is based on one or more hypothetical assumptions and, therefore, should be considered for limited use only. Limited use of PFSs means use by the responsible party and those with whom that party is negotiating directly. Examples of appropriate use include negotiations for a bank loan and submission to a regulatory body. A projection is inappropriate for distribution to those who will not be negotiating directly with the responsible party.

19.5.10. Relative to prospective financial statements, a practitioner may accept an engagement to

	Review	Examination
A.	No	Yes
B.	Yes	Yes
C.	Yes	No
D.	No	No

Answer (A) is correct. *(CPA, adapted)*

REQUIRED: The engagement regarding PFSs that may not be accepted.

DISCUSSION: AT-C 305 does not provide for a review of PFSs but does allow an examination.

Answer (B) is incorrect. AT-C 305 does not provide for a review of PFSs but does allow an examination. Answer (C) is incorrect. AT-C 305 does not provide for a review of PFSs but does allow an examination. Answer (D) is incorrect. AT-C 305 does not provide for a review of PFSs but does allow an examination.

19.5.11. A practitioner may accept an engagement to apply agreed-upon procedures to prospective financial statements provided that

A. Use of the report is restricted to the specified parties.

B. The prospective financial statements also are examined.

C. Responsibility for the sufficiency of the procedures performed is taken by the practitioner.

D. Limited assurance is expressed on the prospective financial statements taken as a whole.

Answer (A) is correct. *(CPA, adapted)*

REQUIRED: The condition for performing an agreed-upon procedures attest engagement regarding PFSs.

DISCUSSION: The following conditions should be met to accept an engagement: (1) The specified parties have participated in determining its nature and scope, and they take responsibility for the adequacy of the procedures; (2) report use is restricted to those parties; and (3) the statements include a summary of significant assumptions.

Answer (B) is incorrect. The practitioner may apply agreed-upon procedures without providing the more extensive services required by an examination. Answer (C) is incorrect. The specified parties must assume the responsibility for the sufficiency of the procedures performed is taken by the practitioner. Answer (D) is incorrect. The practitioner should state his or her findings.

19.6 Reporting on Pro Forma Financial Information (AT-C 310)

19.6.1. In an attestation review engagement, each of the following items should be included in the presentation of pro forma financial statements except

A. The significant assumptions used in developing the pro forma information.

B. The source of the historical information on which the pro forma information is based.

C. An indication that the pro forma information is not necessarily indicative of results.

D. All direct and indirect effects attributed to the related transaction.

Answer (D) is correct. *(CPA, adapted)*

REQUIRED: The presentation of PFFI in an attestation review engagement.

DISCUSSION: Pro forma adjustments are based on management's assumptions. They should include all significant direct effects of the transaction (or event).

Answer (A) is incorrect. The presentation should describe the significant assumptions used in developing the pro forma adjustments and any significant uncertainties about these assumptions. Answer (B) is incorrect. PFFI should be labeled as such to distinguish it from historical financial information. Thus, the presentation should describe the source of the historical financial information on which it is based. Answer (C) is incorrect. The pro forma financial information is not necessarily indicative of the results that would have been achieved if the transaction actually had occurred earlier.

19.6.2. An accountant has been engaged to examine pro forma adjustments that show the effects on previously audited historical financial statements due to a proposed disposition of a significant portion of an entity's business. Other than the procedures previously applied to the historical financial statements, the accountant is required to

	Reevaluate the entity's internal control over financial reporting	Determine that the computations of the pro forma adjustments are mathematically correct
A.	Yes	Yes
B.	Yes	No
C.	No	Yes
D.	No	No

Answer (C) is correct. *(CPA, adapted)*

REQUIRED: The procedure(s), if any, applied in an examination of PFFI.

DISCUSSION: In an examination of PFFI, the practitioner's additional procedures include (1) understanding the underlying transaction or event; (2) discussing the assumptions about the transaction or event with management; (3) evaluating whether adjustments are consistent with each other and the data and are included for all significant effects; (4) gathering sufficient evidence to support the adjustments; (5) evaluating whether the assumptions are sufficiently, clearly, and comprehensively presented; (6) determining that computations are correct and that the pro forma column properly reflects their application to the historical statements; (7) obtaining written management representations; and (8) evaluating the PFFI to determine whether certain matters (the transaction or event, assumptions, adjustments, and uncertainties) have been properly described and the sources of the historical information have been properly identified. Moreover, in a business combination, the practitioner must obtain a sufficient understanding of each part of the combined entity. However, no evaluation of internal control beyond that done in the engagement is performed with respect to the historical statements.

19.6.3. The practitioner's report on an examination of pro forma financial information (PFFI)

A. Should have the same date as the related historical financial statements.

B. Should be added to the report on the historical financial statements.

C. Need not mention the report on the historical financial statements.

D. May state an unmodified, qualified, or adverse opinion.

Answer (D) is correct. *(Publisher, adapted)*

REQUIRED: The true statement about the practitioner's report on an examination of PFFI.

DISCUSSION: The report should include an opinion on whether (1) management's assumptions provide a reasonable basis for the significant effects attributable to the transaction or event, (2) the pro forma adjustments give appropriate effect to the assumptions, and (3) the pro forma amounts reflect the proper application of those adjustments to the historical data. Scope limitations, uncertainties, reservations about the assumptions or the presentation (including inadequate disclosure), and other matters may lead to modification of the opinion or a disclaimer.

Answer (A) is incorrect. The report should be dated as of the completion of procedures. Answer (B) is incorrect. The report may appear separately. Moreover, if it is combined with the report on the historical statements, the combined report may need to be dual-dated. Answer (C) is incorrect. The report should refer to the financial statements from which the historical information is derived and state whether they were audited or reviewed.

19.6.4. A practitioner may report on an examination of pro forma financial information (PFFI) if the related historical financial statements have been

A. Audited.

B. Audited or reviewed.

C. Audited, reviewed, or compiled.

D. Reviewed or compiled.

Answer (A) is correct. *(Publisher, adapted)*

REQUIRED: The service(s) on historical statements permitting an examination of PFFI.

DISCUSSION: A practitioner may examine or review PFFI only if certain conditions are met. One condition is that the level of assurance provided be limited to that given on the historical statements. Accordingly, an examination that provides a basis for positive assurance is appropriate only if the historical statements have been audited.

Answer (B) is incorrect. If the historical statements have been reviewed, only a review of the PFFI is appropriate. Answer (C) is incorrect. A compilation of the historical statements provides no assurance. Thus, it is not a basis for the practitioner to examine or review the PFFI. Answer (D) is incorrect. A compilation of the historical statements provides no assurance. Thus, it is not a basis for the practitioner to examine or review the PFFI.

19.6.5. A practitioner's report on a review of pro forma financial information should include a

A. Statement that the entity's internal control was not relied on in the review.

B. Disclaimer of opinion on the financial statements from which the pro forma financial information is derived.

C. Caveat that it is uncertain whether the transaction or event reflected in the pro forma financial information will ever occur.

D. Reference to the financial statements from which the historical financial information is derived.

Answer (D) is correct. *(CPA, adapted)*

REQUIRED: The statement that should be included in a review of pro forma financial information.

DISCUSSION: A practitioner's report on PFFI should include, among other things, (1) an identification of the pro forma information, (2) a reference to the financial statements from which the historical financial information is derived and a statement as to whether such financial statements were audited or reviewed, (3) a statement that the review was made in accordance with standards established by the AICPA, (4) a caveat that a review is substantially less in scope than an examination and that no opinion is expressed, (5) a separate paragraph explaining the objective of PFFI and its limitations, and (6) the practitioner's conclusion providing limited assurance.

Answer (A) is incorrect. The report should not mention internal control. Answer (B) is incorrect. The practitioner should disclaim an opinion on the pro forma financial information. Answer (C) is incorrect. The transaction may already have occurred.

19.7 Compliance Attestation (AT-C 315)

19.7.1. In an examination compliance attestation engagement,

A. The practitioner provides limited assurance.

B. The practitioner may accept an engagement to examine the effectiveness of internal control over compliance only if an assertion about internal control is provided to the practitioner by the client.

C. The result is a legal determination of an entity's compliance with specified requirements.

D. The practitioner should accept responsibility for the entity's compliance with the specified requirements.

Answer (B) is correct. *(Publisher, adapted)*

REQUIRED: The true statement about compliance attest engagements.

DISCUSSION: A written assertion may take many forms. A precondition of an examination under AT-C 315 is that the practitioner requests a written assertion from management. If the request is refused, the practitioner should withdraw if possible under the applicable law or regulation. However, AT-C 315 does not apply to an examination of internal control over compliance with specified requirements. Such an examination is governed by AT-C 105 and AT-C 205. According to AT-C 205, if the engaging party also is the responsible party and refuses the request for a written assertion, the practitioner should withdraw if possible under the applicable law or regulation.

Answer (A) is incorrect. In an examination, the practitioner expresses an opinion. Answer (C) is incorrect. The report does not provide a legal determination on compliance with specified requirements, but it may be useful to legal counsel or others in making such determinations. Answer (D) is incorrect. The responsible party, typically management, must accept responsibility for the subject matter of the engagement, e.g., compliance.

19.7.2. According to AT-C 315, *Compliance Attestation*, a practitioner may examine compliance with specified requirements. For this purpose, AT-C 205, *Examination Engagements*, states that, to obtain reasonable assurance, the practitioner should obtain sufficient appropriate evidence to limit attestation risk to an appropriately low level. According to AT-C 105, *Concepts Common to All Attestation Engagements*, attestation risk is

A. The susceptibility of the subject matter to material misstatement without regard to related controls.

B. The risk that material misstatement of the subject matter will not be timely prevented, or detected and corrected, by the appropriate party's internal control.

C. The risk that the practitioner may express an inappropriate opinion or conclusion on a materially misstated subject matter or assertion.

D. The risk that the practitioner's procedures will not detect a material misstatement.

Answer (C) is correct. *(Publisher, adapted)*

REQUIRED: The nature of attestation risk.

DISCUSSION: In an examination review, attestation risk is the risk that the practitioner expresses an inappropriate opinion or conclusion when the subject matter or assertion is materially misstated. A misstatement is a difference between (1) the measurement or evaluation of the subject matter by the responsible party and (2) the proper measurement or evaluation based on the criteria. A misstatement may be called a deviation, exception, or instance of noncompliance. The components of attestation risk are similar to those for audit risk: inherent risk, control risk, and detection risk.

Answer (A) is incorrect. Inherent risk is the susceptibility of the subject matter to material misstatement before consideration of any related controls. Answer (B) is incorrect. Control risk is the risk that that a material misstatement that could occur in the subject matter will not be timely prevented, or detected and corrected, by the appropriate party's internal control. Answer (D) is incorrect. Detection risk is the risk that the practitioner's procedures will not detect a material misstatement.

19.7.3. According to AT-C 315, *Compliance Attestation*, a practitioner may accept a compliance attestation engagement to perform

	Agreed-Upon Procedures	An Examination	A Review
A.	Yes	No	Yes
B.	No	Yes	No
C.	Yes	Yes	No
D.	No	No	Yes

Answer (C) is correct. *(Publisher, adapted)*

REQUIRED: The type(s) of compliance attestation engagements.

DISCUSSION: The practitioner may perform agreed-upon procedures related to an entity's (1) compliance with specified requirements of laws, regulations, rules, contracts, or grants or (2) internal control over compliance with specified requirements. But the specified parties must (1) agree to the procedures to be applied and (2) take responsibility for the sufficiency of such procedures for their purposes. The practitioner also may examine (1) an entity's compliance with specified requirements or (2) an assertion about compliance with specified requirements. An engagement to examine internal control over compliance is governed by AT-C 105, *Concepts Common to All Attestation Engagements*, and AT-C 205, *Examination Engagements*. However, AT-C 315 does not provide for a review engagement. The reason is that AT-C 210, *Review Engagements*, prohibits a review of compliance with specified requirements (and also of prospective financial information and internal control).

19.7.4. A practitioner's report on agreed-upon procedures related to an entity's compliance with specified requirements should contain

A. A statement of restrictions on the use of the report.

B. An opinion about whether management complied with the specified requirements.

C. Negative assurance that control risk has not been assessed.

D. An acknowledgment of responsibility for the sufficiency of the procedures.

Answer (A) is correct. *(CPA, adapted)*

REQUIRED: The item in a report on a compliance attestation engagement to apply agreed-upon procedures.

DISCUSSION: The report based on agreed-upon procedures should contain an alert restricting use to specified parties.

Answer (B) is incorrect. The report on agreed-upon procedures should be in the form of a summary of procedures and findings, not an opinion. Answer (C) is incorrect. Negative assurance about whether an entity is in compliance or whether management's assertion is fairly stated is not permitted in reports on applying agreed-upon procedures. Answer (D) is incorrect. The parties who agreed to the procedures are responsible for their sufficiency.

19.7.5. Practitioner was engaged by a group of pension recipients to apply agreed-upon procedures to financial data supplied by Pension regarding Pension's written assertion about its compliance with contractual requirements to pay benefits. The report on these agreed-upon procedures should contain a(n)

A. Disclaimer of opinion about the fair presentation of Employer's financial statements.

B. List of the procedures performed (or reference to them) and Practitioner's findings.

C. Opinion about the effectiveness of Employer's internal control over pension payments.

D. Acknowledgment that the sufficiency of the procedures is solely Practitioner's responsibility.

Answer (B) is correct. *(CPA, adapted)*

REQUIRED: The statement in a report on a compliance attestation engagement to apply agreed-upon procedures.

DISCUSSION: The practitioner's report should be in the form of procedures and findings but should not provide any assurance about whether the entity is in compliance or whether the responsible party's assertion is fairly stated (AT-C 315).

Answer (A) is incorrect. The report should not contain a disclaimer of opinion on the fair presentation of Employer's financial statements. However, it should contain a paragraph stating that the independent accountant was not engaged to and did not perform an examination of the financial data related to the written assertion about compliance with contractual requirements to make pension payments. It also should state that (1) the objective of an examination would have been an expression of opinion on compliance with the specified requirements and (2) no such opinion is expressed. Answer (C) is incorrect. An agreed-upon procedures engagement typically results in a list of the procedures performed and related findings, not an opinion. Answer (D) is incorrect. The specified parties who agreed to the procedures are responsible for their sufficiency.

19.8 Management's Discussion and Analysis (AT-C 395)

19.8.1. Which of the following statements best serves as management's assertion of consistency in an MD&A presentation?

A. Information included in the presentation is properly classified and described.

B. Nonfinancial data have been accurately derived from related records.

C. Reported transactions took place during a given period.

D. Descriptions of transactions are included to understand financial condition.

Answer (B) is correct. *(CPA, adapted)*

REQUIRED: The item that best serves as management's assertion of consistency in MD&A.

DISCUSSION: Assertions are management representations in the MD&A presentation. They relate to (1) occurrence, (2) consistency with the financial statements, (3) completeness, and (4) presentation and disclosure. Assertions about consistency are whether (1) reported transactions, events, and explanations are consistent with the statements; (2) historical financial amounts are accurately derived from the statements and related records; and (3) nonfinancial data have been accurately derived from related records.

Answer (A) is incorrect. An assertion about presentation and disclosure is that information included in the presentation is properly classified and described. Answer (C) is incorrect. An assertion about occurrence is that reported transactions or events took place during a given period. Answer (D) is incorrect. An assertion about completeness relates to, among other things, whether descriptions of transactions and events are necessary to an understanding of the entity's financial condition (e.g., liquidity and capital).

19.8.2. In accordance with AT-C 395, *Management's Discussion and Analysis*, the presentation of an MD&A is a written assertion that

A. May be examined but not reviewed.

B. May be examined or reviewed.

C. A practitioner may attest to only if the entity is an issuer.

D. A practitioner may attest to only if the entity is a nonissuer.

Answer (B) is correct. *(Publisher, adapted)*

REQUIRED: The true statement about an attest engagement performed on the presentation of MD&A.

DISCUSSION: A practitioner may perform an attest engagement regarding MD&A prepared in accordance with SEC rules and presented in an annual report or other document. This presentation is a written assertion that may be examined or reviewed whether the entity is an issuer or a nonissuer. However, a report on a review cannot be filed with the SEC.

Answer (A) is incorrect. MD&A may be reviewed. Answer (C) is incorrect. The entity presenting MD&A may be an issuer or a nonissuer. Answer (D) is incorrect. The entity presenting MD&A may be an issuer or a nonissuer.

STUDY UNIT TWENTY
GOVERNMENTAL AUDITS

The first subunit presents an overview of the basic characteristics of governmental auditing and addresses the generally accepted government auditing standards (GAGAS) that differ from GAAS. The second subunit is based on the AICPA's guidance on auditing compliance with governmental requirements. The third subunit applies to statutory and regulatory requirements.

QUESTIONS

20.1 Government Auditing Standards

20.1.1. Financial audits of certain governmental entities are required to be performed in accordance with generally accepted government auditing standards (GAGAS) as issued in *Government Auditing Standards*. These standards do not require, as part of an auditor's report, the inclusion of

A. A statement as to whether the tests performed provide sufficient appropriate evidence to support an opinion on internal control over financial reporting.

B. The significant deficiencies, with identification of material weaknesses.

C. Sampling methods used to test the controls designed to detect fraud whether or not material fraud is found.

D. A description of the scope of testing of internal control over financial reporting.

Answer (C) is correct. *(CPA, adapted)*

REQUIRED: The item not required by GAGAS to be identified in an audit report.

DISCUSSION: The Government Accountability Office (GAO) issues *Government Auditing Standards* (the Yellow Book). GAGAS apply to financial audits, attestation engagements, and performance audits. GAGAS for financial audits incorporate by reference the AICPA's Statements on Auditing Standards (SAS) and also state requirements. However, they do not require that the report identify specific sampling techniques used to test the controls. Nevertheless, when presenting material fraud, auditors might consider the report contents standards for performance audits that pertain to, among other things, methodology. Thus, if sampling significantly supports the findings, the auditor might describe the sample design and state why it was chosen.

Answer (A) is incorrect. Auditors should state whether tests provided sufficient appropriate evidence to support opinions on internal control over financial reporting and compliance with laws, regulations, contracts, or grant agreements. Answer (B) is incorrect. Auditors should communicate in writing on a timely basis significant deficiencies and material weaknesses identified during the audit. They are included in the GAGAS report on internal control over financial reporting. Answer (D) is incorrect. The report on the financial statements should describe the scope of testing of (1) compliance with laws, regulations, contracts, or grant agreements and (2) internal control over financial reporting. It should present the findings or refer to separate reports containing that information.

20.1.2. When performing an audit of a city that is subject to the requirements of the federal Single Audit Act, an auditor should adhere to

A. Governmental Accounting Standards Board General Standards.

B. Governmental Finance Officers Association Governmental Accounting, Auditing, and Financial Reporting Principles.

C. *Government Auditing Standards*.

D. Securities and Exchange Commission Regulation S-X.

Answer (C) is correct. *(CPA, adapted)*

REQUIRED: The standards for an audit of a city that is subject to the requirements of the federal Single Audit Act.

DISCUSSION: The Single Audit Act establishes audit requirements for recipients of federal awards administered by nonfederal entities. The act requires that audits of such entities be in accordance with *Government Auditing Standards* issued by the GAO. OMB *Audit Requirements for Federal Awards* (2 CFR 200) Compliance Supplement and related GAAS also apply. The act and the OMB guidance state certain requirements that exceed those of the GAO's Standards.

20.1.3. The purpose of performance auditing is to determine if the desired results of a program are being achieved. The first step in conducting such an audit is to

A. Evaluate the system used to measure results.

B. Determine the time frame to be audited.

C. Collect quantifiable data on the program's success or failure.

D. Identify the legislative intent of the program being audited.

Answer (D) is correct. *(CIA, adapted)*

REQUIRED: The first step in conducting a governmental performance audit.

DISCUSSION: Performance audits provide findings or conclusions based on an evaluation of sufficient appropriate evidence against stated criteria, such as specific requirements, measures, or defined business practices. Performance audit objectives vary widely. One example is assessing the extent to which legislative goals are being achieved. It attempts to measure the accomplishments and relative success of the undertaking. However, this measurement depends on the actual intent of the legislation that established the program.

Answer (A) is incorrect. Evaluating the system used to measure results is a subsequent step in a performance audit. Answer (B) is incorrect. Determining the time frame to be audited is a subsequent step in a performance audit. Answer (C) is incorrect. Collecting quantifiable data on the program's success or failure is a subsequent step in a performance audit.

20.1.4. An auditor was engaged to conduct a performance audit of a governmental entity in accordance with *Government Auditing Standards*. These standards do not require the auditor to report

A. The audit objectives and the audit scope and methodology.

B. All significant instances of noncompliance and instances of abuse.

C. The views of the audited program's responsible officials concerning the auditor's findings.

D. A concurrent opinion on the financial statements taken as a whole.

Answer (D) is correct. *(CPA, adapted)*

REQUIRED: The action not required of an auditor engaged in a performance audit of a governmental entity in accordance with *Government Auditing Standards*.

DISCUSSION: Performance audits relate to assessing (1) program effectiveness and results; (2) economy and efficiency; (3) internal control; (4) compliance with legal requirements; or (5) providing prospective analysis, guidance, or summary information. There is no requirement that a financial audit be conducted simultaneously or concurrently with a performance audit.

Answer (A) is incorrect. The audit objectives and the audit scope and methodology is a part of the auditor's report based on a performance audit. Answer (B) is incorrect. All significant instances of noncompliance and instances of abuse are a part of the auditor's report based on a performance audit. Answer (C) is incorrect. The views of the audited program's responsible officials concerning the auditor's findings is a part of the auditor's report based on a performance audit.

20.1.5. In reporting under *Government Auditing Standards*, an auditor most likely would be required to report a falsification of accounting records directly to a federal inspector general when the falsification is

A. Discovered after the auditor's report has been made available to the federal inspector general and to the public.

B. Reported by the auditor to the audit committee as a significant deficiency in internal control.

C. Voluntarily disclosed to the auditor by low-level personnel as a result of the auditor's inquiries.

D. Communicated by the auditor to the auditee and the auditee fails to make a required report of the matter.

Answer (D) is correct. *(CPA, adapted)*

REQUIRED: The time when an auditor is required to report externally under *Government Auditing Standards*.

DISCUSSION: Under *Government Auditing Standards*, auditors should report fraud, noncompliance, and abuse directly to parties outside the auditee (for example, to a federal inspector general or a state attorney general) in two circumstances. These requirements are in addition to any legal requirements for direct reporting. First, if auditors have communicated such fraud, noncompliance, or abuse to the auditee and (s)he fails to report them, the auditors should communicate their awareness of that failure to the auditee's governing body. If the auditee does not make the required report as soon as practicable after the auditor's communication with its governing body, the auditors should report the fraud, noncompliance, or abuse directly to the external party specified in the law or regulation. Second, management is responsible for taking timely and appropriate steps to remedy fraud, noncompliance, or abuse that auditors report to it. When fraud, noncompliance, or abuse involves assistance received directly or indirectly from a government agency, auditors may have a duty to report it directly if management fails to take remedial steps. If auditors conclude that such failure is likely to cause them to depart from the standard report or resign from the audit, they should communicate that conclusion to the auditee's governing body. Then, if the auditee does not report the fraud, noncompliance, or abuse as soon as practicable to the entity that provided the government assistance, the auditors should report directly to that entity.

20.1.6. The services provided by government auditors may extend beyond the expression of an opinion on the fairness of financial presentation to include reporting on

	Performance	Compliance	Economy & Efficiency
A.	Yes	Yes	No
B.	Yes	Yes	Yes
C.	No	Yes	Yes
D.	Yes	No	Yes

Answer (B) is correct. *(CPA, adapted)*

REQUIRED: The scope of a governmental audit.

DISCUSSION: Under *Government Auditing Standards*, the types of engagements addressed include (1) financial audits (financial statement audits and other types, such as compliance with specified regulations for federal award expenditures), (2) performance audits, and (3) attestation engagements (e.g., reporting on compliance with specified laws, regulations, rules, contracts, or grant agreements). Performance audits include many objectives, such as assessing (1) program effectiveness and results, (2) economy and efficiency, (3) internal control, and (4) compliance with legal requirements.

20.1.7. How does Office of Management and Budget *Audit Requirements for Federal Awards* (2 CFR 200) define a subrecipient?

A. As a nonfederal entity that provides a federal award to another entity to carry out a federal program.

B. As an individual who receives and expends federal awards received from a pass-through entity.

C. As a dealer, distributor, merchant, or other seller providing goods or services that are required for the conduct of a federal program.

D. As a nonfederal entity that expends federal awards received from another entity to carry out a federal program.

Answer (D) is correct. *(CPA, adapted)*

REQUIRED: The definition of a subrecipient.

DISCUSSION: OMB *Audit Requirements for Federal Awards* (2 CFR 200) defines a subrecipient as a nonfederal entity that expends federal awards received from another entity, often another governmental body, to carry out a federal program.

Answer (A) is incorrect. A subrecipient expends funds received from another entity. Answer (B) is incorrect. The entity making the award may be, but need not be, a pass-through entity. Answer (C) is incorrect. The subrecipient may be any form of entity that is awarded and expends funds to carry out a federal program.

20.1.8. The financial auditor's report on internal control and compliance in accordance with *Government Auditing Standards* (the Yellow Book) is required to include

I. The scope of the auditor's testing of internal control.

II. Uncorrected misstatements that were determined by management to be immaterial.

A. I only.

B. II only.

C. Both I and II.

D. Neither I nor II.

Answer (A) is correct. *(CPA, adapted)*

REQUIRED: The item(s), if any, included in the report on internal control and compliance in accordance with GAGAS.

DISCUSSION: When providing an opinion or a disclaimer on financial statements, auditors also should report on (1) internal control over financial reporting and (2) compliance with laws, regulations, contracts, or grant agreements that have a material effect on the financial statements. Auditors report on internal control and compliance regardless of whether they identify internal control deficiencies or instances of noncompliance. Auditors should include, either in the same or in separate report(s), a description of the scope of the auditors' testing of (1) internal control over financial reporting and (2) compliance. Auditors also should state in the reports whether the tests they performed provided sufficient appropriate evidence to support opinions on the effectiveness of internal control and on compliance.

Answer (B) is incorrect. The auditor's report is not necessarily required to include uncorrected misstatements that were determined by management to be immaterial. Under the SASs, which are included in GAGAS, the auditor should determine whether uncorrected misstatements are material. Answer (C) is incorrect. The auditor's report is not necessarily required to include uncorrected misstatements that were determined by management to be immaterial. Answer (D) is incorrect. The scope of the auditor's testing of internal control should be included in the auditor's report.

20.1.9. Tell, CPA, is auditing the financial statements of Youth Services Co. (YSC), a not-for-profit organization, in accordance with GAGAS as promulgated in *Government Auditing Standards*. Tell's report on YSC's compliance with laws and regulations is required to contain statements of

	Positive Assurance	Negative Assurance
A.	Yes	Yes
B.	Yes	No
C.	No	Yes
D.	No	No

Answer (D) is correct. *(CPA, adapted)*

REQUIRED: The assurance, if any, provided regarding compliance in a report on a financial statement audit in accordance with GAGAS.

DISCUSSION: An additional GAGAS requirement for reporting on financial audits states, in part, that the report should either (1) describe the scope of the auditors' testing of internal control over financial reporting and of compliance with laws and regulations and present the results of those tests or (2) refer to a separate report containing that information. No statement of assurance is required. However, the auditor should report whether tests provide sufficient appropriate evidence to support an opinion on internal control and on compliance, etc.

20.1.10. Which of the following statements represents a quality control requirement under *Government Auditing Standards*?

A. A CPA who conducts government audits is required to undergo an annual external peer review when an appropriate internal quality control system is not in place.

B. A CPA seeking to enter into a contract to perform an audit should provide the CPA's most recent external peer review report to the party contracting for the audit.

C. An external peer review of a CPA's practice should include a review of the working papers of each government audit performed since the prior external quality control review.

D. A CPA who conducts government audits may not make the CPA's external quality control review report available to the public.

Answer (B) is correct. *(CPA, adapted)*

REQUIRED: The quality control requirement under *Government Auditing Standards*.

DISCUSSION: According to *Government Auditing Standards*, an audit organization conducting an audit in accordance with these standards must have an appropriate internal quality control system in place and undergo an external peer review at least every 3 years. For example, a CPA seeking to enter into a contract to perform an audit should provide the CPA's most recent external peer review report to the party contracting for the audit.

Answer (A) is incorrect. Organizations conducting audits in accordance with the *Government Audit Standards* should have an external peer review at least once every 3 years. Answer (C) is incorrect. An external peer review consists of (1) review of the auditors' quality control practices, (2) consideration of internal monitoring, (3) review of selected auditors' reports and documentation, (4) review of other documentation, and (5) interviews with professional staff. Answer (D) is incorrect. Audit organizations should ordinarily make their external peer review reports available to auditors during their work and to appropriate oversight bodies. The report also should be made available to the public.

20.1.11. Reporting on internal control over financial reporting as part of a financial audit under generally accepted governmental auditing standards (GAGAS) requires a

A. Written report describing the entity's controls specifically designed to achieve the internal control objectives of safeguarding of assets and compliance with laws and regulations.

B. Written report describing each significant deficiency observed, including identification of those considered material weaknesses.

C. Statement of negative assurance that the controls not tested have an immaterial effect on the entity's financial statements.

D. Statement of positive assurance that controls designed to detect material errors and fraud were tested.

Answer (B) is correct. *(CPA, adapted)*

REQUIRED: The requirement of GAGAS regarding reports on internal control.

DISCUSSION: When performing GAGAS financial audits, auditors should communicate in the report on internal control over financial reporting and compliance based upon the work performed. The following are communicated: (1) significant deficiencies and material weaknesses in internal control; (2) instances of fraud and noncompliance with provisions of laws or regulations that have a material effect on the audit, and any other instances that warrant the attention of those charged with governance; (3) noncompliance with provisions of contracts or grant agreements that has a material effect on the audit; and (4) abuse that has a material effect on the audit.

Answer (A) is incorrect. Identification of specific controls in not required under GAGAS. However, under GAGAS, auditors should report the scope of their testing of internal control over financial reporting, including whether the test provided sufficient appropriate evidence to support an opinion on internal control. Answer (C) is incorrect. GAGAS do not require expression of any form of assurance on internal control. Answer (D) is incorrect. GAGAS do not require expression of any form of assurance on internal control.

20.1.12. An auditor most likely will be responsible for communicating significant deficiencies in the design of internal controls

A. To a court-appointed creditors' committee when the client is operating under Chapter 11 of the Federal Bankruptcy Code.

B. To shareholders with significant influence (more than 20% equity ownership) when the deficiencies are deemed to be material weaknesses.

C. To the Securities and Exchange Commission when the client is a publicly held entity.

D. To specific legislative and regulatory bodies when reporting under *Government Auditing Standards*.

Answer (D) is correct. *(CPA, adapted)*

REQUIRED: The circumstance in which an auditor is likely responsible for communicating significant deficiencies in internal control.

DISCUSSION: An auditor is required to include significant deficiencies and material weaknesses in internal control over financial reporting in a report prepared under *Government Auditing Standards*. The report is required to be distributed to those charged with governance, to the appropriate officials of the audited entity, and to the appropriate oversight bodies or organizations requiring or arranging for the audits.

Answer (A) is incorrect. Management is responsible for providing audited financial statements to a creditors' committee. Answer (B) is incorrect. The auditor's report is included with the audited financial statements in the annual report, a document that is available to all shareholders. Answer (C) is incorrect. The opinion on internal control of an issuer discloses material weaknesses but not significant deficiencies.

20.1.13. Which of the following is a documentation requirement that an auditor should follow in a financial audit in accordance with *Government Auditing Standards*?

A. The audit documentation should contain copies of documents examined.

B. The auditor should document the supervisory review of the evidence that supports the findings, conclusions, and recommendations contained in the auditors' report.

C. The auditor should document all deficiencies in internal control discovered during the audit.

D. The audit documentation should contain a caveat that all instances of material errors and fraud may not be identified.

Answer (B) is correct. *(CPA, adapted)*

REQUIRED: The documentation requirement under *Government Auditing Standards*.

DISCUSSION: In addition to the AICPA requirements for audit documentation, auditors should comply with certain requirements when performing a GAGAS financial audit. These requirements include documenting (1) supervisory review, before the report release date, of the evidence that supports the findings, conclusions, and recommendations contained in the auditors' report and (2) any departures from GAGAS and the effects on the audit and on the auditors' conclusions when the audit does not comply with GAGAS due to (a) law, (b) regulation, (c) scope limitations, (d) restrictions on access to records, or (e) other issues.

Answer (A) is incorrect. Auditors are not required to include copies of documents examined or to list detailed information from those documents. Answer (C) is incorrect. The auditor is required to communicate only significant deficiencies and material weaknesses in internal control. Answer (D) is incorrect. This type of caveat is appropriate for the auditor's report, but it need not be stated in the audit documentation.

20.1.14. In accordance with the general standard on independence stated in *Government Auditing Standards*, an audit organization may perform nonaudit services that do not violate the overarching principles that the standard is based on. Thus, the audit organization most likely may do which of the following without impairing its independence with respect to the audited entity?

A. Perform internal audit services.

B. Prepare tax filings.

C. Operate the audited entity's information technology system.

D. Prepare accounting records.

Answer (B) is correct. *(Publisher, adapted)*

REQUIRED: The activity most likely to be permissible under the independence standard.

DISCUSSION: The audit organization and the individual auditor, whether government or public, should be independent in mind and appearance. Audit organizations should not provide nonaudit services involving management functions or making management decisions, and audit organizations should not audit their own work or provide nonaudit services when the services are significant or material to the subject matter of the audits. Accordingly, an audit organization may, for example, prepare and draft financial statements if prepared by management, prepare routine tax filings, advise on IT system design, or advise on control self-assessment.

Answer (A) is incorrect. Audit organizations may not perform internal audit services unless they reasonably conclude that they will not examine their own work during the audit. Answer (C) is incorrect. Prohibited nonaudit services include operating the IT system. Answer (D) is incorrect. Prohibited nonaudit services include preparing and maintaining accounting records.

20.1.15. In a financial audit under *Government Auditing Standards*, procedures have disclosed material instances of noncompliance with regulations. The report should

A. Also disclose immaterial instances of noncompliance.

B. Indicate that the audit was designed to provide reasonable assurance that noncompliance that could result in criminal prosecution would be detected.

C. Express a qualified opinion.

D. Place the findings in proper perspective.

Answer (D) is correct. *(Publisher, adapted)*

REQUIRED: The necessary element of a report on a financial audit given material noncompliance with regulations.

DISCUSSION: To give the reader a basis for judging the prevalence and consequences of deficiencies in internal control, fraud, noncompliance, and abuse, the instances identified should be related to the population or the number of cases examined and be quantified in terms of monetary amounts, if appropriate.

Answer (A) is incorrect. Auditors may detect significant instances of (1) noncompliance with provisions of contracts or grant agreements or (2) abuse that have an effect on the financial statements (or other financial data) that are less than material but warrant the attention of those charged with governance. In such circumstances, they should communicate those findings in writing to audited entity officials. When auditors detect any instances of (1) fraud; (2) noncompliance with provisions of laws, regulations, contracts, or grant agreements; or (3) abuse that do not warrant the attention of those charged with governance, the auditors' determination of whether and how to communicate such instances to audited entity officials is a matter of professional judgment. Answer (B) is incorrect. The auditor's duty regarding noncompliance is defined by AU-C 250, *Consideration of Laws and Regulations in an Audit of Financial Statements*. The auditor's responsibility is to obtain sufficient appropriate evidence about material items in the statements determined by laws and regulations having direct effects on such determinations. For laws and regulations not having such direct effects, the auditor's responsibility is limited to performing specified procedures. Answer (C) is incorrect. Whether the opinion should be modified cannot be determined from the facts given. If noncompliance materially affects the statements and is not adequately reflected in them, a qualified or adverse opinion should be expressed on the statements. In other circumstances, a disclaimer of opinion should be expressed.

20.2 Compliance Audits

20.2.1. Before issuing an unmodified report on a compliance audit, an auditor becomes aware of an instance of material noncompliance occurring after the period covered by the audit. The least appropriate response by the auditor would be to

A. Discuss the matter with management and, if appropriate, those charged with governance.

B. Issue a qualified compliance report describing the subsequent noncompliance.

C. Determine whether the noncompliance relates to conditions that existed as of period end or arose subsequent to the reporting period.

D. Modify the standard compliance report to include a paragraph describing the nature of the subsequent noncompliance.

Answer (B) is correct. *(CPA, adapted)*

REQUIRED: The least appropriate response to subsequent discovery of noncompliance on a compliance audit.

DISCUSSION: In any situation, a material instance of noncompliance occurring before issuance of the report will require disclosure in the report.

Answer (A) is incorrect. Discussing this issue with management and those charged with governance to determine how it might impact the engagement is appropriate. Answer (C) is incorrect. The effect of the noncompliance on the audit report depends on whether the condition existed at the end of the period or after that date. Answer (D) is incorrect. The auditor must determine the effect of the noncompliance before deciding the appropriate report to issue.

20.2.2. In a compliance audit, the auditor's primary objective is to

A. Determine that all instances of noncompliance are discovered and reported.

B. Test and express an opinion on internal control over compliance.

C. Obtain sufficient appropriate evidence to form an opinion on compliance.

D. Provide management with recommendations for improvement over compliance.

Answer (C) is correct. *(Publisher, adapted)*

REQUIRED: The auditor's primary objective in a compliance audit.

DISCUSSION: The auditor's objective in a compliance audit is to obtain sufficient appropriate evidence to form an opinion and report at the level specified in the governmental audit requirement on whether the entity complied, in all material respects, with the applicable compliance requirements.

Answer (A) is incorrect. Only instances of material noncompliance need be reported on. Answer (B) is incorrect. Although the auditor considers internal control in planning the audit, no opinion is required. Answer (D) is incorrect. An audit of compliance does not require the auditor to provide recommendations for improvement over compliance.

20.2.3. In an audit of an entity's compliance with applicable compliance requirements, an auditor obtains written representations from management acknowledging

A. Its responsibilities for compliance, including disclosure of noncompliance.

B. Implementation of controls designed to detect all noncompliance.

C. Expression of positive assurance to the auditor that the entity complied with all applicable compliance requirements.

D. Employment of internal auditors who can report their findings, opinions, and conclusions objectively.

Answer (A) is correct. *(Publisher, adapted)*

REQUIRED: The representations obtained from management in a compliance audit.

DISCUSSION: The auditor obtains written representations from management about its responsibilities for (1) understanding and complying with the compliance requirements and (2) establishing and maintaining controls that provide reasonable assurance that the entity administers government programs in accordance with the compliance requirements. Among other things, the auditor also requests representations that management has disclosed all known noncompliance with the applicable compliance requirements, including that subsequent to the period covered by the auditor's report.

Answer (B) is incorrect. Management should disclose all known noncompliance. Given the inherent limitations of internal control, it cannot be expected to prevent or detect all noncompliance. Answer (C) is incorrect. In a compliance audit, management does not express an opinion that it has complied with all applicable compliance requirements. Answer (D) is incorrect. The entity will decide whether to employ internal auditors.

20.2.4. A material weakness in internal control over compliance arises when

A. At a minimum, a deficiency is important enough to merit attention by those charged with governance.

B. A reasonable possibility exists that material noncompliance will not be prevented or timely detected and corrected.

C. A risk of material noncompliance exists prior to the audit.

D. The design or operation of a control does not allow management or employees to detect noncompliance in the normal course of their duties.

Answer (B) is correct. *(Publisher, adapted)*

REQUIRED: The definition of a material weakness.

DISCUSSION: A material weakness in internal control over compliance is a deficiency, or combination of deficiencies, in internal control over compliance that results in a reasonable possibility that material noncompliance with a compliance requirement will not be prevented, or detected and corrected, on a timely basis.

Answer (A) is incorrect. A significant deficiency in internal control over compliance is a deficiency, or a combination of deficiencies, in internal control over compliance that is less severe than a material weakness yet merits attention by those charged with governance. Answer (C) is incorrect. The risk of material noncompliance prior to the audit is the combination of the inherent risk of noncompliance and the control risk of noncompliance. Answer (D) is incorrect. A deficiency in internal control over compliance exists when the design or operation of a control over compliance does not allow management or employees, in the normal course of performing their assigned functions, to prevent, or detect and correct, noncompliance on a timely basis.

20.2.5. When an auditor is performing a compliance audit and identifies pervasive risks of material noncompliance, the auditor should

A. Withdraw from the engagement.

B. Develop an overall response to such risks.

C. Perform additional analytical procedures.

D. Issue a disclaimer of opinion.

Answer (B) is correct. *(Publisher, adapted)*

REQUIRED: The auditor's response to pervasive risks of noncompliance.

DISCUSSION: The auditor should develop an overall response to such risks. For example, the auditor may use more experienced staff or increase supervision.

Answer (A) is incorrect. The auditor need not withdraw from the engagement and should attempt to mitigate risks by developing an overall response to such risks. Answer (C) is incorrect. The use of analytical procedures to gather substantive evidence is generally less effective in a compliance audit than it is in a financial statement audit. Answer (D) is incorrect. The auditor should attempt to mitigate risks by developing an overall response to such risks.

20.3 Federal Audit Requirements and the Single Audit Act

20.3.1. The Single Audit Act is intended to be the definitive legislation concerning the audit of federal awards administered by nonfederal entities. Which of the following statements is a false statement about the act?

A. The single audit concept changes the focus from individual grants to grant recipients.

B. The act requires federal auditors to rely on single audit findings, to base any supplemental auditing on them, and to pay any additional auditing costs.

C. The auditor must designate one of the grant providers as a cognizant agency to act as a liaison between the auditee and the federal agencies providing funds.

D. Audit reporting should cover an opinion on the fairness of the financial statements, a report on internal control, and a report on compliance with grant requirements.

Answer (C) is correct. *(Publisher, adapted)*

REQUIRED: The false statement about the Single Audit Act.

DISCUSSION: A recipient expending more than $50 million per year in federal awards must have a cognizant agency for audit. The designated agency is the federal awarding agency that provides the predominant amount of direct funding, unless the OMB specifies another cognizant agency or the cognizant agency reassigns cognizance to another federal awarding agency. The cognizant agency overseeing the audit process acts as a liaison among the auditor, the auditee, and the granting agencies. Guidance for the application of the Single Audit Act is provided in OMB *Audit Requirements for Federal Awards* (2 CFR 200). Generally accepted governmental auditing standards (GAGAS) and generally accepted auditing standards (GAAS) apply when appropriate.

Answer (A) is incorrect. The single audit concept changes the focus of audits from individual grants to the grant recipients. Answer (B) is incorrect. The act requires federal auditors to rely on single audit findings. Answer (D) is incorrect. The audit report or reports should cover the financial statements, internal control, and compliance with grant requirements.

20.3.2. In an audit of compliance with requirements governing awards under major federal programs performed in accordance with the Single Audit Act, the auditor's consideration of materiality differs from materiality under generally accepted auditing standards. Under the Single Audit Act, materiality for the purpose of reporting an audit finding is

A. Calculated in relation to the financial statements taken as a whole.

B. Determined in relation to a type of compliance requirement for a major program.

C. Decided in conjunction with the auditor's risk assessment.

D. Ignored, because all account balances, regardless of size, are fully tested.

Answer (B) is correct. *(CPA, adapted)*

REQUIRED: The materiality determination under the Single Audit Act.

DISCUSSION: Under the Single Audit Act, the emphasis of the audit effort is on major programs related to federal awards administered by nonfederal entities. According to OMB *Audit Requirements for Federal Awards* (2 CFR 200) Compliance Supplement adopted under the Single Audit Act, the schedule of findings and questioned costs includes instances of material noncompliance with laws, regulations, contracts, or grant agreements related to a major program. The auditor's determination of whether a noncompliance is material for the purpose of reporting an audit finding is in relation to a type of compliance requirement for a major program or an audit objective identified in the OMB 2 CFR 200 Compliance Supplement. Examples of types of compliance requirements include (1) activities allowed or unallowed; (2) allowable costs/cost principles; (3) cash management; (4) eligibility; (5) matching, level of effort, and earmarking; and (6) reporting.

Answer (A) is incorrect. In a for-profit financial statement audit, materiality is related to the financial statements as a whole. Answer (C) is incorrect. Risk assessment is performed in planning the audit, but once the auditor makes a finding, the decision to report it is contingent on the materiality to the major program. Answer (D) is incorrect. Materiality should be considered in determining the appropriate tests to be applied.

20.3.3. Under the Single Audit Act, the auditor should report on compliance with laws, regulations, and the provisions of contracts or grant agreements, noncompliance with which could have a material effect on the financial statements. This report should also express or disclaim an opinion on whether the auditee complied with laws, etc., that could have a direct and material effect on each major program. In accordance with the act and OMB *Audit Requirements for Federal Awards* (2 CFR 200) Compliance Supplement, which contains policies, procedures, and guidelines to implement the act, the auditor

A. Is not responsible for identifying major federal programs.

B. Should apply a concept of materiality in the audit of major federal programs that is similar to that in an audit under GAAS.

C. Should determine whether the recipient has engaged in activities to which particular types of compliance requirements apply.

D. Is required to restrict control risk and assess inherent and detection risk.

Answer (C) is correct. *(Publisher, adapted)*

REQUIRED: The true statement about compliance auditing of major federal financial assistance programs.

DISCUSSION: OMB guidance lists the types of compliance requirements, e.g., (1) activities allowed or unallowed; (2) allowable costs or cost principles; (3) cash management; (4) eligibility; (5) matching, level of effort, and earmarking; and (6) reporting. The data collection form submitted by the auditee should include, for each federal program, a yes or no statement as to whether there are audit findings for each of the types of compliance requirements and the total of any questioned costs.

Answer (A) is incorrect. The auditor determines whether a federal program is major. The auditor uses a risk-based approach that considers current and prior audit experience, oversight by federal agencies and pass-through entities, and the inherent risk of the program. Most large programs (Type A), except those determined to be low risk, and smaller programs (Type B, i.e., non-Type A programs that meet one of two quantitative thresholds) determined to be high risk are audited as major programs. A federal agency or pass-through entity may also request that a program be audited as a major program. Answer (B) is incorrect. Under the act, the materiality of an instance of noncompliance is in relation to a type of compliance requirement for a major program or an audit objective identified in the OMB guidance. Answer (D) is incorrect. The auditor assesses inherent and control risk and restricts detection risk.

20.3.4. An auditor is auditing a nonfederal entity's administration of a federal award pursuant to a major program under the Single Audit Act. The auditor is required to

	Obtain Evidence Related to Compliance	Express or Disclaim an Opinion on Compliance
A.	Yes	Yes
B.	Yes	No
C.	No	Yes
D.	No	No

Answer (A) is correct. *(Publisher, adapted)*

REQUIRED: The auditor's responsibility in a compliance audit.

DISCUSSION: After an audit of a nonfederal entity that expends federal awards, the audit report on compliance should include an opinion or a disclaimer of opinion as to whether the auditee complied with the applicable compliance requirements, that is, with laws, regulations, rules, and the provisions of contracts or grants. This report also should describe identified noncompliance or refer to an accompanying schedule of noncompliance.

20.3.5. Wolf is auditing an entity's compliance with requirements governing a major federal program in accordance with the Single Audit Act. Wolf detected noncompliance with requirements that have a material effect on the program. Wolf's report on compliance should express

A. No assurance on the compliance tests.

B. Reasonable assurance on the compliance tests.

C. A qualified or adverse opinion.

D. An adverse opinion or a disclaimer of opinion.

Answer (C) is correct. *(CPA, adapted)*

REQUIRED: The assurance about compliance given noncompliance with material requirements.

DISCUSSION: Under the Single Audit Act, the auditor should express an opinion on compliance with requirements having a direct and material effect on a major federal program or state that an opinion cannot be expressed. When the compliance audit detects noncompliance with those requirements that the auditor believes have a direct and material effect on the program, the auditor should express a qualified or adverse opinion. The auditor should state the basis for such an opinion in the report.

Answer (A) is incorrect. The auditor should express an opinion on compliance. Answer (B) is incorrect. The auditor's report should state that the audit was planned and performed to provide reasonable assurance about whether material noncompliance occurred. Answer (D) is incorrect. A disclaimer is not appropriate when the auditor has detected material noncompliance.

STUDY UNIT TWENTY-ONE
INTERNAL AUDITING

The Institute of Internal Auditors (The IIA) governs the professional practice of internal auditing worldwide. Its mission is "[t]o enhance and protect organizational value by providing risk-based and objective assurance, advice, and insight." Accordingly, The IIA has issued an extensive body of professional literature.

The IIA's International Professional Practices Framework (IPPF) contains both mandatory guidance and recommended guidance. The IIA considers adherence to the **mandatory guidance** essential for the professional practice of internal auditing. The mandatory guidance consists of four elements: (1) the Core Principles for the Professional Practice of Internal Auditing, (2) the Definition of Internal Auditing, (3) the Code of Ethics, and (4) the *Standards*. The Definition of Internal Auditing is a concise statement of the role of internal audit within the organization.

Internal auditing is defined as an independent, objective assurance and consulting activity designed to add value and improve an organization's operations. It helps an organization accomplish its objectives by bringing a systematic, disciplined approach to the evaluation and improvement of the effectiveness of risk management, control, and governance processes.

The *Standards* (known formally as the *International Standards for the Professional Practice of Internal Auditing*) serve the following four purposes:

1. Guide adherence to the mandatory elements of the International Professional Practices Framework
2. Provide a framework for performing and promoting a broad range of value-added internal auditing services
3. Establish the basis for the evaluation of internal audit performance
4. Foster improved organizational processes and operations

The *Standards* are of three types.

1. **Attribute Standards**, numbered in the 1000s, describe the professional requirements that apply to the organizations and people who perform internal auditing.
2. **Performance Standards**, numbered in the 2000s, govern the nature of internal auditing and establish quality criteria for evaluating the internal audit function's performance.
   - **Interpretations** are provided by The IIA to clarify terms and concepts referred to in Attribute or Performance Standards.
3. **Implementation Standards** expand upon individual Attribute or Performance Standards.
   - Attribute and Performance Standards apply to all internal audit engagements, but each Implementation Standard describes only the requirements of either an **assurance** or a **consulting** engagement.

The recommended guidance (Implementation Guidance and Supplemental Guidance) was developed by The IIA through a formal approval process. It describes practices for effective application of the Core Principles, the Definition of Internal Auditing, the Code of Ethics, and the *Standards*. Implementation Guidance consists of Implementation Guides, which state internal audit approaches, methods, and matters to be considered. Supplemental Guidance consists of Practice Guides, Global Technology Audit Guides, and Guides to the Assessment of IT Risk. They address detailed internal audit activities, such as procedures, processes, and programs.

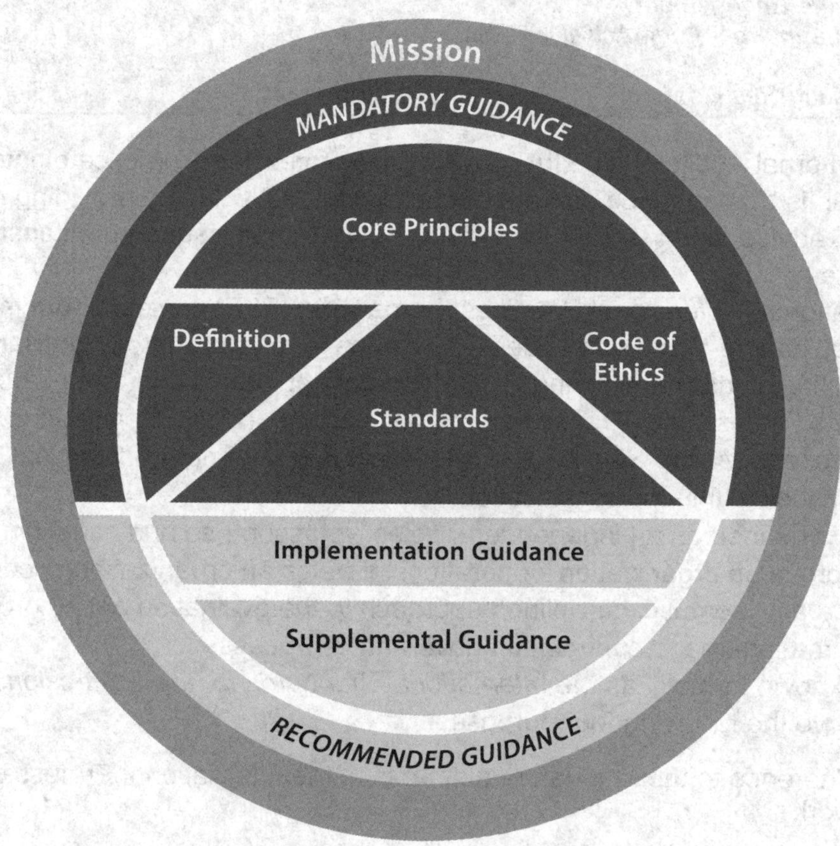

QUESTIONS

21.1 Introduction to Internal Auditing

21.1.1. The proper organizational role of internal auditing is to

A. Assist the external auditor to reduce external audit fees.

B. Perform studies to assist in the attainment of more efficient operations.

C. Serve as the investigative arm of the board.

D. Serve as an independent, objective assurance and consulting activity that adds value to operations.

Answer (D) is correct. *(CIA, adapted)*

REQUIRED: The role of internal auditing.

DISCUSSION: The Definition of Internal Auditing states, in part, “Internal auditing is an independent, objective assurance and consulting activity designed to add value and improve an organization’s operations.”

Answer (A) is incorrect. Reducing external audit fees may be a direct result of internal audit work, but it is not a reason for staffing an internal audit activity. Answer (B) is incorrect. The primary role of internal auditing includes, but is not limited to, assessing the efficiency of operations. Answer (C) is incorrect. Internal auditors serve management as well as the board.

21.1.2. Internal auditing has planned an engagement to evaluate the effectiveness of the quality assurance function as it affects the receipt of goods, the transfer of the goods into production, and the scrap costs related to defective items. The engagement client argues that such an engagement is not within the scope of the internal audit activity and should come under the purview of the quality assurance department only. What is the most appropriate response?

A. Refer to the internal audit activity's charter and the approved engagement plan that includes the area designated for evaluation in the current time period.

B. Because quality assurance is a new function, seek the approval of management as a mediator to set the scope of the engagement.

C. Indicate that the engagement will evaluate the function only in accordance with the standards set by, and approved by, the quality assurance function before beginning the engagement.

D. Terminate the engagement because it will not be productive without the client's cooperation.

Answer (A) is correct. *(CIA, adapted)*

REQUIRED: The response to an assertion that evaluating quality assurance is beyond the scope of internal auditing.

DISCUSSION: The written charter, approved by the board, defines the scope of internal audit activities (Inter. Std. 1000). The risk-based plan of engagements is established after consultation with senior management and the board and is adjusted for changes in the organization (Inter. Std. 2010).

Answer (B) is incorrect. The engagement client does not determine the scope of this type of assurance engagement. A scope limitation imposed by the client might prevent the internal audit activity from achieving its objectives. Answer (C) is incorrect. Other objectives may be established by management and the internal auditors. The engagement is not limited to the specific standards set by the quality assurance department. It considers such standards in the development of the engagement program. Answer (D) is incorrect. The internal auditors must conduct the engagement and communicate any scope limitations to management and the board.

21.1.3. An internal auditor often faces special problems when performing an engagement at a foreign subsidiary. Which of the following statements is false with respect to the conduct of international engagements?

A. The IIA *Standards* do not apply outside of the United States.

B. The internal auditor should determine whether managers are in compliance with local laws.

C. There may be justification for having different organizational policies in force in foreign branches.

D. It is preferable to have multilingual internal auditors conduct engagements at branches in foreign nations.

Answer (A) is correct. *(CIA, adapted)*

REQUIRED: The false statement with respect to the conduct of international audits.

DISCUSSION: Pronouncements by The IIA have no geographic limits. Compliance with the concepts in the *Standards* is essential for the responsibilities of internal auditors to be met, regardless of the national environment.

Answer (B) is incorrect. The internal audit activity must evaluate the adequacy and effectiveness of controls, including those relating to compliance with laws, regulations, policies, procedures, and contracts. Answer (C) is incorrect. Varying laws and customs and other environmental factors justify policy differences. Answer (D) is incorrect. The internal audit activity collectively must possess the knowledge, skills, and other competencies needed to perform its responsibilities.

21.1.4. Internal auditing is an assurance and consulting activity. An example of an assurance service is a(n)

A. Advisory engagement.

B. Facilitation engagement.

C. Training engagement.

D. Compliance engagement.

Answer (D) is correct. *(Publisher, adapted)*

REQUIRED: The example of an assurance service.

DISCUSSION: According to The IIA Glossary, an assurance service is "an objective examination of evidence for the purpose of providing an independent assessment of governance, risk management, and control processes for the organization. Examples may include financial, performance, compliance, system security, and due diligence engagements."

21.1.5. A major reason for establishing an internal audit activity is to

A. Relieve overburdened management of the responsibility for establishing effective controls.

B. Safeguard resources entrusted to the organization.

C. Ensure the reliability and integrity of financial and operational information.

D. Evaluate and improve the effectiveness of control processes.

Answer (D) is correct. *(CIA, adapted)*

REQUIRED: The major reason for establishing an internal audit activity.

DISCUSSION: The internal audit activity helps an organization accomplish its objectives by bringing a systematic, disciplined approach to the evaluation and improvement of the effectiveness of risk management, control, and governance processes (Definition of Internal Auditing).

Answer (A) is incorrect. Management is responsible for the establishment of internal control. Answer (B) is incorrect. Governance, risk management, and control processes ultimately serve to safeguard the organization's resources. Answer (C) is incorrect. Ensuring the reliability and integrity of financial and operational information is a management responsibility.

21.1.6. What is the most accurate term for the procedures used by the board to oversee activities performed to achieve organizational objectives?

A. Governance.

B. Control.

C. Risk management.

D. Monitoring.

Answer (A) is correct. *(Publisher, adapted)*

REQUIRED: The most accurate term for the means of providing oversight of processes administered by management.

DISCUSSION: Governance is the "combination of processes and structures implemented by the board to inform, direct, manage, and monitor the activities of the organization toward the achievement of its objectives" (The IIA Glossary).

Answer (B) is incorrect. Control is "any action taken by management, the board, and other parties to manage risk and increase the likelihood that established objectives and goals will be achieved. Management plans, organizes, and directs the performance of sufficient actions to provide reasonable assurance that objectives and goals will be achieved" (The IIA Glossary). Answer (C) is incorrect. Risk management is "a process to identify, assess, manage, and control potential events or situations to provide reasonable assurance regarding the achievement of the organization's objectives" (The IIA Glossary). Answer (D) is incorrect. Monitoring consists of actions taken by management and others to assess the quality of internal control performance over time. It is not currently defined in the *Standards* or The IIA Glossary. But, in the COSO framework for internal control, it assesses the quality of a system's performance over time. Moreover, the chief audit executive must maintain a system to monitor the disposition of results communicated to management (Standard 2500).

21.1.7. The work of the internal audit activity includes evaluating and contributing to the improvement of risk management systems. Risk is

I. The negative effect of events certain to occur
II. Measured in terms of impact
III. Measured in terms of likelihood

A. I only.

B. I and II only.

C. II and III only.

D. I, II, and III.

Answer (C) is correct. *(Publisher, adapted)*

REQUIRED: The nature of risk.

DISCUSSION: The internal audit activity must evaluate the effectiveness and contribute to the improvement of risk management processes (Perf. Std. 2120). Risk is the possibility of an event's occurrence that will affect the achievement of objectives. Risk is measured in terms of impact and likelihood (The IIA Glossary).

21.1.8. The chief audit executive (CAE) is best defined as the

A. Inspector general.

B. Person responsible for the internal audit function.

C. Outside provider of internal audit services.

D. Person responsible for overseeing the contract with the outside provider of internal audit services.

Answer (B) is correct. *(Publisher, adapted)*

REQUIRED: The best definition of the CAE.

DISCUSSION: The CAE is a person in a senior position responsible for effectively managing the internal audit activity in accordance with the internal audit charter and the mandatory elements of the IPPF (The IIA Glossary).

Answer (A) is incorrect. The specific job title of the chief audit executive may vary across organizations (The IIA Glossary). Answer (C) is incorrect. The internal audit activity may be insourced. Answer (D) is incorrect. The term "chief audit executive" is defined broadly because (1) the internal audit activity may be insourced or outsourced and (2) many different titles are used in practice.

21.1.9. The actions taken to manage risk and increase the likelihood that established objectives and goals will be achieved are best described as

A. Supervision.

B. Quality assurance.

C. Control.

D. Compliance.

Answer (C) is correct. *(Publisher, adapted)*

REQUIRED: The term for actions taken to manage risk and increase the likelihood that established objectives and goals will be achieved.

DISCUSSION: Control is "any action taken by management, the board, and other parties to manage risk and increase the likelihood that established objectives and goals will be achieved" (The IIA Glossary).

Answer (A) is incorrect. Supervision is just one means of achieving control. Answer (B) is incorrect. Quality assurance relates to just one set of objectives and goals. It does not pertain to achievement of all established organizational objectives and goals. Answer (D) is incorrect. Compliance is "adherence to policies, plans, procedures, laws, regulations, contracts, or other requirements" (The IIA Glossary).

21.1.10. The role of the internal audit activity in the promotion of ethics and values in an organization is to

A. Avoid active support of ethics and values because of possible loss of independence.

B. Evaluate the effectiveness of the organization's code of conduct.

C. Assume accountability for the effectiveness of the governance process.

D. Become the chief ethics officer.

Answer (B) is correct. *(Publisher, adapted)*

REQUIRED: The minimum role of the internal audit activity in the promotion of ethics and values in an organization.

DISCUSSION: The internal audit activity assesses and recommends improvements in governance processes for promoting ethics and values in the organization (Perf. Std. 2110). It therefore reviews related objectives, programs, and activities. These may include a code of conduct (IG 2110).

Answer (A) is incorrect. Internal auditors must be active ethics advocates. However, assuming the role of, for example, chief ethics officer may, in some circumstances, impair individual objectivity and the internal audit activity's independence. Answer (C) is incorrect. The organization's board and its senior management are responsible for the effectiveness of the governance process. Answer (D) is incorrect. The internal auditor's basic role is to assess the processes for promoting ethics and values.

21.1.11. Which of the following activities is outside the scope of internal auditing?

A. Evaluating risk exposures regarding compliance with policies, procedures, and contracts.

B. Safeguarding of assets.

C. Evaluating risk exposures regarding compliance with laws and regulations.

D. Ascertaining the extent to which management has established criteria to determine whether objectives have been accomplished.

Answer (B) is correct. *(CIA, adapted)*

REQUIRED: The activity outside the scope of internal auditing.

DISCUSSION: Safeguarding assets is an operational activity and is therefore beyond the scope of the internal audit activity. However, the internal audit activity's assurance function evaluates the adequacy and effectiveness of controls related to the organization's governance, operations, and information systems regarding safeguarding assets (Perf. Std. 2130).

Answer (A) is incorrect. Internal auditors must evaluate risk exposures relating to, among other things, the organization's compliance with laws, regulations, policies, procedures, and contracts. Answer (C) is incorrect. The internal audit activity must evaluate risk exposures relating to, among other things, the organization's compliance with laws, regulations, policies, procedures, and contracts. Answer (D) is incorrect. Ascertaining the extent to which management has established adequate criteria to determine whether objectives have been accomplished is within the scope of internal auditing.

21.1.12. The internal auditors' ultimate responsibility for information security includes

A. Identifying technical aspects, risks, processes, and transactions to be examined.

B. Determining the scope and degree of testing to achieve engagement objectives.

C. Periodically assessing information security practices.

D. Documenting engagement procedures.

Answer (C) is correct. *(Publisher, adapted)*

REQUIRED: The internal auditors' ultimate responsibility for information reliability and integrity.

DISCUSSION: The internal audit activity evaluates the adequacy and effectiveness of controls in responding to risks within governance, operations, and information systems related to the reliability and integrity of financial and operational information (Impl. Std. 2130.A1).

21.1.13. Senior management has requested a compliance audit of the organization's employee benefits package. Which of the following is considered the primary engagement objective by both the chief audit executive and senior management?

A. The level of organizational contributions is adequate to meet the program's demands.

B. Individual programs are operating in accordance with contractual requirements and government regulations.

C. Participation levels support continuation of individual programs.

D. Benefit payments, when appropriate, are accurate and timely.

Answer (B) is correct. *(CIA, adapted)*

REQUIRED: The primary engagement objective of a compliance audit of the employee benefits package.

DISCUSSION: The internal audit activity evaluates risk exposures related to governance, operations, and information systems regarding, among other things, compliance with laws, regulations, and contracts. Based on the risk assessment, the internal audit activity evaluates the adequacy and effectiveness of controls encompassing governance, operations, and information systems. This evaluation should include, among other things, compliance with laws, regulations, policies, procedures, and contracts (Impl. Std. 2120.A1). Operation in accordance with contracts and regulations takes precedence over all other objectives because it relates to the most basic aspects of the programs.

21.1.14. The internal audit activity must evaluate the effectiveness and contribute to the improvement of risk management processes. With respect to evaluating the effectiveness of risk management processes, internal auditors most likely should

A. Recognize that organizations should use similar techniques for managing risk.

B. Determine that risks align with the organization's risk appetite.

C. Determine the level of risks acceptable to the organization.

D. Treat the evaluation of risk management processes in the same manner as the risk analysis used to plan engagements.

Answer (B) is correct. *(Publisher, adapted)*

REQUIRED: The responsibility of internal auditors for assessing the adequacy of risk management processes.

DISCUSSION: Determining whether risk management processes are effective is a judgment resulting from the internal auditor's assessment that (1) organizational objectives support and align with the organization's mission; (2) significant risks are identified and assessed; (3) appropriate risk responses are selected that align risks with the organization's risk appetite; and (4) relevant risk information is captured and communicated in a timely manner across the organization, enabling staff, management, and the board to carry out their responsibilities (Inter. Std. 2120).

Answer (A) is incorrect. Risk management processes vary with the size and complexity of an organization's business activities. Answer (C) is incorrect. Management and the board determine the level of acceptable organizational risks. Answer (D) is incorrect. Evaluating management's risk processes differs from the internal auditors' risk assessment used to plan an engagement, but information from a comprehensive risk management process is useful in such planning.

21.2 Charter, Independence, and Objectivity

21.2.1. An element of authority that must be included in the charter of the internal audit activity is

A. Identification of the organizational units where engagements are to be performed.

B. Identification of the types of disclosures that should be made to the board.

C. Access to records, personnel, and physical properties relevant to the performance of engagements.

D. Access to the external auditor's engagement records.

Answer (C) is correct. *(CIA, adapted)*

REQUIRED: The element of authority that should be included in the charter of the internal audit activity.

DISCUSSION: The charter (1) establishes the internal audit activity's position within the organization, including the nature of the chief audit executive's functional reporting relationship with the board; (2) authorizes access to records, personnel, and physical properties relevant to the performance of engagements; and (3) defines the scope of internal audit activities (Inter. Std. 1000).

Answer (A) is incorrect. The audit schedule is based on a risk assessment; it is thus inappropriate to designate specific engagement areas in the internal audit charter. Answer (B) is incorrect. Disclosure to the board is an obligation, not an element of authority. Answer (D) is incorrect. Access to the external auditor's engagement records cannot be guaranteed.

21.2.2. An external assessment of an internal audit activity contains an expressed opinion. The opinion may apply to

A. Only to the internal audit activity's conformance with the *Standards*.

B. Only to the effectiveness of the internal auditing coverage.

C. Only to the adequacy of internal control.

D. Conformance with the *Standards* and an assessment for each standard.

Answer (D) is correct. *(CIA, adapted)*

REQUIRED: The subject of the opinion expressed in a communication after an external assessment of a quality program.

DISCUSSION: External assessments of an internal audit activity contain an expressed opinion or conclusion on overall conformance with the *Standards* and possibly an assessment for each standard or series of standards. An external assessment also includes, as appropriate, recommendations (corrective action plans) for improvement.

Answer (A) is incorrect. An opinion may be expressed on the *Standards* and an assessment may be made for each standard or series of standards. Answer (B) is incorrect. The scope of an external assessment extends to more than the effectiveness of the internal auditing coverage. Answer (C) is incorrect. An external assessment addresses the internal audit activity, not the adequacy of the organization's controls.

21.2.3. In which of the following situations does an internal auditor potentially lack objectivity?

A. An internal auditor reviews the procedures for a new electronic data interchange (EDI) connection to a major customer before it is implemented.

B. A former purchasing assistant performs a review of internal controls over purchasing 4 months after being transferred to the internal auditing department.

C. An internal auditor recommends standards of control and performance measures for a contract with a service organization for the processing of payroll and employee benefits.

D. A payroll accounting employee assists an internal auditor in verifying the physical inventory of small motors.

Answer (B) is correct. *(CIA, adapted)*

REQUIRED: The situation in which the internal auditor may lack objectivity.

DISCUSSION: Internal auditors must not assess operations for which they were previously responsible. Objectivity is presumed to be impaired if the internal auditor provides assurance services for an activity for which (s)he had responsibility within the previous year (Impl. Std. 1130.A1).

Answer (A) is incorrect. Objectivity is not adversely affected when the internal auditor recommends standards of control for systems or reviews procedures before they are implemented. Answer (C) is incorrect. Objectivity is not adversely affected when the internal auditor recommends standards of control for systems or reviews procedures before they are implemented. Answer (D) is incorrect. Use of staff from other areas to assist the internal auditor does not impair objectivity, especially when the staff is from outside of the area where the engagement is being performed.

21.2.4. A charter is being drafted for a newly formed internal audit activity. Which of the following best describes an appropriate organizational position to be incorporated into the charter?

A. The chief audit executive reports to the chief executive officer but has access to the board.

B. The chief audit executive is a member of the board.

C. The chief audit executive is a staff officer reporting to the chief financial officer.

D. The chief audit executive reports to an administrative vice president.

Answer (A) is correct. *(CIA, adapted)*

REQUIRED: The appropriate organizational position of the internal audit activity.

DISCUSSION: The CAE, reporting functionally to the board and administratively to the organization's CEO, facilitates organizational independence. The CAE must communicate and interact directly with the board (Attr. Std. 1111).

Answer (B) is incorrect. Placing the CAE in a governance position impairs his or her objectivity. Answer (C) is incorrect. Serving as a staff officer and reporting to the CFO limit the influence and independence of the internal audit activity. Answer (D) is incorrect. Reporting to an administrative vice president limits the influence and independence of the internal audit activity.

21.2.5. When faced with an imposed scope limitation, the chief audit executive needs to

A. Refuse to perform the engagement until the scope limitation is removed.

B. Communicate the potential effects of the scope limitation to the board.

C. Increase the frequency of engagements concerning the activity in question.

D. Assign more experienced personnel to the engagement.

Answer (B) is correct. *(CIA, adapted)*

REQUIRED: The appropriate response to an imposed scope limitation.

DISCUSSION: A scope limitation, along with its potential effect, needs to be communicated to the board.

Answer (A) is incorrect. The engagement may be conducted under a scope limitation. Answer (C) is incorrect. A scope limitation does not necessarily require more frequent engagements. Answer (D) is incorrect. A scope limitation does not necessarily require more experienced personnel.

21.2.6. An audit committee of the board of directors of an organization is being established. Which of the following is normally a responsibility of the committee with regard to the internal audit activity?

A. Approval of the selection and dismissal of the chief audit executive.

B. Development of the annual engagement work schedule.

C. Approval of engagement work programs.

D. Determination of engagement observations appropriate for specific engagement communications.

Answer (A) is correct. *(CIA, adapted)*

REQUIRED: The responsibility of an audit committee.

DISCUSSION: Organizational independence is effectively achieved when the CAE reports functionally to the board. One example of functional reporting is the board's approval of the appointment or removal of the CAE (Inter. Std. 1110). The audit committee is a subcommittee of outside directors who are independent of management. The term "board" includes the audit committee.

Answer (B) is incorrect. Development of the annual engagement work schedule is an operational function of the CAE and the internal audit activity staff. A summary of the (1) audit plan, (2) work schedule, (3) staffing plan, and (4) financial budget is submitted annually to senior management and the board. Answer (C) is incorrect. Approval of engagement work programs is a technical responsibility of the internal audit activity staff. Answer (D) is incorrect. The determination of engagement observations appropriate for specific engagement communications is a field operation of the internal audit activity staff.

21.3 Standards and Proficiency

21.3.1. Use of external service providers with expertise in healthcare benefits is appropriate when the internal audit activity is

A. Evaluating the organization's estimate of its liability for postretirement benefits, which include healthcare benefits.

B. Comparing the cost of the organization's healthcare program with other programs offered in the industry.

C. Training its staff to conduct an audit of healthcare costs in a major division of the organization.

D. All of the answers are correct.

Answer (D) is correct. *(CIA, adapted)*

REQUIRED: The reason(s) for using specialists in healthcare benefits.

DISCUSSION: The CAE must obtain competent advice and assistance if the internal auditors lack the knowledge, skills, and other competencies needed to perform all or part of the engagement (Impl. Std. 1210.A1). Thus, external service providers may provide assistance in (1) estimating the liability for postretirement benefits, (2) developing a comparative analysis of healthcare costs, and (3) training the staff to audit healthcare costs.

21.3.2. The purposes of the *Standards* include all of the following except

A. Establishing the basis for the measurement of internal audit performance.

B. Guiding the ethical conduct of internal auditors.

C. Guiding adherence to the mandatory elements of the International Professional Practices Framework.

D. Fostering improved organizational processes and operations.

Answer (B) is correct. *(CIA, adapted)*

REQUIRED: The item not a purpose of the *Standards*.

DISCUSSION: Guiding the ethical conduct of internal auditors is the purpose of the Code of Ethics, not the *Standards*.

Answer (A) is incorrect. Establishing the basis for the evaluation of internal audit performance is one of The IIA's stated purposes of the *Standards*. Answer (C) is incorrect. Guiding adherence to the mandatory elements of the International Professional Practices Framework is one of The IIA's stated purposes of the *Standards*. Answer (D) is incorrect. Fostering improved organizational processes and operations is one of The IIA's stated purposes of the *Standards*.

21.3.3. Internal auditors must possess the knowledge, skills, and other competencies essential to the performance of their individual responsibilities. Consequently, all internal auditors should be competent with regard to

A. Operating within the organization's framework for governance, risk management, and control.

B. Evaluating investments in securities.

C. Applying management principles at the operational level.

D. Performing structured systems analysis.

Answer (A) is correct. *(CIA, adapted)*

REQUIRED: The competency that all internal auditors should possess.

DISCUSSION: The internal audit activity collectively must possess or obtain the knowledge, skills, and other competencies needed to perform its responsibilities (Attr. Std. 1210). Operating within the organization's framework for governance, risk management, and control is a detailed competency supporting the core competency of governance, risk, and control. This detailed competency is recommended for each broad job level (staff, manager, or CAE) of the internal audit activity.

Answer (B) is incorrect. The Competency Framework does not specifically address evaluating investments in securities. Answer (C) is incorrect. The Competency Framework does not specifically address applying management principles at the operational level. Answer (D) is incorrect. The Competency Framework does not specifically address performing structured systems analysis.

21.3.4. Which of the following statements is true with respect to due professional care?

A. An internal auditor should perform detailed tests of all transactions before communicating results.

B. An item should not be mentioned in an engagement communication unless the internal auditor is absolutely certain of the item.

C. An engagement communication should never be viewed as providing an infallible truth about a subject.

D. An internal auditor has no responsibility to recommend improvements.

Answer (C) is correct. *(CIA, adapted)*

REQUIRED: The true statement about due professional care.

DISCUSSION: Due professional care implies application of reasonable prudence and competence, not infallibility (Attr. Std. 1220). Thus, it requires the internal auditor to conduct examinations and verifications to a reasonable extent. Accordingly, internal auditors cannot give absolute assurance that noncompliance or irregularities do not exist.

Answer (A) is incorrect. An internal auditor must conduct reasonable examinations and verifications, but detailed tests of all transactions are not required. Answer (B) is incorrect. Absolute assurance need not, and cannot, be given. Answer (D) is incorrect. An internal auditor must recommend improvements to promote conformance with acceptable procedures and practices.

21.3.5. Assurance engagements must be performed with proficiency and due professional care. Accordingly, the *Standards* require internal auditors to

I. Consider the probability of significant noncompliance

II. Perform assurance procedures with due professional care so that all significant risks are identified

III. Weigh the cost of assurance against the benefits

A. I and II only.

B. I and III only.

C. II and III only.

D. I, II, and III.

Answer (B) is correct. *(Publisher, adapted)*

REQUIRED: The responsibilities of internal auditors regarding proficiency and due professional care.

DISCUSSION: Internal auditors must exercise due professional care by considering the

- Extent of work needed to achieve the engagement's objectives
- Relative complexity, materiality, or significance of matters to which assurance procedures are applied
- Adequacy and effectiveness of governance, risk management, and control processes
- Probability of significant errors, fraud, or noncompliance
- Cost of assurance in relation to potential benefits (Impl. Std. 1220.A1)

Assurance procedures alone, even when performed with due professional care, do not guarantee that all significant risks will be identified (Impl. Std. 1220.A3).

21.3.6. A chief audit executive has reviewed credentials, checked references, and interviewed a candidate for a staff position. The CAE concludes that the candidate has a thorough understanding of internal audit techniques, accounting, and finance. However, the candidate has limited knowledge of economics and information technology. Which action is most appropriate?

A. Reject the candidate because of the lack of knowledge required by the *Standards*.

B. Offer the candidate a position despite lack of knowledge in certain essential areas.

C. Encourage the candidate to obtain additional training in economics and information technology and then reapply.

D. Offer the candidate a position if other staff members possess sufficient knowledge in economics and information technology.

Answer (D) is correct. *(CIA, adapted)*

REQUIRED: The proper hiring decision by a CAE.

DISCUSSION: Each member of the internal audit activity need not be qualified in all disciplines.

Answer (A) is incorrect. The *Standards* do not require each internal auditor to possess a knowledge of all relevant subjects. Answer (B) is incorrect. The internal audit activity's needs may be for additional expertise in economics or information technology. Answer (C) is incorrect. Encouraging the candidate to obtain additional training does not adequately address the internal audit activity's current needs.

21.4 Control

21.4.1. Which of the following best defines control?

A. Control is the result of proper planning, organizing, and directing by management.

B. Controls are statements of what the organization chooses to accomplish.

C. Control is provided when cost-effective measures are taken to restrict deviations to a tolerable level.

D. Control accomplishes objectives and goals in an accurate, timely, and economical fashion.

Answer (A) is correct. *(CIA, adapted)*

REQUIRED: The best definition of control.

DISCUSSION: A control is "any action taken by management, the board, and other parties to manage risk and increase the likelihood that established objectives and goals will be achieved. Management plans, organizes, and directs the performance of sufficient actions to provide reasonable assurance that objectives and goals will be achieved (The IIA Glossary). Thus, control is the result of proper planning, organizing, and directing by management.

Answer (B) is incorrect. Established objectives and goals are what the organization chooses to accomplish. Answer (C) is incorrect. The internal audit activity evaluates the effectiveness and efficiency of controls, but the definition of control addresses effectiveness in achieving objectives and goals. Answer (D) is incorrect. Effective and efficient performance accomplishes objectives and goals in an accurate, timely, and economical fashion.

21.4.2. The procedure requiring preparation of a prelisting of incoming cash receipts, with copies of the prelist going to the cashier and to accounting, is an example of which type of control?

A. Preventive.

B. Corrective.

C. Detective.

D. Directive.

Answer (A) is correct. *(CIA, adapted)*

REQUIRED: The kind of control exemplified by a prelist of cash receipts.

DISCUSSION: A prelisting of cash receipts in the form of checks is a preventive control. It is intended to deter undesirable events from occurring. Because irregularities involving cash most likely take place before receipts are recorded, either remittance advices or a prelisting of checks should be prepared in the mailroom so as to establish recorded accountability for cash as soon as possible. A cash register tape is a form of prelisting for cash received over the counter. One copy of a prelisting will go to accounting for posting to the cash receipts journal, and another is sent to the cashier for reconciliation with checks and currency received.

Answer (B) is incorrect. A corrective control remedies an error or irregularity. Answer (C) is incorrect. A detective control uncovers an error or irregularity that has already occurred. Answer (D) is incorrect. A directive control causes or encourages a desirable event.

21.4.3. In evaluating the effectiveness and efficiency with which resources are employed, an internal auditor is responsible for

A. Determining the extent to which adequate operating criteria have been established.

B. Verifying the existence of assets.

C. Reviewing the reliability of operating information.

D. Verifying the accuracy of asset valuation.

Answer (A) is correct. *(CIA, adapted)*

REQUIRED: The internal auditor's responsibility for evaluating effective and efficient use of resources.

DISCUSSION: Internal auditors must determine the extent to which management has established adequate criteria to determine whether objectives and goals have been accomplished (Impl. Std. 2210.A3).

Answer (B) is incorrect. Verifying existence relates to the safeguarding of assets. Answer (C) is incorrect. The reliability of operating information concerns the reliability and integrity of information. Answer (D) is incorrect. Verifying the accuracy of asset valuation concerns the reliability and integrity of information.

21.4.4. An organization's directors, management, external auditors, and internal auditors all play important roles in creating a proper control environment. Senior management is primarily responsible for

A. Establishing a proper organizational culture and specifying a system of internal control.

B. Designing and operating a control system that provides reasonable assurance that established objectives and goals will be achieved.

C. Ensuring that external and internal auditors adequately monitor the control environment.

D. Implementing and monitoring controls designed by the board of directors.

Answer (A) is correct. *(CIA, adapted)*

REQUIRED: The best description of top management's responsibility.

DISCUSSION: Senior management is primarily responsible for establishing a proper organizational culture and specifying a system of internal control.

Answer (B) is incorrect. Senior management is not likely to be involved in the detailed design and day-to-day operation of a control system. Answer (C) is incorrect. Management administers risk and control processes. It cannot delegate this responsibility to the external auditors or to the internal audit activity. Answer (D) is incorrect. The board has oversight governance responsibilities but ordinarily does not become involved in the details of operations.

21.4.5. The chief audit executive's responsibility for assessing and reporting on control processes most likely includes

A. Communicating to senior management and the board an overall assessment control.

B. Overseeing the establishment of internal control processes.

C. Maintaining the organization's governance processes.

D. Arriving at a single assessment based solely on the work of the internal audit activity.

Answer (A) is correct. *(Publisher, adapted)*

REQUIRED: The chief audit executive's responsibility for assessing and reporting on control processes.

DISCUSSION: To promote continuous improvement in maintaining effective controls, the internal audit activity usually provides an overall assessment or a compilation of control evaluations from individual engagements (IG 2130).

Answer (B) is incorrect. Senior management is responsible for overseeing the establishment of internal control processes. Answer (C) is incorrect. The board is responsible for establishing and maintaining the organization's governance processes. Answer (D) is incorrect. The challenge for the internal audit activity is to evaluate the effectiveness of the organization's system of controls based on the aggregation of many individual assessments. Those assessments are largely gained from internal auditing engagements, management's self assessments, and external assurance providers' work.

21.5 Planning and Supervising the Engagement

21.5.1. Internal auditors must develop and document a plan for each engagement. The planning process should include all the following except

A. Establishing engagement objectives and scope of work.

B. Obtaining background information about the activities to be reviewed.

C. Identifying sufficient information to achieve engagement objectives.

D. Determining how, when, and to whom the engagement results will be communicated.

Answer (C) is correct. *(CIA, adapted)*

REQUIRED: The item not part of the planning process.

DISCUSSION: Internal auditors must develop and document a plan for each engagement, including the engagement's objectives, scope, timing, and resource allocations (Perf. Std. 2200). Identifying sufficient information to achieve engagement objectives is done during field work, not planning.

Answer (A) is incorrect. The planning process includes establishing engagement objectives and scope of work. Answer (B) is incorrect. The planning process includes obtaining background information. Answer (D) is incorrect. The planning process includes determining how, when, and to whom the engagement results will be communicated.

21.5.2. In the planning phase, the scope of an internal audit engagement is defined by the

A. Engagement objectives.

B. Scheduling and time estimates.

C. Preliminary survey.

D. Engagement work program.

Answer (A) is correct. *(CIA, adapted)*

REQUIRED: The factor initially defining the scope of an internal audit engagement.

DISCUSSION: The established scope must be sufficient to satisfy the objectives of the engagement (Perf. Std. 2220).

Answer (B) is incorrect. The scheduling and time estimates are based on the objectives and scope of the engagement. Answer (C) is incorrect. The preliminary survey must be completed and the engagement objectives set before the engagement scope can be established. Answer (D) is incorrect. The engagement work program is the last of the four steps listed.

21.5.3. Which of the following activities represents the greatest risk to a post-merger manufacturing organization and is therefore most likely to be the subject of an internal audit engagement?

A. Combining impress funds.

B. Combining purchasing functions.

C. Combining legal functions.

D. Combining marketing functions.

Answer (B) is correct. *(CIA, adapted)*

REQUIRED: The activity representing the greatest risk.

DISCUSSION: The financial exposure in the purchasing function is ordinarily greater than in, for example, the legal and marketing functions. Also, purchasing functions ordinarily represent the greatest exposure to loss of the items listed and are therefore most likely to be evaluated. After a merger, risk is heightened because of the difficulty of combining the systems of the two organizations. Thus, the likelihood of an engagement is increased.

Answer (A) is incorrect. Imprest funds are typically immaterial in amount. Answer (C) is incorrect. Legal functions do not typically represent a risk of loss as great as the purchasing functions. Answer (D) is incorrect. Marketing functions do not typically represent a risk of loss as great as the purchasing functions.

21.5.4. An external consultant is developing methods for the management of a city's capital facilities. An appropriate scope of an engagement to evaluate the consultant's product is to

A. Review the consultant's contract to determine its propriety.

B. Establish the parameters of the value of the items being managed and controlled.

C. Determine the adequacy of the risk management and control systems for the management of capital facilities.

D. Review the handling of idle equipment.

Answer (C) is correct. *(CIA, adapted)*

REQUIRED: The appropriate scope of an engagement to evaluate a consultant's product.

DISCUSSION: "In planning the engagement, internal auditors must consider:

- The strategies and objectives of the activity being reviewed and the means by which the activity controls its performance.
- The significant risks to the activity's objectives, resources, and operations and the means by which the potential impact of risk is kept to an acceptable level.
- The adequacy and effectiveness of the activity's governance, risk management, and control processes compared to a relevant framework or model.
- The opportunities for making significant improvements to the activity's governance, risk management, and control processes" (Perf. Std. 2201).

Answer (A) is incorrect. The review of the consultant's contract to determine its propriety is related to the procurement decision. Answer (B) is incorrect. The establishment of parameters for values of items being managed and controlled is a management responsibility. Answer (D) is incorrect. Management must determine policies regarding idle equipment. Some equipment may be retained for emergency use.

21.5.5. In planning an assurance engagement, a survey could assist with all of the following except

A. Obtaining engagement client comments and suggestions on control problems.

B. Obtaining preliminary information on controls.

C. Identifying areas for engagement emphasis.

D. Evaluating the adequacy and effectiveness of controls.

Answer (D) is correct. *(CIA, adapted)*

REQUIRED: The planning item not assisted by a survey.

DISCUSSION: Internal auditors may perform a survey to (1) become familiar with activities, risks, and controls to identify areas for engagement emphasis and (2) invite comments and suggestions from stakeholders. A survey is not sufficient for evaluating the adequacy and effectiveness of controls. Evaluation requires testing.

Answer (A) is incorrect. A survey could assist with obtaining client comments and suggestions on control problems. Answer (B) is incorrect. A survey could assist with obtaining preliminary information on controls. Answer (C) is incorrect. A survey could assist with identifying areas for engagement emphasis.

21.5.6. The best control over the work on which internal auditors' opinions are based is

A. Supervisory review of all engagement work.

B. Preparation of time budgets for internal audit activities.

C. Preparation of engagement working papers.

D. Staffing of internal audit activities.

Answer (A) is correct. *(CIA, adapted)*

REQUIRED: The best control over the work on which internal auditors' opinions are based.

DISCUSSION: The engagement must be properly supervised to ensure objectives are achieved, quality is ensured, and staff is developed (Perf. Std. 2340). Supervision includes (1) ensuring the auditors possess the requisite knowledge, skills, and other competencies; (2) providing appropriate instructions during planning and approving the engagement program; (3) ensuring the approved engagement program is complete unless changes are justified and authorized; (4) determining working papers adequately support observations, conclusions, and recommendations; (5) ensuring communications are accurate, objective, clear, concise, constructive, and timely; (6) ensuring objectives are met; and (7) providing opportunities for developing internal auditors' knowledge, skills, and other competencies. Thus, supervision is a control that applies to all aspects of engagements.

Answer (B) is incorrect. Although useful, time budgets do not ensure the adequacy of work. Answer (C) is incorrect. Working papers support the conclusions and engagement results, but supervision is necessary to ensure the adequacy of work. Answer (D) is incorrect. Proper staffing is required, but supervision is essential to ensure the adequacy of work.

21.5.7. Determining that engagement objectives have been met is part of the overall supervision of an engagement and is the ultimate responsibility of the

A. Staff internal auditor.

B. Board.

C. Engagement supervisor.

D. Chief audit executive.

Answer (D) is correct. *(CIA, adapted)*

REQUIRED: The person(s) with ultimate responsibility for determining that engagement objectives have been met.

DISCUSSION: The CAE has overall responsibility for supervising the engagement (Inter. Std. 2340).

21.5.8. Why should organizations require assurance engagement clients to reply promptly and outline the corrective action that has been implemented on reported observations?

A. To remove items from the pending list as soon as possible.

B. To effect savings or to institute compliance as early as possible.

C. To indicate concurrence with the engagement observations.

D. To ensure that the engagement work schedule is kept up to date.

Answer (B) is correct. *(CIA, adapted)*

REQUIRED: The reason clients should promptly reply and state the corrective action that has been implemented on reported observations.

DISCUSSION: Of the choices provided, effecting savings or achieving compliance are the only ones that benefit organizations as a whole.

Answer (A) is incorrect. Removing items from the pending list concerns a mechanical and immaterial aspect of the communication process. Answer (C) is incorrect. The client may not concur with the observations and recommendations. This dispute may or may not be considered in closing the engagement. Answer (D) is incorrect. Ensuring that the engagement work schedule is kept up to date is an administrative function of the internal audit activity.

21.5.9. Upon reviewing the final communication of engagement results, senior management decided to assume the risk of not implementing corrective action on certain engagement observations. Evaluate the following and select the best alternative for the chief audit executive:

A. Notify regulatory authorities of management's decision.

B. Perform additional engagement procedures to further identify the policy violations.

C. Conduct a follow-up engagement to determine whether corrective action was taken.

D. Discuss the matter with senior management and possibly the board if the residual risk accepted is excessive.

Answer (D) is correct. *(CIA, adapted)*

REQUIRED: The best choice when management agrees to assume the risk of not implementing corrective action.

DISCUSSION: A CAE may believe that senior management has accepted a level of risk that may be unacceptable to the organization. The CAE then must discuss the matter with senior management. If the CAE determines that the matter is unresolved, (s)he must report the matter to the board (Perf. Std. 2600).

Answer (A) is incorrect. Regulatory authorities do not need to be notified. Management has decided to assume responsibility, and no regulatory violations were mentioned. Answer (B) is incorrect. Additional procedures are not required unless the CAE believes that the residual risk assumed is too great. Answer (C) is incorrect. A follow-up engagement is not required unless the CAE believes that the residual risk assumed is too great.

21.5.10. Writing an engagement work program most likely occurs at which stage of the engagement?

A. During the planning stage.

B. Subsequent to evaluating risk management and control systems.

C. As the engagement is performed.

D. At the end of each engagement when the standard work program should be revised for the next engagement to ensure coverage of noted problem areas.

Answer (A) is correct. *(CIA, adapted)*

REQUIRED: The stage of the engagement during which the work program most likely is written.

DISCUSSION: During planning, internal auditors start to develop the engagement work program with consideration of (1) budgets, (2) logistics, (3) final communication format, (4) to whom (and how and when) results will be communicated, and (5) needs for direct supervision of audit staff. The last planning step before field work usually involves audit management's approval of the work program. But as in all audits, the engagement plan and work program may require adjustment when new information is obtained (IG 2200).

Answer (B) is incorrect. The work program states the procedures to be followed during the engagement (The IIA Glossary). Answer (C) is incorrect. The work program normally is written during the planning stage, not as the engagement is performed. However, the work program may be modified during the engagement. Answer (D) is incorrect. Although revising the work program at the end of one engagement for the next engagement is allowed, it should still be written during the planning phase.

21.6 Performing the Engagement

21.6.1. Engagement information is usually considered relevant when it is

A. Derived through valid statistical sampling.

B. Objective and unbiased.

C. Factual, adequate, and convincing.

D. Consistent with the engagement objectives.

Answer (D) is correct. *(CIA, adapted)*

REQUIRED: The circumstance in which information is usually considered relevant.

DISCUSSION: Relevant information supports engagement observations and recommendations and is consistent with the objectives for the engagement (Inter. Std. 2310).

Answer (A) is incorrect. Whether sampling is appropriate and the results are valid are issues related to the determination of sufficiency and reliability rather than relevance. Answer (B) is incorrect. Objectivity and lack of bias do not ensure that information will support observations and recommendations and be consistent with the engagement objectives. Answer (C) is incorrect. Sufficient information is factual, adequate, and convincing so that a prudent, informed person would reach the same conclusions as the internal auditor.

21.6.2. What characteristic of information is satisfied by an original signed document?

A. Sufficiency.

B. Reliability.

C. Relevance.

D. Usefulness.

Answer (B) is correct. *(CIA, adapted)*

REQUIRED: The characteristic of information satisfied by an original signed document.

DISCUSSION: Reliable information is the best information attainable through the use of appropriate engagement techniques (Inter. Std. 2310). An original document is the prime example of such information.

Answer (A) is incorrect. Sufficient information is factual, adequate, and convincing. The information contained on the document may be none of those things. Answer (C) is incorrect. Relevance concerns the relationship of the information to some objective of the engagement. No engagement objective is disclosed in the question. Thus, whether the information on the document is relevant to the investigation cannot be determined. Answer (D) is incorrect. Usefulness is achieved if the item helps the organization (the internal auditor, in this case) to accomplish predetermined goals. No such goals are specified.

21.6.3. When sampling methods are used, the concept of sufficiency of information means that the samples selected provide

A. Reasonable assurance that they are representative of the sampled population.

B. The best information that is reasonably obtainable.

C. Reasonable assurance that the information has a logical relationship to the engagement objective.

D. Absolute assurance that a sample is representative of the population.

Answer (A) s correct. *(CIA, adapted)*

REQUIRED: The meaning of sufficiency of information when sampling methods are used.

DISCUSSION: Sufficient information is factual, adequate, and convincing so that a prudent, informed person would reach the same conclusions as the auditor (Inter. Std. 2310). If properly designed and executed, a statistical sample is representative of the sampled population.

Answer (B) is incorrect. The best information reasonably obtainable is reliable information. Answer (C) is incorrect. The logical relationship indicates relevance. Answer (D) is incorrect. Cost-benefit considerations usually preclude absolute assurance.

21.6.4. An adequately documented working paper should

A. Be concise but complete.

B. Follow a unique form and arrangement.

C. Contain examples of all forms and procedures used by the engagement client.

D. Not contain copies of engagement client records.

Answer (A) is correct. *(CIA, adapted)*

REQUIRED: The characteristic of an adequately documented working paper.

DISCUSSION: The matters documented (e.g., information and engagement procedures) should be sufficient, reliable, relevant, and useful to support the engagement objectives, observations, conclusions, and recommendations (IG 2330).

Answer (B) is incorrect. Working papers should be uniform and consistent. Answer (C) is incorrect. Working papers should contain only information related to an engagement objective. Answer (D) is incorrect. Copies of engagement client records should be included whenever necessary.

21.6.5. An inexperienced internal auditor notified the senior auditor of a significant variance from the engagement client's budget. The senior told the new internal auditor not to worry because the senior had heard that there had been an unauthorized work stoppage that probably accounted for the difference. Which of the following statements is most appropriate?

A. The new internal auditor should have investigated the matter fully and not bothered the senior.

B. The senior used proper judgment in curtailing what could have been a wasteful investigation.

C. The senior should have halted the engagement until the variance was fully explained.

D. The senior should have aided the new internal auditor in formulating a plan for accumulating appropriate information.

Answer (D) is correct. *(CIA, adapted)*

REQUIRED: The senior internal auditor's proper response to a significant budget variance.

DISCUSSION: When analytical audit procedures identify unexpected results or relationships, the internal auditor evaluates such results or relationships instead of obtaining information to explain the variance. The senior allowed the identified variance to go unevaluated.

Answer (A) is incorrect. An inexperienced internal auditor should refer this matter to the senior. Answer (B) is incorrect. The facts given do not support the conclusion that accumulating additional information would be wasteful. Answer (C) is incorrect. The variance needs explanation, but the engagement should continue.

21.6.6. The primary purpose of an internal auditor's working papers is to

A. Provide documentation of the planning and execution of engagement procedures performed.

B. Serve as a means with which to prepare the financial statements.

C. Document weaknesses in internal control with recommendations to management for improvement.

D. Comply with the *Standards*.

Answer (A) is correct. *(CIA, adapted)*

REQUIRED: The primary purpose of an internal auditor's working papers.

DISCUSSION: Engagement working papers, among other things, aid in planning, performing, and reviewing the engagement.

Answer (B) is incorrect. Working papers do not provide the means for preparation of the financial statements. Answer (C) is incorrect. Documentation of control weaknesses is only one example of working paper content, not the primary purpose for them. Answer (D) is incorrect. The preparation of adequate working papers is a requirement of the *Standards* but is not the primary purpose for their existence.

21.6.7. Which of the following does not describe one of the functions of engagement working papers?

A. Facilitates third-party reviews.

B. Aids in the planning, performance, and review of engagements.

C. Provides the principal support for engagement communications.

D. Aids in the professional development of the operating staff.

Answer (D) is correct. *(CIA, adapted)*

REQUIRED: The response that does not describe one of the functions of engagement working papers.

DISCUSSION: Engagement working papers generally (1) aid in planning, performance, and review of engagements; (2) provide the principal support for engagement results; (3) document whether engagement objectives were achieved; (4) support the accuracy and completeness of the work performed; (5) provide a basis for the internal audit activity's quality assurance and improvement program; and (6) facilitate third-party review.

Answer (A) is incorrect. The facilitation of third-party reviews is a function of working papers. Answer (B) is incorrect. Working papers aid in the planning, performance, and review of engagements. Answer (C) is incorrect. Working papers provide the principal support for results.

21.6.8. Which of the following actions constitutes a violation of the confidentiality concept regarding working papers? An internal auditor

A. Takes working papers to his or her hotel room overnight.

B. Shows working papers on occasion to engagement clients.

C. Allows the external auditor to copy working papers.

D. Misplaces working papers occasionally.

Answer (D) is correct. *(CIA, adapted)*

REQUIRED: The action violating the confidentiality concept regarding working papers.

DISCUSSION: The internal audit activity controls engagement working papers and provides access to authorized personnel only. By misplacing working papers occasionally, the internal auditor is thus violating the confidentiality concept.

Answer (A) is incorrect. Continuous physical control of working papers during fieldwork may be appropriate. Answer (B) is incorrect. Engagement clients may be shown working papers with the CAE's approval. Answer (C) is incorrect. Internal and external auditors commonly grant access to each others' work programs and working papers.

21.6.9. When reviewing engagement working papers, the primary responsibility of an engagement supervisor is to determine that

A. Each worksheet is properly identified with a descriptive heading.

B. Working papers are properly referenced and kept in logical groupings.

C. Standard internal audit activity procedures are adhered to with regard to working paper preparation and technique.

D. Working papers adequately support the engagement observations, conclusions, and recommendations.

Answer (D) is correct. *(CIA, adapted)*

REQUIRED: The primary responsibility of an engagement supervisor when reviewing engagement working papers.

DISCUSSION: All engagement working papers are reviewed to ensure they support engagement communications and necessary audit procedures are performed.

Answer (A) is incorrect. Descriptive headings are not of primary importance. Answer (B) is incorrect. Proper referencing and logical groupings are not of primary importance. Answer (C) is incorrect. Adherence to procedures is not of primary importance.

21.6.10. Which of the following states an inappropriate policy relating to the retention of engagement working papers?

A. Working papers should be disposed of when they have no further use.

B. Working papers prepared for fraud investigators should be retained indefinitely.

C. Working-paper retention schedules should be approved by legal counsel.

D. Working-paper retention schedules should consider legal and contractual requirements.

Answer (B) is correct. *(CIA, adapted)*

REQUIRED: The inappropriate policy relating to the retention of engagement working papers.

DISCUSSION: The CAE must develop retention requirements for engagement records, regardless of the medium in which each record is stored. These retention requirements must be consistent with the organization's guidelines and any pertinent regulatory or other requirements (Impl. Std. 2330.A2). Although working papers pertaining to fraud investigations might be kept apart from others, no working paper will have to be kept indefinitely.

Answer (A) is incorrect. The duration of retention should be determined by usefulness. Answer (C) is incorrect. Approval by legal counsel is appropriate. Answer (D) is incorrect. Legal and contractual requirements may determine the retention period.

21.6.11. An internal auditing manager is reviewing the engagement working papers prepared by the staff. Which of the following review comments is true?

A. Each working paper should include the actual and the budgeted times related to such engagement work.

B. Including copies of all the forms and directives of the engagement client constitutes over-documentation.

C. Conclusions need not be documented in the working papers when the engagement objectives are achieved.

D. Each working paper should include a statement regarding the engagement client's cooperation.

Answer (B) is correct. *(CIA, adapted)*

REQUIRED: The review comment that is true.

DISCUSSION: All engagement working papers are reviewed to ensure they support engagement communications and necessary audit procedures are performed. However, adequate support includes only those forms and directives that are relevant to the engagement or to the observations, conclusions, and recommendations. Thus, including copies of all the forms and directives of the client constitutes over-documentation.

Answer (A) is incorrect. Actual and budgeted times are documented in the budget section of the working papers and not on each working paper. Answer (C) is incorrect. Conclusions should be documented in the working papers whether or not the engagement objectives are achieved. Answer (D) is incorrect. Only noncooperation is likely to be documented.

21.7 Managing the Internal Audit Activity

21.7.1. Which of the following is most essential for guiding the internal audit staff?

A. Quality program assessments.

B. Position descriptions.

C. Performance appraisals.

D. Policies and procedures.

Answer (D) is correct. *(CIA, adapted)*

REQUIRED: The item most essential for guiding the internal audit staff.

DISCUSSION: The chief audit executive must establish policies and procedures to guide the internal audit activity (Perf. Std. 2040).

Answer (A) is incorrect. Quality program assessments do not provide specific daily guidance to the staff with respect to performance standards. Answer (B) is incorrect. Position descriptions do not provide specific daily guidance to the staff with respect to performance standards. Answer (C) is incorrect. Performance appraisals do not provide specific daily guidance to the staff with respect to performance standards.

21.7.2. When assigning individual staff members to actual engagements, internal auditing managers are faced with a number of important considerations related to needs, abilities, and skills. Which of the following is the least appropriate criterion for assigning a staff internal auditor to a specific engagement?

A. The staff internal auditor's desire for training in the area.

B. The complexity of the engagement.

C. The experience level of the internal auditor.

D. Special skills possessed by the staff internal auditor.

Answer (A) is correct. *(CIA, adapted)*

REQUIRED: The least appropriate criterion for assigning a staff auditor to a specific audit.

DISCUSSION: A staff internal auditor's desire for specific training is necessarily secondary to carrying out the responsibilities of the internal audit activity with regard to proper staffing.

Answer (B) is incorrect. The complexity of the engagement determines the experience and skills required of the assigned staff. Answer (C) is incorrect. Experience is a factor in a staffing decision. Answer (D) is incorrect. Special expertise is a factor in a staffing decision.

21.7.3. The internal auditor is considering making a risk analysis as a basis for determining the areas of the organization where engagements should be performed. Which one of the following statements is true regarding risk analysis?

A. The extent to which management judgments are required in an area could serve as a risk factor in assisting the internal auditor in making a comparative risk analysis.

B. The highest risk assessment should always be assigned to the area with the largest potential loss.

C. The highest risk assessment should always be assigned to the area with highest probability of occurrence.

D. Risk analysis must be reduced to quantitative terms in order to provide meaningful comparisons across an organization.

Answer (A) is correct. *(CIA, adapted)*

REQUIRED: The true statement about risk analysis.

DISCUSSION: Among the common factors used in risk models for establishing the priority of engagements is management competence. Thus, the internal auditor could appropriately consider the extent of management competence, which includes judgment, as a risk factor.

Answer (B) is incorrect. Risk analysis considers both the potential loss (or damages) and the probability of occurrence. An area with the largest potential loss may have a very low likelihood. Answer (C) is incorrect. A high probability of occurrence may be associated with a small potential loss. Answer (D) is incorrect. The concept of risk analysis is not limited to quantitative measures.

21.7.4. The chief audit executive routinely reports to the board as part of the board meeting agenda each quarter. Senior management has asked to review this presentation before each board meeting so that any issues or questions can be discussed beforehand. The CAE needs to

A. Provide the report to senior management as requested and discuss any issues that may require action to be taken.

B. Withhold disclosure of the report to senior management because such matters are the sole province of the board.

C. Disclose to the board only those matters in the report that pertain to expenditures and financial budgets of the internal audit activity.

D. Provide information to senior management that pertains only to completed engagements and observations available in published engagement communications.

Answer (A) is correct. *(CIA, adapted)*

REQUIRED: The action that needs to be taken regarding the review of internal audit reports by senior management.

DISCUSSION: The frequency and content of reporting are determined in discussion with senior management and the board and depend on the importance of the information to be communicated and the urgency of the related actions to be taken by senior management or the board (Inter. Std. 2060).

Answer (B) is incorrect. Reports must be presented to senior management. Answer (C) is incorrect. The report is not restricted to expenditures and financial budgets. Information about significant deviations from the approved audit plan and staffing plans also is included. Answer (D) is incorrect. The information need not be limited to completed engagements and observations available in published engagement communications.

21.7.5. The most important reason for the chief audit executive to ensure that the internal audit department has adequate and sufficient resources is to

A. Ensure that the function is adequately protected from outsourcing.

B. Demonstrate sufficient capability to meet the audit plan requirements.

C. Establish credibility with the audit committee and management.

D. Fulfill the need for effective succession planning.

Answer (B) is correct. *(CIA, adapted)*

REQUIRED: The most important reason for the chief audit executive to ensure that the internal audit department has adequate and sufficient resources.

DISCUSSION: The CAE must ensure that internal audit resources are appropriate, sufficient, and effectively deployed to achieve the approved plan (Perf. Std. 2030).

Answer (A) is incorrect. The decision to outsource the internal audit function is not primarily based on existing resources. Answer (C) is incorrect. The amount of resources is not a significant factor in establishing credibility. Answer (D) is incorrect. Succession planning is not related to the amount of audit resources.

Questions 21.7.6 and 21.7.7 are based on the following information. You are the chief audit executive of a parent organization that has foreign subsidiaries. Independent external audits performed for the parent are not conducted by the same firm that conducts the foreign subsidiary audits. Because the internal audit activity occasionally provides direct assistance to both external firms, you have copies of audit programs and selected working papers produced by each firm.

21.7.6. The foreign subsidiary's auditors would like to rely on some of the work performed by the parent organization's audit firm, but they need to review the working papers first. They have asked you for copies of the working papers of the parent organization's audit firm. What is the most appropriate response to the foreign subsidiary's auditors?

A. Provide copies of the working papers without notifying the parent's audit firm.

B. Notify the parent's auditors of the situation and request that they either provide the working papers or authorize you to do so.

C. Provide copies of the working papers and notify the parent's audit firm that you have done so.

D. Refuse to provide the working papers under any circumstances.

Answer (B) is correct. *(CIA, adapted)*

REQUIRED: The proper response to a request by one external audit firm for another external audit firm's working papers held by the internal auditors.

DISCUSSION: Organizations may use the work of external auditors to provide assurance related to activities within the scope of internal auditing. In these cases, the CAE takes the steps necessary to understand the work performed by the external auditors, including access to the external auditors' programs and working papers. Internal auditors are responsible for respecting the confidentiality of those programs and working papers.

Answer (A) is incorrect. The working papers are the property of the parent's external auditors, and their confidentiality should be respected. Answer (C) is incorrect. The external auditors must give prior authorization for the release of their working papers. Answer (D) is incorrect. The CAE has the responsibility to ensure proper coordination with external auditors.

21.7.7. The foreign subsidiary's external audit firm wants to rely on an audit of a function at the parent organization. The audit was conducted by the internal audit activity. To place reliance on the work performed, the foreign subsidiary's auditors have requested copies of the working papers. What is the most appropriate response to the foreign subsidiary's auditors?

A. Provide copies of the working papers.

B. Ask the parent's audit firm if it is appropriate to release the working papers.

C. Ask the board for permission to release the working papers.

D. Refuse to provide the working papers under any circumstances.

Answer (A) is correct. *(CIA, adapted)*

REQUIRED: The proper response to a request by external auditors for the internal auditors' working papers.

DISCUSSION: Coordination involves access to each other's work programs, working papers, and reports (IG 2050). Access is provided to external auditors for them to be satisfied as to the acceptability, for external audit purposes, of relying on the internal auditors' work.

Answer (B) is incorrect. The working papers are the property of the organization. The responsibility of the CAE is to maintain the security of the working papers and to coordinate efforts with the external auditors. Thus, the decision belongs not to the parent's external auditors but to the CAE. Answer (C) is incorrect. Access to working papers by external auditors is subject to the approval of the CAE. Answer (D) is incorrect. The CAE ensures proper coordination with external auditors by, among other things, granting the external auditors access to the internal auditors' working papers.

21.7.8. The chief audit executive for an organization has just completed a risk assessment process, identified the areas with the highest risks, and assigned an engagement priority to each. Which of the following conclusions most logically follow(s) from such a risk assessment?

I. Items should be quantified as to risk in the rank order of quantifiable monetary exposure to the organization.

II. The risk priorities should be in order of major control deficiencies.

III. The risk assessment process, though quantified, is the result of professional judgments about both exposures and probability of occurrences.

A. I only.

B. III only.

C. II and III only.

D. I, II, and III.

Answer (B) is correct. *(CIA, adapted)*

REQUIRED: The conclusion(s) logically following from a risk assessment process.

DISCUSSION: Any assessment of risk priority and exposure necessarily implies the exercise of professional judgment. Thus, although risk factors may be weighted to determine their relative significance, a ranking based solely on such specific criteria as monetary exposure or control deficiencies is not always indicated.

Answer (A) is incorrect. Quantifiable monetary exposure is not the sole criterion for ranking risk exposures. Answer (C) is incorrect. Major control deficiencies are not the sole criteria for ranking risk exposures. Answer (D) is incorrect. Ranking risk exposures strictly by quantifiable monetary exposure or by major control deficiencies downplays the importance of professional judgment.

21.7.9. External assessment of an internal audit activity is not likely to evaluate

A. Adherence to the internal audit activity's charter.

B. Conformance with the *Standards*.

C. Detailed cost-benefit analysis of the internal audit activity.

D. The internal audit staff's expertise.

Answer (C) is correct. *(CIA, adapted)*

REQUIRED: The purpose not served by external assessment of an internal audit activity.

DISCUSSION: The external assessment has a broad scope of coverage that includes (1) conformance with the Code of Ethics and the Standards evaluated by review of the internal audit activity's charter, plans, policies, procedures, practices, and applicable legislative and regulatory requirements; (2) the expectations of the internal audit activity expressed by the board, senior management, and operational managers; and (3) the efficiency and effectiveness of the internal audit activity (IG 1312). However, the costs and benefits of internal auditing are neither easily quantifiable nor the subject of an external assessment.

Answer (A) is incorrect. Adherence to the internal audit activity's charter is within the broad scope of coverage of the external assessment. Answer (B) is incorrect. Conformance with the *Standards* is within the broad scope of coverage of the external assessment. Answer (D) is incorrect. The efficiency and effectiveness of the internal audit activity, including the internal auditors' knowledge, experience, and expertise, are within the broad scope of coverage of the external assessment.

21.7.10. A quality assurance and improvement program of an internal audit activity provides reasonable assurance that internal auditing work is performed in accordance with its charter. Which of the following are designed to provide feedback on the effectiveness of an internal audit activity?

I. Proper supervision
II. Proper training
III. Internal reviews
IV. External reviews

A. I, II, and III only.

B. II, III, and IV only.

C. I, III, and IV only.

D. I, II, III, and IV.

Answer (C) is correct. *(CIA, adapted)*

REQUIRED: The elements designed to provide feedback on the effectiveness of an internal audit activity.

DISCUSSION: A quality assurance and improvement program (QAIP) is designed to provide reasonable assurance that the internal audit activity conforms with the Standards and the Code of Ethics. QAIP processes include appropriate supervision, periodic internal assessments and ongoing monitoring of quality assurance, and periodic external assessments.

21.7.11. Ordinarily, those conducting internal quality program assessments report to

A. The board.

B. The chief audit executive.

C. Senior management.

D. The internal audit staff.

Answer (B) is correct. *(CIA, adapted)*

REQUIRED: The person(s) to whom those conducting internal quality program assessments report.

DISCUSSION: The CAE establishes a structure for reporting results of internal assessments that maintains appropriate credibility and objectivity. Generally, those assigned responsibility for conducting ongoing and periodic reviews report to the CAE while performing the reviews and communicate results directly to the CAE.

Answer (A) is incorrect. At least annually, the CAE reports the results of internal assessments to the board. Answer (C) is incorrect. The CAE shares information about internal assessments with appropriate persons outside the internal audit activity, such as senior management. Answer (D) is incorrect. Results ordinarily are communicated directly to the CAE. Given a self-assessment, reporting to the internal audit staff essentially involves having the staff report to itself.

21.7.12. Quality program assessments may be performed internally or externally. A distinguishing feature of an external assessment is its objective to

A. Identify tasks that can be performed better.

B. Determine whether internal audit services meet professional standards.

C. Set forth the recommendations for improvement.

D. Provide independent assurance.

Answer (D) is correct. *(CIA, adapted)*

REQUIRED: The distinguishing feature of an external assessment.

DISCUSSION: External assessments must be conducted at least once every 5 years by a qualified, independent reviewer or review team from outside the organization (Attr. Std. 1312). Individuals who perform the external assessment should not (1) have an actual or perceived conflict of interest or (2) be a part of or controlled by the organization (Inter. Std. 1312).

Answer (A) is incorrect. An internal assessment will identify tasks that can be performed better. Answer (B) is incorrect. An internal assessment will determine whether internal audit services meet professional standards. Answer (C) is incorrect. An internal assessment will set forth recommendations for improvement.

21.7.13. Internal auditors may include in their audit report that their activities conform with The IIA *Standards*. They may use this statement only if

A. It is supported by the results of the quality program.

B. An independent external assessment of the internal audit activity is conducted annually.

C. Senior management or the board is accountable for implementing a quality program.

D. External assessments of the internal audit activity are made by external auditors.

Answer (A) is correct. *(Publisher, adapted)*

REQUIRED: The condition permitting internal auditors to report that their activities conform with the *Standards*.

DISCUSSION: The chief audit executive may state that the internal audit activity conforms with the *International Standards for the Professional Practice of Internal Auditing* only if the results of the quality assurance and improvement program support this statement (Attr. Std. 1321).

Answer (B) is incorrect. An independent external assessment of the internal audit activity must be conducted at least once every 5 years. Answer (C) is incorrect. The CAE must develop and maintain a QAIP that covers all aspects of the internal audit activity. Answer (D) is incorrect. Assessments also may be made by others who are (1) independent, (2) qualified, and (3) from outside the organization.

21.7.14. Which of the following is a false statement about the relationship between internal auditors and external auditors?

A. Oversight of the work of external auditors is the responsibility of the chief audit executive.

B. Sufficient meetings are scheduled between internal and external auditors to ensure timely and efficient completion of the work.

C. Internal and external auditors may exchange engagement communications and management letters.

D. Internal auditors may provide engagement work programs and working papers to external auditors.

Answer (A) is correct. *(CIA, adapted)*

REQUIRED: The false statement about the relationship between internal and external auditors.

DISCUSSION: Oversight of the work of external auditors, including coordination with the internal audit activity, is the responsibility of the board. Coordination of internal and external audit work is the responsibility of the CAE (Perf. Std. 2050).

21.7.15. To demonstrate conformance of the internal audit activity with the mandatory guidance of The IIA,

A. The chief audit executive determines the form and content of the results communicated without seeking input from senior management or the board.

B. The results of external assessments are communicated upon their completion.

C. The results of periodic internal assessments are communicated at least monthly.

D. The results of ongoing monitoring are communicated upon their completion.

Answer (B) is correct. *(Publisher, adapted)*

REQUIRED: The true statement about demonstrating conformance with the mandatory guidance of The IIA.

DISCUSSION: "To demonstrate conformance with the Code of Ethics and the *Standards*, the results of external and periodic internal assessments are communicated upon completion of such assessments, and the results of ongoing monitoring are communicated at least annually" (Inter. Std. 1320).

Answer (A) is incorrect. The form, content, and frequency of communicating the results of the quality assurance and improvement program is established through discussions with senior management and the board and considers the responsibilities of the internal audit activity and chief audit executive as contained in the internal audit charter. Answer (C) is incorrect. The results of periodic internal assessments are communicated upon their completion. Answer (D) is incorrect. The results of ongoing monitoring are communicated at least annually.

21.8 IIA Ethics

21.8.1. A primary purpose of establishing a code of conduct within a professional organization is to

A. Reduce the likelihood that members of the profession will be sued for substandard work.

B. Ensure that all members of the profession perform at approximately the same level of competence.

C. Promote an ethical culture among professionals who serve others.

D. Require members of the profession to exhibit loyalty in all matters pertaining to the affairs of their organization.

Answer (C) is correct. *(CIA, adapted)*

REQUIRED: The primary purpose of establishing a code of conduct within a professional organization.

DISCUSSION: The purpose of The IIA's Code of Ethics is "to promote an ethical culture in the profession of internal auditing" (Introduction).

Answer (A) is incorrect. Although this result may follow from establishing a code of conduct, it is not the primary purpose. To consider it so would be self-serving. Answer (B) is incorrect. A code of conduct can help to establish minimum standards of competence, but it is impossible to ensure equality of competence by all members of a profession. Answer (D) is incorrect. In some situations, responsibility to the public at large may conflict with and be more important than loyalty to one's organization.

21.8.2. The IIA Rules of Conduct set forth in The IIA's Code of Ethics

A. Describe behavior norms expected of internal auditors.

B. Are guidelines to assist internal auditors in dealing with engagement clients.

C. Are interpreted by the Principles.

D. Apply only to particular conduct specifically mentioned.

Answer (A) is correct. *(CIA, adapted)*

REQUIRED: The true statement about The IIA Code of Ethics.

DISCUSSION: The IIA's Code of Ethics extends beyond the definition of internal auditing to include two essential components: (1) Principles that are relevant to the profession and practice of internal auditing and (2) Rules of Conduct that describe behavior norms expected of internal auditors (Introduction).

Answer (B) is incorrect. The Rules of Conduct provide guidance to internal auditors in the discharge of their responsibility to all those whom they serve. Engagement clients are not the only parties served by internal auditing. Answer (C) is incorrect. The Rules of Conduct are an aid in interpreting the Principles. Answer (D) is incorrect. The conduct may be unacceptable or discreditable although not mentioned in the Rules of Conduct.

21.8.3. Which of the following is permissible under The IIA's Code of Ethics?

A. Disclosing confidential, engagement-related information that is potentially damaging to the organization in response to a court order.

B. Using engagement-related information in a decision to buy an ownership interest in the employer organization.

C. Accepting an unexpected gift from an employee whom the internal auditor has praised in a recent engagement communication.

D. Not reporting significant observations and recommendations about illegal activity to the board because management has indicated it will address the issue.

Answer (A) is correct. *(CIA, adapted)*

REQUIRED: The action permissible under The IIA Code of Ethics.

DISCUSSION: The principle of confidentiality permits the disclosure of confidential information if a legal or professional obligation exists.

Answer (B) is incorrect. Rule of Conduct 3.2 prohibits internal auditors from using information for personal gain. Answer (C) is incorrect. Rule of Conduct 2.2 prohibits internal auditors from accepting anything that may impair, or be presumed to impair, their professional judgment. Answer (D) is incorrect. Rule of Conduct 2.3 under the objectivity principle requires internal auditors to disclose all material facts known to them that, if not disclosed, might distort the reporting of activities under review.

21.8.4. The IIA's Code of Ethics requires internal auditors to perform their work with

A. Honesty, diligence, and responsibility.

B. Timeliness, sobriety, and clarity.

C. Knowledge, skills, and competencies.

D. Punctuality, objectivity, and responsibility.

Answer (A) is correct. *(CIA, adapted)*

REQUIRED: The qualities internal auditors should exhibit in the performance of their work.

DISCUSSION: Rule of Conduct 1.1 under the integrity principle states, "Internal auditors shall perform their work with honesty, diligence, and responsibility."

Answer (B) is incorrect. Timeliness, sobriety, and clarity are not mentioned in the Code. Answer (C) is incorrect. Knowledge, skills, and competencies are mentioned in the *Standards*. Answer (D) is incorrect. Punctuality is not mentioned in the Code.

21.8.5. An internal auditor working for a chemical manufacturer believed that toxic waste was being dumped in violation of the law. Out of loyalty to the organization, no information regarding the dumping was collected. The internal auditor

A. Violated the Code of Ethics by knowingly becoming a party to an illegal act.

B. Violated the Code of Ethics by failing to protect the well-being of the general public.

C. Did not violate the Code of Ethics. Loyalty to the employer in all matters is required.

D. Did not violate the Code of Ethics. Conclusive information about wrongdoing was not gathered.

Answer (A) is correct. *(CIA, adapted)*

REQUIRED: The ethical implication of failing to gather information about the organization's illegal act.

DISCUSSION: Rule of Conduct 1.3 under the integrity principle prohibits knowingly being a party to any illegal activity. By failing to collect information about a known violation of law, the auditor became party to the illegal act.

Answer (B) is incorrect. The IIA's Code of Ethics does not impose a duty to the general public. Answer (C) is incorrect. The IIA's Code of Ethics does not impose an overriding duty of loyalty to the employer. Answer (D) is incorrect. The internal auditor should have collected and reported such information in accordance with the *Standards*.

21.8.6. An internal auditor discovered some material inefficiencies in a purchasing function. The purchasing manager is the internal auditor's next-door neighbor and best friend. In accordance with The IIA's Code of Ethics, the internal auditor should

A. Objectively include the facts of the case in the engagement communications.

B. Not report the incident because of loyalty to the friend.

C. Include the facts of the case in a special communication submitted only to the friend.

D. Not report the friend unless the activity is illegal.

Answer (A) is correct. *(CIA, adapted)*

REQUIRED: The proper internal auditor action given a conflict between professional duty and friendship.

DISCUSSION: Rule of Conduct 2.3 under the objectivity principle states, "Internal auditors shall disclose all material facts known to them that, if not disclosed, may distort the reporting of activities under review."

21.8.7. The chief audit executive (CAE) has been appointed to a committee to evaluate the appointment of the external auditors. The engagement partner for the external accounting firm wants the CAE to join her for a week of hunting at her private lodge. The CAE should

A. Accept, assuming both their schedules allow it.

B. Refuse on the grounds of conflict of interest.

C. Accept as long as it is not charged to employer time.

D. Ask the comptroller whether accepting the invitation is a violation of the organization's code of ethics.

Answer (B) is correct. *(CIA, adapted)*

REQUIRED: The CAE's response to a social invitation by an external auditor who is subject to evaluation by a committee on which the CAE serves.

DISCUSSION: Rule of Conduct 2.1 under the objectivity principle states, "Internal auditors shall not participate in any activity or relationship that may impair or be presumed to impair their unbiased assessment. This participation includes those activities or relationships that may be in conflict with the interests of the organization." Furthermore, under Rule of Conduct 2.2, "Internal auditors shall not accept anything that may impair or be presumed to impair their professional judgment."

Answer (A) is incorrect. The auditor should not accept. Answer (C) is incorrect. Not charging the time to the company is not sufficient to eliminate conflict-of-interest concerns. Answer (D) is incorrect. The auditor should know that accepting the invitation raises conflict of interest issues.

21.8.8. During an engagement, an employee with whom you have developed a good working relationship informs you that she has some information about senior management that is damaging to the organization and may concern illegal activities. The employee does not want her name associated with the release of the information. Which of the following actions is considered to be unethical?

A. Assure the employee that you can maintain her anonymity and listen to the information.

B. Suggest that the employee consider talking to legal counsel.

C. Inform the employee that you will attempt to keep the source of the information confidential and will look into the matter further.

D. Inform the employee of other methods of communicating this type of information.

Answer (A) is correct. *(CIA, adapted)*

REQUIRED: The action inconsistent with The IIA Code of Ethics and the *Standards*.

DISCUSSION: An internal auditor cannot assure anonymity. Information communicated to an internal auditor is not deemed to be privileged.

Answer (B) is incorrect. Suggesting that the person seek expert legal advice from a qualified individual is appropriate. Answer (C) is incorrect. Promising merely to attempt to keep the source of the information confidential is allowable. This promise is not a guarantee of confidentiality. Answer (D) is incorrect. The employee could be directed to other methods of communicating the information in order to maintain her anonymity.

21.8.9. Which of the following concurrent occupations could appear to subvert the ethical behavior of an internal auditor?

A. Internal auditor and a well-known charitable organization's local in-house chairperson.

B. Internal auditor and part-time business insurance broker.

C. Internal auditor and adjunct faculty member of a local business college that educates potential employees.

D. Internal auditor and landlord of multiple housing that publicly advertises for tenants in a local community newspaper listing monthly rental fees.

Answer (B) is correct. *(CIA, adapted)*

REQUIRED: The concurrent occupations that could create an ethical issue.

DISCUSSION: Rule of Conduct 2.1 under the objectivity principle states, "Internal auditors shall not participate in any activity or relationship that may impair or be presumed to impair their unbiased assessment. This participation includes those activities or relationships that may be in conflict with the interests of the organization." As a business insurance broker, the internal auditor may lose his or her objectivity because (s)he might benefit from a change in the employer's insurance coverage.

Answer (A) is incorrect. The activities of a charity are unlikely to be contrary to the interests of the organization. Answer (C) is incorrect. Teaching is compatible with internal auditing. Answer (D) is incorrect. Whereas dealing in commercial properties might involve a conflict, renting residential units most likely does not.

21.8.10. Internal auditors should be prudent in their relationships with persons and organizations external to their employers. Which of the following activities will most likely not adversely affect internal auditors' ethical behavior?

A. Accepting compensation from professional organizations for consulting work.

B. Serving as consultants to competitor organizations.

C. Serving as consultants to suppliers.

D. Discussing engagement plans or results with external parties.

Answer (A) is correct. *(CIA, adapted)*

REQUIRED: The external relationship most likely not to involve an ethics violation.

DISCUSSION: Professional organizations are unlikely to be employees, clients, customers, suppliers, or business associates of the organization. Thus, the consulting fees are not likely to impair or be presumed to impair the internal auditors' professional judgment (Rule of Conduct 2.2). Moreover, relationships with professional organizations are not likely to create a conflict of interest or impair or be presumed to impair internal auditors' unbiased judgment (Rule of Conduct 2.1). Also, the consulting engagement should not result in the improper use of information (Rule of Conduct 3.2).

Answer (B) is incorrect. Serving as a consultant to competitors might create a conflict of interest. Answer (C) is incorrect. Serving as a consultant to suppliers might create a conflict of interest. Answer (D) is incorrect. Internal auditors should "be prudent in the use and protection of information acquired in the course of their duties" (Rule of Conduct 3.1). Furthermore, such discussion might be "detrimental to the legitimate and ethical objectives of the organization" (Rule of Conduct 3.2).

21.8.11. In some countries, governmental units have established audit standards. For example, in the United States, the Government Accountability Office has developed standards for the conduct of governmental audits, particularly those that relate to compliance with government grants. In performing governmental grant compliance audits, the auditor should

A. Be guided only by the governmental standards.

B. Be guided only by The IIA *Standards* because they are more encompassing.

C. Be guided by the more general standards that have been issued by the public accounting profession.

D. Follow both The IIA *Standards* and any additional governmental standards.

Answer (D) is correct. *(CIA, adapted)*

REQUIRED: The standards an auditor follows when performing governmental grant compliance audits.

DISCUSSION: Rule of Conduct 4.2 of The IIA Code of Ethics states, "Internal auditors shall perform internal auditing services in accordance with the International Standards for the Professional Practice of Internal Auditing." Furthermore, an internal auditor is legally obligated to adhere to governmental standards when performing governmental grant compliance audits.

Answer (A) is incorrect. The internal auditor should not only follow the governmental standards. Answer (B) is incorrect. An internal auditor is legally obligated to adhere to governmental standards when performing governmental grant compliance audits. Answer (C) is incorrect. The internal auditor should follow the standards established for those types of audits.

21.8.12. During the course of an engagement, an internal auditor discovers that a clerk is embezzling funds from the organization. Although this is the first embezzlement ever encountered and the organization has a security department, the internal auditor decides to interrogate the suspect. If the internal auditor is violating The IIA's Code of Ethics, the rule violated is most likely

A. Failing to exercise due diligence.

B. Lack of loyalty to the organization.

C. Lack of competence in this area.

D. Failing to comply with the law.

Answer (C) is correct. *(CIA, adapted)*

REQUIRED: The ethics rule most likely violated.

DISCUSSION: Rule of Conduct 4.1 under the competency principle states, "Internal auditors shall engage only in those services for which they have the necessary knowledge, skills, and experience." Internal auditors may not have, and are not expected to have, knowledge equivalent to that of a person whose primary responsibility is to detect and investigate fraud (Impl. Std. 1210.A2).

Answer (A) is incorrect. The requirement to perform work with diligence does not override the competency Rules of Conduct or the need to use good judgment. Answer (B) is incorrect. Loyalty is better exhibited by consulting with professionals and knowing the limits of competence. Answer (D) is incorrect. The internal auditor may violate the suspect's civil rights as a result of inexperience.

21.8.13. Which situation most likely violates The IIA's Code of Ethics and the *Standards*?

A. The chief audit executive (CAE) disagrees with the engagement client about the observations and recommendations in a sensitive area. The CAE discusses the detail of the observations and the proposed recommendations with a fellow CAE from another organization.

B. An organization's charter for the internal audit activity requires the chief audit executive (CAE) to present the yearly engagement work schedule to the board for its approval and suggestions.

C. The engagement manager has removed the most significant observations and recommendations from the final engagement communication. The in-charge internal auditor opposed the removal, explaining that (s)he knows the reported conditions exist. The in-charge internal auditor agrees that, technically, information is not sufficient to support the observations, but management cannot explain the conditions, and the observations are the only reasonable conclusions.

D. Because the internal audit activity lacks skill and knowledge in a specialty area, the chief audit executive (CAE) has hired an expert. The engagement manager has been asked to review the expert's approach to the assignment. Although knowledgeable about the area under review, the manager is hesitant to accept the assignment because of lack of expertise.

Answer (A) is correct. *(CIA, adapted)*

REQUIRED: The situation most likely to be considered a violation of The IIA Code of Ethics.

DISCUSSION: Rule of Conduct 3.1 under the confidentiality principle states, "Internal auditors shall be prudent in the use and protection of information acquired in the course of their duties." Discussion of sensitive matters with an unauthorized party is the situation most likely to be considered a Code violation.

Answer (B) is incorrect. Approval of the engagement work schedule by the board and senior management is required. Answer (C) is incorrect. Information must be sufficient to achieve engagement objectives. Answer (D) is incorrect. The *Standards* allow use of experts when needed.

21.8.14. Which of the following most likely constitutes a violation of The IIA's Code of Ethics?

A. Auditor A has accepted an assignment to perform an engagement at the electronics manufacturing division. Auditor A has recently joined the internal audit activity. But Auditor A was senior auditor for the external audit of that division and has audited many electronics organizations during the past 2 years.

B. Auditor B has been assigned to perform an engagement at the warehousing function 6 months from now. Auditor B has no expertise in that area but accepted the assignment anyway. Auditor B has signed up for continuing professional education courses in warehousing that will be completed before the assignment begins.

C. Auditor C is content as an internal auditor and has come to look at it as a regular 9-to-5 job. Auditor C has not engaged in continuing professional education or other activities to improve effectiveness during the last 3 years. However, Auditor C feels performance of quality work is the same as before.

D. Auditor D discovered an internal financial fraud during the year. The books were adjusted to properly reflect the loss associated with the fraud. Auditor D discussed the fraud with the external auditor when the external auditor reviewed working papers detailing the incident.

Answer (C) is correct. *(CIA, adapted)*

REQUIRED: The violation of The IIA Code of Ethics.

DISCUSSION: Rule of Conduct 4.3 under the competency principle states, "Internal auditors shall continually improve their proficiency and the effectiveness and quality of their services."

Answer (A) is incorrect. No professional conflict of interest exists per se, especially given that the internal auditor was previously in public accounting. However, the internal auditor should be aware of potential conflicts. Answer (B) is incorrect. An internal auditor must possess the necessary knowledge, skills, and competencies at the time an engagement is conducted, not the time it is accepted. Answer (D) is incorrect. The information was disclosed as part of the normal process of cooperation between the internal and external auditor. Because the books were adjusted, the external auditor was expected to inquire as to the nature of the adjustment.

21.9 Communicating Results

21.9.1. Which of the following is not included in the statement of scope in an engagement final communication?

A. Period covered by the engagement.

B. Engagement objectives.

C. Activities not reviewed.

D. Nature and extent of the work performed.

Answer (B) is correct. *(CIA, adapted)*

REQUIRED: The item not included in the statement of scope in an engagement final communication.

DISCUSSION: Scope statements identify the audited activities and may include supportive information such as time period reviewed and related activities not reviewed to define the boundaries of the engagement. They may describe the nature and extent of engagement work performed. Engagement objectives are included in the purpose paragraph.

21.9.2. Internal auditors realize that at times corrective action is not taken even when agreed to by the appropriate parties. Thus, in an assurance engagement, internal auditors should

A. Decide the extent of necessary follow-up work.

B. Allow management to decide when to follow up because follow-up is management's ultimate responsibility.

C. Decide to conduct follow-up work only if management requests the internal auditor's assistance.

D. Write a follow-up engagement communication with all observations and recommendations and their significance to the operations.

Answer (A) is correct. *(CIA, adapted)*

REQUIRED: The auditor's responsibility to follow up.

DISCUSSION: The chief audit executive determines the nature, timing, and extent of follow-up.

Answer (B) is incorrect. Determining the timing of follow-up is not management's responsibility. It is the responsibility of the CAE. Answer (C) is incorrect. Determining the nature and extent of follow-up is the CAE's responsibility. Management's responsibility is to decide the appropriate action to be taken in response to reported engagement observations and recommendations. Answer (D) is incorrect. The internal auditors must decide the extent of follow-up before submitting a follow-up engagement communication.

21.9.3. Which of the following best defines an internal auditor's overall opinion?

A. A summary of the significant engagement observations.

B. The internal auditor's professional judgment based on multiple engagements.

C. Conclusions that must be included in the final engagement communication.

D. Recommendations for corrective action.

Answer (B) is correct. *(CIA, adapted)*

REQUIRED: The best definition of an internal auditor's overall opinion.

DISCUSSION: An overall opinion is a rating, conclusion, or other description addressing broadly the organization's governance, risk management, or control. It is the professional judgment of the CAE based on multiple engagements and similar activities (e.g., reviews by other service providers). In contrast, a conclusion is based on one engagement stated in an engagement communication. But an overall opinion is communicated separately from an engagement communication.

Answer (A) is incorrect. The summary of significant observations and recommendations is not an overall opinion. An opinion is the internal auditor's professional judgment. Answer (C) is incorrect. The *Standards* do not require the expression of an overall opinion. Answer (D) is incorrect. Recommendations for corrective action are separate from the overall opinion. The overall opinion is the internal auditor's professional judgment.

21.9.4. A *final* communication issued by an internal auditor following an assurance engagement should contain an expression of opinion when

A. The area of the engagement is the financial statements.

B. The internal auditors' work is to be used by external auditors.

C. A full-scope engagement has been conducted in an area.

D. An opinion will improve communications with the readers of the communication.

Answer (D) is correct. *(CIA, adapted)*

REQUIRED: The circumstances in which an engagement final communication issued by an internal auditor should contain an expression of opinion.

DISCUSSION: Final communication of an assurance engagement's results should, if appropriate, contain the internal auditor's opinion (Impl. Std. 2410.A1). Improving communications with the reader satisfies the appropriateness criterion.

Answer (A) is incorrect. The area of the engagement is irrelevant to decisions about whether an overall opinion is appropriate. Answer (B) is incorrect. Whether the internal auditors' work is to be used by external auditors is irrelevant. The external auditors cannot depend on an overall opinion but must examine details and form their own opinion. Answer (C) is incorrect. An overall opinion is not mandatory.

21.9.5. The internal audit activity for a chain of retail stores recently concluded an engagement to evaluate sales adjustments in all stores in the Southeast region. The engagement revealed that several stores are costing the organization substantial sums in duplicate credits to customers' charge accounts. The final engagement communication published 8 weeks after the engagement was concluded incorporated the internal auditors' recommendations to store management that should prevent duplicate credits to customers' accounts. Which of the following standards has been disregarded?

A. The follow-up actions were not adequate.

B. The internal auditors should have implemented appropriate corrective action as soon as the duplicate credits were discovered.

C. Internal auditor recommendations should not be included in the final engagement communication.

D. The final engagement communication was not timely.

Answer (D) is correct. *(CIA, adapted)*

REQUIRED: The standard that was disregarded.

DISCUSSION: Communications must be accurate, objective, clear, concise, constructive, complete, and timely (Perf. Std. 2420). Timely communications are opportune and expedient, depending on the significance of the issue, allowing management to take appropriate corrective action (Inter. Std. 2420). The report, which was not published until 8 weeks after the engagement was concluded, was not issued in a timely fashion, given the significance of the observations and the need for prompt, effective action.

Answer (A) is incorrect. Information is not sufficient to evaluate the effectiveness of follow-up. Answer (B) is incorrect. Internal auditors may properly make recommendations for potential improvements but should not implement corrective action. Answer (C) is incorrect. Internal auditor recommendations are part of the results of the engagement. Final engagement communications include, at a minimum, the purpose, scope, and results of the engagement.

21.9.6. The internal auditor completed work on a segment of the engagement work program. As a result, the internal auditor determined that a modification of the organization's distribution procedures is required. The engagement client agreed and has implemented revised procedures. The internal auditor should

A. Research the problem and recommend in the final engagement communication measures that should be taken.

B. Jointly develop and communicate an appropriate recommendation.

C. Communicate the problem and assume that management will take appropriate action.

D. Indicate in the final engagement communication that the client determined and implemented corrective action.

Answer (D) is correct. *(CIA, adapted)*

REQUIRED: The action an internal auditor should take when an engagement client has implemented changes.

DISCUSSION: The internal auditor may communicate engagement client accomplishments, in terms of improvements since the last engagement or the establishment of a well-controlled operation. This information may be necessary to fairly present the existing conditions and to provide perspective and balance to the final engagement communication.

21.9.7. The final engagement communication regarding supply activities of a division will most likely be circulated to

A. The lowest level of managers with sufficient authority to take action on engagement recommendations because it is their responsibility.

B. The highest level of managers because they should be kept informed.

C. The mid- and lower-level engagement client personnel of the division because they are the ones most affected.

D. The organization's external auditors because they will need the information in performing their own engagement.

Answer (A) is correct. *(CIA, adapted)*

REQUIRED: The most likely recipients of the final operational audit report regarding supply activities of a division.

DISCUSSION: The CAE distributes the final engagement communication to the management of the audited activity and to those members of the organization who can ensure engagement results are given due consideration and take corrective action or ensure that corrective action is taken.

Answer (B) is incorrect. The highest level of managers is likely to receive a summary. Answer (C) is incorrect. Engagement client personnel at lower levels lack authority to act on recommendations. Answer (D) is incorrect. External auditors may see such reports, but the lowest level of managers with authority to take corrective action must see such reports.

21.9.8. Which of the following is false with respect to the use of interim engagement communications? Interim engagement communications

A. Are used to communicate information that requires immediate attention.

B. Are used to communicate a change in engagement scope for the activity under review.

C. Keep management informed of engagement progress when engagements extend over a long period of time.

D. Eliminate the need for issuing final engagement communications.

Answer (D) is correct. *(CIA, adapted)*

REQUIRED: The false statement about interim engagement communications.

DISCUSSION: Interim reports are oral or written and may be transmitted formally or informally. They are used to communicate information that requires immediate attention, to communicate a change in engagement scope for the activity under review, or to keep management informed of engagement progress when engagements extend over a long period. The use of interim reports does not diminish or eliminate the need for a final report.

21.9.9. One purpose of the exit meeting is for the internal auditor to

A. Require corrective action.

B. Review and verify the appropriateness of the engagement communication based upon client input.

C. Review the performance of internal auditors assigned to the engagement.

D. Present the final engagement communication to management.

Answer (B) is correct. *(CIA, adapted)*

REQUIRED: The purpose of the exit meeting.

DISCUSSION: The primary purpose of an exit meeting is to ensure the accuracy of the information used by the internal auditor. Accordingly, client input is solicited to verify the appropriateness of the engagement communication.

Answer (A) is incorrect. Only management can require corrective action. Answer (C) is incorrect. Internal auditor performance is reviewed in private with the individual employee, not at the exit meeting. Answer (D) is incorrect. The exit meeting is normally based on draft communications. The final engagement communication is subject to modification based on the results of the exit meeting.

21.9.10. The scope section of an internal auditor's final engagement communication should identify

A. The engagement techniques used.

B. Any limitations imposed.

C. The sampling methodology employed.

D. Any unresolved differences with engagement clients.

Answer (B) is correct. *(CIA, adapted)*

REQUIRED: The item identified in the scope section of an internal audit report.

DISCUSSION: Because limitations set the boundaries of the engagement, they must be identified in the scope section.

21.9.11. An internal auditor has completed an engagement to review an organization's activities and is ready to issue a final engagement communication. However, the engagement client disagrees with the internal auditor's conclusions. The internal auditor should

A. Withhold the issuance of the final engagement communication until agreement on the issues is obtained.

B. Perform more work, with the engagement client's concurrence, to resolve areas of disagreement. Delay the issuance of the final engagement communication until agreement is reached.

C. Issue the final engagement communication and indicate that the engagement client has provided a scope limitation that has led to a difference as to the conclusions.

D. Issue the final engagement communication and state both the internal auditor and engagement client positions and the reasons for the disagreement.

Answer (D) is correct. *(CIA, adapted)*

REQUIRED: The action to be taken when an engagement client disagrees with an internal auditor's conclusions before the final report is issued.

DISCUSSION: As part of the internal auditor's discussions with the engagement client, the internal auditor obtains agreement on the results of the engagement and on any necessary plan of action to improve operations. If the internal auditor and engagement client disagree about the engagement results, the engagement communications state both positions and the reasons for the disagreement. The engagement client's written comments may be included as an appendix to the engagement report, in the body of the report, or in a cover letter.

Answer (A) is incorrect. If the engagement is complete, the final engagement communication should be issued in a timely manner. Moreover, agreement with the engagement client is not mandatory. Answer (B) is incorrect. If the internal auditor is satisfied with the conclusions drawn from the engagement, there is no reason to perform more work. Answer (C) is incorrect. The disagreement on conclusions is not a scope limitation.

21.9.12. Communication skills are important to internal auditors. The internal auditor should be able to effectively convey all of the following to the engagement client except

A. The engagement objectives for a specific engagement client.

B. The evaluations based on a preliminary survey of an engagement client.

C. The risk assessment used in selecting the area for engagement investigation.

D. Recommendations that are generated in relationship to a specific engagement client.

Answer (C) is correct. *(CIA, adapted)*

REQUIRED: The matter that an internal auditor need not convey to the engagement client.

DISCUSSION: Internal auditors need to be skilled in oral and written communications so that they can clearly and effectively convey such matters as engagement objectives, evaluations, conclusions, and recommendations. The internal auditor's risk assessment is not specifically mentioned.

21.9.13. When a final engagement communication contains a significant error, the *Standards* require the chief audit executive to

A. Issue a written report to individuals who can ensure that engagement results are given due consideration.

B. Issue a written report to individuals who received the original communication.

C. Communicate corrected information to all individuals who received the original communication.

D. Communicate corrected information to all those who might have relied on the original communication.

Answer (C) is correct. *(Publisher, adapted)*

REQUIRED: The duty of the CAE when a final engagement communication contains a significant error.

DISCUSSION: If a final engagement communication contains a significant error or omission, the CAE must communicate corrected information to all who received the original communication (Perf. Std. 2421). Thus, the *Standards* do not require a written report.

21.9.14. Exit meetings serve to ensure the accuracy of the information used by an internal auditor. A secondary purpose of an exit meeting is to

A. Get immediate action on a recommendation.

B. Improve relations with the engagement clients.

C. Agree to the appropriate distribution of the final engagement communication.

D. Brief senior management on the results of the engagement.

Answer (B) is correct. *(CIA, adapted)*

REQUIRED: The secondary purpose of an exit meeting.

DISCUSSION: Discussion of conclusions and recommendations with the engagement client not only provides a quality control review but is also a courtesy that enhances the internal auditor-client relationship. In addition, the exit meeting is an important aspect of the participative approach to internal auditing because it involves the client in the engagement process as well as in any recommended changes arising from the engagement.

Answer (A) is incorrect. An interim engagement communication would have been used to obtain immediate action on a recommendation. Answer (C) is incorrect. The distribution of communications is not a secondary purpose of an exit meeting. Answer (D) is incorrect. Senior management ordinarily should be given a summary of the results.

21.9.15. An internal auditor has just completed an engagement and is in the process of preparing the final engagement communication. The observations in the final engagement communication should include

A. Statements of opinion about the cause of an observation.

B. Pertinent factual statements concerning the control weaknesses uncovered during the course of the engagement.

C. Statements of both fact and opinion developed during the course of the engagement.

D. Statements concerning potential future events that may be helpful to the engagement client.

Answer (B) is correct. *(CIA, adapted)*

REQUIRED: The information included in a final engagement communication.

DISCUSSION: Observations are pertinent statements of fact.

Answer (A) is incorrect. Observations must be statements of fact rather than statements of opinion. Opinions are the internal auditor's evaluations of the effects of observations and recommendations on the activities reviewed. Answer (C) is incorrect. The observations include statements of fact, but not statements of opinion. Answer (D) is incorrect. Observations concern current, not future, factual conditions or events.

STUDY UNIT TWENTY-TWO
INFORMATION SYSTEMS

This study unit covers computers, computer operations, computer systems, and computer controls.

A variety of controls may be performed to ensure the accuracy, completeness, and authorization of transactions. The two broad groupings of information systems control activities are general and application controls.

General controls are policies and procedures that relate to the organization's processing environment as a whole and support the effective functioning of application controls. These include controls over data center operations, system software acquisition and maintenance, applications system development and maintenance, and access security. The controls apply to mainframe, server, and end-user environments.

1. **Data center operation controls** include the plan of the organization and the operation of the computer processing activity. They are concerned with the proper segregation of duties and responsibilities within the computer processing environment. The responsibilities of systems analysts, programmers, operators, file librarians, and the control group should be performed by different individuals, and proper supervision should be provided. Operating controls ensure efficient and effective operation within the computer processing department. These controls also ensure proper procedures in the event of data loss caused by error or disaster. Typical operating controls include the proper labeling of all files, both internally and externally, halt and error procedures, duplicate files, and reconstruction procedures for files.
2. **System software acquisition, application system development, and maintenance controls** are concerned with the proper planning, procurement, testing, and documentation of systems. These controls also provide for security and virus protection of software, including operating systems, utility programs, and application software. Maintenance controls include authorizations, program change controls, and documentation, including proper use of flowcharts.
3. **Access security controls** provide assurance that only authorized individuals have access to computer equipment and data files. These controls include physical safeguards of equipment, proper library security, and passwords.

Application controls apply to the processing of individual applications. These controls help ensure that transactions are valid, properly authorized, and completely and accurately processed. They can be classified into input, processing, and output controls.

1. **Input controls** are designed to provide reasonable assurance that data received for computer processing have been properly authorized and are in a form suitable for processing. Input controls also include those that relate to rejection, correction, and resubmission of data that were initially incorrect.
2. **Processing controls** are designed to provide reasonable assurance that data submitted for processing have been processed appropriately, i.e., that all transactions are processed as authorized, no authorized transactions are omitted, and no unauthorized transactions are added.
3. **Output controls** are designed to ensure that the processing results are accurate and that only authorized personnel receive the output.

QUESTIONS

22.1 Introduction to the Information Systems Environment

22.1.1. A management information system

A. Can exist only with computers.

B. Primarily processes data and produces reports.

C. Supports the operations, management, and decision-making functions in an organization.

D. Is a single large system in an organization.

Answer (C) is correct. *(CIA, adapted)*

REQUIRED: The description of a management information system.

DISCUSSION: A management information system (MIS) is a system of resources within the organization that processes data to generate information useful in operations and management. It provides the most comprehensive support for decision making involving structured tasks.

Answer (A) is incorrect. An MIS rarely exists without computers except in small businesses. Answer (B) is incorrect. The data processing cycle (processing of data and production of reports) generates information for use in the MIS. Answer (D) is incorrect. The MIS consists of many subsystems, including the accounting information system.

22.1.2. Early decision models used with structured decisions, such as inventory reordering and production scheduling, emphasized finding the structure of the decision and programming as much of it as possible. More recent models have been developed to support unstructured decision processes. Models of the latter type are called

A. Decision support systems.

B. Management information systems.

C. Systems analysis techniques.

D. Rational decision models.

Answer (A) is correct. *(CIA, adapted)*

REQUIRED: The term for models developed to support unstructured decision processes.

DISCUSSION: A decision support system (DSS) assists middle- and upper-level managers in long-term, nonroutine, and often unstructured decision making. It is an aid to decision making, not the automation of a decision process.

Answer (B) is incorrect. A MIS does not normally include subsystems that provide support for unstructured decisions. Answer (C) is incorrect. Systems analysis techniques are used to design the DSS. Answer (D) is incorrect. All decision models are rational.

22.1.3. The first phase in the evolutionary development of information systems occurs when

A. Management discovers it is losing money.

B. Resources permit the hiring of a system staff.

C. The decision is made to acquire a computer system.

D. The growth of an enterprise brings about the need for improved administrative planning and control.

Answer (D) is correct. *(CDP, adapted)*

REQUIRED: The first phase in the evolutionary development of an information system.

DISCUSSION: As its information needs change, an organization requires improved methods of processing data to provide information for managerial decisions and to control the implementation of those decisions. When this need is recognized, firms begin systems development activities.

Answer (A) is incorrect. Management may lose money for many reasons other than the lack of systems development. Answer (B) is incorrect. The need for improved processing should be the deciding criterion, not whether resources permit the hiring of additional staff. Answer (C) is incorrect. The need should precede the decision to acquire a computer system.

22.1.4. Who is ultimately responsible for the implementation of cost-effective controls in an automated system?

A. The director of internal auditing.

B. Operating management.

C. The independent auditor.

D. The control group in the computer processing department.

Answer (B) is correct. *(CIA, adapted)*

REQUIRED: The party or parties primarily responsible for the implementation of cost-effective controls.

DISCUSSION: Operating management should ensure that effective controls are implemented in all parts of an organization. Management is ultimately responsible for establishing systems to provide reasonable assurance of achieving organizational objectives and goals.

Answer (A) is incorrect. Internal auditing is responsible for evaluating, but not establishing, internal controls. Answer (C) is incorrect. The independent auditor is responsible for expressing an opinion on the fairness of the financial statements. Answer (D) is incorrect. The control group acts as a liaison between system users and the information processing department and implements many controls on an operational basis, but it is not responsible for the development of controls.

22.1.5. The most common computer-related problem confronting organizations is

A. Hardware malfunction.

B. Input errors and omissions.

C. Disruption to computer processing caused by natural disasters.

D. Fraud.

Answer (B) is correct. *(CIA, adapted)*

REQUIRED: The most common problem confronting an organization using computers.

DISCUSSION: The most common problem confronting an organization in its use of computers is erroneous or incomplete input. Input is especially susceptible to errors and omissions because of the substantial human intervention required. Comprehensive and effective input controls are necessary to ensure that data stored in files or used in processing are not contaminated.

Answer (A) is incorrect. Hardware malfunction is not considered a major problem once the development and testing phase is complete. Answer (C) is incorrect. The second most common problem is the disruption to processing caused by natural disasters, such as fire or power failures. Answer (D) is incorrect. The third most common problem is computer abuse, e.g., fraud.

22.1.6. Which one of the following statements about an accounting information system (AIS) is false?

A. AIS supports day-to-day operations by collecting and sorting data about an organization's transactions.

B. The information produced by AIS is made available to all levels of management for use in planning and controlling an organization's activities.

C. AIS is best suited to solve problems where there is great uncertainty and ill-defined reporting requirements.

D. AIS is often referred to as a transaction processing system.

Answer (C) is correct. *(CMA, adapted)*

REQUIRED: The false statement about an accounting information system (AIS).

DISCUSSION: An AIS is a subsystem of a management information system that processes financial and transactional data relevant to managerial and financial accounting. The AIS supports operations by collecting and sorting data about an organization s transactions. An AIS is concerned not only with external parties, but also with the internal activities needed for management decision making at all levels. An AIS is best suited to solve problems when reporting requirements are well defined. A decision support system is a better choice for problems in which decision making is less structured.

22.1.7. Which of the following risks are greater in computerized systems than in manual systems?

I. Erroneous data conversion
II. Erroneous source document preparation
III. Repetition of errors
IV. Concentration of data

A. I and II.

B. II and III.

C. I, III, and IV.

D. I, II, III, and IV.

Answer (C) is correct. *(CISA, adapted)*

REQUIRED: The risks that are greater in computerized systems than in manual systems.

DISCUSSION: Unlike a manual system, a computer system converts data to machine-readable form so that transactions can be processed. This additional step increases the risk of input error. Moreover, if an error exists in the program, systematic, repetitive errors will occur in processing transactions. Finally, data are typically stored magnetically or optically on disks. This concentration of data increases the risk of loss from natural and other disasters. Source document preparation either precedes processing or is eliminated altogether in a computerized system. Thus, the risk of erroneous source document preparation in computerized systems is the same as or less than the equivalent risk in manual systems.

22.1.8. Management activities can be classified in three levels: strategic planning, management control, and operational control. Information requirements vary with the level of management activity. Which of the following best describes the information requirements for strategic planning?

A. Frequent use, external, aggregate information.

B. Future-oriented, outdated, detailed information.

C. Highly current, accurate, largely internal information.

D. Wide scope, aggregate, future-oriented information.

Answer (D) is correct. *(CIA, adapted)*

REQUIRED: The best description of the information requirements for strategic planning.

DISCUSSION: Strategic planning concerns development of the entity's long-range mission and objectives and the means for accomplishing them. Such plans are often stated in general terms and exclude operational detail because of uncertainty about future conditions. Strategic planning is commonly defined as having a planning horizon of 1 to 10 years. The information needed for strategic planning tends to come from external sources, to be very wide in scope, and to be highly aggregated (not detailed). Moreover, this information is future oriented, much less current than that needed for operational or management control, relatively less accurate, and infrequently used.

Answer (A) is incorrect. Information needed for strategic planning is not frequently used. Answer (B) is incorrect. Information needed for strategic planning is not detailed or necessarily outdated. Answer (C) is incorrect. Information needed for operational control needs to be highly current and accurate and is largely internal.

22.1.9. Compared with closed systems, open systems are characterized by

A. Less expensive components.

B. Decreased interoperability.

C. More dependence on particular vendors.

D. More restricted portability.

Answer (A) is correct. *(CIA, adapted)*

REQUIRED: The item that characterizes open systems.

DISCUSSION: Open systems consist of components produced in conformity with nonproprietary public standards. Since the 1980s, government agencies have demanded that suppliers provide components with interfaces defined by public standards. These standards apply especially to operating systems and telecommunications protocols. Thus, they permit systems from different suppliers to work together (interoperability). Moreover, open systems can be sized to an entity's needs (scalability), relocated to new platforms (portability), and used for years to come (compatibility). Another result of product interchangeability is the formation of a commodity market and a decline in prices. Less product differentiation means that competition is increasingly based solely on price.

Answer (B) is incorrect. Open systems have increased interoperability. Answer (C) is incorrect. Users of open systems have a wider range of vendors available. Answer (D) is incorrect. Open systems are more portable.

22.2 Basic Hardware Concepts

22.2.1. A piece of hardware that takes the computer's digital information and transforms it into signals that can be sent over ordinary communication channels is called a(n)

A. Terminal emulator.

B. Communications control unit.

C. VPN.

D. Modem.

Answer (D) is correct. *(CIA, adapted)*

REQUIRED: The hardware that transforms digital information into analog signals.

DISCUSSION: Modems are used to communicate between different devices across communication channels. The analog modem (modulator-demodulator) converts the digital form of data storage in a computer into sound waves. The modem at the receiving end converts the analog signal back to the digital form used by the computer. A digital modem converts digital signals from one transmission system to another (e.g., a cable modem).

Answer (A) is incorrect. A terminal emulator permits a personal computer to interface with a mainframe. Answer (B) is incorrect. Communications control units include communications processors (front-end processors), multiplexors, and concentrators. Communications processors are small computers that perform communications tasks (storing and moving data, editing, message switching, etc.). Multiplexors combine signals from different terminals into one signal to be sent to the CPU or other point. A concentrator is essentially a more advanced multiplexor. Answer (C) is incorrect. A virtual private network allows for a secure connection to another network over the Internet.

22.2.2. Which of the following is not an element of hardware?

A. Monitors.

B. Application programs.

C. CD-RW drive.

D. Scanners.

Answer (B) is correct. *(Publisher, adapted)*

REQUIRED: The item that is not considered hardware.

DISCUSSION: Computer hardware consists of the configuration of physical equipment. Application software consists of programs written for or by users to perform certain ultimate tasks specified by the users.

Answer (A) is incorrect. Monitors are output devices for display of data or graphics. Answer (C) is incorrect. A CD-RW (compact disk-read/write) is a laser optical disk. It provides high capacity storage, is movable, has a rapid data transfer rate, and is rewritable. Answer (D) is incorrect. Scanners are input devices that digitize documents and,graphics.

22.2.3. Which of the following is a hardware device not usually associated with input?

A. Printer.

B. Optical scanner.

C. Touch screen.

D. Mouse.

Answer (A) is correct. *(Publisher, adapted)*

REQUIRED: The hardware device not usually associated with input.

DISCUSSION: A printer is used to produce a hard copy of information output. Printers may print one character, one line, or one page at a time. They also vary with respect to speed and quality.

Answer (B) is incorrect. An optical scanner reads characters directly from source documents based upon the shapes of the characters. Answer (C) is incorrect. Touch screen technology provides another limited alternative to keyboard input. Commands or data can be entered by touching the sensitized surface of a monitor. Answer (D) is incorrect. A mouse is a pointing device used for input.

22.2.4. Which of the following computer hardware devices allows for an immediate update of merchandise inventory in a retail environment?

A. Inventory control terminal.

B. CD-RW.

C. Digital storage device.

D. Point-of-sale terminal.

Answer (D) is correct. *(CIA, adapted)*

REQUIRED: The computer hardware device that allows for an immediate update of merchandise inventory.

DISCUSSION: Point-of-sale terminals have replaced cash registers in retail stores. They capture data by optical scanning or by keying. The data are then transmitted to a CPU. The system facilitates collection of sales data, updating and ordering of inventory, pricing at the point of sale, and checking of customer credit cards.

Answer (A) is incorrect. The term inventory control terminal is not meaningful in this context. Answer (B) is incorrect. CD-RW is the acronym for a compact disk that is rewritable. Answer (C) is incorrect. A digital storage device is used to store and back up data.

22.2.5. Banks are required to process many transactions from paper documents (e.g., checks, deposit slips) during the course of an average business day. This requires a reliable, yet economical form of input. The most common source automation device used by banks is

A. RFID.

B. Magnetic tape.

C. Bar coding.

D. Magnetic ink character recognition.

Answer (D) is correct. *(CMA, adapted)*

REQUIRED: The most common source automation device used by banks.

DISCUSSION: Magnetic ink character recognition (MICR) is used by banks to read the magnetic ink on checks and deposit slips. An MICR reader is a form of data entry device.

Answer (A) is incorrect. A radio frequency input device (RFID) is not a common source automation device used by banks. Answer (B) is incorrect. Magnetic tape is used as a secondary storage medium. It is low cost and reusable, but data retrieval is relatively slow because it uses sequential access. Answer (C) is incorrect. Bar coding is a data entry technique often used by manufacturers, wholesalers, and retailers, but it is rarely used by banks.

22.2.6. Uninterruptible power supplies are used in computer centers to reduce the likelihood of

A. Failing to control concurrent access to data.

B. Losing data stored in main memory.

C. Dropping data during transmission.

D. Crashing disk drive read-write heads.

Answer (B) is correct. *(CIA, adapted)*

REQUIRED: The reason for uninterruptible power supplies in computer centers.

DISCUSSION: Fully protected systems have generator or battery backup to prevent data destruction and downtime from electrical power disturbances. Loss of electrical power or voltage fluctuations need not disturb the vulnerable contents of main memory if an uninterruptible system is in place.

Answer (A) is incorrect. Concurrency controls serve this purpose. Answer (C) is incorrect. Hardware controls built into the system avoid errors in transmission. Answer (D) is incorrect. Disk drives are currently designed to protect against crashing read-write heads.

22.2.7. When evaluating the downsizing of the plant materials inventory system, data center personnel considered redundant array of inexpensive (or independent) disks (RAID) for the inventory database. One reason to use RAID is to ensure that

A. If one drive fails, all data can still be reconstructed.

B. All data are split evenly across pairs of drives.

C. Before-and-after images are stored for all transactions.

D. Write time is minimized to avoid concurrency conflicts.

Answer (A) is correct. *(CIA, adapted)*

REQUIRED: The reason to use RAID.

DISCUSSION: A disk array expedites data transfer and provides fault tolerance. It combines two or more drives with special controller circuitry and software to execute reads and writes as if only one disk drive existed. When files are stored on RAID, data can be reconstructed even if one drive fails.

Answer (B) is incorrect. Splitting data evenly across pairs of drives (data striping) results in faster reads and writes but reduced reliability. The failure of one drive causes loss of all data. Answer (C) is incorrect. Writing before-and-after images is a means of creating a transaction log for database transactions, which can be implemented with or without RAID. Answer (D) is incorrect. Minimizing write time is not an advantage of RAID.

22.2.8. The location in the central processing unit (CPU) where data and programs are temporarily stored during processing is the

A. USB flash drive.

B. Magnetic tape drive.

C. Random-access memory (RAM).

D. Magnetic disk drive.

Answer (C) is correct. *(CMA, adapted)*

REQUIRED: The location in the CPU where data and programs are temporarily stored during processing.

DISCUSSION: The CPU is the part of the computer system that manipulates numbers, symbols, and letters. Primary storage is the area in the CPU where programs and data are temporarily stored during processing. Internal primary storage is also known as random-access memory because each memory location therein can be randomly accessed in the same amount of time.

Answer (A) is incorrect. A universal serial bus flash drive is a small, portable device that plugs into a computer's USB port and functions as a portable hard drive. Answer (B) is incorrect. A magnetic tape drive is not for temporary storage. Answer (D) is incorrect. A magnetic disk drive is a secondary storage medium for permanent storage of data.

22.2.9. In a computer system, the place where parts of the operating system program and language translator program are permanently stored is

A. Read only memory (ROM).

B. Magnetic disk drive.

C. Random access memory (RAM).

D. Magnetic tape drive.

Answer (A) is correct. *(CMA, adapted)*

REQUIRED: The place where parts of the operating system and language translator are permanently stored.

DISCUSSION: ROM consists of semiconductor chips that come from the manufacturer with programs already stored in them. These chips can be read from but not written to and therefore constitute permanent storage. Start-up instructions are permanently stored in ROM in a personal computer to initiate processing and prevent users from accidentally erasing or changing the system. Some personal computers, however, have erasable, programmable ROM (EPROM). EPROM may be erased by an ultraviolet technique (but not by the computer) after which new instructions may be entered.

Answer (B) is incorrect. A magnetic disk is a temporary storage device. Answer (C) is incorrect. RAM is a temporary storage device. Answer (D) is incorrect. Magnetic tape is a temporary storage device.

22.2.10. Access time in relation to computer processing is the amount of time it takes to

A. Transmit data from a remote terminal to a central computer.
B. Complete a transaction from initial input to output.
C. Perform a computer instruction.
D. Retrieve data from memory.

Answer (D) is correct. *(CMA, adapted)*

REQUIRED: The definition of access time.

DISCUSSION: Access time is the interval between the moment at which an instruction control unit initiates a call for data and the moment at which delivery of the data is completed.

Answer (A) is incorrect. Access time refers to the speed of data retrieval not data transmittal. Answer (B) is incorrect. Throughput time is the time to complete a transaction from initial input to output. Answer (C) is incorrect. Access time is much slower than the time required to execute an instruction.

22.2.11. Which of the following measures indicates the computational power of a microprocessor?

A. Capacity of the hard disk.
B. Main memory storage capacity.
C. Number of bits processed per second.
D. Read only memory.

Answer (C) is correct. *(CIA, adapted)*

REQUIRED: The measure indicating the computational power of a microprocessor.

DISCUSSION: Processing speed is commonly calculated in terms of arithmetic-logic operations performed per second. This measure is a function of the main processing chip's cycle speed stated in gigahertz.

Answer (A) is incorrect. Capacity of the hard disk is a measure of data storage. Answer (B) is incorrect. Main memory storage capacity is a measure of memory. Answer (D) is incorrect. Read only memory is main memory that ordinarily cannot be modified by the user. It is not a performance measure.

22.2.12. A manufacturer is considering using bar code identification for recording information on parts used by the manufacturer. A reason to use bar codes rather than other means of identification is to ensure that

A. The movement of all parts is recorded.
B. The movement of parts is easily and quickly recorded.
C. Vendors use the same part numbers.
D. Vendors use the same identification methods.

Answer (B) is correct. *(CIA, adapted)*

REQUIRED: The reason to use bar codes.

DISCUSSION: Bar code scanning is a form of optical character recognition. Bar codes are a series of bars of different widths that represent critical information about the item. They can be read and the information can be instantly recorded using a scanner. Thus, bar coding records the movement of parts with minimal labor costs.

Answer (A) is incorrect. Any identification method may fail to record the movement of some parts. Answer (C) is incorrect. Each vendor has its own part-numbering scheme. Answer (D) is incorrect. Each vendor has its own identification method, although vendors in the same industry often cooperate to minimize the number of bar code systems they use.

22.3 Basic Software and Data Organization Concepts

22.3.1. Several language interfaces exist in a database management system. These typically include a data-definition language (DDL), a data control language (DCL), a data-manipulation language (DML), and a database query language (DQL). What language interface would a database administrator use to establish the structure of database tables?

A. DDL.
B. DCL.
C. DML.
D. DQL.

Answer (A) is correct. *(CIA, adapted)*

REQUIRED: The language interface used by a database administrator to establish the structure of database tables.

DISCUSSION: The data-definition language defines the database structure and content, especially the schema (the description of the entire database) and subschema (logical views of the database). The schema specifies characteristics such as the names of the data elements contained in the database and their relationship to each other. The subschema defines the logical data views required for applications. Thus, it limits the data elements and functions available to each application.

Answer (B) is incorrect. DCL is used to specify privileges and security rules. Answer (C) is incorrect. DML provides programmers with a facility to update the database. Answer (D) is incorrect. DQL is used for ad hoc queries.

22.3.2. A highly confidential file needs to be properly deleted from a computer. The best way to accomplish this task is to use a(n)

A. Security card.

B. Encryption routine.

C. Disk utility.

D. Multiplexor.

Answer (C) is correct. *(CIA, adapted)*

REQUIRED: The best way to delete a confidential file.

DISCUSSION: Unknown copies of sensitive data may exist on the hard drive or in memory. Most delete utilities erase file pointers but not underlying data. However, some utilities are available for this purpose.

Answer (A) is incorrect. Security cards are used during logons. Answer (B) is incorrect. Encryption routines are mathematical algorithms and keys used to encode sensitive information so that it is unintelligible until decrypted. Answer (D) is incorrect. A multiplexor is used to control multiple transmissions from linked terminals and modems.

22.3.3. Computer manufacturers install software programs permanently inside the computer as part of its main memory to provide protection from erasure or loss if electrical power is interrupted. This concept is known as

A. File integrity.

B. Software control.

C. Firmware.

D. Random access memory (RAM).

Answer (C) is correct. *(CMA, adapted)*

REQUIRED: The term for software installed permanently in the computer.

DISCUSSION: Firmware consists of software programs permanently installed in the computer hardware. Firmware can be used to monitor internal conditions, e.g., by making signal counts (such as accesses to the computer) or taking snapshots of indicators. Thus, ROM (read only memory) is firmware.

Answer (A) is incorrect. File integrity is achieved by implementing controls that protect the completeness, accuracy, and physical security of files. Answer (B) is incorrect. Software control refers to library control of programs. Answer (D) is incorrect. RAM is a computer's main memory.

22.3.4. Software offered to users on a "try before you buy" basis is called

A. Shareware.

B. Firmware.

C. Middleware.

D. Freeware.

Answer (A) is correct. *(Publisher, adapted)*

REQUIRED: The software offered on a "try before you buy" basis.

DISCUSSION: Shareware is commercial software offered to users without initial charge. It is traditionally offered by less established software developers. Shareware often comes with some features disabled. Ordinarily, it can only be used without charge for a limited time. Users pay a fee to "register" the software, in return for which they receive a license to use it with all features enabled.

Answer (B) is incorrect. Firmware is permanently wired into the hardware. Answer (C) is incorrect. Middleware oversees the interaction between disparate systems. Answer (D) is incorrect. Freeware is software that, although usually copyrighted, may be used without any licensing fee on a much less limited basis than shareware.

22.3.5. A program that edits a group of source language statements for syntax errors and translates the statements into an object program is a(n)

A. Interpreter.

B. Compiler.

C. Debugger.

D. Encrypter.

Answer (B) is correct. *(CIA, adapted)*

REQUIRED: The program that edits and translates source language statements into an object program.

DISCUSSION: A compiler is a form of software that performs language translation. It translates human-readable computer language (source code) programs into machine language object programs. The instructions in object code are grouped into modules. Prior to execution, the modules are joined by the linkage editor to form the load module. The load module is what the computer actually executes.

Answer (A) is incorrect. An interpreter translates and executes source language statements one at a time. Answer (C) is incorrect. A debugger is a program that traces program execution or captures variable values for the purpose of helping the developer find program errors. Answer (D) is incorrect. An encrypter is a program that converts ordinary text to encoded text that cannot be deciphered without access to the encryption key and procedure.

22.3.6. A computer program processes payrolls. The program is a(n)

A. Operating system.

B. Application program.

C. Report generator.

D. Utility program.

Answer (B) is correct. *(CIA, adapted)*

REQUIRED: The term associated with a computer program used to perform a business function.

DISCUSSION: Application programs are written to solve specific user problems; that is, they perform the ultimate computer functions required by system users. Thus, a program designed to process payroll is an application program.

Answer (A) is incorrect. An operating system is a set of programs used by the CPU to control operations. Answer (C) is incorrect. A report generator is a component of a database management system that produces customized reports using data stored in the database. Answer (D) is incorrect. Utility programs are standardized subroutines that can be incorporated into other programs.

22.3.7. Specialized programs that perform generalized functions, such as sorting and data comparison, are called

A. Utility programs.

B. Communication programs.

C. Object programs.

D. Source programs.

Answer (A) is correct. *(CISA, adapted)*

REQUIRED: The term describing programs that perform generalized functions such as sorting.

DISCUSSION: Utility programs are standardized subroutines that can be incorporated into other programs, e.g., to alphabetize or to find square roots. These routines are ordinarily supplied by the manufacturer and are part of the operating system.

Answer (B) is incorrect. Communication programs provide interface between remote computer sites. Answer (C) is incorrect. Object programs are not limited to utility functions. Answer (D) is incorrect. Source programs are not limited to utility functions.

22.3.8. Python, FORTRAN, C++, and Ruby are all examples of

A. Application programs.

B. Machine languages.

C. Higher-level languages.

D. Operating systems.

Answer (C) is correct. *(CIA, adapted)*

REQUIRED: The proper classification of Python, FORTRAN, C++, and Ruby.

DISCUSSION: A higher-level programming language allows specification of processing steps in terms of highly aggregated operations. They are ordinarily user-friendly. Translation into machine language (an object program) is performed by a compiler program. Examples include Python, FORTRAN, C++, and Ruby.

Answer (A) is incorrect. All of the answers are languages, not application programs. Answer (B) is incorrect. Machine language is a programming language made up of instructions that a computer can directly recognize and execute. Answer (D) is incorrect. An operating system is a set of programs and routines used by the CPU to control the operations of the computer and its peripheral equipment.

22.3.9. Structured Query Language (SQL) is best defined as a

A. Programming language in which UNIX is written.

B. Report generator used to produce customized business reports.

C. Programming language in which many business applications are written.

D. Data manipulation language used in conjunction with a database management system (DBMS).

Answer (D) is correct. *(Publisher, adapted)*

REQUIRED: The definition of SQL.

DISCUSSION: SQL is the most common standard data manipulation language for relational DBMSs. A data manipulation language is used for accessing and processing data from a database to satisfy requests for data and to create applications.

Answer (A) is incorrect. C is the language used in much of the UNIX operating system. Answer (B) is incorrect. A report generator has a greater emphasis on data formats, organization, and display than a query language. Answer (C) is incorrect. COBOL is the programming language in which many business applications are written.

22.3.10. Regardless of the language in which an application program is written, its execution by a computer requires that primary memory contain

A. A utility program.

B. An operating system.

C. Compiler.

D. Assembly.

Answer (B) is correct. *(D. Payne)*

REQUIRED: The item necessary to execute an application program.

DISCUSSION: An operating system (e.g., UNIX or Windows) is required in all computerized systems to oversee the elements of the CPU and the interaction of the hardware components.

Answer (A) is incorrect. Utility programs are application programs that are usually attached to larger programs. They perform various activities, such as sorting data, merging files, converting data from one medium to another, and printing. Answer (C) is incorrect. A compiler converts (compiles) a program written in a source language, such as FORTRAN, into machine language. Answer (D) is incorrect. An assembler translates an assembly language program into machine language. Assembly language uses mnemonic codes for each machine language instruction.

22.3.11. Computers understand codes that represent letters of the alphabet, numbers, or special characters. These codes require that data be converted into predefined groups of binary digits. Such chains of digits are referred to as

A. Registers.

B. ASCII code.

C. Input.

D. Bytes.

Answer (D) is correct. *(CIA, adapted)*

REQUIRED: The term for the chains of digits that a computer is capable of understanding.

DISCUSSION: A byte is a grouping of bits that can define one unit of data, such as a letter or an integer.

Answer (A) is incorrect. A register is a location within the CPU where data and instructions are temporarily stored. Answer (B) is incorrect. ASCII (American Standard Code for Information Interchange) is the coding convention itself. Answer (C) is incorrect. Input is the data placed into processing (noun) or the act of placing the data into processing (verb).

22.3.12. Computers containing more than one central processing unit (CPU) are increasingly common. This feature enables a computer to execute multiple instructions from multiple programs simultaneously. This process is

A. Time sharing.

B. Multitasking.

C. Multiprocessing.

D. Batch processing.

Answer (C) is correct. *(Publisher, adapted)*

REQUIRED: The term for executing multiple programs with multiple CPUs.

DISCUSSION: Multiprocessing greatly increases system efficiency by executing multiple programs on the same computer at the same time. In systems with only one CPU, although multiple programs may be active simultaneously, program instructions are only executed for one program at a time.

Answer (A) is incorrect. In time sharing, the CPU spends a fixed amount of time on each program. Answer (B) is incorrect. Multitasking is multiprogramming on a single-user operating system. It is the process of having multiple programs active at a given time, although the CPU is executing instructions from only one program at a time. Answer (D) is incorrect. Batch processing entails execution of a list of instructions from beginning to end without interruption.

22.3.13. Structured programming is best described as a technique that

A. Makes the order of the coding reflect as closely as possible the dynamic execution of the program.

B. Reduces the maintenance time of programs by the use of small-scale program modules.

C. Provides knowledge of program functions to other programmers via peer reviews.

D. Controls the coding and testing of the high-level functions of the program in the development process.

Answer (B) is correct. *(CISA, adapted)*

REQUIRED: The best description of structured programming.

DISCUSSION: Structured programming is an approach for creating a series of standardized, interrelated subroutines or modules. Guidelines are followed by programmers to create programs that are easy to read, maintain, and modify because changes in one module do not affect others.

Answer (A) is incorrect. The instructions coded by programmers do not necessarily reflect the actual order of the processing steps performed during execution by the computer. Answer (C) is incorrect. Structured programming does allow other programmers to understand the coding but not via peer reviews. Answer (D) is incorrect. Structured programming does not provide for testing during the development process.

22.3.14. The primary purpose of a macro program in a spreadsheet application is to allow the end user to

A. Reduce keystrokes.

B. Merge files with two different formats.

C. Delete redundant files from the root directory.

D. Rearrange data elements.

Answer (A) is correct. *(CIA, adapted)*

REQUIRED: The purpose of a macro program.

DISCUSSION: A macro program records keystrokes and commands used in repetitious jobs, which reduces the necessary keystrokes.

Answer (B) is incorrect. A merge file is a system software utility. Answer (C) is incorrect. Deleting files is a system software utility. Answer (D) is incorrect. Rearranging data elements is a possible macro application but is not the primary purpose of macros.

22.3.15. In an inventory system on a database, one stored record contains part number, part name, part color, and part weight. These individual items are called

A. Fields.

B. Stored files.

C. Bytes.

D. Occurrences.

Answer (A) is correct. *(CIA, adapted)*

REQUIRED: The term for the data elements in a record.

DISCUSSION: A record is a collection of related data items (fields). A field (data item) is a group of characters representing one unit of information.

Answer (B) is incorrect. A file is a group or set of related records ordered to facilitate processing. Answer (C) is incorrect. A byte is a group of bits (binary digits). It represents one character. Answer (D) is incorrect. "Occurrences" is not a meaningful term in this context.

22.3.16. Block codes

A. Are generally used to identify missing items from a set of documents or records.

B. Allow a user to number items sequentially.

C. Allow a user to assign meaning to particular segments of a coding scheme.

D. Are randomly calculated groups of numbers used as a control check.

Answer (C) is correct. *(CMA, adapted)*

REQUIRED: The true statement about block codes.

DISCUSSION: Coding of data is the assignment of alphanumeric symbols consistent with a classification scheme. Block coding assigns blocks of numbers in a sequence to classes of items. For example, in a chart of accounts, assets may be assigned numbers 100-199, liabilities the numbers 200-299, etc.

Answer (A) is incorrect. Some items in a block code may be unassigned to allow for flexibility. Answer (B) is incorrect. Some items in a block code may be unassigned to allow for flexibility. Answer (D) is incorrect. Block codes are assigned judgmentally, not at random.

22.3.17. An inventory clerk, using a computer terminal, views the following on screen: part number, part description, quantity on hand, quantity on order, order quantity, and reorder point for a particular inventory item. Collectively, these data make up a

A. Field.

B. File.

C. Database.

D. Record.

Answer (D) is correct. *(CIA, adapted)*

REQUIRED: The term for the collection of data described.

DISCUSSION: A record is a collection of related data items (fields). A field (data item) is a group of characters representing one unit of information. The part number, part description, etc., are represented by fields.

Answer (A) is incorrect. Field refers to a single data item. Answer (B) is incorrect. File refers to multiple records. Answer (C) is incorrect. Database refers to multiple files.

22.3.18. A file containing relatively long-term information used as a source of reference and periodically updated with detail is termed a

A. Transaction file.

B. Record layout.

C. Master file.

D. Dump.

Answer (C) is correct. *(Publisher, adapted)*

REQUIRED: The file containing relatively long-term information.

DISCUSSION: A master file containing relatively long-term information, such as an inventory file listing the part number, description, quantities on hand, quantities on order, etc., is used in a file processing run. Transactions are processed against the master file, thus periodically updating it.

Answer (A) is incorrect. A transaction file (detail file) contains current transaction information used to update the master file, such as the number of items shipped to be removed from inventory. Answer (B) is incorrect. A record layout is a representation of the format of the records on the file. It shows the position and length of the fields in the file. Answer (D) is incorrect. A dump is a listing of the contents of memory.

22.4 File Structures and Modes of Processing

22.4.1. The relationship between online, real-time database systems and batch processing systems is that

A. A firm will have only one processing mode because a single computer cannot do both.

B. A firm will not use batch processing if it has a large computer.

C. A firm may use both processing modes concurrently.

D. A firm will always prefer an online, real-time processing system because batch processing is slow.

Answer (C) is correct. *(Publisher, adapted)*

REQUIRED: The relationship between online, real-time database systems and batch processing systems.

DISCUSSION: Firms may find it beneficial to incorporate both processing modes into one system. A database may be established for information that must be obtained quickly, for instance, a sales processing system in which credit information must be available to sales personnel on an ongoing basis. However, other processing requirements may take advantage of the speed and control provided in a batch processing system. For example, payroll transactions may be processed quickly and efficiently in a batch mode.

Answer (A) is incorrect. One computer can operate in both modes. Answer (B) is incorrect. Firms with large computers find it both cost effective and efficient to group transactions and process them periodically. Answer (D) is incorrect. A firm will not automatically prefer an online, real-time system. When transactions, e.g., payroll, can be conveniently grouped, processing is extremely fast and efficient in a batch mode.

22.4.2. Sequential access means that

A. Data must be stored on magnetic tape.

B. The address of the location of data is found through the use of either an algorithm or an index.

C. Each record can be accessed in the same amount of time.

D. To read record 500, records 1 through 499 must be read first.

Answer (D) is correct. *(CIA, adapted)*

REQUIRED: The characteristic of sequential access.

DISCUSSION: Sequential access means that records are stored in logical or physical order, and the only way to retrieve a record is to read the preceding records. Records may be sequentially ordered despite being physically separate. Thus, they may be linked via pointers.

Answer (A) is incorrect. Magnetic tape is not the only medium on which data are stored sequentially. For instance, data storage on disk drives may also be sequential. Answer (B) is incorrect. Locating data through a hashing function or index is a characteristic of direct or random file access. Answer (C) is incorrect. Given sequential access storage, less time is needed to retrieve the first record than subsequent records.

22.4.3. Which of the following features is least likely to be found in a real-time application?

A. User manuals.

B. Preformatted screens.

C. Automatic error correction.

D. Turnaround documents.

Answer (D) is correct. *(CISA, adapted)*

REQUIRED: The feature not likely to be used in a real-time application.

DISCUSSION: Turnaround documents are source documents typically printed by the computer system as output and then later returned for use as machine-readable input. Real-time systems are unlikely to use them.

Answer (A) is incorrect. User manuals are an important component of a real-time system. They explain how to use the system properly. Answer (B) is incorrect. Preformatted screens are usually the means by which users interact with real-time systems. Answer (C) is incorrect. Automatic error correction is a prime advantage of real-time systems. It allows immediate error detection and correction.

22.4.4. Data processing assigns a unique identification code or key to each data record. Which one of the following statements about coding is false?

A. A primary key is the main code used to store and locate records within a file.

B. Records can be sorted, and temporary files created, using codes other than their primary keys.

C. Secondary keys are used when the primary keys cannot be found.

D. Secondary keys are used for alternative purposes, including inverted files, and a given data record may have more than one secondary key.

Answer (C) is correct. *(CMA, adapted)*

REQUIRED: The statement about coding that is false.

DISCUSSION: A primary key is the main code used to store and locate records within a file. Primary keys uniquely identify every record. Secondary keys may not be unique and thus cannot serve the same purposes as primary keys.

Answer (A) is incorrect. A primary key is the main code used to store and locate records within a file. Answer (B) is incorrect. Records can be sorted and temporary files created using codes other than their primary keys. Answer (D) is incorrect. Secondary keys are used for alternative purposes, including inverted files, and a given data record may have more than one secondary key.

22.4.5. Which of the following is most likely characteristic of a direct access file that uses indexes or dictionaries as its addressing technique when processing randomly?

A. A randomizing formula is used.

B. Two accesses are required to retrieve each record.

C. Synonyms will be generated that will result in extra accesses.

D. There will be a high incidence of gaps or unassigned physical records within the file.

Answer (B) is correct. *(CDP, adapted)*

REQUIRED: The most likely characteristic of a direct access file using indexes.

DISCUSSION: Typically, indexed files will use tables or indexes for locating the address of a record. For example, in accessing an alphabetic record, first the index must be accessed and searched (in much the same way as finding a telephone number in a directory) to locate the pointer or address of the record. Next, the record must be accessed at the address location.

Answer (A) is incorrect. A randomizing formula or hashing scheme is used to obtain direct access without consulting an index (direct access method). The procedure determines the address of a record by transforming the primary key of the record into a random number (the desired address). Answer (C) is incorrect. Synonyms may be generated when access is obtained without indexation. If the randomizing formula generates the same address for two different keys (a synonym), the record is placed in the next higher available address. Answer (D) is incorrect. Indexing permits elimination of most gaps. The direct access method leaves gaps because the randomizing procedure may not generate the numbers corresponding to many storage addresses.

22.4.6. Based only on the database file excerpt presented below, which one of the fields or combinations of fields is eligible for use as a key?

Column I	Column II	Column III	Column IV	Column V	Column VI
Florida	Sopchoppy	G9441	6	02/06/2017	$1823.65
Georgia	Hahira	H5277	2	02/06/2017	$412.01
Iowa	Clear Lake	B2021	1	02/06/2017	$6606.53
Iowa	Clear Lake	C2021	14	02/06/2017	$178.90
Kansas	Lawrence	A1714	2	02/06/2017	$444.28
Georgia	Milledgeville	A1713	1	02/06/2017	$195.60

A. Column I and Column II in combination.

B. Column I and Column V in combination.

C. Column III alone.

D. Column IV and Column V in combination.

Answer (C) is correct. *(Publisher, adapted)*

REQUIRED: The field or combination thereof that could be used as a key.

DISCUSSION: Some field or combination of fields on each record is designated as the key. The essence of a key is that it contains enough information to uniquely identify each record; i.e., there can be no two records with the same key. Of the choices presented, only Column III by itself uniquely identifies each record.

Answer (A) is incorrect. Column I and Column II in combination do not uniquely identify each record. Answer (B) is incorrect. Column I and Column V in combination do not uniquely identify each record. Answer (D) is incorrect. Column IV and Column V in combination do not uniquely identify each record.

22.4.7. A system updates master files in batch mode overnight, and duplicated copies of the files are updated and queried during the day. Which of the following best describes this online system?

A. Memo updating.

B. Online updating.

C. Remote job entry.

D. Inquiry.

Answer (A) is correct. *(CISA, adapted)*

REQUIRED: The term for nightly updating master files in batch mode, with duplicated copies updated and queried daily.

DISCUSSION: Memo updating minimizes the risk of damage to the database during processing transactions. A copy of the database is updated upon data entry, but a log of each transaction is also stored. Periodically, the transaction log is used to update the actual database, and a new “memo” copy is established.

Answer (B) is incorrect. Online updating requires master files to be updated a short time after the transaction is entered. Answer (C) is incorrect. Remote job entry is the initiation of an application program from a remote terminal. Answer (D) is incorrect. Inquiry provides users with a response to a request in a timely manner with no file update.

22.4.8. A business uses magnetic disks to store accounts receivable information. What data file concepts underlie the ability to answer customer inquiries as they are received?

A. Sequential storage.

B. Spreadsheets.

C. Record keys, indexes, and pointers.

D. Batch processing.

Answer (C) is correct. *(CIA, adapted)*

REQUIRED: The data file concepts needed to answer customer inquiries as they are received.

DISCUSSION: A record key is an attribute that uniquely identifies or distinguishes each record from the others. An index is a table listing storage locations for attributes, often including those other than the unique record key attribute. A pointer is a data item that indicates the physical address of the next logically related record.

Answer (A) is incorrect. The ability to respond immediately to customers requires direct access. Answer (B) is incorrect. The ability to respond immediately to customers requires direct access. Answer (D) is incorrect. Answering inquiries on a real-time basis requires immediate processing.

22.5 Databases

22.5.1. Of the following, the greatest advantage of a database (server) architecture is that

A. Data redundancy can be reduced.

B. Conversion to a database system is inexpensive and can be accomplished quickly.

C. Multiple occurrences of data items are useful for consistency checking.

D. Backup and recovery procedures are minimized.

Answer (A) is correct. *(CIA, adapted)*

REQUIRED: The greatest advantage of a database architecture.

DISCUSSION: Data organized in files and used by the organization's various application programs are collectively known as a database. In a database system, storage structures are created that render the applications programs independent of the physical or logical arrangement of the data. Each data item has a standard definition, name, and format, and related items are linked by a system of pointers. The programs therefore need only specify data items by name, not by location. A database management system handles retrieval and storage. Because separate files for different application programs are unnecessary, data redundancy can be substantially reduced.

Answer (B) is incorrect. Conversion to a database is often costly and time-consuming. Answer (C) is incorrect. A traditional flat-file system, not a database, has multiple occurrences of data items. Answer (D) is incorrect. Given the absence of data redundancy and the quick propagation of data errors throughout applications, backup and recovery procedures are just as critical in a database as in a flat-file system.

22.5.2. One advantage of a database management system (DBMS) is

A. Each organizational unit takes responsibility and control for its own data.

B. The cost of the data processing department decreases as users are now responsible for establishing their own data handling techniques.

C. A decreased vulnerability as the database management system has numerous security controls to prevent disasters.

D. The independence of the data from the application programs, which allows the programs to be developed for the user's specific needs without concern for data capture problems.

Answer (D) is correct. *(CMA, adapted)*

REQUIRED: The advantage of a DBMS.

DISCUSSION: A fundamental characteristic of databases is that applications are independent of the database structure; when writing programs or designing applications to use the database, only the name of the desired item is necessary. Programs can be developed for the user's specific needs without concern for data capture problems. Reference can be made to the items using the data manipulation language, after which the DBMS takes care of locating and retrieving the desired items. The physical or logical structure of the database can be completely altered without having to change any of the programs using the data items. Only the schema requires alteration.

Answer (A) is incorrect. Each organizational unit develops programs to use the elements of a broad database. Answer (B) is incorrect. Data handling techniques are still the responsibility of the data processing department. It is the use of the data that is departmentalized. Answer (C) is incorrect. The DBMS is not necessarily safer than any other database system.

22.5.3. Which of the following is a false statement about a database management system application environment?

A. Data are used concurrently by multiple users.

B. Data are shared by passing files between programs or systems.

C. The physical structure of the data is independent of user needs.

D. Data definition is independent of any one program.

Answer (B) is correct. *(CISA, adapted)*

REQUIRED: The false statement about data in a DBMS environment.

DISCUSSION: In this kind of system, applications use the same database. There is no need to pass files between applications.

Answer (A) is incorrect. The advantage of a DBMS is that data can be used concurrently by multiple users. Answer (C) is incorrect. When a DBMS is used, the physical structure of the data is independent of user needs. Answer (D) is incorrect. When a DBMS is used, the data are defined independently of the needs of any one program.

22.5.4. In a database system, locking of data helps preserve data integrity by permitting transactions to have control of all the data needed to complete the transactions. However, implementing a locking procedure could lead to

A. Inconsistent processing.

B. Rollback failures.

C. Unrecoverable transactions.

D. Deadly embraces (retrieval contention).

Answer (D) is correct. *(CIA, adapted)*

REQUIRED: The potential problem of a locking procedure.

DISCUSSION: In a distributed processing system, the data and resources a transaction may update or use should be held in their current status until the transaction is complete. A deadly embrace occurs when two transactions need the same resource at the same time.

Answer (A) is incorrect. Inconsistent processing occurs when a transaction has different effects depending on when it is processed. Data locking ensures consistent processing. Answer (B) is incorrect. Rollback failure is the inability of the software to undo the effects of a transaction that could not be run to completion. A rollback failure is not caused by data locking. However, data locking may lead to situations in which rollback is required. Answer (C) is incorrect. Unrecoverable transactions are not a typical symptom of locking procedures.

22.5.5. An internal auditor encounters a batch-processed payroll in which each record contains the same type of data elements, in the same order, with each data element needing the same number of storage spaces. Which file structure most appropriately supports this set of records?

A. Single flat file structure.

B. Hierarchical structure.

C. Network structure.

D. Relational structure.

Answer (A) is correct. *(CIA, adapted)*

REQUIRED: The file structure in which each record has the same type and order of data elements and the same storage requirements.

DISCUSSION: In a single flat file structure, all attributes and field lengths in a record are identical to those in the other records. The structure is typically a table or spreadsheet with records for rows and attributes for columns.

Answer (B) is incorrect. A hierarchical or tree structure is used to express relationships in which one attribute or item is related to many others in layers of subordinate records. Answer (C) is incorrect. A network structure expresses complex relationships in which many attributes are related to many others. Answer (D) is incorrect. A relational structure is not unlike the flat structure but is far more sophisticated. It gives the system the ability to handle many data relationships that were not anticipated by the designers. It uses a series of tables in which each table defines a relationship.

22.5.6. To trace data through several application programs, an auditor needs to know what programs use the data, which files contain the data, and which printed reports display the data. If data exist only in a database system, the auditor could probably find all of this information in a

A. Data dictionary.

B. Database schema.

C. Data encryptor.

D. Decision table.

Answer (A) is correct. *(CIA, adapted)*

REQUIRED: The information source in a database needed to trace data through several application programs.

DISCUSSION: The data dictionary is a file of all data items contained in the database and their length, usage, and ownership. Only certain persons or entities are permitted to retrieve data or to modify data items.

Answer (B) is incorrect. The schema describes the structure of the database. Answer (C) is incorrect. An encryptor encodes data. Answer (D) is incorrect. A decision table is a type of logic diagram that presents in matrix form the decision points and related actions reflected in a computer program.

Questions 22.5.7 through 22.5.12 are based on the following information. Five brand managers in a consumer food products company met regularly to figure out what price points were being lowered by their competitors and how well coupon promotions did. The data they needed to analyze consisted of about 1 terabyte of daily point-of-sale (POS) data from major grocery chains for each month. The brand managers are competent users of spreadsheet and database software on personal computers. They considered several alternative software options to access and manipulate data to answer their questions.

22.5.7. The selected option is unlikely to use a hierarchical database system because

A. A hierarchical database system requires multiple joins.

B. Programming queries for it are too costly and time consuming.

C. Point-of-sale data are too sensitive for routine access.

D. Summarization of point-of-sale data will not answer the questions.

Answer (B) is correct. *(CIA, adapted)*

REQUIRED: The reason the selected option is unlikely to use a hierarchical database system.

DISCUSSION: A hierarchical structure is tree-like. A record is divided into segments that are connected in one-to-many relationships. Because all of the paths through the data must be prespecified, a hierarchical structure is inflexible and does not support ad hoc queries. Thus, programming queries for a hierarchical database are often costly and time consuming.

Answer (A) is incorrect. Hierarchical database systems do not have commands for joins, which are standard features in relational systems. Answer (C) is incorrect. The point-of-sale information is clearly proprietary, but brand managers must use it to manage the business. Answer (D) is incorrect. Point-of-sale data contain precisely the information that, if summarized appropriately, will answer questions about product sales and product use.

22.5.8. The limiting factor in the brand managers' use of a relational database system to answer their ad hoc questions will most likely be

A. Understanding what individual data records represent.

B. Obtaining computer resources for complicated queries.

C. Distinguishing primary and foreign keys in the data.

D. Lack of management interest in using the results.

Answer (B) is correct. *(CIA, adapted)*

REQUIRED: The limiting factor in the use of a relational database to answer ad hoc queries.

DISCUSSION: The limiting factor will likely be the availability of computer resources for complicated queries about the large volume (1 terabyte) of data. The disadvantage of relational databases is low processing efficiency. Many accesses may be needed to execute the select, join, and project commands.

Answer (A) is incorrect. The brand managers understand the data that point-of-sale terminals capture in grocery stores. Answer (C) is incorrect. Distinguishing primary and foreign keys in the data will be relatively straightforward. The brand managers are already familiar with the data. Answer (D) is incorrect. Management is highly interested in the results.

22.5.9. The organization's senior management was pleased that its brand managers were taking the initiative to use sales data creatively. The information systems director, however, was concerned that the brand managers might be creating standard queries that would provide erroneous results for decision making. The best approach for ensuring the correctness of the brand managers' queries is

A. A source code review of the queries.

B. A code comparison audit.

C. A transaction retrieval and analysis.

D. An input-output analysis.

Answer (A) is correct. *(CIA, adapted)*

REQUIRED: The best approach for ensuring correctness of queries.

DISCUSSION: A source code review, that is, a review of the programs written in a high-level language, will detect erroneous queries written by the managers, which may then be corrected.

Answer (B) is incorrect. A code comparison audit is used to compare two versions of the same program to verify that only authorized code is executed. Answer (C) is incorrect. A transaction retrieval and analysis is a sampling approach to collecting data about transactions to verify correct processing. Answer (D) is incorrect. An input-output analysis traces transactions from input to output.

22.5.10. The brand managers tried to import the POS data into personal computer spreadsheets for analysis. Their efforts were unsuccessful, most likely because of

A. The complexity of the mainframe data structure and the large volume of data.

B. The difficulty of establishing access privileges for each subset of the mainframe data.

C. Inconsistencies in the mainframe data due to lack of integrity constraints on the data files.

D. Error-prone transmission links for downloading the data from the mainframe data files.

Answer (A) is correct. *(CIA, adapted)*

REQUIRED: The reason efforts to include POS data in spreadsheets were not successful.

DISCUSSION: The managers' efforts were unsuccessful because of the high complexity of the mainframe data structure and the large volume of data. Because spreadsheets lack SQL (structured query language) query capabilities, there is no way to manipulate the huge volume of data into two-dimensional views that can be readily imported into spreadsheets. SQL is the standard data manipulation language for relational databases. A data manipulation language is used in conjunction with a conventional third- or fourth-generation programming language to extract data from databases and develop applications.

Answer (B) is incorrect. Access privileges for the POS data would have to be established, but this operation is routine. Answer (C) is incorrect. Lack of integrity constraints on data files might result in inaccurate data but would not affect downloading and subsequent analysis. Answer (D) is incorrect. Transmission links for downloading the data from the mainframe data files can be made sufficiently error free to accomplish the downloading.

22.5.11. Eventually, the brand managers chose a data analysis tool and report writer that permitted multidimensional views of the data. The tool could support different views, such as actual versus projected sales by region, actual versus projected sales by product, and projected sales by product and by region. In order to see the data in such views, the brand managers would need to specify

A. A protocol for data transmission.

B. Access privileges by user number.

C. Integrity constraints for the data.

D. Criteria for retrieving the data.

Answer (D) is correct. *(CIA, adapted)*

REQUIRED: The item that must be specified to see the data.

DISCUSSION: In the mainframe database, the data exist in files or tables, not in the formats interesting to brand managers. Thus, before users can see views of the data, the data must be retrieved and reconfigured in appropriate ways.

Answer (A) is incorrect. Protocols for data transmission will be determined by IS and telecommunications personnel, not by users. Answer (B) is incorrect. Different access privileges may be granted to different users, but specifying access privileges by user number does not cause data to be retrieved in a specified format. Answer (C) is incorrect. Integrity constraints will be established for data entering the original database on the mainframe, but they are independent of how data views will be presented to users.

22.5.12. After abandoning spreadsheets as their analysis tool, the brand managers were successful in downloading limited subsets of the POS and using the data to populate relational database files on their personal computers. They could then access the data using a relational query language. One of the downloaded files contained actual sales by product by store, and another contained projected sales by product by store. In order to compare actual and projected sales by product by store, a query would have to include

A. Projecting the two tables on product and store identification codes.

B. Projecting the two tables on product identification codes.

C. Joining the two tables on product and store identification codes.

D. Joining the two tables on product identification codes.

Answer (C) is correct. *(CIA, adapted)*

REQUIRED: The operation required to compare data in relational database files.

DISCUSSION: The join operation combines relational tables. Thus, joining the two tables on product and store identification codes combines the two files containing those codes. The next step is to project a subset of the joined table that includes the desired data.

Answer (A) is incorrect. Projecting is the relational operation that creates column subsets from a file. Projecting the tables on identification codes would still leave actual and projected sales in different files. Answer (B) is incorrect. Projecting is the relational operation that creates column subsets from a file. Projecting the tables on identification codes would still leave actual and projected sales in different files. Answer (D) is incorrect. Joining the two tables on product identification codes does not achieve the necessary combination with store identification codes.

22.5.13. Which of the following database models is considered to be the most versatile?

A. The hierarchical model.

B. The tree model.

C. The network model.

D. The relational model.

Answer (D) is correct. *(CIA, adapted)*

REQUIRED: The most versatile database model.

DISCUSSION: Because data are organized in two-dimensional tables, the relational database models are easier to construct than the complex architectures that result when using the hierarchical and network models. The tables (relations) provide flexibility because they can be combined (joined) in many ways to permit a wide variety of inquiries. They also permit data to be more readily added to or omitted from the data structures.

Answer (A) is incorrect. The hierarchical model organizes data through the development of relationships that are strictly one to many. Construction of this model is difficult because the data are hard coded. When data are added to the database, the index must be completely redefined. Answer (B) is incorrect. The tree model organizes data through the development of relationships that are strictly one to many. Construction of this model is difficult because the data are hard coded. When data are added to the database, the index must be completely redefined. Answer (C) is incorrect. The network model organizes data through the development of relationships that are many to many. Construction is therefore difficult.

22.5.14. A flat file structure is used in database management systems (DBMS) when a

A. Complex network structure is employed.

B. Network-based structure is used and a complex database schema is developed.

C. Simple network structure is employed.

D. Relational database model is selected for use.

Answer (D) is correct. *(CMA, adapted)*

REQUIRED: The situation in which a flat file structure is used with a DBMS.

DISCUSSION: A flat file structure is used with a relational database model. A relational structure organizes data in conceptual tables. One relation (table or file) can be joined together or related to another without pointers or linked lists if each contains one or more of the same fields (also known as columns or attributes). The relational structure has become popular because it is relatively easy to construct and yet very powerful.

Answer (A) is incorrect. A complex network structure requires something more intricate than a flat file structure. Answer (B) is incorrect. A network database structure reduces redundancy by arranging data through development of many-to-many relationships; that is, each item may have multiple antecedent as well as successive relationships, which would preclude a simple flat file structure. Answer (C) is incorrect. "Simple network structure" is oxymoronic. The nature of the multiple relationships within a networked database precludes simplicity.

22.5.15. All of the following are methods for distributing a relational database across multiple servers except

A. Snapshot (making a copy of the database for distribution).

B. Replication (creating and maintaining replica copies at multiple locations).

C. Normalization (separating the database into logical tables for easier user processing).

D. Fragmentation (separating the database into parts and distributing where they are needed).

Answer (C) is correct. *(CIA, adapted)*

REQUIRED: The item not a method for distributing a relational database across multiple servers.

DISCUSSION: Normalization is the term for determining how groups of data items in a relational structure are arranged in records in a database. This process relies on "normal forms," that is, conceptual definitions of data records and specified design rules. Normalization is intended to prevent inconsistent updating of data items. It is a process of breaking down a complex data structure by creating smaller, more efficient relations, thereby minimizing or eliminating the repeating groups in each relation.

Answer (A) is incorrect. The snapshot technique makes duplicates to be stored at multiple locations. Changes are periodically copied and sent to each location. If a database is small, storing multiple copies may be cheaper than retrieving records from a central site. Answer (B) is incorrect. The replication technique makes duplicates to be stored at multiple locations. Changes are periodically copied and sent to each location. If a database is small, storing multiple copies may be cheaper than retrieving records from a central site. Answer (D) is incorrect. Fragmentation or partitioning stores specific records where they are most needed. For example, a financial institution may store a particular customer's data at the branch where (s)he usually transacts his or her business. If the customer executes a transaction at another branch, the pertinent data are retrieved via communications lines.

22.5.16. Users making queries in a relational database often need to combine several tables to get the information they want. One approach to combining tables is known as

A. Joining.

B. Merging.

C. Projecting.

D. Pointing.

Answer (A) is correct. *(CIA, adapted)*

REQUIRED: The approach to combining tables when making database queries.

DISCUSSION: Joining is the combining of two or more relational tables based on a common data element. For example, if a supplier table contains information about suppliers and a parts table contains information about parts, the two tables can be joined using the supplier number (assuming both tables contain this attribute) to give information about the supplier of particular parts.

Answer (B) is incorrect. The three basic operations in a relational database are selecting, joining, and projecting. Answer (C) is incorrect. Projecting is the basic operation in a relational database that results in a subset consisting of columns (fields) in a table. This operation creates a new table containing only the required information. Answer (D) is incorrect. A pointer is a data element attached to a record that gives the address of another record.

22.6 Networks and Data Communication

22.6.1. An electronic meeting conducted between several parties at remote sites is referred to as

A. Teleprocessing.

B. Interactive processing.

C. Telecommuting.

D. Teleconferencing.

Answer (D) is correct. *(CMA, adapted)*

REQUIRED: The process of holding an electronic meeting between several parties at remote sites.

DISCUSSION: Conducting an electronic meeting among several parties at remote sites is teleconferencing. It can be accomplished by telephone or electronic mail group communication software. Videoconferencing permits the conferees to see each other on video screens. The practice has grown in recent years as companies have attempted to cut their travel costs.

Answer (A) is incorrect. Teleprocessing refers to connections in an online system. Answer (B) is incorrect. Interactive processing allows users to converse directly with the system. It requires online processing and direct access to stored information. Answer (C) is incorrect. Telecommuting refers to the practice of individuals working out of their homes by communicating with their office via the computer.

22.6.2. Which of the following statements is true regarding Transmission Control Protocol and Internet Protocol (TCP/IP)?

A. Every TCP/IP-supported transmission is an exchange of funds.

B. TCP/IP networks are limited to large mainframe computers.

C. Every site connected to a TCP/IP network has a unique address.

D. The actual physical connections among the various networks are limited to TCP/IP ports.

Answer (C) is correct. *(CPA, adapted)*

REQUIRED: The true statement regarding TCP/IP.

DISCUSSION: TCP/IP is a suite of communications protocols used to connect computers to the Internet. It is also built into network operating systems. It is the foundation of the Internet protocol as well as numerous other commercial protocols. Every site connected to a TCP/IP network has a unique address.

Answer (A) is incorrect. TCP/IP supports numerous transmissions, not just those involving the exchange of funds. Answer (B) is incorrect. TCP/IP networks can be accessed from both personal computers and large mainframe computers. Answer (D) is incorrect. The physical connections are accessed by the data link connections, which in turn are accessible by numerous network and transport protocols.

22.6.3. Which of the following is considered to be a server in a local area network (LAN)?

A. The cabling that physically interconnects the nodes of the LAN.

B. A device that stores program and data files for users of the LAN.

C. A device that connects the LAN to other networks.

D. A workstation that is dedicated to a single user on the LAN.

Answer (B) is correct. *(CIA, adapted)*

REQUIRED: The server in a local area network.

DISCUSSION: A server is a computer in a network that operates as a librarian. It stores programs and data files for users of the LAN and manages access to them.

Answer (A) is incorrect. The cabling that interconnects the nodes of the LAN is the telecommunications link. Answer (C) is incorrect. A device that connects the LAN to other networks is a network gateway. Answer (D) is incorrect. A workstation dedicated to a single user of the LAN is a client.

22.6.4. Which of the following is not a characteristic of a graphical user interface termed a dashboard?

A. It attempts to provide as much data as possible.

B. It organizes and presents information in a way that is easy to read.

C. It provides a decision maker a sense of the big picture.

D. It helps a user navigate and interpret data.

Answer (A) is correct. *(Publisher, adapted)*

REQUIRED: The statement not characteristic of a dashboard.

DISCUSSION: A dashboard helps prevent a user from drowning in a sea of data. It is a visual way of interacting with a computer using items such as windows, icons, and menus used by most modern systems. It helps a user navigate, organize, and interpret data to make it understandable and useful.

22.6.5. In distributed data processing, a ring network

A. Has all computers linked to a host computer, and each linked computer routes all data through the host computer.

B. Links all communication channels to form a loop, and each link passes communications through its neighbor to the appropriate location.

C. Attaches all channel messages along one common line with communication to the appropriate location via direct access.

D. Organizes itself along hierarchical lines of communication usually to a central host computer.

Answer (B) is correct. *(CMA, adapted)*

REQUIRED: The true statement about a ring network in a distributed data processing system.

DISCUSSION: In a distributed system, an organization's processing needs are examined in their totality. The decision is not whether an application should be done centrally or locally, but rather which parts are better performed by small local computers as intelligent terminals, and which parts are better performed at some other, possibly centralized, site. The key distinction between decentralized and distributed systems is the interconnection among the nodes in the network. A ring network links all communication channels to form a loop and each link passes communications through its neighbor to the appropriate location.

Answer (A) is incorrect. A star network routes all data through the host computer. Answer (C) is incorrect. A bus network attaches all channel messages along one common line with communication to the appropriate location via direct access. Answer (D) is incorrect. A tree configuration is organized along hierarchical lines to a host computer.

22.6.6. When two devices in a data communications system are communicating, there must be agreement as to how both data and control information are to be packaged and interpreted. Which of the following terms is commonly used to describe this type of agreement?

A. Asynchronous communication.

B. Synchronous communication.

C. Communication channel.

D. Communication protocol.

Answer (D) is correct. *(CIA, adapted)*

REQUIRED: The agreement as to how both data and control information are to be packaged and interpreted.

DISCUSSION: A protocol is a set of formal rules or conventions governing communication between a sending and a receiving device. It prescribes the manner by which data are transmitted between these communications devices. In essence, a protocol is the envelope within which each message is transmitted throughout a data communications network.

Answer (A) is incorrect. Asynchronous communication is a mode of transmission. Communication is in disjointed segments, typically character by character, preceded by a start code and ended by a stop code. Answer (B) is incorrect. Synchronous communication is a mode of transmission in which a continuous stream of blocks of characters result in faster communications. Answer (C) is incorrect. A communication channel is a transmission link between devices in a network. The term is also used for a small processor that controls input-output devices.

22.6.7. An insurance firm uses a wide area network (WAN) to allow agents away from the home office to obtain current rates and client information and to submit approved claims using notebook computers and dial-in modems. In this situation, which of the following methods will provide the best data security?

A. Dedicated phone lines.

B. Call-back features.

C. Frequent changes of user IDs and passwords.

D. End-to-end data encryption.

Answer (D) is correct. *(CIA, adapted)*

REQUIRED: The best data security method for a wide area network.

DISCUSSION: Encryption of data is a security procedure in which a program encodes data prior to transmission and another program decodes the data after transmission. Encoding is important when confidential data that can be electronically monitored are transmitted between geographically separated locations. The question defines what is termed "tunneling" or a "virtual private network."

Answer (A) is incorrect. Dedicated phone lines are not available to agents in the field. Answer (B) is incorrect. Call-back features are used to authenticate the user but do not otherwise protect the transmitted data. Answer (C) is incorrect. Frequent changes of user IDs and passwords are used to authenticate the user but do not otherwise protect the transmitted data.

22.6.8. Large organizations often have their own telecommunications networks for transmitting and receiving voice, data, and images. Very small organizations, however, are unlikely to be able to make the investment required for their own networks and are more likely to use

A. Public switched lines.

B. Fast-packet switches.

C. Standard electronic mail systems.

D. A WAN.

Answer (A) is correct. *(CIA, adapted)*

REQUIRED: The telecommunications networks likely to be used by small organizations.

DISCUSSION: Organizations can use public switched lines (phone lines) on a per-transmission basis. This option is the most cost-effective way for low-volume users to conduct telecommunications.

Answer (B) is incorrect. Fast-packet switches receive transmissions from various devices, break the data into packets, and route them over a network to their destination. They are typically installed by telecommunication utility companies and other large companies that have their own networks. Answer (C) is incorrect. Electronic mail systems do not allow for voice transmissions. Answer (D) is incorrect. Large organizations would use a wide area network.

22.6.9. Advantages of using fiber optic cable are that

I. The signal is attenuated.
II. Data are transmitted rapidly.
III. It is small and flexible.
IV. It is unaffected by electrical interference.

A. I and III.

B. I and IV.

C. I, II, and III.

D. II, III, and IV.

Answer (D) is correct. *(CISA, adapted)*

REQUIRED: The advantages of fiber optics.

DISCUSSION: A fiber optic cable uses light impulses that travel through clear flexible tubing half the size of a human hair. Fiber optic cables are not subject to electrical interference and are highly reliable. They provide for extremely flexible and fast data transmission. The signal remains strong across long distances; i.e., it does not tend to weaken (attenuate).

Answer (A) is incorrect. Attenuation of the signal is not an advantage of using fiber optics. Answer (B) is incorrect. Attenuation of the signal is not an advantage of using fiber optics. Answer (C) is incorrect. Attenuation of the signal is not an advantage of using fiber optics.

22.6.10. The practice of using a network of remote servers hosted on the Internet to store, manage, and process data, rather than using a local server or a personal computer, is

A. Web functionality.

B. Cloud computing.

C. Local networking.

D. Time sharing.

Answer (B) is correct. *(Publisher, adapted)*

REQUIRED: The term associated with the use of remote servers hosted on the Internet to store data and provide processing.

DISCUSSION: Cloud computing is offered by service providers to allow for remote storage and processing. This minimizes the resources needed at a user's facility.

Answer (A) is incorrect. Web functionality is the ease with which users can navigate a website and obtain the information they are seeking. Answer (C) is incorrect. Local networking is a group of computers and associated devices that share a common communications line or wireless link to a server. Cloud computing contrasts with local networking. Answer (D) is incorrect. Time sharing is a nonsensical term in this context.

22.6.11. Which of the following statements is(are) correct regarding electronic mail security?

1. Electronic mail can be no more secure than the computer system on which it operates.
2. Confidential electronic mail messages should be stored on the mail server as electronic mail for the same length of time as similar paper-based documents.
3. In larger organizations, there may be several electronic mail administrators and locations with varying levels of security.

A. 1 only.

B. 1 and 2 only.

C. 1 and 3 only.

D. 2 and 3 only.

Answer (C) is correct. *(CIA, adapted)*

REQUIRED: The correct statement about email security.

DISCUSSION: Electronic mail can be no more secure than the computer system on which it operates. Also, in larger organizations, there may be several electronic mail administrators and locations with varying levels of security.

Answer (A) is incorrect. In larger organizations, there may be several electronic mail administrators and locations with varying levels of security. Answer (B) is incorrect. Confidential electronic mail messages may be subject to a different retention period from that of similar paper-based documents. Also, in larger organizations, there may be several electronic mail administrators and locations with varying levels of security. Answer (D) is incorrect. Electronic mail can be no more secure than the computer system on which it operates. Also, confidential electronic mail messages may be subject to a different retention period from that of similar paper-based documents.

22.6.12. The Internet consists of a series of networks that include

A. Gateways to allow networks to connect to each other.

B. Bridges to direct messages through the optimum data path.

C. Repeaters to physically connect separate local area networks (LANs).

D. Routers to strengthen data signals between distant computers.

Answer (A) is correct. *(CIA, adapted)*

REQUIRED: The composition of the Internet.

DISCUSSION: The Internet facilitates information transfer among computers. Gateways are hardware or software products that allow translation between two different protocol families. For example, a gateway can be used to exchange messages between different email systems.

Answer (B) is incorrect. Bridges are used to connect segments of a LAN. Answer (C) is incorrect. Repeaters are used to strengthen data signals. Answer (D) is incorrect. Routers are used to determine the best path for data across the Internet.

22.6.13. Which of the following is true concerning HTML?

A. It is used to translate high-level language commands to computer processor instructions.

B. It is a dynamic programming language which can be used to build web scripts that interact with users.

C. It is independent of hardware and software.

D. It is a style sheet language used to describe the look and formatting of documents written in markup languages.

Answer (C) is correct. *(Publisher, adapted)*

REQUIRED: The true statement concerning HTML.

DISCUSSION: Hypertext Markup Language (HTML) is the most popular language for authoring web pages. It is hardware and software independent, which means that it can be read by several different applications and on many different kinds of computers. HTML uses tags to mark information for proper display in browsers.

Answer (A) is incorrect. This function is performed by a compiler, not HTML. Answer (B) is incorrect. This describes JavaScript rather than HTML. Answer (D) is incorrect. This describes Cascading Style Sheets (CSS) rather than HTML.

22.6.14. XML

A. Is focused on the content of the data.

B. Has become less important as new languages on the Internet are developed.

C. Uses standardized tags.

D. Is useful to display highly unstructured data.

Answer (A) is correct. *(Publisher, adapted)*

REQUIRED: The true statement about XML.

DISCUSSION: XML (eXtensible Markup Language) is useful for putting structured data into a text file. It can be used to extract and tag structured information from a database for transmission and subsequent use in other applications, e.g., display on the Internet or importation into a spreadsheet.

Answer (B) is incorrect. XML has become very popular for use on the Internet. Information tagged in XML can be integrated into HTML and other presentations. Answer (C) is incorrect. XML is very flexible and allows the user to design customized (extensible) tags. Answer (D) is incorrect. The data must conform to a structure to be properly tagged.

22.6.15. Which of the following is a false statement about XBRL?

A. XBRL is freely licensed.

B. XBRL facilitates the automatic exchange of information.

C. XBRL is used primarily in the U.S.

D. XBRL is designed to work with a variety of software applications.

Answer (C) is correct. *(Publisher, adapted)*

REQUIRED: The false statement about XBRL.

DISCUSSION: XBRL (eXtensible Business Reporting Language) was developed for business and accounting applications. It is an XML-based application used to create, exchange, and analyze financial reporting information that was developed for worldwide use.

Answer (A) is incorrect. The AICPA-led consortium that developed XBRL has promoted the language as a freely licensed product. Answer (B) is incorrect. XBRL facilitates the exchange of information, for example, for reporting to the SEC. Answer (D) is incorrect. XBRL allows exchange of data across many platforms and is being integrated into accounting software applications and products.

22.6.16. The most difficult aspect of using Internet resources is

A. Making a physical connection.

B. Locating the best information source.

C. Obtaining the equipment required.

D. Getting authorization for access.

Answer (B) is correct. *(CIA, adapted)*

REQUIRED: Identify the most difficult aspect of using Internet resources.

DISCUSSION: The most difficult aspect of using Internet resources is ocating the best information given the large number of information sources.

Answer (A) is incorrect. There is no limitation on the number access ports. Answer (C) is incorrect. The only equipment required for accessing Internet resources is a computer, a modem, a telephone or other access line, and basic communication software. Answer (D) is incorrect. Organizations routinely provide Internet access to their employees, and individuals can obtain access through individual subscription to commercial service providers.

22.6.17. The firewall system that limits access to a computer by routing users to replicated Web pages is

A. A packet filtering system.

B. Kerberos.

C. A proxy server.

D. An authentication system.

Answer (C) is correct. *(Publisher, adapted)*

REQUIRED: The firewall system that routes users to replicated web pages.

DISCUSSION: A proxy server maintains copies of web pages to be accessed by specified users. Outsiders are directed there, and more important information is not available from this access point.

Answer (A) is incorrect. A packet filtering system examines each incoming IP packet. Answer (B) is incorrect. Kerberos is encryption and authentication software that uses DES encryption techniques. Answer (D) is incorrect. An authentication system verifies a user's identify and is often an application provided by a firewall system, but it is not a firewall system itself.

22.6.18. A network firewall is designed to provide adequate protection against which of the following?

A. A computer virus.

B. Unauthenticated logins from outside users.

C. Insider leaking of confidential information.

D. A Trojan horse application.

Answer (B) is correct. *(Publisher, adapted)*

REQUIRED: The protection provided by a network firewall.

DISCUSSION: A firewall is a device that separates two networks and prevents passage of specific types of network traffic while maintaining a connection between the networks. Generally, a network firewall is designed to protect a system from unauthenticated logins from outside users, although it may provide several other features as well.

Answer (A) is incorrect. A firewall cannot adequately protect a system against computer viruses. Answer (C) is incorrect. Industrial spies need not leak information through the firewall. Telephones or flash drives are much more common means of sharing confidential information. Answer (D) is incorrect. Like a virus, a firewall cannot adequately protect against a Trojan horse or any other program that can be executed in the system by an internal user.

22.7 System Planning and Design

22.7.1. Which one of the following is not considered a typical risk associated with outsourcing (the practice of hiring an outside company to handle all or part of the data processing)?

A. Inflexibility.

B. Loss of control.

C. Loss of confidentiality.

D. Less availability of expertise.

Answer (D) is correct. *(CMA, adapted)*

REQUIRED: The item that is not considered a typical risk associated with outsourcing.

DISCUSSION: Some companies have outsourced their data processing function because of the economies provided, superior service quality, avoidance of changes in the organization's IS infrastructure, cost predictability, the freeing of human and financial capital, avoidance of fixed costs, and the greater expertise offered by outside vendors. The risks of outsourcing include the inflexibility of the relationship, the loss of control, the vulnerability of important information, and often dependency on a single vendor.

22.7.2. The proper sequence of activities in the systems development life cycle is

A. Design, analysis, implementation, and operation.

B. Design, implementation, analysis, and operation.

C. Analysis, design, implementation, and operation.

D. Programming, analysis, implementation, and operation.

Answer (C) is correct. *(CMA, adapted)*

REQUIRED: The sequential steps in a systems development life cycle.

DISCUSSION: The first step in systems development is identification and definition of a need relative to organizational objectives. The next step is to determine the scope of the required study and to proceed with a thorough analysis of the existing system. These steps lead to the general design of a new system. If the new system proves to be justified, the decision is then made to proceed with its implementation. Detailed systems design, including development and design of data files, is part of the implementation phase. Following implementation and operation, systems maintenance must be undertaken by analysts and programmers throughout the life of a system. Maintenance is the redesign of the system and programs to meet new needs or to correct design flaws.

Answer (A) is incorrect. Analysis precedes design. Answer (B) is incorrect. Analysis precedes design. Answer (D) is incorrect. This choice does not include the design step.

22.7.3. An IT manager has only enough resources to install either a new payroll system or a new data security system, but not both. Which of the following actions is most appropriate?

A. Giving priority to the security system.

B. Leaving the decision to the IT manager.

C. Increasing IT staff output in order for both systems to be installed.

D. Having the information systems steering committee set the priority.

Answer (D) is correct. *(CISA, adapted)*

REQUIRED: The appropriate action given inadequate resources.

DISCUSSION: The needs assessment and cost-benefit analysis should be conducted by those responsible for making the decision. In this case, the information systems steering committee is the appropriate decision maker.

Answer (A) is incorrect. Not enough information is given to conclude that priority should be given to the security system. Answer (B) is incorrect. The IT manager should not be the only decision maker. Answer (C) is incorrect. The question indicates that development of both systems is not possible.

22.7.4. The strengths of the bottom-up approach to systems development are that it

I. Supports evolutionary growth of organizational functions

II. Minimizes the cost of systems development and maintenance

III. Incorporates the existing organizational systems

IV. Identifies the factors crucial to organizational success

A. I and III.

B. I and IV.

C. II and III.

D. II and IV.

Answer (A) is correct. *(CIA, adapted)*

REQUIRED: The strengths of the bottom-up approach to systems development.

DISCUSSION: The bottom-up approach begins at the operational level, designs each functional unit, and then ties these units together at each management level of the organization. This approach builds on existing capabilities and allows for evolutionary growth of organizational functions.

Answer (B) is incorrect. Identifying crucial factors at the organizational level is a strength of the top-down approach. It begins with organizational objectives and goals, then breaks them into functional requirements to be implemented at lower levels of the organization. Answer (C) is incorrect. The bottom-up approach may not be the least costly in all circumstances. Answer (D) is incorrect. The bottom-up approach may not be the least costly in all circumstances.

22.7.5. Enterprise resource planning (ERP) software packages, such as SAP ERP Central Component and Oracle e-Business Suite, are all-inclusive systems that attempt to provide entity-wide information. ERP systems provide advantages to an organization's auditors because they

A. Have proven difficult for some firms to install.

B. Typically require firms to reduce the division of duties and responsibilities found in traditional systems.

C. Typically have built-in transaction logs and ability to produce a variety of diagnostic reports.

D. Have been installed by smaller firms so, to date, few auditors have encountered them.

Answer (C) is correct. *(Publisher, adapted)*

REQUIRED: The advantage of an ERP for the auditor.

DISCUSSION: ERP systems have a variety of controls and report generation functions that allow auditors to abstract and monitor data collected and processed. Some ERP systems have built-in audit functions.

Answer (A) is incorrect. The difficulty of installing ERP systems is a disadvantage for the auditors. Answer (B) is incorrect. ERP systems often require the client to depart from the traditional functional division of duties, such as accounting, finance, marketing, etc. The result is increased audit risk. Answer (D) is incorrect. ERP systems are very costly and therefore usually have been implemented by large organizations. However, the trend is for more and more organizations to install these systems.

22.7.6. Which of the following should be reviewed before designing any system elements in a top-down approach to new systems development?

A. Types of processing systems used by competitors.

B. Computer equipment needed by the system.

C. Information needs of managers for planning and control.

D. Controls in place over the current system.

Answer (C) is correct. *(CIA, adapted)*

REQUIRED: The first item to be reviewed when using a top-down approach to application development.

DISCUSSION: The functionality that the system will provide to the end users is always the first consideration.

Answer (A) is incorrect. The systems used by competitors may be inappropriate to the entity's needs. Answer (B) is incorrect. Hardware needs cannot be assessed until the functionality of the system has been specified. Answer (D) is incorrect. Controls over the current system may be completely irrelevant to the new system.

22.7.7. Using a telecommunications provider affects in-house networks. To prepare for changes resulting from enhanced external network services, management should

A. Optimize in-house networks to avoid bottlenecks that would limit the benefits offered by the telecommunications provider.

B. Plan for rapid implementation of new capabilities in anticipation of ready acceptance of the new technology.

C. Downsize the company's disaster recovery plan to recognize the increasing role of the telecommunications provider.

D. Enhance the in-house network management to minimize dependence on the telecommunications provider for network management.

Answer (A) is correct. *(CIA, adapted)*

REQUIRED: The appropriate action to prepare for changes resulting from enhanced external network services.

DISCUSSION: To prepare the company for changes resulting from the enhanced external network services, management should take appropriate action. A number of bottlenecks may limit the benefits that can be derived from the external network. Furthermore, applications, systems software, and communications protocols must be able to process information in a format and in a manner acceptable to end users.

Answer (B) is incorrect. Resistance to change, inflexible organizational structures, and skepticism about the technology should be expected and must be successfully managed if the company is to reap the benefits. Answer (C) is incorrect. A company's disaster recovery plan should be enhanced to ensure the reliability of the network. Answer (D) is incorrect. Network management may now be primarily a function, yet it will become more of a partnership arrangement with the communications carrier.

22.7.8. Even though an organization is committed to using its mainframe for its manufacturing plant operations, it has been looking for ways to downsize other applications. The purpose of downsizing is to

A. Improve reliability.

B. Improve security.

C. Reduce complexity.

D. Decrease costs.

Answer (D) is correct. *(CIA, adapted)*

REQUIRED: The purpose of downsizing.

DISCUSSION: The purpose of downsizing is to reduce costs of applications by abandoning larger, more expensive systems in favor of smaller, less expensive systems that are more versatile.

Answer (A) is incorrect. Downsizing is not likely to impact reliability. Answer (B) is incorrect. Security is usually better on a mainframe. Answer (C) is incorrect. Downsizing applications often increases their complexity. The data files become fragmented across multiple systems.

22.7.9. Many companies and government organizations would like to convert to open systems in order to

A. Get volume discounts from equipment vendors.

B. Achieve more economies of scale for equipment.

C. Use less expensive computing equipment.

D. Facilitate the integration of proprietary components.

Answer (C) is correct. *(CIA, adapted)*

REQUIRED: The reason for converting to open systems.

DISCUSSION: Open systems are those for which suppliers provide components whose interfaces are defined by public standards. For example, the U.S. government specifies that its suppliers adhere to the Unix operating system and the telecommunications protocols developed for the Internet. In contrast, a closed system's components are built to proprietary standards so that the equipment made by other suppliers cannot interface with the existing system. Accordingly, converting to open systems increases the number of vendors from which substitutable components can be acquired, which increases price competition for equipment.

Answer (A) is incorrect. Running open systems tends to increase the number of vendors and decrease the amount of the average purchase from any one vendor. The result is a decrease in the opportunities for volume discounts from vendors. Answer (B) is incorrect. In general, running open systems allows organizations to scale their computing facilities to a precise size, which may be inconsistent with attempting to achieve economies of scale due to larger volumes concentrated in fewer sites. Answer (D) is incorrect. Running open systems tends to reduce an organization's reliance on proprietary components and reduce the need for their integration into existing systems.

22.7.10. The implementation of a client-server architecture offers significant potential benefits but also introduces certain management and control issues. For this architecture, which of the following is true?

A. The client part of the application should be designed to peripheral devices.

B. Organizations with decentralized information technology staff are best suited to meet the challenges of managing this architecture.

C. The training needs of end users are reduced because the client workstations will support graphical user interfaces, which are self-explanatory.

D. The diagnosis and resolution of system problems may be difficult because client-server systems can rarely be constructed without products from a number of vendors.

Answer (D) is correct. *(CIA, adapted)*

REQUIRED: The true statement about implementation of a client-server architecture.

DISCUSSION: A client-server system divides processing of an application between a client machine on a network and a file server. This division depends on which tasks each is best suited to perform. However, user interaction is ordinarily restricted to the client part of the application. This portion normally consists of the user interface, data entry, queries, and receipt of reports. The file server customarily manages peripheral hardware and controls access to shared databases. Thus, a client-server application must be designed as separate software components that run on different machines but appear to be one application. Multiple vendors are ordinarily involved in the many facets of client-server systems, and problems with the systems often cannot be traced easily to a single vendor's product or service.

Answer (A) is incorrect. The file server customarily manages peripheral hardware. Answer (B) is incorrect. Due to the need to obtain consensus regarding the management of client-server systems and to coordinate information technology expertise and end-user initiatives, organizations with strong, centralized IT departments are less likely to experience severe management problems. Answer (C) is incorrect. Training needs of end-user staff may be substantial. The client-server platform extends certain development capabilities to the users and increases the ability of users to access and manipulate data.

22.7.11. Object technology provides a new and better way of enabling developers and users to build and tailor applications. In light of this technology, what action should management take with respect to its older (legacy) systems?

A. Plan for rapid migration of legacy systems to object-based applications.

B. Consider the more stable legacy systems as initial candidates for conversion.

C. Investigate the integration of object-based capabilities with legacy systems.

D. Defer the use of object technology until the legacy systems need replacement.

Answer (C) is correct. *(CIA, adapted)*

REQUIRED: The approach to introducing object technology.

DISCUSSION: Object technology is an approach to writing computer programs that expedites development. Objects are self-contained, reusable parts that are especially helpful for developing interactive and graphical programs. A legacy system is an older system that has been operating for years. Legacy systems represent a significant investment and may still provide adequate service. To balance the need for meeting changes in the corporate and technical environments with the economic imperative represented by the investment in legacy systems, information systems departments should seek opportunities to add object-oriented capabilities to existing systems.

Answer (A) is incorrect. The costs of migrating legacy systems and retraining the personnel who are to develop and maintain them preclude rapid transition. Answer (B) is incorrect. Legacy systems that are difficult to modify and maintain are better candidates for conversion to object technology. Answer (D) is incorrect. Object technology should be explored as a better approach for implementing business applications.

22.7.12. Object technology has become important in companies' strategic use of information systems because of its potential to

A. Permit quicker and more reliable development of systems.

B. Maintain programs written in procedural languages.

C. Minimize data integrity violations in hierarchical databases.

D. Streamline the traditional "waterfall" systems development methodology.

Answer (A) is correct. *(CIA, adapted)*

REQUIRED: The reason object technology is likely to become more important in companies' strategic use of information systems.

DISCUSSION: An object-oriented approach is intended to produce reusable code. Because code segments can be reused in other programs, the time and cost of writing software should be reduced.

Answer (B) is incorrect. Object technology has the potential to support faster maintenance of programs written in object-oriented, but not procedural, languages. Answer (C) is incorrect. Object technology is being applied to relational, but not hierarchical, databases. Answer (D) is incorrect. Object technology is typically implemented in a prototyping environment.

22.7.13. Two major retail companies, both publicly traded and operating in the same geographic area, have recently merged. The companies are approximately the same size and have audit departments. Company A has little EDI experience. Company B has invested heavily in information technology and has EDI connections with its major vendors. Which of the following is the least important risk factor when considering the ability to integrate the two companies' computer systems?

A. The number of programmers and systems analysts employed by each company.

B. The extent of EDI connections with vendors.

C. The compatibility of existing operating systems and database structures.

D. The size of company databases and the number of database servers used.

Answer (A) is correct. *(CIA, adapted)*

REQUIRED: The least important risk factor when integrating two companies' computer systems.

DISCUSSION: The number of systems personnel employed may reflect differences in operating philosophy (outsourcing vs. in-house development of applications). However, the number of personnel in each company is a less serious concern than the compatibility of hardware and software.

Answer (B) is incorrect. Company A has little EDI experience. Hence, the greater the number of vendors that must be connected with Company A, the greater the risk exposure. Answer (C) is incorrect. The difficulty and expense of conversion will be increased if the computer systems have significant compatibility problems. Answer (D) is incorrect. The greater the complexity of the systems to be integrated, the greater the risk exposure.

22.7.14. An electronics company has decided to implement a new system through the use of rapid application development techniques. Which of the following would be included in the development of the new system?

A. Deferring the need for system documentation until the final modules are completed.

B. Removing project management responsibilities from the development teams.

C. Creating the system module by module until completed.

D. Using object development techniques to minimize the use of previous code.

Answer (C) is correct. *(CIA, adapted)*

REQUIRED: The implementation of a new system using rapid application development techniques.

DISCUSSION: The new system would be developed module by module until completed.

Answer (A) is incorrect. System documentation is not eliminated or deferred by using rapid application development. Answer (B) is incorrect. Project management involves development teams. Answer (D) is incorrect. Object development might not be of use; if it were, it would increase usage of previous code.

22.7.15. Which of the following risks is more likely to be encountered in an end-user computing (EUC) environment as compared with a centralized environment?

A. Inability to afford adequate uninterruptible power supply systems.

B. User input screens without a graphical user interface (GUI).

C. Applications that are difficult to integrate with other information systems.

D. Lack of adequate utility programs.

Answer (C) is correct. *(CIA, adapted)*

REQUIRED: The risk more likely to be encountered in an EUC environment.

DISCUSSION: The risks arising from allowing end users to develop their own applications are the risks associated with decentralization of control. These applications may lack appropriate standards, controls, and quality assurance procedures.

Answer (A) is incorrect. Inability to afford adequate uninterruptible power supply systems is a risk in all computing environments. Answer (B) is incorrect. Almost all EUC environments have some form of GUI. Answer (D) is incorrect. Lack of adequate utility programs is a risk in all computing environments.

Questions 22.7.16 through 22.7.18 are based on the following information. The state administration has just appointed a new director of the Department of Information Systems (DIS). DIS is responsible for information systems for state functions and maintains large computers located in the state capital and distributed facilities in each county. In cooperation with staff in other state departments and agencies, DIS oversees the contracting process for outside contractors who develop major systems. After major systems have been installed and accepted, DIS is responsible for their maintenance.

One major system installed just as the new director of DIS was being appointed was the Integrated Public Assistance System (IPAS), which integrated recordkeeping, collections, and disbursements for food stamps, welfare, and child support for over one million recipients. At the time this system was developed, most of the costs for information systems for public assistance were paid by the federal government if a state's system met federal requirements. IPAS was designed for online entry of case information in county offices and overnight batch generation of checks to recipients.

Initially, when only a few counties had been converted to the system, response time on terminals in county offices was about 3 seconds. Now, with about half the counties converted, response time is at least 30 seconds and sometimes as long as 10 minutes. All data records appear to be correct despite the response time, and transmission errors have been negligible. The same computer also supports other online application systems that have been operating normally.

The long response times have delayed conversion of existing cases to the new system. During the conversion period, any new cases for public assistance were to be entered into the new system, but the lengthening response time has caused many new applicants to wait several months before their cases were entered, thus delaying the start of their authorized benefits.

The governor of the state is aware of the status of IPAS and has asked the new director of DIS to propose remedies for the situation. Realizing the need for assessing the system, the director of DIS has asked the state's internal auditing department to investigate the system configuration and recommend ways to improve online response.

22.7.16. If the slow response times were caused by application software, the most likely cause would be application programs that

A. Make erroneous updates of transactions to the master files.

B. Require more printing than the installed printers can accommodate.

C. Invoke more input-output operations than are necessary for the specified functions.

D. Contain infinite loops that degrade response time.

Answer (C) is correct. *(CIA, adapted)*

REQUIRED: The most likely cause of slow response time if application software is to blame.

DISCUSSION: Processing is relatively more rapid than input and output. Thus, invoking more input-output operations than are necessary for the specified functions is the most likely application software cause of lengthening response time.

Answer (A) is incorrect. Despite the response time, all data records appear to be correct, so the programs are not likely to make erroneous updates of transactions to the master files. Answer (B) is incorrect. Requiring more printing than the installed printers can accommodate does not appear to be the problem. Online terminal response is independent of printer use. Answer (D) is incorrect. The presence of infinite loops in application programs would cause the program to stop rather than just run more slowly.

22.7.17. If the response time is caused by central site hardware, the most likely cause is

A. A malfunctioning CPU.

B. Inadequate disk access.

C. Defective disk volumes.

D. Failing disk channels.

Answer (B) is correct. *(CIA, adapted)*

REQUIRED: The most likely cause of slow response time if central site hardware is to blame.

DISCUSSION: As more records are added to the system, the disk space becomes saturated and degrades the system. Overhead time related to management of disk space takes more and more computer cycles and can degrade response time.

Answer (A) is incorrect. The symptom of a malfunctioning CPU is complete failure or unusual results, neither of which is present here. Answer (C) is incorrect. A symptom of defective disk volumes is unrecoverable or erroneous data on disk files, neither of which occurred here. Answer (D) is incorrect. A symptom of failing disk channels is unrecoverable or erroneous data on disk files, neither of which occurred here.

22.7.18. If the response time is a function of the communications network, the most likely cause is

A. Defective terminals in county offices.

B. Insufficient transmission capacity.

C. A malfunctioning front-end controller.

D. Transient errors in transmission lines.

Answer (B) is correct. *(CIA, adapted)*

REQUIRED: The most likely cause if the response time is a function of the communications network.

DISCUSSION: As more and more sites (counties) are added to the network, the transmission capacity may be overloaded. Transmission capacity is based on the technology used, e.g., telephone lines, microwave, and satellite. Directly tied to the technology is the communication equipment, e.g., the use of concentrators and front-end processors (controllers).

Answer (A) is incorrect. A symptom of defective terminals in county offices would be transmission errors, which are not present. Answer (C) is incorrect. A symptom of a malfunctioning front-end controller would be transmission or data errors, which are not present. Answer (D) is incorrect. A symptom of transient errors in transmission lines would be transmission errors, which are not present.

22.7.19. A systems development approach used to quickly produce a model of user interfaces, user interactions with the system, and process logic is called

A. Neural networking.

B. Prototyping.

C. Reengineering.

D. Application generation.

Answer (B) is correct. *(CIA, adapted)*

REQUIRED: The approach used to produce a model of user interfaces, user interactions with the system, and process logic.

DISCUSSION: Prototyping produces the first model(s) of a new system. This technique usually employs a software tool for quick development of a model of the user interface (such as by report or screen), interaction of users with the system (for example, a menu-screen approach or data entry), and processing logic (the executable module). Prototyping stimulates user participation because the model allows for quick exploration of concepts and development of solutions with quick results.

Answer (A) is incorrect. Neural networking involves hardware or software that imitates the processing activities of the human brain. Answer (C) is incorrect. Reengineering salvages reusable components of existing systems and restructures them to develop new systems or to improve the old systems. Answer (D) is incorrect. An application generator is software that can be used to develop an application simply by describing its requirements to the computer rather than by writing a procedural program.

22.7.20. Which of the following is not an audit objective in the review of hardware acquisition?

A. Ensuring that adequate information for sound management decision making is available prior to contracting for the purchase, rent, or lease of new equipment.

B. Ensuring that vendors are provided with appropriate and uniform data for submission of bids according to management approved specifications and guidelines.

C. Ensuring that appropriate hardware is selected, installed, and tested in accordance with management approved specifications.

D. Ensuring that provisions are made to minimize damage or abuse to hardware and to maintain the hardware in good operating condition.

Answer (D) is correct. *(CISA, adapted)*

REQUIRED: The audit objective not related to the review of hardware acquisition.

DISCUSSION: Determining whether controls are in place to minimize damage or abuse to equipment is considered in the evaluation of the firm's operating environment. This step occurs subsequent to the acquisition of the equipment.

Answer (A) is incorrect. Ensuring that adequate information for sound management decision making is available is an objective of a hardware acquisition review. Answer (B) is incorrect. Ensuring that vendors are provided with appropriate and uniform data is an objective of a hardware acquisition review. Answer (C) is incorrect. Ensuring that appropriate hardware is selected, installed, and tested is an objective of a hardware acquisition review.

22.7.21. All of the following are included in the systems implementation process except

A. Training.

B. Documentation.

C. Systems design.

D. Testing and conversion.

Answer (C) is correct. *(CMA, adapted)*

REQUIRED: The item not included in the systems implementation process.

DISCUSSION: Systems implementation includes training and educating users, documenting the systems, testing the systems' programs and procedures, systems conversion (including final testing and switchover), and systems follow-up. General systems design is not a part of the implementation stage of the life cycle; the detailed systems design, such as the line-by-line coding of computer programs, is accomplished at this stage.

22.7.22. Management's enthusiasm for computer security seems to vary with changes in the environment, particularly the occurrence of other computer disasters. Which of the following concepts should be addressed when making a comprehensive recommendation regarding the costs and benefits of computer security?

1. Potential loss if security is not implemented
2. Probability of occurrences
3. Cost and effectiveness of the implementation and operation of computer security

A. 1 only.

B. 1 and 2 only.

C. 3 only.

D. 1, 2, and 3.

Answer (D) is correct. *(CIA, adapted)*

REQUIRED: The concept(s) that should be addressed in an analysis of cost-benefit considerations.

DISCUSSION: Potential loss is the amount of dollar damages associated with a security problem or loss of assets. Potential loss times the probability of occurrence is an estimate (expected value) of the exposure associated with lack of security. It represents a potential benefit associated with the implementation of security measures. To perform a cost-benefit analysis, the costs should be considered. Thus, all three items need to be addressed.

Answers (A), (B), and (C) are incorrect. Potential loss, the probability thereof, and the cost and effectiveness of security measures are important elements of the analysis.

22.7.23. Which of the following is not an important element in deciding whether to lease or purchase computer equipment?

A. Cost of money.

B. Tax considerations.

C. Maintenance expense.

D. Parallel operations cost.

Answer (D) is correct. *(CDP, adapted)*

REQUIRED: The unimportant element in deciding whether to lease or purchase computer equipment.

DISCUSSION: Any cost that is not affected by the decision need not be considered. Parallel operations costs (costs of operating both the old and new systems during the checkout period of the new system) are incurred whether the firm leases or purchases the equipment.

Answer (A) is incorrect. High interest rates may favor the lease option. Answer (B) is incorrect. The amount and availability of the investment tax credit, deductions for interest and depreciation, and other tax-planning factors will vary depending on the option chosen. Answer (C) is incorrect. Maintenance expense will vary depending on the terms of the lease or purchase.

22.7.24. The cost-effectiveness of information technology is affected by how efficiently it is used. One procedure designed to help ensure efficiency is to

A. Control access to sensitive output.

B. Provide for backup and disaster recovery.

C. Monitor the change environment for software in use.

D. Delete copies of data files when the information is no longer needed.

Answer (D) is correct. *(CIA, adapted)*

REQUIRED: The procedure designed to ensure the cost-effectiveness of information technology.

DISCUSSION: Efficiency is not achieved when facilities are underused, work is nonproductive, or procedures are uneconomical. Efficiency will be improved by freeing media and disk space for other uses, thus reducing data storage costs.

Answer (A) is incorrect. Access to sensitive output is a security concern. Answer (B) is incorrect. Backup and disaster recovery is an operational integrity issue. Answer (C) is incorrect. The change environment is a security and independence concern.

22.8 System and Application Software Acquisition and Maintenance

22.8.1. Which of the following is an indication that a computer virus is present?

A. Frequent power surges that harm computer equipment.

B. Unexplainable losses of or changes to data.

C. Inadequate backup, recovery, and contingency plans.

D. Numerous copyright violations due to unauthorized use of purchased software.

Answer (B) is correct. *(CIA, adapted)*

REQUIRED: The indicator of a computer virus.

DISCUSSION: The effects of computer viruses range from harmless messages to complete destruction of all data within the system. A symptom of a virus would be the unexplained loss of or change to data.

Answer (A) is incorrect. Power surges are caused by hardware or power supply problems. Answer (C) is incorrect. Inadequate backup, recovery, and contingency plans are operating policy weaknesses. Answer (D) is incorrect. Copyright violations represent policy or compliance problems.

22.8.2. In the computer program development process, a problem will most likely result when

A. Programmers take a longer amount of time to perform programming tasks than expected.

B. Written specifications from the user are used to develop detail program code.

C. Programmers use specialized application tools to simulate the system being programmed.

D. User specifications are inadvertently misunderstood.

Answer (D) is correct. *(CMA, adapted)*

REQUIRED: The most likely cause of a problem during computer program development.

DISCUSSION: Program development entails coding programs in accordance with the specifications established in the physical design phase of the systems development life cycle. The physical system design includes creating specifications for, among other things, work flow and programs (but not coding) that are consistent with the general or conceptual design. The general design incorporates user descriptions of the applications. Accordingly, a misunderstanding about user specifications can have fundamental and far-reaching consequences.

Answer (A) is incorrect. Although a programming delay is undesirable, it does not necessarily impair the achievement of objectives. Answer (B) is incorrect. User specifications are the foundation of the program development process. Answer (C) is incorrect. Using specialized application tools should avert problems.

22.8.3. Each of the following will help ensure development of an effective application system except

A. Active participation by user departments in the development stage.

B. Management involvement in the development stage.

C. Prioritization of applications to be developed.

D. Post-implementation reviews.

Answer (C) is correct. *(CISA, adapted)*

REQUIRED: The step that would not help ensure the development of an effective system.

DISCUSSION: Effectiveness relates to the ability to meet the objectives set forth by the organization. The nature of the applications themselves, not necessarily the order in which they are implemented, would influence their effectiveness.

Answer (A) is incorrect. Active participation by user departments in the development stage helps ensure that the objectives of the system are identified. Answer (B) is incorrect. Management involvement helps ensure that proper resources are directed to development. Answer (D) is incorrect. Post-implementation reviews are important for ensuring that a newly developed application includes the appropriate controls and effectively meets management's needs. If the system is not controlled or effective, the post-implementation review should identify the weaknesses for further correction.

22.8.4. Use of unlicensed software in an organization

1. Increases the risk of introducing viruses into the organization
2. Is not a serious exposure if only low-cost software is involved
3. Can be detected by software checking routines that run from a network server

A. 1 only.

B. 1 and 2 only.

C. 1, 2, and 3.

D. 1 and 3 only.

Answer (D) is correct. *(CIA, adapted)*

REQUIRED: The true statement(s) about unlicensed software.

DISCUSSION: Antivirus measures should include strict adherence to software acquisition policies. Unlicensed software is less likely to have come from reputable vendors and to have been carefully tested. Special software is available to test software in use to determine whether it has been authorized.

22.8.5. An insurance company that has adopted cooperative processing is planning to implement new standard software in all its local offices. The new software has a fast response time, is very user friendly, and was developed with extensive user involvement. The new software captures, consolidates, edits, validates, and finally transfers standardized transaction data to the headquarters server. Local managers, who were satisfied with existing locally written personal computer applications, opposed the new approach because they anticipated

A. Increased workloads.

B. Centralization of all processing tasks.

C. More accountability.

D. Less computer equipment.

Answer (C) is correct. *(CIA, adapted)*

REQUIRED: The reason for opposing introduction of new software.

DISCUSSION: Cooperative processing implies a tighter coupling than previously existed between the personal computers and the server. The result may threaten the managers' perceived autonomy by increasing the control exercised by headquarters and therefore the accountability of local managers.

Answer (A) is incorrect. Given that only existing systems would be converted, the transaction volume would likely remain relatively constant. Answer (B) is incorrect. In a cooperative processing environment, different computers execute different parts of an application. Answer (D) is incorrect. Compared with mainframe-only processing, cooperative processing typically requires more computer equipment at distributed locations.

22.8.6. Effective internal control for application development should provide for which of the following?

I. A project steering committee to initiate and oversee the system

II. A technical systems programmer to evaluate systems software

III. Feasibility studies to evaluate existing systems

IV. The establishment of standards for systems design and programming

A. I and III only.

B. I, II, and IV only.

C. I, III, and IV only.

D. II, III, and IV only.

Answer (C) is correct. *(CISA, adapted)*

REQUIRED: The components of effective internal control for application development.

DISCUSSION: Effective systems development requires participation by top management. This can be achieved through a steering committee composed of higher-level representatives of system users. The committee approves or recommends projects and reviews their progress. Studies of the economic, operational, and technical feasibility of new applications necessarily entail evaluations of existing systems. Another necessary control is the establishment of standards for system design and programming. Standards represent user and system requirements determined during systems analysis.

Answer (A) is incorrect. Standards must be established. Answer (B) is incorrect. A technical systems programmer has a role in the development and modification of the operating system but not necessarily in applications development. The technical support in this area would be provided by systems analysts rather than programmers. Answer (D) is incorrect. A technical systems programmer has a role in the development and modification of the operating system but not necessarily in applications development.

22.8.7. A benefit of using computer-aided software engineering (CASE) technology is that it can ensure that

A. No obsolete data fields occur in files.

B. Users become committed to new systems.

C. All programs are optimized for efficiency.

D. Data integrity rules are applied consistently.

Answer (D) is correct. *(CIA, adapted)*

REQUIRED: The benefit of CASE.

DISCUSSION: CASE is an automated technology (at least in part) for developing and maintaining software and managing projects. A benefit of using CASE technology is that it can ensure that data integrity rules, including those for validation and access, are applied consistently across all files.

Answer (A) is incorrect. Obsolete data fields must be recognized by developers or users. Once recognized, obsolete data fields can be treated consistently in CASE procedures. Answer (B) is incorrect. Using CASE will not ensure user commitment to new systems if they are poorly designed or otherwise do not meet users' needs. Answer (C) is incorrect. Although it has the potential to accelerate system development, CASE cannot ensure that all programs are optimized for efficiency. In fact, some CASE-developed modules may need to be optimized by hand to achieve acceptable performance.

22.8.8. Program documentation is a control designed primarily to ensure that

A. Programmers have access to production programs.

B. Programs do not make mathematical errors.

C. Programs are kept up to date and perform as intended.

D. No one has made use of the computer hardware for personal reasons.

Answer (C) is correct. *(CMA, adapted)*

REQUIRED: The purpose of program documentation.

DISCUSSION: Complete, up-to-date documentation of all programs and associated operating procedures is necessary for efficient operation of a computer installation. Maintenance of programs is important to provide for continuity and consistency of data processing services to users. Program documentation (the program run manual) consists of problem statements, systems flowcharts, operating instructions, record layouts, program flowcharts, program listings, test data, and approval and change sheets.

Answer (A) is incorrect. Programmers should not have access to production programs. Answer (B) is incorrect. Editing routines check for arithmetic errors prior to processing, and debugging should uncover errors in programs. Answer (D) is incorrect. Documentation cannot ensure computer security.

22.8.9. The process of monitoring, evaluating, and modifying a system as needed is referred to as

A. Systems analysis.

B. Systems feasibility study.

C. Systems maintenance.

D. Systems implementation.

Answer (C) is correct. *(CMA, adapted)*

REQUIRED: The term for the process of monitoring, evaluating, and modifying a system.

DISCUSSION: Systems maintenance must be undertaken by systems analysts and applications programmers continuously throughout the life of a system. Maintenance is the redesign of the system and programs to meet new needs or to correct design flaws. Ideally, these changes should be made as part of a regular program of preventive maintenance.

Answer (A) is incorrect. Systems analysis is the process of determining user problems and needs, surveying the organization's present system, and analyzing the facts. Answer (B) is incorrect. A feasibility study determines whether a proposed system is technically, operationally, and economically feasible. Answer (D) is incorrect. Systems implementation involves training and educating system users, testing, conversion and follow-up.

22.8.10. CASE (computer-aided software engineering) is the use of the computer to aid in the development of computer-based information systems. Which of the following could not be automatically generated with CASE tools and techniques?

A. Information requirements determination.

B. Program logic design.

C. Computer program code.

D. Program documentation.

Answer (A) is correct. *(CIA, adapted)*

REQUIRED: The item not automatically generated by CASE.

DISCUSSION: CASE applies the computer to software design and development. It maintains on the computer a library of standard program modules and all of the system documentation, e.g., data flow diagrams, data dictionaries, and pseudocode (structured English); permits development of executable input and output screens; and generates program code in at least skeletal form. Thus, CASE facilitates the creation, organization, and maintenance of documentation and permits some automation of the coding process. However, information requirements must be determined prior to using CASE.

Answer (B) is incorrect. CASE may generate program logic design. Answer (C) is incorrect. CASE may generate computer program code. Answer (D) is incorrect. CASE may generate program documentation.

22.8.11. The accountant who prepared a spreadsheet model for workload forecasting left the company, and the accountant's successor was unable to understand how to use the spreadsheet. The best control for preventing such situations from occurring is to ensure that

A. Use of end-user computing resources is monitored.

B. End-user computing efforts are consistent with strategic plans.

C. Documentation standards exist and are followed.

D. Adequate backups are made for spreadsheet models.

Answer (C) is correct. *(CIA, adapted)*

REQUIRED: The best control to permit new employees to understand internally developed programs.

DISCUSSION: The accountant's successor could not use the forecasting model because of inadequate documentation. By requiring that documentation standards exist and are followed, the company will enable new employees to understand internally developed programs when the developer leaves the organization.

Answer (A) is incorrect. Monitoring concerns controlling the use of resources. Answer (B) is incorrect. Consistency with strategic plans concern evaluation of the system. Answer (D) is incorrect. Maintaining adequate backups for spreadsheet models is necessary, but lack of adequate backup is not the reason the accountant's successor could not use the forecasting model.

22.8.12. Which of the following controls will best protect production programs from unauthorized modification?

A. Requiring two operators to be present during equipment operation.

B. Implementing management review of daily run logs.

C. Limiting program access solely to operators.

D. Restricting programmer access to the computer room.

Answer (C) is correct. *(CISA, adapted)*

REQUIRED: The best control to provide protection against unauthorized changes in production programs.

DISCUSSION: Operators require access to production programs in order to run the programs. However, systems programmers and others should be denied access to the resident production programs to limit the risk of unauthorized changes.

Answer (A) is incorrect. Unauthorized modifications can be made by programmers at terminals regardless of whether two operators are present during operation. Answer (B) is incorrect. An effective control would be a management review of console logs, not run logs. Answer (D) is incorrect. Unauthorized modifications can be made by programmers at terminals regardless of whether programmers are denied access to the computer room.

22.8.13. An entrepreneur purchases a copy of spreadsheet software for use on a single office personal computer. Which of the following actions would most likely not violate the software license agreement?

A. Making a backup copy.

B. Installing the spreadsheet software on a multi-user network.

C. Using the spreadsheet software at home for personal business.

D. Reselling the spreadsheet software.

Answer (A) is correct. *(CIA, adapted)*

REQUIRED: The action that would not violate a software license agreement.

DISCUSSION: A software agreement usually allows one backup copy to be made. Installing the software on multiple computers and making additional copies are likely copyright violations.

Answer (B) is incorrect. Installing the spreadsheet software on a multi-user network makes it available to multiple users. Answer (C) is incorrect. Not all software vendors allow use on different machines. Answer (D) is incorrect. Agreements typically prohibit resale.

22.8.14. Managers at a consumer products company purchased personal computer software from only recognized vendors and prohibited employees from installing nonauthorized software on their personal computers. To minimize the likelihood of computer viruses infecting any of its systems, the company should also

A. Restore infected systems with authorized versions.

B. Recompile infected programs from source code backups.

C. Institute program change control procedures.

D. Test all new software on a stand-alone personal computer.

Answer (D) is correct. *(CIA, adapted)*

REQUIRED: The best protection against viruses.

DISCUSSION: Software from recognized sources should be tested in quarantine (for example, in a test/development machine or a stand-alone personal computer) because even vendor-supplied software may be infected with viruses. The software should be run with a vaccine program and tested for the existence of logic bombs, etc.

Answer (A) is incorrect. If viruses infect a system, the company should restore the system with authorized software, but this procedure does not minimize the likelihood of initial infection. Answer (B) is incorrect. If viruses infect programs that the company created, it should recompile the programs from source code backups, but this procedure does not minimize the likelihood of initial infection. Answer (C) is incorrect. Instituting program change control procedures is good practice but does not minimize the likelihood of the system being infected initially.

22.8.15. Which of the following operating procedures increases an organization's exposure to computer viruses?

A. Encryption of data files.

B. Frequent backup of files.

C. Downloading public-domain software from websites.

D. Installing original copies of purchased software on hard disk drives.

Answer (C) is correct. *(CIA, adapted)*

REQUIRED: The procedure that increases exposure to viruses.

DISCUSSION: Viruses are spread through shared data. Downloading public-domain software carries a risk that contaminated data may enter the computer.

Answer (A) is incorrect. Viruses are spread through the distribution of contaminated programs. Answer (B) is incorrect. Backing up files does not increase the chances of a virus entering the computer system. Answer (D) is incorrect. Original copies of purchased software on hard disk drives should be free of viruses.

22.8.16. An organization installed antivirus software on all its personal computers. The software was designed to prevent initial infections, stop replication attempts, detect infections after their occurrence, mark affected system components, and remove viruses from infected components. The major risk in relying on antivirus software is that antivirus software may

A. Not detect certain viruses.

B. Make software installation overly complex.

C. Interfere with system operations.

D. Consume too many system resources.

Answer (A) is correct. *(CIA, adapted)*

REQUIRED: The major risk in relying on antivirus software.

DISCUSSION: Antivirus software designed to identify and remove known viruses is sometimes known as a vaccine. A vaccine works only for known viruses and may not be effective for variants of those viruses or new viruses.

Answer (B) is incorrect. Having antivirus software is unlikely to make software installation overly complex. Answer (C) is incorrect. Antivirus software need not interfere with system operations. Its execution can be scheduled in advance so as not to interfere with running programs. Answer (D) is incorrect. Antivirus software can be set to execute at times when it would not consume too many system resources, e.g., at startup.

22.9 Access and Security Controls

22.9.1. An equipment manufacturer maintains a secure website for access to its order-entry system for the convenience of its pre-approved customers worldwide so they may order parts. Because of the cost and sensitive nature of certain electronic parts, the manufacturer maintains secure access to its order-entry system. The best technique for monitoring the security of access is

A. Integrated test facility for the order-entry system.

B. Tracing of transactions through the order-entry system.

C. Transaction selection of order-entry transactions.

D. Logging of unsuccessful access attempts.

Answer (D) is correct. *(CIA, adapted)*

REQUIRED: The best technique for monitoring the security of access.

DISCUSSION: Pre-approved customers should be assigned passwords. An access log should be used to record all attempts to use the system. The date and time, codes used, and data involved are recorded. The system should monitor unsuccessful attempts because repeated attempts suggest that someone is trying random or patterned character sequences in order to identify a password.

Answer (A) is incorrect. An integrated test facility (ITF) is a technique by which an auditor selects transactions and processing functions and applies the transactions to a fictitious entity during a normal processing cycle along with regular transactions. Answer (B) is incorrect. Tracing follows the path of a transaction during processing. Answer (C) is incorrect. Transaction selection uses an independent computer program to monitor and select transactions for internal audit review. Like tracing, it fails to determine whether a transaction is legitimate. It would be an appropriate technique to apply to transactions suspected to be illegitimate.

22.9.2. The primary objective of security software is to

A. Control access to information system resources.

B. Restrict access to prevent installation of unauthorized utility software.

C. Detect the presence of viruses.

D. Monitor the separation of duties within applications.

Answer (A) is correct. *(CIA, adapted)*

REQUIRED: The primary objective of security software.

DISCUSSION: The objective of security software is to control access to information system resources, such as program libraries, data files, and proprietary software. Security software identifies and authenticates users, controls access to information, and records and investigates security related events and data.

Answer (B) is incorrect. Security software will control the use of utilities, not their installation. Answer (C) is incorrect. Antivirus software detects the presence of viruses. Answer (D) is incorrect. Security software may be a tool to establish, but does not monitor, separation of duties.

22.9.3. Assigning passwords to computer users is a control to prevent unauthorized access. Because a password does not conclusively identify a specific individual, it must be safeguarded from theft. A method used to protect passwords is to

A. Require that they be displayed on computer screens but not printed on hard copy output.

B. Set maximum character lengths.

C. Require passwords to be changed periodically.

D. Eliminate all records of old passwords.

Answer (C) is correct. *(Publisher, adapted)*

REQUIRED: The password security technique.

DISCUSSION: Security measures include changing passwords frequently, that is, establishing a relatively short maximum retention period; not displaying or printing passwords; setting minimum lengths; prohibiting the use of certain words, character strings, or names; mandating a minimum retention period so users cannot promptly change passwords back to their old and convenient values; and retaining old passwords to prevent their use.

Answer (A) is incorrect. A password should not be displayed. Answer (B) is incorrect. A minimum length requirement is more likely. Answer (D) is incorrect. Retention of old passwords prevents their reuse.

22.9.4. The duties properly assigned to an information security officer could include all of the following except

A. Developing an information security policy for the organization.

B. Maintaining and updating the list of user passwords.

C. Commenting on security controls in new applications.

D. Monitoring and investigating unsuccessful access attempts.

Answer (B) is correct. *(CIA, adapted)*

REQUIRED: The duty not properly assigned to an information security office.

DISCUSSION: The information security officer should not know user passwords. They are normally stored on a computer in encrypted format, and users change them directly.

22.9.5. Which of the following is a control that will prevent accessing the accounts receivable files from a hardwired terminal located in a manufacturing department?

A. An echo check.

B. A device authorization table.

C. Providing only dial-up terminals.

D. Using data encryption.

Answer (B) is correct. *(J. Brooks)*

REQUIRED: The control that will prevent access via a hardwired terminal.

DISCUSSION: A device authorization table restricts file access to those physical devices that logically need access. Because it is illogical for anyone to access the accounts receivable file from a manufacturing terminal, the device authorization table will deny access even when a valid password is used.

Answer (A) is incorrect. An echo check relates to the accuracy of signals sent from or to a terminal. Answer (C) is incorrect. Dial-up terminals provide less security than hardwired terminals. Any terminal may dial into the communications port using public telephones. Answer (D) is incorrect. Although data encryption (transmitting data in code form) might make the data unusable, it would not prevent access.

22.9.6. Authentication is the process by which the

A. System verifies that the user is entitled to enter the transaction requested.

B. System verifies the identity of the user.

C. User identifies himself or herself to the system.

D. User indicates to the system that the transaction was processed correctly.

Answer (B) is correct. *(CISA, adapted)*

REQUIRED: The definition of authentication.

DISCUSSION: Identification is the process of uniquely distinguishing one user from all others. Authentication is the process of determining that individuals are who they say they are. For example, a password may identify but not authenticate its user if it is known by more than one individual.

Answer (A) is incorrect. Authentication involves verifying the identity of the user. This process does not necessarily confirm the functions the user is authorized to perform. Answer (C) is incorrect. User identification to the system does not imply that the system has verified the identity of the user. Answer (D) is incorrect. This procedure is an application control for accuracy of the transaction.

22.9.7. The use of message encryption software

A. Guarantees the secrecy of data.

B. Requires manual distribution of keys.

C. Increases system overhead.

D. Reduces the need for periodic password changes.

Answer (C) is correct. *(CIA, adapted)*

REQUIRED: The effect of message encryption software.

DISCUSSION: The machine instructions necessary to encrypt and decrypt data constitute system overhead. As a result, processing speed may be slowed.

Answer (A) is incorrect. No encryption approach absolutely guarantees the secrecy of data. Answer (B) is incorrect. Keys may also be distributed electronically via secure key transporters. Answer (D) is incorrect. Periodic password changes are needed. Passwords are the typical means of validating users' access to unencrypted data.

22.9.8. The encryption technique that requires two keys, a public key that is available to anyone for encrypting messages and a private key that is known only to the recipient for decrypting messages, is

A. Rivest, Shamir, and Adelman (RSA).

B. Advanced encryption standard (AES).

C. Modulator-demodulator.

D. A cypher lock.

Answer (A) is correct. *(CIA, adapted)*

REQUIRED: The encryption technique requiring two keys.

DISCUSSION: RSA is an encryption standard licensed to hardware and software vendors. Compared with AES, RSA entails more complex computations and therefore has a higher processing overhead. RSA requires two keys: the public key for encrypting messages is widely known, but the private key for decrypting messages is kept secret by the recipient.

Answer (B) is incorrect. AES is a shared private-key method developed for the U.S. government. It encrypts data using a choice of three key sizes: 128, 192, and 256 bits. AES requires only a single key for each pair of parties that want to send each other encrypted messages. Answer (C) is incorrect. A modem is used for telecommunications. Answer (D) is incorrect. A cypher lock is a physical device.

22.10 Application and Processing Controls

22.10.1. Application control objectives do not normally include assurance that

A. Authorized transactions are completely processed once and only once.

B. Transaction data are complete and accurate.

C. Review and approval procedures for new systems are set by policy and adhered to.

D. Processing results are received by the intended user.

Answer (C) is correct. *(CISA, adapted)*

REQUIRED: The assurance not provided by an application control.

DISCUSSION: Application controls provide reasonable assurance that the recording, processing, and reporting of data are properly performed. Review and approval procedures for new systems are among the general controls known as system software acquisition and maintenance controls.

Answer (A) is incorrect. An objective of application controls is that authorized transactions are completely processed once and only once. Answer (B) is incorrect. An objective of application controls is that transaction data is complete and accurate. Answer (D) is incorrect. An objective of application controls is that processing results are received by the intended user.

22.10.2. Many customers, managers, employees, and suppliers have blamed computers for making errors. In reality, computers make very few mechanical errors. The most likely source of errors in a fully operational computer-based system is

A. Operator error.

B. Systems analysis and programming.

C. Processing.

D. Input.

Answer (D) is correct. *(CMA, adapted)*

REQUIRED: The most common cause of error.

DISCUSSION: GIGO is the acronym for garbage-in, garbage-out. Inappropriate input results in inappropriate output.

Answer (A) is incorrect. Although there is a chance of operator error, operators are typically guided by run manuals. Answer (B) is incorrect. If programs are properly designed and tested before implementation, most bugs (errors) can be removed. Answer (C) is incorrect. Once programs are operationally tested, the processing usually does not result in errors.

22.10.3. The most valuable information for detecting unauthorized input from a processing facility is provided by the

A. Console log printout.

B. Transaction journal.

C. Automated suspense file listing.

D. User error report.

Answer (B) is correct. *(CISA, adapted)*

REQUIRED: The control to detect unauthorized input from a terminal.

DISCUSSION: A transaction log records all transactions received by the computer processing facility. The log can be subsequently compared with authorized transactions (e.g., authorized source documents) to ensure validity of the transactions.

Answer (A) is incorrect. A console log does not record the individual transactions transmitted from a terminal. Answer (C) is incorrect. The suspense file only lists transaction activity if an edit error occurs. Answer (D) is incorrect. A user error report lists only input that results in an edit error.

22.10.4. A wholesaling firm has a computerized billing system. Because of a clerical error while entering information from the sales order, one of its customers was billed for only three of the four items ordered and received. Which of the following controls could have prevented, or resulted in prompt detection and correction, of this situation?

A. Matching line control counts produced by the computer with predetermined line control counts.

B. Periodic comparison of total accounts receivable per accounts receivable master file with total accounts receivable per accounts receivable control account.

C. A completeness check that does not allow a sales invoice to be processed if key fields are blank.

D. Prenumbered shipping documents together with a procedure for follow-up any time there is not a one-to-one relationship between shipping documents and sales invoices.

Answer (A) is correct. *(CIA, adapted)*

REQUIRED: The control to prevent, or promptly detect and correct, the clerical error.

DISCUSSION: Detective controls, such as a line control count, identify undesirable events as they occur. A line control count counts individual line items on documents. These counts are compared to predetermined line control counts for each document to detect missing lines.

Answer (B) is incorrect. A comparison of the accounts receivable master file and the control account will show no discrepancy. Both would be based on the three-item invoice. Answer (C) is incorrect. A completeness check could not be used to catch the billing error. Many invoices would properly include three or fewer items. Answer (D) is incorrect. All four items were included in the same shipment, so a sales invoice corresponding to the shipping document would exist.

22.10.5. If, in reviewing an applications system, it is noted that batch controls are not used, which of the following statements by the user of the system is acceptable as a compensating control?

A. "The supervisor must approve all inputs."

B. "We do a 100% key verification of all data input."

C. "We do a 100% physical review of the input document to the output document."

D. "The volume of transactions prohibits batching."

Answer (C) is correct. *(CISA, adapted)*

REQUIRED: The control that compensates for the lack of batch controls.

DISCUSSION: If the application provides for matching each input document with an output document, the need for batch totals is minimized. The physical review provides evidence that all records were processed.

Answer (A) is incorrect. Approval of input does not ensure that all input records are processed. Answer (B) is incorrect. Key verification does not ensure that the initial keypunching was done for all records. Answer (D) is incorrect. The greater the volume, the more appropriate batch totals become.

22.10.6. A company's labor distribution report requires extensive corrections each month because of labor hours charged to inactive jobs. Which of the following data processing input controls appears to be missing?

A. Completeness test.

B. Validity test.

C. Limit test.

D. Control total.

Answer (B) is correct. *(CIA, adapted)*

REQUIRED: The data processing input control not performed when labor hours are charged to inactive jobs.

DISCUSSION: Validity tests are used to ensure that transactions contain valid transaction codes. Before hours are assigned to a job, a programmed control should determine that the job code is active.

Answer (A) is incorrect. Completeness tests are used to ensure that the input has the prescribed amount of data in all data fields. Answer (C) is incorrect. Limit tests are used to determine whether the data exceed certain predetermined limits. Answer (D) is incorrect. Control totals are used to reconcile computer input to the source document totals.

22.10.7. An online bank teller system permitted withdrawals from inactive accounts. The best control for denying such withdrawals is a

A. Proof calculation.

B. Check-digit verification.

C. Master file lookup.

D. Duplicate record check.

Answer (C) is correct. *(CIA, adapted)*

REQUIRED: The best control for denying withdrawals from inactive accounts.

DISCUSSION: The master file will contain information about the status of bank accounts (i.e., active or inactive). By looking up the account numbers in the master file, the teller can verify that the account is active.

Answer (A) is incorrect. A proof calculation is the use of a predefined algorithm to be performed on the information in a telecommunications transmission to verify that no transmission errors occurred. Answer (B) is incorrect. A check-digit verification is used to control the accuracy of input of reference numbers but does not deny access to an inactive but valid account. Answer (D) is incorrect. A duplicate record check ensures that duplicate records are not processed.

22.10.8. Omen Company is a manufacturer of men's shirts. It distributes weekly sales reports to each sales manager. The quantity 2R5 appeared in the quantity sold column for one of the items on the weekly sales report for one of the sales managers. The most likely explanation for what has occurred is that the

A. Output quantity has been stated in hexadecimal numbers.

B. Computer has malfunctioned during execution.

C. Printer has malfunctioned and the "R" should have been a decimal point.

D. Program did not contain a data checking routine for input data.

Answer (D) is correct. *(CMA, adapted)*

REQUIRED: The probable reason for reporting a quantity item using an alphabetic character.

DISCUSSION: The probable explanation for reporting a quantity using a character other than a digit is that the data were incorrectly encoded and the computer program did not perform a field check, which would have detected the error. A field check tests whether a field consists of the proper characters, whether alphabetic, numeric, special, or combinations thereof.

Answer (A) is incorrect. R is not a hexadecimal character. Hexadecimal characters are 0-9 and A-F representing 0 to 15 in decimal. Answer (B) is incorrect. The probability of a computer malfunction resulting in the printing of an R is slight. Answer (C) is incorrect. The number 2.5 would not be appropriate for a quantity of shirts sold.

22.10.9. The online data entry control called preformatting is

A. A program initiated prior to regular input to discover errors in data before entry so that the errors can be corrected.

B. A check to determine if all data items for a transaction have been entered by the person entering the data.

C. A series of requests for required input data that requires an acceptable response to each request before a subsequent request is made.

D. The display of a document with blanks for data items to be entered by the person entering the data.

Answer (D) is correct. *(CMA, adapted)*

REQUIRED: The definition of preformatting.

DISCUSSION: To avoid data entry errors in online systems, a preformatted screen approach may be used. It is a screen prompting approach that involves the display on a monitor of a set of boxes for entry of specified data items. The format may even be in the form of a copy of a transaction document. This technique is best suited to conversion of data from a source document.

Answer (A) is incorrect. An edit routine is a program initiated prior to regular input to discover errors in data before entry so that the errors can be corrected. Answer (B) is incorrect. A completeness check tests whether all data items for a transaction have been entered by the person entering the data. Answer (C) is incorrect. The dialogue approach is another screen prompting method for data entry. It is most appropriate when information is received orally, e.g., by phone.

22.11 Artificial Intelligence

22.11.1. Expert systems consist of

A. Software packages with the ability to make judgment decisions.

B. A panel of outside consultants.

C. Hardware designed to make judgment decisions.

D. Hardware and software used to automate routine tasks.

Answer (A) is correct. *(CIA, adapted)*

REQUIRED: The definition of expert systems.

DISCUSSION: Artificial intelligence and its subfield, expert systems, have been identified as one of the major issues facing the accounting profession. Expert systems enable a computer to make decisions in a human way. An expert system is an interactive system that asks a series of questions and uses knowledge gained from a human expert to analyze answers and come to a decision, that is, to exercise judgment. Expert systems were originally developed to make decisions in areas that did not have enough human experts to satisfy the need to make decisions. Some of the earliest expert systems were used by doctors to diagnose diseases. Work is being done with expert systems in taxation, financial accounting, managerial accounting, and auditing.

Answer (B) is incorrect. Expert systems do not require outside consultants. Answer (C) is incorrect. Hardware does not make judgment decisions. Answer (D) is incorrect. Automation of routine tasks is not the purpose of expert systems.

22.11.2. For which of the following applications would the use of a fuzzy logic system be the most appropriate artificial intelligence (AI) choice?

A. Assigning airport gates to arriving airline flights.

B. Forecasting demand for spare auto parts.

C. Ventilating expressway tunnels.

D. Diagnosing computer hardware problems.

Answer (C) is correct. *(CIA, adapted)*

REQUIRED: The most appropriate use for fuzzy logic.

DISCUSSION: Fuzzy logic is a superset of conventional (Boolean) logic that has been extended to handle the concept of partial truth. Because they use nonspecific terms (membership functions) characterized by well-defined imprecision, fuzzy logic systems can create rules to address problems with many solutions. Fuzzy logic can be used when values are approximate or subject and data are incomplete or ambiguous. These systems have been applied successfully to applications such as ventilating expressway tunnels, selecting companies for business combinations, or detecting fraud in medical insurance claims.

Answer (A) is incorrect. Assigning airport gates to arriving airline flights requires an expert system that uses precise data for quick and consistent decisions. Answer (B) is incorrect. Neural networks provide the technology to undertake sophisticated forecasting and analysis. They emulate the processing patterns of the brain and therefore can learn from experience. Answer (D) is incorrect. Diagnosing problems with computer hardware could be accomplished by an expert system.

22.11.3. The processing in expert systems is characterized by

A. Algorithms.

B. Deterministic procedures.

C. Heuristics.

D. Simulations.

Answer (C) is correct. *(CIA, adapted)*

REQUIRED: The characteristic of processing in knowledge-based systems.

DISCUSSION: Knowledge-based (expert) systems contain a knowledge base for a limited domain of human expertise and inference procedures for the solution of problems. They use symbolic processing based on heuristics rather than algorithms. A heuristic procedure is an exploratory problem-solving technique that uses self-education methods, e.g., the evaluation of feedback, to improve performance. These systems are often very interactive and provide explanations of their problem-solving behavior.

Answer (A) is incorrect. Algorithms are defined procedures used in typical computer programs. Answer (B) is incorrect. Deterministic procedures are procedures used in computer programs that permit no uncertainty in outcomes. Answer (D) is incorrect. Simulations are computer programs that permit experimentation with logical and mathematical models.

22.11.4. Prudent managers will recognize the limits within which expert systems can be effectively applied. An expert system is most appropriately used to

A. Compensate for the lack of certain technical knowledge within the organization.

B. Help make customer-service jobs easier to perform.

C. Automate daily managerial problem-solving.

D. Emulate human expertise for strategic planning.

Answer (B) is correct. *(CIA, adapted)*

REQUIRED: The most appropriate use for an expert system.

DISCUSSION: Expert systems are systems that allow a computer to make decisions in a human way. Expert systems allow even small companies to perform activities and provide services previously only available from larger firms. The use of expert systems has helped to improve the quality of customer service in applications such as maintenance and scheduling by automating them and making them easy to perform.

Answer (A) is incorrect. Expert systems codify and apply existing knowledge, but they do not create knowledge. Answer (C) is incorrect. Expert systems do best in automating lower-level clerical functions. Answer (D) is incorrect. Expert systems concern problems with relatively few possible outcomes that are all known in advance.

22.11.5. A bank implemented an expert system to help account representatives consolidate the bank's relationships with each customer. The expert system has

A. A sequential control structure.

B. Distinct input-output variables.

C. A knowledge base.

D. Passive data elements.

Answer (C) is correct. *(CIA, adapted)*

REQUIRED: The component of an expert system.

DISCUSSION: An expert system relies on a computer's ability to make decisions in a human way. There are three components to an expert system: a knowledge base, an inference engine, and a user interface. The knowledge base contains the rules used when making decisions.

Answer (A) is incorrect. Traditional programs, not expert systems, have sequential control structures. Answer (B) is incorrect. Traditional programs, not expert systems, have distinct input-output variables. Answer (D) is incorrect. Traditional programs, not expert systems, have passive data elements.

22.12 CISA Concepts

NOTE: The CISA exam is offered each year and consists of 150 multiple-choice questions that cover the five job practice areas created from the most recent CISA job practice analysis. The practice areas and percentages below indicate the emphasis of questions that will appear on the exam:

The Process of Auditing Information Systems	Provide audit services in accordance with IS audit standards to assist the organization in protecting and controlling information systems	21%
Governance and Management of IT	Provide assurance that the necessary leadership and organization structure and processes are in place to achieve objectives and to support the organization's strategy	16%
Information Systems Acquisition, Development, and Implementation	Provide assurance that the practices for the acquisition, development, testing, and implementation of information systems meet the organization's strategies and objectives	18%
Information Systems Operations, Maintenance, and Service Management	Provide assurance that the processes for information systems operations, maintenance, and service management meet the organization's strategies and objectives	20%
Protection of Information Assets	Provide assurance that the organization's security policies, standards, procedures, and controls ensure the confidentiality, integrity, and availability of information assets	25%

22.12.1. Which of the following are typical responsibilities of a Certified Information Systems Auditor?

I. Evaluation of the IS strategy and the processes for its development
II. Evaluation of the IS policies, standards, and procedures
III. Evaluation of management practices

A. I and III.

B. I and II.

C. II and III.

D. I, II, and III.

Answer (D) is correct. *(CISA, adapted)*

REQUIRED: The responsibilities of an IS auditor.

DISCUSSION: According to the Information Systems Audit and Control Association (ISACA), the responsibilities of a CISA include all items listed.

22.12.2. Which of the following statements best describes the computer processing technical requirements for IS auditors? IS auditors should

A. Be as technically proficient as the people they audit.

B. Conduct audits in accordance with generally accepted IS audit standards.

C. Only possess a limited amount of technical knowledge, mainly in the area of current buzzwords.

D. Only possess a knowledge of auditing and controls.

Answer (B) is correct. *(CISA, adapted)*

REQUIRED: The statement that best describes the technical requirements of IS auditors.

DISCUSSION: According to ISACA, the IS auditor should conduct audits in accordance with generally accepted IS audit standards and guidelines to ensure that the organization's information technology and business systems are adequately controlled, monitored, and assessed.

Answer (A) is incorrect. IS auditors can rely on the work of technical specialists in those areas for which they are not as proficient as the people they are auditing. Answer (C) is incorrect. IS auditors need more than a limited amount of data processing knowledge. Answer (D) is incorrect. IS auditors need more than knowledge of auditing and controls.

22.12.3. The first step the IS audit manager should take when preparing the annual IS audit plan is to

A. Meet with the audit committee members to discuss the IS audit plan for the upcoming year.

B. Ensure that the IS audit staff is competent in areas that are likely to appear on the plan and provide training as necessary.

C. Assess the overall risks and develop objectives.

D. Begin with the prior year's IS audit plan and carry over any IS audit steps that have not been completed.

Answer (C) is correct. *(CISA, adapted)*

REQUIRED: The first step in the annual audit plan.

DISCUSSION: The first step in an IS audit is to assess the overall risks and develop an audit program that consists of control objectives and audit procedures that should satisfy those objectives.

Answer (A) is incorrect. The IS audit manager would not meet with the audit committee until a risk analysis of areas of exposure has been completed. Answer (B) is incorrect. The IS audit manager does not know what areas are to appear on the IS audit plan until a risk analysis is completed and discussions are held with the audit committee members. Answer (D) is incorrect. A risk analysis would be the first step before any IS audit effort is expended.

22.12.4. In which of the following areas is an internal IS auditor expected to draw upon the work of an external auditor?

A. Safeguarding of company assets.

B. Accuracy and reliability of accounting records.

C. Promotion of operational efficiency.

D. Adherence to company policies and legal obligations.

Answer (B) is correct. *(CISA, adapted)*

REQUIRED: The area in which the IS auditor would draw on the work of the external auditor.

DISCUSSION: External auditors express opinions on the fairness of the financial statements. Thus, the internal IS auditor would most likely draw on the work of the external auditor for assurances about the reliability of the accounting records.

Answer (A) is incorrect. An external auditor would not be relied upon to safeguard company assets. Answer (C) is incorrect. External auditors typically do not evaluate operational efficiencies unless specifically engaged to do so. External auditors' procedures are limited to those considered necessary to form an opinion on the fairness of the financial statements. Answer (D) is incorrect. Whereas external auditors may review adherence to company policies and legal obligations in specific situations, their review is limited to those procedures considered necessary to express an audit opinion.

22.12.5. Monitoring environmental controls includes which of the following?

I. Evaluating digital signature techniques

II. Evaluating fire suppression systems

III. Evaluating the uninterruptible power supply (UPS)

A. I and III.

B. I and II.

C. I, II, and III.

D. II and III.

Answer (D) is correct. *(CISA, adapted)*

REQUIRED: The activities related to environmental controls.

DISCUSSION: Environmental controls relate to the physical aspects of the IT infrastructure and include fire suppression and the uninterruptible power supply.

22.12.6. The audit objective of an IS resource management evaluation is to provide assurance that

A. The IS manager practices effective, efficient, and economic support to the organization's business objectives.

B. Organizational resources of time and money are used in the most economical manner during the acquisition of hardware and software.

C. Appropriate control features are included in systems hardware and software.

D. All tasks have been computerized.

Answer (A) is correct. *(CISA, adapted)*

REQUIRED: The audit objective of an IS resource management evaluation.

DISCUSSION: The audit objective of an IS resource management evaluation is to analyze and evaluate the information systems (IS) strategy, policies and procedures, management practices, and organization structures. The process includes evaluation of management's actions relating to the use of resources.

Answer (B) is incorrect. The audit objective of an IS resource management review is not limited to acquisition of hardware and software. Answer (C) is incorrect. Whether appropriate control features are included in systems hardware and software does not relate to resource management but to control issues. Answer (D) is incorrect. Proper processing methods should be evaluated using cost and benefit criteria.

22.12.7. A primary purpose of an input-output control module in an operating system is to ensure that

A. Read and write requests are properly executed.

B. A record is maintained of all file accesses.

C. Control modules are held to near size.

D. Hardware errors are recorded promptly.

Answer (A) is correct. *(CISA, adapted)*

REQUIRED: The purpose of an input-output control module in an operating system.

DISCUSSION: Input-output controls are concerned with the reading and writing of data. They should be used to determine if read and write requests are properly executed.

Answer (B) is incorrect. A console log is used to record file accesses and processing. Answer (C) is incorrect. Holding control modules to near size is nonsensical in this context. Answer (D) is incorrect. Hardware errors are detected by hardware controls, not by input-output controls.

22.12.8. To ensure privacy in a public-key encryption system, knowledge of which of the following keys is required to decode the received message?

I. Private
II. Public

A. I only.

B. II only.

C. Both I and II.

D. Neither I nor II.

Answer (A) is correct. *(CISA, adapted)*

REQUIRED: The key(s) required to decode messages in a public-key system to ensure privacy.

DISCUSSION: In a public-key system, the public key is used to encrypt the message prior to transmission. The private key is needed to decrypt (decode) the message.

Answer (B) is incorrect. The private key, not the public key, is needed to decrypt (decode) the message. Answer (C) is incorrect. The public key is needed to encode, not decode, the message. Answer (D) is incorrect. The private key is needed to decrypt (decode) the message.

22.12.9. Which of the following types of transmission media are most secure against unauthorized access or tapping?

A. Copper wire.

B. Twisted pair.

C. Fiber-optic cables.

D. Coaxial cables.

Answer (C) is correct. *(CISA, adapted)*

REQUIRED: The most secure transmission medium.

DISCUSSION: Unlike metallic-based systems, the non-conducting nature of optical fiber makes it virtually impossible to remotely detect the signal being transmitted within the cable. There must be physical access to the cable to intercept the transmission.

Answer (A) is incorrect. Copper wire can be tapped easily with inexpensive equipment. Answer (B) is incorrect. Twisted pair is made of copper and thus can be tapped easily with inexpensive equipment. Answer (D) is incorrect. Coaxial cables can be tapped easily with inexpensive equipment.

22.12.10. Each of the following statements about distributed data processing (DDP) systems is true except

A. From the IS auditor's perspective, it is a desirable trend in DDP systems design to off-load operating system and communication functions from software into hardware or microcode.

B. DDP systems are essentially unauditable because of the complexity of network software.

C. DDP systems increase the need for effective risk analysis.

D. An important design goal of DDP systems is to provide more power and flexibility to the end users even though inadequate controls may exist in some of the end-user software.

Answer (B) is correct. *(CISA, adapted)*

REQUIRED: The false statement concerning DDP systems.

DISCUSSION: Technical complexity is not a valid reason for failing to audit a processing system. The IS auditor should have sufficient technical knowledge and training to audit complex networks.

Answer (A) is incorrect. Hardware or microcode functions have the advantage of being less prone to unauthorized modification than software. Answer (C) is incorrect. Processing may be distributed to numerous user areas, each with varied risk levels and degrees of control, requiring an effective risk analysis methodology to ensure adequate audit coverage for critical functions. Answer (D) is incorrect. End-user software is usually designed for rapid development and ease of modification. It could be susceptible to errors in the hands of an inexperienced user.

22.12.11. An IS auditor is called as an expert witness by the plaintiff in litigation involving the misuses of a service bureau's computer by an unauthorized individual who used another's password to manipulate data. The IS auditor's testimony regarding security issues should include descriptions of each of the following except the

A. Access control.

B. Method of assignment of passwords.

C. Methods that could prevent similar misuse.

D. Controls that were overridden to gain access.

Answer (C) is correct. *(CISA, adapted)*

REQUIRED: The inappropriate testimony by an IS auditor in a case involving unauthorized access to a plaintiff's files.

DISCUSSION: The IS auditor is not likely to be able to provide testimony that another method of control would have prevented the unauthorized action. Such testimony is mere speculation by the auditor.

Answer (A) is incorrect. Access control concerns procedures germane to the litigation. The auditor's assessments will be important to the plaintiff's case. Answer (B) is incorrect. The method of assignment of passwords is germane to the litigation. Answer (D) is incorrect. Controls that were overridden to gain access are germane to the litigation.

22.12.12. A data center that has installed online communications, a database management system, access control software, and a sophisticated network is planning its first test at the hot site. The first test should include recovery of

A. All systems and application software.

B. Only the operating system.

C. All system software and the network.

D. Only the access control software.

Answer (B) is correct. *(CISA, adapted)*

REQUIRED: The purpose of an initial test at a data center's hot site.

DISCUSSION: A hot site is typically a service bureau where a data center can obtain processing services in case of a disaster. The more common commercial hot sites limit the amount of time a subscriber can be present to perform testing. Thus, an organization's best approach is to attempt to recover the operating system first because it is the nucleus of all processing.

Answer (A) is incorrect. The operating system should be recovered before other software. Answer (C) is incorrect. The operating system should be recovered before the network. Answer (D) is incorrect. The operating system should be recovered before the access control software.

22.12.13. Which of the following is of most concern when contracting for a hot site as the alternative processing facility?

A. The number of other subscribers to the hot site.

B. Possession by the hot site of the most current version of the operating system software.

C. Location of the hot site's offsite storage facility.

D. Number of years the hot site has been in operation.

Answer (A) is correct. *(CISA, adapted)*

REQUIRED: The item of most concern when contracting for a hot site.

DISCUSSION: The number of other subscribers would affect the availability of facilities at the hot site. The computer resources provided should be adequate to perform necessary processing.

Answer (B) is incorrect. The ability of the hot site to process the current application software is more important than consideration of the operating system version. Answer (C) is incorrect. Assurance as to adequate protection of files, rather than the location of the hot site's offsite storage facility, are of concern. Answer (D) is incorrect. Capabilities of a hot site are of greater concern.

22.12.14. The IS auditor finds that data communications are subject to message encryption and that effective controls have been designed for the encryption and decryption processes. Based on this finding, tests of controls should be carried out to ensure that

A. The network has an effective mechanism for determining whether all parts of a message sent are received.

B. The X.25 interface standard is being correctly applied during encryption and decryption.

C. Authorized encryption and decryption procedures are being adhered to in practice.

D. Messages sent by way of satellite transmissions are not dispersed over too wide a receiving area.

Answer (C) is correct. *(CISA, adapted)*

REQUIRED: The appropriate control in an encrypted data communications environment.

DISCUSSION: Tests of controls evaluate the effectiveness of the operation of controls. The auditor has concluded that the encryption controls have been adequately designed, but tests must be conducted to see if they are being applied as intended.

Answer (A) is incorrect. Whether all parts of a message sent are received is not related to data encryption. Answer (B) is incorrect. The X.25 interface standard is only used in packet-switched networks. Answer (D) is incorrect. Determining that messages sent by way of satellite transmissions are not dispersed over too wide a receiving area is not related to data encryption.

22.12.15. Which of the following are features of security software packages?

I. Provision of an audit trail
II. Backup of critical files
III. Establishment of various levels of protection
IV. Monitoring of accesses to protected resources

A. I and IV.

B. II and III.

C. I, III, and IV.

D. I, II, III, and IV.

Answer (C) is correct. *(CISA, adapted)*

REQUIRED: The control features included in security software packages.

DISCUSSION: Security software packages typically provide audit trails of access attempts, the capability of assigning degrees of protection to data elements, and monitoring of systems accesses. File backup is typically not a function of security software.

Answer (A) is incorrect. Establishment of various levels of protection is also a feature of security software packages. Answer (B) is incorrect. Security software packages typically do not provide for backing up critical files. However, there may be a feature for backing up the security software files. Answer (D) is incorrect. Security software packages typically do not provide for backing up critical files.

22.12.16. The critical recovery time period is the length of time

A. The company will process at the alternative site before returning to the data center.

B. The company can do without IS services before business is significantly affected.

C. Covered by the offsite rotation cycle for backup files.

D. The recovery team will need to work together in a disaster condition.

Answer (B) is correct. *(CISA, adapted)*

REQUIRED: The definition of critical recovery time.

DISCUSSION: The critical recovery time period is the time in which the company must recover IS services before the disaster has a significant negative effect on its ability to continue in existence.

Answer (A) is incorrect. The time the company will process at the alternative site before returning to the data center is less critical than the time the company can do without IS services before business is significantly affected. Answer (C) is incorrect. The time covered by the offsite rotation cycle for backup files is less critical than the time the company can do without IS services before business is significantly affected. Answer (D) is incorrect. The time the recovery team will need to work together in a disaster condition is less critical than the time the company can do without IS services before business is significantly affected.

22.12.17. An appropriate control technique for a data communications security review is to ensure that

A. Messages transmitted over secure media are always encrypted.

B. User authentication mechanisms are used with stand-alone personal computer installations.

C. Telecommunication system commands can be entered only from the master console.

D. Sensitive messages are always transmitted bit by bit, enclosed between a start bit and a stop bit.

Answer (C) is correct. *(CISA, adapted)*

REQUIRED: The appropriate technique for a data communications security review.

DISCUSSION: To ensure security, systems commands should be made only from the master control console. In addition, a computer-generated log should be maintained of all systems modifications.

Answer (A) is incorrect. Encryption may not be cost beneficial for nonsensitive data. Answer (B) is incorrect. User authentication mechanisms should be used on all systems, not just personal computer installations. Answer (D) is incorrect. Transmissions are usually in packets of data rather than bit by bit.

22.12.18. As transactions to update an online sales order system are processed, the transactions are copied to a transaction log. At the end of the day, the sales order entry disk files are copied to a backup tape. During the backup procedure, the disk file containing the sales order system failed, and the file was lost. Which, if any, of the following are required to restore the online sales order system?

I. The previous day's backup file.
II. The previous day's transaction log.
III. The current day's transaction log.
IV. None. The system cannot be restored.

A. IV only.

B. I and III.

C. I and II.

D. I, II, and III.

Answer (B) is correct. *(CISA, adapted)*

REQUIRED: The file(s) required to restore the online sales order system.

DISCUSSION: The previous day's backup file will be the most current backup of the result of processing up until that time. The current day's transaction log will contain all of the activity since that time. The combination of these two files will allow restoration of the system.

Answer (A) is incorrect. Restoration is possible. Answer (C) is incorrect. The previous day's transaction file includes the activity that has been included on the previous day's system backup file. Answer (D) is incorrect. The previous day's transaction file includes the activity that has been included on the previous day's system backup file.

22.12.19. Why would the IS auditor of a company that is considering contracting its computer processing needs to a service bureau request a copy of each candidate bureau's financial statements?

A. To evaluate the fairness of each service bureau's charges on the basis of relative profit margins.

B. To determine whether each service bureau is affiliated with a company that might represent a conflict of interests.

C. To evaluate each service bureau's financial stability and ability to fulfill the contract.

D. To obtain an understanding of the processing performed by each service bureau and the controls within the system.

Answer (C) is correct. *(CISA, adapted)*

REQUIRED: The purpose of requesting financial statements from a service bureau.

DISCUSSION: A primary concern of a company contracting for its data processing needs is whether the service bureau has the financial stability to perform its contract. One means of assessing financial stability is to analyze the bureau's financial statements.

Answer (A) is incorrect. The financial statements do not disclose the relative profit margins by types of service provided. Answer (B) is incorrect. The financial statements are not the best source of such information. Answer (D) is incorrect. Marketing literature of the service bureau provides a description of the services offered.

22.12.20. The results of a generalized audit software simulation of the aging of accounts receivable revealed substantial differences in the aging distribution, even though grand totals reconciled. Which of the following should the IS auditor do first to resolve the discrepancy?

A. Recreate the test, using different software.

B. List a sample of actual data to verify the accuracy of the test program.

C. Ignore the discrepancy because the grand totals reconcile and instruct the controller to correct the program.

D. Create test transactions and run test data on both the production and simulation programs.

Answer (B) is correct. *(CISA, adapted)*

REQUIRED: The first step an IS auditor should take when illogical results are obtained from a GAS package.

DISCUSSION: Actual data are easily obtained and can be compared with the aging schedule to assess the integrity of the simulation program's logic.

Answer (A) is incorrect. Only if it were determined that the program was corrupted would substitute software be required. Answer (C) is incorrect. The auditor has reason to believe that errors may exist and should determine the reasons for the discrepancy. Answer (D) is incorrect. This expensive procedure will not be justified until the data from the simulation have been checked.

22.12.21. An auditor should review the procedures within a program change control group to determine whether it does which of the following?

A. Makes programs available to programmers for change only on receiving proper authorization.

B. Reviews user documentation for any necessary changes resulting from a program change.

C. Codes the necessary program changes.

D. Estimates the time and cost involved in a program change.

Answer (A) is correct. *(CISA, adapted)*

REQUIRED: The function of a program change control group.

DISCUSSION: A program change control group is responsible for determining that proper procedures are carried out relative to controlling programming changes. This includes ensuring that proper authorizations are received for changes. To avoid fraud and to ensure compatibility with other programs, programmers should not be able to make unauthorized changes.

Answer (B) is incorrect. The systems analyst has the operational responsibility to ensure that documentation is changed to reflect the modification. Answer (C) is incorrect. Programmers, not the control group, should code the necessary changes. Answer (D) is incorrect. The systems analyst, in conjunction with management, should estimate the time and cost involved in a program change.

APPENDIX A
SUBUNIT CROSS-REFERENCES TO AUDITING TEXTBOOKS

This section contains the tables of contents of current auditing textbooks with cross-references to the related subunits or study units in this study manual. Systems topics are all covered in Gleim Study Unit 22, “Information Systems,” so we did not list systems textbooks in this cross-reference. The auditing texts are listed in alphabetical order by the first author. As you study a particular chapter in your auditing textbook, you can easily determine which subunit(s) to study in your Gleim EQE material.

AUDITING TEXTBOOKS

Arens, Elder, Beasley, and Hogan, *Auditing and Assurance Services*, Sixteenth Edition, Prentice Hall, Inc., 2016.

Boynton and Johnson, *Modern Auditing: Assurance Services and the Integrity of Financial Reporting*, Eighth Edition, John Wiley & Sons, Inc., 2005.

Guy, Carmichael, and Whittington, *Audit Sampling: An Introduction to Statistical Sampling in Auditing*, Fifth Edition, John Wiley & Sons, Inc., 2001.

Hall, *Information Technology Auditing*, Fourth Edition, Cengage Learning, 2016.

Hooks, *Auditing and Assurance Services: Understanding the Integrated Audit*, First Edition, John Wiley & Sons, Inc., 2010.

Johnstone, Gramling, and Rittenberg, *Auditing: A Risk-Based Approach to Conducting a Quality Audit*, Tenth Edition, Cengage Learning, 2015.

Knechel and Salterio, *Auditing: Assurance & Risk*, Fourth Edition, Routledge, 2016.

Louwers, Blay, Sinason, Strawser, and Thibodeau, *Auditing & Assurance Services*, Seventh Edition, McGraw-Hill, Inc., 2017.

Messier, Glover, and Prawitt, *Auditing & Assurance Services: A Systematic Approach*, Tenth Edition, McGraw-Hill, Inc., 2017.

O’Reilly, McDonnell, Winograd, Gerson, and Jaenicke, *Montgomery’s Auditing*, Twelfth Edition, John Wiley & Sons, Inc., 1999.

Reding, Sobel, et al., *Internal Auditing: Assurance & Advisory Services*, Fourth Edition, The Institute of Internal Auditors, 2017.

Ricchiute, *Auditing*, Eighth Edition, South-Western, 2005.

Sawyer, et al., *Sawyer’s Guide for Internal Auditors*, Sixth Edition, The Institute of Internal Auditors, Inc., 2012.

Stuart, *Auditing and Assurance Services: An Applied Approach*, First Edition, McGraw-Hill/Irwin, 2011.

Whittington and Pany, *Principles of Auditing and Other Assurance Services*, Twentieth Edition, McGraw-Hill, Inc., 2016.

AUDITING TEXTBOOKS

Arens, Elder, Beasley, and Hogan, *Auditing and Assurance Services*, Sixteenth Edition, Prentice Hall, Inc., 2016.

Part 1: The Auditing Profession
- Chapter 1 - The Demand for Audit and Other Assurance Services - 1.1-1.4
- Chapter 2 - The CPA Profession - SU 1
- Chapter 3 - Audit Reports - SUs 15-17
- Chapter 4 - Professional Ethics - 2.1-2.7
- Chapter 5 - Legal Liability - 2.8, 3.6-3.7

Part 2: The Audit Process
- Chapter 6 - Audit Responsibilities and Objectives - SU 1
- Chapter 7 - Audit Evidence - SU 10
- Chapter 8 - Audit Planning and Materiality - 3.1-3.5
- Chapter 9 - Assessing the Risk of Material Misstatement - 8.1
- Chapter 10 - Assessing and Responding to Fraud Risks - 3.3, 3.6-3.7
- Chapter 11 - Internal Control and COSO Framework - 1.1, 5.1-5.3
- Chapter 12 - Assessing Control Risk and Reporting on Internal Controls - 3.2-3.3, 8.3, 9.3
- Chapter 13 - Overall Audit Strategy and Audit Program - SUs 3-4

Part 3: Application of the Audit Process to the Sales and Collection Cycle
- Chapter 14 - Audit of the Sales and Collection Cycle: Tests of Controls and Substantive Tests of Transactions - SU 6, SU 11
- Chapter 15 - Audit Sampling for Tests of Controls and Substantive Tests of Transactions - SU 14
- Chapter 16 - Completing the Tests in the Sales and Collection Cycle: Accounts Receivable - 10.2, 11.1
- Chapter 17 - Audit Sampling for Tests of Details of Balances - SU 14

Part 4: Application of the Audit Process to Other Cycles
- Chapter 18 - Audit of the Acquisition and Payment Cycle: Tests of Controls, Substantive Tests of Transactions, and Accounts Payable - 7.1-7.3, 12.1
- Chapter 19 - Completing the Tests in the Acquisition and Payment Cycle: Verification of Selected Accounts - 7.1-7.3, 12.1
- Chapter 20 - Audit of the Payroll and Personnel Cycle - 7.4-7.5, 12.7
- Chapter 21 - Audit of the Inventory and Warehousing Cycle - 7.1-7.2, 12.2
- Chapter 22 - Audit of the Capital Acquisition and Repayment Cycle - 4.4, 7.6, 12.3-12.6
- Chapter 23 - Audit of Cash and Financial Instruments - 5.2, 11.2, 12.4

Part 5: Completing the Audit
- Chapter 24 - Completing the Audit - SU 4, 9.1-9.2, SU 13

Part 6: Other Assurance and Nonassurance Services
- Chapter 25 - Other Assurance Services - SUs 17-19, 2.8-2.9
- Chapter 26 - Internal and Governmental Financial Auditing and Operational Auditing - SUs 20-21

Boynton and Johnson, *Modern Auditing: Assurance Services and the Integrity of Financial Reporting*, Eighth Edition, John Wiley & Sons, Inc., 2005.

Part I: The Auditing Environment
- Chapter 1 - Auditing and the Public Accounting Profession – Integrity in Financial Reporting - SU 1, 2.8-2.9
- Chapter 2 - Auditors' Responsibilities and Reports - SUs 15-16
- Chapter 3 - Professional Ethics - 2.1-2.5
- Chapter 4 - Auditors' Legal Liability - 2.7, 3.3, 3.6-3.7

Part II: The Decision Making of Auditing Planning
- Chapter 5 - Overview of the Financial Statement Audit - 3.1-3.5
- Chapter 6 - Audit Evidence - SU 10
- Chapter 7 - Accepting the Engagement and Planning the Audit - SUs 3-4
- Chapter 8 - Materiality Decisions and Analytical Procedures - 3.3, 3.5
- Chapter 9 - Audit Risk: Including the Risk of Fraud - 3.3, 3.6, SU 8
- Chapter 10 - Understanding Internal Control - SU 5, 9.4

Part III: The Decision Making of Collecting and Evaluating Evidence
- Chapter 11 - Audit Procedures in Response to Assessed Risks: Tests of Controls - SU 8
- Chapter 12 - Audit Procedures in Response to Assessed Risks: Substantive Tests - SU 8, SU 10
- Chapter 13 - Audit Sampling - SU 14

Part IV: Auditing the Transaction Cycles and Completing the Audit
- Chapter 14 - Auditing the Revenue Cycle - SU 6, SU 11
- Chapter 15 - Auditing the Expenditure Cycle - SU 7, 12.1-12.2
- Chapter 16 - Auditing the Production and Personnel Services Cycles - 7.3-7.5, 12.2-12.3, 12.7
- Chapter 17 - Auditing the Investing and Financing Cycles - 7.6, 12.4-12.6
- Chapter 18 - Auditing Investments and Cash Balances - 6.4, 11.2
- Chapter 19 - Completing the Audit/Postaudit Responsibilities - 9.1-9.3, SU 13

Part V: Other Attest and Assurance Services
- Chapter 20 - Attest and Assurances Services and Related Reports - SUs 17-19
- Chapter 21 - Internal, Operational, and Governmental Auditing - SUs 20-21

Guy, Carmichael, and Whittington, *Audit Sampling: An Introduction to Statistical Sampling in Auditing*, Fifth Edition, John Wiley & Sons, Inc., 2001.

- Chapter 1 - Overview of Audit Sampling - 14.1
- Chapter 2 - Selecting a Representative Sample - 14.1
- Chapter 3 - Attribute Sampling - 14.2
- Chapter 4 - Using Variable Sampling for Accounting Estimation - 14.3
- Chapter 5 - Using Variable Sampling for Audit Hypothesis Testing - 14.3
- Chapter 6 - Probability-Proportional-to-Size Sampling - 14.4
- Chapter 7 - Nonstatistical Audit Sampling - 14.1

Hall, *Information Technology Auditing*, Fourth Edition, Cengage Learning, 2016.

- Chapter 1 - Auditing, Assurance, and Internal Control - 1.1-1.3, SUs 5-8
- Chapter 2 - IT Governance - 22.1, 22.7-22.8
- Chapter 3 - System Security I -- Networks and Operating Systems - 22.1, 22.6, 22.9
- Chapter 4 - System Security II -- Data Management - 22.4-22.5, 22.9-22.10
- Chapter 5 - Systems Development and Program Change Procedures - 22.8
- Chapter 6 - Overview of Transaction Processing and Financial Reporting Systems - 5.5, SUs 6-7
- Chapter 7 - Computer-Assisted Audit Tools and Techniques - 10.4
- Chapter 8 - CAATTs for Data Extraction and Analysis - 10.4
- Chapter 9 - Application Controls and Substantive Testing I -- The Revenue Cycle - SU 6, SU 11
- Chapter 10 - Application Controls and Substantive Testing II -- The Expenditure Cycle - SU 7, SU 12
- Chapter 11 - Enterprise Resource Planning Systems - 22.7
- Chapter 12 - Ethics, Fraud Schemes, and Fraud Detection - SU 2, 3.6-3.7

Hooks, *Auditing and Assurance Services: Understanding the Integrated Audit*, First Edition, John Wiley & Sons, Inc., 2010.

Part I: Introduction
- Chapter 1 - An Introduction to Auditing - SU 1
- Chapter 2 - Overview of an Integrated Audit - 1.2, 10.1

Part II: The Audit Environment
- Chapter 3 - The Auditor's Role in Society - 1.1
- Chapter 4 - Legal Environment Affecting Audits - 3.6-3.7, SU 2

Part III: Executing an Integrated Audit
- Chapter 5 - Client Acceptance and Continuance and Preliminary Engagement Procedures - 3.1-3.2
- Chapter 6 - Audit Planning and Risk Assessment - 3.3-3.7, SU 4
- Chapter 7 - Internal Control, Understanding Internal Control over Financial Reporting and Auditing Design Effectiveness - SU 5
- Chapter 8 - Planning and Testing Operating Effectiveness of Internal Control over Financial Reporting - 5.5, SU 8, 14.1-14.2
- Chapter 9 - Substantive Procedures and the Financial Statement Audit - 3.5, 10.1-10.2, 14.1, 14.3-14.4
- Chapter 10 - The Revenue Process Cycle: Sales, Billing, and Collection in the Health-Care Provider and Retailing Industries - SU 6, SU 11
- Chapter 11 - Completing the Integrated Audit and Reporting - SU 9, SU 13, SUs 15-16

Part IV: Additional Transaction Cycles and Other Topics

Chapter 12 - Auditing Acquisition and Payments Processes: Purchases, Cash Disbursements and Related Activities in the Automotive Industry - SU 7, 12.1-12.2
Chapter 13 - The Human Resources Cycle Process and Related Accounts: Personnel and Payroll in the Service Industries - SU 7, 9.4, 12.7
Chapter 14 - The Inventory Cycle and Related Accounts: Tracking and Costing Products in the Land Development and Home Building Industry - SU 7, 12.2
Chapter 15 - Assets, Liabilities, and Equity Related to the Financing Cycle - 7.6, SU 12
Chapter 16 - Topics Beyond the Integrated Audit - SUs 17-20

Johnstone, Gramling, and Rittenberg, *Auditing: A Risk-Based Approach to Conducting a Quality Audit*, Tenth Edition, Cengage Learning, 2015.

Chapter 1 - Auditing: Integral to the Economy - SU 1
Chapter 2 - The Risk of Fraud and Mechanisms to Address Fraud: Regulation, Corporate Governance, and Audit Quality - 1.5, 3.6, 5.1, 8.1
Chapter 3 - Internal Control over Financial Reporting: Management's Responsibilities and Importance to the External Auditors - 5.1-5.3
Chapter 4 - Professional Liability and the Need for Quality Auditor Judgments and Ethical Decisions - 2.1-2.6
Chapter 5 - Professional Auditing Standards and the Audit Opinion Formulation Process - 1.1-1.4, SU 15
Chapter 6 - A Framework for Audit Evidence - SU 10
Chapter 7 - Planning the Audit: Identifying and Responding to the Risks of Material Misstatement - SU 3, 8.2
Chapter 8 - Specialized Audit Tools: Sampling and Generalized Audit Software - 10.4, SU 14
Chapter 9 - Auditing the Revenue Cycle - SU 11
Chapter 10 - Auditing Cash and Marketable Securities - 5.2, 11.2, 12.4
Chapter 11 - Auditing Inventory, Goods and Services, and Accounts Payable: The Acquisition and Payment Cycle - 12.1-12.2
Chapter 12 - Auditing Long-Lived Assets: Acquisition, Use, Impairment, and Disposal - 12.3
Chapter 13 - Auditing Debt Obligations and Stockholders' Equity Transactions - 12.5-12.6
Chapter 14 - Activities Required in Completing a Quality Audit - SU 9
Chapter 15 - Audit Reports on Financial Statements - SUs 15-17
Chapter 16 - Advanced Topics Concerning Complex Auditing Judgments - N/A
Chapter 17 - Other Services Provided by Auditing Firms - SUs 18-19

Knechel and Salterio, *Auditing: Assurance & Risk*, Fourth Edition, Routledge, 2016.

Chapter 1 - Assurance and Auditing - SU 1, 2.8-2.9
Chapter 2 - Managing Risk: The Role of Auditing and Assurance - 3.1-3.4, 8.1
Chapter 3 - The Building Blocks of Auditing - 3.5, 10.1
Chapter 4 - The Audit Process - 9.3
Chapter 5 - Understanding the Client's Industry and Business: Strategic Analysis and Management Controls - SU 3
Chapter 6 - Understanding the Client's Industry and Business: Processes and Process Controls - SU 3
Chapter 7 - Risk Mitigation and the Audit: Internal Control over Financial Reporting in a GAAS Audit - 3.3, SU 5, 8.1
Chapter 8 - Internal Control over Financial Reporting in an Integrated Audit - SU 8
Chapter 9 - Inquiry and Analytical Evidence Including Auditing of Accounting Estimates - 3.5, SU 4, 10.1
Chapter 10 - Designing Substantive Tests: Responses to Residual Risks - SU 10
Chapter 11 - Audit Testing for the Sales and Customer Service Process - SU 6, SU 11
Chapter 12 - Audit Testing for the Supply Chain and Production Process - SU 7, 12.1-12.2, 12.7
Chapter 13 - Auditing Resource Management Processes - SU 7, 12.3-12.6
Chapter 14 - Completing the Audit I: Final Evidence Aggregation and Analysis - SU 9, SU 13
Chapter 15 - Completing the Audit II: Audit Reporting - SUs 15-16
Chapter 16 - The Ethical Auditor: Factors Affecting Auditor Decision-Making - 2.1-2.5
Chapter 17 - Interpreting Sample-Based Audit Evidence - SU 14

Louwers, Blay, Sinason, Strawser, and Thibodeau, *Auditing & Assurance Services*, Seventh Edition, McGraw-Hill, Inc., 2017.

Part I: The Contemporary Auditing Environment
- Chapter 1 - Auditing and Assurance Services - 1.1-1.4
- Chapter 2 - Professional Standards - 1.1, 1.5

Part II: The Financial Statement Audit
- Chapter 3 - Engagement Planning - 3.1-3.5, 4.1-4.2, 10.1-10.3
- Chapter 4 - Management Fraud and Audit Risk - 3.3, 3.6-3.7, 8.1-8.2
- Chapter 5 - Risk Assessment: Internal Control Evaluation - 3.3-3.4, 5.1-5.3, 8.1-8.2, 9.3-9.4
- Chapter 6 - Employee Fraud and the Audit of Cash - 3.6, 6.4, 11.2
- Chapter 7 - Revenue and Collection Cycle - SU 6, SU 11
- Chapter 8 - Acquisition and Expenditure Cycle - SU 7, 12.1-12.2, 12.7
- Chapter 9 - Production Cycle - SU 7, 12.2
- Chapter 10 - Finance and Investment Cycle - 4.4, 7.6, 12.3-12.7
- Chapter 11 - Completing the Audit - SU 4, 9.1-9.2, SU 13
- Chapter 12 - Reports on Audited Financial Statements - SUs 15-16

Part III: Stand-Alone Modules
- Module A - Other Public Accounting Services - 1.3-1.4, 2.8-2.9, SUs 17-18
- Module B - Professional Ethics - 2.1-2.7
- Module C - Legal Liability - 2.8
- Module D - Internal Audits, Governmental Audits, and Fraud Examinations - SUs 20-21
- Module E - Overview of Sampling - 14.1
- Module F - Attributes Sampling - 14.2
- Module G - Variables Sampling - 14.3-14.4
- Module H - Auditing and Information Technology - 5.5, 6.4, 7.2-7.3, 7.5, 8.3, 10.4, SU 22

Messier, Glover, and Prawitt, *Auditing & Assurance Services: A Systematic Approach*, Tenth Edition, McGraw-Hill, Inc., 2017.

Part 1: Introduction to Assurance and Financial Statement Auditing
- Chapter 1 - An Introduction to Assurance and Financial Statement Auditing - 1.1-1.4
- Chapter 2 - The Financial Statement Auditing Environment - 1.1, 1.5, 3.1

Part 2: Audit Planning and Basic Auditing Concepts
- Chapter 3 - Audit Planning, Types of Audit Tests, and Materiality - SUs 3-4
- Chapter 4 - Risk Assessment - 3.3
- Chapter 5 - Evidence and Documentation - SU 10

Part 3: Understanding and Auditing Internal Control
- Chapter 6 - Internal Control in a Financial Statement Audit - SU 5, SU 8
- Chapter 7 - Auditing Internal Control over Financial Reporting - 9.3-9.4

Part 4: Statistical and Nonstatistical Sampling Tools for Auditing
- Chapter 8 - Audit Sampling: An Overview and Application to Tests of Controls - 14.1-14.2
- Chapter 9 - Audit Sampling: An Application to Substantive Tests of Account Balances - 14.1, 14.3-14.4

Part 5: Auditing Business Processes
- Chapter 10 - Auditing the Revenue Process - SU 6, SU 11
- Chapter 11 - Auditing the Purchasing Process - 7.1-7.3, 12.1-12.2
- Chapter 12 - Auditing the Human Resource Management Process - 7.4-7.5, 12.7
- Chapter 13 - Auditing the Inventory Management Process - 12.2
- Chapter 14 - Auditing the Financing/Investing Process: Prepaid Expenses, Intangible Assets, and Property, Plant and Equipment - 7.6, 12.3
- Chapter 15 - Auditing the Financing/Investing Process: Long-Term Liabilities, Stockholders' Equity, and Income Statement Accounts - 7.6, 12.5-12.6
- Chapter 16 - Auditing the Financing/Investing Process: Cash and Investments - 11.2, 12.4

Part 6: Completing the Audit and Reporting Responsibilities
- Chapter 17 - Completing the Audit Engagement - 9.1-9.2, SU 13
- Chapter 18 - Reports on Audited Financial Statements - SUs 15-17

Part 7: Professional Responsibilities
- Chapter 19 - Professional Conduct, Independence, and Quality Control - 2.1-2.6
- Chapter 20 - Legal Liability - 2.8

Part 8: Assurance, Attestation, and Internal Auditing Services
- Chapter 21 - Assurance, Attestation, and Internal Auditing Services - 2.8-2.9, SUs 18-19, SU 21
- Chapter 22 - Advanced Module: Professional Judgment Framework - Understanding and Developing Professional Judgment in Auditing - 1.2, 2.1

O'Reilly, McDonnell, Winograd, Gerson, and Jaenicke, *Montgomery's Auditing*, Twelfth Edition, John Wiley & Sons, Inc., 1999.

Part I: The Audit Environment
- Chapter 1 - An Overview of Auditing - 1.1
- Chapter 2 - Organization and Structure of the Auditing Profession - SU 1
- Chapter 3 - Auditing Standards and Professional Conduct - 1.1, 2.1-2.6
- Chapter 4 - Auditors' Professional Responsibility - SU 1, 9.1-9.2
- Chapter 5 - Auditors' Legal Liability - 2.7

Part II: Theory and Concepts
- Chapter 6 - The Audit Process - SU 3
- Chapter 7 - Engagement Planning and Management - SU 3
- Chapter 8 - Obtaining Information About the Entity - SU 4
- Chapter 9 - Overview of Internal Control - SU 5
- Chapter 10 - Understanding Entity-Level Controls - SU 5
- Chapter 11 - Understanding Activity-Level Controls - SU 5
- Chapter 12 - Assessing Control Risk and Developing the Audit Strategy - 3.6-3.7, SU 8, SU 10
- Chapter 13 - Auditing the Revenue Cycle - SU 6, SU 11
- Chapter 14 - Auditing the Purchasing Cycle - SU 7, SU 12
- Chapter 15 - Substantive Tests - SU 10
- Chapter 16 - The Use of Audit Sampling - SU 14

Part III: Auditing Specific Accounts
- Chapter 17 - Auditing Cash and Cash Equivalents - 5.2, 11.2
- Chapter 18 - Auditing Accounts Receivable and Related Revenue Cycle Accounts - SU 6, SU 11
- Chapter 19 - Auditing Inventories and Cost of Sales - 12.2
- Chapter 20 - Auditing Prepayments and Accruals - SU 7, 12.7
- Chapter 21 - Auditing Investment in Debt and Equity Securities and Related Income - 7.6, 12.4
- Chapter 22 - Auditing Property, Plant, and Equipment, and Intangible Assets and Deferred Charges - 7.6, 12.3
- Chapter 23 - Auditing Accounts Payable and Related Purchasing Cycle Accounts - SU 7, SU 12
- Chapter 24 - Auditing Income Taxes - 7.6
- Chapter 25 - Auditing Debt and Equity - 7.6, 12.5-12.6
- Chapter 26 - Auditing Financial Statement Disclosures - SU 13

Part IV: Completing the Work and Reporting the Results
- Chapter 27 - Completing the Audit - SU 9, SU 13
- Chapter 28 - Reporting on Audited Financial Statements - SUs 15-16
- Chapter 29 - Other Reporting Situations Related to Audits - SU 18
- Chapter 30 - Reporting on Nonaudit Services - 2.8-2.9, SU 18
- Chapter 31 - Attestation Engagements - 1.3, SU 19
- Chapter 32 - Compliance Auditing - 19.7

Reding, Sobel, et al., *Internal Auditing: Assurance & Advisory Services*, Fourth Edition, The Institute of Internal Auditors, 2017.

Fundamental Internal Audit Concepts
- Chapter 1 - Introduction to Internal Auditing - 21.1
- Chapter 2 - The International Professional Practices Framework: Authoritative Guidance for the Internal Audit Profession - 21.1
- Chapter 3 - Governance - N/A
- Chapter 4 - Risk Management - N/A
- Chapter 5 - Business Processes and Risks - N/A
- Chapter 6 - Internal Control - 5.1-5.2, 21.4
- Chapter 7 - Information Technology Risks and Controls - 5.5, SU 22
- Chapter 8 - Risk of Fraud and Illegal Acts - 3.6, 5.1
- Chapter 9 - Managing the Internal Audit Function - 21.7
- Chapter 10 - Audit Evidence and Working Papers - SU 10, 21.6, SU 22
- Chapter 11 - Audit Sampling - SU 14

Conducting Internal Audit Engagements
- Chapter 12 - Introduction to the Engagement Process - 21.1, 21.5
- Chapter 13 - Conducting the Assurance Engagement - 21.6
- Chapter 14 - Communicating Assurance Engagement Outcomes and Performing Follow-up Procedures - 21.9
- Chapter 15 - The Consulting Engagement - N/A

Ricchiute, *Auditing*, Eighth Edition, South-Western, 2005.

Part One: Responsibilities and Reporting
- Chapter 1 - An Introduction to Audit and Other Assurance Services - SU 1
- Chapter 2 - Standards, Materiality, and Risk - 1.1, 3.3
- Chapter 3 - Audit Reports - SUs 15-16
- Chapter 4 - Professional Ethics - 2.1-2.6
- Chapter 5 - Legal Liability - 2.7, 3.6-3.7

Part Two: The Audit Process and Internal Control
- Chapter 6 - Evidence - SU 10
- Chapter 7 - The Audit Process and Detecting Fraud - SUs 3-4
- Chapter 8 - Internal Control - SU 5, SU 8

Part Three: Auditing the Revenue/Receipt and the Expenditure/Disbursement Cycles
- Chapter 9 - Audit Sampling - SU 14
- Chapter 10 - Sales and Cash Receipts Transactions - SU 6
- Chapter 11 - Accounts Receivable and Cash Balances - SU 11
- Chapter 12 - Purchases and Cash Disbursements Transactions - 7.1-7.3
- Chapter 13 - Accounts Payable, Prepaids, and Accrued Liabilities - SU 12

Part Four: Auditing Other Cycles and Completing an Audit
- Chapter 14 - Personnel and Payroll - 7.4-7.5, 12.7
- Chapter 15 - Inventory and Fixed Assets - 7.6, 12.2-12.3
- Chapter 16 - Investments, Debt, and Equity - 7.6, 12.4-12.6
- Chapter 17 - Completing an Engagement - SU 9, SU 13

Part Five: Assurance and Attestation Services, Compliance and Internal Auditing
- Chapter 18 - Other Assurance and Attestation Services - SUs 17-19
- Chapter 19 - Compliance and Internal Auditing - 19.7, SU 21

Sawyer, et al., *Sawyer's Guide for Internal Auditors*, Sixth Edition, The Institute of Internal Auditors, Inc., 2012.

Volume 1: Internal Audit Essentials
- Chapter 1 - Nature of Modern Internal Auditing - 21.1
- Chapter 2 - Control and Risk Models - 21.4
- Chapter 3 - Assurance and Consulting Services - 21.1
- Chapter 4 - Audit Process Management - 21.7
- Chapter 5 - Stakeholder Relationships - 21.5

Volume 2: Internal Audit Processes and Methods
- Chapter 6 - Defining the Audit/Risk Universe - N/A
- Chapter 7 - Entity-wide Risk Assessment - SU 3, 21.5
- Chapter 8 - Entity-wide Assurance Projects - N/A
- Chapter 9 - Planning an Assurance Engagement - SU 3, 21.5
- Chapter 10 - Evaluating Design of Controls and Other Risk Management Techniques - SU 3, 22.9-22.10
- Chapter 11 - Testing Effectiveness of Controls and Other Risk Management Techniques - SU 10, SU 14, SU 22
- Chapter 12 - Documentation - 10.3, 21.6
- Chapter 13 - Communication of Results - 21.9
- Chapter 14 - Consulting Activities - N/A

Volume 3: Governance, Risk Management, and Compliance Essentials
- Chapter 15 - Governance, Risk Management, and Compliance Essentials - N/A
- Chapter 16 - Governance - N/A
- Chapter 17 - Risk Management - N/A
- Chapter 18 - Compliance - N/A
- Chapter 19 - Fraud, Ethics, and People Risk - 3.6, 21.5, 21.8
- Chapter 20 - Corporate Social Responsibility and Sustainability - N/A

Stuart, *Auditing and Assurance Services: An Applied Approach*, First Edition, McGraw-Hill/Irwin, 2011.

Chapter 1 - What Is Auditing? - 1.1-1.3
Chapter 2 - The Auditing Planning Process: Understanding the Risk of Material Misstatement - 1.5, 3.1-3.5, 3.7, 4.1-4.3, 8.1-8.3
Chapter 3 - Internal Controls - 5.1-5.3, 5.5, 9.1-9.2
Appendix A - Information Systems Auditing - SU 22
Chapter 4 - Auditing the Revenue Business Process - SU 6, 10.2, 10.4, 11.1
Chapter 5 - Audit Evidence and the Auditor's Responsibility for Fraud Detection - 3.6, 10.1, 10.3
Chapter 6 - Auditing the Acquisition and Expenditure Business Process - 3.5, SU 7, SU 12
Chapter 7 - Auditing the Inventory Business Process - 7.1-7.3, 12.2
Chapter 8 - Audit Sampling: Tests of Controls - 14.1-14.2
Chapter 9 - Audit Sampling: Substantive Tests of Details - 14.3-14.4
Chapter 10 - Cash and Investment Business Processes - 11.2, 12.4
Chapter 11 - Long-Term Debt and Owners' Equity Business Process - 12.5-12.6
Chapter 12 - Completing the Audit - 9.1-9.3, SU 13
Chapter 13 - Audit Reports - 4.5, SUs 15-16
Chapter 14 - The Auditing Profession - 2.1-2.6

Whittington and Pany, *Principles of Auditing and Other Assurance Services*, Twentieth Edition, McGraw-Hill, Inc., 2016.

Chapter 1 - The Role of the Public Accountant in the American Economy - SU 1
Chapter 2 - Professional Standards - 1.1
Chapter 3 - Professional Ethics - 2.1-2.6
Chapter 4 - Legal Liability of CPAs - 2.7, 3.6-3.7
Chapter 5 - Audit Evidence and Documentation - SU 4, SU 10
Chapter 6 - Audit Planning, Understanding the Client, Assessing Risks, and Responding - SU 3, SU 8
Chapter 7 - Internal Control - SU 5, SU 8
Chapter 8 - Consideration of Internal Control in an Information Technology Environment - 5.5, 6.4, 7.2-7.3, 7.5, 8.3
Chapter 9 - Audit Sampling - SU 14
Chapter 10 - Cash and Financial Investments - 5.2, 11.2, 12.4
Chapter 11 - Accounts Receivable, Notes Receivable, and Revenue - SU 6, SU 11
Chapter 12 - Inventories and Cost of Goods Sold - SU 7, 12.2, 12.7
Chapter 13 - Property, Plant, and Equipment: Depreciation and Depletion - 7.6, 12.3
Chapter 14 - Accounts Payable and Other Liabilities - SU 7, 12.1
Chapter 15 - Debt and Equity Capital - 7.6, 12.5-12.6
Chapter 16 - Auditing Operations and Completing the Audit - SU 9, SU 13
Chapter 17 - Auditors' Reports - SUs 15-16
Chapter 18 - Integrated Audits of Public Companies - 9.3
Chapter 19 - Additional Assurance Services: Historical Financial Information - SUs 17-19
Chapter 20 - Additional Assurance Services: Other Information - 1.3-1.4, SU 9
Chapter 21 - Internal, Operational, and Compliance Auditing - 19.7, SU 21

APPENDIX B
AUTHORITATIVE PRONOUNCEMENTS: COVERAGE AND CROSS-REFERENCES

The following pages provide two-way cross-references:

- Pronouncement sections organized by study unit
- Pronouncement sections referenced to study units

BY STUDY UNIT

The listing below and on the following pages indicates coverage by study unit in this book.

Study Unit 1 Engagement Responsibilities

AU-C Preface Principles Underlying an Audit Conducted in Accordance With Generally Accepted Auditing Standards
AU-C 200 Overall Objectives of the Independent Auditor and the Conduct of an Audit in Accordance With Generally Accepted Auditing Standards
AU-C 220 Quality Control for an Engagement Conducted in Accordance With Generally Accepted Auditing Standards
AT-C 105 Concepts Common to All Attestation Engagements
AT-C 205 Examination Engagements
AT-C 210 Review Engagements
AT-C 215 Agreed-Upon Procedures Engagements
AR-C 60 General Principles for Engagements Performed With Statements on Standards for Accounting and Review Services
AR-C 70 Preparation of Financial Statements
AR-C 80 Compilation of Financial Statements
AR-C 90 Review of Financial Statements
PR 100 Standards for Performing and Reporting on Peer Reviews
QC 10 A Firm's System of Quality Control
AS 1001 Responsibilities and Functions of the Independent Auditor
AS 1101 Audit Risk
AS 1110 Relationship of Auditing Standards to Quality Control Standards
AS 1201 Supervision of the Audit Engagement
AS 1220 Engagement Quality Review

Study Unit 2 Professional Responsibilities

AICPA *Code of Professional Conduct*
Sarbanes-Oxley Act of 2002
Consulting Services: Definitions and Standards
Statements on Standards for Tax Services
AS 1005 Independence
AS 1010 Training and Proficiency of the Independent Auditor
AS 1015 Due Professional Care in the Performance of Work

Study Unit 3 Planning and Risk Assessment

AU-C 200 Overall Objectives of the Independent Auditor and the Conduct of an Audit in Accordance With Generally Accepted Auditing Standards
AU-C 210 Terms of Engagement
AU-C 240 Consideration of Fraud in a Financial Statement Audit
AU-C 250 Consideration of Laws and Regulations in an Audit of Financial Statements
AU-C 300 Planning an Audit
AU-C 315 Understanding the Entity and Its Environment and Assessing the Risks of Material Misstatement
AU-C 320 Materiality in Planning and Performing an Audit
AU-C 330 Performing Audit Procedures in Response to Assessed Risks and Evaluating the Audit Evidence Obtained
AU-C 450 Evaluation of Misstatements Identified During the Audit
AU-C 510 Opening Balances—Initial Audit Engagements, Including Reaudit Engagements
AU-C 520 Analytical Procedures
AS 1101 Audit Risk
AS 1201 Supervision of the Audit Engagement
AS 2101 Audit Planning
AS 2105 Consideration of Materiality in Planning and Performing an Audit
AS 2110 Identifying and Assessing Risks of Material Misstatement
AS 2301 The Auditor's Responses to the Risks of Material Misstatement
AS 2305 Substantive Analytical Procedures
AS 2401 Consideration of Fraud in a Financial Statement Audit
AS 2405 Illegal Acts by Clients
AS 2610 Initial Audits—Communications Between Predecessor and Successor Auditors
AS 2810 Evaluating Audit Results

Study Unit 4 Strategic Planning Issues

AU-C 540 Auditing Accounting Estimates, Including Fair Value Accounting Estimates, and Related Disclosures
AU-C 550 Related Parties
AU-C 585 Consideration of Omitted Procedures After the Report Release Date
AU-C 610 The Auditor's Consideration of the Internal Audit Function in an Audit of Financial Statements
AU-C 620 Using the Work of an Auditor's Specialist
AS 1105 Audit Evidence
AS 1210 Using the Work of a Specialist
AS 2410 Related Parties
AS 2501 Auditing Accounting Estimates
AS 2502 Auditing Fair Value Measurements and Disclosures
AS 2503 Auditing Derivative Instruments, Hedging Activities, and Investments in Securities
AS 2605 Consideration of the Internal Audit Function
AS 2810 Evaluating Audit Results
AS 2901 Consideration of Omitted Procedures After the Report Date

Study Unit 5 Internal Control Concepts and Information Technology

AU-C 315 Understanding the Entity and Its Environment and Assessing the Risks of Material Misstatement
AS 2110 Identifying and Assessing Risks of Material Misstatement

Study Unit 6 Internal Control -- Sales-Receivables-Cash Receipts Cycle

AU-C 315 Understanding the Entity and Its Environment and Assessing the Risks of Material Misstatement
AS 2110 Identifying and Assessing Risks of Material Misstatement

Study Unit 7 Internal Control -- Purchases, Payroll, and Other Cycles

AU-C 315 Understanding the Entity and Its Environment and Assessing the Risks of Material Misstatement
AS 2110 Identifying and Assessing Risks of Material Misstatement

Study Unit 8 Responses to Assessed Risks

AU-C 315 Understanding the Entity and Its Environment and Assessing the Risks of Material Misstatement
AU-C 330 Performing Audit Procedures in Response to Assessed Risks and Evaluating the Audit Evidence Obtained
AU-C 450 Evaluation of Misstatements Identified During the Audit
AS 2110 Identifying and Assessing Risks of Material Misstatement
AS 2301 The Auditor's Responses to the Risks of Material Misstatement
AS 2810 Evaluating Audit Results

Study Unit 9 Internal Control Communications and Reports

AU-C 260 The Auditor's Communication With Those Charged With Governance
AU-C 265 Communicating Internal Control Related Matters Identified in an Audit
AU-C 402 Audit Considerations Relating to an Entity Using a Service Organization
AU-C 940 An Audit of Internal Control over Financial Reporting That Is Integrated with an Audit of Financial Statements
AS 1301 Communications with Audit Committees
AS 1305 Communications About Control Deficiencies in an Audit of Financial Statements
AS 2201 An Audit of Internal Control Over Financial Reporting That is Integrated with an Audit of Financial Statements
AS 2601 Consideration of an Entity's Use of a Service Organization
AS 6115 Reporting on Whether a Previously Reported Material Weakness Continues to Exist
AT-C 320 Reporting on an Examination of Controls at a Service Organization Relevant to User Entities' Internal Control Over Financial Reporting

Study Unit 10 Evidence -- Objectives and Nature

AU-C 230 Audit Documentation
AU-C 330 Performing Audit Procedures in Response to Assessed Risks and Evaluating the Audit Evidence Obtained
AU-C 500 Audit Evidence
AU-C 501 Audit Evidence—Specific Considerations for Selected Items
AU-C 505 External Confirmations
AU-C 510 Opening Balances—Initial Audit Engagements, Including Reaudit Engagements
AS 1105 Audit Evidence
AS 1215 Audit Documentation
AS 2301 The Auditor's Responses to the Risks of Material Misstatement
AS 2310 The Confirmation Process
AS 2810 Evaluating Audit Results

Study Unit 11 Evidence -- The Sales-Receivables-Cash Cycle

AU-C 240 Consideration of Fraud in a Financial Statement Audit
AU-C 500 Audit Evidence
AU-C 501 Audit Evidence—Specific Considerations for Selected Items
AU-C 505 External Confirmations
AS 1105 Audit Evidence
AS 2310 The Confirmation Process
AS 2810 Evaluating Audit Results

Study Unit 12 Evidence -- Purchases, Inventory, Payroll, and Other Cycles

AU-C 240 Consideration of Fraud in a Financial Statement Audit
AU-C 500 Audit Evidence
AU-C 501 Audit Evidence—Specific Considerations for Selected Items
AU-C 540 Auditing Accounting Estimates, Including Fair Value Accounting Estimates, and Related Disclosures
AS 1105 Audit Evidence
AS 2501 Auditing Accounting Estimates
AS 2502 Auditing Fair Value Measurements and Disclosures
AS 2503 Auditing Derivative Instruments, Hedging Activities, and Investments in Securities
AS 2510 Auditing Inventories
AS 2810 Evaluating Audit Results

Study Unit 13 Evidence -- Key Considerations

AU-C 500 Audit Evidence
AU-C 501 Audit Evidence—Specific Considerations for Selected Items
AU-C 560 Subsequent Events and Subsequently Discovered Facts
AU-C 570 The Auditor's Consideration of an Entity's Ability to Continue as a Going Concern
AU-C 580 Written Representations
AS 1105 Audit Evidence
AS 2415 Consideration of an Entity's Ability to Continue as a Going Concern
AS 2505 Inquiry of a Client's Lawyer Concerning Litigation, Claims, and Assessments
AS 2801 Subsequent Events
AS 2805 Management Representations
AS 2810 Evaluating Audit Results
AS 2905 Subsequent Discovery of Facts Existing at the Date of the Auditor's Report

Study Unit 14 Evidence -- Sampling

AU-C 530 Audit Sampling
AS 2315 Audit Sampling

Study Unit 15 Reports -- Opinions and Disclaimers

AU-C 700 Forming an Opinion and Reporting on Financial Statements
AU-C 705 Modifications to the Opinion in the Independent Auditor's Report
AU-C 905 Alert That Restricts the Use of the Auditor's Written Communication
AS 2815 The Meaning of "Present Fairly in Conformity with Generally Accepted Accounting Principles"
AS 2820 Evaluating Consistency of Financial Statements
AS 3101 The Auditor's Report on an Audit of Financial Statements When the Auditor Expresses an Unqualified Opinion
AS 3105 Departures from Unqualified Opinions and Other Reporting Circumstances
AS 3110 Dating of the Independent Auditor's Report
AS 3320 Association with Financial Statements

Study Unit 16 Reports -- Other Modifications

AU-C 560 Subsequent Events and Subsequently Discovered Facts
AU-C 570 The Auditor's Consideration of an Entity's Ability to Continue as a Going Concern
AU-C 600 Special Considerations—Audits of Group Financial Statements (Including the Work of Component Auditors)
AU-C 700 Forming an Opinion and Reporting on Financial Statements
AU-C 705 Modifications to the Opinion in the Independent Auditor's Report
AU-C 706 Emphasis-of-Matter Paragraphs and Other-Matter Paragraphs in the Independent Auditor's Report
AU-C 708 Consistency of Financial Statements
AS 1205 Part of the Audit Performed by Other Independent Auditors
AS 2415 Consideration of an Entity's Ability to Continue as a Going Concern
AS 2801 Subsequent Events
AS 2815 The Meaning of "Present Fairly in Conformity with Generally Accepted Accounting Principles"
AS 2820 Evaluating Consistency of Financial Statements
AS 2905 Subsequent Discovery of Facts Existing at the Date of the Auditor's Report
AS 3101 The Auditor's Report on an Audit of Financial Statements When the Auditor Expresses an Unqualified Opinion
AS 3105 Departures from Unqualified Opinions and Other Reporting Circumstances
AS 3110 Dating of the Independent Auditor's Report

Study Unit 17 Related Reporting Topics

AU-C 720 Other Information in Documents Containing Audited Financial Statements
AU-C 725 Supplementary Information in Relation to the Financial Statements as a Whole
AU-C 730 Required Supplementary Information
AU-C 800 Special Considerations—Audits of Financial Statements Prepared in Accordance With Special Purpose Frameworks
AU-C 805 Special Considerations—Audits of Single Financial Statements and Specific Elements, Accounts, or Items of a Financial Statement
AU-C 806 Reporting on Compliance With Aspects of Contractual Agreements or Regulatory Requirements in Connection with Audited Financial Statements
AU-C 810 Engagements to Report on Summary Financial Statements
AU-C 905 Alert That Restricts the Use of the Auditor's Written Communication
AU-C 910 Financial Statements Prepared in Accordance With a Financial Reporting Framework Generally Accepted in Another Country
AU-C 915 Reports on Application of Requirements of an Applicable Financial Reporting Framework
AU-C 920 Letters for Underwriters and Certain Other Requesting Parties
AU-C 925 Filings With the U.S. Securities and Exchange Commission Under the Securities Act of 1933
AU-C 930 Interim Financial Information
AS 2701 Auditing Supplemental Information Accompanying Audited Financial Statements
AS 2705 Required Supplementary Information
AS 2710 Other Information in Documents Containing Audited Financial Statements
AS 3105 Departures from Unqualified Opinions and Other Reporting Circumstances
AS 3310 Special Reports on Regulated Companies
AS 3315 Reporting on Condensed Financial Statements and Selected Financial Data
AS 4101 Responsibilities Regarding Filings Under Federal Securities Statutes
AS 4105 Reviews of Interim Financial Information
AS 6101 Letters for Underwriters and Certain Other Requesting Parties
AS 6105 Reports on the Application of Accounting Principles

Study Unit 18 Preparation, Compilation, and Review Engagements

AR-C 60 General Principles for Engagements Performed With Statements on Standards for Accounting and Review Services
AR-C 70 Preparation of Financial Statements
AR-C 80 Compilation of Financial Statements
AR-C 90 Review of Financial Statements
AR-C 100 Special Considerations—International Reporting Issues
AR-C 120 Compilation of Pro Forma Financial Information

Study Unit 19 SSAEs – Examination, Review, and Agreed-Upon Procedures Engagements

AT-C 105 Concepts Common to All Attestation Engagements
AT-C 205 Examination Engagements
AT-C 210 Review Engagements
AT-C 215 Agreed-Upon Procedures Engagements
AT-C 305 Prospective Financial Information
AT-C 310 Reporting on Pro Forma Financial Information
AT-C 315 Compliance Attestation
AT-C 395 Management's Discussion and Analysis

Study Unit 20 Governmental Audits

AU-C 935 Compliance Auditing
AS 6110 Compliance Auditing Considerations in Audits of Recipients of Governmental Financial Assistance
Government Auditing Standards (Yellow Book)

Study Unit 21 Internal Auditing

The Institute of Internal Auditors' International Professional Practices Framework
- Mandatory Guidance
  - Definition of Internal Auditing
  - Code of Ethics
  - Core Principles for the Professional Practice of Internal Auditing
  - *International Standards for the Professional Practice of Internal Auditing (Standards)*

Recommended Guidance
- Implementation Guidance (Implementation Guides)
- Supplemental Guidance (Practice Guides)

Study Unit 22 Information Systems

Information systems, operations, and controls
CISA Concepts

BY PRONOUNCEMENT

The following list relates AU-C and other auditing pronouncements to the Gleim study unit(s) where they are addressed.

Section No.	Gleim Study Unit	Statements on Auditing Standards
AU-C 200–299		**General Principles and Responsibilities**
200	1, 3	Overall Objectives of the Independent Auditor and the Conduct of an Audit in Accordance With Generally Accepted Auditing Standards
210	3	Terms of Engagement
220	1	Quality Control for an Engagement Conducted in Accordance With Generally Accepted Auditing Standards
230	10	Audit Documentation
240	3, 11, 12	Consideration of Fraud in a Financial Statement Audit
250	3	Consideration of Laws and Regulations in an Audit of Financial Statements
260	9	The Auditor's Communication With Those Charged With Governance
265	9	Communicating Internal Control Related Matters Identified in an Audit
AU-C 300–499		**Risk Assessment and Response to Assessed Risks**
300	3	Planning an Audit
315	3, 5-8	Understanding the Entity and Its Environment and Assessing the Risks of Material Misstatement
320	3	Materiality in Planning and Performing an Audit
330	3, 8, 10	Performing Audit Procedures in Response to Assessed Risks and Evaluating the Audit Evidence Obtained
402	9	Audit Considerations Relating to an Entity Using a Service Organization
450	3, 8	Evaluation of Misstatements Identified During the Audit
AU-C 500–599		**Audit Evidence**
500	10-13	Audit Evidence
501	10-13	Audit Evidence—Specific Considerations for Selected Items
505	10-11	External Confirmations
510	3, 10	Opening Balances—Initial Audit Engagements, Including Reaudit Engagements
520	3	Analytical Procedures
530	14	Audit Sampling
540	4, 12	Auditing Accounting Estimates, Including Fair Value Accounting Estimates, and Related Disclosures
550	4	Related Parties
560	13, 16	Subsequent Events and Subsequently Discovered Facts
570	13, 16	The Auditor's Consideration of an Entity's Ability to Continue as a Going Concern
580	13	Written Representations
585	4	Consideration of Omitted Procedures After the Report Release Date
AU-C 600–699		**Using the Work of Others**
600	16	Special Considerations—Audits of Group Financial Statements (Including the Work of Component Auditors)
610	4	The Auditor's Consideration of the Internal Audit Function in an Audit of Financial Statements
620	4	Using the Work of an Auditor's Specialist
AU-C 700–799		**Audit Conclusions and Reporting**
700	15-16	Forming an Opinion and Reporting on Financial Statements
705	15-16	Modifications to the Opinion in the Independent Auditor's Report
706	16	Emphasis-of-Matter Paragraphs and Other-Matter Paragraphs in the Independent Auditor's Report
708	16	Consistency of Financial Statements
720	17	Other Information in Documents Containing Audited Financial Statements
725	17	Supplementary Information in Relation to the Financial Statements as a Whole
730	17	Required Supplementary Information
AU-C 800–899		**Special Considerations**
800	17	Special Considerations—Audits of Financial Statements Prepared in Accordance With Special Purpose Frameworks
805	17	Special Considerations—Audits of Single Financial Statements and Specific Elements, Accounts, or Items of a Financial Statement
806	17	Reporting on Compliance With Aspects of Contractual Agreements or Regulatory Requirements in Connection with Audited Financial Statements
810	17	Engagements to Report on Summary Financial Statements

Section No.	Gleim Study Unit	Statements on Auditing Standards
AU-C 900–999		**Special Considerations in the United States**
905	15, 17	Alert That Restricts the Use of the Auditor's Written Communication
910	17	Financial Statements Prepared in Accordance With a Financial Reporting Framework Generally Accepted in Another Country
915	17	Reports on Application of Requirements of an Applicable Financial Reporting Framework
920	17	Letters for Underwriters and Certain Other Requesting Parties, as Amended
925	17	Filings With the U.S. Securities and Exchange Commission Under the Securities Act of 1933
930	17	Interim Financial Information
935	20	Compliance Audits
940	9	An Audit of Internal Control Over Financial Reporting That is Integrated with an Audit of Financial Statements
945	17	Auditor Involvement With Exempt Offering Documents
		Statements on Standards for Attestation Engagements
AT-C 105	1, 19	Concepts Common to All Attestation Engagements
AT-C 205	1, 19	Examination Engagements
AT-C 210	1, 19	Review Engagements
AT-C 215	1, 19	Agreed-Upon Procedures Engagements
AT-C 305	19	Prospective Financial Information
AT-C 310	19	Reporting on Pro Forma Financial Information
AT-C 315	19	Compliance Attestation
AT-C 320	9	Reporting on an Examination of Controls at a Service Organization Relevant to User Entities' Internal Control Over Financial Reporting
AT-C 395	19	Management's Discussion and Analysis (Not clarified)
		Statements on Standards for Accounting and Review Services
AR-C 60	1, 18	General Principles for Engagements Performed With Statements on Standards for Accounting and Review Services
AR-C 70	1, 18	Preparation of Financial Statements
AR-C 80	1, 18	Compilation of Financial Statements
AR-C 90	1, 18	Review of Financial Statements
AR-C 100	18	Special Considerations—International Reporting
AR-C 120	18	Compilation of Pro Forma Financial Information
		Statements on Quality Control Standards
QC 10	1	A Firm's System of Quality Control
		Standards for Performing and Reporting on Peer Reviews
PR 100	1	Standards for Performing and Reporting on Peer Reviews
		Statements on Standards for Consulting Services
CS 100	2	Consulting Services: Definitions and Standards
		Statements on Standards for Tax Services
TS 100	2	Tax Return Positions
TS 200	2	Answers to Questions on Returns
TS 300	2	Certain Procedural Aspects of Preparing Returns
TS 400	2	Use of Estimates
TS 500	2	Departure From a Position Previously Concluded in an Administrative Proceeding or Court Decision
TS 600	2	Knowledge of Error: Return Preparation and Administrative Proceedings
TS 700	2	Form and Content of Advice to Taxpayers
		Other Standards and References
	2	AICPA *Code of Professional Conduct*
	2	Sarbanes-Oxley Act of 2002
	20	*Government Auditing Standards* (Yellow Book)
	21	The Institute of Internal Auditors
	22	CISA Concepts

Section No.	Gleim Study Unit	Public Company Accounting Oversight Board Standards
General Auditing Standards		
1000		**General Principles and Responsibilities**
1001	1	Responsibilities and Functions of the Independent Auditor
1005	2	Independence
1010	2	Training and Proficiency of the Independent Auditor
1015	2	Due Professional Care in the Performance of Work
1100		**General Concepts**
1101	1, 3	Audit Risk
1105	4, 10-13	Audit Evidence
1110	1	Relationship of Auditing Standards to Quality Control Standards
1200		**General Activities**
1201	1, 3	Supervision of the Audit Engagement
1205	16	Part of the Audit Performed by Other Independent Auditors
1210	4	Using the Work of a Specialist
1215	10	Audit Documentation
1220	1	Engagement Quality Review
1300		**Auditor Communications**
1301	9	Communications with Audit Committees
1305	9	Communications About Control Deficiencies in an Audit of Financial Statements
Audit Procedures		
2100		**Audit Planning and Risk Assessment**
2101	3	Audit Planning
2105	3	Consideration of Materiality in Planning and Performing an Audit
2110	3, 5-8	Identifying and Assessing Risks of Material Misstatement
2200		**Auditing Internal Control over Financial Reporting**
2201	9	An Audit of Internal Control over Financial Reporting That Is Integrated with an Audit of Financial Statements
2300		**Audit Procedures in Response to Risks – Nature, Timing, and Extent**
2301	3, 8, 10	The Auditor's Responses to the Risks of Material Misstatement
2305	3	Substantive Analytical Procedures
2310	10, 11	The Confirmation Process
2315	14	Audit Sampling
2400		**Audit Procedures for Specific Aspects of the Audit**
2401	3	Consideration of Fraud in a Financial Statement Audit
2405	3	Illegal Acts by Clients
2410	4	Related Parties
2415	13, 16	Consideration of an Entity's Ability to Continue as a Going Concern
2500		**Audit Procedures for Certain Accounts or Disclosures**
2501	4, 12	Auditing Accounting Estimates
2502	4, 12	Auditing Fair Value Measurements and Disclosures
2503	4, 12	Auditing Derivative Instruments, Hedging Activities, and Investments in Securities
2505	13	Inquiry of a Client's Lawyer Concerning Litigation, Claims, and Assessments
2510	12	Auditing Inventories
2600		**Special Topics**
2601	9	Consideration of an Entity's Use of a Service Organization
2605	4	Consideration of the Internal Audit Function
2610	3	Initial Audits – Communications Between Predecessor and Successor Auditors
2700		**Auditor's Responsibilities Regarding Supplemental and Other Information**
2701	17	Auditing Supplemental Information Accompanying Audited Financial Statements
2705	17	Required Supplementary Information
2710	17	Other Information in Documents Containing Audited Financial Statements

Section No.	Gleim Study Unit	Public Company Accounting Oversight Board Standards
2800		**Concluding Audit Procedures**
2801	13, 16	Subsequent Events
2805	13	Management Representations
2810	3, 4, 8, 10-13	Evaluating Audit Results
2815	15, 16	The Meaning of "Present Fairly in Conformity with Generally Accepted Accounting Principles"
2820	15, 16	Evaluating Consistency of Financial Statements
2900		**Post-Audit Matters**
2901	4	Consideration of Omitted Procedures After the Report Date
2905	13, 16	Subsequent Discovery of Facts Existing at the Date of the Auditor's Report
Auditor Reporting		
3100		**Reporting on Audits of Financial Statements**
3101	15, 16	The Auditor's Report on an Audit of Financial Statements When the Auditor Expresses an Unqualified Opinion
3105	15, 16	Departures from Unqualified Opinions and Other Reporting Circumstances
3110	15, 16	Dating of the Independent Auditor's Report
3300		**Other Reporting Topics**
3305	17	Special Reports
3310	17	Special Reports on Regulated Companies
3315	17	Reporting on Condensed Financial Statements and Selected Financial Data
3320	15	Association with Financial Statements
Matters Relating to Filings Under Federal Securities Laws		
4101	17	Responsibilities Regarding Filings Under Federal Securities Statutes
4105	17	Reviews of Interim Financial Information
Other Matters Associated with Audits		
6101	17	Letters for Underwriters and Certain Other Requesting Parties
6105	17	Reports on the Application of Accounting Principles
6110	20	Compliance Auditing Considerations in Audits of Recipients of Governmental Financial Assistance
6115	9	Reporting on Whether a Previously Reported Material Weakness Continues to Exist

INDEX